THE WORLDWIDE GUIDE TO
MOVIE LOCATIONS

TONY REEVES

D1331784

TITAN BOOKS

The Worldwide Guide to Movie Locations
ISBN: 1 84023 207 2
ISBN-13: 9781840232073

Published by
Titan Books
A division of
Titan Publishing Group Ltd
144 Southwark Street
London SE1 0UP

First edition February 2001
Second revised edition February 2003
Third revised and expanded edition March 2006
10 9 8 7 6 5 4 3

ACKNOWLEDGEMENTS
Thanks to the following people for their invaluable help: Ian Aegis; Alabama Bureau of Travel & Tourism (Peggy Collins); Frank Anzalone; Arizona Film Commission; London Borough of Barnet; Geoffrey Bayldon; Simon Bosanquet; London Borough of Camden; Ian Carmichael; James Cary-Parkes; Chicago Film Office; George Cole; Simon Cork; Stephen K Crocker; Simon Crook; Dallas Convention & Visitors Bureau (Veronica Lynch,); Malcolm Davis; Terry Deal; Dallas Denton-Cox; Dan Dusek; Harvey Edgington, Film London; The Edmonton Hundreds; Peter Elford; Assheton Gorton; Ben Greenacre; Greenwich Film Unit; Peter Hannan BSC; Jon Hardy; Nigel Hatton; Hawaii Film Commission; Herts Filmlink; Matthew Hodson; HRH Group of Hotels (Sabina Bailey); Japan National Tourist Organization (Kylie Clark); Peter Jaques; Pat Karam; Ken Littleton of Cowboy Country; Lockwood-Mathews Mansion Museum Inc, Norwalk; Steen Mangen; Oliver Mantel; Sir Alec McCowen; Louise McManus Fernandes; Christian McWilliams; Melbourne Film Office (Lucy Chancellor Weale); Mono Lake Committee; City of Monrovia; Angus More Gordon; Munich Tourism; Tony Nuttall; Ontario Film Development Corporation; City of Oshawa (Julie Nixon); City of Palm Springs; Carolyn Partrick; Greater Philadelphia Film Office; Pittsburgh Film Office; Glen Platts; Vicky Powell; Kevin Priest; M&G Priest; Paul Raphael; Nils Reucker; Adam Richards; Colin Richardson; Ridgecrest Film Commission (Ray Arthur); Ritz-Carlton, Half Moon Bay; Simon Robson; Gillian Rodgerson; San Antonio Public Library (Cammie Gunter); Santa Barbara Conference & Visitors Bureau and Film Commission (Emma Thomas); Shoreditch Town Hall Trust; Donald Spicer; Trois Estate, Austin (Crisene Casper); Brian Tunstill; Norman Warwick; Kevin Wellard; West London Film Office; Westin Palace Madrid (Marta Aguilar Benavides); Alison Williams, Film London; Russ Williamson; Working Title Films; Wyoming Film Office.

PUBLISHER'S NOTE
Every effort has been made to ensure that the information given in this book was correct at the time of going to press. However, details such as travel information and phone numbers can change. The publishers cannot accept responsibility for any consequences arising from the use of this book.
We would be delighted to receive any corrections for incorporation into the next edition.

PRIVACY
Please note that many of the locations detailed in this book are private property, and are not open to the general public. Please respect the privacy of the owners, and be aware that access of any kind is often prohibited.

Visit our website: **www.titanbooks.com**

Did you enjoy this book? We love to hear from our readers. Please e-mail us at:
readerfeedback@titanemail.com or write to Reader Feedback at the above address.
To subscribe to our regular newsletter for up-to-the-minute news, great offers and competitions, email:
titan-news@titanemail.com

A CIP catalogue record for this title is available from the British Library.

Printed and bound in Great Britain by MPG, Bodmin, Cornwall.

CONTENTS

IF YOU FILM IT, THEY WILL COME...

I kicked off the intro to the first edition of *The Worldwide Guide to Movie Locations* with a few statistics about the phenomenon of movie tourism:

"In 1994, the Queen Elizabeth Suite of the Crown Hotel, Amersham in Buckinghamshire, suddenly became booked up for years ahead. Since 1977, the number of visitors to America's oldest national park, Devil's Tower in Wyoming, has increased by three quarters. And in 1989, the tiny town of Dyersville, Iowa (population 3,825) became a major tourist mecca.

There's a simple connection. All three places had recently appeared in successful films. The Crown was the hotel where Hugh Grant rattled the four-poster with Andie MacDowell in *Four Weddings and a Funeral*; Steven Spielberg picked the peculiar rock monolith of Devil's Tower as the alien rendezvous in *Close Encounters of the Third Kind*; and it was near Dyersville that Kevin Costner built his supernatural baseball pitch in *Field of Dreams*. By 1992, 60,000 visitors had motored out to see the field, and with each passing year the numbers have increased. Movie locations have become today's historic sites. Romantics queued to spend their honeymoons in Amersham, awestruck stargazers looked up to Devil's Tower, and dads swung a bat with their sons out in Dyersville."

Almost five years later, and following the effect that the global phenomenon of *The Lord of the Rings* trilogy had on New Zealand tourism, this book no longer needs a lengthier justification.

The seed of the book was sown when I moved down to London from a dull Midlands town and found I'd landed in the heart of 'movie gothic' territory. Around the corner from my Earl's Court bedsit, John Landis was filming *An American Werewolf in London*. On the way to the local shops, I'd pass the gloomy apartment block where Catherine Deneuve went murderously batty in *Repulsion*. A few minutes walk in the opposite direction I found the house where sinisterly camp gentleman's gentleman Dirk Bogarde played mindgames with aristocrat James Fox in *The Servant*. And my journey to work took me past the extravagant blue-tiled mansion where Joseph Losey shot his bizarre psychodrama *Secret Ceremony* with Elizabeth Taylor and Mia Farrow, and the site of Carl Boehm's home in *Peeping Tom*.

Okay, I was a bit of a movie freak, but this fascination with the landscape of cinema would probably never have taken root if, a few years later, I'd not had the chance to visit America. The magic name of Hollywood had me taking out a whopping bank loan and heading for West Coast USA. San Francisco was my first destination, and it was a strange sensation to find that I already knew this city. These were the hills Steve McQueen bounced down in *Bullitt*, the zigzag streets navigated by *The Love Bug*, the square where Gene Hackman eavesdropped on *The Conversation* and, of course, the prison island where Burt Lancaster served time as *The Birdman of Alcatraz*. But above all, the cool pastel colours and misty coastal light marked the city out as the backdrop to Hitchcock's *Vertigo*. This was unmistakably the dreamy world of Scottie and Madeleine, overlooked by Coit Tower, the landmark Kim Novak uses to trace James Stewart's flat.

The next stop, Los Angeles, and its excitingly seedy suburb, Hollywood, turned out to offer more glimpses of movie heaven. The gleaming white Griffith Observatory is forever haunted by the image of a tearful James Dean holding out the handful of bullets at the climax of *Rebel Without a Cause* (they're savvy enough to have erected a bust of the actor in the grounds). The old carousel on the Santa Monica pier is instantly recognisable from *The Sting*, despite the studio's best efforts to relocate it to Chicago. And, among the tourist tat and strip malls, I found wistfully evocative glimpses of the *noir* world of *Chinatown*.

Apart from tantalisingly arbitrary guidebook tidbits, there was precious little detail on California's awesome film history. Even here, at the very heart of the movie industry, it seemed the boisterous, extrovert young member of the arts family was not yet mature enough to merit serious attention. In the UK, it wasn't until 1996, when this pushy little newcomer had actually reached the age of 100 and could be regarded as respectable, that the first plaques recording cinema history began to appear.

So, in the best tradition of "let's put on the show right here...", I began to compile the worldwide guide myself, expecting to catalogue maybe a hundred or so iconic locations (the *Godfather* mansion, the *Chariots of Fire* beach, the *Exorcist* house and the like). But soon I began to discover the unexpected: dystopian settings for *Blade Runner* dotted around LA; *Lawrence of Arabia*'s 'Middle East' in Seville; alien planetscapes of the *Star Trek* movies in the California desert – and the book began to grow into something much larger.

We're all familiar with the thrill of visiting the site of events – whether real or fictional – that have affected us. And what medium affects us more than film, drawing us directly into the story so that we experience sights and sounds first hand? The revolution in home entertainment has fostered an even closer relationship with movies. When once we were content to go to the cinema and see a film once, video and DVD collections render backdrops to our favourite scenes more familiar, and more inviting, than ever. Ease of travel makes it possible to step through the screen and into those scenes.

So, of course, this is primarily a travel guide, but even if you're staying at home, *The Worldwide Guide to Movie Locations* is a fascinating look at the trickery and the expertise that go into movie-making. Practical problems or budgetary restrictions often prevent filmmakers from shooting on the locations they'd ideally like. There's an unsung genius in the way an inventive director (or location scout) can reorder the world's geography to suit a picture's needs. The Coen brothers, needing a New York restaurant for *Barton Fink*, which was made in Los Angeles, used the gleaming deco interior of the Queen Mary, the old liner permanently berthed at Long Beach. The spectacular Id Club in *Species* is in reality the wildly elaborate foyer of a Hollywood cinema. And when Laurence Olivier returns to his Roman villa in *Spartacus*, the camera misses by inches the kitschily twenties marble statue at the monumental swimming pool of newspaper magnate William Randolph Hearst, where the scene was shot. The list goes on...

But the real joy of this book is for travellers, and I hope you get the chance to visit at least some of the sites. Do go and see. These places may not be here forever: Norma Desmond's *Sunset Blvd.* mansion was bulldozed in the sixties. Since taking photos for this book, the Hawthorne Grill, held up by Honey-Bunny and Pumpkin in *Pulp Fiction*, has been torn down, as has the Ambassador Hotel, a location for films from the 1937 *A Star Is Born* to Tony Scott's *True Romance*. And Glasgow's Volcano nightclub, where Ewan McGregor picked up Kelly Macdonald in *Trainspotting*, is no more.

Where's *Oliver!*?

Five years down the line from the first edition of the *Worldwide Guide* and a frequent question is: "Where's *Oliver!*, or *My Fair Lady*, or *Mary Poppins*? No, these films weren't forgotten, but they were made entirely in the studio, so there are no locations to visit. The famous crescent in Carol Reed's *Oliver!* is not Bath's Royal Crescent, as many people seem to believe. It was built on the backlot of Shepperton Studios. Likewise, every frame of *My Fair Lady* was filmed on soundstages at Burbank, where both Covent Garden and Royal Ascot were (not too faithfully) recreated. The 'London' landmarks of *Mary Poppins* are pure Hollywood, and both *Singin' in the Rain* and *The King and I* were studio-bound.

Studio filming has excluded many classic Hollywood titles of the 30s, 40s and 50s, when equipment was cumbersome, and it was often more convenient to recreate locations within the controllable confines of the studio. A small crew (known as a second unit) would be dispatched to the story's setting, say New York, to film background shots which would then be edited into the final cut to establish the locale. There seems little point including these films, unless the second unit filming goes beyond the basic establishing shot (the Empire State Building, Big Ben...).

A typical example of the way films were put together is *All About Eve*. Set in New York's Theatreland, the film was made largely in the studio, where theatre and night-club interiors were recreated in Hollywood. Only the exteriors needed to be filmed in New York, so why go to the expense of flying stars, along with their hairdressers, make-up artists, psychics, hangers-on and pampered pooches, to the East Coast merely to film them slipping in and out of doorways? The answer was to film the scenes with stand-ins (you'll have no problem distinguishing the carefully-lit studio scenes from the 'newsreel' style New York exteriors). And when a real theatre lobby was needed, the cast was asked to stray no farther than a trip up the coast to San Francisco.

By the 50s, technical advances led to a film-making revolution, with audiences expecting a greater degree of realism. Cinema opened up the world, to show us the streets of New York (*The Naked City*, 1948), the canals of Venice (*Summer Madness*, 1955), the cafés of Paris (*A Bout de Souffle*, 1959) or the north of England (*Billy Liar*, 1963). The subsequent growth in travel has meant that it's no longer enough to watch. We want to visit. Cinema has become the greatest travel brochure you could wish for.

And this is your guide book.

I hope you enjoy the wealth of travel opportunities as much as I have. My top pleasures fall into two categories. There's the buzz that comes with a box-office classic, the instantly recognisable cinematic icon. It's hard to beat the excitement of standing in Luke Skywalker's sunken homestead from *Star Wars*; lingering before the white wooden church, unchanged since Gary Cooper pleaded for help in *High Noon*; or cycling over the bridge that Bruce the Shark swam under to get into the 'safe' inlet in *Jaws*.

But no less exciting are the more personal favourites: exploring the dank, narrow waterways of Venice, every bit as spooky as they appeared in *Don't Look Now*; enjoying a burger and fries in the wonderfully quirky *Bagdad Cafe*; and resisting the urge to tango at the vegetable counter in the supermarket from *Go*. But for me, tops would have to be the tiny Californian coastal resort where Hitchcock filmed *The Birds*. Settling down in front of the TV to watch the Oscars, with a balcony view over Bodega Bay, was close to my idea of movie heaven.

Whatever your tastes, the adventure starts here. Going to the movies will never be quite the same again.

Tony Reeves

London, December 2005

HOW TO USE THE GUIDE

The *Worldwide Guide to Movie Locations* is listed alphabetically by film title – taking note of word spaces (*The Man Who Knew Too Much* comes before *Manhattan*), the only exception being numbered sequels, which are listed in numerical order. Foreign language films are generally listed in the original language (Visconti's *The Leopard* is listed as *Gattopardo, Il*), but there is an alternative titles index at the back of the book. For handy recognition, the year, director and main stars of each film are included at the beginning of the entry. After these details, but before the full entry, the main locations – city, county, US state or country – are listed. Since you might want to check out the movie sites in a particular area, these locations are cross-referenced with a gazetteer at the back of the book.

Apart from listing the key locations you can see and visit, I've also included a record of those which have gone and a note of those which never existed. Fans still turn up in Atlanta hoping to visit Tara, unaware that Scarlett's mansion was no more than a wood and plaster frontage on the Selznick backlot in Culver City. The places you can actually see are picked-out in **bold type**. Since opening hours and admission charges are constantly subject to change, I've not included the details but, wherever possible, I've listed a phone number (with area but not international code) or a website address. If you are planning to visit a particular location, it's always advisable to check ahead. Historic houses in the UK are often closed during winter months, and there's always the possibility that commercial establishments such as hotels, restaurants and bars may have changed name, or ceased business altogether.

Many of these locations advertise themselves and welcome visitors; however just as many are private properties. Feel free to visit and take a discreet look but please don't ever disturb residents or trespass on private property. Any disturbance of people's privacy can only hinder future listings.

To accommodate the slew of new films released since 2001, and not to blow the book up to elephantine proportions, there have had to be some deletions. Don't worry. These titles have been put into storage, alongside Mrs Bates in the Fruit Cellar. You can access this archive online at *www.movie-locations/filmarchive.html*. Corrections and updates can be viewed at *www.movie-locations/updates.html*.

You can find more information – and more photographs – of London-set films in the companion volume *The Worldwide Guide to Movie Locations Presents: London*.

A

A BOUT DE SOUFFLE (aka *Breathless*)
(1959, dir: Jean-Luc Godard)
Jean-Paul Belmondo, Jean Seberg, Daniel Boulanger.
● PARIS, FRANCE; MARSEILLES, FRANCE

Godard's first full-length feature was one of the key films in the move from the confines of the studio, and was shot – apart from the opening scene of Belmondo hotwiring a car in the **Vieux Port of Marseille** – on the streets of **Paris**.

Seberg's hotel: Les Rives de Notre Dame

Seberg's Left Bank hotel, the riverfront Hotel de Suede – as it was in 1959 – lies in the shadow of Notre Dame, and was used as a make-do studio for most of the film's interiors. One of the film's sites that's been given a substantial revamp and, with an eye to its location, a change of name, **Les Rives de Notre Dame** can be seen at **15 quai St Michel** at the junction of rue Xavier Privas (© *42.21.32.76, www.rivesdenotredame.com; metro: St Michel*).

The café, where Belomondo orders a breakfast he can't afford, is now a drugstore. It was Le Royale St Germain, at the intersection of the boulevard St Germain and the rue de Rennes opposite the St Germain des Pres metro station. Wannabe-journalist Seberg is out selling the *New York Herald Tribune* on the **Champs Elysées**, where Belmondo catches up with her. The old office of the *Trib*, out of which Seberg works, has undergone a major facelift (it now houses a pensions company), but the brass plaque to the left of the doorway still records that from 1930 to 1978 this was the paper's home. In front of the office, Godard puts in a cameo appearance as the weaselly snitch who tips off the law. You can see the new frontage just off the Arc de Triomphe end of the Champs, at **21 rue de Berri** (*metro: George V*).

Much of the subsequent action centres around the Champs. The entrances to the **George V metro** station itself are where Belmondo gives the slip to the detectives before striking poses in front of Humphrey Bogart stills in a movie house lobby. The much-modernised cinema is the **Cinema Normandie, 116 bis Champs Elysées**, next to the Lido de Paris. At the top of the Champs stood the Pergola, the spacious first floor café where Seberg meets journalist Van Doude, and southwest is the avenue Montaigne, home of Paris' swishest designer stores. Here, in front of the **Christian Dior store, 30 avenue Montaigne**, Seberg dreams of posh frocks while

The old *New York Herald Tribune* office: Rue de Berri

Belmondo shows off his savvy, knowing that this is the place to make phone calls for free.

Briefly leaving the city centre, Seberg interviews novelist M Parvulesco on the terrace of what was, in 1959, Paris' main airport, **Orly**, about 45 minutes south of the city.

Back on the Champs, it's Seberg's turn to be tailed, through crowds watching a (real) visit of General de Gaulle and President Eisenhower to the Tomb of the Unknown Soldier beneath the Arc de Triomphe. Like Belmondo, Seberg's evasive action also ends, unsurprisingly, in a movie house. She leaves the cops flummoxed, ducking through the **Cinema Mac-Mahon, 5 avenue Mac-Mahon** (© *43.80.24.82*), just off L'Étoile, which is still very much in business and pretty much unchanged.

Seberg dodges the cops: Cinema Mac-Mahon

The photographer's apartment: Rue Campagne Première, Montparnasse

The night scenes shift south of the Seine to the pseud's paradise that was the Left Bank. Belmondo and Seberg take off for St Germain in a stolen car, taking time to admire the sparkling lights of **Place de la Concorde** *en route*. They end up further south in the midst of the clutch of famously arty hangouts on the **boulevard Montparnasse** at its junction with boulevard Raspail (*metro: Vavin*). The

Belmondo gets breathless: Rue Campagne Première, Montparnasse

Kosmos (it's lost the quaint K to become **Le Cosmos**) at **101 boulevard Montparnasse**, and **Le Select** at **99**, the two bars used as backdrop to the scene, are still serving, as is **La Rotonde**, which the couple drive past on the way to the haven of 'Zumbach's girlfriend's place'.

This is the photographer's apartment where the pair spend their last night, only a couple of blocks south of boulevard Montparnasse, at **11 rue Campagne Première**. Running northeast from boulevard Raspail, the quiet side-street has long been a magnet for artists. Modigliani, Miro, Picasso, Ernst, Giacometti and Kandinsky have all, at some time, called it home. Belmondo makes his doomed attempt to outrun a police bullet down the centre of the red-brick road, ending up literally breathless at the southern T-junction with boulevard Raspail (*metro: Raspail*). See also *Breathless*, the LA-set remake.

A.I. ARTIFICIAL INTELLIGENCE
(2001, dir: Steven Spielberg)
Haley Joel Osment, Jude Law, Frances O'Connor.
● **CALIFORNIA; OREGON**

Spielberg is at his best when he's Spielberg, and not trying to be David Lean or, in this case, Stanley Kubrick. This adaptation of Brian Aldiss's sci-fi story *Super Toys Last All Summer Long* trundles tiresomely from one seemingly arbitrary and sentimental ending to another, until you want to go into the projection booth with scissors and put an end to it all. By its nature, most of the film was shot in the studio, where the Gondola and Flesh Fair sets were built in the huge **Spruce Goose Dome** in Long Beach, south LA. Built in 1983 to house Howard Hughes's famous plane, it's been used as a makeshift film studio since the Goose was whisked off to Seattle (interiors for *Batman Forever* and the awful remake of *The Haunting* were shot here). At 415 feet in diameter and 100 feet high, it's the largest geodesic dome in the world.

Henry Swinton (Sam Robards) drives a futuristic car through the Oregon foothills of **Oxbow Regional Park**, in the Sandy River Gorge, eight miles east of Gresham, Multnomah County.

Á PROPOS DE NICE
(1930, dir: Jean Vigo)
● **NICE, FRANCE**

The first of Vigo's three surreal, experimental movies (he died four years later at the age of 29) is a wickedly satirical documentary contrasting the lives of the rich and the poor in France's Riviera city, a favourite resort of the well off since the 19th century. While Cannes and Monaco, flanking Nice on either side, have prospered, and thus suffered from crass redevelopment, Nice – although hardly downmarket – has an endearing, somewhat decaying, down-at-heel feel.

Haunt of the rich: Hotel Negresco, Promenade des Anglais

Vigo, though, turned his camera toward the monied grotesques of the thirties on the **Promenade des Anglais**, the grand seaside parade that was built in the 1820s and supposedly paid for by the local English community to provide work for the

Extravagant grave monuments: Protestant Cemetery

unemployed after the failure of the 1822 orange crop. Of the sumptuous hotels seen here, including the Hotel Ruhl and the Palais de la Mediterranée, only the mega-grandiose **Hotel Negresco, 37 Promenade des Anglais** (© *93.16.64.00, www.hotel-negresco-nice.com*), still lords it over the seafront. This temple to opulence, which houses an enormous chandelier whose twin hangs inside the Kremlin, boasted the presence of twelve kings at its opening. Incidentally, it was outside the Negresco that dancer Isadora Duncan came to a terrible end when a trailing scarf snagged in the wheels of her Bugatti. The Ruhl has been demolished to make way for the bland Casino Ruhl, while the Mediterranée is merely a gutted shell.

Vigo constructs his film around Nice's carnival, still held over the twelve days of Lent until Shrove Tuesday, when King Carnival is ceremonially burned. It's a raucous but good-natured event, with parades and a Battle of the Flowers.

The impressionist jigsaw also takes in the naval fleet, filmed in the beautiful bay at **Villefranche**, just east of Nice, and the extravagantly tasteless grave monuments of the **Protestant Cemetery** on the hill overlooking the old town.

ABOMINABLE DR PHIBES, THE
(1971, dir: Robert Fuest)
Vincent Price, Joseph Cotten, Peter Jeffrey.
● **HERTFORDSHIRE; LONDON**

Dr Phibes' mansion: Immanuel College, Elstree Road

Style and wit triumph over a shoe-string budget and speed of shooting in this horror outing, filmed mostly on campy thirties sets built at Elstree Studios. To see the exterior of Phibes' mansion, head for the Elstree Road between Bushey and Elstree in Hertfordshire. At the junction with the A409 you can't miss the looming tower of the **Immanuel College, 87-91 Elstree Road** – a Victorian gothic extravaganza set in an 11-acre campus, that used to be the Rosary Priory High School, and before that, the Caldecote Towers Hotel. The building can also be seen in Tom Selleck actioner *High Road to China*. But there'll be no more filming, as its grotesque charm has been sabotaged by some horribly inappropriate modern additions (*rail: Elstree or Stanmore*). The cemetery where Phibes and his wife were supposedly laid to rest is the overgrown and creepy old section of **Highgate Cemetery**, on the west side of **Swain Road**, London N6 (*tube: Archway*). The newer section of Highgate is generally open (*admission charge*), but you can only see the much more impressive older section with a guided tour on Sundays.

ABOUT A BOY

(2002, dir: Chris Weitz, Paul Weitz)
Hugh Grant, Nicholas Hoult, Toni Collette.
● LONDON

Meeting single mothers at SPATs: Woodbridge Chapel, Clerkenwell

In theory the teaming of *American Pie* bakers the Weitz brothers with Grant to bring Nick Hornby's novel to the screen seemed positively gruesome. Yet this one works.

The neighbourhood, where Will Freeman (Grant) flouts John Donne (or is that Jon Bon Jovi) with his solitary island life is **Clerkenwell**, once radical working-class (Lenin once edited the Bolshevik newspaper *Iskra* at 37a Clerkenwell Green), now media-darlingville. You won't find the entrance to his no-frills, techno-head flat, though, which was built for the movie at the St James Walk side entrance to **16-18 St James Walk**, at the corner of Sekforde Street. Will shops at **Comptoir Gascon, 63 Charterhouse Street** (℗ *020.7608.0851*), a mouthwatering French deli (an offshoot of restaurant Club Gascon and Cellar Gascon at 57 West Smithfield, alongside the Church of St Bartholomew, where Grant famously didn't get married at the climax of *Four Weddings*. **St James Clerkenwell, Clerkenwell Close**, is the church where Will doesn't volunteer to help at the drop-in centre (you can see the church again in *Dance With a Stranger*), and the nearby **Woodbridge Chapel, Haywards Place**, is where he does attend SPATs (Single Parents Alone Together) as a cheesy ploy to meet single mothers.

Marcus sets up a date for his mum: Otto Dining Lounge, Sutherland Avenue, Maida Vale

Grant's 'island' apartment: St James Walk, Clerkenwell

Will waits for his date outside the **BFI London IMAX Cinema, South Bank, 1 Charlie Chaplin Walk, Waterloo**, SE1 (℗ *020.7902.1234, www.bfi.org.uk/imax*). You can't miss the giant illuminated cinema in what used to be the old concrete 'bullring' in front of Waterloo Station. Big, big, big is the order of the day. Overwhelming cinematic experience or monumental headache? Your call. Part of the BFI, the 477-seat cinema, with the UK's largest screen (20 by 26 metres), opened in 1999, with the emphasis on spectacular travelogues, occasional 3D features and showings of classic movies (which don't occupy the full giant screen).

Home of Marcus and his hippy mum: Oseney Crescent, Kentish Town

Grant tries to come clean: Hakkasan, Hanway Place

He splits up with a series of increasingly enraged women at the spacious, minimalist **Otto Dining Lounge, 215 Sutherland Avenue**, at **Maida Vale** (℗ *020.7266.3131*).

31 Oseney Crescent, Kentish Town, north of Camden, was home to terminally depressed thrift-shop hippy Fiona (Collette) and her son Marcus (Hoult). By the Penguin Pool of **London Zoo**, Will and Marcus chat about guy stuff. The hairdresser, where Grant gets a call from Hoult, is **Parsons Skott, 243 Westbourne Grove, Notting Hill** (℗ *020.7243.0939, www.parsonsskott.co.uk*). **1 St Stephen's Crescent**, opposite St Stephen's Church at Talbot Road, Notting Hill, is home to single mother Rachel (Rachel Weisz). Will tries to unravel his web of deceit in **Hakkasan, 8 Hanway Place** (℗ *020.7927.7000*). Forget the rather dingy sidestreet, it's high, high style in this Chinese restaurant from the creators of the Wagamama noodle chain – the interior did scoop a design award. The school concert, where Will risks his cool to accompany Marcus's shaky version of 'Killing Me Softly', is in **Acton Town Hall, Acton High Street**.

ABRE LOS OJOS (aka *Open Your Eyes*)

(1997, dir: Alejandro Amenábar)
Eduardo Noriega, Penélope Cruz, Najwa Nimri.
● SPAIN

Remade in Hollywood as *Vanilla Sky* by Cameron Crowe with Tom Cruise and Penélope Cruz. This original was filmed in **Madrid**.

ABYSS, THE

(1989, dir: James Cameron)
Ed Harris, Michael Biehn, Mary Elizabeth Mastrantonio.
● SOUTH CAROLINA

Close encounters of the submarine kind when an oil rig crew aboard the *Deepcore* submersible drilling platform in the Caribbean investigate something very strange under the sea. The nightmarish production (which star Ed Harris refused to talk about) fared poorly on initial release, but was finally rewarded with a successful second life on video, which at last makes sense of the plot by restoring the vital tsunami – giant tidal wave – climax.

Cameron's locations reflect the hard, industrial feel of his movies – *Aliens* used a power station, *T2* disused steel mills – *The Abyss'* underwater scenes were filmed in an uncompleted nuclear power station. The Duke Power Company's Cherokee Power Station never went on line and was subsequently abandoned only to be snapped up by movie entrepreneur Earl Owensby – owner of the Owensby Studios in North Carolina. He rented the facility out to *The Abyss'* production company, who built the film's *Deepcore* sets inside the two gigantic concrete tanks. When filled, they became, at 7.5 million gallons and 2.6 million gallons, two of the largest freshwater containers in the world. You can see them just outside **Gaffney**, 45 miles east of Greenville on Route 29, South Carolina.

ACCATTONE

(1961, dir: Pier Paolo Pasolini)
Franco Citti, Franca Pasut, Silvana Corsini.
● **ROME, ITALY**

Pasolini's first film, the relentlessly downbeat story of doomed thief and pimp Vittorio (*aka* Accattone – 'Scrounger'), starred the then-unknown non-actor Franco Citti, who went on to be a Pasolini regular and appeared as a Sicilian minder in the *Godfather* movies. Contributions to the script came from Citti's younger brother Sergio (who actually plays his brother in the movie) and director-to-be Bernardo Bertolucci. Filming in Rome, the movie studiously avoids the *Roman Holiday* sights and picturesque ruins in favour of the dismal slums and concrete tower blocks of the suburbs. The one touch of Ancient Romanesque is Stella's tearful meeting with her manipulative pimp among the statues of the **Via Appia Antica** after a disastrous first attempt at prostitution. Most of the movie was filmed in the middle of the **Pigneto district**, east of the city. The first shots were filmed in the slums of **Via Fanfulla da Lodi**, which runs between Via Prenestina and Via del Pigneto.

ACCIDENT

(1967, dir: Joseph Losey)
Dirk Bogarde, Stanley Baker, Michael York.
● **OXFORDSHIRE; SURREY; LONDON**

Cool observation rules in one of the major Pinter/Losey/Bogarde collaborations of the sixties, as the car-crash death of aristocratic student Michael York triggers off a series of flashbacks charting the status games played on a university campus. It was filmed largely around **Oxford University**, though the site of the titular accident is miles to the south in Surrey.

The university locations include Oxford's **St John's College** on **St John's Street**, where mousy don Bogarde experiences a bout of mid-life angst. The quads here are open to the public, usually on weekday afternoons, but check in advance for opening times. The entrance to Bogarde's rooms can be seen at the southeast corner of the elaborately gargoyled inner **Canterbury Quad**. In the grounds of **Magdalen College** (*admission charge*) you

can see the bridge where Michael York invites Bogarde for an ultimately humiliating punt along the Cherwell. The entrance is on the High Street toward Magdalen Bridge. Being a Pinter adaptation, the boys have to play their little games, and here it's a bizarre 'football game', which must still give the film's insurers nightmares. The rough and tumble – roughly based on the Eton Wall Game – was shot in

Bogarde's rooms: Canterbury Quad, St John's College, Oxford

the classical grandeur of Robert Adams' Great Hall of **Syon House, Brentford**, where Bogarde keeps goal in front of the cast of a Dying Gladiator (even in 1773 this bronze copy cost a cool £300 when bought in Rome). Syon House, set in grounds landscaped by Capability Brown, is on the north bank of the Thames eight miles west of London, off the A4 between Brentford and Isleworth (*tube/rail: Gunnersbury Park*). The Great Hall is open to the public (© 020.8560.0881, *www.syon-park.co.uk; admission charge*). You can see more of its elegant rooms and corridors in *The Madness of King George*. Bogarde's house, scene of the accident, is **Norwood Farm Hall,** on **Elveden Road** north of the Esher bypass, Cobham, Surrey (*rail: Oxshott*).

ACE IN THE HOLE (aka *The Big Carnival*)

(1951, dir: Billy Wilder)
Kirk Douglas, Jan Sterling, Porter Hall.
● **NEW MEXICO; LOS ANGELES, CALIFORNIA**

Washed up in the Mid-West, wise-ass New York hack Kirk Douglas sees a chance to break back into the big-time by milking the human interest story of a cave-in victim, even when it means holding off a rescue attempt. The hick town home of Douglas' paper, the *Sun-Bulletin*, is **Albuquerque**, central New Mexico, where director Wilder grabbed verité-style shots using a concealed camera mounted on a truck.

Although the underground scenes were filmed on a mock-up back at the **Paramount Studios** on **Melrose Avenue** in Hollywood, the desert location really is New Mexico. You won't be able to follow the trail to the old Indian Cliff Dwellings at the Minosa Trading Post where Richard Benedict was entombed, though. The film used a gigantic set, claimed at the time to be the largest constructed for any movie other than a war film. Towering 237 feet into the air and covering an area 1,200 by 1,600 feet, it incorporated the cliff dwellings, the Indian settlement and the ensuing carnival. You can visit the breathtaking New Mexico desert where the mammoth set was built some 20 miles to the west of **Gallup**, I-40, on the Arizona border. I-40, incidentally, is part of the old Route 66.

ACE VENTURA, PET DETECTIVE

(1994, dir: Tom Shadyac)
Jim Carrey, Sean Young, Courteney Cox.
● **MIAMI, FLORIDA**

Ace Ventura's apartment: Campton Apartments, Washington Avenue

Udo Kier's seafront estate: Villa Vizcaya, Coconut Grove

Jim Carrey shot to overnight megabucks stardom with his love-it-or-loathe-it manic shtick, as the animal-friendly 'tec tracking down the Miami Dolphins' kidnapped mascot Snowflake. It was filmed around Miami, Florida, where Carrey keeps a secret menagerie in his 'Surfside' apartment, the **Campton Apartments, 1455 Washington Avenue** – alongside the artsy rock venue Cameo Theatre at 1445 near Espanola West – in the newly-revitalised art deco district of South Beach.

The football stadium Snowflake disappears from is the real home of the Miami Dolphins, the **Pro Player Stadium** (formerly and famously the Joe Robbie Stadium), **2269 NW 199th Street**, a hi-tech 73,000 seater sports arena about 16 miles northwest of downtown Miami. If you fancy catching a game, there's a Metro-Dade Transit Authority bus from town (© *305.638.6700, www.proplayerstadium.com*).

You can also visit the exclusive seafront villa of fish-collector Udo Kier, where Carrey skips the party to find a shark in the cellar. It's **Villa Vizcaya, 3251 South Miami Avenue** at 32nd Road in Coconut Grove on the coast of South Miami, built in 1916 as the winter home of magazine founder James Deering. A smaller-scale Xanadu, the Italian Renaissance mansion is packed with European artefacts – Roman sarcophagi, Catherine de Medici's fireplace, the contents of Italian villas. There are formal gardens and tours of the building (© *305.579.2708, www.vizcayamuseum.org*; admission charge). A frequently-used location, you can also see the villa in *Absence of Malice*, *Airport '77* and *Any Given Sunday*.

The African villages of the dismal sequel, *Ace Ventura: When Nature Calls*, were constructed on the **777 Ranch**, at **Hondo** near San Antonio, Texas (© *830. 426.3476*). A 15,000 acre wildlife reserve, the ranch is open to the public for safari tours and, yes, you can ride the same zebra-striped jeep seen in the movie. More scenes were shot in Texas, at **Camp Waldemar**, **Botany Bay Plantation** and **Cherokee Plantation** in South Carolina; and in Canada, at the **Panorama Resort**, British Columbia.

ACROSS 110th STREET

(1972, dir: Barry Shear)
Anthony Quinn, Anthony Franciosa, Yaphet Kotto.
● NEW YORK CITY

Quentin Tarantino pays homage to this classic seventies actioner by playing Bobby Womack and JJ Johnson's theme tune over the credits of *Jackie Brown*. Black and Italian gangs vie for control of Harlem, while black and Italian cops jockey for control of the precinct, in this gritty, documentary-style thriller. Taken from the novel *Across 110th* by Wally Ferris, the movie makes terrific use of real locations. The opening credits sequence sets the tone as the white mobsters' '68 Cadillac drives north through Manhattan to **110th Street**, the northern boundary of Central Park, dividing the Upper West Side from Harlem (the road sign which metamorphoses into the title credit is 'Lenox Avenue/110th Street'), then on to **125th Street**, past Harlem landmark the **Apollo Theater**, at **253 West** (see *Malcolm X* for full details). The Italians' party was shot at Central Park's southern boundary, **Central Park South**.

Of the 60 or so locations used, the majority were in Harlem itself, where the production shot in real police stations, bars and private apartments. There's not much to search out as many of the buildings were already condemned, a boon to film-makers who wanted to pepper walls with bullet holes. Still under construction at the time of filming, though, was the half-built high-rise from which Tony Franciosa and his henchmen dangle the hapless Ed Bernard. It's the **Federal Building, 125th Street** at Lenox Avenue, Harlem. The final, bloody shoot-out is on **Lenox Avenue** between 141st and 142nd Streets.

ADAM'S RIB

(1949, dir: George Cukor)
Katharine Hepburn, Spencer Tracy, Judy Holliday.
● LOS ANGELES, CALIFORNIA; NEW YORK CITY

One of the great Tracy-Hepburn comedies, with lawyer Hepburn defending Judy Holliday against a charge of attempted murder, while husband Tracy acts for the prosecution. Set in New York, it was filmed mainly on MGM's

Tracy and Hepburn clash in court: Criminal Courts Building, Centre Street

stages in Culver City, LA, using a few location scenes to add authenticity. The office, outside which Holliday waits for erring husband Tom Ewell before following him down into the subway, is on **Bowling Green, Broadway** at Battery Place, Lower Manhattan. Tracy and Hepburn drive to court on **Franklin D Roosevelt Drive** alongside the East River – courtesy of a little back projection. The forbidding court exterior, with its ironic motto, 'Equal and exact justice to all men of whatever state or persuasion', can still be seen in Manhattan's Chinatown. It's the **Criminal Courts Building**, known as 'The Tombs', **100 Centre Street** between Leonard and White Streets.

Hepburn and Tracy make up at the tax office: Bayard Street

The accountant's office, where Tracy and Hepburn reunite while filing their tax returns, is on **Bayard Street**, in the shadow of The Tombs, beneath the Bridge of Sighs, which linked the Municipal Prison to the courthouse.

ADDAMS FAMILY, THE

(1991, dir: Barry Sonnenfeld)
Raul Julia, Anjelica Huston, Christopher Lloyd.
● LOS ANGELES, CALIFORNIA

Coen brothers' cinematographer Sonnenfeld turned first-time director with the movie version of the sixties TV show of the fifties cartoons. It was shot at the **Hollywood Center Studios, 1040 Las Palmas Avenue**, mainly on Stage 3/8, which coincidentally happened to be the studio where the original TV series was filmed. This studio, built in 1919 as the Jasper Studio, survived under various names until, in 1980, it became the ill-fated Zoetrope Studios as part of Francis Ford Coppola's scheme to run a large independent production facility.

Sadly, there's no Addams Mansion to see. The frontage of the house was built for the film on a mountain overlooking the Burbank Hills at **Toluca Lake**. (The TV pilot did use a real house, on Adams Boulevard, just south of Hollywood. You can still see it during the show's opening credits, but a painting was substituted for the run of the series.) The film's locations include the charity auction, where the Addamses buy back their own finger trap, which was filmed in LA's 1927 club and theatre complex, the **Ebell of Los Angeles, 4401 Wilshire Boulevard** at South Lucerne Boulevard, midtown (see *Forrest Gump* for full details). The school theatre, where Wednesday and Pugsley stage a Peckinpahesque version of Shakespeare, is the **Brentwood Theatre** on the grounds of the **Sawtelle Veteran's Administration Medical Center, 11301 Wilshire Boulevard** in Westside (© 800.233.3123, www.brentwoodtheatre.com). The Wampum Court Motel, to which the family are exiled, was in **Sylmar**, northern LA, off the Golden State Freeway in the San Fernando Valley.

The sequel, Addams Family Values, was shot around California: the very WASP Camp Chippewa – America's Foremost Facility for Privileged Young Adults – is **Sequoia Lake, Sequoia National Forest**; though the arrival of the campers was shot at **Camp Sequoia** itself; while the cheesy Thanksgiving musical pageant, gloriously subverted by Wednesday, was staged on the other side of the lake at **Camp Tulequoia**.

"Tack-o-rama…": Mario's Palace, Broken Hill, inside…

ADVENTURES OF PRISCILLA, QUEEN OF THE DESERT, THE

(1994, dir: Stephan Elliott)
Terence Stamp, Hugo Weaving, Guy Pearce.
● NEW SOUTH WALES, AUSTRALIA; SOUTH AUSTRALIA; NORTHERN TERRITORY, AUSTRALIA

The Abba-inspired three-pack of drag queens in this feelgood

…and outside

Aussie road movie take a journey through the outback in a silver-painted bus, christened 'Priscilla', to a booking in Alice Springs. The trip starts out from **Sydney** – oohs and aahs for the **Opera House** and the **Harbour Bridge** – before striking out across the inhospitable desert of New South Wales. The first major stop-off is **Broken Hill**, an outback mining town about 750 miles west of Sydney, where Mitzi, Felicia and Bernadette raise eyebrows when they go shopping on **Argent Street**, the main drag (pun definitely intended).

The eccentric hotel the girls check into is **Mario's Palace, 227 Argent Street** at Sulphide Street (yes, all the street names – Bromide, Chloride, Oxide, reading like a chemistry textbook – reflect the town's mining history) (© 80.88.1699). Mario, who appears as himself in the movie, is likely to be presiding. If you're in the area, a few miles northwest of Broken Hill is the ghost town of Silverton, one of the most used Australian locations (see *Mad Max 2* for details), and a few miles further on from here you'll find the next stop, the **Mundi Mundi Plain Lookout**, where the dragsters find themselves stranded after Priscilla breaks down.

Help appears in the shape of good-hearted Bob and his strange wife, Cynthia, who give the three a lift to **Coober Pedy**, a further 500 miles west in central South Australia. Another mining town, Coober Pedy is tougher, rougher and even hotter than Broken Hill. The terrain is so inhospitable, in fact, that most dwellings are built underground (the name means 'white man in a hole'). The strange mining-scarred landscape is another favourite location, providing the post-apocalyptic wastelands of *Mad Max Beyond Thunderdome* and Wim Wenders' *Until the End of the World*. If you want to try out the subterranean accommodation, the stopover here is the three-star **Underground Motel, Catacomb Road** (© 86.72.5324), to the north of town.

From here the journey heads north a few hundred miles into Northern Territory, finally arriving at the ostensible destination, **Alice Springs**, where it's best bib and tucker for the dressy nightspot they perform at – **Lasseter's Casino** on **Barrett Drive**.

King's Canyon is the site of Felicia's triumphant climb. The spectacular gorge, a cousin of the USA's Grand Canyon, is in the **Watarrka National Park** at the western end of **Ernest Giles Road**, a couple of hundred miles west of Alice Springs. The original script specified the much more iconic Ayers Rock – and what an image that would have been – but Ayers (Uluru)

Felicia fulfils her dream: King's Canyon, Watarrka National Park

is a significant feature of Aboriginal culture, and the idea of three drag queens traipsing over it was a complete no-no.

ADVENTURES OF ROBIN HOOD, THE

(1938, dir: William Keighley; Michael Curtiz)
Errol Flynn, Olivia de Havilland, Basil Rathbone.
● CALIFORNIA

This great Errol Flynn vehicle cost $1.9 million, yet surprisingly recouped only $1.5 million at the box office. It proved enormously expensive because, as well as the sets, they used the spanking new Technicolor system.

Sherwood Forest is **Bidwell Park, Chico**, with its authentic oaks and sycamores. And its less authentic wild vines. Not to mention the plaster trees and rocks imported by art director Carl Jules Weyl.

Chico, 30 miles east of I-5 and halfway between Sacramento and Redding, Northern California, is actually built around the ten mile-long park, which was donated by the widow of city founder William Bidwell. Here is the spot where Flynn's men stage the raid on Basil Rathbone's treasure caravan. At **Big Chico Creek**, running through **Chico Canyon** in the park, Robin challenges Little John to a longstaff fight and duels with Friar Tuck in the creek.

Robin Hood's camp, site of the huge banquet following the treasure raid, when Olivia de Havilland begins to thaw out, was about a mile from the park entrance, around Hooker, the world's largest oak tree – 92 feet tall, 149 feet across its branches and named after British naturalist Sir Joseph Hooker. Bidwell Park was also used for some exterior shots in *Gone With the Wind*. Chico is on the Seattle-Sacramento railway line, and also on the north-south Greyhound route (© *Visitors Bureau: 916.342.4258*).

The archery tournament, where the too-cocky Robin gets arrested, was filmed in Busch Gardens, Pasadena. Don't bother to look for them. The gardens, seen also in *Citizen Kane*, have long since gone the way of many of LA's great landmarks. Extra shots for the attack on the treasure caravan were filmed in the **Sherwood Lake** and **Sherwood Forest** area. No, not on a location trip to England – this Sherwood Forest can be found about 15 miles west of LA, south of Westlake Village on Potrero Road, just off Highway 101 near the Santa Monica Mountains. The name is no coincidence, as it comes from the area's use as a location in the 1922 Douglas Fairbanks Robin Hood movie.

The lower part of Nottingham Castle (its upper reaches are a matte painting) was built on the old Warners' Calabasas Ranch. This too has gone. The area is now a golf course and housing development south of Ventura Freeway on the road toward Westlake. The streets of Nottingham are 'Dijon Street' on the Warners' Burbank backlot, and the interiors were shot here too. In the Lighting Prop Shop on the **Warners' Studio Tour** you can still see the chandeliers from the production, along with other treasures, such as the lamps from Rick's Bar in *Casablanca*. This tour, unlike the Universal Studios theme park, is the real thing – a small-scale guided tour around the surprisingly unchanged and low-tech lot where Jack Warner kept

his stars on a short leash and his movies on a tight budget. You need to book ahead (© *818.954.1951*) and you'll find the tour entrance at **4000 Warner Boulevard** off the Ventura Freeway, Burbank.

ADVISE AND CONSENT

(1962, dir: Otto Preminger)
Don Murray, Charles Laughton, Henry Fonda.
● WASHINGTON DC; LOS ANGELES, CALIFORNIA

A cracking cast, including Charles Laughton in his last role as a scheming Southern senator, have a ball in the White House when there's trouble as President Franchot

Charles Laughton investigates: Treasury Building, Washington DC

Tone attempts to appoint liberal Henry Fonda as Secretary of State. The astonishing amount of co-operation Preminger managed to get from government departments for a film exposing chicanery, blackmail and closet homosexuality seems to indicate an unhealthy pride in their Machiavellian image.

The movie was filmed almost entirely on real DC locations; virtually the only purpose-built set is the thoroughly convincing full-size recreation of the Senate Chamber (a long-standing rule forbids photography here), at Columbia Studios on Gower Street in Hollywood. Alan Drury, author of the original book, sits behind one of the hundred desks.

The centre of all the game-playing and manipulating is, of course, the **Capitol**, home of the US Congress, where scenes were filmed in the **Great Rotunda** beneath the capitol's dome, and in the historic **Reception Room** just off the Senate Chamber. The building is open to the public (© *202.225.6827*) and there are free guided tours (though when the Senate or House are in session you'll need to show ID and get a pass from the Appointment Desk for the Senate side or the Doorkeeper's office for the House side). The tour entrance is on East Capitol Street, Capitol Hill (*metro: Capitol South, Union Station*).

Charles Laughton arranges a clandestine meeting with the mysterious 'Mr Fletcher' on the Ellipse of the **Mall**, the two-mile stretch of lawn neatly separating DC into north and south, in front of the **Washington Monument**, the 555-foot obelisk on the Mall at 15th Street (there's a free elevator to the top if you're willing to queue) (*metro: Smithsonian*). He investigates the employment record of weaselly Burgess Meredith at the **Treasury Building, Pennsylvania Avenue NW** at 15th Street. If you book in advance (© *202.622.0896*; *metro: Farragut West, McPherson Square*) you can tour the magnificent interior of this imposing Greek Revival building. The canteen, where Don Murray receives one of the series of threatening phone calls, is also in the Treasury Building.

The hearing of the 'Sub-committee of the Senate Foreign Relations Committee' – which tries, unsuccessfully, to discredit Fonda – was filmed in the **Caucus Room**.

Political machinations: US Capitol Building, Washington DC

The airport, used by Murray for his stealthy trip to New York, is **DCA**, Washington National, over the Potomac, three-and-a-half miles south of downtown on the George Washington Memorial Parkway. Franchot Tone's address to the White House Press Corps was shot in the ballroom of the Sheraton-Park Hotel, now the **Sheraton Carlton, 923 16th Street NW** at K Street (*© 202.638.2626 or 800.325.3535; metro: Farragut West, McPherson Square*), in the Crystal Room, where DC journos do regularly interview politicians.

AFRICAN QUEEN, THE

(1951, dir: John Huston)
Humphrey Bogart, Katharine Hepburn, Robert Morley.
● **ZAIRE; UGANDA; LONDON; LOS ANGELES, CALIFORNIA**

As WWI breaks out, Hepburn takes Bogart gunning for the beastly Hun, who've caused the death of her preacher-brother in German East Africa. There's a surprising amount of location filming in Africa for the period – seemingly as an excuse for macho director Huston to go hunting elephants (see Peter Viertel's thinly-disguised book of the shoot, *White Hunter, Black Heart*, or Clint Eastwood's film version). Katharine Hepburn has also penned her own wonderfully idiosyncratic version of events in *The Making of The African Queen, or How I Went to Africa with Bogart, Bacall and Huston and Almost Lost My Mind*.

Even so, much of the African jungle was recreated at Worton Hall Studios in Isleworth, southwest London. The interior of Robert Morley's First Methodist Church at Kungdu was built here, to match an exterior constructed in Africa. A none-too-convincing double stands in for Morley, who never left England – just look at the cross-cutting between Hepburn with Morley in London and Hepburn with the congregation in Africa. The doomed church and the village of Kungdu were built on the shore of Lake Albert at **Port Butiaba, Uganda**, up near the border with Zaire. Morley's funeral was filmed in Zaire itself (then the Congo), on a hillside about two-and-a-half miles upriver from the village of **Biondo**, on the **Ruiki** – the river which stands in for the Ulanga in the early scenes of the *Queen* chugging down to confront the Germans.

The *Queen* going over the falls is a model made by monks from the local monastery at Ponthierville in Zaire

Still in service: the *African Queen*, Key Largo, Florida

(nuns made the tiny Bogart and Hepburn), filmed on the falls above the town, while the German fort at Shona was shot back at Worton Hall.

The reedy lake where a becalmed Hepburn and Bogart finally confront the *Louisa* is a small offshoot of Lake Albert at Murchison Falls, up the Nile among the crocs and the hippos, now **Kabalego Falls** in Uganda's National Park of the same name. They've changed since the movie filmed here. Once, the Nile was forced under pressure through a tiny gap in the rocks, but flooding in 1961 burst through the rocks and there are now two falls. Although the area suffered greatly during Uganda's recent troubled history, the park – Uganda's largest – is now open again. Paraa Safari Lodge and Chobe Safari Lodge, the two camps nearest the Falls are once again functioning after having been destroyed and looted. If you plan to visit, it's still a good idea to check ahead on local conditions.

The ending, with the scuppered little steamer finally blowing the gunboat to smithereens, filmed back in Isleworth again. The *African Queen* itself wasn't really blown up at all. It still exists and you can see it at Key Largo, first of the Florida Keys on Route 1 at Florida's southern tip. It's been berthed outside the **Holiday Inn, 99701 Overseas Highway, Key Largo, Oceanside** since the early eighties, though it does occasionally scuttle off to appear in parades around the US (*© 305.451.2121, www.holidayinnkeylargo.com*).

AFTER HOURS

(1985, dir: Martin Scorsese)
Griffin Dunne, Rosanna Arquette, Verna Bloom.
● **NEW YORK CITY**

The Terminal Bar: The Emerald Pub, Spring Street, SoHo

Manhattan's SoHo district is the setting for the best of eighties 'yuppie nightmare' genre movies. Word processor Griffin Dunne ventures down to this expensive, if rundown, artsy enclave to meet the goofy Rosanna Arquette. If you really want to follow him, take the subway down to **Spring Street**, the station where the near-penniless Dunne fails to talk his way onto the platform when ticket prices are suddenly hiked up. **28 Howard Street** at Crosby Street is the spacious loft of dour sculptress Kiki Bridges where Arquette inconsiderately conks out.

A few blocks west you can sample burgers in the wonderfully stylish stainless-steel diner which Dunne scuttles back to through the course of an increasingly frantic night. It's the **Moondance Diner, 80 Sixth Avenue** at Grand Street in SoHo (see *Spider-Man* for details).

Further west still is the Terminal Bar, where John Heard pours beer and Dunne keeps company with a brace of leather queens. If you want to try a

Rosanna Arquette conks out: Howard Street, SoHo

Griffin Dunne finds shelter: Moondance Diner, Sixth Avenue, SoHo

Dunne's workplace: Metropolitan Life Tower, Madison Avenue

beer here, it's an Irish tap room, the **Emerald Pub, 308 Spring Street** at Renwick Street, and over the road at **307** you can see the apartment of 'Miss Beehive 1965', disaffected barmaid Teri Garr. Heard's place, where Dunne's problems escalate after he's mistaken for a burglar, was further along the road on the corner of Greene Street at 128 Spring Street. The site has since been redeveloped. The elaborate iron gates of Dunne's workplace, outside which he's finally dumped, are those of the **Metropolitan Life Tower, Madison Avenue** between 23rd and 24th Streets by Madison Square Park.

AGE D'OR, L'

(1930, dir: Luis Buñuel)
Gaston Modot, Lya Lys, Max Ernst.
● **PARIS, FRANCE; SPAIN**

Riots at the film's release: Le Studio 28, Montmartre

Buñuel and his co-writer Salvador Dali set out to top the eye-slitting and sexual symbolism of their first collaboration, *Un Chien Andalou*, with a provocatively incendiary mix of sex, scatology and blasphemy (originally titled *La Bête Andalouse*). They succeeded in spades. During the film's first run, at Studio 28 in Paris, riots broke out, led by an unholy alliance of outraged rightwing Catholics, patriots and anti-Semites. The screen was showered with ink and the foyer exhibition of Surrealist art was destroyed. Nevertheless, more than 60 years on, **Le Studio 28** (named after the year it opened) is still showing movies, and you can visit it at **10 rue de Tholoze** in Montmartre (*metro: Blanche or Abesses*). *L'Age d'Or* itself was immediately banned, and it remained virtually unshown until the early seventies.

It's been claimed that the villa seen in the movie is the home of the Vicomte de Noailles, the wealthy aristocrat who funded many Surrealist projects, but although the movie was conceived and written here, it was largely filmed in Paris. Nevertheless, the Villa de Noailles was the centre of the hi-jinks and zany parties with which Dali, Picasso and others tried desperately to shock the bourgeoisie. And Man Ray did shoot one of his surreal films here. You'll find the Villa de Noailles in Parc St-Bernard,

The Dali-esque coastline: Cabo de Creus, Cataluña

Hyères, in the south of France, on the N96 between Toulon and St Tropez. Built for the Noailles in 1923, and recently restored, there are guided tours around the villa on Friday afternoons from mid-June to mid-September (book in advance from the Tourist Office, © 04.94.65.18.55).

A mixture of silent and sound footage, much of *L'Age d'Or* is studio-shot. The silent scenes were shot at the **Billancourt Studios, 50 Quai du Pont-du-Jour** on the Seine's north bank in southwest Paris (*metro: Billancourt or Marcel Sembat*), and the sound sequences at the Studios de la Tobis, Epinay-sur-Seine. Exteriors were also filmed at Montmorency, Seine-et-Oise, and in the 16th Arrondissement.

The striking, Dali-esque landscape of the opening scene is **Cabo de Creus**, on the Costa Brava, Cataluña. The rocky outcrop is the tail-end of the Pyrenees, trailing out to form Spain's most easterly point. The young Dali holidayed at nearby Cadaques, and in later life lived at Port Lligat.

AGE OF INNOCENCE, THE

(1993, dir: Martin Scorsese)
Daniel Day-Lewis, Michelle Pfeiffer, Winona Ryder.
● **NEW YORK; PENNSYLVANIA; PARIS, FRANCE**

Scorsese's lush film of Edith Wharton's novel used a variety of period locations around New York State to conjure up the pre-high-rise Manhattan of the 1870s, including frat houses, yacht clubs, gravel pits, private homes and clubs, although the New York Academy of Music, where Daniel Day-Lewis first claps eyes on Michelle Pfeiffer during a performance of *Faust*, was actually filmed in Philadelphia. The impressive red and gilt opera house is the **Philadelphia Academy of Music, South Broad Street** and **Locust Street** (© 215.893.1999, www.academyofmusic.org), home of the Philadelphia Orchestra. An ideal setting, the opulent interior of the building, which dates from 1857, is modelled after La Scala in Milan.

Back in New York, the Beauforts' house, to which everyone retires for the post-opera ball, can be found bang in the centre of Manhattan. It's the **National Arts Club, 15 Gramercy Park South** (© 212.475.3424, www.national-artsclub.org) at Irving Place in the Gramercy district (*subway: 23rd Street or 14th Street and Union Square, Routes 4, 5 and 6*).

Previously known as the Tilden House, the Victorian gothic building was home to Samuel J Tilden, the city Governor who

The opera house: Philadelphia Academy of Music, South Broad Street

Daniel Day-Lewis and Winona Ryder in the white aviary: Enid A Haupt Conservatory, Bronx Park

brought about the downfall of the notoriously corrupt 'Boss' Tweed, builder of the New York County Courthouse. In 1874 the house was remodelled by the co-designer of Central Park, Calvert Vaux, while the period redecoration added for the movie so pleased the members that they kept it. If you're lucky, you may get a peek inside as the club occasionally houses exhibitions. Be aware, there's a surprisingly strict dress code: no Spandex or Lycra (fair enough), no T-shirts or tank tops, no stirrup pants or capri pants, and 'no denim of any type or in any color'. So there. (© *212.475.3424, www.nationalartsclub.org*). You can see more of it, including the exterior, in Woody Allen's *Manhattan Murder Mystery*. Filming also took place at **Old Westbury Gardens** on Long Island (see *North by Northwest* for details).

The town of **Troy**, on the Hudson River's east bank across from Albany, upstate New York, stood in for 19th century New York. Once a thriving business centre to rival Manhattan, the town failed to achieve the same success and, fortunately for the film-makers, missed out on the high-rise redevelopment. 23rd Street exteriors were filmed here, while **River Street**, downtown Troy, stands in for turn-of-the-century Wall Street. Mrs Mingott's pooch-filled salon in 'a wilderness near Central Park' is the **Phi Kappa Phi Fraternity House, 49 Second Street**, of Troy's Rensselaer Polytechnic Institute (Troy is in Rensselaer County).

Daniel Day-Lewis' parents' house is the **Federal Gale House, First Street**, a Hall of Residence of another of Troy's three colleges, the Russell Sage College. The law office is the **Rice Building** at First and River Streets. **Washington Park** stands in for Manhattan's Gramercy Park. Troy has a Visitor Information Center which you'll find at 251 River Street (© *518.270.8667*). The stretch of River Street south of the centre was period dressed for the movie and, although most of the stores are empty, the set decoration has been kept.

Over in the Bronx you can find the delicate white aviary in which Day-Lewis walks with Winona Ryder. The **Enid A Haupt Conservatory of Bronx's Botanical Gardens, 200th Street** at Bronx Boulevard in Bronx Park (© *718.220.8700, www.nybg.org; admission charge*) might look familiar to Londoners, since its design is based on Kew Gardens' Great Palm House.

Other US locations in the New York area included the Boston park where Day-Lewis casually bumps

The Beauforts' house: National Arts Club, Gramercy Park South

into Pfeiffer (in Brooklyn) and the formal garden in Florida, where he tries to gee-up the marriage plans (actually Long Island). The European scenes, however, really were shot in Paris, including inside the **Louvre**.

AGONY AND THE ECSTASY, THE
(1965, dir: Carol Reed)
Charlton Heston, Rex Harrison, Diane Cilento.
● **ITALY**

It's all agony and little ecstasy in this dull 15th century sitcom, as slow and temperamental interior designer Charlton Heston tussles with tightwad Pope Rex Harrison. Heston is meant to be Michelangelo, commissioned to paint the ceiling of the Sistine Chapel. The real chapel was, not surprisingly, out of the question for filming, and was duplicated in Rome's Cinecittà Studios, where sections of the plaster set were gradually removed to reveal a huge photographic reproduction of Michelangelo's original. The 'wet plaster' which constantly drips into Heston's mouth is chocolate pudding, by the way.

Heston chooses the marble for his sculptures from the quarries actually used by Michelangelo at **Carrara**, southeast of La Spezia up in the Apuan Alps of Tuscany. You can take a trip up to see some of the 400 separate quarries in three valleys – Fantiscritti, Collonata and Torano – which have supplied the best quality marble since Roman times. St Peter's Square, circa 1508, was recreated in one of Italy's finest Medieval squares, the **Piazza del Popolo** at **Todi**, 25 miles south of Perugia off the E45 in Umbria.

AGUIRRE, WRATH OF GOD
(1972, dir: Werner Herzog)
Klaus Kinski, Ray Guerra, Helena Rojo.
● **PERU**

Kinski is one of Pizarro's lieutenants taking a raft party down river to discover El Dorado but instead discovering megalomania. You'll need to be an adventurous traveller to follow in his footsteps. Herzog's wild epic was filmed, spectacularly, in the near-inaccessible **Andes of northwest Peru**, literally hundreds of miles from the nearest city, on the lands of the Aguaruna and the Lauramarca Indians.

AIRPLANE!
(1980, dir: Jim Abrahams; David Zucker; Jerry Zucker)
Robert Hayes, Julie Haggerty, Peter Graves.
● **LOS ANGELES, CALIFORNIA**

A wild hit'n'miss spoof, based not on *Airport* but on Arthur Hailey's play *Flight Into Danger* (filmed as *Zero Hour!* in 1957 with Dana Andrews as the shell-shocked pilot having to land a plane after the crew goes down with food poisoning). The featured airport is **Los**

"It's a big pretty white plane with red stripes…": Los Angeles International Airport

Angeles International (LAX), southwest of the city at the end of **Sepulveda Boulevard**, where the 747s really do press their noses alarmingly close to the departure lounge windows. The space shuttle in *Airplane II: The Sequel* still takes off from LAX.

AIRPORT

(1970, dir: George Seaton)
Burt Lancaster, Dean Martin, George Kennedy.
● MINNESOTA; CALIFORNIA

First of the major airliner-in-danger movies that spawned so many imitations throughout the seventies. Lincoln International Airport, where a frazzled Burt Lancaster has to cope with blizzards, a suicide bomber and Oscar-winning stowaway Helen Hayes, is **Minneapolis-St Paul International Airport** on **Cedar Avenue** just to the south of Minneapolis where, rather than resorting to models, a real Boeing 707, rented at a cost of $18,000 a day, was actually landed in a snowstorm at -43°F as the film froze in the camera. The interiors were shot inside a grounded 707 installed at Universal Studios in Hollywood.

In the first sequel, *Airport '75*, stewardess Karen Black takes the controls of a stricken 747. The doomed flight takes off from **Dulles International Airport**, which serves Washington DC but is actually about 20 miles to the west on Dulles Access, Route 267, in Virginia. Charlton Heston and George Kennedy are flown in to **Salt Lake City Airport**, west of the city, to take charge. The mid-air helicopter-to-747 transfer stunt was filmed over the Heber Valley, east of the Wasatch Range in Utah. Other airports used in the production include **Los Angeles International**; the old **Van Nuys Airport** (also seen in *Casablanca*), **6590 Hayvenhurst Avenue**, Van Nuys, northwest LA; and **Edwards Airforce Base** north of LA in the Mojave desert.

To add variety to the midair crisis plot, the plane in *Airport '77* plummets to the bottom of the ocean. A cast of Hollywood stalwarts gamely bounce about on a jet set mounted on cantilevers in the Universal Studio, Hollywood. Millionaire James Stewart's museum-home is in Florida. It's **Villa Vizcaya, 3251 South Miami Avenue**. A familiar location, you can also see this Italianate mansion in *Any Given Sunday*, and its grounds in *Absence of Malice*. For further details, see *Ace Ventura, Pet Detective*. Filming also took place at **Burbank Airport**; **Los Angeles international**; and **Dulles International** in Virginia. The offshore filming was, as usual, around the San Diego area, while underwater scenes were filmed on the Universal backlot at **Wakulla Springs** near Tallahassee, Florida (a regular sub-aqua location – see also *Creature From the Black Lagoon*).

For the third sequel, *Airport '80: The Concorde*, it's the supersonic luxury jet in trouble as arms dealer Robert Wagner tries to prevent passenger Susan Blakely publishing damning evidence against him. The Concorde touches down and takes off from **Dulles International Airport** near DC, in Virginia. It's heading for Charles de Gaulle Airport in Paris, but missile and F-15 fighter plane attacks mean an emergency landing with nets at **Le Bourget**, Paris' original airport, north of the city. Hotel scenes

were shot back in LA at our old friend the **Biltmore Hotel, 506 South Grand Avenue**, downtown (see *The Fabulous Baker Boys* for details). The final forced landing in the Alps was filmed at **Alta** in Utah, southeast of Salt Lake City.

ALAMO, THE

(1960, dir: John Wayne)
John Wayne, Laurence Harvey, Richard Widmark.
● TEXAS

Wayne's lumbering epic, a long, long way from the historical truth, actually began filming in Mexico – there's not much of the real Alamo left – but this proved too expensive. Even so, at $7,500,000, *The Alamo* was the costliest movie made at the time. The production was closed down and restarted at **Brackettville** on Highway 90, about 100 miles west of San Antonio toward Del Rio, West Texas, where Wayne leased 400 acres of a 22,000 acre ranch belonging to one JT 'Happy' Shahan, and the Alamo was rebuilt. The full-sized facsimile, which took two years to complete, used the original plans, the traditional adobe techniques and, without any apparent irony, a largely Mexican workforce of 5,000. It was claimed at the time to be the biggest movie set outside Hollywood.

The Alamo: the full-size facsimile was rebuilt in Brackettville, Texas...

And it's still there, as a tourist attraction as well as a location for many subsequent movies. Extensions acquired over the years include a section of San Antonio which metamorphoses over its length to become Fort Worth of the 1880s. Alamo Village, open May to September, can be found just north of Brackettville itself, on Route 674 (© *512.563.2580*). It was put on the market in March 2004.

The real **Alamo**, in **San Antonio**, was founded as the Mission San Antonio de Valero in 1718, the first in a chain of missions built along the San Antonio River to extend the frontier of the Spanish empire and convert the Native Americans to Catholicism. It was closed down in 1793 and its lands given to the 39 mission Indians, then occupied on and off by the various forces in control of Texas until it achieved immortality in 1836 when 1,888 Texan volunteers were massacred, rather pointlessly, by Santa Ana's troops. Among those who perished in the massacre were American folk heroes Jim Bowie and Davy Crockett, hence Hollywood's fascination with this bit of US history. The only survivor of the massacre was a black servant found hiding in the chapel and played, memorably, by blonde Joan O'Brian in

...only part of the real complex still stands on Alamo Plaza in San Antonio

The Alamo.

Although the town of San Antonio is shaded by alamo (cottonwood) trees, the name actually comes from a Spanish Cavalry unit from the pueblo of El Alamo de Parras who occupied the old mission in 1801. The chapel, built in 1756, and the Long Barrack are virtually all that remain of the fortified complex, though the site now also contains the extensive Alamo Memorial Museum (*©* *210.225.1391, www.thealamo.org*), which occupies a 4.2 acre site on Alamo Plaza. Entry is free, but watch your dress and behaviour here – the place has taken on the status of a holy shrine. Bare chests and loud shirts are out, hushed voices and solemn patriotism very much in.

For John Lee Hancock's 2004 remake with Billy Bob Thornton and Dennis Quaid, a new set (purportedly even more authentic – it faces in the right direction for a start) was built at Reimer's Ranch, Hamilton Pool Road, Dripping Springs, Highway 290, a hunting-rock-climbing ranch about 25 miles west of Austin, Texas.

ALEXANDER
(2004, dir: Oliver Stone)
Colin Farrell, Angelina Jolie, Anthony Hopkins.
● MOROCCO; THAILAND; MALTA

The wedding feast in the Hindu kush: Atlas Mountains

Another view of the wedding feast: Atlas Mountains

Years in the planning, Stone's epic resolutely stayed on to be filmed in Morocco after the Casablanca bomb attacks when other productions fled the country. The massive sets for the Hindu Kush were built in the Atlas Mountains about an hour's drive outside Marrakech. Alexander's palace grounds are the gardens of the grand **La Mamounia Hotel** (see *The Man Who Knew Too Much*, 1956, for full details). The production moved to Thailand for scenes involving elephants. The **Grand Harbour** of **Valletta**, in Malta, was shot, prior to principal photography, from **Fort St Elmo** (where *Midnight Express*, scripted by Stone, was shot), **Upper Barrakka** and **Senglea Port**, to represent (with a little CGI) the port of Alexandria.

ALEXANDER NEVSKY
(1938, dir: Sergei Eisenstein)
Nikolai Cherkassov, Nikolai Okhlopkov, Andrei Abrikosov.
● RUSSIA

13th century Prince Nevsky defeats Teutonic knights in a battle on the ice of Lake Peipus in Northern Russia, to music by Prokofiev. This state-funded film is set largely in the city of Novgorod, about 100 miles south of St Petersburg, but the city had changed too much to allow location filming. Although the 13th century cathedral is still there, it's surrounded by modern buildings and no longer as gleaming white as it once was. The city sets were built just outside Moscow, at enormous expense. Despite the film's wintry look, *Nevsky* was actually filmed during the summer, with snow simulated by white sand shipped in from the beaches of the Baltic Sea, cotton wool perched in the tree branches and the actors showered with salt. Lake Peipus was also mocked-up on the set, with the artificial ice floes supported by collapsible pontoons that gave way on cue.

As an homage, Ken Russell virtually recreates this sequence at the end of his 1967 thriller *Billion Dollar Brain* (the third film to feature Michael Caine as Harry Palmer), where it's the private army of batty General Midwinter disappearing beneath the ice.

ALFIE
(1966, dir: Lewis Gilbert)
Michael Caine, Shelley Winters, Millicent Martin.
● LONDON

Caine shot to stardom as a callous cockney womaniser forced to face up to mortality, abortion and formidable American matrons. The various locations are, unsurprisingly, around London. The opening scene ("I suppose you think you're goin' to see the bleedin' titles now…"), despite establishing shots of Westminster, was actually filmed on **Camley Street**, NW1, behind King's Cross station, with the famous Victorian gasometers much in evidence in the background. The industrial buildings where Alfie's steamed-up car is parked have gone, and the site is currently Camley Street Natural Park, a wildlife preserve, but not for long. The site is up for re-development and even the gasometers are scheduled to be moved. Catch it while you can.

You'll find Alfie's seedy bedsit in Notting Hill Gate, at **22 St Stephen's Gardens** off Chepstow Road, W2 (*tube: Royal Oak*). It hasn't really changed at all, apart from a little pedestrianisation of the area, which means that Jane Asher would no longer be able to jump straight onto a convenient bus. Over the Thames from World's End, Chelsea, you can see the green spire of **St Mary's, Battersea Parish Church** on **Battersea Church Road**, SW11, where Julia Foster spends her lunchbreaks with nerdy but dependable bus conductor Graham Stark, and Alfie balefully watches her baby's christening.

The sanatorium where Alfie recuperates after a shadow is found on his lung, and where he seduces fellow patient's wife Vivien Merchant, is **York House and Gardens, York Street** (the A305), Twickenham, conveniently close to the film studios (*rail: Twickenham*). The 17th century mansion, alongside the new

Alfie recuperates in the sanatorium: York House, Twickenham

The christening: St Mary's, Battersea

Civic Centre, is now council offices, but the ornamental gardens are open to the public (entrance to the left of the house on Sion Road).

Alfie and his friend Murray Melvin take a walk along side the **Grand Union Canal** by the Lock-Keeper's cottage at King's Cross, with the gasometers in the background. He photographs voracious Shelley Winters at the Tower of London, while the lobby of Winters' apartment (complete with Tretchikoff 'Green Lady' painting) is actually the **Dorchester Hotel, Park Lane**, W1 (a *huge* £15 a week).

ALICE DOESN'T LIVE HERE ANY MORE
(1974, dir: Martin Scorsese)
Ellen Burstyn, Kris Kristofferson, Billy Green Bush.
● **LOS ANGELES, CALIFORNIA; ARIZONA**

After being widowed, Ellen Burstyn determines to return to her roots in Monterey and resume her career as a singer. With her young son, she eventually fetches up in **Tucson**, Arizona, where she lowers her sights a little to work in a diner. Mel and Ruby's Bar-B-Q was filmed in a real Tucson diner, and all the other joints where Burstyn tries to get work as a lounge singer are genuine Tucson bars, too. The giant cow skull-fronted restaurant where Burstyn stops off *en route* from Phoenix to Tucson is actually the **Longhorn Bar and Grill, 28851 South Nogales Highway, Amado** (*© 520.398.3955*) on I-9, a good 30 miles to the south of Tucson (seen also in *Boys on the Side*).

The Monterey Dining Room billboard seen at the end of the movie, when Burstyn decides to stay on and give her relationship with farmer Kristofferson another chance, is not a piece of heavy-handed 'happiness-in-your-own-backyard' symbolism, but an actual Tucson sign that strayed into the closing shot by luck.

ALICE IN DEN STADTEN (aka *Alice in the Cities*)
(1974, dir: Wim Wenders)
Rudiger Vogler, Yella Rotlander, Lisa Kreuzer.
● **WUPPERTAL, GERMANY; NEW YORK CITY; AMSTERDAM**

The cities being New York, Amsterdam and Wuppertal, as burnt out photographer Vogler journeys from America to Germany after being lumbered with a little girl. The Boardwalk where the movie opens is in Queens, New York, at **Rockaway Beach** by Beach 67th Street. Also in Queens, Vogler sells his car within earshot of the organ at **Shea Stadium, 126th Street**, Flushing, and has to catch the subway at **Willet's Point/Shea Stadium** station on the Main Street-Flushing Line 7. He takes the young Alice to see the view from the outside Observation Deck of the **Empire State Building, 350 Fifth Avenue**, before they depart for Europe from **JFK Airport**. The European destination is Amsterdam's **Schiphol Airport**, and there's a brief jaunt around the canals of the

city centre before the last leg of the journey takes them to Germany. If you fancy a ride on the creaky old suspension railway the pair take to find Alice's Grandma's house, you'll find it in **Wuppertal**, about 30 miles north of Cologne. The railway – amazingly, built in 1900 – rattles along for eight miles, 39 feet above the city's streets, linking eighteen stations between Vohwinkel and Oberbarmen, and has reputedly never had an accident in its history.

ALIEN
(1979, dir: Ridley Scott)
Sigourney Weaver, John Hurt, Tom Skerritt.
● **BERKSHIRE**

Not surprisingly, there's nothing to see of this movie, set as it is entirely aboard a space freighter, with weirdly effective alien planet sets – and the creature itself – based on designs by Swiss artist HR Giger. It was shot at Shepperton Studios, west of Shepperton Green off the B376 in Surrey, and at longtime home of Hammer Films, Bray Studios, Down Place in Berkshire

ALIENS
(1986, dir: James Cameron)
Sigourney Weaver, Michael Biehn, Carrie Henn.
● **LONDON**

Director Cameron's penchant for industrial locations (see *The Abyss* and the *Terminator* movies) takes him from Pinewood Studios to the cavernous disused **Acton Lane Power Station** on Acton Lane, W3.

ALIEN³
(1992, dir: David Fincher)
Sigourney Weaver, Charles Dance, Paul McGann.
● **NORTHUMBERLAND**

Filmed mostly at Pinewood Studios, the surface of the alien planet was **Blast Beach, Seaham**, alongside **Dawdon Colliery** on the Northumberland coast, blackened with years of detritus from the Seaham Harbour Blast Furnace. The area was recently cleaned up in an extensive restoration programme. There was more filming at the nearby, now defunct, **Blyth Power Station** in **Bedlington**. The station's four landmark chimneys were finally demolished in December 2003.

ALL ABOUT EVE
(1950, dir: Joseph L Mankiewicz)
Bette Davis, George Sanders, Anne Baxter.
● **NEW YORK CITY; SAN FRANCISCO, CALIFORNIA; NEW HAVEN, CONNECTICUT**

Clever use of location adds a little East Coast authenticity to this largely studio-bound story of ruthless ambition, set in Manhattan's theatreland, which got a record fourteen Oscar nominations, and

The New York theatre: John Golden Theater, West 45th Street

bagged six of them, including biggies Best Picture, Direction and Screenplay.

Manipulative Eve Harrington, first seen as a sweet, unassuming little mite, hangs around the stage door of New York's **John Golden Theater, 252 West 45th Street** at 8th Avenue (© *212.239.6200*), for a glimpse of her idol, Margo Channing. Though the alley beside the Golden, where helpful Celeste Holm offers to take Eve backstage, is a studio set, the establishing longshot is real. Doubles stood in for the two stars, who remained back at the Fox studios in Hollywood, a standard technique of the period used throughout the film.

The cast did make it a little further up the West Coast, though, to San Francisco to film theatre interiors, where a pre-stardom Marilyn Monroe appears as George Sanders' protégé – Miss Caswell, 'a graduate of the Copacabana school of acting.' The Golden's interior is the **Curran Theater, 445 Geary Street**, downtown San Francisco (© *415.551.2000, www.bestofbroadway-sf.com/curran.html*). Built in 1922, the theatre is still a popular venue for the latest big musicals.

Celeste Holm gets a stand-in for her entrance into New York's famous **21 Club, 21 West 52nd Street** near Fifth Avenue (© *212.582.7200, www.21club.com*), where she bumps into Eve. The real 21, a pretty exclusive drinking club which started up during Prohibition as a speakeasy, was given a new lease of life in 1987 when, after years of decline, it was renovated. It features frequently as a symbol of worldly success in such films as Oliver Stone's *Wall Street* and Woody Allen's *Manhattan Murder Mystery* – where you can see the club's jockey-covered frontage.

Footsteps on the Ceiling, in which Eve finally gets the plum role, opens at the **Shubert Theater, 247 College Street, New Haven**, Connecticut (© *203.562.5666, www.shubert.com*), a traditional out-of-town try-out venue for Broadway-bound shows (*A Streetcar Named Desire* premièred here in 1947, launching Marlon Brando to stardom), and the hometown of Yale University. Once again, doubles are used for the long shots, while Anne Baxter and George Sanders stroll past rear projection of the Shubert and the nearby Taft Hotel.

...and the West Coast interior: Curran Theater, Geary Street, San Francisco

The swanky apartment to which Eve finally retires, clutching her Sarah Siddons award, was shot on New York's **Fifth Avenue**, again with a stand-in.

ALL OR NOTHING

(2002, dir: Mike Leigh)
Timothy Spall, Lesley Manville, Alison Garland.
● **LONDON**

So relentlessly glum it starts to feel more like a wallow than observation and, underneath the surface grit, isn't this just the old 'family drawn together by adversity' TV

movie? Like Leigh's *Naked*, a central performance holds the screen. The locale is **Greenwich**, southeast London, though not the touristy Greenwich of Naval

Spall's cab office: Lassell Street, Greenwich

College and maritime history. The cab office of hangdog Phil (Spall) is **73 Lassell Street** in Greenwich. The local boozer was the British Sailor, which also stood on Lassell Street, until it was demolished. The estate is the **Haddo Estate**, north of Greenwich Station, and about to be demolished. The graffiti is real. The hospital, where son Rory (James Corden) suffers the consequences of his junk food lifestyle, is **Greenwich District Hospital, Woolwich Road**.

ALL QUIET ON THE WESTERN FRONT

(1930, dir: Lewis Milestone)
Lew Ayres, Louis Wollheim, John Wray.
● **CALIFORNIA**

WWI seen through the eyes of young soldiers from the German side, this anti-war epic still packs a punch. The huge sets were constructed on Universal's backlot, and recycled over the years (you can catch them again in James Whale's classic *Frankenstein*). The trench scenes were filmed at the **Irvine Ranch** near Santa Ana, Route 405 in Orange County southeast of LA, while more scenes were shot at **Balboa**, on the southern California coast between Newport and Laguna Beaches. With only 150 extras, Milestone was forced to employ bravura techniques for the battle scenes. And in the classic final shot, it's the director's own hand reaching for the butterfly.

ALL THE KING'S MEN

(1949, dir: Robert Rossen)
Broderick Crawford, Joanne Dru, John Ireland.
● **CALIFORNIA**

An initially decent man finds political fame, corruption and, ultimately, assassination in this *film à clef* based on the career of Louisiana Governor Huey Long. Set in the South, it was shot largely on location around northern California. The city of **Suisun**, off I-80 to the northeast of San Francisco, was used for the election scenes, and the locale given a more folksy, funky feel with 50 tons of topsoil dumped onto the paved streets. Nearby **Fairfield** and **Stockton**, Route 5, east of San Francisco, stood in for Southern towns.

ALL THE PRESIDENT'S MEN

(1976, dir: Alan J Pakula)
Robert Redford, Dustin Hoffman, Jason Robards.
● **WASHINGTON DC; LOS ANGELES, CALIFORNIA**

The third of Pakula's excellent paranoia trilogy (following *Klute* and *The Parallax View*) which manages to make the potentially uncinematic uncovering of the Watergate story truly gripping, is brilliantly photographed around a

Woodward and Bernstein's office: The Washington Post Building

spookily benighted DC by Gordon Willis. (It's worth remembering that, post 9/11, there may be restrictions on visiting certain buildings, and security arrangements are subject to change.)

Authenticity is all. The break-in was actually filmed in the **Watergate Complex** (not far from the Georgetown house used for *The Exorcist*), with Frank Wills – the very security guard who discovered the taped door – recreating the moment on the exact spot (the arresting officer, by the way, is future *Amadeus* Oscar-winning actor F Murray Abraham). The Democratic offices were on the sixth floor of the complex at **2600 Virginia Avenue NW**, west of downtown DC (*metro: Foggy Bottom*). If you feel like a souvenir, you can pick up a bottle of Watergate Whisky from the store in the complex.

Base 1, the lookout, is stationed – as he was in reality – on the balcony of Room 723 directly opposite, which is now **Hall on Virginia Avenue, 2601 Virginia Avenue NW** at New Hampshire Avenue – student housing for George Washington University. Until 1999 this was the Howard Johnson Motor Lodge but, sadly, you can no longer book the room used by the burglars.

Washington Post reporters Bob Woodward (Redford) and Carl Bernstein (Hoffman) work out of the paper's building at **1150 15th Street NW** between L and M Streets, downtown DC (*metro: Farragut North*). On Mondays, between 10am and 3pm, there's a tour of the building, which takes in the actual newsroom (*©* *bookings: 202.334.6000*). The movie's city room, in which the pair worry away at the burglary story, is, however, an elaborate set built on soundstages at Warner Brothers' Burbank lot. The 32,000 square-foot set cost half a million dollars, and the obsessive detail went further than just reproducing all 250 of the reporters' and editors' desks in their correct positions and the graphics on the walls – it went as far as filling the wastepaper baskets with real waste from the actual *Post* offices, *correctly assigned to each department.*

Genuine DC locations include, of course, the **Capitol Building** – the entrance for tours is on East Capitol Street, Capitol Hill (*©* *202.225.6827; metro: Capitol South, Union Station*).

The magnificent circular reading room, where the duo sort through the White House book-request slips, is the domed, marble Main Reading Room in the Jefferson Building of the **Library of Congress, First Street SE** between East Capitol Street and Independence Avenue (*©* *202.707.5000;*

The burglary: The Watergate complex, Virginia Avenue NW

metro: Capitol South, Union Station).

The concert building outside which Redford catches a cab for his first assignation with enigmatic insider Deep Throat is the **John F Kennedy Center for the Performing Arts, 2700 F Street, NW** (*©* *202.467.4600, www.kennedy-center.org; metro: Foggy Bottom*). The complex, which opened in 1971, houses two theatres, a concert hall and an opera house (*©* *202.416.8000*). The highrise wilderness where Redford keeps the rendezvous can be found over the Potomac River in **Arlington**, Virginia, though, if you want to see the car park itself, you'll need to visit LA. The sinister garage was beneath the former ABC Entertainment Center, 2000 Avenue of the Stars at Constellation Boulevard in Century City, currently being redeveloped.

Hoffman meets up with his phone company contact at the site of all those sixties anti-war demos, **Lafayette Park**, north of the White House, on Pennsylvania Avenue and H Street NW between Jackson and Madison Places (*metro: Farragut West*). The lead takes him to the County Justice Building of Miami where he tricks his way into meeting official Ned Beatty. The building is no more Miami than it is DC. It's **Los Angeles City Hall, 200 North Spring Street**, downtown, the home of *Dragnet* and *Superman*. Also in LA, you'll find the burger joint where Redford and Hoffman hatch the plot to get Sloane to confirm Haldeman's name (McDonald's in **Santa Monica**), and disgraced lawyer Donald Segretti's apartment, overlooking the Marina in **Marina del Rey**.

The FBI works out of the **J Edgar Hoover FBI Building, 10th Street and Pennsylvania Avenue NW**, downtown DC, though the interior of the building, where Woodward and Bernstein badger the agent, is, surprise, not the real FBI HQ at all, but once again City Hall, LA. Due to security concerns, public tours of the FBI Building have been suspended indefinitely (*metro: Metro Center, Gallery Place, Federal Triangle*).

ALMOST FAMOUS

(2000, dir: Cameron Crowe)
Patrick Fugit, Billy Crudup, Frances McDormand.
● LOS ANGELES, CALIFORNIA; SAN DIEGO, CALIFORNIA; NEW YORK CITY

Crowe's semi-autobiographical movie (he was a *Rolling Stone* reporter). The fictitious band Stillwater is based on The Allman Brothers (with whom Crowe toured) and Led Zeppelin, though Russell Hammond (Crudup) is supposedly based on Glenn Frey of The Eagles. The film opens on **Newport Avenue, Ocean Beach, San Diego**, by the long-closed Strand Theatre at 4948-52. Behind the credits you can see **Balboa Park**. The opening venue, where William Miller (Fugit) gets to meet Stillwater for the first time, is the **San Diego Sports Arena**. The

The lookout: Hall on Virginia Avenue

King of the Road Motor Lodge, Tempe: Roosevelt Hotel, Hollywood Boulevard

The 'Riot House': Continental Hyatt, Sunset Boulevard

Cleveland Arena is the **Hollywood Palladium, 6215 Sunset Boulevard**. Following the band to LA, Miller stays in the Continental Hyatt House, now the **Continental Hyatt, 8401 Sunset Boulevard**, on the Strip – nicknamed the 'Riot House'. Celeb rioters include Led Zeppelin, who trashed it, the Stones, who trashed it (see the documentary *Cocksucker Blues*), and Jim Morrison, who dangled out of a window (a scene moved to the Chateau Marmont in Oliver Stone's *The Doors*). Little Richard called the place home for many years. The hotel's rooftop pool can be seen in *This Is Spinal Tap*. The King of the Road Motor Lodge, Tempe, Arizona, where William gets a message from his mother ("DON'T TAKE DRUGS"), and where the band expresses doubts about consorting with the enemy before deciding that the cover of *Rolling Stone* would be cool, is unmistakably the lobby of the venerable **Roosevelt Hotel, 7000 Hollywood Boulevard** (see *Catch Me If You Can* for full details). Filming also occurred at the **Chateau Marmont 8221 Sunset Boulevard** in West Hollywood, the **Western Dunes Motor Hotel, 4300 Wilshire Boulevard**, and the **Ambassador Hotel, 3400 Wilshire Boulevard**, both midtown.

Over on the East Coast, Penny Lane (Kate Hudson) ODs in the **Plaza Hotel, West 59th Street** at Fifth Avenue (see *North by Northwest* for full details). Stillwater checks into the **Gramercy Park Hotel, 2 Lexington Avenue** (*© 212.505.0535, www.gramercyparkhotel.com*), and the celebration dinner is at the now-gone Max's Kansas City Diner (also seen in *Driller Killer*),which stood at **213 Park Avenue South**, just north of Times Square.

ALPHAVILLE

(1965, dir: Jean-Luc Godard)
Eddie Constantine, Anna Karina, Akim Tamiroff.
● **PARIS, FRANCE**

Lemmy Caution's hotel: Scribe Hotel, Paris

Sci-fi fantasy with special agent Lemmy Caution travelling across space (by car, naturally) to investigate the bleak futuristic city of Alphaville, represented by a quirkily photographed sixties Paris. The Electricity Board building is used as an ominous computer centre. Caution's hotel is the **Scribe Hotel, 1 rue Scribe** (*©*

44.71.24.24), by the Place de l'Opéra. This rather grand edifice, which was the Allied Forces' press HQ during WWII, has another place in cinema history. An inscription round the corner, at the hotel's boulevard des Capucines entrance (no. 14) records that here, in the Salon Indien of the Grand Café, the Lumière Brothers first demonstrated cinematic projection on 28 December, 18-95.

Quentin Tarantino pays homage to the director by naming the diamond shop, site of the robbery, in *Reservoir Dogs* Karina's, after *Alphaville*'s co-star who was at the time married to Godard, and also by calling his production company, A Band Apart, after Godard's 1964 movie, *Bande à Part*.

ALTERED STATES

(1980, dir: Ken Russell)
William Hurt, Blair Brown, Bob Balaban.
● **NEW YORK CITY; MASSACHUSETTS; LOS ANGELES, CALIFORNIA; MEXICO**

No love lost between scriptwriter Paddy Chayevsky (who took his name off the film) and director Ken Russell in this story of an obsessed scientist using a mix of drugs and sensory deprivation to investigate primal states of consciousness. The faculty where William Hurt conducts his first tentative experiments is New York's **Columbia University**, between Amsterdam Avenue and Broadway, West 114th and West 120th Streets up towards Mornington Heights. Popular with wacko paranormal investigators, it spawned the trio of *Ghostbusters* a few years later.

Hurt relocates to Boston, where he lives in the **Beacon Hill** district and continues his experiments at **Harvard Medical School**. The bizarre rock formations he flies out to are in Mexico (they're for real – the *Fantasy Island* set at Burbank which the studio wanted to use was too Disneyfied for Russell), and he returns via Boston's Logan Airport. The evolutionarily regressed Hurt visits the animals in **Bronx Zoo**, the largest urban zoo in the States, **Bronx Park** on **Southern Boulevard**, New York. The scenes with Hurt regressing further to some kind of primal blob were filmed at the **Biltmore Hotel, 506 South Grand Avenue**, downtown LA (see *Ghostbusters* for details).

AMADEUS

(1984, dir: Milos Forman)
F Murray Abraham, Tom Hulce, Simon Callow.
● **CZECHOSLOVAKIA**

Shaffer's fantasia on the rivalry between composers Salieri and Mozart was filmed almost entirely in real castles and palaces throughout Czechoslovakia. Only four sets were built for the movie – Schikander's Volkstheater, where Simon Callow stages a surreal comedy; Salieri's hospital room; the interior of Mozart's apartment; and the staircase where he meets his father, at Prague's **Barrandov Studios**. The famous studios, in the suburb of Hlubocepy, were founded in 1933 by President Vaclav Havel's uncle Milos.

The relatively unchanged **Old Town** (Staré Mesto) of **Prague** stands in for 18th century Vienna. The opera

The Emperor's palace: Arcibiskupsky Palác, Hradcanské námestí

The opera performances: Tyl Theatre, Prague

performances, *Seraglio, Marriage of Figaro* and *Don Giovanni*, were filmed here in the unchanged **Tyl Theatre, Zelezna ulice** (Zelezna Street) **11** at Havirska Street. Built in 1783 for Count Anton von Nostitz-Rieneck, as the Nostitz Theatre, it became the German Theatre in the mid-19th century until 1945, when it was renamed for Czech dramatist and actor Josef Kajetan Tyl. It's now Czechoslovakia's National Theatre. During his lifetime, Mozart was always more appreciated in Prague than in Vienna, and the composer actually chose to stage the première of *Don Giovanni* at the Tyl, on 29 October 1787.

To the west, reached by the Karluv Most (Charles Bridge) over the Vltava River, you'll find the **Malá Strana** (Lesser Town), a picturesque quarter of winding streets, taverns and old houses which provided more period backdrops. North of the Mala Strana is the residential district of Hradcany, where the aristocracy built their swish palaces. Here you can see the Emperor's Palace – actually the recently restored **Arcibiskupsky Palác** (Archbishop's Palace, formerly Gryspek Palace), the Prague residence of Cardinal Tomasek, in **Hradcanské námestí** (Hradcany Square) opposite St Vitus Cathedral. Originally a Renaissance mansion, it was bought by Ferdinand I from the Royal Private Secretary – Florian von Gryspek – and presented to the Catholic Archbishop of Prague. During the 16th century it was rebuilt and extended before being remodelled in the Baroque style between 1675 and 1688. In 1764 Johan Joseph Wirch reworked it into Rococo style and decorated the interior in sumptuous splendour. You can see the results, but it's not easy. The Palace is only open to the public one day a year, between 9am and 5pm on Maundy Thursday.

Salieri's first encounter with the brattish Mozart uses the equally lavish interior of the Baroque palace at **Kromeriz**, northern Moravia in the eastern part of the Czech Republic. The palace and its gardens are open for guided tours, or you can take a virtual your at *www.kromeriz.biz/kromeriz_castle_tour.html* or *www.azz.cz*. More austere interiors for Salieri were found in the former **Palace of the Grand Prior of the Knights of Malta, Maltézské námestí** (Maltese Square). For a while Prague's Museum of Musical Instruments, it's now home to the Anglo-American College, a private liberal arts college.

AMANTS, LES (aka *The Lovers*)
(1958, dir: Louis Malle)

Jeanne Moreau, Alain Cuny, Jean-Marc Bory.

● **FRANCE**

Jeanne Moreau is married to stuffy old Alain Cuny and carrying on an affair in Paris too, when she suffers a sudden Gallic attack of *amour fou* and takes off with a younger hunk, in Malle's early New Wave movie. Moreau and Cuny's villa is a composite of an actual villa in **Dijon** – as it's supposed to be – together with exteriors shot near Paris. The neighbouring roads were filmed around Burgundy, while the grounds were actually way to the south in Provence. The small village where Moreau and her beau-to-be stop off en route to Dijon is **Montbard**, 45 miles northwest of the city on the River Brenne and the Canal du Bourgogne.

AMANTS DU PONT NEUF, LES (aka *The Lovers on the Bridge*)
(1990, dir: Leos Carax)
Juliette Binoche, Denis Lavant, Klaus-Michael Gruber.

● **FRANCE**

The real thing: Pont Neuf, Paris

A bizarre romance between middle-class artist Binoche, who's losing her sight, and nihilist fire-eating street-punk Lavant, set on the Pont Neuf in Paris during the 1989 Bicentennial celebrations. The Paris locations you can see include the street where Lavant is hit by a car at the beginning of the movie – **boulevard Sebastopol**, which runs north/south from Strasbourg St Denis Metro to Chatelet – and the **Nanterre Night Refuge** to which he's taken.

The metro station, inside which Lavant impresses Binoche with his acrobatics, is **Pont Neuf** itself; while the one with the illuminated pavement, where Binoche is chased, is **Montparnasse Bienvenue**. Beyond Pont Neuf, the iron-latticed bridge to which Binoche retires after drugging café patrons, is the wooden-planked **Pont des Arts** leading from the Institut de France to the Louvre. And it really is the **Louvre** Binoche steals into at night for a private viewing of the Rembrandt self-portrait. The shot of Binoche taking an uncomfortably close peek at the painting with a cigarette lighter was reputedly snatched while the ever-present Louvre guard had popped out to the toilet.

The Pont Neuf itself was closed for renovations from 1989 to 1991, and its turrets provide shelter for the movie's down-and-out characters. If the Paris background looks sparsely populated, though, that's because, for the most part, the film was made on a giant set which recreates the Seine river fronts in forced perspective. Which also explains why, until Claud Berri's mammoth adaptation of *Germinal* came along in 1993, *Pont Neuf* was the most expensive French movie ever made. The real bridge was scheduled to be used for filming, with a set taking over for the spectacular night-time scenes, but when Denis Lavant injured a tendon in his wrist the production moved full-time to the set, which had then to be extended to accommodate daytime shooting.

40 bulldozers set to shifting a quarter of a million cubic tons of earth to recreate the River Seine in a field near **Montpellier**, in **Lansargues**, southwest of Nîmes down toward the south coast. But money ran out, and in December 1988 the production closed down. After an aborted five week shoot in 1989, a new producer and even rumours of Elia Kazan or Robert De Niro taking over as director, the production finally wrapped in January 1990, with a final cost rumoured at between 100 and 160 million francs.

The real **Pont Neuf** – the New Bridge, actually the oldest existing bridge across the Seine, completed in 1607 – crosses the river in a series of twelve arches by the western tip of the Ile de la Cité, dividing it neatly into two sections (*metro: Pont Neuf*).

AMARCORD
(1974, dir: Federico Fellini)
Puppella Maggio, Magali Noel, Armando Brancia.
● **ITALY**

Fellini's typically imaginative, anecdotal look at small-town Italian life in the thirties won the 1973 Best Foreign Picture Oscar. Like all of his later films, it was shot on the huge Stage 5 at Cinecittà outside Rome. The town of Borgo, built in the studio by Art Director Danilo Donati, is based on Rimini on Northern Italy's Adriatic coast. The Grand Hotel of Rimini exterior, though, where Bisceine has a dubious adventure with the sheik's wives, was too large even for Cinecittà. It's the five-storey, art nouveau **Paradiso sul Mare**, which you can see in **Anzio**, on the coast 35 miles south of Rome. Built in the early twenties as a casino, it was closed on the orders of Pope Pius X, who couldn't entertain the notion of gambling so close to the Vatican. The owner was financially ruined and the building is now a wholesome catering school. It's owned by the town of Anzio and you can occasionally attend events.

AMATEUR
(1994, dir: Hal Hartley)
Martin Donovan, Isabelle Huppert, Elina Lowensohn.
● **NEW YORK CITY**

Fiercely indie director Hartley deserts his usual Long Island locales for central Manhattan, and even ventures, quirkily, into thriller territory as amnesiac heavy Donovan gets involved with virgin nymphomaniac nun Huppert and a pair of oddball hitmen.

The café where Elina Lowensohn meets Damian Young and puts in a fateful phone call to Amsterdam was **Angelika Café** in the six-screen arthouse cinema **Angelika Film Center, 18 West Houston Street** at Broadway in Greenwich Village (*©* *212.995.2000, www.ange-likafilmcenter.com/newyork*).

The café: Angelika Film Center, Greenwich Village

The couple are subsequently tracked down to the concourse of **Grand Central Station**. The public phone where a manic Young, suffering the after-effects of a little improvised electro-convulsive therapy, gets arrested, is at the corner of **Fifth Avenue and 19th Street**, just northwest of Union Square.

Donovan is finally gunned down when he accompanies Huppert back to her convent. This normally quiet haven is a blissfully useful escape from Manhattan. A cluster of Medieval European buildings transported to and rebuilt in the US, **The Cloisters** overlook the Hudson River in Fort Tryon Park north of Washington Heights. If you need to chill out, The Cloisters are open every day except Mondays from 9.30am to 4.45pm, entrance on **West 193rd Street** at Fort Washington Avenue (*© 212.923.3700; subway: 190th Street*).

AMAZING COLOSSAL MAN, THE
(1957, dir: Bert I Gordon)
Glenn Langan, Cathy Downs, William Hudson.
● **NEVADA**

The fallout from a nuclear explosion in the Nevada desert causes colonel Glenn Langan to grow ten feet a day in this sci-fi flick from cheapo FX merchant Bert Gordon. A combi-

The end of the Colossal Man: Hoover Dam, Nevada

nation of real location work and model shots has Langan wreaking havoc on the endearingly modest **Las Vegas Strip**, as it appeared in 1957. Although some of the fifties Vegas landmarks are no more, including the crown he rips from the roof and the revolving Silver Slipper, 48-feet-tall Las Vegas Vic, whom Langan apparently crumples up, still towers over the **Pioneer Club, 25 East Fremont Street**, even if he's not puffing away on a cigarette any more. He's now enclosed within the Fremont Street Experience, a four-block electronic canopy that delivers an eye-and-ear-popping *son et lumière* show. The Colossal Man is eventually toppled from the edge of the **Hoover Dam**, east of Vegas near Boulder City. The spectacular dam, which blocks the Colorado River to form Lake Mead and power all that neon, was built between 1930 and 1935 and took some 96 lives in the process. It's 30 miles east of Vegas, and Route 93 – the Flagstaff road from where Mr Colossal plummets into the waters of the Colorado – runs along the top. The Visitor Centre, from which you can descend 44 storeys to the base on a guided tour, features in *Lost In America*, and there's a new one scheduled to open.

AMERICAN BEAUTY
(1999, dir: Sam Mendes)
Kevin Spacey, Annette Bening, Wes Bentley.
● **CALIFORNIA**

Although set in the Chicago suburbs, the film was shot in California. The aerial shots of the neat, bland chequer-

The high school: South High School, Torrance

Mr Smiley: "You are so-o-o-o busted": Carl's Jr, Canoga Park

board neighbourhood in Sam Mendes' Oscar-winning drama, are the suburbs of California state capital, **Sacramento**, as are the streets where Lester Burnham (Spacey) jogs with his neighbours. Sadly though, you won't be able to visit the Burnham family house. The very specific sightlines needed as the characters constantly peer into each other's houses, meant that (although real houses in Brentwood and Canoga Park were used for interior shots) the houses seen in the film are on the controlable environment of the studio backlot on the Warner Ranch in Burbank. Lester lusts after his daughter's friend Angela (Mena Suvari) at **South High School, 4801 Pacific Coast Highway, Torrance**, in LA's South Bay area, and Mr Smiley, where Lester gets a job serving up burgers – "I think you'll remember me this time." – is **Carl's Jr, 20105 Saticoy Street, Canoga Park**, in the San Fernando Valley.

AMERICAN GIGOLO

(1980, dir: Paul Schrader)
Richard Gere, Lauren Hutton, Hector Elizondo.
● CALIFORNIA

Gere's neighbourhood: Westwood Village

High-class rent boy Julian Kaye (Gere) discovers the downside of Tinseltown when he's framed for murder. Borrowing its striking visual style from Bertolucci's *Il Conformista*, Schrader's movie was filmed round a cool, slick, pastel LA – particularly **Westwood Village**, a one-time exclusive enclave between Hollywood and Bel-Air, where Kaye's stylish home, the Westwood Hotel Apartments, is supposedly sited. The building was actually the Sunset Plaza Apartments, which stood at 1220 Sunset Plaza Drive, Mount Olympus, to the north of Beverly Hills. It has been home to Mitzi Gaynor, Katharine Hepburn and James Dean, but lost the fight for preservation as part of Hollywood's history and was demolished in 1987. The diner where Kaye is questioned by Detective Sunday (Elizondo) really was in Westwood, and was the Me & Me, 10975 Weyburn Avenue, in the shadow of Mann's Village Theatre, the white Spanish-Moderne tower in the background at 961 Broxton Avenue. It's on the main

Gere appeals for help: Perino's, Wilshire Boulevard

drag, **Westwood Plaza**, that bored society wife Michelle Stratton (Hutton) takes Kaye until 'accidentally' bumping into him in **Tower Records**. The white Spanish-domed structure seen here is a Westwood landmark dating from 1929 and currently housing **Eurochow, 1099 Westwood Boulevard**, (*©* *310.209.0066, www.eurochow.com*), one of Mr Chow's drop-dead stylish designer restaurants. Westwood is home to the University of California, and the quiet wooded glade where Hutton tells him she's going away for a while is the University's **Mildred E Mathias Botanical Garden** (*© 310.825.1260, www.botgard. ucla.edu*), a seven-acre tree-shaded canyon southeast of the campus, off Hilgard and Le Conte Avenues.

Gere gets an alibi: Probe, now A.D., North Highland Avenue

Kaye drives a couple of miles east to Beverly Hills, where he takes clients to legendary 'Pink Palace', the **Beverly Hills Hotel**, recently reopened after extensive renovation. The Mission Revival-style building, dating from 1912, which in its time has been home to Howard Hughes, Gable and Lombard, Chaplin and – reputedly – site of Monroe's liaisons with the Kennedy brothers, is tucked discreetly away behind thick shrubbery at **9641 Sunset Boulevard** near Rodeo Drive (*© 310.276.2251, www.the-beverlyhillshotel.com*). The open air café where Kaye gets an ominous warning was itself on **Rodeo Drive**, opposite the Polo Ralph Lauren store at 444, but establishments on this image-obsessed strip come and go as fashion dictates. Further east, in Hollywood, is the gay disco where he has to go to fix up an alibi, **A.D.** (formerly, and famously, Probe, one of LA's oldest gay discos), **836 North Highland Avenue** (*© 323.467.3000*), near Melrose Avenue. The glitzy restaurant where our dishevelled hero gets short shrift when he pleads for help was **Perino's, 4101 Wilshire Boulevard** at Norton Avenue. This classic Hollywood restaurant is now closed (see *Mommie Dearest* for details). Kaye takes Route 111 east out of LA for his assignment with the creepy voyeur and his wife, which was filmed in **Palm Springs**.

AMERICAN GRAFFITI

(1973, dir: George Lucas)
Richard Dreyfuss, Ronny Howard, Paul LeMat.
● CALIFORNIA

Dismissed as 'a disgrace' and 'unreleasable' by the suits who know the business, *Graffiti* not only grossed millions and spawned a wave of pale imitations, but earned a pair of Oscar nominations for George Lucas as both

The movie theatre: Mystic Theater, Petaluma

writer and director. The film was inspired by Lucas' own adolescent years cruising the Strip in Modesto, on Highway 99 between Stockton and Fresno in central California.

And Modesto is the town to head for if you've got the wheels and want to show them off. The regular cruise has moved from its sixties location – Tenth Street between G and K Streets – to McHenry Avenue. There is actually a 'Graffiti night' on the first Saturday after graduation day (some time in the middle of June – call the visitors' bureau [© 209.577.5757] to check the date). Modesto now even boasts roller-skating waitresses at the A&W Root Beer Drive-In, close to the cruise strip, at 1404 G Street.

Despite all this razzmatazz, Modesto is not where the movie was shot. The two towns used, which had barely changed since the sixties, were **Petaluma** in Sonoma County and **San Rafael** in Marin County, on Highway 101 north of San Francisco. San Rafael, now all rather gentrified, was the first choice for filming but the disruption caused by initial shooting on **Fourth Street**, downtown, led to the production being moved to another location. You'll instantly recognise Petaluma as Graffiti-town. Proud of its varied and well-preserved architecture, Petaluma has provided the backdrop for a whole slew of movies including Francis Coppola's Peggy Sue Got Married, Joe Dante's Explorers, Paul Verhoeven's Basic Instinct, legendary turkey Howard the Duck and the controversial nineties remake of Lolita. You can take a walking tour of the town's many movie sites, with a guide from the tourist information office at 799 Baywood Street (© 707.762.2785). The boys drive up and down **Petaluma Boulevard North**, on **D Street** and **Washington Street**, the main drag used in the movie.

Richard Dreyfuss is drafted into the Pharaohs gang in front of the **Old Opera House, 149 Kentucky Street**.

Dreyfuss joins the Pharaohs: Kentucky Street, Petaluma

The cop car stunt: Petaluma Boulevard North

And the used car lot, where Dreyfuss chains the axle of the police car, can still be recognised. It's a vacant lot alongside the **McNear Building, 15-23 Petaluma Boulevard North**. The State Movie Theater (showing Dementia 13, the horror movie a young Francis Ford Coppola directed for Roger Corman) is the

Mystic Theater in the McNear at number 23. The high school is **Tamalpais High School, 700 Miller Avenue, Mill Valley**.

Sadly, the film's most

The teens cruise the main drag: Petaluma Boulevard North, Petaluma

famous location, Mel's Drive-In, with its rollerskating waitresses, no longer exists. It was real, and actually situated in the city of San Francisco itself, on the corner of South Van Ness and Mission Street. It closed down and was, amazingly, demolished. The good news is, it was one of a chain, and a surviving classic Mel's can be found at 3355 Geary Boulevard.

AMERICAN HISTORY X
(1998, dir: Tony Kaye)
Edward Norton, Edward Furlong, Fairuza Balk.
● LOS ANGELES, CALIFORNIA

There was controversy when Ed Norton allegedly re-edited the movie to increase his role. Tragedy ensues when reformed Derek Vinyard (Norton) finds his White Supremacist past hard to shake off. The neighbourhood of the Vinyard family is **Venice Beach**, LA's Bohemian beachfront community increasingly troubled by gang-related problems. Danny Vinyard (Furlong) attends Venice Beach High, actually **Venice High School, 13000 Venice Boulevard, Venice** (see Grease for details). Oddly, for inhabitants of Venice Beach, Derek and Danny stop off, on the way to Venice High, at **Johnie's Coffee Shop, 6101 Wilshire Boulevard** at Fairfax Avenue, opposite the golden cylinder of the old May and Co department store in midtown LA. This streamlined fifties coffee shop is also where Anthony Edwards receives news of the impending apocalypse in the underrated thriller Miracle Mile, and features in both The Big Lebowski and Reservoir Dogs.

AMERICAN PIE
(1999, dir: Paul Weitz)
Jason Biggs, Chris Klein, Natasha Lyonne.
● LOS ANGELES, CALIFORNIA

Hormonally-fuelled teen comedy, with four high school boys vowing to lose their virginity before graduation. Set in the fictitious town of East Great

Jim's house: Cedar Drive, Long Beach

Falls, Michigan, the high school interiors were filmed at **Long Beach Polytechnic High School, 1600 Atlantic Avenue** at Pacific Coast Highway in Long Beach, southern LA, though the exterior is nearby **Millikan High School, 2800 Snowden Avenue**. Dog Years (based on Yesterdog, 1505 Wealthy Street, Eastown, in Grand

Dog Years: South Myrtle Avenue, Monrovia

Rapids, Michigan), the coffee shop hangout, was created in an empty property, which has since become a real coffee house, the **Caffe Opera, 402 South Myrtle Avenue** (© *626.301.0317*), in **Monrovia**, LA's eastern suburb.

But the Great Falls neighbourhood is largely **Long Beach**. The house of permanently frustrated Jim Levinstein (Biggs), where the pie of the title gets some serious abuse, is **4153 Cedar Drive**.

AMERICAN PIE 2

(2001, dir: JB Rogers)
Jason Biggs, Seann William Scott, Alyson Hannigan.
● **CALIFORNIA; MICHIGAN**

Michelle's house: Cedar Avenue, Long Beach

On to college, and a little more crudity without the Weitz brothers. Apart from a couple of second unit shots of the gang driving through Michigan (it's not really them), once again, the whole movie was made around LA. Jim's home is once again **4153 Cedar Drive**, Long Beach. Deceptively dweeby bandster Michelle (Hannigan) lives nearby at **3925 Cedar Avenue**. East Great Falls Regional Airport is **Long Beach Airport, 4100 Donald Douglas Drive**, and the hospital where Jim gets taken after supergluing himself to, erm, himself, is **Long Beach Community Hospital, 1720 Termino Avenue**, which was also the hospital in *Spider-Man*.

School this time around is **UCLA (University College of Los Angeles)** and, although the exterior of Dog Years is the **Coffee Bean & Tea Leaf** again, the interior had to be recreated in the studio. Vicky and Jessica get a summer job in **Aardvark's Vintage Clothing Store, 1253 East Colorado Boulevard** in Pasadena.

For the arrival in Michigan, **Main Street, Seal Beach** became Grand Harbor, where the bridge is **Davies Bridge** on **East Second Street**. The lakefront resort is **Paradise Cove**, Malibu. Tall Oaks Band Camp, where Jim sneaks out to meet Michelle, is **Camp JCA Shalom, 34342 Mulholland Highway** in Malibu (*www.campjcashalom.com*), though the band show was filmed up in **Altadena**, north of Pasadena. The house the lads

Redecorating the house: Country Club Drive, Long Beach

get a summer job redecorating, where Paul Finch (Eddie Kaye Thomas) explains the joys of tantric sex, is **4165 Country Club Drive**, back in Long Beach.

The New York street, from which Nadia (Shannon Elizabeth) phones, is downtown LA, with the Twin Towers matted in, and Spain, despite the elaborate dressing, is clearly **Pasadena City Hall, 100 North Garfield Avenue** at Holly Street, Pasadena, seen in Chaplin's *The Great Dictator*, *A Walk In the Clouds* and *Beverly Hills Cop II*.

AMERICAN PSYCHO

(2000, dir: Mary Harron)
Christian Bale, Jared Leto, Reese Witherspoon.
● **ONTARIO, CANADA; NEW YORK CITY, NEW YORK**

New York style in Ontario: Senator, Victoria Street, Toronto

Bret Easton Ellis' notorious eighties-set slasher satire gets a stylish but restrained treatment from director Harron. Set in the exclusive bars and restaurants of New York's yuppie circuit, the movie was actually shot largely in Toronto, Ontario, with the real new York featured only in a sprinkling of establishing shots.

Harry's Bar, where the guys compare cards and where Patrick Bateman finally confesses all to a disbelieving lawyer, was the upper crust Boston Club, **4 Front Street East**, which is now closed. The other supposedly-New York upper-crust hangouts are

Another New York eaterie: Montana, John Street, Toronto

Comparing cards in Harry's Bar: the Boston Club, Front Street, Toronto

forties-style diner the **Senator, 249 Victoria Street**; kitschy Pacific Rim restaurant **Monsoon, 100 Simcoe Street**; old dance hall-turned theatre space, the **Phoenix, 410 Sherbourne Street**; the wood-beamed Wild West roadhouse **Montana, 145 John Street**; and the aptly-named **Shark City, 117 Eglinton Avenue East**. Street scenes were filmed around Toronto's Cabbagetown district, while the spectacular shoot-out with the police was shot on **Pearl Street** between Simcoe and Duncan Streets, just around the corner from Monsoon.

AMERICAN SPLENDOR

(2003, dir: Shari Springer Berman; Robert Pulcini)
Paul Giamatti, Hope Davis, Harvey Pekar.
● **OHIO; NEW YORK CITY; CALIFORNIA**

Professional grump Harvey Pekar supplied the words, Robert Crumb (who defined the look of the late-sixties counterculture with *Mr Natural* and *Fritz the Cat*) provided the scruffy, uncouth visuals for *American Splendor* comic books. Although the Pekars live in Cleveland Heights, the movie was filmed around **Lakewood**, Ohio. Pekar pitches his comic strip idea to Crumb in **Shay's Pizza Shop, 4007 Saint Clair Avenue** (© *216.431.6339*). Ultra-nerd Toby Radloff takes Harvey and Joyce to see *Revenge of the Nerds* at the **Detroit Theatre, 16407 Detroit Avenue** (© *216.521.2245*), and it's in the **Elmwood Home Bakery, 15204 Madison Avenue** (© *216.221.4338*) that Pekar meets Alice Quinn. Harvey, naturally, doesn't join in when Joyce skates with their adopted daughter Danielle at the **Halloran Ice Rink, West 117th** at Linnet (© *216.664.4187*).

There are even brief glimpses of the **Pacific Resident Theatre, 703 Venice Bouilevard** in LA (where *Splendor* is dramatised) and the **NBC Building, Rockefeller Plaza**, New York, as Harvey makes his legendary appearances on *Letterman*.

AMERICAN WEDDING

(2003, dir: Jesse Dylan)
Jason Biggs, Seann William Scott, Alyson Hannigan.
● **LOS ANGELES, CALIFORNIA**

The bar: Clancy's Crab Broiler, Glendale

'American Pie 3' has less Long Beach, though Jim still lives at **4153 Cedar Drive** and he's taught to dance by Stifler in the gym of **St Anthony High School, 620 Olive Avenue**.

This time, there's more of **Orange**, southeast of LA, where you'll find the flower shop at East Great Falls Hospital in the lobby of **Chapman University, 1 University Drive, downtown Orange**. There are walking tours (*www.chapman.edu*) but, Piesters, remember, this is a Christian institution. The university was also seen in *Surviving Christmas*, with Ben Affleck and Christina Applegate.

The airport, where Finch and Michelle greet Michelle's sister, Cadence (January Jones), is **Ontario Airport**, not in Canada but in California, on I-10 east of LA. The bar is **Clancy's Crab Broiler, 219 North Central Avenue, Glendale** (© *818.242.2722*), a Boston-style seafood house, and with live jazz at weekends.

The seaside hotel: Ritz-Carlton, Half Moon Bay

If you want to relive the full *American Wedding* experience... Zyskowski Flowers, where Stifler gets the wedding blooms, is **Radio Shack, 101 South Glassell Street** on the SE corner of the **Circle, Orange** (OK, you can't really get flowers here). The Chicago wedding dress shop is **Cantu and Castillo, 7415 Beverly Boulevard** in Los Angeles (© *323.931. 8325, www.cantucastillo.com*). The seaside hotel where the wedding is finally celebrated is the wonderful **Ritz-Carlton, 1 Miramontes Point Road, Half Moon Bay**, about 30 miles south of San Francisco (© *650.712.7000, www.ritzcarlton.com/resorts/half_moon_bay*), while the reception garden (you wouldn't want to miss out on the dog poo) is **Huntington Library and Gardens, 1151 Oxford Road, San Marino**, east of Pasadena (see *Indecent Proposal* for details).

AMERICAN WEREWOLF IN LONDON, AN

(1981, dir: John Landis)
David Naughton, Jenny Agutter, Griffin Dunne.
● **LONDON; SURREY; WALES**

A pub full of character actors rhubarbing away on the Yorkshire Moors can only mean bad news for two American backpackers. The moors were filmed around the Black Mountains in Wales, and East Proctor is in reality the tiny village of **Crickadarn**, about six miles southeast of Builth Wells off the A479. If you want to join the locals here for a pint at The Slaughtered Lamb, you'll have quite a journey. Although the

Jenny Agutter's flat: Coleherne Road

exterior is an empty cottage dressed up for the movie, the interior, where Lila Kaye tends bar and a frighteningly young Rik Mayall plays chess, is in Surrey. It's **The Black Swan, Old Lane** at the junction with Ockham Lane, **Martyr's Green**, about a mile northwest of Effingham Junction (*rail: Effingham Junction*) between Guildford and Leatherhead.

The hospital where David Naughton recovers from a nasty wolf bite was the **Princess Beatrice Maternity Hospital on Finborough Road** at Lillie Road in Earl's Court, London SW5. The building is still there, and is now a hostel for the homeless. Around the corner at **64 Coleherne Road**, SW10, you can see nurse Jenny Agutter's flat, where Naughton does some shape-shifting to 'Bad Moon Rising' (*tube: Earl's Court*).

Unusually, the tube station, where the city gent gets chomped, was filmed, during the wee small hours, at **Tottenham Court Road tube** (London Transport's all-purpose location, the closed Aldwych Station in the Strand, is almost invariably used for filming). The undead victims pop up in a studio recreation of the old Eros News Cinema (now a GAP clothes store) on

The Slaughtered Lamb, interior: The Black Swan, Martyr's Green

the corner of Shaftesbury Avenue in Piccadilly Circus. And once again Landis demonstrates his talent for staging major set-pieces in impossible locations by setting the climactic mayhem smack in the middle of **Piccadilly Circus** itself, although, if you look carefully, you can see a wobbly street sign. In fact, some of this sequence was filmed on a mock-up of the Circus at Twickenham Studios. The dark alley, where the wolf is finally cornered, which seems to be in the West End, is **Winchester Walk**, off the familiar location of Park Street in Borough (*tube: London Bridge*).

The dull and belated sequel, *An American Werewolf in Paris*, was shot largely in Luxembourg.

AMERIKANISCHE FREUND, DER (aka *The American Friend*)

(1977, dir: Wim Wenders)
Dennis Hopper, Bruno Ganz, Gerard Blain.
● GERMANY; FRANCE; NEW YORK CITY

Ripley's mansion: Saulenvilla, Hamburg

Wenders films Patricia Highsmith's *Ripley's Game* as a Hitchcockian thriller, with Dennis Hopper as shady wheeler-dealer Tom Ripley turning essentially decent picture framer Zimmerman (Ganz) into a contract killer. The book's French location, Fontainebleau, is shifted to the scuzzy harbour area of Hamburg.

A few miles west of downtown Hamburg on the grand Blankenese road you'll find Ripley's grand, if dilapidated, mansion, where shifty French crook Raoul Minot calls to hire a killer. It's **Saulenvilla, Elbchaussee 186**, overlooking the riverside suburb of Ovelgonne high, above the north bank of the Elbe.

Back in Hamburg itself, you can see Zimmerman's picture-framing shop – actually a hat shop, and still in existence – it's **Lange Strasse 22**, on the corner of Kleine Pinnes, just to the south of the S-bahn Reeperbahn Station near the sleazy St Pauli district. A little to the east, on the corner of **Davidstrasse** and the waterside road of St Pauli-Hafenstrasse, near to the old St Pauli Fishmarkt, is Zimmerman's waterfront apartment. And it's on Hamburg's **U-bahn railway** that Minot makes his proposition to Zimmerman, on the stretch from St Pauli at the eastern end of the Reeperbahn along the Elbe waterfront to Rodingsmarkt in the Altstadt.

Convinced he's suffering from a terminal blood disease, Zimmerman's increasingly panicky visits to his doctor take him down the endless escalators (there's a giant lift now) to the oppressive **Old St Pauli Elbtunnel** (a new motorway

Zimmerman's shop: Lange Strasse, Hamburg

tunnel a couple of miles to the west was completed in 1974). Built between 1907 and 1911 to relieve the pressure on the Elbe ferry to the docks of Steinwerder, the twin tunnels are not for claustrophobes. 490 yards long, the carriageways are a mere six feet wide. They're closed at night and on Sundays, but the rest of the time there's free entry (on foot – vehicles pay a toll). The funfair Zimmerman takes his family to is

The road tunnel: St Pauli-Elbtunnel, Hamburg

the **Hamburger Dom**, held every year in November/December in the **Heiligengeistfeld**, also in the St Pauli district.

Zimmerman is taken to Paris for a second opinion on his illness. The hospital where he undergoes tests is the **American Hospital, 63 boulevard Victor-Hugo, Neuilly-sur-Seine**, northwest Paris (*metro: Anatole France*). Convinced he's on the way out, Zimmerman agrees to carry out a hit on the Paris Metro as his victim changes trains at Etoile. He actually manages to complete the task one station further west on the RER 'A' line, on an escalator at **La Defense Station**, west of the city centre.

His second assignment is to whack the mob boss (a cameo from movie director Samuel Fuller), on the no-longer operating Munich-Hamburg Express, where Ripley turns up to help out. The flight of steps down which Sam Fuller (or his stunt double, at least) finally takes a tumble are further away from Saulenvilla than they appear in the movie, toward the waterfront.

The opening scene, which was filmed in New York City, features another cameo appearance, from veteran movie-maker Nicholas Ray, who directed Hopper alongside James Dean in *Rebel Without a Cause*.

AMITYVILLE HORROR, THE

(1979, dir: Stuart Rosenberg)
James Brolin, Margot Kidder, Rod Steiger.
● NEW JERSEY

The true (!) story of a family hounded out of their Long Island home by apparently supernatural phenomena. The lesson for potential housebuyers is to make sure that a) the previous owner was not your double and responsible for slaughtering his entire family, and b) that your house isn't built over a festering pit of demonic slime. The home of the real George and Kathleen Lutz at 112 Ocean Avenue, Amityville, proved such popular attraction for tourists that the local mayor imposed a parking ban on the street. The movie, though, didn't use the actual location, but was filmed at **18 Dock Street, Tom's River**, a riverside house on the Garden State Parkway, Ocean County, about 20 miles south of Asbury Park on the New Jersey coast. There was more filming at **Scotch Plains**, New Jersey. The prequel, *Amityville II: The Possession*, returned to the Tom's River house for the exteriors, but was largely shot at the **Churubuscu Studios** in **Mexico City**.

ANALYZE THIS

(1999, dir: Harold Ramis)
Robert De Niro, Billy Crystal, Lisa Kudrow.
● **NEW YORK; NEW JERSEY; FLORIDA**

When mob boss Paul Vitti (De Niro) begins to get anxiety attacks, hapless shrink Dr Sobel (Crystal) is hired to cure him in Ramis's satire, filmed around New York, including **Todt Hill, Staten Island** (near to the *Godfather* mansion and, allegedly, home to a number of figures involved in organised crime – allegedly, that is), and **Sing Sing Penitentiary, Ossining**. The hospital, where Vitti's 'heart failure'turns out to be an anxiety attack, is **Elmhurst Hospital Center, 79-01 Broadway, Elmhurst**, Queens. The neighbourhood joint, where Vitti meets fellow mobsters, is the **Old Lion Social Club**, Little Italy.

The Appalachin mafia meeting was filmed in **Katonah**, New York State. New Jersey locations include **Montclair** and **Jersey City**, site of the shootout. **Fort Lauderdale**, Florida, was also used. Lisa Kudrow's (first) wedding takes place at the expensive **Sheraton Bal Harbour Hotel, 9701 Collins Avenue** at 96th Avenue, **Bal Harbour, Miami Beach**, Florida (*© 305.865.7511*).

Easter celebrations: Cathedral of St Alexander Nevsky, Paris

ANASTASIA

(1956, dir: Anatole Litvak)
Ingrid Bergman, Yul Brynner, Helen Hayes.
● **PARIS, FRANCE; HERTFORDSHIRE; COPENHAGEN**

Lavish filming of Marcelle Maurette's play, with Ingrid Bergman winning an Oscar as the woman who might or might not be the surviving daughter of the slaughtered Romanov family. Bergman is discovered in Paris' Russian neighbourhood between the Arc de Triomphe and Parc Monceau. The Russian Orthodox church, where Easter is being celebrated at the beginning of the film, is the **Cathedral of St Alexander Nevsky, 12 rue Daru** (*metro: Courcelles*). 'Anastasia' contemplates suicide at the foot of the steps below **Pont Alexandre III** over the Seine.

The final seal of approval needs to be given by crusty-but-lovable Dowager Empress Helen Hayes. In the real life incident on which the play was based, Anastasia's visit to the Empress was conveniently delayed so many times that the old woman died before the claim could be tested. In the movie, however, Bergman is taken to visit the Empress in Copenhagen. Second unit filming, including **Copenhagen Railway Station** and the nearby **Tivoli Gardens**, can't disguise the fact that the Empress' palace is none other than **Knebworth House**, near Stevenage, Hertfordshire (see Tim Burton's *Batman* for details).

ANATOMY OF A MURDER

(1959, dir: Otto Preminger)
James Stewart, Ben Gazzara, Lee Remick.
● **MICHIGAN**

As Hollywood moved toward more realistic, 'adult' sub-

jects in the late fifties, the glossy artifice of the studios began to look increasingly inappropriate. While scouting exterior locations, Otto Preminger made the bold decision to dispense with studio filming and move the entire production up to the book's setting of Michigan's water-hemmed Upper Peninsula, filming on real locations when possible. Although Robert Traver's book was based on actual events – the trial of a soldier accused of shooting the man he believes raped his wife – the blue-collar town of Iron City and the nearby lakeside resort of Thunder Bay are fictional. Their real life counterparts, where Preminger filmed, are **Ishpeming** and **Marquette**. Marquette is on the Lake Superior coast of Michigan's Upper Peninsula, I-41, and Ishpeming about 15 miles west.

Behind the 'Traver' pseudonym was Michigan Supreme Court Justice John Voelker, and Voelker's house in Ishpeming became the home and law office of his alter ego Paul Biegler (Stewart). Similarly, the 1905 red sandstone **Marquette County Courthouse** was used for the courtroom scenes. Transformed into a temporary studio, the entire second floor of the building was taken over by the film company, with defendant Ben Gazzara held in the cells there. Also in Marquette was the waterfront lunchstand where Stewart and old soak Arthur O'Connell debate whether to defend Gazzara, and the hospital, where O'Connell ends up after a road smash.

Barney Quill's bar, scene of the murder, is two different places – the interior is the Tripoli Bar in Ishpeming (supposedly where the actual shooting occurred and, legend has it, where the bullet holes were preserved by the proprietor). In the movie, it's the bar of the Thunder Bay Inn, which was actually Marquette's Big Bay Inn (though a contemporary photograph of the location clearly shows the sign 'Bay View Inn'). The motel didn't have a bar, so the one-storey Tavern Bar extension was built, and subsequently preserved as a tourist attraction.

Over in Ishpeming are the law library, where Stewart digs out legal precedent – not a law library at all but **Ishpeming Public Library** on **Main Street** – and **Ishpeming Railroad Depot**, the station where Arthur O'Connell meets the army psychiatrist. The Thunder Bay trailer park where Gazzara and Lee Remick live, and the scene of the rape, is a real trailer camp about 25 miles west of Ishpeming at **Michigamme** on I-41.

ANDERSON TAPES, THE

(1971, dir: Sidney Lumet)
Sean Connery, Dyan Cannon, Martin Balsam.
● **NEW YORK CITY**

Sean Connery is an ex-con unprepared for the modern world of surveillance as he heads a gang out to rob an entire luxury apartment block. Lumet's paranoid thriller was filmed on location around Manhattan. Connery is released from the notorious **Riker's Island** in

The lavish apartment block: East 91st Street, Upper East Side

Queens (see *Carlito's Way* for details), and he arrives in Manhattan at the **Port Authority Bus Terminal** on **Eighth Avenue**. The lavish Italianate palazzo they set their sights on is at **1 East 91st Street** on Fifth Avenue, overlooking Central Park. One of New York's largest private houses, the last on Millionaire's Row, it was built in 1918 for banker Otto Kahn and became the Convent of the Sacred Heart (if you're going to take a vow of poverty, you might as well do it in a millionaire's mansion on the Upper East Side), and is now a girls' school. Some interiors were shot at the **New York Production Center Studios**, 221 West 26th Street, but the mansion's oval staircase is the real thing.

ANDREI ROUBLEV

(1966, dir: Andrei Tarkovsky)
Anatoly Solonitsin, Ivan Lapikov, Nikolai Grinko.
● RUSSIA

Epic life of the 15th century artist, virtually the inventor of Russian icon painting who freed the art form from its foreign influences.

At the beginning of the film, Rublev works at the **Church of the Holy Trinity**, part of the **Monastery of the Trinity St Sergius** in **Zagorsk**, 50 miles northeast of Moscow. Zagorsk, now an industrial town, grew up around the Monastery, which houses the remains of the Saint and, in the Church of the Assumption, the remains of usurper tsar Boris Godunov. Rublev's *Icon of the Trinity* here is a copy – the original is in the Tretyakov Gallery, south of the Moskva in the Zamoskvarechye district of Moscow.

The painter spends most of his life at the **Andron-nikov Monastery** in Moscow – which now houses the Andrei Rublev Museum. It's north of Ulianovskaya Street, east of the city centre by the Yaouza River (*rail: Kursk Station*). He decorates the Cathedral of the Dormition in Vladimir, the city which is sacked,100 miles east of Moscow.

You can also see an early icon by Rublev in the Cathedral of the Annunciation in the Kremlin. It was painted in 1405 for a smaller church on the site, which was demolished to make way for the cathedral. These are the places where the events actually took place, and can be visited.

ANGEL (aka *Danny Boy*)

(1982, dir: Neil Jordan)
Stephen Rea, Veronica Quilligan, Ray McAnally.
● IRELAND

Neil Jordan's first film, a fable set against the Troubles in Northern Ireland, was filmed largely in the town of **Bray**, on the Irish coast, about ten miles

The seafront of the unnamed town: Bray

south of Dublin.

ANGEL HEART

(1987, dir: Alan Parker)
Mickey Rourke, Robert De Niro, Lisa Bonet.

● NEW YORK CITY; NEW YORK; NEW ORLEANS, LOUISIANA

De Niro hires PI Mickey Rourke to track down a debtor, but since their respective characters are called Lou Ciphre and Angel, it's clear we're not in for a straight crime film.

Despite the fifties setting, Parker makes great use of real locations in New York and Louisiana. The scuzzy New York of the time was recreated around the 19th century tenements of **Eldridge Street**, on Manhattan's Lower East Side, where the 1955 prices in the shop windows nearly led to riots. Although the same area is also used for some of the Harlem scenes, the Mission and the procession are the real **Harlem**, as is the Lincoln Presbyterian Hospice where Rourke visits bandleader Spider, which was shot at the **Harlem Hospice** on **138th Street**.

Down in the East Village, you can find the bar where Rourke gets hold of pictures of Johnny Favorite. It's **Vazak's Bar, 108 Avenue B** at the corner of Tomkins Square. Vazak's is a familiar 'lowlife atmosphere' bar seen in plenty of other movies, including *"Crocodile" Dundee* and *The Godfather Part II*.

The Poughkeepsie nursing home where Rourke impersonates a hospital inspector is **Rhinebeck**, in Albany, upstate New York toward the Catskills, which had been home to the former secretary, recently deceased, to Franklin D Roosevelt. The neighbourhood of sweaty junkie Dr Fowler, supposedly at 419 Kitteredge, was filmed over on **Staten Island**. In Brooklyn, the venerable **Coney Island, West 10th Street** at Surf Avenue on the South Shore, repainted glumly to suit the film's monochrome look, serves as the rundown, rat-infested amusement park where Rourke looks for Madame Zora.

And on to New Orleans, sort of. Rourke's arrival in Louisiana by train was shot at **Hoboken Railway Station**, just over the Hudson from Lower Manhattan.

The real Big Easy shooting was largely around the Victorian houses and shops in the old Irish section along **Magazine Street**, New Orleans. The streetcar was filmed on the main **St Charles Avenue track**. Charlotte Rampling's house was a boarded-up property behind Royal Street, while the slave quarters at the back doubled as Rourke's hotel. The touristy shots of New Orleans take in the arches by the market on **Decatur Street, St Peter Street** alongside St Louis Cathedral.

The church where Rourke indulges in a little profane language is **St Alphonsius, 2029 Constance Street**, parallel to Magazine Street. The racetrack, though, doesn't exist – it was specially built in an empty field. The gumbo shack where Rampling's father gets his face boiled is a disused New Orleans bus depot and the flashbacks to a post-war Times Square were also, confusingly, filmed in New Orleans. If you want to visit the plantation village where Rourke meets up with Lisa Bonet, it's the **Laurel Valley Village Museum, 595 Highway 308** (*© 985.446.8111*), a perfectly preserved sugar plantation dating from 1832, two miles south of Thibodoux. The plantation, still in use in the 21st century, once covered 5,000 acres and is pretty much as seen in the movie – only the cemetery is faked. Thibodoux is on Route 1, 50 miles west of New Orleans on the Bayou Lafouche. The Red

Rooster, where Rourke meets up with Toots Sweet, is actually the popular **Maple Leaf Club, 8316 Oak Street**, New Orleans (© *504.866.9359*), a smallish, tin-ceilinged music bar with the best of local blues, Cajun and R&B.

ANGELA'S ASHES
(2000, dir: Alan Parker)
Robert Carlyle, Emily Watson, Joe Breen.
● IRELAND

The ashes of controversy were fanned into flame when Alan Parker decided to film Frank McCourt's grim, poverty-ridden autobiography on the actual locations in **Limerick**, in the west of Ireland. In the end, much of the movie was shot in **Cork**, at **Cobh Harbour**, and on sets in Dublin.

ANGST ESSEN SEELE AUF (aka *Fear Eats the Soul*)
(1973, dir: Rainer Werner Fassbinder)
Brigitti Mira, El Hedi Ben Salem, Barbara Valentin.
● MUNICH, GERMANY

Loosely based on Douglas Sirk's 1955 melodrama *All That Heaven Allows*, Fassbinder's film deals with the prejudice surrounding the relationship between Mira's older charwoman and Ben Salem's younger Moroccan immigrant. It was shot in Munich.

ANNA KARENINA
(1935, dir: Clarence Brown)
Greta Garbo, Fredric March, Basil Rathbone.
● CALIFORNIA

A second stab at Tolstoy's novel (Garbo starred in a 1927 silent version called *Love*), filmed largely in a Hollywood studio, though the racetrack and steeplechase scenes were shot up the coast on the beautiful **Monterey Peninsula**.

ANNÉE DERNIÈRE À MARIENBAD, L' (aka *Last Year in Marienbad*)
(1961, dir: Alain Resnais)
Delphine Seyrig, Giorgio Albertazzi, Sacha Pitoeff.
● MUNICH, GERMANY

If, in the sixties, you saw a serious bunch of students hunched over a table mysteriously moving matchsticks around, chances are they were high society members playing out Sacha Pitoeff's fiendish game from this art house movie *par excellence*. Well, was it Marienbad? Or Frederiksbad? Or neither? Sorry to be so prosaic, but it was **Munich**. Three overwrought baroque castles were knitted together to make a single, vast, labyrinthine hotel. You could go crazy trying to untangle Resnais' sinuous jigsaw, one location flowing seamlessly into another, the layout of the garden endlessly changing and doors not always opening onto the same room. Not surprisingly, the major location, a gigantic rococo palace where elegantly attired guests play arcane games, was once home to the famously extravagant King Ludwig I. It's **Schloss Nymphenburg**, 200 years in the building and half a mile from wingtip to wingtip, in a northwest suburb of the city. Ludwig, while struggling with his sexuality, managed to scandalise society by commissioning a series of portraits of women – including notorious courtesan Lola Montes

Interior of the Marienbad hotel: Schloss Nymphenburg, Munich

– which now hang in the palace's Schönheitengalerie (The Gallery of Beauties). The largest of its kind in Germany, the palace is set in 500 acres of parkland, varying from the wild to the geometrically formal French-style gardens seen in the film. Nymphenburg can be reached by the number 12 streetcar or the 41 bus from downtown Munich. It's open Tuesdays to Sundays.

In the grounds is the hunting lodge, **Amalienburg**, second of the movie's locations. If 'hunting lodge' conjures up images of rustic simplicity, you're in for a surprise. The interior is even more florid than Nymphenburg; a white, green and gold rococo fantasy centered around the sumptuous Spiegelsaal, the Hall of Mirrors. Resnais has loads of fun here with the endless reflections, seen over the opening monologue and used as the setting for the concert on Seyrig and Albertazzi's final evening.

The plainer exterior, seen as Frederiksbad in Albertazzi's memories and in the framed pictures throughout the film, is the **Neues Schloss** of **Schloss Schleissheim**, housing the Bayerische Staatsgalerie collection of baroque art. Find it to the northwest of Munich, on the S-1 urban line and the 292 bus to Oberschleissheim. You won't be able to see the classical statue of Charles III and his wife, which appears to move constantly about the gardens, though. Based on characters in a painting by Poussin, it was built specially for the movie. You can pose in the formal gardens, but if you want to appear as stylish as the cast, the trick is to organise your own accessories. Unlike the trees, the humans cast impossibly long, dramatic shadows – these were actually painted onto the ground.

The real Marienbad, by the way, or more properly Marianske Lazne, which has no connection with the movie at all, is a spa town in the Czech Republic about 80 miles west of Prague, south of Karlovy Vary.

ANNIE HALL
(1977, dir: Woody Allen)
Woody Allen, Diane Keaton, Shelley Duvall.
● NEW YORK CITY; LOS ANGELES, CALIFORNIA

Oscar-winner for Best Picture, and seen by many as his best film, Allen's innovative, episodic account of the on/off relationship between East Coast Jewish intellectual Alvy Singer and the WASPish Annie, who eventually takes root on the West Coast, was filmed mainly around New York. The young Alvy's childhood home is under the Cyclone Ride at **Coney Island**, entrance on **West 10th Street** at Surf Avenue on Brooklyn's South Shore, subway lines D, Q, N, B and F. The wooden house actually burned down in May 1991, but the Cyclone is still there. Steve's Famous Clam Bar, seen in the flashback, which stood at 515 Atlantic Avenue at Third Avenue, is now a diner.

As usual, Allen visits a clutch of New York cinemas.

The picture house showing Bergman's *Face to Face*, where Alvy is recognised from TV as he waits for Annie, is the **Beekman Cinema, 1254 Second Avenue** at

The LA health food restaurant: Cabo Cantina, Hollywood

East 65th Street (*© 212.737.2622*) on the East Side, and now part of the Clearview chain. He conjures Marshall McLuhan out of the air to silence a loudmouth pseud in the queue at the New York Theater, now demolished, which stood at 1514 Broadway. The final movie house, where Alvy bumps into Annie taking her new guy to see *The Sorrow and the Pity*, was the Thalia Cinema, which closed in 1987. The theatre is now Symphony Space, an arts project, at **2537 Broadway**, on the Upper West Side. Annie's apartment is on **70th Street**, between Lexington and Park Avenues (the number remains a mystery as we don't see the exterior). The beach and the beach house, where Alvy and Annie have problems with lobsters, is **The Hamptons**, the exclusive South Shore enclave at the far eastern end of Long Island on Route 27, while the sporty club where Alvy and Annie first meet is the **Wall Street Tennis Club**. The inevitable visit to **Central Park** sees the couple mocking nerdy passers-by.

Over on the West Coast – anathema to Woody Allen – was the health food restaurant where Alvy tries the alfalfa sprouts with mashed yeast, before Annie turns down his proposal. Then it was the Source Restaurant, but food fads change, it was for a long time the Cajun Bistro, but it's now Mexican restaurant **Cabo Cantina, 8301 Sunset Boulevard** at Sweetzer Avenue (*© 323.822.7820*) in west Hollywood.

ANY GIVEN SUNDAY

(1999, dir: Oliver Stone)
Al Pacino, Jamie Foxx, Cameron Diaz.
● **FLORIDA; TEXAS**

Oliver Stone's power-playing drama of American football treads familiar territory and spends too much time on the football pitch. Set largely in Florida, the home of the fictitious Miami Sharks is the **Orange Bowl Stadium, 1501 NW 3rd Street**, Miami (*© 305.643.7100*). The mayor's party is held in that familiar old standby of Miami movies, **Villa Vizcaya, 3251 South Miami Avenue** at 32nd Road, an Italianate mansion south of Miami in Coconut Grove (for details, see *Ace Ventura, Pet Detective*). The nightspot where Jamie Foxx bumps into his ex is the **Cardozo Hotel, 1300 Ocean Drive**, South Beach (see *There's Something About Mary* for details). More scenes were shot in Miami's southern suburb of **Homestead**, and the home of the Dallas Knights, scene of the climactic game, is in the real Lone Star state – it's the **Texas Stadium, Irving**.

APARAJITO (aka *The Unvanquished*)

(1956, dir: Satyajit Ray)
Kanu Banerjee, Karuna Banerjee, Pinaki Sen Gupta.

● **INDIA**

The second of Ray's acclaimed Apu trilogy, based on the novels by Bibhutibhusan Banerjee, follows the life of the young village boy determined to pursue his education in the city as first his father, and then his mother, die.

Aparajito opens in **Varanisi**, the post-independence name of Benares in the northern province of Uttar Pradesh (confusingly, Varanisi is also referred to by the old name of Kashi), to which Apu's family move at the end of *Pather Panchali*, the first film of the trilogy. Varanisi is the major Hindu holy city (home to over two thousand temples and shrines), built on the sacred Ganga River. The opening sequence gives a picture of bustling life on the ghats, the stepped landings on the river banks, where priests recite, a muscleman swings a club and bodies are burned. Young Apu passes the time on the ghats and it's here, negotiating the steps, that his father Harihar collapses. Apu returns to the landings to fetch a bowl of Ganga water for the dying Harihar. 81 ghats line this four mile stretch of the Ganga's western bank.

The incense-filled temple to which Apu accompanies his mother is Varanisi's chief shrine, the **Vishvanath Temple** (Vishvanath is an alternative name for Shiva, Lord of the Dance). Built in 1750, the gilded decoration from 1939 has earned it the name of the Golden Temple. It's set back from the Ganga between Dasashwarnedh and Manikarnika Ghats, and is not open to non-Hindus. You can get the best view from the roof of the house opposite, which makes a small charge for the privilege.

After Harihar's death, Apu and his mother leave the city for a remote village in Bengal (the name is given as Mansapota, and the nearby school Apu attends in Arboal), but Apu has ambitions beyond life as a village priest and takes the train to Calcutta where he studies at the university. He arrives at eastern India's main rail terminal, **Howrah Station** on the north bank of the Hooghly River, and sees the English street sign on Harrison Road.

APARTMENT, THE

(1960, dir: Billy Wilder)
Jack Lemmon, Shirley MacLaine, Fred MacMurray.
● **NEW YORK CITY**

Wilder's snappy satire scooped Best Picture, Writer and Director Oscars. Jack Lemmon features as an insurance clerk obliged to let out his apartment to philandering boss Fred MacMurray. The Consolidated Life of New York, where Lemmon works, was a brand new (in 1960) $13 million skyscraper in Manhattan's commercial district, which provided the exterior and lobby scenes. When Lemmon waits in vain for Shirley MacLaine (while she's being wined and dined by sleazeball MacMurray), it's outside the **Majestic Theater, 247 West 44th Street** between Broadway and 8th Avenue, where the hit musical of the day, *The Music Man*, was playing (*© 212.239.6200*). It's a real New York bar where a morose Lemmon builds up an impressive collection of cocktail olives, on the West Side at **205 Columbus Avenue**, between West 69th and West 70th Streets. The address of the titular brownstone house itself is given as 51 West 57th Street, on the West

Side close to Central Park, though the apartment used was actually on **59th Street**.

APOCALYPSE NOW

(1979, dir: Francis Ford Coppola)
Martin Sheen, Marlon Brando, Robert Duvall.
● **PHILIPPINES**

Coppola films Joseph Conrad's *Heart of Darkness* as a total Vietnam experience, a series of overwhelming cinematic set-pieces. Filmed on the island of **Luzon** in the Philippines, the nightmare shoot was recorded in Eleanor Coppola's book *Notes* and her amazing documentary film, *Hearts of Darkness*.

The Wagnerian helicopter attack on the quiet village was filmed at **Baler** on the northeastern coast of Luzon (the northern island of the Philippines, home to the capital, Manila). The helicopters, provided by President Marcos, were being used to put down Filipino insurgents at night, and occasionally during the day too, when they would suddenly veer off mid-shot. The surfing beach, fresh with the smell of napalm, subsequently commandeered by Robert Duvall is **Baler Bay**, and is indeed just being discovered as *the* place to ride the waves in the Philippines. Baler is about 120 miles northeast of Manila, reachable by a seven-hour bus journey.

As the disaster toll mounted (star Harvey Keitel was replaced by Martin Sheen, who suffered a heart attack) the sets, originally located at **Iba**, on Luzon's west coast, northwest of Manila, were wrecked by Hurricane Olga. Many had to be recreated at **Pagsanjan**, about an hour and a half's drive southeast of Manila. The trippy Do Long bridge was built here, on the Magdapio River, as was Kurtz's compound. Pagsanjan is worth the visit – to reach it, take the South Expressway from Manila as far as you can go, turn left to Calamba, then right, and it's signposted. Alternatively, there's a bumpy three-hour bus ride. There's also a thrilling, and extremely wet, boat trip up the rapids to Pagsanjan Falls (also known as Magdapio Falls). Check with the local travel agencies, as some of the boatmen have been known to rip off tourists. The four mile paddle upriver to the falls passes the site of Brando's nightmare empire, and it's followed by a scary, white-water ride back over fourteen sets of rapids.

The local Ifugaos were recruited to play extras and disembodied heads (their bodies concealed in boxes buried beneath the set) in Kurtz's kingdom, and the climactic hacking to death of a water buffalo – which Coppola managed to capture on film – is part of their ritual celebration, though whether an elaborate set and romantic backlighting are part of the tradition isn't made clear.

APOLLO 13

(1995, dir: Ron Howard)
Tom Hanks, Bill Paxton, Kevin Bacon.
● **LOS ANGELES, CALIFORNIA; TEXAS; FLORIDA**

Very special FX in this surprisingly gripping account of the ill-fated 1970 moonflight. There's far less location filming than you might imagine, since the gigantic Saturn V rockets, which carried the moon missions from Cape Kennedy, have long since been replaced by recy-

clable shuttles. As a consequence, much of the movie was tricked up in Hollywood. The Saturn V launched in the movie is a one-twentieth scale model, while most of the sequence is computer generated. Mission Control, too, was filmed in the studios at Universal.

To achieve the authentic feeling of weightlessness, director Howard filmed the Apollo capsule scenes on a set built inside a KC-135 cargo plane used for NASA training flights. The jet followed a 30,000 feet parabolic trajectory before going into a roller-coaster dive, giving 23 seconds of weightlessness to get a shot in the can. The effect on stomach contents of ten days filming under these conditions earned the KC-135 the nickname the Vomit Comet. The plane flew from **Ellington Field**, about 15 miles south of **Houston, Texas**.

Rather like some enormous dinosaur, NASA's moving parts are a long, long way from its brain, though, fortunately for space buffs who'll doubtless want to explore the real thing, both sites can be visited. The launch site, which provided backgrounds for the faked take-off, is of course the **Kennedy Space Center, Merritt Island, Florida** (© *321.867.5000*, *www.ksc.nasa.gov/visit/visitor.htm*). Merritt Island, most of which is a wildlife reserve, can be reached by I-405 from Titusville, on the coast 50 miles east of Orlando, or Route 3 north on Bennett Causeway from the town of Cocoa. Two bus tours, Red and Blue, cover the site – the Red Tour takes in the Space Center, where you can see the 52-storey Vehicle Assembly Building. This massive structure, where the Saturn rockets were built, is seen in the movie, but the open door is another piece of computer generated trickery. Even if NASA had been persuaded to open the 400-foot-high doors for filming, there wouldn't have been a Saturn inside. Sophisticated motion-control techniques were used to add the rocket to a genuine helicopter shot. You can see one of the old Saturn rockets on the Space Center tour, though. The other place to see a Saturn V is in the Rocket Park at the Lyndon B Johnson Space Center in Houston, site of the real Mission Control. You can tour most of this facility, including Shuttle training vehicles, laboratories, samples of moon rock and, if it's not closed for a launch, the actual Mission Control Room itself. Open every day except Christmas, 9am to 4pm, entrance is free. It's about 20 miles south of Houston on I-45 (© *713.244.2100*).

You can also visit the Florida motel with an ocean view where Mrs Lovell spends the night before the launch, and where she ominously loses her wedding ring in the shower. It's actually in Los Angeles: the **Safari Inn Motel, 1911 Olive Avenue, Burbank** (© *818.845.8586*). This sixties themed motel with illuminated 'African' sign can also be seen as Clarence and Alabama's hideaway in Tony Scott's film of Quentin Tarantino's *True Romance*. Gary Sinise's and Kevin

Saturn V rocket: Lyndon B Johnson Space Center, Houston

Bacon's apartments were in the **Ambassador Hotel, 3400 Wilshire Boulevard**, midtown LA. The hotel closed in 1989 and is now used only as a movie location. It's currently under threat of demolition.

ARABESQUE

(1966, dir: Stanley Donen)
Gregory Peck, Sophia Loren, Alan Badel.
● **LONDON; BERKSHIRE; OXFORDSHIRE; SOUTH WALES**

Gregory Peck's college: St John's, Oxford

Veteran director Donen invests this lightweight sub-Hitchcock comedy thriller with lurid sixties visuals, as Professor Gregory Peck is marked for death after he deciphers some mysterious Egyptian hieroglyphics. The university where Peck lectures is, of course, Oxford, and you can see the rather grand quad where he's propositioned at **St John's College** on St Giles Street. It's the inner Canterbury Quad (which also appears in Joseph Losey's *Accident*).

Touristy locations include **Regents Park Zoo**; **Trafalgar Square** (unable to use a helicopter shot, Donen took his camera up Nelson's Column using block and tackle); the **British Museum**; the Royal Enclosure at **Ascot Racetrack** in Berkshire; and **Waterloo Station**.

The climactic chase, with helicopter-borne villains pursuing Peck and Loren under a railway viaduct, was filmed at **Crumlin**, on the railway line between Newport and Abertillery, Gwent, in South Wales. The viaduct was demolished after filming. According to studio publicity, road, rail, gas and electricity were cut off during the stunt filming, and 350 people from a nearby village had to be evacuated – though £2 'disturbance money' was handed out to each family. Ms Loren's wardrobe, by comparison, cost £53,500.

ARABIAN NIGHTS

(1974, dir: Pier Paolo Pasolini)
Ninetto Davoli, Franco Citti, Franco Merli.
● **NORTH AFRICA; MIDDLE EAST; NEPAL; INDIA**

Final part of Pasolini's Trilogy of Life, following *The Decameron* and *The Canterbury Tales*, beautifully filmed in North Africa and the Middle East. The African scenes were shot in the northeast of the continent in **Ethiopia** and **Eritrea**, and over the Red Sea in **Yemen**. Filming also took place in **Nepal** and **India**. The wedding scene was shot at **Esfahan** in central **Iran** in the courtyard of the spectacular pale-blue tiled **Mesjed-e Imam** (formerly the Mesjed-e Shah), completed in 1638 after 26 years of work. It's on the south side of the Meidun-e Imam, the huge square in the centre of Esfahan.

ARACHNOPHOBIA

(1990, dir: Frank Marshall)
Jeff Daniels, John Goodman, Julian Sands.

● **CALIFORNIA; VENEZUELA**

Jaws with spiders. The fictional Californian coastal town of Canaima, where the house and barn were built for the movie, is **Cambria**, which you'll find ten miles south of San Simeon toward San Luis Obispo on Highway 1. The jungle scenes were shot near Angel Falls in Venezuela, at a place actually called **Canaima**.

ARMAGEDDON

(1998, dir: Michael Bay)
Bruce Willis, Ben Affleck, Steve Buscemi.
● **NEW YORK CITY; LOS ANGELES, CALIFORNIA; TEXAS; SOUTH DAKOTA; WASHINGTON DC; FLORIDA; NEW MEXICO; FRANCE; TURKEY; INDIA; CHINA**

Asteroid fragments rain down on New York...: Grand Central Station

The saving grace of Michael Bay's gung-ho epic, as an asteroid the size of Texas threatens total oblivion, is the ragtag line-up of quirky characters whose price tag for saving the world is never to pay taxes again – ever. The Space Shuttle launch is for real, filmed at the **Kennedy Space Center** in Florida (see *Apollo 13* for details). Filming also took place at NASA's six million-gallon neutral buoyancy tank at the **Lyndon B Johnson Space Center, Houston**, Texas (*www.spacecenter.org*). Establishing reaction shots were taken in New York, Washington DC and at **Pilot Point, Aubrey** and **Denton**, Texas. The surface of the asteroid, where the shuttles *Independence* and *Freedom* crash-land, was in the **Badlands National Park**, South Dakota (*www.nps.gov/badl*). Director Bay also used **Edwards Air Force Base**, north of LA; the **Shrine Auditorium, 665 West Jefferson Boulevard** (see *A Star Is Born* for details); and the **Fletcher Oil Refinery, 24721 Main Street, Carson** between Sepulveda and Lomita Boulevard. Filming also occured at the, imaginatively-named, **Very Large Array National Radio Astronomy Observatory** (*www.aoc.nrao.edu/AOC*) on the San Augustin Plains at **Socorro**, New Mexico, 27 dishes arranged along three 13-mile arms. The visitor centre is on Route 52, and there's a walking tour of the site.

The lively nightclub, from which Buscemi and Owen Wilson get ejected after celebrating their last night on Earth, is the lobby of the wildly elaborate **Los Angeles Theatre, 615 South Broadway**, downtown Los Angeles (a very popular location, see *Chaplin* for details). Harry Stamper (Willis) visits his ageing dad at the **RR Blacker House, 1177 Hill-**

...but land in LA: Main Street

Willis bids goodbye to his old dad: RR Blacker House, Pasadena

crest Avenue, **Oak Knoll**, Pasadena – though only in the restored Director's Cut (seen also in *Back to the Future*).

More global atmosphere shots were filmed in **San Michele**, France; the **Blue Mosque** and **Ortakoy**, Istanbul, Turkey; at the **Taj Mahal** and the **Red Fort**, India; and in **Shanghai**, China. The opening meteor shower blitzing 53rd Street, New York was actually filmed in Los Angeles, around **Fourth Street** and **Main Street**, by the old **Barclay Hotel** (seen also in *As Good As It Gets*).

The church where Liv Tyler and Affleck get hitched at the end of the movie is **St Brendan's, 310 South Van Ness Avenue** at Third Street, Hancock Park, midtown LA, which may (or may not) be a nod to classic 50s sci-fi *The War of the Worlds*, which also filmed at the church.

ARMY OF DARKNESS
(1993, dir: Sam Raimi)
Bruce Campbell, Embeth Davidtz, Marcus Gilbert.
● CALIFORNIA

The third *Evil Dead* movie goes back to the Middle Ages for this bloody romp, filmed mainly on the La Brea Stage in Hollywood. The 13th century English castle was constructed in the, no doubt, geographically accurate High Desert of California at **Acton**, just off Route 14 north of LA. Filming also took place at **Vasquez Rocks** (see *Blazing Saddles* for details).

AROUND THE WORLD IN EIGHTY DAYS
(1956, dir: Michael Anderson)
David Niven, Cantinflas, Shirley MacLaine.
● LONDON; PARIS, FRANCE; SPAIN; INDIA; HONG KONG, CHINA; JAPAN; CALIFORNIA; COLORADO; OKLAHOMA

Cantinflas and the pennyfarthing: Upper Cheyne Row, Chelsea

Statistics first: 50 guest stars; 68,894 people on screen (count 'em); eight different countries filmed; four million air-passenger miles travelled; 112 exterior locations; 140 sets in six Hollywood studios, plus studios in England, Hong Kong and Japan; 34 species of animal; 33 assistant directors. The plan was to use a director from each country to direct each sequence, but Brit director Anderson, who kicked off with an efficient – if uninspired – job in London was handed the whole assignment by producer Mike Todd. Associate Producer William Cameron Menzies, the brilliant production designer who storyboarded *Gone With the Wind*, was responsible for the exterior locations in Europe, Colorado and Oklahoma.

The opening scenes were shot in London, beginning with **Rotten Row, Hyde Park**. The Scots Guards parade was filmed at **Wellington Barracks**, the unofficial shots taken by a camera hidden in a vegetable stall. Niven accepts the challenge to travel around the world at the **Reform Club**, a real London club still going strong, at **104 Pall Mall**, SW1 (though, along with Baggott's Employment Office and Lloyd's of London, the interiors were recreated at Elstree). Cantinflas pedals his penny-farthing along **Upper Cheyne Row** off Oakley Street just north of Albert Bridge, Chelsea, SW3, to **Victoria Square**, a quiet square tucked away to the northwest of Buckingham Palace Road, SW1 (where the Schlegel sisters live in Merchant-Ivory's film of *Howards End*). The building used as Hesketh-Baggott's Employment Office, where John Gielgud complains to agency boss Noël Coward, is unchanged. It's **5 Lower Grosvenor Place** on the corner of Victoria Square, SW1 (*tube: Victoria*).

Niven and Cantinflas arrive in Paris at the **Gare du Nord**, rue du Faubourg Saint Martin. They travel by taxi to Thomas Cook's in the arcades of the **rue de Rivoli**, via **Place Vendôme** and rue de Castiglione. The film ran into a spot of trouble with the law here when around forty out-of-period cars were spirited away out of camera range without permission. Don't bother trying to look for the dinky French village from which Niven and Cantinflas make their balloon ascent – it's simply a studio set.

The Spanish seaport where the balloon lands is also a studio set, though some scenes were filmed on the road near **Toledo**, and the bullfight was staged in **Chinchon**, about 25 miles southeast of Madrid on the M311 Valencia road. The arcaded town square, Plaza Mayor, with its photogenic wooden loggias was dressed up for a fiesta and the 6,500 inhabitants were togged up in period gear. Plaza Mayor is actually used for bullfights in the late summer, but a more civilised way to see the square is to try the many little restaurants overlooking it.

The Suez docks were recreated on a soundstage at the RKO Studios in Hollywood, were we get the first sight of the HMS *Mongolia*, which takes Niven and co to Bombay. With a bit of ingenuity from the art department, the same boat reappears throughout the movie, as the SS *Rangoon* from Calcutta to Hong Kong, the SS *General Grant* to San Francisco, and finally the ill-fated *Henrietta* from New York to Liverpool.

The Indian train journey is real enough, but the Bombay street and the Pagoda of Pillaji, where a browned-up Shirley MacLaine escapes ritual suttee are pure Hollywood. The waterfront dive on the Calcutta to Hong Kong leg is back at RKO – the junk journey to Yokohama features real views of Mount Fuji, but RKO again provides the Japanese theatre where Cantinflas performs. The San Francisco election rally and Clancy's, the Barbary coast

Noël Coward's employment agency: Lower Grosvenor Place, Victoria

dive, where George Raft pairs up with Marlene Dietrich as Frank Sinatra tinkles the ivories, are all Hollywood.

The transcontinental railway journey, with Buster Keaton (talking!) as a guard, was filmed on the **Durango and Silverton Narrow Gauge Railway**, running 45 miles between Durango and Silverton alongside Route 550 through the spectacular 3,000 foot San Juan Mountains in southwest Colorado. You can ride on the train – travel to Silverton by bus and make the one-way journey back – or you can get further information from 479 Main Avenue, Durango, Colorado (© *303.247.2733, www.durangotrain.com*), but the return journey will take up a whole day. The railroad is also seen in *Across the Wide Missouri, Butch Cassidy and the Sundance Kid, How The West Was Won* and *Ticket to Tomahawk*. The stampede of buffalo (2,448 of them – go ahead, doubters, count them) was shot in Oklahoma, as was the Indian pow-wow with Cantinflas being burned at the stake, at **Lawton**, about 70 miles southwest of Oklahoma City on I-44 in the southwest of the state.

The final sea journey from New York to Liverpool, with the *Henrietta* dismantled to feed its own furnace, was filmed offshore at **Newport Beach**, just south of LA.

Arthur and the hookers: Plaza Hotel, Fifth Avenue

ARTHUR

(1981, dir: Steve Gordon)
Dudley Moore, John Gielgud, Liza Minnelli.
● **NEW YORK CITY; NEW YORK**

Any pretensions Steve Gordon may have had toward saying something about alcoholism are scuppered by Moore's (unbelievably Oscar-nominated) one-note, end-of-the-pier drunk, and it's left to waspish butler Gielgud to walk off with the Academy Award, and the film.

If you're in the same tax bracket, why not enjoy a meal at the classy restaurant where Moore shocks fellow diners with hooker Gloria, the **Oak Room** at the **Plaza Hotel, Fifth Avenue** at 59th Street (© *212.759.3000, www.fairmont.com/theplaza*). See *North by Northwest* for full details. But please don't imitate Liza Minnelli by shoplifting at **Bergdorf-Goodman's** posh department store, **754 Fifth Avenue** between 57th and 58th Streets. On the Upper East Side, visit Moore's Grandma's house, the **Carnegie**

Liza Minnelli shoplifts: Bergdorf-Goodman, Fifth Avenue

Opting out of the wedding: St Bartholomew's, Fifth Avenue

Mansion, 2 East 91st Street, familiar from *Marathon Man, Working Girl* and Sean Connery thriller *The Next Man*.

Over on Long Island, the swanky country homes of

Arthur's Grandma's: Carnegie Mansion, Upper East Side

Arthur's fiancée Susan and her father can be found in **Glen Cove** and **Manhasset**. Filming also took place at the **Knole Estate, Old Westbury** on Long Island, and the stables were at **Caumsett**, on the Marshall Field III estate, now a State Park. You can find the church, where Moore opts out of the arranged marriage, on Park Avenue, naturally. It's the Byzantine-styled, Episcopalian **St Bartholomew's, 109 Fifth Avenue**.

AS GOOD AS IT GETS

(1997, dir: James L Brooks)
Jack Nicholson, Helen Hunt, Greg Kinnear.
● **NEW YORK CITY; LOS ANGELES, CALIFORNIA**

Oscars for Nicholson and Hunt in this enjoyable but soft-centred feel-good movie, as waitress Helen Hunt, gay neighbour Greg Kinnear and Verdell the dog soften up bigotted obsessive-compulsive writer Nicholson. Nicholson and Kinnear's apartment block is **31-33 12th Street** between Fifth and Sixth Avenues in

The Cafe 24 Heures: Barclay Hotel, Fourth Street

Nicholson's apartment: 12th Street, West Village

the West Village, New York. Helen Hunt lives at **1 Windsor Place** in the rather nice Prospect Park district of Brooklyn. The Café 24 Heures, where Hunt works, is actually way over on the west coast. It was constructed on the ground floor of the rundown **Barclay Hotel**, on the corner of **Fourth Street** and **Main Street**, in a decrepit area of downtown (the junction appears as New York again in *Armageddon*). The seafront restaurant, supposedly in Chesapeake Bay, Baltimore, can be found down in Long Beach, south of LA. It's **Khoury's Restaurant, 110 North Marina Drive** on the Alamitos Bay Landing Center (© *562.598.6800, www.khourys.net*). The pier is **Seal Beach Pier, Main Street, Seal Beach**.

ASCENSEUR POUR L'ECHAFAUD (aka *Lift to the Scaffold/Frantic*)

(1957, dir: Louis Malle)
Maurice Ronet, Jeanne Moreau, Georges Poujouly.

Dumping the Merc: Pont de Bir-Hakeim

The suicide pact:
Boulevard de Grenelle

● **PARIS, FRANCE**

Louis Malle's first feature is a tightly-made thriller with a cool Miles Davis score. Ronet plots with Moreau to kill her husband – his boss – but their scheme goes awry when a local tearaway takes Ronet's car for a murderous joyride while Ronet is trapped in a lift overnight. The innovative camera-work shows a distracted Moreau walking down the **Champs Elysées** at night, illuminated only by the light from shop windows. The motel where the joyriders kill the German tourists was in Normandy, as there were none in Paris then.

They dump the car on the **Pont de Bir-Hakeim**, the double-decker road and rail bridge just west of the Eiffel Tower. Originally the Passy Viaduct, the bridge was renamed in 1949 to commemorate the Free French Army's battles against Rommel in the Libyan Desert in 1942 (*metro: Bir-Hakeim, Passy*). You'll probably be more familiar with it from Bertolucci's *Last Tango in Paris*. The subsequent botched suicide pact at the girlfriend's apartment is just south of the Pont de Bir-Hakeim, at **55 boulevard de Grenelle**. The art nouveau building is largely unchanged, but is slightly more upmarket, and probably not home to many teenage shop assistants these days.

ASPHALT JUNGLE, THE
(1950, dir: John Huston)
Sterling Hayden, Louis Calhern, Marilyn Monroe.
● **LOS ANGELES, CALIFORNIA; KENTUCKY**

The inner-city setting of Huston's prototype caper movie was intended to be non-specific. Locations scouted included St Louis and Cincinnati, but in the end the crew simply filmed around **LA**, apart from the final sequence, shot at horse-racing capital **Lexington** in Kentucky.

ASSAULT ON PRECINCT 13
(1976, dir: John Carpenter)
Austin Stoker, Darwin Joston, Laurie Zimmer.
● **LOS ANGELES, CALIFORNIA**

Precinct 13: Social and Public Art Resource Center, Venice Boulevard

Carpenter's reworking of Howard Hawks' *Rio Bravo* sees an unlikely mixed-race street gang besieging a near-deserted police station. The precinct is actually Precinct 9, in the fictitious Anderson, and the movie was originally called *The Anderson Alamo*. The title was changed to *The Siege*, before distributor Irwin Yablans came up with the final catchy, if inaccurate, moniker.

Shot on a shoestring, the movie uses a patchwork of locations around LA, and the interiors were filmed at the Producers Studio, now **Raleigh Studios**. The streets near the station are in Watts, LA's troubled South Central area, and the view across the street from the precinct is North Hollywood. However, Anderson Police Station, Division 14 itself is the old Police and Fire Station of Venice, which was the only art deco police station in LA and is now the **Social and Public Art Resource Center, 685 North Venice Boulevard** (*www.sparcmurals.org*), on the northest corner of Pisani Drive, Venice, devoted to LA's excellent tradition of multi-ethnic public art. Murals, that is.

ATALANTE, L'
(1934, dir: Jean Vigo)
Jean Dasté, Dita Parlo, Michel Simon.
● **FRANCE**

Vigo's dreamy, poetic movie, with Dita Parlo as barge captain Jean Dasté's wife, seduced away from romantic shipboard life by the lure of Paris. The dozen or so cats aboard the barge, so much a part of the movie's feel, were Vigo's idea, replacing the dog specified in the script.

The opening wedding scene was staged at the village of **Maurecourt** on the Oise, just north of the Seine, about 20 miles northwest of Paris. Canal scenes were filmed at nearby **Conflans-Sainte-Honorine**, a centre for river navigation on the Seine (there's a River Craft Museum here). The journey to Paris continues along the **Canal de Ourcq**, northeast of the city, into the marina at **Bassin la Villette** (also seen in Jean-Jacques Beineix's *Diva*) and on to the Canal St Martin, where the barge docks at the **Quai de la Loire**, northeast from Jaures metro station. The cabaret where Dita Parlo is tempted toward city life by a pedlar is the Charentonneau Dance Hall in **Maisons Alfort** to the southeast of Paris (though the interior is a set). The railway station where Parlo is robbed is the **Gare d'Austerlitz**, which had to be shot in the closed station after midnight, populated with friends of Vigo dragged from the bars of St-Germain-des-Pres.

ATLANTIC CITY
(1980, dir: Louis Malle)
Burt Lancaster, Susan Sarandon, Michel Piccoli.
● **ATLANTIC CITY, NEW JERSEY; CANADA**

Enjoyably quirky low-life comedy drama, scripted by playwright John Guare and filmed in the famed old East Coast resort as the grand old hotels were being demolished and the quaint seaside tradition metamorphosed into a flash-trash ersatz Vegas (casino gambling was legalised in 1977). The action, of course, centres on the famous **Boardwalk**. Originally a temporary structure built to prevent sand being trampled into the elegant seafront hotels, the Boardwalk now defines the resort. The elephant-shaped building seen at the beginning, as Susan Sarandon's disreputable relatives ride into town, is **Lucy the**

Margate Elephant, a Victorian folly, originally built of wood and tin. She's six-storeys high, has spiral stairs in her legs and houses a museum of Atlantic City memorabilia. You'll find Lucy at **9200 Atlantic Avenue** (© *609.823.6473, www.lucytheelephant.org; admission charge*). Sarandon trains to be a dealer at the Resorts International Casino, now **Merv Griffin's Resorts Casino Hotel, 1133 Boardwalk** at North Carolina Avenue (© *609.344.1133*), Atlantic City's first casino. The seafood restaurant where she shares a celebration meal with Lancaster is the rather pricey 1912 landmark **Knife and Fork Inn, 29 South Albany Avenue** at Atlantic Avenue (© *609.344.1133*). The constantly moving car park where Sarandon's ne'er-do-well husband meets his end is the **Park Mobile**. The film was a Canadian 'tax shelter' movie, which is why most of the supporting cast are Canadian, and the interiors were filmed in **Montreal**.

ATTACK OF THE KILLER TOMATOES!

(1978, dir: John de Bello)
David Miller, George Wilson, Sharon Taylor.
● **SAN DIEGO, CALIFORNIA**

Sadly, this promisingly-titled shocker turns out to be just a deliberate spoof. The town menaced by the fiendish fruits is **San Diego**, Southern California. The sequel, *Return of the Killer Tomatoes!* (1988), also filmed in San Diego, is famous for an early appearance by George Clooney.

AU REVOIR LES ENFANTS

(1987, dir: Louis Malle)
Gaspard Manesse, Raphael Fejto, Francine Racette.
● **LOIRE, FRANCE**

The newcomer at a Catholic boarding school in Occupied France has to hide the fact that he's Jewish. Filming took place in the town of **Provins**, 50 miles southeast of Paris in the Loire district, at the **Institution Sainte-Croix, rue St Thibault**, where the church of Saint-Croix was enlarged in the 13th century to house a piece of the true cross (no, really), brought back from the Crusades. This is the movie, the apocryphal story goes, that Quentin Tarantino, in his days working in a video store, struggled to pronounce, subsequently giving rise to the name *Reservoir Dogs*. His mum swears it's true…

AUSTIN POWERS: INTERNATIONAL MAN OF MYSTERY

(1997, dir: Jay Roach)
Mike Myers, Elizabeth Hurley, Michael York.
● **LOS ANGELES, CALIFORNIA; LAS VEGAS, NEVADA**

Mike Myers' spoof of swingin' sixties spy movies covers such clichéd territory that it has no right to be as funny as it is. Apart from a couple of stock second-unit shots, there was no filming in England, though a neat process shot manages to place a Bob's Big Boy smack in the middle of Piccadilly Circus. The London scenes were filmed on the Paramount backlot in LA. The opening shot is of the **Valley of Fire State Park**, near Las Vegas, Nevada (see *Star Trek: Generations* for details). The action swift-

ly moves to Las Vegas proper, where Myers and Elizabeth Hurley arrive at the **Stardust Resort and Casino, 3000 Las Vegas Boulevard South** (© *702. 732.6111, www.stardustlv.com*), though the casino interiors were filmed in the

Lotte Fagina's place: Imperial Palace, Las Vegas

Riviera Hotel and Casino, 2901 Las Vegas Boulevard South (©*702. 732.5110, www.rivierahotel.com*), seen also in Doug Liman's *Go* and Scorsese's *Casino*. Sixties musical legend Burt Bacharach, who used to score the kind of camp romp being parodied – think *Casino Royale* or *What's New, Pussycat?* – plays piano

Powers' stays in Vegas: Stardust Casino, Las Vegas

on the upper deck of Myers' red double-decker on the glittering Vegas Strip. Alotta Fagina's penthouse is in the Oriental-themed **Imperial Palace, 3535 Las Vegas Boulevard South** (© *702.731.3311, www.imperialpalace.com*). The Imperial's other gimmick is a vast collection of some 700 vintage cars (© *702.794.3174*), including motors owned by Elvis, Hitler and Al Capone. The interiors are a bit less glamorous – they were filmed at a sewage filtration plant at Van Nuys. The final escape from Dr Evil's underground complex was shot in **Vasquez Rocks County Park, Escondido Road**, northeast of Newhall, California. For details see *Blazing Saddles*.

AUSTIN POWERS: THE SPY WHO SHAGGED ME

(1999, dir: Jay Roach)
Mike Myers, Heather Graham, Michael York.
● **CALIFORNIA**

The joke hasn't stretched as thin as you might have anticipated. The Secret Projects Room, where Basil Exposition (York) equips Powers with his psychedelic VW 'Swingers 2' time machine, is the enormous Blimp Hangar at **Tustin**, southeast of LA, seen also in *Pearl Harbor*. The lovely English countryside, which looks nothing like southern California, is the **San Marcos Pass**, on Route 154 near West Camino Cielo in Los Padres National Forest. And if, for a second, you thought that was the real Carnaby Street in London, take a look at the Hollywood Hills in the distance.

AUSTIN POWERS IN GOLDMEMBER

(2002, dir: Jay Roach)
Mike Myers, Beyoncé Knowles, Michael Caine.
● **LOS ANGELES, CALIFORNIA; UTAH**

With an inexplicably irritating villain, this really is a sequel too far. Apart from the opening stunt, with Powers shooting down a helicopter in the fantastic landscape of **Moab**, Utah, it's all California. The interior of Buckingham Palace, where Nigel Powers (Caine) fails to turn up for Austin's investiture, is the familiar Crystal Ballroom of the **Millennium Biltmore Hotel, 506 South Grand Avenue** (see *Beverly Hills Cop* for details). The magic of movie FX puts Powers' pad on the roof of **County Hall** on London's South Bank (see the real thing in Hitchcock's *Frenzy*). The British Intelligence Academy, 1958, is the **Greystone Mansion, 905 Loma Vista Drive** in Beverly Hills. For details of this popular location, see *The Loved One*. Dr Evil's submarine (created by CGI) is berthed in the docks at **San Pedro**, south LA.

The première of *Austinpussy* appears to be at **Grauman's Chinese Theatre, 6925 Hollywood Boulevard** in Hollywood, but the beautiful interior is actually that of the **Orpheum Theatre, 842 South Broadway** (see *Last Action Hero* for details).

AVANTI!
(1972, dir: Billy Wilder)
Jack Lemmon, Juliet Mills, Clive Revill.
● **ITALY**

Blackish comedy with Jack Lemmon in Italy collecting the body of his recently deceased father and falling for the daughter of his father's similarly deceased mistress. The aeroplane scene, with Lemmon swapping his golf pants for a suit and tie, was filmed aboard an Alitalia DC8 at Rome's **Leonardo da Vinci Airport (Fiumicino Airport)**, 22 miles southwest of the city. His problems with immigration were shot in the Main Terminal.

The sun-baked resort island where Lemmon and Juliet Mills overcome their grief is **Ischia**, largest of the Neapolitan islands, off Italy's Amalfi coast, south of Naples (although most of the interiors were shot in Rome's Palatino Studios). If you want to visit Ischia like Jack Lemmon, fast and expensively, take the hydrofoil from Naples. Better, though, to take a boat to the island, famous mostly for its spa waters and mud baths. You won't find Lemmon's elegant, old-world hotel on Ischia at all, but back on the Italian mainland, south of the Bay of Naples on the Sorrentine Peninsula. It's the pricey 1834 **Hotel Excelsior Vittoria, Piazza Tasso, Sorrento** (*© 081.807.1044, www.exvitt.it*), where tenor Enrico Caruso once stayed, immortalising the town in the song 'Return to Sorrento'.

AVIATOR, THE
(2004, dir: Martin Scorsese)
Leonardo DiCaprio, Cate Blanchett, Kate Beckinsale.
● **CALIFORNIA; QUÉBEC, CANADA**

No, your DVD player doesn't need adjusting – the first half-hour of Scorsese's biopic of Howard Hughes recreates the old magenta-and-turquoise, two-strip Technicolor look of 30s Hollywood. Set, naturally enough, around LA, the studio filming was in Canada, at Mel's Cité du Cinema, Montréal, and at Saint-Hubert, Québec. Here, the façade of Grauman's Chinese (for the première of Hughes's *Hell's Angels*) and the interior of the Ambassador Hotel's Coconut Grove, were recreated.

Mystery Mesa, a remote area south of **Vasquez Canyon Road** between Sierra Highway and Bouqet Canyon Road at **Santa Clarita**, northwest of LA, was peppered with bi-planes to become the desert set of *Hell's Angels*. The same location has been seen in *The Scorpion King*, *Hidalgo* and *Spider-Man*, and hosted battle scenes for Spielberg's *War of the Worlds*.

At **San Bernardino**, east of LA, a hangar of **San Bernardino International Airport** was emblazoned with the 'Hughes' name on one side, and rival 'TWA' on the other for airport scenes. The Lockheed Constellation was borrowed from the Airline History Museum, Hangar 9, 201 NW Lou Holland Drive, Kansas City (*© 816.421.3401, www.airlinehistorymuseum.com*).

The Hollywood nightclub, outside which Hughes' car is rammed by a furious Faith Domergue, is the rear (parking lot) entrance to the **Southwestern Law School, 3050 Wilshire Boulevard**, in midtown LA, which was once the famous Bullocks Department Store (see *Topper* for details). Hughes (DiCaprio) meets Katharine Hepburn (Blanchett) when he comes ashore by the jetty at **72nd Place** in Long Beach. **Woodland Hills Golf Course, 21150 Dumetz Road, Woodland Hills** (*© 818.347.1476*) stands in for the Wilshire Country Club, where Hughes and Hepburn play a round or two.

The wrap party for *Hell's Angels*, and the celebration as Hughes announces his plans to build the biggest seaplane ever, were both filmed in the exquisite deco lounges of the **Queen Mary** in Long Beach.

Authentic LA locations include **Pantages Theater, 6233 Hollywood Boulevard** (previously seen in *Species*, *Batman Forever*, *Ed Wood* and *The Bodyguard*), where Hughes attends a première with Hepburn; Hughes' headquarters, where *Hell's Angels* and *The Outlaw* were edited, at **7000 Romaine Street** in West Hollywood; and Hughes' seven-bedroom house at **211 Muirfield Road, Hancock Park**, alongside his favourite Wilshire Country Club golf course. The interiors of both HQ and home were recreated in the studio.

The house of Ava Gardner (Beckinsale) is Frank Lloyd Wright's 1926 **Sowden House, 5121 Franklin Avenue**, between Western and Normandie Avenues, Los Feliz.

AVVENTURA, L'
(1960, dir: Michelangelo Antonioni)
Monica Vitti, Gabriele Ferzetti, Lea Massari.
● **ROME, ITALY; SICILY, ITALY**

A group of middle and upper class Italians visit a deserted volcanic island. When one of them disappears, the ensuing search drifts into indolence, and the mystery is never solved.

The opening scene, outside Anna's father's villa, was filmed on the outskirts of **Rome** – that's the dome of St Peter's in the background. Her boyfriend Sandro's home is Lady Montague's apartment, on **Isola Tiberina**, a tiny island in the Tiber between Palatino and the Trastevere district. It's reached by **Ponte Fabricio**, the oldest surviving bridge over the river. Sandro's apartment is just to the left of the bridge (which you can glimpse though the open window in the film). In front of it is the tiny square

The staircase of the customs house: Villa Palagonia, Bagheria

where Claudia waits.

From here, it's south to the Tyrrhenian Sea and a yacht cruise around the volcanic **Lipari**, or Aeolian, islands. There are fourteen islands, seven of them inhabited. Panarea, smallest of the inhabited islands, is where the cast and crew stayed during filming. Anna disappears from **Lisca Bianca**, a deserted, jagged volcanic rock about three miles east, where the futile search begins. A couple of miles north is the steeply conical island of **Basiluzzo**, the first the party encounters *en route* to Lisca Bianca.

Sandro and Claudia report Anna's disappearance to the authorities on the Sicilian mainland at Milazzo (the nearest Sicilian port to the Liparis, and where you'll depart from if you want to visit). The grand, if faded, Customs House is definitely worth a visit, but you won't find it in Milazzo. It's actually the **Villa Palagonia** in **Bagheria**, way to the west near Palermo. This bizarre confection, designed by Palatino, has a garden which was initially populated by 200 grotesque statues – giants, dwarves, hybrids – commissioned by the clearly mad Francesco Ferdinando Gravina e Alliata (grandson of the man who originally commissioned the villa) as caricatures of his wife's supposed lovers. The interior of the villa was equally crazy – chairs with legs of unequal length, cushions containing hidden spikes and mirrors hung at weird angles. The cushions and chairs have gone, and the number of lovers is down to 62, but the building is being restored and you can visit. It's on **Piazza Garibaldi**, along Corso Umberto, a short walk from Bagheria railway station. Alternatively, there's an AST bus from Palermo's Piazza Lolli to Bagheria every half hour. The villa is open daily between 9am and 1pm, then 4pm and 7pm (*www.villa-palagonia.it*).

Sandro and Claudia begin travelling around Sicily, following up possible sightings of Anna. First, they take the train from **Milazzo** along the northern coast. Sandro alights at **Castoreale**, although once he hits the platform, the location becomes the more atmospheric **Cefalu**, overshadowed by the great rocky headland, further west along the coast toward Palermo. He continues the search on the island's northeast tip, in **Messina**, where he encounters publicity-hungry 'writer' Gloria Perkins. Claudia, meanwhile, rests up at the Villa Montaldo (or Montalto in the published script), where Giulia is seduced by the Princess'

The decayed interior of the customs house: Villa Palagonia, Bagheria

grandson. It's actually the **Villa Niscemi** near Palermo, home to Princess Lampedusa, who plays Princess Montaldo in the movie. The villa, on **Piazza Niscemi**, Via di Fante near the entrance to the Parco Della Favorita north of Palermo towards Mondello, was the inspiration for the house of Tancredi in Giuseppe de Lampedusa's *The Leopard*, filmed in 1963 by Luchino Visconti – see *Gattopardo, Il*). It's since been acquired by the Comune. The villa's terrace looks out to the distant heights of San Ferracavallo and Monte Gallo to the west, and the Gulf of Palermo to the east. Sandro moves on to Troina to question the pharmacist who may have seen Anna, though the scene was shot on the **Catanian Plain**.

Before the journey: Ponte Fabricio, Rome

Here, Claudia catches up with him and together they travel south toward the town of **Noto**. The eerily deserted modern town they stop at is one of the newly-built Cassa del Mezzogiorno towns near **Caltanisetta**, in the centre of the island. The railway tunnel, where Sandro and Claudia finally get it together is **Santa Panagia**, just north of Siracusa (Syracuse) on the southeast coast.

Even further south and inland a little is their destination, the impressively Baroque town of Noto, where they stay at the fictitious Trinacria Hotel. Noto was built of honey-coloured limestone at the end of the 17th century, when the existing town was destroyed in an earthquake. It looks, as Sandro observes, like an elaborate stage set. From the tower of the **Chiesa del Collegio**, the Collegio church where Claudia rings the bells, there's a view of the stunning **Piazza Municipio** overlooked by the **Duomo** and its wide, stepped approach. Sandro tries to get into the **Museo Civico**, housed in the Convent of Santissimo Salvatore to the right of the Duomo. He doesn't have much luck, but you might fare better. In the Piazza Municipio he accidentally-on-purpose spills ink over the student's architectural drawing. The building used as the Trinacria is behind the Museo Civico, its balcony overlooking the imposing facade of the **Church of San Francesco** on **Piazza Immacolata**.

The movie ends in **Taormina**, amid the lavish surroundings of an impossibly grand hotel, where Sandro, having betrayed the missing Anna with Claudia, now cheats on Claudia with the dreadful Gloria Perkins. The **San Domenico Hotel, Piazza San Domenico 5**, Taormina (© *0942.613111, www.sandomenico.thi.it*) is one of the world's most famous luxury hotels, housed in a 15th century monastery. The final scene, a wordless, numb acceptance between Claudia and Sandro, takes place on one of the hotel's terraces before the ruined tower of the church of San Domenico, with the peak of Mount Etna on the horizon.

B

BABE

(1995, dir: Chris Noonan)
James Cromwell, Magda Szubanski, Christine Cavanaugh.
● **NEW SOUTH WALES, AUSTRALIA**

An irresistible animal fantasy written by George Miller, who made the *Mad Max* movies. Hoggett's Farm was built in the rolling green countryside of **Robertson**, 80 miles south of Sydney, on the Illawara Highway in the Southern Highlands of New South Wales.

The sequel, *Babe, Pig in the City*, returned to Robertson. The Flealands Hotel neighbourhood was constructed at the Fox Studios in Sydney. The Metro Theatre is a copy of **624 George Street**, central Sydney, which also happens to house the film company's production offices.

BABETTE'S FEAST

(1987, dir: Gabriel Axel)
Stephane Audran, Birgitte Federspiel, Bodil Kjer.
● **DENMARK**

Exiled Parisian chef Audran manages to bring unwanted gastronomic pleasure into the lives of an austere Danish religious community by cooking the mother of all banquets. Filmed in **Vendsyssel**, the northernmost island of Jutland, Denmark. Filming also at **Dragsholm** chateau, and at **Marup** church. The military scenes were shot at the garrison town of **Naestved**, 50 miles southwest of Copenhagen, Sjaelland – home of the Royal Guard Hussars.

BABY DOLL

(1956, dir: Elia Kazan)
Carol Baker, Karl Malden, Eli Wallach.
● **MISSISSIPPI**

'The dirtiest American picture ever legally exhibited' squealed *Time* magazine of this Tennessee Williams adaptation, which sparked a boom in shortie-nighties. Director Kazan likes to work on real locations, so the movie was shot in the South, at the small town of **Benoit, Mississippi**, on Route 1, about 20 miles north of Greenville close to the Arkansas border.

BACK TO THE FUTURE

(1985, dir: Robert Zemeckis)
Michael J Fox, Christopher Lloyd, Lea Thompson.
● **LOS ANGELES, CALIFORNIA**

Marty McFly (Fox) has to engineer his own parents' romance after being whisked back to the 1950s in this enjoyably slam-bang fantasy. The setting of Mill Valley is fictitious, and the town square is a much-

Doc's house, 1985: North Victory Boulevard, Burbank

Doc Emmett's house: Gamble House, Westmoreland Place.

re-used set on the Universal lot, but many of the other locations can be found around LA. Doc Emmett's house, 1640 Riverside Drive, Mill Valley, is one of LA's great architectural joys, the 1908 **Gamble House, 4 Westmoreland Place** in Pasadena, just a little to the south of the Pasadena Historical Society. Built for the Gamble family (as in Proctor and…), this charming, Japanese-influenced wood shingle house is open to the public (© *818.793.3334*). The Doc's workshop, where the time-travelling DeLorean is stored, is actually the **Gamble House bookshop**, alongside the main house. The front door on which Fox knocks, though, and the house interior, is the 1907 **RR Blacker House**, a similar Japanese-inspired design by Charles and Henry Greene, at **1177 Hillcrest Avenue, Oak Knoll**, Pasadena. If you've seen the deleted scenes on the *Armageddon* DVD, you'll also recognise the Blacker as the house where Bruce Willis bids goodbye to his dad.

The fifties neighbourhood of Fox's Mom-to-be is also Pasadena. Lea Thompson's house, where Fox gets hit by a car, is **1727 Bushnell Avenue** in South Pasadena. And big lummock Biff lives just down the road at **1809 Bushnell Avenue**. A few miles further south you'll find Mill Valley High School, down in Whittier, southeastern LA, hometown of Richard Milhaus Nixon. And indeed the school, **Whittier Union High School, 12417 Philadelphia Street** at Pierce Avenue, is where Tricky Dickie graduated in 1930. The 'Enchantment Under The Sea' dance, though, where Fox finally unites his parents and invents rock 'n' roll, was filmed in Hollywood, in the gymnasium of the **First United Methodist Church of Hollywood, 6817 Franklin Avenue**.

Back to the eighties. The Doc's house in 1985 (the garage of the old mansion, which supposedly burned down) was constructed for the film behind **Burger King, 535 North Victory Boulevard, Burbank** (a stretch of road seen in *Memento*). The McFly home is beneath the power pylons of **Arleta** in the Valley. It is **9303 Roslyndale Avenue**, a quiet sidestreet off

The McFly home in the 80s: Roslyndale Avenue, Arleta

43

Marty McFly's mother's house: Bushnell Avenue, Pasadena

Sunburst Street.

To the east of Whittier, in the anonymous sprawl of industrial estates aptly called City of Industry, is the Twin Pines Mall where Doc Emmett gets gunned down by irate Libyans. It's the **Puente Hills Mall** on the southeast corner of the Pomona Freeway exit, Highway 60, at **Azusa Avenue**.

BACK TO THE FUTURE PART II

(1989, dir: Robert Zemeckis)
Michael J Fox, Christopher Lloyd, Lea Thompson.
● CALIFORNIA

The confusing sequel (shot back-to-back with *Part III*), which flips from past to future, revisits many of the familiar locations. The school is, once again, **Whittier High** in Pasedena, and the 'Enchantment' dance was carefully recreated at the **First United Methodist Church of Hollywood**. The Mill Valley town square at Universal was dressed to represent alternative futures – one good, one nightmarish – while Biff's Vegas-style 'Pleasure Palace', in the nightmare future, is no more than a nine-foot model.

BACK TO THE FUTURE PART III

(1990, dir: Robert Zemeckis)
Michael J Fox, Christopher Lloyd, Mary Steenburgen.
● ARIZONA; CALIFORNIA

The final part of the trilogy sends Fox zooming back to the Wild West, and what location could be more iconic than **Monument Valley**, Arizona? See *Stagecoach* for details of this familiar, but still breathtaking, Western backdrop. The railroad scenes were shot on the **Sierra Railroad** between Jamestown and Sonora – a stretch of track also seen in films such as *Bad Day at Black Rock* and *High Noon*. It's on Route 108 east of Stockton, California. The 1885 version of the Mill Valley square was reconstructed up here. Once again, Doc Emmett's place is the **Gamble House** (see *Back to the Future*), though this time the interiors were on a Universal soundstage.

BACKBEAT

(1993, dir: Iain Softley)

Hamburg's Star Club: National Club, Kilburn

Stephen Dorff, Sheryl Lee, Ian Hart.
● HAMBURG, GERMANY; LONDON; LIVERPOOL; WALES

The story of Stu Sutcliffe, a founder member of the Beatles, who left the group and died of a brain haemorrhage before they hit the big time.

Set, unsurprisingly, in Liverpool and Hamburg, much of the film was actually shot in

London. The opening scene, where Sutcliffe and Lennon get involved in a fight at the Anchor Pub, Liverpool, filmed on the familiar cobbles of **Cheney Street**,

The Top Ten Club, Hamburg: The Dome, Tufnell Park

London NW1, behind King's Cross Station. A location seen in many films including *The Ladykillers* (1955), *Chaplin* and *Richard III*, its days are numbered as the area is sadly due for extensive redevelopment.

The Hamburg trip takes the boys to the notorious **Reeperbahn**, where the band starts out playing cruddy basement clubs. Interiors, though, are largely London again. The Kaiserkeller filmed in a sidestreet off Ladbroke Grove, W10; the Top Ten Club is **The Dome, Dartmouth Park Road, Tufnell Park**, N19, on Junction Road opposite Tufnell Park tube station; while the deco-ish Polydor Record Company where the band signs a record deal, is a private residential block in Highgate, **High Point, North Road**, N1. Success, after Sutcliffe's death, takes the boys to the Star Club for the *Twist and Shout* number, which filmed in the **National Club, 234 Kilburn High Road**, London NW6. The remote lighthouse they escape to for a little r&r can be seen at **Point of Air**, three miles east of Prestatyn off the A548, on the coast of North Wales.

BAD BOYS

(1995, dir: Michael Bay)
Will Smith, Martin Lawrence, Tea Leoni.
● FLORIDA

Will Smith's apartment: Tyler Adams Hotel and Apartments

Another slambang Simpson-Bruckheimer actioner, with mismatched cops Lawrence and Smith tracking down a mega-stash of heroin lifted from the cop station. The druggy party, where Tea Leoni dives into the pool after witnessing a double murder, is at the **Biltmore Hotel, 1200 Anastasia Avenue** at De Soto Boulevard, Coral Gables, southwest Miami (*© 305.445.1926*). Built in 1926, and designed by the architects of the Waldorf-Astoria and Grand Central Station in New York, the hotel has had a chequered history, closing down and being resold several times. It's now a national historic landmark and offers one-hour walking tours. Will Smith's stylish apartment is in the **Tyler Adams Hotel and Apartments** (previously the Collins Park Hotel), **2030 Park Avenue** in

Trouble at the party: Biltmore Hotel, Anastasia Avenue, Coral Gables

Miami's art deco district.

BAD DAY AT BLACK ROCK
(1955, dir: John Sturges)
Spencer Tracy, Robert Ryan, Anne Francis.
● CALIFORNIA

Tracy arrives in a small town with a big secret in this excellent, pared-down suspenser. 'Black Rock' has nothing to do with it – the script was called *Bad Day at Hondo* until John Wayne turned up in 1953 with a movie called *Hondo*. Writer Millard Kaufman stopped for gas in the tiny town of Black Rock, Arizona, and a new title was born. Most of the film was shot on the lot at MGM, though some exteriors were lensed on the edge of Death Valley, at **Lone Pine** on Route 395, California (also the location for 1989 horror comedy *Tremors* and Bogart's *High Sierra*, among many others).

BAD LIEUTENANT
(1992, dir: Abel Ferrara)
Harvey Keitel, Frankie Thorn, Zoe Lund.
● NEW YORK CITY

Although Keitel is frighteningly intense as a doomed Catholic cop who witnesses the rape of a nun, the movie plays like Andy Warhol filming a rejected Scorsese script on a grant from the Catholic Truth Society. It was filmed around New York's Little Italy area, in the Bronx and in Jersey City. The grocery store where

Keitel finds redemption: Port Authority Bus Terminal, Eighth Avenue

Keitel deals with the robbery: Median Foods, Seventh Avenue

Keitel sorts out the robbery is **Median Foods, 461 Seventh Avenue** near 35th Street, midtown Manhattan. He finally attains redemption, handing over the money which would have saved his life, to the two rapists, at the **Port Authority Bus Terminal** on **Eighth Avenue** between West 40th and West 42nd Streets.

BAD TASTE
(1988, dir: Peter Jackson)
Peter Jackson, Mike Minett, Peter O'Herne.
● NEW ZEALAND

The road to the *Rings* started here, with Peter Jackson's semi-pro exercise in gross-out schlock, made over four years on a budget of twopence. The house where aliens package up fat-free humans for intergalactic consumption is a protected colonial homestead, the **Gear House, Okowai Road, Papakowhai, Porirua** (© *04.237.8540*), in a picturesque harbour town about 20 minutes north of Wellington, New Zealand. Filmed also at **Titahi Bay**;

Pukerua Bay; and **Makara Beach**, Wellington.

BAD TIMING
(1980, dir: Nicolas Roeg)
Art Garfunkel, Theresa Russell, Harvey Keitel.
● VIENNA; LONDON; MOROCCO; NEW YORK CITY

Garfunkel is a psychoanalyst whose obsessive infatuation with Russell leads to tragedy. Fittingly, the movie filmed mainly in the home of psychoanalysis, the cluttered, elegant Jugendstil city of Vienna where Freud himself probed tortured psyches.

Theresa Russell's florid apartment building is on **Schoenebroene Schlosstrasse**. The gallery she visits with Garfunkel to see the Klimt paintings is the **Neue Galerie**, on the second floor of the **Stallburg**, the stables of the famous Riding School in the Hofburg Palace complex. The entrance is at Reitschulgasse 2, on the northern corner of Josepfsplatz between Stallburgasse and Braunerstrasse. The Klimts, Schieles and other paintings were moved in the late-eighties though, and they're now on display in the Österreichisches Galerie Belvedere Sammlungen des 19. und 20. Jahrhunderts (the Austrian Gallery Belvedere Collections of 19th and 20th Century Art) in the Belvedere Palace (*www.belvedere.at*), which stands on a hill southeast of the Schwarzenberg Palace overlooking Vienna in acres of formal gardens.

The large, elegant coffee house, where Art Garfunkel meets Daniel Massey, is the landmark **Cafe Landtmann, Dr Karl Lueger Ring 4**, a historic hangout for politicians, next to Vienna's Burgtheater.

The flashback scenes to Morocco were filmed at **Ouarzazate**, a favourite North African location. The area can be seen in films as diverse as *The Jewel of the Nile*, *The Last Days of Sodom and Gomorrah* and Bertolucci's *The Sheltering Sky*. The film's coda was shot in New York.

BADLANDS
(1973, dir: Terrence Malick)
Martin Sheen, Sissy Spacek, Warren Oates.
● COLORADO

The first film from the enigmatic Malick who, after one more feature (*Days of Heaven* in 1978) didn't release a film for over twenty years until 1999's *The Thin Red Line*. *Badlands* is clearly an influence on *Natural Born Killers* and Malick's style was shamelessly ripped off for the Tarantino-scripted, Tony Scott-directed *True Romance*. The film was inspired by the case of Charles Starkweather and his fourteen-year-old girlfriend, Caril Fugate, who killed ten people in 1958, including Fugate's mother, stepfather and half-sister. The real events took place in Lincoln, Nebraska, but although Malick's version is transposed to the Badlands of South Dakota, it was shot in **La Junta**, I-50, Otero County, southeast Colorado, and at **Las Animas**, about 25 miles to the east.

BAGDAD CAFE
(1988, dir: Percy Adlon)
Marianne Sägebrecht, CCH Pounder, Jack Palance.
● CALIFORNIA

The Bagdad Cafe: Bagdad Cafe, Newberry Springs

German tourist Sägebrecht brings a touch of magic to a humble roadside stop-off in Adlon's whimsical fantasy. The cafe was the Sidewinder Cafe, now – unsurprisingly – renamed the **Bagdad Cafe**, on the famed old Route 66 between the east and west off-ramps of I-40 at **Newberry Springs**, east of Barstow on Highway 40, California. It's every bit as friendly and eccentric as its movie counterpart. Don't forget to sign the visitor book. The strange light reflections come from the 100-acre field of mirrors of the Department of Energy's **Solar One Power Plant** at **Daggett**, east on the main highway I-40 out of Barstow.

BALLAD OF CABLE HOGUE, THE
(1970, dir: Sam Peckinpah)
Jason Robards, Stella Stevens, David Warner.
● **NEVADA; ARIZONA**

Peckinpah followed up *The Wild Bunch* with this slow, eccentric, likeable and gentle Western. The film's base was at Echo Bay, 53 miles northeast of Las Vegas near to Lake Mead, but the actual location is the **Valley of Fire**, a few miles to the north off I-15. Hogue's castle is a real hotel bought and transported, complete with furniture, from Bishop, just over the border in Central California. The interiors lensed at **Apache Junction**, a Western movie town east of Phoenix, Arizona.

BARRY LYNDON
(1975, dir: Stanley Kubrick)
Ryan O'Neal, Marisa Berenson, Patrick Magee.
● **IRELAND; WILTSHIRE; SUSSEX; GLOUCESTERSHIRE; YORKSHIRE; GERMANY**

Barry travels to Potsdam: Sans Souci, Potsdam

To achieve the breathtaking painterly look, Kubrick pushed the technology of the time, demanding specially ground lenses which enabled him to film on real locations using available light and even, amazingly, to film by candlelight. The production was initially based at Waterford in southeast Ireland. **Carrick-on-Suir**, 15 miles to the northwest, is where Redmond Barry (O'Neal) – as the hero starts out – joins the English militia. The stone walls and towers of **Kells**, nine miles south of Kilkenny, are the backdrop to the scenes of the English Redcoats, while the German encampment, where Barry meets Captain Potzdorf, is **Cahir Castle**, ten miles west of Clonmel in Tipperary. **Dublin Castle** is used for the elegant hotel and the casino, where he pursues his career as a card player.

After terrorist threats, the production decamped to England, where interiors were shot in two grand Wiltshire houses: **Wilton House**, two-and-a-half miles west of Salisbury on the A30, and the Marquis of Bath's pile, **Longleat House** in Warminster.

Redmond Barry becomes Barry Lyndon when he marries rich widow the Countess of Lyndon in the chapel of **Petworth House** in the centre of Petworth, five-and-a-half miles east of Midhurst, West Sussex. The exterior of the vast estate he marries into is **Castle Howard** (the familiar setting for UK TV's *Brideshead Revisited*), 15 miles northeast of York off the A64 in Yorkshire. The interior, where Barry scuppers his chance of being awarded a title after an ugly scuffle with his stepson, is one of the lavish state rooms of **Corsham Court**, four miles west of Chippenham off the A4, and also in Wiltshire.

For the Berlin exteriors, the film uses the complex of elegant palaces and parks at **Potsdam**. Although geographically southwest of Berlin, the town was, until 1990, part of East Berlin.

BARTON FINK
(1991, dir: Joel Coen)
John Turturro, John Goodman, Judy Davis.
● **LOS ANGELES, CALIFORNIA**

The lobby of Fink's Hotel Earle: Wiltern Centre, Wilshire Boulevard

The Coen Brothers' cryptic movie sends a Left-ish, Odets-style Broadway playwright to a literal Hollywood hell. There's no real East Coast here though. New York's Belasco Theater (the real location for Woody Allen's *Bullets Over Broadway*), where Fink's drama of the common working man triumphs, is actually LA's beautifully preserved 1926 **Orpheum Theater, 842 South Broadway**, downtown LA (a popular location seen also in *Dead Again, Ed Wood, Last Action Hero* and *The Doors*). The stylish 'Sardi's'-type restaurant and bar, where Fink gets the call to the West Coast, was filmed in the deco bowels of the **Queen Mary** at her dry dock on **Pier J** at the end of Long Beach Freeway, Long Beach.

Moving to Hollywood, Fink checks into the dismally claustrophobic Hotel Earle. Although the hotel room and corridors are sets, the lobby is the entrance of the restored 1931 grand movie palace the **Wiltern Theater**, in the **Wiltern Center, 3790 Wilshire Boulevard** at Western Avenue, midtown LA.

The studio commissary of Capitol Pictures, where Fink meets the cynical director, filmed in the now closed and shuttered **Ambassador Hotel, 3400 Wilshire Boulevard** at Catalina Street, midtown (see the 1954 *A Star Is Born* for details). The 'adjoining' men's toilet where burned-out writer Mayhew loses his lunch, is about a mile to the east in the **Park Plaza Hotel, 607 South Park View Street** overlooking MacArthur Park. Its toilets obviously have a strange fascination, as they also feature as the scene of Tim Roth's dope cover story in *Reservoir Dogs*. The USO dance, where a celebratory Fink inadvertently starts a brawl, was also filmed at the Park Plaza,

Fink celebrates at the USO dance: Ballroom, Park Plaza Hotel, South Park View Street

in the wood-panelled Ballroom (a familiar venue seen in *Chaplin, New York, New York, Hook* and many other films).

The exterior corridor leading up to Bill Mayhew's bungalow on the Capitol lot is on the **Columbia Pictures' lot** (previously the MGM Studio), **10202 West Washington Boulevard**, Culver City, though the interior of the bungalow is once again the Ambassador Hotel. The office of production executive Ben Geisler is a bungalow on the lot of the **Hollywood Center** (previously Francis Coppola's ill-fated Zoetrope Studios) at **1040 North Las Palmas Avenue** off Romaine Street in Hollywood.

The bizarre closing scene was shot near **Zuma Beach** on the west side of Point Dume, west of Malibu.

BASIC INSTINCT

(1992, dir: Paul Verhoeven)
Sharon Stone, Michael Douglas, George Dzundza.
● SAN FRANCISCO, CALIFORNIA

By wrapping a potentially interesting idea (role-reversal serial killer movie) in a Hitchcock pastiche, Verhoeven's movie comes over as a confused piece of homophobic misogyny. The director chooses a *Vertigo*-esque San Francisco, with Sharon Stone sporting the inappropriate Hitchcock uniform of sexual repression, all tightly-clenched hair and severe grey suit. The apartment of Detective Nick Curran (Douglas) – where even the staircase is modelled on that of the belltower in *Vertigo* – is **1158 Montgomery Street**. After grilling writer Catherine Tramell (Stone) in the film's most notorious scene, teetotal Curran decides to desert the Evian at **Tosca, 242 Columbus Avenue**, a pricey media persons' hangout (this is obviously a well paid police force). The Police HQ where Stone does for knickers what Clark Gable did for vests, filmed at Warners' studio in Hollywood, as did Johnny Boz's churchified rock club – a set based on New York's Limelight Club.

The Stetson Bar, though, is real. It's **Raw Hide II, 280 Seventh Street**, south of Market, a lesbian C&W bar in San Francisco. The exterior, and the diner next door, were false fronts constructed in a deserted alley beneath the **Transbay Terminal Deck**, Mission Street at First Street. Tramell's luxurious house is **2930 Vallejo Street** at Baker Street, east of the Presidio in Pacific Heights. The Salinas Medical Center is **Rohnert Park Healthcare Center, 1450 Medical Center Drive**; and there was filming at the Dominican College in Marin

Michael Douglas' apartment: Montgomery Street

County.

Det Curran tails Tramell to **Petaluma** (the northern Californian town where *American Graffiti* filmed), where Tramell is visiting murderer Hazel Dobkins (Dorothy Malone), at **26 Liberty Street**, opposite St Vincent Church. The car chase filmed up **Kearney Street**'s steep sidewalk steps on Telegraph Hill. Tramell's swish Stinson pad was actually shot south of San Fran at a beachfront estate on a rocky bluff, on **Spindrift Road, Carmel Highlands** (which is why it seems to be reached via the **Bixby Bridge** on Highway 1, California's Big Sur coastline). The plush home, on the same road as Clint Eastwood's place in *Play Misty For Me*, is not visible from the street, but you can visit **Garrapatta State Beach**, Route 1 about eight miles to the south, where the beach scenes were shot.

The climax, with Beth Garner (Jean Tripplehorn) taking the bullet, was staged at **2201 Broadway, Oakland**, just over the Bay Bridge from San Francisco.

BASKET CASE

(1982, dir: Frank Henelotter)
Kevin Van Hentenryck, Terri Susan Smith, Beverly Bonner.
● NEW YORK

Enjoyably grungy horror comedy with Duane and his evolutionarily challenged, ex-conjoined twin Belial, out for revenge on the doctors who separated them. Shot

The Hotel Broslin: Franklin Street, Tribeca

in countless locations around New York City, primarily around Times Square, on the kind of budget that barely runs to shoestrings, studio work was out of the question. The movie was filmed in friends' houses at **Glens Falls**, on the Hudson River north of Albany, I-87, as well as New York lofts, offices and private apartments. Don't believe the end credits. There was no Hotel Broslin. Duane (Van Hentenryck) and his trusty basket wander the old **42nd Street** of porno theatres before the big clean-up. The exterior of the seedy hotel is **80 Franklin Street**, Tribeca, where the service elevator was converted into a hotel reception desk. The neon 'Broslin' sign, from which Duane dangles, was attached to a fire escape on **Hubert Street** at Hudson Street, a few blocks east. The bar is an amalgam of two Greenwich Village bars, both seen in *Cruising*: **Badlands, 388 West Street** at Christopher Street, and what was, for a while, the notorious S&M Hellfire Club. It's now classy Italian restaurant **Vento, 14th Street** at Ninth Avenue in the Red Triangle Build-

Douglas falls off the wagon after grilling Sharon Stone: Tosca, Columbus Avenue ing, West Village. It also became Ed Harris's apartment block in *The Hours*.

BATMAN

(1989, dir: Tim Burton)
Michael Keaton, Jack Nicholson, Kim Basinger.
● **LONDON; HERTFORDSHIRE; BEDFORDSHIRE**

Chase Meridian's office, exterior: Surrogate's Court, Chambers Street

Burton's Gotham City, a nightmare fantasy of New York, was actually built in England. The late Anton Furst's set covered most of the 18 soundstages at Pinewood Studio. Wayne Manor, though, is real, and is a conflation of two buildings. The exterior is **Knebworth House**, a gothicised Tudor

Wayne Manor: Knebworth House

manor house 28 miles north of London on the A1 (© *01438.812661; admission charge; rail: Stevenage*). It also provided gloomy Gothic mansions for, among others, Ken Russell's *Lair of the White Worm*, Gene Wilder's *Haunted Honeymoon* and Ingrid Bergman's Oscar-winning *Anastasia*. The interiors are **Hatfield House, Hatfield**, a Jacobean pile (© *01707.262823; admission charge; rail: Hatfield*). The gaming room, where Kim Basinger asks, "Who's Bruce Wayne?" was filmed in the Long Gallery here. Wayne's arsenal, with its two-way mirror, was shot in the Marble Hall, while the library, where Alfred advises Bruce Wayne to get married, is the library.

The Axis Chemical Works, where Jack Nicholson plunges into the chemical sludge, was shot at a disused power station in **Acton Lane**, west London. The exploding exterior was **Little Barford Power Station**, a couple of miles south of St Neots in Bedfordshire.

The first sequel, 1992's *Batman Returns*, was shot in the US, and was completely studio-bound, taking up all seven of Warner's large LA soundstages, plus one at Universal, where the Penguin's lair was built.

BATMAN BEGINS

(2005, dir: Christopher Nolan)
Christian Bale, Michael Caine, Ken Watanabe.
● **CHICAGO, ILLINOIS; LONDON; ICELAND; BUCKINGHAMSHIRE**

Arkham Asylum interior: St Pancras Chambers, King's Cross

Nolan promised a more realistic take than previous incarnations. Gotham City this time is Chicago, though there was substantial filming

around London. Wayne Manor, after its previous sojourns in the US, returns to the UK. It's **Mentmore Towers** in Mentmore, Buckinghamshire (for details see *Brazil*). Bruce Wayne (Bale) meets Rachel (Katie Holmes) in **Plateau**, Canary Wharf, London. The Batmobile is seen at **ExCel, the Exhibition and**

Arkham Asylum exterior: The Ridgeway, Mill Hill

Gotham City Law Courts: Senate House, University College London

Conference Centre at **Canning Town**. The City of Gotham State Courts is **Senate House, University College London**, seen as New York in *The Hunger*, and the king's bunker in *Richard III*. Arkham Asylum is the severe forties-style **National Institute for Medical Research, the Ridgeway** at Burtonhole Lane, **Mill Hill** (*tube: Mill Hill East*), north London. The interior is **St Pancras Chambers** in the old **St Pancras Station, Euston Road**, NW1 (see *Chaplin* for details). Filming also occurred at **The Hippodrome, Leicester Square**, and outside **City Point**, opposite Moorgate Station. Some interiors were filmed in St Pancras Chambers. The secret ninja lair is **Coalhouse Fort, Tilbury Docks**, east London. The Tibetan Himalayas scenes, where Wayne flees to seek counsel with Ra's Al Ghul (Watanabe) were shot in Iceland, at **Orsaefasveit, Vatnajokuls** and **Svinafellsjokuls**.

Chicago locations include the **Samuel Cole Building, 233 West Lake Street**; Alexander White Building, 227 West Lake Street; the Batmobile garage chase in the **Randolph and Lake Parking Garage**; and the **Franklin Street Bridge, North Franklin Street**, over the Chicago River; Lower Wacker Drive.

BATMAN FOREVER

(1995, dir: Joel Schumacher)
Val Kilmer, Chris O'Donnell, Jim Carrey.
● **LOS ANGELES, CALIFORNIA; NEW YORK**

As the directorial reins were handed over to Joel Schumacher, the series came up with an eclectic mix of East and West Coast locations. Wayne Manor undergoes another transformation, to Long Island mansion. This time it's the **Webb Institute of Naval Architecture** (previously The Braes), **Welwyn Preserve** on **Crescent Beach**, Glen Cove on the north shore of Long Island.

Pan-Asia Town, scene of Two-Face's opening robbery, is over on the West Coast. It's a section of **Figueroa Street**, downtown LA, dressed with a flurry of neon signs. The Gotham backstreets where O'Donnell takes the Batmobile for a spin and encounters the dayglo street-gang, filmed on the old Hennessy Street set, a section of New York's Greenwich Village built on the backlot at Warner

Gotham City: Exchange Place

Bros' Burbank Studios. But more Gotham Cityscapes were found in New York, on **Exchange Place**, the ultimate concrete canyon, running between Broadway and William Street, a block north of Wall Street in Lower Manhattan.

Not far away is the grandiose entrance to the Ritz Gotham Hotel, where Edward Nygma (Carrey) holds his wild bash. It's the **Smithsonian Museum of the Native American** – previously the old US Customs House – **Broadway** at Bowling Green, Lower Manhattan (seen also in *Ghostbusters II* and *The Royal Tenenbaums*). In a flash, it's back to the West Coast for the 'Ritz' interior, which is the foyer of the venerable **Pantages Theater, 6233 Hollywood Boulevard**, Hollywood (see *The Bodyguard* for details). The office of Chase Meridian (Nicole Kidman) is New York. The exterior, where the Batmobile arrives, and the imposing arched marble foyer with its double staircase, are those of the 1911 **Surrogate's Court, 31 Chambers Street** at Center Street, Lower Manhattan, also the site of the climax of *Romeo Is Bleeding*. The building is open to the public. Meridian's bizarre nouveau-ish apartment is a studio set, but you can see the room it's based on in Prague Castle. Similarly with the Gotham City Police headquarters rooftop, where the bat-signal is located. Although this is a set, you can see the two real art deco buildings that inspired it: one in lower Manhattan, at **60 Wall Street**, the other over in downtown Los Angeles – the turquoise terra-cotta **Eastern Columbia Building, 849 South Broadway** (for details see *Predator 2*, which featured this architectural gem as a location). Still on the west coast Broadway is the dazzling **Los Angeles Theatre, 615 South Broadway**, whose glittering lobby is used as Gotham's Excelsior Grand Casino (see *Chaplin* for details). The exterior of Two-Face's lair is the monumental façade of New York's **Manhattan Bridge**, while the Riddler's Claw Island lair is a, slightly enhanced, view of **Alcatraz Island** in the bay at San Francisco in longshot, and the old **ARCO Refinery, Carson**, California, for closer views.

BATTAGLIA DI ALGERI, LA (aka *Battle of Algiers*)
(1965, dir: Gillo Pontecorvo)
Brahim Haggiag, Jean Martin, Yacef Saadi.
● ALGERIA
___

The first feature film made in Algeria (and nominated for an Academy Award as Best Foreign Film) covers the final days of the country's struggle against French rule in 1954. Despite the utterly convincing documentary style, no actual newsreel footage was used. Pontecorvo filmed entirely on location, and with a non-professional cast, largely in the **Casbah** of Algiers, where the events depicted had taken place. When houses needed to be blown up, full-size buildings were erected in the narrow streets, largely from expanded polystyrene. Ali's house, where he dies when it's destroyed the end of the movie, was reconstructed on the site of the real house.

BATTLE OF THE SEXES, THE
(1960, dir: Charles Crichton)
Peter Sellers, Constance Cummings, Robert Morley.
● SCOTLAND
___

The tobacconist: Lawnmarket, Edinburgh

Blackish comedy, based on a Thurber story, filmed by veteran director Crichton who later made *A Fish Called Wanda*. Efficiency expert Constance Cummings, American *and* female, is dispatched to shake up traditional Scottish tartan weavers, The House of MacPherson. She arrives at Edinburgh's **Waverley Station**, just off Princes Street. The House of MacPherson itself is on **George Street**, Edinburgh, but the film plays with the city's geography, giving it a photogenic view across Princes Street to Waverley Bridge and the Balmoral

The car shunt: Grassmarket, Edinburgh

Hotel. The tobacco shop, where Sellers buys cigarettes, is on **Lawnmarket** opposite St Giles Cathedral. The car shunt was filmed on **Grassmarket** at **King Stable's Road** beneath Edinburgh Castle. The remote Scottish Highlands, where the crofters work, were actually in **Holyrood Park** Edinburgh.

BATTLESHIP POTEMKIN (aka *Potemkin*)
(1925, dir: Sergei Eisenstein)
A Antonov, Grigori Alexandrov, Vladimir Barsky.
● UKRAINE
___

Eisenstein's silent classic is a fictionalised account of the 1905 revolutionary uprising in the Black Sea port of **Odessa**. The massacre on the steps (an episode invented by Eisenstein) is one of cinema's most innovatory sequences, and probably runs second only to *Psycho*'s shower murder as the most referenced of movie images – just watch those prams bouncing down steps in movies as diverse as Terry Gilliam's *Brazil* or Brian de Palma's *The Untouchables*. Odessa is a charming Ukranian resort on the northern shore of the Black Sea, though as the area gets more industrialised, the sea is becoming increasingly polluted.

The steps – originally the Richelieu Steps, named for Odessa's first governor, the Duke of Richelieu, whose statue stands at the top of them – were built between 1837 and 1841, and designed in perspective, reducing from 21 metres wide at the base to 13 at the top, to look more imposing from below. They run from the grand 19th century buildings of **Primorsky Bulvar** (Primorsky

Boulevard) to the now-busy road of **ulitsa Suvorova** along the seafront. If you can't manage the steps, there's now an Odessa escalator running alongside, though it's yet to feature in a movie. Odessa is about two hours by air from Moscow, or 24 hours by express train.

BEACH, THE
(1999, dir: Danny Boyle)
Leonardo DiCaprio, Tilda Swinton, Robert Carlyle.
● THAILAND

Notoriously filmed on **Phi Phi Leh Island**, near Phuket, Thailand, amid allegations of ecological vandalism when imported palms were planted to make the 'perfect' beach even more perfect. DiCaprio's naïve traveller sets out to find the fabled beach from the bustling backpack chaos of **Khao San Road**, downtown Bangkok. **Khao Yai National Park**, **Krabi** and **Phuket** were also used.

BEACH BLANKET BINGO
(1965, dir: William Asher)
Annette Funicello, Frankie Avalon, Deborah Walley.
● LOS ANGELES, CALIFORNIA

This archetypal beach movie, and many others of the period, was shot at **Surfrider Beach** – the surfers' paradise, alongside Malibu Pier, and at **Zuma Beach**, Malibu, LA.

BEAST FROM TWENTY THOUSAND FATHOMS, THE
(1953, dir: Eugene Lourié)
Paul Christian, Paula Raymond, Cecil Kellaway.
● NEW YORK CITY; LOS ANGELES, CALIFORNIA

Inspired by Ray Bradbury's short story 'The Foghorn' (about a surviving prehistoric lizard mistaking the sound of a foghorn for the mating call of another dinosaur), this monster-on-the-loose pic was animated by stop-motion genius Ray Harryhausen and directed by production designer Lourié, who designed *La Grande Illusion* and *La Regle du Jeu*, among many others, for Jean Renoir. Made quickly and cheaply, it's set in New York, but filmed mostly in the studio in Hollywood. The real New York locations include the **Fulton Fishmarket**, where the rhedasaurus comes ashore from the East River, and **Wall Street**, Lower Manhattan. The climax, with the monster being killed at Coney Island, filmed in the Amusement Park at **Long Beach**, LA.

The dinosaur skeleton dominating the museum set is the one Cary Grant painstakingly assembled in Howard Hawks' *Bringing Up Baby*, which was discovered in an old RKO warehouse.

BEAT THE DEVIL
(1954, dir: John Huston)
Humphrey Bogart, Jennifer Jones, Gina Lollobrigida.
● ITALY

Campy, culty spy spoof – or, as Bogart put it, "only the phonies liked it." It filmed in the small Medieval town of **Ravello**, high on a mountainside about four miles above Amalfi, south of Naples, in Campania, Italy. The ill assorted bunch of shady characters sit around bars in the **Piazza Duomo**. Bogart's villa is the **Villa Cimbrone** here.

The terrace decorated with marble busts, where Bogart takes Jennifer Jones, is the Terrace of Infinity, the villa's famous Belvedere overlooking the Amalfi coast – "the most beautiful view in the world" according to Gore Vidal, who took up residence in Ravello. The villa, dating from before the 11th century, has included DH Lawrence and Greta Garbo – who famously conducted an affair with conductor Leopold Stokowski here – among its guests. And for trivia buffs, the clapper-boy on the movie was composer and lyricist-to-be Stephen Sondheim.

BEAUTIFUL MIND, A
(2001, dir: Ron Howard)
Russell Crowe, Ed Harris, Jennifer Connelly.
● NEW YORK CITY; NEW YORK; NEW JERSEY

In the movies there's no affliction, physical or mental, that can't be overcome by sheer willpower and the lurve of a good woman. Ron Howard puts the struggle of brilliant mathematician John Nash (Crowe) through the Hollywood blender and – hey presto – nabs the triumph over adversity Oscars (Best Picture, Best Director), while James Horner's score raises the possibility that perhaps Princeton University is going to hit an iceberg. And, yes, it is **Princeton University, New Jersey**, filmed in three separate visits as the movie was shot largely in sequence. The Princeton clapboard house is in **East Orange**, New Jersey. The house of John and Alicia Nash is a three-storey brownstone on **Grand Street**, off Washington Street, next to Paulus Hook Park, East Orange.

The aerial shot of the Pentagon is real, but the Pentagon office is **Keating Hall, Fordham University** in the Bronx. Harvard is **Manhattan College, Riverdale**, New York State, and **Union Theological Seminary, 3041 Broadway**, on the Upper East Side, New York, was also used for college scenes.

There is no Wheeler Defense Laboratory at MIT (Massachusetts Institute of Technology), and the film didn't shoot there. The lab exterior is an abandoned wing of the **Garden State Cancer Center, BelleVille**, New Jersey. MIT's Great Dome is the **Gould Memorial Library** of **Bronx Community College**, which also became the hospital. The Governor's ball was filmed in **Lenfell Hall** of **Florham Mansion**, now the **College at Florham Campus** of **Fairleigh Dickinson University, Madison**, New Jersey.

The grand mansion, where Nash leaves his top secret code-breaking results, is **Alder Manor, 1061 North Broadway, East Front** in **Yonkers**, about 20 miles from New York, seen also in *The Royal Tenebaums, Mona Lisa Smile* and, um, *Flesh For the Beast*. After lying abandoned for many years, the mansion is currently being restored as an Irish Cultural Centre.

John Nash finally receives his Nobel Prize in **Prudential Hall, New Jersey Performing Arts Center, Newark**, New Jersey.

Studio filming was at the **Peninsula at Bayonne Harbor**, formerly the Military Ocean Terminal, a former military base off the east coast of Bayonne into New York Bay (sets for *Far From Heaven* were also built here).

BEDAZZLED

(1967, dir: Stanley Donen)
Dudley Moore, Peter Cook, Eleanor Bron.
● **LONDON**

Stanley Moon (Moore), longing for waitress Margaret (Bron), is given seven wishes by devil Peter Cook in this hit and miss but inventive Faustian satire. Heaven finally turns out to be the **Great Conservatory** at **Syon Park, Brentford** (*tube: Gunnersbury*). See *Accident* for full details.

BEDAZZLED

(2000, dir: Harold Ramis)
Brendan Fraser, Elizabeth Hurley, Frances O'Connor.
● **CALIFORNIA; LONDON**

Disappointing remake, heavy on the FX, with Fraser excellent as the innocent, geeky Elliot Richards, but Hurley a poor substitute for Peter Cook's cynically petulant sadist. Set in San Francisco.

The Synedyne Building, where Elliot works, is the **McKesson Building, 600 Market Street** at Post Street. He plummets from his first wish onto the bonnet of a car at **Washington Square Park**, and the subsequent traffic pile-up was filmed at **Columbus and Vallejo Street**. After the beach wish, Elliot materialises in the **Vaillancourt Fountain**, a tumble of ruins tastefully resembling San Francisco after the Big One, at **Justin Herman Plaza** on **Embarcadero**.

It's not all the real Bay City, though. Some of the movie was shot in LA, at the **Los Angeles State and County Arboretum** (see *Anaconda* for details). Elliot becomes a strangely tall, though sadly lacking, pro-basketball player at the **Forum, 3900 West Manchester Boulevard, Inglewood**. Being San Francisco, it's hard to avoid *Dirty Harry* connections, and *Bedazzled* features two of the film's locations: Elliot wants to dispute his 'Big Mac and Coke' wish with God at **Saints Peter and Paul Church, 666 Filbert Street**, and finally gets to keep his soul in **San Francisco City Hall**.

And, surprisingly, some of the film was even shot in England. Ford's Theatre, in Washington DC, where Elliot becomes Abe Lincoln, is **Richmond Theatre, The Green, Richmond** in southwest London (see *The Krays* for details).

BEETLEJUICE

(1988, dir: Tim Burton)
Michael Keaton, Alec Baldwin, Geena Davis.
● **VERMONT**

Keaton is full-tilt hyperactive as the exorcist-in-reverse, evicting unwanted living souls from the home of newly-deads Baldwin and Davis. The dinky little town nestling in the rolling green hills, where Baldwin and Davis set up home, just has to be New England. And it is. The location is **East Corinth**, Vermont, just off highway 25 near the New Hampshire border.

BEGUILED, THE

(1971, dir: Don Siegel)
Clint Eastwood, Geraldine Page, Elizabeth Hartman.

● **LOUISIANA**

Great fun, as the priceless Geraldine Page grimly saws off injured soldier Clint Eastwood's leg, in a Confederate Ladies' school. Actually, it's the **Ashland-Belle Helene House** (also used in the Clark Gable-Yvonne de Carlo melodrama *Band of Angels*), one of the many beautiful plantation houses on the Mississippi between New Orleans and Baton Rouge, Louisiana. It's at **7497 Ashland Road**, off the River Road, about five miles north of Darrow. Bought by the Shell Oil company, it's sadly no longer open to the public.

BEING JOHN MALKOVICH

(1999, dir: Spike Jonze)
John Cusack, John Malkovich, Cameron Diaz.
● **NEW YORK CITY; LOS ANGELES, CALIFORNIA**

If you've not seen this determinedly perverse fantasy, with down-at-heel puppeteer Craig Schwartz (Cusack) discovering a portal into the head of the actor, I can't

John Horatio Malkovich's home: Park Avenue, Manhattan

explain the plot here. The home of John Horatio Malkovich is **620 Park Avenue** on New York's prestigious East Side. After visiting the inside of Malkovich's head, tourists drop out by the side of the **New Jersey Turnpike Interchange 14C**. Though set in New York, some of the movie was shot in LA, at the **Bing Theatre**, on the campus of the **University of Southern California**, at the **Colorado Street Bridge** in Pasadena, and at the old **Ambassador Hotel, 3400 Wilshire Boulevard**, midtown.

BEING THERE

(1979, dir: Hal Ashby)
Peter Sellers, Shirley MacLaine, Melvyn Douglas.
● **NORTH CAROLINA; LOS ANGELES, CALIFORNIA; WASHINGTON DC**

Downbeat, deadpan Sellers, as Chance the naïve gardener, becomes a major celeb as his tiddly little gardening homilies are taken for deep wisdom in this over-long satire. The interior of the dowdy Washington house, where Chance suddenly finds himself unemployed and homeless on the death of his employer, filmed in the **Fenyes Mansion, 470 West Walnut Street, Pasadena**, northeast of LA. You can visit the house – it's the headquarters of the Pasadena Historical Society.

After wandering the streets of Washington DC, the grandiose mansion he finds himself guest in after a minor accident is **Biltmore House** on the

The Washington Mansion: Fenyes Mansion, West Walnut Street, Pasadena

The grand mansion: Biltmore House, Asheville

Biltmore Estate, **Asheville**, western North Carolina (*www.biltmore.com*). The Biltmore House is a 255-room French Renaissance-style chateau built in the 1890s for the Vanderbilts (see it also as Mason Verger's estate in *Hannibal*), and now open to the public. It was designed by Richard Hunt Morris, whose other claim to fame on the design front is the plinth for the Statue of Liberty. The grounds were landscaped by Edward Law Olmos, who also landscaped New York's Central Park. The house contains the Vanderbilt's collection of paintings and it's open to the public. It's on Route 25, three blocks north from Route 40. More interiors were shot in the **Craven Estate, 430 Madeline Avenue**, west of Orange Grove Boulevard, Pasadena (seen also in *Enemy of the State*).

The big clinch: Flatiron Building, Fifth Avenue

BELL, BOOK AND CANDLE

(1958, dir: Richard Quine)
James Stewart, Kim Novak, Jack Lemmon.
● NEW YORK CITY

Adaptation of John Van Druten's stage comedy with James Stewart as a New York publisher slowly coming to the conclusion that girlfriend Novak and her weird family are witches. Set largely in a studio-reconstruction of Greenwich Village. Stewart and Novak are magically transported to the roof of the **Flatiron Building, 175 Fifth Avenue**, the oddly-shaped skyscraper occupying the triangular block where Broadway crosses East 23rd Street. Built in 1902, it was, in its day, the tallest building in the world.

BELLBOY, THE

(1960, dir: Jerry Lewis)
Jerry Lewis, Alex Gerry, Bob Clayton.
● MIAMI, FLORIDA

Jerry Lewis, who wrote and directed, is, well, a bellboy who is, well, clumsy. Filmed at Miami's Fontainbleu Hotel (also seen in *Goldfinger* and *The Bodyguard*) – now the **Fontainbleau Hilton Resort and Spa, 4441 Collins Avenue**, Miami Beach.

BELLE DE JOUR

(1967, dir: Luis Buñuel)
Catherine Deneuve, Michel Piccoli, Genevieve Page.
● PARIS, FRANCE

Buñuel supposedly hated Joseph Kessel's novel about a bored, masochistic wife of a wealthy Parisian surgeon who spends her afternoons working in a brothel, but nevertheless turned it into a surreal masterpiece. The elegant

café terrace, where Catherine Deneuve is picked up for the Duc's incestuously necrophilic fantasy, is the **Chalet de la Grande Cascade** by the Second Empire artificial waterfall near the Longchamp Crossroads in the **Bois de Boulogne**. It's a very glitzy restaurant, and if you don't have a car it's

Deneuve meets the necrophile: Chalet de la Grande Cascade, Bois de Boulogne

The brothel: Square Albin-Cachot

quite a schlep (*metro: Ranelagh*) along Route de l'Hippodrome. Behind Deneuve on the restaurant terrace you can see Buñuel talking business with Robert and Raymond Hakim – producers of the movie. And it's their office, with the movie stills outside, where Pierre Clementi robs a deliveryman in the lift. The building, since gutted and turned into an Italian restaurant, can be seen at **79 Champs Elysées**.

Madame Anais', the classy brothel where ice-cool Deneuve confronts a bizarre spectrum of sexualities, is at **1 square Albin-Cachot**, a tiny cul-de-sac south of rue Leon Maurice Nordmann between rue de la Sante and rue de la Glacière (*metro: Glacière*).

BELLE ET LA BÊTE, LA (aka *Beauty and the Beast*)

(1946, dir: Jean Cocteau)
Jean Marais, Josette Day, Mila Parely.
● FRANCE

Cocteau's surreal and visually dazzling version of the old fairy tale. The merchant's house is **Rochecorbon**, a tiny manor built below the level of the road at Tours. Don't confuse this with Roche Courbon Chateau, between La Rochelle and Saintes in the Poitou-Charentes area, which is famed – confusingly – as the 'Sleeping Beauty' castle. The Beast's castle is the 17th century **Chateau Raray** in Picardy, about six miles northeast of Senlis. It's not open to the public, but any interior could only be a disappointment after seeing Cocteau's imaginative anthropomorphic architecture, though you can view the exterior.

BEN HUR

(1926, dir: Fred Niblo)
Ramon Novarro, Francis X Bushman, Carmel Myers.
● ITALY

Much troubled epic filming of General Lew Wallace's religiose tome, which began filming in Egypt – though none of the Egyptian footage was eventually used – but decamped to Italy. The impressive sea battle filmed off **Livorno** on Italy's northeastern coast.

BEN HUR

(1959, dir: William Wyler, Andrew Marton)

Charlton Heston, Stephen Boyd, Jack Hawkins.
● **ITALY**

Elephantine remake of the 1926 epic, filmed at Rome's enormous Cinecittà Studios, where the stupendous chariot race was shot by second unit director Marton. The gigantic Circus, modelled on the circus at Antioch, was cut out of a huge rock quarry and filled with 40,000 tons of white sand, imported from Mediterranean beaches. Full-sized galleys were floated on a titanic man-made lake. So who says size isn't important? The film took a record eleven Oscars, and gave birth to a wonderfully entertaining feud between star Heston and writer Gore Vidal, who claims he added a homosexual subtext to the script, which Heston denies. Watch the movie.

The Nazareth scenes were shot in **Fiuggi**, famous as a spa town since the 11th century, 50 miles east of Rome. Hur's camel journey from the galleys back to Judea, was shot at **Nettuno**, famed for its Medieval town walls, on the coast 30 miles south of Rome. The oasis, where he meets up with Scot Finlay Currie and Welsh sheik Hugh Griffith, is **Folliano**. The valley of lepers, where Hur's mother and sister serve out their time, is a rock quarry in Rome.

BEND IT LIKE BECKHAM
(2002, dir: Gurinder Chadha)
Parminder K Nagra, Keira Knightley, Jonathan Rhys Meyers.
● **LONDON; HAMBURG, GERMANY**

Jess's home: Sutton Square, Heston

Feelgood romance with Jess (Nagra) defying cultural conventions to play women's soccer. **Soccer Scene, 46 Carnaby Street**, is where Jess secretly buys soccer boots. After buying her boots, she relaxes in the **Three Greyhounds, 25 Greek Street** at Old Compton Street, Soho. The gleaming, golden-domed Sikh temple, where the boisterous wedding takes place, is **Central Gurdwara, 62 Queensdale Road** at the corner of Norland Road, in Notting Hill. **Yeading FC, Beaconsfield Road, Southall**, is the ground where Jess trains with Joe (Rhys Meyers), and **Barra Park**, to the west in **Hayes**, is the park where she proves she's more than a match for the lads. Jess's home is **33 Sutton Square, Heston**, beneath the Heathrow Airport flight path. During the trip to Germany, the team stays at **Hotel Steigenberger, Heilingengelstbrucke 4, Hamburg**.

BÊTE HUMAINE, LA (aka *Judas Was a Woman/The Human Beast*)
(1938, dir: Jean Renoir)
Jean Gabin, Simone Simon, Fernand Ledoux.
● **PARIS, FRANCE**

Melodramatic filming of Emil Zola's novel, with Gabin as the doomed train driver plotting with *femme fatale* Simon to murder her station-master husband. Gabin's engine breaks down at **Le Havre Station**, where there was much location filming.

A section of Simone's apartment was built on a raised platform in the railroad

Jean Gabin plans murder: Gare St-Lazare, rue St Lazare

yard at Le Havre to allow views of the sidings from the window. Similarly, Gabin's Paris apartment overlooks the exit of the enormous **Gare St-Lazare**, the third largest railway station in the world, rue St Lazare. The rail journey filmed was from Evreux to Le Havre. The village where Gabin stops off to see his godmother, is **Breaute-Beuzeville** in Normandie.

BEVERLY HILLS COP
(1984, dir: Martin Brest)
Eddie Murphy, Judge Reinhold, Steven Berkoff.
● **DETROIT, MICHIGAN; LOS ANGELES, CALIFORNIA**

Eddie Murphy's first outing as Axel Foley helps out the Motortown economy by writing off any number of cars in the opening chase through picturesque Detroit.

Upmarket cop shop: City Hall, Beverly Hills

Once in Beverly Hills we get the establishing tourist shots of the **Beverly Hills Hotel** and **Rodeo Drive**, before Murphy bullshits his way into the fictional Beverly Palms Hotel, supposedly on Wilshire Boulevard, in actuality the 700-room **Millennium Biltmore Hotel, 506 South Grand Avenue** (© *213.624.1011*), a smart Spanish-Italian Renaissance landmark, not in Beverly Hills at all but downtown LA. Built in 1923, it's been a frequent movie location over the years (*Beverly Hills Cop III* returns to the Biltmore for the Private Security Agent's Convention), from *The Sting* and *Ghostbusters*, to *Independence Day* and *Daredevil*. It hosted the Oscars, too, during the thirties. Murphy pulls off the banana-in-the-exhaust-pipe gag opposite the Biltmore, on **Pershing Square**. Being Beverly Hills, the cop station is no ordinary precinct, but the splendid 1932 Spanish-Baroque **Beverly Hills City Hall, North Crescent Drive** at Santa Monica Boulevard, also used for parts *II* (along with **Pasadena City Hall, 100 North Garfield Avenue**) and *III*.

The exclusive club, in which Murphy embarrasses drug lord Maitland (Berkoff), is the **Athenaeum**, the

Maitland's estate: East Channel Road, Santa Monica Canyon

The Beverly Palms Hotel: Biltmore Hotel, South Grand Avenue

dining club of the California Institute of Technology, at **551 South Hill Avenue** in Pasadena, seen in plenty of other movies including part II (as the Beverly Hills Gun Club) and *The X-Files*. Maitland's estate, site of the shootout finale, is **609 East Channel Road** in the Santa Monica Canyon.

The 1987 Tony Scott directed *Beverly Hills Cop II* also features the **Hollywood Historical Museum, 1666 North Highland Avenue** (also seen in *The Two Jakes*) as the robbed jewellery store; the 'nodding donkey' oil wells at **Baldwin Hills**; **614 Walden Drive** as Foley's 'squat'; a shoot-out at Mexican restaurant **Acapulco, 385 North La Cienega Boulevard** in Hollywood; and Hugh Hefner's **Playboy Mansion, 10236 Charing Cross Road** off Mapleton Drive, at the end of the concrete mixer chase.

In the 1994 Landis directed part *III*, Wonderworld amusement park is Paramount's **Great America Amusement Park, Great America Parkway, Santa Clara**, though the Alien Attack ride is the Earthquake attraction on the Universal Studio Tour: **Universal Studios, 100 Universal City Plaza** (© *818.508.9600*).

BIG

(1988, dir: Penny Marshall)
Tom Hanks, Elizabeth Perkins, Robert Loggia.
● NEW YORK CITY; NEW YORK; NEW JERSEY

The toyshop: FAO Schwarz, Fifth Avenue

Best of the clutch of eighties body-swap movies, and originally meant to star Robert De Niro, though the boy-man Josh now seems a part Tom Hanks was born to play. The home of young Josh Baskin is over the Hudson River from Manhattan, in New Jersey at **Cliffside Park**, where he attends **Cliffside Park High School**. At the fair at **Ross Dock** on the **Palisades Interstate Park**, beneath the **George Washington Bridge**, he gets his wish to be big granted by Zoltar and promptly relocates to central Manhattan, fetching up in standard sleazy **Times Square**. The hotel he stays in is the **St James Hotel, 109 West 45th Street** (a two-star hotel, not nearly as shabby as it appears in the movie). The office of MacMillan Toys is the old Hasbro Toy Company Building at **32 West 23rd Street**. Josh celebrates his birthday at the red-walled **Asti Restaurant, 13 East 12th Street** (© *212.741.9105*). Ultra-competitive Paul (John Heard) challenges Josh at squash in the **Thompson Playground**, on the northwest corner of **Thompson and Spring Streets** in Greenwich Village. The toyshop, where the grown-up Josh gets to dance on the fab giant keyboard, is **FAO Schwarz, 745 Fifth Avenue** at 58th Street. Sea Point Park, the spookily deserted deco funfair, where he finally gets to reverse the growing-up process, is **Playland, Playland Parkway, Rye** (*www.ryeplayland.org*), on the banks of Long Island Sound, New York State, west of Yonkers on Highway 95, and seen also in *Fatal Attraction* and Woody Allen's *Sweet and Lowdown*.

BIG CHILL, THE

(1983, dir: Lawrence Kasdan)
Kevin Kline, William Hurt, Glenn Close.
● SOUTH CAROLINA

Kevin Costner, who's suicide brings together a bunch of erstwhile sixties students, ended up being cut from the movie. Kevin Kline's smart white mansion, where everyone gathers for the wake and to rake over old ashes, is **Tidalholm, 1 Laurens Street, Beaufort** on the coast of South Carolina. A private house, not open to the public, Tidalholm was built in 1853 for cotton merchant Edgar Fripp, and is one of many mansions in the area reflecting the wealth made by Sea Island cotton.

BIG EASY, THE

(1987, dir: Jim McBride)
Dennis Quaid, Ellen Barkin, Ned Beatty.
● NEW ORLEANS, LOUISIANA

Ellen Barkin hates Dennis Quaid so much that you just know they're going to end up together while investigating corruption in a touristy New Orleans.

A body is discovered in the fountain of the **Piazza d'Italia** on **Poydras Street**, near Tchoupitoulas Street, one of several 'European' – French, Spanish, British – themed piazzas in the area. Quaid takes Barkin to a recreation of the famous Tipitina's, a music joint and local institution. Visit the real thing at 501 Napoleon Avenue. Ellen Barkin, obviously doing pretty well for herself, later receives a phone call at **Antoine's**, a very expensive French-Creole restaurant – and the oldest eatery in the US under continuous family ownership – at **713 St Louis Street** in the French Quarter.

BIG FISH

(2003, dir: Tim Burton)
Ewan McGregor, Albert Finney, Billy Crudup.
● ALABAMA; GEORGIA; PARIS, FRANCE

Lacking the darkness that anchored Burton's earlier films, this story of Will Bloom's attempt to reconcile with his fantasist father is just too whimsical to pack an emotional punch. Apart from a brief excursion to Paris, where Will (Crudup) works, the movie was shot entirely in the vicinity of Montgomery, central Alabama.

The fictitious town of Ashton is downtown **Wetumpka** (where *The Grass Harp* [1996] and

Ed Bloom's house: Collier House, East Bridge Street, Wetumpka

Racing the Dodge Charger: Bibb Graves Bridge, Wetumpka

Ashton: Wetumpka

TV movie *The Rosa Parks Story* were filmed), on Route 231, about 15 miles north of Montgomery. The grand Victorian house of the older Ed Bloom (Finney) and his wife (Jessica Lange) is the old **Collier House, East Bridge Street** (with the addition of a second story), on the Coosa River overlooking downtown Wetumpka.

Young Ed (McGregor) tells the story of catching the big fish to a bunch of kids around the campfire in **Jackson Lake Park**. He demonstrates his prowess at baseball on the football field of **Capitol Heights Junior High School, 206 Federal Drive, Montgomery**, and at basketball in the gym of **Cloverdale Junior High**. He courageously rescues the doggy from a fire on **James Street, Tallassee**, a few miles to the east. Ed is "the biggest thing Ashton had ever seen" until Karl the Giant (Matthew McGrory) shows up. Karl's cave is on the banks of the Tallapoosa River at the **Lower Boat Ramp** behind **2171 Highway 229, Tallassee**. After befriending Karl, Ed is given the Key to the City on the steps of Ashton Courthouse, which is **Elmore County Courthouse, 100 Commerce Street**. The parade for Ed and Karl as they leave town, is on **East Bridge Street** and **Court Street**, Wetumpka.

The picture-perfect town of Spectre was a set built by designer Dennis Gassner and, yes, that really is Billy Redden, the boy from *Deliverance*, playing 'Duelling Banjos' on the porch.

Auburn University campus, where Ed goes to find Sandra Templeton (Alison Lohman) is the gothic **Huntingdon College, East Fairview Avenue, Montgomery** itself.

Back in Wetumpka, Ed and Norther (Steve Buscemi) rob the Horizon Savings and Loan Bank, which is **Thames Pharmacy, 121 East Bridge Street**, on the outside, and the **Old First National Bank Building**, on **Company Street**, on the inside. The getaway was shot on **Company Street**. The Felder Hotel is **Rose's Discount Store, 100 Court Street**.

There was also filming at **Millbrook**; **Prattville**; **Pike Road** (a tiny town outside Montgomery); at the **Gunn Farm** in **Tallassee**; and at the church in **Lowndesboro**.

Will races the red Dodge Charger with his ailing dad along **Commerce Street** and over the 1930s downtown **Bibb Graves Bridge**, spanning the Coosa River, downtown. Ed's funeral was filmed at the church in **Deatsville**, northwest of Wetumpka.

BIG LEBOWSKI, THE
(1998, dir: Joel Coen)
Jeff Bridges, John Goodman, Steve Buscemi.
● **LOS ANGELES, CALIFORNIA**

The vaguely retro bowling alley, where Goodman and Buscemi hang out in the Coens' goofball spin on *The Big Sleep*, was Hollywood Star Lanes, 5227 Santa Monica Boulevard, Hollywood, but unfortunately it's been demolished.

The bowling alley: Hollywood Star Lanes, Santa Monica Boulevard, Hollywood

The German nihilists drink with the toeless woman: Dinah's, Culver City

If there's a Beverly Hills mansion featured in a Hollywood movie, chances are it will have been filmed in the eastern suburb of Pasadena, which is packed to bursting with lavish estates but charges only a fraction of the rate for film permits. Perversely, *The Big Lebowski*'s Pasadena mansion is a conflation of two Beverly Hills estates. The exteriors are a grand estate on Charing Cross Road, just northwest of Los Angeles Country Club. The interiors are the **Greystone Mansion, 905 Loma Vista Drive**. The mansion, and its expansive landscaped grounds, are a frequently used location. See *The Loved One* for details. Julianne Moore's artist's loft is above the Palace Theater, at **630 South Broadway**, downtown LA. Bridges and Goodman discuss the possible provenance of Bunny's toe at **Johnie's, 6101 Wilshire Boulevard** at Fairfax Avenue (see *American History X* for details), opposite the huge golden cylinder of the old May & Co department store. The café, where the German nihilists drink with the toeless woman, is **Dinah's, 6521 South Sepulveda, Culver City**. The final scattering of ashes is on a bluff at **Palos Verdes**, south of LA.

BIG SLEEP, THE
(1946, dir: Howard Hawks)
Humphrey Bogart, Lauren Bacall, Elisha Cook Jr.
● **LOS ANGELES, CALIFORNIA**

General Sternwood hires Philip Marlowe to protect his wild daughter in the classic noir treatment of Raymond Chandler's novel. Filmed entirely in the studio, but many locales are based on real locations. Marlowe's Cahuenga Building was the Guaranty Building, now the Bank of America, 6331 Hollywood Boulevard, down the road from Mann's Theater. Geiger's shifty bookshop is actually Book Treasury, 6707 Hollywood Boulevard, and the apartment at which Joe Brody is murdered is on the corner of Palmerston Place and Kenmore near Franklin Avenue.

BILL & TED'S EXCELLENT ADVENTURE

(1989, dir: Stephen Herek)
Keanu Reeves, Alex Winter, George Carlin.
● ARIZONA

Likeably dorky fun with the Valley Boys zizzing about in time for a school history project. And for once, it's somewhere else pretending to be California. San Dimas (east of LA) was in reality filmed in Arizona, at **Phoenix** and **Scottsdale**, plus **Cococino National Forest**, around Flagstaff. For the sequel, *Bill & Ted's Bogus Journey* (originally intended to be *Bill & Ted Go to Hell*), the locale becomes a real LA suburb, **Northridge** in the San Fernando Valley. The spectacular landscape where B&T come face to face with Death is **Vasquez Rocks County Park, Escondido Road**, northeast of Newhall (see *Blazing Saddles* for details).

Harry Palmer's squalid digs: Pentonville Road, King's Cross

BILLION DOLLAR BRAIN

(1967, dir: Ken Russell)
Michael Caine, Oscar Homolka, Francoise Dorleac.
● LONDON; FINLAND

Third of the Harry Palmer (Caine) films has the seedy agent delivering a flask full of eggs to a European destination and becoming involved with a Right-wing American loony's plan for world domination. Palmer's dingy digs, over the surgical appliance shop, are at **297 Pentonville Road** at the junction with Gray's Inn Road, opposite King's Cross Station, N1 (*tube: King's Cross*). He views the contents of the flask with the aid of a pedoscope (remember those foot X-ray machines that every upmarket shoe shop once had?) at **Whiteley's** in Queensway, W2, the Bayswater mega-department store recently given a new lease of life with a major overhaul (*tube: Bayswater*). His Finnish assignment takes him to the capital, **Helsinki**, and 85 miles west at the frozen Baltic port of **Turku**. The Texan scenes were shot in the studio in England.

BILLY ELLIOT

(2000, dir: Stephen Daldry)
Jamie Bell, Julie Walters, Gary Lewis.
● COUNTY DURHAM; LONDON

Stephen Daldry's surprise smash was filmed mainly in **Easington** in County Durham in the north of England, and in **Lynemouth**. Featuring **Dawdon Miners Welfare**. The interior of the youth centre where Billy practises is

Billy rehearses: Hanwell Community Centre, Hanwell

Hanwell Community Centre, Westcott Crescent, Hanwell, W7, once a Victorian poor school where Charlie Chaplin was a resident. Billy's

proud dad and brother go to see the grown-up Billy (in the person of Adam Cooper) in Matthew Bourne's radical all-male-swans production of *Swan Lake*, at the **Theatre Royal Haymarket, Haymarket**, London.

BILLY LIAR

(1963, dir: John Schlesinger)
Tom Courtenay, Julie Christie, Wilfred Pickles.
● YORKSHIRE; LONDON

When the New Wave of the sixties shifted the focus of British cinema from the middle class Home Counties to the working class inner cities, it wasn't all grim up north. Schlesinger incorporated fantasy sequences and broad satire into this adaptation of Keith Waterhouse and Willis Hall's play

The undertaker's: Southgate, Bradford

Billy chickens out at Bradford Central: Marylebone Station, London

about an undertaker's clerk who lives a rich fantasy life but ultimately blows his chance of real escape with swinging free spirit Julie Christie. Filmed mainly around Bradford, where Tom Courtenay clowns about on the city's war memorial on **Prince's Way** (shockingly disrespectful, less than twenty years after the end of WWII). The shop which served as the undertakers where Billy works can be found nearby, at the foot of the steps on **Southgate**, off Sunbridge Road. The pompous Victorian cemetery he walks in, with one of his two fiancées, can be found northeast of the city centre. The grimy monuments of **Undercliffe Cemetery** overlook Bradford, on **Undercliffe Lane**, off Otley Road. Although he appears to walk to the city centre in a couple of minutes, Billy's home is in one of the nicer suburbs, about four miles north of the city, at **37 Hinchcliffe Avenue, Baildon**, north of Shipley (*rail: Baildon*).

The dance hall, where Billy's romantic entanglements catch up with him, was the old Locarno, now gone, which stood on Manningham Lane. Billy's review of the victorious troops in the fantasy realm of 'Ambrosia'

Billy's house: Hinchcliffe Avenue, Baildon

Billy and his girlfriend: Undercliffe Cemetery, Bradford

filmed at **Leeds Town Hall**. Look out for director Schlesinger, in a characteristic Hitchcock-style cameo, as a Russian officer in one of the fantasy sequences. The final scene, set on Central Station, Bradford, with Christie leaving for the Big City, was shot in the capital itself, ironically, on London's **Marylebone Station**.

BIRDMAN OF ALCATRAZ

(1962, dir: John Frankenheimer)
Burt Lancaster, Karl Malden, Thelma Ritter.
● **CALIFORNIA**

Longtime home of the Birdman: Alcatraz Island

The Federal Bureau of Prisons was not best pleased with the idea of filming the story of Robert Stroud, and offered no cooperation, so Leavenworth (where Stroud was originally imprisoned) and Alcatraz were constructed on studio backlot. Strangely, the original director was the veteran of Ealing comedies, Charles Crichton, who made a belated comeback with *A Fish Called Wanda*, but he left after just three weeks of work.

The real **Alcatraz Island**, which once housed 'Machine Gun' Kelly and Al Capone, is seen in a long shot from San Francisco Bay. See *Escape From Alcatraz*, which did film at the real location, for details on visiting the national monument.

BIRDS, THE

(1963, dir: Alfred Hitchcock)
Tippi Hedren, Rod Taylor, Suzanne Pleshette.
● **CALIFORNIA**

The attack on the school: Bodega Lane, Bodega

Hitchcock's film of the Daphne du Maurier short story (originally set in Cornwall) uses lots of process shots, but, as usual, he plays fair with the geography. Melanie (Hedren) is first seen in San Francisco's **Union Square**, heading to the pet shop – where Hitch puts in his cameo with a pair of fluffy dogs. Notice the crafty edit here, covered by the news-stand flashing by the camera, from the real San Francisco to the pet shop, which was a set at Universal studios in Hollywood.

Mitch (Taylor) drives north up the California coast to **Bodega Bay**, centre of the bird attacks. Bodega Bay, once a small fishing village on the coast 50 miles north of San Francisco, really is a centre for bird migration, and the air can be disconcertingly thick with squawking and chattering. It's a great place for birdwatching, and even amateurs can check out the different species on a chart at the tourist office. The Tides Restaurant, in which the assort-

ed locals shelter from the bird attacks, has expanded into an unrecognisable hotel complex. The big surprise is that there is no town. No post office, no gas sta-

Sheltering from the bird attacks: Tides Hotel, Bodega Bay

tion, little more than a cluster of holiday accommodation. The aerial view of Bodega Bay is largely a painting. In fact, many of the Bodega Bay scenes, including the post office itself, were shot on a set back at the Universal lot, where Hitchcock felt more in control of the elements.

A few miles inland is the quaint village of **Bodega**, where you can see the schoolhouse of Annie (Pleshette) at **17110 Bodega Lane**, which, in the movie, appears to be just up the hill from the bay. The house was originally a schoolhouse, a local community centre and for a while a guest house. It's now a private residence.

BIRDY

(1984, dir: Alan Parker)
Matthew Modine, Nicolas Cage, John Harkins.
● **PHILADELPHIA, PENNSYLVANIA; CALIFORNIA; NEW JERSEY**

Much friendlier birds here. Modine is a traumatised war vet who's retreated into silence, Cage his physically damaged friend. Set in Philadelphia, which certainly provides the city backdrops, much of the movie was filmed around northern California. The hospital in which Modine is incarcerated is **Agnew's State Hospital** at **Santa Clara**, just south of San Francisco (the sets were built here). The elevated railway, where Cage and Modine clamber among the girders to catch pigeons, really is Philly: **46th Street Station** at the corner of Market Street and 46th Street to the west of the city. The pair take a renovated '53 Ford to the coast, but Atlantic City, where the scene is set, has been extensively redeveloped. The fairground scenes actually filmed 30 miles south of Philadelphia at **Wildwood** on the Jersey coast. The Atlantic City jail, where they end up, is a wing of the women's prison at Philadelphia's House of Correction. The statue of William Penn can be seen atop the rather overblown **Philadelphia City Hall, Penn Square** at Broad and Market Streets (seen also in *Twelve Monkeys*).

BIRTH OF A NATION, THE

(1915, dir: DW Griffith)
Henry B Walthall, Mae Marsh, Miriam Cooper.
● **LOS ANGELES, CALIFORNIA**

Griffith's Civil War epic and hymn of praise to the Ku Klux Klan was filmed around LA long before Hollywood became the centre of the film industry. The 'Battle of Petersburg' was staged north of the city in LA's San Fernando Valley. Much of the location shooting took place around the area now occupied by Forest Lawn Hollywood Hills Cemetery, the last resting place of Charles Laughton, George Raft, Stan Laurel, Buster Keaton and Liberace,

6300 Forest Lawn Drive in Burbank.

BLACK HAWK DOWN
(2001, dir: Ridley Scott)
Josh Hartnett, Ewan McGregor, Jason Isaacs.
● **MOROCCO**

Scott's jittery, bleached-out account of the 1993 US mission to capture Somalian warlords that went so disastrously wrong is set in Mogadishu, pretty much a no-go area. The film was made in Morocco, largely around **Rabat** and the nearby city of **Sale**, across the Bou Regreg River, on the Atlantic coast. Sale was deemed to be pretty similar to Mogadishu, where the working class district of **Sidi Moussa** was transformed into the Somali capital. **Avenue Nasser**, the main strip, became Hawlwadig Road. The 'Target Building' was built from scratch on a football ground (don't worry, the film company built the city a new football stadium), and Mogadishu's Bakara Market was reconstructed in a courtyard off the **Rue de Consuls** shopping street of the 17th century Rabat medina.

The first Black Hawk is downed in the **Hay Arrahma** district of Sale, about two miles from Avenue Nasser. The US military base is the Royal Moroccan Air Force field at **Kenitra**, on the coast 20 miles north of Rabat, and the firing range was constructed on the beach at nearby **Mehdiya**.

BLACK NARCISSUS
(1947, dir: Michael Powell; Emeric Pressburger)
Deborah Kerr, Kathleen Byron, David Farrar.
● **SUSSEX**

Director Powell turns this unlikely melodrama, about a group of nuns attempting to set up a convent in the Himalayas, into a bizarrely beautiful experience. Amazingly, the far eastern locations were created almost entirely in the studio at Pinewood, while the jungle scenes filmed in deepest Sussex. The lush forest is **Leonardslee Gardens**, one of the largest woodland gardens in the UK, planted with exotic blooms. It's about four miles from Horsham in Sussex (*rail: Horsham Station*), and is open from the beginning of April to the end of October (*℗ 01403.891212, www.leonardslee.com; admission charge*).

BLACK RAIN
(1989, dir: Ridley Scott)
Michael Douglas, Andy Garcia, Ken Takakura.
● **OSAKA; NEW YORK CITY; CALIFORNIA**

The seething, industrial city of Osaka is a gift to the man who directed *Blade Runner*, as semi-sleazy New York cop Douglas tracks a Yakuza-style mobster to Japan. Scott gets much the same feeling of a polluted Oriental urban nightmare blasted by banks of neon. Osaka is home to several enormous underground shopping malls, and the extravagant mall with pretensions to being a cathedral

The sinister underground mall: Hankyu Umeda Mall

where Andy Garcia unwisely responds to the taunting of a sinister biker, is the **Hankyu Umeda Mall**, near to Umeda and Osaka Stations.

The house of the mob chief isn't a Japanese location at all, but at Los Feliz in the heart of LA. Previously featured as Harrison Ford's apartment block in *Blade Runner*, it is Frank Lloyd Wright's **Ennis-Brown House, 2607 Glendower Avenue**, a concrete Mayan temple-style home on the slopes below the Griffith Park Observatory. For details of this much-filmed landmark, see *The House on Haunted Hill*. The climactic motorbike chase sequence also filmed back in California, when the money for Japanese filming ran out. It was shot in the **Napa Valley** region of Northern California.

BLACKMAIL
(1929, dir: Alfred Hitchcock)
Anny Ondra, Donald Calthrop, John Longden.
● **LONDON**

Hitchcock's first talkie (it started out as a silent), with Anny Ondra killing her assailant after fighting off an attempted rape. The climactic chase takes place

The climactic chase: Drinking fountain at the British Museum

in the **British Museum**, mocked up in the studio with huge photographs of the galleries, though the exterior is real enough, with blackmailer Calthrop stopping at the stone drinking fountain at the museum's entrance.

BLADE
(1998, dir: Stephen Norrington)
Wesley Snipes, Stephen Dorff, N'Bushe Wright.
● **LOS ANGELES, CALIFORNIA; BRITISH COLUMBIA, CANADA**

Blood-drenched cartoon strip, filmed with bags of style and energy on some spectacular sets and downtown LA locations. The interior of the hospital, where N'Bushe Wright is attacked by the crispy fried vampire, and from which Snipes makes a flying escape, is a disused facility in Boyle Heights, but the exterior is the elaborate white terracotta building at **610 South Broadway**, coincidentally one of the buildings Harold Lloyd dangled from in *Safety Last*. Wright's apartment is the **Chester Williams**

The hospital: South Broadway

The Pearl vampire club: South Broadway

Building, 215 Fifth Street, which became a New York subway station in *Phone Booth* (and is directly opposite John Doe's apartment from *Se7en*). The Pearl vampire club is a dressed-up shop front on **South Broadway** at the northwest corner of 8th Street, just opposite the ornate Tower Theater at 802. Studio filming was in Vancouver.

BLADE RUNNER

(1982, dir: Ridley Scott)
Harrison Ford, Rutger Hauer, Sean Young.
● **LOS ANGELES, CALIFORNIA**

The futuristic police station: Union Station, Alameda Street

Somehow, Ridley Scott's film of Philip K Dick's novel *Do Androids Dream of Electric Sheep?* has mutated in critical opinion from so-so spectacle to a classic of modern cinema. More to do with 20/20 hindsight than the release of the, admittedly far superior, Director's Cut which restores the equivocal unicorn while removing Harrison Ford's deliberately dirgy voiceover (he hoped it would prove unusable) and the tacked-on happy ending (which consists of some second unit footage from Stanley Kubrick's *The Shining*). Harrison Ford is a Blade Runner (a title taken from William Burroughs, replacing Dick's box-office killer), a tracker-down and eliminator of very human looking replicants. Rutger Hauer is the replicant in love with life.

The polluted, rainswept, Orientalised LA futurescape, which has provided the pattern for countless dystopian fantasies, is the old Warners' backlot gangster street transformed with miles of neon and acres of glass. The excellent model shots incorporate existing LA landmarks including the cylindrical towers of the Bonaventure Hotel (itself a fave LA location) at 404 South Figueroa Street, downtown LA. The cop station of the future, to which Ford is hauled, is an office set built within the vast concourse of another

The tunnel to Deckard's home: Second Street Tunnel, Figueroa Street

Deckard's apartment building: Ennis-Brown House, Glendower Avenue, Silverlake

favourite LA location, the 1939 Spanish Revival-style **Union Station, 800 North Alameda Street**, downtown, seen in many films, including *The Way We Were*, *The Driver*, *The Replacement Killers* (which shares many of *Blade Runner*'s locations), *Pearl Harbor*, *Charlie's Angels: Full*

Throttle and *Catch Me If You Can*.

The waterlogged home of toymaker Sebastian, where Ford is menaced by androids and has the final showdown with Rutger Hauer, is the **Bradbury Building, 304 South Broadway** at Third Street. Outside, it's an unremarkable red-brick block, but the central courtyard, illuminated by sky-

Sebastian's waterlogged home: Bradbury Building, South Broadway

lights (through which the illuminated blimp is seen in the movie), is a joyous fantasy of wrought-iron grillwork, marble and brickwork surrounding open-cage elevators. It was a bit decrepit when *Blade Runner* was filmed, but it's since been lovingly restored and now houses offices. The ground floor is open to the public. The exterior of the Bradbury Building filmed at the junction of **Broadway and Third Street**, but there's plenty of set dressing so don't look for the massive pillars. The interior of the scuzzy Yukon Hotel is the **Pan Am Building, South Broadway** at Third Street, opposite the Bradbury Building, downtown LA. You may recognise it as the apartment of the comatose 'Sloth' victim in *Se7en*.

The tunnel through which Harrison Ford approaches his apartment is the **Second Street Tunnel**, running between Figueroa Street and Hill Street, downtown LA. His home turns out to be Frank Lloyd Wright's terrific **Ennis Brown House, 2607 Glendower Avenue**, Silverlake, below Griffith Park. A few storeys were added optically, and casts taken from the building's trademark concrete blocks to be used for the interior studio shots. See William Castle's classic fifties schlocker *The House on Haunted Hill* for details of the house.

BLAIR WITCH PROJECT, THE

(1999, dir: Daniel Myrick; Eduardo Sánchez)
Heather Donahue, Michael C Williams, Joshua Leonard.
● **MARYLAND**

The surprise smash hit of 1999 was a made-for-peanuts fake documentary, supposedly edited down from amateur footage of three student filmmakers who disappeared in the Black Hills Forest near Burkittsville, Maryland, while following up a local legend about the titular witch. Filmed in **Burkittsville**, Maryland. Don't expect a warm welcome, though, if you visit. Locals are not best

"We have shot the first scene...": Burkittsville

"an unusually high number of children laid to rest": Burkittsville Cemetery pleased with the attention their town has received – even booing the filmmakers out of town when they returned to discuss filming a sequel. Joshua Leonard's house is in **Wheaton**, Maryland, just north of Washington D.C. The Black Hills Forest is **Seneca Creek State Park**, about 25 miles west of Burkittsville. The 200-year-old house featured in the film has been saved from demolition by the film's distributors. It's the **Griggs House** in **Patapsco State Park**, western Baltimore County.

BLAZING SADDLES
(1974, dir: Mel Brooks)
Cleavon Little, Gene Wilder, Harvey Korman.
● **LOS ANGELES, CALIFORNIA**

Bedrock: Vasquez Rocks County Park

The last really sidesplitting Mel Brooks movie, graced with a smidgeon of antiracist sentiment. The climax, with Hedley Lamarr (Korman) commanding allegiance from his assorted bad guys, is at **Vasquez Rocks County Park, 10700 West Escondido Canyon Road**,

Escaping the studio...: Warner Bros lot, Warner Boulevard, Burbank

California. Named after 19th century outlaw Tiburcio Vasquez, who hid out here, the spectacular 745-acre location – an outburst of the San Andreas fault where spurs of rock have been

...to the cinema: Grauman's Chinese Theatre, Hollywood Boulevard

thrust out of the earth – has been used in hundreds of Westerns and sci-fi movies, including *Bill And Ted's Bogus Journey*, *Blazing Saddles*, *The Flintstones* and *Austin Powers*. The park is in the high desert north of LA, between Newhall and Acton, off Route 14 (© *661.268.0840, parks.co.la.ca.us/vasquez_narea.html*). The backlot at **Warner Bros, 4000 Warner Boulevard** in Burbank gets a starring role in the big fight scene. Lamarr gets a cab at the studio entrance – "Drive me off this picture!" – to the fabulous **Grauman's Chinese Theatre, 6925 Hollywood Boulevard** (© *323.464.8111*). The theatre opened in 1929 with the première of DeMille's *King of Kings* and you'll hardly need reminding of the 180 or so hand-, foot-, nose- and whatever-prints of the famous gracing its forecourt, the tradition begun accidentally (oh yeah), by Norma Talmadge, Mary Pickford or Douglas Fairbanks Sr, according to which version of the legend you choose to believe.

BLITHE SPIRIT
(1945, dir: David Lean)
Rex Harrison, Kay Hammond, Constance Cummings.
● **BUCKINGHAMSHIRE**

Noël Coward considered his play "the best thing I ever wrote", but was far from pleased with David Lean's movie version. Harrison's marriage is threatened by the appearance of the ghost of his former wife (coated in dreadful green make-up). The opened-up countryside scenes filmed near the studios around the village of Denham, on the A40, Buckinghamshire. The house is **Fairway, Denham**.

BLOB, THE
(1958, dir: Irvin S Yeaworth Jr)
Steven McQueen, Aneta Corseau, Olin Howlin.
● **PENNSYLVANIA**

Low budget sci-fi with carnivorous jello from space feasting on bit part players in a small town until a young (well, 28) Steven McQueen pops it in the freezer. The terrorised town is **Valley Forge**, 15 miles west of Philadelphia, Pennsylvania, on I-76. Most of the movie interiors and exteriors were filmed in the Valley Forge Studios. Real locations include **Jerry's Supermarket** (where the Blob is played by a weather balloon – for much of the rest of the time it's a chunk of silicone wobbling about on miniature sets); the exterior of the **Colonial Theater** – the town's terrorised cinema; the doctor's office; and the **Downington Diner**, scene of the movie's climax and (in 1989 at least) still the town's main tourist attraction. The not-half-bad updated 1988 remake (*The Blob*, directed by *The Mask*'s Chuck Russell), with spectacularly gloopy FX and a fine cast of character players, was filmed in **Abbeville**, on Route 14, 20 miles south of Lafayette in Lafayette County, southern Louisiana.

BLOCKHEADS
(1938, dir: John G Blystone)
Stan Laurel, Oliver Hardy, Billy Gilbert.
● **LOS ANGELES, CALIFORNIA**

Ollie finds Stan still guarding a WWI trench twenty years after the end of the war, at an 'old soldiers' home', the Veterans Administration complex in

The final chase: West 8th Street

LA. The entrance of the complex, used for filming, has been demolished but it stood at the junction of Sawtelle Boulevard and Ohio Avenue, west of the San Diego Freeway between Westwood Village and West LA (it's also the hospital where hundred-and-something Dustin Hoffman rasped out the story of *Little Big Man*). Shotgun-wielding Billy Gilbert chases the pair down an alleyway between two buildings in the final scene. The pretty-much unchanged alleyway can still be seen between the **St Arthur Apartments, 2014 West 8th Street** and the **Westmont, 807 South Westlake Avenue**, just south of MacArthur Park in Midtown LA.

BLOOD ON SATAN'S CLAW (aka *Satan's Skin*)

(1970, dir: Piers Haggard)
Patrick Wymark, Linda Hayden, Barry Andrews.
● **OXFORDSHIRE**

In 17th century rural England a mysterious claw is ploughed up, and soon something nasty is taking over the local children. Original and scary period horror from the director of Dennis Potter's landmark TV series *Pennies From Heaven*. It was filmed northwest of Henley-on-Thames, at **Bix Bottom** on the A423 west of Maidenhead, at an isolated farmhouse – the remnant of a village wiped out by the plague.

BLOOD SIMPLE

(1984, dir: Joel Coen)
John Getz, Frances McDormand, Dan Hedaya.
● **TEXAS**

Dan Hedaya hires the hitman: Mount Bonnell Park, Austin

The Coen brothers' dazzling post-noir début film was shot in the area of state capital Austin and nearby Round Rock, Texas. The movie's $1.5 million budget was raised by hawking around a three-minute trailer while younger brother and producer Ethan Coen worked as a statistical typist at Macy's.

Dan Hedaya's Neon Boots bar no longer exists. It was the Starliner on Little Cisco Road off Braker Lane at North Lamarr in the Walnut Forest area of northeast Austin (there's now a mall on the site). The overlook, where Hedaya instructs M Emmet Walsh to kill John Getz, is **Mount Bonnell Park**, above Lake Austin – not a lake at all but a stretch of the Colorado River – on Mount Bonnell Road at the western end of 35th Street, Austin, behind Camp Mabry National Guard Installation. Walsh traces the illicit lovers to the **Heart Of Texas Motel, 5303 W Highway 290** (*© 512.892.0644*) down in southwest Austin near Oak Hill on Route 71/290, the Fredericksburg Road.

Hutto is a little town, population 659, about 20 miles northeast of Austin on Route 79 and it's two miles south of Hutto on **Farm Road 1660** you can find the ploughed field where the victim of the botched murder is buried. The darkroom where Walsh burns the incriminating photos is the **Old Grove Drug Building** on **Sixth Street**, Austin. Also on Sixth Street, above a restaurant, is the apartment building McDormand moves into, which is the scene of the bloody climax.

BLOWUP

(1966, dir: Michelangelo Antonioni)
David Hemmings, Vanessa Redgrave, Sarah Miles.
● **LONDON**

Antonioni's landmark mystery, with photographer Thomas (Hemmings, in a role earmarked for Terence Stamp) accidentally capturing something suspicious on film. The eerie park where Thomas may or may not have photographed something is **Maryon Park**, south of Woolwich Road, SE7 (*rail: Woolwich Dockyard*). Antonioni notoriously manipulated reality to achieve his visual effects, painting paths black and grass green. The bushes, where the 'body' was hidden, were added, and houses overlooking the park were false flats. The tennis court, where students mimed the surreal tennis match in the park, is still there, unchanged. The antique shop (it was a grocery store) was in Clevely Close, at the park's northeast corner, but has since been demolished and the corner redeveloped.

David Hemmings' studio, exterior: Pottery Lane, Holland Park

The white-face students: Economist Plaza, St James's Street

Economist Plaza, a hidden courtyard immediately north of Ryder Street, off Piccadilly in London's West End, housing the tower block of the *Economist* magazine offices, appears deceptively large as the rather creepy white-face students career around the tiny space in a truck at the beginning of the movie.

David Hemmings shows the portfolio to his publisher: El Blason, Blacklands Terrace, Chelsea

Beneath the railway arch over **Consort Road**, just east of Peckham Rye Station, southeast London, Thomas mingles with the down-and-outs, but it's in **El Blason, 8-9 Blacklands Terrace** (*© 020.7823.7383*), a classy Spanish restaurant off the King's Road in Chelsea, that he shows the portfolio of images of working class men to his publisher Ron (Peter Bowles).

Steps up to the mysterious site: Maryon Park

Thomas's studio scenes filmed in the studio of John Cowans, **49 Princes Places**, off Princedale Road, Notting Hill, although the exterior is nearby **77 Pottery Lane**, W11, next to the Earl of Zetland pub, north of Holland Park Avenue (*tube: Holland Park*).

BLUE HAWAII

(1961, dir: Norman Taurog)
Elvis Presley, Joan Blackman, Nancy Walters.
● **HAWAII**

The Elvis of the movie years rarely ventured beyond the soundstage, so there aren't too many Presley locations, but he could always be tempted out to Hawaii, where this story of a GI turned beachcomber was shot. Featured is the **Coco Palms Resort, 241 Kuhio Highway, Kapaa** (© *808.822.4921*), which opened in 1953, on Coconut Coast, on the east of the island of Kauai between Lihue and Anahola, and the **Hanauma Bay Beach Park** on the southeastern point of Oahu.

BLUE LAGOON, THE

(1949, dir: Frank Launder)
Jean Simmons, Donald Houston, Noel Purcell.
● FIJI

H de Vere Stacpole's novel about two shipwrecked children growing up on a desert island and discovering (discreet) sex, was shot half in the studio at Pinewood and half on an island north of **Vitu Levu**, the main island of the Fiji archipelago. The 1980 Hollywood remake, replacing the Britishly chaste Simmons and Houston with Brooke Shields and Christopher Atkins, was photographed by veteran cinematographer Nestor Almendros, seemingly under the impression it was some contribution to the art of cinema, again in Fiji, on the deserted island of **Nanuya Levu**.

BLUE LAMP, THE

(1949, dir: Basil Dearden)
Jack Warner, Jimmy Hanley, Dirk Bogarde.
● LONDON

Site of Bogarde's hideout: Lord Hills Road

Hanley is the idealistic young police officer, and Warner his older mentor, PC Dixon, gunned down by young hoodlum Bogarde, only to rise from the dead for a long-running TV series. *The Blue Lamp* was one of the first British movies to move out onto the streets for much of its filming, around Ladbroke Grove, Paddington Green and Edgware Road.

Many of the west London locations have now gone, including the old Harrow Road Police Station out of which Dixon works, although the Blue Lamp of the title has been retained and you can see it still hanging outside the new station on Harrow Road, W9. The bridge, where Dixon passes the time with a little improvised verse, can still be seen in Little Venice, the **Westbourne Terrace Road Bridge** over the Grand Union Canal. Bogarde's hideout has been demolished but the site is still recognisable on **Lord Hills Road** at the Canal in W9.

Dixon's beat: Westbourne Terrace Road Bridge, Little Venice

The Metropolitan Theatre, where Bogarde establishes his alibi by ostensibly watching Tessie O'Shea's act, closed in 1962 and has been demolished. It stood at 267 Edgware Road. The Coliseum Cinema where Dixon gets shot has also been demolished – the site is now occupied by council buildings. The car chase, around Notting Hill and North Kensington, climaxes at the White City dog stadium on White City Road, off Wood Lane W12, Shepherds Bush. The stadium was torn down in the 1980s and BBC offices now stand on the site.

BLUE VELVET

(1986, dir: David Lynch)
Kyle McLachlan, Laura Dern, Isabella Rossellini.
● NORTH CAROLINA

Disturbed, disturbing, visually glorious, nastily sadistic, but one of Lynch's most satisfying movies to date. The apparently sweet and easy Lumbertown – "at the sound of the falling tree" – is the movie city (it's home to several movie studios) of **Wilmington**, North Carolina, and many of the locations can easily be recognised.

Isabella Rossellini's Deep River apartment: Carolina Apartments, Market Street, Wilmington

Lumbertown – at the sound of the falling tree: Wilmington, across the Cape Fear River

The general vista of Lumbertown is the view of Wilmington across the Cape Fear River toward Water Street. Arlene's Restaurant, where MacLachlan and Dern hatch their plan to uncover Lumbertown's secrets, isn't a restaurant at all, but the **New Hanover Human Resources Office** at **4th and Chestnut Streets**. Laura Dern's school is the **New Hanover High School, 1307 Market Street**. The police station, where Kyle McLachlan first glimpses the strange Man in Yellow, is the **Wilmington Police Headquarters, 115 Redcross Street**. Isabella Rossellini's gloomy Deep River apartment block, where McLachlan wit-

Arlene's Restaurant: New Hanover Human Resources, Fourth Street

Lumbertown Police Station: Wilmington Police HQ, Redcross Street

nesses one of the creepiest sex scenes in film history, is the **Carolina Apartments, Market Street** at Fifth Avenue.

BLUES BROTHERS, THE

(1980, dir: John Landis)
John Belushi, Dan Aykroyd, Carrie Fisher.
● ILLINOIS; WISCONSIN; LOS ANGELES, CALIFORNIA

Enormously overblown and expensive slapstick chase movie went from box office disaster to cult status mainly because of the terrific soundtrack, the great array of

Site of the brothers' hotel: West Van Buren Street

soul stars on display and Belushi's charisma. It was filmed, of course, around Chicago, employing Landis' usual breathtaking knack of persuading the authorities to allow him to stage major set pieces in busy public places.

John Belushi is released from the **Joliet Correctional Center**, north of the suburb of Joliet on Highway 53, itself south of the city. The new Bluesmobile demonstrates its prowess by leaping across the **East 95th Street Bridge** over the Calumet River at Calumet Harbor, south Chicago, down near the Indiana border. The brothers' digs, 'Hotel For Men Only. Transients Welcome', no longer exists. It wasn't blown up by Carrie Fisher (that was a large photograph of the building pasted on to flyaway polystyrene blocks), but it has since been demolished. It stood at **22 West Van Buren Street**, at the last check, still a vacant lot beneath the el-train.

The Soul Food Restaurant, where the waitress is Aretha Franklin and John lee Hooker plays outside, is on **Maxwell Street**, centre of the bustling Maxwell Street flea market at the junction with South Halstead Street, just southeast of the University of Illinois campus. Much of the area has since been demolished. The Nazis turn up at the brothers' official address, **1060 West Addison Street** – which just happens to be the home of the Chicago Cubs, **Wrigley Field**. The shopping mall the brothers drive their car through is the **Dixie Mall, Harvey**, a suburb of south Chicago over the Little Calumet River.

The Palace Hotel Ballroom, "up north on Lake Wazupumani," where the Blues Brothers get their first major gig, is actually down south. it's the **South Shore Country Club, South Shore Drive** at East 71st Street. The 1916 Mediterranean-style building, on the coast toward Calumet Harbor, was recently renovated. The interior, though, is the **Hollywood Palladium, 6215 Sunset Boulevard**, at El Centro Avenue, seen also in *Galaxy Quest* and *Million Dollar Baby*. See *Day of*

The expensive climax: Richard J Daley Center

the Locust for details.

The climactic chase through central Chicago, under the el, ends up at the prestigious **Richard J Daley Center** building (named for Mayor Daley, who died in office in 1976). The building stands on the block bounded by Randolph, Dearborn and Clark Streets and Washington Boulevard. On the open plaza south of the Center on Washington Boulevard is the 50-foot-tall **Chicago Picasso Sculpture**, the cubist head Jake and Elwood use for a landmark. Amazingly, Landis got permission for the Bluesmobile to crash through the Daley Center windows. The brothers' ultimate destination, **City Hall-County Building**, is west of the Daley Center over Clark Street. It's here they barricade themselves in while the National Guard abseil down the side of the building. The 'Cook County' clerk, who receives their payment, is that other expert in expensive, lumbering monsters, Steven Spielberg.

Other locations used by the movie include the northwestern suburb of **Park Ridge**; **Wauconda**, 25 miles northwest of Chicago on Route 12; **Waukegan**, 25 miles north on the coast near the Wisconsin border; and **Milwaukee**, on the coast over the border in Wisconsin itself.

After the death of Belushi, a sequel was never a good idea. And choosing to film much of *Blues Brothers 2000* in Canada didn't help. Chicago sets the scene, but much of the filming was done in **Toronto** and **Kingston**, Ontario. The Kentucky fairground is **Markham Fairgrounds**, Toronto.

BODY HEAT

(1981, dir: Lawrence Kasdan)
William Hurt, Kathleen Turner, Richard Crenna.
● FLORIDA; HAWAII

Steamy near-remake of *Double Indemnity*, with lawyer Hurt plotting with Turner to kill her husband. Originally set in Atlantic City, the locale was changed to Florida for the movie. It was shot around the **Lake Worth** area of Palm Beach, southern Florida. The bridge is at **Delray Beach**, the boardwalk is **Hollywood Beach**, south of Fort Lauderdale down toward Miami. Filming also took place on the glorious Garden Isle of **Kauai**, Hawaii.

BODYGUARD, THE

(1992, dir: Mick Jackson)
Kevin Costner, Whitney Houston, Gary Kemp.
● LOS ANGELES, CALIFORNIA; FLORIDA

Costner is the bodyguard hired to protect performer Houston from a murderous nut.

The wild, pre-Columbian nightmare of a theatre, where Houston defies the threats to perform (and in the ensuing chaos provides the image for the movie poster) is the **Mayan Theater, 1038 South Hill Street**, downtown LA. It's followed the standard pattern of grand

Houston performs after the death threat: Mayan Theater, South Hill Street

The Oscar ceremony was filmed in the Pantages Theater, Hollywood Boulevard

...but the arrival was shot downtown: Park Plaza Hotel

'themed' movie theatre in the twenties (along with the Chinese and the Egyptian), a sixties slump into porno house and revival as a nightclub. You can see its incarnation as an XXX movie dive in the 1973 Jack Lemmon Oscar-winner *Save the Tiger*.

The working class bar where Costner and Houston stop off for a drink, is the venerable institution **Joe Jost's, 2803 East Anaheim Street** in Long Beach.

Houston nips off to perform an Aids charity benefit (with not a red ribbon in sight?) at the **Fontainebleau Hilton Hotel, 4441 Collins Avenue**. Yes, that's where Bond stymied the crooked poolside card game in *Goldfinger*. The killer pursues Houston to a wintery retreat at **Fallen Leaf Lake, Fallen Leaf Road** running south from Route 89 at the southern tip of Lake Tahoe, on the California side of the Nevada border.

The climactic Academy Awards ceremony was filmed at two different locations. You won't find the imposing exterior with its enormous Egyptian statues in any guide book to Hollywood: it's the imposing frontage of the **Park Plaza Hotel**, overlooking MacArthur Park. The 37-foot tall statues were added by Production Designer Jeffrey Beecroft. And to confuse things further, the luscious black and gold zigzag *moderne* interior is a few miles away in Hollywood. It's the 1929 **Pantages Theater, 6233 Hollywood Boulevard**, which, in the fifties, actually was home to the Academy Awards ceremony. The Rotary Club dinner epilogue filmed in the familiar Crystal Ballroom of LA's **Biltmore Hotel** (seen in *The Fabulous Baker Boys* and *Splash* among many other films), **506 South Grand Avenue**, on Pershing Square, downtown.

BOILER ROOM

(2000, dir: Ben Younger)
Giovanni Ribisi, Vin Diesel, Nia Long.
● **NEW YORK CITY**

Seth (Ribisi) is seduced by Jim Young's (Ben Affleck) get-rich-quick brokering pitch in this snappy re-run of *Wall Street*. The employees of JT Marlin descend like locusts on the **Roosevelt Hotel, East 45th Street** (see *The French Connection* for details), where it is announced that the firm has unlimited trading authorisation. The midtown deco Roosevelt is also featured in *Maid in Manhattan* and in *Quiz Show*. Seth has a fruitless meeting with his disapproving dad at the **Gemini Diner, 641 Second Avenue** at 35th Street (℃ *212.532.2143*), Murray Hill, and walks out of a family dinner at **Ratner's, 138**

Delancey Street (℃ *212.677.5588*), on the Lower East Side, another *French Connection* location.

The Marlin lads indulge in a little tribal sparring with the big boys from JP Morgan in **Killarney Rose, 80 Beaver Street** at Pearl Street (℃ *212.422.1486*), a brokers' hangout in, naturally enough, the Financial District. Another fun-packed night ends up in a macho altercation at Irish pub **Fiddler's Green, 58 West 48th Street** (℃ *212.819.0095*). It doesn't get beyond verbal conflict with a bunch of gay guys who give as good as they get in wood-pannelled restaurant **The Odeon, 145 West Broadway** at Thomas Street, Tribeca (℃ *212.233.0507*).

BOMBSHELL (aka *Blonde Bombshell*)

(1933, dir: Victor Fleming)
Jean Harlow, Lee Tracy, Franchot Tone.
● **LOS ANGELES, CALIFORNIA**

Wisecracking Hollywood-set farce. The nightclub scene filmed in the famous, but sadly now closed, Cocoanut Grove of the **Ambassador Hotel, 3400 Wilshire Boulevard** at Catalina Street, midtown (see *Barton Fink* for details).

BONFIRE OF THE VANITIES, THE

(1990, dir: Brian De Palma)
Tom Hanks, Melanie Griffith, Bruce Willis.
● **NEW YORK CITY; LOS ANGELES, CALIFORNIA**

Fatally miscast and drastically cut down, De Palma's film is little more than a trot through the plot of Tom Wolfe's satirical novel. The whole story of the making of the movie is chronicled with painful detail in Julie Salamon's fascinating *The Devil's Candy* (and what a movie that would make).

'Master of the Universe' Hanks lives at **800 Park Avenue** near 75th Street, naturally on Manhattan's prestigious East Side (*subway: 77th Street*), although his lobby filmed in number 77, way down south of Midtown. His workplace is the Bond Trading Room at **Merrill-Lynch** in **Two, World Financial Center**, the tallest of architect Cesar Pelli's asymetrical four-tower complex occupying the landfill site at Manhattan's southern tip. Merrill Lynch cooperated with this less-than-sympathetic portrayal of New York life on condition that their name was not mentioned. Oops.

Lost in a controversial caricature of the Bronx in the High Bridge district on **167th Street**, between Sherman and River Avenues (*subway: 167th Street Station, Green Route to Woodlawn*), Hanks and Griffith get involved in the fateful hit-and-run accident under the **Third Avenue Bridge**, where Third Avenue crosses the East River north of East Harlem. Hanks finds himself taken to the austere deco fortress of the **Bronx County Courthouse Building, 851 Grand Concourse** at the south-west corner of East 161st

Home of the 'Master of the Universe': Park Avenue, East Side

Street. The local subway station is 161st Street/Yankee Stadium a couple of blocks west, but this is not the one Willis hustles Hanks into, which was a fake entrance built on the sidewalk to keep the action flowing smoothly.

Rev Bacon (a caricature of Al Sharpton) exploits the case with a demo for the media at a housing project on **171st Street** between Fulton and Third Avenues, just west of Crotona Park in the Bronx. Out on bail, Hanks attends a post-opera party, which was filmed way across on the West Coast, among the stuffed predators in the **Los Angeles County Museum of Natural History**, part of the Exposition Park complex of museums and galleries, downtown LA on Exposition Boulevard.

Back on the East coast, the courthouse used for Hanks' – much cut-down – trial scene is over in Queens. It's the **Queens County Courthouse** on **Sutphin Boulevard** in the Jamaica District. The lionisation of Willis, which opens and closes the movie, is held in the Grand Central-sized Plaza of the **Winter Garden** with its enormous arched window overlooking the Hudson River. Coincidentally, it's part of the same lavish Battery Park City complex housing the Merrill-Lynch offices.

BONNIE AND CLYDE
(1967, dir: Arthur Penn)
Warren Beatty, Faye Dunaway, Gene Hackman.
● TEXAS

This stylish and violent mythologising of two much uglier gangsters was filmed around Dallas, Texas, at many of the sites where the actual events happened. The three banks raided are the real banks, which had been left unchanged after closing down during the Depression in the thirties. They're at **Pilot Point**, 50 miles north of Dallas on Route 377; **Red Oak**, just south of Dallas; and **Venus**, Route 67 about 20 miles southwest of Dallas (a town also seen in *The Trip to Bountiful*). The other locations, Arcadia, Louisiana, Dexter, Iowa and Joplin, Montana, also filmed in Texas. Among the small, unmodernised towns used are **Midlothian** and trusty old **Waxahachie** (the location for *Places in the Heart* and *Tender Mercies*), both also just south of Dallas; **Rowlett**; **Maypearl** (south of Venus); **Garland** (Route 66, northeast of Dallas); and **Ponder** (Route 156, 25 miles north of Fort Worth).

The real-life killing of Parker and Barrow took place in Dexter, about 80 miles northwest of Des Moines, just north of Route 30 in Carroll County, Iowa. The bloody 'Ring of Fire' shooting was filmed at **Lemmon Lake**, a privately-owned preserve on Trinity River a few minutes from downtown Dallas.

BOOGIE NIGHTS
(1997, dir: Paul Thomas Anderson)
Mark Wahlberg, Burt Reynolds, Julianne Moore.
● LOS ANGELES, CALIFORNIA

Anderson's rose-tinted look at the fall of the porn film industry in the seventies bursts with style and energy. It was filmed largely in the San Fernando Valley north of LA. The Hot Traxx disco, where film director Jack Horner (Reynolds) spots Eddie Adams (Wahlberg) working as a

waiter, has cleaned up its act a little, and is in fact a church, **Iglesia Cristiana Nuevo Empezar, 18419 Sherman Way** at Canby Avenue, **Reseda**.

The Hot Traxx disco: Sherman Way, Reseda

Just west, on Sherman Way, you can see the now-closed Reseda picture house used for the opening credits. Horner's house is in **West Covina**, and his porno warehouse is the real thing, **Gourmet Video** in Van Nuys.

The dubious scam: El Royale Motel, Studio City

Eddie, transformed into porn legend Dirk Diggler and down on his luck, is reduced to showing off his spectacular endowment for bucks in front of **St Catherine's of Siena Church, 18115 Sherman Way** at Lindley Avenue, where he gets beaten up by a carload of surfer punks. A little further west along Sherman Way, Buck Swope (Don Cheadle) witnesses the bloodily bungled robbery at **Miss Donuts, 18231 Sherman Way**, near Etiwanda Avenue. Todd Parker (Thomas Jane) ropes Dirk and Reed (John C Reilly) into

Buck witnesses the bloodily bungled robbery: Miss Donuts, Sherman Way

Dirk gets beaten up: St Catherine's of Siena Church, Sherman Way

his dubious scam to rip off Rahad (Alfred Molina) at the **El Royale Motel, 11117 Ventura Boulevard**, Studio City.

BOOMERANG
(1947, dir: Elia Kazan)
Dana Andrews, Jane Wyatt, Lee J Cobb.
● CONNECTICUT; NEW YORK

Innovative semi-doc melodrama based on a true story of murder in small-town USA. An innocent man is saved but, unusually, the real killer is not unmasked. Also unusually for this period, it was shot entirely on location, a Kazan trademark. The street scenes were filmed in **Stamford**, Connecticut, the court scenes in the courthouse of **White Plains**, New York.

BOOT, DAS (aka *The Boat*)
(1981, dir: Wolfgang Petersen)

Jürgen Prochnow, Herbert Gronemeyer, Klaus Wennemann.
● **GERMANY; FRANCE**

Wolfgang Petersen's epic (the TV version is six hours long) and excruciatingly claustrophobic account of life beneath the waves aboard a German U-boat during WWII was shot on a deliberately cramped set at the **Bavaria Studios** in Munich. The opening Bar Royal was also a studio set. The studio, built back in the silent era in 1919, was also used for such disparate movies as Stanley Kubrick's *Paths of Glory*, Ingmar Bergman's *The Serpent's Egg*, Uli Edel's controversial *Last Exit to Brooklyn*, Wolfgang Petersen's *The Neverending Story* and Bob Fosse's *Cabaret*. You can tour the famous studio, with the spaceship from *Enemy Mine* and sets from *Astérix et Obélix Contre César*, at **Bavariafilmplatz 7, 82031 Geiselgasteig** on the southern border of Munich (© *089.64.99.23.04*).

The submarine pens the sub sets out from, and site of the tragic air raid at the end, are real. They are at the **La Pallice** naval base, built by the German Command in 1941 at **La Rochelle** near Rochefort-sur-mer on the Atlantic coast of France. The same base was used in *Raiders of the Lost Ark*, which also borrowed *Das Boot*'s submarine.

The sea scenes were shot in the North Atlantic around **Heligoland** and in **Bodensee** (Lake Constance) in Bavaria.

BORN FREE
(1966, dir: James Hill)
Virginia McKenna, Bill Travers, Geoffrey Keen.
● **KENYA**

The Adamsons raise lion cubs, and have to train Elsa the grown lioness to live in the wild. This was filmed on the actual location, at **Naro Moru** in Meru National Park, surprisingly the least spoiled, least visited of Kenya's parks. A replica of the Adamsons' house was built on a 750-acre equatorial farm here in the Kenya Highlands, with filming on the surrounding plains and along the **Naro Moro River**.

BORN ON THE FOURTH OF JULY
(1989, dir: Oliver Stone)
Tom Cruise, Raymond J Barry, Willem Dafoe.
● **TEXAS; PHILIPPINES; MEXICO**

Cruise makes a bid for the traditional disability Oscar, complete with lank hair and a beard, as real-life Vietnam veteran Ron Kovic, who led opposition to the Vietnam War after being paralysed from the waist down. The movie was made at Los Colinas Studios in Dallas, Texas, and both Kovic's neighbourhood of Massapequa, Long Island, and the Miami scenes were filmed around the Dallas area. The Vietnam scenes were shot in the Philippines.

The Kovics' Long Island home is on **Creekside Drive**, off Houghton Road, southwest Dallas, near the Hawn Freeway. Young Ron's high school is **Henderson Elementary School, 2200 South Edgefield Avenue, Elmwood** in **Oak Cliff**, Dallas. After the killings at Kent State University, Abbie Hoffman leads protests at **Dallas Hall**, home of **Dedman College, Boaz Lane** off Daniel Avenue,

on the campus of **Southern Methodist University**. The Chicago Convention Center is the **Dallas Convention Center, 650 South Griffin Street**.

BOUCHER, LE (aka *The Butcher*)
(1969, dir: Claude Chabrol)
Stephane Audran, Jean Yanne, Antonio Passalia.
● **FRANCE**

A typically Hitchcockian thriller from Chabrol, as a serial killer haunts a small French town. It's filmed around the Dordogne area of France. The town is **Tremolat**, a beautiful little village close to the Cingle de Tremolat, a great bend in the Dordogne River about 70 miles east of Bordeaux.

BOUDU SAUVÉ DES EAUX (aka *Boudu Saved From Drowning*)
(1932, dir: Jean Renoir)
Michel Simon, Charles Granval, Marcelle Hainiaa.
● **PARIS, FRANCE**

Boudu (Simon) is the tramp rescued from a watery death who makes life hell for the family who take him in. Sound familiar? It was remade by Hollywood in 1985 as *Down and Out in Beverly Hills*. In Renoir's original, Boudu falls into the Seine from the **Pont des Arts**, the wooden-planked pedestrian link between the Lou-

Boudu saved from drowning: Pont des Arts

The bookshop: Arenthon, quai Malaquais

vre on the Right Bank and the Institut de France on the Left (the bridge was featured more recently in *Le Fabuleux Destin d'Amélie Poulain*). The shop belonging to Lestingois (Granval), who saves him, is a real bookstore, and still in business. It's **Arenthon, 3 quai Malaquais**, on the Left Bank between the Pont des Arts and the Pont Neuf. Boudu was lucky to have been saved, though – you can't see the Pont des Arts from the shop's windows.

BOUND
(1996, dir: Larry Wachowski; Andy Wachowski)
Jennifer Tilly, Gina Gershon, Joe Pantoliano.
● **LOS ANGELES, CALIFORNIA**

Taut little off-centre noir from the Wachowski brothers, who went on to make the phenomenally successful *The Matrix*. Like the sci-fi blockbuster, the

The apartment block: Talmadge Apartments

brothers set the action in their home town of Chicago while filming elsewhere. The deco apartment block where neighbours Tilly and Gershon enjoy what readers of one magazine voted the most popular kiss in screen history is actually the **Talmadge Apartments, 3278 Wilshire Boulevard** at Berendo Street, midtown LA.

Bligh's home: Montpelier Row, Twickenham

BOUNTY, THE

(1984, dir: Roger Donaldson) Anthony Hopkins, Mel Gibson, Laurence Olivier.
● TAHITI; NEW ZEALAND; LONDON; MIDDLESEX; WILTSHIRE

The old *Mutiny on the Bounty* warhorse, told in flashback from Bligh's court martial. Scripted by Robert Bolt and slated to be directed by David Lean, it was finally helmed by Donaldson, who has since hived off into empty bozo movies like *Species* and *Dante's Peak*. You can find the building used for Lieutenant Bligh's

The court martial exterior: Royal Naval College, Greenwich

home in Twickenham. It's one of the elegant terraced houses running along the western edge of Marble Hill Park. Built in 1721, it was once home to poet Alfred Lord Tennyson, and you can see it at **15 Montpelier Row**, south of Richmond Road to the southwest of Richmond Bridge (*tube: Richmond, rail: St Margaret's*).

The galleried club, where Bligh invites Fletcher Christian to sail with him, is the **Reform Club** in Pall Mall, St James, SW1. Bligh's court martial filmed at two separate locations. The exterior is the **Royal Naval College** at Greenwich, SE10 (*rail: Greenwich*), but the grand interior, where Laurence Olivier presides, is the Double Cube Room of **Wilton House, Wilton**, two-and-a-half miles west of Salisbury on the A30 in Wiltshire. It's open to the public (*admission charge*).

The South Seas location is the island of **Moorea**, close to Tahiti. Four sets, the landing site, the Polynesian village where Bligh meets the King, the Dutch port of Coupand in Timor and the breadfruit gardens, were built here. The *Bounty* itself was built at **Whangarei** on the North Island of New Zealand, and here and further south at **Gisbourne**, most of the boat's scenes and the Pitcairn Island scenes were shot.

BOURNE IDENTITY, THE

(2002, dir: Doug Liman) Matt Damon, Franka Potente, Chris Cooper.
● PARIS, FRANCE; PRAGUE, CZECH REPUBLIC; ITALY; GREECE

The opening scene is the harbour of **Imperia**, and Jason

Bourne (Damon) disembarks in the neighbouring harbour of **Oneglia** in Liguria, northern Italy. Bourne's apartment is on **Avenue Kléber**, near the Arc de Triomphe in Paris. Wombosi's mansion is on **Place des Etats-Unis**. The Treadstone safehouse is on **Place du Marché Sainte Catherine**. Filming also occurred at the **Hotel Regina**, the **Jardin des Tuileries**, the banks of the Seine, the **l'Ile St Louis**, the futuristic **La Defense** and the **Place des Pyramides**. Zurich is Prague, where the interior and exterior of the United States Consulate was a defunct branch of HypoBank about to be redeveloped as a luxury hotel. Some Paris locations were also tricked up in Prague, including the art nouveau **Imperial Café** and **Kampa Park** (in which Bourne battles Zurich policemen). The Alps are **Cesky Sibir** (Czech Siberia), outside the city. The French farmhouse is in the village of **Suchdol**, not far from Ruzyne, Prague's international airport. The final scenes were shot on **Mykonos**, Greece.

BOURNE SUPREMACY, THE

(2004, dir: Paul Greengrass) Matt Damon, Joan Allen, Brian Cox.
● GERMANY; INDIA; RUSSIA; ITALY; NEW YORK

At the start of the movie, Jason Bourne (Damon) and Marie (Franka Potente) are lying low in **Goa**, a long-time hippie beach paradise on the west coast of

Kirill reports to his control at the airport motel: Motel Avus, Halensee

India that still carries signs of its many years under Portuguese rule. Their hideaway is on the isolated white sand **Palolem Beach**, about 3km from Canacona railway junction in southern Goa. If you want more luxury – you're not on a budget – stay, like Damon, at the Intercontinental Grand Resort Goa, Raj Baga, Canacona (© *91.832.266.7777*).

The market town, though, is not as close as it appears. It's the Goan capital, **Panaji** (previously Panjim), way to the north, where hired killer Kirill (Karl Urban) tries to trace Bourne at the telegraph office, the **Communidade Building** on **Church Square**. He chases Bourne's Suzuki Gypsy through the old **Fontainhas Heritage Precinct** and **Candolim**, before it plunges off the **Nerul Bridge** into the River Nerul. Still craving that movie star experience? The star's

CIA Berlin HQ: Karl-Liebknecht Allee

The Naples customs house: Eingangsbereich Nord building of Messe Berlin

Bourne's first hit, in the fictitious Hotel Brecker: Haus Cumberland, Kurfurstendamm, Berlin

Landy's hotel: The Westin Grand Berlin, Friedrichstrasse

hotel here was the Taj Fort Aguada Beach Resort, Sinquerim (*© 91.832.564.5858*).

The rest of the film flits between Germany, Italy, Russia and the Netherlands, but most of it was filmed in **Berlin**. The deal set up to flush out a CIA mole, sabotaged by Kirill to frame Bourne, is at **Kantstrasse / Hardenbergstrasse**, alongside Zoologischer Garten Station. Kirill reports to his control, Yuri, at **Motel Avus, Halenseestrasse 51, Halensee** (*© 030.30.10.570*), at the end of the famous Avus racetrack opposite the ICC (International Congress Centre).

As Bourne returns to Europe, there's the briefest glimpse of the real **Naples** harbour (courtesy of a seaborne second unit), but the Stazione Marittima di Napoli, the Italian customs office at which Bourne is held, is the **Eingangsbereich Nord** building of **Messe Berlin**, the northern entrance to the Berlin Exhibition Grounds, **Messedamm 22**. Likewise, although there's an establishing shot of Moscow's **Sheremetyevo International Airport** as Kirill arrives in Russia, his meeting with Yuri was filmed in the parking area beneath the **ICC**, part of the same complex.

When Ward Abbott (Cox) travels to Amsterdam to find Nicky (Julia Stiles), it's in Berlin – on **Walter-Benjamin-Platz** – that he contacts her. And the flight back from Amsterdam to Berlin's **Templehof Airport** must be the shortest on film, since it also begins at Templehof. By now it should come as no surprise that the Munich house of Jarda, the other remaining Treadstone operative, is also Berlin, on **Kaiserstrasse**, in the **Wannsee** district.

Bourne arrives in Berlin at **Ostbahnhof**, one of east Berlin's two major termini, and takes a cab into the city, crossing the elaborately turretted **Oberbaum Bridge** (a quick homage to *Run, Lola, Run*, which starred Potente). He tracks US agent Pamela Landy (Allen) to the **Westin Grand Berlin, Friedrichstrasse 158-164** (*© 030.2027.0; www.westin-grand.com*), and tails her to the CIA hub, which is an empty office block on **Karl-Liebknecht Allee**.

Bourne leaps onto the boat: Friedrichstrasse Bridge over the Spree

Setting up a meeting with Nicky under the **World Clock (Weltzeituhr)** in **Alexanderplatz**, Bourne takes evasive action amid a student demo.

Don't make plans quite yet to check in to the Hotel Brecker, Kurfurstendamm 288, where Bourne begins to remember his disastrous first mission – to kill Russian politician Neski. Although there's no such hotel, there are plans to turn the location used, **Haus Cumberland, Kurfurstendamm 193**, into a luxury hotel. As

The last Treadstone agent, in the Munich house: Kaiserstrasse, Wannsee, Berlin

Bourne looks for Neski's daughter in Moscow: Scharrenstrasse, Berlin

the police arrive, Bourne makes his escape on foot. The police motorbike crashes into a taxi on **Kantstrasse**. Bourne depends on the precision of the Berlin railway system to make his escape on **S-Bahnhof Friedrichstrasse** (try that one in London…), leaping onto a boat from tthe **Friedrichstrasse Bridge** over the Spree.

Bourne takes the train to Moscow, arriving at **Moscow Kievskiai** rail station (the real thing, which serves the Ukraine); but the Moscow disco, where Yuri finds Kirill to inform him that Bourne is still alive, is the, now closed, **Cafe Moskau, Karl Marx Allee 34** (part of the Kino International complex) in Berlin. The Moscow street where Bourne looks for Neski's daughter is **Scharrenstrasse**, south of Alexanderplatz in Spittelmarkt. The police arrive on **Friedrichsgracht**, and Kirill is temporarily arrested on **Spittelmarkt** at **Leipziger Strasse**. Part of the subsequent car chase is indeed Moscow, but much was still Berlin, in the suburb of **Potsdam**, and on **Karl Marx Allee**, which was covered in snow. The final crash is at the **Potsdamer Platz** exit to Berlin's **Tiergarten Tunnel**.

BOYS DON'T CRY

(1999, dir: Kimberley Peirce)
Hilary Swank, Chloe Sevigny, Peter Sarsgaard.
● **TEXAS**

Based on a true story, which happened in Falls City, Nebraska, when Brandon Teena, a popular, handsome new boy in town, was brutally murdered and found to be Teena Brandon, a lesbian living as a boy. Shot in and around **Austin**, Texas, the courthouse was in **Greeneville**, Texas.

BOYS' TOWN

(1938, dir: Norman Taurog)
Spencer Tracy, Mickey Rooney, Henry Hull.
● **NEBRASKA**

Tracy pulls all the stops out (he really wanted to be a priest) as Father "There's no such thing as a bad boy" Flanagan in this teary true-life biopic filmed on location in the real **Boys' Town** on the western edge of Omaha,

Nebraska.

BOYZ N THE HOOD

(1991, dir: John Singleton)
Cuba Gooding Jr, Larry Fishburne, Ice Cube.
● LOS ANGELES, CALIFORNIA

23-year-old Singleton's film, about the vicious circle of black-on-black violence, was filmed in the area he grew up in, LA's South Central district. The focus of the movie is Inglewood, an area just east of LA International Airport. The opening scene, where a pool of blood becomes a source of fascination to the schoolkids, took place at the junction of **Lawrence Street and Woodworth Avenue**, south of Hollywood park in southern Inglewood. If you need to visit, take care in this area of transients' apartment buildings. Young Tré Styles (Gooding) attends director Singleton's old school, **Clyde Woodworth Elementary School, 3200 West 104th Street, Inglewood**. A block east is the notorious north-south cruising strip of **Crenshawe Avenue**, the setting for the piddling slight that escalates into tragedy.

The rather anaemic-looking Westside restaurant, where 'Furious' Styles (Fishburne) and Reva Devereaux (Angela Bassett) have a heart-to-heart, is **Coley's Kitchen Jamaican Restaurant, 4335 Crenshaw Boulevard** (© *213.290.4010*), a wildly colourful Jamaican restaurant where you can get such traditional West Indian fare as jerk chicken and curried goat.

BRAINDEAD (aka *Dead Alive*)

(1992, dir: Peter Jackson)
Timothy Balme, Diana Penalver, Elizabeth Moody.
● NEW ZEALAND

More wildly emetic schlock-horror from the director of *Bad Taste*, filmed in **Wellington**, New Zealand, and at the **Pinnacles**.

BRAVEHEART

(1995, dir: Mel Gibson)
Mel Gibson, Patrick McGoohan, Sophie Marceau.
● IRELAND; SCOTLAND

Best Film and Best Director, according to the Academy Awards. Hmmm. There was much controversy when it was admitted that this story of Scottish independence was to be filmed largely in Ireland, but the Republic is on the ball with tax breaks and the use of its army. The village of Lanark, where William Wallace lives as a child and later falls in love with Murron, was one of the few locations actually in Scotland. The Medieval Scottish village was constructed in the **Glen Nevis Valley** at the foot of Britain's highest peak, Ben Nevis. The village set was completely dismantled and the area returned to its former state, though the Braveheart Car Park, constructed to service the location, has been retained. The filming site is up the glen, past the car park, and below the road's highest point. The design of the village houses was based on those of St Kilda, a tiny island off the Scottish coast, inhabited until the late 18th century, but now a tourist attraction.

More Scottish landscapes were filmed at **Loch Leven**

and **Glen Coe**. Wallace's trek up to the spectacular peak was shot on the **Mamores**. The interior of Mornay's castle is another Scots location, filmed in the **Edinburgh Council Chamber**.

Everything else in the movie was filmed in Ireland, within a 30 mile radius of Dublin. The fortified English town of York is **Trim Castle**, a massive ruin kitted out for the movie with wooden buttresses and a seven-ton gate. The London square was also created at Trim, on the other side of the castle wall. (Trim Castle can be seen in Sam Fuller's war movie, *The Big Red One*). The town of Trim is about 26 miles northwest of Dublin on the River Boyne, Co Meath. About five miles northeast of Trim is **Bective Abbey**, which was used as the courtyard of Longshanks' castle and the dungeons, where Wallace is imprisoned.

Edinburgh Castle is tall, square-towered **Dunsoghly Castle**, dating from 1450 and the only castle in Ireland to retain its original Medieval trussed roof. It's about two miles northwest of Finglas, northern Dublin off the N2 between Kilshane Bridge and Pass If You Can. Another English stockade was constructed around an old hunting lodge at **Coronation Plantation**. Westminster Abbey is **St Nicholas Church, Dunsany Castle**. The escape from Mornay's castle, after bloodily crushing his skull, filmed at **Blessington Lakes**, where a 45-foot tower was specially constructed. Most interiors filmed in Dublin's Ardmore Studios. The battles of Stirling and Falkirk were staged at the **Curragh and Ballynmore Eustace**, a large, privately-owned stretch of land, and on the studio lot at Ardmore.

BRAZIL

(1985, dir: Terry Gilliam)
Jonathan Pryce, Michael Palin, Robert De Niro.
● LONDON; KENT; CUMBRIA; BUCKINGHAMSHIRE; PARIS, FRANCE

The glum, fifties-style setting of Terry Gilliam's visually stunning fantasy is a mixture of elaborate sets built at Lee Studios, and cunning location work. The vast

Katharine Helmond's plastic surgery: Leighton House, Kensington

clerks pool in the Department of Records, where Sam Lowry (Pryce) works, and the deserted corridors of the Expediting Department are the interior of the old deserted CWS Flour Mill at the Royal Victoria Dock. The mill also provided the grim passageways and stairwells, as well as the exterior of Shangri La Towers, the unfortunate Buttle's tower block.

Mentmore Towers, in the village of **Mentmore**, Buckinghamshire, was built in the 1850s for the Rothschild family. Designed by Sir Joseph Paxton, the architect of Crystal Palace, it's modelled on the Elizabethan Wollaton Hall near Nottingham. In 1977 the house hit the headlines when the entire contents were sold by Sothebys. A hidden stash of silverware was discovered beneath

The chase through the apartment block: Palacio d'Abraxas, Noisy-le-Grand

The apartment block chase: Palacio d'Abraxas, Noisy-le-Grand

a trapdoor. The house became headquarters of the Maharishi University of Natural Law, but was recently put up for sale. It is no longer open to the public. The house's grand Entrance Hall, with its white marble staircase leading up to the glass-roofed Grand Hall, is used as the pompous restaurant where Pryce meets his mother, oblivious to a pyrotechnic terrorist attack.

The flamboyant setting for Katharine Helmond's facial surgery is the famous Arab Hall of **Leighton House, 12 Holland Park Road**, London W14, albeit camped up with Michelangelo's David in its alcoves. This Victorian gem, decorated in gilt and blue Islamic tiles – the fantasy creation of Royal Acadamician Frederick Lord Leighton – is part of the Leighton House Museum (© *020.7602.3316, www.rbkc.gov.uk/leighton housemuseum; tube: High Street Kensington*), open free of charge every day except Sundays. It contains more restored Victorian interiors, along with paintings by Leighton himself and contemporaries Burne-Jones, Millais and Watts. Find it north of the western reaches of Kensington High Street.

Helmond's cluttered home is the Billiard Room of the old **National Liberal Club, 1 Whitehall Court** at Whitehall Place, seen in many old movies, including *The Elephant Man*. The dramatic spiral staircase is also here. The club has since been incorporated into the **Royal Horseguards Hotel**. The industrial complex is the **BP Oil Refinery** on the **Isle of Grain**, Kent.

Pryce's neighbourhood is **Noisy-le-Grand**, a self-consciously modern satellite town in the district of Marne-la-Vallée, east of Paris, en-route to Euro-Disney on the RER line. The bizarre apartment block is architect Ricardo Bofill's 1984 **Palacio d'Abraxas Apartments, Place d'Abraxas**, off Boulevard du Mont d'Est, west of the town centre. The delirious pathway to the funeral parlour in Pryce's climactic fantasy is the central court of the same complex. A great showpiece when built, it doesn't seem to have been well maintained. The pink deco interior of the Chapel of Our Lady of the Checkout Counter itself is the **Rainbow Room**, on the top floor of the old Biba store, **99 High Street Kensington**, entrance

The entrance to the funeral parlour: Palacio d'Abraxas, Noisy-le-Grand

on Derry Street (*www.roofgardens.com*).

The brief country idyll filmed in the Lake District in Cumbria. The torture chamber is the interior of one of the giant cooling towers of Croydon Power Station. The complex has since been demolished, though the names of the new streets on the site – Ampere, Volta, Faraday, Galvani – record its history, and there's even a Brazil Close. The station also provided the exterior of the Ministry, and though most, including the imposing entrance, has gone, you can still see some of the monumental deco brickwork at the foot of the two huge chimneys now on the site of the IKEA Superstore on Ampere Way.

BREAKFAST AT TIFFANY'S
(1961, dir: Blake Edwards)
Audrey Hepburn, George Peppard, Mickey Rooney.
● **NEW YORK CITY**

A film of the book would have been nice, but this cleaned-up jaunt through the edited highlights is jolly enough to be going on with, and Audrey Hepburn is, as always, a treat. Holly Golightly is the flighty social butterfly with a past, who enjoys nothing more than an alfresco breakfast gazing in the window of swish jewellery store, **Tiffany's, 727 Fifth Avenue** at 57th Street.

Coffee and Danish at the ready?: Tiffany's, Fifth Avenue

Holly Golightly's apartment: East 71st Street

The green and white candy-striped awning of Golightly's apartment building, where Mickey Rooney donned rubber eyelids as an an unlikely Japanese landlord, may have gone, but you'll still recognise the townhouse at **169 East 71st Street**, on the East Side, New York.

BREAKFAST CLUB, THE
(1985, dir: John Hughes)
Emilio Estevez, Judd Nelson, Molly Ringwald.
● **CHICAGO, ILLINOIS**

Archetypal Hughes teen-movie with the five principals whiling away an afternoon's detention. This being John Hughes, the setting is inevitably Chicago, in this case Des Plaines, and featuring **Main North** and **Glenbrook North High Schools**.

BREAKING AWAY
(1979, dir: Peter Yates)
Dennis Christopher, Dennis Quaid, Daniel Stern.
● **INDIANA**

Enormously likeable little middle-America movie, a sort of *Rocky* for cyclists, but done with wit and style. Made by a Brit director, it got a surprise Oscar nomination for

Best Picture, and actually picked up the Academy Award for Steve Tesich's quirky script. The movie was made entirely on location in **Bloomington**, Indiana, 40 miles southwest of Indianapolis, and on the campus of the screenwriter's Alma Mater, **Indiana University, 107 South Indiana Avenue**. The area's old limestone quarries, where Christopher and his buddies hang out, are a legacy of the town's past, hence Cutters, the students' term for locals.

BREAKING THE WAVES
(1996, dir: Lars Von Trier)
Emily Watson, Stellan Skarsgard, Katrin Cartlidge.
● **SCOTLAND; DENMARK**

Beautifully shot and affectingly acted, this story of a virginal bride sexually degrading herself to please her paralysed husband is horribly miscalculated. Danish scenes were filmed in **Hellerup** and **Lyngby**, while the Scottish scenes were shot at **Mallaig** and **Glendale** on the Isle of Skye, and at **Morar**.

BREATHLESS
(1983, dir: James McBride)
Richard Gere, Valerie Kaprinsky, Art Metrano.
● **LOS ANGELES, CALIFORNIA**

Brilliantly good-looking (with great LA locations) and bravely unlikeable remake of Godard's trash-culture landmark *A Bout de Souffle*, gaining oodles of cool credentials courtesy of Tarantino, who lists it as one of his faves. The action is transferred from sixties mono Paris to eighties pastel California. Locations included the **University of California**, Los Angeles; **Westwood**; and **Venice Beach**. The terrific murals, a feature of LA's Venice area, are the ones near **Windward Avenue** and **Speedway**. The nightmarishly futuristic hotel is the **Westin Bonaventure, 404 South Figueroa**, downtown LA.

BRIDE OF CHUCKY
(1998, dir: Ronny Yu)
Jennifer Tilly, Brad Dourif, Alexis Arquette.
● **ONTARIO, CANADA**

"Well, hello dolly" – Jennifer Tilly picks up Chucky: Parliament Street

The motel: Hillcrest Motel, Lakeshore Boulevard West, Toronto

Fourth in the series, with tongue very firmly in cheek, filmed in Ontario, Canada, at **Brampton**; **Pickering**; and Toronto itself. Jennifer Tilly kills the cop and first picks up the Chucky doll in the derelict, but landmark structure at **45 Parliament Street**. The pair hide out in Room 121 of the wonderfully fifties **Hillcrest**

Motel, 2143 Lakeshore Boulevard West on the shore of Lake Ontario (℗ *416.255.7711*). The gorgeous wedding chapels can be found on the strip near sideshows and waxworks of the gloriously tacky **Clifton Hill** in Niagara Falls. Sets were constructed in warehouses at **373 Front Street East, 15 Fraser Avenue** and **153 Eastern Avenue**. Filming also took place at an old army camp in **Oshawa**.

BRIDE OF THE MONSTER
(1955, dir: Edward Wood Jr)
Bela Lugosi, Tor Johnson, Tony McCoy.
● **LOS ANGELES, CALIFORNIA**

Another classic from the widely acknowledged Worst Director of All Time (it's the film with the fake octopus seen in Tim Burton's *Ed Wood*), shot, exotically, in **Griffith Park**, Los Angeles.

BRIDGE ON THE RIVER KWAI, THE
(1957, dir: David Lean)
Alec Guinness, William Holden, Sessue Hayakawa.
● **SRI LANKA**

The first of Lean's large-scale epics, *Bridge* was filmed on location in Sri Lanka, in the small community of **Kitulgala** on the Kelani River. The bridge itself, 425 feet long and rising 90 feet above the water, cost $250.000 to build. The cast and crew stayed at the **Government Rest House** in Kitulgala, which overlooks the site of the bridge. A few stumps from the movie bridge still remain on either side of the river. The British HQ, from which Jack Hawkins leads a force to blow up the bridge, is the **Peradeniya Botanic Gardens** on the outskirts of **Candy**, Sri Lanka, where Mountbatten did indeed have his station command from 1943 to 1945. There was more filming in the Sri Lankan capital of Colombo, at the **Mount Lavinia Hotel, 104 Hotel Road** (℗*0094.1717.450*). The real River Kwai itself can be seen in the 'Vietnam' sequences of *The Deer Hunter*. The real Bridge on the River Kwai, still standing, looks nothing like Lean's romanticised version. It's a concrete and girder structure standing, not amongst Sri Lanka's lush jungle vegetation, but on a scrubby Thai plain. You can take a River Kwai excursion, plus train ride, from Bangkok.

BRIDGE TOO FAR, A
(1977, dir: Richard Attenborough; Sidney Hayers)
Dirk Bogarde, James Caan, Michael Caine.
● **NETHERLANDS**

Long, long account of the disastrous WWII Allied parachute drop into the Netherlands, filmed at **Deventer**, 40km north of Arnhem, and at **Nijmegen**, south of Arnhem. Filming also took place at **Brinkhorst**; **Bemmel**; **Lent**; and **Grave**, all in the Netherlands.

BRIDGET JONES'S DIARY
(2001, dir: Sharon Maguire)
Renée Zellweger, Hugh Grant, Colin Firth.
● **LONDON; BUCKINGHAMSHIRE; GLOUCESTERSHIRE**

Daniel (Grant) takes Bridget (Zellweger) on a mini-break

to the **Stoke Poges Golf Club, Park Road, Stoke Poges**, in Buckinghamshire (*© 01753.717171*). Yes, this is the golf club seen in *Goldfinger* and used as the interior of the Hamburg hotel in *Tomorrow Never Dies*. Daniel's flat is a wharf conversion on **Clink Street**, SW1. Bridget's parents' home, where she first meets Mark (Firth) during a Christmas break – filmed in June with loads of fake snow – is in **Snowshill**, off the A46 about 12 miles north-east of Cheltenham, Gloucestershire. The church there is **St Barnabas**.

In the newspaper column, Bridget's London home was in Holland Park, and her locals included **The Pharmacy**, **Coffee Republic** on Portobello Road (outside which Hugh Grant bumps into Julia Roberts in *Notting Hill*), **192** and **Café Rouge**. For the movie, however, she's been relocated south of the river to Borough. Bridget's flat is above **The Globe, Bedale Street** at Green Dragon Court (a location for *The French Lieutenant's Woman*). Across Bedale Street you can see the shops which were tranformed into the cab office, the newsagent and, of course, the fictitious Greek restaurant where Grant and Firth slug it out during a birthday party. The restaurant where Zellweger and Grant have a date is **Cantina, 36 Shad Thames** (*© 020.7403.5403*). They have a clinch beneath the walkways of **Shad Thames** itself (see *The Elephant Man* for details). Other London locations include **St James's Square**, **St Pancras**, **King's Cross** and **Liverpool Street Station** (seen also in *The Elephant Man* and *Mission: Impossible*).

BRIEF ENCOUNTER

(1945, dir: David Lean)
Celia Johnson, Trevor Howard, Joyce Carey.
● LANCASHIRE; BUCKINGHAMSHIRE; LONDON

The railway station: Carnforth

Milford Junction railway station, supposedly in Kent, where Howard and Johnson meet up for their chastely clandestine afternoons, is **Carnforth Station** in Lancashire, about five miles north of Lancaster. The station is still standing and in use, though much of it is closed and boarded up. The tea room (the interior of which was recreated in the studio at Denham) is gone, but the platform tunnels and platform one, where Celia nearly takes a dive under the boat train, are still recognisable. Carnforth was chosen because of its distance from the German airfields and the subsequent relax-ation of the black-out regulations so far north (this was early 1945). You can plainly see station signs with the names of northern towns in the film. The

Milford High Street: Station Parade, Beaconsfield

lugubrious voice of the station announcer, by the way, is writer Noël Coward himself.

The rest of the film was shot in the Home Counties, with some of the busier railway shots filmed at Watford Junction. Milford High Street can be found in **Beaconsfield**, Buckinghamshire. The barrel organ on the

The accident on the boating lake: Long Bridge, Regent's Park

Celia Johnson bumps into Trevor Howard: Burke's Parade, Beaconsfield

corner by Harris's plays on **Station Parade**, alongside Beaconsfield Station, and Celia bumps into Trevor outside Boots, a few hundred yards south on **Burke's Parade**.

The cinema where they see the trailer for *Flames of Passion* was a picture house in Victoria, London, though the deco exterior was an entrance to the Denham Studios, since demolished, on the North Orbital Road, Denham. The hospital where Howard works is a set built for Alexander Korda's 1945 Robert Donat-Deborah Kerr comedy, *Perfect Strangers*. The boating lake is slap in the middle of London's **Regent's Park**. You can see the **Long Bridge**, which Trevor Howard clings to, in the bird sanctuary in the centre of the park, northwest of the Inner Circle opposite the entrance to the Open Air Theatre.

BRIGHTON ROCK (aka *Young Scarface*)

(1947, dir: John Boulting)
Richard Attenborough, Hermione Baddeley, William Hartnell.
● SUSSEX

Cuddly Attenborough is surprisingly menacing as baby-faced teenage hoodlum in Graham Greene's adaptation of his own book, which was filmed mostly on location in a seedy forties **Brighton**. Opening at **Brighton Station**. Pinkie and the mob catch up with Kolley Kibber at the Star and Garter pub, now **Dr Brighton's** on the sea front at Little East Street. Kibber flees through **The Lanes**, up **Queens Road** and back to the station, where the gang is waiting for him. He

The Star and Garter pub: Dr Brighton's, Little East Street

Kibber flees for his life: Queens Road

catches a number six bus and gets off at the **Clock Tower**. Running down **Church Street** to **Brighton Pavilion**, he's finally killed on **Palace Pier**. The racecourse is, of course, **Brighton Racecourse**.

BRING ME THE HEAD OF ALFREDO GARCIA
(1974, dir: Sam Peckinpah)
Warren Oates, Gig Young, Isela Vega.
● MEXICO

Peckinpah continued his love affair with the dusty south in this strange, slow movie, which was shot entirely on atmospheric Mexican locations, many around Mexico City. 'El Jefe', who gives the command of the title, rules from the **Hacienda de San Juan**, a 200-year-old fortress north of Mexico City near to Teotihuacan (Place of the Gods), an amazing area of pyramids and temples covering seven square miles. Oates works in the **Tlaquepaque Bar** in Plaza Garibaldi, Mexico City. The bizarrely colourful graveyards are in Mexico City.

BRITANNIA HOSPITAL
(1982, dir: Lindsay Anderson)
Leonard Rossiter, Graham Crowden, Joan Plowright.
● LONDON

Britannia Hospital: Friern Barnet Hospital, New Southgate

Last, and by far the least, of Lindsay Anderson's trilogy, which began so brilliantly with *If....*, wobbled a bit with the eccentric *O Lucky Man!* but finally crashed to earth with this cringingly banal, state-of-the-nation allegory, filmed at the huge, sprawling **Friern Hospital, Friern Barnet Road**, just west of New Southgate Station in London N11. True to the spirit of the movie and the times, it's now closed.

BROADWAY DANNY ROSE
(1984, dir: Woody Allen)
Woody Allen, Mia Farrow, Nick Apollo Forte.
● NEW YORK CITY; NEW JERSEY

The deli where the group of old comics recounts the tale of failed theatrical agent Danny Rose is the **Carnegie Delicatessen & Restaurant, 854 Seventh Avenue**, near West 54th Street, New York. *The* New York deli, it claims to serve the best pastrami and corned beef in the world, and they do serve a Broadway Danny Rose sandwich. Check out the mouthwatering website, complete with virtual tour and soundbites, at *www.nyctourist.com/ivrs/carndeli_1*. Danny signs up his woeful clients at the **Brill Building, 1619 Broadway** between West 49th and West 50th Streets.

BROWNING VERSION, THE
(1951, dir: Anthony Asquith)
Michael Redgrave, Jean Kent, Nigel Patrick.
● DORSET

A film version of Terence Rattigan's venerable play, about crusty teacher Crocker-Harris facing up to personal crises on his premature retirement. Filmed at **Sherborne School, Sherborne** in Dorset. In 1994 Mike Figgis (*Leaving Las Vegas*) filmed a decent remake with Albert Finney taking over the schoolmaster's gown. The school interiors were again shot at **Sherborne**, though the exteriors are **Milton Abbey School, Milton Abbas**, also in Dorset.

BRUCE ALMIGHTY
(2003, dir: Tom Shadyac)
Jim Carrey, Morgan Freeman, Jennifer Aniston.
● NEW YORK; ONTARIO, CANADA; LOS ANGELES, CALIFORNIA

Set in Buffalo, this crude comedy, which never fully explores the possibilties of the set up, was mostly filmed on the Universal backlot, including the *Back to the Future* square, the New York Street and the Brownstone Street. The real **Buffalo** and **Niagara Falls** are seen briefly, captured by a second unit team.

Frustrated Bruce Nolan (Carrey) wrecks his car, and challenges God, on **Harbor Drive, San Diego**. Omni Presents, the old building where he subsequently meets his maker (Freeman) is the **Rykoff Building** at **Seventh and Alameda**, downtown LA. The lavish restaurant, where Tony Bennett croons 'If I Ruled the World' for Bruce and Grace Connelly (Aniston), is **Cicada, 617 South Olive Street** (see *Indecent Proposal* for details).

BUCKET OF BLOOD, A
(1959, dir: Roger Corman)
Dick Miller, Barboura Morris, Antony Carbone.
● LOS ANGELES, CALIFORNIA

Before he made the cult *Little Shop of Horrors*, Corman directed this little number from the same scriptwriter, Chuck Griffith. After accidentally killing his landlady's cat, nerdy sculptor Miller (now a permanent fixture of Joe Dante's movies) covers it in clay, calls it 'Dead Cat', becomes a proto-Damien Hirst and moves on to human sculptures. The film was shot in five days, mainly on studio sets, but with location filming around **Venice Beach**.

BUFFY THE VAMPIRE SLAYER
(1992, dir: Fran Kazui)
Kristy Swanson, Luke Perry, Paul Reubens.
● LOS ANGELES, CALIFORNIA

Swanson is a California airhead destined to be the Ms Van Helsing of the West Coast in this witty spoof horror which didn't set the box office alight but nonetheless spawned a TV series. It was shot around LA. Buffy works out in the frequently filmed ballroom of the **Park Plaza Hotel, 607 South Park View Street**, midtown LA. Her school is the familiar old **John Marshall High School, 3939 Tracy Street**, Silverlake, which numbered the

Buffy's school: John Marshall High School

young Leonardo DiCaprio among its students.

BULL DURHAM

(1988, dir: Ron Shelton)
Kevin Costner, Susan Sarandon, Tim Robbins.
● **NORTH CAROLINA**

Sarandon is a baseball obsessive who makes a point of initiating new players, which sounds tacky but it all works. It was filmed around North Carolina with locations in **Raleigh**; **Greensboro**; **Asheville**; **Burlington**; and **Wilson**. The ball games were shot at **Durham Athletic Park, 426 Morris Street, Durham**.

BULLETS OVER BROADWAY

(1994, dir: Woody Allen)
John Cusack, Chazz Palminteri, Dianne Wiest.
● **NEW YORK CITY**

The old comics reminisce: Broadway Deli, Seventh Avenue

The stables: Claremont Riding Academy, West 89th Street

Once again, Woody Allen manages to turn the mean streets of New York into a warmly glowing visual treat. The theatre where Woody stand-in John Cusack gets his play staged with dubious finances is the **Belasco Theater, 111 West 44th Street** between 6th and 7th Avenues. You might recognise the hotel lobby of Cusack's mob backer, Nick Valenti, as the place where Luca Brasi gets garrotted in *The Godfather*. It's been renovated since the seventies, but the **Edison Hotel, 228 West 47th Street** (© *212. 840.5000*) is still a deco delight.

On the Upper West Side you'll find the stable where gangster-cum-playwright Cheech is quizzed: the **Claremont Riding Academy, 175 West 89th Street** between Amsterdam and Columbus Avenues (where the hippies got their horses for the Central park ride in Milos Forman's film of *Hair*). Even further north is Helen Sinclair's penthouse apartment, on **110th Street at Riverside Drive**, though the beautiful early 20th century roof, with its rare view of a skyscraper-free Manhattan skyline is an office building on **Nassau Street**, down in Lower Manhattan. The Three Deuces nightclub was filmed in central Manhattan, in the ballroom of the **New Yorker Hotel, 481 Eighth Avenue** (© *212.971.0101*). The ballroom also appeared, albeit differently decorated, in Woody Allen's *Radio Days*. The old movie theatre, under the elevated railway tracks, is over the East River in Williamsburg, Brooklyn.

BULLITT

(1968, dir: Peter Yates)
Steve McQueen, Robert Vaughn, Jacqueline Bisset.

● **SAN FRANCISCO, CALIFORNIA**

Bullitt meets up with an informant: Enrico's, Broadway

Brit director Yates set the industry standard for car chases in this SF based police actioner. Detective Frank Bullitt has to track down killers before the fact leaks out that a prize witness has been offed. The doomed witness, Johnny Ross, is first spotted by the baddies in the lobby of the de-luxe **Mark Hopkins Hotel, 1 Nob Hill** at California Street (© *415.392.3434, hotels.sanfran cisco.interconti.com*). As you might deduce from the address, this grand SF institution was built on the site of one of the city's most prestigious mansions. See it also in *The Betsy* and *Daddy's Gone a-Hunting*. But it's downhill for Ross from here: the rather less grand hotel where he is installed stood on Embarcadero, at the foot of the double-deck **Oakland Bay Bridge**, and has since been demolished

Robert Vaughn serves a writ: Grace Cathedral

You can see Bullitt's apartment, unchanged, at **1153-1157 Taylor Street**, a stylish 1906 three-story frame building at the corner of Clay Street. Over the road you can still shop at **VJ Groceries**, where Bullitt stocks up on TV dinners. The church, where Robert Vaughn

Frank Bullitt's apartment: Taylor Street

...and the shop where he stocks up: VJ Groceries, Taylor Street

serves a writ of habeas corpus on the police chief, is **Grace Cathedral, 1051 Taylor Street**, a couple of blocks south of Bullitt's home. The bar where Bullitt meets up with informant Eddie is also still in existence. It's **Enrico's, 504 Broadway** at the corner of Kearney Street. The car chase (the car is a Mustang Shelby) was filmed largely on **Fillmore Street**, between Broadway and Vallejo Street. The climactic shoot-out took place in **San Francisco International Airport**.

BUNNY LAKE IS MISSING

(1965, dir: Otto Preminger)
Carol Lynley, Keir Dullea, Laurence Olivier.
● **LONDON**

Laurence Olivier takes Carol Lynley for a drink: Warrington Arms

Frognall End, Keir Dullea's mansion: Cannon Hall, Hampstead

The Little People's Garden School: Netherhall Gardens, Hampstead

Preminger's weird black comedy, with a wonderful cast of eccentrics, filmed on location around London as policeman Olivier tries to track down the missing, but possibly imaginary, daughter of possibly batty Carol Lynley. Lynley's flat, where Noël Coward is the grossly lubricious landlord, was just off Trafalgar Square but has since been demolished. The Little People's Garden School, from which Bunny disappears, is still there, however. It's **South Hampstead High School, 5 Netherhall Gardens**, near Finchley Road, Hampstead, NW3 (*tube: Finchley Road*). Don't be fooled by the 'Frognal End NW3' street signs – there's no such place. The glorious art nouveau pub where Olivier takes the distraught Lynley for a drink is the **Warrington Arms, 93 Warrington Crescent** – once a favourite haunt of Marie Lloyd – in Maida Vale, W9 (*tube: Maida Vale*). The grand Hampstead home of Keir Dullea, and scene of the climax, was once home to actor Gerald du Maurier. It's **Cannon Hall, 14 Cannon Place** at Squire's Mount tucked away off East Heath Road, NW3, just off Hampstead Heath (*tube: Hampstead*).

BUS STOP

(1956, dir: Joshua Logan)
Marilyn Monroe, Don Murray, Betty Field.
● ARIZONA; IDAHO

The film of William Inge's play, about a dim macho cowboy's attempt to woo a singer during a bus stop in a small Western town was shot on location in **Phoenix**, Arizona, and at **Sun Valley** and **Ketchum**, close together on Route 75, the scenic highway north from Twin Falls by the Sawtooth National Forest, Idaho. The **North Fork Store**, seen in the movie, is about ten miles north of Ketchum on Route 75 in the National Forest itself. During Arizona filming, MM stayed at the Sahara Motor Hotel, 401 North 1st Street, Phoenix.

BUSY BODIES

(1933, dir: Lloyd French)
Stan Laurel, Oliver Hardy, Tiny Sandford.
● LOS ANGELES, CALIFORNIA

Laurel and Hardy change the record: Canon Drive, Beverly Hills

This short features Laurel and Hardy working in a sawmill, and driving to work with the phonogram under the car bonnet. They motor along **Canon Drive** in Beverly Hills – stopping to change the record of course, outside **517 North Canon Drive**, which is still unchanged today.

BUTCH CASSIDY AND THE SUNDANCE KID

(1969, dir: George Roy Hill)
Paul Newman, Robert Redford, Katharine Ross.
● UTAH; COLORADO; MEXICO

A spiffing romantic Western, originally written for Jack Lemmon (Butch) and Paul Newman (Sundance). Butch's first (real life) bank hold-up was at **Telluride** in the spectacular Uncompahgre National Forest, Route 550, southwest Colorado, and the **New Sheridan Hotel, 231 West Colorado Avenue** boasts a bar used in the movie.

The railway robberies filmed on the **Durango-Silverton Narrow Gauge Railroad** in southwest Colorado (see *Indiana Jones and the Last Crusade* for details). The breathtaking leap into the river was a less than breathtaking hop six feet onto a hidden platform (apparently Redford has a fear of heights). It was filmed at **Trimble Bridge** on the **Animas River**, near Durango, southwest Colorado.

The spectacular landscapes filmed in southwest Utah, at **St George**, on Route 15 in Washington County; **Snow Canyon** a few miles north on Route 18 (also, notoriously, locations for John Wayne's disastrous Genghis Khan pic *The Conqueror*); and in **Zion National Park**. Katharine Ross' house, site of the famous but rather twee musical interlude, was built for the movie and still stands in **Grafton**, a crumbling ghost town near Rockville, also Washington County.

The New York scenes were to have been shot on the *Hello Dolly* set at Twentieth Century-Fox in Hollywood, but since *Dolly* was yet to be released, studio head Richard Zanuck objected to revealing the expensive new showpiece, so the montage of period photos was used. The Bolivian scenes were shot in **Taxco** and **Curenavaca** to the south of Mexico City, Mexico.

BUTCHER BOY, THE

(1997, dir: Neil Jordan)
Eamonn Owens, Stephen Rea, Fiona Shaw.
● IRELAND

Jordan's imaginative film of Patrick McCabe's novel, about a psychotic young boy troubled by bizarre visions, was filmed in the author's home town of **Clones**, Co. Monaghan, on the A34 about 35 miles west of Dundalk.

C

CABARET
(1972, dir: Bob Fosse)
Liza Minnelli, Joel Grey, Michael York.
● GERMANY

Toned down from the stage musical, this is still a stylish filming of Christopher Isherwood's stories of pre-war Berlin. The Kit Kat Club was built in Munich's Bavaria Studios. Michael York's arrival in Berlin Hauptbahnhof station was shot on the old railway station at **Lubeck**, northeast of Hamburg. The baron's castle is **Schloss Eutin**, about 20 miles from Lubeck in Schleswig-Holstein. The lake district exteriors and interiors were shot on the estate of the Duke of Oldenburg. Filming also occurred in the Berlin suburb of **Dohlem**, with street scenes shot around **Berlin** and in the **Tiergarten**, as well as in **Munich**.

CADDYSHACK
(1980, dir: Harold Ramis)
Chevy Chase, Rodney Dangerfield, Bill Murray.
● FLORIDA

Clumpy farce set around a golf course, filmed at the **Rolling Hills Golf and Tennis Club, 3501 West Rolling Hills Circle** at South West 36th Street, Davie, about ten miles from downtown Fort Lauderdale, Florida. The waterside hi-jinks filmed at the **Boca Raton Hotel and Country Club, 501 East Camino Real** in the wealthy coastal resort of **Boca Raton**, north of Fort Lauderdale.

CAGE AUX FOLLES, LA (aka *Birds of a Feather*)
(1978, dir: Edouard Molinaro)
Ugo Tognazzi, Michel Serrault, Michel Galabru.
● ST TROPEZ, FRANCE

Tognazzi and Serrault argue: Place de l'Ormeau, St Tropez

Molinaro's amiable farce, centering around a gay nightclub (remade by Hollywood as *The Birdcage*) was shot on the charming, and surprisingly unspoilt, waterfront of St Tropez on the French Riviera. There is no Cage Aux Folles club, of course, but you will recognise the **Place de l'Ormeau**, at the end of **rue de l'Ormeau**, as the spot behind the club where Tognazzi and Serrault argue after stomping out.

CANDYMAN
(1992, dir: Bernard Rose)
Virginia Madsen, Tony Todd, Xander Berkeley.
● CHICAGO, ILLINOIS

Clive Barker's horror story is transposed from its UK setting of Liverpool to Chicago, where the vengeful spirit of an executed slave is traced to the troubled housing projects of **Cabrini Green**, on Division Street in the south-west area of Old Town. Once regarded as notoriously dangerous, much has been demolished and gentrification seems to be underway.

CANTERBURY TALE, A
(1944, dir: Michael Powell; Emeric Pressburger)
Eric Portman, Sheila Sim, Dennis Price.
● KENT

Wartime oddity from the Powell-Pressburger team with Price, Sim and John Sweet undertaking a latterday pilgrimage to Canterbury, while an unhinged magistrate pours glue onto women's hair during the wartime blackout.

The railway station, where the pilgrims meet up, is **Selling**, the stop before Canterbury East on the Kent Coast line from Victoria. The village of Chillingbourne is fictitious – a composite of several villages in the area around Canterbury. Eric Portman's house is **Wickhambreux Court** in the village of **Wickhambreux**, about five miles east of Canterbury, north of the A257. Just southeast of Wickhambreux on the A257 itself is the village of **Wingham**, where you'll find the **Red Lion Hotel, Canterbury Road**. The blacksmith's shop was at **Shottenden**, six miles west of Canterbury, off the A28. The hall, where Eric Portman delivers his lecture on the Pilgrim's Way, is the town hall at **Fordwich**, a couple of miles northeast of Canterbury.

The exterior of **Canterbury Cathedral** is real enough, but the organ sound is that of St Alban's Cathedral (Canterbury's having been dismantled for wartime safety reasons), and the nave was rebuilt in the studio at Denham (the stained glass windows at Canterbury had been boarded up).

CANTERBURY TALES, THE
(1971, dir: Pier Paolo Pasolini)
Pier Paolo Pasolini, Hugh Griffith, Laura Betti.
● AVON; ESSEX; GLOUCESTERSHIRE; SUFFOLK; SUSSEX; SICILY, ITALY

All the exuberance of Chaucer with, happily, *all* of the concomitant crudities of his period. The second part of Pasolini's folksy Medieval 'Trilogy of Life' (coming between *The Decameron* and *The Arabian Nights*), was filmed on location around real English villages including: **Chipping Campden**, ten miles south of Stratford-upon-Avon on the B4035 in Gloucestershire; **Lavenham** (the site of the witch burning in *Witchfinder General*), ten miles south of Bury St Edmunds on the A1141 in Suffolk; **St Osyth**, a couple of miles west of Clacton-on-Sea on the B1027 in Essex; **Bath** in Avon; **Battle**, five miles northwest of Hastings in Sussex; and **Rye**, eight miles northeast of Hastings, also in Sussex.

The 'Hell' scenes, with the giant Devil farting friars from his arse (I told you it contained the crudities of his period), were shot in the volcanic landscapes of Sicily.

CAPE FEAR
(1962, dir: J Lee-Thompson)
Robert Mitchum, Gregory Peck, Polly Bergen.
● **GEORGIA**

Psycho con Mitchum terrorises the family of lawyer Peck, whom he blames for a long prison stretch. Cape Fear River is actually in movie-heavy North Carolina (you can see it in *Blue Velvet* and Nicolas Roeg's film of Dennis Potter's TV play *Track 29*) but this movie was shot in and around **Savannah**, Georgia.

CAPE FEAR
(1991, dir: Martin Scorsese)
Robert De Niro, Nick Nolte, Jessica Lange.
● **FLORIDA**

Scorsese's first studio genre picture is a big, violent, widescreen remake of the 1962 thriller with De Niro as the crazy con, Nolte protecting his family and cameos from the stars of the original. It was shot in Florida, around **Fort Lauderdale** and its southern suburb **Dania**, I-95 north of Miami, and in the subtropical wilderness of the **Everglades**, down on Florida's southern tip. If you want to visit, the main entrance to the Everglades National Park is on Route SR 9336 from Florida City, or off Route 41 at Shark Valley and Everglades City.

You'll find the college, where De Niro seduces Juliette Lewis into a bout of finger-sucking, in **West Broward County**, just east of *Caddyshack*'s Rolling Hills Golf Club. It's **Broward Community College, 3501 SW Davie Road**. De Niro clings to the underside of the family car at **Seminole Indian Truck Stop, North US Highway 27**.

The attack on De Niro, where he taunts Nolte, filmed on **Brickel Avenue**. New Essex is **Hollywood Boulevard** in West Broward, where the ice cream store is the **Rainbo Cafe, 1909 Hollywood Boulevard**.

CAPTAIN CORELLI'S MANDOLIN
(2001, dir: John Madden)
Nicolas Cage, Penélope Cruz, John Hurt.
● **GREECE**

Louis de Bernières' novel was disappointingly brought to the screen by the director of *Shakespeare in Love*, and filmed on the island of **Cephallonia**, one of the Ionian Islands.

Site of the car wash: Rampart Boulevard

CAR WASH
(1976, dir: Michael Schultz)
Franklin Ajaye, Sully Boyar, Richard Pryor.
● **LOS ANGELES, CALIFORNIA**

Hi jinks at a car wash in LA scripted by Joel Schumacher, and causing major traffic problems when the Pointer Sisters did their big number. The De Luxe Car Wash, an existing facility kitted out with all modern gimmicks, stood on **Rampart Boulevard** at Sixth Street, near Lafayette Park, downtown LA. It's since been demolished.

CARLITO'S WAY
(1993, dir: Brian De Palma)
Al Pacino, Sean Penn, Penelope Ann Miller.
● **NEW YORK CITY**

Pacino is the ex-con trying, unsuccessfully, to go straight in De Palma's gutsy thriller. Scuzzy lawyer Penn involves him in a crazy plot to spring a client from the notorious **Riker's Island Prison Barge**. The island, in the East River north of Astoria, Queens, is reached by the Riker's Island Bridge from Hazen Street in Steinway just west of La Guardia Airport. The nightclub where a coked-up Penn lets slip about the prison break was the **Copacabana, 10 East 60th Street** at Madison Avenue on the east Side (it's now closed, but see *Goodfellas* for details). Pacino, released from prison, watches old flame Miller from a rainswept roof. The dance class is at the **Joffrey Ballet School** on the corner of **Sixth Avenue** and 10th Street in Greenwich Village. Nearby, the turreted gothic building past which Pacino follows Miller is the old **New York Public Library** on Sixth Avenue; and in **Le Figaro Café, 168 Bleecker Street** at MacDougal Street, Pacino and Miller talk over old times. Miller's apartment is **17 Gay Street**, also in the village, and it's at the end of **Gay Street**, at

Pacino watches Miller: Joffrey Ballet School, Sixth Avenue

Penelope Ann Miller's Greenwich Village apartment: Gay Street

Pacino and Miller mull over old times: Le Figaro Café, Bleecker Street

The elaborate shootout: Grand Central Station

the junction with **Waverly Place**, that Pacino is arrested.

Dodging the bad guys, Pacino jumps onto the South Ferry subway train at **125th Street Station** on Park Avenue in Harlem. The final bravura confrontation takes place all over **Grand Central Station**, 42nd Street at Park Avenue, with a shoot-out on the Park Avenue elevator.

Nicholson and Garfunkel meet up: Wollman Skating Rink, Central Park

CARNAL KNOWLEDGE

(1971, dir: Mike Nichols)
Jack Nicholson, Ann-Margret, Art Garfunkel.
● VANCOUVER, BRITISH COLUMBIA, CANADA; NEW YORK CITY; MASSACHUSETTS

Top notch directing and acting of a brilliantly cynical Jules Feiffer sex comedy. Largely New York set, it was mainly shot in and around Vancouver, Canada. The skating rink, where a lone white-clad skater signals the passing of time and Nicholson and Garfunkel meet up to mull over their lives, is Central Park's **Wollman Memorial Skating Rink**, 59th Street at 6th Avenue. The rink was recently rebuilt, courtesy of Donald Trump.

Nicholson and Garfunkel's college years were filmed at **Smith College, Northampton**, Massachusetts (see *Who's Afraid of Virginia Woolf?* for details).

CARNIVAL OF SOULS

(1962, dir: Herk Harvey)
Candace Hilligoss, Frances Feist, Sidney Berger.
● KANSAS; UTAH

Weird, offbeat little indie horror movie – a one-off from the director Harvey – made, apart from the lead role, with a non-professional cast. It was shot around Harvey's hometown of **Lawrence**, Kansas, about 30 miles west of Kansas City on Highway 70. The opening car smash filmed at **Kaw Bridge, Lawrence**. The bizarre carnival itself was a rundown funfair, the **Saltair Pavilion**, I-80, west of Salt Lake City, Utah. The wooden pavilion seen in the film has since been replaced by a tacky Vegas-style complex, but it does contain a scale-model of the original.

CAROUSEL

(1956, dir: Henry King)
Gordon Macrae, Shirley Jones, Cameron Mitchell.
● MAINE

Macrae returns from the dead to make amends for his wasted life in a muted version of Rodgers and Hammerstein's superb musical, which unwisely changes key scenes for the cinema. Based on Ferenc Molnar's play *Liliom*, *Carousel* transposes the action from Hungary to the New England seaside. One of the few musicals of the period to pop its head out of the studio gates, it was shot mainly at the prettified Maine coastal port of **Boothbay Harbor**, off I-1, around 30 miles south of Augusta. Filming also took place at **Newcastle**, Maine.

CARRIE

(1976, dir: Brian De Palma)
Sissy Spacek, Piper Laurie, William Katt.
● LOS ANGELES, CALIFORNIA

Arguably the best filming of a Stephen King story so far, with repressed teen Spacek wreaking revenge on her cruel classmates and her religious-nut mom Laurie. Bates High

Bates High School: Hermosa Beach Community Center, Hermosa Beach

School (what else would it be called in a De Palma movie?) is a conflation of **Hermosa Beach Community Center** (which used to be the Pier Avenue School), **Pier Avenue** at Pacific Coast Highway, Hermosa Beach between Manhattan Beach and Redondo Beach, Highway 1 south of LA International Airport, and **Pacific Palisades High School, Temescal Canyon Road** in Santa Monica. The interior of the gym was reconstructed at **Culver City Studios, 9336 Washington Boulevard**, Culver City, for the final conflagration – the same studio where they burned Atlanta for *Gone With the Wind*.

The bucket of blood that ends Carrie's night out is obtained by John Travolta and co from a pig farm in the industrial town of Vernon, southeast LA. The farm coyly hides behind images of porkers scampering in green meadows. It's the cutesy **Farmer John's Pig Mural**, one of the biggest murals in the world. Covering an entire city block, it was begun in 1957 by movie industry artist Les Grimes, who died in a fall from scaffolding while working on the project. You can glimpse it in Antonioni's *Zabriskie Point*, but see it for real at **3049 East Vernon Avenue, Vernon**, LA.

CARRY ON AGAIN DOCTOR

(1969, dir: Gerald Thomas)
Jim Dale, Kenneth Williams, Charles Hawtrey.
● BERKSHIRE

Ooh, Doctor Nookey! Bodily functions always gave the hospital Carry Ons a head start, and this is one of the best. Long Hampton Hospital is the Ceremonial Entrance to **Maidenhead Town Hall, St Ives Road, Maidenhead**, also used in *Carry On Doctor* and *Carry On Behind*. The Moore-Nookey Clinic (go on, say it out loud) is Heatherden Hall, the building at the

Dr Nookey's surgery: Park Street, Windsor

Long Hampton Hospital: Maidenhead Town Hall

heart of the Pinewood Studios complex, regularly drafted in for the low-low-budget series (it was the hospital in *Carry On Nurse*, for example). It's actually the studio administrative building. After returning from the tropical island with a lucrative slimming cure, Dr Nookey sets up his consulting rooms at **12 Park Street, Windsor**, just a few doors away from the familiar location seen in *Carry On Loving* and *Carry On Regardless*.

CARRY ON AT YOUR CONVENIENCE
(1971, dir: Gerald Thomas)
Sidney James, Kenneth Williams, Charles Hawtrey.
● **BUCKINGHAMSHIRE; SUSSEX**

Filming took place at **Black Park Country Park**, Buckinghamshire, and in **Brighton**.

CARRY ON CAMPING
(1969, dir: Gerald Thomas)
Sidney James, Barbara Windsor, Bernard Bresslaw.
● **BUCKINGHAMSHIRE**

The camping shop: High Street, Maidenhead

The shop, where Charles Hawtrey is shown how to stick the pole up (sigh), was Courts (now closed), **19 High Street, Maidenhead**, at the corner of St Ives Road. Sid James and Bernard Bresslaw look into the St Ives Road window and, yes, that's Maidenhead Town Hall – the hospital from *Carry On Doctor* and *Carry On Again Doctor* – in the background. The holiday camp scenes were filmed at cold, wet **Burnham Beeches**. Chayste Place, the finishing school for young ladies, is, once again, Heatherden Hall, the Pinewood studios administration building.

CARRY ON DICK
(1974, dir: Gerald Thomas)
Sidney James, Barbara Windsor, Kenneth Williams.
● **BERKSHIRE; BUCKINGHAMSHIRE**

The Reverend Flasher's church: St Mary's, Hitcham Lane, Burnham

The countryside is, naturally, the much-used **Black Park**, alongside Pinewood Studios, and **Maidenhead Thicket**. The church of Reverend Flasher (James), aka Dick Turpin, is **St Mary's, Hitcham Lane**, just west of **Burnham** in Buckinghamshire, but its prominently-featured WWI war memorial is never really explained. The stocks (the ever-patrician Williams refused to do the movie if this scene remained) are at **Stoke Poges**, north of Slough.

CARRY ON – DON'T LOSE YOUR HEAD
(1967, dir: Gerald Thomas)

Kenneth Williams, Sidney James, Jim Dale.
● **BUCKINGHAMSHIRE; SURREY**

Set, of course, in the French Revolution. The French Chateau, which is about as near as you'll get to the real thing in the UK, is **Waddesdon Manor**, at the west end of Waddesdon village, on the A 41 six miles northwest of Aylesbury. This French Renaissance-style chateau was built for the Rothschild family. It's now owned by the National Trust and open to the public (*© 01296.651142, www.waddesdon.org.uk; admission charge*). It features also in *Isadora* and *Never Say Never Again*. More period scenes used **Cliveden** near Taplow, Buckinghamshire (see *Help!* for details), and **Clandon Park**, West Clandon, east of Guildford, Surrey (*© 01483.222482, recorded info: 01483.223479; rail: Clandon; admission charge*).

CARRY ON GIRLS
(1973, dir: Gerald Thomas)
Sidney James, Bernard Bresslaw, Kenneth Connor.
● **BUCKINGHAMSHIRE; SUSSEX**

Tired old formula jokes as 'Women's Libbers' attempt to disrupt a seaside Beauty Contest. The town of Fircombe is, of course, Brighton and the hotel, significantly grander than it's supposed to be in the film, is Brighton's **Grand Hotel** on the seafront, now most famous as the site of the IRA's 1984 bomb attack on members of the Conservative party, it's featured also in *Quadrophenia*.

CARRY ON LOVING
(1970, dir: Gerald Thomas)
Sidney James, Hattie Jacques, Richard O'Callahan.
● **BERKSHIRE**

Once again, most of the filming is around **Windsor**, Berkshire (the castle walls are a pretty recognisable backdrop to many scenes). Much Snogging-on-the-Green railway station, where Charles Hawtrey gets arrested for following Sid James into the gents toilet, is the **Windsor and Eton Station**, which looks very different now. The Wedded Bliss Agency was on the fourth floor of **15 Park Street** at Sheet Street – back in 1961, Sid James' Helping Hands employment agency operated out of the basement of the same building. The Parkway Hotel, where nerdy Richard O'Callahan meets the photographer's model, is the side entrance, Garter's Bar, to **Ye Harte and Garter**

The Parkway Hotel: Ye Harte and Garter, Windsor

Hotel, Jubilee Arch, at the entrance to Windsor Station off Sheet Street. Kenneth Williams' rather posh home can be seen halfway

Kenneth Williams' house: Adelaide Square, Windsor

along **Adelaide Square**.

CARRY ON REGARDLESS
(1961, dir: Gerald Thomas)
Sidney James, Kenneth Connor, Joan Sims.
● **BERKSHIRE; LONDON; SCOTLAND**

Number five in the series consists of unconnected sketches linked by an Employment Agency gimmick: Helping Hands Ltd, which operates from the basement of **15 Park Street** at Sheet Street, just to the south of Windsor Castle, Windsor. The sinister man who wants a fourth at bridge is supposedly staying at the **Dorchester Hotel, Park Lane**, London. His garbled phone call sends Kenneth Connor to the **Forth Bridge** (courtesy of back-projection) in a parody of *The 39 Steps*. Kenneth Williams and monkey are barred from the bus in front of the railway arch on **Goswell Road**, Windsor. The zoological gardens across the road, that Williams takes the chimp to, is **Alexandra Park**.

CARRY ON SERGEANT
(1959, dir: Gerald Thomas)
William Hartnell, Kenneth Williams, Bob Monkhouse.
● **SURREY**

Little post-war conscription comedy that unexpectedly spawned the seemingly endless series of increasingly bawdy romps. Dour army officer Hartnell (the original *Doctor Who*) licks a shower of conscripts into shape. Filmed at the home of the Queen's Royal West Surrey Regiment (HM took her driving lessons here), the Victorian Stoughton Barracks, which in 1995 was converted into luxury housing and renamed **Cardwells Keep, Stoughton Road**, Stoughton, north of Guildford, Surrey.

CARRY ON UP THE KHYBER
(1968, dir: Gerald Thomas)
Sidney James, Bernard Bresslaw, Kenneth Williams.
● **WALES; SCOTLAND; BUCKINGHAMSHIRE**

This *Carry On* seemed to have a slightly higher budget. The Himalayas were shot in Snowdonia, around the **Llanberis Pass**. The British colonial home is, of course, **Heatherden Hall**, the old Pinewood studio building.

CARS THAT ATE PARIS, THE
(1974, dir: Peter Weir)
Terry Camillieri, John Meillon, Melissa Jaffa.
● **NEW SOUTH WALES, AUSTRALIA**

The début movie of Peter Weir, who went on to make *The Truman Show*, is a black comedy about a small, out-of-the-way town where the inhabitants make a living from engineering road accidents and selling the spare parts. The little town of Paris is **Sofala**, an old gold-rush town in the Turon River Valley, about 30 miles from Bathurst in the Western Plains, west of Sydney, New South Wales.

CASABLANCA
(1942, dir: Michael Curtiz)
Humphrey Bogart, Ingrid Bergman, Paul Henreid.
● **LOS ANGELES, CALIFORNIA**

Based on an unproduced play (*Everybody Comes to Rick's*

by Murray Burnett and Joan Alison), this confused production, with a script changing from day to day and no ending decided, was never likely to produce one of the

The runway of Casablanca Airport: Waterman Drive, Van Nuys

great weepies of all time. Yet, finally, all the pieces fell into place perfectly.

Casablanca is almost entirely studio-bound, shot on Warner's Burbank lot, and, with Jack Warner's customary thrift, recycling sets from previous productions. Eastern sets were rehashed from *The Desert Song*, while the railway station was leftover from the Bette Davis weepie *Now Voyager*. If you want to see the original plane from the movie, and you're willing to suspend your disbelief, it's rumoured that it's included in the *Casablanca* tableau at the Disney-MGM Studios Theme Park in Orlando, Florida, where audio-animatronics recreate 'great scenes from the movies'. You can see locations from the large hanging lamps from Rick's Bar in the Lighting Prop Shop and Sam's surprisingly tiny piano on the **Warner Bros Studios VIP Tour**. This is not like the Universal theme park, it really is an intimate and technical 2 1/4 hour tour of the determinedly lo-tech studio (© *818.846.1403, www.warnerbros.com*). You can see locations from *Spider-Man*, *Minority Report* and *Gremlins* among many others, along with TV faves such as *E.R.* and *The West Wing*. There's always the chance of glimpsing real filming (although television stuff is most likely). Numbers are limited, so book ahead. There's also a DeLuxe tour, a couple of hours longer and including lunch in the studio commissary. The farewell on the tarmac was filmed, not at an actual airport, but at Warner's, on Stage 21 or Stage 1 – according to which version you believe.

There is one location to be visited, though. The arrival of Captain Strasser (the splendidly nasty Conrad Veidt) was filmed at the old Metropolitan Airport at Van Nuys near Burbank. The site has since been incorporated into **Van Nuys Airport, 6590 Hayvenhurst Avenue**, occupying the area between Woodley Avenue to the east, Balboa Boulevard to the west, and Roscoe Boulevard and Vanowen Street. The art deco control tower has sadly been demolished, but you can still see one of the old hangars from the movie. When the airport was realigned, the two hangars no longer stood within the terminal boundaries. Used as engineering workshops, they stood on **Waterman Drive**, a tiny private street running west from Woodley Avenue between Blythe and Arminta streets, to the northeast of the airport lot. Sadly, one has already been demolished, but one remaining trace of *Casablanca* still survives.

CASINO
(1995, dir: Martin Scorsese)
Robert De Niro, Sharon Stone, Joe Pesci.
● **LAS VEGAS, NEVADA; CALIFORNIA**

The fictitious Tangier casino: Riviera Hotel and Casino, Las Vegas Boulevard

Joe Pesci enjoys a fling with Sharon Stone: La Concha, Las Vegas Boulevard

Scorsese's crackling account of the takeover of Vegas by faceless corporations suffered by coming hard on the heels of the magnificent *Goodfellas*. It was filmed largely, of course, in Vegas itself. The fictitious Tangier casino is the **Riviera Hotel and Casino, 2901 Las Vegas Boulevard South** (© 702.732.5110), seen also in Doug Liman's *Go*. Pesci's death scene was filmed in **Fresno**, California. Filming also took place at **Baker**, in the Mojave Desert, and **Hanford**, California. The kitschy motel, where Pesci (Santoro) enjoys a brief fling with Ginger (Stone), is **La Concha, 2955 Las Vegas Boulevard South** (© 702.735.1255).

CAST AWAY
(2000, dir: Robert Zemeckis)
Tom Hanks, Helen Hunt, Lari White.
● **FIJI; RUSSIA; TENNESSEE; TEXAS**

Tom Hanks' home is in **Memphis**, Tennessee. His troubleshooting mission takes him to **Moscow**. The South Pacific island he spends four years surviving on is **Monu-riki**, one of the Fijian islands. The attempted raft escape filmed at the island of **Namotu**, on its way to Moscow, is picked up in the tiny town of **Canadian**, Texas, where the film company found a crossroads stretching uninterrupted to the horizon.

CAT BALLOU
(1965, dir: Eliot Silverstein)
Jane Fonda, Lee Marvin, Michael Callan.
● **COLORADO**

Fonda hires drunken has-been gunslinger Marvin to kill a villain (Marvin again) in revenge for the death of her father in this spoof Western made at the **Buckskin Joe Frontier Town, 1193 Fremont County Road** (© 719.275.5149, www.buckskinjoes.com) a theme park in the Greenhorn Mountains, west of Cañon City, Colorado. Other films which used Buckskin Joe include *The Cowboys*, *Comes a Horseman*, *True Grit* and *Lightning Jack*.

CAT ON A HOT TIN ROOF
(1958, dir: Richard Brooks)
Elizabeth Taylor, Paul Newman, Burl Ives.
● **NEW YORK**

Bowdlerised Tennessee Williams adaptation, buoyed up by a great cast on top form. The Deep South mansion is actually the elegant 1920s red-brick **Coleman Mansion, Muttontown**, near Oyster Bay, one of Long Island's grand North Shore mansions, seen also in Elaine May's *A New Leaf*.

CAT PEOPLE
(1982, dir: Paul Schrader)
Natassja Kinski, Malcolm McDowell, John Heard.
● **NEW ORLEANS, LOUISIANA**

Schrader makes explicit the themes hinted at in Val Lewton's understated 1942 classic. Natassja Kinski turns into a panther at the zoo in **Audobon Park**, New Orleans. Her house is on the corner of **Chartres** and **Esplanade**, opposite the Germaine Wells Mansion.

CATCH ME IF YOU CAN
(2002, dir: Steven Spielberg)
Leonardo DiCaprio, Tom Hanks, Nathalie Baye.
● **NEW YORK CITY; LOS ANGELES, CALIFORNIA; NEW JERSEY; QUÉBEC, CANADA**

Spielberg's return to form continues with this bouncy, pastel-coloured period piece, tracing the incredible career of opportunist con artist Frank Abagnale Jr. Montréal and

Frank's mother's house: East California Boulevard, Pasadena

Québec stood in for France. **Place Royale**, Québec City, stood in for the square of Montrichard where Abagnale (DiCaprio) is arrested, with **Notre Dame des Victoires** in the background.

Union Station, 800 North Alameda Street, downtown LA (see *Blade Runner* for details), became the grandiose Miami Mutual Bank, where Frank comes on to the cashier, who helpfully explains the workings of the system. The Tropicana Motel, where Abagnale has a really close encounter with FBI Agent Hanratty (Hanks), is the rear of the **Roosevelt Hotel, 7000 Hollywood Boulevard** (© 323.466.7000, www.hollywoodroosevelt.com), opened in 1927 on the site of strawberry fields. In 1929, the first Academy Awards (all three of them) were presented in the Blossom Room (now the Academy Room), when *Wings* picked up the first Best Picture statuette. Janet Gaynor and Emil

Poolside at the Tropicana: Roosevelt Hotel, Hollywood Boulevard

Hanratty catches up with Frank at the Tropicana Motel: Rear of the Roosevelt Hotel, Hawthorn Avenue

Frank's narrow escape: Roosevelt Hotel, Hollywood Boulevard

Looking for Frank: Tropicana Bar, Roosevelt Hotel, Hollywood Boulevard

Jannings picked up the other two awards, for Best Actress and Actor. The rooms don't actually look out onto the street. The poolside area, where Abagnale stays, is a forties addition to the hotel. The poolside **Tropicana Bar** is real. Filming also occurred at **Rose City High School, 325 South Oak Knoll Avenue** in Pasadena, also seen in *Stuart Little 2*, *Legally Blonde* and *Pleasantville*. The Strong family home in New Orleans is in Altadena. The white house, where Hanratty informs Frank's mother that he owes $1.3 million, is **3077 East California Boulevard, Pasadena**. Frank makes a phone call on **Park Avenue at East 50th Street** in front of what was the old Pan Am Building. Monroe High School is actually Bellarmine Jefferson High School, Burbank. College Co-Ed, off Wilshire. The courthouse is **Old Orange Courthouse, 211 West Santa Ana Boulevard, Santa Ana**, California.

The university, where Frank recruits 'eight young ladies' as stewardesses, is the Fine Arts Auditorium of the **Ebell of Los Angeles, 743 South Lucerne Boulevard**, midtown (see *Forrest Gump* for full details). Miami International Airport, where Abagnale evades the FBI by escorting a chorus line of flight attendants, is **Ontario Airport**, on I-10 east of LA (seen also in *American Wedding*). The FBI offices are the old **Boeing-Aerospace** facility in **Downey**. The sleekly 60s New York airport is the real deal, the 1962 **TWA Building** at **JFK Airport**, which stood conveniently empty at the time of filming.

The smaller apartment that Frank and his family move to after they lose their home, is on **Buena Vista Avenue**, downtown **Yonkers**. And also in Yonkers are the Washington DC square, which is **Larkin Park**, and the **Launderland Laundromat, Lake Avenue**, where the rather down-at-heel Hanratty does his laundry while Frank lives the high life. The hotel where he's enjoying himself with model Cheryl Ann (Jennifer Garner) is the **Ambassador Hotel, 3400 Wilshire Boulevard**. The Ambassador is also the Miami hotel, where Frank forges Pan Am cheques with model plane labels. The cathedral-like Chase Bank is **Brooklyn Borough Hall**. There was also filming at the **Waldorf-Astoria Hotel**, New York; the Brooklyn bank and courthouse buildings; and in Orange, NJ.

CATCH 22

(1970, dir: Mike Nichols)
Alan Arkin, Jon Voight, Richard Benjamin.
● MEXICO

For years, Orson Welles wanted to film Joseph Heller's surreal anti-war novel, but – as with *Moby Dick* – he had to settle for playing a cameo role in someone else's film. This was filmed at **Guayamos**, a seaport and fishing village on the west coast of northern Mexico, Route 15, about 300 miles south of the border at Nogales.

C'EST ARRIVÉ PRES DE CHEZ VOUS (aka *Man Bites Dog*)

(1992, dir: Remy Belvaux; Andre Bonzel; Benoit Poelvoorde)
Benoit Poelvoorde, Remy Belvaux, Andre Bonzel.
● BELGIUM; FRANCE

This very nasty black comedy takes no prisoners, as a documentary crew follows extrovert serial killer Poelvoorde around suburban Belgium. Shot around **Namur**, 35 miles southeast of Brussels, Belgium. Poelvoorde dumps his victims into the marble quarry at **Neuville**, five miles north of Lyon, France.

CET OBSCUR OBJET DU DÉSIR (aka *That Obscure Object of Desire*)

Conchita's apartment: Calle Vida, Seville

(1978, dir: Luis Buñuel)
Fernando Rey, Carole Bouquet, Angela Molina.
● FRANCE; SPAIN;

On a journey from Seville to Madrid, Mathieu (Rey) tells the story of his sexual obsession with the changeable Conchita (played alternately by Bouquet and Molina). The opening scenes, where Rey pours a bucket of water over Conchita, were shot at **Seville Railway Station** (now completely rebuilt). Mathieu is robbed, and meets up again with Conchita, at his hotel in Lausanne, Switzerland. Back in Seville, where Mathieu meets up – yet again – with Conchita, he goes of to see **Seville Cathedral** (the third largest in Europe, after St Peter's in Rome and St Paul's in London) and the adjoining **Giralda Tower**, originally a minaret. The apartment, where Mathieu visits Conchita, is **7 Calle Vida** off Calle Agua, behind the Real Alcazar. And it's in **Madrid** that Mathieu and Conchita go off to an explosive future.

CHAN IS MISSING

(1982, dir: Wayne Wang)
Wood Moy, Marc Hayashi, Laureen Chew.
● SAN FRANCISCO, CALIFORNIA

The first feature-length US movie to be produced entirely by a Chinese-American cast and crew was also Wang's first US movie (before *The Joy Luck Club* and *Smoke*). Two taxi drivers fruitlessly try to track down Chan, who's disappeared with $2,000. It was shot around San Francisco's Chinatown, the largest Chinese community in the US outside of New York, which grew up in the early 19th century around Portsmouth Square when Chinese immigrants fled war and famine in Canton. It covers the area between Broadway, Bush Street, Powell Street and

Looking for Chan: Ross Alley, Chinatown

Kearny Street to the east. Grant Avenue, running north-south through the area, is tourists' Chinatown. **Stockton Street**, running parallel and just to the west, is its real heart. Much of *Chan Is Missing* was filmed around **Ross Alley**, a small street between Grant and Stockton.

CHANT OF JIMMIE BLACKSMITH, THE

(1978, dir: Fred Schepisi)
Tommy Lewis, Freddy Reynolds, Angela Punch.
● NEW SOUTH WALES, AUSTRALIA

The casual racism of turn-of-the-century Australia explodes in shocking violence. Filmed in New South Wales, at **Armidale**, around the **Bundarra Dorrigo State Forest**; at **Dubbo**; **Gulgong**; **Mudgee**; **Rylstone**; and at **Kempsey, Port Macquarrie**.

The Aldershot theatre: Wilton's Music Hall

CHAPLIN

1992, dir: Richard Attenborough)
Robert Downey Jr, Dan Aykroyd, Geraldine Chaplin.
● CALIFORNIA; LONDON; SUSSEX; SWITZERLAND

Attenborough's bio-pic is a disappointing skim through the life of the great sentimentalist, but it uses a slew of interesting locations.

The early life of Chaplin (Downey Jr) in London's Lambeth, south London, was actually filmed in north London, behind King's Cross Station at the junction of the cobbled **Cheney Road** and **Battle Bridge Road**, NW1. The houses – including Charlie's home – were a vast set which took four months to build, though the gasometers are real enough (they probably look familiar, having been seen in the original *The Ladykillers* and *Alfie*, *Backbeat* and *Shirley Valentine,* as well as many other films, ads and TV shows). The site is being redeveloped as the King's Cross channel tunnel terminal, and the gasometers have been removed. Their future is uncertain.

The scene of little tot Chaplin saving the day when his mother's stage act takes a nose dive, set in Aldershot, was

Chaplin returns to the London pub: The Salisbury, Harringay

filmed in the famous **Wilton's Music Hall, 1 Grace's Alley, Wellclose Square**, off Cable Street, E1. The hall, built in 1858, was the first and

one of the most successful of London's music halls. It was taken over by scandalised Methodists in the 1880s, and run as a mission until 1956, when it became a rag warehouse. For many years it lay dilapidated, used only for film shoots (including *Isadora* and *The Krays*) and music videos (Frankie Goes To Hollywood's 'Relax' must have had the Methodists whizzing round in their graves). It's now home to the Broomhill Opera. Chaplin's first comic success, crashing the stage as a belligerent drunk, was filmed at the beautiful **Hackney Empire, 291 Mare Street**, E8 (© 020.8985.2424, www.hackneyempire.co.uk). The stageside box, in which he makes his appearance was built especially for the movie. The Cane Hill Asylum, where Chaplin's disturbed mother is incarcerated, was shot inside the disused **St Pancras Station, Euston Road**, NW1, alongside the King's Cross location. Closed for years, it is occasionally open to the public (one day a year) to view the stunning Victorian interior, recently used for Christopher Nolan's *Batman Begins*.

Chaplin's Lambeth home: Cheney Road, Kings Cross

The riverside audition for music hall impresario Fred Karno was filmed in the grounds of the former Astor estate at **Cliveden** (see *Help!* for details). After being snubbed at a snobbish restaurant, Chaplin takes his first love, Hetty Kelly, for a cup of tea at the old Covent Garden vegetable market, where it was possible to get a cuppa at any hour of the day or night – or even get a beer at seven in the morning, due to the special license arrangements for the Garden porters. In the seventies, the market moved to a modern site in Nine Elms, so the scene was actually shot at **Smithfield Meat Market** between Charterhouse Street and Long Lane, EC1. You can see the real Covent Garden market, as it was in its heyday, in Hitchcock's *Frenzy*.

Chaplin soon takes off for the fledgling movie industry of the States. Mack Sennett's Keystone Studio, where Chaplin got his first job, stood at 1712 Allessandro Street. Chaplin's own studio, where he made *The Immigrant*, *The Floorwalker* and *Easy Street* in 1916 and 1917, was located at 1025 Lillian Way, south of Santa Monica Boulevard between Eleanor and Romaine Streets. No trace of either remains. Hollywood in the twenties was still a town of citrus groves, so the studios were recreated north of LA at **Fillmore**, Route 126 between Ventura and Valencia. The 'Hollywoodland' sign, where Chaplin plays with Fairbanks, was recreated too.

The mock-Tudor studio is a recreation of the one Chaplin

Chaplin's first comic success: Hackney Empire

Baiting J Edgar Hoover: Ballroom of the Park Plaza Hotel

used from 1918 onwards, though this, amazingly, has survived. It's now the home of Jim Henson's production company, and is currently graced with a giant Kermit the Frog, at **1416 La Brea Avenue**, south of Sunset Boulevard. Chaplin's footprints are preserved in concrete on Stage 3. Charlie's home was on Summit Drive in Beverly Hills, but the film utilises a house built by the same architect, Wallace Neff, in the monied LA suburb of **San Marino**.

William Randolph Hearst's post-WWII party, where Chaplin upstages FBI boss J Edgar Hoover with his bread-roll dance, is held in the much-used Ballroom of the **Park Plaza Hotel, 607 South Park View Street** overlooking Macarthur Park in downtown LA (see *New York New York* for details of this legendary movie location).

Returning to England, the train journey from Southampton to London was filmed on the dependable old **Bluebell Line** – a five mile stretch of track between Horstead Keynes and Sheffield Park, northeast of Haywards Heath in Sussex. The enthusiastic welcome to the capital, which actually took place at Waterloo Station, was filmed on **St Pancras Station**, one of the least changed of London's great termini. The Covent Garden pub, where Chaplin discovers he's no longer just one of the lads, is the grand, but rather faded, **Salisbury, Green Lanes** at the corner of St Ann's Road, Harringay, N15 (seen also in *The Long Good Friday* and in David Cronenberg's *Spider*).

The shipbound scene, of Chaplin heading back to the States, was shot aboard the **Queen Mary** at her berth on Pier J in Long Beach, LA – the Manhattan skyline was added later. The première of *Limelight* was filmed in the dazzling foyer of the 1931 Second Empire-style **Los Angeles Theatre, 615 South Broadway** (www.losangelestheatre.com) in the vibrant – if a bit down at heel – Hispanic centre of downtown LA. The theatre's gorgeous interior can also be seen in *Batman Forever*, *New York New York*, *Charlie's Angels* and its sequel, as a raunchy casino in *Armageddon*, and as the Vatican, no less, in *End of Days*.

The première of *Limelight*: Los Angeles Theater

Anthony Hopkins' fictional biographer interviews the elderly Chaplin at the real Chaplin estate, courtesy of his widow Oona, who had given the film her blessing. It's in **Vevey**, 12 miles east of Lausanne on the north shore of Lake Leman in Switzerland. The closing scenes, of Chaplin's belated Lifetime Achievement Oscar award, though shot on a set at Shepperton Studios, were inter-cut with shots of the actual ceremony at the current home of the Academy Award ceremonies, the **Dorothy Chandler Pavilion**, part of the Music Center, **135 North Grand Avenue** between First and Temple Streets in LA's Bunker Hill district.

CHARADE
(1963, dir: Stanley Donen)
Audrey Hepburn, Cary Grant, Walter Matthau.
● PARIS, FRANCE

Lightweight, blackish comedy thriller of the kind they can't seem to make anymore (see *The Truth About Charlie* if you don't believe me), set in Paris. Hepburn and Grant stay at the **Hotel Saint Jacques, 35 rue des Ecoles** (℃ 44.07.45.45) in the Latin Quarter (where Grant famously takes a shower in his suit), near the St Jacques metro. Hepburn is lured to the Centre Gardens of the **Palais Royal**, while the movie climaxes in the **Comedie Français, 2 rue de Richelieu** (*metro: Palais-Royal*).

Hepburn and Grant stay at the Hotel Saint Jacques, rue des Ecoles

CHARGE OF THE LIGHT BRIGADE, THE
(1936, dir: Michael Curtiz)
Errol Flynn, Olivia de Havilland, David Niven.
● CALIFORNIA

Exciting adventurer, with little or nothing to do with the Crimea. A full-scale replica of the Chukoti Garrison, the Indian fortress, was built at Lasky Mesa, a desolate windswept spot, dry, covered in tumbleweed and crawling with tarantulas, according to de Havilland's autobiography. Lasky Mesa, a 7,000 acre tract of land north of LA, was bought up by the studio for filming, and many movies were shot here. The area, between Agoura and Woodland Hills, is now known as the **Ahmanson Ranch**, and is scheduled for redevelopment. See *Gone With the Wind*, part of which filmed here, for details.

CHARGE OF THE LIGHT BRIGADE, THE
(1968, dir: Tony Richardson)
Trevor Howard, John Gielgud, David Hemmings.
● TURKEY; LONDON

This vastly underrated, darkly iconoclastic sixties version, with a quirky script from Charles Wood and stunning animated sequences from Richard Williams, could hardly be more different from the Curtiz version. There were endless legal wrangles over the script, which was accused of borrowing heavily from Cecil Woodham-Smith's book *The Reason Why*. Laurence Harvey, who owned rights to the book, was given a role, but eventually cut from the movie.

The office of Lord Raglan (Gielgud), the Horseguards HQ, was filmed in the Governor's Office of the old **Royal Mint** (before its function was moved to south Wales), **Cartwright Street**, E1, northeast of the Tower of London (*tube: Tower Hill*). The arrival of the troops was shot in **Istanbul**, Turkey. The charge itself, the 'Valley of Death', was filmed near the villages of **Saraycik** and **Pacenek**, about 30 miles from Ankara in central Anatolia.

CHARIOTS OF FIRE
(1981, dir: Hugh Hudson)
Ben Cross, Ian Charleson, Nigel Havers.
● SCOTLAND; MERSEYSIDE; BERKSHIRE; BUCKINGHAMSHIRE; YORKSHIRE

This overrated flagwaver is purportedly based on truth but traditionally Hollywoodised, hence the Best Picture Oscar. Although set partly in France, it was shot entirely in the UK. The famous slo-mo run along the beach which opens the movie, supposedly at Broadstairs, Kent, is **West Sands** at St Andrews on the Fife coast, where the Carlton Hotel is actually the **clubhouse** of the **Royal and Ancient Golf Club.**

Sensitive to accusations of anti-Semitism, Caius (pronounced 'Keys') College, Cambridge, the alma mater of Harold Abrahams (Cross), refused permission to film on its property, and **Eton College** in Windsor stands in. A familiar location, Eton is also seen in *Henry VIII and His Six Wives*, *Young Sherlock Holmes* and *The Madness of King George*. Abrahams' 'College Dash' around the Great Court of Trinity College is around the School Quad.

Meanwhile, the zealous Eric Liddell (Charleson) is awarding prizes at the Highland games, a scene shot at **Sma Glen**, on the A822 a few miles north of Crieff, Perthshire. **Inverleith**, in Edinburgh, is the rugby ground where Liddell preaches to the crowd after the Scotland-Ireland meet, while the Scotland-France International shot at **Goldenacre**, the grounds of Heriot's Rugby Club on **Bangholm Terrace, in Edinburgh**.

The London restaurant, to which Abrahams takes singer Sybil Gordon after seeing her in *The Mikado*, is the **Oyster Bar** of Edinburgh's **Café Royal, 17 West Register Street** at Rose Street. Liddell, his obsession with running vying with his faith, is late for the religious meeting at the **Assembly Hall** on the **Mound** in Edinburgh, and afterwards, with his sister Jennie, looks out over the city from **Holyrood Park**. The vast estate, where aristocratic Lord Lindsay comforts Sybil before leaping over hurdles topped with glasses of champagne, is **Hall Barn**, south of Beaconsfield in Buckinghamshire. A 17th century private house built for poet Edmund Waller, the estate can also be seen in the 1994 film of *Black Beauty*. The relatively

Liddell runs to the religious meeting: Assembly Hall, Edinburgh

Abrahams' romantic dinner: Café Royal, Edinburgh

unchanged **York Station** stands in for London's King's Cross, while Dover Station, from which the athletes leave for the Olympic Games in France, is the

The race around Trinity College, Cambridge: Eton College, Windsor

port of **Birkenhead**, over the Mersey from Liverpool.

Much of Paris is actually Merseyside. The British Embassy ball, where the Prince of Wales tries to persuade Liddell to run on the Sabbath, is **Liverpool Library and Town Hall**, and the French café is the no-longer-used chapel of the **Royal Hospital**, Liverpool. The Church of Scotland in Paris, where Liddell preaches, really is in Scotland. It's the **Broughton McDonald Church, Broughton Place** in Edinburgh. The Paris Stade des Colombes, venue for the climactic Olympics, is the **Bebington Oval Sports Centre, Old Chester Road, Wirral** on Merseyside.

CHARLEY VARRICK
(1973, dir: Don Siegel)
Walter Matthau, Andy Robinson, Joe Don Baker.
● NEVADA

Matthau is a small time bank robber finding himself with a stash of mob money in this tight little thriller from the dependable Siegel. The town of Tres Cruces is **Genoa**,

The Tres Cruces bank: Courthouse Museum, Genoa

a few miles south of Carson City in Nevada, close to the California border. The Tres Cruces Western Fidelity Bank is Genoa's **Courthouse Museum, 191 First Street**.

CHARLIE'S ANGELS
(2000, dir: McG [aka Joseph McGinty Nichol])
Cameron Diaz, Drew Barrymore, Lucy Liu.
● CALIFORNIA

As tempting or as sickly as dayglo candies on a supermarket shelf, McG's light-as-froth confection is kept afloat by the sheer enthusiasm of the three leads. The time trials (budgetary constraints nixed the full race as planned) were filmed under dodgy weather conditions (look at the way the sky changes) at the **California Speedway, 9300 Cherry Avenue**, Fontana. The subsequent chase leads to the familiar **Vincent Thomas Bridge**, San Pedro.

Madame Wong's House of Blossoms is the Japanese garden of the **Huntington Library and Gardens, 1151 Oxford Road, San Marino**, where the fencing scene was also shot. See *Indecent Proposal* for full details of the estate.

Cameron Diaz's fantasy dance number, 'Heaven Must Be Missing An Angel', was filmed in the lobby of the

Diaz's canalside house: Carroll Canal Court, Venice

wildly elaborate **Los Angeles Theatre, 615 South Broadway**, downtown Los Angeles (see *Chaplin* for full details). Diaz's house, where she informs the bemused mailman that he can feel free to stick things in her slot, is **410 Carroll Canal Court** in the quiet and beautiful remnant of Venice's canals, though the frontage has been remodelled slightly.

The HQ of Red Star Technologies is the great white block of **Federal Building, 11000 Wilshire Boulevard,** overshadowing **Westwood Village**, but the facility's rooftop café was created on the roof of the **LA Center Studios, 1202 West Fifth Street**, downtown.

The malfunctioning burger stand is **Foster Freeze, 1624 Cravens Avenue**, Torrance. The tower hideout of villain Knox (Sam Rockwell) is on **Marineland of the Pacific, Palos Verdes Estates**, where scenes for *Pirates of the Caribbean* were shot. The final scenes, of Knox's helicopter being blown up, Charlie's house and the Hawaii beach, were all filmed at **Sycamore Cove, Malibu**.

CHARLIE'S ANGELS: FULL THROTTLE
(2003, dir: McG)
Cameron Diaz, Drew Barrymore, Lucy Liu.
● **CALIFORNIA**

Like hyperactive kids, the enthusiasm can get just a wee bit wearing, and you'd be forgiven for wanting all concerned to chill out and lie down in a darkened room. The beach, where the Angels check out Sex Wax and come across fallen Angel Madison Lee (Demi Moore), is the familiar **Zuma Beach** in **Malibu**. The dirt bike chase uses a real coalfield on **Terminal Island**, down south of LA in San Pedro. And, naturally, the harbour scenes were filmed in **San Pedro** itself.

Cameron Diaz has moved from the canals of Venice to **2028 The Strand, Hermosa Beach** (helpfully written on the letter she and Luke Wilson receive). Lucy Liu, though, lives in architect John Lautner's still futuristic-looking (though it was built in 1963) **Sheats-Goldstein Residence, Benedict Canyon**, which was seen also in *Playing God* and *The Big Lebowski*. Beneath the elaborate dressing, the lair of Madison Lee is none other than **Union Station, 800 North Alameda Street**, downtown LA (see *Blade Runner*). Another celebrity house: the orphanage, where the Angels, in nun drag, check out the past of the Thin Man (Crispin Glover). It's as far from a convent as you could imagine. It's Hugh Hefner's **Playboy Mansion, 10236 Charing Cross Road** off Mapleton Drive (which you can see as itself in *Beverly Hills Cop II*), running between the western reaches of Sunset Boulevard and Los Angeles Country Club. The dance at Rydell High (a namecheck for *Grease*) is **Birmingham High School, 17000 Haynes Street, Van Nuys**, seen also in schlocker *Society*. Dylan (Barrymore) loses her

mojo and hares off to Mexico, where she receives wisdom from former Angel Jaclyn Smith. The Mexican bar is **El Carmen, 1838 West Third Street**.

The climax of the movie centres around **Hollywood Boulevard**. *Maximum Extreme 2* is premièring at **Grauman's Chinese Theatre, 6925 Hollywood Boulevard**. The gang gets the map from the foyer of the **Guinness World of Records, 6764 Hollywood Boulevard**, hands over the suitcase in the classic old **Musso and Frank Grill, 6667 Hollywood Boulevard** (seen also in *Ed Wood* and the remake of *Ocean's Eleven*), and marches through the foyer of the **Roosevelt Hotel, 7000 Hollywood Boulevard** (see *Catch Me If You Can* for details). The roof of the Roosevelt, with its landmark red neon sign, was recreated in the studio, as was the roof of Disney's flagship **El Capitan Theatre, 6838 Hollywood Boulevard**. Madison Lee (who's specialist subject is flying mammals, remember) flies off down Hollywood Boulevard. Well, not quite. The tattoo parlors, Goth shops and memorabilia stores of Hollywood are suddenly replaced by the gutted old edifices of downtown LA. The chase roars past the distinctive marquee of the **Orpheum Theatre, 842 South Broadway**, before climaxing in the gorgeous auditorium of the **Los Angeles Theatre, 615 South Broadway** (see *Chaplin* for details), where Lee goes down to flaming hell.

CHARME DISCRET DE LA BOURGEOISIE, LE
(aka *The Discreet Charm of the Bourgeoisie*)
(1972, dir: Luis Buñuel)
Fernando Rey, Delphine Seyrig, Stephane Audran.
● **PARIS, FRANCE**

A group of ever-so-well-mannered bourgeois are constantly frustrated in their attempts to get together for a meal in Buñuel's surreal black comedy, filmed around Paris. The house

Fernando Rey's house: rue de Franqueville, Passy-La Muette

of super-cynical Fernando Rey, smuggling cocaine in his diplomatic bag, is on **rue de Franqueville** at rue Verdi, near Ranelagh Gardens in the embassy-infested Passy-La Muette district, 16th arrondissement.

CHASING AMY
(1997, dir: Kevin Smith)
Ben Affleck, Joey Lauren Adams, Jason Lee.
● **NEW JERSEY; NEW YORK CITY**

Kevin Smith's pan-sexual love story is set, like his earlier *Clerks* and *Mallrats*, on the western tip of the New Jersey coast, around Red Bank, Leonardo and Asbury Park, with just a glimpse of Manhattan. Ben Affleck and Jason Lee's apartment is **30 Broad Street, Red Bank**, above Jack's Music Shop. The Manhattan Comicon convention, where Affleck first meets Joey Lauren Adams, is held in the **Berkely Cartaret Hotel and Convention Center, Ocean Avenue** at Deal Lake Drive on the **Asbury**

Park shorefront. The park, where they open up to each other, is **Victory Park, River Road, Rumson** out on the westernmost tip. Lee's motormouth pal reveals the story behind Adams' Fingercuffs nickname outside **Quick Stop, 58 Leonard Avenue** in **Leonardo** – the famous location for Smith's breakthrough movie, *Clerks*. Affleck grills Adams at the ice hockey match at **Ocean Ice Palace, 197 Chambersbridge Road, Brick**. And of course, Jay and Silent Bob put in their trademark appearance, at the **Marina Diner, Highway 36** at **East Road, Belford**.

CHEYENNE AUTUMN
(1964, dir: John Ford)
Richard Widmark, Carroll Baker, Karl Malden.
● **UTAH; COLORADO; WYOMING**

With this story of the forced resettlement of the Cheyenne nation in the 1860s, John Ford tries to make amends for years of whooping savages. The Cheyenne, played by Navajos and Dolores Del Rio, are dispossessed of their grassland home and relocated 1,500 miles away in the harsh north. The effect of this dislocation is somewhat dissipated by the fact that they hardly ever seem to leave **Monument Valley**. At this point in his career, Ford was tending toward the slipshod in some of his movies, and the Kennedy assassination, which occurred during filming, added to Ford's mood of disaffection. Much of the Monument Valley location work was simply filmed in front of the crew's base at **Goulding's Lodge**. Ford also used the area around **Moab**, Utah, including **White's Ranch, Castle Valley, Professor Valley, Fisher Canyon, Arches National Park** and **Mexican Hat**. Filming also took place at **Gunnison Canyon** in Colorado and **Fort Laramie**, Wyoming.

CHICAGO
(2002, dir: Rob Marshall)
Renée Zellweger, Catherine Zeta-Jones, Richard Gere.
● **TORONTO, ONTARIO, CANADA; CHICAGO, ILLINOIS**

I know it's Fred Ebb and Bob Fosse again, but there's just a little too much borrowing from *Cabaret* to justify the Best Picture Oscar. Set in the titular city, the movie was filmed in Toronto, where the prison and the ornate Onyx Theatre sets were built at the old **Gooderham & Worts distillery buildings**, where *X-Men*

Toronto, where most of Chicago was shot: Elgin Theatre, Yonge Street

and *The Recruit*, among many others, were filmed.

The few real locations (all in Toronto too) include **Union Station, 65 Front Street, Old City Hall**, the **Legislative Building** in Queen's Park, **Osgoode Hall**, and the now-closed **Danforth Music Hall, 147 Danforth Avenue**. The office of Billy Flynn (Gere) is in **Casa Loma, 1 Austin Terrace** at Spadina Road (see *X-Men* for details). Velma and Roxie's final number is set in the **Chicago Theatre, 175 North State Street** at

East Lake Street. There's only the briefest glimpse of the exterior, heavily dressed to disguise the modern skyline (see the real Chicago's elaborate lobby in *The Untouchables*). The interior is Toronto's sumptuous **Elgin Theatre, 189 Yonge Street**.

CHIEN ANDALOU, UN
(1928, dir: Luis Buñuel)
Simone Mareuil, Pierre Batcheff, Jaime Miravilles.
● **PARIS, FRANCE**

Buñuel and Salvador Dali's classic surreal short filmed in Paris' Ursuline Studios, and at **Le Havre**.

CHILD'S PLAY
(1988, dir: Tom Holland)
Catherine Hicks, Chris Sarandon, Brad Dourif.
● **CHICAGO, ILLINOIS**

A superior jokey shocker, directed by the writer of *Psycho II*, with dying killer Brad Dourif possessing the 'Good Guy' doll, leading to a string of sequels. Catherine Hicks' quartzite stone-clad apartment block, in which the creepy Chucky doll goes on the rampage, is the **Brewster, 2800 North Pine Grove Avenue** at West Diversey Parkway in Chicago's Lake View district.

House of Chucky: North Pine Grove Avenue

CHIMES AT MIDNIGHT
(1966, dir: Orson Welles)
Orson Welles, Keith Baxter, John Gielgud.
● **SPAIN**

Welles' adaptation of both parts of *Henry IV* (incorporating bits of *Henry V*) was made under impossible conditions in Spain, and contains the best battle scene in any movie, ever. Typical of his underfunded European movies, Welles cobbles together various locations. Backgrounds were filmed against the oldest and best preserved Medieval walls in Spain, at **Avila**, 50 miles northwest of Madrid on the Salamanca road. The two miles of wall are defended by 88 towers. The battle and the Gadds Hill robbery used the **Casa de Campo** – once a royal hunting area, it's now a huge, popular park in Madrid, reached by metro or bus (route 33).

Henry IV's palace is mostly **Castillo de Montjuich**, situated in Parque de Montjuich on a hill overlooking Barcelona. Built as a castle in 1640, it now houses the Military Museum. Further scenes of Henry's court were filmed at the castle of **Cardona**, which was also used for Henry V's coronation. The rear of Cardona became Hotspur's castle. Cardona is about 50 miles northwest of Barcelona, and the castle is now a lavish parador (hotel). The remainder of the coronation scene was shot in a Madrid church. The snow scenes were staged to the north at **Soria** and in the Basque region. Soria's Romanesque 12th century (though largely rebuilt in the 16th century) **Cathedral of San Pedro** was also used.

Other villages used include **Calatanazor**, a Medieval town about 12 miles west of Soria; **Colmenar Viejo**, north of Madrid; **Guipuzcoa**; and **Puerto de San Vicente**, 65 miles west of Toledo. Street scenes were filmed in **Pedraza**, an old town about 55 miles north of Madrid. The Plaza Mayor here is one of Castile's most beautiful squares, and there are many preserved old streets as well as the town's Medieval walls.

CHINA SYNDROME, THE

(1979, dir: James Bridges)
Jack Lemmon, Jane Fonda, Michael Douglas.
● CALIFORNIA

Timely thriller with a message, which was about to be written off as anti-nuke eco-hysteria when Three Mile Island went into an 'impossible' meltdown. Not surprisingly, there was no location filming in a real nuclear plant, but three conventional power plants in the LA area stood in (despite a large amount of hostility, directed particularly at 'Hanoi Jane'). The main exterior is the **Scattergood Power Plant, 12700 Vista del Mar** – the coast road running by Los Angeles Airport – at Playa del Rey.

CHINATOWN

(1974, dir: Roman Polanski)
Jack Nicholson, Faye Dunaway, John Huston.
● LOS ANGELES, CALIFORNIA

"It's Chinatown": Ord Street, Chinatown

It was reportedly a fraught production, but Polanski added bags of atmosphere and a tragic ending to Robert Towne's brilliant script (based on the corruption involved in LA's water programme) and a classic neo-noir resulted. Although the film uses plenty of period LA locations, there are some stunning sets: the interior of the Hall of Records, the Department of Water and Power, Gittes' living room and the interior of the old house in Pasadena are all fake.

The lake at the centre of the intrigue is the real thing. **Lake Hollywood**, a reservoir built by Water Commissioner William Mulholland in 1925 as part of the water programme, can be reached by entrances on Lake Hollywood Drive (north) and Weidlake Drive (south). JJ Gittes (Nicholson) tails the water commissioner in a rowing boat across the palm-fringed fifteen-acre lake in Echo Park, at Glendale Boulevard and Park Avenue, Silver Lake. The

The fake Mrs Mulwray: East Kensington Road, Echo Park

dry river bed, where mysterious flows of water indicate that something fishy is going on, is the **Big Tujunga Wash** at Foothill Boulevard,

Sunland. Gittes gets his nose sliced open (by director Polanski) at **Point Fermin**, Point Fermin Park, Gaffey Street at Paseo del Mar, San Pedro, south LA. He goes to see Noah Cross (Huston), the power behind the plotting, on **Catalina Island**, just off the LA coast. That's the 1928 white Spanish-Moderne

The Brown Derby: The Windsor, West Seventh Street

The sinister Mar Vista Rest Home: Eastern Star Home, Sunset Boulevard

Avalon Casino by the landing stage at the northwest end of Crescent Bay (it contains a beautiful 1,000 seater cinema, a grand ballroom plus a small museum and art gallery), **1 Casino Way, Avalon**.

The mansion of Evelyn Mulwray (Dunaway) is supposedly one of Pasadena's grand houses on **South Oakland Avenue**, though I've not been able to find it. She meets up with Gittes at the old Brown Derby restaurant, but the scene was actually shot in one-time French restaurant, now Korean restaurant (but, thankfully, unchanged) **The Prince, 3198 West Seventh Street, Koreatown** (© 213.389.1586). Gittes discovers the body of the fake Mrs Mulwray in the apartment complex at **848 1/2 East Kensington Road** in the Echo Park district, near to locations seen in *LA Confidential* and *The Fast and the Furious*. The Mar Vista Rest Home, where the pair go to "find a place for dad" and discover a whole load of unwittingly rich inmates, is the **Eastern Star Home, 11725 Sunset Boulevard**, on the road's western reaches in Brentwood. The uncompromisingly downbeat climax was filmed in LA's real Chinatown, on **Spring Street** near **Ord Street**, which has since been largely redeveloped.

CHITTY CHITTY BANG BANG

(1968, dir: Ken Hughes)
Dick Van Dyke, Sally Anne Howes, Lionel Jeffries.
● BUCKINGHAMSHIRE; AUSTRIA; FRANCE; GERMANY

Straightforward musical film of Ian Fleming's children's story about the eccentric inventor who transforms a clapped-out racing car into a magical toy. In-joke spotters will have twigged that the original owner of of the dilapidated racer is James Bond's Q, Desmond Llewellyn.

The windmill

Dick Van Dyke's home: Smock Windmill, Cadmore End

The kingdom of Vulgaria: Schloss Neuschwanstein

home of Caractacus Potts (Van Dyke) is the **Smock Windmill**, a genuine restoration still at **Cadmore End** on the B482 about four miles west of High Wycombe in Buckinghamshire. It seems the car has pretty miraculous powers already. When Van Dyke drives Sally Anne Howes and the kids down to the beach from Cadmore End, they end up by the sea at **St Tropez** in the South of France. Gert Frobe's airship hovers over the hillside near the village of **Turville**, just southwest of Cadmore End.

Followed by Chitty, the balloon flies to the mythical child-hating kingdom of Vulgaria. The town square, where Robert Helpmann's creepy Childcatcher and the cavalry (with horses from the famous stud farm near Munich) search for the kiddies, is **Rothenburg ob der Tauber**. Rothenburg was fortunate enough to be both economically devastated by the Thirty Years War and hidden away from major commercial routes, which meant that over the years it has never been modernised. Now, although a bit of a tourist trap, it's a perfectly preserved 17th century wonder, about 45 miles west of Nurnberg toward Stuttgart, in Bavaria.

Baron Bomburst's Vulgarian castle, subliminally familiar as the model for Disneyland's Sleeping Beauty castle, is Ludwig II's marvellously kitsch fantasy of **Schloss Neuschwanstein**, about 150 miles to the south of Rothenburg. Built between 1870 and Ludwig's mysterious death in 1886, not by an architect but by a theatrical set designer (one C Jank, who was responsible for designing the original production of Wagner's *Tannhauser*) high above the Schwansee and the Alpsee. There are guided tours (there's a bus service from Schwangau, about a mile away), but in summer it can get mighty packed.

CHUNGKING EXPRESS

(1994, dir: Wong Kar-wai)
Takeshi Kaneshiro, Brigitte Lin, Tony Leung Chiu-wai.
● **HONG KONG, CHINA**

All the rough energy of *A Bout de Souffle* in Wong Kar-wai's brace of stories set in flashy, frenetic downtown Hong Kong, as two lovelorn cops (in separate stories) cope with being dumped. The teeming tourist hotel, which provides the movie's title, is the **Chungking House** (aka Chungking Mansions), **40 Nathan Road** in the **Tsim Sha Tsui** district of Kowloon. The house, a 75-room traditional stopover for backpackers, is an old apartment block, divided up into guest houses of varying quality. The public areas are a bit grubby and, some say, rife with petty crime (© *852.2366.5362*). The bar where Kaneshiro meets mysterious, blonde-wigged drug-dealer Lin, is **Bottoms Up**, in the **Mohan's Building**, also in Tsim Sha Tsui. The fast food place, where Kaneshiro hangs out and site of the second story, is **Midnight Express, 3 Lan Kwai Fong** in

the Central District.

CINCINNATI KID, THE

(1965, dir: Norman Jewison)
Steve McQueen, Edward G Robinson, Karl Malden.
● **NEW ORLEANS, LOUISIANA**

McQueen is the Kid, an itinerant card player in this Depression era poker movie shot in **New Orleans** Louisiana. The film was begun by Sam Peckinpah who was fired by the studio when he insisted on filming (albeit fleetingly) nudity – a definite no-no for a major studio in 1965.

CINEMA PARADISO

(1988, dir: Giuseppe Tornatore)
Philippe Noiret, Jaques Perrin, Salvatore Cascio.
● **SICILY, ITALY**

Lushly-scored wallow in cinematic nostalgia, with Noiret as the old picture palace projectionist who bequeaths a love of movies, literally, to his young assistant. Much of the filming was around the town of **Bagheria**, birthplace of the director Tornatore, a short bus ride to the east of Palermo in northern Sicily (the Villa Palagonia here was featured in Antonioni's *L'Avventura*). The town square, where the old cinema frontage stood, is in the village of **Palazzo Adriano**, about 30 miles south of Palermo, and close to the towns of Prizzi and Corleone, both of which have passed their names on to Hollywood.

More Sicilian scenes were filmed at **Palermo** itself; **Cefalu**; **Castelbuono**; and **Lascari**.

CITADEL, THE

(1938, dir: King Vidor)
Robert Donat, Rosalind Russell, Ralph Richardson.
● **WALES**

Donat is an idealistic young doctor in a mining village, tempted by the easy life of London in this film of AJ Cronin's novel. The village scenes filmed in **Abertillery**, north of Pontypool, Gwent, south Wales.

CITIZEN KANE

(1941, dir: Orson Welles)
Orson Welles, Joseph Cotten, Everett Sloane.
● **LOS ANGELES, CALIFORNIA; NEW YORK**

Another classic from the heyday of the studio film, *Kane* was shot almost entirely in the old **RKO Studio, 780 Gower Street** at Melrose Avenue, Hollywood. The studio, built in 1920 as the Robertson-Cole Studios, was bought by Howard Hughes in 1948, and subsequently by Lucille Ball in 1957. It has since been incorporated into the Paramount Studios, but you can't miss the giant RKO globe built onto the corner of the soundstage on the northwest corner of Gower Street and Melrose Avenue.

The original Xanadu: Hearst Castle, San Simeon

The old RKO Studio, Gower Street, Hollywood

As an economy measure, Welles incorporated what had supposedly been 'film tests' into the finished movie. Thus, the projection room, where the opening newsreel is shown, was the real RKO projection room (with Joseph Cotten and a then-unknown Alan Ladd among the reporters); Susan Alexander's nightclub was an old Western set; and her attempted suicide had no set at all, just a couple of flats.

For real interest, though, check out Hearst Castle (*www.sansimeonsbest.com/hearst_castle*), the original architectural hotchpotch on which Kane's 'Xanadu' was based, in idea if not visually. The building was never completed and now never will be. Away from the impressive façade, at the rear of the building, the elaborate decoration and the thin coating of stone runs out to reveal the concrete structure beneath. Just like a movie set, in fact. Hearst Castle is on Coastal Highway 1, on the central California coast near to San Simeon, just about halfway between Los Angeles and San Francisco. It's now owned by the state, is more properly known as the Hearst State Historical Monument, and is open to the public for four tours every day except Thanksgiving, Christmas Day and New Year's Day.

Views of Xanadu in the fake documentary at the beginning of the movie are shots of **Oheka Castle, 135 West Gate Drive, Huntington**, on Long Island, New York (© *631.692.2707, www.oheka.com*). Built in 1919 for tycoon Otto Hermann Kahn (hence the name), who also commissioned the lavish Manhattan mansion used for *The Anderson Tapes*, it's now a hotel and banqueting centre.

The grounds of Xanadu were filmed in Busch Gardens, Pasadena, an estate built by the Busch brewing family. These vast, landscaped gardens have long since vanished, but portions of the old layout can be glimpsed in back gardens of some of the grand houses in the area. You can see the remnants of the landscaping in the gardens of properties around **Arroyo Boulevard** between Bellefontaine Street and Madeline Drive.

CITY SLICKERS
(1991, dir: Ron Underwood)
Billy Crystal, Daniel Stern, Jack Palance.
● **NEW YORK CITY; NEW MEXICO; COLORADO**

In New York, city boy commuter Crystal takes the **East River Tram, Second Avenue** between East 59th and East 60th Streets, to Roosevelt Island, now famous as the site of the climactic confrontation in

Crystal travels to work: East River Tram, East Side

Sam Raimi's *Spider-Man*. The western scenes were filmed in Northern New Mexico, and at **Steward's Ranch** on Lightner Creek near Durango on Route 160, southwest Colorado.

CLASH BY NIGHT
(1952, dir: Fritz Lang)
Barbara Stanwyck, Paul Douglas, Robert Ryan.
● **CALIFORNIA**

Melodramatic complications occur when Barbara Stanwyck returns from the big city to the fishing town where she grew up, takes up with an old flame and is soon a-cheatin' on him. Lang, who always preferred studio filming, for once took a film crew up the coast to **Monterey**, where he filmed location shots on **Cannery Row**.

CLERKS
(1994, dir: Kevin Smith)
Brian O'Halloran, Jeff Anderson, Marilyn Ghigliotti.
● **NEW JERSEY**

Kevin Smith's micro-budget indie production, famously financed by credit cards and filmed in the convenience store where the director was working, **Quick Stop Groceries, 58 Leonard Avenue, Leonardo**, on the western tip of New Jersey. The video store is **RST Video**, next door at number 60. The undertaker's is **Postens Funeral Home, 59 East Lincoln Avenue, Atlantic Highlands**.

CLIENT, THE
(1994, dir: Joel Schumacher)
Susan Sarandon, Tommy Lee Jones, Brad Renfro.
● **TENNESSEE; ARKANSAS; LOUISIANA**

Another legal thriller from the John Grisham production line, with Susan Sarandon acting for underage witness Brad Renfro. Inevitably, it was filmed in the South, in Memphis and New Orleans. The movie kicks off in Memphis. Sneaking a furtive smoke with his little brother, young Renfro is involved in the suicide of a mob lawyer who lets slip where the body of a senator is buried. The woods where the lawyer shoots himself are in the **John F Kennedy Park, 4575 Raleigh-LaGrange Road** in Memphis. Renfro and his traumatised brother are whisked off to the Elvis Presley Wing of the Saint Peter Charity Hospital, actually the **Memphis Regional Medical Center, 877 Jefferson Avenue**, known as 'the Med'.

In Hollywood, no matter how poor someone is, there'll always be a high flying lawyer willing to work for nothing, and sure enough, Renfro stumbles across Sarandon, who works out of the high-rise **Sterick Building, 9 North Third Street**, a location actually specified by Grisham in the book. The seedy café, where the bad guys hire a PI to keep an eye on the kid, is a familiar Memphis location seen in Jim Jarmusch's *Mystery Train* and in Jerry Lee Lewis biopic *Great Balls of Fire*, the **Arcade Restaurant, 540 South Main Street**. Ossie Davis' courthouse is the **Memphis County Courthouse, 140 Adams Avenue**, and the Women's Detention Hall, where Renfro gets banged up, is the **Criminal Justice Center, 201 Poplar Avenue**.

The bad guys operate out of New Orleans. LaPaglia and his uncle are bugged in the **Germanic Red Room** of **Antoine's Restaurant, 713 St Louis Street** (© *504.581.4422*), another Grisham favourite, also seen in *The Pelican Brief*. The movie's climax supposedly takes place in New Orleans, with Sarandon driving over the Huey P Long Bridge, but the boathouse, where the senator is buried, is a country inn on **Horseshoe Lake**, near **Hughes**, Arkansas, about 30 miles west of Memphis.

CLOCKERS

(1995, dir: Spike Lee)
Harvey Keitel, Mekhi Phifer, Delroy Lindo.
● **NEW YORK CITY**

Richard Price's novel of 24-hour drug dealers – the 'Clockers' of the title – was set in New Jersey, and was due to be filmed by Martin Scorsese. Scorsese subsequently stepped back to become producer with Spike Lee taking over direction and so, naturally, the location leapt across Manhattan to Brooklyn. It was filmed on the **Gowanus Housing Projects**, between Wyckoff and Baltic Streets, Hoyt and Bond Streets in the Boerum Hill section of Brooklyn. The little park where the Clockers hang out, and Delroy Lindo runs his business, is on the south side of **Wyckoff Street** between Hoyt and Bond Streets. Strike's apartment, Rodney's grocery store and the church where Victor turns himself in can all be found in the immediate area. Don't bother looking for Moby's restaurant, where the murder takes place, or the Kool Breeze bar opposite. Along with the police station, they were simply abandoned buildings dressed up for the movie

CLOCKWORK ORANGE, A

(1971, dir: Stanley Kubrick)
Malcolm McDowell, Patrick Magee, Adrienne Corri.
● **LONDON; HERTFORDSHIRE; BUCKING-HAMSHIRE; MIDDLESEX**

The Ludovico Medical Facility: Lecture Centre, Brunel University, Uxbridge

For many years, Kubrick's refusal to allow the film to be shown in the UK gave his blackly comic version of Anthony Burgess' novel about free will and control an undeserved reputation as a fearsome video nasty. Set vaguely in the north, judging by the accents, the film was made almost entirely on location around London and the Home Counties, with the notoriously travel-phobic Kubrick choosing locations from architectural guides. Virtually the only purpose-built set, the Korova Milk Bar, was constructed in a factory just off Borehamwood High Street near to the MGM Studios (where *2001* had been shot).

Alex's estate is part of the unspeakable concrete disaster that is **Thamesmead South**, a vast, grim, windswept collection of tower blocks connected by intimidating walkways. The benighted subway, where the Droogs attack the old tramp, can be found over in west London. It's the northern subway beneath the huge circular advertising installation on **Trinity Road, Wandsworth** – deserted, unswept and extremely unnerving.

The tramps' revenge: Albert Bridge, Chelsea Embankment

The Flat Block Marina is Thamesmead's artificially created **Southmere Lake**. Alex reasserts his dominance over fellow Droogs here by dumping Dim in the water and slicing his outstretched hand at **Binsley Walk** on the lake's western shore overlooked by the blocks of Yarnton Way. More futuristic cityscapes filmed in the sixties concrete shopping centre of **Friar's Square** in **Aylesbury**, Buckinghamshire. Another urban disaster, the centre was closed down in 1990 and drastically remodelled as a much more friendly redbrick indoor mall.

Alex's apartment in Municipal Flat Block 18A, Linear North is a flat in the village of Elstree. Kubrick was ever the perfectionist: the couple who lived here moved out while £5,000 was spent on redecoration. With filming over and the flat restored to its original state, they returned only to be moved out again so two close-ups could be shot. The cat woman's house is a real mansion in the Hertfordshire countryside. Also in Hertfordshire is 'Home', Patrick Magee's futuristic pad and site of the notorious 'Singin' in the Rain' rape of Adrienne Corri (when the two met in Hollywood, Gene Kelly allegedly snubbed Kubrick for the use of this number in the scene). The house is **Skybreak**, tucked invisbly away in the tiny village of **Warren Radlett**, Hertfordshire.

Fast sex to fast food: the *très* sixties chrome and glass Chelsea Drugstore, which stood on the King's Road at the northwest corner of Royal Avenue, became a record shop, where Alex picks up two girls for a spot of high speed 'in and out'. The shop closed in the seventies and is now a McDonald's.

The Ludovico Medical Facility, where Alex undergoes the gross aversion therapy, is the campus of **Brunel University** in **Uxbridge**, Middlesex. The giant overhanging concrete monstrosity is the Lecture centre in the middle of campus, opposite which Alex is received into the Art Centre. The campus is on Kingston Lane off Hillingdon Hill about a mile south of Uxbridge (*tube: Uxbridge*).

The newly defenceless Alex meets an earlier victim on the **Chelsea Embankment** at Oakley Street, SW3, and it's under **Albert Bridge** that the tramps take their revenge.

CLOSE ENCOUNTERS OF THE THIRD KIND

(1977, dir: Steven Spielberg)
Richard Dreyfuss, Melinda Dillon, François Truffaut.
● **ALABAMA; WYOMING; CALIFORNIA; WASHINGTON DC, WASHINGTON; INDIA; MEXICO**

Spielberg resurrected the Cinema of Awe not seen since the days of the great religious epics (just count the references to *The Ten Commandments*) as earth is visited by friendly aliens. The opening sandstorm, and the ship stranded in the Sahara Desert seen in the Special Edition, were filmed in California's Mojave Desert. More desert scenes were shot at **Tequisquiapan** and **Bernal**, Querétaro, Mexico. Howard K Smith, the news anchorman, shot his scenes in **Washington DC**. The footage of Truffaut making recordings in India was filmed in **Bombay**. The air traffic control center is in **Palmdale**, California.

Most of the filming, however, was in Alabama, where dirigible hangars, larger than any Hollywood soundstage, were found to house the enormous sets. Consequently, the whole production moved to the south. The landing site was the biggest indoor set ever built, constructed at the former air force base, now an industrial complex in Mobile. The hangars are numbers 5 and 6, Building 17 of the **Brookley Field Industrial Complex, Old Bay Street, Mobile**. Other sets built in the hangars include the road bend where the cop cars attempt to follow the alien craft into space, and the interior of the Dreyfuss house. The mountainside scenes used artificial boulders, with only twelve basic shapes carefully placed at differing angles to prevent patterns becoming obvious. Dreyfuss' house is a real house in Mobile, while Jillian's mother's house is in **Baldwin County** to the east of Mobile. The big evacuation scene filmed at **Bay Minette** over the Mobile and Tensaw Rivers, 30 miles northeast of Mobile on Route 31.

PHOTOGRAPH COURTESY NORTHEAST WYOMING

The landing site: Devil's Tower, Black Hills National Forest

Apart from the 'strip' itself, the landing site is real and has since become a major tourist attraction. The striking sawn-off peak of **Devil's Tower National Monument** can be found in the northeast corner of Wyoming in the **Black Hills National Forest**. According to native legend, the strange formation was made by giant bears clawing at a mountain to reach a princess on the summit. According to science, it's the plug of an extinct volcano. Devil's Tower was designated the US' first national monument, in 1906. It's open all year round, and there's a visitor centre open from April to October, about three miles from the entrance. It's 33 miles northeast of Moorcroft, I-90. Nearest airports are Gillette, Wyoming, and Rapid City, South Dakota. Details at *www.gorp.com/gorp/resource/us_ nm/wy_ devil.htm*.

CLOSELY OBSERVED TRAINS (aka *Closely Watched Trains*)
(1966, dir: Jiri Menzel)
Vaclav Neckar, Jitka Bendova, Vladimir Valenta.
● CZECHOSLOVAKIA

An apprentice railway guard at a small country station in Czechoslovakia discovers sex and love during WWII, but when he becomes a saboteur this small, closely observed comedy takes a tragic turn. It was shot on the railway station at **Lodenice** in Czechoslovakia.

CLUELESS
(1995, dir: Amy Heckerling)
Alicia Silverstone, Stacey Dash, Brittany Murphy.
● LOS ANGELES, CALIFORNIA

Spot-on updating of Jane Austen's *Emma* (and closer to the spirit of the original than the 1996 straightforward period version), set in Beverly Hills. Alicia Silverstone's school is **Occidental College, 1600 Campus Road** in Eagle Rock, which you may recognise as California University from TV's *Beverly Hills 90210*. She shops, of course, on Rodeo Drive – the steps and fountain are **Rodeo II**, opposite the Wilshire Beverly Hotel. The shopping mall is **West Side Pavilion, 10800 Pico Boulevard**, and the skateboarding scene uses the parking lot of **Shoreline Village, 407 Shoreline Village Drive**, Long Beach. The bizarre gingerbread fairytale cottage Silverstone wanders past in Beverly Hills is the **Spadena House, 515 Walden Drive**, off Santa Monica Boulevard. Built in 1921 as combined production offices and movie set for the Irving C Willat movie company, it stood originally at 6509 West Washington Boulevard, Culver City and was moved to its present location in the thirties.

COAL MINER'S DAUGHTER
(1980, dir: Michael Apted)
Sissy Spacek, Tommy Lee Jones, Levon Helm.
● KENTUCKY; VIRGINIA; TENNESSEE

Brit director Apted's biopic of C&W singer Loretta Lynn won Spacek an Oscar for the title role. It was filmed in **Whitesburg** and **Jenkins**, Kentucky, and just over the border at **Wise** in western Virginia. Spacek also gets to perform at the Grand Ol' Opry in the **Ryman Auditorium, 116 Opry Place**, Fifth Avenue North between Broadway and Commerce Street, Nashville, Tennessee.

COCOON
(1985, dir: Ron Howard)
Don Ameche, Wilford Brimley, Hume Cronyn.
● FLORIDA; BAHAMAS; CALIFORNIA

Enjoyably hokey, feelgood fantasy as alien Brian Dennehy and pals unwittingly rejuvenate a bunch of oldsters. Filming took place in the retirement haven of St Petersburg on Florida's west coast. The old folks' home is the **Sunny Shores Rest Home, 125 56th Avenue South**, while the 'magical' pool is part of a large neo-Spanish estate on **Park Street**, St Petersburg, where the poolhouse was specially built. The scenes on the Manta III boat were shot offshore at **Tierra Verde** in the **Boca Ciega Bay**, and at **Nassau** in the Bahamas. The ballroom, where the old folks strut their stuff, is the old Mediterranean revival style **Coliseum Ballroom, 535 Fourth Avenue North**, downtown St Petersburg (℡ *813.892.5202*). Brimley is rejected when he applies for his driving licence at the **St Petersburg Municipal Building**.

The lame, quick cash-in sequel, *Cocoon: The Return*, moved from St Petersburg to Miami, with more filming in San Francisco – the old folks' bungalows are the Sunrise Court Apartments, Miami. Jack Gilford and Elaine Stritch have a date at the **Desiree Supper Club, 9674 Coral Way** (℡ *305.559.0969*) in Miami, and filming also took place at the **Miami Seaquarium, 4400 Rickenbacker Causeway**, Virginia Key (*© 305.361.5705*).

COLD MOUNTAIN
(2003, dir: Anthony Minghella)
Jude Law, Nicole Kidman, Renée Zellweger.
● **SOUTH CAROLINA; ROMANIA**

Set in North Carolina – the Blue Ridge Mountains in Asheville, home of the peak in the original novel's title – it was actually largely filmed in the remote village of **Potigrafu**, Romania, about 25 miles north of the capital, Bucharest. The average monthly salary in Romania is around $100, quite an incentive for the production company, along with the fact that powerlines and modern buildings don't have to be digitally removed. And the script called for snow, which can't be guaranteed in the Carolinas. More scenes were shot in the mountainous region of Transylvania.

The **College of Charleston's Cistern, Charleston**, South Carolina, provided the backdrop for the slave market. The library became an Auction House, while Church Street above Broad Street became a street scene with wooden sidewalks and hitching posts. Two churches, **St Philip's** and the **French Huguenot Church**, were also used. There was also filming at **Cypress Garden, 3030 Cypress Gardens Road, Moncks Corner**s, Charleston (*© 843.553.0515, www.cypressgardens-sc.org*), seen also in *The Patriot* and *Radio*.

COLLATERAL
(2004, dir: Michael Mann)
Tom Cruise, Jamie Foxx, Jada Pinkett Smith.
● **LOS ANGELES, CALIFORNIA**

New York was the original setting for the story of an unwitting cab driver hired to ferry a hitman from job to job, but once Mann took over direction, the action was switched to Los Angeles. As in *Heat*, the director relishes the look of the city and its architecture, this time filming almost entirely at night on high-definition video.

Coolly professional killer Vincent (Cruise) picks up his instructions in a clandestine bag switch as he arrives at **LAX (Los Angeles International Airport)**. Cabbie Max (Foxx) supposedly drops off prosecutor Annie (Pinkett Smith) and picks up Vincent at 312 Spring Street, downtown, which would be the United States Courthouse. The building certainly is downtown LA, but it's the **Gas Company Building, 555 West Fifth Street** at Grand Avenue (previously seen in *Speed* and *Charlie's Angels*).

It all starts to go wrong for Max when a dead body plummets onto his cab. The site of what turns out to be the first hit is given as 1039 South Union Street, but is **1839 South Union Avenue** at West Washington Boulevard, southwest of downtown. Although Max prides himself on his knowledge of LA thoroughfares, when they head off to 7565 Fountain Avenue, in West Hollywood, they're pulled over by the cops on **Franklin Avenue** at Cahuenga. Max seems to have overshot a little – this is north of Hollywood (and the Fountain apartment itself appears to look out over downtown LA).

The jazz club, in which the unfortunate Daniel becomes

Vincent's second job after retailing his Miles Davis anecdote, is **Cheerio's, 4333 Leimert Boulevard, Leimert Park** (*© 323.298.8672*). Max makes off with Vincent's precious laptop, throwing it onto the I-10 Freeway from the footbridge at **City Terrace**, east of downtown.

It's down to the refineries of **Wilmington**, south LA, for the next hit. The club in which Max is obliged to pass himself off as Vincent, though, is in east LA. It's **El Rodeo, 8825 East Washington Boulevard, Pico Rivera** (*© 562.942.0755, www.elrodeonightclub.com*).

Next stop is Koreatown, in midtown LA, to take out the Korean gangster in Fever disco. The exterior of the club is **Bliss, 3465 West Sixth Street** at South Kenmore Avenue (*© 213.365.1222*). Don't be disappointed. The interior was recreated in the studio at seven times the size of the real thing.

Max puts his foot to the floor on **Figueroa Street**, south past Arco Plaza, 505 South Flower Street, and the football mural on Hotel Figueroa, 939 South Figueroa Street, before flipping the cab at the intersection of **Figueroa and 10th**, outside the **Staples Center**. He legs it off up **Flower Street**, grabbing a cellphone from a man outside the downtown branch of the excruciatingly hip **Standard Hotel, 550 South Flower Street**.

Figuring out that (coincidence!) Annie is Vincent's final target, Max tries to call her from the roof of the parking garage of the 52-story **777 Tower, 777 South Figueroa Street** at West 8th Street. Mann needed a roof overlooked by skyscrapers but, unfortunately, the 777 garage, which fitted the bill perfectly, is used by the secret service. The film company persuaded the spooks to allow them, under strict supervision, two hours to grab the scene and clear out.

Next door is **Ernst & Young Plaza** (previously Citicorp Plaza), **725 Figueroa Street**, which became the lobby of Annie's office. Conveniently, it's adjacent to the **Seventh and Figueroa Metro Station**, into which Max and Annie are pursued. Supposedly heading south on the Blue Line, the train is actually a Green Line, heading west, stopping briefly at **Harbor Freeway Station**, before they leave Vincent behind at **Marine-Redondo Station, 2406 Marine Avenue** in Redondo Beach – the station where *Heat* opens.

COLLECTOR, THE
(1965, dir: William Wyler)
Terence Stamp, Samantha Eggar, Mona Washbourne.
● **LONDON; KENT; LOS ANGELES, CALIFORNIA**

Stamp is far too attractive to be the repressed and unhinged butterfly collector who kidnaps art student Eggar to add to his 'collection' in this psychological thriller. Stamp stalks Eggar in Hampstead, kidnapping her in the tiny **Mount Vernon Lane**, off Holly Hill just up the hill from Hampstead tube station. The house

The kidnapping: Mount Vernon Lane, Hampstead

where Stamp holds Eggar prisoner is a 400-year-old farmhouse in Tudor style in a vast estate near **Edenbridge**, ten miles northwest of Tunbridge Wells on the B2026 in west Kent. The local village is **Westerham**, five miles to the north. The interiors, however, were reconstructed on soundstages in the US, at Columbia's Gower Street Studio in Hollywood.

COLOR OF MONEY, THE

(1986, dir: Martin Scorsese)
Paul Newman, Tom Cruise, Mary Elizabeth Mastrantonio.
● **ILLINOIS; NEW JERSEY**

'Crossing the US' – in Chicago: Zum Deutschen Eck, Southport Avenue

Scorsese's kinetically thrilling follow up to Robert Rossen's 1961 *The Hustler* has Newman coming back to the role of pool hall king Fast Eddie Felson, ostensibly grooming talented tyro Cruise for pool stardom. Though the story takes off from Chicago and heads across the States to the Atlantic City tournament, it was filmed on real locations almost entirely in the city of Chicago.

The pool hall where Cruise first grabs Newman's attention by trashing John Turturro is **Fitzgerald's, 6615 West Roosevelt Road** in Berwyn, west of the city (*rail: Berwyn*). Established as a pool hall in 1915, you can see Fitzgerald's as the Suds Bucket, site of the raucous dance, in *A League of Their Own*. The Sir Loin Inn, where Newman takes Cruise and Mastrantonio for a meal and a lesson in human moves, is **O'Brien's Steakhouse, 1528 North Wells Street** near West North Avenue in the Old Town district (*©312.787.3131*).

Another Chicago bar turned into a pool hall for the movie was the **Gingerman Tavern, 3720 North Clark Street** at West Waveland Avenue northwest of Wrigley Field in Wrigleyville. Real pool halls include **St Paul's Billiards** (it was formerly the Vaudeville Theatre), **1415**

Cruise first grabs Newman's attention: Fitzgerald's, Berwyn

The Nine-ball Classic in Atlantic City: Navy Pier, Chicago

West Fullerton Avenue in Lincoln Park-De Paul, where Cruise gets beaten up; **Chris's Billiards, 4637 North Milwaukee Avenue** between Laurence and Montrose in northwest Chicago; the **Gaslight, 2858 North Halsted** at West Diversey; and **North Center Bowl, 4017**

North Lincoln Avenue, where a disillusioned Newman finally ditches Cruise. More scenes were filmed at German oompah restaurant **Zum Deutschen Eck, 2924 North Southport Avenue** at Diversey in north Chicago.

Studying human moves: O'Brien's Steakhouse, North Wells Street

The Nine-ball Classic Tournament is held at the oft-used **Resorts International Hotel** on the Boardwalk at Atlantic City, New Jersey, but even this turns out to be Chicago. Although there are establishing shots of the hotel, the giant arched hall of the climactic poolathon is the **Navy Pier**, east of the Streeterville district. This 3,000 foot pier was built in 1916 (it was intended to be one of a pair but its partner never materialised) when Lake Michigan was used for commercial shipping. Post-thirties it fell into decline, until major renovations in 1976. The pier entrance is on **Streeter Drive** at 600 East Grand Avenue near Lake Shore Drive just north of the Chicago River.

Bar-cum-pool hall: Gingerman Tavern, North Clark Street

Similarly, Tom Cruise's Atlantic City hotel can be found in the Windy City. It's the **Blackstone Hotel, 636 South Michigan Avenue** at East Balbo Drive (*© 312.427.4300*), the same venue that hosted the bloody banquet in Brian De Palma's *The Untouchables*.

COLOR PURPLE, THE

(1985, dir: Steven Spielberg)
Whoopi Goldberg, Margaret Avery, Oprah Winfrey.
● **NORTH CAROLINA; CALIFORNIA**

Spielberg in worthy David Lean mode, aiming for Oscars but missing again, films a tidied-up version of Alice Walker's novel about an abused black woman who finally finds her own freedom. Set in Georgia, it was filmed in the area around **Wadesboro** in North Carolina, including the old **Wadesboro Courthouse**, and in the towns of **Marshville**, **Ansonville** and **Lilesville**, all about 30 miles east of Charlotte (most of the African scenes were shot in North Carolina, too).

COMMITMENTS, THE

(1991, dir: Alan Parker)
Robert Arkins, Andrew Strong, Michael Aherne.
● **IRELAND**

Raucous filming of Roddy Doyle's novel about a Dublin soul band. Doyle's fictitious Barrytown was based on Kilbarrack, a working class estate in Dublin's Northside, and the movie was shot on no fewer than 44 locations, mixing Dublin's bland Northside estates with the older, char-

Getting rid of the keyboard player: Bray Head Hotel, Bray

The band splits up at Gallagher's: Sir John Rogerson's Quay

acterful city centre. The opening scene, with Jimmy Rabette trying to offload cassettes, filmed on **Sherriff Street**, Dublin. Rabette's home is in **Darndale**. Joey the Lips' mother's house is on **Pembroke Road** in Ballsbridge. The concert, where Jimmy decides to get rid of the keyboard player, is the **Bray Head Hotel** in **Bray**, on the coast south of Dublin. The church, where 'A Whiter Shade of Pale' is played on the organ, is **St Francis Xavier's, Gardiner Street**. The Commitments' rehearsal room is above a Snooker Hall on **Lower Camden Street**. The local hall where the band starts out is the **Guide Hall** in **Synge Street**. The music bar, Gallagher's, where the band finally falls apart during a gig while waiting for Wilson Pickett to turn up, is the **Waterside Rock Bar** on **Sir John Rogerson's Quay**, and it's on the quay that Jimmy finally encounters Pickett's limo.

CON AIR

(1997, dir: Simon West)
Nicolas Cage, John Malkovich, John Cusack.
● **LAS VEGAS, NEVADA; UTAH; LOS ANGELES, CALIFORNIA**

Another hi-octane thriller, and an A-list cast, from the Jerry Bruckheimer stable, with a whole psycho ward of super-convicts hijacking a plane. The initial boarding, supposedly at Oakland Airport, over the bay from San Francisco, is **Salt Lake City** in Utah. Likewise, the desert landing, where serial killer Steve Buscemi gets added to the mix, at Carson City, Nevada, uses the local airport at **Ogden**, Utah. The desert landing in Death Valley is at **Wendover**, on the formless salt flats of the Utah-Nevada border.

The plane is finally brought to earth on the Strip in Las Vegas and, as in *Mars Attacks!*, the cameras incorporate the last moments of a Vegas landmark into a fictitious scenario. This time it's the demolition of the venerable Sands Hotel, which is seemingly trashed when the plane careers through its lobby. To complete the illusion, 250 feet of the Vegas Strip were also mocked up, with the plane wing apparently clipping the neon guitar of the Hard Rock Café. The road tunnel is LA's **Second Street Tunnel**, between Hill Street and Figueroa Street, downtown. Filming also took place around **Moab**, Utah, at **Determination Towers** in **Mill Canyon**.

CONAN THE BARBARIAN

(1981, dir: John Milius)
Arnold Schwarzenegger, Sandahl Bergman, James Earl

Jones.
● **SPAIN**

Self-styled 'Zen fascist' Milius' po-faced and pompous film of the pulp character was shot in Spain, at freezing **Segovia** and the blazing desert of **Almeria**. The slightly more enjoyable sequel, *Conan the Destroyer*, was filmed in Mexico, at **Samalayuca**, 50 miles south of El Paso on Route 45, and at **Juarez**.

CONFORMISTA, IL (aka *The Conformist*)

(1969, dir: Bernardo Bertolucci)
Jean-Louis Trintignant, Stefania Sandrelli, Pierre Clementi.
● **PARIS, FRANCE; ROME, ITALY**

Trintignant's hotel: Gare d'Orsay, rue de Bellchasse

Strange psycho-political thriller from Bertolucci, with a deeply repressed Trintignant succumbing to fascism in thirties Italy. Trintignant's hotel, where he awaits orders from his fascist bosses to kill an anti-Nazi professor, is part of Paris' old **Gare d'Orsay, 1 rue de Bellechasse**, (see Orson Welles' *The Trial*, which filmed within the station, now an art museum). The professor's address and phone number in the movie are actually those of Jean-Luc Godard, included as a joke after the two directors had fallen out.

In Rome, Trintignant crosses the **Sant'Angelo Bridge** to the **Colosseum**. And it's inside the Colosseum that Trintignant comes face to face with the chauffeur he thought he had killed years before.

CONVERSATION, THE

(1974, dir: Francis Ford Coppola)
Gene Hackman, John Cazale, Allen Garfield.
● **SAN FRANCISCO, CALIFORNIA**

The Godfather and *Apocalypse Now* not withstanding,

Recording the conversation: Union Square

Hackman's dream: Alta Plaza Park, Steiner Street

this is arguably Coppola's masterpiece, an audio reworking of Antonioni's *Blowup* with surveillance expert Harry Caul (Hackman) apparently uncovering a plan to kill a pair of illicit lovers. It's set in San Francisco, where the crucial conversation is recorded in **Union Square**. Caul's workshop is one of the old warehouses in San Francisco's South of Market district, and his bizarre confessional dream (originally intended to be the ending of the film) was filmed in **Alta Plaza Park, Steiner Street**, site of the car-down-the-steps stunt in *What's Up, Doc?*. The forbidding, black, X-braced building, where Harry frets after being dismissed by a young Harrison Ford, is the **Alcoa Building, 1 Maritime Plaza** on Battery Street between Clay and Washington Streets. The Jack Tar Hotel, where Harry fears he's uncovered a murder plot, has had a bit of a revamp since the seventies, and is now the **Cathedral Hill Hotel, 1101 Van Ness Avenue** at Geary Street (© *415.776.8200, www.cathedralhillhotel.com*).

COOGAN'S BLUFF

(1968, dir: Don Siegel)
Clint Eastwood, Lee J Cobb, Don Stroud.
● **NEW YORK CITY; CALIFORNIA**

A western sherriff rides into the Big Apple and shows the city boys how things get done. It's the old loner against the system story again, which Siegel had already tried in *Madigan* with Richard Widmark, and returned to with Eastwood in *Dirty Harry*. Where possible, Siegel liked to avoid studios and film on location. The opening scene, set in Arizona, was shot in the **Mojave Desert** near Mojave itself, California.

From here on, it's New York City, with Clint arriving (and departing at the end of the movie) by helicopter on the helipad of the **Pan Am Building**, towering over Grand Central Station at **200 Park Avenue**. You won't be able to make a similar entrance, though. The noisy, unpopular pad was closed down in 1977 after a fatal accident, in which, incidentally, the director of the notorious (but faked) movie *Snuff*, Michael Findlay, was apparently decapitated.

The cop station is New York's **23rd Precinct**. The ghastly, homophobic Pigeon Toed Orange Peel Disco scene did film in the studio. It's Universal's old opera house set, built for the 1925 Lon Chaney *Phantom of the Opera*. Coogan and Julie's love scene was filmed in **Fort Tryon Park**, north of Washington Heights overlooking the Hudson River. The final motorbike chase was shot around **The Cloisters**, a collection of architectural bits from various monasteries in southern France and Spain, in Fort Tryon Park, **West 193rd Street** at Fort Washington Avenue towards Inwood.

COOL HAND LUKE

(1967, dir: Stuart Rosenberg)
Paul Newman, George Kennedy, Jo Van Fleet.
● **CALIFORNIA**

An Academy Award for George Kennedy, and a nomination for Newman in this Christ-ish allegory with Newman suffering on a chain gang. Shot in the **San Joaquin River delta** area near **Stockton**, California.

COTTON CLUB, THE

(1984, dir: Francis Coppola)
Richard Gere, Gregory Hines, Diane Lane.
● **NEW YORK CITY**

Diane Lane's luxury pad: Apthorp Apartments, Broadway

The potentially fascinating story of Harlem's legendary nightclub where, in the twenties, all-white audiences flocked to watch black performers, suffered from a horribly troubled production. Producer Robert Evans, who was to have directed, was replaced by script doctor Coppola. Al Pacino and Sylvester Stallone were considered for the role that eventually went to Richard Gere. Richard Pryor was replaced by Gregory Hines. Roy Radin, a vaudeville producer, offered to raise finance from contacts in Puerto Rico, but subsequently turned up shot dead in a canyon north of LA.

The Cotton Club was meticulously recreated by designer Richard Sylbert at the **Kaufmann-Astoria Studios, 34-12 36th Street** in Queens. Original menus were copied, authentic flowers of the period were used and the superb Art Direction got a well-deserved Oscar nomination.

Location shooting took place around Manhattan. The rather sinister party to which Gere is invited by Dutch Schultz, and where rival mobster Flynn is bloodily stabbed, filmed in the **Plaza Hotel, Fifth Avenue** at 59th Street. The grand block where Lane is kept in luxury by Schultz is the **Apthorp Apartments, 2211 Broadway** between West 78th and West 79th Streets.

The Abyssinian church, where Hines proposes to Lonette McKee, is the ballroom of **Grand Prospect Hall, 263 Prospect Avenue, Park Slope** in Brooklyn (*www.grandprospect.com*), seen also in *Prizzi's Honor*, *Last Exit to Brooklyn* and *The Royal Tenenbaums*. Another section of the hall is used for the Hoofers' club, where the old troupers go through their paces, and also the scene in the black bar where Hines tells Laurence Fishburne that he wants Mike the bouncer killed. The machine gun revenge attack by Cage's men on Julian Beck, which backfires horribly when children are mown down, was filmed on **West 131st Street** in Harlem.

The elaborately theatrical finale was staged in **Grand Central Terminal** (aka *Station*), 89 East 42nd Street.

COUNTY HOSPITAL

(1932, dir: James Parrott)
Stan Laurel, Oliver Hardy, Billy Gilbert.
● **LOS ANGELES, CALIFORNIA**

The Laurel and Hardy pic where Stan visits Ollie in hospital and nearly wrecks the place. The hospital is actually **City Hall, 9770 Culver Boulevard** at Duquesne Avenue, Culver City in LA. The city hall has

Stan and Ollie's hospital: Culver City Hall, Culver City

been rebuilt, but the old frontage has been incorporated into the new design and is still recognisable.

CRASH
(1997, dir: David Cronenberg)
James Spader, Deborah Kara Unger, Holly Hunter.
● **ONTARIO, CANADA**

Cronenberg's controversial film of JG Ballard's perverse novel about people getting sexual excitement from car wrecks, filmed on stretches of highway in **North York**, northern Toronto.

CREATURE FROM THE BLACK LAGOON
(1954, dir: Jack Arnold)
Richard Carlson, Julie Adams, Ricou Browning.
● **FLORIDA; LOS ANGELES, CALIFORNIA**

Way up the Amazon, a group of scientists discover a scaly creature, half-man, half-amphibian, in the daddy of all fifties creature-features. Much of the Amazon lagoon is Park Lake on the Universal backlot in Hollywood, where the *Rita* explores the creepy backwaters. The opening 'Creation of the World' sequence filmed on the **Will Rogers State Beach** at Pacific Palisades, where Sunset Boulevard reaches the ocean. Dr Maia's camp, where the fossilised man and the mangled native bodies are found (and the creature makes a grab for Julie Adams' ankle) is **Sierra Canyon**, Chatsworth, northwest of LA.

Julie peers at fish in the **Hermosa Beach Aquarium**, **Route 1** south of LA toward Palos Verdes. The speedboat, supposedly in Brazil's Morajo Bay, was filmed at **Portuguese Bend**, an area of spectacular rock faults on **Palos Verdes Drive South** on the south coast of the Palos Verdes Peninsula.

The second unit location filming of the excellent underwater scenes (it's diver Ricou Browning in the rubber monster suit) was at **Wakulla Springs**, 14 miles south of Tallahassee on Route 267 in northern Florida. Wakulla Springs has an unknown depth – no diver has yet reached the bottom – 'Wakulla' is a Native word which means 'Mysterious Waters'. It's been the setting for countless underwater film sequences, including the old *Tarzan* movies.

CREEPSHOW
(1982, dir: George A Romero)
Carrie Nye, Viveca Lindfors, Leslie Nielsen.
● **PENNSYLVANIA; NEW JERSEY**

Compendium of Stephen King (who also stars in one episode) stories in slam-bang comic book style, filmed, like almost all of Romero's work, near Pittsburgh. The main location was the **Penn Hall Academy**, set in wooded grounds near **Monroeville** (the mall location for Romero's *Dawn of the Dead*). The interiors were shot in the academy's gymnasium.

Father's Day: John Amplas returns from the dead to wreak vengeance on his family. Filmed at a gothic-style mansion in **Fox Chapel**, a swanky suburb of Pittsburgh a couple of miles to the north, just off I-28, with the grounds dressed as the overgrown cemetery.

Something to Tide You Over: Ted Danson and Gaylen Ross come back from the dead to wreak vengeance on Leslie Nielsen. It's away from Pittsburgh, which sadly doesn't have a coastline, for the beach scenes, which were filmed at **Island Beach State Park** on the New Jersey Coast.

The Crate: The creepy science lab and college campus are Penn Hall itself.

The Lonesome Death of Jordy Verrill: Stephen King mutates into a giant plant. A meteor crater and a house overrun by mutoid plants were constructed on a hillside near to Penn Hall.

They're Creeping Up on You: More Penn Hall interiors, overrun this time by 28,000 (go ahead, count 'em) giant five-inch cockroaches, bussed in from bat-guano caves in Trinidad.

Creepshow II followed, with three more Stephen King chillers. King, having his say this time around, insisted that one of the episodes, *The Hitchhiker*, was shot in his hometown, **Bangor**, Maine.

CRIMES AND MISDEMEANORS
(1989, dir: Woody Allen)
Woody Allen, Martin Landau, Mia Farrow.
● **NEW YORK CITY**

Parallel stories, one satiric, one deadly serious, as media nerd Allen struggles to make documentaries and eye surgeon Landau rids himself of his mistress.

Site of the Bleecker Street Cinema: Bleecker Street, Greenwich Village

Woody Allen retires to the Bleecker Street Cinema with his niece, to watch Hitchcock's only screwball comedy *Mr and Mrs Smith*, the 1937 Edward G Robinson movie *The Last Gangster*, Betty Hutton in 1943's *Happy Go Lucky* and Alan Ladd in *This Gun for Hire*. The movie house stood at **144 Bleecker Street** in Greenwich Village, but has since closed down – in 1996 it was a video store. It was, incidentally, also the cinema where Aidan Quinn worked as projectionist in *Desperately Seeking Susan*. Smug Alan Alda offers Woody Allen a directing job during a party at the swanky restaurant **Tavern On The Green, Central Park West** at 67th Street, in Central Park itself on the West Side (see *Ghostbusters* for details).

Allen and Joanna Gleason make up a foursome with Alan Alda and Mia Farrow at the One Fifth Restaurant, which was at **1 Fifth Avenue** at Eighth Street, just to the north of Washington Square in the Village, but has now gone. Take a look at the deco highrise that housed the restaurant. This was the original choice for Sigourney Weaver's possessed apartment block in *Ghostbusters*. The wedding party that ends the movie was filmed in the **Waldorf-Astoria Hotel, 301 Park Avenue** between East 49th and East 50th Streets, midtown.

"CROCODILE" DUNDEE
(1986, dir: Peter Faiman)
Paul Hogan, Linda Koslowski, John Meillon.

Mick Dundee's hotel: Plaza Hotel

The fight scene: Cortlandt Alley

● QUEENSLAND, AUSTRALIA; NORTHERN TERRITORY, AUSTRALIA; NEW YORK CITY

Aussie bumpkin comes to the big city – with hilarious consequences! And that's about it for this inexplicably successful bore. The town of Walkabout Creek is **McKinlay** in Queensland. The Federal Hotel here had a new façade built to become the Walkabout Creek Bar. It has since changed its name to the **Walkabout Creek Hotel**, which doubled the price of the property when it was subsequently sold. The outback scenes were filmed in **Kakadu National Park**, Northern Territory, including at the **UDP Falls**. All very wild and beautiful, until you realise that UDP stands for Uranium Development Project. Kakadu National Park begins 93 miles east of Darwin and stretches for 62 miles to the western border of Arnhem Land, an area set aside solely for the use of Aboriginals, and from the northern coast 50 to 120 miles south. To get there, head south 22 miles from Darwin to Humty Doo then turn east onto the Arnhem Highway which leads through the park to Park Headquarters at Jabiru.

The New York hotel where Hogan stays is, of course, the ubiquitous **Plaza Hotel, Fifth Avenue** at 59th Street. The interior was recreated in the studio – Plaza bathrooms don't actually have bidets, but as it's such a hilarious joke, who cares? Hogan scares off muggers with his huge knife on the plaza in front of the **Municipal Building, 1 Center Street** at Chambers Street. The alley where he gets into a fight is the oft-used **Cortlandt Alley**, running between Canal and Franklin Streets alongside Broadway in Lower Manhattan.

The bar, where Dundee – hilariously – gets fixed up with a man dressed as a woman, is **Vazac's**, called the Seven and B, **108 Avenue B** on the corner of Tomkins Square in the East Village (see it also in, amongst many other films, *Godfather II*, where the Rosato Brothers attempt to garotte Pentangeli).

The happy-ending subway is **Columbus Circle**, at the SW corner of Central Park – geographically nonsensical as the nearest subway to the Plaza, but it does allow cute views of Central Park for the climax.

The equally 'hilarious' sequel reversed the formula, starting out in New York before heading Down Under.

CROSS OF IRON

(1977, dir: Sam Peckinpah)
James Coburn, James Mason, Maximillian Schell.
● YUGOSLAVIA

Peckinpah's only war movie, shot in what was northern Yugoslavia, in the area between Trieste and Zagreb. A deserted factory complex at **Obrov**, about 20 miles southeast of Trieste, was the setting for the scenes in the trenches.

CROW, THE

(1994, dir: Alex Proyas)
Brandon Lee, Ernie Hudson, Michael Wincott.
● NORTH CAROLINA

Dark, gothic thriller, notorious for the on-set accident which killed Brandon Lee. The Detroit setting was recreated almost entirely on the backlot of the De Laurentiis Studio, **Wilmington**, North Carolina. A few interiors were found in Wilmington itself, the town familiar as Lumbertown in David Lynch's *Blue Velvet*.

CRUEL INTENTIONS

(1999, dir: Roger Kumble)
Sarah Michelle Gellar, Ryan Phillippe, Reese Witherspoon.
● NEW YORK; LOS ANGELES, CALIFORNIA

The Valmont house: Fifth Avenue

First-time director Roger Kumble's updating of *Les Liaisons Dangereuses* as a dark teen movie is set in New York high society, but much of it was actually filmed in LA. Mrs Rosemont's house, the country estate, is **Old Westbury Gardens** on Long Island (see *North By Northwest* for details). The interior of the house filmed in two mansions and a hotel on the West Coast. The interiors are both in the exclusive Hancock Park district of LA – one the **Otis Chandler Mansion**, the other the home of screenwriter Shane Black; while the indoor swimming pool, where Sebastian Valmont (Phillippe) gives innocent virgin Annette Hargrove (Witherspoon) an eyefull, is the **Biltmore Hotel, 506 South Grand Avenue**, downtown LA (see *Ghostbusters* for details of this familiar location). Also in Hancock Park is the old people's home, where Sebastian and Annette do good works, which is the **Ebell Club, 743 South Lucerne Boulevard** (see *Forrest Gump* for details of this popular location). The interior of Cecile's (Selma Blair), where she takes cello lessons, is on **Blue Jay Way** in the Hollywood Hills. The shrink's office of the opening scene is downtown LA, and Blaine Tuttle's (Joshua Jackson) modern place is in **Brentwood**.

The Valmont house is the **Ukranian Cultural Center, Fifth Avenue** at 79th Street. The interior of Witherspoon's home is the **Marriott Essex House Hotel, 160 Central Park South**. The dress shop, where Kathryn Merteuil (Gellar) passes on a bit of gossip, is on **Robertson Boulevard**, LA; while Penn Station, where Sebastian enjoys a moist-eyed reconciliation with Annette, is actually one of the stations on the new subway system in downtown LA.

Kathryn finally gets her comeuppance at Sebastian's

memorial service at **All Saints Church, 132 North Euclid Avenue, Pasadena** (seen also in *Legally Blonde* and *The Other Sister*).

CRUISING
(1980, dir: William Friedkin)
Al Pacino, Karen Allen, Paul Sorvino.
● **NEW YORK CITY**

Pacino goes into the closet as an undercover cop investigating a series of bloody murders connected to New York's gay S&M scene in this voyeuristic, homophobic exploitationer from the director of the gay self-loathefest, *Boys in the Band*. It was filmed on location around New York, despite much noisy disruption from gay activist groups who got wind of the project.

Friedkin did manage to film in real leather bars, many of which are still in existence, including the **Badlands, 388 West Street** at Christopher Street in Greenwich Village. The gay sex shop is next door, the **Underground Erotic Emporium, 390 West Street** at Dock Strip. Other locales include the **Eagle's Nest, 142 Eleventh Avenue** at West 21st Street in Chelsea; and around the famous gay areas of Christopher Street and West Street in the Village. The notorious S&M Hellfire Club (seen in *Basket Case*) became one of the leather bars. Gentrification continues in the West Village and the building now houses classy Italian restaurant **Vento, 14th Street** at Ninth Avenue in the Red Triangle Building (which became Ed Harris's apartment block in *The Hours*). Police scenes were filmed at **Police Plaza** in the **Municipal Building, 1 Center Street** at Chambers Street.

CRY-BABY
(1990, dir: John Waters)
Johnny Depp, Amy Locane, Ricki Lake.
● **BALTIMORE, MARYLAND; MARYLAND**

Mainstream, post-Divine Waters without the shock value of the earlier pictures but still with a great sense of camp and a cast including Joe Dallesandro, Patty Hearst, Willem Dafoe and former porn star Traci Lords. It's a pastiche of fifties teen flicks, centring on the running battle between the Straights and the Drapes, with Depp as the badboy crybaby leader of the Drapes. And, of course, it has to be Baltimore. Turkey Point, the redneck Riviera hangout of the Drapes, is the **Milford Mill Swim Club, 3900 Milford Mill Road, Windsor Mill**. Depp ends up incarcerated in the **Maryland House of Correction**.

CRY FREEDOM
(1987, dir: Richard Attenborough)
Kevin Kline, Penelope Wilton, Denzel Washington.
● **ZIMBABWE**

Attenborough follows *Gandhi* with another liberal epic, charting Donald Woods' escape from South Africa after the death in custody of his friend Steve Biko. It was not shot in South Africa. According to Woods, an irate South African film producer announced he was filming his own version – *Biko: the True Story* – thus demonstrating the country's freedom of expression. The producer's offices were raided by the Security Police and the film was never made.

Location filming for *Cry Freedom* was in neighbouring Zimbabwe, largely in and around the capital Harare. It was here, in the well-to-do suburb of **Avondale**, that the exterior of the Woods' house was built on a vacant lot on **Ridge Road** (interiors were filmed back at Shepperton Studios). Woods' newspaper office is in central Harare; the flashback to Biko's cross-examination at the SASO trial was shot in the **High Court, Harare**; the Soweto demonstrations were staged in **Bulawayo**; Biko (Washington) takes Woods (Kline) to see how South African blacks live at **Mbare township**; he addresses football game spectators at **Gweru**; Biko's fatal incarceration was shot in real police cells in Harare. The King Williams Town mortuary, where Woods views Biko's body, is a gymnasium in **Mutare**, and the funeral, involving 15,000 Shona extras, was shot in the **Chibuku Stadium**, a soccer ground in the Harare suburb of **Chitungwiza**.

Woods begins hitching to freedom from **Gweru**; the town of **Shurugwi** stands in for Stutterheim – the **Grand Hotel** here, closed for more than a year, was partly renovated for the New Year's Eve party; the border post at Telle Bridge was constructed by the **Macheke River**, near the border with Mozambique; Woods' arrival at Maseru was shot at Mutare. Maseru Airport is the **Charles Prince Airport**, a small civil airfield for charter flights about 11 miles west of Harare; Johannesburg Airport is in fact **Sandown Racetrack** in England.

CRYING GAME, THE
(1992, dir: Neil Jordan)
Stephen Rea, Jaye Davidson, Miranda Richardson.
● **IRELAND; LONDON**

IRA man Rea becomes involved with the partner of the British soldier he was supposed to kill. The opening Irish scenes were filmed on location at **Laytown** in South Armagh. Rea moves to London and meets up with hairdresser Dil

The attack on the judge: Eaton Place

(Davidson's Oscar nomination was for Best Actor, giving away the big plot twist) at Millie's Hairdressing Salon, Spitalfields, in reality an empty clothing factory at **3 Fournier Street**. The Metro Bar, where Davidson sings the title song, was the London Apprentice pub, a famous gay bar at **333 Old Street**, now a straight pub simply called **333**. The exterior, however, is an empty property behind the pub on the corner of the quaintly cobbled **Coronet Street** and Boot Street, Hoxton, N1. The 'Metro'

logo is still visible. The wasteland behind, where Rea sorts out Davidson's problem, has since been built up. The gardens where he skulks to

Dil's salon: Fournier Street, Spitalfields

Exterior of the Metro Bar: Coronet Street, Hoxton

Jaye Davidson's apartment: Hoxton Square

watch Davidson are in nearby **Hoxton Square**. Davidson's apartment, where the goldfish meet a sad end on the pavement, is **9 Hoxton Square**.

Irish terrorist Miranda Richardson spies on the couple at the **Clifton Restaurant, 126 Brick Lane**, E1. Davidson follows Rea to the, now closed, Lowndes Arms, **37 Chesham Street**, SW1 (now a private home), northeast of Sloane Square, which happens to be opposite the 'discreet knocking shop' where the IRA carry out their bloodily bungled attack on the judge, **100 Eaton Place**.

CUL-DE-SAC

(1966, dir: Roman Polanski)
Donald Pleasence, Lionel Stander, Jack MacGowran.
● **NORTHUMBERLAND**

Absurdist black comedy, with Stander and MacGowran as unlikely gangsters terrorising Donald Pleasence, sporting an even more unlikely frock, in his remote island castle. Shot in bleak monochrome on the island of **Lindisfarne**, off the coast of Northumberland.

CURSE OF FRANKENSTEIN, THE

(1957, dir: Terence Fisher)
Peter Cushing, Christopher Lee, Hazel Court.
● **BUCKINGHAMSHIRE**

The movie that put Hammer films on the map, when the studio decided to remake the 1931 Universal classic in colour, with splodges of gore and body parts. After a spate of legal wrangling with Universal, who jealously guarded their contribution to the story and copyrighted the make-up design (which is why Lee looks such a mess), Hammer began their production line of horrors. Baron Frankenstein's Swiss chateau, steeped in gloom to disguise its Englishness, is Oakley Court, now the **Oakley Court Hotel**, next door to Hammer's Bray Studios in Buckinghamshire, where the rest of the movie – and most of their subsequent output – was shot. See *The Rocky Horror Picture Show*, which also filmed here, for details of Oakley Court. And, yes, that is Melvyn Hayes playing the young Frankenstein.

CURSE OF THE CRIMSON ALTAR

(1968, dir: Vernon Sewell)
Boris Karloff, Christopher Lee, Rupert Davies.
● **MIDDLESEX; HERTFORDSHIRE**

Great cast, and a good photographer in John Coquillon – who did such an excellent job on the English countryside

in *Witchfinder General* – are wasted in this occult thriller from the team who brought you giant moths in *The Blood Beast Terror*. And wouldn't you know it, it's the very same location. The 1870 Norman Shaw house was once home to lyricist W S Gilbert (of Gilbert and Sullivan), who ultimately drowned in its lake. It's now the **Grim's Dyke Hotel, Old Redding** at Harrow Weald north of Harrow off the A409 (*www.grimsdyke.com*). Apart from horror movies, the house has been used for *The Prime of Miss Jean Brodie* and the semi-documentary *It Happened Here*. The local village in the movie is **Ridge Village**, three miles west of Potters Bar in Hertfordshire.

The cursed house: Grim's Dyke Hotel

CYRANO DE BERGERAC

(1990, dir: Jean-Paul Rappeneau)
Gerard Depardieu, Anne Brochet, Vincent Perez.
● **FRANCE; HUNGARY**

Lavishly filmed version of Edmund Rostand's verse drama – the precursor of all Hollywood self-sacrificing 'women's weepies' – with Depardieu in excellent form as the poet-swordsman afraid to declare his love because of his spectacularly outsize nose. The movie was shot in various picturesque towns around France.

The town on the river, where Cyrano first reveals his feelings for Roxane, is **Moret-sur-Loing**, about 45 miles southeast of Paris, near Fontainebleau in the Ile-de-France region. Impressionist Alfred Sisley lived here until his death in 1899 and it features in many of his paintings. The streets where Cyrano acts mad and stalks de Guiche are in **Le Mans** (home of the 24-hour Grand Prix), 125 miles southwest of Paris on the River Sarthe in the Loire valley. The gothic walls and flying buttresses in the background are the superb Medieval **Cathedral of Saint-Julien**, last resting place of Richard the Lionheart's widow, Queen Berengaria. Other period backgrounds include the town of **Dijon**, the capital of Burgundy in the Côte d'Or; and **Uzes**, 15 miles north of Nimes in the Languedoc-Rousillon area.

The abbey where the dying Cyrano is finally reunited with Roxane is the **Abbey de Fontenaye**, three miles northeast of the little industrial town of Montbard, northwest of Dijon. Founded by St Bernard in 1118, the abbey was turned into a paper mill during the Revolution but restored in 1906.

The interiors and the balcony scene were filmed in **Budapest Studios**, Hungary, while the Battle of Arras was staged on Budapest's outskirts.

D

DAHONG DENGLONG GAOGAO GUA (aka
Raise the Red Lantern)
(1991, dir: Zhang Yimou)
Li Gong, Jingwu Ma, Caifei He.
● SHANXI PROVINCE

Yimou's ravishingly beautiful movie was shot in the old preserved **Qiao family villa** in **Qiaojiabao** near **Taiyuan**, the capital of Shanxi province, China. It's open as a museum. You can find details of a tour to the mansion from Shanghai at *www.shanghaitonight.com*.

DAM BUSTERS, THE
(1954, dir: Michael Anderson)
Michael Redgrave, Richard Todd, Ursula Jeans.
● LINCOLNSHIRE; LAKE DISTRICT, CUMBRIA; WALES

Michael Redgrave is Barnes Wallis, inventor of the bouncing bomb which effectively destroyed German dams during WWII. The airfield scenes were filmed on the actual location of **Scampton** (also used for the 1990 WWII airborne movie *Memphis Belle*), about five miles north of Lincoln in Lincolnshire, and at the village of **Hemswell**, a few miles further north. The testing of the bouncing bombs was staged at **Gibraltar Point**, on the Lincolnshire coast near Skegness, while a second unit crew filmed attacks on the dams at **Lake Windemere** in the Lake District and at **Elan Valley** in Powys, Wales.

DAMNED, THE (aka *These Are the Damned*)
(1961, dir: Joseph Losey)
Macdonald Carey, Shirley Anne Field, Oliver Reed.
● DORSET

Strange, creepy sci-fi about a bunch of radioactive kids kept sealed underground. An English film from American director Losey, made for Hammer Films, and shot around the seaside resort of **Weymouth** in Dorset, where the children are imprisoned in caves within the cliffs to the north of the town.

DANCE WITH A STRANGER
(1985, dir: Mike Newell)
Miranda Richardson, Rupert Everett, Ian Holm.
● LONDON

Straightforward account of the case of Ruth Ellis (Richardson), the last woman to be hanged for murder in Britain, after shooting her wastrel upper class boyfriend David Blakeley (Everett). Set in the fifties, the street exteriors were mostly filmed in tight close-up to avoid the necessity of extensive period dressing. The entrance to the nightclub ("These places are glori-

The shooting at the Magdala Tavern: Three Kings, Clerkenwell

The West End nightclub: Wellington Court, Knightsbridge

fied brothels...") where the sadly devoted Desmond Cussen (Holm) introduces Blakeley to Ellis, is the side entrance to the grand **Wellington Court**, in the tiny passageway of **Park Close**, Knightsbridge.

It was outside the Magdala Tavern, South Hill Park, NW3, opposite Hampstead Heath railway station that David Blakeley was gunned down. The pub still exists, and bullet holes can still be seen in the tiles of its frontage. The Magdala is not a particularly photogenic pub though, and the film substitutes the much more picturesque **Three Kings, 7 Clerkenwell Close, Clerkenwell** (close to many of the locations of *About A Boy*), where Ellis lurks with her pistol behind the railings of **St James Clerkenwell Church**.

DANCES WITH WOLVES
(1990, dir: Kevin Costner)
Kevin Costner, Mary McDonnell, Graham Greene.
● SOUTH DAKOTA; WYOMING; KANSAS

'Kevin's Gate' jeered the cynics during this first directorial effort, but a Best Picture Oscar got Costner the last laugh. The soft-centred but well-meaning tear-jerker was filmed on location in South Dakota, mainly near the **Triple U Standing Butte Ranch** outside **Pierre**, on Route 14 at the Missouri River, central South Dakota, where 3,500 buffalo constitute the world's largest privately-owned herd. The herd dictated the location, and the location in turn necessitated changing the subjects of the story from the Comanche of Oklahoma and Texas – as in Michael Blake's original novel – to the Sioux.

The Tennessee civil war battle was also filmed outside Pierre. The winter camp is **Spearfish Canyon** outside Rapid City, Route 90 in southwest South Dakota. Native Americans were recruited as extras from the Rosebud, Pine Ridge and Eagle Butte Reservations.

Costner sets out from Fort Hays, Kansas, about 100 miles west of Salina on I-70. A purpose-built set was constructed about four miles south of Rapid City, and the buildings have since been re-sited as a tourist attraction on Tomahawk Drive.

The wagon ride from Fort Hayes to Fort Sedgewick was filmed in the **Sage Creek Wilderness Area** of **Badlands National Park**, while a Second Unit shot the spectacular scenery of **Jackson**, Wyoming.

DANGEROUS LIAISONS
(1988, dir: Stephen Frears)
John Malkovich, Glenn Close, Michelle Pfeiffer.
● FRANCE

Lush adaptation of Christopher Hampton's play of Laclos' novel, *Les Liaisons Dangereuses*. The thuddingly literal title translation was a reaction to the assumption that foreign movies are box office poison in the US. It was filmed largely at the **Chateau de Champs-sur-Marne**, overlooking the Marne about 12 miles east of Paris. The 18th century chateau was rented by Madame de Pompadour, who spent a small fortune on improvements (the original owner, who had gone bankrupt, keeled over and died on its steps as he was about to be arrested).

The country house of Mme de Rosemonde (Mildred Natwick) is **Chateau Maisons-Lafitte**, a superb 17th century French Renaissance chateau about 12 miles northwest of Paris, in which Louis XIV, XV and XVI stayed.

The theatre where the Gluck opera is performed is the **Theatre Montansier**, alongside the Palace of Versailles.

Des Moulins' printing shop: Cour de Commerce St Andre

Moulins (played by brilliant opera and theatre director Patrice Chereau), closed down by the revolutionary guards, is the Via Gallery on the **Cour de Commerce St Andre** opposite the rear entrance to the historic Le Procope café (one of the world's oldest cafés, its patrons have included Rousseau, Voltaire, Balzac and Benjamin Franklin as well as revolutionaries Marat, Napoleon and the real Robespierre and Danton. The entrance is at 13 rue l'Ancienne Comedie). A prototype guillotine was supposedly set up outside number 9 Cour de Commerce St Andre, St Germain-des-Pres (*metro: Odeon*).

DAREDEVIL
(2003, dir: Mark Steven Johnson)
Ben Affleck, Jennifer Garner, Colin Farrell.
● NEW YORK CITY, NEW YORK; LOS ANGELES, CALIFORNIA

Director Johnson has a fanboy's enthusiasm and knowledge of Stan Lee's comic strip, but he doesn't have the cinematic technique to light up the screen. That job is left to Colin Farrell's Bullseye, with the kind of scenery-chewing brio not witnessed since Bette Davis hurricaned through the fifties. And isn't this exactly the same plot as

DANTON
(1982, dir: Andrzej Wajda)
Gerard Depardieu, Wojciech Pszoniak, Patrice Chereau.
● FRANCE

Veteran Polish director Wajda filmed an adaptation of the play *The Danton Affair* by Stanislawa Przybszewska, about the rift between revolutionary puritan Robespierre and the libertarian Danton, shot around Paris. The printing shop belonging to Camille Des

Batman? Set in New York's notorious, and largely gone, 'Hell's Kitchen' district, the filming locale is largely downtown LA, on rooftops surounding **Fifth Street** and **Broadway**.

Matt Murdock's apartment block: Arcade Building, South Broadway

LA's Olympic Auditorium is usually the venue for boxing or wrestling scenes in the movies (see *Ed Wood*, *Rocky* and *Raging Bull* for starters) and,

Bullseye plays darts in the English pub: Ye Olde King's Head, Santa Monica Boulevard

seemingly true to form, the Red Devil wrestles at the Olympic. The frontage seen, though, is the old (and closed) **Olympic Theater, 313 West 8th Street**, downtown LA (where Charlton Heston watches *Woodstock* in 1971 horror flick *The Omega Man*), while the backstage scenes use the bowels of the **Ambassador Hotel, 3400 Wilshire Boulevard** (see *A Star Is Born*, 1937 and 1954, for details),

The Olympic venue: The Olympic Theater, West Eighth Street

The apartment of Matt Murdock (Affleck) is the **Arcade Building, 542 South Broadway** between Fifth and Sixth Streets (which also served as the movie's HQ). The black and white party, where Murdock takes the opportunity to confront Kingpin (Michael Clarke Duncan) is the **Millennium Biltmore Hotel, 506 South Grand Avenue** (see *Beverly Hills Cop* for full details). Even the English pub, where Bullseye demonstrates the lethal potential of the humble paperclip, is LA. You can test your accuracy at the dartboards of **Ye Olde King's Head, 116 Santa Monica Boulevard**, a British expat watering hole in Santa Monica.

DARK PASSAGE
(1947, dir: Delmer Daves)
Humphrey Bogart, Lauren Bacall, Agnes Moorehead.
● SAN FRANCISCO, CALIFORNIA

A framed convict escapes, meets Lauren Bacall and is transformed by plastic surgery into Humphrey Bogart. To avoid showing the pre-Bogie face, the entire opening sequence of the movie uses a radical subjective point-of-view.

The prison Bogart escapes from, in a barrel, is **San Quentin**, Marin County, across the bay from San Francisco. If you want to visit this notorious facility, there's a Visitor Center and Museum. You'll need to call

Lauren Bacall's stunning apartment: Montgomery Street

ahead to book (© *415.454.8808*), and remember to take along photographic ID. The impressive spinning barrel shot is repeated in another San Fran-based movie, *Foul Play*.

On the road south, Bacall is stopped and questioned by the law, in a scene adapted this time by Hitchcock for *Psycho*. Crossing the Golden Gate Bridge, she gets an attack of paranoia by the marvellous art deco toll gates. The gates have, however, been updated since the forties. Amazingly unchanged is Bacall's impossibly stylish deco apartment, where Bogart hides out. It looks like an art director's fantasy, but you can still see the silver, white and glass marvel at **1360 Montgomery Street** at Filbert Street. When the house was up for sale in 1996, a lifesize cutout of Bogart was cheekily exhibited in the window. It's at the top of the **Filbert Steps**, the endless stairs Bogart struggles up after his plastic surgery at the beginning of the movie.

DARKMAN

(1990, dir: Sam Raimi)
Liam Neeson, Frances McDormand, Larry Drake.
● **LOS ANGELES, CALIFORNIA**

It didn't bust any blocks, but Raimi's zingy comic strip adventure put the director on the road to *Spider-Man*. Raimi had wanted to make *The Shadow* but, when he couldn't get the rights to the character, invented his own damaged anti-hero: Peyton Westlake (Neeson), hideously scarred and left for dead, but – happily – working on a formula for artificial skin.

The Strack HQ, where Julie Hastings (McDormand) investigates corruption, is, of course, the familiar **Westin Bonaventure Hotel, 404 South Figueroa Street**, downtown LA. Darkman spies on henchman Pauly, and later impersonates him, at **Erny's Best Deli, 1645 Vine Street** at Hollywood Boulevard, Hollywood. The unfortunate Pauly is subsequently flung from an upper window of the **Hotel Rosslyn, 112 West 5th Street**, downtown LA. The Strack Industries City of the Future ball is held in the **Wilshire Ebell Theatre**. You can see the building's Renaissance-style façade at **4401 West 8th Street** near Lucerne Boulevard, midtown (see *Forrest Gump* for full details). Darkman (in the guise of villain Durant) visits Hung Fat at **Hong Kong Low, 425 Gin Ling Way** in Chinatown, downtown LA.

DARLING

(1965, dir: John Schlesinger)
Julie Christie, Dirk Bogarde, Laurence Harvey.
● **LONDON; BUCKINGHAMSHIRE; SURREY; FLORENCE, ITALY**

An Oscar for Christie as the ambitious actress ending up as – would you believe? – 'Princess Diana', trapped in a loveless marriage, in this cynical satire from Schlesinger.

Diana Scott (Christie) flirts with TV producer Robert Gold (Bogarde, in a part originally written as a US columnist and intended for Montgomery Clift) on the

Bogarde's home: South End Road, Belsize Park

Thames foreshore by **Strand on the Green** at Chiswick, W4. Bogarde's family home is on **South End Road**, Belsize Park overlooking Hampstead Heath, NW3.

Christie retreats to the country at **Skindles** in Maidenhead. She meets Miles Brand (Harvey) at his pad at **40-41 Wimpole Street**, W1, goes shoplifting with Roland Curram at **Fortnum and Mason's** in Piccadilly and lives unhappily ever after in Rome, actually a palazzo in Florence.

DAWN OF THE DEAD (aka *Zombies*)

(1978, dir: George A Romero)
David Emge, Ken Foree, Scott Reiniger.
● **PENNSYLVANIA**

Second of Romero's zombie trilogy finds the crumbly flesh-eaters taking over a suburban shopping mall – cue satire on consumerism. The mall is the huge 143-shop **Oxford Developments Mall, Monroeville**, 30 miles southeast of Pittsburgh, Pennsylvania, on I-76. Surprisingly, 130 of the stores in the mall cooperated with shooting. One local bank even loaned $20,000 in notes for the scene where now-useless money flutters through the air (it was covered by a cheque to cover losses). The rooftop hideout (there isn't one in the mall) was an empty warehouse in downtown Pittsburgh.

DAY AT THE RACES, A

(1937, dir: Sam Wood)
The Marx Brothers, Margaret Dumont, Allan Jones.
● **LOS ANGELES, CALIFORNIA**

The racetrack: Santa Anita Racetrack, Arcadia

This mid-period Marx-ism, with the brothers causing chaos at the races, was shot at the **Santa Anita Racetrack, 285 West Huntington Boulevard, Arcadia**, between LA and Pasadena. With its towering palms and distinctive green and yellow wrought ironwork, the Santa Anita has been a favourite with Hollywood punters since 1934 (it's where James Mason fell off the wagon in the 1954 *A Star Is Born*).

DAY OF THE DEAD

(1985, dir: George A Romero)
G Howard Klar, Ralph Marrero, John Amplas.
● **PENNSYLVANIA; FLORIDA**

Third of Romero's zombie trilogy finds the zombies vastly outnumbering the living, who are holed up in an underground bunker and indulging in some nastiness of their own. Most of the filming took place in a limestone mine at **Wampum**, 35 miles northwest of Pittsburgh, toward New Castle, Pennsylvania. The giant elevator to the underground compound was the Nike missile base outside Pittsburgh, though the entrance (the elevator platform) was built in a field on **Sanibel Island**, off the west coast of Florida, near Fort Myers. Sanibel Island was also used for the beach from which the heroes manage to escape at the end of the movie. The city of the dead, rendered suitably decayed for the filming, is **Fort Myers** itself.

DAY OF THE JACKAL, THE

(1973, dir: Fred Zinnemann)
Edward Fox, Michel Lonsdale, Eric Porter.

● FRANCE; AUSTRIA; ITALY; LONDON

In 1963, the OAS hires a professional hitman to assassinate General de Gaulle. Zinneman's detailed, episodic filming of Frederick Forsyth's novel was filmed all over Europe.

Fox, the coldly professional gunman, initially meets up with the OAS leaders in Vienna's **Prater** park, home of the familiar Big Wheel, seen in *The Third Man*.

The assassination attempt on De Gaulle: Rue de Rennes, Montparnasse

The UK locations are now largely defunct: Fox consults *Le Figaro* in the old circular **Reading Room** at the **British Museum Library**. He gets a false birth certificate at **Somerset House** in the **Strand**, where all UK births, marriages and deaths were recorded until the register moved to St Catherine's House. Somerset House has since found fame as a regular movie location, in *GoldenEye* (as St Petersburg), *Portrait of a Lady*, *Wilde* and others. The British police operate from the old **Scotland Yard** building on **Victoria Embankment** north of Westminster Bridge, SW1.

The town where Fox collects his customised packaway gun from Cyril Cusack and his fake ID from Ronald Pickup, is **Genova** on the coast of northern Italy. His fraught border crossing back into France is at **Ventimiglia** on the coast road a few miles east of Monaco. He meets up with Delphine Seyrig in a hotel, supposedly near Grasse, ten miles northwest of Cannes on the N85, but actually a dilapidated chateau near Paris, and he catches his train to Paris at **Tulle**, arriving at the **Gare d'Austerlitz**, Place Valhubert on the Quai d'Austerlitz.

The Jackal makes his attempt on de Gaulle from a hotel window opposite the Montparnasse Bienvenue metro station. The hotel can be seen virtually unchanged at **150 rue de Rennes** on the place du 18 Juin 1940, at the boulevard du Montparnasse.

DAY OF THE LOCUST, THE

(1975, dir: John Schlesinger)
William Atherton, Karen Black, Burgess Meredith.

● LOS ANGELES, CALIFORNIA

The madness of Hollywood in the thirties leads naïve art director Tod Hackett (Atherton) to apocalyptic visions of the burning of LA. Schlesinger's film

The movie producer's home: Ennis-Brown House, Glendower Avenue

of Nathanael West's bitingly satirical novel so perfectly captures the feel of thirties LA that, like *Chinatown*, it's surprising to find that much of the movie was filmed on the Paramount lot, including the apartments of Atherton and Black. The design of Atherton's San Bernardino Arms apartment was based on the home of author West, where he wrote *Day of the Locust*, the mock-Tudor Parva Sed Apartments, 1817 North Ivar Street, Hollywood (which are just down the road from the Alto Nido Apartments, at 1851, where scribe William Holden tapped the keys in *Sunset Blvd.*).

Karen Black's kitschy pink stucco cottage is also on the Paramount backlot, the blue sky behind it no more than a painted backdrop, which meant that filming had to be ended each day when shadows of telegraph poles began to creep across the 'sky'.

And as ever, the Hollywood sign is not real. It is, in reality, quite inaccessible. You certainly can't drive up to it. Two letters of the sign were erected in a more convenient area of the Hollywood Hills.

But there are real locations: the posh bordello, which supplies wannabe-actress Faye (Black) with a little part-time work, is a mansion, **1240 Cerro Crest Drive** in Beverly Hills, once owned by stripper Gypsy Rose Lee. The movie producer's house, with a horse in the swimming pool, is Frank Lloyd Wright's glorious Mayan pyramid-style **Ennis-Brown House, 2607 Glendower Avenue** below Griffith Park in Los Feliz (for details of this much-used location, see *The House on Haunted Hill*). Harry Greener (Meredith) attempts to sell his patent medicine in the scarily exclusive neighbourhood of **Whitley Heights**, modelled on an Italianate village, and reputedly where Bette Davis lived in *Now, Voyager*. If it's not yet gated, as many exclusive streets now are, it can be reached by Milner Road off Highland Avenue, south of the Hollywood Bowl.

When Meredith succumbs to a heart attack, his funeral service is conducted at the 1930s deco Mausoleum of **Inglewood Memorial Park Cemetery**, northeast corner of **Manchester Avenue** at Prairie Avenue, Inglewood, south Central LA. Big Sister's Temple, where Geraldine Page works miracles, is the ballroom of the old **Hollywood Palladium**, big band mecca of the forties, at

Big Sister's Temple: Hollywood Palladium, Sunset Boulevard

6215 Sunset Boulevard, and site of the geeky fan convention in sci-fi spoof *Galaxy Quest*.

The movie studio at the centre of the action is, of course, **Paramount, 5451 Marathon Street**. See that other great exposé of Tinseltown, *Sunset Blvd.* for further details of the Paramount lot.

The climactic riot is triggered by Homer Simpson. Yes, that's the name of Donald Sutherland's sad, simmering loner who finally flips out and attacks a ghastly child star in front of a horrified crowd. The ensuing apocalypse uses not the real Hollywood Boulevard but a gigantic studio recreation of three blocks, centring on Grauman's Chinese Theatre, 6925 Hollywood Boulevard, which allowed for the addition of a convenient, if nonexistent, street directly opposite the famous movie palace.

DAY OF THE TRIFFIDS, THE
(1962, dir: Steve Sekely)
Howard Keel, Nicole Maurey, Kieron Moore.
● **LONDON; SPAIN**

Disastrous filming of John Wyndham's sci-fi novel about killer plants from space. The troubled production all but ended the director's career. Of the 300 mechanical triffids built, only seven full-sized monsters eventually made it onto the screen. Plus, when the assembled film ran a mere 55 minutes, veteran Freddie Francis was brought in to shoot a totally unconnected subplot about Moore and Janette Scott trapped in a Cornish lighthouse. The dazzling meteor shower blinds most of the world's population, apart from Howard Keel who is recovering from an eye operation in London's **Moorfield Eye Hospital, City Road**, EC1. The blinded train driver crashes into, and causes a panic at, **Marylebone Station**, NW1. Keel goes to find his ship via **Piccadilly Circus**, **Charing Cross** and **Westminster Bridge**. The climax of the movie takes place in **Alicante**, Spain.

DAY THE EARTH CAUGHT FIRE, THE
(1961, dir: Val Guest)
Edward Judd, Janet Munro, Leo McKern.
● **LONDON**

A surprisingly downbeat and detailed sci-fi, with global warming going to extremes after nuclear tests tilt the earth's axis – it also contains the priceless credit: 'Beatnik music by Monty Norman'. Much of the realism comes from the decision to film in the old black glass, deco office of the *Daily Express*, **121 Fleet Street**, EC4. The newspaper editor is actually played by Arthur Christiansen, the *Express'* editor for 25 years, who also acted as technical advisor. Although the *Express* has moved out, the office still stands on Fleet Street. Peer in at the dazzling gold lobby, to glimpse a bit of Manhattan sophistication in the City. Gone, though, is Harry's, the real bar where the journalists gather, which stood across the street.

The Met Centre, where reporter Judd tries to ferret out the truth, is actually the **Board of Trade Building** in Westminster. The CND rally filmed, of course, in **Trafalgar Square**, in the days when anti-bomb protesters regularly marched from Aldermaston, between Reading and Newbury. Judd takes his son to the old

Battersea Funfair. The famous fair finally closed for good in the 1970s, but you can still visit the site in Battersea Park on the south bank of the Thames across from Chelsea.

DAY THE EARTH STOOD STILL, THE
(1951, dir: Robert Wise)
Michael Rennie, Patricia Neal, Hugh Marlowe.
● **WASHINGTON DC**

"Klaatu barada nikto": Ellipse

"Klaatu barada nikto" intones Klaatu (Rennie), famously, as he arrives on Earth accompanied by robot Gort, on a mission to stop all wars. Wise's classic was filmed in Washington DC, with the flying saucer touching down on the **Ellipse**, the 52-acre green oval between the White House and the Mall.

DAYS OF HEAVEN
(1978, dir: Terrence Malick)
Richard Gere, Brooke Adams, Sam Shepard.
● **ALBERTA, CANADA**

Hardships of farmlife in the Texas panhandle during the early 1900s. Visually one of the most stunning movies ever, with the cinematography of the late Nestor Almendros picking up a well-deserved Oscar. Reclusive director Malick had made only one other movie, the superb *Badlands*, and didn't make another until *The Thin Red Line* in 1998.

Days of Heaven was filmed, not in Texas at all, but at **Banff** and **Lethbridge** in Alberta, Canada, among an Amish-like people called Hutterites whose way of life, set apart from modern society, pretty much approximated the period of the movie. Authentic grain silos and steam driven farm machines were loaned by private collectors.

Unbelievably, the original 70mm prints of this visual masterpiece were lost forever when a studio employee, ordered to trash unwanted reels of the Tom Cruise boyracer flop *Days of Thunder*, destroyed the wrong title.

DAYS OF WINE AND ROSES
(1962, dir: Blake Edwards)
Jack Lemmon, Lee Remick, Charles Bicford.
● **CALIFORNIA**

John Frankenheimer directed the original television version of JP Miller's heavy-handed script about a young couple's plunge into alcoholism, but Edwards was hired to leaven the gloom with a little humour. Set in, and largely filmed around, San Francisco, the home of Joe and Kirsten Clay (Lemmon and Remick) is **1800 Pacific Avenue**, between Franklin Street and Gough Street.

DAZED AND CONFUSED
(1993, dir: Richard Linklater)
Jason London, Joey Lauren Adams, Milla Jovovich.
● **TEXAS**

More Texan slackers from Linklater, and once again the location is the state capital, Austin, along with **Georgetown**, about 20 miles north on I-35. Robert E Lee High is **Bedichek Middle School, 6800 Bill Hughes Road** in Austin, and the local burger joint is the **Top Notch Restaurant, 7525 Burnet Road**. The alfresco party filmed in **West Enfield Park**, beneath the Moontower that the lads attempt to climb, the towering lighting system built for the local power plant.

DEAD, THE

(1987, dir: John Huston)
Angelica Huston, Donal McCann, Rachael Dowling.
● **DUBLIN, IRELAND; CALIFORNIA**

Director John Huston was seriously ailing when he came to film this James Joyce story, and the interiors for what turned out to be his final film were shot in a warehouse north of LA in Valencia, on I-5. The exteriors, though, really are Dublin. The house is **15 Ushers Island**. Other genuine Irish locations include the **Halfpenny Bridge** over the Liffey; **Temple Bar**; **Anglesea Street**; and **Henrietta Street**.

House of the dead: Ushers Island

DEAD CALM

(1989, dir: Philip Noyce)
Nicole Kidman, Sam Neill, Billy Zane.
● **QUEENSLAND, AUSTRALIA**

Shipbound suspenser, with wacko Zane threatening Kidman and Neill aboard their yacht, filmed at **Hamilton Island**, Queensland, and at **Whitsunday Passage** on the Great Barrier Reef.

DEAD MAN

(1996, dir: Jim Jarmusch)
Johnny Depp, Gary Farmer, Lance Henriksen.
● **ARIZONA; OREGON; WASHINGTON**

Strange black and white Western from Jarmusch, shot in **Cococina National Forest, Sedona**; **Camp Verde** and **Peoria**, Arizona; **Grants Pass**, Oregon; and **Neah Bay**, Washington State.

DEAD MEN DON'T WEAR PLAID

(1982, dir: Carl Reiner)
Steve Martin, Rachel Ward, Carl Reiner.
● **LOS ANGELES, CALIFORNIA**

Since Reiner's homage to *films noir* ingeniously incorporates clips from Hollywood classics, most of the movie is filmed on sets which accurately match up to their forties counterparts, but there are a couple of real LA locations, notably **Union Station, 800 North Alameda Street**, downtown, where Martin is followed onto the train by Cary Grant (in a clip from Hitchcock's *Suspicion*). See *Blade Runner* for details of Union Station. Martin researches at **Los Angeles Central Library South Flower Street** at West Fifth Street, downtown LA (see *Ghostbusters* for details). There was also filming at **Mayfield School, 500 Bellefontaine** (seen also in *Devil in a Blue Dress* and *The Lost World: Jurassic Park*).

DEAD OF NIGHT

(1945, dir: Cavalcanti; Charles Crichton; Robert Hamer; Basil Dearden)
Mervyn Johns, Roland Culver, Frederick Valk.
● **BUCKINGHAMSHIRE**

Brilliant compendium of ghost stories framed by a recurring nightmare. Light relief is provided by a golfing ghost story with Basil Radford and Naunton Wayne (the Char-

The ghostly wedding: St Mary the Virgin, Turville

ters and Caldicott team from Hitchcock's *The Lady Vanishes*). The golf course, supposedly the Royal and Ancient at St Andrews in Scotland, is **Stoke Poges Golf Course, Stoke Poges**, (for details, see *Goldfinger*, which uses the same location for Bond's game with Auric Goldfinger). The church where the deceased Wayne haunts Radford's wedding is **St Mary the Virgin** at **Turville**, Buckinghamshire – the village and church also used in the excellent wartime drama, *Went the Day Well*.

DEAD POETS SOCIETY

(1989, dir: Peter Weir)
Robin Williams, Robert Sean Leonard, Ethan Hawke.
● **DELAWARE**

Delaware's only claim to movie fame, so far, is this well-done, if mechanically predictable, tearjerker from the 'inspiring teacher who formed me' genre. Welton Academy is **St Andrew's School, Noxontown Pond Road, Middletown**, a private school situated in 2,000 acres of farmland about two miles from Noxontown Pond, between Wilmington and Dover, northern Delaware.

The theatre where Robert Sean Leonard plays Puck (elevated to "the lead role") in *A Midsummer Night's Dream*, is the historic **Everett Theatre** of St Andrew's, which was renovated specially for the film. The town is the old colonial town of **New Castle**, six miles south of Wilmington on Route 9, where Leonard's father's house is situated, in the affluent suburb of **Westover Hills**. The cave, where the society meets, is **Wolf Cave**, a registered historic landmark, although the interior was recreated in a New Castle warehouse.

DEAD RINGERS

(1988, dir: David Cronenberg)
Jeremy Irons, Genevieve Bujold, Heidi Von Palleske.
● **ONTARIO, CANADA**

Cronenberg's understated but weird drama about identical twin gynaecologists (which should have won Irons the Oscar he later picked up for *Reversal of Fortune*) was filmed in Toronto. You won't be able to eat at either of

Bujold makes a disturbing discovery: The elegant conservatory of Casa Loma

The ending, outside the twins' apartment: Trinity Square Park, Toronto

the film's restaurants. Giannino's, the swanky Italian joint with the elaborate murals has now closed, while the elegant place where Genevieve Bujold discovers she's been dating two men is simply the conservatory of **Casa Loma, 1 Austin Terrace** (for details, see *X-Men*, where this faux-Medieval folly became Professor Xavier's academy). The twins' apartment is **Bell Trinity Square, 483 Bay Street** behind the Eaton Place shopping complex, and it's just outside, in **Trinity Square Park**, that the movie ends.

DEATH IN VENICE

(1971, dir: Luchino Visconti)
Dirk Bogarde, Bjorn Andresen, Silvana Mangano.
● **ITALY**

Aschenbach's hotel: Hotel des Bains, Venice Lido

Suggested by Thomas Mann's slim novella, Visconti's film works as a superb romantic tearjerker with immaculate production design. As in the book, Gustav von Aschenbach's sumptuous hotel is, of course, the **Grand Hotel des Bains, Lungomare Marconi 41**, on the east shore of Venice's Lido, though interiors were filmed at Cinecittà Studios in Rome. The Lido, a narrow sliver of land, nine miles long but barely a mile wide, is a ten minute boat ride from Piazza San Marco. To reach the hotel from the vaporetto stop on the Lido, take Gran Viale Santa Maria Elizabetta across the island to the sandy eastern shore. The Hotel des Bains is is on the corner of Santa Maria Elizabetta, over the main road from the private beach – surprisingly, it's not actually on the beach as it seems to be in the film (don't confuse it with the elaborate Moorish Hotel Excelsior, which *is* on the beach further to the south).

Aschenbach stalks Tadzio: Dietro la Fenice

The hotel is closed during winter months, from November to March (*© 5260201*).

The obsessed Von Aschenbach

follows Tadzio through the maze of tiny canalside paths behind La Fenice opera house, **dietro la Fenice**. The tiny campo, where Aschenbach's questions elicit no more than stony silence, is the **Campiello dei Calegheri**, just west of the opera house. The bank, where the English manager is more forthcoming, is the **Banca Commerciale Italiana**, in the northeast corner of Piazza San Marco. The flashbacks to von Aschenbach's marriage were filmed in a plum orchard about 100 miles northwest of Venice at **Bolzano** in the Dolomites.

Questioning the locals: Campiello dei Calegheri

The truth from the bank manager: Banca Commerciale Italiana, Piazza San Marco

DEATH ON THE NILE

(1978, dir: John Guillermin)
Peter Ustinov, David Niven, Bette Davis.
● **EGYPT; WARWICKSHIRE**

Leaving on the Nile cruise: Hotel Pullman Cataract, Aswan

Forget the plot, enjoy the cast, in this second of the stylishly period, star-studded Agatha Christie adaptations which followed the success of *Murder on the Orient Express*. The country home of ghastly rich bitch, and victim-to-be, Lois Chiles, is **Compton Wynyates** – also the country estate in *Candleshoe* – eight miles west of Banbury in Warwickshire. It's now a private home, and not open to the public.

Chiles and Simon MacCorkindale take off on honeymoon to Egypt, where jilted Mia Farrow follows them to the giant pyramids at **Giza**. You too can follow in their footsteps and climb the Great Pyramid, though be aware it's not officially allowed, and it is quite dangerous. People are regularly killed bouncing down the stone steps. Poirot is first seen here, by the **Sphinx**.

The grand Nile hotel, where everyone assembles and from which the 'Karnak' departs, is the **Hotel Pullman Cataract** (previously and better known as the Old Cataract Hotel), **Sharia Abtal el Tahrir, Aswan** (*© 316000*). The stop-off, where the first attempt at murder on Chiles life occurs when a chunk of rock plummets from an ancient temple, is **Luxor**. The huge temple complex is **Karnak**, where you can see the avenue of ram-headed sphinxes, and the **Temple of Amun** where Chiles is nearly killed. Farrow turns up again at **Abu Simbel**.

DEATH WISH

(1974, dir: Michael Winner)
Charles Bronson, Hope Lange, Vincent Gardenia.
● **NEW YORK CITY, NEW YORK; ARIZONA**

A huge box-office success, but the casting of grizzly tough guy Bronson scuppered the potentially interesting concept of a drippy-liberal conscientious

Bronson's apartment: Riverside, East Side

objector transformed into a vigilante anti-hero only after his wife and daughter have been viciously attacked. Set, and largely filmed, in New York. Bronson's apartment is **33 Riverside** at 75th Street on the East Side, and it's in nearby **Riverside Park**, overlooking the Hudson River, that he blasts his first mugger. The architectural office, where he works, is **2 Park Avenue** at 32nd Street in the Murray Hill district.

Bronson's crusade was originally to have been inspired by a viewing of *High Noon*. When it proved impossible to use clips from Fred Zinnemann's classic, Bronson's inspiration became a business trip to Tucson, Arizona, where he watches an Old West shoot-out at the **Old Tucson Studios, 201 South Kinney Road**, a movie-lot turned tourist attraction near Tucson.

DEER HUNTER, THE

(1978, dir: Michael Cimino)
Robert De Niro, John Cazale, John Savage.
● **PENNSYLVANIA; WEST VIRGINIA; OHIO; WASHINGTON; THAILAND**

The controversial Vietnam movie, accused of both racism and of inaudible dialogue (though it received an Oscar nomination for its sound, and an even more inexplicable nomination for its totally unbelievable script), is nominally set in the blue-collar steeltown of Clairton, about ten miles south of Pittsburgh, Pennsylvania. The town, however, is an amalgamation of eight different locales. Three are in Pennsylvania: the real **Clairton**; **McKeesport**, over the Monongahela River; and **Pittsburgh** itself. Two are towns to the west in the sliver of West Virginia between the Ohio River and Pennsylvania: **Weirton** and **Follansbee**. And three more are just over the Ohio River down in Ohio State: **Steubenville** and **Mingo Junction** on Route 7, and **Struthers**, which is about 25 miles north, near to Youngstown. Similarly, the steelworks, dominating the town, is a different plant from scene to scene. The opening steel factory scenes were shot in US Steel's **Central Blast Furnace, Cleveland**, though only after a nervous studio insured its stars to the tune of $5million – the plant is known locally as the Widowmaker.

The church where John Savage weds Rutanya Alda is Cleveland's **St Theodosius Russian Orthodox Cathedral, 733 Starkweather Avenue**, claimed to be an exact replica of the Czar's cathedral inside the Kremlin, Moscow.

The raucous reception is held in the same city's **Lemko Hall, 2335 West 11th Street**. The Eagle Supermarket, where Meryl Streep works, is also on Starkweather Avenue.

Welsh's Bar, where De Niro and his macho pals play pool, was built behind an existing storefront on **Commercial Street** in **Mingo Junction**. Plenty of product placement here, with all the bottles of Rolling Rock neatly turned to face camera, and De Niro's ringing endorsement, "A good beer – it's the best around." To be fair, it is the local brew, from the Latrobe Brewery between Pittsburgh and Johnstown, Southern Pennsylvania. The bowling alley is the **Bowladrome Lanes, 56 State Street, Struthers**, Ohio.

The deer hunt itself, set in the Allegheny Mountains, was shot 10,000 feet above sea level in the **Heather Meadows** area of **Mount Baker**, Washington State, close to the British Columbian border.

The Vietnam scenes filmed in Thailand, with **Bangkok** standing in for Saigon, and in the **Katchanburi** district of north Thailand near to the Burmese border. The prison camp, where the VC obligingly allow the boys to play Russian roulette with three bullets (with one bound they're free...) was built on the **River Kwai** (as in *Bridge On...*). The 1973 evacuation of downtown Saigon was staged on **Throng Wad Road** in Bangkok, with 6,000 enthusiastic extras responding to a call for 800. The US Airfield is Bangkok's main international terminal, **Don Muang Airport**.

Back in the States, De Niro finds Savage an embittered patient in Cleveland's (real) **Veteran's Administration Hospital**. Walken is buried (after a pretty impressive run as a professional Russian Roulette player) in the **Pennsylvania Versailles Cemetery, McKeesport**.

The hugely successful theme music was originally written for the 1970 David Hemmings-Samantha Eggar tear-jerker *The Walking Stick*, where it was heard by practically no one.

DEFIANT ONES, THE

(1958, dir: Stanley Kramer)
Sidney Poitier, Tony Curtis, Theodore Bikel.
● **CALIFORNIA**

Typically worthy Kramer melodrama, with white racist Curtis escaping from a chain gang only to find himself manacled to Sidney Poitier. The film is set, of course, in the Deep South, but the movie was filmed largely on the Newhall Land and Farming Company, a 40,000 acre movie lot on the northern border of LA. **Newhall** is still popular – the 'raptor attack in the long grass in *The Lost World: Jurassic Park* was shot there. It's a couple of miles to the west of I-5 on Route 126 up toward Valencia. The railroad scenes, with Poitier and Curtis clambering aboard the freight train, were filmed around 15 miles to the northwest at **Piru** (where Judy Garland and James Mason flee to get married in *A Star Is Born*). The hazardous river crossing scene was shot even further north up in Kern County, on the Kern River (another popular location – it was the same river crossed in John Ford's *Stagecoach*).

DEJEUNER SUR L'HERBE (aka *Lunch on the Grass*)

(1959, dir: Jean Renoir)
Paul Meurise, Catherine Rouvel, Jacquline Moran.
● **FRANCE**

Renoir's whimsical romance sees a scientist specialising in artificial insemination taking off for a country idyll, and practising a spot of the real thing with the maid. Of course, he's humanised and finally marries her. It was filmed at **Les Collettes** forest in the Auvergne area, and in and around **Cagnes-sur-Mer** on the Côte d'Azur.

DELIVERANCE

(1972, dir: John Boorman)
Jon Voight, Burt Reynolds, Ned Beatty.
● **GEORGIA**

What's more disturbing, the backwater hell that the four city guys find themselves in, or the fact that the movie generated a whitewater rafting tourist boom in the area? *Deliverance* was filmed at **Rabun Gap** and in Rabun County, up in the northeastern corner of Georgia. The river down which Reynolds and co canoe is the **Chattooga River**, defining the border of South Carolina, near **Clayton**. The waterfall is the **Tallulah Falls**. The lake at the end is **Lake Jocassee**, a mountain lake created by the Duke Power Company, with waterfalls and sheer rock faces in Oconee County. You can raft here but, be warned, this truly is a seriously dangerous river.

DERNIER METRO, LE (aka *The Last Metro*)

(1980, dir: François Truffaut)
Catherine Deneuve, Gerard Depardieu, Jean Poiret.
● **PARIS, FRANCE**

Truffaut's claustrophobic drama has Depardieu hiding out from the Nazis during the occupation. It was shot in Paris on a very tight budget, largely on sets built in a disused chocolate factory in **Clichy**.

DESERTO ROSSO, IL (aka *The Red Desert*)

(1964, dir: Michelangelo Antonioni)
Monica Vitti, Richard Harris, Rita Renoir.
● **ITALY**

Beautiful to look at, with fascinating use of colour, and filmed in the industrial landscape of **Ravenna** in northern Italy.

DESPERADO

(1995, dir: Robert Rodriguez)
Antonio Banderas, Salma Hayek, Joaquim de Almeida.
● **MEXICO**

Banderas becomes the itinerant guitarista as Rodriguez luxuriates in a studio budget with a virtual revamp of his low-budget calling card *El Mariachi*. Long on visual pyrotechnics and short on narrative, it was shot at the same location, **Ciudad Acuna**, over the Rio Grande from Del Rio, Texas.

DESPERATELY SEEKING SUSAN

(1985, dir: Susan Seidleman)
Rosanna Arquette, Madonna, Aidan Quinn.
● **NEW YORK CITY, NEW YORK; NEW JERSEY**

Spying on Madonna: Gangway 1, Battery Park

Screwball romantic comedy with bored Arquette chasing up Madonna's cryptic personal ads. New Jersey coastal resort Atlantic City is the site of the hotel where La Ciccone takes polaroids of herself. Arriving in New York, she deposits her luggage at the world's largest and busiest bus terminal, the **Port Authority Bus Terminal, 8th Avenue** between 40th and 42nd Streets. Arquette lives over the Hudson River in New Jersey, where her pricy-looking apartment overlooks the George Washington Bridge. She reads Madonna's ad while at the hairdressers, **Nubest Salon and Spa, 1482 Northern Boulevard, Manhasset** on Long Island, spies on Madonna's tryst at **Gangway 1, Battery Park** on Manhattan's southernmost tip, and subsequently follows her to the East Village. The lively hippy-punk shopping street where Arquette upsets the street stall is **St Mark's Place**, the stretch of 8th Street between Third Avenue and Tomkins Park Square, and she buys Madonna's jacket at funky second-hand store **Love Saves The Day, 119 Second Avenue** at East 7th Street.

Aidan Quinn worked as a projectionist at the old Bleecker Street Cinema, which stood at **144 Bleecker Street** between Thompson Street and La Guardia

The shopping street: St Mark's Place, Greenwich Village

Place, Greenwich Village, seen also in Woody Allen's *Crimes And Misdemeanors*. It's now a video store. Also gone is the dance club where Arquette's husband gets to meet up with Madonna, which was Danceteria, at 30 West 21st Street in the heart of Chelsea.

New Jersey locations include **Tenafly** and **Edgewater**, northern New Jersey, north of New York, west of the Hudson; and **Lakehurst**, between New York and Atlantic City. Shooting also took place at **Roslyn Heights**, Nassau County, Long Island.

DEVIL IN A BLUE DRESS

(1995, dir: Carl Franklin)
Denzel Washington, Jennifer Beals, Don Cheadle.
● **CALIFORNIA**

A stylish private eye movie from Walter Mosley's novel, set in 1948 Los Angeles, and filmed entirely on location around LA, in **Malibu**, **Pasadena** and in **Piru**, 40 miles to the north. The forties black centre of Central Avenue was recreated in a frequently used, and run-down, area of downtown Los Angeles, along four blocks of **Main Street**, around the **Regent Theater, 448 South Main Street**. As few photographs of Central Avenue survive,

Central Avenue of the forties: Main Street

the store names, Lovejoy's Breakfast Club, Bluebird Market, Waters and Sons Record Shop, were taken from a period directory of black businesses. The mansion is **Mayfield Senior School, 500 Bellefontaine Street,** Pasadena, the interior of which became Richard Attenborough's house in *The Lost World: Jurassic Park*.

DEVIL RIDES OUT, THE

(1968, dir: Terence Fisher)
Christopher Lee, Charles Gray, Patrick Mower.
● HERTFORDSHIRE; BUCKINGHAMSHIRE

The night in the chalk circle: Edgwarebury Hotel, Elstree

Disappointingly ordinary filming of a potentially scary story, with Lee as an aristocrat, on the side of the angels for once, rescuing his friends from a devil-worshipping cult. The conjuring of Satan was filmed in **Black Park Country Park**, Buckinghamshire. The house of villain Mocata (Gray) is **High Canons, Buckettsland Lane, Well End**, a couple of miles to the north of Borehamwood in Herfordshire (a much used location seen in *Half Moon Street*, *Rentadick*, *Murder on the Orient Express* and lots of TV shows). Close to Elstree-Borehamwood Studios, it's a private house and not visible from the road.

The faux half-timbered home of Paul Eddington and Sarah Lawson, where the four characters spend the night besieged in the chalk circle, is the **Edgwarebury Hotel, Edgwarebury Lane** off Barnett Lane, **Elstree** (*℃ 0870.609.6151, wwwcorushotels.com/edgwarebury*). Conveniently close to Elstree and Borehamwood Studios, this veteran location can also be seen in *School For Scoundrels*, *Sons of the Sea*, the rather dated Agatha Christie mystery *Endless Night*, the 1970s black comedy *Hawks*, *Hide and Seek* (1963) and the farce *Not Now, Comrade*.

DEVILS, THE

(1970, dir: Ken Russell)
Oliver Reed, Vanessa Redgrave, Gemma Jones.
● NORTHUMBERLAND

Brilliantly cinematic, pitch black comedy account of John Whiting's play, based in turn on Aldous Huxley's book *The Devils of Loudun*. One of Russell's, and Britain's, greatest movies. The walled city of Loudun was built, from terrific designs by Derek Jarman, at **Pinewood**. The exterior, seen behind the rotting corpses of the opening scenes, is the 12th century Norman keep of **Bamburgh Castle**, 16 miles north of Alnwick in Northumberland.

It's open Easter to October (*℃ 01669.620314; admission charge*).

DIAMONDS ARE FOREVER

(1971, dir: Guy Hamilton)
Sean Connery, Jill St John, Charles Gray.
● LAS VEGAS, NEVADA; CALIFORNIA; AMSTERDAM; GERMANY

Connery returned as Bond, for his last appearance in the mainstream series, in one of the better films, unfortunately hampered by production problems and soured by a streak of gratuitous homophobia.

The diamond smuggling plot naturally takes Bond to Europe's gem capital, Amsterdam, where shocked sightseers see the body of the old lady being hauled from the **Amstel Canal** at the **Skinny Bridge**. Bond girl Tiffany Case's apartment is on the third floor of **Reguliersgracht 36**.

But, of course, Bond is soon off to glossier locations, in this case Las Vegas. Apart from the car chase through the parking lot of the Mint, which was filmed on the Universal lot, the Vegas exteriors were shot in the casino city itself. The Slumber Mortuary, where Bond nearly gets cremated, is the **Las Vegas Visitors Bureau** building on Highway 10. Although there was no shortage of over-the-top decor in Vegas, the designers decided to built the fantasy interior at Pinewood. Full advantage was taken of the 'theme' casinos though, with Bond and Tiffany Case meeting up in **Circus Circus, 2880 Las Vegas Boulevard South**, where trapeze artists dangle over the heads of the punters.

Willard Whyte's Whyte House is the **Las Vegas Hilton** (then the Las Vegas International Hotel). At the **Riviera Hotel and Casino, 2901 Las Vegas Boulevard South** (*℃ 702.732.5110*) (the major location for Martin Scorsese's *Casino*), Bond wins $50,000 and Plenty O'Toole, though Sammy Davis Jr's cameo ended up on the cutting room floor. Bond stays, naturally, at the home of the bare-breasted Folies Bergère revue, **The Tropicana, 3801 Las Vegas Boulevard South**. The car chase, filmed on **Fremont Street**, meant that Vegas' main drag had to be cordoned off for three nights.

The Techtronics Missile Laboratories are the **Johns Manville Gypsum plant** on the outskirts of Vegas. Whyte's winter villa is a private home, the **Elrod Residence, 2175 Southridge Drive, Palm Springs**, designed by Frank Lloyd Wright acolyte John Lautner. Blofeld launches his satellite from the **Vandenberg Air Force Base**, on the coast between San Luis Obispo and Santa Barbara, I-1, southern California. The anti-aircraft guns were mounted on a temporary oil rig which was installed off the coast of Southern California near Oceanside, Route 5, between Los Angeles and San Diego.

It was a confused and troubled production, leading to some eccentric continuity as the disparate shots were matched up. The most famous blooper is the stunt car careering down a narrow alley on its two left-hand wheels and emerging from the alley on its right side.

DIARIOS DE MOTOCICLETA (aka *The Motorcycle Diaries*)

(2004, dir: Walter Salles)

Gael Garcia Bernal, Rodrigo de la Serna, Mercedes Moran.

● **ARGENTINA; CHILE; PERU; CUBA**

Che Guevara was either (a) an inspiring visionary who helped liberate Cuba from a corrupt dictatorship (if you're on the Left), (b) a ruthless ideologue who helped enslave Cuba under a totalitarian dictatorship (if you're on the Right) or (c) that guy on the posters who sang with The Doors and overdosed on a speedball at the Marmont (if you're under 25).

Salles' film (shot on a 16-week schedule, in sequence, and wherever possible, at the real locations) focuses on the journals of the young Ernesto Guevara (Bernal), nick-named Fuser ('furious', for his no-holds-barred approach to rugby), travelling around Latin America with his pal, Alberto Granado (de la Serna) and witnessing firsthand the inequity and poverty which fuelled his later revolutionary zeal. If you want to recreate Guevara's journey authentically, you'll need a 1939 Norton 500 in good working order. Otherwise, cheat and use a tour company. The trip covers around 5,000 miles, west from **Buenos Aires**, through **Patagonia** and into Chile, north along the Andes to **Machu Picchu** and finally to the **Guajira Peninsula** in Venezuela.

Ernesto and Alberto, and their long-suffering Norton, La Poderosa, start out from Buenos Aires, Argentina, passing through the city's **Plaza Once**, and stopping at first to visit Ernesto's posh girlfriend, Chichina, who's staying in **Miramar**, on the coast about 200 miles south of Buenos Aires which, in the fifties, was a rich, and exclusively white, resort.

The journey proper finds the pair heading west toward the Chilean border. The film skips quickly across Argentina to the beautifully photogenic **Lake District** and the lakeside village of **Villa la Angostura**, in the south of Neuquen province, at the northeastern shore of **Lago Nahuel Huapi**. At the lake's southern tip, at **San Carlos de Bariloche**, Ernesto is taken ill after wading into the freezing water to retrieve the duck shot down by Alberto and they spend the night at the railway station, before crossing the border into Chile at **Lago Frias**, where mountains rise dramatically from the lake's waters.

There's a less-than-grand entrance to the town of **Temuco**, pushing the ailing bike, but fleeting fame follows a bogus interview with the newspaper *El Diario Austral*. Scenes were filmed at **Freire**, to the south; and in **Lautaro**, just to the north, where the bike gets fixed for free, but where Ernesto and Alberto are chased out of town after coming on to the local womenfolk (an incident apparently invented for the film).

As La Poderosa finally gives up the ghost and the two continue on foot, the lives of the people they meet begin to encroach and the film's tone darkens. At **Valparaiso**, the historic port west of Chile's capital, Santiago, there's bad news for Ernesto, and he and Alberto glumly descend in the funicular railway running between the surrounding hills and the lower town. As much a feature of the city as San Francisco's cable cars, there are 15 of these 'ascensores', built between 1883 and 1916, still operating.

The Inca city: Machu Picchu, the Andes

From Valparaiso, they tramp through the barren, lunar landscape of the **Atacama Desert**, where the plight of a Communist couple, on the road looking for work after being evicted from their land, only deepens their awareness of injustice.

The Atacama, incidentally, stretches north into Peru, where, between Arequipa and Lima, you'll find the mysterious Nazca lines. These giant, stylised drawings – birds, spiders, lizards – etched on the plains, are best seen from the air (which led to the kind of barking mad theories expounded in cable documentaries at four in the morning). The strange patterns were clearly made, not by aliens, but by the indigenous Nazca people, between 1,500 and 2,000 years ago, though why still remains a riddle.

The search for casual labour brings Ernesto and Alberto's travelling companions to the US-owned Anaconda Copper Company, the real mine visited by Guevara, and still operating. It's at **Chuquicamata**, about ten miles from Calama, east of Antofagasta. "This is not a tourist attraction" scowls the foreman, but, ironically, it now is. One of the world's largest open-cast mines, it is now state owned. You can visit from 10am daily: you'll need to produce your passport and make a donation. Head for **Oficina Ayuda a la Infancia**, at the top of **Avenida JM Carrera**.

Following the Andes north, the pair enter Peru, and the city of **Cuzco**, "the heart of America". In an improvised scene, they are given cocoa leaves to chew – which helps alleviate effects of high altitude. Actually, most of the Cuzco scene was filmed in the village of **Ollantaytambo**, in the Sacred Valley of the Incas. If you're travelling from Cuzco to Machu Picchu, stop off at Ollantaytambo, not only for the unique village, but for its fortified temple, the only Inca stronghold to withstand Spanish attack.

Arriving at the fortified Inca city 45 miles northwest of Cuzco, Ernesto is understandably awestruck by his first glimpse of Machu Picchu ('old mountain' in the local language). It seems to have been something of a royal retreat, built between 1460 and 1470. Remote and little-known, it fell prey to disease and internal strife, and by the time of the Spanish conquest in 1532 it was already forgotten. The complex of terraces was rediscovered by American explorer Hiram Bingham in 1911. It's best to visit during the dry season, between May and September. If you're not doing the motorcycle trip, fly to Cuzco (allow a couple of days to acclimatise to the altitude) and take the train to Aguas Calientes (not forgetting to stop off at Ollantaytambos). From here, there's a bus ride, with 13 hair-raising hairpin curves, to Machu Picchu.

Moving on to **Lima**, Dr Pesce sets the two medical

students on the final part of their journey, along the Amazon to **San Pablo**, and what was a 'leper colony' when Guevara visited. It's a hospice for what is now termed Hansen's Disease, 250 miles east of **Iquitos**. You can visit and, from a gift shop, buy handicrafts made by the residents. For the film, the hospital was recreated at **Santa María del Ojeal**, at the end of Sinchiquy Creek. The set has remained, and is now local authority offices.

The epilogue, featuring the real Alberto Granado, was filmed in **Havana**, Cuba.

DIE ANOTHER DAY

(2002, dir: Lee Tamahori)
Pierce Brosnan, Halle Berry, Judi Dench.
● **LONDON; CORNWALL; HAMPSHIRE; WALES; SPAIN; ICELAND**

Tamahori brings a touch of grittiness and – almost – realism to the early scenes, but is let down by some cheesy effects and downright silly gimmicks (invisible cars!). The opening surfing scene features what are claimed to be the biggest waves in the world at a place called '**Jaws**' on the coast of **Maui**, Hawaii. Bond comes ashore at **Holywell Bay**, near Newquay in Cornwall. North Korea is largely the Pinewood backlot, though airborne scenes were filmed at the army base in **Aldershot** in Hampshire.

Hong Kong was faked on sets, and the US blockade of Cuba meant that the real Havana was out of the question. **Cadiz**, on the Atlantic coast of Spain (where it rained constantly), stood in for the Cuban capital, but the interior of the cigar factory, where Bond drops the magic name Universal Exports in his search for terrorist Zao, is **Simpson House, 92 Stoke Newington Road**, north London.

And how times change. Remember Connery's Bond dissing pop music in *Goldfinger* ("like listening to the Beatles without earplugs")? Now Bond arrives in the capital to the accompaniment of The Clash. The entrance to the abandoned (and fictitious) Vauxhall Cross Underground Station can be seen at the southern end of **Westminster Bridge**, alongside County Hall. (The long-suffering guys who work there are heartily sick of gullible fans wanting to see the fictitious station.) The station itself, though based on the much-used Aldwych Station on the Strand, is a studio set.

Gustav Graves (Toby Stephens) makes a spectacular entrance, parachuting down in front of **Buckingham Palace**. Gentlemen's club Blades is mainly a set, as you can tell from the way the surroundings are treated, but the central section of the fencing duel and the lobby, where Bond receives the mysterious key, are the **Reform Club, 104 Pall Mall**, seen in the original *Around the World In Eighty Days*, the 2002 remake of *The Four Feathers*, Lindsay Anderson's *O Lucky Man!* and *The Bounty*.

Graves' ice palace is in Iceland, where the ice chase was filmed on the frozen **Lake Jokulsarlon**, near **Hofn**. The biodome interior is based on the **Eden Project, Bodelva**, a complex of three geodesic domes, four miles east of St Austell in Cornwall (*www.edenproject.com*). It's an ambitious biosphere project designed to promote the relationship between plants, people and resources.

The real Eden Project is briefly glimpsed as Jinx (a stunt double, not Halle Berry) rappels down.

The exotic beach house, where Bond and Jinx finally get it together among the diamonds, is **Penbryn**, between Aberystwyth and Cardigan, Wales. The 'love nest' took a team of eight several days to construct, though it appears on screen for seconds, and neither Brosnan nor Berry appeared at the location.

DIE HARD

(1988, dir: John McTiernan)
Bruce Willis, Alan Rickman, Bonnie Bedelia.
● **LOS ANGELES, CALIFORNIA**

John McClane (Willis), armed with only a sweaty singlet, saves an office block from a bunch of terrorists, but the whole movie gets hijacked by histrionic villain Alan Rickman anyway. The block is on Fox's

The Nakatomi tower: Fox Plaza, Avenue of the Stars

ex-backlot again; the Nakatomi tower is the 34-story **Fox Plaza, 2121 Avenue of the Stars**, part of the Century City complex, where thousands of dollars worth of Italian marble were imported to replace any glitzy Fox marble that got chipped during the slam-bang climax.

DIE HARD II: DIE HARDER

(1990, dir: Renny Harlin)
Bruce Willis, Bonnie Bedelia, William Atherton.
● **WASHINGTON DC; COLORADO; MICHIGAN; CALIFORNIA**

"How can this be happening again?" wonders McClane, as he tackles terrorists once more, this time at **Washington Dulles International Airport**, some 26 miles west of downtown DC along Route 66 at Harndon (which is actually in East Virginia). Much of the movie was shot at Colorado's **Stapleton International Airport**, at the eastern end of East 32nd Avenue in Denver, and in **Breckenridge**, Route 9, south of I-70 west of Denver in the Rocky Mountains. The plane crash, which called for stiff winds, was staged at **Tehachapi Pass** in the Mojave Desert, and the search for survivors at **Alpena**, on the shore of Lake Huron, northern Michigan, Route 23.

The little church taken over to become the baddies' HQ is **Highland Lake Church**, in **Mead**, on I-35 about 30 miles north of Denver, Colorado (the steeple and front of the church destroyed in the explosion were fakes added for the movie).

DIE HARD WITH A VENGEANCE

(1995, dir: John McTiernan)
Bruce Willis, Samuel L Jackson, Jeremy Irons.
● **NEW YORK CITY; SOUTH**

"As I was going to St Ives…": Broadway at 72nd Street

Jeremy Irons robs the bank: Federal Reserve Bank, Liberty Street

CAROLINA; MARYLAND

Alan Rickman turns out to have a brother who's almost, but not quite, as theatrical, and bent on revenge. Part three is set in New York, where Irons sets up a disaster to divert attention while he robs the **Federal Reserve Bank, 33 Liberty Street** in Manhattan's Financial District. Willis and Jackson play Simon Says, following instructions at **Tomkins Square Park**, East Village, solving the "As I was going to St Ives…" riddle on **Broadway** at **72nd Street**, and careering through Central Park in a commandeered taxi. Filming also took place at **Yankee Stadium** in the Bronx and in **Charleston**, South Carolina. The ending was filmed at the **Truckers Inn, 7401 Assateague Drive, I-95 and Route 175, Jessup**, Maryland.

DINER

(1982, dir: Barry Levinson)
Steve Guttenberg, Daniel Stern, Mickey Rourke.
● **BALTIMORE, MARYLAND**

Levinson's ensemble piece sees a group of college students gather to talk through problems at their local diner in 1959. The eaterie was shipped in from a diner graveyard in Oakland, New Jersey, after the owner of an existing establishment upped his asking price. It was installed on a vacant lot at Boston Street and Montford Avenue, overlooking the North West Harbor south of Patterson Park. The art department thought it would look great facing the rippling water, but director Levinson favoured logic over appearance and had it turned to face the street. The area has since been redeveloped, but you can still see the diner, which was relocated to **400 East Saratoga Street** at Holliday Street.

Guttenberg celebrates his wedding at the **Engineer's Society, 11 West Mount Vernon Place**. The diner is quite a star. Apart from appearing in two other Levinson films, *Tin Men* and *Avalon* (where it's shown being lowered into place), it was featured as the Capitol Diner in *Sleepless in Seattle*.

DINOSAURUS

(1960, dir: Irvin S Yeaworth)
Ward Ramsay, Paul Lukather, Greg Martell.
● **VIRGIN ISLANDS**

A bunch of dinosaurs and a caveman are brought back to life on a tropical island, filmed at **St Croix**, in the Virgin Islands.

DIRTY DANCING

(1987, dir: Emile Ardolino)
Jennifer Grey, Patrick Swayze, Jerry Orbach.
● **VIRGINIA; NORTH CAROLINA**

This teen coming-of-age movie, set in the sixties, queasily drags in serious issues as flippant plot devices. The

Catskills setting is actually the Appalachians, where the main location is the **Mountain Lake Hotel, Mountain Lake**, off I-460 west of Roanoke, Virginia. There was more filming at **Lake Lure**, southeast of Asheville, North Carolina, a picturesque area which had been a major location during the silent movie era.

DIRTY DOZEN, THE

(1967, dir: Robert Aldrich)
Lee Marvin, Ernest Borgnine, Robert Ryan.
● **HERTFORDSHIRE**

12 convicted GIs in WWII Britain are given a chance to avoid the death sentence or a life stretch by undertaking a suicide mission behind enemy lines.

Manoevres in the Devon village: Aldbury, Hertfordshire

The fictitious Marston-Tyne Military Prison, where Lee Marvin chooses his recruits, is **Ashridge Management College**, once a Tudor manor house (and home

Marston-Tyne Military Prison: Ashridge College, Little Gaddesden

to the young Elizabeth I), but greatly added to over the years and now a huge Victorian gothic complex. It's down a toll road from the village of **Little Gaddesden**, about six miles northeast of Hemel Hempstead in Hertfordshire (*rail: Tring*).

'Major' Donald Sutherland seriously pisses off Robert Ryan while inspecting troops at a military airbase, which is **Hendon Aerodrome**, 15 miles north of London. The Devon village, Red Force Division 1 HQ, where the Dozen disrupt military manoevres and capture the commanding officers. It's the historic village of **Aldbury**, with its duckpond and stocks on the village green, a couple of miles to the west of Little Gaddesden in Herfordshire. This popular location can also be seen in Gainsborough Picture's colourful 1947 period melodrama *Jassy* and in the Swinging Sixties comedy thriller *Crossplot*.

You won't, however, be able to visit the French chateau, target of the mission. Solid and imposing as it looks, the entire building was no more than a giant set, 2400 feet across and 50 feet high, built on the backlot at MGM Studios in Borehamwood.

DIRTY HARRY

(1971, dir: Don Siegel)
Clint Eastwood, Andy Robinson, Harry Guardino.
● **SAN FRANCISCO, CALIFORNIA**

Some peculiarly right-wing tub-thumping mars this brilliantly made thriller, gratuitously linking CND peace symbols to the psycho-villain, Scorpio (Robinson).

The threat to kill a priest: Saints Peter and Paul, Filbert Street

The search for Scorpio: Broadway

The movie was shot almost entirely around San Francisco, where Scorpio starts off taking potshots at SF citizens from the rooftop of the **Bank of America World HQ, 555 California Street** at Kearney Street (the building, incidentally, used for the entrance to *The Towering Inferno*). The rooftop pool, where the first victim splashes about, is on top of the **Holiday Inn at Chinatown, 750 Kearny Street** between Washington and Merchant Streets.

Detective Harry Callahan is soon summoned to the mayor's office – and it is the real Mayor's Office in San Francisco's **City Hall**, conveniently empty over a Memorial Day weekend. The imposing dome can be seen on **Polk Street** between McAllister and Grove.

The shootout around the café, when Harry spots a robbery in progress and gets to use his "How lucky do you feel?" spiel for the first time, is the only studio section. It was filmed at **Warner Bros Burbank** lot in LA, where car crashes are easier to set up, which is why San Francisco suddenly looks so *flat*.

The Police Department Harry works out of was the old **Pacific Gas and Electric Building, 245 Market Street** in the Financial District. The helicopter discovers Scorpio on the rooftop of **1606 Stockton Street**, overlooking Washington Square, where he's choosing another victim. The twin-spired Italianate church over the way is **Saints Peter and Paul, 666 Filbert Street**, to which he returns to carry out his threat of blowing away a Catholic priest.

The night-time search for the killer takes Harry and his college kid partner down **Broadway**, past such local colour as **Big Al's** and the **Roaring Twenties** clip joints. The railway station is **Forest Hill MUNI Station**, between Twin Peaks and Mount Davidson.

Harry is lead around town to meet with Scorpio at the 100-foot tall concrete cross which tops **Mount Davidson**, San Francisco's highest peak, at 398 feet. The path up to the peak begins at the corner of Myra Way and Sherwood Court. He eventually tracks the killer down to **Kezar Stadium, Kezar Drive** in Golden Gate Park. And when the suspect is released, Harry tails him to a strip joint – the Roaring Twenties again, on Broadway.

Scorpio is spotted on the rooftop: Stockton Street

The hijacked school bus is taken over the **Golden Gate Bridge** onto **Sir Francis Drake Boulevard** and through the **Waldo Tunnel** on Highway 101. The final showdown, where Scorpio is famously wasted was at the old rock quarries of **Larkspur**, about ten miles north of the Golden Gate Bridge. The area has since been completely redeveloped as Larkspur Landing.

DIRTY PRETTY THINGS

(2002, dir: Stephen Frears)
Chiwetel Ejiofor, Audrey Tautou, Sergi López.
● LONDON

Nasty discovery at the Baltic Hotel: Whitehall Court, Westminster

The contrived thriller elements sit uneasily against the interesting milieu of London's semi-legal immigrant underclass. It's never really explained why anyone would attempt to flush away a human heart, is it? The entrance to the fictitious Baltic Hotel, where Okwe (Ejiofor) finds the surplus organ blocking the toilet, is **4 Whitehall Court** at Horseguards Avenue. Although the rooms and corridors are studio sets, the lavish lobby is that of **Wandsworth Town Hall, High Street**. Okwe reveals to Senay (Tautou) that he's married as they walk in **Bunhill Burial Ground, 38 City Road**. Originally much larger than the remnant left today, the cemetery has been restored after being severely bomb-damaged during WWII. Established in 1315, it was, unusually, not consecrated, which meant that it became the last resting place for non-conformists and liberal humanists. It was closed in 1853 when occupancy reached 120,000. Famous graves include those of John Bunyan (author of *Pilgrim's Progress*), Daniel Defoe (author of *Robinson Crusoe* and *Moll Flanders*) and mystic poet and painter William Blake.

DIRTY ROTTEN SCOUNDRELS

(1988, dir: Frank Oz)
Michael Caine, Steve Martin, Glenne Headly.
● FRANCE

A remake of 1964's *Bedtime Story*, with Caine and Martin taking over from David Niven and Marlon Brando as two conmen vying for the hand of Glenne Headly on the French Riviera. The setting of Beaumont-sur-Mer is fictitious, represented by **Beaulieu-sur-Mer**, an elegant Edwardian resort east of Nice, where the **Grand Hotel de Cap-Ferrat** stands in for Beaumont's Grand. More Riviera locations were found at **Nice** itself; the fishing port of **Villefranche-sur-Mer** to the east; and at **Antibes**, between Nice and Cannes. Beaumont's airport is the **Aerodrome International Cannes-Mandelieu**, while its casino is Beaulieu-sur-Mer's glass-enclosed **Rotonde**. The harbour is the yacht harbour at **Juan les Pins**, the art gallery, the **Fondation Ephrussie de Rothschild, Villa Ile-de-Frances, Cap Ferrat**. **Villa Hier**, a private home on the coast of **Cap d'Antibes**, was used for Caine's luxury pad, and tons of sand were brought in to bury the naturally stony beach.

The pirated concert: Theatre des Bouffes du Nord

DIVA

(1981, dir: Jean-Jacques Beineix)
Frederic Andrei, Wilhelmenia Wiggins Fernandez, Richard Bohringer.
● PARIS, FRANCE

Parisian postman Andrei secretly tapes a concert by his heroine, opera diva Fernandez, and finds the bootleg cassette becoming the MacGuffin in a drugs'n'prostitution racket…

The remains of Bohringer's warehouse: Quai de la Seine

but forget the plot, this is Paris and style is all.

Fernandez's bootlegged concert filmed at the **Theatre des Bouffes du Nord, 37 bis, boulevard de la Chappelle** in the 18th arrondissement. Long abandoned and used as a warehouse, it was taken over by the legendary Peter Brook as the base for his international rep company. Though the theatre was renovated, it was not redecorated, hence the quaintly distressed look.

The woman who plants the compromising cassette in Andrei's postbag gets a stiletto in the back at the **Gare St Lazare** (the world's third largest railway station), on **rue St-Lazare**, while another witness gets the stiletto treatment on **boulevard Barbes**, alongside the boulevard de la Chappelle.

The opera singer's hotel: Hotel Royal Monceaux, avenue Hoche

Andrei meets Deruaz shoplifting at the **Lido Musique** record store on the **Champs Elysées**, and returns a stolen frock to Ms Fernandez at her suite in the impossibly luxurious **Hotel Royal Monceaux, 35-39 avenue Hoche**, just off the place Charles de Gaulle. He escapes assassins by riding his bike into the Paris Metro. The moving pavement is at the **Opera Station**.

Bohringer's warehouse apartment has since been demolished – it stood on **quai de la Seine** at rue de Crimée in the Bassin de la Villette. Andrei's meeting with a prostitute was

The chase: Étoile-Foch entertainment complex

filmed by one of Hector Guimard's few remaining glass art nouveau 'butterfly roof' metro stations on the **avenue Foch**. He is chased into the nearby **Étoile-Foch** entertainment complex with its arcades and bowling alley.

DJANGO

(1966, dir: Sergio Corbucci)
Franco Nero, José Bódalo, Eduardo Fajardo.
● SPAIN

Paella Western, filmed at **Colmenar Viejo**; **La Pedriza**; and **Torremocha de Jarama**, Madrid.

D.O.A.

(1950, dir: Rudolph Maté)
Edmond O'Brien, Pamela Britton, Neville Brand.
● SAN FRANCISCO, CALIFORNIA; LOS ANGELES, CALIFORNIA

O'Brien is slipped a fatal dose of slow poison and sets out to track down his own killer before the inevitable end in this noir thriller made on location in San Francisco and Los Angeles. O'Brien finally meets up with his murderer at the magnificent **Bradbury Building, 304 South Broadway**, downtown LA (see *Blade Runner* for details of this landmark building).

DO THE RIGHT THING

(1989, dir: Spike Lee)
Danny Aiello, Spike Lee, Ossie Davis.
● NEW YORK CITY

Racial tensions erupt during a blistering New York heatwave in Lee's controversial polemic, shot in the Bedford-Stuyvesant area of Brooklyn. Sal's Famous Pizzeria stood on **Stuyvesant Street** between Quincy and Lexington. A metal plaque was set into the sidewalk to mark the location but, apparently, it's since disappeared.

DOCTOR DOLITTLE

(1967, dir: Richard Fleischer)
Rex Harrison, Samantha Eggar, Anthony Newley.
● WILTSHIRE; WEST INDIES; CALIFORNIA

Astonishingly, this dreadful, big budget, musicalised version of Hugh Lofting's story got an Oscar nomination as Best Film. What had the Academy been

Puddleby-on-the-Marsh: Castle Combe

watching that year? To portray the little coastal town of Puddleby-on-the-Marsh, the filmmakers chose the 'prettiest village in England', **Castle Combe** in Wiltshire. From the start, this was destined to be a troubled production. Castle Combe, smack in the middle of Wiltshire, is miles from the sea, so a seafront had to be built on the bank of the tiny river which runs through the village, and the unspoiled loveliness of the location, which had attracted 20th Century-Fox in the first place, was transformed. The subsequent disruption, along with the constant high-decibel playback of the music tracks, resulted in

The doctor's house: Castle Combe

plummeting relations with the locals. One villager, who had the intention of removing the set once and for all, was intercepted carrying sticks of dynamite. Nevertheless, in the main street you can still recognise the seafront, the jail, and the Doctor's house.

The UK's lack of constant sunshine seemed to take everyone by surprise and, as the already poor weather continued to deteriorate, the production was closed down and moved to LA, where the village was recreated on a Hollywood soundstage.

Then it was time to move to the tropical splendour of the West Indies for the beach scenes with the giant snail, which were filmed at **Marigot Bay, Santa Lucia**. The crew arrived just in time for the rainy season.

DR. DOLITTLE

(1998, dir: Betty Thomas)
Eddie Murphy, Ossie Davis, Oliver Platt.
● CALIFORNIA

Out with the music, in with Eddie Murphy and elaborate special effects for this update set in San Francisco, where the doctor's apartment is on **Webster Street**. The carnival is at **Aquatic Park** near Fisherman's Wharf, and the scene with the tiger was filmed at **Coit Tower** (see *Vertigo* for details). Filming also took place in **Pacific Heights**; and out of San Fran at **Big Bear**; Pasadena; and **Lake Sherwood**, California.

DOCTOR IN THE HOUSE

(1954, dir: Ralph Thomas)
Dirk Bogarde, Kenneth More, Donald Sinden.
● LONDON

St Swithin's Hospital: University College, Gower Street

First of many film and TV adaptations of Richard Gordon's *Doctor* books, with Bogarde, More, Sinden and Donald Houston as suspiciously elderly medical students (33, 40, 31 and 31 years old respectively) romping through every bedpan and thermometer joke known to mankind. St Swithin's Hospital is played by **University College, Gower Street**, south of Euston Road by Euston Square tube station (also seen in *The Mummy* and *Batman Begins*). The fairground is the old Battersea Funfair which, until the 1970s, was in Battersea Park over Albert or Chelsea Bridges from Chelsea Embankment.

DR NO

(1962, dir: Terence Young)
Sean Connery, Joseph Wiseman, Ursula Andress.
● WEST INDIES; LONDON

Ian Fleming's sadistic, humourless snob disappeared for all time when Sean Connery adopted the name James Bond. First of a series of campy villains is veteran stage actor Wiseman hiding behind rubber eyelids, operating out of the fictional Crab Key in the West Indies.

The opening scenes are in **Kingston, Jamaica**, where the 'three blind mice' amble through **Harbour Street**, downtown. John Strangway is gunned down by the 'mice' and spirited away after a bridge game at the Queens Club, now the **Liguanea Club**, a fitness club in **New Kingston** (*© 926.8144*). Strangway's cottage, where his secretary is offed and Bond later picks up a clue, stood on **Kinsale Street**, north of Kingston in the foothills of the Blue Mountains. It's now gone.

Time to bring in 007. Bond's first big-screen appearance is at the chemin-de-fer table of Le Cercle, at **Les Ambassadeurs, Hamilton Place**, behind the Hilton Hotel, off Park Lane, London (recreated in the studio, though a couple of years later the Beatles would be bopping the night away in *A Hard Day's Night* in the real thing). If you fancy your luck, the club is still going.

After a little banter with Miss Moneypenny, Bond begins a long tradition by swanning off to the West Indies. He is met by the impostor 'Mr Jones' at **Norman Manley International Airport**, halfway along the Palisadoes, the ten-mile spit which protects the harbour at **Kingston**, Jamaica. The meeting with the Colonial Secretary, at Government House filmed at the Governor General's mansion, **King's House**, in central Kingston. The waterfront where Bond searches out Quarrel is **Morgan's Harbour**, near Port Royal at the western tip of the Palisadoes.

Miss Taro's bungalow on the fictitious Magenta Drive is a villa at the pricy **SuperClub Grand Lido Sans Souci Hotel**, in Ocho Rios – a convenient location, since the crew were staying there – in the foothills of the Blue Mountains. 96 suites, eight deluxe rooms and seven penthouses. Even in low season it will knock you back $250 a night, and no kids – it's couples and over-16s only (*© 876.974.2353*).

The waterfalls outside **Ocho Rios** provide Crab Key's shore, where Bond and Quarrel arrive. The beach where bikini-clad Andress famously rises from the the waves to grace countless schoolboys' bedroom walls, is **Laughing Waters**, then a private section of Roaring River which was the hideaway estate of recluse, and Bond fan, Mrs Minnie Simpson. You'll find the cascades a mile west of Dunn's River, three miles west of Ocho Rios, near to the hydroelectric power station.

Dr No's bauxite mine on Crab Key is a real bauxite mine, the **Kaiser Terminal** on the A3 coast road near Ocho Rios on the north shore, and the mangrove swamp where the dragon tank captures Bond and Honey is **Falmouth**, about 40 miles to the west.

DR STRANGELOVE OR: HOW I LEARNED TO STOP WORRYING AND LOVE THE BOMB

(1963, dir: Stanley Kubrick)
Peter Sellers, George C Scott, Sterling Hayden.
● SURREY

Kubrick's black farce filmed almost entirely in the studio at **Shepperton**. The airborne shots were taken from a B-17 bomber over the Arctic, Greenland, Iceland, Canada's Northwestern Territories and the Rockies. Location filming took place at London Airport. The computer scenes were filmed in the computer room at IBM, where the IBM 7090 – one of only three in the world – was insured by the film company for four million dollars. New York shutterbug WeeGee (played by Joe Pesci in biopic *The Public Eye*) acted as advisor to the stills photographer on the movie.

DOCTOR ZHIVAGO

(1965, dir: David Lean)
Omar Sharif, Julie Christie, Alec Guinness.
● SPAIN; FINLAND; CANADA

Lean's lumbering, sugarcoated romance, loosely based on bits of Boris Pasternak's novel, always seems to teeter on the verge of being a musical. Despite the endless snowscapes, most of the film was shot in Spain, with the major sets constructed in **Canillas**, a little suburb of Madrid. The Christmas card cottage, with its dinky icicles and plaster snow, was built in the mountainous region 100 miles northeast of Madrid at **Soria**. Other Spanish locations included **Granada**; **Guadalajara**; **Aljalvir**; and **Aranjuez**.

The train sequence was filmed in Finland, on the railway laid during the 1940 Russian invasion, at the town of **Joensuu**, some 400 miles north of Helsinki. The refugees' trek filmed at **Lake Phyhaselka** in Finland, 100 miles from the real Russian border. There was even a little second unit filming in the Canadian Rockies, providing more mountain views for the train sequence. The giant hydroelectric dam, which bookends the story, is **Aldeadavila Dam** on the Douro River, 55 miles west of Salamanca.

DOG DAY AFTERNOON

(1975, dir: Sidney Lumet)
Al Pacino, John Cazale, Chris Sarandon.
● NEW YORK CITY

Writer Frank Pierson picked up an Oscar for his screenplay, while Pacino, Sarandon and Lumet got nominations, for this based-on-real-life story of incompetent bank robbers, one of whom was trying to get money to finance his boyfriend's sex change. The Brooklyn bank where the couple are holed up was actually a garage on **10th Street** in Flatbush, Brooklyn.

DOGMA

(1999, dir: Kevin Smith)
Ben Affleck, Linda Fiorentino, Matt Damon.
● PENNSYLVANIA; NEW JERSEY

The Catholic Church got pretty upset over Kevin Smith's rambling but imaginative satire, which sees Affleck and Damon as a pair of dispossessed angels attempting to re-enter Heaven via a loophole in Catholic doctrine.

There are only glimpses of Smith's usual stomping ground of **Red Bank** and **Asbury Park** (where the old man is battered at the opening of the movie), for, although the movie is set in New Jersey and Illinois, most of it was in fact shot around Pittsburgh. For instance, General Mitchell Airport, Milwaukee, where Affleck and Damon tempt a nun to go AWOL, is **Pittsburgh International Airport**, and the Mexican restaurant, in which Linda Fiorentino's supernatural mission is explained by angel Alan Rickman is the **Franklin Inn, 2313 Rochester Road, Franklin Park** (© 412.366.4140), northwest Pittsburgh.

On Pittsburgh's North Side, muse Salma Hayek wows 'em as a stripper in silver bra and specs at the **Park View Cafe, 2 East North Avenue** at Federal Street. Down southwest of the city in **Dormont** you'll find the **Dormont Cafe, 2887 West Liberty Avenue**, where demonic Jason Lee is dispatched by a holy golf club. Also in Dormont was Mooby's Fast Food joint, an old Burger King restaurant, site of Chris Rock's revelations about the real Christ, now a Rite Aid drugstore at **3210 Banksville Road**, Highway 19, opposite Dormont Park.

In Pittsburgh itself you can't miss the Mooby Corp Building, **USX Tower, 600 Grant Street** – Pittsburgh's tallest skyscraper – and the Software Engineering Institute of **Carnegie Mellon University, 4500 Fifth Avenue** between Dithridge and Craig Streets, which was used for the Mooby boardroom, where Matt Damon guns down the directors. The posh restaurant where Rickman makes the astonishing revelation that God has gone missing, is the **Grand Concourse Restaurant** (© 412.261.1717), the restored waiting room of Pittsburgh's old P & LE railway station in **Station Square**. St Michael's Church, supposedly in Red Bank, NJ, where Cardinal Glick's Catholicism WOW! movement replaces the depressing crucifix with the upbeat Buddy Christ – and site of the apocalyptic climax – is the **Everlasting Covenant Cathedral, 130 Larimer Avenue** in **East Liberty** (watch out though, this isn't a particularly comfortable section of town).

DOLCE VITA, LA (aka *The Sweet Life*)

(1960, dir: Federico Fellini)
Marcello Mastroianni, Anita Ekberg, Anouk Aimée.
● ROME, ITALY

If it had no other significance, Fellini's first non-narrative delirium would be remembered for coining the word *paparazzi*. The film's major location, Rome's **Via Veneto**, was recreated on sets at Cinecittà Studios outside Rome, and from this point on Fellini virtually forsook real locations whenever possible for the more controllable environment of the studio. The gardens of the millionaire's estate are the baths of **Hadrian's Villa** at **Tivoli**, outside Rome. The jazz club used the ruins of the **Caracalla Baths**. Anita Ekberg's much-publicised frolic in the fountain was filmed on a real location. Like Marilyn Monroe's subway-grating scene in *The Seven Year Itch*, the shoot mysteriously received mountains of advance publicity. Hotel

Ekberg's frolic: Trevi Fountain

rooms overlooking the site were snapped up and, in a freezing January, some 5,000 onlookers watched Ms Ekberg fondle her kitten in the **Trevi Fountain**.

DONNIE BRASCO

(1997, dir: Mike Newell)
Al Pacino, Johnny Depp, Anne Heche.
● **NEW YORK CITY**

Pacino and Depp first meet: Mare Chiaro, Mulberry Street, Little Italy

The director of the enjoyable, if overrated, *Four Weddings and a Funeral* changed genres radically to helm this small masterpiece, based on the true story of FBI agent Joe Pistone (Depp) who, in the seventies, under the name Donnie Brasco, infiltrated the mob. An uncharacteristically subdued Pacino turns in one of his

Pistone and Brasco meet, interior: Mare Chiaro, Mulberry Street

best performances as the doomed middle-ranker who unwittingly signs his own death warrant by vouching for the fraudulent Brasco.

It's set mostly in New York, and was all shot there – even the short Miami episode. The Little Italy bar where Pacino and Depp first meet is **Mare Chiaro, 176 Mulberry Street** between Broome and Grand Streets. The bar, also known as **Tony's**, has been seen in many movies including *Nine 1/2 Weeks*, *State of Grace* and *The Godfather, Part III* – a list of its film credits hangs on the wall. Although photos of the owner with the likes of Frank Sinatra decorate the bar, the relentless encroachment of Chinatown on the area of the old Little Italy means that this once-Italian bar is now Chinese run.

Filming *Donnie Brasco* on Mott Street

Depp meets up with his contacts in **Katz's Delicatessen, 205 East Houston Street** between Ludlow and Orchard Streets in the East Village, most famous as the restaurant where Meg Ryan faked it for Billy Crystal in *When Harry Met Sally…*. Depp and Pacino meet up with the mob boss on **Mott Street** in Little Italy, where the Genco olive oil company had its offices in *The Godfather*.

DONNIE DARKO

(2001, dir: Richard Kelly)
Jake Gyllenhaal, James Duval, Patrick Swayze.
● **LOS ANGELES, CALIFORNIA**

Strange and dark, the stuff of cults, with Donnie Darko (Gyllenhaal) haunted by Harvey's evil twin, Frank the giant bunny. Set in

The jet engine falls on Donnie Darko's house: Country Club Drive, Long Beach

Virginia, it was filmed around LA. Darko's school, Middlesex High School, is **Loyola High School, Venice Boulevard** just east of Normandie

The rabbit appears in the cinema: Aero Theater, Montana, Santa Monica

Avenue. It's at the **Aero Theater, 1328 Montana at 14th Street, Santa Monica**, that Frank the Rabbit instructs Darko to burn down the mansion of oleaginous sleazebag Jim Cunningham

Slimy Jim Cunningham's mansion: Country Club Drive, Long Beach

(Swayze). The art deco cinema (seen also in *Get Shorty*), opened in 1939, was where the young Robert Redford watched movies and was almost taken over

Donnie's school: Loyola High School, Venice Boulevard

by his Sundance organisation. It's being restored by the American Cinematheque. Cunningham's mock-Tudor mansion is **4252 Country Club Drive** down in Long Beach, south LA. You might recognise the grand house as the home of 'popular jock' Jake Wyler in *Not Another Teen Movie*. Darko's house is nearby at **4225 Country Club Drive**.

DONOVAN'S REEF

(1963, dir: John Ford)
John Wayne, Elizabeth Allen, Lee Marvin.
● **HAWAII**

John Ford's clumpingly macho comic knockabout is set on a South Seas island, but was filmed on the island of **Kauai**, Hawaii (see *Jurassic Park* for details). "I believe in God, as we all do, but I respect the beliefs and customs of my people," says the native woman, hedging her bets, as she prays to the god of the canyon.

You can find the stunning **Waimea Canyon**, 'the Grand Canyon of the Pacific', in the wilderness on the west side of the island. Take Kaumualii Highway

(Highway 50), running along the south coast, to Waimea, then head north on Waimea Canyon Road. Two lookouts on the road, Waimea Canyon Lookout and Puu Hinahina, both give breath-taking views across the mile-wide valley.

Sutherland and Christie's hotel – exterior: Hotel Gabrielli Sandwirth, Riva degli Schiavoni

...and the interior: Hotel Bauer Grunwald, Campo San Moise

DON'T LOOK NOW

(1973, dir: Nicolas Roeg) D o n a l d Sutherland, Julie Christie, Hilary Mason.
● VENICE, ITALY

Dank, crumbling, off-season Venice provides the setting for Roeg's reinvention of a Daphne du Maurier short story as a dazzling cinematic mosaic. Sceptical architect John Baxter (Sutherland), doomed by a refusal to accept his own extrasensory powers, and his wife Laura (Christie) stay at the Europa Hotel, a conflation of two classy – and pricy – Venetian establishments. The lobby and the exteriors are the **Hotel Gabrielli Sandwirth, Castello 4110, Riva degli Schiavoni**, (© 5231580), a converted gothic

The church Sutherland restores: San Nicolo dei Mendicoli, Campo San Nicolo

The church interior: San Nicolo dei Mendicoli

The detective trails Sutherland around the city: San Polo

palace overlooking the San Marco Canal just east of the Piazza San Marco. The hotel interior – location for one of cinema's most convincing sex scenes – is over to the west of Piazza San Marco, the expensive **Bauer Grunwald, San Marco 1459, Campo San Moise** (© 5207022).

The church Baxter is restoring is way down in the southwest of the city. It's **San Nicolo dei Mendicoli**, one of the oldest in Venice and restored – in real life – during the seventies (though you

won't see the mosaic worked on in the movie, which was nothing more than a prop). The church, which is open to the public from 10 till noon in the mornings and 4.30 to 7.30 in the afternoon, is on **Campo San Nicolo**, a small square surrounded on three sides by the Rio di San Nicolo and the Rio delle Terese. To get to

The sisters' hotel: La Fenice et des Artistes, Campiello Fenice

Sutherland follows the mysterious little figure: Calle di Mezzo

it, you need to follow the Canale della Giudecca waterfront, the Fondamenta delle Zattere, west past the Stazione Marittima toward the rather glum, industrial San Marta area.

The suspicious detective follows Baxter through the **San Polo** district in the centre of the northern curve of the Grand Canal's reverse 'S', to the southwest of Venice's second largest square, the Campo San Polo: the **Calle di Castel Forte** and the **Ponte Vinanti**.

The restaurant in which John and Laura meet the two strange sisters is the **Ristorante Roma**, near to the Ponte Scalzi over the Grand Canal by the railway station, Stazione Ferrovia Santa Lucia.

After Laura collapses, she's taken to hospital from the landing stage on the north side of the Grand Canal here. The sisters stay at **La Fenice et des Artistes, San Marco 1936, Campiello Fenice** alongside, and serving, the Fenice Opera House which burned to the ground in such mysterious circumstances, west of Piazza San Marco.

The narrow canal, to which Baxter finally follows the tiny red-coated figure, is the **Calle di Mezzo**, northeast of Piazza San Marco, to the gates of the **Palazzo Grimani** (at the junction of Rio di Santa Maria Formosa and Rio di San Severo – don't confuse it with the *other* Palazzo Grimani on the Canal Grande), where he finds out that – oops! – it's not his daughter after all. The Palazzo has been deserted for years, but in 1998 was in the process of being renovated. The gated

The funeral: Church of San Stae, Campo San Stae

Sutherland finally meets the mysterious figure: Palazzo Grimani, Calle di Mezzo

entrance to the Palazzo, through which Baxter enters, can be seen on Calle di Mezzo.

The funeral, which ends the film, is at the 17th century **Church of San Stae** (a contraction of San Eustachio) at **Campo San Stae** on the northern curve of Canal Grande.

Morrison on auto-destruct: Chateau Marmont

DOORS, THE

(1991, dir: Oliver Stone)
Val Kilmer, Meg Ryan, Frank Whaley.

● **CALIFORNIA; NEW YORK CITY; PARIS, FRANCE**

The shaman/Native American mysticism of Stone's biopic of Doors singer/songwriter/poet Jim Morrison somehow never quite gels, but it beats a straightforward fame 'n' drugs drama any day. It was shot at almost 80 locations, mainly around California. The Doors first come together at LA's Bohemian hangout, **Venice Beach**. Getting out of LA for a couple of scenes, they visit **San Francisco**, in its full sixties incarnation, and outrage Ed Sullivan in **New York** (though Morrison didn't actually sing "Girl we couldn't get much *higher*" on live TV after being ordered to change the line).

In LA, quite a few of the city's venerable institutions are seen. The band performs at the **Whisky-a-Gogo, 8901 Sunset Boulevard** in West Hollywood, which was repainted vibrant red and had its striped awnings restored for the movie. The legendary London Fog club (now part of rock hangout Duke's Coffee Shop, 8909 Sunset Boulevard), where the Doors were house band, is actually the **Viper Room, 8852 Sunset Boulevard** (℗ *310.358.1881, www.viperroom.com*), owned by Johnny Depp and, yes, destined to be remembered forever as the spot where River Phoenix overdosed in 1993.

The bar, where bad boy Morrison takes a pee against the counter, is **Barney's Beanery, 8447 Santa Monica Boulevard** (℗ *323.654.2287, www.barneys-beanery.com/barneysbeanery*), a West Hollywood drinking hole since 1927, when it served up beans on the old Route 66 into the city. It's alleged that Jean Harlow used to pick up men here, and it's where Janis Joplin spent her last evening. It's enjoyably raucous,

Morrison pees against the bar: Barney's Beanery, Santa Monica Boulevard

The band performs at the legendary Whisky-a-Gogo, Sunset Boulevard

and where else but in Hollywood is the karaoke evening likely to end with a movie star turn? Barney's is also featured in 1986 thriller *Out of Bounds*, with Anthony Michael Hall.

The London Fog nightclub: The Viper Room, Sunset Boulevard

After his breakdown, Morrison enjoys a drink on the window ledge above the traffic at the **Chateau Marmont, 8221 Sunset Boulevard** (℗ *323.656.1010, www.chateaumarmont.com*), built in 1929 and long a residential hotel for the likes of Boris Karloff, Greta Garbo, Errol Flynn and Harlow again. But most famously, it was here in 1982 that another personality programmed to auto-destruct, John Belushi, overdosed on coke and heroin. The legendary hotel also appears in *Myra Breckinridge*, provided the hotel exterior of (and the inspiration for) the Mon Signor Hotel in the disastrous *Four Rooms*, and was seen in the Mark Wahlberg heavy metal vehicle *Rock Star*. The New Haven concert, brought to a halt when Morrison is arrested for abusing the cops, filmed in the beautiful **Orpheum Theater, 842 South Broadway**, downtown LA (see *Last Action Hero* for details). More footage was filmed at the disused **Ambassador Hotel, 3400 Wilshire Boulevard**, midtown LA.

The desert scenes were shot in **Providence Mountains State Park**, a 5,900 acre recreation area on a mountain slope overlooking a vast expanse of desert. Way out in the middle of nowhere, take I-40 about 100 miles east of Barstow, then turn northwest on the Essex Road. There was trouble for the movie company when the fake Native American pictographs painted for the movie proved more difficult to remove than had been promised.

The final scene was filmed at Morrison's grave in Paris' largest cemetery, the **Père Lachaise, 65 boulevard de Menilmontant** in the 20th arrondissement.

Morrison's grave: Père Lachaise cemetery

The much-graffitied grave is in the 16th section. From the main entrance, take the Avenue Principale to the Avenue de Puits, turn right and follow the Avenue Casimir-Perier. Other celeb graves seen in the movie include Oscar Wilde (Jacob Epstein's sphynx), Bizet, Marcel Proust, Sarah Bernhardt, Balzac and Rossini. You can also find the tomb of Abelard and Heloise, and the graves of Simone Signoret, Edith Piaf, Gericault, Chopin, Colette, Isadora Duncan, director Max Ophuls, Marie Walewska (Bonaparte's mistress, played on screen by Garbo in *Conquest*) and cinema pioneer Georges Méliès.

DOUBLE INDEMNITY

(1944, dir: Billy Wilder)

Barbara Stanwyck, Fred MacMurray, Edward G Robinson.

● LOS ANGELES, CALIFORNIA

Barbara Stanwyck's house: Quebec Drive, Hollywood Hills

Insurance sales-man Walter Neff (MacMurray) is ensnared by femme fatale P h y l l i s D i e t r i c h s o n (Stanwyck) to bump off her – well-insured – hubby in Wilder's classic *noir*. Dietrichson's house, sup-posedly in Los Feliz, can be found in the maze of tiny winding lanes in the Hollywood Hills, at **6301 Quebec Drive**, off Beachwood, north from Franklin Avenue. In the movie it stood alone, overlooking Hollywood, but now, although unchanged, it is packed into a densely built up area of pricy properties. Pasadena Station was filmed at the **Glendale Amtrak Station on Cerritos Avenue** off Vassar Avenue by Forest Lawn Memorial Park.

DOUBLE VIE DE VÉRONIQUE, LA (aka *The Double Life of Véronique*)

(1991, dir: Krzysztof Kieslowski)
Irène Jacob, Wladyslaw Kowalski, Philippe Volter.

● POLAND; FRANCE

Irène Jacob picked up the Best Actress award at Cannes for her dual role in this story of two identical women, one Polish, one French, whose lives mysteriously cross. It was filmed in **Krakow**, Poland, and in **Clermont-Ferrand**, France.

DRACULA

(1931, dir: Tod Browning)
Bela Lugosi, Helen Chandler, Edward Van Sloan.

● LOS ANGELES, CALIFORNIA

The first Hollywood version of Bram Stoker's vampire story, though it had been filmed, unofficially, in Germany in 1921 by FW Murnau, as *Nosferatu*. *Dracula*, kicking off Universal's cycle of stylish, atmospheric horror movies of the thirties and forties, is basically a filming of the British stage adaptation by Hamilton Deane, which had opened in London in 1927 with 23 year-old Raymond Huntley (the pompous civil servant of the *St Trinian's* and dozens of other British movies) as the Count. The role was created on Broadway by the Hungarian classical actor Lugosi, who went on to land the film role after Lon Chaney Sr, who was terminally ill, and Conrad Veidt, who returned to his native Germany, passed over the project.

The Transylvania and Yorkshire sets were all built, and subsequently much recycled, at Carl Laemmle's **Universal Studios**, north of Hollywood (see *Frankenstein* for details of the studio).

The exteriors of Castle Dracula are cunningly revamped from the 'Medieval' style sets of old Universal silents by assistant designer Herman Rosse. The sets for the Transylvanian inn and its yard were built at Universal on what is now the site of the Studio Tour tram stops. Arriving in England, Dracula contrives an invitation to Lucy and Mina at the Albert Hall – actually the old *Phantom of the Opera* set (which was still in use in 1973 – see it as the burlesque house in *The Sting*). One real location, the opening shots of Renfield's coach careering through the eerie Mittel-European landscape, was filmed at **Vasquez Rocks**, the area of tortured sandstone forma-tions near to LA seen in so many Westerns and, later, in sci-fi movies (see *Blazing Saddles* for details of Vasquez Rocks).

DRACULA (aka *Horror of Dracula*)

(1958, dir: Terence Fisher)
Christopher Lee, Peter Cushing, Melissa Stribling.

● BERKSHIRE; BUCKINGHAMSHIRE

Hammer Films repeated the Universal pattern and, after their successful remake of *Frankenstein*, set out to refilm all the thirties classics with colour and gore. *Dracula* filmed almost entirely on the lot at Hammer's **Bray Studios, Down Place**, between Maidenhead and Windsor. The Transylvanian countryside filmed alongside Pinewood Studios in **Black Park Country Park**.

DRACULA

(1979, dir: John Badham)
Frank Langella, Laurence Olivier, Kate Nelligan.

● CORNWALL

Dracula's castle: St Michael's Mount

Frank Langella put in the fangs (after playing the role in a Broadway ver-sion) with Olivier wielding the gar-lic and stake in this lush, romantic melodrama.

Though made in England, the film doesn't use the book's setting of Whitby in Yorkshire, but filmed in Corn-wall. Count Drac-

Seward's asylum: King Arthur's Castle Hotel, Tintagel

ula's castle is **St Michael's Mount**, half a mile offshore – it's connected by a causeway – from **Marazion**, three miles east of Penzance in Cornwall. Home of Lord St Levan, the 17th century castle is a National Trust prop-erty and open to the public, Monday to Friday, April to October (*© 01736.710507*).

Seward's asylum, run by Donald Pleasence, is the mock-gothic **King Arthur's Castle Hotel, Tintagel**. The village, where Dracula tries to board ship, is **Mevagissey**, a fishing village way to the west, five miles south of St Austell.

DRACULA AD 1972

(1972, dir: Alan Gibson)
Christopher Lee, Peter Cushing, Christopher Neame.

● LONDON; HERTFORDSHIRE

The groovy seventies coffee bar: King's Road, Chelsea

Gruesomely enjoyable (for all the wrong reasons) attempt to update the fag end of the Hammer series to the Swinging Seventies, set around the King's Road, Chelsea, years after Chelsea's sixties heyday. The church is obviously a set, but the groovy coffee bar where the trendy young things gather is now Italian restaurant **La Bersagliera, 372 King's Road** up towards World's End. The country scenes filmed at **Tykes Water Lake** at **Aldenham** Country Park, west of Elstree between Bushey and Borehamwood, Hertfordshire.

DRAGONHEART

(1996, dir: Rob Cohen)
Dennis Quaid, voice of Sean Connery, David Thewlis.
● **SLOVAKIA**

A period fantasy adventure filmed in Slovakia. The opening scene was shot at the ruin of **Cachtice Hrad**, once home to the notorious Erzsebet Bathory, the legendary Blood Countess, alleged to have bathed in the blood of virgins, whose story was wildly mythologised in Hammer's *Countess Dracula*. The ruined tower can be found above the town of Cachtice. The movie uses the beautiful landscapes of the Slovakian National Park near the Medieval town of **Levoca**, while Einon's castle is **Spis Castle** in eastern Slovakia, one of the largest castles in Europe, set against the backdrop of the Tatra Mountains, overlooking the protected ancient towns of Spisska Kapitula and Spisska Podhradie.

DRAUGHTSMAN'S CONTRACT, THE

(1982, dir: Peter Greenaway)
Anthony Higgins, Janet Suzman, Anne Louise Lambert.
● **KENT**

The first of Greenaway's elegant, game-playing features, with Higgins as the draughtsman, commissioned by Janet Suzman to produce a series of drawings, but subsequently drawn into an enigmatic murder plot. The country house is **Groombridge Place** (✆ *01892.861444, www.groom bridge.co.uk*), a 1655 moated house set in landscaped grounds, four miles southwest of Royal Tunbridge Wells on the Kent/Sussex border. The grounds (but not the house itself) are open to the public daily from Easter to the end of October (✆ *01892. 863999, admission charge*).

DRILLER KILLER

(1979, dir: Abel Ferrara)
Jimmy Laine (Abel Ferrara), Carolyn Marz, Baybi Day.
● **NEW YORK CITY**

One of the legendary 'video nasties' that caused a moral panic in the early eighties. Ferrara went on to direct the stunning *King of New York* and the intense *Bad Lieutenant*. The film was shot almost entirely around **Union Square** in New York. Early on, Ferrara (under the acting pseu-

donym Jimmy Laine) sees a stabbing on **Union Square West** from his rooftop. The club, where Tony Coca-Cola and the Roosters – the dreadful punk band that's driving him crazy – play, is the legendary hangout of the Warhol set, Max's Kansas City, which stood at **213 Park Avenue South** just north of the Square.

DRIVER, THE

(1978, dir: Walter Hill)
Ryan O'Neal, Bruce Dern, Isabelle Adjani.
● **LOS ANGELES, CALIFORNIA**

Site of the famous Torchy's: West Fifth Street

Dern is 'The Cop' (it's an existential thriller, so the characters have no names) determined to lock up 'The Driver', a speedy getaway expert. Walter Hill's fast-paced, pared-down thriller was filmed on the streets of LA.

The bar Dern operates out of was Torchy's, **218 1/2 West Fifth Street**, downtown LA. Obviously a fave Hill location, you can see Torchy's as the San Francisco redneck bar of *48 Hours*. Torchy's has since closed and the premises is currently an electrical goods store. You can glimpse it in *Spider-Man* as Spidey swings along a supposed New York street. O'Neal meets up with Adjani on the illuminated walkways of LA's futuristic **Westin Bonaventure Hotel, 404 South Figueroa Street** (see *In the Line of Fire* for details of the Bonaventure). The luggage deposit boxes, where bags are stored and switched and Dern sets up O'Neal for the climax, are at **Union Station, 800 North Alameda Street**.

DRIVING MISS DAISY

(1989, dir: Bruce Beresford)
Jessica Tandy, Morgan Freeman, Dan Aykroyd.
● **GEORGIA**

Worthy middlebrow sentimentality, centering on the growing friendship between wealthy Miss Tandy and chauffeur Freeman, filmed around the stately homes of Atlanta, Georgia. Miss Daisy's gracious mansion is **822 Lullwater Road** in the **Druid Hills** area of the city.

DRUGSTORE COWBOY

(1989, dir: Gus Van Sant)
Matt Dillon, Kelly Lynch, James Remar.
● **OREGON**

Set in 1971, this small scale study of the lives of a group of drug addicts was filmed in Portland, Oregon. Dillon and Lynch's apartment is the **Irving Apartments, 2127 Northwest Irving Street** in the centre of town. The pharmacy they rob is **Nob Hill Pharmacy, 2100 Northwest Glisan Street** at Northwest 21st Avenue, a couple of blocks south.

DUCK SOUP

(1933, dir: Leo McCarey)
The Marx Brothers, Margaret Dumont, Louis Calhern.

● LOS ANGE-
LES, CALIFOR-
NIA

Groucho is Rufus
T Firefly, who
becomes President
of Freedonia in
one of the best of
the Marx film out-

Freedonia: Entrance to the Arden Villa,
Arden Road, Pasadena

ings. Although deco-ish Freedonia is firmly set in
Paramount Studios, the garden party of rival Sylvania,
where Groucho (surprise!) insults Margaret Dumont ("All
I can offer you is a Rufus over your head.") filmed at the
Arden Villa, 1145 Arden Road. You might recognise
the villa as the Carrington mansion from TV's *Dynasty*
and as George Cukor's estate in the James Whale biopic
Gods and Monsters. It's a private home in Pasadena, east
of LA, not visible from the street.

DUEL

(1971, dir: Steven Spielberg)
Dennis Weaver, Jacqueline Scott, Eddie Firestone.
● CALIFORNIA

Spielberg's first theatrical feature (though it was originally made for American TV) remains one of the great
cinematic débuts, despite being made in a mere two weeks.
The simple plot has nerdy driver Weaver threatened by a
monster truck and its unseen driver. The movie opens in
downtown LA where Weaver drives down **South
Broadway**, and heads north on Highway 5, the Golden
State Freeway toward Bakersfield. Most of the filming
is on **Route 14** and in the **Angeles National Forest** just
north of LA. The gas station where he gets the warning
about the radiator hose, and phones his wife from the
launderette, is **Acton**, just south from Route 14. He finally trashes the monster at **Soledad Canyon**, off Route 14
toward Ravenna.

DUEL IN THE SUN

(1946, dir: King Vidor; Josef Von Sternberg; William
Dieterle; B Reeves Eason; David O Selznick)
Jennifer Jones, Joseph Cotten, Gregory Peck.
● CALIFORNIA; ARIZONA

Massive, lurid vanity project from Selznick, intended to
outwind *Gone With the Wind* and to showcase his pro-
tegée Jennifer Jones. Jones is the 'half-breed' Indian girl
who falls in love with the son of the ranch family she lives
with and sparks off family feuds. It was filmed out in the
blazing desert of Arizona, on the Texas Ranch, now the
Triangle T Ranch near **Dragoon**, and at **Lasky Mesa**,
west of the San Fernando Valley in California (see *The
Charge of the Light Brigade* for details). Original director Vidor walked off the movie, fed up, like many another director, with Selznick's relentless 'hands on' approach
to producing. Dieterle took over, with contributions from
veterans Josef von Sternberg and Reeves Eason, along
with – naturally – Selznick himself.

DUELLISTS, THE

(1977, dir: Ridley Scott)

Keith Carradine, Harvey Keitel, Edward Fox.
● FRANCE; SCOTLAND

Scott's first feature, complete with trademark atmospheric
mists and lush visuals, is Joseph Conrad's story about a
series of obsessive duels fought between two officers during the Napoleonic Wars. It was filmed around the beautiful Medieval village of **Sarlat La Caneda**, 35 miles
southeast of Perigueux in the Dordogne. There was also
some filming at **Aviemore**, on the A9 southeast of
Inverness, Scotland.

DUMB AND DUMBER

(1994, dir: Peter Farrelly)
Jim Carrey, Jeff Daniels, Lauren Holly.
● COLORADO; UTAH; RHODE ISLAND

Carrey and Daniels travel from Providence to Aspen, to
return Lauren Holly's money-packed briefcase, in the
film that launched the Farrelly brothers' brand of hi-jinx,
lo-taste filmmaking.

Most of the film was shot in Colorado and Utah. There
is a little scene-setting in Providence, Rhode Island, but
Mary Swanson's New England mansion is actually in
Utah. It's **La Caille**, a 20-acre estate built in 1975, at **Quail
Run, Little Cottonwood Canyon** in the city of **Sandy**.
Most of the transcontinental journey, the highways, fast-
food joints and truckstops, were filmed around **Fort
Morgan** (boyhood home of bandleader Glenn Miller) on
the eastern plains of Colorado.

The arrival of Carrey and Daniels in Aspen actually
filmed on **Main Street, Breckenridge**, which is at a higher altitude than the swanky ski resort, and more likely to
be snow-covered in late spring. It's not unlikely that
Breckenridge was a damn sight cheaper too. The mini-
bike ride through Aspen was shot on **Main Street, Park
City** in Utah. The lavish Danbury Hotel, where Carrey
and Daniels dip into the case of money to buy a
Lamborghini and stay in the Presidential Suite, is the
**Stanley Hotel, 333 West Wonder View Avenue, Estes
Park** (℃ *001.970.586.3371*) in Colorado. The grandly
imposing hotel became the inspiration for the Overlook
in *The Shining* after Stephen King stayed there in 1973.
The Kubrick movie didn't film here, but the TV remake,
sanctioned by King (who hated the big screen version)
did. The Avalanche Bar & Grill, where Carrey waits in
vain for Lauren Holly, is the Stanley's bar. Daniels is
meanwhile meeting up with her at **Copper Mountain
Resort** in Breckenridge, which is where he licks the frost
on the ski lift.

The Snowy Owl Benefit was filmed in the **Union
Pacific Railroad Depot, 400 West South Temple** (℃
801.595.3600), a former train station, built in 1909, and
now a historic landmark building in **Salt Lake City**, Utah.
The Aspen chalet and the home of baddie Nicholas Andre
both filmed in **Dee Valley**, adjoining Park City, Utah.
Most interiors were filmed, by the way, in **Intermountain
Studios**, Orem in Utah, the studio built by the Osmonds
for *The Donnie and Marie Osmond Show*....

E

Elliot's house: Dos Rios Drive, Tujunga

E.T. THE EXTRA-TERRESTRIAL
(1982, dir: Steven Spielberg)
Henry Thomas, Drew Barrymore, Peter Coyote.
● LOS ANGELES, CALIFORNIA

In its day, the biggest-grossing movie ever, Spielberg's tearjerking fantasy was filmed largely on the soundstages at **Culver Studios** (previously Pathe, Pathe-de Mille and RKO-Pathe Studios), **9336 Washington Boulevard** in Culver City, where many other movie greats, including *King Kong* and *Gone With the Wind*, were shot. Interiors, apart from the high school, were filmed here, but so were some exteriors too, including the rear of the house and the backyard where Elliot leaves a trail of M&Ms to tempt the alien.

The redwood forest scenes are in the **Redwood National Park** at **Crescent City**, Route 101 in far northern California near the Oregon border. You'll find Elliot's frog-infested school in LA; it's **Culver City High School, Elenda Street** at Franklin Avenue. The principal was played by Harrison Ford, whose role ended up on the cutting room floor, though the back of his head and shoulder are supposedly still in the finished film.

The flying bikes: White Oak Boulevard, San Fernando Valley

The neighbourhood chosen for the movie was Northridge – the epicentre of 1994's disastrous quake – northwest LA in the San Fernando Valley. The Halloween and chase scenes filmed in the **Porter Ranch** district and the flying bicycle chase on **White Oak Boulevard** between Tribune and San Fernando Mission Roads, but Elliot's house is about 15 miles to the east. Spielberg wanted a more dramatic backdrop and headed off to the foothills of the San Gabriel Mountains. The actual house is **7121 Dos Rios Drive, Tujunga**, a suburb north of Burbank.

EARTHQUAKE
(1974, dir: Mark Robson)
Charlton Heston, Ava Gardner, Genevieve Bujold.
● LOS ANGELES, CALIFORNIA

Sunset-Vine Tower, Sunset Boulevard

The San Andreas Fault finally writes off LA in this unexpectedly downbeat addition to the seventies disaster movie genre, shot in the short-lived, headache-inducing gimmick of Sensurround. The movie was filmed in and around LA, apart from the opening scene of the San Andreas fault which shot at **Carrizo Plains**, about 100 miles to the north. The first ominous traces of impending disaster are discovered at the **Mulholland Dam** on Lake

Survivors congregate at Wilson Plaza: Ahmanson Center, Wilshire Boulevard

Hollywood up in the Hollywood Hills (see *Chinatown* for details). The city of LA itself was conjured up from a mixture of models, sets and real locations. Among the landmark buildings reproduced in miniature were the Taft Building at the corner of Hollywood and Vine (which for many years was HQ of the hated puritanical Hays Office) and the Capitol Records Tower, 1750 Vine Street, an architectural stack of 45s with a stylus jutting from its roof, destroyed again in *The Day After Tomorrow*.

The street scenes are largely in Hollywood, around the famous Hollywood and Vine intersection (though much of the action was filmed on the New York Street on the Universal backlot), and just south is Charlton Heston's office block, the **Sunset-Vine Tower, 6290 Sunset Boulevard** at Vine. At 20 storeys, it's Hollywood's tallest structure, built in 1964, after the abolition of height restrictions. Wilson Plaza, the disaster centre, is the **Ahmanson Center Building, 3701 Wilshire Boulevard** at Oxford Avenue, though the shopping mall was the **Broadway Plaza, 700 West Seventh Street** at Broadway, downtown. The cantilevered houses, where Genevieve Bujold is caught in the quake, can be seen on **Coldwater Canyon** north of Hollywood. The devastated roadway was a stretch of unfinished freeway near Glendale.

EAST OF EDEN
(1955, dir: Elia Kazan)
James Dean, Raymond Massey, Julie Harris.
● CALIFORNIA

This adaptation of John Steinbeck's epic novel was largely made in the book's setting of northern California, around **Salinas** and the coastal town of **Mendocino** (standing in for much-changed Monterey). The family mansion is no more, however. The Denslow-Morgan-Preston Mansion burned down a year after filming, and the site at 45200 Little Lake Street now houses the Mendocino Art Center and Gallery. It's close to Angela Lansbury's house from TV's *Murder, She Wrote*, at the corner of Little Lake and Ford Streets. **Salinas Valley** hosted most of the location shooting (the beanfields and the ice-house of the Trask farm filmed here), and there was more filming near the city of Salinas, at the Spreckels Sugar Factory, to the southeast. In its day, the largest sugar refinery in the world, it was damaged in the 1989 earthquake and demolished a few years later. The funfair was built back on the Warner's lot in Burbank.

EASY RIDER
(1969, dir: Dennis Hopper)
Peter Fonda, Dennis Hopper, Jack Nicholson.
● **LOS ANGELES, CALIFORNIA; ARIZONA; NEW MEXICO; NEW ORLEANS, LOUISIANA**

This surprise low-budget sixties smash, revolution-ising the studios and launching dozens of variable quality imitations, was shot in sequence, apart from the New

Fonda dumps the Rolex: Ballarat ghost town

Orleans Mardi Gras scene, which was actually first in the can. Always know where you're heading.

The cross-country journey, which follows much of the famed old Route 66, begins in LA. The opening druggy deal (a cameo from legendary record producer Phil Spector) was shot at **Los Angeles International Airport**, but from there on the movie filmed on the hoof across the American southwest. The key scene of Fonda tossing his Rolex to the ground was staged in the ghost town of **Ballarat**, east of Route 178, between Trona and Stovepipe Wells on the western edge of Death Valley. But it's way south again, heading east on I-40, that Fonda and Hopper cross the Colorado River into Arizona at **Topock**. From here, the journey takes Route 95 alongside the Colorado River before turning south along I-60 to Routes 71 and 89, the scenic route into **Flagstaff** going through the towns of Prescott and Cottonwood.

From Flagstaff, it's north on 89, where you can find the **Magic Mountain gas station** (no longer operational) and the geological wonders of the **Painted Desert** and **Monument Valley**. The town parade was filmed in **Las Vegas** – not the glitzy casino city of Nevada but the tiny frontier town in New Mexico. Thrown into jail for "parading without a licence", the pair meet up with star-to-be Jack Nicholson. Although the exterior of the old jail can be seen in Las Vegas, at **157 Bridge Street**, the interiors filmed in **Taos**, once home to DH Lawrence, and the writer's last resting place. The town jail is now an art gallery, **Bryans Gallery, Camino de la Placitas** in the town square.

Next stop is the scary redneck café, also long gone,

which stood in the small town of **Morganza**, Louisiana, by the Mississippi, about 30 miles northwest of state capital Baton Rouge. From here, it's just a short hop, past the clutch of plantation houses familiar from so many other movies, to New Orleans and Mardi Gras.

ECLISSE, L' (aka *The Eclipse*)
(1962, dir: Michelangelo Antonioni)
Alain Delon, Monica Vitti, Francesco Rabal.
● **ROME, ITALY**

Another of Antonioni's cool, classic sixties studies of bourgeois alienation, along with *L'Avventura* and *La Notte*, set in the soulless suburbs of Rome. After leaving her husband, Monica Vitti dives into an affair with heartless young stockbroker Alain Delon, whom she meets in the bustle of the **Rome Stock Exchange**.

ED WOOD
(1994, dir: Tim Burton)
Johnny Depp, Martin Landau, Sarah Jessica Parker.
● **LOS ANGELES, CALIFOR-NIA**

Burton's surprisingly moving tribute to the legendary 'Worst Director of All Time' filmed at 68 real locations around LA. Amazingly, Burton managed to find period locations, including the suburbs of **Torrance**; **Sierra**

The funeral home: North Cherokee Avenue

Madre; **Long Beach**; **Norwalk**; **Gardena**; and **Eagle Rock**; and even discovered unchanged corners among the tacky, redeveloped streets of Hollywood.

Wood's appalling stage venture filmed at **Theatre/ Theater, 1713 Cahuenga Boulevard** at Hollywood Boulevard. The fledgling director finds encouragement in the reviews with the rest of the cast at **Boardner's Bar, 1652 North Cherokee Avenue**, a traditional old Hollywood hangout since the 1940s, just off Hollywood Boulevard, seen also in *LA Confidential*, *Leaving Las Vegas*, and as the after-work hangout of Harrison Ford and Josh Hartnett in *Hollywood Homicide*. To the left of Boardner's you can see the vacant shop premises dressed as the Hollywood Funeral Home, where Wood first sees Bela Lugosi testing coffins. Wood begins to assemble his extended family of oddballs when he encounters wrestler Tor Johnson at the **Olympic Auditorium, Grand Avenue** at Olympic Boulevard, downtown LA – it's the venue where the boxing scenes from the *Rocky* movies and *Raging Bull* were filmed. The Brown Derby restaurant, where Wood hosts a fundraiser, is long gone. It was recreated

in the grounds of the Ambassador Hotel on Wilshire Boulevard, opposite which you can actually see the shell of the famed hat-shaped landmark. You can

Wood meets Welles: Musso and Frank's Grill, Hollywood Boulevard

Wood gets funding for his masterpiece: Toluca First United Methodist Church, Burbank

Wood reads the reviews: Boardner's Bar, Hollywood

also see the church attended by the cast of *Plan 9* when Wood gets some unorthodox funding. It's the **Toluca Lake First United Methodist Church, 4301 Cahuenga Boulevard** in Burbank.

There were a couple of authentic locations: the *Bride of the Monster* sequence, with Lugosi battling a rubber octopus, was filmed where the real Ed Wood actually shot his classic in **Griffith Park**, and Wood's home in the movie is the director's last apartment in Hollywood. His inspirational meeting with idol Orson Welles was shot in another classic Hollywood landmark, the oldest restaurant in the city, **Musso and Frank's Grill, 6667 Hollywood Boulevard** (opposite Boardner's and the funeral home, and recently seen in Steven Soderbergh's *Ocean's Eleven* and in *Charlie's Angels: Full Throttle*). Pretty unbelievably, Wood's film premières at the wonderful **Pantages Theater, 6233 Hollywood Boulevard** at El Centro, though the cinema interior is actually the slightly less grandiose **Orpheum Theater, 842 South Broadway**, downtown Los Angeles, seen in *Dead Again, The Doors* and *Last Action Hero*.

EDUCATING RITA

(1983, dir: Lewis Gilbert)
Michael Caine, Julie Walters, Michael Williams.
● DUBLIN, IRELAND

Academy nominations for the two leads in Willy Russell's adaptation of his own Liverpool-set play. Though still ostensibly set in Liverpool, the movie was shot entirely

Caine's rooms at college: Graduates Memorial Building

The grim family singalong, exterior: The Dame Tavern, Dame Court

around Dublin, where the university campus is **Trinity College**, and Caine's rooms are in the **Graduates Memorial Building**. The pub, where Rita begins to feel alienated from her family at a dismal singalong, is a conflation of two Dublin institutions. The interior is the hangout of Trinity students, the

Stag's Head, 1 Dame Court, while the exterior is just over the road, the **Dame Tavern, 18 Dame Court**. Twenties, the restaurant where Rita waits tables alongside ditsy Maureen Lipman, is **Dobbins Wine Bistro, 15 Stephens Lane**. A very drunk Caine looks for Rita at the old Flamingo disco, now gone, which was sited in the revamped **Stillorgan Park Hotel, Stillorgan Road** in Blackrock. Rita leaves for sum-

But the interiors filmed over the street: Stag's Head, Dame Court

mer school from Dublin's **Pearse Street Station**, while the wedding of Rita's pregnant younger sister was filmed at the **Church of the Holy Family, Aughrim Street**, in an area often used as a location – scenes for *Michael Collins, My Left Foot* and *The Boxer* were shot in the church's parish district.

EDWARD SCISSORHANDS

(1990, dir: Tim Burton)
Johnny Depp, Winona Ryder, Dianne Wiest.
● FLORIDA

The twee little pastel neighbourhood where Scissorhands sculpts bushes is **Tinsmith Circle, Carpenter's Run** in **Lutz**, about five miles north of Tampa on Route 41, Florida. 44 houses here were made over for the movie. Sadly, they're not always candy-coloured, nor do they sport quirky topiary. The dinosaur, elephant, Elvis and penguin shaped bushes were metal and chickenwire frames covered with greenery. The beauty salon, where Kathy Baker tries to seduce Edward, is in the **Southgate Shopping Center, 2500 South Florida Avenue**, Lakeland, east of Tampa.

8 MILE

(2002, dir: Curtis Hanson)
Eminem, Kim Basinger, Mekhi Phifer.
● MICHIGAN; NEW YORK CITY

'B-Rabbit' (professional badboy and mediabater Eminem) struggles to make it as a white rap artist from the wrong side of 8 Mile Road, the divide between Detroit central and its northern suburbs, where Eminem grew up. Filming occurred in Detroit, Highland Park, Southfield, Southgate, Sterling Heights and Warren, Michigan, plus New York and Queens. The exterior of the WJLB Building is the Penobscot Building, Detroit (the interiors were shot in the studio). The trailer park is a block from 8 Mile, and Eminem boards a bus on **8 Mile Road** itself. The Shelter is a real club, in the basement of St Andrew's Hall, but the scenes were actually filmed in a warehouse at **240 Chene Street**. The exterior is **30 Clifford**. The club where Eminem performs to the hyped-up crowd was an abandoned **Rite Aid store** at **Michigan and Griswold**. The **Chin Tik, 2121 Cassi**, downtown, a popular hangout in the fifties and sixties, had been closed for nearly twenty years, though interest in the film has caused speculation that it may reopen. The fight in the parking garage is on

Grand River Road. There is a brief scene on Chene Street, East Side, and Eminem and his stupid friend hide out in an East Side house. The house burning scene was picketed by locals, concerned at the negative image of the city being portrayed. Eminem works at the stamping plant, **950 East Milwaukee** at Hastings. The trailer park is **20785 Schultes, Warren**.

84 CHARING CROSS ROAD
(1987, dir: David Jones)
Anthony Hopkins, Anne Bancroft, Judi Dench.
● **LONDON; NEW YORK CITY**

This transatlantic romance, conducted entirely by letter, between American bibliophile Bancroft and English bookseller Hopkins, was based on true events. The bookshop at number 84, on the northeast corner of Cambridge Circus, has been modernised and is now a restaurant – for the film it was mocked up at **Shepperton Studios**. Hopkins's north London Muswell Hill home and neighbourhood was actually filmed in the southwest of the city in **Richmond**. The mock-Tudor pavilion alongside which Hopkins sits can be seen in **Soho Square**. Period accuracy demanded that **Madison Avenue**, in the New York scenes, be returned to its original two-way traffic system.

EL (aka *This Strange Passion*)
(1953, dir: Luis Buñuel)
Arturo De Cordova, Delia Garces, Luis Beristain.
● **MEXICO**

De Cordova is the bourgeois gentleman who whisks Delia Garces off her feet (and it is her feet he first falls for – this being a Buñuel movie), only to descend into dangerous paranoia. The movie, hailing from the Spanish director's period of Mexican exile, was shot in **Mexico City**. The less-than-happy couple spend their fraught honeymoon in **Guanajuato**, an elegant, muy-European city about 200 miles northwest of Mexico City.

EL CID
(1961, dir: Anthony Mann)
Charlton Heston, Sophia Loren, Herbert Lom.
● **SPAIN**

From the golden age of epics, this ranks as one of the best, unusually deserting toga country for the story of legendary Spanish hero Don Rodrigo de Bivar.

The movie was shot at three studios around Madrid, **Chamartin**, **Sevilla** and **Cea**, as well as on real Spanish locations. Burgos Cathedral, site of the coronation scene, has seen quite a few changes since the 11th century and a full-sized mock-up was built at the Sevilla Studios.

The tournament, where an embittered Sophia Loren gives her favour to Heston's opponent, was filmed in front of the 15th century gothic castle of **Belmonte**, built for writer and warrior Don Juan Manuel. One of the best preserved of its kind in Spain, and now declared a national monument, the castle is perched on a hilltop overlooking the province of La Mancha about 75 miles southeast of Madrid on the road between Alcazar de San Juan and Olivares.

The Cid's exile filmed in the **Guadarrama**

Mountains, north of Madrid, and more period scenes were shot around **Valladolid** – known as 'castle country' – in Old Castile, 100 miles northwest of Madrid.

For the final battle scenes Valencia was played by the walled city of **Peñiscola**, an old fortress town built on a promontory surrounded by the sea on three sides. It's on Spain's east coast 60 miles north of Valencia itself. The fortress walls, dating from the time of Phillip II, are emblazoned with his coat of arms and the castle once served as the papal court of Pope Benedict XIII, whose chapel and rooms can be visited. The giant Moorish gates, out of which the Cid ultimately rides, were installed for the movie and left behind as a gift to the city.

EL DORADO
(1967, dir: Howard Hawks)
John Wayne, Robert Mitchum, James Caan.
● **ARIZONA**

Hawks' solid Western filmed at the **Old Tucson Studios, 201 South Kinney Road**, Tucson. Built for the 1940 Western *Arizona*, the studio is still in use – *Tombstone* was filmed here in 1993 – and also functions as a Western theme park, open daily (© *602.883.6457*).

ELECTION
(1999, dir: Alexander Payne)
Matthew Broderick, Reese Witherspoon, Chris Klein.
● **NEBRASKA**

A high-school re-working of Budd Schulberg's *What Makes Sammy Run?*. George Washington Carver High School is **Papillion-La Vista High School, 402 East Centennial Road, Papillion**, Nebraska. The motel, at which teacher Jim McAllister (Broderick) sets up a fruitless assignation with Linda, is **American Family Inn, 1110 East Crook Road South, Bellevue** (© *402.291.0804, www.americanfamilyinn.com*). Tammy finds peace contemplating the chimneys of the **OPPD North Omaha Power Station, 7475 John J Pershing Drive**, on the Missouri River.

ELECTRA GLIDE IN BLUE
(1973, dir: James William Guercio)
Robert Blake, Billy Green Bush, Jeannine Riley.
● **UTAH; ARIZONA**

Cult biker/cop movie, following in the wake of *Easy Rider*, the only movie from Guercio, the manager of the rock band Chicago – he wrote the music for the film too. Filmed at **Phoenix** and **Carefree** in Arizona, it features a great mythic final shot of **Monument Valley**.

ELEPHANT MAN, THE
(1980, dir: David Lynch)
John Hurt, Anthony Hopkins, John Gielgud.
● **LONDON**

One of Lynch's more mainstream films, this eerie romantic fantasy is overlaid with an obsessive attention to the detail of industrial Victoriana. There's little left to see of the film's London locations; Lynch seems to have been one step ahead of the developers all the way.

The smoke-wreathed opening London street scenes

"I am a man!": Liverpool Street Station

Dr Carr Gomm's office: Liberal Club, Whitehall Place

filmed on the South Bank by London Bridge along **Shad Thames**, a familiar location – seen also in *The French Lieutenant's Woman* – now lost to inevitable gentrification as the warehouses are converted into wine bars and restaurants; and in the tiny knot of cobbled streets off **Clink Street** and **St Mary Overies Dock** behind Southwark Cathedral and Borough Market, SE1. Here, too, the atmosphere is long gone. The warehouses have actually been demolished, though the old street plan and cobbled roads have been retained. The area is worth a visit, having the remains of the Bishop of Winchester's 14th century Palace banqueting hall and the old Clink prison (which became the generic name for all subsequent lock-ups), now open as a museum.

Gone, too, is the old Eastern Hospital on Homerton Row, Lower Clapton, E9, replaced by the spanking new Homerton Hospital. The Eastern stood in for the London Hospital on Whitechapel Road, E1, where the real John Merrick actually stayed. This hospital still exists, opposite Whitechapel Tube Station, but its modern annexes rendered it unsuitable for filming. The corridors of the hospital and the office of Dr Carr Gomm (Gielgud) are the **Liberal Club, 1 Whitehall Court** at Whitehall Place, SW1, now incorporated into the Royal Horseguards Hotel.

The wonderfully decrepit Victorian railway station where Merrick arrives back in London after his escape from the freak show is the old **Liverpool Street Station, Bishopsgate**, EC2. Since filming the station has been thoroughly gutted. The wooden walkways, photogenic grime and white-tiled toilets have gone, but if you look up at the sparkly clean brick walls above the entrance to Platform 1 you'll recognise the shell of the building seen in the movie. The walkway, where Merrick was pursued by the mob, followed roughly the same path as its replacement above the platform entrances. The bright new Liverpool Street station can be seen in Brian De Palma's *Mission: Impossible*.

ELIZABETH
(1997, dir: Shekhar Kapur)
Cate Blanchett, Joseph Fiennes, Kathy Burke.
● **DERBYSHIRE; NORTHUMBERLAND; COUNTY DURHAM; YORKSHIRE; BERKSHIRE; MIDDLESEX**

Power politicking in the Tudor court, using real locations all over England. **Haddon Hall**, south of Bakewell, Derbyshire (℃ *01629.812855*), is substituted for Hatfield House, Elizabeth's childhood home, and itself a frequent

location, though much altered during the Jacobean period.

Several locations were found in Northumberland. The burning of the martyrs at Bishopsgate, London is **Alnwick Castle** (℃ *01665.510777*), as is Leith Castle, where Mary Queen of Scots rides after the battle. Alnwick has, of course, since found fame as one of the Hogwarts locations in the *Harry Potter* films. Not far away you'll find the hunting lodge, where Elizabeth and Dudley meet, and also the Leith Castle apartment of Mary of Guise, which are both **Chillingham Castle** (℃ *01668.215359*). Seven miles south of Alnwick is **Warkworth Castle** (℃ *01665.711423*), seat of the Percy family, in which the cells of the Tower of London were filmed, while the torture chamber and the apartment of Walsingham were **Aydon Castle**, near Corbridge (℃ *01434.632450*).

County Durham provided the Whitehall Palace river pageant, which is **Raby Castle**, Staindrop, about 12 miles west of Darlington (℃ *01833.660202*); and **Durham Cathedral** (another *Potter* location), the **Chapter House** of which became the Whitehall Palace State Room, and its nave, the queen's royal court.

North Yorkshire stands in for the Tower of London courtyard, the French bordello and the armoury, which are **Bolton Castle** (where the real Mary, Queen of Scots was imprisoned for six months), six miles from Leyburn (℃ *01969.623981*), while Elizabeth's coronation takes place in **York Minster**. Lord Arundel's home is **Dorney Court**, a Tudor manor house near Maidenhead, Berkshire (℃ *01628.604638*), which also featured in a slightly different genre of British film, *Lock, Stock and Two Smoking Barrels*. The final scene, and the coronation party, are **St Alban's Church, Teddington**, Middlesex, now a community arts centre.

ELVIRA MADIGAN
(1967, dir: Bo Widerberg)
Pia Degermark, Thommy Berggren, Lennart Malmer.
● **SWEDEN**

Lovingly photographed tragedy that seemed like the ultimate doomed romance back in the sixties. Army officer Berggren runs off with tightrope-walker Degermark, but their idyll is short lived, and, rather than be parted, the pair opt for a suicide pact. Filmed in **Skane**; **Nordsjallend**; and **Karlbergs slott och Solliden** in Stockholm.

EMERALD FOREST, THE
(1985, dir: John Boorman)
Powers Boothe, Meg Foster, Charley Boorman.
● **BRAZIL; LINCOLNSHIRE**

After searching for eleven years in the Brazilian jungle, dam engineer Boothe meets up with the young son taken by Indians. This wonderful-looking drama was filmed on location in Brazil. Boothe's Amazco office is a government building on the waterfront of **Belem**, on the south of the Amazon delta. The dam being constructed is over the Araguaia River at **Tucurui**, about 200 miles to the south. For the dam burst sequence, a scaled down model was built across a stream in the rather less exotic location of **Spilsby**, Lincolnshire. Jungle locations are **Paraty** and **Carajas**, while the waterfall, where Boothe finally meets his son, is at **Itatiata**.

EMMA
(1996, dir: Douglas McGrath)
Gwyneth Paltrow, Toni Collette, Jeremy Northam.
● **DORSET; BUCKINGHAMSHIRE; HAMPSHIRE; MIDDLESEX**

Straightforward filming of the Jane Austen novel, upstaged by the more spirited nineties update, *Clueless*. The fictional village of Highbury is **Evershot**, eight miles south of Yeovil in Dorset, where scenes were filmed on **Fore Street** and at the **Old Manor**, standing in for the schoolhouse. Mrs Weston's house, Randalls, is **Mapperton**, five miles northeast of Bridport, Dorset, and seen also in *Restoration*. The gardens here are open to the public in summer (© *01308.862645*). Other period locations include **Stratfield Saye**, home of the Duke of Wellington, between Reading and Basingstoke (© *01256.882882*); **Claydon House**, Middle Claydon, 13 miles northwest of Aylesbury in Buckinghamshire – an 18th century house with rococo decoration (© *01296.730349*); and **Stafford House** at West Stafford, east of Dorchester. Filming also occurred ar **Breakspear House, Breakspear Road North**, a disused old people's home southeast of harefield in Middlesex. For a while home to librettist WS Gilbert, the Grade I listed building is being redeveloped as flats.

EMMANUELLE
(1974, dir: Just Jaeckin)
Sylvia Kristel, Marika Green, Alain Cuny.
● **SEYCHELLES**

The wife of a French Embassy official explores the possibilities of soft-focus sex in Siam in this classic of seventies softcore kitsch, which actually filmed in **l'Union Estate**, the old colonial house of a coconut plantation on the island of **La Digue** in the Seychelles. The house stands on the road between the main, and only, town of La Reunion and the main beach at Grand Anse.

EMPIRE OF THE SUN
(1987, dir: Steven Spielberg)
Christian Bale, John Malkovich, Miranda Richardson.
● **SHANGHAI; SPAIN; BERKSHIRE; LONDON; CALIFORNIA**

Spielberg's Leanian epic, based on JG Ballard's autobiographical novel, has Bale as a boy surviving on his wits after being separated from his parents during the WWII Japanese invasion of Shanghai. It was filmed largely on location in Shanghai, and in Spain.

Bale's colonial home in Shanghai did film in that city's English settlement. The style was so similar to stockbroker belt England that it proved possible to shoot interiors in a bungalow at Sunningdale, on the A30 between Egham and Camberley, on the exotic Berkshire/Surrey border, southwest of London.

The downtown Shanghai scenes were filmed in the old colonial financial district overlooking the Huangpu River waterfront, a virtually unchanged area of the city, where Spielberg coordinated the enormous crowd scenes of mass panic around the **Bund** (now called the Zhongshan

Dongyilu).

The hotel, from which Bale signals to the Japanese warship, is the **Peace Hotel**, called the Cathay in the forties. This grand deco building, dating from the twenties, with its distinctive pyramid roof, is at **20 Nanjiang Dong Lu** (Nanjing Street). One of the famous stopovers for the English abroad, it was here that Noël Coward wrote *Private Lives* (© 8621.63216888, *www.shanghaipeacehotel.com*). The bridge, clogged with panicking crowds below the hotel, is the **Waibaidu Bridge** over Suzhou Creek, flowing into the Huangpu by Huangpu Park, the small green area once notoriously barred to the native Chinese.

The Japanese detention centre filmed inside part of the huge, abandoned gasworks complex at **Beckton** on the Thames in east London, where Kubrick famously filmed the Vietnam scenes for *Full Metal Jacket*. The prison camp set was built near **Jerez**, 80 miles northwest of Seville in southwest Spain.

END OF THE AFFAIR, THE
(1999, dir: Neil Jordan)
Ralph Fiennes, Julianne Moore, Stephen Rea.
● **LONDON; SUSSEX**

The church: St Mark's, Myddleton Square, Islington

Jordan brings a convincingly shabby period feel to this version of the Graham Greene novel. The Café Royal is the art deco bar of the **Sheraton Park Lane Hotel, Piccadilly** (© 020.7499.6321), which also appears in *Mona Lisa* and *Gangster No.1*. The gleaming wood and glass bar where Maurice Bendrix (Fiennes) receives evidence of supposed 'intimacy' from private detective Parkis (Ian Hart) is the **Prince Alfred, 5a Formosa Street**, Maida Vale (© 020.7286.3287), seen also in Michael Radford's pretentious *B Monkey* and in *King Ralph*. Sarah Miles (Moore) remonstrates with God in the Church of **St Bartholomew the Great, Smithfield**, while Parkis and his son spy on her (see *Four Weddings and a Funeral* for details).

63-65 Myddleton Square, on the west side at Inglebert Street, near Angel, Islington, is the home of Father Smythe (Jason Isaacs), Sarah's priestly confidant. The normally elegant square, dating from 1827, is made to look weedy and grubby. Across the street is **St Mark's Church**, where Sarah finds the investigator's boy asleep in the doorway. Bendrix's house, supposedly on Clapham Common, is **Abingdon House, 61 Kew Green**. The corrugated iron alongside the house masks, not a bombed site, but Kew Gardens' Herbarium. You can catch a

Bendrix's house on Clapham Common: Abingdon House, Kew Green

The V1s fall on Clapham Common: Kew Green

Father Smythe's house: St Mark's, Myddleton Square, Islington

glimpse of the entrance to the gardens in the background as Bendrix runs across the green to stop Sarah's cab. The church, where the V1s (flying bombs) fall, is the **Parish Church of St Anne** on the green. **Battersea Park** on the south bank of the Thames across from Chelsea, also stands in for Clapham Common scenes.

Maurice and Sarah spend a weekend in Brighton, where they visit **Brighton Pavilion** (see *Richard III* for details). **Kensal Green Cemetery, Harrow Road**, was used for Sarah's funeral, where Bendrix is told of the miraculous disappearance of the investigator's boy's birthmark.

ENFANTS DU PARADIS, LES (aka *Children of Paradise*)

(1945, dir: Marcel Carné)
Jean-Louis Barrault, Arletty, Pierre Brasseur.
● **FRANCE**

Carné's great classic of theatre life in 1840s Paris was filmed during the German occupation, amid accusations of collaboration. It's set on Paris' Boulevard du Temple, near the working-class districts of Sainte-Antoine and Saint-Denis in the 3rd and 10th arrondissements, named after the Order of the Knights Templar who were once associated with the area. The Boulevard was a strolling area, with pedlars and showmen's booths and, though it was suppressed after the 1789 Revolution, it boomed again after the restoration, becoming the 'Boulevard du Crime', after the number of theatres presenting melodramas, or the shifty mountebanks operating outside. Only one of the original theatres remains, the Theatre Dejazet.

The Boulevard was recreated, at a cost of five million francs, by designer Alexander Trauner on the studio lot at the **Studios la Victorine** in Nice, where close on 50 building and theatre façades were erected. The site of this vast outdoor set is now the studio parking lot. Most of the interiors filmed at Victorine too, though some scenes were shot at the **Joinville and Francoeur Studios in Paris**. The Studios la Victorine are still there (they feature in Truffaut's *Day for Night*), at **16 avenue Edouard Grinda**, Nice.

ENGLISH PATIENT, THE

(1996, dir: Anthony Minghella)
Ralph Fiennes, Juliette Binoche, Kristin Scott Thomas.
● **ITALY; TUNISIA**

Minghella's visually lush adaptation of Michael Ondaatje's

Ralph Fiennes Egyptian desert camp: Camel's Neck

WWII romance is set in Italy and Egypt, though the dazzling desertscapes are in fact Tunisia. 1940s Cairo is **Tunis**, the Egyptian original being a much more developed city these days, while the the city's Medina filmed in **Sfax**, on the Tunisian coast. The invasion of Tobruk shot in the port of **El Mahdia**, between Sfax and Sousse. Ralph Fiennes' desert camp is in the western Tunisian desert near to **Nefta**, not too far from the set of *Star Wars Episode I: The Phantom Menace*, beneath the strange rock formation called, for obvious reasons, the **Camel's Neck**. A guided desert safari with four-wheel drive vehicle is the only practical way to see the location. The huge shimmering salt lake is **Chott el Jerid**, the dry lake you'll need to cross to reach Nefta, and the cave where Kristin Scott Thomas dies, which is near the old Bedu caravan post of **Tozeur**. Locations can be easily reached on expeditions or tours available to those based at the beach resorts of Hammamet, Sousse or Monastir (Tunisian Tourist Office: © 020.7224.5561).

The old Shepheard's Hotel, Cairo – the wartime watering hole for explorers, diplomats and spies which was destroyed in the fifties – is not Egypt either. Nor Tunisia. It's the **Grand Hotel des Bains** in Venice, the setting for Visconti's *Death in Venice*. The actual Italian locations include the village, which is **Pienza** in Tuscany, and the chapel where Binoche studies the frescoes. This is the 13th century **Bacci Chapel** in the church of **San Francesco** at **Arezzo**, also in Tuscany. The frescoes, painted between 1453 and 1466 by Piero Della Francesca, have recently been restored. Reservations are required to view them, and, no, you can't light flares or dangle from the ceiling.

ENTER THE DRAGON

(1973, dir: Robert Clouse)
Bruce Lee, John Saxon, Jim Kelly.
● **HONG KONG, CHINA**

British Intelligence enlists the aid of martial arts master Lee in Hollywood's first flirtation with the martial arts genre, made, on a minuscule budget, at Kowloon's **Golden Harvest Studios** – a former textile mill. The museum and dungeon sets were built here, with Hong Kong's drunks and vagrants drafted in as extras. And since no respectable Hong Kong woman would play a hooker, real prostitutes were brought in from the city's Maze Nightclub.

The location filming took place around Hong Kong itself, and Kowloon. The opening credits record the bustle of Hong Kong's **Barker Street**. Jim Kelly wanders through the narrow streets of the city's giant produce markets. The trip through the junks and sampans to the island fortress of villain Han was shot in **Aberdeen Harbour**, behind a small strip of land on the ocean side of Hong Kong. Han's Castle still overlooks Aberdeen Harbour, and though it's now surrounded by highrises, the steps up from the harbour can still be seen. The tournament fields were actually the tennis courts of Hong Kong attorney MW Lo. Surrounded by eight-foot walls, they're built into the hillside above **Tai Tam Bay**, prime site of the Japanese invasion of 1941.

The old music hall: Alhambra Theatre, Bradford

ENTERTAINER, THE

(1960, dir: Tony Richardson)
Laurence Olivier, Joan Plowright, Roger Livesey.
● **LANCASHIRE; YORKSHIRE**

Olivier recreates his Royal Court stage role, as failed seaside comedian Archie Rice, in John Osborne's bilious state-of-the-nation play. It's set and was mainly filmed on the blowsy seafront of now-faded resort **Morecambe**, the two-week-holiday escape for workers of the industrial north, where the theatre scenes were shot in Morecambe's **Alhambra Music Hall**. Featured is **Hart's Restaurant, 271 Marine Parade**, opposite the clocktower (© *01524.410307, www.harts-restaurant.co.uk*).

ENTERTAINING MR SLOANE

(1969, dir: Douglas Hickox)
Beryl Reid, Harry Andrews, Peter McEnery.
● **LONDON**

Beryl Reid's cemetery home: Camberwell Old Cemetery, Honor Oak

Joe Orton it's not, but an enjoyable black comedy anyway with priceless performances. The Midlands semi, sited by a rubbish tip, becomes a gothic folly in a London cemetery. The movie filmed in **Camberwell Old Cemetery** at **Honor Oak** in south London. The lodge where Beryl Reid entertains Peter McEnery is at the cemetery entrance on **Forest Hill Road**, opposite Marmora Road, SE22. A Grade II listed building, the 1856 house (put on the market by owners Southwark Council for £100,000 in 1993) has since been renovated.

ERASERHEAD

(1978, dir: David Lynch)
Jack Nance, Charlotte Stewart, Jeane Bates.
● **PHILADELPHIA, PENNSYLVANIA; LOS ANGELES, CALIFORNIA**

Lynch's first full-length movie is a claustrophobically oppressive nightmare of sexual guilt, filmed in a grim, industrial cityscape around Philadelphia. The interiors were shot in the stables of the American Film Institute, then at the **Greystone Mansion, 501 North Doheny Road**, Beverly Hills. The mansion itself, and the extensive grounds, are familiar locations seen in *The Loved One*, *The Disorderly Orderly*, *Death Becomes Her* and

Spider-Man. This grand estate was built for oil magnate EL Doheny. In 1929, Doheny's son and his male secretary were discovered shot here, in an assumed murder/suicide.

ERIN BROCKOVICH

(2000, dir: Steven Soderbergh)
Julia Roberts, Albert Finney, Aaron Eckhart.
● **CALIFORNIA**

"What have medical records to do with real estate transactions?" asks untutored law clerk Erin Brockovich, thus opening a can of expensive and deadly worms. Pacific Gas & Electric had reassured the good folk of Hinkley, California, that chromium, used as a corrosion inhibitor in its cooling towers and leaking into the town's water supply, was yummy and nutritious, rather than revealing the truth: it was lethal hexavalent chromium. The brash, uneducated Brockovich (Oscar-winning Roberts) relentlessly uncovers the truth and paves the way for the biggest ever settlement for a civil class action lawsuit.

It's in the nature of movies that the story of one charismatic individual eclipses the tragedy of a community, but the trustworthy Soderbergh avoids either sentimentality or glamour. "I push for the actual locations, unless there is a compelling reason not to," he says, and, indeed, the real Judge LeRoy A Simmons agrees to allow actions against PG&E, at the real **Barstow Courthouse, 235 East Mountain View Avenue, Barstow**.

There's obviously scene setting at **Hinkley** itself, about 20 miles west of Barstow in the Mojave Desert, but changes to the town (not least of which is the buying up of contaminated land by PG&E – which is what connected real estate to medical records in the first place) meant shifting some of the scenes to **Boron**, a further 30 miles west, including the barbecue, in **Boron City Park**, and the town meeting, which was filmed in Boron's firehouse.

Erin first gets to meet law firm chief Ed Masry (Finney) after her car is hit by a Jaguar as she drives along **Magnolia Boulevard**, at **Lankershim Boulevard**, North Hollywood. Erin visits the campus of **UCLA** in **Westwood**, LA, to find out more about chromium. Interior sets, built for the film, still stand, at prestigious film school, the Brooks Institute of Photography, 5301 North Ventura Avenue, Ventura, between LA and Santa Barbara.

ESCAPE FROM ALCATRAZ

(1979, dir: Don Siegel)
Clint Eastwood, Patrick McGoohan, Roberts Blossom.
● **SAN FRANCISCO, CALIFORNIA**

Dark, downbeat account of the only documented escape from the notorious Rock, though the escapers' implied survival remains a moot point. Some interiors had to be recreated at Paramount in Hollywood, but much of the movie was actually shot at the disused prison of **Alcatraz Island** in San Francisco Bay (*www.nps.gov/alcatraz*). Extensive renovations were made to the crumbling structure, which have helped to preserve it as a tourist attraction. The paint used to restore the site to its earlier appearance needed to be easily removable so as not to obscure graffiti left from the 1969-71 occupation of the island by

The real interior of Alcatraz Prison

Native Americans, which is now regarded as a legitimate part of the island's history.

The island functioned as a Federal prison, in effect little more than a dumping ground for problematic convicts, from 1934. Despite the prison's fame, most inmates were not household names, though celeb inmates included "Machine Gun" Kelly, Robert Stroud, The Birdman (see *Birdman of Alcatraz*), and of course, Al Capone. Capone, who was moved to the Rock after continuing to run his empire from behind bars in Atlanta, still sought to buy influence by offering to pay for an extension to the exercise yard. His kind offer wasn't taken up and the King of Crime was relegated to working in the prison laundry.

By 1963, when the concept of confinement without hope of reformation had become outdated and the cost of maintaining the island prohibitive, the prison was closed. Alcatraz is now a national park and can be visited by boat from Fisherman's Wharf in San Francisco.

ESCAPE FROM NEW YORK
(1981, dir: John Carpenter)
Kurt Russell, Lee Van Cleef, Donald Pleasence.
● ST LOUIS, MISSOURI; NEW YORK CITY

Kurt Russell is sent in to rescue President Donald Pleasence, after his plane is downed in the island of Manhattan, now (in the distant future of 1997) a maximum security prison. Most of the the futuristic New York of John Carpenter's cult thriller is not the Big Apple at all, but St Louis, Missouri. The fight scene, ostensibly in the Big Apple's Madison Square Garden, is the **Grand Hall** of **Union Station, 1 St Louis Union Station**, a then-vacant railway terminus, now been renovated as a vast mall/hotel complex. 59th Street Bridge is St Louis' **Chain of Rocks Bridge**. Russell finds cabby Ernest Borgnine happily singing along to the shabby remnants of a Broadway show at the **Fox Theater, Grand Avenue** at Washington. Brain's hideout is the **Civil Courts Building, 12th** at Market. The plane crash site is the corner of **Broadway and St Charles Street**, downtown St Louis, an area which had recently been devastated by a huge fire.

ET DIEU... CREA LA FEMME (aka *And God... Created Woman*)
(1957, dir: Roger Vadim)

The newsagent where Bardot worked: San Tropez

Brigitte Bardot, Curt Jurgens, Jean-Louis Trintignant.
● FRANCE

Director Roger Vadim put not only Bardot on the map, as the orig-

inal 'Sex Kitten', but also **St Tropez**, in this widescreen sex melodrama. Considering its reputation, the tiny fishing port is, visually at least, astonishingly unchanged since the fifties and you'll recognise most of the film's locations. Bardot's home is in the **La Ponche** district, north of the Old Town, but most of the film was shot

Site of Curt Jurgens' office: Quai Jean Jaurès, St Tropez

Site of the bar: Quai Frédéric Mistral, San Tropez

on the picturesque waterfront. It's still a jumble of tiny pastel-coloured cafés, and you can see Curt Jurgens' office on **Quai Jean Jaurès**. The sea wall and steps, where La Bardot pouted and wiggled, are on **Môle Jean Réveille**, across the port from Belvedere de la Marine. Nearby is the gentle slope of **Quai Frédéric Mistral**, which was the site of the Bar des Amis, outside which Jean-Louis Trintignant gets involved in a fistfight and in the basement of which the movie climaxes. The bar is now a souvenir shop, Bleu Continu. Tucked away behind the cafés here is the newsagent where Bardot worked, now a vacant building, **2 rue du Cepoun Louis Sanmartin**, at the junction with Montée Honnorat Coste.

EVERY WHICH WAY BUT LOOSE
(1978, dir: James Fargo)
Clint Eastwood, Sondra Locke, Ruth Gordon.
● CALIFORNIA; NEW MEXICO; COLORADO

This bozo knockabout comedy, featuring a lovable orangutan alongside Clint, was a surprise box office smash, spawning an equally dumb sequel, *Any Which Way You Can*. It was shot around the southwest, from LA's **San Fernando Valley** through **Santa Fe** and **Taos**, New Mexico, to **Denver**, Colorado.

EVIL DEAD, THE
(1982, dir: Sam Raimi)
Bruce Campbell, Ellen Sandweiss, Betsy Baker.
● TENNESSEE; MICHIGAN

Raimi's influential, gory, energetic shocker, with five benighted teensters stuck in a cabin in a possessed forest. was filmed in 16mm and financed by Detroit dentists. The location is near a campground area at **Morristown**, north of I-81, about 40 miles northeast of Knoxville in East Tennessee. The animation sequences were filmed in a basement in Raimi's hometown, **Detroit**, Michigan.

EVIL DEAD II
(1987, dir: Sam Raimi)
Bruce Campbell, Sarah Berry, Dan Hicks.
● NORTH CAROLINA; MICHIGAN

More fun in the woods. The little cabin is now at **Wadesboro**, 40 miles east of Charlotte on Highway 74, North Carolina. Studio filming was at the **De Laurentiis Studios** in **Wilmington**, North Carolina, with additional work in **Detroit**, Michigan once again.

EVITA

(1996, dir: Alan Parker)
Madonna, Jonathan Pryce, Antonio Banderas.
● **ARGENTINA; HUNGARY; LONDON**

Alan Parker brings visual grandeur to the ropey old Lloyd Webber-Rice cart-horse. The production managed to film in **Buenos Aires** (in the face of much artificially induced anti-Madonna hysteria), but it's often **Budapest** standing in for the Argentinian capital. The great coup, of course, was filming 'Don't Cry For Me Argentina' on the balcony of the **Casa Rosada, Government House**, on the **Plaza de Mayo**. The railway station is in Argentina too; the **British Victorian Retiro Station**.

The modernisation of Buenos Aires sent the production company to Europe, however. The tank invasion was filmed in **Liberty Square**, Budapest. Evita's grandiose funeral was shot, not on Buenos Aires' Avenida de Mayo, but on Budapest's **Constitution Avenue** near the Parliament building. But even Budapest presented problems. Evita's lying in state wasn't staged in the Basilica of St Stephen as had been planned, but in the city's **Museum of Ethnography**.

The *boliche* (bar/restaurant) where Magaldi performs, and the various nightclubs and hotels where Eva Duarte (Madonna) works her way to the top, are sets at Shepperton. The real Evita, by the way, appeared at the Colon Opera House in Buenos Aires, and is buried in the Recoleta Cemetery.

Some of the movie was even shot in London: the Buenos Aires theatre where Eva first meets Juan Peron (Pryce), is **Richmond Theatre, The Green, Richmond** (© 020.8940.0088, www.theambassadors.com/richmond). The Richmond Theatre is a frequent screen star, seen in the Peter Sellers black comedy *The Naked Truth*, *Bugsy Malone*, *The Krays*, George Sluizer's *Crimetime*, *Jack & Sarah*, Mike Leigh's *Topsy Turvy*, *Wilde*, *Finding Neverland* and the 2000 remake of *Bedazzled*.

EXCALIBUR

(1981, dir: John Boorman)
Nigel Terry, Helen Mirren, Nicol Williamson.
● **IRELAND**

Boorman's Arthurian fantasy eschews real castles as too naturalistic, and films in the wild landscapes of southern Ireland in Wicklow, Kerry and Tipperary. The forests are the 400-year-old natural oak woods at **Lough Dan** in the Wicklow Mountains, 20 miles south of Dublin, and **Childer's Wood**, near Roundwood for jousting scenes and for Arthur and Guinevere's wedding. Battle scenes feature the primaeval settings of **Wicklow Head**, on the east coast at Wicklow, and **Lamb's Head**, County Kerry.

Cahir Castle, seen in Stanley Kubrick's *Barry Lyndon* is used for the early 'dark ages' scenes.

EXORCIST, THE

(1973, dir: William Friedkin)
Linda Blair, Ellen Burstyn, Max von Sydow.
● **WASHINGTON DC; NEW YORK CITY; IRAQ**

Massively hyped on release, picketed by fundamentalist Christians – the kind of publicity you just can't buy – *The Exorcist* set new standards for gross-out horror movies.

The possessed house: Prospect Avenue, Georgetown

Author William Peter Blatty's stated intention was a movie about Catholic faith. Director Friedkin wisely dumped Blatty's flakily religiose 'Thousand Points of Light' ending, with souls twinkling in Heaven.

The opening scene of Father Merrin (Bergman regular von Sydow) confronting the demon Pazuzu, is pre-Saddam Hussein Iraq. The location was a real archaeological dig near **Al Mawsil**, and the town where Father Merrin suffers is **Hatra**.

The desecrated church: Dahlgren Chapel, Georgetown

Movie actress Chris MacNeil (a character supposedly based on Shirley MacLaine) is shooting a movie about student protest on the campus of **Georgetown University**, Washington DC (also used for *The Exorcist III*) – author Blatty's alma mater. It's on campus that the **Dahlgren Chapel** is obscenely desecrated. Father Karras visits his sick mother in New York's **Goldwater Memorial Hospital** on Roosevelt Island in the East River (for a long time the site of madhouses and prisons – it was here Mae West served her eight day sentence in the 1930s for appearing in her play *Sex*). The hospital appeared again in the very different *Exorcist II: The Heretic*. The aerial **East River Tram** that takes you to Roosevelt Island is featured in *City Slickers* and hijacked by the Green Goblin in *Spider-Man*.

The possessed house itself stands at **3600 Prospect Avenue** at 36th Street NW (used again for *The Exorcist III*), close to the Potomac River in Georgetown, southwest DC, but it's not quite as seen in the movie. You won't be able to spot the window of Regan's room, from which the ominous shaft of light floods in the poster image. This wing of the house was no more than a false front built for the movie. You can, though, find the flight of steps down which Father Karras hurtles, alongside the

Burstyn's student protest movie: Georgetown University

The flight of steps: M Street

house, leading down from Prospect Avenue to **M Street** (see them again in *The Exorcist III*).

The complex interior set, with moving walls and refrigeration, was built at the Ceco Studios (now called Cameramart), **450 West 54th Street** between 9th and 10th Avenues in New York.

The Exorcist III follows on from the original rather than part *II* and is, incidentally, quite horrific. Directed by *The Exorcist*'s writer, some filming occurred at the disused **Ideal Cement Factory building** at **Wilmington, North Carolina**.

EXORCIST II: THE HERETIC

(1977, dir: John Boorman)
Richard Burton, Linda Blair, Louise Fletcher.
● **NEW YORK; ARIZONA; LOS ANGELES, CALIFORNIA**

Not remotely similar in style or content to *The Exorcist*, and the Georgetown house was mocked up at Warner Bros' Burbank studios. Fletcher's clinic, where she investigates Blair's nightmares, was the disused **Goldwater Hospital, Roosevelt Island** in the East River, New York. The hospital also featured in *The Exorcist*. Blair's New York apartment is the black, accordion-pleated **CBS Building, Sixth Avenue** between 52nd and 53rd Streets, although the rooftop terrace, where Blair teeters 35 stories up, is the **Warner Communications Building, between Fifth and Sixth Avenues** overlooking 51st Street and St Patrick's Cathedral.

The African Mission Center is at **Lone Rock**, on the shore of the artificially-created Lake Powell, near Page in northern Arizona. Also near Page is the village at the base of the Ethiopian Rock Church, at **Crazy Canyon**. Both *The Greatest Story Ever Told* and *Planet of the Apes* used the same spectacular rockscapes. The mud city of Jepti was a set built at the Burbank studios, based on the real African villages of Mopti and Djenne in Mali.

EXPLORERS

(1985, dir: Joe Dante)
Ethan Hawke, River Phoenix, Jason Presson.
● **CALIFORNIA**

Dante's enjoyable, satirical sci-fi has Hawke, Phoenix (in his first movie) and Presson as three schoolkids who, in their homemade spacecraft, visit aliens whose knowledge

Ethan Hawke spies on his dream girl: D Street, Petaluma

of Earth is derived entirely from stray TV signals. The small US town the kids take off from is **Petaluma**, in Sonoma County, Route 101, 30 miles north of San

Francisco, and also the location for *American Graffiti*. The movie opens on Petaluma's D Street, and the house where Hawke spies on his dream girl is **920 D Street**. The drive-in, where the spacecraft crashes into the snack bar, is the **Pickwick Drive-In Theater** in the **Pickwick Recreation Center, 1001 West Riverside Drive**, Burbank.

EYES WIDE SHUT

(1999, dir: Stanley Kubrick)
Tom Cruise, Nicole Kidman, Sydney Pollack.
● **LONDON; BEDFORDSHIRE**

After all the hype and the secrecy, Kubrick's final movie was greeted with a strangely muted reception, but there's no denying how gorgeous it all looks. Although it's set in New York, there are only the most fleeting glimpses of the real city, courtesy of a second unit.

Greenwich Village, New York: Hatton Garden

The masked orgy, exterior: Mentmore Towers

The big party scene, where Cruise attends to host Pollack's hooker after she ODs on a speedball, filmed at **Luton Hoo** (see *Four Weddings and a Funeral* for details). Most of the Greenwich Village streets were constructed at Pinewood, but a few shots were London streets dressed as New York. After leaving the apartment of hooker Vinessa Shaw, Cruise is stalked by a sinister man as he walks along **Hatton Gardens**, where New York-style payphones were installed between numbers 32 and 38. The stalker, apparently across the street, is actually on **Worship Street**, EC2, just off City Road in the City (look out for the real **Nicon House, 21 Worship Street**, in the background). **Berner Street** and **Eastcastle Street** also became Greenwich Village. The interior of Club Sonata, the New York jazz club, is **Madame Jo-Jo's, Brewer Street**, in Soho. The Royal Suite of the **Lanesborough Hotel, 1 Lanesborough Place**, SW1, was the site of the edgy meeting between Cruise and Pollack.

Knebworth House (Wayne Manor in Tim Burton's *Batman*) was screentested and rejected for the masked 'orgy' scene. In the end, two separate locations were used. The exterior is **Mentmore Towers**, in the village of **Mentmore**, Buckinghamshire (see *Brazil* for details). It is no longer open to the public. The exotic interior, with its Indian-style carvings, is **Elveden Hall**, a private house on the A11 about four miles west of Thetford in Suffolk. The final Christmas shopping reconciliation scene was filmed on the ground floor of the famous toyshop **Hamley's, Regent Street**, London W1.

F

FABULEUX DESTIN D'AMÉLIE POULAIN, LE
(aka *Amélie*)
(2001, dir: Jean-Pierre Jeunet)
Audrey Tautou, Mathieu Kassovitz, Serge Merlin.
● PARIS, FRANCE; GERMANY

Jeunet jettisons the darkness of his previous, studio-bound *Delicatessen* and *City of Lost Children* to tread the fine line between charmingly whimsical and sick-inducingly twee. He just about manages to stay on the right side, turning Paris, and particularly **Montmartre**, his home turf, into a brightly-coloured fantasy (though interiors were shot in the studio in Cologne). The film opens with a bluebottle buzzing along **rue Saint Vincent**, behind Sacre Coeur in Montmartre.

It's not all sweetness and light: Amélie's mother is killed by a plummetting Canadian tourist in front of **Notre Dame Cathedral** (an incident based, like many of the film's vignettes, on a true event). The railway station from which Amélie embarks to see her emotionally and geographically distant father is **Gare du Nord**, and she skims stones along the **Canal St Martin**. Amélie's apartment is at **56 rue des Trois-Frères**, around the corner from the greengrocers, **Le Marche de la Butte, Passage des Abbesses**.

Amélie searches for Bretodeau, to return his box of precious mementoes, at a phone booth on **rue Mouffetard** at rue Clovis, in the Latin Quarter. The bar where she overhears the result is to the south, **Le Verre a Pied, 118 bis rue Mouffetard**. She gets a surge of love and the desire to help mankind while crossing the wooden **Pont des Arts**, by the Louvre (seen in *Boudu Sauvé des Eaux*).

Although the metro station where Amélie first sees Nino (Kassovitz) groping about under a photobooth seems to be Abbesses, the scene was filmed at **Lamarck-Caulaincourt**, outside which the blind man experiences a moment of transcendence after Amélie has described the sights and sounds of the bustling market on **rue Lamarck** for him. The porn shop where Nino works is **Palace Video, 37 boulevard de Clichy** in the raunchy Pigalle district (where you'll find the original Moulin Rouge nightclub). Amélie sets up a complicated assignation with Nino on the steps in front of **Sacre Coeur**; and solves the riddle of the mystery man who's been leaving his photo everywhere in the ticket hall of **Gare de l'Est**. The stairs where Amélie sees Nino's 'Où et quand?' posters are at the overground Line 6 station of **La Motte-Picquet-Grenelle**, south of Champ de Mars – also the station Amélie stands beneath when she scratches the name of the first Dominique Bredoteau from her list.

But the location you really want to see is the lovely art deco café where Amélie works, which is, surprisingly, real. It's **Café les Deux Moulins, 15 rue Lepic** at rue Cauchois. Rue Lepic winds down from Place du Tertre and turns sharply south at rue des Abbesses. And yes, you can sample the *creme brulee* here, which is now named after Amélie.

FABULOUS BAKER BOYS, THE
(1989, dir: Steve Kloves)
Jeff Bridges, Beau Bridges, Michelle Pfeiffer.
● SEATTLE, WASHINGTON; LOS ANGELES, CALIFORNIA

The resort hotel: Greystone Mansion, Loma Vista Drive, Beverly Hills

Though this story of two cheesy lounge pianists, who find success but fall apart when they hook up with singer Michelle Pfeiffer, is set in **Seattle**, Washington, it was made far from the rains and the mist, largely in sunny Los Angeles. The real Pacific Northwest is used to set the scene: Jeff Bridges is first seen leaving a one-night-stand on **First Avenue** at Vine Street in Seattle's Bohemian Belltown district. His apartment is a third-floor warehouse overlooking the city's famous Pioneer Square, above **Masin's Furniture Co, 220 Second Avenue South** at South Main Street. After the split-up, he thinks he sees Pfeiffer outside the **West Coast Roosevelt Hotel, 1531 Seventh Avenue** at Pine Street (seen also in the biopic of France Farmer, *Frances*).

The piano showroom, where the auditions are conducted, is down south in Los Angeles' eastern suburb of **Pasadena**, and the deli in LA's **Fairfax** district. The brothers' gigs take in such familiar LA venues as the **Ambassador Hotel, 3400 Wilshire Boulevard**, which doubled as a number of sites (see the 1954 *A Star Is Born* for details); the **Variety Arts Theatre, 940 South Figueroa Street**, downtown; and the **Hollywood Roosevelt Hotel, 7000 Hollywood Boulevard**, Hollywood. The upscale resort hotel is a combination job. The exterior is the **Greystone Mansion, 905 Loma Vista Drive**, Beverly Hills (see *The Loved One* for details), while you'll no doubt recognise the imposing lobby and the **Crystal Ballroom**, where Pfeiffer stops the show with her piano-lolling 'Makin' Whoopee', as the **Biltmore Hotel, 506 South Grand Avenue**, downtown (see *Beverly Hills Cop*).

FACE, THE (aka *The Magician*)
(1958, dir: Ingmar Bergman)
Max Von Sydow, Gunnar Bjornstrand, Ingrid Thulin.
● SWEDEN

Dry old stick Bjornstrand subjects charlatan Von Sydow's theatrical show to official scrutiny and lives to regret it. In keeping with the film's theme of theatricality, it's mostly studio-shot, but you can find Bjornstrand's house and the cobbled street in the **Skansen Open Air Museum, Djurgardsslaten 49-51, Stockholm**. The museum, a collection of around 150 period buildings (and a zoo) has been a Stockholm attraction since 1891. It's open every day except Christmas (✆ 08.442.8000).

Bogus priest Cage plants the bomb: New LA Convention Center

FACE/OFF
(1997, dir: John Woo)
John Travolta, Nicolas Cage, Joan Allen.
● **LOS ANGELES, CALIFORNIA**

Woo's first real American success since relocation from Hong Kong, with Travolta and Cage having huge fun impersonating each other's mannerisms in this brazenly ludicrous face-swap thriller. The vast atrium, where bogus priest Nicolas Cage plants a bomb, is the **New Los Angeles Convention Center, Figueroa Street** between 11th Street and Venice Boulevard, downtown LA. See it also as the spaceport in *Starship Troopers*. The futuristic lab, where the face-swap takes place, is a private house in Agoura Hills, designed in 1993 by Ed Niles which, coincidentally, was also used for *Starship Troopers* (as Casper Van Dien's home).

The exterior of the high-security Erewhon prison, where Travolta taunts Cage, is a private oil platform three miles off the coast of **Carpenteria**, while the interior is the power substation of **Eagle Rock**, LA.

The 'Somewhere Over the Rainbow' slo-mo shootout was filmed in the loft of the old **Pacific Electric Building, 610 South Main Street**. A frequent location, its third floor became police HQ in *Se7en* and the DA's office in *L.A. Confidential*, while the building also provided the apartment in *Grace of My Heart*, the laboratory in *Paulie* and the newspaper office in *Spider-Man*. The speedboat climax was shot in **San Pedro Harbor**, south of the city.

FAHRENHEIT 451
(1966, dir: François Truffaut)
Oskar Werner, Julie Christie, Cyril Cusack.
● **LONDON; FRANCE**

Ray Bradbury's sci-fi novel filmed by Truffaut, with music by Bernard Herrmann and photography by Nicolas Roeg, was shot mostly at Pinewood studios in England. The monorail, however, was a stretch of experimental line in France, at **Chateauneuf-sur-Loire**, about 15 miles from Orleans. The futuristic (for 1966) housing is the **Alton Estate** in Roehampton.

FALL OF THE ROMAN EMPIRE, THE
(1964, dir: Anthony Mann)
Stephen Boyd, Alec Guinness, Christopher Plummer.
● **SPAIN**

Last of the great sixties epics, looking terrific because of the decision to build expensive three-dimensional sets, and likely to be oddly familiar to a new generation of filmgoers as much of the film was recycled as *Gladiator*. A vast reconstruction of the Roman Forum was built at the site of another Samuel Bronston production, *55 Days at Peking*, on the ranch of the Marques de Villabragima at **Las Matas**, 16 miles from Madrid.

The opening scenes, of Marcus Aurelius' campaign against the barbarians, are in the **Sierra de Guadarrama** mountains above Segovia, north of Madrid. The battle against the Persians was shot 100 miles to the south of Madrid on a plain near **Manzanares El Real**. Sagunto, on the east coast, 20 miles north of Valencia, stood in for the Roman city of Ravenna. Coincidentally, Sagunto is one of the towns taken from the Moors by the subject of another Bronston epic, El Cid. Lakeside scenes were shot on the shore of **Lake Santillana**.

FALLEN IDOL, THE (aka *The Lost Illusion*)
(1948, dir: Carol Reed)
Bobby Henrey, Ralph Richardson, Michele Morgan.
● **LONDON**

The Embassy, where butler Ralph Richardson comes close to being falsely arrested for murder in this adaptation of a Graham Greene short story,

The Embassy: Belgrave Square

is the headquarters of the St John's Ambulance organisation at the northeast corner of **Belgrave Square**, on Wilton and Grosvenor Crescents (*tube: Hyde Park Corner*). The maze of narrow mews streets where Richardson clandestinely meets with Michele Morgan, and where young Bobby Henrey gets lost, have moved seriously upmarket from the pub'n'café atmosphere of the movie. They are **Belgrave Mews** and **Kinnerton Street**, just to the north of Belgrave Square. The day out was filmed at **Regents Park Zoo**, at the old refreshment stand in front of the **Mappin Terraces**.

FAME
(1980, dir: Alan Parker)
Irene Cara, Lee Curreri, Gene Anthony Ray.
● **NEW YORK CITY**

The trials and tribulations of a bunch of aspiring hopefuls at New York's **High School of Performing Arts**. The school used to be at **120 West 46th Street**, until 1984,

The High School of Performing Arts: West 46th Street

when the facility transferred to the Lincoln Center. The building, gutted by fire in 1988, but restored as the Jacqueline Kennedy Onassis High School, was used only for exteriors. Most of the actual filming took place in the disused Haaren High School, 10th Avenue at 59th Street, which closed down in 1976. It was also used for 1967's *Up the Down Staircase*. The Haaren has since been demolished.

FAMILY PLOT
(1976, dir: Alfred Hitchcock)

Kidnapping the bishop: Grace Cathedral, Taylor Street

Barbara Harris leaves a message: Fairmont Hotel, Mason Street

The department store: Southwestern Law School

Karen Black, Bruce Dern, Barbara Harris.

● **CALIFORNIA**

Hitchcock's last film, a lightweight comedy thriller, is set in San Francisco, but it's no *Vertigo*. Among the real San Francisco landmarks is the **Fairmont Hotel, 950 Mason Street** (© 415.772.5000, www.fairmont.com), seen also in *Petulia* and *The Rock*, where Barbara Harris leaves a message for cabby Bruce Dern at the hotel's *porte cochere*. The cathedral, where Hitch stages the bravura sequence in which a bishop is kidnapped in full view of his congregation, is also for real. It's **Grace Cathedral, 1051 Taylor Street**, also used in *Bullitt*.

But many of the locations are down the coast in LA. The department store, where Dern quizzes the chauffeur's daughter, was Bullock's, the 1928 art deco gem in midtown Los Angeles. Although the store has closed, the building lives on as the **Southwestern Law School, 3050 Wilshire Boulevard** (for details see *Topper*). Barlow Creek Cemetery, where Katherine Helmond is tailed, is **Pioneer Cemetery** in **Sierra Vista Park, Sierra Madre Boulevard**, Sierra Madre, just northeast of Pasadena. The tiny cemetery was booked for filming months in advance and allowed to become wild and overgrown. Cathleen Nesbitt's Rainbird Mansion, supposedly in Pacifica, is a grand house in South Pasadena, while the out-of-control car chase was shot on **Angeles Crest**, LA.

FANNY AND ALEXANDER

(1982, dir: Ingmar Bergman)
Gunn Walgren, Ewa Froeling, Erland Josephson.

● **SWEDEN**

Surprisingly benign Dickensian drama from Bergman, with stern pastors, kindly old relatives and a happy ending. The major location is **Uppsala**, 40 miles north of Stockholm.

FAR FROM THE MADDING CROWD

(1967, dir: John Schlesinger)
Julie Christie, Alan Bates, Terence Stamp.

● **DORSET; WILTSHIRE**

Schlesinger brought all the naturalistic innovations of six-

ties new wave cinema, along with the atmospheric photography of Nicolas Roeg, to Thomas Hardy's tragic novel. Set in fictional Weatherbury (based on

Gabriel Oak arrives in Weatherbury: Gold Hill, Shaftesbury

Puddletown, five miles northeast of Dorchester on the A35), the movie was shot in Dorset and Wiltshire.

The caravan of shepherd Gabriel Oak (Bates), where the tragedy is set in motion when a rogue sheepdog drives his flock over a cliff, stood on the cliffs at **Scratchy Bottom**, between Worbarrow Bay and Osmington, close to the spectacular sea-arch of **Durdle Door**, on the Dorset Coast Path (seen also in *Wilde*). Bathsheba Everdene's (Christie) humble farm was a disused farm building beneath the Hardy Monument (that's Captain Hardy, of "kiss me" fame, not the novelist) at **Portesham**, west of Dorchester. As Oak's fortunes are plummeting, Bathsheba's rise when she inherits Weatherbury Farm (based, in the book, on Waterston Manor in Puddletown), which in the movie is represented by **Bloxworth House**, a 17th century brick house near **Bere Regis** (it's occasionally open to the public).

Oak arrives in Weatherbury to look for work. The steep cobbled street is **Gold Hill**, familiar to a generation of British TV viewers from the 'Hovis' ad. It's behind the Town Hall of **Shaftesbury**, Wiltshire, on the A30 about 20 miles west of Salisbury. The hiring fair itself, though, is **Market Place, Devizes**, almost 30 miles to the north. On the square you can see the **Bear Hotel** (© 01380.722444), where the farm-owners relax, and the **Corn Exchange**, where Bathsheba proves she's more than a match for the local traders. Also in Devizes is **St John's Church**, used as All Saints, where Fanny fatally misses her wedding to Captain Troy (Stamp).

The interior of Squire Boldwood's (Peter Finch) home is in Wiltshire, too; **Thornhill House** at the village of Sturminster Newton, between Shaftesbury and Sherborne, but its exterior is back in Dorset at **Friar Waddon House**, near Weymouth. Other locations near to Dorchester include Fanny's grave, in the graveyard of **St Nicholas** at **Sydling St Nicholas**, seven miles northwest of Dorchester (*rail: Maiden Newton*); the all-night party which is the **Tithe Barn, Abbotsbury**, near the coast, eight miles southwest of Dorchester; and the grassy, stepped hillocks, where Captain Troy demonstrates his swordsmanship. This is **Maiden Castle**, a ten-acre neolithic camp a mile or two southwest of Dorchester on the road to Martinstown. The camp, which became a hill fort, was the site of a bloody battle

Captain Troy shows off his swordsmanship: Maiden Castle, Dorchester

during the Roman invasion. It subsequently became a Roman encampment.

The cockfight was shot in the six-storey 18th century folly **Horton Tower**, just outside **Horton**, about ten miles north of Bournemouth.

FAREWELL MY LOVELY

(aka *Murder My Sweet*)
(1944, dir: Edward Dmytryk)
Dick Powell, Claire Trevor,
Mike Mazurki.
● LOS ANGELES,
CALIFORNIA

Marlowe is drugged up at Jules Amthor's: Sunset Boulevard, Hollywood

The alternative title was meant to warn audiences expecting a musical, when crooner Dick Powell changed gear to become Philip Marlowe in one of the first films noir, an adaptation of Raymond Chandler's novel. Jules Amthor's apartment is the **Argyle, 8358 Sunset Boulevard, West Hollywood** (see *The Player* for details), where Marlowe is kept drugged up.

FAREWELL MY LOVELY

(1975, dir: Dick Richards)
Robert Mitchum, Charlotte Rampling, Sylvia Miles.
● LOS ANGELES, CALIFORNIA

Atmospheric, and more explicit, remake with Mitchum a bit of a softie. Jules Amthor has become butch dyke Francis Amthor, "LA's famous madam" (with a young Sylvester Stallone as henchman). Her brothel is now the **Milbank and McFie Residence, 3340 Country Club Drive** at Arlington Avenue, between Pico and Olympic Boulevards, midtown (not open to the public). The swishy gilt White Orchid nightclub where Marlowe meets corrupt official Burnett, is the old Myron's Ballroom, now renamed **Grand Avenue, 1024 South Grand Avenue**, downtown LA (which you can also see in *New York New York*). Also featuring the, now closed, **Far East Café, 347 1st Street**, Little Tokyo, downtown LA.

FARGO

(1996, dir: Ethan Coen)
Francis McDormand, William H Macy, Steve Buscemi.
● MINNESOTA; NORTH DAKOTA

The Coens' inventive thriller (based on a 'true story'), was shot mainly around **Brainerd**, Minnesota, but, as luck would have it, a particularly mild winter meant that filming had to move north for snow scenes, as far as **Fargo** itself, and **Grand Forks**, North Dakota. Also featured is **Embers Restaurant, 7525 Wayzata Boulevard** at Pennsylvania Avenue South in the St Louis Park area of Minneapolis. Although there *is* a giant Paul Bunyan statue in Brainerd (it's in the Paul Bunyan Amusement Center on the west edge of town, billed as 'The World's Largest Talking Animated Man', and he's seated), the statue seen in the movie was erected on **Pembina County Highway 1**, four miles west of **Bathgate**, North Dakota, up towards the Canadian border.

The Racer's Edge: North Orange Drive, Hollywood

FAST AND THE FURIOUS, THE

(2001, dir: Rob Cohen)
Paul Walker, Vin Diesel, Michelle Rodriguez.
● CALIFORNIA

Rob Cohen's street-racing movie belts along with the power and speed of a rice rocket. It opens with Paul Walker testing his car in the parking lot of **Dodger Stadium, 1000 Elysian Park Avenue**.

Cohen wanted to emphasise LA's overlooked neighbourhoods and sets Vin Diesel's world in a picturesque and popular area of **Echo Park**, north of downtown LA. Diesel's house is **722 East Kensington Road**, and Toretto's market and diner, where Walker insinuates himself into the community, is the nearby friendly local grocery store **Bob's Market, 1234 Bellevue Avenue** at Kensington Road. The Racer's Edge, the garage where Walker works, is an anonymous red-brick building at **1046 North Orange Drive**, just south of Santa Monica Boulevard in Hollywood and, no, there's no car on the roof.

The motorbike gang scenes were shot in Little Saigon. The white statues are the **Vietnamese Cultural Court, 9221 Bolsa Avenue, Westminster**. The Asian gateway is at **9631 Bolsa Avenue**. The first big car rally was filmed on **Prairie Avenue**, between 120th Street and 118th Street. Jordana Brewster and Paul Walker go on a date at **Cha Cha Cha, 656 North Virgil Avenue** at Melrose Avenue in the Virgil Village district of Silverlake. Walker and Diesel stop at **Neptune's Net, 42505 Pacific Coast Highway**, Malibu. The final race, with the train, is on **Terminal Way, Terminal Island**. The 'Race Wars' rally was filmed at **San Bernardino International Airport, East Third Street** at Del Rosa Drive, San Bernardino. Walker is arrested at **Seventh Street and Valencia Street**. El Gato Negro was nothing more than a set built on a vacant lot in **El Segundo**. In an

Toretto's market and diner: Bob's Market, Bellevue Avenue, Echo Park

Vin Diesel's house: East Kensington Road, Echo Park

homage to *Bullitt*, Walker chases the bikers down the slope of **Micheltorena Street** in Echo Park (where you can find the mansion of both *Scream 3* and *Halloween H20*) and on to **Glendale Boulevard**.

FAST TIMES AT RIDGEMONT HIGH
(1982, dir: Amy Heckerling)
Sean Penn, Jennifer Jason Leigh, Judge Reinhold.
● **LOS ANGELES, CALIFORNIA**

All American Burger: the Coffee Bean & Tea Leaf, San Vicente Boulevard

Intended to be a movie of the times, *Fast Times* has become *American Graffiti* for the eighties and, I suspect, much of its cult following is down to the nostalgia factor. There's an amazing array of soon-to-bes on display, with a script from *Jerry Maguire* director Cameron Crowe, Sean Penn as iconic stoner

Ridgemont High: Van Nuys High School, Cedros Avenue

Spicoli, plus early appearances by Anthony Edwards, Nicolas Cage (as Nicolas Coppola), Forest Whitaker, Eric Stoltz and Martin Brest (who went on to direct *Beverly Hills Cop*, *Midnight Run* and – erm – *Gigli*). Ridgemont High is a combination of two valley schools: **Canoga Park High School, 6850 Topanga Canyon Boulevard** at Vanowen Street, and **Van Nuys High School, 6535 Cedros Avenue**, which has included Robert Redford and Jane Russell among its pupils, and, for a short while, Marilyn Monroe. The exterior of Ridgemont Mall is **Santa Monica Place Mall, Broadway** at Third Street, Santa Monica (see *The Terminator*), but the interior is the old Sherman Oaks Galleria, **15303 Ventura Boulevard**. The famous galleria, Valley Girl central, seen also in *Commando*, was damaged in the 1994 Northridge earthquake and subsequently demolished. A new, open-air galleria now stands on the site. Perry's Pizza was real and Jennifer Jason Leigh, in pure Method fashion, took a job here as preparation for her role. All American Burger, from which Judge Reinhold gets fired, is now the **Coffee Bean & Tea Leaf, 11698 San Vicente Boulevard** at Barrington Avenue in **Brentwood**.

FATAL ATTRACTION
(1987, dir: Adrian Lyne)
Michael Douglas, Glenn Close, Anne Archer.
● **NEW YORK CITY; NEW YORK**

Flashy re-run of vengeful-ex thriller *Play Misty for Me*, set in New York. The restaurant where Michael Douglas first claps eyes on Glenn Close is **Mr Chow of New York, 324 East 57th Street**, midtown, a branch of the snobby Beverly Hills restaurant. Close's warehouse apartment is

Michael Douglas' fatal mistake: Mr Chow of New York, East 57th Street

675 Hudson Street, in the **Red Triangle Building** between 13th and 14th Streets (which was also home to Ed Harris in *The Hours*), but the lift they make out in is actually around the corner, at **400 East 14th Street**. The funfair Close takes the kiddie to is **Rye Playland, Playland Parkway, Rye**, New York State

Close's warehouse apartment: the Red Triangle Building, Hudson Street

(where Josh gets his wish reversed in *Big*).

Douglas' out-of-town house is a conflation of two properties: the exterior is in **Bedford**, just east of I-684 in Westchester County, New York State, where the new ending for the movie was shot (it's the old Irene Selznick estate), while interiors were filmed at a house in **Mt Kisco**. The medical centre is the **Westchester Medical Center, Valhalla**, New York State.

FEET FIRST
(1930, dir: Clyde Bruckman)
Harold Lloyd, Barbara Kent, Robert McWade.
● **LOS ANGELES, CALIFORNIA; HAWAII**

Revisiting his famous silent *Safety Last*, Harold Lloyd plays a shoe salesman getting mixed up with crooks and – surprise! – ending up dangling from a tall building. This skyscraper can still be seen at **848 South**

Harold Lloyd dangles again: South Broadway

Broadway, on the corner of 9th Street, by the Orpheum Theater, downtown LA, and is still there unchanged. Filming also took place in the **Aloha Tower** area of **Oahu**, Hawaii.

FELLINI SATYRICON
(1970, dir: Federico Fellini)
Martin Potter, Hiram Keller, Max Born.
● **ITALY**

Fellini, as usual, conjures up most of his surreal, satiric images at **Cinecittà** studios in Rome. However, the shipboard scenes, with the giant fish and a one-eyed Alain Cuny marrying the hero, filmed at **Fregene** on the coast west of Rome, and on the **Isle of Ponza**, 35 miles out in the Tyrrhenian Sea from Gaeta – between Rome and Naples. Some scenes with Potter and Keller in the subterranean grotto, which couldn't be recreated at Cinecittà, were shot in the caverns beneath Rome's **Coliseum**.

FELLINI'S ROMA

(1972, dir: Federico Fellini)
Peter Gonzales, Stefano Majore, Anna Magnani.
● ROME, ITALY

Brilliantly inventive kaleidoscopic collage of memories and images of Rome, filmed almost entirely on the soundstages at **Cinecittà**. The hallucinatory motorway ride into Rome is for real – apart from the terminal traffic jam at a very deliberately artificial Coliseum – as is the closing motorbike tour of the city.

FEMALE TROUBLE

(1974, dir: John Waters)
Divine, Edith Massey, David Lochary.
● BALTIMORE, MARYLAND

The tragic life of Dawn Davenport, shot, naturally, around the less salubrious areas of Waters' native Baltimore. Dawn enjoys a traditional Christmas carol singing with Mom and Dad at her home in the **Orchard Hills** district. She strolls with resolutely heterosexual hairdresser and husband-to-be Gator around romantic **Fell's Point**, at the south end of Broadway overlooking North West Harbor. At Fell's Point and Broadway is the bridal shop where she purchases her ravishing see-through wedding gown, and she performs as 'The Most Beautiful Woman in the World' at the **Theater Club Theater**.

FEMME EST UNE FEMME, UNE (aka *A Woman Is a Woman*)

(1961, dir: Jean-Luc Godard)
Jean Paul Belmondo, Jean-Claude Biraly, Anna Karina.
● PARIS, FRANCE

Tribute to the Hollywood musical: Porte St Denis, rue du Faubourg St Denis

Always unpredictable, Godard followed up his groundbreaking *A Bout De Souffle* with this oddball tribute to the Hollywood musical. Filmed on the streets of Paris, at **Porte St Denis, rue du Faubourg St Denis**.

FERRIS BUELLER'S DAY OFF

(1986, dir: John Hughes)
Matthew Broderick, Alan Ruck, Mia Sara.
● CHICAGO, ILLINOIS; LOS ANGELES, CALIFORNIA

Matthew Broderick became a cult role model to the slacker generation when he bunked off school to spend a day

The parade: Dearborn Street

bumming around Chicago. Set, like many of Hughes' films, in the fictitious Illinois town of Shermer – Shermerville was the name of Hughes' neighbourhood of Northbrook until 1923 – Broderick's school is **Glenbrook North High School, 2300 Shermer Road**, Northbrook (previously used by

Ferris Bueller's Chicago home: Country Club Drive, Long Beach

Hughes in *The Breakfast Club*). Windy City landmarks visited include the Skydeck Observatory on the 103rd floor of the (then) tallest building in the world, the **Sears Tower**, between West Adams Street, West Jackson Boulevard, South Franklin Street and South Wacker Drive in the Loop (© *312.875.9696*); **Wrigley Field**, home of the Chicago Cubs, **1060 West Addison Street** at North Clark Street in Wrigleyville; and the **Art Institute of Chicago, South Michigan Avenue** at East Adams Street in the Loop (© *312.443.3600*). The parade Broderick joins with a rendition of 'Twist And Shout' is a real annual German-American parade filmed on **Dearborn Street**, intercut with a restaging for the movie on the following Saturday, when 10,000 locals turned up in response to ads on the radio and in newspapers. But even in a John Hughes movie, it's not all Chicago: Matthew Broderick's house is in LA. It's **4160 Country Club Drive**, just south of Virginia Country Club in Long Beach, a popular house seen also in *Red Dragon* and as the home of Preston Wasserstein (Robert Patrick Benedict) in the *Risky Business* parody of *Not Another Teen Movie*.

FEW GOOD MEN, A

(1992, dir: Rob Reiner)
Tom Cruise, Demi Moore, Jack Nicholson.
● CALIFORNIA; WASHINGTON DC

There was precious little co-operation from the US Marines, who objected strongly to the near-psychotic Jack Nicholson character in Aaron Sorkin's adaptation of his

The US Naval Academy: St Elizabeth's Hospital

own stage drama. As a result, much of the movie was filmed on Warner's Burbank backlot. The US naval base at Guantanamo Bay, Cuba consists of several locations: the 'fenceline' is at **Crystal Cove State Park**, between Newport and Laguna Beaches south of LA, while other parts of the base filmed at **Fort McArthur** and the **Point Magu Naval Air Station**. The meeting on the verandah of Nicholson's home was filmed at the home of the Coast Guard Commander in **San Pedro**, overlooking the harbour.

The real Washington DC does put in an appearance, though. Landmark sights include the **Memorial Bridge** over the Potomac, between the Lincoln memorial and Arlington Cemetery. Cruise's apartment is on a quiet street just to the northwest in Georgetown, but you'll look in vain for the newsstand on **18th Street**, where he picks up a paper. It was created purely for the movie. The US Naval Academy is actually **St Elizabeth's Hospital, 2700 Martin Luther King Jr Avenue SE**.

FIDDLER ON THE ROOF

(1971, dir: Norman Jewison)
Topol, Norma Crane, Leonard Frey.
● YUGOSLAVIA

The Broadway musical, based on the stories of Sholom Aleichem, survives the transition to the screen with the help of some pretty authentic European locations. The fictitious village of "Anatevka, just south of somewhere" is a skilful conflation of two former-Yugoslavian villages, **Lakenik** and **Mala Gorica**, in Croatia about 30 miles from Zagreb. Some buildings were constructed from scratch, and others built up with false fronts, but the film used many of the houses unchanged.

FIELD OF DREAMS

(1989, dir: Phil Alden Robinson)
Kevin Costner, James Earl Jones, Amy Madigan.
● IOWA; MASSACHUSETTS

"If you build it, they will come," promised the supernatural voices, and come they did. Kevin Costner's supernatural baseball feelgood weepie has provided Iowa with a major tourist attraction. The baseball field, now well signposted, is about four miles northeast of **Dyersville**, just off Highway 20, west of Dubuque. The diamond straddled two properties and after filming, half of it was ploughed up and returned to farming. But as tourists came, the farmer relented, and the field was restored. The baseball ground, where Costner and James Earl Jones receive subliminal messages on the scoreboard, is home of the Boston Red Sox, **Fenway Park, Boston**, in Massachusetts. The smallest major league ground in the States (and the site of Babe Ruth's first professional appearance in 1914), it's on **Yawkey Way** – the ticket office is at no. 4.

FIFTH ELEMENT, THE

(1997, dir: Luc Besson)
Bruce Willis, Milla Jovovich, Gary Oldman.
● LONDON; MAURITANIA

Luc Besson trips out again in this explosion of sci-fi flavoured eye candy. Largely studio-bound, Fhloston Paradise, where the blue alien diva performs, is London's **Royal Opera House, Covent Garden** (*www.royal-opera.org*), filmed during the building's renovation.

FIGHT CLUB

The exterior of the Clifton Cafeteria: West Eighth Street

(1999, dir: David Fincher)
Edward Norton, Brad Pitt, Helena Bonham Carter.
● LOS ANGELES, CALIFORNIA

As in *Se7en*,

The scuzzy hotel: Bristol Hotel, West Eighth Street

Fincher turns the normally sunny environs of LA into a dank, grim nightmare for this blacker-than-pitch adaptation of Chuck Palahniuk's satirical novel, nominally set in Wilmington, Delaware.

The luxurious Pearson Towers condo, in which unnamed narrator Norton indulges his IKEA nesting instinct (slogan: 'A Place to Be Somebody'), is **Promenade Towers, 123 South Figueroa Street** (*www.promenadetower.com*), between First and Second Streets, downtown LA. When it's blown to bits, he moves into the dismal squat of anarchic Tyler Durden (Pitt). There's nothing to see: the house on Paper Street (a Wilmington address) was nothing more than a temporary set constructed down in LA's San Pedro harbour area, and the nearby Lou's Tavern – though a real bar – has since been demolished.

The film, coincidentally, shares a couple of locations with the 1953 *War of the Worlds*. First is the St Francis of Assisi Religious Center, where Norton's support group evenings are disrupted by the chain-smoking Marla Singer (Bonham Carter), which is **St Brendan's, Third Street** at Van Ness Avenue, south of Hollywood.

The restaurant of the "luxurious" Pressman Hotel, where Durden did something unspeakable to the cream of mushroom soup, is the **Emerald Ballroom** of the familiar **Millennium Biltmore Hotel, 506 Grand Avenue** (see *Beverly Hills Cop* for details). Look out for a glimpse of Tyler Durden in the same location, among the hotel staff on the corporate video welcoming Norton to his hotel room. Also downtown LA, but slightly less classy, Marla's digs were the (now closed) **Bristol Hotel, 423 West Eighth Street**. Trust me, you wouldn't have wanted to stay there – during filming, cinematographer Jeff Cronenweth was hospitalised after being hit on the head by a beer-bottle flung down by a disgruntled resident.

During the 'homework assignment' to start a fight with a complete stranger, you may recognise the forecourt with the geometric metal sculptures as **444 South Flower Street** at Fifth Street, downtown: it's the bank robbed by De Niro's crew in *Heat*. The computer store blown up by Durden's Project Mayhem space monkeys is on the corner of the 500 block of **Sixth Street** at South Olive Street, southwest of Pershing Square, downtown.

The old Clifton's Silver Spoon Cafeteria, **515 West Seventh Street**, downtown LA, which had closed in 1998, became the restaurant in which a confused Norton warns Marla to get out of town. The exterior, where he puts her on the bus, is faked at **325 West Eighth Street**, not far from the Bristol (also the downtown section of street Gene Barry seems constantly to be running down in *War of the Worlds*).

FINAL DESTINATION

(2000, dir: James Wong)
Devon Sawa, Ali Larter, Seann William Scott.

● BRITISH COLUMBIA, CANADA

James Wong's neat horror thriller, adapted from an unused *X-Files* script, is chock full of in-jokes and spot-em references. Most of the characters' names derive from classic horror movies (Hitchcock, Chaney, Lewton, Waggner etc), the same joke used in Joe Dante's *The Howling*. New York's JFK Airport is **Vancouver International Airport, Sea Island, Richmond**. There was also filming at **Squamish**, British Columbia.

The sequel filmed around **Vancouver**, including Campbell River on Vancouver Island.

FIRM, THE

(1993, dir: Sydney Pollack)
Tom Cruise, Gene Hackman, Jeanne Tripplehorn.
● MEMPHIS, TENNESSEE; CAYMAN ISLANDS; MASSACHUSETTS; WASHINGTON DC; ARKANSAS

There's trouble ahead when ambitious young Harvard grad Tom Cruise lands a job with a powerful but dubious law firm in Memphis. The opening Harvard scenes were actually filmed at **Harvard University, East Cambridge** and **Harvard Square**, Massachusetts. The impossibly luxurious hotel suite used for Bendini, Lambert and Locke's interview is in Boston's **Copley Plaza Wyndham Hotel, 138 St James Avenue** in Copley Square.

In Memphis, the rooftop party is atop the **Peabody Hotel, 149 Union Avenue** (*www.peabodymemphis.com*), home of the marching ducks who troop down from their penthouse to splash about in the lobby fountain every morning. It's also in the Peabody that Cruise confronts the mob brothers at the end of the movie. Other Memphis locations include **Elmwood Cemetery**, scene of the funeral of the Firm's ex-employees; and Gary Busey's detective agency, which is in the **Cotton Exchange Building, 65 Union Avenue**. The greyhound track, where FBI agent Ed Harris is set up, is the **Southland Greyhound Park, 1550 North Ingram Boulevard** just over the Mississippi on I-40 or I-55 in West Memphis, Arkansas.

The firm's luxury getaway is on **Grand Cayman**, largest of the three Cayman Islands (*The Firm* was the first movie to be shot in these islands). The 'tax avoidance' meeting takes place at the grand 240-room **Hyatt Regency Grand Cayman Resort and Villas** at **Seven Mile Beach** on West Bay Road, north of Georgetown (*© 345.949.1234, grandcaymanhyatt.com*). And though Abanks Diving Lodge was a set, built on the island's North Sound, it was intended to be kept as a tourist attraction. The company's condo itself is the **Great House** on **Seven Mile Beach**. The night-time party, which leads to Cruise's little indiscretion on the beach, is at **The Planet** (formerly Rumheads), the beachside bar of the Holiday Inn.

On to Washington, where Cruise attends a seminar at the **Hotel Washington, 15th Street** at Pennsylvania Avenue NW (*© 202.638.5900*), used also in *Contact*; and a furtive meeting with the FBI takes place by the **Reflecting Pool** in front of the Lincoln Memorial, at the foot of the Mall.

Mud Island in Memphis is the setting for the climactic chase. The 52-acre park contains the **Mississippi River Museum**, where Cruise tries to hide himself, as well as River Walk, a five-block long scale model of the Mississippi itself. The **Monorail**, and footbridge above, which lead to the island, both feature in the climax, and begin at **125 Front Street** at Adams Avenue, downtown.

FISH CALLED WANDA, A

(1988, dir: Charles Crichton)
John Cleese, Jamie Lee Curtis, Kevin Kline.
● LONDON; OXFORD; SURREY

Jamie Lee Curtis comes on to barrister John Cleese: Osney Lane

Superbly crafted black comedy, directed by Ealing veteran (*The Lavender Hill Mob*) Crichton. Kipling Mansions, the pad of Ken Pile (Michael Palin) and home to Wanda the fish, is **Aubrey House, 7 Maida Avenue**, W2, on the Grand Union Canal (if you're in the area, a few doors up you can see the flat shared by Lynn Redgrave and Charlotte Rampling in *Georgy Girl*).

The jewel robbery is staged in the centre of London's diamond trading district, **Hatton Garden**, EC1, north of Holborn, where Wanda Gershwitz (Curtis) checks out **Diamond House, 37-38 Hatton Garden**. Hatton Garden, also a backdrop for *Snatch* and *High Heels and Low Lifes*, became Greenwich Village in Stanley Kubrick's *Eyes Wide Shut*. The getaway filmed quite a distance away, in Clerkenwell. Moustachioed Wanda waits with the car in **Clerkenwell Green**, EC1, where Mrs Coady (Patricia Hayes) is walking her dogs. The flight of steps where the robbers swap cars can be seen between **Roberts Place and Clerkenwell Close**, just to the north of Clerkenwell Green. The gateway where Pile disposes of the evidence is **St John's Gate** on Clerkenwell Road at St John's Square. Mrs Coady's house, where Pile makes a disastrous attempt on her life, is **69 Onslow Gardens**, South Kensington. The pet cemetery, where the little doggies get buried, is a real one: **Silvermere** at **Cobham** in Surrey.

Archie Leach's office: New Square, Lincoln's Inn Fields

The legal scenes were filmed around the **Old Bailey**, EC4, and the olde worlde legal offices of **Lincoln's Inn** (also a backdrop for the Boulting brothers *Brothers In Law*). The office of barrister Archie Leach (Cleese), where Wanda

The Old Bailey interiors: Oxford Town Hall, St Aldgate's

Wanda Gershwitz checks out Diamond House, Hatton Garden

Kipling Mansions: Maida Avenue, Maida Vale

breaks all the rules by calling on him, is **2 New Square**, in the southeast corner. New Square can also be seen as 19th century London in Tony Richardson's *Tom Jones*. The interior of the Old Bailey, however, is actually **Oxford Town Hall**, St Aldgate's at Carfax in the centre of town. The prison, too, is in Oxford. The rusticated entrance to **HM Prison Oxford**, where Otto (Kline) and Wanda first catch sight of Leach, is on New Road, alongside Castle Mound. The side street, where Wanda makes her move on Leach, you can find a couple of blocks west behind Morrell's Brewery. It's **Osney Lane** between Woodbine Place and The Hamel.

St Trevor's Wharf, where Leach borrows the luxurious pad for a doomed tryst with Wanda, is the **New Concordia Wharf, Bermondsey Wall West**, one of those renovated Thames-side warehouses, with a terrific view of Tower Bridge. The window-hanging stunt was filmed a couple of blocks down, in then undeveloped **Reed's Wharf**.

FISHER KING, THE

(1991, dir: Terry Gilliam)
Jeff Bridges, Robin Williams, Mercedes Ruehl.
● **NEW YORK CITY; LOS ANGELES, CALIFORNIA**

Ex-DJ Jack Lucas (Bridges), plagued with guilt that he may have inadvertently caused a mass killing, finds redemption through winsomely mad tramp Henry Sagan (Williams), in Gilliam's twee Arthurian fantasy set in Manhattan.

A drunken Jack talks to himself at the base of the gilt equestrian statue of General William Tecumseh Sherman, on the west side of **Fifth Avenue** by the Plaza Hotel. Sagan and his army of vagrants save Jack from vigilantes at the foot of Manhattan Bridge. Sagan watches the object of

The red castle: Hunter High School, Madison Avenue

his affections, Lydia (Amanda Plummer), at her place of work, the **Metropolitan Life Building, Madison Avenue** between 23rd and 24th Streets. Commuters break into a romantic waltz for Gilliam's big conceit in the Concourse of **Grand Central Station**. The Red Knight chasing Sagan down Fifth Avenue was actually filmed on **Amsterdam Avenue** (where the traffic flows in the opposite direction). The 'red castle', where the Grail is kept, is the Squadron A and Eighth Regiment Armory, now **Hunter High School, Madison Avenue** at 94th Street on the Upper East Side. Sagan's basement hideout is the boiler Room of the **Park Plaza Hotel, 607 South Park View Street**, downtown LA. All the interiors, apart from the Chinese restaurant which was a set in New York, were filmed in Los Angeles.

FISTFUL OF DOLLARS, A

(1964, dir: Sergio Leone)
Clint Eastwood, Gian Maria Volonté, Marianne Koch.
● **SPAIN; ROME, ITALY**

First of the Spaghetti Westerns, which is a bit of a misnomer, since – apart from interiors at **Cinecittà** studios in **Rome** – the locations were filmed in Spain. The opening scene, of Eastwood stopping at the well as he rides into the grim town of San Miguel, is **Cortijo El Sotillo**, near the resort of San Jose in the Cabo de Gata, the coastal strip of southeastern Spain east of Almeria. The Western landscapes are the familiar arid deserts of the area, used in countless movies since *Lawrence of Arabia* was shot here in 1962. The main street of San Miguel is **Hoyo de Manzanares**, near Colmenar, about 20 miles north of Madrid, a Western town built as a movie location whose sad state of disrepair exactly conveyed the death-haunted look Leone needed. The estate of the villainous Rojo brothers is part of the the museum of traditional life in Madrid's **Casa de Campo** park.

FITZCARRALDO

(1982, dir: Werner Herzog)
Klaus Kinski, Claudia Cardinale, Jose Lewgoy.
● **PERU; BRAZIL**

Kinski is the obsessed turn-of-the-century Irishman Fitzgerald, determined to build an opera house in the Amazonian jungle, even if that means physically dragging his ship over a mountain. The making of the movie is chronicled in Les Blank's documentary *Burden of Dreams*.

Kinski and Cardinale arrive at **Manaus**, at the junction of the Negro and Amazon Rivers in northern Brazil, to hear a concert by Caruso. Their skiff docks at the Manaus waterfront landing, below the **Mercado** municipal market. The opera house is the **Teatro Amazonas**, built at the height of the rubber boom between 1896 and 1910, when local Indians and poor whites were used as slave labour to make vast fortunes for the rubber barons. This dazzling palace, whose fountains flowed with French champagne on first nights, once hosted the likes of Jenny Lind, the Ballet Russes and Sarah Bernhardt – who, bizarrely, would mime to great arias as a stand-in soprano warbled away in the orchestra pit. It's on Manaus' **Placa Sao Sebastio**, and has recently been restored to all its glory.

Fitcarraldo returns to his house, which is about 900 miles up the Amazon in **Iquitos**, Peru. The house used to stand on the **Plaza de Armas**, the town centre of Iquitos, capital of the Department of Loreto. The square also contains the metal house of M. Eiffel, of Tower fame, and the boats from *Fitzcarraldo* are moored in the nearby port.

Two boats, with reinforced hulls, were used in filming: one to navigate the rapids (yes, they did it for real) and one to be dragged over the mountain. Herzog in fact went one better than the real Fitzcarraldo, who sensibly dismantled his boat and had it taken over the mountain in pieces. The *Molly Aida* was dragged by 500 Indian extras for over a mile, to a height of 600 feet. The launch, with the ship careering down into the river, was a one-take shot. The river scenes were filmed in an inaccessible region of the River Urubamba near **Rio Comisea**, in the territory of the Machiguenges and the neighbouring Campas, several hundred miles to the south of Iquitos, with supplies brought in from the nearest town of Pucallpa, hundreds of miles downriver. The site of the actual boat-towing, Istmo de Fitzcarrald, is about 300 miles further south.

Peru can be a risky country to travel in, but most of the cities are safe enough (though robbery remains a constant danger). All the roads from Iquitos peter out a short way into the jungle; it's accessible only by air or water. If you really want to follow in Kinski's footsteps, there are jungle cruises up the Amazon from Iquitos.

FIVE EASY PIECES

(1970, dir: Bob Rafelson)
Jack Nicholson, Karen Black, Susan Anspach.
● OREGON; CALIFORNIA

Easygoing drama with a disaffected Nicholson giving up middle class life to drift across the US. Nicholson works at the oilfields near **Taft**, Kern County, California. Filming also took place at **Eugene**, **Portland** and **Florence**, Oregon.

FLASHDANCE

(1983, dir: Adrian Lyne)
Jennifer Beals, Michael Nouri, Lilia Skala.
● PENNSYLVANIA

Beals is a welder with ambitions to be a dancer in this movie, co-written by Joe Eszterhas and filmed in **Pittsburgh**, Pennsylvania. Beals runs into problems at Pittsburgh's famous **Carnegie Institute, 4400 Forbes Avenue, Oakland** (© *412.622.3131*), home of the Museum of Art and the Carnegie Museum of Natural History.

FLESH EATERS, THE

(1964, dir: Jack Curtis)
Martin Kosleck, Rita Morley, Byron Sanders.
● NEW YORK

Gungy little indie low-budget shocker, with Kosleck breeding carnivorous plankton who chomp their way through the extras with a grossness rare for the time. It was filmed, with that sleazily effective air of cheapness, around the famous beaches of **Montauk**, last village of the Hamptons, way out at the far eastern tip of Long Island, Route 27.

FLY, THE

(1986, dir: David Cronenberg)
Jeff Goldblum, Geena Davis, John Getz.
● ONTARIO, CANADA

Goldblum mutates into a giant insect in Cronenberg's visceral remake of the 1958 culty sci-fi. Filmed in Toronto, mainly at the **Kleinburg Studios** to the north of the city. The

Geena Davis meets nerdy Goldblum: Walker Court, Art Gallery of Ontario

opening conference, where Goldblum and Davis meet, was staged in **Walker Court**, at the **Art Gallery of Ontario, 317 Dundas Street W** at McCaul Street, downtown Toronto. The clinic, where Davis tries to get an emergency abortion after the horrendous maggot dream, is the **Chinese Consulate, 240 St George Street**, Yorkville, north of downtown. Goldblum's lab is a turn-of-the-century brick warehouse in a

Goldblum abducts Davis: Chinese Consulate, St George Street

derelict section of Toronto that's since been gentrified.

FOG, THE

(1979, dir: John Carpenter)
Adrienne Barbeau, Jamie Lee Curtis, Hal Holbrook.
● CALIFORNIA

Enjoyable early Carpenter spookster, with the long-drowned crew of a wrecked ship returning to wreak what the undead tend to wreak best. Filmed in the towns of **Port**

The fogbound light: Point Reyes Lighthouse

Reyes Station and **Inverness** in Marin County, on the coast north of San Francisco, Highway 1. The lighthouse is the **Point Reyes Lighthouse**. Filming also took place at **Bodega Bay**, location of Hitchcock's *The Birds*.

FOLLOW THAT CAMEL (aka *Carry On – Follow That Camel*)

(1967, dir: Gerald Thomas)
Phil Silvers, Jim Dale, Charles Hawtrey.
● KENT

Basically 'Carry On Legionnaire', with Silvers as guest star. The desert location is **Camber Sands**, west of Dungeness on the south Kent coast.

FOOTLOOSE

(1984, dir: Herbert Ross)
Kevin Bacon, Lori Singer, John Lithgow.
● UTAH

Bacon is the young newcomer who scandalises the small US town of Bomont, and upsets hellfire blatherer Lithgow with the godless concept of dancing. Fittingly, the town of **Payson**, which stood in for the fictitious Bomont, lies just south of Provo, the seat of Utah County on the shore of Lake Utah – more white, conservative and Mormon than the state capital itself. You can find Payson 15 miles to the south on I-15. Filming also took place in **Provo** itself; in **American Fork**; and at the **Lehi Roller Mills, Lehi** for the dance sequences.

FOR WHOM THE BELL TOLLS
(1943, dir: Sam Wood)
Gary Cooper, Ingrid Bergman, Akim Tamiroff.
● **CALIFORNIA**

The near-inaccessible location for this epic Hemingway adaptation was in the **Sierra Nevada Mountains** north of Yosemite National Park, 50 or 60 miles west of Sacramento, and two hours north of Sonora, the nearest town.

FOR YOUR EYES ONLY
(1981, dir: John Glen)
Roger Moore, Carole Bouquet, Topol.
● **GREECE; ITALY; SPAIN; BAHAMAS; LONDON**

One of the better of the later Moore Bonds, with a ghastly opening teaser, with a 'wacky' Blofeld character being dumped into an industrial chimney – using the North Thames gasworks site at **Becton** in London, which was also Vietnam in Kubrick's *Full Metal Jacket*.

The mining of a spy ship in the Ionian Sea upsets the British Ministry of Defence. Those are the MoD's reassuringly solid doors on **Whitehall Court**, SW1. Melina's parents are gunned down on their yacht in **Corfu Harbour**. At north Italian winter sports resort **Cortina d'Ampezzo** (location for the original *Pink Panther*), in the Dolomites, Bond stays at the **Miramonte Majestic Grand, localita Pezzie 103** (*☎ 3936.4201*). He meets arch-baddie Kristatos at the **Olympic Ice Rink**, built, like many of Cortina's facilities, for the 1956 Winter Olympics. As was the now unused **Olympic Ski Jump** and the **Bobsleigh Run** which feature in the ensuing chases.

After a brief sojourn in Corfu, Bond and Melina set off in search of St Cyril's. First stop is a wedding party staged at **Bouas-Danilia Village**, an authentic-looking, but fake, tourist attraction 9km north of Corfu, off the Paleokastrita Road (it's very well advertised, and not as Disneyfied as it might sound). But the location used for St Cyril's is far less accessible. The dazzling mountaintop monastery is **Meteora**, just over a mile north of Kalambaka in central Greece. There are actually five of the original 24 monasteries remaining perched on vertiginous pinnacles. They were built in such inaccessible places during the Serbian-Byzantine wars of the 14th century, when the only access was by removable wooden ladders. They can now be visited (by those with a good head for heights and suitably restrained clothing – which can be hired, if your bermuda shorts are a bit too *risqué*) via steps and ramps. The monastery featured in the film is **Aghia Triatha** (Holy Trinity), reached by a circular staircase of 139 steps. The inhabitants of the other monasteries, none too keen on the intrusion of a film crew, reportedly hung out their washing to disrupt shooting.

FOREIGN CORRESPONDENT
(1940, dir: Alfred Hitchcock)
Joel McCrea, Laraine Day, Herbert Marshall.
● **LOS ANGELES, CALIFORNIA**

Hitchcock's wartime drama was, by necessity, almost totally studio-bound, filming at the independently-owned studios of Samuel Goldwyn. Almost 100 sets were built, ranging from a square in Amsterdam (needing a diversion of the Colorado River and a sewer system to provide the rainstorm); an 80-foot, three-tiered windmill; the cabin of a crashing plane (which alone cost $160,000 and was suspended

Rowley plummets from the campanile: Westminster Cathedral, Victoria Street

on wires to plunge into the studio tank); to a gigantic mock up of London's Waterloo Station. Cuddly retired assassin Rowley (Edmund Gwenn) plummets from the campanile of **Westminster Cathedral, Victoria Street**, Victoria, in a shot captured by a second unit.

FORREST GUMP
(1994, dir: Robert Zemeckis)
Tom Hanks, Robin Wright, Gary Sinise.
● **SOUTH CAROLINA; GEORGIA; WASHINGTON DC; LOS ANGELES, CALIFORNIA; UTAH; MAINE**

Moving affirmation of simple values or a reactionary celebration of bone-headed sentimentality? The Academy decided on the former and doled out a second Best

The New Year party: Cole's restaurant, Pacific Electric Building, South Main Street

Actor award to Hanks. The bench, on which Gump collars anyone who'll listen, was erected in **Chippewa Square, Savannah**, Georgia, and removed afterwards. If you really do want to ponder exactly how much like a box of chocolates life is, there's a similar seat nearby.

Many of the film's locations were found in a small area of South Carolina around **Beaufort**. The Vietnam scenes used **Fripp Island** and **Hunting Island State Park**, off the Beaufort coast. The fictitious town of Greenbow, Alabama, where the young Gump grows up, is **Varnville**, on Route 68 about 35 miles northwest of Beaufort. Many of the main street shops dressed for the movie have elected to retain the Gump look. The Gump boarding house, Jenny's house and the bus stop were constructed on the **Bluff Plantation, Twickenham Road**, just southeast of Yemassee, on the Combahee River between Varnville and Beaufort. The Four Square Baptist Church, where Gump prays for shrimp with the choir, is **Stoney Creek Chapel, McPhersonville**, Hampton County. In Beaufort itself, the

University of South Carolina stood in for the University of Alabama, where Gump unwittingly gets involved with Governor George Wallace's attempt to prolong segregation, while its **Beaufort Performing Arts Center, 801 Carteret Street**, became the Bayou le Batre Hospital. Bubba's Louisiana home was not in the fictitious Bayou La Batre, but at **Lucy Creek**, just southeast of Beaufort on **Ladys Island**. There was more filming at **Hampton Street Elementary School, Walterboro**, north of Beaufort.

Gump's marathon run takes him first to **Santa Monica Yacht Harbor** on the west coast, then to the **Marshall Point Lighthouse**, near **Point Clyde**, Maine, on the east. Three years, two months, fourteen days and sixteen hours later, he decides to go home at **Monument Valley** in Utah.

In Washington DC to meet Richard Nixon, Gump stays at the **Watergate Hotel, 2650 Virginia Avenue NW**, and reports mysterious men with torches in the building opposite (see *All the President's Men* for details of this location). He addresses the crowd at the **Lincoln Memorial** in DC, before meeting Jenny in the **Reflecting Pool**. After the anti-war demo, Gump hands over his Congressional Medal of Honor to Jenny on **Maine Avenue SW**, in front of the **Jefferson Memorial** in East Potomac Park.

The New Year party was filmed in **Cole's** restaurant, in the **Pacific Electric Building, 610 South Main Street** (a building used also in *L.A. Confidential*, *Se7en* and *Face/Off*). The hospital scenes were shot in the **Ebell of Los Angeles, 743 South Lucerne Boulevard**, midtown LA (© 323.937.0272, www.ebellla.com). This complex is comprised of a women's club and the Wilshire Ebell Theatre (the entrance of which is at 4401 West 8th Street). The Ebell can also be seen in *The Addams Family*, *Air Force One*, *Catch Me If You Can*, *Cruel Intentions*, *Darkman*, *Death Becomes Her*, *The General's Daughter*, *Ghost*, *Very Bad Things* and *The Wedding Planner*.

FORT APACHE

(1948, dir: John Ford)
John Wayne, Henry Fonda, Shirley Temple.
● **UTAH**

Typical Fordian cavalry pic, with Fonda as a stiff-backed officer leading his men to defeat against those damn Injuns. Filmed at **Monument Valley** in Utah; also at nearby **Mexican Hat** and **Gooseneck**, on the San Juan River.

48 HOURS

(1982, dir: Walter Hill)
Eddie Murphy, Nick Nolte, Annette O'Toole.
● **CALIFORNIA**

Con Murphy is let out of jail to team up with cop Nolte in Hill's frantic comedy thriller, set in San Francisco, though mostly filmed around LA. The redneck C&W bar, where Murphy embodies its patrons' worst nightmares – "a nigger with a badge" – was **Torchy's, 218 1/2, West Fifth Street**, downtown LA. A favourite location with Hill (among others), it was Bruce Dern's hangout in *The Driver*. It's since closed down, and the property is currently an electrical goods store. Nolte and Murphy slug it out at the corner of **Fifth Street** and **Spring Street**,

downtown LA.

The 1990 sequel, *Another 48 Hours*, was once again set, but this time also filmed, in San Francisco. The racetrack where Nolte shoots – and burns – a suspect is at **Hunter's Point**, a few miles south of downtown on Highway 101 – it's where you'll find Candlestick Park, the major league baseball stadium shaken up during a game in the 1989 quake. Much of the action centres around the sleazy **Tenderloin district**, between Union Square and the Civic Center. The final confrontation with the biker hitmen and the Ice Man filmed in the **Bird Cage Club**, one of the many strip joints on the Bay City's answer to Soho, and 42nd Street, **Broadway**.

FOUL PLAY

(1978, dir: Colin Higgins)
Goldie Hawn, Chevy Chase, Dudley Moore.
● **CALIFORNIA**

Sub-Hitchcock, but enjoyable, comedy thriller, with Hawn and Chase thwarting an assassination attempt on a strangely vacuous Pope. Filmed in the movie-makers'

The assassination attempt: San Francisco War Memorial Opera House

dream city of San Francisco, with the inevitable, but pretty good, bouncy car chase, heading for a climax at the **San Francisco War Memorial Opera House** during a performance of *The Mikado*. The grand opera house building and the lavish entrance hall are at **401 Van Ness Avenue**, at Grove Street, though the interior seen in the movie is that of the **Shrine Auditorium, 665 West Jefferson Boulevard**, downtown Los Angeles (see *King Kong*, 1933, for details). Goldie Hawn's apartment is **430 Vallejo Street**.

FOUR FEATHERS, THE

(1939, dir: Zoltan Korda)
Ralph Richardson, John Clements, C Aubrey Smith.
● **SUDAN**

AEW Mason's story of the man who becomes a hero after being sent the white feathers of cowardice, was filmed, in colour, partly in the Sudan. The lavish battle scenes have been recycled over the years, even reappearing in the 1955 Cinemascope remake *Storm Over the Nile*.

FOUR WEDDINGS AND A FUNERAL

(1994, dir: Mike Newell)
Hugh Grant, Andie MacDowell, Simon Callow.
● **LONDON; HERTFORDSHIRE; ESSEX; BEDFORDSHIRE; SURREY; BUCKINGHAMSHIRE; HAMPSHIRE**

The lightweight romantic comedy which turned out to be the most successful British film of all time (until the Sheffield unemployed started dropping their trousers) was filmed entirely in London and the Home Counties.

You can find Hugh Grant's London flat at **22 Highbury Terrace**, on the northwest corner of Highbury

Reception No. 1: Goldington's, Church End

Fields at the junction of Highbury Terrace Mews, N5.

Wedding No. 1 (Angus and Laura, at St John's Church, Stoke Clandon, Somerset) is held at **St Michael's Church** in the village of **Betchworth**, a couple of miles to the west of Reigate, Surrey (*rail: Betchworth; closed Sundays*). The reception, with the sheep, is **Goldington's**, a private home set in 52 acres of rolling Hertfordshire countryside. You can see the Georgian mansion just off **New Road**, **Church End** between Chorleywood and the village of Sarratt, north from the A404, Hertfordshire (*rail: Chorleywood*).

The black and white Tudor exterior of the Lucky Boatman, where Grant and MacDowell first get it together after the reception, is the half-timbered **King's Arms, Amersham** (the northernmost terminus of the Metropolitan line) in Buckinghamshire, also in *Murder at the Gallop*. At the time of filming it was only a bar, but it has since closed and is scheduled to reopen as a hotel. The interior is the **Crown Hotel**, a few doors along, at number 16, where you'll find the very four-poster in the hotel's Queen Elizabeth I honeymoon suite (though it's always been booked well in advance since the release of the film).

Wedding No. 2 (Bernard and Lydia at the Catholic St Mary of the Fields, Cripplegate, EC2) was filmed in the (Anglican) **Royal Naval College Chapel, King William Walk, Greenwich**, SE10. Although the future of the college is in doubt, the chapel is open to the public, and likely to stay that way (*rail: Greenwich*). The second reception (The Holbein Place) was staged at **Luton Hoo** (then a stately home), a couple of miles south of Luton and 30 miles north of London off the M1, Bedfordshire. It's now a hotel, but the 1767 Robert Adam house was, until recently, open to the public, and housed a fascinating collection of Romanov memorabilia. A frequent movie location, it's been seen in *A Shot in the Dark*, *Eyes Wide Shut*, *Never Say Never Again* and *Wilde*, and was recently put up for sale.

The Lucky Boatman exterior...: King's Arms, Amersham

...and the interior: The Crown Hotel, Amersham

The restaurant, where MacDowell catalogues her sexual track record, was the Dome in **Wellington Street**, Covent Garden (now the **Café Rouge**). Grant hares off to meet his brother at the entrance to the **National Film Theatre** on the South Bank, and it's on the terrace of the South Bank that Grant explains to MacDowell about David Cassidy and the Partridge Family. MacDowell tries on wedding dresses at **Albrissi**, an interior design service at **1 Sloane Square** – actually at the start of Cliveden Place by Sloane Square.

Wedding No. 3, where MacDowell marries the stiff in the skirt at the chapel of Glenthrist Castle, Perthshire, was actually filmed in Surrey at **Albury Park**, just southeast of Guildford, which is open May to September (© *01483.202964; admission charge*). The kilt-swirling interior of the castle is the Victorian gothic house, home of Sir James Scott, Lord Lieutenant of Hampshire, **Rotherfield Park, East Tisted** on the A32 south of Alton, Hampshire (and, yes, it is available for wedding receptions). It's occasionally open to the public on Sundays and Bank Holidays during the summer (© *01420.588204*).

Simon Callow's funeral is held at **St Clement, West Thurrock**, Essex. This 'redundant' church – stranded in the wastes of an industrial estate – was restored by soap giants Procter and Gamble (whose giant formless grey cube overshadows it) in 1987 as part of the company's 150th anniversary. It's a nature reserve and pretty fiddly to get to. From West Thurrock (a couple of miles west of Grays railway station), take the Stoneness Road south from London Road, turn east into Headley Avenue and south again into St Clement's Road where the tiny church is tucked away between the titanic industrial monsters. The spectacular bridge in the background is the **Queen Elizabeth II Bridge** over the Thames alongside the Dartford Tunnel. Non-wedding No. 4, at St Julian's, the church where Grant has second thoughts, is **St Bartholomew the Great, Smithfield**, hidden away behind its

Wedding No. 2: Royal Naval Chapel, Greenwich

The funeral: St Clement, West Thurrock

Hugh Grant's flat: Highbury Terrace, Highbury Fields

Non-wedding No. 4: St Bartholomew the Great, Smithfield

gatehouse *(tube: Farringdon or Barbican)*. The interior can also be seen in *Robin Hood, Prince of Thieves* and in Neil Jordan's *The End of the Affair*.

1492: CONQUEST OF PARADISE
(1992, dir: Ridley Scott)
Gerard Depardieu, Sigourney Weaver, Fernando Rey.
● COSTA RICA; SPAIN

Columbus' landfall, in this version of the story, takes place on a beach near to **Jaco**, Costa Rica. Ten major sets were constructed here, including the city of Isabel. Back in Spain, the production used several of the genuine historical locations in the cities of **Caceres**; **Trujillo**; **Seville**; and **Salamanca**. In Salamanca, scenes were filmed in the **Old Cathedral** (the city has twin cathedrals fused together as part of the same complex in the centre of town); in the **Convento of San Esteban**, a Dominican monastery built at the end of the 16th century; and also on the **Plaza Mayor**. In Seville, filming took place in the **Alcazar** – the royal palace – and in the **Casa de Pilatos** on **Plaza de Pilatos**, a lavish palace, supposedly a copy of Pontius Pilate's residence.

FRANKENSTEIN
(1931, dir: James Whale)
Boris Karloff, Colin Clive, Mae Clarke.
● LOS ANGELES, CALIFORNIA

Mary Shelley's gothic novel was turned into a classic movie by gay director Whale, starring his lover Colin Clive as the original doctor, and shot almost entirely on the Universal lot and stages. The European village was left over from Lewis Milestone's *All Quiet on the Western Front*. The beautifully designed, and much copied, laboratory set survived for *Flash Gordon* serials, which also nicked the music from *Bride of Frankenstein*. The lakeside scene, where the Creature hurls the little girl into the water to see if she floats, was shot at **Sherwood Lake**, in Sherwood Forest northwest of LA.

FRANKENSTEIN MUST BE DESTROYED
(1969, dir: Terence Fisher)
Peter Cushing, Freddie Jones, Simon Ward.
● MIDDLESEX

Baron Frankenstein hides out: Stanmore Hall

No monster this time, but a spot of brain-swapping leaves poor old Freddie Jones with a stitched head. The house where Peter Cushing hides out is **Stanmore Hall, Wood Lane**, north of Stanmore off the A4140, Middlesex. The hall, with some modern additions, is now home to the Anglo-Swedish Consulting Service, and though it can be glimpsed through the gates on Wood Lane, it's not open to the public.

FRANTIC
(1988, dir: Roman Polanski)

Harrison Ford, Emmanuelle Seigner, Betty Buckley.
● PARIS, FRANCE

Harrison Ford's Paris hotel: Grand Hotel, rue Scribe

Harrison Ford is an American in Paris whose wife is kidnapped. The posh hotel the couple stay in is the **Grand Hotel, 2 rue Scribe** (© *40.07.32.32; metro: Opéra*), designed in 1860 by Charles Garnier, the man responsible for the ludicrously over the top Opera House nearby. It's been radically renovated since and now looks blandly modern in spite of being one of Europe's oldest luxury hotels.

Ford arranges an assignation with the kidnappers on the Yellow Level of the underground car park of the **Centre George-Pompidou, rue Saint Martin**, 4th arrondissement.

FRENCH CONNECTION, THE
(1971, dir: William Friedkin)
Gene Hackman, Roy Scheider, Fernando Rey.
● NEW YORK CITY; WASHINGTON DC; FRANCE

The greatest car chase in cinema?: New Utrecht Avenue, Brooklyn

The doomed detective (though you need to read the script to find out that's what he is – the movie offers no clue) follows Fernando Rey and Marcel Bozzuffi through the streets of **Marseilles** at the beginning of the film. From here on in, though, it's New York. The lowlife bar where Hackman gets plastered is on **South Street** at Market Street at the foot of Manhattan Bridge on the Lower East Side. The toll bridge, where Tony Lo Bianco is tailed, is the **Triborough Bridge** to Randall's Island at the east end of 125th Street. At seven in the morning, Hackman and Scheider stake out **Ratner's Restaurant, 138 Delancey Street** (seen also in *Boiler Room*) on the Lower East Side at the entrance to the Williamsburg Bridge, once a hangout – allegedly – for the likes of Meyer Lansky and Bugsy Siegel.

Scheider first bumps into Rey, 'Frog One', at the entrance to the **Roosevelt Hotel, East 45th Street** at Madison Avenue (© *212.661.9600*). The midtown deco Roosevelt also features in *Boiler Room, Maid in Manhattan* and *Quiz Show*. Frog One's hotel is the **Westbury, 15 East 69th Street** at Madison

Start of the chase: Bay 50th Street Station, Brooklyn

Frog One's hotel: Westbury, East 69th Street

The stake-out: Ratner's, Delancey Street

Avenue on the East Side. He gives Hackman the slip by ducking into the fancy flower shop, **Ronaldo Maia Flowers**, a couple of blocks away at **27 East 67th Street** at Madison, and slips away with the on-off routine on the subway at **Grand Central**. Lo Bianco and Rey meet up in Washington DC, in front of the **Capitol Building**.

Hackman's home is the **Marlboro Housing Project**, on Avenues V, W and X off Stillwell Avenue in Brooklyn, where Frog Two takes pot shots at him. He requisitions a passing car and begins the movie's famous chase sequence at **Bay 50th Street Station**. The car chase filmed (over five weeks) beneath the **Bensonhurst Elevated Railway** – 26 blocks (count 'em) of Brooklyn's Stillwell Line from Bay 50th Street Station along **Stillwell Avenue**, into **86th Street** and finally right into **New Utrecht Avenue**, ending at **62nd Street Station**, where Frog Two gets shot. The chase was filmed, unusually and not entirely legally, at full speed, with real pedestrians and traffic, though there are five staged stunts too.

French TV celeb 'Devereaux' stays at the **Doral Park Avenue Hotel, 70 Park Avenue** at 38th Street in the Murray Hill district. Lo Bianco picks up the drug-stuffed car from the hotel's underground car-park just around the corner on **37th Street**. It's back to the Triborough Bridge for the final drug deal and shoot-out on **Wards Island**, where Lo Bianco's brother works.

The superior sequel, *French Connection II*, was filmed on location around **Marseille**.

FRENCH LIEUTENANT'S WOMAN, THE
(1981, dir: Karel Reisz)
Meryl Streep, Jeremy Irons, Leo McKern.
● **DORSET; DEVON; BERKSHIRE; LONDON**

A box office smash but a not too successful filming of John Fowles' novel, replacing the literary commentary with a present day parallel relationship. But the abiding image is of Meryl Streep (or rather, a stunt double) in a big cloak standing on the **Cobb** in **Lyme Regis**, Dorset. The Cobb is a curving 13th century breakwater built by Edward I to improve the harbour. Filming on location around Lyme Regis included the aban-

Jeremy Irons' London House: St James's Gardens, Holland Park

doned **railway station**, which actually closed in 1965; the **Undercliff**, the coastal area between Lyme Regis and Axmouth; and

Meryl's stunt double: Cobb, Lyme Regis

Broad Street, including the **Royal Lion Hotel** and **Mr Chapman's Bookshop**, which has been left as it was dressed for the movie.

The Exeter scenes were actually filmed at **Kingswear**, over the River Dart from Dartmouth, in Devon. The bar and the bedroom scenes of the Endicott's Family Hotel were shot at the **Steam Packet Inn, Fore Street**, while the **Royal Dart** was repainted in brown and cream to suit the 1867 setting. Exeter St David's Station was **Windsor Central Station**, Berkshire, which has since been radically modernised.

Jeremy Irons searches for Meryl Streep among the whores in **Green Dragon Court**, the dark, pillared space used as a carpark behind the Globe pub (where *Bridget Jones* lives in the first movie) in Borough. Period street scenes were filmed in the narrow all-purpose byways between the warehouses of **Bermondsey** in London. The dock office was an elaborate set built on the Thames waterfront at **Shad Thames**. Virtually all that is seen of the real location are the warehouses opposite. Irons' London house is **2 St James's Gardens**, opposite St James Norlands Church, **Holland Park** (which, at the time of filming, was home to TV presenter Robin Day).

FRENZY
(1972, dir: Alfred Hitchcock)
Jon Finch, Barry Foster, Barbara Leigh-Hunt.
● **LONDON**

A disappointing collision between Anthony Shaffer's blackly humorous script and the director's virulent misogyny, with Hitchcock, returning to film in London for the first time in many years, seemingly stuck in a thirties time warp.

A body is found in the Thames alongside **County Hall**, while a politician blathers on about pollution to an audience including a prurient, bowler-hatted Hitch, but most of the action centres around the old Covent Garden in the days when it was still a thriving fruit and veg market. In the mid-seventies, the market moved to Nine

Discussing the murders: Nell of Old Drury, Drury Lane

The home of doomed Brenda Blaney: Ennismore Gardens Mews, Knightsbridge

Barry Foster's flat: Henrietta Street, Covent Garden

Elms near Vauxhall, and Covent Garden became a prettified tourist trap.

Many of the locations are still recognisable, however. **The Globe, Bow Street**, the public house from which Blaney (Finch) is sacked from his job as a barman, can still be seen, though it's been completely renovated. The pub where he overhears the city gents drooling over the wave of sex killings remains unchanged. It's the **Nell of Old Drury, 29 Catherine Street**, WC2, opposite the Drury Lane Theatre. The flat of 'necktie strangler' Robert Rusk (Foster), where Hitch pulls off the eerie silent tracking shot up and down the stairs, is **3 Henrietta Street**. There's a barely perceptible cut as someone passes the camera – the interior is a studio set. Blaney takes Babs (Anna Massey) to the **Hilton Hyde Park** (formerly the Coburg Hotel), **129 Bayswater Road**, opposite Hyde Park. **31 Ennismore Gardens Mews**, behind Brompton Oratory in Knightsbridge, was home to doomed Brenda Blaney (Leigh-Hunt). Brenda's marriage bureau, where she is raped and strangled, has now gone. The narrow alleyway where it stood, which ran south from Oxford Street, is now incorporated into a shop, though you can still see its elaborate wrought-iron arch above **119 Oxford Street**.

FRESHMAN, THE
(1990, dir: Andrew Bergman)
Matthew Broderick, Marlon Brando, Frank Whaley.
● NEW YORK CITY; ONTARIO, CANADA

Brando's Italian-American club: Hester Street, Chinatown

Naïve film student Clark Kellogg (Broderick) manages to become entangled with the mob and a revoltingly decadent gourmet club when he arrives in New York. His college is the **Tisch School of the Arts**, part of New York University, southeast corner of Washington Square Park at **La Guardia Place**, Greenwich Village.

Predating *Scream*'s knowing post-modernism, Marlon Brando is cast as Carmine Sabatini, the man on whom *The Godfather* was supposedly based, while *The Godfather Part II* is the movie Clark studies. Clark reaches Sabatini's Italian-American social club via **Mulberry Street** (another little in-joke: Mulberry Street was a main Little Italy location for *The Godfather* movies). The club itself is **175 Hester Street**, an area now absorbed into Chinatown.

Clark's first job for Sabatini is to deliver a Komodo dragon lizard from the JFK Cargo Terminal to New Jersey. Although it's set in New York, much of *The Freshman*

was actually filmed in Canada. The shopping mall where the lizard escapes and gets to ride the glass elevator is the **Woodbine Centre**, Toronto, near to the Woodbine Racetrack. Clark evades FBI agents by driving into the goods lift on **East 12th Street**, opposite Cinema Village in the East Village. Other Toronto locations include **Front Street East; Wellington Street East; Dunvegan Road; St Joseph Street;** and **Seaton Street**.

FRIDAY THE 13TH
(1980, dir: Sean S Cunningham)
Betsy Palmer, Adrienne King, Harry Crosby.
● NEW JERSEY

Archetypal cheapo slasher, starting a series that seems to have run and run, and featuring an early appearance from Kevin Bacon. Camp Crystal Lake is **Camp No Be Bo Sco, 11 Sand Pond Road**, a boy scout camp founded in 1927, on **Lake Cedar**, just south of Blairstown on Route 818, northwest New Jersey.

FRIED GREEN TOMATOES AT THE WHISTLE STOP CAFÉ
(1991, dir: Jon Avnet)
Mary-Louise Parker, Mary Stuart Masterson, Kathy Bates.
● GEORGIA

Set in Birmingham, Alabama, this story of women's self-reliance and self-discovery, though toned down from the novel (in which the central friendship is explicitly lesbian), was filmed in **Juliette**, 60 miles southeast of Atlanta, Georgia, east off I-75 toward Macon. The café was the general store on McCrackin Street. And guess what? Yes, it's since been renamed the **Whistle Stop Cafe**, and it's still in business. Drop by at **443 McCrackin Street** (© *478.992.8886, www.thewhistlestopcafe.com*). The rail depot, however, was a dilapidated structure found in the middle of nearby woods, which was excavated, repaired and transported to sit alongside an existing track.

The Rose Hills Nursing Home, where Bates visits her mother and strikes up a life-changing friendship with Jessica Tandy, is the **Starcrest Nursing Home**, formerly a blacks-only hospital, in **Newman**, 30 miles southwest of Atlanta off I-85.

FRIENDLY PERSUASION
(1956, dir: William Wyler)
Gary Cooper, Dorothy McGuire, Anthony Perkins.
● CALIFORNIA

Cooper is the patriarch of a pacifist Quaker family caught up in the US Civil War. This was filmed in **Bidwell Park**, central California (see *The Adventures of Robin Hood*, for details) and on the **M and T Ranch**, Butte County.

FROM DUSK TILL DAWN
(1996, dir: Robert Rodriguez)
George Clooney, Quentin Tarantino, Harvey Keitel.
● CALIFORNIA

Mexico? No. But although the Tarantino-scripted, all-stops-out Western vampire splatterfest was made in the more accessible California, you won't be able to visit the Titty Twister bar. The elaborate trucker hangout was

Site of the Titty Twister bar: Calico Dry Lake Bed, Mojave Desert

constructed from scratch, telegraph poles and all, on the featureless salt flats of **Calico Dry Lake Bed**, beneath the touristy Calico Ghost Town, on I-15 about a mile east of Barstow in the Mojave Desert.

FROM HERE TO ETERNITY

(1953, dir: Fred Zinneman)
Burt Lancaster, Deborah Kerr, Frank Sinatra.
● HAWAII; CALIFORNIA

Honolulu soaper centring around Pearl Harbor. That the army comes out significantly better than in the book is not entirely unconnected with the need to film in Hawaii's **Schofield Barracks**, **Wilkina Drive**, about ten miles north of Honolulu. But the film's most enduring image has to be Burt and Deborah rolling in the surf on **Kuhio Beach**, now helpfully called the 'From Here to Eternity Beach', at **Halona Cove** by the Halona Blow Hole, east of Diamond Head, Waikiki, on Kalanianaole Highway.

FROM RUSSIA WITH LOVE

(1963, dir: Terence Young)
Sean Connery, Robert Shaw, Lotte Lenya.
● SCOTLAND; TURKEY; VENICE, ITALY

Much of the second Bond movie, which was still on a shoestring budget, was filmed in the grounds of Pinewood Studios, with the studio's main administration building standing in for SPECTRE headquarters in the opening scene.

Bond travels to Istanbul to collect potential defector Tatiana Romanova, whom he meets clandestinely on the picturesque **Bosphorus Ferry**. The mosque, where Donald Grant kills the agent, is the **Mosque of Saint Sophia**. Also in Istanbul is agent Krilencu's apartment, in the industrial section of the city. In Ian Fleming's book, the apartment has a huge billboard advertising *Niagara* outside, with a trapdoor in Marilyn's mouth. In the movie, the advert is for the Broccoli/Saltzman production *Call Me Bwana*, the mouth belonging to Anita Ekberg. Enough said.

The Orient Express leaves from Istanbul's **Sirkeci Station**, which also stands in for Belgrade and Zagreb stations. The motorboat chase was begun off the coast of Turkey, at a small village called **Pendik** near the Greek border, but delays and hassles led to it being abandoned and completed at **Crinan**, on the west coast of Scotland. The helicopter chase was filmed at **Lochgilphead** in Scotland. The final shot, of Bond sailing under the Bridge of Sighs in Venice, was captured by a second unit.

FUGITIVE, THE

(1993, dir: Andrew Davis)
Harrison Ford, Tommy Lee Jones, Sela Ward.
● ILLINOIS; NORTH CAROLINA

Ford makes a narrow escape: City Hall-County Building, Chicago

Big screen version of the long-running TV series, set in, and largely filmed around, Chicago. Harrison Ford, before being accused of his wife's murder, attends a charity fundraiser at the city's deluxe **Four Seasons Hotel, 120 East Delaware Place** (℗ *312.280.8800, www.fourseasons.com/chicagofs*), at North Michigan Avenue on the Magnificent Mile. The hospital he works at is the **University of Chicago Hospital**, on the campus of the University of Chicago between East 57th and East 59th Streets and South University and South Ellis Avenues in the Hyde Park-South Kenwood district.

The charity ball: Four Seasons Hotel, East Delaware Place

The breathtakingly staged train crash, which sets Ford free, was filmed on the Great Smoky Mountains Railway at **Dillsboro**, about 40 miles west of Asheville in the far western tip of North Carolina. A further 30 miles west at the Tennessee border is the **Fontana Dam** on the Little Tennessee River at **Lake Cheoah**, where Ford makes his spectacular dive into the white water (the drainage pipe was constructed for the movie).

Ford confronts the villain: Chicago Hilton, South Michigan Avenue

Ford checks out prosthetic limbs at **Cook County Hospital, Harrison Street** at South Wood Street, and makes a narrow escape from Chicago's **City Hall-County Building** after visiting a prisoner in the lock-up. The building, which also figures in the climax of *The Blues Brothers*, is on the block bounded by North Clark, North LaSalle, West Randolph and West Washington Streets. Ford escapes across the plaza outside, past the Picasso sculpture, to lose himself in a (real) St Patrick's Day Parade on **Dearborn Street**.

The climax of the movie, with Ford finally confronting the real villain, occurs in the plush Grand Ballroom of the **Chicago Hilton and Towers, 720 South Michigan Avenue** at East Balbo Drive in the South Loop (℗ *312.922.4400*).

FUGITIVE KIND, THE

(1959, dir: Sidney Lumet)
Marlon Brando, Anna Magnani, Joanne Woodward.
● NEW YORK

The Deep South, festering with lushes, repression and

terminal illness, is just waiting for Brando to drift into town. Yes, it's Tennessee Williams' play, *Orpheus Descending*. Director Lumet, like Woody Allen, doesn't like to stray too far from New York if he can help it, so this Mississippi town is actually in upstate New York. It's **Milton**, a small Hudson Valley town on Highway 9W near Poughkeepsie.

FULL METAL JACKET

(1987, dir: Stanley Kubrick)
Matthew Modine, Adam Baldwin, Vincent d'Onofrio.
● LONDON; CAMBRIDGESHIRE; NORFOLK

Kubrick's strange Vietnam movie, actually two films in one, looks like no other. No lush foliage or rolling green hills, but the bombed out ruins of a far eastern city. The first half, the training sequence on Paris Island, filmed at PEA **Bassingbourn Barracks, Bassingbourn**, north of Royston on the A505 between Cambridge and Letchworth in Cambridgeshire. The Vietnam scenes famously filmed in the vast abandoned gasworks at **Beckton**, on the north bank of the Thames, dressed by designer Anton Furst (who designed the brilliant Gotham City for Tim Burton's *Batman*) and planted with (wilting) palm trees. The delta helicopter scenes were filmed, not on the Mekong River, but over the **Norfolk Broads**.

FULL MONTY, THE

(1997, dir: Peter Cattaneo)
Robert Carlyle, Tom Wilkinson, Mark Addy.
● YORKSHIRE

Owing more to the spirit of Ealing than to radical politics, this amiable story of redundant steelworkers exploit-

Lomper's suicide attempt: Pickering Road

ing their natural assets was made around **Sheffield**, Yorkshire. The closed steelworks is **Sanderson Special Steels, Newhall Road**, in Newhall to the northwest of the city centre. A little to the south is the **Sheffield and Tinsley Canal**, where Gaz and Dave get stranded atop a sinking car alongside the **Bacon Lane Bridge** in Attercliffe. West a couple of miles, in Hillfoot, is the school where Gaz drops off his son, now the **Sheffield Boxing Centre, 73 Burton Street** off Langsett Road.

Gerald's gnome-infested house: Whirlow Park Road

Site of the real Monty: Shiregreen Working Men's Club, Shiregreen Lane

The **Langsett Music Centre** became the Job Centre where the lads' practice routine livens up the dole queue. The area is overlooked by Sheffield's Ski Village, and it's on **Pickering Road**, opposite this swanky new amenity, that Lomper's suicide attempt is thwarted. You can find the tiny park, where the lads make amends to Gerald after disrupting his job interview, southwest, over the A61 Penistone Road in front of the **Blake Pub, 53 Blake Street**.

Gaz stranded on the sinking car: Sheffield and Tinsley Canal, Attercliffe

Gaz's son's school: Burton Street

The 'Full Monty': Idsworth Road

Crookes Cemetery, where Lomper's mum is laid to rest, is west of the city at Crookes, north of the A57 Manchester Road. Down to the southwest, in Whirlow, is Gerald's gnome-infested house, at **34 Whirlow Park Road**.

Millthorpe Working Men's Club, where the lads finally perform, is a combination of **Shiregreen Working Men's Club, 136 Shiregreen Lane**, in Shiregreen to the north of the city, where the routine was actually performed, and **Regency House, Idsworth Road**, off Firth Park Road, a furniture warehouse which supplied the club's exterior.

G

GALAXY QUEST
(1999, dir: Dean Parisot)
Tim Allen, Sigourney Weaver, Alan Rickman.
● **UTAH; LOS ANGELES, CALIFORNIA**

Enjoyably wicked, but one-joke, send up of *Star Trek* as aliens contact the crew of a seventies TV show. The *Galaxy Quest* convention is held at the **Hollywood Palladium, 6215 Sunset Boulevard** (see *The Day of the Locust* for details). The alien planet is the quirky, knobbly landscape of the tiny (one mile by two) **Goblin Valley State Park**, southeast Utah. The park is southwest from Green River, five miles west of Highway 24, and seven miles south on a dirt road.

GALLIPOLI
(1981, dir: Peter Weir)
Mark Lee, Mel Gibson, Bill Kerr.
● **SOUTH AUSTRALIA; EGYPT**

Peter Weir's account of the tragic WW1 campaign (when the Australian and New Zealand Army Corps suffered shocking casualties after a badly organised attempt to secure the tactically important Dardanelles Strait in Turkey) was made mainly in Australia. Mark Lee's west Australia home is **Beltana**, in the Flinders Mountain Range, south Australia. The western Australian desert he crosses with Mel Gibson is the salt flat of **Lake Torrens**, to the west of the Flinders range. Anzac Cove, site of the disastrous battle, is **Port Lincoln**, down on the southern tip of the Eyre Peninsula on Spencer Gulf. The Egyptian bazaar scenes, though, really are **Cairo**.

Gandhi stays in London's East End: Kingsley Hall, Powis Road

GANDHI
(1982, dir: Richard Attenborough)
Ben Kingsley, Candice Bergen, Edward Fox.
● **INDIA; LONDON**

Ben Kingsley's performance and the big set pieces enliven this worthy, coffee-table epic biopic, which was made almost entirely in India, including the South African scenes. General Smuts' office is **Hyderabad House, New Delhi**, built by Edwin Lutyens as a residence for the ruler of Hyderabad. Regarded as too Western in style, it was used as a guesthouse for visiting dignitaries. The enormous funeral procession, as with so many other scenes, was filmed on the actual location of the real event, from **Rashtrapati Bhavan** – the Viceroy's Palace in Delhi – down **Rajpath** to **India Gate**. Scenes were also shot at **Porbandar**, Gandhi's birthplace. The protest at the salt works and the Calcutta riots were shot in Bombay, with the shipboard scenes shot on board the *MS Dwarka* in the city's port. More filming took place at the **Aga Khan Palace, Pune Nagar Highway, Pune**, southeast of Bombay, where Gandhi was interred during the Quit India Movement in 1942. It's now designated as a Gandhi Memorial and is open to the public (© *26680250; admission charge*). Also in Pune were the South African mosque scene and the protest in the Imperial Theatre. **Patna** in the northeast was the setting for the Champaran indifo farmers' riots, and the train scenes were staged in **Udaipur**. The assassination was filmed on the spot where Gandhi was actually shot, in the gardens of **Gandhi Smriti** (formerly Birla House), **5 Tees January Marg, New Delhi**, also a national memorial (© *3011480*).

English locations included **Kingsley Hall, Powis Road**, Bromley-by-Bow, E3, in the East End, where the real Gandhi stayed on his visit to London in 1931, and the **Institute of Directors Club, 116 Pall Mall** (seen also in the 1956 *Around the World in 80 Days*). The **Old Town Hall Arts Centre, Market Square, Staines** in Berkshire, used to be the council HQ. It was restored and in 1994 opened as a theatre and function room. It became the Indian courtroom where Judge Broomfield (Trevor Howard) sentences Gandhi to six years imprisonment for sedition. It's since been seen in *Ali G Indahouse*.

GANGS OF NEW YORK
(2002, dir: Martin Scorsese)
Leonardo DiCaprio, Daniel Day-Lewis, Cameron Diaz.
● **ROME, ITALY**

Scorsese's epic recreation of New York's Five Points district was designed by Dante Ferretti (who had already worked for Pier Paolo Pasolini and Federico Fellini) on the backlot of Cinecitta Studios in Rome. The real Five Points stood at the intersection of Mulberry, Anthony (now Worth), Cross (now Park), Baxter and Water Streets. According to Charles Dickens, who visited in 1842, "This is the place: these narrow ways diverging to the right and left, and reeking everywhere with dirt and filth… Debauchery has made the very houses prematurely old. See how the rotten beams are tumbling down, and how the patched and broken windows seem to scowl dimly, like eyes that have been hurt in drunken frays." There's nothing left of the old neighbourhood, which stood in the area north of the present New York City Courthouse.

GARDEN STATE
(2004, dir: Zach Braff)
Zach Braff, Natalie Portman, Ian Holm.
● **NEW JERSEY; LOS ANGELES, CALIFORNIA**

Braff writes, directs and stars in this sweetly soft-centred Sundance award-winner. You might detect a hint of autobiography as smalltime actor Andrew Largeman (Braff) flees Tinseltown to connect with his roots in New Jersey, as it's filmed around Braff's hometown of **South Orange**, as well as **Wallington, Dumont, Cranford, Morristown, Tenafly** and **Mahwah**, New Jersey.

The disappointment: you won't be able to bellow into

the echoing chasm. It was digitally created for the movie. The good news: you can eat at the exotic Beverly Hills restaurant, though you'll find it in Brooklyn. Sample seafood under the gaze of a golden Buddha at **SEA Thai Bistro, 114 North 6th Street** between Berry and Wythe Streets, Williamsburg, Brooklyn (© *718.384.8850*).

GATTOPARDO, IL (aka *The Leopard*)

(1963, dir: Luchino Visconti)
Burt Lancaster, Claudia Cardinale, Alain Delon.
● **SICILY, ITALY**

Site of the lavish ball: Palazzo Valguarnero Gangi, Palermo

The location for Visconti's lavish version of Giuseppe di Lampedusa's epic novel could only be Sicily.

Visconti initially wanted to use the Medieval village of Palma di Montechiaro to represent Donnafugata, the family home of the princes of Salina, but this would have meant building a road, and that's where the men in dark glasses stepped in (allegedly) to ask for their piece of the action. Visconti wisely moved the production to the decaying village of **Ciminna**, 30 miles south of Palermo. The Piazza of Donnafugata is Ciminna's square, where the façade of Salina's palace was constructed.

More of the movie was filmed in the gorgeous palazzo of **Villa Boscogrande, Via T Natale 91, Mondello**, a seaside resort north of Palermo. The villa is now a swish hotspot. The grand ball was staged in the **Palazzo Valguarnera Gangi, Piazza Croce dei Vespri** in **Palermo** itself. The ballroom is not open to the public, but the palazzo now houses a restaurant. And though the red-shirted Garibaldini filmed on the real streets of Palermo, a section of the town was rebuilt for the film.

GENERAL, THE

(1926, dir: Buster Keaton; Clyde Bruckman)
Buster Keaton, Marion Mack, Glen Cavender.
● **OREGON**

Keaton's classic is based on real events during the Civil War (also filmed – straight – by Disney in 1956 as *The Great Locomotive Chase*), when Union soldiers stole a train from Atlanta, Georgia, and attempted to drive it to Chattanooga, Tennessee. Striving for authenticity, Keaton wanted to use the real train, which was then still housed at the station in Chattanooga (Chattanooga Choo-Choo and Terminal Station, 1400 Market Street, now commemorates the first major public passenger service between the north and south), but Tennesseans didn't take kindly to their history being the subject of a comedy and refused permission. The railroad finally used for filming was at **Cottage Grove**, about 20 miles south of Eugene, off I-5, western Oregon.

GENEVIEVE

(1953, dir: Henry Cornelius)
Dinah Sheridan, John Gregson, Kay Kendall.

● **BUCKINGHAMSHIRE; BERKSHIRE; LONDON**

Stopping for a drink: One Pin Pub, Hedgerley

Two couples enter their vintage cars in the London to Brighton car race in this classic, irresistible comedy. In fact, most of the race was shot, not on the road to Brighton, but around Pinewood Studios.

The movie kicks off in London, where

The two couples stop for ice cream: De Burgh Arms, High Street, Yiewsley

you can see the house of Alan and Wendy McKim (Gregson and Sheridan) at **17 Rutland Mews South**, Knightsbridge. The newsreel crew films the race in front of the gates of **Moor Park Golf Course, Anson Walk**, on the A404, between Rickmansworth and Northwood in Buckinghamshire. The **One Pin Pub**, where the couples stop for a hair of the dog, can be found on **Parish Lane** at One Pin Lane in **Hedgerley**, Buckinghamshire. The **De Burgh Arms, High Street, Yiewsley**, just south of West Drayton Station, is the pub where the two couples stop for ice cream and end up bickering again. Amazingly, the very fifties **People's Café**, opposite the pub, is still thriving. And **The Jolly Woodman** stands on **Littleworth Road, Burnham**, north of Maidenhead, Berkshire.

Collinswood Road, also in Hedgerley, and **Common Road, Fulmer**, provided more stretches of country road. By the time of shooting, the old tramlines that used to run across Westminster Bridge had long gone, which meant that the close-ups of jammed car wheels had to be shot on lines in **Lewisham**, south London.

GENOU DE CLAIRE, LE (aka *Claire's Knee*)

(1971, dir: Eric Rohmer)
Jean-Claude Brialy, Aurora Cornu, Béatrice Romand.
● **HAUTE-SAVOIE, FRANCE**

Another of Rohmer's navel-gazing moral tales among the young, middle-classes, filmed in the Haute-Savoie region of France, by **Lake Annecy**, some 60 miles east of Lyon at the foot of the Alps.

GEORGY GIRL

(1966, dir: Silvio Narizzano)
Lynn Redgrave, Alan Bates, Charlotte Rampling.
● **LONDON**

The clanking metal staircase leading up to the top-floor flat shared by Lynn Redgrave and Charlotte Rampling, in this Swinging Sixties comedy, could still be seen in the alley off **Maida Avenue**, alongside the Grand Union Canal at the corner of Edgware Road (it's actually the rear of **449 Edgware Road**), until the next door restaurant added an extension. Further down Maida Avenue,

James Mason's house: Harley Road, Primrose Hill

The stairs to Georgy's flat: Maida Avenue

between numbers 15 and 22, is **St Mary's Church**, where James Mason finally proposes to Redgrave. Maida Avenue is also the site of Michael Palin's flat in *A Fish Called Wanda*.

Mason's grand home, where Redgrave entertains nursery classes, is the former home of opera singer Dame Clara Butt, near Primrose Hill, at **7 Harley Road**, NW3. The registry office where Rampling finally marries Alan Bates is **Hampstead Town Hall, Rosslyn Hill** at the corner of Belsize Avenue, Belsize Park, currently being renovated as an arts centre.

GERMINAL

(1993, dir: Claude Berri)
Gérard Depardieu, Renaud, Miou-Miou.
● FRANCE

Berri's epic filming of Zola's novel, set in the Wallers-Arenberg mine, was made in the region of the **Lewarde Mining Museum**, east of Douai, south of Lille in the Nord-Pas-de-Calais region near the Belgian border.

GET CARTER

(1971, dir: Mike Hodges)
Michael Caine, Ian Hendry, Britt Ekland.
● TYNESIDE, NORTHUMBERLAND

It was definitely grim up north when Jack Carter (Caine) took the train to Newcastle to sort out the murder of his brother. No longer. The city has perked up no end since the dismal seventies and many of the locations are either gone or have been smartly renovated. Arriving at **Newcastle Central Station**, Jack heads for – almost – the nearest pub for a pint ("in a thin glass"), but the bar is no more. Baron House, on Neville Street at Grainger Street, now stands on the site of the pub which once boasted the longest bar in Europe. The nearest pub to the sta-

Jack stays at the Las Vegas boarding house: Coburg Street, Gateshead

Thorpe gets cornered in Oxford Gallerie: Klub Ikon, Newbridge Street, Newcastle

tion is **O'Neill's, 38 Neville Street**, a branch of the ubiquitous chain of Oirish theme pubs, which was once the Vick and Comet, the bar where Keith (Alun Armstrong) tends bar. Just to the left of O'Neill's is tiny, crooked **Pink Lane**, where you'll find the Gotham Town club, which was once Bower's Café, where Jack gives his niece some advice. Another lost location is the demolished Frank Street, where Jack's brother lived, in **Benwell**, to the west of the city centre.

Unchanged filming sites include **West Road Crematorium, Silverhill Drive** off West Road, where the funeral of Jack's brother is held, and **Newcastle Racecourse** (*www.newcastleracecourse.com*), in **High Gosforth Park**, north of the city, where Jack meets devious chauffeur Eric (Hendry).

South of the Tyne, dominating Gateshead town centre, stands the huge concrete bulk of **Gateshead Car Park, Trinity Square**, the highrise atop which Cliff Brumby had plans to open a restaurant. Odd as it may seem, that's indeed what was intended for this unloved concrete monster. Threatened with demolition for years, it's still hanging on, which is more than Brumby did, as Jack hurled him from the top level to splat on a car roof in Trinity Square. Further along West Street brings you to Coburg Street. On the right, **25 Coburg Street** was the Las Vegas Boarding House (far smarter than it appears on screen), where Jack stays, and famously shocks the neighbours by seeing off a brace of hitmen with nothing more than his proudly brandished weapon.

It's outside the Coburg Street house that Jack is attacked by the snivelly Thorpe, who somehow manages to sprint through Gateshead town centre, across the High Level Bridge and through Newcastle city centre, to scuttle into the Oxford Galleries club where he's cornered in the gents. The nightclub still thrives, in its new incarnation as **Klub Ikon, 49 Newbridge Street** at Oxford Street, in front of the Holiday Inn.

Jack crosses the river to **Hebburn**, where the betting shop behind which he knifes Albert once stood. On his return he shoots it out with the boys from London at the defunct

Brumby plummets from the empty highrise: Gateshead Car Park, Trinity Square

Jack drinks at the Vick and Comet: O'Neill's, Neville Street, Newcastle

Wallsend Ferry terminal. Newcastle's famed bridges are of course featured: Carter meets Margaret on the gloomy walkway of the **High Level Bridge**, gets chased down the steps at **Queen's Lane** and under the **Swing Bridge** to **Watergate**, where he's met by his fairy godmother. He later buys heroin, which he uses to kill Margaret, on the Swing Bridge, catching up with her at the bingo hall on St James Street. The site is now occupied by St James metro station, but you can recognise the Strawberry pub (nuns once brewed strawberry wine from fruit they grew here, honestly) which still stands in the shadow of St James' Park football club.

Outside the city centre is the house of Brumby ("You're a big man, but you're out of shape"), in **Carrville**, way to the south, and the home of villain Cyril Kinnear (playwright John Osborne), the real-life house of a local fruit machine king, who was involved in a slot-machine scam linked to a local murder. It's **Dryderdale Hall, Hamsterley** in County Durham, now a hotel (*© 1388.488494, www.dryderdalehall.co.uk*). The bleak ending is at **Blackhall Colliery** on **Blackhall Rocks Beach** between Seaham and Hartlepool – near the location used for *Alien 3*. The mine machinery and coal waste has gone and the location is now barely recognisable.

A 1972 black remake, *Hit Man*, with Bernie Casey and Pam Grier, was made around LA, featuring the astonishing **Watts Towers, 1765 107th Street, Watts**, in South Central, and the **Milbank and McFie Residence, 3340 Country Club Drive** (see the 1975 *Farewell My Lovely* for details); while the latest remake, with Sylvester Stallone, was shot around Seattle, Vancouver and Las Vegas.

GET SHORTY

(1995, dir: Barry Sonnenfeld)
John Travolta, Rene Russo, Gene Hackman.
● **LOS ANGELES, CALIFORNIA**

Gene Hackman's office: UTB Building, Hollywood Boulevard

Loan enforcer John Travolta finds his vocation in movie production when he relocates from Miami to Hollywood, in Elmore Leonard's satirical thriller. The movie was actually made entirely in LA, including the Miami scenes, which were shot in the **Westside** neighbourhood and at an Italian eaterie in **Santa Monica**.

Travolta arrives at **LAX** airport, where much of the plot

Travolta and Hackman spot DeVito: Café Med, West Sunset Boulevard

centres around the left-luggage boxes in the Southern Terminal, and stays at **Sunset Towers, 8358 Sunset Boulevard**, West Hollywood (see *The*

Player for details). The **UTB Building, 6605 Hollywood Boulevard**, opposite celebrated underwear palace Frederick's of Hollywood, became the office of schlock movie producer Gene Hackman. When Travolta and Hackman drive along the western reaches of Sunset Boulevard, they spot egomaniac movie star Danny DeVito dining at **Café Med, 8615 West Sunset Boulevard**. Rene Russo's house is on **Carbon Canyon, Malibu**.

GETAWAY, THE

(1972, dir: Sam Peckinpah)
Steve McQueen, Ali MacGraw, Ben Johnson.
● **TEXAS**

McQueen and MacGraw on the lam: River Walk, San Antonio

A crooked deal gets Steve McQueen released from **Huntsville State Penitentiary**, Highway 190, about 60 miles north of Houston, to pull a bank job. He goes on the run with partner Ali MacGraw to **San Marcos**, northeast of San Antonio; **San Antonio** itself, on **River Walk**; and finally to **El Paso**, with a climactic shootout at the old Laughlin Hotel, before the couple ride off to Mexico. Shortly after filming, the Laughlin was demolished to make room for the Sheraton.

The 1994 remake, with Alec Baldwin and Kim Basinger, relocated the action to **Phoenix** and **Prescott, Arizona**.

GHOST

(1990, dir: Jerry Zucker)
Patrick Swayze, Demi Moore, Whoopi Goldberg.
● **NEW YORK CITY; LOS ANGELES, CALIFORNIA**

Demi Moore's New York pad: Prince Street, SoHo

The unfeasibly spacious New York pad of Molly (Moore) is one of Tribeca's impressive and trendy cast iron apartment buildings, at **104 Prince Street** between Greene and Mercer Streets. Sam Wheat (Swayze) gets a bullet on **Crosby Street** between Prince and Spring Streets, only to return and follow his murderer onto the subway at **Franklin Street** station, and then to **Myrtle Avenue Station** in Brooklyn. The cool Italian restaurant, where medium Oda Mae Brown (Goldberg) has to convince Molly of Sam's presence ("Ditto") is **Mezzogiorno, 195 Spring Street** at Sullivan Street (*© 212.334.2112, www.mezzogiorno.com*). 42nd Street subway station, where another ghost (Vincent Schiavelli) teaches Sam poltergeist stuff, is a set built, like most of the interiors, in the studio in LA. Also in LA is the bank, where Sam accompanies Oda Mae to open a new account, which is the old Bank of America Building, **650 South Spring Street**, downtown (see *Se7en* for details). But the bank where they close the account with Lyle Ferguson is not a bank at all but the Lounge of the **Ebell of Los Angeles, 4401 West Eighth Street** at Lucerne Boulevard, midtown LA (see *Forrest Gump* for details). Oda Mae reluctantly donates the four million dollars to "a bunch o' nun's" at the base of the statue of George Washington in front of **Federal Hall, 28 Wall Street**.

GHOSTBUSTERS

(1984, dir: Ivan Reitman)
Bill Murray, Dan Aykroyd, Harold Ramis.
● **NEW YORK CITY; LOS ANGELES, CALIFORNIA**

The firestation exterior...:
North Moore Street,
Tribeca

The phenomenally successful horror comedy is set in New York, but its locations are divided between the east and west coasts. The first of many supernatural appearances occurs in the **New York Public Library**, where the marble lions in the opening shots flank the wide flight of steps along **Fifth Avenue** between 40th and 42nd Streets. The haunted stacks, though, were filmed across the continent in the **Los Angeles Central Library, Fifth and Hope Streets**.

...and interior: Firestation
No. 23, East Fifth Street

After getting the boot from New York's **Columbia University** (which doesn't have a Department of Parapsychology, or a Weaver Hall), Murray, Aykroyd and Ramis conceive their ghostbusting plan on the steps of the university's **Low Memorial Library**, on the **Upper Quadrangle** of the campus, north of College Walk, between Amsterdam Avenue and Broadway, West 114th and West 120th Streets, seen more recently in *Spider-Man*. The fictitious Manhattan City Bank that hands out the loan is the **Irving Trust Building, 1 Wall Street**.

The dinky little firestation (yes, it is a real one) that serves as HQ can be seen at **14 North Moore Street**, off West Broadway in the Tribeca area, but the interior is a disused firestation on the west coast, in downtown LA. It's **Firestation No. 23, 225 East Fifth Street**, seen also in *The Mask* , *Big Trouble in Little China* and *Flatliners*. Built in 1910, the station has been closed since the sixties. Be aware that this isn't the most salubrious area of town.

The university campus: Columbia
University

Also in LA is the fictitious Sedgewick Hotel, where the Ghostbusters capture their first apparition in the ballroom. It's that old

favourite, the **Biltmore Hotel, 506 South Grand Avenue**, downtown LA.

Back in New York, 'Spook Central', Sigourney Weaver's troubled apartment block, is **55 Central Park West** at 65th Street, with

The haunted library, inside: Los Angeles
Central Library, Fifth Street

a few upper storeys added in by the studio art department. The chosen location was originally to have been 1 Fifth Avenue in Greenwich Village, an art deco apartment tower block with gothic trimmings and stylised gargoyles, but local residents finally nixed the idea. The building housed the One Fifth restaurant, a location for Woody

The possessed apartment
block: Central Park West

Allen's *Crimes and Misdemeanors*. Just across from Weaver's apartment, in Central Park, you can see the restaurant where Rick Moranis pounds on the window to escape a ravening hellhound. It's another much-used location, the **Tavern on the Green, Central Park West** at 67th Street. The Ghostbusters vehicles can be seen on the Warners' Burbank lot if you take the Studio Tour of **Warner Bros, 4200 Warner Boulevard** (© *818.972.8687*).

The sequel, *Ghostbusters II*, features the **Museum of the Native American, Broadway** at Bowling Green.

GIANT

(1956, dir: George Stevens)
James Dean, Elizabeth Taylor, Rock Hudson.
● **TEXAS**

Edna Ferber's Texas family saga lives up to its name with a massive George Stevens production. The studio filming, on what turned out to be James Dean's last

Memorabilia display in the lobby:
Paisana Hotel, Marfa

movie, was at Warners' Burbank studio, but the Texas landscapes were filmed at **Marfa**, a tiny town out on Route 90 in the West Texas desert between El Paso and Del Rio. Here the Reata ranch house set stood, until most of it finally crumbled away in the eighties. The ruins stand on the **Ryan Ranch**, west of Marfa. The land is private property, but the scaffold skeleton can be seen on the left from I-90, on the road toward Valentine. Little Reata can also be seen a few miles west of Marfa, on the right of I-90 – look for the windmill. Robert Altman's film *Come Back to the 5 & Dime Jimmy Dean, Jimmy Dean* featured a group of Deanophiles in the (fictitious) nearby town of McCarthy who collect bits of the old set, and in *Fandango* Kevin Costner and chums visit its crumbling remains.

The recently renovated Hotel Paisano in Marfa (*www.hotelpaisano.com*) contains a lobby display of signed photos and memorabilia from the movie. Although only lesser cast and crew members stayed at the Paisano, the leads did hang out here in the evenings. And if you're visiting the town, you'll doubtless want to investigate Marfa's other claim to fame – the Marfa Mystery Lights.

GIARDINO DEI FINZI-CONTINI, IL (aka *The Garden of the Finzi-Contins*)
(1970, dir: Vittorio De Sica)
Dominique Sanda, Lino Capolicchio, Helmut Berger.
● ITALY

The Oscar for Best Foreign Language Film went to De Sica's study of an aristocratic Jewish family in pre-WWII Italy hiding their heads in the sand as Fascism threatens, which was shot in **Ferrara**.

GIGI
(1958, dir: Vincente Minnelli)
Leslie Caron, Maurice Chevalier, Louis Jourdan.
● PARIS, FRANCE; LOS ANGELES, CALIFORNIA

Louis Jourdan's house: Musée Jacquemart-Andre

Real location filming around the French capital adds bags of atmosphere to the musical version of Colette's novel about a young girl in *fin-de-siècle* Paris. The opening and closing scenes were filmed in the **Bois de Boulogne**, the vast tract of forested parkland to the west of the city. The scenes in **Maxim's, 3 rue Royale**, were actually filmed in the famed restaurant (*www.maxims-de-paris.com*), while the ice skating scene uses the **Palais des Glaces, 37 rue du Faubourg du Temple**.

The ice skating scene: Palais de Glace, rue du Faubourg du Temple

Louis Jourdan's elegant house is the **Musée Jacquemart-Andre, 158 boulevard Haussmann** in the 8th arrondissement (*www.musee-jacquemart-andre.com*). A luxurious 19th century classical mansion, with paintings and a furniture collection, it was bequeathed to the Institut de France and is open to the public. Bad weather meant that the beach scenes, scheduled to be filmed at Trouville, were shot later in Los Angeles, at **Venice Beach**.

GLADIATOR
(2000, dir: Ridley Scott)
Russell Crowe, Joaquin Phoenix, Oliver Reed.
● SURREY; MOROCCO; MALTA

The savage opening battle, set in Germania, was staged at **The Bourne** near **Farnham**, Surrey, and caused ructions among environmentalists after

The African arena: Aït Ben Haddou

swathes of forest were cleared for filming – although this was an area scheduled for clearing by the Forestry Commission. The African town, where Russell Crowe is sold into slavery, is **Aït Ben Haddou**, near Ouarzazate in Morocco. The provincial arena was added to the existing village, which had already hosted films such as *Lawrence of Arabia*, *The Last Days of Sodom and Gomorrah* and *Jewel of the Nile*.

The vast Roman sets (with CGI additions) were constructed on the massive remains of **Fort Ricasoli** on **Malta**.

GLENN MILLER STORY, THE
(1954, dir: Anthony Mann)
James Stewart, June Allyson, Harry Morgan.
● CALIFORNIA

Biopic of the bandleader, and his search for 'the sound', featuring the ballroom of the **Santa Monica Pier**, at the foot of Colorado Avenue. The pawn shop stood on Clay

Glenn Miller goes to the pawn shop: Angel's Flight

Street, alongside **Angel's Flight**, downtown LA's tiny funicular railway, a much-loved landmark railway, demolished in 1969, which ran from Hill Street up to Clay Alley. The structure was kept in storage and was restored, but after a fatal accident it has closed again and its future remains uncertain. The surrounds are unrecognisable – the railway now runs up a grassy green slope.

GLORY
(1989, dir: Edward Zwick)
Matthew Broderick, Denzel Washington, Morgan Freeman.
● GEORGIA; MASSACHUSETTS

Matthew Broderick in a story of the first black regiment in the US army. The Boston scenes filmed in **Savannah**, Georgia. Once a great cotton port, Savannah slid into deep decline until the 1950s, when a giant restoration project was begun. The beautiful downtown area is now the USA's largest Urban Historic Landmark district.

The location for the parade, when the 54th finally gets its blue coats, is **River Street**, running along the south bank of the Savannah River, Savannah. Broderick's mansion is the Italianate **Hugh W Mercer House, 429 Bull Street** on Monterey Square, then a private home but now open to the public. It was the real home of Jim Williams, central character of *Midnight in the Garden of Good and*

Evil (played by Kevin Spacey in Clint Eastwood's movie, which also filmed at the house) Readville Camp, Massachusetts was filmed in **Battlefield Park**.

The assault on Fort Wagner was shot 60 miles south on **Jekyll Island**, once the private playground of the stinking rich – we're talking Vanderbilts, Rockefellers and Astors – it was bought by the state of Georgia in 1947 (for $650,000 if you must know). The Battle of Antietam was staged near **McDonough**.

Jons supermarket: South Central Avenue

The Vegas hotel: Frontier Hotel and Casino, Las Vegas Boulevard South

GO

(1999, dir: Doug Liman)
Sarah Polley, Desmond Askew, Scott Wolf.
● **LOS ANGELES, CALIFORNIA; NEVADA**

LA checkout clerks get involved with drug busts, guns and stolen cars in Liman's dazzling, blackly funny follow-up to *Swingers*, made almost entirely on location around Los Angeles and Las Vegas. The store is **Jons, South Central Avenue** at East Adams Boulevard in LA, which was chosen for its unmodernised appearance. The film-makers were horrified to find out that the owner had used the location fee to – you guessed it – smarten up his store before filming started. The inspiration for the store came from Ralph's Grocery in LA, known as 'rock'n'roll Ralph's', as it's sited in the middle of the stretch of guitar shops and academies on Sunset Boulevard in Hollywood. The Vegas locations are the **Riviera Hotel and Casino, 2901 Las Vegas Boulevard South** at Riviera Boulevard (© *702.734.5110*); and the **Frontier Hotel and Casino, 3120 Las Vegas Boulevard South** (© *702.794.8200*).

GO-BETWEEN, THE

(1970, dir: Joseph Losey)
Dominic Guard, Julie Christie, Alan Bates.
● **NORFOLK**

The shopping expedition: Tombland Alley, Norwich

Set in a golden Edwardian summer, Losey's film of the LP Hartley story (adapted by Harold Pinter) was made on location in Norfolk. Michael Redgrave, in one of the movie's ominous flash-forwards to a dull, grey present, arrives at **Norwich Station, Thorpe Road**. In hap-

Leo is sent to amuse himself: Norwich Cathedral

pier times, his younger self is taken on a shopping expedition to Norwich by Julie Christie. While young Dominic Guard is sent to amuse himself in **Norwich Cathedral**, Christie clandestinely meets up with hunky farmer Alan Bates at the horsefair on **Tombland**. Off Tombland is **Tombland Alley**,

Julie Christie's cottage: Heydon

along which Christie and Guard walk. The ghoulish name comes from the fact that bodies of plague victims are buried behind its walls.

The local village is **Heydon**, just west of the B1149, about eight miles west of Aylsham (*BR: Aylsham*). Here you'll find the **Church of St Peter and St Paul**, where the locals gather and where the older Redgrave walks in the graveyard. On the green opposite stands Julie Christie's cottage, where Redgrave is asked to carry one last message. The cricket match, though, is not in Heydon. You can see the green, now rough, overgrown and planted with a couple of decrepit goalposts, just south of the village of **Thornage**. The three skeletal trees overlooking the green are still recognisable, as are the farm outbuildings. The B1110 runs right through the green.

The country house: Melton Constable Hall, Melton Constable

Southwest of Thornage is Melton Constable on the B1354, and a couple of miles south on the road to Hindolveston is a large unmarked gate which is the entrance to **Melton Constable Hall**, now a private residence.

GO WEST

(1940, dir: Edward Buzzell)
The Marx Brothers, John Carroll, Diana Lewis.
● **CALIFORNIA**

The railway commandeered by Groucho and co in this Wild West caper is the old Sierra Railroad in northern California, seen in dozens of movies including *High Noon, My Little Chickadee* and *Unforgiven*. It still operates, as **Railtown 1897**

The old railroad: Jamestown

State Park, part of the California State Railroad Museum at **Fifth** and **Reservoir Street, Jamestown**, on Route 49 about 50 miles east of Stockton. At weekends from April through October, you can take a 40-minute round trip (© *916.445.6645, www.csrmf.org/railtown.html*).

GODFATHER, THE
(1972, dir: Francis Ford Coppola)
Marlon Brando, Al Pacino, Diane Keaton.
● NEW YORK CITY; LONG ISLAND, NEW YORK; LOS ANGELES, CALIFORNIA; LAS VEGAS, NEVADA; SICILY, ITALY

Luca Brasi is garrotted: Sofia's Restaurant, Edison Hotel, 47th Street

With mafia movies out of fashion and a relatively unknown director at the helm, Paramount was keen to cut costs by updating the movie to the present day and filming on its Hollywood lot. But as paperback sales hit 12 million copies, the studio reluctantly conceded to Coppola's demands, and much of the film was shot on real locations in New York.

Even the studio filming was done on the east coast, at New York's Filmways Studios, **246 East 127th Street, East Harlem** at Second Avenue. The studio has since closed down, and is now a huge supermarket called Foodways.

The wedding scene, at the Corleone compound on Long Island, did film on an island over the water from New York – not on Long Island, but **Staten Island**. The outdoor festivities were staged in the garden of **120 Longfellow Road**, in the affluent neighbourhood of Emerson Hill. The Corleone Mansion itself is next door at **110 Longfellow Road**. The Staten Island Rapid Transit Railway will take you from St George Station, four stops to Grasmere. From here, it's about a half hour's walk north to Longfellow Road, a leafy cul-de-sac running east from Ocean Terrace. Numbers 110 and 120 are the last houses at the end of the road.

When Don Corleone sends his consigliore, Tom Hagen, to Hollywood, to make the studio head the infamous 'offer he can't refuse', there's a great newsreel shot of the old Hollywood, with **Hollywood United Methodist Church** on Highland Avenue (see *What Price Hollywood?* for details) and **Grauman's Chinese Theatre** (as it then was) on Hollywood Boulevard still recognisable from the days before the area became swamped by tacky tourist shops.

The Genco Olive Oil office: Mietz Building, Mott Street

The Paramount lot, **5451 Marathon Street** at Bronson Avenue behind Melrose Avenue in Hollywood stands in for Woltz International

The Corleone Mansion: Longfellow Road, Staten Island

Pictures' (see *Sunset Blvd* for details of the studio). After Woltz eventually agrees to meet up with Hagen, it's a rare case of an East Coast residence standing in for Hollywood. The bedroom of Woltz's villa, where the studio boss finds the head of his unfortunate horse, is the living room of **Falaise**, on **Sands Point Preserve**, the Guggenheim estate way out at **95 Middleneck Road** on Long Island. You can visit the Preserve, which also houses mansions seen in the 1998 update of *Great Expectations* and *Scent of a Woman* in the summer months. It's about four miles north of Point Washington (there's a cab firm near the station), on the Long Island Railroad from New York's Pennsylvania Station, Seventh Avenue. The exterior of Woltz's mansion, seen also as Whitney Houston's estate in *The Bodyguard*, really is LA. It's supposedly the enormous Beverly Hills estate of silent star Harold Lloyd, **Greenacres, 1740 Green Acres Drive**. See *Westworld* for details.

Michael and Kay are staying at the grand St Regis Hotel, now the **St Regis-Sheraton, 2 East 55th Street** (© *212.767.0525*) on the corner of Fifth Avenue. Nearby stood Best & Co, the New York department store where they do their Christmas shopping, on Fifth Avenue between 51st and 52nd Streets in the fashionable stretch of 'Ladies' Mile'. Although already closed, the store briefly blazed back to life for filming before being demolished. Sadly, the model-train heaven, Polk's Hobby Shop, which stood at 314 Fifth Avenue near 31st Street, is also gone. This is where Tom Hagen stocks up on presents when Sollozzo's men invite him for a car ride. It has now been replaced by a pizza joint.

The bar, where Sollozzo meets up with Luca Brasi, is the **Edison Hotel, 228 West 47th Street** (*www.edison-hotelnyc.com*). You'll recognise the slightly redecorated corridor with its circular mirrors in Woody Allen's *Bullets Over Broadway*. It's inside what is now **Sophia's Restaurant**, the Edison's coffee shop, that Brasi is pinned down to the counter and garrotted.

The Genco Olive Oil premises, supposedly on Mulberry Street, outside which the Don is gunned down, was the **Mietz Building, 128 Mott Street**, a then-unchanged area between Little Italy and Chinatown. The relentless encroachment of Chinatown into Little Italy means that the building has since been gutted and has become a Chinese market, though the 'Mietz' name is still visible on the frontage. The art deco entrance was created especially for the movie. With astonishing speed, the news hits the papers while Michael and Kay watch *The Bells of St Mary's* at **Radio City Music Hall, 1260 Sixth Avenue** at 50th Street. The exterior of hospital where Michael visits his wounded father is the **Lincoln Medical Center, 234 East 149th Street** in the Bronx, though the deserted interior is the **New York Eye and**

SWINGING LONDON

WEST LONDON: On the Thames at **Strand-on-the-Green**, Chiswick, W4, stands the historic **City Barge** pub (**1a**), where the Beatles discovered a tiger in the cellar in *Help!*. East of the railway bridge, Julie Christie dallied with Dirk Bogarde on the muddy waterfront in John Schlesinger's *Darling* (**1b**). In nearby Hammersmith, stands the 'White Pad' at **1 Melrose Terrace**, W6 (**2**), centre of all the frenetically surreal happenings in *The Knack*, while the normally bustling **Shepherd's Bush Market** on **Goldhawk Road** (**3**) was the dark passageway where unfortunate Rocker Ray Winstone took a bloody beating from the Mod gang in *Quadrophenia*. Notting Hill has more than its share of classic locations. Michael Caine's *très* sixties pad, jammed with thrift shop bric-a-brac in *The Italian Job* (1969) was **18 Denbigh Close** (**4a**), off Portobello Road. At **25 Powis Square** (**4b**) stands the now-gentrified home of burned-out rock star Mick Jagger in *Performance*, and on **Lancaster Road** at St Mark's Grove stands the pub which became Camden's legendary (then fictitious, but now real) **The Mother Black Cap** (**4c**) in *Withnail & I*. Further east is the home of compulsive

womaniser *Alfie*, at **22 St Stephen's Gardens**, W2 (**4d**). David Naughton did some shape-shifting in Earl's Court to become *An American Werewolf in London* in the flat of nurse Jenny Agutter at **64 Coleherne Road**, SW10 (**5**).

CENTRAL LONDON: Although the old vegetable market has moved south of the river, you can still down a pint at **The Globe, Bow Street**, WC2 (**6**), where Jon Finch worked in Hitchcock's *Frenzy*. And while the old Scala Theatre, used for the concert scenes in *A Hard Day's Night*, has gone, the alleyway opposite the site on **Charlotte Street** (**7**), from which the Fab Four emerge in time for their TV appearance, still remains.

THE CITY AND EAST LONDON: Near to Smithfield Market is **Vic Naylor, 40 St John Street**, EC1 (**8**), which became JD's Bar in Guy Ritchie's *Lock, Stock and Two Smoking Barrels*. The eerie park, where David Hemmings might or might not have witnessed a murder in Antonioni's *Blowup* is **Maryon Park** (**9**), south of Woolwich Road, SE7. Finally, at **Binsley Walk** in **Thamesmead South** (**10**), you'll find the Flat Block Marina, home to Alex and the Droogs in *A Clockwork Orange*.

STAR WARS WORLD TOUR

TUNISIA: George Lucas took the architecture of Tunisia as the basis for the look of the desert planet Tatooine in the original *Star Wars* movie – *Episode IV: A New Hope*. Perhaps the most famous location is in the desert town of **Matmata**, where the dwellings are carved from the soft sandstone to escape the blistering desert heat. The interior of Luke Skywalker's homestead is the circular inner courtyard of the **Sidi Driss Hotel** (**1a**,**1b** & **1c**), where you can see the breakfast nook (**1d**) with murals and tiling added for the film. The Mos Eisley cantina was shot in the sponge-fishing town of **Ajim** on the Ile de Jerba off the central coast. The exterior of Luke's home and the featureless desert wastes are the vast, white salt lake of **Chott el Jerid** (**1e**), to the west, occupying the centre of the country all the way to the Algerian border. On the western edge of the Chott is the oasis town of Nefta. You'll need a four-wheel-drive vehicle, and probably a guide, to visit the dunes of **Chott el Gharsa**, north of Nefta, where the Mos Espa sets (**1f** & **1g**) for *Episode I: The Phantom Menace* still stand. The remains of two sets can be seen here, along with the strange, angular rock formations from the desert fight with Darth Maul. Young Anakin's slave quarter home can be found behind the main square of **Medenine** (**1h**), a town about 35 miles southeast of Matmata. The rear of the slave-quarters, where he works on the pod racer with Jar Jar, and where his mother drops portentous hints about a virgin birth, is the deserted **Hotel Ksar Hadada, Ksar Hadada** (**1i** & **1j**) near Ghomrassen, south of Medenine toward Tataouine.

CALIFORNIA: Since the bantha of *A New Hope* was in reality a disguised elephant hired from Marine World, its scenes were shot in California's **Death Valley** (**2**). The desert of the second sequel, *Return of the Jedi*, is also California, the endless sand dunes of **Buttercup Valley** (**3**), near Yuma, in the southeast corner of the state. At the opposite end of the state you'll find the monster trees from the Moon of Endor on the temperate Pacific coast, almost at the Oregon border. They are the giant Redwood groves of the **Jedediah Smith Redwood State Park, 4241 Kings Valley Road, Crescent City** (**4**).

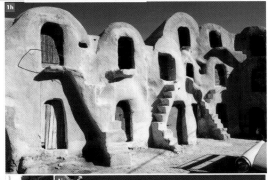

ITALY: The staterooms and staircases of Queen Amidala's palace for *The Phantom Menace* are the overwhelming marble interiors of **Palazzo Reale**, the Royal Palace, on **Piazza Carlo III, Caserta** (**5a** & **5b**), directly opposite the railway station, about 15 miles north of Naples.

GUATEMALA: The rebel base of *A New Hope*, on the fourth moon of Yavin, is the giant Mayan temple complex at **Tikal** (**6**), in the 222-square-mile rainforest of the **Parque Nacional Tikal**, northern Guatemala.

NORWAY: The ice planet Hoth, in *The Empire Strikes Back*, is the **Hardanger Jøkulen Glacier** at **Finse** (**7**).

STAR TREK, USA

As you'd expect from a series set in space, the first three *Star Trek* movies were almost entirely studio-bound, but there's been an increasing use of real locations, almost always in California.

SAN FRANCISCO: The original TV series ended in 1969, but it wasn't until 1979 that *Star Trek* made it to the big screen. That film was nearly all shot in a studio, but it did site the Starfleet Academy alongside the Golden Gate Bridge in San Francisco. The Golden Gate academy was seen again in *Star Trek VI: The Undiscovered Country*. In *Star Trek IV: The Voyage Home* the *Enterprise* crew zoom back to 1986 San Francisco. They split up at the junction of **Columbus, Kearney** and **Pacific Avenues** (**1**).

NOVATO: The lakeside campus of Camp Khitomer, site of the climactic peace conference of *Star Trek VI: The Undiscovered Country*, is the **Fireman's Fund Building, 777 San Marin Drive** (**2**), in the town of Novato in Marin County, north of San Francisco.

MONTEREY: On the coast 115 miles south of San Francisco is the **Monterey Bay Aquarium, 886 Cannery Row** (**3**), which became the Sausalito Cetacean Institute where Kirk and the crew find the humpback whales in *Star Trek IV: The Voyage Home*.

BISHOP: In central California, toward the Nevada border, the foothills of the spectacular Sierra Nevada range become distinctly Alpine in character. Nineteen miles west of Bishop, up in the Inyo National Forest, is the peaceful reservoir of **Lake Sabrina** (**4a** & **4b**). A near-inaccessible peak overlooking the lake was used as the mountaintop refuge of the Ba'ku people in *Star Trek: Insurrection*.

OWENS LAKE (**5**): South of Lone Pine on I-395, central California, this vast, dry lake bed became the Planet of Galactic Peace in *Star Trek V: The Final Frontier*.

TRONA: South toward Ridgecrest in the Mojave Desert are the **Trona Pinnacles** (**6**), an area of bizarre tufa spires formed when the area was beneath a long-vanished sea, which became the surface of the planet Shakari, where Captain Kirk has a close encounter with 'God' in *Star Trek V: The Final Frontier*.

LOS ANGELES: The superbly art deco **Union Station, 800 North Alameda Street** (**7**), in downtown LA, was transformed into the thirties nightclub for the holodeck scene in *Star Trek: First Contact*. The snowy wastes of the Knik Glacier in Alaska were used as the surface of Rura Penthe, the penal asteroid Kirk is banished to in *Star Trek VI: The Undiscovered Country*, but the penal colony was built in **Bronson Canyon** in LA's Griffith Park.

VALLEY OF FIRE: Over the border in Nevada, about 50 miles east of Las Vegas, is the dazzling red **Valley of Fire State Park** (**8**), which became Viridian 3, where James T Kirk finally passed into history in *Star Trek Generations*.

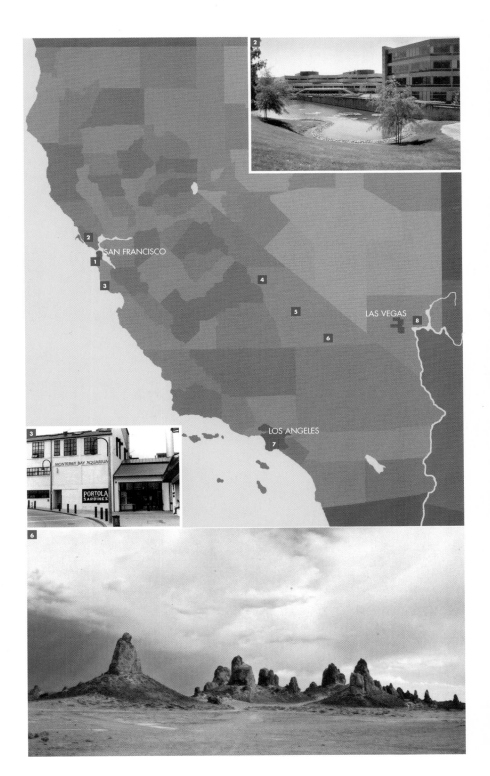

2

SAN FRANCISCO

1

3

4

5

LAS VEGAS

8

6

3

MONTEREY BAY AQUARIUM

PORTOLA
SARDINES

LOS ANGELES

7

6

THE WORLD OF JAMES BOND

AMSTERDAM: The gem capital of Europe naturally featured in *Diamonds Are Forever*. A canal trip may take you past the **Skinny Bridge**, where the old lady's body is dragged from the water. Bond girl Tiffany Case lives in one of the city's elegant, narrow canal houses at **Reguliersgracht 36 (1)**.

PARIS: In *A View to a Kill*, villainess May Day parachutes from the **Eiffel Tower**, but its Jules Verne Restaurant was recreated in the studio. Risk a Seine boat trip under the elaborate **Pont Alexandre III (2)**, from which Bond leaps into the pleasure cruiser.

COTE D'AZUR: A natural Bondian haunt. There's usually a casino scene, and in *GoldenEye*, Bond plays at the most famous of all, the **Casino de Monte-Carlo (3a)** in Monaco. It's from the **Bay of Monte Carlo (3b)** that Xenia Onatopp steals the super-dooper helicopter. Visit at night when the lights twinkle and gleam… Monte Carlo by day is a grimly ugly example of unbridled development. Take the coast road west to the beautiful little fishing village of **Villefranche-sur-Mer**, a popular filming location used for the motorbike chase in the non-mainstream Bond, *Never Say Never Again*, a remake of *Thunderball*. Largo's Palmyra fortress is **Fort Carré d'Antibes** at Antibes, a little further west along the coast.

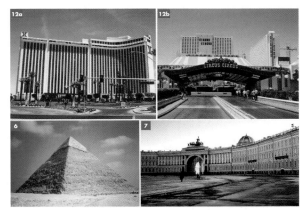

SPAIN: The stylish new **Guggenheim Museum, Bilbao** (**4**), is used as a backdrop to the opening teaser of *The World Is Not Enough*.

VENICE: Featured in two Bond movies, though blink and you'll miss its appearance at the end of *From Russia With Love*, when Bond's gondola passes under the **Bridge of Sighs** and out to the Canal Grande. He spends more time in the city in *Moonraker*. The entrance to Drax's glassworks is **Venini, 314 Piazzetta dei Leoni** (**5**), northeast of San Marco. The boat chase ends with Bond hovering across **Piazza San Marco**, where you can see the **Torre dell'Orologio**, the clock tower in which Bond slugs it out with the baddies.

CAIRO: Stop off to witness the touristy *son et lumière* at the **Pyramid of Cheops** (**6**), as seen in *The Spy Who Loved Me*.

ST PETERSBURG: True, most of *GoldenEye*'s spectacular tank chase was shot on a set in Hertfordshire, but the imposing square is the real **Palace Square** (**7**).

UDAIPUR: The Maharani converted two of his spectacular palaces into luxury hotels, both of which are seen in *Octopussy*. Bond stays at the **Shiv Niwas Hotel** (**8a**) on the lake shore, but a short boat ride will take you out to the fabulous **Lake Palace Hotel** (**8b**), Octopussy's floating palace, in the middle of

Lake Pichola. You may not have a barge rowed by handmaidens, but even the movie cheated by using a hidden motor.

THAILAND: Bond makes a spectacular descent down the side of the **Westin Banyan Tree Hotel**, Bangkok, in *Tomorrow Never Dies*, while south at Phuket you can see **Khow-Ping-Kan** (**9**), the island lair of Scaramanga from *The Man With the Golden Gun*, in **Phang Nga Bay**, Phuket, on the Malay Peninsula.

JAPAN: The Ninja Training School of *You Only Live Twice* is **Himeji Castle, Himeji** (**10**), 33 miles west of Kobe.

SAN FRANCISCO: The State Office Building in *A View to a Kill* is **San Francisco City Hall** (**11a**). While the opening of the **Lefty O'Doul Bridge, Third Street** (**11b**), provides an ending for the firetruck chase.

LAS VEGAS: The Whyte House of *Diamonds Are Forever* is the **Las Vegas Hilton** (**12a**). Spend a few bucks in **Circus Circus** (**12b**), the themed casino with acrobats performing overhead.

NEW ORLEANS: The French Quarter (**13**) of New Orleans is used for the Jazz funeral of *Live and Let Die*.

BAHAMAS: Finally, to the Bahamas for the original *Thunderball*, and Largo's other Palmyra estate, on **New Providence Island** (**14**).

SALZBURG'S SOUND OF MUSIC

MIRABELL GARDENS (1): Behind the Mirabell Palace. At the northern end of the gardens are the 'Do Re Mi' steps and the Pegasus Fountain, to the south the 'leaping' entrance statues (2).

RESIDENZPLATZ (3): Where Maria splashes in the Residenzbrunnen (Residence Fountain) on her way to the Von Trapp house and, later, Nazi troops march after the Anschluss.

ROCK RIDING SCHOOL (4): The family performs 'Edelweiss' at the song festival before escaping over the border.

WINKLER TERRACE (5): Take the lift to this restaurant terrace overlooking the city. The kids begin 'Do Re Mi' here, and it is also used as the convent terrace (the abbey actually looks south over the non-descript suburbs). Follow the path south-east along the Monchsburg Cliffs.

NONNBERG ABBEY (6): You can peek into the courtyard (seen in the film) and the chapel (which isn't). Go west to Leopoldskroner Teich. From the west shore of the lake look across to the palace of Leopoldskron.

LEOPOLDSKRON (7): A private establishment, which supplied the Von Trapp mansion's lakeside terrace.

SCHLOSS FROHNBURG (8): To see the front entrance of the Von Trapp mansion, head south on the small cycle track of Hellbrunner Allee. Soon you'll recognise the yellow-painted wall where Maria alights from the bus ('I Have Confidence in Me') and pauses before the forbidding gates.

SCHLOSS HELLBRUNN (9, off the map): To avoid constant trespassing, the '16 Going On 17' pavilion was moved from the grounds of Leopoldskron to Schloss Hellbrunn.

MONDSEE (10, about 15 miles east of Salzburg): The cathedral of Mondsee was used for the wedding of Maria and Captain Von Trapp.

The Christening: Mount Loretto, Staten Island

Ear Infirmary, 310 East 14th Street in the East Village.

Michael is subsequently picked up outside Jack Dempsey's Broadway Bar (another long-gone venue mocked up in New York for the movie), and taken towards New Jersey, which ought to mean taking the George Washington Bridge over the Hudson. The bridge used for the U-turn scene, however, is the **Queensboro Bridge** over the East River. Louis' Restaurant, where Sollozzo and McCluskey are gunned down over the veal, was the old Luna restaurant under the elevated White Plains Road IRT in **Belmont**, New York's largest Italian community.

Fleeing to Sicily, Michael goes to ground in the village of Corleone. The real Corleone, south of Palermo, has been modernised, so it's actually a combination of two villages a few miles northwest of Taormina. In **Forza**, a small medieval community dominated by the ruins of a 16th century castle, you'll find the church seen when Michael first walks into Corleone. A few miles north, in **Savoca**, you can see the small, wood-panelled **Bar Vitelli**, at which Michael meets innkeeper's daughter Apollonia, as well as **Chiesa di Santa Lucia**, the church at which he marries her. The villa Michael is staying at when his car is blown up, is the 18th century **Castello degli Schiavi** (Castle of Slaves), near **Fiumefreddo**, about six miles south of Taormina (seen again in *Godfather III*).

Back in New York, Sonny beats up bullying brother-in-law Carlo at **118th Street and Pleasant Avenue**, east of First Avenue in East Harlem, but soon gets his payback, blown away in a spectacular hail of bullets at tollbooths supposedly on the Jones Beach Causeway, Long Island, but actually built on the disused airfield **Floyd Bennett Field**, southeast of Brooklyn at the end of Flatbush Avenue. Bonasera's funeral parlour is the morgue at **Bellevue Hospital, First Avenue** at East 29th Street by the East River in the Gramercy district.

The summit meeting of the Five Families takes place in the boardroom of the Penn Central Railroad above **Grand Central Station**, 42nd Street and Park Avenue, while Michael's foray into Las Vegas was filmed at the **Tropicana, 3801 Las Vegas Boulevard South** at Tropicana Avenue, on the Strip. After Don Corleone's lavish funeral, at the **Calvary Cemetery, Greenpoint Avenue** in Queens, overlooked by the Queens Expressway bridge crossing Newton Creek, Michael becomes Godfather in a ritual brilliantly intercut with the bloody murders of the family heads. Clemenza blasts Stracci and Cuneo in the lift of the **St Regis-Sheraton**

Michael Corleone learns that the Don has been shot: Radio City Music Hall

(where Michael and Kay spent their night in New York); Moe Greene is shot through the eye in the steamroom of the **McBurney YMCA, 215 West 23rd Street** (*©

Michael becomes the Godfather: St Patrick's Cathedral, Mulberry Street

212.741.9226*); and arch-enemy Barzini is gunned down by fake cop Al Neri on the steps of the **New York County Courthouse, 60 Center Street** at Pearl Street, Lower Manhattan (see *Twelve Angry Men* for details of this popular location).

The christening itself took place inside New York's **Old St Patrick's Cathedral, 264 Mulberry Street** between East Prince and Houston Streets in Little Italy, though the exterior is the **Mission of the Immaculate Virgin, Hylan Boulevard, Mount Loretto**, down in the southwest corner of Staten Island (*rail: Pleasant Plains*).

GODFATHER PART II, THE

(1974, dir: Francis Ford Coppola)
Robert De Niro, Al Pacino, Lee Strasberg.
● **NEW YORK CITY; CALIFORNIA; NEVADA; FLORIDA; ITALY; DOMINICAN REPUBLIC**

Arguably superior to part one, *The Godfather Part II* was the first sequel ever to win Best Picture at the Oscars.

The village of Vito Andolini's

The attack on Pentangeli: PH Vazac's, Avenue B, East Village

youth is supposedly Corleone, a real town about 20 miles south of Palermo in western Sicily, though the locale seen in the movie is around Taormina in the northeast. New York's Ellis Island, point of arrival for all the European immigrants during the first half of the century, where Vito Andolini becomes Vito Corleone, still exists but has long since fallen into disrepair. The film uses the **Old Fish Market** at **Trieste**, on the Adriatic, northern Italy.

The Corleone lakeside estate is **Fleur du Lac**, the **Henry Kaiser estate** on the western California shore of **Lake Tahoe**. The lakeside area has been developed and the Corleone compound is now the boathouse of a private, gated, community.

De Niro's Little Italy, 1917 scenes were shot on **Sixth Street** in the East Village between Avenues A and B, tricked out in period dressing. A block north is the bar where the Rosato brothers try to garotte Pentangeli, **PH Vazac's, 108 Avenue B** at Seventh Street (known as 'Seven and B'), at the southeast corner of Tompkins Square Park in the East Village. A popular 'lowlife' bar, Vazac's can also be seen in *"Crocodile" Dundee* and *Angel Heart*, among many others. The ensuing shoot-out was filmed outside on **East 7th Street**.

Caffe Reggio, MacDougal Street, Greenwich Village

When Michael Corleone visits Hyman Roth in Miami it's the real thing, but Cuba was obviously out of the question. The pre-revolutionary scenes were shot in the Dominican Republic, the eastern part of the island of Hispaniola (Gulf & Western, Paramount's parent company conveniently owns property in there). **Santo Domingo**, the island's capital on the southern coast, stood in for Havana, where Roth's hotel is **El Embajador Hotel, Avenue Sarasota** (© *809.221.2131*), and Batista's palace, where the New Year's Party is cut short by revolution, is Santo Domingo's **Presidential Palace**.

The army post, where the FBI protect Pentangeli, is the **California Institute for Men, Central Avenue**, three miles south of **Chino**, Highway 60 to the east of LA.

Two other places claiming to have been used as locations, but not instantly recognisable, are the **Doheny Mansion, Chester Place**, on the campus of Mount St Mary's College, off West Adams Boulevard in Los Angeles and venerable coffee house **Caffe Reggio, 19 MacDougal Street** at West 3rd Street in Greenwich Village.

GODFATHER PART III, THE

(1990, dir: Francis Ford Coppola)
Al Pacino, Andy Garcia, Diane Keaton.
● **NEW YORK CITY; ROME, ITALY; NEW JERSEY; SICILY, ITALY**

The operatic climax: Teatro Massimo, Palermo

Locations for the overambitious end to what became the *Godfather* trilogy are split between New York and Italy, where studio interiors were shot at the famous Cinecittà Studios in Rome. Michael Corleone is awarded the Order of St Sebastian the Martyr at **Old St Patrick's Cathedral, 264 Mulberry Street**, Little Italy (site of the christening in *The Godfather*). The Italian-American street festival, during which Joey Zasa (Joe Mantegna) is gunned down, is on **Elizabeth Street**, which runs parallel to Mott Street, the Little Italy location where Don Corleone was shot in the first film, and in fact, more filming took place at the **Mietz Building, 128 Mott Street**, which served as the Genco Olive Oil company in part one. Vincent (Garcia) and Mary Corleone (Sofia Coppola) drink at **Mare Chiaro, 176 Mulberry Street** between Broome and Grand Streets (see *Donnie Brasco* for details). The neighbourhood lady is Martin Scorsese's mother, Catherine. Palazzo Azzurro, site of the helicopter attack on the mob convention is **Trump Castle Casino Resort, Atlantic City**,

New Jersey (though the interior was recreated in the studio at Cinecittà). Family lawyer Harrison (George Hamilton) visits shifty Archbishop Gilday (Donal Donnelly), staying modestly at the **Waldorf Astoria Hotel, 301 Park Avenue**. The Immobiliare takeover meeting is the **Old US Customs House**, now housing the **National Museum of the American Indian, One Bowling Green** at Broadway, Lower Manhattan, seen in *Ghostbusters II*, *Batman Forever* and *The Royal Tenenbaums*.

The long-disused **Palermo Town Hall** was opened up and refurbished for Michael's return to Sicily. Sicilian locations from the previous *Godfather* movies were revisited, including the village of **Forza d'Agro** north of Taormina. When Kay visits Sicily for her son's opera debut, she's met by Michael at **Bagheria Railway Station**, near Palermo (in Bagheria you can visit the extravagant villa seen in Antonioni's *L'Avventura*). The toast to Anthony was filmed at **Villa Malfitano, Via Dante 167**, Palermo (open to the public, mornings Monday to Saturday; © *091.6816133*). The archbishop's office is the map room of the pentagonal **Villa Farnese** (open to the public), at **Caprarola**, a small village near Viterbo, about 30 miles north of Rome. Michael is absolved by Cardinal Lamberto, the future Pope John Paul I, at the **Church of Santa Maria della Quercia** in **Viterbo**. The grandly operatic climax was filmed at the **Teatro Massimo, Piazza Verdi** in **Palermo**, and though renovation work meant that the interior opera scenes had to be filmed at Cinecittà, the tragic conclusion to the saga is staged on the opera house steps.

The Sicilian villa of Don Tommasino, where Michael finally dies, is **Castello degli Schiavi**, near **Fiumefreddo**, where Apollonia was killed in the first of the trilogy (see *The Godfather*).

GODS AND MONSTERS

(1998, dir: Bill Condon)
Ian McKellen, Brendan Fraser, Lynn Redgrave.
● **LOS ANGELES, CALIFORNIA**

Fictionalised account of the last days of the classic Hollywood director James Whale, and a putative relationship with hunky gardener Brendan Fraser. James Whale's actual house stands on Amalfi Drive in Pacific Palisades, but a similar house in **Altadena**, an eastern suburb of LA, was used for the movie exteriors. George Cukor's estate, site of the garden party where a ditsy Princess Margaret mistakes Whale for Cecil Beaton, is the **Arden Estate, 1145 Arden Road**, Pasadena – a frequently used location seen also in the Marx Brothers' *Duck Soup* and in TV's *Dynasty*. The villa is a private home, not visible from the street.

GODZILLA

(1998, dir: Roland Emmerich)
Matthew Broderick, Jean Reno, Hank Azaria.
● **HAWAII; NEW YORK CITY**

Nuclear fallout gives birth to a gigantic monster the size of a skyscraper which somehow manages to go to ground in New York City. The tropical island, where the giant footprint is originally discovered, is the **Kualoa Ranch**,

Godzilla's nest: Madison Square Gardens

4 9 - 5 6 0 Kamehameha Highway on **Oahu**, one of the Hawaiian islands (see *Jurassic Park* for details). In New York, the monster stomps around **Fifth Avenue** at 42nd Street before making its nest inside **Madison Square Gardens**, Seventh Avenue between West 31st and West 33rd Streets.

GODZILLA, KING OF THE MONSTERS

(1954, dir: Terry Morse; Inoshiro Honda)
Raymond Burr, Takashi Shimura, Momoko Kochi.
● JAPAN

The daddy of all creature features, with the radioactive lizard first appearing on the fictitious Odo Island, supposedly off the Izu Peninsula. The Odo scenes were filmed around **Toba City**, entrance to the Ise-Shima National Park on the Shima peninsula. The monster naturally heads for Japan's capital, and trashes **Tokyo**. Godzilla comes ashore at eastern Tokyo Bay, destroying a train at **Shinagawa Railway Station**, the large station serving the south and Yokohama. He stomps through Minato-Ku and Shimbashi on his way to the central shopping district, Ginza. He torches **Matsuzakaya Department Store, 6-10-1 Ginza, Chuo-ku** (*Subway: Ginza*), tears down the clock on the **Wako Department Store, 4-5-11 Ginza, Chuo-ku** at the main Ginza crossing, Yonchome, and heads northeast across **Sukiya Bridge**. He destroys the **Tokyo Marion Building** (previously the Nichigeki Theatre)**, 2-5-1 Yurakucho, Chiyoda-ku**, and crosses into the Akasaka district, home to the major government and media buildings, where he smashes the national assembly hall, the **Diet Building, Nagatacho 1-chome** (*Subway: Kokkaigijido*). Don't worry, the 1936 building still stands, and you can take a peek inside to watch a debate in progress (*admission free*). He then destroys **Kachidoki Bridge** at the mouth of the Sumida River, before returning to the ocean.

GOING MY WAY

(1944, dir: Leo McCarey)
Bing Crosby, Barry Fitzgerald, Rise Stevens.
● LOS ANGELES, CALIFORNIA

St Dominic's: Santa Monica Catholic Church, California Avenue

The Best Picture of 1944, apparently, was this sentimental story of young priest Bing Crosby taking over a tough New York parish. St Dominic's is actually **Santa Monica Catholic Church, 715 California Avenue**, Santa Monica.

GOLD RUSH, THE

(1925, dir: Charles Chaplin)
Charles Chaplin, Georgia Hale, Mack Swain.
● CALIFORNIA

Chaplin is a Yukon prospector who finally gets rich. The film includes the classic bread roll dance and shoe-eating scene. The snowy locations are at **Truckee**, in the Sierra Nevadas of California, Route 80, northwest of Lake Tahoe.

GOLDENEYE

(1995, dir: Martin Campbell)
Pierce Brosnan, Sean Bean, Izabella Scorupco.
● LONDON; HERTFORDSHIRE; SURREY; ST PETERSBURG; PUERTO RICO; FRANCE; SWITZERLAND; MONACO

Exterior of the Russian church: Brompton Cemetery, Earl's Court

The increasingly moribund series was on the verge of retirement when it got a new lease of life with Pierce Brosnan. The opening teaser, Bond's spectacular bungee jump, at the 'Arkangel Chemical Weapons Facility – USSR', is actually the **Tusker Dam, Lake Verzasca**, at **Hittnau** in Switzerland. Bond's race with Xenia Onatopp, supposedly in the hills above Monte Carlo, uses the mountain roads around **Thorenc**, about 20 miles north of Grasse, way to the northwest. Nevertheless, Bond arrives at the **Casino de Monte Carlo**, Monaco, and it's from the bay at **Monte Carlo** that Onatopp steals the Stealth helicopter.

M's office is, finally, MI6's real HQ, in the spanking new building on the Thames by **Vauxhall Bridge**. Although there is some real filming in **St Petersburg** in Russia, much of the tank chase was filmed on a massive set, built at the old Rolls Royce aircraft plant in **Leavesden**, Hertfordshire.

Many of the other Russian locations were shot around the southeast of England: St Petersburg Airport, where Bond is met by Jack Wade, is actually the **Queen's Stand, Epsom Racecourse, Epsom**, Surrey, while the St Petersburg square where Wade fixes the motor is the courtyard of the recently restored **Somerset House** on the **Strand**. The interior of the Russian church, where N a t a l y a (Scorupco) takes

The Russian cathedral: St Sofia's Greek Cathedral, Bayswater

St Petersburg: Somerset House, The Strand

The Grand Hotel Europe, St Petersburg: Langham Hilton, Portland Place

shelter, is **St Sofia's Greek Cathedral, Moscow Road**, Bayswater, W2; and the exterior is the rear (the Fulham Road side) of the 1839 chapel in the extravagantly Victorian **Brompton Cemetery, Old Brompton Road**, Earl's Court, SW5. You might also recognise this as the cemetery where Rowan Atkinson disrupts the funeral in Bond spoof *Johnny English*. Despite those flags, the Grand Hotel Europe, St Petersburg, is the **Langham Hilton, 1c Portland Place** (© 020.7636.1000, www.langham.hilton.com), opposite the BBC's Broadcasting House. The forbidding gilt and wood council chamber, where General Ourumov learns that Natalya has survived the GoldenEye detonation, is the **Draper's Hall, Throgmorton Street**, EC2, in the City of London. It became a Russian interior again for *The Saint*.

The massive radio telescope dish isn't in London. It's at **Arecibo**, in Puerto Rico (you might recognise it from *Contact*).

GOLDFINGER

(1964, dir: Guy Hamilton)
Sean Connery, Gert Frobe, Honor Blackman.

● MIAMI, FLORIDA; KENTUCKY; SWITZERLAND; BUCKINGHAMSHIRE

Bond plays Goldfinger at golf: Stoke Poges Golf Club, Slough

The budget was still relatively modest for the third Bond, and, apart from a week's filming in Switzerland, all Sean Connery's scenes were shot in England. When Goldfinger cheats at cards at the Fountainebleau Hotel, now the **Fountainebleau Hilton Resort and Spa, 4441 Collins Avenue, Miami**, Florida, Connery was filming his scenes on a mock-up of the hotel at Pinewood. In fact, a lot of the filming was done not far from Pinewood in Buckinghamshire. The South American Holdings of the pre-credits sequence are a storage tank complex at **Stanwell**, west of London between Staines and Hounslow; the cliff over which the Merc plummets is **Harefield Quarry**; while the Blue Grass Airfield, Kentucky, is **Northolt Aerodrome**. Likewise, the golf match between Bond and Goldfinger, supposedly at Royal St George's, Sandwich in Kent,

Goldfinger cheats at cards: Fountainebleau Hilton, Miami

uses **Stoke Poges Golf Club**, on the A332 a couple of miles north of Slough. The clubhouse, in front of which Oddjob decapitates a statue with his lethal hat, is **Stoke Park Club, Stoke Road, Stoke Poges** in Buckinghamshire (© 01753.717171, www.stokepark-club.com). See *Tomorrow Never Dies* for details.

Though the exterior of the real **Fort Knox**, Kentucky, south of Louisville near the Indiana border, is briefly seen, the fort was recreated at **Black Park Woodland** behind the studio at Pinewood. A wholly fantastic interior (the problems of storing gold bullion make vaults boringly unphotogenic) was created on a soundstage. Bond trails Goldfinger's Rolls along Alpine roads and encounters Tilly Masterson at **Andermatt**, a small Swiss village, 50 miles south of Zurich in the shelter of the Leopontine Alps near the Simplon Tunnel. And although the long shots of Auric Enterprises are the **Pilatus Aircraft Factory** outside **Lucerne**, Switzerland, the scenes set in Goldfinger's complex use the familiar Pinewood studio buildings.

GONE IN 60 SECONDS (aka *Gone in Sixty Seconds*)

(1974, dir: HB Halicki)
HB Halicki, Marion Busia, Jerry Daugirda.

● LOS ANGELES, CALIFORNIA

Pretty much a one-man show from car-crash fanatic and first-time director Halicki (who was killed in a stunt-gone-wrong in 1989). Eleanor, the 1973 Mustang, is parked in the **International Towers Apartments, 700 Ocean Boulevard East**, Long Beach, as she is in the 2000 remake. The block is also seen in *Lethal Weapon*. The film was shot around the South Bay area, in **Carson, Torrance** and **Redondo Beach**, with an extended chase through the centre of Long Beach, filmed on a quiet Sunday morning. One of the 'shopping list' of classic cars is stolen from the elaborate apartment block alongside International Towers, the **Villa Riviera, 800 Ocean Boulevard East**, Long Beach. The dirt track is the old Ascot Speedway, which was also featured in Howard Hawks's *Red Line 7000* and in *The Killers*. The Orange Mustang leap was shot on the **Vincent Thomas Bridge**.

GONE IN 60 SECONDS (aka *Gone in Sixty Seconds*)

(2000, dir: Dominic Sena)
Nicolas Cage, Giovanni Ribisi, Angelina Jolie.

● LOS ANGELES, CALIFORNIA

There's little in common with the 1974 version except for the delight in smashing up cars, the scene where the exhaust blows drugs away, and a couple of filming locations. The café, where Randall Raines (Cage) goes to consult his mum, is the **Quality Coffee Shop, 1238 West Seventh Street**, downtown, a

Chaos in the car chase: St Vincent's Court, Seventh Avenue

familiar location also seen in *Se7en*, *Training Day* and *Ghost World*. The bar where Sway (Jolie) works to make ends meet is **Joe Jost's, 2803 East Anaheim Street** at Temple Avenue, Long Beach (*www.joejosts.com*), also seen in *The Bodyguard*.

Shannon is stolen from outside the **Frolic Room, 6245 Hollywood Boulevard** (see *LA Confidential* for details). Randall and Sway steal Stacy from outside **Johnie's Coffee Shop, Wilshire Boulevard** at Fairfax Avenue. Another of the shopping list is whisked away by a fake valet parker from **Yamashiro, 1999 North Sycamore Avenue** in Hollywood (see *Sayonara* for details). Raines is warned off ("The ladies are dirty") outside the 1994 neon deco of the **Hollywood Park Casino, 3883 West Century Boulevard, Inglewood** (© *310.330.2800, www-playhpc.com*), located at the famous Hollywood Park Racetrack. As in the original, Eleanor is parked beneath the **International Towers Apartments**, Long Beach but, oddly, the subsequent chase is through the backstreets of downtown LA, many miles north, with Randall causing major traffic mayhem by shooting out of **St Vincent's Court** onto **Seventh Avenue**. He's suddenly back to the south, being chased along the concrete channel of the Los Angeles River toward Freb's workshop beneath the **Sixth Street Bridge** (seen also in *Repo Man*). Eleanor makes a speactacular leap over the cop cars on the **Vincent Thomas Bridge**. The final chase scenes were filmed in the old **Naval Shipyard, Long Beach**

GONE TO EARTH (aka *The Wild Heart*)
(1950, dir: Michael Powell; Emeric Pressburger)
Jennifer Jones, David Farrar, Cyril Cusack.
● SHROPSHIRE

Powell and Pressburger's wildly overblown period romance uses the Shropshire villages of **Much Wenlock**, 12 miles southeast of Shrewsbury on the A458; **Church Stretton**, 12 miles south of Shrewsbury on the A49; and **Craven Arms**, a further seven miles south on the A49.

GONE WITH THE WIND
(1939, dir: Victor Fleming; George Cukor; Sam Wood)
Vivien Leigh, Clark Gable, Olivia de Havilland.
● CALIFORNIA

Although people still arrive in Atlanta expecting to visit Scarlett's estate, not a frame was shot in Georgia. Virtually all the movie was filmed at what was then the Selznick International Studios. This studio, built by DW Griffith's contemporary and early innovator Tom Ince in 1916, passed into various hands over the years. In 1924 it was Pathe Studios, in 1925 the DeMille Studios (*King of Kings* was made here in 1927), in 1931 RKO-Pathe. Later, in 1957, it became Desilu-Culver and later still just **Culver Studios**. You can see the original studio building, unchanged, at **9336 Washington Boulevard** between Ince and Van Buren, Culver City. The Washington Boulevard frontage of the studio was used for the entrance to Twelve Oaks.

One of the earliest shots in the can was the burning of Atlanta, so early, in fact, that Scarlett O'Hara hadn't yet been cast. Legend has it that Vivien Leigh arrived during

The entrance to Twelve Oaks: Culver Studios, Washington Boulevard

filming and instantly secured the part. What went up in flames was the old Selznick backlot, in a massive space-clearing operation. You can plainly see the giant gates of King Kong's Skull Island – bizarrely out of place in Atlanta – during the conflagration.

The few locations include the barbecue at Twelve Oaks, which used the long-gone Busch Gardens in Pasadena, an estate built by the Busch brewing family. Remnants of the landscaping can still be seen in gardens of the houses around Arroyo Boulevard between Bellefontaine Street and Madeline Drive (see *Citizen Kane* for details).

When Scarlett vows never to go hungry again, it's an early morning sunrise at **Lasky Mesa, Calabasas**, in the Simi Valley. Loads of movies were shot here, including the 1936 *The Charge of the Light Brigade*. The area, between Agoura and Woodland Hills, is now known as the **Ahmanson Ranch**, and is currently scheduled to be redeveloped. Gerald O'Hara's last ride was also filmed at Calabasas. The attack in Shantytown is at **Big Bear Lake** at San Bernardino, east of LA. Gerald's walk with Scarlett was shot on the **Reuss Ranch, Malibu Lake**.

The cotton fields of Tara and O'Hara's first horse ride are around **Chico**, way up in northern California, some 80 miles north of Sacramento. Filming took place around **Bidwell Park, Pentz Road,** and **Paradise Apple Orchard**.

Various estates lay claim to be the inspiration for Tara. The staircase was supposedly based on an original at Cretien Point Plantation, about four miles from Sunset, between Lake Charles and Baton Rouge, Louisiana, while the avenue of oaks is based on one at Boone Hall Plantation, seven miles north of Charleston, near US17, South Carolina.

GOOD MORNING, VIETNAM
(1987, dir: Barry Levinson)
Robin Williams, Forest Whitaker, Tung Thanh Tran.
● THAILAND

Thalang, in Phuket Province, stood in for Saigon in Levinson's black comedy.

GOOD WILL HUNTING
(1997, dir: Gus Van Sant)
Matt Damon, Robin Williams, Ben Affleck.
● BOSTON, MASSACHU-SETTS; TORON-TO, ONTARIO, CANADA

Co-stars Matt Damon and Ben Affleck picked up an Oscar for their

The South Boston Bar: Woody's L Street Tavern, Eighth Street

The toy store: Ontario Specialty Co, Church Street

Damon explains his gift: Au Bon Pain, Harvard Square

screenplay, set around South Boston and Harvard Square. Although the publicity made great play of the Boston locales, much of the movie was actually made in Toronto. Real Boston locations include the college, where underachiever Damon works as janitor, which is **Massachusetts Institute of Technology, Cambridge** – the exterior is MIT's **McLaurin Building**. Robin Williams' college is the **Bunker Hill Community College, Rutherford Avenue, Charlestown**, while Minnie Driver's college room is over the Charles River, **Dunster House, Harvard University**, Cambridge. Harvard Square is the site of **Au Bon Pain, 27 Brattle Street,** where Damon tries to explain his gift to Driver, and also the now closed Tasty Café, where the two share a very messy pickle. Off Massachusetts Avenue was Harvard student hangout the Bow and Arrow Pub, now gone. The working class bar where Damon hangs out with Affleck and his buddies is **Woody's L Street Tavern, 658 East Eighth Street A**. Williams takes Damon for a heart-to-heart in the **Boston Public Garden**, southwest of downtown.

The University of Toronto supplied many of the film's interiors: **Knox College, Whitney Hall, St Michael's College** and **McLennan Hall**; while the **Central Technical High School** was also used. Dorm interiors were filmed at **Wycliffe College, Hoskin Avenue**. In downtown Toronto are the **Ontario Specialty Co, 133 Church Street** at Queen Street, the toy store where Damon demonstrates his magic trick, and the **Crown Life Building, 120 Bloor Street East**, the glossy corporate environment Damon rejects. The interior of the college bar, where Damon humiliates the history student, is the **Upfront Bar and Grill, 106 Front Street East**, downtown Toronto.

GOODBYE MR CHIPS

(1939, dir: Sam Wood)
Robert Donat, Greer Garson, Paul von Hernreid.
● **DERBYSHIRE**

Classic tearjerker from James Hilton's novel, following the life of a shy schoolmaster from 1870 to WWI. Made by MGM with an American director, Sam Wood, it was filmed in England. Brookfield School is **Repton School**, Repton, between Derby and Burton-upon-Trent, though the school was recreated in the studio for most scenes.

The 1969 musical remake used **Sherborne**, in Dorset. Sian Phillips' waterfront house is **59 Strand-on-the-Green**, on the north bank of the Thames just east of Kew

Bridge, London W4. The Alpine holiday is replaced by an Italian jaunt, taking in the ruins of **Pompeii** at the foot of Vesuvius; **Positano**, about 15 miles to the south; and, further south, **Paestum**.

GOODFELLAS

(1990, dir: Martin Scorsese)
Ray Liotta, Joe Pesci, Robert De Niro.
● **NEW YORK CITY; NEW JERSEY; LONG ISLAND, NEW YORK**

Scorsese's classic tracking shot: the old Copacabana, East 60th Street

"Being a gangster was better than being President of the United States": there's no trace of special pleading in Scorsese's hard-eyed look at the career of Henry Hill, shot entirely on location around New York City, the borough of Queens and New Jersey. The home of young Henry (Christopher Serrone), where he enviously watches the sharp-suited wiseguys, is **2409 32nd Street**, just south of 24th Avenue, **Astoria**, in Queens.

The Idlewild Airport scenes used the cargo buildings of **Kennedy Airport**. Idlewild is now LaGuardia, near to which you'll find the Airline Diner, where the grown-up Hill (Liotta) and pal Tommy DeVito (Pesci) steal a truck. It's now part of the Jackson Hole franchise. Confusingly, but thankfully, it keeps the famous old neon 'Airline' sign. You can grab a burger in the classic pink and chrome interior of the **Jackson Hole Diner, 69-35 Astoria Boulevard** at 70th Street in Queens (© *718.204.7070*). The kitschy Bamboo Lounge, where Tommy does his scary "funny guy" turn, was the Hawaii Kai Restaurant, **49th Street** at Broadway. It's now a stylish Japanese restaurant and the glorious South Seas decor is only a memory.

Karen is distinctly unimpressed with Hill on the first disastrous double date, at **Salerno's Restaurant, 11711 Hillside Avenue** at Myrtle Avenue, Richmond Hill, Queens (© *718.846.9332*). But Hill goes on to make a little more of an impression, whisking her through the kitchen entrance of the old Copacabana Nightclub (now closed), **10 East 60th Street** at Fifth Avenue in Manhattan. You can still see the entrance used for the electrifying tracking shot. The posh beach club, where Hill relaxes

Henry Hill's house: 32nd Street, Astoria

The bodies in the Cadillac: Long Island Railroad trestle, Babbage Street

Hill and DeVito steal a truck: Jackson Hole Diner, Astoria Boulevard

Billy Batts gets stomped at the Suite Lounge: Sogdiana Restaurant, Grand Avenue, Queens

with Karen after his first big airport job, is the **Catalina Beach Club, 2041 Park Street** in **Atlantic Beach** (*©* *516.239.2150)*, on Long Island's southwest coast.

Hill's Suite Lounge, where Billy Batts gets stomped into a bloody pulp to the gentle hippie strains of Donovan's 'Atlantis', is **Sogdiana Restaurant** (formerly the Spartan), **7320 Grand Avenue** at 73rd Place, Maspeth, Queens. Although it's still recognisable, the streamlined fifties exterior has been somewhat remodelled since filming,

As Jimmy Conway (De Niro) cuts the links between himself and the airline robbery, bodies start to turn up all over. Kids discover the bloody couple in a pink cadillac under the trestle of the Long Island Railroad tracks on **Babbage Street**, alongside Salerno's in Richmond Hills. Karen's edgy meeting with the increasingly paranoid Conway was filmed on **Smith Street** at 9th Street, alongside the Gowanus Canal, under the elevated railway F Line in Brooklyn's dodgy Red Hook district.The shopping mall, where a coked-out Hill makes a phone call about being followed by a helicopter, is on **Richmond Avenue, Staten Island**.

Filming also took place on the **Palisades Parkway**, which runs along the west bank of the Hudson River in New Jersey; at **Fort Lee**, just over the George Washington Bridge in New Jersey; at **New Rochelle** on Route 95 north of New York City; on **Coney Island Avenue** in Brooklyn; in Brooklyn's **Prospect Park**; and at **Valley Stream**, Long Island. Henry Hill's trial, where he finally informs on Jimmy and boss Paulie, was shot in **New York County Courthouse, 60 Centre Street**.

GORILLAS IN THE MIST

(1988, dir: Michael Apted)
Sigourney Weaver, Bryan Brown, John Omirah Miluwi.
● RWANDA

Powerful and moving biopic of anthropologist Dian Fossey, her battle to save Africa's mountain gorillas and her murder in 1985. The movie's location was determined by the habitat of the remaining 650 gorillas, which can be found in just two colonies, on the borders of Rwanda, Congo and Uganda. Fossey's **Karisoke Research Centre** struggles on in the **Virunga Conservation Area**, about ten miles west of Ruhengeri, Rwanda. Sigourney Weaver was so affected during the making of the movie (it was made less than three years after Fossey's murder) that she

became Honorary Chairperson of the Dian Fossey Gorilla Fund International. While the conservation area remains so unstable, it might be better to just visit the DFGFI website at *www.gorillafund.org*.

GÖTTERDÄMMERUNG (aka *The Damned*)

(1969, dir: Luchino Visconti)
Dirk Bogarde, Ingrid Thulin, Helmut Berger.
● GERMANY; AUSTRIA; ITALY

The fall of a decadent Krupp-like family in Nazi Germany, filmed by Visconti as a wildly operatic melodrama.

The German locations include the Rhineland cities of **Dusseldorf** and **Essen**, both just north of Cologne. The steel mill scenes were filmed in Italy at the industrial city of **Terni** in Umbria, 50 miles north of Rome. The lakeside hotel setting for the 'Night of the Long Knives' orgy and massacre, set in Wiessee, were actually filmed on the southwestern tip of the **Atter See**, 20 miles southeast of Salzburg in Unterach.

GRADUATE, THE

(1967, dir: Mike Nichols)
Dustin Hoffman, Anne Bancroft, Katharine Ross.
● CALIFORNIA

The Taft Hotel, where graduate Benjamin conducts an illicit affair with neighbour Mrs Robinson, is actually the **Ambassador Hotel, 3400 Wilshire Boulevard**, midtown LA. The hotel has been closed since 1989 and is currently under threat of demolition (see the 1954 *A Star Is Born* for details).

The Taft Hotel: Ambassador Hotel, Wilshire Boulevard

The university, attended by Benjamin's real love, who happens to be Mrs Robinson's daughter Elaine, is supposedly Berkeley, over the Bay from San Francisco. For the most part, though, it's the spacious Romanesque campus of the **University of Southern California (USC)**, **Jefferson Boulevard**, bounded by Vermont Avenue, Exposition Boulevard and Figueroa Street, downtown LA. The fountain, where Benjamin mopes about waiting for Elaine, is in front of the **Edward L Doheny Jr Memorial Library**, between Hoover Boulevard and Childs Way. Elaine's dorm is the **Von Kleinsmid Center of International and Public Affairs** at USC.

The real Berkeley makes a showing, though. Benjamin drives south over the double-decker **Oakland Bay Bridge**, which is actually *away* from Oakland. If he had driven *toward* Oakland he would have been invisible on the bridge's lower deck. Elaine walks through

Waiting at the Berkeley fountain: USC Campus, Los Angeles

The disrupted wedding: United Methodist Church, La Verne

Sproul Plaza, and the frat house is **Theta Delta Chi Fraternity House, 2647 Durant Avenue** between Rowditch and College. Benjamin follows Elaine to her meeting by the Monkey House in **San Francisco Zoo**, south of the Sunset district.

The gas station, where Benjamin tries to find out where Elaine is getting married by posing as a priest, is at **Winchester Canyon**, north of Santa Barbara. The church, where the wedding is finally disrupted, is not in Santa Barbara at all. It's the **United Methodist Church of La Verne, 3205 D Street, La Verne**, east of Los Angeles.

GRAND BLEU, LE (aka *The Big Blue*)
(1988, dir: Luc Besson)
Rosanna Arquette, Jean-Marc Barr, Jean Reno.

● FRANCE; SICILY; ITALY; GREECE; PERU

Besson's beautiful, if somewhat pretentious, hymn to diving looks like a fabulously glossy travelogue. Insurance official Johana (Arquette) first claps eyes on dolphinesque diver Jacques (Barr) at **La Raya**, a train stop 4,000 feet up on the Altiplano plateau of Peru. She contrives to follow him to **Taormina**, on the east coast of Sicily, where he takes part in the world championships. Jacques and arch-rival Enzo (Reno) stay at the impossibly grand **San Domenico Palace Hotel, Plazza San Domenico 5**. This cloistered 15th century building, built as a monastery, was used for the climax of Antonioni's sixties classic of alienation *L'Avventura*.

The aquarium, where Jacques takes presents to the dolphins (aaaaah) is **Marineland** in **Antibes** on the French Riviera. Nearby is the venerable **Carlton Hotel** on the **Croisette** at **Cannes** (see Hitchcock's *To Catch a Thief* for details), where Jacques and Johana briefly stay. The stranded boat is on **Amorgos**, one of the Greek Cyclades Islands, where there was filming at **Le Grand Bleu** bar, naturally, and also on **Manganari**, an out of the way Greek island in the Mediterranean where Luc Besson spent some of his childhood, and which inspired the film.

GRANDE ILLUSION, LA (aka *Grand Illusion*)
(1937, dir: Jean Renoir)
Jean Gabin, Pierre Fresnay, Erich von Stroheim.

● FRANCE

The Hallbach POW camp for officers, where Jean Gabin is initially incarcerated, is the army barracks at **Colmar**, in Alsace, toward the German border. Winterborn, the fortress prison commanded by Erich von Stroheim that he's transferred to, is **Haut-Koenigsbourg Castle**, overlooking the village of St Hippolyte, about 60 miles to the southwest.

GRAPES OF WRATH, THE
(1940, dir: John Ford)
Henry Fonda, John Carradine, Jane Darwell.

● CALIFORNIA; OKLAHOMA; NEW MEXICO

John Ford's moving, but politically softened, filming of Steinbeck's story of migrating farmers in the thirties was shot mainly on the Fox backlot on **Pico Boulevard, LA**, where the Hooverville settlement was built. Real Californian locations included the San Fernando Valley, and the river scene, which was shot at **Needles** on I-40 at the the Arizona border, but that's as far as the cast got. The Weedpatch migrant camp was at **Lamont**, California. A second unit did the location work, filming doubles leaving the farm in **McAlester**, Oklahoma, Highway 69, 100 miles south of Tulsa. The courthouse was at **Sayre**, Oklahoma. The service station, diner, bridge and train sequence filmed at **Laguna Pueblo, Gallup** and **Santa Rosa**, New Mexico.

GREASE
(1978, dir: Randal Kleiser)
John Travolta, Olivia Newton-John, Stockard Channing.

● LOS ANGELES, CALIFORNIA

The movie was softened up from the stage version (the roll of cling-film in the 'Greased Lightning' number remains unexplained in the film), and all-

Rydell High: Venice High School, Venice Boulevard, Venice

American Sandy Dubrwski was airbrushed into Aussie Sandy Olsen to accommodate Newton-John, it remains one of the most successful musicals of all time. Rydell High is a conflation of three schools. The art deco façade is **Venice High School, 13000 Venice Boulevard** (seen also in *American History X*). The school interiors, including the dance contest in the gym, are **Huntington Park High School, 6020 Miles Avenue** in Huntington Park, southeast of downtown LA. The 'You're the One That I Want' carnival finale is staged on the sports fields of **John Marshall High School, 3939 Tracy Street** in **Silverlake**, north of downtown (seen also in the genuine 1957 juvenile delinquent movie *The Young Stranger* and lots of others, including the original *Buffy the Vampire Slayer* movie).

The car racing sequence, where Sandy decides she

Car racing: Spillways of the Los Angeles River, between First and Seventh Street Bridges

'You're The One That I Want': Sports fields of John Marshall High School, Tracy Street, Silverlake

doesn't want to be Sandra Dee any more, is along the concrete spillways of the Los Angeles River between the **First and Seventh Street Bridges**, east of downtown, a location used in fifties sci-fi classic *Them!* and more recently in *S.W.A.T.*.

Grease II, the disappointing sequel with Maxwell Caulfield replacing Travolta and pre-stardom Michelle Pfeiffer stepping into Olivia Newton-John's stilettoes, used the **Excelsior High School** at **Norwalk**, southeast LA on Route 5.

GREAT DICTATOR, THE
(1940, dir: Charles Chaplin)
Charles Chaplin, Jack Oakie, Paulette Goddard.
● CALIFORNIA

Chaplin contributed to the WWII war effort with a debunking of Hitler and Mussolini, by playing a Jewish barber mistaken for fascist dictator Adenoid Hynkel. Oakie is fellow fascist Napaloni. Mostly studio-bound in Hollywood of course, but Hynkel's oratory was shot up north in the **San Fernando Valley** and the war scenes and duck hunt were filmed around **Malibu Lake**, south of Mulholland Highway near Cornell in the Santa Monica Mountains. The exterior of Hynkel's palace, seen when Jack Oakie arrives, is **Pasadena City Hall, 100 North Garfield Avenue**, Pasadena (see *American Pie 2* for details of this popular location).

GREAT ESCAPE, THE
(1963, dir: John Sturges)
Steve McQueen, James Garner, Richard Attenborough.
● GERMANY

After scouting locations around California, Stalag Luft III was eventually recreated in a pine forest behind the **Geiselgasteig** studios near Munich. The railroad scenes were filmed on a stretch of line running between Munich and Hamburg. Steve McQueen's motorbike scenes were shot at **Fussen** on the Austrian border.

GREAT EXPECTATIONS
(1946, dir: David Lean)
John Mills, Bernard Miles, Valerie Hobson.
● KENT; LONDON

Perhaps the greatest Dickens adaptation, filmed mostly in the studio at Denham. The opening scenes used **St Mary's Marshes** on the south side of the Thames Estuary a few miles northeast of Rochester. It's here too, at high tide, that Pip and Herbert Pocket arrive and depart in a rowboat, and about a mile inland that Joe Gargery's forge was built. The Rotterdam Paddle Boat plied the **River Medway**. Pip's arrival in London was filmed in front of the real **St Paul's Cathedral**, the shots carefully angled to exclude modern buildings and bomb damage.

GREAT GATSBY, THE
(1974, dir: Jack Clayton)
Robert Redford, Mia Farrow, Bruce Dern.
● RHODE ISLAND; NEW YORK CITY

Scott Fitzgerald's novel is set on Long Island, centering on the uncrossable class divide between East Egg and West Egg, old and new money, separated by Long Island Sound. The encroaching urbanisation of new money forced Paramount to look elsewhere for locations, finally settling for Rhode Island.

Daisy's childhood home, where she meets Gatsby, is a white-pillared, Southern-style mansion on **Hope Street, Bristol**, about ten miles north of Newport off Route 114. The Gatsby Mansion is in **Newport**, Rhode Island. It's **Rosecliffe, Bellevue Avenue**, an imitation of the Petit Trianon at Versailles, built in 1909. The interior of Bellevue featured as the Swiss chateau gatecrashed by Arnold Schwarzenegger at the opening of *True Lies*.

The area is pretty damn exclusive – the stars of the movie rented cottages on the Hammersmith Farm Estate, owned by Jackie Onassis' parents, the Auchincloss family. The Kennedy wedding reception was held here, and it became the presidential hideaway during the early sixties. Ironically, **Hammersmith Farm, Ocean Drive**, ended up slumming it in the movie as Gatsby's West Egg Mansion. Both Rosecliffe and Hammersmith Farm are open to the public.

Other locations included **Marble House** in Rhode Island; and two grand New York hotels, the **Waldorf-Astoria Hotel, 301 Park Avenue** between East 49th and East 50th Streets and the **Plaza Hotel, Fifth Avenue** at 59th Street. Interiors were shot at **Pinewood Studios** in England, where the Conservatory, built as an extension to Pinewood's original building, Hertherden Hall, still stands.

GREAT RACE, THE
(1965, dir: Blake Edwards)
Jack Lemmon, Tony Curtis, Peter Falk.
● AUSTRIA; CALIFORNIA; OREGON

Elaborate, big-budget farce centering on the 1908 New York to Paris car race. Potsdorf is **Salzburg** in Austria. The railway scenes utilised the Sierra Railroad, which you can visit in **Jamestown**, northern California. Other US locations included the **Alabama Hills, Lone Pine**, central California and **Gearhart**, Oregon.

GREATEST SHOW ON EARTH, THE
(1952, dir: Cecil B DeMille)
Charlton Heston, Betty Hutton, James Stewart.
● FLORIDA; PENNSYLVANIA; WASHINGTON DC

DeMille's irresistible circus hokum, filmed in part at **Sarasota**, south of Tampa, on Florida's west coast, headquarters of the Ringling Brothers Barnum and Bailey Circus. The recently renovated Ringling Museum, which includes John Ringling's mansion, based on the Doge's Palace in Venice, is half a mile south of the Sarasota-Bradenton Airport on US41 (*© 813.355.5101*).

GREATEST STORY EVER TOLD, THE
(1965, dir: George Stevens)
Max von Sydow, Charlton Heston, Carroll Baker.
● UTAH; NEVADA; CALIFORNIA

The vast budget of this underrated epic demanded stars, stars, stars, but since the main roles went to relative unknowns, a series of absurdly distracting cameos disrupts the film.

Stevens wanted to film in Israel, but practical considerations, and the sway of unions, resulted in a decision to film entirely on US soil. So, lo and behold, it was discovered that 'Utah looks more like the Holy Land than the Holy Land'. In truth the locations are stunning, if geographically inaccurate, and the visuals fall apart only with the horribly studio-bound crucifixion, filmed at **Culver City Studios** after bad weather closed down location shooting.

The southwest US forms the backdrop for most of the movie, with the Colorado River standing in for the River Jordan and Navajo taking time off from playing Sioux, Cheyenne and Apaches to become the Roman army.

Kane County, on Utah's southern border, stood in for the Holy Land. The town of Bethlehem was reconstructed near **Moab**, between the spectacular Arches and Canyonlands National Parks. The Sea of Galilee, though, is some way off in western Nevada. It's **Pyramid Lake**, within Pyramid Lake Indian Reservation, 30 miles north of Reno. Capernaum was built on the lake's shore. The cast and crew stayed in the town of Page, Arizona, near the Glen Canyon Dam. The opening of the dam had been held up for the shoot, and after filming, the area was flooded. Many of the film's locations now lie under the waters of Lake Powell.

McTeague's dentist office: Laguna Street, San Francisco

GREED
(1924, dir: Erich von Stroheim)
Gibson Gowland, Zasu Pitts, Jean Hersholt.
● CALIFORNIA

Having rebuilt Monte Carlo on the Universal lot for *Foolish Wives*, extravagant genius Erich von Stroheim took an entirely different approach to his epic adaptation of Frank Norris' novel *McTeague* and made the movie on real locations, largely around San Francisco. Virtually taking over an entire city block, he not only used exteriors but filmed inside houses too, with his cast living and sleeping on the sets. The resulting 96 hours of film were edited down to a nine hour picture, then to five. Eventually the studio stepped in and slashed the movie down to little more than two hours.

McTeague's Polk Street dentist office can still be recognised at **611 Laguna Street** on the corner of Hayes Street. The church attended by McTeague and his new bride is St Paulus Lutheran Church, which stood at the corner of Eddy and Gough Streets (that's the church you can see in *Vertigo* opposite Mckittrick's Hotel) until it was destroyed by fire a few years ago. The famously shocking desert climax, with the treacherous McTeague handcuffed to the dead body of his one-time friend, was shot out in the blistering wilderness of **Death Valley**.

GREEN MILE, THE
(1999, dir: Frank Darabont)
Tom Hanks, David Morse, Bonnie Hunt.
● TENNESSEE; NORTH CAROLINA

Another Stephen King prison drama from the director of *The Shawshank Redemption*, set in Cold Mountain Penitentiary, South Georgia, but made largely in Tennessee. The prison exterior is the old **Tennessee State Penitentiary, Nashville**, seen also in Sharon Stone's *Last Dance*. More scenes were shot at **Lewisburg**; **College Grove**; **Columbia**; **Nolensville**; and **Shelbyville**.

Georgia Pines nursing home is **Flat Top Manor** (*admission free*), the turn-of-the-century home of businessman Moses Cone, in the **Moses Cone National Park** on the Blue Ridge Parkway at **Blowing Rock**, between Asheville and Winston-Salem, North Carolina.

GREGORY'S GIRL
(1981, dir: Bill Forsyth)
Gordon John Sinclair, Dee Hepburn, Clare Grogan.
● SCOTLAND

The Scots town is **Cumbernauld**, a new town just north of Glasgow, where Gregory's school is **Abronhill High School**, in the Abronhill district. Gregory waits by the huge clock in the **New Town Plaza**. Filming also took place at **Partick Thistle FC** and at the **Cumbernauld Theatre**.

GREYSTOKE: THE LEGEND OF TARZAN, LORD OF THE APES
(1984, dir: Hugh Hudson)
Christopher Lambert, Ralph Richardson, Ian Holm.
● SCOTLAND; HERTFORDSHIRE; OXFORDSHIRE; LONDON; CAMEROONS

Good-looking but clumsy retelling of the old warhorse. The screenplay credit goes to PH Vazak – the script was originally written by Robert Towne who, on seeing the movie, insisted on giving the writing credit to his dog. The dog in turn is named after PH Vazak's bar in Greenwich Village, itself a famous movie location (*The Godfather Part II*). The African scenes filmed in **Cameroons**.

The Greystoke Mansion is **Floors Castle**, north of **Kelso** in Scotland, about 25 miles southwest of Berwick-upon-Tweed. It's open to the public (© *01573.23333, www.floorscastle.com; admission charge*). Floors provides the exterior and the ballroom, but the other interiors were filmed at **Hatfield House, Hatfield** in Hertfordshire (*www.hatfield-house.co.uk*), also seen as the Great House in Sally Potter's time-shifting, gender-shifting film of Virginia Woolf's *Orlando*, as Wayne Manor in *Batman*, and in period pieces such as *Shakespeare in Love* and *Henry VIII and His Six Wives*. The grand entrance hall, where Ralph welcomes Tarzan on his arrival and where James Fox proposes to Andie MacDowell in front of a blazing fire, is Hatfield's magnificent Marble Hall (see *Batman* for details). The elaborate staircase, down which Ralph Richardson famously slides on a tea tray, is also at Hatfield. It's the Grand Staircase, one of a few surviving Jacobean wooden staircases and a marvel of carving. And yet more interiors were provided by **Blenheim Palace, Woodstock** in Oxfordshire (*www.blenheimpalace.com*), also seen in Kenneth Branagh's *Hamlet*.

Tarzan is unwisely invited to the opening of the Greystoke Wing of the **Natural History Museum, Cromwell Road** (℃ *020.7942.5011, www.nhm.ac.uk*), in the Dinosaur Hall. The museum also features in *Loch Ness* and the excellent, low-key 1950 thriller *Seven Days to Noon*. Tarzan liberates the captive ape, which has the good taste to head directly for Gilbert Scott's marvellously kitschy, and recently restored, **Albert Memorial**, down the road in **Kensington Gardens** opposite the Royal Albert Hall.

GRIFTERS, THE

(1990, dir: Stephen Frears)
Anjelica Huston, John Cusack, Annette Bening.
● **CALIFORNIA; PHOENIX, ARIZONA**

Neo noir from British director Frears, with Huston, Cusack and Bening as three con-artists involved in a queasily incestuous relationship. The hotel in LA where Cusack hangs out is the **Bryson, 2701 Wilshire Boulevard**, downtown (it also served as the rather seedier hotel that Mickey Rourke and Faye Dunaway dive into to avoid the cops in *Barfly* and was seen in the opening sequence of Paul Thomas Anderson's *Magnolia*). Filming also took place in **San Diego**. The race track is the **Turf Paradise Race Horse Track, 19th Avenue** at Bell Road, Phoenix, Arizona, and the airport is the **Sky Harbor Airport**, at Phoenix.

GROSSE POINTE BLANK

(1997, dir: George Armitage)
John Cusack, Minnie Driver, Alan Arkin.
● **MICHIGAN; CALIFORNIA**

The coffee shop: South Myrtle Avenue, Monrovia

There's a little scene-setting in **Detroit** and its classy suburb of **Grosse Pointe** itself, for this black comedy, but most of the movie was shot in LA's eastern suburbs of Pasadena, Duarte and Monrovia. The Grosse Pointe neighbourhood, where Cusack rekindles romance with old flame Minnie Driver, is the 400 block of **South Myrtle Avenue**, Monrovia. The café, where he meets up with rival hitman Dan Aykroyd, is **Natick's Hobby Shop, 405 South Myrtle Avenue**. Pointes High is **John Marshall High School, 3939 Tracy Street, Silverlake**, a familiar filming location seen in *Buffy the Vampire Slayer*, body-swap comedy *Like Father, Like Son* and fifties teen-flick *The Young Stranger*

GROUNDHOG DAY

(1993, dir: Harold Ramis)
Bill Murray, Andie MacDowell, Chris Elliott.
● **ILLINOIS**

Murray's stylus gets stuck in the groove of time, living the same day over and over again in smalltown USA. Punxsutawney, Pa. is actually **Woodstock**, 45 miles north-

west of Chicago on Route 14, Illinois. The movie makes use of the old pre-Civil War courthouse and jail, the restored turn-of-the-century opera house and town square with its bandstand and gazebo.

GUNFIGHT AT THE O.K. CORRAL

(1957, dir: John Sturges)
Kirk Douglas, Burt Lancaster, Jo Van Fleet.
● **ARIZONA**

Another version of the legendary showdown between Wyatt Earp, Doc Holliday and the Clantons. The OK Corral was reconstructed at the Western facsimile town of **Old Tucson, 201 South Kinney Road**, (℃ *602.883.6457, www.oldtucson.com*), Arizona, now a major tourist attraction. The set was built for the 1940 Western *Arizona*, and has been seen in films such as *Rio Bravo*, *El Dorado* and *The Quick and the Dead*. The crew also ventured south to the town of **Elgin**, another favourite location, just down the road from the real Tombstone.

GUNGA DIN

(1939, dir: George Stevens)
Cary Grant, Victor McLaglen, Douglas Fairbanks Jr.
● **CALIFORNIA**

Spectacular epic set on India's North West frontier, with the ubiquitous **Alabama Hills**, at Lone Pine, on I-395, central California, standing in for the Himalayas. The location was put to similar use in, amongst other films, *The Charge of the Light Brigade* (1936) and *The Lives of a Bengal Lancer*. The Hills, striking rock formations, are west of the town of Lone Pine off Whitney Portal Road. The huge English fort was built on **Indian Springs Road**, south of Whitney Portal, against the backdrop of the Sierra Nevadas. The Temple of Kali was constructed in a hollow now known as **Temple Pocket** on **Horseshoe Meadow Road** – where a stone marker commemorates the shoot.

Site of the temple: Temple Pocket, Horseshoe Meadow Road

Site of the English fort: Indian Springs Road, Alabama Hills

GUNS OF NAVARONE, THE

(1961, dir: J Lee Thompson)
Gregory Peck, David Niven, Stanley Baker.
● **RHODES**

A jolly adventure, but being a Carl Foreman-scripted movie, there's plenty of moral philosophising before we reach the bangs and crashes. Set on the island of Rhodes, the interiors were filmed at Shepperton Studios, the exteriors at – believe it or not – **Navarone**, on Rhodes.

H

HAINE, LA (aka *Hate*)
(1995, dir: Mathieu Kassovitz)
Vincent Cassel, Hubert Kounde, Saïd Taghmaoui.
● **PARIS, FRANCE**

Kassovitz' tough film about racism looks at a side of Paris rarely seen on screen, made on the streets of the **Chanteloupe-les-Vignes** estate.

HAIRSPRAY
(1988, dir: John Waters)
Divine, Ricki Lake, Colleen Fitzpatrick.
● **BALTIMORE, MARYLAND; PENNSYLVANIA**

Divine's last movie is a blow for Chubby Lib and racial integration, set in a fictitious day-glo sixties, and filmed, of course, in Baltimore. Ricki Lake is Tracy Turnblad, a hefty teenager desperate to bop in the audience of the grossly white *Corny Collins Show*, Divine, her even heftier Mom. Tracy's high school is **Merganthaler Vocational Technical School, 3500 Hillen Road**. The library is **Perry Hall High School, 4601 Ebenezer Road, Perry Hall**. "Are you big-boned, got a glandular problem but you still want the glamour?": Mr Pinky's Hefty Hideaway shop, where Tracy shops for outsize fashions, is **3311 Eastern Avenue** (which used to be Pacey's bridal store) at South Clinton in the Highlandtown neighbourhood. Tilted Acres, the segregated amusement park, is **Dorney Park, 3830 Dorney Park Road, Allentown** (*www.dorneypark.com*) in Pennsylvania.

The hardware store: Mission Street, South Pasadena

The old Myers house: Mission Street, South Pasadena

The high school: South Pasadena High School, Lyndon Street

HALLOWEEN
(1978, dir: John Carpenter)
Jamie Lee Curtis, Donald Pleasence, Nancy Loomis.
● **LOS ANGELES, CALIFORNIA**

The original, and best, stalk'n'slash, with more scary stalking than gratuitous slashing. Set in the fictitious Illinois suburb of Haddonfield (producer Debra Hill grew up in Haddonfield, New Jersey), the movie blends locales in Hollywood and South Pasadena. Jamie Lee Curtis' house is in South

Site of the murders: Orange Grove Avenue, Hollywood

Pasadena, on **Oxley Street** at the corner of Fairview Avenue, South Pasadena. Haddonfield High is **South Pasadena High School, Lyndon Street** at Fremont Avenue. Nichol's Hardware Store, robbed by Michael Myers ("just some rope, a knife and a Halloween mask… must be kids") is **The Frame Shop, 964 Mission Street** at Meridian Avenue in South Pasadena. And on the opposite corner of Meridian is **Century House, 1000 Mission Street**, the now-bright-and-nicely-renovated Myers house. If the angle of the house looks a little odd, that's because the entire building was actually moved from its former position around the corner at 707 Meridian Avenue.

The Doyle and Wallace houses can be found in Hollywood, on the 1500 block of Orange Grove Avenue between Sunset Boulevard and Selma Avenue. The

Jamie Lee Curtis babysits: Orange Grove Avenue, Hollywood

house where Jamie Lee Curtis babysits is **1530 Orange Grove Avenue**, and the scene of the murders is across the street at **1537 Orange Grove Avenue**.

HALLOWEEN H20: 20 YEARS LATER
(1998, dir: Steve Miner)
Jamie Lee Curtis, Adam Arkin, Josh Hartnett.
● **LOS ANGELES, CALIFORNIA**

Twenty years after the events of the original *Halloween*, Michael Myers tracks down his sister, now the disturbed alcoholic head of a private school. The fictitious town of Summer Glen is **La Puente**, LA. The school is a mansion complex built for film star Antonio Moreno in the twenties. For many years it was a Franciscan convent, and it's now abandoned. Only the wrought iron gates and the gate-

Myers haunts the private school: Micheltorena Street, Silverlake house are visible. The **Canfield-Moreno Residence and Complex** is at **1923 Micheltorena Street, Silverlake**, LA (used also in *Scream 3*).

HAMLET

(1990, dir: Franco Zeffirelli)
Mel Gibson, Glenn Close, Alan Bates.
● **SCOTLAND; KENT**

Solid, traditional Shakespeare utilising real castle exteriors. Elsinore is a conflation of two British castles. The main one is **Dunnottar Castle** (© *01569.762173, www.dunechtestates.co.uk*), set on a striking sandstone outcrop on Scotland's east coast, almost cut off from the mainland. It was one of the most impregnable of Scottish fortresses. To find it, head south from Aberdeen, through Stonehaven on the A92. The battlements where the ghost appears and Ophelia's funeral were filmed here. The "To be or not to be…" soliloquy uses **Dover Castle**, overlooking Dover in Kent. it's open to the public from March to the end of October (© *01304.211067; admission charge*). The castle also appears in *To Kill a King*. Another location was **Blackness Castle** (© *01506.834807*), on the B903 east of Falkirk in West Lothian.

HAMLET

(1996, dir: Kenneth Branagh)
Kenneth Branagh, Julie Christie, Derek Jacobi.
● **OXFORDSHIRE**

Big, big widescreen production (the first British movie in years to be filmed in 70mm) shot largely in the studio. The exteriors of Elsinore are **Blenheim Palace**, in **Woodstock** village, eight miles north of Oxford. Home to the Duke of Marlborough, the house is open mid-March to the end of October (© *0993.811325, www.blenheimpalace.com; admission charge*).

HANNAH AND HER SISTERS

(1986, dir: Woody Allen)
Mia Farrow, Dianne Wiest, Michael Caine.
● **NEW YORK CITY; ITALY**

The mock-Tudor village: Pomander Walk

Another tour of Manhattan from Allen, revolving around the various relationships of sisters Mia Farrow, Barbara Hershey and Dianne Wiest, between three Thanksgiving dinners. Farrow's apartment is at the **Langham, 135 Central Park West**. Architect Sam Waterston takes Wiest and Carrie Fisher for a tour of his (and so, we presume, Allen's) favourite New York buildings, including the **Dakota Apartments, 172nd Street** at Central Park West (see *Rosemary's Baby*); the old bulging windows on West 44th Street; the glistening, deco **Chrysler Building, 405 Lexington Avenue** at East 42nd Street (see *Q – The Winged Serpent*); Abigail Adams' old stone house, **421 East 61st Street** at York and First Avenues on the East

Side (it's now a museum and open to the public); and the **Waldorf-Astoria Hotel, 301 Park Avenue** between East 49th and East 50th Streets. He also takes them through the charming little mock-Tudor village of **Pomander Walk, 260-266 West 95th Street** to 94th Street. You'll be lucky to take such a romantic stroll through it, though – the street is generally locked to the public.

When Michael Caine 'accidentally' bumps into Barbara Hershey in the East Village, she takes him to the Pageant Print and Book Store – now the **Pageant Bar and Grill, 109 East Ninth Street**. They conduct their affair at the **St Regis-Sheraton Hotel, 2 East 55th Street** (seen in *The Godfather*) on the southeast corner of Fifth Avenue.

Allen takes a deeply unimpressed Wiest, who prefers coke'n'punk, to hear Bobby Short, regular jazz entertainer in the **Cafe Carlyle** in the **Carlyle Hotel, 35 East 76th Street** at Madison Avenue (© *212.744.1600, www.carlyle.com*) on the East Side. After her terrible singing audition, Wiest meets Carrie Fisher outside the **Booth Theater, 222 West 45th Street** between Broadway and Eighth Avenue. The production briefly leaves New York when Waterston takes Wiest to the opera. The performance of *Manon Lescaut* was filmed at the **Regio Theatre, Turin** (*www.teatroregio.torino.it*), Italy.

When hypochondriac Allen is found not to have a brain tumour, he dances out of the **Mount Sinai Hospital, East 98th to East 101st Streets** between Fifth and Madison Avenues on the Upper East Side. His brush with death takes him on a search for religion to the **Church of the Transfiguration, 1 East 29th Street** near Madison Square, but eventually he finds solace watching the Marx Brothers' *Duck Soup* at the **Metro Cinema, 2626 Broadway** at 99th Street on the Upper West Side.

HANNIBAL

(2001, dir: Ridley Scott)
Anthony Hopkins, Julianne Moore, Ray Liotta.
● **FLORENCE, ITALY; NORTH CAROLINA; WASHINGTON DC; VIRGINIA**

Lecter gives himself away at the carousel: Union Station, Massachusetts Avenue NE

Ridley Scott jettisoned the procedural authenticity of *The Silence of the Lambs* for a more 'operatic' approach, and managed to turn the terrifying psychopath into a cuddly wisecracker. The film looks good, though.

Much of the film was shot around Richmond, Virginia. The fishmarket, site of the shoot-out with Evelda Drumgo, was a set built on a parking lot behind the Canal Club under the freeways at the renovated former industrial **Shockoe Bottom** in Richmond (and don't worry – the blood-spattered baby was animatronic). Clarice Starling's basement and Lecter's cell used Richmond's old **Virginia State Library** on **Capitol Square** at 11th Street. Clarice's home is on **Park Avenue**, while Krendler's is at **Grove and Harrison**. The finale, with the ravenous hogs, was filmed on the **Montpelier Estate**, Virginia (*www.mont-pelier.org*), former home of James Madison, fourth President of the USA.

Hannibal Lecter is lying low as 'Dr Fell' in **Florence**, where he lives and works in the library of the **Palazzo Capponi, via dei Bardi 36**. Avaricious cop Pazzi spies on Fell as he sips coffee in a café on **Piazza della Republica**, and the doctor is spotted on security cameras at the **Pharmacy of Santa Maria Novella, via delle Scala 16**. Pazzi buys a silver bracelet (on which to collect Lecter's fingerprints) on the **Ponte Vecchio**, over the River Arno. It's beneath the **Loggia del Mercato Nuovo** that Lecter foils (and guts) the pickpocket, and that Pazzi washes the blood from his hands in the wild boar fountain, **Il Porcellino**. The opera (written specially for the film) was staged, coincidentally, in the courtyard of the **Pazzi Chapel**, next to the monastery of **Santa Croce**. The square with the monumental sculptures is, of course, **Piazza della Signoria** (seen also in *A Room With a View*) overshadowed by the **Palazzo Vecchio**. The interior of the palazzo was reconstructed in a warehouse just outside Florence, but it's the real exterior from which the unfortunate Pazzi is ejected: "Bowels in or bowels out?"

Back in the USA, the carousel, where Lecter gives himself away with the merest touch of Clarice's hair, was in DC's beautifully restored **Union Station, Massachusetts Avenue NE** between First and Second Streets (also the scene of the chase in *The Recruit*). The vast estate of Mason Verger is **Biltmore House** on the Biltmore Estate in **Asheville**, North Carolina (see *Being There* for details).

HARD DAY'S NIGHT, A

(1964, dir: Richard Lester)
The Beatles, Wilfrid Brambell, Victor Spinetti.
● LONDON; WEST COUNTRY

Lester, who started out making films with the Goons, set the style for pop movies for decades to come with his freewheeling, machine-gun edited, surreal day-in-the-life musical. The opening scenes of teen hysteria, presumably meant to be in Liverpool, were filmed at London's **Marylebone Station**. The journey shunts between Paddington Station, Minehead, Taunton and Newton Abbot in the West Country. The scene where the boys run alongside the train to annoy a grumpy commuter, is **Crowcombe**, north Somerset. And the final destination of the journey? Why, it's Marylebone Station, London.

The Beatles are driven to the Scala Theatre, which used to stand on **Charlotte Street**, just off Tottenham Court Road. A block of flats, Scala House, now occupies the site, but opposite you can still see the alleyway from which the Beatles emerge in time for the final concert.

The groovy nightclub: Les Ambassadeurs, Hamilton Place

Wilfred Brambell, as Paul's grandad, excuses himself to go gambling at **Les Ambassadeurs** n i g h t c l u b, **Hamilton Place**, behind the Hilton Hotel (see *Dr No*

for details). The club's **Garrison Room** served as the nightclub where the group demonstrate those great sixties dances.

The TV studio, where the band

Ringo goes walkabout: Turk's Head, Twickenham

rehearse and perform the climactic concert, is the Scala again, but when the four escape down the fire escape for a moment of pixilated fun, it's the iron staircase behind the **London Apollo Hammersmith, Queen Caroline Street** (*© 0870.606.3400*), when it was the Hammersmith Odeon, a legendary music venue. They hurry down the steps, only to land on the helicopter pad at **Gatwick Airport**, where their scamperings about are matched up with extra footage filmed on the **Thornbury Road Playing Fields**, south of the Great West Road, A4 (*tube: Osterley*).

Ringo takes off for a spot of meandering along the **Putney Towpath**, the south bank of the Thames just west of Kew Bridge. He samples pub sandwiches in the **Turk's Head, Winchester Road** at the corner of St Margaret's Grove, St Margaret's, Twickenham, conveniently close to the film studios. The chase sequence is around Notting Hill Gate, with the since-demolished St John's Secondary School, 83 Clarendon Road, used as the police station.

HARRY POTTER AND THE PHILOSOPHER'S STONE (aka *Harry Potter and the Sorcerer's Stone*)

(2001, dir: Chris Columbus)
Daniel Radcliffe, Rupert Grint, Emma Watson.
● LONDON; BERKSHIRE; WILTSHIRE; SCOTLAND; GLOUCESTERSHIRE; YORKSHIRE; OXFORDSHIRE; DURHAM; NORTHUMBERLAND; MIDDLESEX

The first of the *Harry Potter* saga uses locations the length and breadth of the UK, starting out in Berkshire, where the house of the dreadful Dursleys, at 4 Privet Drive, is **12 Picket Post Close, Martins Heron**, one rail stop away from Bracknell.

In London, it's at the **Reptile House** of **Regent's Park Zoo** (*www.londonzoo.co.uk*) that Harry learns he can speak to snakes and liberates the boa constrictor (though what kind of life can it expect in Regents Park?). The entrance to The Leaky Cauldron was an empty shop, now optician store **The Glass House, 42 Bull's Head Passage** in **Leadenhall Market** beneath the Lloyds Building in the City. The crazily angled exterior of Gringott's Bank is obviously a set, but the interior is the imposing **Exhibition Hall** of **Australia House**, with its chandeliers and Australian marble columns. It's not generally open to the public but there are daily tours. Find it at the eastern end of the traffic island where **Aldwych** meets the **Strand**. The Hogwarts Express supposedly departs from Platform 9$\frac{3}{4}$ of **King's Cross Station**, which is actually the arched wall between **Platforms 4** and **5**.

North to Yorkshire, where Hogsmeade Station is **Goathland Station** on the North Yorkshire Moors Railway (*www.nymr.demon.co.uk*).

And this is where it gets complicated. Hogwarts is a dizzying assembly of different locations. The richly-vaulted cloisters of **Gloucester Cathedral, Gloucester** (*www.gloucestercathedral.org.uk*), down in the southwest of England, became the corridors leading to Gryffindor House, where the lady in the oil painting asks for the password. The cloisters of **Durham Cathedral, Durham**, in the northeast, became the snowy quadrangle where Harry sets the owl flying. Then it's back south, to **Lacock Abbey**, in Lacock, a gothicised 13th century abbey three miles south of Chippenham in Wiltshire, which supplied many of the classrooms. The **Sacristy** became Professor Snape's Potions Class: "How to bottle fame, brew glory and even put a stopper in death." The **Warming Room**, which really does contain a genuine cauldron, is Professor Quirrell's Defence Against the Dark Arts classroom. And it's in the **Chapter House** that Harry stumbles upon the miraculous Mirror of Erised. The house, home of the Talbot family, including the Medieval cloisters seen in the movie, is open daily (except Tuesday) from the beginning of April to the end of October (✆ *01249.730227; admission charge*). You can also see it in the 1958 melodrama *The Moonraker*. The **Outer Bailey** of **Alnwick Castle** (*www.alnwickcastle.com*), Northumbria (seen also in Disney's *The Spaceman and King Arthur*), is the site of Madame Hooch's flying lesson. Professor Flitwick's Charms Class, where Hermione (Watson) manages to levitate a feather – "Wingardium Leviosa!" – is the **Fourth Form Rooms** of **Harrow Old Schools, Harrow-on-the-Hill**. The **Bodleian Library** of **Oxford University** (seen also in *The Madness of King George*) supplied two locations: **Duke Humphrey's Library**, where Harry tries to find out about Nicholas Flamel; and the elaborately fanvaulted **Divinity School**, which became Hogwarts School's hospital.

HARRY POTTER AND THE CHAMBER OF SECRETS

(2002, dir: Chris Columbus)
Daniel Radcliffe, Rupert Grint, Emma Watson.
● DURHAM; OXFORDSHIRE; GLOUCESTERSHIRE; YORKSHIRE; SCOTLAND; LONDON

Unsurprisingly, there are plenty of the same locations: the Hogwarts Express departs from **King's Cross Station**, though the exterior is the more photogenic **St Pancras Station** just to the west. Hogsmeade Station is again **Goathland**, north Yorkshire and, once again, **Gloucester Cathedral, Gloucester, Durham Cathedral**, Durham, and **Duke Humfrey's Library, Oxford**, become the wizard school. The express travels over **Glenfinnan Viaduct** in Scotland, and Hogwarts landscapes were filmed around **Glencoe**.

HARRY POTTER AND THE PRISONER OF AZKABAN

(2004, dir: Alfonso Cuaron)
Daniel Radcliffe, Rupert Grint, Emma Watson.
● HERTFORDSHIRE; LONDON; SURREY; SCOTLAND

More spectacular scenery filmed around **Glencoe**, and Hogwarts Lake is **Loch Shiel**, but the lake where Harry sees the Hippogriff and confronts the Dementors is **Virginia Water** in Surrey. Magnolia Way, where the Knight Bus picks up Harry after he runs away from the Dursleys, is **Dowding Way**, off **Aerodrome Way** opposite the Leavesden Studios in Hertfordshire (where the movie was based). The bus races along

The Leaky Cauldron mark II: Stoney Street, Borough

Harry accidentally hails the Knight Bus: Dowding Way

Green Lanes, between **Bourne Hill** and **Fox Lane** in **Palmers Green**, north London, before delivering Harry to The Leaky Cauldron, which has moved from Leadenhall Market – but I guess that's magic. It can now be seen opposite Borough Market (a frequent location, seen in *Bridget Jones's Diary*, *Lock, Stock and Two Smoking Barrels* and *Howards End*, among others) at **7 Stoney Street**. Next door, **8 Stoney Street**, became the Third Hand Bookshop.

HARRY POTTER AND THE GOBLET OF FIRE

(2005, dir: Mike Newell)
Daniel Radcliffe, Rupert Grint, Emma Watson.
● DEVON; SCOTLAND; HERTFORDSHIRE

Although there's some second-unit filming at **Black Rock Gorge, Evanton**, in Scotland, poor weather around Glencoe for the previous productions persuaded the filmmakers to substittute **Exmoor** in Devon. The Portkey scene was filmed at **Beacon Hill** near Berkhamsted.

HATARI!

(1962, dir: Howard Hawks)
John Wayne, Hardy Kruger, Elsa Martinelli.
● TANZANIA

Comedy-actioner with Wayne on the loose in Africa, rounding up animals for incarceration in zoos, filmed in the **Serengeti National Park**, Tanzania, around the foothills of Kilimanjaro's little twin, **Mount Meru**.

HAUNTING, THE

(1963, dir: Robert Wise)
Julie Harris, Claire Bloom, Richard Johnson.
● WARWICKSHIRE

A genuinely scary, low-key haunted house suspenser. Set in the United States, Hill House was supposedly 'built in the most remote part of New England he could find'. The great gothic house is actually about five miles southeast of Stratford-upon-Avon in Warwickshire. Supposedly the most haunted house in Britain, the 60-room mansion has been converted into a hotel. The **Ettington Park Hotel**, is on the A34 in **Alderminster** (✆ *01789.450123*).

De Niro studies metallurgy: Broadway Deli, Third Street, Santa Monica

HEAT

(1995, dir: Michael Mann) Robert De Niro, Al Pacino, Val Kilmer.

● LOS ANGELES, CALIFORNIA

Stylemeister Michael Mann remakes his own *LA Takedown* seven years on as a conscious love-letter to the architecture of LA. The hospital where Neil McCauley (De Niro) steals an ambulance is **St Mary Medical Center, 1050 Linden Avenue** in Long Beach and, while Chris Shiherlis (Kilmer) seems to be buying dynamite in Arizona, he's no further away than **Whittier**, southeast of LA. The bearer bonds robbery, where the security guards are cold-bloodedly executed, is on **Venice Boulevard** at **Convention Center Drive** beneath the Santa Monica freeway, behind the LA Convention Center, south of downtown. In the fraught aftermath, loose cannon Waingro is lucky to escape the wrath of McCauley during a confrontation at **Johnie's Broiler, 7447 Firestone Boulevard, Downey**. The classic 1958 restaurant, seen also in *Reality Bites, Short Cuts* and *What's Love Got To Do With It?* is closed and has been under threat of demolition for some time.

McCauley buys a book on metallurgy at the now-closed Hennessey and Ingalls bookstore, which stood at **1254 Third Street Promenade** in Santa Monica. The nearby restaurant, where Eady (Amy Brenneman) comes on to McCauley while he's studying 'Stress Fractures in Titanium', is the **Broadway Deli, 1457 Third Street** at Broadway at the pedestrianised Third Street Promenade in Santa Monica (don't confuse it with the Broadway Bar and Grill on the opposite corner). Not far away, on the Santa Monica sea front, is the Japanese restaurant Pacino stakes out, **Zen Zero, 1535 Ocean Avenue**.

The deserted drive-in, where Van Zant's men set up a double cross, was the Centinela Drive-In, which stood at 5700 West Centinela Avenue, Inglewood, before being demolished and replaced by apartments.

McCauley and cop Vincent Hanna (Pacino) meet up (the legendary first appreance of the two on screen together) in upscale Beverly Hills restaurant **Kate Mantilini, 9101 Wilshire Boulevard** (*©* *310.278.3699*). When Breedan (Dennis Haysbert) is recruited by McCauley as a driver, he throws in his job as dishwasher in one of the few remaining original **Bob's Big Boy** burger bars, at **4211 Riverside Drive** in Burbank. A brass plaque by one of the tables commemorates the filming.

Pacino and De Niro meet on screen: Kate Mantilini, Wilshire Boulevard

The major bank job is at **444 South Flower Street** at Fifth Street, downtown (you can see the abstract silver sculptures on the forecourt again in

The shoot-out: South Figueroa Street

Fight Club), and the subsequent mother of all shoot-outs spills out onto the stretch of **South Figueroa Street** between Fifth and Fourth Streets.

McCauley calls Nate (Jon Voight) to get Van Zant's address at **The Blue Room, 916 South San Fernando Road, Burbank** (see *Memento* for

Robbing the bank: Flower Street

details). When his relationship falls apart, Hanna moves into the **Holiday Inn, 170 North Church Lane**, overlooking the freeway in **Brentwood**. The airport hotel at which Waingro finally gets his dues is the **Hilton Los Angeles Airport, 5711 West Century Boulevard** (*©* *310.410.4000*), and it's on the runways of **LAX (Los Angeles International Airport)**, that the final shoot-out is staged.

HEAT AND DUST

(1983, dir: James Ivory) Julie Christie, Christopher Cazenove, Shashi Kapoor.

● INDIA; LONDON

More Forsterish Anglo-Indian culture clashing from the Merchant-Ivory-Jhabvala team, shot, of course, on location. The palace is **Hyderabad**, and the house featured in the modern story is in the centre of the old city of Hyderabad, near the **Char Minar**. The club is in **Secunderabad** and the little bungalow is in **Gulmarg** in Kashmir. The views of England seen during the Indian duststorm are of **Richmond Park**.

HEATHERS

(1989, dir: Michael Lehmann) Christian Slater, Winona Ryder, Shannen Doherty.

● LOS ANGELES, CALIFORNIA

Teenage fantasies of revenge on the revolting, snobby 'Heathers' and the macho jocks are cranked up to murderous heights when mean'n'moody crackpot Slater moves to Ryder's high school. This superb black comedy would have been even blacker had the original ending been kept. Set in Sherwood, Ohio, Westerburg High is a conflation of several schools, but the main location was the old Corvalis High School, now **Osaka Sangyo University of Los Angeles, 2921 Laurel Canyon Boulevard** at Maxwellton Road about half a mile from Ventura Boulevard, Studio City in the San Fernando Valley. The gym is **Verdugo Hills High School, Tujunga**, seen in many other movies, including *The Craft, one eight seven* and *River's Edge*. The **John Adams Middle School, 2425 16th Street, Santa Monica** was also used. The name Westerburg is a nod to Paul Westerberg, lead

Westerburg High: Osaka Sangyo University of Los Angeles, Studio City

Oxford Road, San Marino (see *Indecent Proposal* for details). The jocks' 'cow pushing' takes place in a quiet corner of **Griffith Park**, LA.

HEAVEN'S GATE
(1980, dir: Michael Cimino)
Kris Kristofferson, Christopher Walken, John Hurt.
● MONTANA; IDAHO; OXFORDSHIRE

March to the graduation ceremony: New College Lane, Oxford

As a film, *Heaven's Gate* is not the disaster that legend would have it, but it lost serious money and all but finished United Artists. The whole story is recounted in Stephen Bach's fascinating book *Final Cut*.

The prologue is set in Harvard University, but after the college refused permission for filming, Cimino amazingly decided on Oxford University as a stand-in, and the production decamped to England. The opening sunrise shot is **Tom Tower, Christ Church**. The band marches to the graduation ceremony under the **Bridge of Sighs** on **New College Lane**, to the **Sheldonian Theatre**, where Joseph Cotten gives the address. The alfresco dance uses the spacious quad of **Mansfield College, Mansfield Road**.

The major location for the movie, though, is **Kalispell**, Montana, in Flathead County, where the roller rink was built. Kalispell is the gateway to Glacier National Park, Blackfoot Indian Territory. The town of Sweetwater was

The Harvard graduation: Sheldonian Theatre, Oxford

built over a parking lot in Glacier National Park on the edge of **Two Medicine Lake**. The mountain opposite is **Painted Teepee**. The Main Street of Casper, Wyoming is **Wallace**, Idaho, on I-90, a nondescript mining town, whose other claim to fame is as the home of Sweater Girl Lana

The alfresco dance: Mansfield College Quad, Mansfield Road

singer of Ryder's fave band of the time, The Replacements.

The opening croquet match was filmed in the statue garden of the **Huntington Library, 1151**

Turner.

HELL IN THE PACIFIC
(1968, dir: John Boorman)
Toshiro Mifune, Lee Marvin.
● SOUTH PACIFIC

Boorman's allegorical two-hander has a US pilot and a Japanese officer marooned together on a tropical island. The location is **Palau Islands**, in the southwestern corner of Micronesia. The film used the wartime Japanese communication centre at **Airai** on the largest island of **Babelthuap**, alongside Palau's airport.

HELLRAISER
(1987, dir: Clive Barker)
Andrew Robinson, Clare Higgins, Sean Chapman.
● LONDON

The movie that launched the Cenobites, perverse pleasure-seekers from Hell, especially Pinhead. In the film, the house where Clare Higgins disposes of

66 Lodovico Street: Dollis Hill Lane

casual pick-ups to revive Sean Chapman with fresh blood is 66 Lodovico Street. The real house is actually much grander, and less dilapidated, than it appears in the movie, and it's the rear of the house that's seen. It's actually **187 Dollis Hill Lane**, NW2, high on the hill, the rear overlooking Cricklewood, where the interiors filmed at the Production Village Studio, 100 Cricklewood Lane.

HELP!
(1965, dir: Richard Lester)
The Beatles, Eleanor Bron, Leo McKern.
● LONDON; WILTSHIRE; BUCKINGHAMSHIRE; AUSTRIA; BAHAMAS

The Beatles' second cinematic outing, this time in colour, is a more surreal, freewheeling affair. The four terraced houses, behind which the Fab Four inhabit a single luxury suite, are numbers **5, 7, 9** and **11 Ailsa Avenue**, west of St Margaret's Road just over Twickenham Bridge in St Margaret's, near Twickenham Studios. Ringo attempts, unsuccessfully, to have a sacrificial ring removed at classy jewellers **Asprey's, 165 New Bond Street**, W1. The Rajahama Indian restaurant was the Dolphin Restaurant, now the **California Pizza Company, 8 Blandford Street**, W1, by Marylebone High Street.

The Beatles perform in the middle of a circle of Chieftain tanks, while being protected by the army, at **Knighton Down** on the B3086 about ten miles north of Salisbury at Larkhill on Salisbury Plain. When they hide out at Buckingham Palace, it's really **Cliveden** (site of the actual events recounted in *Scandal*), three miles northeast of Maidenhead on the B476 Hedsor road (*rail: Taplow*). Cliveden, a National Trust property once home to the Astor family, is open to the public (*© 01628.605069; admission charge*).

The 'terraced' luxury pad: Ailsa Avenue, St Margaret's

The riverside pub, with the Beethoven-loving tiger in the basement, is the historic **City Barge, 27 Strand-on-the-Green, Gunnersbury**, W4, east of Kew Bridge by Post Office Alley. The 15th century pub is named for the Lord Mayor's barge, which was moored nearby. For a really surreal experience, visit during high tide when the riverside terrace disappears and the front bar is awash with Thames water.

The ski scenes were filmed on the slopes at **Obertrauen** in Austria, while the sun-drenched beaches are at **Nassau** and on the surroundings of **New Providence Island** in the Bahamas. The airport is Nassau's itself. 'Another Girl' is performed on **Paradise Island** – a more appealing name to tourists than the original Hog Island. A major location for *Thunderball*, the island is off New Providence's northeastern coast and is now linked by a concrete bridge. The upmarket eaterie is Paradise Island's famous **Cafe Martinique** (also seen in *Thunderball*), once the guesthouse of Dr Axel Wenner-Gren, the man who bought an estate on, and developed, Hog Island. It's on the shore of the man-made Paradise Lake (*© 809.326.3000*). The featured beaches are **Cabbage Beach**, the white sand behind Paradise Towers and Grand Hotel, and **Victoria Beach**, scene of the climactic chaos, down **Casuarina Drive** on the island's northwest shore.

HENRY: PORTRAIT OF A SERIAL KILLER

(1990, dir: John McNaughton)
Michael Rooker, Tom Towles, Tracy Arnold.
● **CHICAGO, ILLINOIS**

Controversial, low-key documentary-style film about a motiveless mass murderer, shot around Chicago, where Henry's neighbourhood is just west of the Chicago River from DePaul. He takes his pal Otis to stalk victims on **Lower Wacker Drive**. The bar is **Lassen's Tap, 2121 183rd Street** at Morris Avenue, **Homewood** (*© 708.935.0996*), south of Chicago, where director McNaughton once tended bar.

HENRY V

(1944, dir: Laurence Olivier)
Laurence Olivier, Leslie Banks, Robert Newton.
● **IRELAND**

Olivier's heroic wartime version of Shakespeare, filmed largely on stylised sets at the Rank Studios in Denham in England. Starting out in Shakespeare's Globe, the action becomes increasingly more naturalistic up to the thrilling set-piece Battle of Agincourt. Half a mile of track was laid on the estate of Lord Powerscourt in **Enniskerry**, near Dublin, for the famous shot following the charge of the French knights.

HESTER STREET

(1975, dir: Joan Micklin Silver)
Steven Keats, Carol Kane, Mel Howard.
● **NEW YORK CITY**

Hester Street: Morton Street, Greenwich Village

Quiet study of the life of Jewish immigrants on New York's East Side in the 1890s. The Lower East Side was recreated on the small block of **Morton Street**, between Seventh Avenue and Bleeker Street in the heart of Greenwich Village. The picnic was shot in **the Rambles** in **Central Park**. The Great Hall of Ellis Island, where the immigrants arrive in the US, is actually the **Tweed Courthouse, 52 Chambers Street**, another favourite New York location (see *Kramer vs Kramer* for details).

HIGH FIDELITY

(2000, dir: Stephen Frears)
John Cusack, Iben Hjejle, Todd Louiso.
● **CHICAGO, ILLINOIS**

Nick Hornby's novel is transposed from London to Chicago, filming mainly around the **Wicker Park** and **Buck Town** area. Championship Vinyl, the record store of pop geek and serial rejectee Rob Gordon (Cusack) was an empty store on the corner of **North Milwaukee Avenue and North Honore Street** (the interior was a studio set). Rob's high school is **Lane Technical High School, 2501 West Addison Street**, and he waits on the **Armitage Street Station** for a train to work.

The bar where Rob goes to hear Marie DeSalle (Lisa Bonet) was Lounge Ax, **2438 North Lincoln Avenue**, which closed in early 2000. The space is now called **Gramercy**. It's across from the **Biograph Theatre** where, as Rob points out, John Dillinger was shot.

He sees a movie with Rejection No. 2, film critic Penny (Joelle Carter), at **The Music Box Theatre, 3733 North Southport Avenue** (*© 773.871.6604*), and they drink afterwards at **Strega Nona, 3747 North Southport Avenue**, next door (*© 773.244.0990*). **Hi Ricky Restaurant, 3730 North Southport Avenue**, is where he takes Rejection No. 4, messed-up Sarah (Lili Taylor).

It's in jazz club **The Green Mill Cocktail Lounge, 4802 North Broadway Avenue** at Lawrence, with its 'Al Capone drank here often' sign (*© 773.878.5552*), that Rob reminisces about Laura (Hjejle). Meanwhile, Laura tells Rob's sister Liz (real-life sister Joan Cusack) four pieces of uncomfortable information in steakhouse **Smith & Wollensky, 318 North State Street, Marina City** (*© 312.670.9900*).

On the **Kinzie Street Bridge**, Rob lists the things he misses about Laura, before tentatively proposing to her over a lunchtime drink at **The Rainbo Club, 1150 North Damen** (*© 312.489.5999*). The launch party for 'I Sold My Mom's Wheelchair', where Barry (Jack Black) finally gets to perform, is **Double Door, 1572 North**

Milwaukee Avenue (© *773.489.3160, www.double-door.com*).

Davis and Sheen's flat: Stanley Passage, King's Cross

HIGH HOPES

(1988, dir: Mike Leigh)
Philip Davis, Ruth Sheen, Edna Dore.
● LONDON; ESSEX

Glum comedy of manners from Mike Leigh. Philip Davis and Ruth Sheen's flat is on **Stanley Passage**, behind King's Cross Station, N1. It runs between Pancras Road and the famous stretch of Cheney Road by the now-gone gasometers, seen in *The Ladykillers* and *Chaplin* among many others. Davis and Sheen visit Karl Marx's tomb in **Highgate Cemetery**. Richard Rodgers' loved-or-loathed **Lloyd's Building** also puts in an appearance.

HIGH NOON

(1952, dir: Fred Zinnemann)
Gary Cooper, Thomas Mitchell, Grace Kelly.
● CALIFORNIA

The original choice for Hadleyville: Columbia State Park

Sheriff Will Kane stands alone against the baddies, but fortunately wife Amy does not forsake him. The opening scenes, under the credits, were shot at the **Iverson Ranch** near Chatsworth, north of LA, but the fictitious Hadleyville, New Mexico, was to have been played by the Main Street of Columbia State Park, a preserved gold-rush town in northern California. By the time the crew arrived, however, spring had arrived and the bleak, bare main street of Columbia had burst into green leafiness. In the end, they used the Western Street at, by coincidence, Columbia Pictures in **Burbank**. Some of the real mining town remains in the picture, though. You can't miss the white picket fence of Sam Fuller, the cowardly friend who sends his wife to claim he's not at home. This is the **Wilson House** on Main Street, a few doors away from the Visitor Center, and the last privately-owned home in the town. **Columbia State Historic Park** is east of the town of Columbia, 45 miles northeast of Modesto in Tuolumne County (© *209.532.4301; open daily*).

Cowardly Sam Fuller's home: Columbia State Historic Park

A few miles southeast of Columbia you'll find the church where Kane pleads for special deputies to face Frank Miller. It's **St Joseph's Catholic Church, Gardner Avenue** at Tuolumne Road in **Tuolumne City**, not a city at all but a tiny town just off Route 108. The railroad station was built alongside a watertower

Will Kane appeals for help: St Joseph's, Tuolumne City

at **Warnerville**, a little to the southwest, about 14 miles east of Oakdale on the narrow gauge Sierra Railroad (see *Go West* for details of the railroad).

HIGH PLAINS DRIFTER

(1972, dir: Clint Eastwood)
Clint Eastwood, Verna Bloom, Marianna Hill.
● CALIFORNIA; NEVADA

Site of Lago: Mono Lake

Surreal revenge Western. The fictitious town of Lago was built, complete with interiors, at the strange lunar-like landscape of **Mono Lake**, east of Yosemite National Park at the foot of the Sierra Nevadas. It's on Highway 395, central California. The opening and closing scenes of barren emptiness were filmed at **Winnemuca Dry Lake** near Fallon, east of Carson City, Nevada.

PHOTOGRAPH COURTESY GREG REIS, MONO LAKE COMMITTEE

HIGH SIERRA

(1941, dir: Raoul Walsh)
Humphrey Bogart, Ida Lupino, Arthur Kennedy.
● CALIFORNIA

The climactic chase: Whitney Portal Road, Lone Pine

Bogart is 'Mad Dog' Earle, on the lam in this classic chase movie, which sees Bogie holed up in the mountains above **Lone Pine**, Route 395 in central California. **Cedar Lake** in the San Bernardino Mountains was also used. The final car chase takes off from Lone Pine, west along the winding **Whitney Portal Road** up toward the snow-capped High Sierras and Mount Whitney itself, which in 1941 (before Alaska joined) was the highest point in the US.

HIGH SOCIETY

(1956, dir: Charles Walters)
Bing Crosby, Grace Kelly, Frank Sinatra.
● RHODE ISLAND

The Philadelphia Story, laced with Cole Porter songs, is relocated to Rhode Island. The mansion, where Sinatra and Crosby vie for Grace Kelly, is **Clarendon Court, Bellevue Avenue, Newport**. It's a private house, not open to the public, and was home to Claus von Bulow, the millionaire businessman cleared of the attempted murder of his wife, Sunny. The von Bulow story is told in *Reversal of Fortune* which, not surprisingly, wasn't filmed at Clarendon Court.

HIGHLANDER

(1986, dir: Russell Mulcahy)
Christopher Lambert, Sean Connery, Clancy Brown.
● SCOTLAND; LONDON; NEW YORK CITY

The confrontation with Kurgan: Silvercup Studios, Queens

McLeod meets Kurgan in the New York church: St Augustine's, Kilburn

A gobsmacking jumble of accents: Frenchman Lambert plays titular immortal Scotsman Connor MacLeod, while Scot Connery plays Spanish nobleman Juan Sanchez Villa-Lobos Ramirez in this flashy nonsense made by a director of TV ads (and does it show). MacLeod's home is the 13th century **Eilean Donan Castle** on an islet in **Dornie**, eight miles east of Kyle of Lochalsh on the A87, Wester Ross (© *01599.555202; admission charge*). The battle between the tribes was staged at **Glencoe**, on the A82 in Argylleshire. The beach, where MacLeod experiences the Quickening, is **Refuge Bay, Curtaig** near Morar, while the spectacular jagged peak where Ramirez teaches swordplay is **Cioch** in the **Cuillin Hills** on the Isle of Skye. In present day New York, MacLeod decapitates a rival swordsman in the carpark of **Madison Square Garden**. The scuzzy backstreet is the all-purpose fighting alley, **Cortlandt Alley**, between Canal and Franklin Streets alongside Broadway in Lower Manhattan (it's where "Crocodile" Dundee fights off muggers).

The New York church, where MacLeod meets the insinuatingly blasphemous Kurgan (Brown), is the huge, rather severe, red-brick **St Augustine's Kilburn, Kilburn Park Road**, opposite Rudolph Road, London. The church is open to visitors on Saturday mornings between 10 and 12, and Tuesdays between 9 and 12. The final confrontation with Kurgan is, conveniently, atop the **Silvercup Studios, 42-25 21st Street** in Queens, where the film's interiors were shot.

The first sequel, *Highlander II: The Quickening*, was made in **Buenos Aires**, Argentina, while *Highlander III: The Sorcerer* (aka *Highlander – The Final Dimension*) returned to Scotland, filming at **Glencoe, Glen Nevis** and **Ardnamurchan**.

HILLS HAVE EYES, THE

(1977, dir: Wes Craven)
Susan Lanier, Robert Houston, Virginia Vincent.
● CALIFORNIA

Wes Craven's second movie, now something of a classic, has a suburban family turning out to be a fair match for the cannibalistic primitives who menace them after they're stranded in the Nevada desert. It was filmed in **Apple Valley**, outside of Victorville, in the San Bernardino area.

HIMMEL ÜBER BERLIN, DER (aka *Wings of Desire*)

(1987, dir: Wim Wenders)
Bruno Ganz, Solveig Dommartin, Peter Falk.
● BERLIN, GERMANY

Angels' perch: The Siegessäul

Wenders' romantic fantasy (remade in California as *City of Angels*) with Bruno Ganz as one of a pair of angels hovering above Berlin who yearns to exchange his wings for humanity. Beautifully shot (in black and white until Ganz enters the human realm) around the then still-divided city. Ganz is first seen perched atop the symbol of Berlin's war damage, the shattered spire of **Kaiser Wilhelm Gedächtniskirche** on **Breitscheidplatz**, and later alongside the golden Winged Victory statue atop the **Siegessäule** column on **Strasse des 17 Juni** in the Tiergarten. Much of the movie was shot around **Potsdammer Platz** and the dismal wastelands alongside the wall, now unrecognisable as the city's development races ahead. You can still find the little second-hand shop where the newly-human Ganz picks up his colourful outfit, at **Goebenstrasse 6**, near the Yorkstrasse S-Bahn station.

HITCHER, THE

(1986, dir: Robert Harmon)
Rutger Hauer, C Thomas Howell, Jennifer Jason Leigh.
● CALIFORNIA

There's just no peace in the California desert, is there? Chances are you will never *ever* give anyone a lift after seeing this creepy chiller with hapless motorist Howell picking up psycho Hauer. The featureless desertscapes are around **Amboy, Barstow** and in **Death Valley**, California. The building where Hauer stalks Howell is the same **Death Valley Junction** building, on Route 127, used as the motel exterior in David Lynch's *Lost Highway*.

HOBSON'S CHOICE

(1953, dir: David Lean)
Charles Laughton, Brenda de Banzie, John Mills.
● MANCHESTER

Yorkshireman Laughton's great hammy turn as a tyrannical Lancashire patriarch, with some wonderfully grimy location filming around **Salford**, near Manchester, on the banks of the River Irwell.

HOME ALONE

(1990, dir: Chris Columbus)
Macaulay Culkin, Joe Pesci, Daniel Stern.
● CHICAGO, ILLINOIS

The house of Kevin McAllister (Culkin) is to the north of Chicago, at **671 Lincoln Avenue, Winnetka** (rail: Winnetka, Metra Commuter line from North-

The McAllister home: Lincoln Avenue, Winnetka

western Station). Nearby is the green where Culkin visits Santa Claus, in front of **Winnetka Village Hall, Green Bay Road**. The green with the bandstand, where Culkin shops for a toothbrush, is one stop north of Winnetka, **Hubbard Woods**, while the church is way over in the western suburb of **Oak Park**. The airport from which the family leave is, of course, **Chicago O'Hare**. And the Paris airport at which they land? That's O'Hare too.

HOME ALONE 2: LOST IN NEW YORK

(1992, dir: Chris Columbus)
Macaulay Culkin, Joe Pesci, Daniel Stern.
● NEW YORK CITY; CHICAGO, ILLINOIS

Once again Culkin gets separated from his family, as they head for Florida and he catches a plane for New York. **671 Lincoln Avenue** and **Chicago O'Hare** reprise their roles from the first movie. Culkin stays at the **Plaza Hotel, Fifth Avenue** at 59th Street, New York, but this is a John Hughes-produced movie, and if it can be shot in Chicago, it will be. The luxury suite, in which the family is reunited at the end of the movie, supposedly overlooking Central Park, is the Conrad Hilton Suite of the **Chicago Hilton and Towers, 720 South Michigan Avenue** (see *The Fugitive*). Likewise, Eddie Bracken's toyshop is the unmistakable rusticated arch of the **Rookery Building, 209 South La Salle Street** at West Adams Street in the Loop (see *The Untouchables* for details).

HONDO

(1953, dir: John Farrow)
John Wayne, Geraldine Page, Ward Bond.
● MEXICO

Wayne defends Geraldine Page and her kid from Indians in New Mexico. Actually, it's old Mexico, at **Camargo** just over the Rio Grande, south of Laredo. When *Hondo* was released, a movie slated to be called *Bad Day at Hondo* needed a rethink, and so became *Bad Day at Black Rock*.

HORSE FEATHERS

(1932, dir: Norman Z McLeod)
The Marx Brothers, Thelma Todd, David Landau.
● LOS ANGELES, CALIFORNIA

Huxley College, where Professor Quincy Adams Wagstaff (Groucho) presides, is **Occidental College, 1600 Campuis Road, Eagle Rock**, seen also in *Clueless* and *Jurassic Park III*.

HÔTEL DU NORD

(1938, dir: Marcel Carné)
Jean-Pierre Aumont,
Annabella, Louis Jouvet.
● PARIS, FRANCE

Marcel Carné's beautifully atmospheric, romantic tragedy, set in a canalside Parisian hotel, was made largely in the studio, but you can see the real hotel, which still exists: **Hôtel du Nord, 102 quai de Jemappes**, on the Canal St-Martin.

The real hotel: Hôtel du Nord, quai de Jemappes

HOTEL NEW HAMPSHIRE, THE

(1984, dir: Tony Richardson)
Beau Bridges, Rob Lowe, Jodie Foster.
● QUÉBEC, CANADA

John Irving's novel may not make a successful movie, but individual episodes are fun. The province of Québec, Canada, stands in for New Hampshire. The hotel is the 140-room **Hotel Tadoussac, 165 rue Bord de l'Eau** (© *418.235.4421*). Tadoussac is on Route 138 on the north shore of the St Lawrence (there's a free ferry), about 170 miles east of Québec.

HOURS, THE

(2002, dir: Stephen Daldry)
Meryl Streep, Nicole Kidman, Julianne Moore.
● LONDON; HERTFORDSHIRE; LEICESTERSHIRE; NEW YORK CITY; FLORIDA

Michael Cunningham's novel interweaves three stories, set in England, Los Angeles and New York, linked by Virginia Woolf's *Mrs Dalloway*. Richmond Station, the pivotal scene where Leonard Woolf (Stephen Dillane) acquiesces to Virginia Woolf's (Kidman) desire to return to London, was filmed on **Lough-borough's Great Central Railway's Quorn Station**, Leicestershire. The 1951 Los Angeles neighbourhood of Laura Brown (Moore) is the Miami suburb of **Hollywood**, Florida. The hotel Laura books into to read *Mrs Dalloway*, and to commit suicide, is the **Biltmore**

Clarissa's New York apartment: West 10th Street, Greenwich Village

Richard's apartment: The Red Triangle Building, 14th Street

Hotel, **1200 Anastasia Avenue** at De Soto Boulevard, Coral Gables, southwest Miami (*©305.445.1926*). See *Bad Boys* for full details.

London's **Richmond Hill** is one of the few real locations, though the Richmond house is the director's own home, **Hogarth House** near Luton, Hertfordshire.

The New York subway is **23rd Street Station**, and the Village florist shop, where Clarissa Vaughan (Streep) buys flowers, supposedly on 23rd Street, is **Sanbrano Inc, 370 Bleecker Street**, in the West Village (the florist is played by Eileen Atkins, who adapted *Mrs Dalloway* for Marleen Gorris's film). Clarissa's New York apartment is **12 West 10th Street** (next door to Mark Twain's house at number 14). The loft apartment of her ailing friend Richard (Ed Harris) is the **Red Triangle Building, 14th Street at Ninth Avenue**, in New York's Meat Packing district, although the interior, like all the film's interiors, was filmed at Pinewood Studios. The building (also seen in *Serpico*) now houses Vento, a trattoria, replacing the notorious Hellfire S&M club, which used to be based in the basement (and was used as a location for both *Basket Case* and *Cruising*). The Triangle apartment alongside Richard's was home to Glenn Close in *Fatal Attraction*.

The possessed house: Melrose Avenue, Monrovia

HOUSE
(1986, dir: Steve Miner)
William Katt, Kay Lenz, George Wendt.
● CALIFORNIA

William Katt inherits the spooky house where an old lady died and gets hounded by his dead buddy from Vietnam. The outrageously gingerbread Victorian house can be found at **329 Melrose Avenue, Monrovia**, east of Pasadena, California.

The sequel, *House II: The Second Story*, uses another folly, the Romanesque **Stimson House, 2421 South Figueroa Street, Exposition Park**, south of downtown LA, now owned by the nuns of Mount St Mary's College.

HOUSE OF USHER, THE (aka *The Fall of the House of Usher*)
(1960, dir: Roger Corman)
Vincent Price, Myrna Fahey, Mark Damon.
● LOS ANGELES, CALIFORNIA

The first of Corman's stylish, low-budget Poe adaptations, this was all studio shot of course, using matte paintings for the house exteriors. Canny as ever, though, Corman took advantage of a fire that swept through the Hollywood Hills to get the shots of Damon's journey through 'blighted' countryside with ashes and charred trees. For the final conflagration, Corman got permission to burn down a huge barn, on the verge of demolition, in Orange County, south LA. The spectacular footage of blazing rafters collapsing was to become a familiar favourite over the years as it cropped up with alarming regularity at the climax of Corman movies.

HOUSE ON HAUNTED HILL, THE
(1958, dir: William Castle)
Vincent Price, Richard Long, Carol Ohmart.
● LOS ANGELES, CALIFORNIA

Price is the millionaire holding an all-night party in the supposedly haunted house cared for by jittery Elisha Cook Jr, in William Castle's classic gimmicky schlocker. The

The house on 'Haunted Hill': Ennis-Brown House, Los Feliz

gimmick this time, Emergo, had a plastic skeleton trundled out from behind the screen over the heads of the audience. Pretty scary. Castle eschews standard gothic, and uses Frank Lloyd Wright's superb **Ennis-Brown House**, a Mayan-temple influenced structure built of precast concrete blocks. The house, built in 1924, suffered years of neglect. After the release of the movie, it was nightly besieged by bozos, hurling bottles. It was slightly damaged in the 1994 quake, too. A frequent location for movies, ads and music videos, you can see the house as a movie producer's home in *Grand Canyon* and *Day of the Locust*, as a villain's hideout in *Black Rain* and *The Karate Kid III*, but perhaps most famously as Harrison Ford's futuristic home in *Blade Runner*. It's a private home now, and struggling to be preserved. There are occasional tours. The house is on a slope below Griffith Park, at **2607 Glendower Avenue**, Los Feliz, LA (*© 213.660.00607*).

For the campy 1999 remake, the amusement park was largely a model, based on a real park in Orlando, Florida. The house itself consisted of miniatures and matte paintings. Only the entrance is real. It's the art deco frontage of the **Griffith Observatory, 2800 East Observatory Road** in Griffith Park, LA (see *Rebel Without a Cause* for details).

HOUSE ON 92nd ST., THE
(1945, dir: Henry Hathaway)
William Eythe, Lloyd Nolan, Signe Hasso.
● NEW YORK CITY

Highly influential documentary-style drama, with the FBI rooting out Nazi spies in New York, this was one of the first Hollywood movies to get right out of the studio. The house, supposedly on the north side of 92nd Street near Madison Avenue, where Elsa Gowns fronted for the spy ring, was actually 53 East 93rd Street. It's now demolished, but its twin, 55, is still standing. Other New York locations include the **Brill Building, 1141 Broadway** (see *The Sweet Smell of Success* for details).

HOW GREEN WAS MY VALLEY
(1941, dir: John Ford)
Walter Pidgeon, Maureen O'Hara, Donald Crisp.
● LOS ANGELES, CALIFORNIA

John Ford's romanticised dream of life in a Welsh mining village was to have been directed by William Wyler, who prepared the movie and worked on the script. Its heart is sort of in the right place, but sentimentality wins out. The village was a huge set built at the Fox Ranch, **Malibu Creek State Park, Las Virgenes Road**, off Mulholland Highway, Calabasas.

HOW THE WEST WAS WON

(1962, dir: Henry Hathaway; John Ford; George Marshall)
Carroll Baker, Henry Fonda, Gregory Peck.
● **SOUTH DAKOTA; COLORADO; KENTUCKY; UTAH**

Site of Fonda's homestead: Lone Pine Campground

Long, sprawling history of the West, filmed as a Cinerama spectacular. The giant format caused all sorts of headaches, including the problem of where to place the microphones in such a wide-open, spacious frame.

The Henry Fonda section – the railroad and the buffalo stampede directed by George Marshall – was shot at **Custer State Park**, near Rapid City, South Dakota. Fonda's cabin, though, was in California, just off **Whitney Portal Road**, above **Lone Pine**, Route 395, against the breathtaking backdrop of Mount Whitney and the High Sierras. The site is now the Lone Pine Campground, a couple of miles west of the town. The Indian attack used the **Alabama Hills**, the striking red rock formations above Lone Pine (see *Gunga Din* for details). The Civil War section, directed by John Ford, naturally uses **Monument Valley**, Utah.

Other locations included **Paducah** on Route 24 in West Kentucky, and **Duck Creek Village**, 30 miles east of Cedar City, Utah (also the location for TV series *My Friend Flicka* among many others). There is a bit of padding, too, from other movies to bulk out the epic. You can see Santa Ana's army from John Wayne's *The Alamo* and battle scenes from Edward Dmytryk's 1958 *Raintree County*, while the modern day epilogue, with Spencer Tracy's voiceover lauding the wonders of the freeway system, is taken from the travelogue demo *This Is Cinerama*.

HOW TO MARRY A MILLIONAIRE

(1953, dir: Jean Negulesco)
Lauren Bacall, Marilyn Monroe, Betty Grable.
● **NEW YORK CITY**

Betty, Betty and Norma Jean share an apartment at **36**

Where to marry a millionaire: Sutton Place South, East Side

Sutton Place South, by the East River in New York. Fred Clark is less than thrilled to be greeted as driver of the fifty millionth vehicle across New York's

George Washington Bridge, West 178th Street crossing the Hudson River to Fort Lee, New Jersey. Also featured is the **Rockefeller Center, West 48th to West 51st Streets** between Fifth and Sixth Avenues, then only partially completed. It was Marilyn who, in 1957, ceremonially detonated the first dynamite charge to begin the excavation of the Time-Life Building.

HOWARDS END

(1992, dir: James Ivory)
Emma Thompson, Vanessa Redgrave, Anthony Hopkins.
● **LONDON; OXFORDSHIRE; SURREY; SHROPSHIRE; DEVON; WORCESTER, WORCESTERSHIRE**

The third of Merchant-Ivory 's impeccably produced Forster adaptations uses a slew of real locations. Starting off in London: the cream-painted home of the Schlegel sisters (Thompson and Helena Bonham Carter) – the fictitious 6 Wickham Place – is **6 Victoria Square**, a quiet square hidden away just

Howards End: Peppard Cottage, Peppard Common, Rotherfield Peppard

Emma Thompson's home, Wickham Place: Victoria Square

north of Victoria Station, SW1, whose photogenic charm was also used in the 1956 *Around the World in Eighty Days*. Not far away, the courtyard of a converted Edwardian apartment block, **51 Buckingham Gate** (℡ *020.7769.7766, www.51-buckinghamgate.com*), previously the St James's Court Hotel, became the exterior of the London home of Henry Wilcox (Hopkins). You can glimpse the landscaped courtyard, with its Shakespearian figures and central fountain, through the hotel's imposing gateway. The interior staircase, where Wilcox proposes to Ruth (Redgrave), is **2 South Audley Street** in Mayfair, which was the office of James Bond producer Albert Broccoli's Eon Productions. See the exterior in *Wilde*.

At the other end of the social scale, the modest home of Leonard Bast (Samuel West) is on **Park Street** behind Borough Market, Borough, SE1 – another popular (though threatened) location you'll probably recognise from *Lock, Stock and Two Smoking Barrels* and *Keep the Aspidistra Flying*. The rainswept exterior of the Ethical Hall is near the Bank of England in the City of Lon-

Sam West's modest home: Park Street, Southwark

Emma Thompson meets her brother: Magdalen College, Oxford

Wilcox tells the Schlegels about Porphyrion: Strawberry House, Chiswick Mall

don, but the interior, where West picks up the wrong umbrella, is **Oxford Town Hall, St Aldgate's** at Carfax in the centre of town (another favourite, it featured as the interior of the Old Bailey in *A Fish Called Wanda*).

The row of houses along **Chiswick Mall** stood in for the Chelsea Embankment, where Wilcox gives a bit of disastrous insider info about the Porphyrion company to the Schlegels, as they leave their weekly discussion group at **Strawberry House**. The same house is home to James Fox and Anjelica Huston in another Merchant-Ivory production, *The Golden Bowl*. And see *Victim* for a neighbouring location.

The Porphyrion Insurance Company, where Mr Bast initially works, is the **Renaissance London Chancery Court Hotel, 252 High Holborn** (© 020.7829.9888), housed in the magnificent old Pearl Assurance Building, which was also used for the offices of Wilcox's Rubber Company. Having stood empty for years, the grandiose marble interior saw frequent service as a film location in such films as *Richard III* and *The Saint*. The bank where he subsequently applies for a job is the **Baltic Exchange, St Mary Axe** off Leadenhall Street, EC3, severely damaged by the IRA bomb attack on the City, now the site of the Swiss Re 'gherkin' building.

The exterior of the London home of Henry Wilcox: Buckingham Gate, Victoria

More venerable landmarks abound: Margaret Schlegel and Ruth are driven from the Mall through London's **Admiralty Arch** at the southwest corner of Trafalgar Square in a gasp-inducing money-shot, which seems to include every horse-drawn period carriage in the British Isles. The station where they buy tickets to Hilton is **St Pancras Station**, Euston Road, NW1, and Thompson takes lunch with Hopkins at **Simpsons-in-the-Strand**.

Out of London, Emma Thompson's brother studies at **Magdalen College, Oxford**, where she meets

Buying the railway tickets: St Pancras Station ticket hall

him on the bridge over the Cherwell (you can explore the grounds – for details see Joseph Losey's *Accident*). The country cottage to which she retreats is at **Blackpool Sands**, where it overlooks the English Channel near Dartmouth, Devon.

Ruth Wilcox expires: Royal Holloway and Bedford New College, Englefield Green

In Surrey, south of **Englefield Green** on the A30 west of Egham, you can't miss the chimneyed and turretted outline of the **Royal Holloway and Bedford New College**, which was used for the nursing home in which Ruth expires. Built in 1887 as a women's college for pill manufacturer Thomas Holloway, and now part of the University of London, its elaborate design was inspired by France's Chateau de Chambord. Howards End itself, in the fictional village of Hilton, is **Peppard Cottage** on Peppard Common just off the B481, in the village of **Rotherfield Peppard** just to the west of Henley-on-Thames, Oxfordshire. Not nearly as remote as it appears in the movie – it's only a couple of doors from the village pub – the cottage was once owned by Lady Ottoline Morrell, who entertained members of the Bloomsbury group here around the turn of the century. Hilton was filmed in Worcestershire: the George Tavern can be found in the village of **Upper Arley**, west off the A442 about six miles northwest of Kidderminster, and Hilton Station is **Bewdley**, a couple of miles to the south, on the Severn Valley Railway.

Margaret takes lunch with Wilcox: Simpsons-in-the-Strand

Wilcox's country mansion, where all the chickens come home to roost at the nightmarish wedding reception, is **Brampton Bryan**, on the A4113 about 12 miles west of Ludlow, Shropshire.

HOWLING, THE

(1981, dir: Joe Dante)
Dee Wallace, Patrick Macnee, Dennis Dugan.
● **CALIFORNIA**

Movie-buff Dante's in-jokey werewolf movie (most of the characters are named after classic horror film directors), was filmed around LA. The hot tub scene was shot in **Griffith Park**, where the tiny tennis pro shop became the office of sheriff Slim Pickens. The opening scenes and the porno store were filmed in a section of west LA which no longer exists. The woods scenes were shot in the **Mendocino Forest** near Fort Bragg.

HUD

(1963, dir: Martin Ritt)
Paul Newman, Patricia Neal, Melvyn Douglas.
● **TEXAS**

Melodrama on a Texas ranch, with reckless son Newman and stern father Douglas, from a novel by Larry McMurtry, author of *The Last Picture Show*. It was filmed in **Claude**, Route 287, about 20 miles east of Amarillo in the north Texas panhandle.

HUDSON HAWK
(1991, dir: Michael Lehmann)
Bruce Willis, Danny Aiello, James Coburn.
● NEW YORK CITY; HUNGARY; ITALY; LONDON

Big-budget misfire from the director of the wonderful *Heathers*. Set partly in New York, it features a 'wacky' chase over the **Brooklyn Bridge**. The prison is the notorious **Sing Sing Prison**, on the Hudson River, north of New York City. Filming also took place in **Budapest**, **Rome**, London and at **Castello di San Leo**, the gigantic Medieval fortress, where Cagliostro was imprisoned and died, about 15 miles southwest of Rimini, Italy.

HUDSUCKER PROXY, THE
(1994, dir: Joel Coen)
Tim Robbins, Jennifer Jason Leigh, Paul Newman.
● CHICAGO, ILLINOIS

The Hudsucker Building: Merchandise Mart

Set in 1950s New York, *Hudsucker* relies mainly on huge stylised sets, but for authentic deco locations the movie decamped to Chicago. The Hudsucker Building is Chicago's **Merchandise Mart**, on the north bank of the Chicago River between Wells and Orleans Streets. Built by Marshall Field in 1931, the Mart boasted the largest floor area of any building in the world until the construction of the Pentagon in Washington DC. The charity ball was filmed in the ballroom of the **Blackstone Hotel, 636 South Michigan Avenue** (see *The Untouchables* for details).

HULK
(2003, dir: Ang Lee)
Eric Bana, Jennifer Connelly, Sam Elliott.
● CALIFORNIA; UTAH

Dispense those nanomeds. Ang Lee continues to confound genre extectations, and with Danny Elfman's thunderous score, he brings an expressive comic book dynamic to the legendary Marvel story.

Nerdy Bruce Banner (Bana) works at the **Lawrence Berkeley National Laboratory** (for the first time at the Advanced Light Source, a giant contraption which generates intense light for scientific and technological research), and **Berkeley Campus**. His father's (Nick Nolte) funky neighbourhood is an industrial area of **Oakland**, over the Bay from San Francisco.

The house of Betty Ross (Connelly) was on the Universal lot, and can also be seen in *To Kill A Mockingbird*. The restaurant where she meets her father (Elliott) is on the artificially-created **Treasure Island** in the Bay, with one of the best views of the city skyline. The cabin in the flashback sequence was built at **Balch County Road** in **Mountain Home Demonstration State Forest**, in Sequoia National Park, near **Springville** (it was dismantled immediately after filming). The airport and barracks are at **Wendover**, Utah (where the atom bomb-carrying Enola Gay was based toward the end of WWII), a location also used for *The Core*. The helicopter shots of the desert are around **Lake Powell, Page**, Arizona, and helicopters chase the Hulk as he bounds across the spectacular red rock formations of **Arches National Park**, Utah.

The dilapidated town, with the abandoned ice-cream parlor, is a set built on the east of I-15 at **Yermo**, in the Mojave, though the overlook, and the little girl's swing are in Utah. The entrance to the army facility is **China Lake Naval Weapons Center**, near **Bakersfield**, California, and the final interior is the huge Stage 12 at Universal, one of the largest in LA. Night exteriors were shot in the sequoia forests of **Porterville**, California.

Hulk leaps and bounds his way back to San Francisco, via the **Golden Gate Bridge**, before popping up through the tarmac in the posh **Telegraph Hill**, at the corner of **Sansome and Vallejo Streets**, a location chosen for the view down to the **Oakland Bay Bridge**. Residents had to be evacuated as the helicopters came in at a height of a mere 75 feet (way below the regulation 500 feet).

HUNCHBACK OF NOTRE DAME, THE
(1939, dir: William Dieterle)
Charles Laughton, Cedric Hardwicke, Maureen O'Hara.
● LOS ANGELES, CALIFORNIA

One of Laughton's really great performances, in a totally irresistible film. This RKO movie uses the set built at Universal in Hollywood for the 1923 Lon Chaney silent version. The bell tower interior is supposedly the Tuscan-style campanile of the **Mudd Hall of Philosophy, University Avenue** at Exposition Boulevard, on the campus of the **University of Southern California**, south of downtown LA (see *The Graduate* for details). The university claims it was also used for the Lon Chaney version, but Mudd Hall wasn't built until 1928, so it's not likely.

HUNGER, THE
(1983, dir: Tony Scott)
Catherine Deneuve, Susan Sarandon, David Bowie.
● LONDON; NEW YORK CITY

Deneuve and Bowie are fashion-plate vampires staving off the years with lashings of the red stuff in this design-led horror. Set in New York, much of the movie was made in the UK. The disco is **Heaven**, the vast gay dance-spot under the arches at Charing Cross in

The New York clinic: Senate House, Malet Street

London. The art deco New York clinic is the foyer of **Senate House, the University of London, Malet Street**, seen also as the king's neo-fascist bunker in Ian McKellen's thirties-set *Richard III*.

HUNT FOR RED OCTOBER, THE

(1990, dir: John McTiernan)
Sean Connery, Alec Baldwin, Scott Glenn.
● **CALIFORNIA; WASHINGTON; NORTH CAROLINA; LIVERPOOL**

Soviet admiral Connery hijacks his own 'invisible' submarine and attempts to defect, in this Cold War thriller made around **San Diego**, California, and at **Port Angeles** on Route 101, north of Seattle, on the Strait of Juan de Fuca, Washington State. The Russian Embassy, where shifty Joss Ackland bluffs and sweats, is actually **Sessions House**, a courtroom in Liverpool. Studio filming was at **Wilmington Studios**, North Carolina, and scenes were also shot in the Function Room of the **Park Plaza Hotel, 607 South Park View Street**, midtown LA.

HURRICANE, THE

(1999, dir: Norman Jewison)
Denzel Washington, Vicellous Reon Shannon, Liev Schreiber.
● **NEW JERSEY; TORONTO, ONTARIO, CANADA**

Dubious biopic of the wrongly-jailed boxer Rubin 'Hurricane' Carter, filmed in New Jersey, on many of the real locations, and in Toronto, Ontario. Jail scenes were shot at **Rahway State Penitentiary, Woodbridge Road, Rahway** (seen also in *Malcolm X*) on Route 1 on the River Rahway, and at **Trenton State Prison**, New Jersey. The robbery scene used the real **Lafayette Bar and Grill, Patterson**, New Jersey, which had to be restored for filming. Much of the movie, though, was shot north of the border in Toronto, at: **Dupont Street** at Dundas Street; the **Harbourfront**; **Kingswood Road; 15 and 53 Fraser Avenue**; **Riverside Drive**; **St Joseph's Health Centre, 30 The Queensway**; **Booksworth, 347 Bay Street**; the **Old City Hall**; the **Winchester Hotel, 537 Parliament** at Gerrard; **11 King Street West**; and **Branksome Hall School, 10 Elm Avenue**.

HUSBANDS AND WIVES

(1992, dir: Woody Allen)
Woody Allen, Mia Farrow, Judy Davis.
● **NEW YORK CITY**

Multi-focused drama of marital, post-marital and extra-marital relationships, recorded semi-documentary style. Mia Farrow has lunch with newly-single Judy Davis at the **Dean & DeLuca Cafe, 121 Prince Street** between

Wooster and Greene Streets in SoHo. The café is run by Dean & DeLuca, the nearby gourmet food store. Woody Allen teaches creative writing to

Shakespeare's 'King Leo': 68th Street Playhouse, Third Avenue

Juliette Lewis at **Barnard College**, part of the familiar **Columbia University**, over Broadway, west of the main campus, **West 116th Street and 120th Streets** between Claremont Avenue and Broadway in Morningside Heights. Sydney Pollack and his ditsy new girlfriend see Kurosawa's version of Shakespeare's '*King Leo*' at the **68th Street Playhouse, Third Avenue** at 68th Street.

HUSH... HUSH, SWEET CHARLOTTE

(1964, dir: Robert Aldrich)
Bette Davis, Olivia de Havilland, Joseph Cotten.
● **LOUISIANA**

This troubled follow-up to the hugely successful *What Ever Happened to Baby Jane?* was all but completed with the re-teaming of Bette Davis and Joan Crawford,

The Southern mansion: Houmas House, Burnside

when Crawford's persistent illnesses brought production to a halt (read Shaun Considine's wickedly gossipy book, *Bette and Joan: The Divine Feud* for the fascinating details). The company aimed high for a replacement: not surprisingly, grandes dames Vivien Leigh and Katharine Hepburn both turned down the role in this southern gothic melodrama, which eventually went to Olivia de Havilland.

The Greek Revival mansion with its three-storey spiral staircase (mind those bouncing heads) is the **Houmas House, 40136 Highway 942**, just west of **Burnside** (© *504.891.9494, www.houmashouse.com*) on Route 44 between New Orleans and Baton Rouge. The house – which has also been seen in *Moon of the Wolf*, *Mandingo* and *Fletch Lives* among others – is open for tours, conducted by impressively knowledgeable guides in Antebellum costume.

HUSTLER, THE

(1961, dir: Robert Rossen)
Paul Newman, Jackie Gleason, George C Scott.
● **NEW YORK CITY; LOS ANGELES, CALIFORNIA**

Ten Academy nominations for Rossen's downbeat, lowlife pool-hall movie, with Newman as 'Fast' Eddie Felson – the character he returned to 25 years later in *The Color of Money*. Apart from the apartment interior, almost all of the film was shot on location around New York. The pool hall, where Fast Eddie squares off against Minnesota Fats (Gleason), was Ames Pool Hall, on the second floor of the Claridge Hotel, Broadway at Times Square (the hotel in which Joe Buck stays in *Midnight Cowboy*). Look out for boxer Jake La Motta (played by De Niro in *Raging Bull*) as a bartender.

I CONFESS

(1953, dir: Alfred Hitchcock)
Montgomery Clift, Anne Baxter, Karl Malden.
● QUÉBEC, CANADA

When Hitchcock needed a deeply Catholic environment to make this story of a priest riddled with sexual guilt and bound by the rules of the confessional, he headed north to Canada, filming in French Québec, around the narrow streets of the old quarter. Anne Baxter's politician husband speechifies at Québec's **Parliament Building, Grande Allée est** at avenue Dufferin (*guided tours, admission free*). She meets up with Clift on the **Lévis Ferry**, crossing the St Lawrence River from Lower Town (why do characters in films always meet furtively aboard ferries?). After Clift's inconclusive trial in the **Halls of Justice**, the real murderer hides out in the city's magnificent landmark **Chateau Frontenac Hotel, 1 rue des Carrieres** (© *418.692.3861*). Clift's church, Sainte Marie, is **Eglise Saint-Zéphirin de Stadacona** (Stadacona was the name of the native village which stood on the site Québec City now occupies).

I KNOW WHAT YOU DID LAST SUMMER

(1997, dir: Jim Gillespie)
Jennifer Love Hewitt, Sarah Michelle Gellar, Ryan Phillippe.
● NORTH CAROLINA; CALIFORNIA

This Kevin Williamson-penned slasher used mostly real locations – the fishing village is just what it says, **Southport**, North Carolina, also the location for *Crimes of the Heart* and *The Birds II: Lands End* (the disappeared-without-trace TV movie sequel to the Hitchcock classic), as well as Williamson's TV series, *Dawson's Creek*. The Shivers store is a real department store on the town square.

The car accident was filmed on a scary stretch of the Pacific Coast Highway, **Meyers Grade** and **Timber Cove Roads**, north of **Jenner**, northern California. Other northern California locations include **Campbell Cove** at **Bodega Bay** (the famous setting for Hitchcock's *The Birds*); **Kolmer Cove**, north of Fort Ross; and **Schoolhouse Beach** near Carmel. The college is **Duke University, Durham**, North Carolina.

The inevitable sequel, *I Still Know What You Did Last Summer*, moved down to Mexico, to be shot at **El Tecuan Marina Resort** and at **El Tamarindo, Jalisco**, on Mexico's Gold Coast. Filming also took place at the **University of Southern California**, in the Exposition park area of downtown LA.

I KNOW WHERE I'M GOING!

(1945, dir: Michael Powell; Emeric Pressburger)
Wendy Hiller, Roger Livesey, Pamela Brown.
● SCOTLAND

Wendy Hiller travels out to the Hebrides to marry a rich old man, but finds love on the way. Filmed in the Western Isles and Mull, the house, Erraig, where Wendy Hiller first stops, is the house of **Carsaig**, on the south coast of Mull. Livesey shows Hiller **Moy Castle** at **Lochbuie**, a few miles east. Hiller moves out of Erraig to stay at Sorne, actually a Victorian castle set in Italianate grounds, called **Torosay**. The isle of Kiloran is the small isle of **Colonsay**, to the south of Mull. The whirlpool is **Corrievrechan**, between Scarba and Jura.

I, ROBOT

(2004, dir: Alex Proyas)
Will Smith, Bridget Moynahan, James Cromwell.
● VANCOUVER, BRITISH COLOMBIA, CANADA

Enjoyable enough sci-fi but, apart from the title and the Three Laws of Robotics, there's not a lot of Isaac Asimov. Set in 'Chicago 2035', the movie was filmed in Vancouver, mostly on CGI-enhanced sets. The opening scenes, of Del Spooner (Smith) chasing what he thinks is a robot 'thief', is, ironically, Antique Alley, a row of shops specialising in collectibles and antiques, the 600 block of **Front Street** (also featured in Jackie Chan's *Rumble in the Bronx*) in **New Westminster**, Vancouver's eastern suburb.

The attempted takeover by the new breed of NS5 robots is at the new **West Cordova Viaduct** in front of the Shaw Tower (claimed to be Vancouver's tallest building), 1077 West Cordova Street at Burrard Street, Coal Harbour. A couple of other futuristic locations are the **ICBC (Insurance Corporation of British Columbia) Building, 152nd Street**, in **Surrey** to the southeast; and **Pier 94** in north Vancouver (where the Brooklyn Bridge set was built for *The Fantastic Four*).

Surprisingly, the old-fashioned **Ovaltine Cafe**, where Spooner chats to Lt Bergin, is the real thing, a 1942 café, **251 East Hastings Street** near Main Street.

ICE COLD IN ALEX (aka *Desert Attack*)

(1958, dir: J Lee Thompson)
John Mills, Sylvia Syms, Anthony Quayle.
● LIBYA

Desert suspenser shot on location just outside the Libyan capital, Tripoli, in pre-Gaddhafi days, though the famous bar scene – later ripped off for a beer ad – was filmed in the studio at Elstree. And, yes, it *was* real lager, six pints of which were downed by John Mills before the shot was in the can.

ICE STORM, THE

(1997, dir: Ang Lee)
Kevin Kline, Joan Allen, Sigourney Weaver.
● CONNECTICUT; NEW YORK CITY

The soulless neighbourhood of Ang Lee's seventies-set family drama is **New Canaan**, on the northeast fringe of Stamford, Connecticut, home to seventies architects like Philip Johnson, who designed the original 'glass house'. Both the stunning seventies-built glass-walled home of Sigourney Weaver and the fifties-style house of Kevin Kline and Joan Allen can be found here. Filming also took place in **Greenwich**, Connecticut. Katie Holmes' New

York apartment is on Park Avenue.

IF....

(1968, dir: Lindsay Anderson)
Malcolm McDowell, David Wood, Richard Warwick.
● GLOUCESTERSHIRE; HERTFORDSHIRE

Dazzling first part of the trilogy that slid spectacularly downhill from the patchy but enjoyable *O Lucky Man!* to the dire *Britannia Hospital*. The public school where McDowell leads a revolt, set against a surreal background of the British class system, is **Cheltenham College**, on **Bath Road (A46)** between Sandford Road and Thirlestaine Road, south of Cheltenham town centre, Gloucestershire. Some of the school interiors, though, were filmed at **Aldenham School, Aldenham** in Hertfordshire.

The school: Cheltenham College

IM LAUF DER ZEIT (aka *Kings of the Road*)

(1975, dir: Wim Wenders)
Rudiger Vogler, Hanns Zischler, Lisa Kreuzer.
● GERMANY

Wenders' long, rambling road movie, with Vogler and Zischler travelling from town to town fixing movie projectors. The 80 cinemas in the original script were eventually whittled down to twelve as the journey from **Luneburg** to **Passau** passes through **Lower Saxony**, **Hessen** and **Bavaria**. The VW factory is in **Wolfsburg**.

IMITATION OF LIFE

(1959, dir: Douglas Sirk)
Lana Turner, Juanita Moore, Susan Kohner.
● LOS ANGELES, CALIFORNIA

Lush, glossy melodrama with Lana Turner as a Hollywood actress and Juanita Moore her black maid whose daughter, Susan Kohner, passes for white. Kohner gets to perform at Hollywood's old Moulin Rouge nightspot. It opened in 1938 as the Earl Carroll Theatre, with the first double revolving stage – 90 feet in diameter. It became the Moulin Rouge in 1953, and later the Aquarius Theatre, now **Nickelodeon on Sunset, 6230 Sunset Boulevard** between Argyle and El Centro, Hollywood. The theatre also appears in the Tina Turner biopic *What's Love Got To Do With It*.

IN A LONELY PLACE

(1950, dir: Nicholas Ray)
Humphrey Bogart, Gloria Grahame, Frank Lovejoy.
● LOS ANGELES, CALIFORNIA

Bogart is an embittered Hollywood scriptwriter suspected of murder. **Beverly Hills City Hall, North Crescent**

Drive at Santa Monica Boulevard (see *Beverly Hills Cop* for details) is featured, and filming supposedly took place at the secluded European-style **Villa Primavera, 1300-1308 North Harper Avenue**, west Hollywood.

Bogart's place: Villa Primavera, North Harper Avenue, Hollywood

IN COLD BLOOD

(1967, dir: Richard Brooks)
Robert Blake, Scott Wilson, John Forsythe.
● KANSAS; MISSOURI; NEVADA; COLORADO; TEXAS; MEXICO

Filming of the true story, as written by Truman Capote, of the murder of a family by two young punks. The semi-documentary style used the real-life locations, following the killers'

The real courthouse, used in the film: Finney County Courthouse, Garden City

flight from the scene of the murder, at **River Valley Farm, River Road, Holcomb**, Kansas, across Missouri, Nevada, Colorado, Texas and Mexico. The trial takes place in the actual courthouse used, **Finney County Courthouse, Garden City**, Kansas.

IN THE HEAT OF THE NIGHT

(1967, dir: Norman Jewison)
Sidney Poitier, Rod Steiger, Warren Oates.
● ILLINOIS

Detective Poitier ends up earning the respect of redneck bigot Rod Steiger in this worthy odd-couple cop movie, which won the Oscar for Best Picture (in the year of *The Graduate* and *Bonnie and Clyde*). Sparta, Mississippi, really is **Sparta**, but in Illinois, about 40 miles southeast of St Louis. More scenes were filmed in the towns of **Belleville** and **Freeburg** on Route 15, the road to St Louis.

IN THE LINE OF FIRE

(1993, dir: Wolfgang Petersen)
Clint Eastwood, John Malkovich, Rene Russo.
● WASHINGTON DC; LOS ANGELES, CALIFORNIA

It's the old psycho-developing-an-affinity-with-unorthodox cop story again, with Malkovich taunting and seducing presidential guard Eastwood. Set, not surprisingly, in Washington DC, where Eastwood drinks at traditional hack hangout the **Old Ebbitt**

Clint's DC hangout: Old Ebbitt Grill, Fifteenth Street

Clint chills out: The Lincoln Memorial

Grill, 675 Fifteenth Street NW (© 202.347.4800, www.ebbitt.com). He chills out with an ice cream on the steps of that inevitable DC location the **Lincoln Memorial**, in front of the Reflecting Pool.

The Denver hotel, where Eastwood stays with Rene Russo, is the familiar old **Biltmore Hotel, 506 South Grand Street** on Pershing Square, downtown LA (see *Beverly Hills Cop* for details). He follows the Pres to LA, where the assassination attempt, and final shoot-out, take place at the futuristic high-rise glass-towered **Westin Bonaventure Hotel, 404 South Figueroa Street**, downtown LA (© 213.624.1000). Another old favourite location, here showing off its **California Ballroom** – the largest in LA – the Bonaventure has been seen in plenty of movies including real-time thriller *Nick of Time*, *Rain Man*, *Strange Days*, classic mockumentary *This Is Spinal Tap* and *True Lies*.

IN THE MOUTH OF MADNESS
(1995, dir: John Carpenter)
Sam Neill, Julie Carmen, Jürgen Prochnow.
● **ONTARIO, CANADA**

The library: Saulter Street Library, Toronto

Set in New York, but made around Ontario, at **Scarborough**, east Toronto; and **King City**, north of Toronto. The New England village of Hobbs End is **Unionville**, about 20 miles from Toronto. Carpenter once more sneaks in an homage to Nigel Kneale – who wrote the script for *Halloween III* – by naming the village after the fictitious London tube station in *Quatermass and the Pit*. The library is the **Saulter Street Library**, Toronto.

IN THE NAME OF THE FATHER
(1993, dir: Jim Sheridan)
Daniel Day-Lewis, Pete Postlethwaite, Emma Thompson.
● **LIVERPOOL, MERSEYSIDE; MANCHESTER; DUBLIN, IRELAND**

Slightly dramatised but basically true story of Gerry Conlon and his father Guiseppe, two of the 'Guildford Four', wrongly imprisoned for the 1974 pub bombing. The Guildford, Surrey, pub is actually the **Brunswick Vaults, 69 Tithebarn Street**, Liverpool – with a specially built addition blown up. The Old Bailey court is a conflation of **Liverpool Museum** (at the front) and **Manchester Town Hall** (at the rear), while the interior is **St George's Hall**, Liverpool. The gaol, with the familiar metal stair, is **Kilmainham Gaol, Dublin** (see it also as

Noël Coward's place of incarceration in *The Italian Job*). Exterior shots used **St Patrick's Institution** courtyard and **Mountjoy Prison**.

IN WHICH WE SERVE
(1942, dir: David Lean; Noël Coward)
Noël Coward, Bernard Miles, John Mills.
● **HERTFORDSHIRE**

Lightly-disguised story of Lord Mountbatten, in the best stiff-upper-lip tradition. Mostly studio-bound, but the flashback picnic is on **Dunstable Downs**, Hertfordshire.

INDECENT PROPOSAL
(1993, dir: Adrian Lyne)
Demi Moore, Woody Harrelson, Robert Redford.
● **CALIFORNIA; LAS VEGAS, NEVADA**

Harrelson loses his cool: The Oviatt Building, South Olive Street

Not surprisingly, all sorts of problems ensue for David (Harrelson) and Diana Murphy (Moore) when filthy rich John Gage (Redford) offers a cool million dollars for one night with Diana. The Vegas casino, where the couple try to recoup their money and get Gage's modest proposal, is the **Las Vegas Hilton, 3000 Paradise Road**. The 1,500 room hotel adjoins the Las Vegas Convention Center, about three quarters of a mile east of the Strip (it was the Whyte House in *Diamonds Are Forever*). The restaurant with the bizarre singing statues, similar to Disneyland's kitschy Enchanted Tiki Room, is the Hilton's **Benihana Village**, a (very) stylised Japanese village setting. The images of Diana haunt her distraught hubby on the 46 television screens of the casino's **Race and Sports Room**. The waterfalls and volcanic flames can be seen a couple of miles south of the Hilton, outside the **Mirage Hotel, 3400 Las Vegas Boulevard South**.

Gage's Mediterranean-style estate is the rear of the **Huntington Library, 1151 Oxford Road, San Marino**, east of Pasadena (© 626.405.2100, www.huntington.org). The gardens became the Japanese Garden of Golden Gate Park, San Francisco, in *The Wedding Planner*, and have also been seen in *Midway*, *Heathers*, *Coming to America*, *Charlie's Angels* (briefly) and *Anger Management*. Diana's real estate office is in the glorious deco **Crossroads of the World, 6671 Sunset Boulevard** at Cherokee, Hollywood. Designed to look like a stately liner docking among a fantasy of Spanish, French, Moorish and English villages, it was built in 1936 as an outdoor shopping mall. See it also as one of the great period backdrops for *L.A. Confidential*. The property she

Redford's estate: Huntington Library, San Marino

Kiss and make up: Paradise Cove Pier, Malibu

shows Redford around is the **Greystone Park and Mansion, 905 Loma Vista Drive, Beverly Hills** (see *The Loved One* for details).

The art deco restaurant, outside which Harrelson confronts Moore and Redford, is **Cicada** (previously the Rex II Ristorante), in the **Oviatt Building, 617 South Olive Street** (© *213.488.9488, www.cicadarestaurant.com*) at Sixth Street just off Pershing Square, downtown LA. More liner-inspired design – the interior of the restaurant was based on thirties floating luxury palace the *Rex*. See the drop-dead stylish interior in Phil Joanou's ditzy thriller *Final Analysis* and *Bruce Almighty*.

The kiss'n'make up ending was shot on the pier at **Paradise Cove**, a private beach west of Malibu, entrance on the 28100 block of the Pacific Coast Highway.

The aliens' target: First Interstate World Center

INDEPENDENCE DAY

(1996, dir: Roland Emmerich)
Will Smith, Jeff Goldblum, Bill Pullman.
● **CALIFORNIA; NEVADA; WASHINGTON DC**

A youthful fighter pilot president, a rainbow coalition of heroes and flying saucers 15 miles wide in this surprise smash. The First Lady's hotel is the **Biltmore Hotel, 506 South Grand Street**, downtown LA, from which she escapes in the chopper (see *Beverly Hills Cop* for details). The desert airforce base is **Wendover Airport** in Nevada, where Will Smith drags the captured alien across **White Sands**. The skyscraper on which the new-agers gather to welcome the aliens, and which is the first target to get zapped, is the roof of the **First Interstate World Center**, north side of 5th Street west of Grand Avenue, downtown LA. The tunnel traffic jam was filmed in LA's **Second Street Tunnel** between Hill Street and Figueroa Street, downtown.

INDIANA JONES AND THE TEMPLE OF DOOM

(1984, dir: Steven Spielberg)
Harrison Ford, Kate Capshaw, Ke Huy Quan.
● **SRI LANKA; CALIFORNIA; MACAU**

The 'Shanghai, 1935' opening of the second Indiana Jones adventure, is the **Rua de Felicidade**, near to the Floating Casino in the rather sleazy Inner Harbour district of Macau, over the Pearl River Estuary from Hong Kong (see *The Man With the Golden Gun* for details). The Pink City of Jaipur was chosen as the Maharajah's abode, but the Indian authorities demanded script changes, so the

palace was finally built at **Elstree Studios**. There was some filming, though, in Sri Lanka, where the Indian village was built amid the tea bushes on the **Hantane Tea Estate** high above the town of **Kandy**. The rope-bridge sequence was also filmed in Sri Lanka, on a 300 foot-deep gorge near a dam construction site (which meant a convenient supply of engineers and equipment to string the bridge).

The Himalayas: Mammoth Lakes

Shanghai Airport is actually the **Hamilton Air Force Base**, at **Novato**, north of San Francisco, California. Also in

Thirties Shanghai: Rua de Felicidade

California, just south of Yosemite National Park, **Mammoth Mountain**, a ski area, stands in for the Himalayas. Other locations include the **Tuolumne River**, which runs through Yosemite in its own 'Grand Canyon', and the **American River**, running from Lake Folsom to Sacramento.

INDIANA JONES AND THE LAST CRUSADE

(1989, dir: Steven Spielberg)
Harrison Ford, Sean Connery, River Phoenix.
● **UTAH; COLORADO; VENICE, ITALY; JORDAN; SPAIN**

The third Indiana Jones film begins in **Moab**, Utah. It's **Sevenmile Canyon**, in the spectacular **Arches National Park**, where young Indy (Phoenix), spends the movie's prologue. But why are the fantastic rock formations suddenly replaced by featureless grassland the moment the train appears? Well, that's because the railway scenes were filmed on the **Cumbras and Toltec Railroad** in southern Colorado. And it's a railroad you can travel, too. The return journey, taking a whole day, runs from Antonito, Route 285, south of Alamosa in southern Colorado, 30 miles southwest through the San Juan Mountains to Chama in northern New Mexico.

Berlin Airport: New Horticultural Hall, Westminster

The school where adult Indy (Ford) teaches is **Rickmansworth Masonic School,**

Indiana Jones takes class: Rickmansworth Masonic School

The Venetian church: Church of San Barnaba, Campo San Barnaba

Home of the Grail, Canyon of the Crescent Moon: Petra

Chorleywood Road (A404) just a couple of minutes north of Rickmansworth Station. Also in the UK is the classically grand setting for the Berlin rally, where Indy manages to get the Führer's autograph, which is **Stowe School** in Buckinghamshire. This former home of the Duke of Buckinghamshire, set in grounds landscaped by Capability Brown, is four miles north of Buckingham town and usually open to the public for the first two weeks in April and from July through to the beginning of September (℮ *0280.813650*). The stern interior of Berlin Airport is the **New Royal Horticultural Hall**, on the corner of **Greycoat** and **Elverton Street** in Westminster, SW1. It's occasionally open for exhibitions. See it as Berlin again in *The Saint* and looking similarly fascist for Ian McKellen's rally in *Richard III*.

The search for the Grail takes Indy to Venice, where he finds a clue in the **Church of San Barnaba, Campo San Barnaba**, south of Rio di San Barnaba off the Canal Grande southeast of the campo Santa Margherita in the Dorsoduro district. If you want to see the real interior, the 1749 church is open daily from 7.30am to noon and 4.30pm to 7pm. And although the Venice waterfront starts out as real, we're soon back in England, chasing around **Tilbury Docks** in Essex.

The fictitious Iskenderun (it was, apparently, a small sultanate south of Turkey and north of Syria) is **Granada** in Spain. The railway station, where Denholm Elliott is besieged by beggars, is **Guadix Station**, about 30 miles east of Granada on the N342.

The Grail, it turns out, resides in the Canyon of the Crescent Moon, in actuality, **Al Khazneh**, the Treasury of the rock city of **Petra** in the Edom Mountains of southwest Jordan. Petra is a three-hour drive from the Jordanian capital of Amman (though you can reach it more easily from Aqaba or from Eilat in Israel), at the end of a three-quarter-mile trek (on foot, camel or horse) through the Siq, a narrow rock fissure in the cliffs.

INN OF THE SIXTH HAPPINESS, THE

(1958, dir: Mark Robson)
Ingrid Bergman, Curt Jurgens, Robert Donat.
● WALES; HAMPSHIRE; LONDON

Missionary Gladys Aylward (Bergman) cheerfully leads a bunch of orphans over the Himalayas. The original intention was to film in Taiwan, China, but derogatory references to the practice of foot-binding upset the Chinese authorities. Snowdonia stands in for the Himalayas, around the villages of **Beddgelert** and **Capel Curig**. The walled city was built at **Nantmor**, at the foot of the Cwm Bychan Valley near Beddgelert.

The China Missionary Office, where Aylward first applies, unsuccessfully, to become a missionary, is the small gatehouse at the right of **Westminster City School, Palace Street** near Victoria Street, Victoria.

The China Missionary Office: Westminster City School, Palace Street

INNERSPACE

(1987, dir: Joe Dante)
Martin Short, Dennis Quaid, Meg Ryan.
● CALIFORNIA

Comedy take on *Fantastic Voyage*, set in San Francisco. The angular glass church, used for Quaid and Ryan's wedding at the end of the movie, is Frank Lloyd Wright's **Wayfarer's Chapel, 5755 Palos Verdes Drive South**, Portuguese Bend at Abalone Cove, **Rancho Palos Verdes**. It was designed in 1949 to blend in with a grove of redwood trees, which have now gone. Filming also took place in **Northridge**, in the San Fernando Valley, north of LA.

INNOCENTS, THE

(1961, dir: Jack Clayton)
Deborah Kerr, Megs Jenkins, Michael Redgrave.
● SUSSEX

Creepily atmospheric adaptation of Henry James' *The Turn of the Screw*. Are the kiddies possessed, or is it the festering imagination of prissy governess Deborah Kerr? The house and grounds are **Sheffield Park**, 40 acres of gardens and lakes designed by Capability Brown, at **Dane Mill**, five miles northwest of Uckfield, on the east side of the A275 between East Grinstead and Lewes in Sussex. The gardens are open to the public on certain days of the week (℮ *01825.790231; admission charge*). A bizarre prequel, *The Nightcomers* starring Marlon Brando, was filmed by Michael Winner.

INSOMNIA

(1997, dir: Erik Skjoldbjærg)
Stellan Skarsgård, Sverre Anker Ousdal, Bjørn Floberg
● NORWAY

The permanent daylight of an Arctic summer is an ingeniously cinematic metaphor for a nagging conscience in Skjoldbjærg's bleak thriller. No pretty scenery here. It's the **Tromsø**, the director's hometown, above the Arctic Circle in northern Norway.

INSOMNIA

(2002, dir: Christopher Nolan)
Al Pacino, Martin Donovan, Robin Williams.
● BRITISH COLUMBIA, CANADA; ALASKA

Nolan's remake moves the action to Alaska and the

fictitious town of Nightmute, though most of the movie was shot in British Columbia. The strangely lunar landscape flown over during the opening scenes is the **Columbia Glacier** near **Valdez**, Alaska. The town of Nightmute is **Squamish**. The cemetery, for the funeral, was constructed for the film on **The Spit**, a finger of land outside Squamish (and the most popular windsurfing spot in BC). Unkumuit, where Walter Finch (Williams) lives, is **Port Alberni**, on Vancouver Island, where the paper mill chase scene was filmed. The fogbound stakeout, which goes tragically awry for Detective Dormer (Pacino), is **Indian Arm**, a landslide site near Vancouver. Finch's lake house was built on a frozen lake in the mountain valley of **Bear Glacier** near the tiny hamlet of **Stewart** (pop. 500) on the northwest Alaskan border.

INTERNAL AFFAIRS
(1990, dir: Mike Figgis)
Richard Gere, Andy Garcia, Laurie Metcalf.
● **LOS ANGELES, CALIFORNIA**

Mike Figgis' dark and uncomfortable police corruption thriller is a riff on *Othello*, with Gere cast against type as a nasty Iago character. Set around LA, where the LAPD HQ is naturally **City Hall, 200 North Spring Street**. Andy Garcia spies on his wife's furtive lunch with Gere at the restaurant of the venerable **Hollywood Roosevelt Hotel, 7000 Hollywood Boulevard**, Hollywood (see *Catch Me If You Can* for details).

Garcia spies on Gere: Hollywood Roosevelt Hotel

INTERVIEW WITH THE VAMPIRE: THE VAMPIRE CHRONICLES

St Martin's Hotel: Market Street

(1994, dir: Neil Jordan)
Tom Cruise, Brad Pitt, Kirsten Dunst.
● **SAN FRANCISCO, CALIFORNIA; LOUISIANA; PARIS, FRANCE**

You can see the disused building used as St Martin's Hotel, where Christian Slater gets Brad Pitt's story, at the corner of **Market Street** with **Golden Gate Avenue** and **Taylor Street** in San Francisco. Pitt's estate is **Oak Alley Plantation, 3645 Los Angeles Highway 18, Vacherie** in Louisiana. One of the restored mansions between

Pitt's estate: Oak Alley Plantation, Vacherie

New Orleans and Baton Rouge (it was also used for the remake of *The Long, Hot Summer*), Oak Alley, built in 1839, takes its name from the avenue of 28 oaks leading up to it. The house is open to the public most days, from 9am to 5pm (© *504.523.4351; admission charge*). The Parisian hotel is actually the **Paris Opera House**.

INTRUDER, THE (aka *The Stranger*)
(1961, dir: Roger Corman)
William Shatner, Frank Maxwell, Beverly Lunsford.
● **MISSOURI**

Roger Corman's message pic about racism in the Deep South was filmed in southeast Missouri at **Sikeston**, on Highways 55 and 57. Initially co-operative locals were given watered down and edited versions of the script, but once the full story began to leak out, enthusiasm declined somewhat. The film company managed to grab a bit more location shooting at **East Prairie High School, 304 East Walnut Street, East Prairie**, just to the southeast, and **Mississippi County Courthouse, Charleston**, to the east, before hotfooting it out of the area.

INVASION OF THE BODY SNATCHERS
(1956, dir: Don Siegel)
Kevin McCarthy, Dana Wynter, King Donovan.
● **LOS ANGELES, CALIFORNIA**

Despite the tacked-on 'safe' ending, Don Siegel's sci-fi noir remains a classic. The fictional town of Santa Mira was based on Mill Valley, on Highway 1 over the Golden Gate Bridge from San Francisco, which is where the director wanted to film. But wouldn't you know it, Allied Artists discovered that the area around their East Hollywood studio in Silverlake looked just

Escaping the pod people: Westshire Drive

like Mill Valley. The studio, now KCET TV Studios, still stands at **4401 Sunset Boulevard**. Much of the movie was shot in the studio, in a mere 23 days. The studio entrance itself features as Santa Mira's hospital. Location shooting was at nearby **Glendale; Chatsworth** in northwest LA; and the neighbourhood of **Los Feliz**. Santa Mira town square is the square of **Sierra Madre**, a sweet little community to the east of Pasadena. Much revamped, you can still recognise the square at the junction of **Sierra Madre Boulevard** and **Baldwin Avenue**.

More of Santa Mira was shot at **Beachwood Canyon** and **Belden Drive** in the maze of roads east of the Hollywood freeway south of Hollywood Reservoir. The flight of steps, up which McCarthy and Wynter escape from the pod people, can be seen at **2744 Westshire Drive**, at the corner of **Beach-**

Santa Mira town square: Sierra Madre

wood Drive and **Woodshire Drive**. At the top of the steps, they hide out in the **Bronson Canyon Caves**, to the north in Griffith Park.

INVASION OF THE BODY SNATCHERS
(1978, dir: Philip Kaufman)
Donald Sutherland, Brooke Adams, Leonard Nimoy.
● SAN FRANCISCO, CALIFORNIA

The updated remake, set and filmed in San Francisco. Don Siegel, director of the original, puts in an appearance, and Kevin McCarthy repeats his role in a tiny cameo, before being run down by a car at the corner of **Leavenworth** and **Turk**. Donald Sutherland lives on **Union Street** near Castle, and works at the **Department of Public Health, 101 Grove Street**. Brooke Adams lives at **720 Steiner Street**, one of the bunch of cutesy Victorian houses overlooking Alamo Square, and backed by the San Francisco skyline, that are used in countless Bay City movies. The humans escape down Montgomery Street to the **Filbert Steps**.

A third version, called *Body Snatchers*, was made by Abel Ferrara at an abandoned army base, **Craig Field**, in **Selma**, Alabama.

IPCRESS FILE, THE
(1965, dir: Sidney J Furie)
Michael Caine, Guy Doleman, Nigel Green.
● LONDON

The Dalby Domestic Employment Bureau: Grosvenor Gardens, Victoria

First of three Harry Palmer spy movies from Len Deighton's books (a series revived in straight-to-video productions years later). Director Furie had little faith in the script, and tricks the movie out with modish sixties angles and framings.

The film was made on location around London. The station from which the scientist is abducted at the opening is **Marylebone Station**, NW1. When Palmer (Caine) consults his cop pal for the lowdown on "Grantby – a right master criminal", it's at the original **Great Scotland Yard** building at **Derby Gate** on the Victoria Embankment, before the Met Police moved to Victoria.

The **Foreign and Commonwealth Office Building**, the old Admiralty Building, at the foot of the Mall alongside Admiralty Arch, became the Ministry of Defence building where Palmer is summoned to the office of Colonel Ross (Doleman) to be transferred to Major Dalby's outfit. **Birdcage Walk**, along the southern border of **St James's Park**, is where Dalby (Green) and Ross plot their devious strategies. T108, the bench used for clandestine meetings, stood on **Rotten Row** in Hyde Park.

30 Grosvenor Gardens at Ebury Street, Victoria, was the Dalby Domestic Employment Bureau, the staffing agency used as a front for Major Dalby's outfit, to which Harry Palmer gets transferred. Much of the movie was shot within the building, which was entirely taken over

for the production.

It's at the **Science Museum Library, Prince Consort Road, South Kensington**, that Palmer makes contact with 'Bluejay'. The library is open to the public for personal research. Furie perks up a fight scene by filming through the glass panes of a phone booth on the south side of the **Royal Albert Hall** (there is no phone booth there).

IRON HORSE, THE
(1924, dir: John Ford)
George O'Brien, Madge Bellamy, Cyril Chadwick.
● NEVADA

In 1923, Paramount had a great hit with its epic Western *The Covered Wagon*, and Fox determined to repeat the success with a grand-scale picture of its own. At $450,000, the story of the building of the first transcontinental railroad turned out to be Fox's most expensive movie at the time. It was made on location at **Wadsworth**, 30 miles east of Reno on Route 80, Nevada. Three shack towns, which became instant ghost towns once shooting was over, were built to house the crew, the cooks and the 5,000 extras.

ISADORA (aka *The Loves of Isadora*)
(1968, dir: Karel Reisz)
Vanessa Redgrave, Jason Robards, James Fox.
● LONDON; DEVON; BUCKINGHAMSHIRE; FRANCE; ITALY; YUGOSLAVIA

Reisz's episodic biopic of the eccentric American dancer (inspired by Ken Russell's delirious TV movie, *Isadora, the Biggest Dancer in the World*, which starred the sublime Vivian Pickles) takes in locations around the world.

The US theatre, where the dancer (Redgrave), under the name 'Peppy Dora', earns $300 with high kicks to take her family to Europe, is **Wilton's Music Hall, 1 Grace's Alley, Wellclose Square**, off Cable Street, E1. Long disused but recently rediscovered, see *Chaplin* for details. Bellevue, the French school "ten miles from Paris", bought for Isadora by sewing machine heir Paris Singer (Robards), can be found in Buckinghamshire. It's the extraordinary **Waddesdon Manor**, a Victorian mansion built atop a Home Counties hill in the style of a Loire Valley chateau for Ferdinand de Rothschild. You can see it at the west end of Waddesdon village, six miles northwest of Aylesbury on the A41. Owned by the National Trust, the house and grounds are open to the public from March to December (© *01296.822850; rail: Aylesbury; admission charge*). You can also see the chateau in *Never Say Never Again* and in *Carry On – Don't Lose Your Head*. Paris Singer's dazzling English home is the real thing – **Oldway Mansion, Paignton** in Devon. It's now Paignton's Civic Centre, though the grounds and tennis courts are open to the public. It's been more recently used as Buckingham Palace in *Churchill: The Hollywood Years*. Theatre scenes were shot at the **Theatre Royal, Drury Lane**, WC2. More London filming took place in the **British Museum, Great Russell Street**, WC1, where Isadora is enthralled by the Parthenon's Elgin Marble.

The Berlin Theatre is the National Theatre at **Rijeka** in the former Yugoslavia. The Nice scenes, set during the twenties at the end of Isadora's career, were shot at **Opatija** on the Croatian coast. Henri's Bar, the beach bar where Isadora finally meets Mr Bugatti, was built at **Mostenica Beach**, Yugoslavia. It was so popular, and sturdy, that locals asked to keep it. Filming also took place at **Ptuj** and **Zagreb** in the former Yugoslavia.

The grotesque car accident – far more spectacular and unbelievable than the movie version – actually occurred outside the Hotel Negresco on the seafront at Nice, itself a movie location seen in Jean Vigo's *A Propos De Nice* and *The Day of the Jackal*.

ISLAND OF LOST SOULS

(1933, dir: Erle C Kenton)
Charles Laughton, Bela Lugosi, Richard Arlen.
● **CALIFORNIA**

Remade twice as *The Island of Dr Moreau*, the chilling first adaptation of HG Wells' novel uses **Catalina Island**, off the coast of LA, as Moreau's kingdom.

IT ALWAYS RAINS ON SUNDAY

(1947, dir: Robert Hamer)
Googie Withers, John McCallum, Jack Warner.
● **LONDON**

Downbeat crime melodrama set in the slummy, post-war East End of London. Most of the film was shot around the **Petticoat Lane** area, but Withers' home, on Coronet Grove, Bethnal Green, is on **Hartland Road**, Chalk Farm, NW1, with Holy Trinity Church in the background. Close by, **60 Hawley Road** was the house of weaselly fence Mr Neesley. Over forty years later, the same house was home to Jeff Goldblum in Richard Curtis's *The Tall Guy*. The final chase was shot in the **Temple Mills Railway Yard, Stratford**, E15.

IT HAPPENED AT THE WORLD'S FAIR

(1963, dir: Norman Taurog)
Elvis Presley, Gary Lockwood, Joan O'Brien.
● **SEATTLE, WASHINGTON**

Presley and Lockwood are a couple of pilots letting loose in Seattle, at the World Fair. Featuring now-famous Seattle landmarks like the **Space Needle** (see *The Parallax View* for details) and the city's **Hallweg Monorail**, which were built specially for the fair.

ITALIAN JOB, THE

(1969, dir: Peter Collinson)
Michael Caine, Noël Coward, Benny Hill.
● **TURIN, ITALY; LONDON; IRELAND**

The interior of Wormwood Scrubs where Mr Bridger (Coward) masterminds the job, is actually **Kilmainham Gaol, Dublin** (seen also in *In the Name of the Father*). Caine's coming out do is at the **Royal Lancaster Hotel, Lancaster Terrace, Bayswater** (© *020.7262.6737, www.royallancaster.co.uk*). His oh-so-sixties bric-a-brac cluttered flat is **18 Denbigh Close**, off the north end of Portobello Road, W11, next to Alice's junk shop. The job is organised in the luxurious highrise of **Peninsula Heights** (formerly Alembic House), **Albert Embankment**, also seen in *Sweeney!*, *A Touch of Class* and *Theatre of Blood*.

The robbery takes place in Turin during a massive traffic jam. The jam starts by the **Palazza Madama** on **Piazza Castello**. Unlike BMC, manufacturers of the Mini, who offered minimal co-operation, Fiat offered limitless help. The rooftop leap, in fact, was filmed on the roof of the Fiat factory, dressed to look like a Turin street. The chase through the sewer was staged in England. Although the entrance and exit were filmed in Turin, the length of sewer used was a new pipe system being installed in Coventry.

The famous ending, dreamed up by a Paramount executive in Hollywood, hated by director Collinson and star Caine, and assigned to a second unit, was shot above a reservoir at **Ceresole Reale**, about 40 miles northwest of Turin.

ITALIAN JOB, THE

(2003, dir: F Gary Gray)
Mark Wahlberg, Edward Norton, Charlize Theron.
● **VENICE, ITALY; LOS ANGELES, CALIFORNIA**

There's only a tenuous link between this film's robberies and that of the sixties favourite: the Minis, and the fact that the opening robbery is, indeed, Italian. It takes place in Venice

The Hollywood mansion of villainous Steve: North San Rafael Avenue, Pasadena

and, yes, that's the familiar **Campo San Barnaba** again (previously seen in *Summer Madness* and *Indiana Jones and the Last Crusade*). The rooftop, where Charlie Croker (Wahlberg) and the crew plan their revenge, is the **Argyle, 8358 Sunset Boulevard, West Hollywood** (see *The Player* for details). The Hollywood mansion of villainous Steve (Norton) is tucked away in leafy privacy at **295 North San Rafael Avenue**, north of Colorado Boulevard in Pasadena. For the final revenge, Lyle "the real Napster" (Seth Green) directs Steve's bullion truck west from Highland onto **Hollywood Boulevard**. The Minis get driven down into the **Hollywood Highland Metro Station**, and if you're going to blow up a section of Hollywood Boulevard, well, you're going to do it directly outside **Grauman's Chinese Theatre**, aren't you? The scary helicopter stunt, with Steve's chopper hovering over Charlie's car, was filmed for real beneath **Lower Grand Street**, downtown.

IT'S A MAD MAD MAD MAD WORLD

(1963, dir: Stanley Kramer)
Spencer Tracy, Jimmy Durante, Milton Berle.
● **CALIFORNIA**

Zillions of stars fill out three hours-plus of Cinerama slapstick, concerning a stash of buried loot. The movie was shot all over southern California, in millionaires' desert playground **Palm Springs**, and south of LA in **Long Beach**. The 'W' everybody is looking for, which turns out to be four palm trees, was in the park at **Portuguese**

Point, on the southwest tip of the Palos Verdes Peninsula.

IT'S A WONDERFUL LIFE
(1946, dir: Frank Capra)
James Stewart, Henry Travers, Donna Reed.
● LOS ANGELES, CALIFORNIA

The dance-hall-swimming pool: Swim-gym, Beverly Hills High School

Hard to believe that this classic was a box office failure on its first release. The town of Bedford Falls, where elderly angel Travers convinces suicidal Stewart that life hasn't been in vain, was totally recreated with a huge 3-block-long set on RKO's **Encino Ranch** in the San Fernando Valley. The gym floor which opens up to reveal a swimming pool is still in action at **Beverly Hills High School, 255 South Lasky Drive**, at Moreno Drive in Beverly Hills, where the 'Swim-Gym' is still signposted.

IVANHOE
(1952, dir: Richard Thorpe)
Robert Taylor, Joan Fontaine, Elizabeth Taylor.
● NORTHUMBERLAND

Colourful historical fluff, including filming at **Bamburgh Castle**, east of Belford in Northumberland. The castle is open daily from April to October (*© 01669.620314; admission charge*).

J

The lone gunman?: Texas Book Depository, Dealey Plaza

JFK

(1991, dir: Oliver Stone)
Kevin Costner, Joe Pesci, Gary Oldman.
● DALLAS, TEXAS; NEW ORLEANS, LOUISIANA;
WASHINGTON DC

Somehow, Oliver Stone got permission to use many actual sites for his contentious film about the Kennedy assassination, including **Dealey Plaza** itself, in Dallas, where the President was murdered by persons unknown. The sixth floor of the Texas Book Depository, now the **Dallas County Administration Building, 411 Elm Street**, is a fascinating museum telling the various stories of the assassination. Vast amounts of background detail are available on self-operated videos and recorded commentaries. The museum is open seven days a week (*© 214.747.6660, www.jfk.org/home.htm*). The movie actually filmed on the seventh floor, which not only interfered less with the museum, but compensated for the growth of the tree outside, over which Lee Harvey Oswald is supposed to have shot.

Other genuine locations include the boarding house Oswald occupied in 1962, to which he returned after the shooting (and where police officer Tippit was killed), at **1026 North Beckley Avenue**; the **Texas Theater, 231 West Jefferson Street**, where Oswald was arrested; and the old **Dallas City Jail, Main Street** at Harwood, where he was shot by Jack Ruby.

Not every location is so real, however. Parkland Hospital, where JFK's body is taken immediately after the shooting, is actually **St Joseph's Hospital, 5909 Harry Hines Boulevard, Fort Worth**, Texas. Jack Ruby's seedy nightclub, The Carousel, is, ironically, represented by the elegant Venetian Room of the **Fairmount Hotel, 1717 North Akard Street** at Ross Avenue, downtown Dallas. The New Orleans bar in which DA Costner watches the TV news reports of the shooting is the arty, laidback **Napoleon House, 500 Chartres Street** at the corner of St Louis Street in the French Quarter. Sleazeball Ed Asner's office is at **531 Lafayette Street**, with the other entrance around the corner at **544 Camp Street**, just west of the French Quarter.

Costner's office is in the **Louisiana Supreme Court Building, 400 Royal Street**, New Orleans. His con-

frontation with lawyer John Candy takes place over a meal at **Antoine's Restaurant, 713 St Louis Street**, New Orleans. The climactic court scene was filmed in the actual location of the Clay Shaw trial, the **Criminal Courts Building, Tulane and Broad Streets**.

Washington DC filming includes JFK's last resting place, **Arlington National Cemetery** at Arlington Memorial Bridge (*metro: Arlington Cemetery*); and Costner's clandestine meeting with Donald Sutherland at the **Lincoln Memorial**, 23rd Street NW (*metro: Foggy Bottom*).

JABBERWOCKY

(1977, dir: Terry Gilliam)
Michael Palin, John Le Mesurier, Warren Mitchell.
● WALES

Gilliam's imaginative, blood and mud-soaked Dark Ages fantasy will appeal to fans of *Monty Python and the Holy Grail*. The Medieval locales are **Chepstow Castle**, Chepstow, Gwent, near the M4 Severn Bridge on the England-Wales border; and **Pembroke Castle**, Pembrokeshire, down towards Wales' southwest tip; as well as **Bosherston Quarry**, about seven miles south.

JACKIE BROWN

(1997, dir: Quentin Tarantino)
Pam Grier, Samuel L Jackson, Robert Forster.
● LOS ANGELES, CALIFORNIA

Apart from the occasional directorial flourish, you'd hardly recognise this Elmore Leonard adaptation as the work of the man who made *Pulp Fiction*. The bar 'near the airport', where Jackson and Robert De Niro hang out, is the **Cockatoo Inn, 4334 West Imperial Highway** at Hawthorne Boulevard, which is indeed not far from Los Angeles International. The vast shopping mall, further south in the South Bay area, is the **Del Amo Fashion Center, Hawthorne Boulevard**. Robert Forster's Cherry Bail Bonds office is **724 East Carson Street**,

The shopping mall: Del Amo Fashion Center, Hawthorne Boulevard

The airport bar: The Cockatoo Inn, West Imperial Highway, Hawthorne

Robert Forster's Cherry Bail Bonds office: East Carson Street, Carson

Carson.

JANE EYRE

(1996, dir: Franco Zeffirelli)
Charlotte Gainsbourg, William Hurt, Anna Paquin.
● DERBYSHIRE; YORKSHIRE

Unlike the studio-bound forties Hollywood version, starring Joan Fontaine and Orson Welles, florid Italian director Zeffirelli went on location for Thornfield Hall, using **Haddon Hall**, just south of Bakewell in Derbyshire. Open to the public from March to September (© *01629.812855; admission charge*). Haddon Hall is also seen as Edward VI's estate in *Lady Jane*. Jane Eyre meets Rochester at **Brimham Rocks**, near Pateley Bridge, north Yorkshire.

JASON AND THE ARGONAUTS

(1963, dir: Don Chaffey)
Todd Armstrong, Honor Blackman, Niall MacGinnis.
● ITALY

Jason goes in search of the Golden Fleece in this showcase for the animation of Ray Harryhausen, with a music score by the magnificent Bernard Herrmann. Location filming took place at **Palinuro**, Italy.

JASSY

(1947, dir: Bernard Knowles)
Margaret Lockwood, Dennis Price, Patricia Roc.
● HERTFORDSHIRE

The village: Aldbury

The mansion: Moor Park Golf Club, Batchworth Heath

Colourful Gainsborough melodrama with gypsy servant Lockwood falling for her master and the priceless Esma Cannon swooning in the witness box. The local village is **Aldbury**, off the A41, six miles northwest of Hemel Hempstead (see *The Dirty Dozen* for details). The grand house is **Moor Park Golf Club, Anson Walk** in Batchworth Heath on the A404 north of Northwood.

JAWS

(1975, dir: Steven Spielberg)

The *Orca* sets out: Menemsha Harbor

Roy Scheider, Richard Dreyfuss, Robert Shaw.
● MASSACHU-SETTS

Dazzlingly directed thriller that launched the Spielberg phenomenon and spawned a shoal of sloppy sequels and copies. The fictitious Amity island is swanky holiday retreat **Martha's Vineyard**, off the coast of Massachusetts. The prestigious resort remains relatively unspoiled since its heyday as a whaling centre in the 19th century, and

Amity Island: Edgartown, Martha's Vineyard

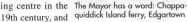

The Mayor has a word: Chappaquiddick Island ferry, Edgartown

the movie's loca-tions remain unchanged. The town centre, where Chief Brody (Scheider) gets materials for the 'Beach closed' signs, is the junction of **Water Street** and **Main Street, Edgartown**, the one-time whaling town on the east coast. At the end of Daggett Street, at the northern end of town, you'll find the **Chappaquiddick Island Ferry**, where the Mayor has a quiet word about boating accidents. The ferry takes pedestrians, bikes and up to three cars at a time.

West of the coast road north from Edgartown toward the popular resort of Oak Bluffs is **Joseph A Sylvia State Beach**, where the swimmers are panicked by the attack on the Kintner boy. Alongside is the **American Legion Memorial Bridge**, under which the shark swims to the 'safe' inlet, **Sengekontacket Pond**, where Brody's son is traumatised by the attack.

Across the island, toward the southwest tip, is the tiny fish-ing port of **Menemsha**. It was here, at the end of the harbour inlet between the General Store and the Galley Restaurant, that the workshed of old seadog Quint (Shaw) was built. As a permanent structure would have had to meet the island's strict building regulations, the area was restored to its original state after shooting, back to an empty lot. The *Orca*'s scenes were filmed over 155 days at sea between Oak Bluffs and East Chop, under well-documented nightmare conditions.

The 'safe' inlet: Sengekontacket Pond

The great shock moment, when Matt Hooper (Dreyfuss) discovers the old fisherman's nibbled head in the wrecked boat, was

The site of Quint's workshop: Menemsha Harbor

added as an afterthought. The 'head' shot was staged in the swimming pool of the movie's editor, Verna Field.

JAWS 2
(1978, dir: Jeannot Szwarc)
Roy Scheider, Lorraine Gary, Murray Hamilton.
● MASSACHUSETTS; FLORIDA

Without Spielberg's genius for staging set pieces, this is a boring plod from one chomping to the next. It's back to **Martha's Vineyard** again, but this time just about encompassing the whole island – **Edgartown**; **Chappaquiddick**; **Oak Bluffs**; **Menemsha**; **Gay Head**; **East Chop**; **Squibnocket**; **Vineyard Haven**; **Sengekontacket**; **Harthaven**; **Katama**; **Mattekeeset**; **Takemmy Trail**; **Chilmark**; **Pohognut**, and **Mayhew Lane**. As if that weren't enough, production delays meant that some of the beach scenes had to be shot at **Navarre Beach**, off Route 98 between Pensacola and Fort Walton beach, northern Florida.

JAY AND SILENT BOB STRIKE BACK
(2001, dir: Kevin Smith)
Jason Mewes, Kevin Smith, Ben Affleck.
● CALIFORNIA; NEW JERSEY

At $20 million, the final Viewaskewniverse movie might be the most expensive in-joke ever. It opens, inevitably, at **Quick Stop Groceries, 58 Leonard Avenue, Leonardo**, in New Jersey, where Smith's directing career began with *Clerks*. Brodie's Secret Stash is, of course, **Jay and Silent Bob's Secret Stash, 35 Broad Street, Red Bank** (© *732.758.0508, www.viewaskew.com/jsbstash*), Kevin Smith's own (geek-free) comic store in New Jersey.

But the rest of the movie is California, largely around LA. The Provasik facility is a corporate park in **Valencia**, north of LA. The Arena Diner, where Jay and SB are surrounded by Will Ferrell and Judd Nelson, was erected at **Vasquez Rocks Natural Area Park, 10700 West Escondido Canyon Road**, near Agua Dulce Springs, north of LA, where the 'Arena' episode of *Star Trek* was filmed (see *Blazing Saddles* for details of Vasquez Rocks). The *Planet of the Apes* homage was filmed on 'almost' the same beach with *Fugitive* pastiche, is largely computer generated, but the top of the dam is **Pyramid Lake**, on I-5 in Los Padres National Forest north of LA.

Jay and SB arrive in Hollywood. There is no Miramax studio gate (Miramax is a production company but doesn't have its own studio). The gate is the **CBS Radford Studio, 4024 Radford Avenue, Studio City** in the San Fernando Valley, where the movie was shot. The première of *Bluntman and Chronic* is at the **El Rey, 5515 Wilshire Boulevard** (© *323.936.6400*), midtown LA (though since 1994 it's not been a cinema but a live music venue).

JAZZ SINGER, THE
(1927, dir: Alan Crosland)
Al Jolson, May McAvoy, Warner Oland.
● LOS ANGELES, CALIFORNIA

The legendary 'first sound film', with Jolson blacked up as the cantor's son bent on a singing career, was shot in Warner Bros' old Hollywood facility before the company moved to its Burbank lot in 1929. The building still stands, and is now home to independent TV channel KTLA, at **5858 Sunset Boulevard** between Bronson and Van Ness Avenue.

JEAN DE FLORETTE
(1986, dir: Claude Berri)
Gérard Depardieu, Yves Montand, Daniel Auteuil.
● PROVENCE, FRANCE

Depardieu is the hunchbacked city boy, blindly determined to make a success of his inherited patch of Provençal farmland. What he doesn't know is that greedy neighbour Montand has blocked up the spring that would feed his plot, and has thus set tragedy in motion. The film was made back to back with *Manon des Sources*, less a sequel than a second half, which reaches the tragic conclusion. Both movies were made on location around Provence in the south of France, mainly in the village of **Cuges les Pins**, and at nearby **Sommieres**. Other locations included **Mirabeau**, **Vaugines** and **Ansouis**.

JEEPERS CREEPERS
(2001, dir: Victor Salva)
Gina Philips, Justin Long, Jonathan Breck.
● FLORIDA

For the most part, a genuinely creepy horror, filmed near **Dunnellan**, Marion County. The church was St James, west of Ocala, Florida. It was deserted at the time of filming and has since been demolished.

JEREMIAH JOHNSON
(1972, dir: Sydney Pollack)
Robert Redford, Will Geer, Stefan Gierasch.
● UTAH

Originally titled *Liver Eatin' Johnson*, from a story by Edward Anhalt and John Milius, the movie was shot around **Alpine Loop** and in **Provo Canyon**, Utah. The area is now part of Redford's Sundance Resort.

JERK, THE
(1979, dir: Carl Reiner)
Steve Martin, Bernadette Peters, Catlin Adams.
● LOS ANGELES, CALIFORNIA

Martin's first starring role, as the dorkish white son of black sharecroppers who makes, and then loses, a fortune. The millionaire mansion he buys stood at 9561 Sunset Boulevard, Beverly Hills. It shot to fame in 1978 when the then-owner, Sheikh Al-Fassi, stopped the traffic by having its classical nude statues painted in anatomically correct colours. The mansion was badly damaged by fire in 1979 and has since been demolished.

JERRY MAGUIRE
(1996, dir: Cameron Crowe)
Tom Cruise, Cuba Gooding Jr, Renée Zellweger.
● LOS ANGELES, CALIFORNIA; ARIZONA; NEW YORK CITY

Crowe's tale of a sports agent undergoing a crisis of conscience used 70 locations around Los Angeles, plus

A meeting or a date?: Paco's Mexican Restaurant, Culver City

scenes filmed in **Tempe** and **Phoenix**, Arizona. The headquarters of Sports Management International is a huge set built at Sony Studios in **Culver City**, an homage to the vast, impersonal office of Billy Wilder's *The Apartment*. Jerry (Cruise) gets talking to Dorothy Boyd (Zellweger) when she loses her son on the luggage carousel at **John Wayne Airport, Santa Ana** in LA (which became the Louisville airport for Michael Mann's *The Insider*). She lives in **Manhattan Beach**, south of LA. The rather OTT Mexican restaurant where Jerry and Dorothy blur the line between an office meeting and a first date, with the help of a Mariachi band, is **Paco's Mexican Restaurant, 4141 South Centinela Avenue**, Culver City (© *310.391.9616*).

The climactic football game, where Rod Tidwell (Oscar-winning Gooding Jr) gets knocked out cold, was played in the **Sun Devil Stadium**, on the campus of **Arizona State University**, between First and Fifth Streets and Rural and Mill Avenues, downtown **Tempe**.

JESUS CHRIST SUPERSTAR
(1973, dir: Norman Jewison)
Ted Neeley, Carl Anderson, Yvonne Elliman.
● ISRAEL

A bunch of flared seventies tourists act out Lloyd-Webber's dire, dated musical in the middle of the desert. Jesus is a wimp and the villains are camp. Judas gets the best role and rises from the dead. To cap it all, Tim Rice wrote the lyrics. Filmed in Israel, at the ruins of **Pratzim**.

JÉSUS DE MONTRÉAL (aka *Jesus of Montréal*)
(1989, dir: Denys Arcand)
Lothaire Bluteau, Catherine Wilkening, Remy Girard.
● MONTRÉAL, QUÉBEC, CANADA

A powerhouse performance from Bluteau as an actor playing Christ in a radical passion play, performed on the **Way of the Cross, St Joseph's Oratory, 3800 chemin Queen Mary**, Mont-Royal, overlooking the city, it's the highest point of Montréal.

JEWEL OF THE NILE, THE
(1985, dir: Lewis Teague)
Michael Douglas, Kathleen Turner, Danny DeVito.
● FRANCE; MOROCCO; UTAH

The sequel to *Romancing the Stone* sees novelist Joan Wilder (Turner) accepting an invitation from a Middle Eastern potentate and getting involved in a Holy War. The opening

The plane runs amok: Aït Ben Haddou

scenes were shot at **Nice** on the French Riviera.

The Middle Eastern scenes filmed in Morocco. The village is **Aït Ben Haddou**, near Ouarzazate, a location familiar from *Gladiator, The Last Days of Sodom and Gomorrah* and seen in *Lawrence of Arabia*. The gateway Douglas crashes the jet plane through was built for the movie and can still be seen – complete with jet plane-shaped hole. The climax, at the royal city of Khadir, used the **Royal Square** of **Meknes** in northern Morocco. It was a trouble-ridden production: sets built in the desert were washed away by freak floods; posters and flags for the rally scene had to be remade when it was discovered that the words on them were blasphemous; while the original production designer and location manager were killed in a plane crash. More desert shots used **Zion National Park** in Utah.

JOHNNY BELINDA
(1948, dir: Jean Negulesco)
Jane Wyman, Lew Ayres, Charles Bickford.
● CALIFORNIA

Gushy melodrama, with deaf and dumb Wyman on trial for the murder of her rapist. Set on the island of Cape Breton, the movie was shot around **Mendocino** on the northern California coast, and at the **Pebble Beach-Pacific Grove** waterfront of central California.

JOHNNY GUITAR
(1954, dir: Nicholas Ray)
Joan Crawford, Mercedes McCambridge, Sterling Hayden.
● ARIZONA

Bizarre Freudian Western, in lurid colour, with a glorious face-off between Crawford and McCambridge. Filmed at Republic's standing Western set in **Sedona**, Route 89A, south of Flagstaff, Arizona, and at **Oak Creek Canyon** between Flagstaff and Sedona.

JOHNNY SUEDE
(1991, dir: Tom DiCillo)
Brad Pitt, Calvin Levels, Alison Moir.
● NEW YORK CITY

Retro-style, silly hair, surreal humour: a cult film-by-numbers, filmed around 44 separate locations in **Williamsburg**, a tough section of north Brooklyn by the East River. DiCillo went on to make *Living in Oblivion*, about the making of a cheapo cult movie with a pretentious, preening, temperamental Hollywood star.

JOUR DE FÊTE
(1948, dir: Jacques Tati)
Jacques Tati, Guy Decomble, Paul Frankeur.
● FRANCE

Tati's début feature-length film, about a village postman embarking on an American-style efficiency drive. The cute little village is **Sainte-Severe-sur-Indre**, about 40 miles south of Bourges in the **Loire**. The village is just south of the D943 Tours-Montlucon road (*rail: Le Châtre*).

JOURNAL D'UNE FEMME DE CHAMBRE, LE
(aka *The Diary of a Chambermaid*)
(1964, dir: Luis Buñuel)

Jeanne Moreau, Michel Piccoli, Georges Geret.
● FRANCE

Moreau is the maid working for a family of bourgeois sexual misfits with a fascist manservant, in this adaptation of Octave Mirbeau's novel (previously filmed, in a softer version, in the studio, by Jean Renoir in 1946). The little town is **Milly-la-Foret**, 12 miles west of Fontainebleau. Film director Jean Cocteau lived here, and decorated its Chapelle Saint-Blaise-des-Simples, where his tomb now lies.

JOURNEY TO THE CENTER OF THE EARTH
(1959, dir: Henry Levin)
James Mason, Pat Boone, Arlene Dahl.
● SCOTLAND; NEW MEXICO

The military parade: Mound Place, Edinburgh

Professor Lindenbrook sets off from (and returns to) **Edinburgh University**, South Bridge. The scenes were shot in the university's **Old Quad**. He absent-mindedly gets mixed up in a military parade at **Mound Place**. Some of the more spectacular underground scenes of this Jules Verne adaptation were filmed in the

The centre of the earth: Carlsbad Caverns, New Mexico

Carlsbad Caverns, Carlsbad, in the southeast corner of New Mexico (see *The Spider* for details).

JOY RIDE (aka *Roadkill*)
(2001, dir: John Dahl)
Paul Walker, Steve Zahn, Leelee Sobieski.
● NEVADA; UTAH; CALIFORNIA

There's more than a nod to *Duel*, Spielberg's début feature, as brothers Fuller (Zahn) and Lewis (Walker) are menaced by an unseen trucker after a practical joke goes horribly wrong.

The Colorado motel, where Rusty Nail gets mad when 'Candy Cane' turns out to be not what he expected, is the **Lone Star Motel, 650 6th Street, Wells** (℗ 775.752.3632), on I-80, northeast Nevada. The gas station, where Walker gets spooked while trying to phone the sherriff, is at the tiny stop of **Delle** ("a two-pump gas station and a café"), 44 miles west of Salt Lake City, Utah.

The college campus, where the pair pick up Venna (Sobieski) is the **University of Redlands, 1200 East Colton Avenue, Redlands**, on I-10 east of LA. They stop at the Z Stop gas station in **Battle Mountain**, on I-80, northern Nevada, where they realise Rusty has caught up with them at the **Owl Motel, 72 East Front Street** (℗ 775.635.5155). The café, where Fuller and Lewis are ordered to buy "six cheeseburgers each – naked", is a dis-

used truckstop outside **Winnemucca**, northern Nevada. Fuller has to hotwire the car at **Lancaster**, California. The ending was filmed on sets built at **Long Beach**, LA

JUBILEE
(1978, dir: Derek Jarman)
Jenny Runacre, Little Nell, Toyah Wilcox.
● LONDON

Jarman's contribution to the Queen's Silver Jubilee year, this bilious view of seventies punk, seen through the eyes of a time-travelling Queen Elizabeth, filmed at **Rotherhithe**. Queen Bess and her astrologer, John Dee, wander along the cliffs at **Winspit**. The nightclub, which is **Westminster Cathedral** (seen in Hitchcock's *Foreign Correspondent*) on the outside, is the now-defunct Catacomb, a once-notorious gay club on Finborough Road at the junction of Old Brompton Road in Earls Court, SW10. Jordan performs 'Rule Britannia' on stage at the **Theatre Royal, Drury Lane**, in front of the mirrored set for *A Chorus Line*.

JULES ET JIM
(1961, dir: François Truffaut)
Oskar Werner, Jeanne Moreau, Henri Serre.
● FRANCE

The 'hidden' garden: Villa Castel, Paris

Truffaut's classic triangular affair between Jean Moreau, Frenchman Henri Serre and German Oskar Werner before and after WWII, filmed in Paris and the South of France. Paris scenes were shot in the hidden gardens of **Villa Castel** behind passage Plantin, up a narrow flight of steps at **83 rue Couronnes** in Belleville (*metro: Couronnes*). On rue du Transvaal, at the top of passage Plantin, is a wrought iron gate through which you can catch a glimpse of these very private gardens.

Filming also took place near to the German border in Alsace and on the Côte d'Azur in the picturesque town of **St Paul-de-Vence**, about 12 miles north of Cannes. The final cremation and funeral was staged in Paris' **Père Lachaise** cemetery (see *The Doors* for details).

JULIA
(1977, dir: Fred Zinnemann)
Jane Fonda, Vanessa Redgrave, Jason Robards.
● NORFOLK; CUMBRIA; OXFORDSHIRE; FRANCE

Fonda plays Lillian Hellman in a dubious account of her friendship with anti-Nazi activist Julia during the 1930s. The American scenes were shot in the UK, with **Winterton-on-Sea**, nine miles north of Great Yarmouth in Norfolk, standing in for Nantucket. Hellman and Dashiell Hammett's beach house was built on the sand dunes here. The Adirondack Mountains were actually around **Keswick** in the Lake District, Cumbria. The boating scenes take place on **Lake Derwentwater**. The Oxford University scenes used **St John's College, New College** and the **University Library, Oxford**.

The Vienna hospital: Hôpital Villemin, Paris

The Badlands dig: Red Rock Canyon, near Ridgecrest

Isla Nublar: Kauai

In Paris, Julia stays at the swanky **Hotel Meurice, 228 rue de Rivoli**, home over the years to King Alphonse XIII of Spain and to Salvador Dali (who stayed for 30 years). During WWII, it actually served as Nazi HQ (*metro: Tuileries; Concorde*). Over the rue de Rivoli, in the **Jardin de Tuileries**, alongside the Place de la Concorde, Maximilian Schell asks Fonda to smuggle $50,000. The 1934 Paris riots were filmed in the preserved city of **Versailles**, the town built alongside the more famous chateau (an early example of town planning, with a grid-like layout). Fonda walks in the small hours in the six-acre **Jardin du Palais Royal**, between the rue de Montpensier and rue de Valois (*metro: Palais Royal*). The railway station she departs from is the **Gare du Nord**, dressed to be circa 1937.

The Vienna Hospital is played by the **Hôpital Villemin**, a now-disused military hospital still standing alongside Paris' Gare de l'Est on the **rue du Faubourg Saint Denis**, built to take wounded WWI soldiers direct from the railway station. Austria and Berlin scenes were both filmed in **Strasbourg**, with **Strasbourg Station** standing in for Berlin's railway terminal and **Strasbourg University** passing itself off as the University of Vienna. The streets of Strasbourg were also used for the Florisdorf riots. The German frontier checkpoint is **Shirmack Station**, 40 miles west of Strasbourg.

JUNIOR BONNER

(1972, dir: Sam Peckinpah)
Steve McQueen, Ida Lupino, Robert Preston.
● **ARIZONA**

Low-key family drama, with ageing rodeo star McQueen returning to his hometown. The movie was filmed in **Prescott**, Arizona, the setting of screenwriter Jeb Rosebrook's story, with the real Prescott Rodeo as background.

The bar to which everyone retires between sessions, and the setting for the brawl, is the **Palace Bar**. The railway station is, naturally, **Prescott Railroad Station**. Robert Preston and Ida Lupino's reconciliation was shot on the back stairs of the **Palace Hotel**.

JURASSIC PARK

(1993, dir: Steven Spielberg)
Sam Neill, Laura Dern, Jeff Goldblum.
● **HAWAII; CALIFORNIA**

Spielberg's blockbuster was filmed mainly on **Kauai**, smallest and most beautiful of the major Hawaiian islands, despite the best efforts of Hurricane Iniki, which flattened the sets.

The Badlands archaeological dig filmed on mainland USA, in a section of **Red Rock Canyon** near **Ridgecrest**, only accessible to four-wheel drive vehicles in California's **Mojave Desert**, but the Isla Nublar locations are all in Hawaii. The waterfall, where John Hammond's helicopter touches down (the helipad was a temporary structure for the movie), is inaccessible by land, but most of the Kauai helicopter tours will point out the **Manawaiopuna Falls** in **Hanapepe Valley**. The site of the giant 'Jurassic Park' gates is almost as hard to get to. They stood alongside **Blue Hole**, a water-filled canyon near the centre of Kauai, which you can reach via a five-hour hike from Wailua, on the eastern coast. The electrified fence was erected in Kauai's **Olokele Valley**, while more scenes were shot at **Lawai**. The Gallimus stampede, where the leaping herd of dinosaurs move like a flock of birds, used the most populous and developed of the islands, Oahu – specifically at the **Kualoa Ranch, Kamehameha Highway, Ka'a'awa Valley**. The ranch is open to visitors, and the fallen tree, under which Sam Neill and the kids sheltered, is still there as a great photo opportunity. Take Kamehameha Highway north from Honolulu, about 20 miles. The entrance is on the left, opposite the Kualoa Regional Park (*© 800.231.7321*).

JURASSIC PARK III

(2001, dir: Joe Johnston)
Sam Neill, William H Macy, Téa Leoni.
● **HAWAII; CALIFORNIA**

Trouble on set, with rumours of unfinished scripts and dissatisfied actors. Despite the FX, this is the weakest of the series. There's a little LA: the Washington DC home of Dr Ellie Sattler (Laura Dern) is in **South Pasadena**; Dr Alan Grant (Neill) lectures in **Thorne Hall, Occidental College, Eagle Rock** (the setting for *Clueless*); and the InGen breeding tanks are a warehouse east of downtown LA.

But it's back to Hawaii for most of the film, though the opening scene, of young Erik paragliding onto Isla Sorna, is a combination of **Palos Verdes**, south of LA, and the coast of the island of **Molokai**, Hawaii. The rest of the filming sites are on the islands of **Kauai** and **Oahu**. The abandoned jungle airfield, where the party touches down on Isla Sorna, is **Dillingham Airfield** on the north shore of Oahu near Waialua. The other Oahu locations are the **Heeia Kea Ranch** and the rain forests of **Manoa Valley**, about two miles north of Waikiki. Kauai locations include the **Mary Lucas Estate** (site of the old reservoir from *Jurassic Park*), the **Wailua River** on the east side, and the **Hanalei Valley**, on the north of the island.

K

KABHI KHUSHI KABHIE GHAM...

(aka *Sometimes Happiness, Sometimes Sorrow...*)
(2001, dir: Karan Johar)
Shah Rukh Khan, Hrithik Roshan, Amitabh Bachchan.
● LONDON; OXFORDSHIRE; BUCKINGHAMSHIRE; KENT; ESSEX; EGYPT

Johar brings together the biggest stars of Hindi cinema and pulls out all the stops to deliver a truckload of industrial strength soap, and the sheer verve is irresistible. Rohan (Roshan) conjures up a bevy of dancing girls for the 'Vande Mataram' number outside the **UCI Empire Leicester Square, 5-6 Leicester Square** (℡ *0870.010.2030, www.uci-cinemas.co.uk*). The newly-roofed, sparkling white **Great Court** of the **British Museum, Great Russell Street**, became the college interior for the 'Deewana Hai Dekho' number. The school concert, where Krishi is supposed to sing 'Do Re Mi', is **Osterley Park House, Jersey Road, Isleworth** (see *The Grass Is Greener* for details). Rohan and Pooja sit on the riverside terrace of **Cantina del Ponte, Butlers Wharf Building, 36c Shad Thames** (see *Bridget Jones's Diary* for details). There was also filming at **Chandni Chowk**, the bazaar of Old Delhi.

KAGEMUSHA (aka *Shadow Warrior*)

(1980, dir: Akira Kurosawa)
Tatsuya Nakadai, Tsutomo Yamazaki, Kenichi Hagiwara.
● JAPAN

The shadow warrior is a lookalike hired to impersonate a clan chief in this stirring period epic. Kurosawa filmed at several castles around Japan, using low-angle shots to avoid intrusive modern surroundings. The spectacular battle scenes were shot on the north island of **Hokkaido**. The tiered white castle is **Himeji Castle**, the 'White Heron' castle, situated on a bluff overlooking the town of Himeji, 33 miles west of Kobe. It's about ten minutes walk from Himeji Station, from where you can see it clearly. It is seen also in *Ran*, Kurosawa's version of *King Lear*, and in the Bond movie *You Only Live Twice*.

KAKUSHI TORIDE NO SAN-AKUNIN (aka *The Hidden Fortress*)

(1958, dir: Akira Kurosawa)
Minoru Chiaki, Kamatari Fujiwara, Toshiro Mifune.
● JAPAN

Widescreen historical drama, with much of the action seen from the point of view of two comic minor rogues, one short, one tall. Remind you of anything?. This is the movie that apparently inspired the structure of *Star Wars*. The landscape is the black volcanic slopes of **Mount Fuji**.

KANAL (aka *They Loved Life*)

(1956, dir: Andrzej Wajda)
Teresa Izewska, Tadeusz Janczar, Emil Kariewicz.
● WARSAW

A fact-based story of Polish patriots hiding in the sewers from the Nazis during the 1944 Warsaw uprising. The manhole cover is at the corner of **Dluga** and **Miodowa** streets, down from the Krasinski Palace, Warsaw. A nearby wall plaque commemorates the events depicted.

KARATE KID, THE

(1984, dir: John G Avildsen)
Ralph Macchio, Noriyuki 'Pat' Morita, Elisabeth Shue.
● LOS ANGELES, CALIFORNIA; ARIZONA

Rocky remade as a teen movie, and by the same director, too. **19223 Saticoy Street, Reseda**, is Macchio's home. The high school is **Charles Evans Hughes Junior**

The kid's South Seas apartment: Saticoy Street, Reseda

High School, 5607 Capistrano at Philiprim Street, **Woodland Hills**. There was more filming at **Sedona**, Arizona.

In *The Karate Kid Part II*, Pat Morita flies back to Japan to see his ailing father, and finds there are old scores to settle. The island of **Oahu, Hawaii**, stands in for Japan. Old rivalries are warmed over again in the second sequel, *The Karate Kid III*. Villain Thomas Ian Griffith's stylish home is the Frank Lloyd Wright-designed **Ennis-Brown House, 2607 Glendower Avenue, Los Feliz, LA**. For full details of this concrete Mayan temple, see *The House on Haunted Hill*.

KES

(1969, dir: Ken Loach)
David Bradley, Colin Welland, Lynne Perrie.
● YORKSHIRE

No-hope life in the industrial north, shot in Loach's effective semi-documentary, semi-improvisational style around the tiny village of **Tankersley**, at Junction 36 of the M1 between Sheffield and Barnsley, and **Barnsley** itself, Yorkshire. The countryside where David Bradley learns to train the kestrel is **Hoyland Common, Hoyland Road, Hoyland**, just northeast of Tankersley. He goes to school at **St Helen's County Secondary School, St Helen's Way, St Helen's**, northeast Barnsley.

KEY LARGO

(1948, dir: John Huston)
Humphrey Bogart, Lauren Bacall, Claire Trevor.
● LOS ANGELES, CALIFORNIA; FLORIDA

A disparate bunch of people are holed up in a Key Largo hotel while a devastating hurricane threatens. Largo is one of the Florida Keys, the curving chain of islands linked by a coral reef, running from Miami to Key West. It's claimed that the movie was filmed at the recently rebuilt Caribbean Club bar, but this might be a bit of wishful thinking by the owners. Director Huston maintained that the whole film was shot at **Warners, Burbank**, including the sea sequences in the studio tank. The only kosher locations are some establishing shots, near the beginning of the movie, of Florida's **Overseas Highway**, which runs between the islands.

KID FOR TWO FARTHINGS, A

(1955, dir: Carol Reed)
David Kossoff, Celia Johnson, Diana Dors.

● **LONDON**

Colourful and sentimental fable set in the old Jewish East End, with young Jonathan Ashmore convinced his one-horned goat is a unicorn, shot around **Mansford Street**, which has since been completely redeveloped, and **Hackney Road**, with St Paul's Cathedral looming strangely large and seemingly just at the end of the road.

KIDNAPPED

(1960, dir: Robert Stevenson)
Peter Finch, James MacArthur, Peter O'Toole.

● **SCOTLAND**

This vesion of the Robert Louis Stevenson adventure, also filmed in 1938 and 1948 in Hollywood, was shot by Disney at Pinewood studios and on location in Scotland. The Scots locations are **Ardgour**; in the remote wilderness near Fort William; **Ballachulish**, near Glencoe in Argyll and **Glen Nevis**. A further remake, in 1971 with Michael Caine and Trevor Howard, used **Seil Island**, about ten miles southwest of Oban; and **Stirling Castle, Stirling** (*admission charge*).

KILL BILL: VOLUME 1

(2003, dir: Quentin Tarantino)
Uma Thurman, Lucy Liu, Vivica A Fox.

● **JAPAN; CALIFORNIA; CHINA**

Tarantino's fanboy collage of Chop Suey and Spaghetti isn't as integrated as the director's previous outings, dulling the impetus of the revenge epic. When The Bride/Black Mamba (Thurman) wakes from her four year coma and takes the Pussy Wagon to the home of Vernita Greene (Fox) in Pasadena, she doesn't have far to go. The hospital where the comatose Bride is abused by the sleazoid Buck is **St Luke's Medical Center, 2632 East Washington Boulevard**, near Altadena Drive, north Pasadena, which closed in February 2002 and is now used exclusively as a movie set.

Kiddo lies comatose: St Luke's Medical Center, East Washington Boulevard, Pasadena

In Tokyo, The Bride, on her bike, trails O-Ren (Liu) on **Rainbow Bridge** (seen also in *Lost In Translation*) to **Odaiba** (man-made islands in the Bay of Tokyo) and surrounding island roadways. O-Ren's House of Blue Leaves, where Thurman sees off the Crazy 88, was a set built in the **Beijing Film Studios**, as was the lurid pink interior of the Tokyo bar and the Okinawa sushi parlour of Hatori Hanzo (Sonny Chiba). The Beijing studio, where *The Last Emperor* was also shot, was built in 1949 under the aegis of Chairman Mao ostensibly to produce propaganda movies, but seems to have been a pet project of Madam Mao, who's tastes supposedly leaned more to *The Sound of Music*.

KILL BILL: VOLUME 2

(2004, dir: Quentin Tarantino)
Uma Thurman, David Carradine, Daryl Hannah.

● **CALIFORNIA; CHINA; MEXICO**

The 'Massacre at Two Pines', supposedly in El Paso, Texas, was filmed in the Mojave Desert, outside **Lancaster**, north of Los Angeles. The trailer of Budd (Michael Madsen) was at **Mule Canyon** in the Calico Hills, about 20 miles east of Barstow. After bursting out of the 'Lonely Grave of Paula Schultz', Beatrix Kiddo/The Bride (Thurman) nonchalantly orders a glass of water at **Emma Jean's Holland Burger Cafe, 17143 D Street**, the old Route 66 between **Victorville** and Oro Grande (*© 760.243.9938*). It's famed as the Home of the Brian Burger. The what? Quite. Emma Jean's is a traditional forties diner with generous portions (it's closed Sundays).

The retreat of Pai Mei (Chia Hui Liu), where Kiddo learns the Five-Point-Palm Exploding Heart technique, is the **Gao Temple** (Gao Miao) on the east side of **Miao Gao Mountain** in **Zhongwei**, 170 km southwest of Yinchuan. You can get a train from Beijing to Zhongwei. The temple complex is in the centre of Zhongwei, reached from the northern end of Gulou Beijie. The exterior of Bill's hacienda was on the coast of Mexico.

KILLER ELITE, THE

(1975, dir: Sam Peckinpah)
James Caan, Robert Duvall, Mako.

● **SAN FRANCISCO, CALIFORNIA**

The English novel *Monkey in the Middle* by Robert Rostand, transposed to San Francisco because Caan wouldn't make the picture outside the US. But it looks good, and uses plenty of locations including, inevitably, **Chinatown**; the **Bethlehem Steel Pier**; and **San Francisco International Airport**, where, to placate the airlines worried about an apparent breach of security, Peckinpah convinced them that a character falling down dead had suffered a heart attack. Of course, he added the gunshot later. The climactic fight takes place at **Suisun Bay**, where the Navy's 'mothball fleet' is stationed.

KILLERS, THE

(1964, dir: Don Siegel)
John Cassavetes, Lee Marvin, Angie Dickinson.

● **LOS ANGELES, CALIFORNIA**

Remake of the 1946 movie of the Hemingway story, and

Ronald Reagan's last movie. Set around LA, where Angie Dickinson's house is at **Toluca Lake**. The jalopy race was filmed at the old Ascot Speedway in Gardena, also seen in the original 1974 *Gone in 60 Seconds*.

KILLING FIELDS, THE

(1984, dir: Roland Joffe)
Sam Waterston, Haing S Ngor, John Malkovich.
● **THAILAND; CALIFORNIA**

New York Times reporter Sidney Schanberg escapes the fall of Phnom Penh in 1975, but his photographer, Dith Pran, left behind and presumed killed, survives the Pol Pot regime. Tragically, Dr Haing S Ngor, who won the Best Supporting Actor Oscar as Pran, was gunned down in a robbery outside his LA home in 1996. It's another film with Thailand standing in for Vietnam (as well as Cambodia), with much of the film being shot around **Phuket**. The French Embassy is the **Colonial Town Hall, Narisarn Road** at Toh Sae Road in Phuket Town, southeast of the island. The Phnom Phen Penh Hotel is the **Railway Hotel, Hua Hin**, which you can reach by narrow gauge train from Hua Lampong station, Bangkok. There was also filming in **San Francisco**.

KILLING OF SISTER GEORGE, THE

(1968, dir: Robert Aldrich)
Beryl Reid, Susannah York, Coral Browne.
● **LONDON**

This crass commercialisation of Frank Marcus' black comedy, about a TV soap star on the verge of losing her job and her young female lover, is saved by terrific performances, especially from Beryl Reid, who originated the role on stage. The film has the distinction of having been banned in Norwich. The club Reid invites snooty BBC lady Coral Browne to, with its mix of genuine butch dykes and femme movie extras, was the Gateways, the legendary but now long-gone lesbian club which stood in Bramerton Gardens, just off the King's Road, Chelsea, SW10. The pub, The Marquis of Granby, which Reid drinks in at the opening of the movie, is actually the wonderful old **Holly Bush, 22 Holly Mount**, NW3, tucked away behind Heath Street in Hampstead (*tube: Hampstead*). It's still there, and virtually unchanged. Over the opening credits, Reid stomps through the narrow stepped passages between **Heath Street** and **Hampstead Grove**, before popping out on the other side of London at the **Embankment**, near Chelsea.

The Paris hotel: Mondrian Hotel, West Hollywood

KILLING ZOE

(1994, dir: Roger Avary)
Eric Stoltz, Jean-Hugues Anglade, Julie Delpy.
● **PARIS, FRANCE; LOS ANGELES, CALIFORNIA**

This heist movie is set in Paris, but the French capital is seen only in establishing shots. The rest of the movie is faked up in Los Angeles, around **Long Beach** (where the gang HQ

used a penthouse suite) and in the downtown area (where the bank hold-up was staged). The coolly chic Parisian hotel where Eric Stoltz meets Julie Delpy is West Hollywood's exclusive **Mondrian Hotel, 8440 Sunset Boulevard** (*© 213.650.9999*).

KIM

(1950, dir: Victor Saville)
Errol Flynn, Dean Stockwell, Paul Lukas.
● **INDIA; CALIFORNIA**

Indian landscapes: Alabama Hills, California

Colourful adventure from the Rudyard Kipling novel, with plenty of actual filming in India, at **Jaipur** and **Bundi**, as well as use of the spectacular **Alabama Hills**, overlooking Lone Pine in central California. The Hills, striking rock formations set against the dramatic backdrop of the snow-capped Sierra Nevada range, have featured in countless movies, often, as here, doubling for India and the Himalayas (see *Gunga Din*, *King of the Khyber Rifles* and *The Lives of a Bengal Lancer*) as well as Western landscapes for *How the West Was Won* and *Joe Kidd*. An annual Lone Pine Film Festival celebrates the area's cinematic legacy, and even the place names reflect the importance of the movie industry. The track leading up to the most frequently used area is called Movie Road. For detailed maps of film locations in the area, check out Dave Holland's invaluable guide *On Location in Lone Pine*, available locally.

KIND HEARTS AND CORONETS

(1949, dir: Robert Hamer)
Dennis Price, Alec Guinness, Valerie Hobson.
● **KENT**

Chalfont, family seat of the D'Ascoynes: Leeds Castle

Best, and blackest, of the Ealing comedies has embittered Price killing off the eight members of the D'Ascoyne family standing between him and his inheritance. Chalfont, the family seat, is **Leeds Castle**, four miles east of Maidstone on the B2163 (*rail: Bearsted*). The Norman castle was turned into a royal palace by Henry VIII, and stands in the middle of a lake surrounded by 500 acres of parkland. It's open to the public daily, except Christmas Day (*© 01622.765400, www.leeds-castle.com; admission charge*). You can also see the castle in period adventure *The Moonrake*).

KIND OF LOVING, A

(1962, dir: John Schlesinger)
Alan Bates, June Ritchie, Thora Hird.

● LANCASHIRE; MANCHESTER

Stan Barstow's novel of northern working class life is set in the fictitious Cressley, Yorkshire, but was filmed in Lancashire. The house newly-weds Alan Bates and June Ritchie share with disapproving mother-in-law Thora Hird is on **Radcliffe New Road, Radcliffe**. The wedding takes place at **St John's Church**, Radcliffe, Manchester. Also in Radcliffe is Beacon's Park, where Bates and Ritchie spend their evenings, which is actually the town's **Coronation Park**. The arcade where the couple go on a date with an unwanted third party is the **Miller Arcade** in **Preston** (which now sports one of the plaques erected in 1996 to mark the centenary of cinema).

KING KONG

(1933, dir: Merian C Cooper; Ernest B Schoedsack)
Fay Wray, Robert Armstrong, Bruce Cabot.

● LOS ANGELES, CALIFORNIA; NEW YORK CITY

The New York theatre: Shrine Auditorium

The landing on Skull Island was filmed at **San Pedro**, home of LA harbour, south LA near Long Beach – the mountains were painted on glass.

Several left-over sets were used by penny-pinching RKO, including the native village (from King Vidor's 1932 *Bird of Paradise*, and the giant wall from DeMille's 1927 *King of Kings*) on the lot at the **Culver Studios, 9336 Washington Boulevard** in Culver City. In turn, the giant Skull Island gates were reused for *Gone With the Wind*, where – bizarrely – they can clearly be seen during the burning of Atlanta. Skull Island itself was shot in Hollywood's own wilderness, the caves at **Bronson Canyon**, about a quarter of a mile from the end of Canyon Drive in Griffith Park.

The interior of the New York theatre where Kong is exhibited is LA's **Shrine Auditorium, 649 West Jefferson Boulevard**, south of downtown LA (see the 1954 film *A Star Is Born* for details). And, of course, it's atop the **Empire State Building, 350 Fifth Avenue** (*www.esb-nyc.com*) at 34th Street, New York, where Kong finally meets his end.

KING KONG

(1976, dir: John Guillermin)
Jeff Bridges, Charles Grodin, Jessica Lange.

● NEW YORK CITY; HAWAII

Skull Island: Na Pali Coast, Kauai

A knowing, campy remake which misses by miles the juddery charm of the original. Skull Island is the inaccessible **Na Pali Coast** on the northern shore of **Kauai**, Hawaii, where camp is set up on **Honopu Beach**. In New York, the deserted downtown bar, where Lange and Bridges grab a few minutes peace, thinking Kong is over in Queens, is Wall Street institution **Harry's at Hanover Square, 1 Hanover Square** in the Financial District (*© 212.425.3412, www.harrystogo.com*). Kong climbs one of the twin towers of the now gone World Trade Center, finally plummeting into the World Trade Center Plaza.

KING KONG

(2005, dir: Peter Jackson)
Naomi Watts, Adrien Brody, Andy Serkis.

● NEW ZEALAND

When he came to film *The Lord of the Rings*, Peter Jackson realised that his native New Zealand was a dead ringer for Tolkien's Middle Earth. So guess where he found '1933 New York' and Kong's tropical island for his remake? Correct. It's New Zealand, mainly around Wellington, on the southern tip of the North Island.

Ocean scenes aboard the *SS Venture* were filmed around **Kapiti Island Nature Reserve**, a bird sanctuary off the coast of Paraparaumu, about 30 miles north of Wellington (*www.kapiti.org.nz/kapiti.html*). The island is a protected environment, so there's a limit of 50 visitors per day. You'll need to get a landing permit and book a commercial launch service (private boats are not permitted to land). The *Venture* berths at **Miramar Wharf, Cobham Drive**, on Wellington's eastern peninsula, **Miramar**, (where you'll find Jackson's Weta FX studio). Skull Island scenes were filmed at one of Wellington's most popular surfing beaches, **Lyall Bay**, southwest of Miramar; and the island's giant wall was built on the northern tip of the Miramar Peninsula, above the Massey Memorial (commemorating Prime Minister William Massey), at **Shelly Bay**.

New York of the 30s, including sections of Times Square (economically redressed to double as Herald Square), Broadway and Fifth Avenue, was built on vacant land at **Seaview, Hutt Valley**, Wellington. The theatre rehearsals, before Carl Denham (Jack Black) exhibits the 'Eighth Wonder of the World' are in the **Opera House, 111-113 Manners Street, Wellington** (*© 64.0.802.4060*). The interior of the New York theatre, in which Kong is exhibited, is the **Civic Theatre, Queen Street** at Wellesley Street, **Auckland** (*© 64.4.385.0162*).

KING OF COMEDY, THE

(1983, dir: Martin Scorsese)
Robert De Niro, Jerry Lewis, Sandra Bernhard.

● NEW YORK

Jerry Lewis' office: Paramount Plaza, 51st Street

Vastly underrated character piece, with De Niro excruciating as a smalltime comic who kidnaps a surprisingly low-key Lewis to get a spot on TV. It's

213

New York-set, where Lewis' office is **Paramount Plaza, 51st Street** at Broadway and the bar is **Club 478, 9th Avenue** between 36th and 37th Streets in the Theater-Garment district. The restaurant scene is, naturally, at showbiz hangout **Sardi's, 234 West 44th Street** at Broadway. Lewis' country retreat is in Nassau County, Long Island.

KING OF KINGS
(1927, dir: Cecil B DeMille)
HB Warner, Jacqueline Logan, Ernest Torrence.
● **LOS ANGELES, CALIFORNIA**

DeMille's life of Christ is heavy on Magdalen's debauchery, but maybe a tad lacking in Christian humility. The Sea of Galilee was filmed at **Catalina Island**, off the coast of LA. The Garden of Gethsemane was, modestly, built in the backyard of CB's East Hollywood home, at **2000 DeMille Drive**, off Los Feliz, which has remained completely unchanged since the old showman's death there in 1959.

KING OF MARVIN GARDENS, THE
(1972, dir: Bob Rafelson)
Jack Nicholson, Bruce Dern, Ellen Burstyn.
● **NEW JERSEY; PENNSYLVANIA**

Nicholson is a radio talk show host, Dern his flaky, ambitious brother, in this downbeat character study filmed mainly around the sadder parts of the East Coast's flash gambling capital, **Atlantic City**, New Jersey. Filming also took place in **Philadelphia**, Pennsylvania.

KING OF NEW YORK
(1990, dir: Abel Ferrara)
Christopher Walken, David Caruso, Larry Fishburne.
● **NEW YORK CITY**

Frank White (Walken) is released from the notorious **Sing Sing Penitentiary, Ossining**, on the Hudson River, 30 miles north of New York (see *20,000 Years at Sing Sing* for details). He runs his criminal empire from a suite in the **Plaza Hotel, 59th Street** at Fifth Avenue (see *North by Northwest* for details). Frank watches Eugene O'Neill's *The Emperor Jones* at the **Lunt Fontanne Theatre, 205 West 46th Street** (℡ 212.575.9200), from the bar of which he's hauled away by the cops. The restaurant where cop Bishop confronts Frank's attack on Larry Wong's gang is at **Doyers and Pell Streets** in Chinatown (a location seen in Woody Allen's *Radio Days*). White's lawyer is at the elegant **Barbetta Restaurant, 321 West 46th Street**, New York's oldest Italian restaurant, celebrating 100 years of business in 2006 (℡ 212.246.9171, *www.barbettarestaurant.com*). It's a favourite of Woody Allen's, seen in *Alice* and *Celebrity*. The cops' unofficial raid on Frank's club, at the foot of the **Brooklyn Bridge**, goes horribly wrong and the ensuing rainsoaked car chase is on the **Queensboro Bridge**. The climactic shoot out was staged in **Times Square**, with Frank slowly expiring alone in the back of a cab.

KING SOLOMON'S MINES
(1950, dir: Compton Bennett; Andrew Marton)
Stewart Granger, Deborah Kerr, Richard Carlson.

● **KENYA; TANGANYIKA; BELGIAN CONGO; UGANDA; NEW MEXICO; CALIFORNIA**

Classic adventure, shot on location in Africa, in Kenya; Tanganyika; the Belgian Congo and Uganda. Also partly filmed in **Death Valley**, California. The underground mines are the breathtaking **Carlsbad Caverns, Carlsbad**, on I-285, southeast New Mexico (see *The Spider*).

KISS ME DEADLY
(1955, dir: Robert Aldrich)
Ralph Meeker, Albert Dekker, Cloris Leachman.
● **CALIFORNIA**

Bizarrely arty filming of the Mike Hammer thriller, with location filming at **Malibu**, north of LA, and in the decrepit area which was Bunker Hill, now massively rebuilt. The strange glow from the suitcase in *Pulp Fiction* is an homage to *Kiss Me Deadly*'s final scene, when the radioactive briefcase is finally opened.

KISS ME, STUPID
(1964, dir: Billy Wilder)
Dean Martin, Kim Novak, Ray Walston.
● **CALIFORNIA; NEVADA**

Sour satire from Wilder. Set in the fictitious Climax, Nevada, it was shot around **Twentynine Palms** in Nevada and in the **Aquarius Theatre, 6230 Sunset Boulevard** between Argyle and El Centro, Hollywood, in the days when it was the Moulin Rouge (see *Imitation of Life* for details).

KNACK... AND HOW TO GET IT, THE
(1965, dir: Richard Lester)
Rita Tushingham, Michael Crawford, Ray Brooks.
● **LONDON**

Flashy, surreal filming of Ann Jellicoe's stylised stage play, set in a very Swinging Sixties London. Naïve Rita Tushingham arrives in the city at **Victoria Coach Station**, SW1. The street scenes are around Shepherd's Bush and Notting Hill Gate; the swimming pool is **Ruislip Lido, Ruislip**, west London; and Ray Brooks' wildly sexist fantasy takes place at the **Royal Albert Hall, Kensington**. The famous 'white pad', where much of the movie is set, is **1 Melrose Terrace**, W6.

KNIGHTS OF THE ROUND TABLE
(1953, dir: Richard Thorpe)
Robert Taylor, Ava Gardner, Mel Ferrer.
● **CORNWALL; DEVON**

Hollywoodised Arthurian legend, with filming at **Tintagel** on the northern coast of Cornwall. The castle was built atop **Haytor Vale** on Dartmoor, Devon.

KNIGHT'S TALE, A
(2001, dir: Brian Helgeland)
Heath Ledger, Paul Bettany, Laura Fraser.
● **CZECH REPUBLIC**

A gleefully goofy 14th-century jousting movie, set to an eighties rock soundtrack, directed by the writer of *L.A. Confidential*. The settings are various French cities and Medieval London, but the jousting fields of Rouen, Lagnysur-Marne and London were built on the backlot of Prague's **Barandov Studio** (with the skyline of the contemporary city removed digitally). The banqueting hall and the interiors of Notre Dame and Rouen cathedrals were built in a huge ice-hockey arena on an island in the Vlatva River in central Prague.

KRAMER VS KRAMER

(1979, dir: Robert Benton)
Dustin Hoffman, Meryl Streep, Jane Alexander.
● **NEW YORK CITY**

The school: PS6, Madison Avenue

Tug-of-love tearjerker, mostly set around the swanky Upper East Side of New York. Hoffman and Streep's son attends **PS6 (Public School 6)**, **Madison Avenue** at 82nd Street, near to the Metropolitan Museum of Art. The Copper Kettle, opposite, from which Streep watches, is now gone. Hoffman runs four blocks with his son to the **Lenox Hill Hospital, 100 East 77th Street** at Park Avenue. Also featuring the marvellous silver art deco **Chrysler Building, 405 Lexington Avenue** at East 42nd Street and the **Tweed Courthouse, 52 Chambers Street** in the Civic Center district. The courtroom (unusually, both inside and out) where Streep and Hoffman slug it out for custody of the close-ups, is **Federal Hall, 26 Wall Street** at Nassau Street in the Financial District.

KRAYS, THE

(1990, dir: Peter Medak)
Gary Kemp, Martin Kemp, Billie Whitelaw.
● **LONDON**

Shooting up the pub: Royal Oak, Hackney

'Fortress Vallance', the Krays' actual home, stood at 178 Vallance Road, Bethnal Green, E2, but the area has since been redeveloped. The search for a suitably unchanged terraced street for the Kray's house led to a sidestreet off Trafalgar Road: **32 Caradoc Street**, Greenwich, SE10. The imposing exterior of the Krays' nightclub is **Richmond Theatre, The Green, Richmond** (© *020.8940.0088*), see *Evita* for details. The interior, though, is **Wilton's Music Hall, 1 Grace's Alley, Wellclose Square**, off Cable Street, E1, seen also in *Chaplin* and *Isadora*.

Cornell is gunned down in the Blind Beggar: Bacchus, Hoxton Street, Hoxton

Fortress Vallance, Bethnal Green: Caradoc Street, Greenwich

Currently closed and up for sale, **The Fleece, 160 Abbey Street** at Neckinger, is the pub where the pathetic Jack 'the Hat' gets steaming drunk, before being dragged off by Ronnie's boyfriend Steve, past the **Marquis of Wellington, Druid Street**, under the railway bridge at **Gedling Place**, to the party to end all parties. The pub that gets smashed up is the **Royal Oak, Columbia Road**, by the famous flower market (also seen in *Lock, Stock and Two Smoking Barrels* and *Honest*).

The Krays' club: Richmond Theatre

Off Kennington Road, **Walcot Square** at Sullivan Road is where Reggie Kray's violent reaction to two guys admiring his car sends his wife Frances into hysterics. The real Blind Beggar, where Ronnie, having grown cocky enough, shot Cornell in a pub full of witnesses, much changed and spruced up, can still be seen in Whitechapel. **Bacchus, 177 Hoxton Street**, stands in for it in the movie. **Woolwich Cemetery** is the site of the funeral of Violet Kray.

KUMONOSU-JO (aka *Throne of Blood/Cobweb Castle*)

(1957, dir: Akira Kurosawa)
Toshiro Mifune, Isuzu Yamada, Takashi Shimura.
● **JAPAN**

Kurosawa's terrific adaptation of *Macbeth*. Macbeth's castle was constructed high up on **Mount Fuji**, though the courtyard (complete with sand brought in from Fiji) was recreated in the studio. The mansion is on Japan's **Izu Peninsula**.

KUNDUN

(1997, dir: Martin Scorsese)
Tenzin Thuthob Tsarong, Gyurme Tethong, Tulku Jamyang Kunga Tenzin.
● **MOROCCO**

Scorsese's film about the early life of the Dalai Lama was never going to be an easy prospect, and it put the director on the list of people banned from Tibet. With the actual locations out of the question, Scorsese returned to the country where he filmed his previous controversial film, *The Last Temptation of Christ*, Morocco. The village where the Dalai Lama is born is **Timlougite**, between Ouarzazate and Marrakech. Dungkhar Monastery is actually **La Kasbah de Toubkal**, a field study centre at **Imlil**.

L

The movie première drug bust: Gramercy Place, Hollywood

L.A. CONFIDENTIAL
(1997, dir: Curtis Hanson)
Russell Crowe, Guy Pearce, Kevin Spacey.
● LOS ANGELES, CALIFORNIA

Hanson's stylish fifties-set cop corruption actioner was filmed almost entirely on real locations around LA. Only the decrepit Victory Motel, site of the final shoot-out, is a purpose-built set, constructed among the 'nodding donkey' wells of the **Baldwin Hills** oilfields near Culver City. The *Badge of Honor* TV show is obviously based on *Dragnet*, and similarly uses **LA City Hall** on the LAPD badge as its logo. It's out of City Hall that the cops operate: **200 North Spring Street**, downtown. The office of sleazy journo Sid Hudgens is beneath the illuminated spire and revolving globe of the **Crossroads of the World, 6671 Sunset Boulevard** in Hollywood, a glorious thirties shopping mall designed as an ocean liner, complete with portholes (see *Indecent Proposal* for details). Hudgens sets up the 'movie première pot bust' in a bungalow at **1714 Gramercy Place**, west of Western Avenue just off Hollywood Boulevard in Hollywood. The impressive-looking El Cortez theater, where *When Worlds Collide* is premièring, was an illuminated marquee built onto the front of an imposing, but abandoned, bank building at **5620 Hollywood Boulevard**. Also in Hollywood is the bar where Captain Smith gives back Bud White's gun and badge: **Boardner's, 1652 North Cherokee Avenue** at Hollywood Boulevard (see *Ed Wood* for details).

Vincennes drowns his sorrows: Frolic Room, Hollywood Boulevard

Just a little to the west is Nick's Liquor Store, where Bud (Crowe) first sees Veronica Lake lookalike Lynn Bracken, which

Exley insults Lana Turner: Formosa Cafe, Santa Monica Boulevard

Patchett's house: Lovell House, Dundee Drive

was recreated on **Larchmont Boulevard**, just south of the Paramount Studios on Melrose Avenue. The Nite Owl Cafe, site of the massacre, is in downtown LA: the **J&J Sandwich Shop, 119 East 6th Street**, opposite the **Pacific Electric Building, 610 South Main Street**, where Bud dangles the terrified DA from a window.

The terraced home of Bracken's high-class pimp is Richard Neutra's 1929 **Lovell House**. Neutra's masterpiece was built for vegetarian health freak Lovell (it's known as the Lovell Health House). It's a private residence, **4616 Dundee Drive, Los Feliz**, below the Griffith Observatory, which you can see on the skyline in the movie. The house where the prostitute is being held, supposedly Avalon Street, in South Central, was on **Avenue 28** in the Lincoln Heights district.

Vincennes (Spacey) and Exley (Pearce) pump boxer Leonard Bidwell for info with a bogus promise at **Bellevue and Marion**, in the Echo Park district, opposite Bob's Market, seen in *The Fast and the Furious*. Vincennes downs a drink at the **Frolic Room, 6245 Hollywood Boulevard**, a surviving forties neon-lit bar alongside the Pantages Theater, before finding the body of the murdered actor-cum-hustler in room 203 of the **Hollywood Center Motel, 6720 Sunset Boulevard**, an original twenties motel, enlarged in the 1950s. The Hollywood bar, festooned with celebrity photos, where White and Exley hassle Johnny Stompanato and the 'real' Lana Turner, is another famous landmark, the **Formosa Cafe, 7156 Santa Monica Boulevard** near La Brea Avenue. This Chinese restaurant was a regular hangout for Bogart, Monroe and Gable, among others. You can see it in Frank Darabont's Hollywood blacklist drama *The Majestic*. Stompanato, by the way, was the underworld hood stabbed to death in the bedroom of Turner's Beverly Hills mansion in 1958 – allegedly by her daughter Cheryl Crane.

Mrs Leffert's house, where a body is found in the crawl space, is in **Elysian Park**, while Bracken's 1927 house is on **Wilcox Avenue**, next to the Wilshire Country Club in the Rossmore district of Hollywood. Navarette's hideout, supposedly on the now-redeveloped Bunker Hill, filmed on **San Marino Street** near the intersection of Olympic Boulevard and Hoover Street west of Macarthur Park. Bidwell's house, 'south of Jefferson', was in

The Nite Owl Cafe: J&J Sandwich Shop, East 6th Street

Angelino Heights near Echo Park.

L.A. STORY
(1991, dir: Mick Jackson)
Steve Martin, Victoria Tennant, Sarah Jessica Parker.
● LOS ANGELES, CALIFORNIA

The TV studio: KCET, Sunset Boulevard

The hotdog stand: Tail o'the Pup, San Vicente Boulevard

Amiable romantic satire, set in a determinedly cosy, whitebread Los Angeles. TV station KYOY, where Steve Martin works as a wacky weatherman, is **KCET, 4401 Sunset Boulevard**. Although now devoted to television, it used to be Allied Artists' film studio, and before that, Monogram Pictures. You can see the building in Don Siegel's original *Invasion of the Body Snatchers*. L'Idiot restaurant, with Patrick Stewart as the fearsome maitre d', is the **Ambassador Hotel, 3400 Wilshire Boulevard** (see the 1954 *A Star is Born* for details). The bank is an old Bank of America building at **650 South Spring Street**, a frequently used location seen in another Steve Martin vehicle, *All of Me*, *Marathon Man*, *The Mask* and *Se7en*, among others. The art gallery Martin rollerskates through is the **Los Angeles County Museum of Art, 5905 Wilshire Boulevard**, midtown (*©* 213.857.6000; admission charge), while the gallery where he critiques abstract art is the Museum of Contemporary Art, 250 South Grand Avenue (*©* 213.626.6222). Richard E Grant grabs a bite to eat at the **Tail o'the Pup, 329 San Vicente Boulevard** at Beverly Boulevard, midtown – the fast-food stand in the shape of a giant hot-dog. The 'full service' garage is the **Gilmore Service Station, Auto Repair & Snack Shop, 859 Highland Avenue** at Willoughby.

LACOMBE, LUCIEN
(1974, dir: Louis Malle)
Pierre Blaise, Aurore Clement, Holger Lowenadler.
● FRANCE

Lacombe is a young peasant who, on being turned down by the Resistance, drifts into collaboration with the Nazis and pays the price. The town is **Figeac**, on the Cele River. Standing at the junction of the N140, N122, D122 and D653 roads in the north of the Midi-Pyrenees region, 45 miles northwest of Rodez, the town has an 11th century church and a mint dating from the 13th century.

LADRI DI BICICLETTE (aka *The Bicycle Thieves*)
(1948, dir: Vittorio De Sica)
Lamberto Maggiorani, Enzo Staiola, Lianella Carell.
● ROME, ITALY

Long-term unemployed worker Maggiorani finally manages to get a bill-posting job, only to find his much-needed bike has been stolen. De Sica's neo-realist classic, a staple of earnest film societies for decades, was shot on the streets of Rome. Maggiorani's home is in the dismal government housing project of **Citta Valmelaina** on the Via Salaria in Rome's northern outskirts. Maggiorani drops off his son at **Porta Pingiana**, and picks him up at night at the piazza at **Porta Pia** in the Montesacro district. Together, they look for the stolen bicycle in the market at **Piazza Vittoria**, before glimpsing the thief at the market of **Porta Portese** to the south of the Trastevere district.

LADY FROM SHANGHAI, THE
(1948, dir: Orson Welles)
Orson Welles, Rita Hayworth, Everett Sloane.
● MEXICO; CALIFORNIA

Welles' weird film noir used locations in Mexico and northern California. The yacht scenes were shot on board Errol Flynn's boat, the *Zaca*, at **Acapulco Bay**, in Mexico.

The aquarium: Steinhart Aquarium, Golden Gate Park

Rita Hayworth dives into the ocean from the landmark **Morro Rock**, Morro Bay, northwest of San Luis Obispo on the southern California coast.

The restaurant was Sally Stanford's Valhalla, since taken over by the Chart House chain. It's still in existence as the **Chart House, 201 Bridgway**, Sausalito (*©* 415.332.0804), over the Golden Gate Bridge from San Francisco. The aquarium is the **Steinhart Aquarium, Music Concourse**, part of the California Academy of Sciences in Golden Gate Park (*©* 415.750.7145, www.cal-academy.org/aquarium). The most famous sequence, the dazzling Hall of Mirrors shoot out, was of course filmed in the studio, where a near-full-size funhouse was built at Columbia Studios. The exteriors, though, were Playland, now gone, which used to stand at the western end of Golden Gate Park.

LADYKILLERS, THE
(1955, dir: Alexander Mackendrick)
Alec Guinness, Katie Johnson, Herbert Lom.
● LONDON

Classic Ealing black comedy, with little old lady Katie Johnson unwittingly giving houseroom to Alec Guinness (in a role intended for Alistair Sim) and his gang of robbers, posing as a string quintet. The locale is London's King's Cross, in the days before the area

The robbery: Battle Bridge Road, King's Cross

Dumping the bodies: Copenhagen Tunnel, King's Cross

became synony-mous with drugs and prostitution. The robbery begins by the Victorian gasometers in **Goods Way**, behind King's Cross Station, and actually takes place in **Battle Bridge Road**. The stretch of cobbled road is a familiar location seen in films as diverse as *The Missionary*, *L'accompagnatrice*, *Alfie*, *Backbeat* and *Chaplin*. The area is sadly threatened by redevelopment.

Johnson's house seems to be at the end of a cul-de-sac facing St Pancras Station in Euston Road, NW1. From the view of the station, the house is clearly meant to be in Argylle Street, running south from Euston Road. Yet Argylle Street is not a cul-de-sac, and the railway lines run north. Although the view *from* the house is Argylle Street, the house itself was in Frederica Street, about a mile to the north, running west from Caledonian Road facing Pentonville Prison. It was no more than a set at the end of this small cul-de-sac, built, in keeping with the off-kilter storyline, with no true right-angles. Regrettably, the whole street has since been redeveloped as a housing estate and no trace remains of the old houses seen in the movie.

The tunnel entrance where the bodies are dropped into goods trailers was indeed behind Frederica Street. It's the entrance to the **Copenhagen Tunnel**. There are three separate tunnels, and the one used for the movie conveniently serves the line to the King's Cross goods yards. It can't be seen any longer from Frederica Street, but Vale Royal, a cul-de-sac running east from York Way, N7, leads to a car park from which you can see the weed covered plot of land where Alec Guinness and Herbert Lom had their final shoot out, and the decayed grandeur of the tunnel entrances. The lethal old-fashioned signals have gone.

The Coen brothers' 2004 remake transfers the action to **Natchez**, Mississippi.

LAND THAT TIME FORGOT, THE

(1974, dir: Kevin Connor)
Doug McClure, John McEnery, Susan Penhaligon.
● **CANARY ISLANDS**

A shipwrecked crew find themselves on an island of pre-historic monsters, in this adventure taken from an Edgar Rice Burroughs story. The prehistoric landscape can be found at **La Palma**, Santa Cruz de Tenerife, Canary Islands.

LARA CROFT TOMB RAIDER

(2001, dir: Simon West)
Angelina Jolie, Iain Glen, Noah Taylor.
● **LONDON; SUFFOLK; CAMBODIA; ICELAND; VENICE, ITALY; BERKSHIRE**

The exterior of Lara Croft's mansion is **Hatfield House** (see Tim Burton's *Batman* for details), though the lavish interior is a studio set. Lord Croft's stone 'tent' tomb in the grounds was added for the film, inspired by the tomb of explorer Sir Richard Burton, which you can see in Mortlake Cemetery. The council of the Illuminati appears to be held in the

The London home of villainous lawyer Manfred: Willis Faber, Trinity Court, Trinity Square Gardens

church of **Santa Maria Della Salute, Venice**, but you'll no doubt recognise the chamber as the **Painted Hall** of **Greenwich Naval College** (see *The Madness of King George* for details). Lara rides her bike across **Tower Bridge** on the way to the auction house, and returns roaring through **Leadenhall Market**. The market stands at the foot of the new Lloyds Building (*tube: Bank*), close to The Leaky Cauldron in the first *Harry Potter* film, and opposite Pizza Express, once the Thai restaurant where Russell Crowe was assigned his mission in *Proof of Life*.

The London home of villainous lawyer Manfred (Glen) is the vast and elaborate office of insurance company **Willis Faber, 10 Trinity Court** (formerly the Port of London Authority building), near the Tower of London. It featured in *Two Way Stretch* and *Sweeney!*. The exotic interior, with its Indian-style carvings, is **Elveden Hall**, a private house on the A11 about four miles west of Thetford in Suffolk, the site of the eerie orgy in Stanley Kubrick's *Eyes Wide Shut*.

The Cambodian temple complex, where Croft must retrieve half of the triangular MacGuffin, is at **Siem Reap** in Cambodia, where she arrives, with game-style ease, onto **Phnom Bakheng**, a hill topped by a Hindu temple (though the site later became a Buddhist centre). She tools up and scoots off in her Land Rover in front of the sacred **Bayon** temple, in **Angkor Thon**, its 54 towers each bearing four enigmatic smiling faces. The most spectacular temple of all, entwined with enormous trees, where Croft encounters the mysterious girl, is **Ta Prohm**. The most famous, **Angkor Wat** itself (the largest religious monument in the world and a World Heritage site), looms over the Cambodian village (no more than a set built around a small ornamental pond). The 1965 film of Joseph Conrad's *Lord Jim*, with Peter O'Toole, is one of the few other films to be shot at Angkor Wat. As Cambodia recovers from its troubled past, a modest tourism industry is beginning to blossom, learning to balance economic gain with inevitable concerns about the effect on the ancient buildings. There's no public transport between the monuments, so check for guided tours.

Lara boards the helicopter for Siberia at **RAF Odiham**, in north Hampshire. It's not a terribly long flight – the arrival was filmed on **Salisbury Plain** in Hampshire (it's costly to fly choppers out to Iceland, which was standing in for Siberia). Another bit of British fakery has **Windsor Great Park**, Berkshire, briefly standing in for the steamy Cambodian jungle as Lara sprints through the undergrowth.

LARA CROFT TOMB RAIDER: THE CRADLE OF LIFE

(2003, dir: Jan de Bont)
Angelina Jolie, Gerard Butler, Ciarán Hinds.
● **LONDON; GREECE; HONG KONG, CHINA; KENYA; WALES**

As with *The Inn of the Sixth Happiness* and *The Most Dangerous Man in the World*, north Wales stands in for the Far East, with filming at a disused slate quarry near **Carmel** and the craggy slopes at **Llyl Gwynant**, where a fantastic thatched village was built. Real Chinese locations include **Hong Kong**, at the the **Times Square** shopping mall, **Causeway Bay**; **Ocean Terminal Mall**; and the double decker tram on **Hennessy Road**. There was more filming at **Mount Kilimanjiro** in Kenya, and in Nairobi. The opening scenes, wedding, earthquake and the appearance of an underwater city is **Santorini**, Greece.

LASSIE COME HOME

(1943, dir: Fred M Wilcox)
Roddy McDowall, Donald Crisp, Elizabeth Taylor.
● **CALIFORNIA; WASHINGTON**

First of the Lassie movies, although, as everyone now knows, Lassie was a laddie. Filming took place at the glorious **Point Lobos State Reserve**, a stretch of rocky coastline four miles south of Carmel on Highway 1, central California, and also at **Lake Chelan**, Washington State.

LAST ACTION HERO

(1993, dir: John McTiernan)
Arnold Schwarzenegger, Art Carney, Charles Dance.
● **NEW YORK CITY; LOS ANGELES, CALIFORNIA**

Mega-hype, mega-budget, mega-star, even ads on NASA rockets, but this surprisingly witty in-joke of a movie still bombed in the summer of dino-mania. The interi-

Interior of the Pandora Theater: Orpheum Theater, South Broadway

or of the Pandora Theater, where Austin O'Brien uses his magic ticket to enter the movie world, is the beautifully preserved 1926 **Orpheum Theater, 842 South Broadway**, downtown LA, still functioning as a movie house (and seen in plenty of films from *Ed Wood* to *Dead Again*). Schwarzenegger's fictitious blockbuster, *Jack Slater IV*, premières on the other coast, at the **RKO Twin Theater, Times Square** in New York, where a giant inflatable Arnie sways about on the sidewalk.

The house where Schwarzenegger almost gets blown up is on the **1100 block of Angelina Street**, downtown LA. In a re-run of *Terminator*

Jack Slater IV première: RKO Twin Theater, Times Square

2's road-into-flood channel leap, a car flies into the LA River channel at the **First Street Bridge**. Leo the Fart's lavish mob funeral filmed atop the roof of the 502-room **Hyatt Regency Hotel, 200 South Pine Avenue** at Shoreline Drive in Long Beach, south LA. The La Brea Tar Pits, in reality on Wilshire Boulevard, midtown, were recreated alongside the Hyatt. O'Brien's school, Lincoln Elementary, is a standing set built on the Culver City lot during the twenties, while Elsinore in the *Hamlet* fantasy scene is the castle built for Francis Coppola's *Bram Stoker's Dracula*.

LAST DETAIL, THE

(1973, dir: Hal Ashby)
Jack Nicholson, Otis Young, Randy Quaid.
● **VIRGINIA; NEW HAMPSHIRE; MASSACHUSETTS; WASHINGTON DC; NEW YORK CITY**

Nicholson and Young are naval officers escorting Quaid to jail, and giving him one last night of freedom on the way. Quaid is taken from the US naval base at **Norfolk**, Virginia, to **Portsmouth**, New Hampshire. Quaid visits his mother's house in Washington DC. Next stop is New York City; then Quaid loses his virginity in a brothel in Boston, Massachusetts, with filming at **South End** and **Boston Common**.

LAST EMPEROR, THE

(1987, dir: Bernardo Bertolucci)
John Lone, Joan Chen, Peter O'Toole.
● **CHINA; ITALY**

Bertolucci's visually luscious epic, charting the life of Pu Yi, the last imperial ruler of China, scored a first in being able to use the **Forbidden City** in **Beijing**. The young

The emperor's childhood: The Forbidden City, Beijing

emperor gets the first intimation of his awesome position when he runs from **The Hall of Supreme Harmony**, under the dazzling yellow canopy, to glimpse assembled masses on the **Courtyard of Supreme Harmony**. The lakes of the Forbidden City were in a state of disrepair, so the lakeside scene was filmed at the **Kunming Lake** in the gardens of **Yiheyuan**, the **Summer Palace**, in the Haidian District, about eight miles northwest of downtown Beijing (*admission charge*). Studio sets, including the young emperor's home and the Dowager Empress's bedroom, were built in the Beijing Studios (where Tarantino would later film much of *Kill Bill*).

The opening, 'Manchuria, 1950', is the railway station at **Changchun**, capital of Jilin Province, an industrial city in the northeast. Here you can also find **Manchukuo Palace**, where Pu Yi is installed as a puppet ruler by the Japanese.

The arrival of Johnson (O'Toole), cut from the theatrical release, and his departure, were filmed at the port of **Dalian**, dubbed 'the Hong Kong of the North'. More scenes were shot around the colonial buildings of **Zhongshan Square**.

After the 1967 Cultural Revolution, the freed Pu Yi sees his old prison governor being marched off for re-education in a street alongside **Tian'anmen Square**. He eventually finds some kind of redemption working as a gardener in the **Beijing Botanical Garden, Wo Fo Si Road**, east of Xinshan Park in the Haidian District (*www.beijingbg.com/engjbg1.htm*).

It's not all China, though. Sets were built at the famous Cinecitta Studios outside Rome, and the prison courtyard is alongside the **Centro Sperimentale di Cinomatogtafia, via Tuscolana 1524**, built nearby in 1935 at the behest of Mussolini. The Tientsin palace, where Pu Yi enjoys a gilded lifestyle in the twenties, is the **Moorish Salon** of the **Palazzo dei Congressi** (Palace of Congress), **Salsomaggiore** (✆ *0524.571664, www.salsocongressi.it*), near to Parma. Built as the Grand Hotel des Thermes in the city famed for its thermal baths, the palace is now a conference and exhibition centre.

LAST HOUSE ON THE LEFT, THE

(1972, dir: Wes Craven)
Sandra Cassel, Lucy Grantham, David Hess.
● **CONNECTICUT; NEW YORK CITY**

Wes Craven's first movie, a cult shocker loosely based on Ingmar Bergman's *The Virgin Spring*, was made on a shoestring, guerilla-style, in **Westport**, I-95, on the southwest coast of Connecticut. The woods belong to a public reservoir just outside town. More scenes were shot in **Manhattan**.

LAST OF THE MOHICANS, THE

(1992, dir: Michael Mann)
Daniel Day-Lewis, Russell Means, Madeleine Stowe.
● **NORTH CAROLINA**

The climactic fight: Hickory Nut Falls, Chimney Rock Park

Fenimore Cooper's story of the French-Indian wars, made on location in the Blue Mountains of North Carolina, at **Massacre Valley** in Burke County, and further west on Highway 40, in the grounds of the **Biltmore Estate, Asheville** (see *Being There* for details). Much of the filming took place in **Chimney Rock Park**, US 74 and 64, 25 miles southeast of Asheville, where you'll find **Inspiration Point**, site of the love scene between Day-Lewis and Stowe, and **Hickory Nut Falls**, where the climactic fight takes place. The park's map lists the movie sites.

A 1936 Hollywood version, with Randolph Scott, didn't stray much further than standard Hollywood locales the **Iverson Ranch, Iverson Lane, Chatsworth**, about 30 miles north of LA; **Kern River**; and **Sherwood Lake**.

LAST ORDERS

(2001, dir: Fred Schepisi)
Michael Caine, Tom Courtenay, Bob Hoskins.

● **LONDON; KENT**

Two pubs are used to represent Graham Swift's fictitious Bermondsey bar, the Coach and Horses. The exterior is **The Wishing Well, 79 Choumert Road** at Bellenden Road, Peckham, but the interior was the defunct **Larkhall Tavern, Larkhall Lane**, Clapham, which served up its last pint in 1999 and is being converted into luxury flats. Jack (Caine) passes on the arcane mysteries of the butcher trade to his son in the, now disused, western section of **Smithfield Market** (seen also in *Catch Us If You Can*), and his butcher shop, Dodds and Son, was at **192 Bellenden Road** at Danby Street, now much smartened up. Across the street stood Vic's (Courtenay) funeral home, at **157 Bellenden Road**. Ray (Hoskins) and Amy (Helen Mirren) reminisce in the grounds of **St Thomas Hospital**, on the Thames Embankment opposite Westminster.

Jack's ashes are taken to be scattered, via a brief tour of **Canterbury Cathedral**, and a stop for a liquid lunch at 400 year-old coaching inn **The Royal Victoria and Bull Hotel, 16-18 High Street, Rochester** (✆ *01634.846266, www.rvandb.co.uk*). The **Chatham War Memorial**, on Great Lines, northeast of the town overlooking Chatham, is the stop-off which triggers wartime memories, on the road to **Margate Pier**, where Jack's mates say their last goodbyes.

LAST PICTURE SHOW, THE

(1971, dir: Peter Bogdanovich)
Jeff Bridges, Timothy Bottoms, Cloris Leachman.
● **TEXAS**

Bogdanovich never came close to equalling this achingly atmospheric evocation of smalltown life in the fifties, from Larry McMurtry's novel. The one-street town of

The picture house, Anarene: Archer City

Anarene, Texas, is actually **Archer City**, Texas – "one street and a traffic light" as a local described it. The burned-out shell of the Royal picture house is still crumbling away, at **115 East Main Street**.

LAST SAMURAI, THE

(2003, dir: Edward Zwick)
Tom Cruise, Ken Watanabe, William Atherton.
● **JAPAN; NEW ZEALAND; LOS ANGELES, CALIFORNIA**

Zwick's account of the passing of the Bushido code with the Western opening-up of Japan is predictable, but he brings the emotional epic sweep of *Glory* to this blending of *Kagemusha* and *The Wild Bunch*.

Katsumoto's temple: Sho-sha-zan Engyo-ji Temple, Himeji City

The Imperial Palace of the emperor Meiji in Tokyo: Chion-In Temple, Kyoto

Katsumoto's (Watanabe) temple is **Sho-sha-zan Engyo-ji Temple** in **Himeji City**, 50km west of Kobe. The temple is atop Mount Shosa. There's a 20 minute bus ride from Himeji, a short cable car ride and a 15 minute walk. The Imperial Palace of the emperor Meiji in Tokyo is the 400 year-old **Chion-In Temple, Kyoto**, where you can see the imposing flight of steps.

Much of the filming was in New Zealand, on the hillsides of the **Uruti Valley**, where the Japanese village was constructed, with **Mount Taranaki** standing in for Mount Fuji. The port where the dissipated Nathan Algren (Cruise) arrives in Japan is a set built at **New Plymouth**, and the parade ground, where the Japanese troops are trained and Algren invites a young recruit to shoot him, is the **Pukekura Sports Ground, Pukekura Park**, New Plymouth. The battle in the fog was filmed in **Mangamahoe Forest**, outside the town.

The restaurant, where Algren is introduced to the Japanese gentlemen, is the **Moorish Room** of the amazing **Castle Green Apartments, 99 South Raymond Avenue, Pasadena** (*www.castlegreen.com*). For full details, see *The Sting*.

There was more filming on the Warner Bros backlot in Burbank. If you want to see how the sophistication of CGI is making location spotting difficult, look at the scene set in San Francisco at the opening, when Algren walks past the cable cars. This was filmed on the New York Street of the Warner Bros Burbank lot. The view of the bay was added digitally.

LAST TANGO IN PARIS

(1972, dir: Bernardo Bertolucci)
Marlon Brando, Maria Schneider, Jean-Pierre Léaud.
● PARIS, FRANCE

The last tango: Salle Wagram, avenue de Wagram

Bertolucci's tragic romance was lusciously photographed on location around Paris by Vittorio Storaro. Tormented widower Brando meets Schneider on the **Pont de Bir-Hakeim**, in the 15th and 16th arrondissements. Originally the Passy Viaduct, the bridge was renamed in 1949 to commemorate battles against Rommel in the Libyan desert. See it also in *Ascenseur Pour l'Echafaud* and *Trois Couleurs: Bleu*.

1 rue Jules Verne, the apartment in which Brando and Schneider energetically consummate the perversely anonymous romance, is **1 rue de l'Alboni** at the end of the bridge in Passy. The wrought iron doorway can be seen at the top of the steps at the northern end of the bridge.

At the foot of the steps you'll recognise, somewhat revamped, the bar from which Schneider makes a phone call. It's the **Kennedy Eiffel Bar, avenue du President Kennedy**.

The apartment: Rue de l'Alboni, Passy

More drastically changed is the salon where Brando and Schneider disrupt the tango competition at the movie's climax. The old, neo-Classical **Salle Wagram** has been remodelled as a disco. You can find it just down the road from the Arc de Triomphe at **39 avenue de Wagram**.

LAST TEMPTATION OF CHRIST, THE

(1988, dir: Martin Scorsese)
Willem Dafoe, Harvey Keitel, Barbara Hershey.
● MOROCCO

Scorsese's absurdly controversial, but actually quite reverential, version of Nikos Kazantzakis' fantasia on the life of Christ took years to get off the ground, and was obliged to use Morocco as a stand-in for the Holy Land. Nazareth and Magdala were both filmed in the village of **Oumnast** (Umnast), about 15 miles south of Marrakech.

Jerusalem was going to be a set until the filmmakers discovered **Mekenes** (Meknes), which provided the **Moulay Ismael Stables** for the interior of the Temple, the Passover baths and the palace of Pontius Pilate. Sultan Moulay Ismael ruled Mekenes for 55 years, from 1672 to 1727, during which time he embarked on a massive building programme and turned the city into a spectacular walled capital with over 50 palaces. The stables are part of his Villa Imperiale, a huge complex of palaces, gardens, barracks and the stables below Mekenes' Medina. From the Ville Nouvelle, cross the River Oued Boufekrane which divides the city, and take the Rue Rouamzine and Rue Dar Smen to the gateway, Bab Mansour. Moulay Ismael's Mausoleum is here, but past that, a corridor leads to the Heri as-Souani (or the Dar el-Mar). Called the 'stables', these high-vaulted rooms were, in all probability, store rooms and granaries.

The final 35-minute 'temptation' sequence was filmed in the Atlas Mountains and around the Roman ruins of **Volubilis**, about 20 miles north of Mekenes.

LAVENDER HILL MOB, THE

(1951, dir: Charles Crichton)
Alec Guinness, Stanley Holloway, Sidney James.
● LONDON; MIDDLESEX; PARIS, FRANCE

Mild-mannered Alec Guinness masterminds a daring bullion robbery in this Ealing classic, and as the

The police chase ends in chaos: Bramley Arms, Notting Hill

plot involves smuggling gold disguised as Eiffel Tower souvenirs, there's filming in Paris, but most of the movie was shot around post-war London. The airport scene was originally scripted as Victoria Station, but it cost ten times as much to close down a major London terminus than to close a small Home Counties airfield, and the scene was shot at **Northolt Airport**, Middlesex.

Queen Victoria Street is the site of the bullion robbery, in front of the burned out shell of Wren's **St Nicholas Cole Abbey**. The film was made in 1951 and the ravaged city shows the damage inflicted during the Blitz (the spire of the church has now been restored). Guinness later escapes from the stolen police car by running off down **Cheapside**, past another damaged Wren church, **St Mary-le-Bow**. The London chase ends at the **Bramley Arms** in Notting Hill, seen also in Harold Pinter's reverse-timescale drama *Betrayal*, as well as cult rock movies *Quadrophenia* and *Sid and Nancy*.

LAWN DOGS

(1998, dir: John Duigan)
Kathleen Quinlan, Sam Rockwell, Mischa Barton.
● KENTUCKY

Lawn man Rockwell's friendship with a ten year-old girl is misunderstood in Duigan's smalltown drama, made in **Prospect**, on the Cincinnati Highway, Route 42, about five miles north of Louisville, Kentucky.

LAWRENCE OF ARABIA

(1962, dir: David Lean)
Peter O'Toole, Omar Sharif, Alec Guinness.
● JORDAN; SPAIN; MOROCCO; LONDON;
SURREY; CALIFORNIA

The Cairo hotel: Palaçio Español, Seville

Lean's last really great movie, before his taste for the overblown ballooned. The opening scene, of Lawrence's fatal motorbike ride (supposedly in Wales), is **Chobham**, Surrey. Lawrence's memorial service did actually use the steps in front of **St Paul's Cathedral** in London, but the interior was recreated in a Spanish studio. In fact, all the interiors, and much of the rest of the film, was shot in Spain. The town of Aqaba was built at a beach called **Playa del Algorocibo** near Carboneros, close to Almeria in southern Spain. The attack on the train filmed at **Genovese Beach, San Jose** on **Cabo del Gato** (Cape of the Cat) nearby.

The courtyard of the Officers' Club, Cairo: Alfonso XIII Hotel, San Fernando, Seville

For many of the Middle Eastern settings, Lean used the heavily Moorish city of **Seville**, particularly the vast complex of buildings in the **Parque de**

Maria Luisa, Avenida de Isabel la Catolica, built for the disastrous 1929 Spanish-American exhibition. Here you can find the Cairo hotel, where Lawrence's companion is refused a drink after the desert crossing, which is the, currently empty and rather dilapidated, **Palaçio Español**, a semi-circular arcaded building in the **Plaza de España** (seen more recently in *Star Wars Episode II: Attack of the Clones*). Jerusalem's civic buildings are the **Plaza of the Americas** (seen in John Milius's *The Wind and the Lion*) just to the south, while Damascus town hall, the Arab council chamber, is the nearby circular **El Casino, Avenida de Maria Luisa**. Also in Seville is the courtyard of the Officers' Club, Cairo, which is the central court of the luxurious **Alfonso XIII Hotel, 2 San Fernando 41004** (© *5422.2850*). Lawrence and Allenby meet in another Seville landmark, the **Casa de Pilatos, Plaza de Pilatos** (© *5422.5055; admission charge*), built in 1519, and supposedly a copy of Pontius Pilate's surprisingly 16th century Jerusalem house.

Lawrence and Allenby meet: Casa de Pilatos, Plaza de Pilatos, Seville

The Arab council chamber: El Casino, Avenida de Maria Luisa

But of course, the real visual splendour of *Lawrence* lies in its breathtaking Jordanian desertscapes. Lawrence's first introduction to the desert is the black basalt landscape of **Jebel Tubayq**, near the Saudi Arabian border, as is much of the trekking and the caravan across the Nefud. Feisal's camp and the well where Lawrence first gets his Arab drag, are the spectacular red cliffs of **Wadi Rumm**, 20 miles north of the Gulf of Aqaba.

Omar Sharif's spectacular camel ride entrance (of course, Sharif wasn't actually in this, his most famous scene) used the mudflats at **Jafr** in Jordan, as did the rescue of the lost Arab boy, Gasim. More scenes were filmed in Morocco, at **Ait Benhaddou**, a spectacular village made up of several small kasbahs (fortresses), about 15 miles northwest of Ouarzazate. Its red towers have been seen in *Gladiator*, *The Last Days of Sodom and Gomorrah* and *The Jewel of the Nile*. Just outside Ouarzazate, the giant Glaoui Kasbah was converted into a hotel, now the Kasbah Tifoultoutte, specially to house the cast. It's about three miles from Ourzazate on the P31 (© *04.88.46.36*).

Extra desert

Jerusalem's civic buildings: Plaza of the Americas, Seville

shots were filmed in the States, on the **Imperial Sand Dunes**, Highway 78, east of El Centro, southern California close to the Mexican border.

LAYER CAKE

(2004, dir: Matthew Vaughn)
Daniel Craig, Michael Gambon, Colm Meaney.
● **LONDON; BUCKINGHAMSHIRE; SURREY; AMSTERDAM**

Daniel Craig's home: Queen's Gate Mews, Kensington

The opening school-of-Ritchie voiceover didn't bode well, but while Mr Madonna plumbed the depths with *Swept Away*, then found a shovel and kept digging with *Revolver*, his one-time producer pulls off the unbelievable feat of producing a watchable London gangster movie. There's little new (apart from the new James Bond, of course), but it's carried off with more attention to plot and character than "cor look at me, ain't I 'ard" slang.

Although loudmouth Duke and even louder Slasher are briefly seen in Amsterdam, the film is shot in, and around, London. Craig (the character remains unnamed throughout the movie) lives at **7 Queen's Gate Mews, Kensington**, SW7. The mews has already featured in two screen classics: it's where the unfortunate chauffeur gets his head shaved in *Performance* and the location for the video of Benny Hill's 'Ernie, Fastest Milkman in the West'. Oh, and that flat used to belong to Guy Ritchie (OK, that's definitely the last mention).

Craig is summoned by Jimmy Price to **Stoke Park House, Stoke Poges** near Slough in Buckinghamshire (coincidentally, twice used as a Bond location: see *Tomorrow Never Dies* for details). His mission, to track down the missing wild-child daughter of crime boss Eddie Temple (Gambon).

The nightclub where Craig bumps into Duke's pushy nephew Sidney and the eager Tammy is **Pacha, Terminus Place, Victoria**, SW1 (© *0795.824.0926, www.pacha-london.com*). He watches helplessly as sidekick Morty indulges in a bit of the old ultra-violence (tea as a lethal weapon – how did *The Avengers* miss that one?) in the lovely black-tiled, 30s-style **Regency Cafe, 17-19 Regency Street** at Page Street, Victoria.

Craig invites Tammy for a spot of afternoon delight at the swish, Philippe Starck-designed **St Martins Lane Hotel, 45 St Martin's Lane, Covent Garden**, WC2 (© *020.7300.5500, www.stmartinslane.com*). Unfortunately, while Tammy is slipping into her perfectly gratuitous sus-

Sidekick Morty indulges in a bit of ultra-violence: Regency Cafe, Regency Street, Victoria

pender belt, Craig is abducted in a laundry trolley, finding himself dangled upside-down from the roof of a half-built highrise. The rooftop, where he's filled in on

Meeting Eddie Temple in the library: Athenaeum Club, Pall Mall

Jimmy's duplicity by kingpin Eddie himself, is **1 West India Quay** at Hertsmere Road, E14, near Canary Wharf, Docklands (the lower floors now house the Marriott International Hotel).

Settling the score with Jimmy at his luxurious house at **St George's Hill, Weybridge**, Surrey, Craig impresses Temple at a meeting in the library of the **Athenaeum Club, 107 Pall Mall** – though its entrance is on the northwest corner of Waterloo Place, SW1. One of the more staid and severe of the London gentlemen's clubs, this august establishment had previously been featured in Lindsay Anderson's anarchic *O Lucky Man!*, SAS actioner *Who Dares Wins* and David Drury's dark paranoia thriller *Defence of the Realm*, as well as providing interiors for *Wilde*.

Trying to rid himself of fearsome Serbian killer Dragan, Craig greets northern hitman Mr Lucky from the train at **Paddington Station**, and sets a trap, which goes horribly wrong, alongside the statue of General Wolfe at **Royal Observatory** in **Greenwich** Park (*www.rog.nmm.ac.uk*).

There's a great nighttime helicopter shot of Craig and his crew driving south over **Southwark Bridge**, before the resolution at Temple's office, which was built in the vast Heinz Storage Facility at **Premier Park, Park Royal**, Stonebridge Park, west London. Fittingly, it's the largest of its kind in the country.

LE MANS

(1971, dir: Lee H Katzin)
Steve McQueen, Siegfried Rauch, Elga Andersen.
● **FRANCE**

The racetrack through Le Mans was taken over for twelve weeks for McQueen's car race movie. The old historic town of **Le Mans** lies 125 miles southwest of Paris on the River Sarthe. An excellent motor museum is attached to the racing circuit. You can see another side of this historic town in *Cyrano De Bergerac*.

LEAGUE OF EXTRAORDINARY GENTLEMEN, THE

(2003, dir: Stephen Norrington)
Sean Connery, Peta Wilson, Stuart Townsend.
● **CZECH REPUBLIC; MALTA**

Norrington's film of the graphic novel is too compromised and too slam-bang to do justice to the fascinating conceit that all late Victorian fantasy fiction actually happened. It was shot entirely in the Czech Republic, even the opening Kenya scene, where the Britannia Club was built on farmland about an hour from Prague (though the basic set was much enhanced with CGI).

The entrance to the London club to which Allan Quartermaine (Connery) is summoned is the home of the Czech Philharmonic Orchestra, concert hall **Rudolfimun, Palachovo namesti 1** (1 Palach Square). The library, where M (Richard Roxburgh) begins to assemble the league, is the **Strahov Library** in the **Strahov Monastery** on the route to Prague Castle, but Dorian Gray's (Townsend) library is no more than a studio set, as was the city of Venice, built outdoors at **CKD**, a former heavy machinery factory in Prague.

LEAGUE OF THEIR OWN, A

(1992, dir: Penny Marshall)
Geena Davis, Tom Hanks, Madonna.
● **ILLINOIS; INDIANA; KENTUCKY; NEW YORK**

The dance: Fitzgerald's, West Roosevelt Road, Berwyn

Davis leads a women's baseball team in this comedy, made largely in **Chicago** and its northern suburb, **Evanston**. Harvey Field is **Wrigley Field, 10060 West Addison Street** at North Clark Street, home of the Chicago Cubs in the Wrigleyville district of northern Chicago. Racine Field is **Bosse Field, Garvin Park** between North Main Street and Heidelbach Street, Evanston. The bar, where the team lets rip at the dance, is **Fitzgerald's, 6615 West Roosevelt Road, Berwyn,** a western suburb of Chicago. This popular bar can also be seen in *The Color of Money* and *Adventures in Babysitting*. To find it, take the Des Plains A Branch 'el' to Harlem Avenue, Berwyn.

Garry Marshall's estate is the **Cantigny Mansion, One South 151 Winfield Road, Wheaton**, two miles north of I-88, west of Chicago. Formerly home to the publisher of the *Chicago Tribune*, the mansion is open to the public (*www.rrmtf.org/cantigny*). The various small towns were found around Indiana, while the boarding house is on the corner of **Fifth Street and Main Street, Henderson**, Kentucky. The movie ends tearily at the **National Baseball Hall of Fame and Museum, 25 Main Street, Cooperstown**, New York State (© *607.547.7200, www.baseballhalloffame.org/index.htm*).

LEATHER BOYS, THE

(1963, dir: Sidney J Furie)
Colin Campbell, Dudley Sutton, Rita Tushingham.
● **LONDON; SUSSEX**

The biker hangout: Ace Café, North Circular Road

Slice of working class sixties life, filmed entirely on location by Canadian Furie. Campbell's marriage to Tushingham is rocky enough, when gay biker

Sutton comes along to confuse the poor lad. The holiday camp is the old Butlin's Camp at **Bognor Regis** on the south coast of Sussex. The biker café is the **Ace Café** (*www.ace-cafe-london.com*) on London's **North Circular Road**, A406, near Stonebridge Park tube station. Built as a lorry stop in 1938, and rebuilt in 1949, its 24-hour service led to it becoming a legendary biker hangout. The café closed its doors in 1969, but has recently been restored and reopened after a long campaign.

LEAVING LAS VEGAS

(1995, dir: Mike Figgis)
Nicolas Cage, Elisabeth Shue, Julian Sands.
● **NEVADA; CALIFORNIA**

Shue and Cage talk beneath the Circus Circus clown

Nicolas Cage gives it all up to drink himself to death in Las Vegas. The LA bar of the opening scenes is **Boardner's, 1652 North Cherokee Avenue** at Hollywood Boulevard (see *Ed Wood* for details). He takes a hooker to the **Saharan Motor Hotel, 7212 Sunset Boulevard** at Alta Vista Boulevard in Hollywood (see *Species* for details).

And although the Vegas exteriors are real enough, the casino interiors were shot 90 miles south in **Laughlin**, on the Arizona border. Founded in 1966 by Don Laughlin, the town has grown to become a mini-Vegas with small-scale counterparts of its big sister's casinos. The movie was shot in the Gold River Casino and Resort. Since bought up by entrepreneur Alan Paulson, it's now the **River Palms Resort Casino, 2700 South Casino Drive** (© *702.298.2242*).

Leaving LA, Cage takes one of the world's great drives, the six-hour trip on I-15 through the Mojave Desert to Vegas. The movie makes up for its Laughlin interiors by setting key scenes in front of a slew of Strip landmark casinos. Cage first bumps into hooker Elisabeth Shue at a stop light on Las Vegas Boulevard outside the **Flamingo Hilton and Tower, 3555 Las Vegas Boulevard South**, the starting point of the new Las Vegas, opened in 1946 by 'Bugsy' Siegel (see *Bugsy* for the history). Shue, in turn, finds Cage in front of **Bally's, 3645 South Las Vegas Boulevard**. They talk in front of the giant illuminated clown of **Circus Circus,**

Shue is picked up by college jocks: Excalibur, Las Vegas Boulevard South

Cage bumps into Shue: The Flamingo, Las Vegas Boulevard South

2880 Las Vegas Boulevard South. Shue is picked up by the college jocks on the aerial walkway in front of the toytown turrets of **Excalibur, 3850 Las Vegas Boulevard South**. The waterfall, where she hails a cab after the rape, is at **Mirage, 3400 Las Vegas Boulevard South**.

The Harvard square: All Saints Church, North Euclid Avenue, Pasadena

Neptune's Beauty Nook: South Myrtle Avenue, Monrovia.

LEGALLY BLONDE

(2001, dir: Robert Luketic)
Reese Witherspoon, Luke Wilson, Selma Blair.

● **LOS ANGELES, CALIFORNIA; MASSACHUSSETS; LONDON**

Superficially ditsy Beverly Hills blonde Elle Woods (Witherspoon) proves she can cut it with the blue bloods at Harvard Law School in this female bonding comedy. Although there are a few establishing shots around Harvard – **Harvard Square**, as Witherspoon arrives – the movie was almost entirely shot in LA.

The romantic restaurant where Warner Huntington III (Matthew Davis) dumps Elle is **Il Cielo, 9018 Burton Way**, Beverly Hills, though the fairy-lit exterior is the campus of **UCLA**, on LA's Westside. Much of the filming was around Pasadena, east of LA, where the **CalTech Campus, 1200 East California Boulevard**, stood in for the fictitious CULA. The gothic Harvard square is the rector's house of **All Saints Church, 132 North Euclid Avenue** (seen also in *Cruel Intentions* and *The Other Sister*), while the hallways and classrooms are **Rose City High School, 325 South Oak Knoll Avenue, Pasadena** (seen also in *Catch Me If You Can*). **345 South Hill Avenue** became the Gamma Theta sorority house. East of Pasadena, Neptune's Beauty Nook is **625 South Myrtle Avenue, Monrovia**. The exterior of the courthouse is **Orange County Law Office** (the interior is a set built at Sylmar for Clint Eastwood's *Midnight in the Garden of Good and Evil*).

The final graduation ceremony was added after test screenings left audiences unsatisfied. By then, Reese Witherspoon was in London filming *The Importance of Being Earnest*, so the rousing finale was filmed in **Dulwich College, College Road, Dulwich Village**, SE21.

LEGENDS OF THE FALL

(1994, dir: Edward Zwick)
Anthony Hopkins, Brad Pitt, Aidan Quinn.
● **ALBERTA, CANADA; BRITISH COLUMBIA, CANADA; JAMAICA**

Set in Montana, Hopkins' homestead retreat was a ranch in the **Ghost River** area, 40 miles west of Calgary, Alber-

ta. The WW1 trenches were also filmed here. Brad Pitt's African travels are actually **Ocho Rios** in Jamaica, and the town of Helena, where Aidan Quinn sets up his business, is Vancouver's Gastown area, east of downtown. **Powell Street** and **Maple Leaf Square** were period dressed. The **Hotel Europe**, on Helena's main street, is at **43 Powell Street**.

Helena: Powell Street, Vancouver

LÉON (aka *The Professional*)

(1994, dir: Luc Besson)
Jean Reno, Gary Oldman, Natalie Portman.
● **NEW YORK CITY; NEW JERSEY; PARIS, FRANCE**

Luc Besson's stylish thriller with hitman Reno versus rampantly OTT crooked cop Oldman is set in New York, but most of the studio shooting took place in Paris. Real New York sites include Spanish Harlem, Chinatown and Wall Street; plus **Hoboken** and **West New York**, New Jersey. Tony's,

Natalie Portman's hotel: 97th Street

...and inside: Hotel Chelsea, West 23rd Street

Danny Aiello's restaurant, supposedly in Little Italy, is **Guido's, 511 9th Avenue** at West 38th Street (© 212.564.8074) south of the Port Authority Bus Terminal. The exterior of Natalie Portman's hotel is **71 97th Street** at Park Avenue on the Upper East Side, but the stairwell and corridors are those of the **Hotel Chelsea, 222 West 23rd Street**, between Seventh and Eighth Avenues (© 212.243.3700), see *Sid and Nancy* for details.

LETHAL WEAPON

(1987, dir: Richard Donner)
Mel Gibson, Danny Glover, Gary Busey.
● **LOS ANGELES, CALIFORNIA**

First in the hugely successful series of actioners pairing suicidally on-the-edge Gibson with staid, middle-aged Glover. The movie was shot all over LA – on the southwest peninsula of **Palos Verdes**; the beachside community of **Santa Monica**; **Studio City** in the San

The opening leap: International Tower, Long Beach

The shootout: Hollywood Boulevard

The successful leap: Emser Building, west Hollywood

Fernando Valley; and **Inglewood** in South Central – as well as at **El Mirage**, the dry lake bed about 20 miles west of Victorville in the Mojave Desert.

The circular apartment block, where a drugged-out woman plummets to her death in the opening scene, is the **International Tower, 700 Ocean Boulevard East**, a block of condominiums in Long Beach, and featured in both versions of *Gone In 60 Seconds*. The rooftop from which Gibson survives a leap with the unwilling suicide, is the **Emser Building, 8431 Santa Monica Boulevard** in west Hollywood. The villains' nightclub, where Gibson is tortured, is the – now closed – **Ritz Theater** on Hollywood Boulevard. The shoot-out is on **Hollywood Boulevard** outside the Vogue Cinema.

LETHAL WEAPON 2

(1989, dir: Richard Donner)
Mel Gibson, Danny Glover, Joe Pesci.

● LOS ANGELES, CALIFORNIA

Glover and Gibson protect Pesci from nasty South Africans, while causing maximum mayhem around LA. Villain Joss Ackland's stilt house, demolished by Gibson, still survives (a mock-up was erected above Valencia, north of LA, for the destruction scene). The real house, designed by John Lautner, can be seen at **7436 Mulholland Drive** in the Hollywood Hills. And Mulholland Drive was convenient for the thrilling car chases. The tunnel chase is through the much-used **Second Street Tunnel**, downtown LA. The hotel, from which Gibson makes a leap into the pool, is the **Park Hyatt Los Angeles** (previously the JW Marriott Hotel), **2152 Avenue of the Stars**, Century City. Danny Glover's house stands on the **Warner Bros Ranch, 3701 West Oak Street** (not generally open to the public). Filming also took place at the **Westin Bonaventure Hotel, 404 South Figueroa Street**, downtown LA.

In *Lethal Weapon 3*, one of the first films to use LA's new subway system, Gibson and Glover are demoted to uniform patrol in the Plaza at **Olvera Street**.

For the opening of *Lethal Weapon 4* a fake gas station was built on **First Street** at Elm Street. Much of the subsequent action takes place around LA's **Chinatown**, though the highway chase used **I-215** between **Pecos Road** and **Windmill Lane**, Las Vegas, Nevada.

LICENCE TO KILL

(1989, dir: John Glen)
Timothy Dalton, Carey Lowell, Robert Davi.

● MEXICO; FLORIDA

Perhaps the most 'serious' of the Bonds. Bond's old buddy Felix Leiter marries Della Churchill at **St Mary's Star of the Sea Catholic Church, 1010 Windsor Lane, Key West** in Florida. Also in Key West, though supposedly in Bimini in the Bahamas, is the fictitious Barrelhead Bar. It's the **Harbor Lights Bar, 711 Eisenhower Drive**. You can see the real Bimini at the end of *Silence of the Lambs*. After Bond decides to go it alone when Leiter loses a leg to villain Sanchez's sharks, he gets his licence to kill revoked during a confrontation with M at the **Ernest Hemingway Museum, 907 Whitehead Street** at Truman Avenue, Key West. The 1851 Spanish-Colonial house was home to the writer from 1931 until his death in 1961. It's open daily, 9am to 5pm (*© 305.296.5811; admission charge*). Other Florida locations include **Garrison Bight Marina** on **Garrison Bight Causeway**; **Overseas Highway**, where the police escort plunges into the sea; and **Key West International Airport, South Roosevelt Boulevard**, where Bond learns of Sanchez's escape.

Most of the movie was made in Mexico (at Churubuscu Studios). Villain Sanchez's house is the **di Portanova Estate**, on the beach near **Las Brisas** in Acapulco. Isthmus City is fictitious, most of it being filmed around **Mexico City**. Banco De Isthmus is the main Post Office of Mexico City. Bond's El Presidente hotel is, on the inside, the splendid art nouveau **Gran Hotel de la Ciudad de Mexico, Calle 16 de Septiembre** (*© 5510.4040*) at the Zocale, the city's gigantic square. It was built in 1899 to accommodate the Centro Mercantil, Mexico City's first shopping centre. The exterior is the **Biblioteca de la Banca de Mexico** (Library of the Bank of Mexico), while the exterior of Sanchez's office is **El Teatro de la Ciudad, 36 Donceles**.

The Isthmus Casino, where Taliso Soto helps Bond out, is the **Casino Espagnol**, Mexico City. Televangelist Wayne Newton's home, the Olimpatec Meditation Institute, is the **Otomi Ceremonial Center**, a bizarre structure built for the native Otomi people in 1980 at **Toluca**, 35 miles west of Mexico City on Route 15. Bond and Leiter find Sanchez at **Isla de Mujeres**, near Cancun, where all the underwater sequences were shot. The climactic chase, at Paso El Diablo, the drug runners' rendezvous, is **Rumorosa Pass**, a winding stretch of road about 50 miles west of Mexicali, just over the border from California.

LIFE AND DEATH OF COLONEL BLIMP, THE

(1943, dir: Michael Powell; Emeric Pressburger)
Roger Livesey, Deborah Kerr, Anton Walbrook.

● LONDON

Powell and Pressburger's masterpiece proved enormously controversial at the time, not least for Walbrook's sympathetic German character. The film is almost totally setbound.

Blimp's London home: Ovington Square, Knightsbridge

For the opening raid on Blimp's Royal Bathers' Club, the army trucks ('borrowed' for the movie) thunder down **Western Avenue**, round **Marble Arch** and into **Berkeley Square**. Blimp's London house, despite being demolished by a bomb in the movie, still stands unchanged, at **15 Ovington Square**, SW3, off the Brompton Road, Knightsbridge (*tube: South Kensington*). The tiny tree-filled square opposite is Ovington Square.

LIGHT SLEEPER
(1992, dir: Paul Schrader)
Willem Dafoe, Susan Sarandon, Dana Delany.
● **NEW YORK CITY**

The third part of Schrader's loose trilogy, which began with *Taxi Driver* and *American Gigolo*. Willem Dafoe is the insomniac drug dealer in New York, where piles of rubbish, deliberately positioned by the design department to indicate moral decay, were constantly removed by the city's too-diligent sanitation department. Filming took place at the **Hotel Pennsylvania, West 32nd Street** by Penn Station; expensive restaurant **Palio, 151 West 51st Street** in the Equitable Center; the **Paramount Hotel, 235 West 46th Street**, between Broadway and 8th Street; and La Côte Basque, the French restaurant to which Sarandon takes Dafoe, which has now gone. It stood at 5 East 55th Street.

LION IN WINTER, THE
(1968, dir: Anthony Harvey)
Peter O'Toole, Katharine Hepburn, Anthony Hopkins.
● **WALES; FRANCE; IRELAND**

James Goldman's play, about the stormy relationship between Henry II and Eleanor of Aquitaine, may not make for the most cinematic experience, but a crackling script bursting with everybody's favourite quotes and some blistering performances make for high-octane entertainment. The interiors were filmed at Bray Studios near Dublin.

The beach scenes are **Marloes Sands**, west of Milford Haven, Pembrokeshire. Various castles around Wales and in the south of France provided the exteriors. The main location is the **Abbey of Montmajour**, near Fontvieille in the south of France. Eleanor's landing was staged on the River Rhone. The ending was shot at **Tarascon**, France.

LITTLE BIG MAN
(1970, dir: Arthur Penn)
Dustin Hoffman, Chief Dan George, Faye Dunaway.
● **MONTANA; ALBERTA, CANADA; CALIFORNIA**

Arthur Penn's picaresque tale of the hundred-and-something survivor of Little Big Horn. The Battle of Little Big Horn itself was shot on the actual site, now the **Custer Battlefield National Monument**, on the Little Big Horn River, Route 94, about 60 miles east of Billings, Montana, and the neighbouring Crow Reservation on Route 90. The winter scenes were filmed in Canada, at **Morley** near Calgary, Alberta. The present-day hospital bookend scenes, with a wheezy centenarian Hoffman, were filmed in the now-demolished Sawtelle Veterans Hospital, west Los Angeles.

LITTLE SHOP OF HORRORS, THE
(1960, dir: Roger Corman)
Dick Miller, Jonathan Haze, Jack Nicholson.
● **LOS ANGELES, CALIFORNIA**

The original, low-budget spoof horror that inspired the campy musical was shot almost entirely on a tiny studio set in two days, between Christmas and New Year, 1959. The second unit filmed exteriors on skid row and at the **Santa Fe rail yards** in downtown LA, with the real inhabitants acting up for the cameras.

LITTLE VOICE
(1998, dir: Mark Herman)
Jane Horrocks, Brenda Blethyn, Michael Caine.
● **YORKSHIRE**

Slim vehicle (from the play originally directed by *American Beauty*'s Sam Mendes) for Jane Horrocks as a seriously introverted northern girl with an uncanny flair for vocal impersonation. Set, and filmed, in **Scarborough**, on the Yorkshire coast, where Horrocks and Blethyn's house is on the corner of **Barwick Terrace** and **Barwick Street**. Boo's Nightclub, where Horrocks is cajoled into performing, is the disused **Haven Holidays** site at **Clayton Bay**, on the A165 a few miles to the south of Scarborough.

Boo's Nightclub: Clayton Bay

LITTLE WOMEN
(1933, dir: George Cukor)
Katharine Hepburn, Joan Bennett, Paul Lukas.
● **NEW HAMPSHIRE**

Louisa May Alcott's book about four sisters growing up, filmed by 'women's director' Cukor, with location filming in **Concord**, New Hampshire.

LITTLE WOMEN
(1994, dir: Gillian Armstrong)
Susan Sarandon, Winona Ryder, Gabriel Byrne.
● **BRITISH COLUMBIA, CANADA; MASSACHUSETTS**

Remake, filmed in **Cobble Hill**, Vancouver and Victoria, British Columbia. More period settings were found at **Historic Deerfield, Deerfield**, the museum of New England history housed in a 330 year-old village in Massachusetts, off I-91 about ten miles south of Greenfield (© *413.774.5581, www.historic-deerfield.org*).

LIVE AND LET DIE
(1973, dir: Guy Hamilton)
Roger Moore, Yaphet Kotto, Jane Seymour.
● **LOUISIANA; JAMAICA; NEW YORK CITY**

One of the better Moore Bonds, playing like an homage to *North by Northwest*, opening with a murder at the United Nations, the hero hiding from an aerial attack in an overgrown field and a final scene on a train. The **United Nations Building** is on **46th Street** at First Avenue, New

York, and Bond is duly dispatched to the Big Apple.

The New York consulate of the fictitious San Monique is on **69th Street**, midtown Manhattan. Bond tails a lead from the Oh Cult Voodoo Store, **33 East 65th Street** on the East Side, up Fifth Avenue to the Fillet of Soul on Lenox Avenue and 124th Street in Harlem. The Fillet actually filmed on the Upper East Side on **Second Avenue at 94th Street**. The ensuing fight scene was shot on **118th Street**, edging towards the real Harlem, with more Harlem scenes using **117th Street**.

The trail leads to the island of San Monique which is, inevitably for a Bond movie, in the West Indies. Bond's hotel, where Baron Samedi performs his tourist-voodoo nightclub act, is the **Sans Souci Hotel, 2171 Magenta Drive** in **Ocho Rios**, Jamaica (which featured as Miss Taro's home in the first Bond movie, *Dr No*). The cemetery was a set built on a hill three miles north of the Montego Bay-Falmouth road. The bus chase (it's a London double-decker under the San Monique logo), used the **Montego Bay-Lucea Highway**. The derelict wharf, where Bond and Rosie try to board Quarrel's yacht, is at **Montego Bay**. Rosie's breakfast veranda is a bungalow at **Half Moon Bay**.

To New Orleans International Airport (**Moisant Field** in **Kenner**, 15 miles east of the Big Easy itself), where Bond is spirited away to the Bleeker Flying School – in actuality the **Lakefront Airport** – where several planes get thoroughly trashed. The crocodile farm (the 'Trespassers will be eaten' sign is actually for real) is Ross Kananga's farm, home to 300 crocs and 'gators, not in Louisiana at all but back in Jamaica, some 20 miles from Montego Bay. Kananga himself, whose name was confusingly nicked for the film's villain, performs the running-over-the-crocs stunt.

Bond escapes by boat, ready for the big set piece chase through the Louisiana bayous. The boat jumps over Highway 11 at the **Crawdad Bridge**, just outside Phoenix on the Mississippi, south of New Orleans. The interrupted wedding was filmed at the **Treadway Estate**, a former Indian reservation in Louisiana's Bayou country, 30 miles from New Orleans. The boats scoot over the lawn at the **Baldwin Estate**, Lousiana. The police riverblock is at **Miller's Bridge**. Adam dies among the rusting wrecks of the boatyard at **Slidell**. The Southern Yacht Club marina is on the shores of **Lake Pontchartrain**.

LIVES OF A BENGAL LANCER, THE
(1935, dir: Henry Hathaway)
Gary Cooper, Franchot Tone, Richard Cromwell.
● CALIFORNIA

Heroics on India's Northwest Frontier, a project originated some years earlier by *King Kong* co-creator Ernest Schoedsack and intended to be made on location, but little of the Indian footage remains. The film was shot on the fantastic rocky outcrops of the **Alabama Hills** above **Lone Pine**, I-395, central California (see *Kim* for details).

LIVING DAYLIGHTS, THE
(1987, dir: John Glen)
Timothy Dalton, Maryam d'Abo, Jeroen Krabbe.
● MOROCCO; AUSTRIA; GIBRALTAR; LONDON

First of the po-faced Bonds, reacting against the increasingly flip Moore movies. The opening war games teaser filmed on **Gibraltar**. Bond's HQ, Universal Exports, is on the south side of London's **Trafalgar Square**. Bond meets Saunders at the **Prater Café** in Vienna's Prater Park, alongside the fairground with *The Third Man*'s Big Wheel, which of course has to be incorporated into the action. The Vienna hotel is the **Hotel Im Palais Schwarzenberg, Schwarzenbergplatz 9**. Situated in 15 acres of park in the heart of Vienna. it was built 300 years ago as a palace, and gutted by the Nazis. Part of the building is now the hotel. The theatre is the **Sofiensale Theater**, and filming also took place in the grounds and palace of **Schonbrunn**. The Afghan airport is **Ouarzazate Airfield** in Morocco (an often-used location – for details of Ouarzazate see *Lawrence of Arabia*). The militaristic villa of villain Joe Don Baker is the **Forbes Museum, Palace El Mendoub, Tangier** (though the interior was recreated in the studio) which was founded by and belonged to millionaire Malcolm Forbes.

LOCAL HERO
(1983, dir: Bill Forsyth)
Denis Lawson, Peter Riegert, Burt Lancaster.
● SCOTLAND; TEXAS

Canny locals of a small Scottish village exploit a Texan oil company in a movie that harks back to the great days of the Ealing comedy. The fictitious Scots village of Ferness is a conflation of two separate locations. The beach is **Morar Beach**, at **Camusdarrach**, 37 miles from Fort William. The village is **Pennan**, over on the other side of Scotland, on the north Grampian coast, 36 miles north of Abberdeen on the B9032. It's at Pennan that you'll find the phone box, which is now the subject of a preservation order. The church is simply a cottage with added set dressing, though the interior is **Our Lady of the Braes Roman Catholic Church** at **Polnish**. The hotel, likewise, was filmed at a private house. The interior is the **Lochailort Inn, Lochailort** on the A861, Invernesshire. The village shop is at **Pole of Itlaw**, south of Banff on the B9121 in Banffshire and the village hall is in **Hilton** on the A948, about 15 miles north of Aberdeen. Skywatching Burt Lancaster heads Knox Oil at its HQ in **Houston**, Texas.

LOCH NESS
(1995, dir: John Henderson)
Ted Danson, Joely Richardson, Ian Holm.
● SCOTLAND; LONDON

Most of the filming is actually on the real **Loch Ness** itself, though it's prettied up with a few extra locations. The ruined castle is **Urquhart Castle**, which *is* on Loch Ness (and can be seen in Billy Wilder's excellent *The Private Life of Sherlock Holmes*), although it's intercut with shots of the more striking **Eilean Donan Castle** (seen also in *Highlander*). The pier and the bay are at **Lower Diabag** on **Loch Torridon**, along with Joely Richardson's hotel. Filming also took place at the villages of **Dores; Foyers**; and **Fort Augustus** on Loch Ness. Danson gets a, not entirely unexpected, attack of conscience at the **Natural History Museum, Cromwell Road** in South Kensington,

London (see *Greystoke* for details).

LOCK, STOCK AND TWO SMOKING BARRELS

(1998, dir: Guy Ritchie)
Jason Flemyng, Dexter Fletcher, Nick Moran.

● LONDON; BERKSHIRE

Winston's dope business: Stables Market, Chalk Farm Road, Camden

Before his laddishness became terminally irritating, Guy Ritchie assembled this great black comedy from bits of *Performance*, *The Long Good Friday*, *Pulp Fiction* and *The Italian Job*, among scores of other movies. As the film opens, Eddie (Moran) and Bacon leg it down the rather intimidating steps to the railway bridge at the end of the tunnel on **Pedley Street** (also seen in *Gangster No.1*). The gang's hang-out is **15 Park Street**, SE1 (also used in *Howards End*), a wonderfully undeveloped street opposite Borough Market. Dog's place, next door, is **13 Park Street**. JD's bar is **Vic Naylor, 40 St John Street**, Smithfield, EC1.

Stables Market, Chalk Farm Road, Camden, is where Winston runs a sadly low-security dope business. Just inside the Chalk Farm Road entrance, on the left, you can see the metal staircase up to the dope den, where the lads take an unfortunate traffic warden along for the ride. The den itself is another warehouse opposite.

The Royal Oak, 73 Columbia Road at Ezra Street, in the heart of the famous flower market, became Samoan Jo's, the South Seas theme pub where Bacon is served a bleedin' rainforest. It also features in *The Krays*, and as the East End boozer in David A Stewart's *Honest*.

Repton Boys Club, Cheshire Street at Ramsey Street, where the boxing-mad Krays once worked out, is the site of the catastrophic 3-card-brag game (it also features in *The Young Americans*). **Blackman's Shoes, 42-44 Cheshire Street**, on the corner of Grimsby Street, is the exterior of 'Hatchet' Harry's office ("Harry Lonsdale: Porn King").

The catastrophic 3-card-brag game: Repton Boys Club, Cheshire Street

JD's bar: Vic Naylor, St John Street, Smithfield

The wood-panelled interior, though, is in **Bethnal Green Town Hall, Cambridge Heath Road** at Patriot Square, which also became Benicio Del Toro's tailor's in another Guy Ritchie film, *Snatch* (it also appears in *Velvet Goldmine*, *The Criminal* and *I Capture the Castle*). And, conveniently, this frequently-seen location happens to house the London Film Office.

The country house robbed by the inept Scousers is **Dorney Court** (✆ *01628.604638*, *www.dorney-court.co.uk*), a Tudor manor house near Maidenhead in Berkshire, also seen in Shekhar Kapur's *Elizabeth*, *Mountains of the Moon* and *Circus*.

Hatchet Harry's porn empire: Blackman's Shoes, Cheshire Street

LOLA RENNT (aka *Run Lola Run*)

(1998, dir: Tom Tykwer)
Franka Potente, Moritz Bleibtreu, Herbert Knaup.

● BERLIN, GERMANY

Tykwer brings a videogame sensibility to this snappy, breathless thriller as Lola (Potente) has 20 minutes to find and deliver 100,000 Deutschmarks to her desperate boyfriend. He does play fast and loose with Berlin's geography, though. Lola's apartment is **13-14 Albrechtstrasse** at Schiffbauerdamm, just across the Spree from Friedrichstrasse Station in the Mitte district, behind the Berliner Ensemble

Lola's apartment, and the start of her run: Albrechtstrasse

theatre. Boyfriend Manni (Bleibtreu) loses the bag of money at **Deutsche Oper** subway station, way to the west in Charlottenburg. He calls Lola from a phone box at the junction of **Tauroggener Strasse** and **Osnabrücker Strasse** just north of Schloss Charlottenburg (*U-bahn: Mierendorffplatz*), but you won't be able to make a phone call here: the box was added for the movie, as was the Vortex sign (one of the film's many references to *Vertigo*) and the clock. You can, though, shop at the **Spar** grocery on the southwest corner, which Manni holds up in the first version of events. Lola heads for her father's Deutsch Transfer Bank, just a short way to the south of her apartment, but when she crosses the Spree, she uses the quaintly turretted and covered **Oberbaumbrücke** in the far east of the city, a pre-Wende crossing point into East Berlin (*U-bahn:*

Manni holds up the Bolle store: Spar, Tauroggenerstrasse

The covered bridge Lola crosses: Oberbaumbrücke

Lola crosses the square: Gendarmenmarkt

Lola finally gets the money: Deutsches Historisches Museum, Zeughaus, Unter den Linden

Castle Quilty: Hilfield Castle, Hilfield Lane, Bushey

Schlesisches Tor, U-bahn-S-bahn: Warschauer Strasse). In no time at all, she's back on **Friedrichstrasse**, chasing over the **Französische Strasse U-Bahn** station before turning into **Behrenstrasse** and on to **Bebelplatz**. Bebelplatz, formerly Opernplatz, is the vast open square in front of Humboldt University where an imaginative below-ground installation of empty shelves commemorates the notorious Nazi book-burning of 1933. **39 Behrenstrasse**, on the square's south side, was dressed to be the bank. The stylish square, seen from above in the first two versions but finally from ground level in the third, is **Gendarmenmarkt**, one of Berlin's most beautiful – and magnificently restored – squares, a couple of blocks to the south. Lola is almost hit by a truck on **Unter den Linden** at Hinter den Giesshaus, just to the northeast of Bebelplatz, before spotting the casino, where she finally wins the money. Although the interior is a government building, with the addition of a hastily improvised version of the Carlotta Valdes portrait from *Vertigo*, the exterior is the **Deutsches Historisches Museum** in the **Zeughaus, Unter den Linden 2** at Oberwallstrasse. And in minutes, Lola arrives at Tauroggener Strasse for the third, final and happy denouement.

LOLITA

(1962, dir: Stanley Kubrick)
James Mason, Sue Lyon, Peter Sellers.
● **BUCKINGHAMSHIRE; HERTFORDSHIRE; RHODE ISLAND**

Lolita's New Hampshire home: Highbury House, Gerrards Cross

Kubrick couldn't have filmed Nabokov's controversial novel in the US, so he moved to the UK. And stayed. Although the story is set in urban America, it was made almost entirely at Elstree Studios. A second-unit in the States provided the briefest of establishing shots and the back-projection sequences. These were filmed in **Westerly**, Rhode Island, and include the RR station (train pulling in) and a cab (with Humbert Humbert in it) traveling on a downtown street. Landmarks are clear and most remain after these 40 plus years. It occurs about five minutes into

the film.

The rest is England. Shelley Winters' lodgings in West Ramsdale, New Hampshire, where James Mason develops an obsession with nymphet Sue Lyon, is **Highburgh House, Packhorse Road, Gerrards Cross** (*rail: Gerrards Cross*), about half a mile north of the railway station, in Buckinghamshire. And it's on Packhorse Road that Shelley Winters gets hit by a car.

Castle Quilty, where Humbert Humbert (Mason) tracks down Quilty (Sellers) is **Hilfield Castle, Hilfield Lane**, just off the A41 north of Bushey in Hertfordshire, seen also in *Murder at the Gallop*. It's a (very) private residence which you can just glimpse from the road.

LONELINESS OF THE LONG DISTANCE RUNNER, THE

(1962, dir: Tony Richardson)
Tom Courtenay, Michael Redgrave, James Fox.
● **SURREY**

The borstal: Ruxley Towers, Claygate

Courtenay is the borstal boy with stamina in this dour character study filmed on location around London. The borstal is **Ruxley Towers**, which until recently could be seen disused and crumbling away at the end of **Ruxley Ridge**, off Common Road, **Claygate**, just southeast of Esher in Surrey (*rail: Claygate*). The facility had been used by the army as a NAAFI facility, but recently it has been substantially renovated and is enjoying a new lease of life as a private and very luxurious home.

LONELY ARE THE BRAVE

(1962, dir: David Miller)
Kirk Douglas, Walter Matthau, Gena Rowlands.
● **NEW MEXICO**

A sombre passing-of-the-old-West movie, adapted by Dalton Trumbo from Edward Abbey's novel *Brave Cowboy*. Shot in the **Manzano Mountains** south of Albuquerque, New Mexico.

LONG GOOD FRIDAY, THE

(1980, dir: John Mackenzie)
Bob Hoskins, Helen Mirren, Derek Thompson.
● **LONDON; SCOTLAND**

One of the few British thrillers that can stand up against the best from the US, as gangland boss Harold Shand (Hoskins) is unwittingly caught up in shady deals with the IRA. The film opens in Northern Ireland, with Shand's right-hand man Colin (Paul Freeman) getting involved in

Harold Shand's casino, where the bomb is discovered: Villa Elephant on the River, Grosvenor Road

The Boulevard Restaurant: It's, Wigmore Street

some very shady financial dealing. In fact, the movie was shot entirely in London (with a little Irish scenery shot in Scotland), and Fagan's, the bar in which Colin hits on the doomed Irish lad, is Grade II listed boozer **The Salisbury, Green Lanes**, at the corner of St Ann's Road, Harringay. Its slightly faded ambience can also be seen in *Chaplin*, and more recently, the pub appears under its own name as the big, bustling pub where Miranda Richardson looks for Gabriel Byrne in David Cronenberg's *Spider*.

The **Aegean Pools, 2 Hale Lane, Mill Hill**, NW7 (*©020.8959.6845*) is the dive pool where Colin is first seen doing high dives before he's offed by a young Pierce Brosnan (in his first screen appearance), though the murder was filmed in **Ladywell Leisure Centre, Lewisham High Street** (*© 020.8690.2123; rail: Ladywell*).

St Patrick's Church, Green Bank, off Dundee Street, running south to Wapping High Street, is the site of the Good Friday service where Harold Shand's mum narrowly escapes being blown up, triggering the chain of events. The street runs down to the Thames near Wapping New Stairs at a stretch known as the **Pool of London** which, not surprisingly, was the backdrop to the semi-documentary drama *Pool of London*, shot around the then bomb-damaged and now largely rebuilt area. It was on the riverfront here that the Lion and Unicorn pub was built – and blown up. Legendary waterfront boozer the **Waterman's Arms, 1 Glenaffric Avenue** (*DLR: Island Gardens*) became The Governor General, where Harold goes looking for Billy – "Walk to the car Billy, or I'll blow your spine off!" – while Victoria (Mirren) is placating the Americans.

Much of the action centres around London's **St Katherine's Dock**, just downstream from Tower Bridge, where Shand's yacht is moored. **33 Villa Road**, Brixton, is the house of Erroll the grass (Paul Barber, now more famous as Horse in *The Full Monty*), who gets cut up by Razors (PH Moriarty). It's, **56-60 Wigmore Street** (*© 020.7224.3484*) alongside Easley's Mews, was the Boulevard Restaurant. Hopefully, you'll enjoy your meal here more than Jeff (Thompson), who gets spat on during his clandestine meeting with the shady

Harold goes looking for Billy: Waterman's Arms, Glenaffric Avenue

Councillor Harris (Bryan Marshall). Opposite Dolphin Square, Italian restaurant **Villa Elephant on the River, 135 Grosvenor Road** (*© 020.7834.1621*), supplied the interior of Shand's casino, where the bomb is discovered, and the lads collect their guns. The Mafia contacts stay at the **Savoy Hotel, 1 Savoy Hill**, on the **Strand** (*© 020.7836.4343, www.savoy-group.com/savoy/savoy.asp*), where Hoskins is abducted during the cracking ending.

LONG GOODBYE, THE

(1973, dir: Robert Altman)
Elliott Gould, Nina Van Pallandt, Sterling Hayden.
● **LOS ANGELES, CALIFORNIA; MEXICO**

Updating of Chandler's novel by veteran screenwriter Leigh Brackett, who also worked on the screenplay for the 1946 *The Big Sleep*. Reviled on release, it's now regarded as a classic. Made almost entirely on location around LA, at **Malibu** Sheriff's office; a rest home in **Pasadena**; the new skyscraper at **9000 Sunset Boulevard**; offices in **Westwood** and **Hollywood**; and **Lincoln Heights Jail**. Nina Van Pallandt's home is Robert Altman's own **Malibu Colony** beachfront house. Elliott Gould's apartment is the beautiful Italianate **High Tower, High Tower Drive** off Camrose Avenue, north Hollywood, where the tower houses an outdoor elevator. Filming also took place in Mexico.

Elliot Gould's apartment: High Tower

LONG, HOT SUMMER, THE

(1958, dir: Martin Ritt)
Paul Newman, Joanne Woodward, Orson Welles.
● **LOUISIANA**

An overheated, in every sense, Deep South melodrama from stories by William Faulkner. The town of Frenchman's Bend, where drifter Newman settles, is **Clinton**, 30 miles north of Baton Rouge. Woodward's mansion is **Asphodel, East Felicia Parish**, one of the many plantation houses along the Mississippi between New Orleans and state capital Baton Rouge (*www.asphodelplantation.com*). The church, where Newman wins a picnic with Woodward at the fundraiser, is **St Andrew's Episcopal Church**.

LONG KISS GOODNIGHT, THE

(1996, dir: Renny Harlin)
Geena Davis, Samuel L Jackson, Brian Cox.
● **ONTARIO, CANADA; NEW JERSEY**

Slam-bang actioner, with happily married Davis waking from an eight-year bout of amnesia to discover that she was previously a lethal CIA assassin. Set in New Jersey, the film was shot mainly in Canada, although when Davis and incompetent PI Jackson hide out in **Atlantic City**, New Jersey, they stay in the **Taj Mahal**. Canadian locations included **Collingwood**, on Nottawasaga Bay, northwest of Toronto; **Hamilton**, south Toronto; **Historic Unionville**,

Jackson's home: Heward Avenue, Toronto

Davis dumps Jackson: Front Street East at Cherry Street

in **Markham**, north Toronto; **Milton**, west Toronto; **Concord**; **Dundas**; **Halton Hills**; **Milford Bay**; **Scarborough**; **Uxbridge**; **Wasaga Beach**; **Windmere**; and **York Region**. Samuel Jackson's home is **134 Heward Avenue**, off Queen Street East, eastern Toronto. Geena Davis dumps him from the car in front of the **Canary Restaurant, 409 Front Street East** at Cherry Street (a regular location, seen in Jean-Claude Van Damme's *Maximum Risk* and Bette Midler weepie *Stella*) down toward the Port of Toronto. Chesterman Station, site of the massive shoot-out and the leap into the frozen canal, is **Old Hamilton Train Station**, which you might recognise as the station where Magneto demonstrates his powers in *X-Men*. The climax was filmed at **Niagara Falls**, though the bridge is actually unharmed.

LONG RIDERS, THE

(1980, dir: Walter Hill)
The brothers Carradine, Keach, Quaid and Guest.
● GEORGIA; TEXAS; CALIFORNIA

Hill's excellent Western casts four sets of Hollywood brothers as the James gang. It utilises excellent locations around **Parrott**, Georgia, as well as Texas and northern California.

LONGEST DAY, THE

(1962, dir: Andrew Marton; Ken Annakin; Bernhard Wicki)
John Wayne, Rod Steiger, Robert Ryan.
● FRANCE

Mitchum, Fonda, Connery, Burton, Steiger, not to mention John Wayne… the Germans never stood a chance, did they? Four nations, four directors: Ken Annakin filmed the British, Bernhard Wicki the Germans, Andrew Marton (and, unofficially, Zanuck himself) the Americans. The French? Well, they were permitted to supply the locations. Publicity for *The Longest Day* makes great play of the fact that it was filmed on the beaches where the allied invasion actually took place, along the **Normandy** coast: codename 'Utah' was the furthest west, on the southeast coast of the Cotentin Peninsula; 'Omaha' covered four miles from Vierville-sur-Mer to Port-en-Bessin; 'Gold', from Port-en-Bessin to La Rivière; 'Juno', from La Rivière to to St-Aubin-sur-Mer; and 'Sword', stretching to the Orne estuary at Ouistreham. Despite the film's claims, most of the Omaha footage was filmed at **Saleccia**, on

Corsica, a famously beautiful beach, east of St Florent on the island's northern coast, but tough to access by land. More of the landing scenes, with Robert Mitchum shaming hesitant extras by plunging recklessly from the landing craft, were staged at **Île-de-Ré** near **La Rochelle**, down on the Bay of Biscay on France's western coast (also home to the submarine pens seen in *Das Boot* and *Raiders of the Lost Ark*). The gun emplacement above Omaha beach, which turns out to be empty, is the real thing, though, at **La Pointe du Hoc**, west of Vierville.

There's a little licence taken with the raid on Ouistreham, lying between the sea and Caen, as the elaborate casino building seen in the movie had already been destroyed by the Germans themselves (in 1952 it was rebuilt with a cinema and disco). And, no, there were no spunky nuns braving enemy fire to tend the wounded. The action was re-staged at **Port-en-Bessin** (to the west, between Gold and Omaha beaches), but Annakin (good name, somebody should nick that for a movie character) does pull off a helicopter shot of staggering virtuosity.

The famous bridge over the Caen Canal at **Bénouville**, a couple of miles south of Ouistreham, was renamed Pegasus Bridge in honour of the 6th Airborne (whose insignia was a flying horse), who took and held the bridge until the Allies arrived. Still in operation, alongside the bridge, stands Café Gondrée, the first building in France to be liberated. The current bridge is a similar design (and significantly larger), but the original can be seen in the grounds of Mémorial Pégasus in nearby Ranville. Major Howard, charged with taking and holding the bridge, is played by Richard Todd, who really was part of this operation.

Perhaps the most famous scene in the movie, the disastrous nighttime parachute drop into a Nazi-occupied village, with Red Buttons witnessing the ensuing massacre as he dangles helplessly from a church steeple, is another of the film's real locations, **Sainte-Mère-Eglise**, way to the west, on the N-13 road to Cherbourg.

The German HQ is **Chateau de Chantilly**, 20 miles north of Paris on the N16 in the Picardy region (see *A View To A Kill* for details).

LOOK BACK IN ANGER

(1959, dir: Tony Richardson)
Richard Burton, Mary Ure, Claire Bloom.
● LONDON

John Osborne's bilious attack on, well, everything. The original kitchen sink drama, transferred from the Royal Court stage to film. London location filming was at **Deptford Market**, **Dalston Junction** and **Stratford East**. Jimmy Porter (Burton) accompanies Edith Evans as she tends the grave of her husband at **St Mary's Roman Catholic Cemetery**, the western section of **Kensal Green Cemetery**, overlooking Scrubs Lane, Kensal Green, NW10 (see *Theatre of Blood* for details).

LOOK WHO'S TALKING

(1989, dir: Amy Heckerling)
John Travolta, Kirstie Alley, Olympia Dukakis.
● BRITISH COLUMBIA, CANADA

Kirstie Alley's New York apartment: Thurlow Street, Vancouver

Bruce Willis voices Mikey the Talking Baby in this one-joke movie, and Travolta's career gets a false restart. Set in New York, where Travolta is a Yellow Cab driver, but the Big Apple has never looked so clean, bland and anonymous. No art deco, and no quirky skyscrapers. That's because it was filmed in Canada, on the streets of downtown **Vancouver**, British Columbia, with barely an establishing shot of New York City. As Travolta's cab rushes Kirstie Alley to hospital, he races along **Hornby Street**, past Vancouver Art Gallery, and along **Burrard Street**, downtown Vancouver. When Travolta drives Alley to Grandpa's they pass the **Hotel Georgia, 801 West Georgia Street**, and a couple of minutes later pass it again in the opposite direction. Some cab driver. Kirstie Alley's apartment building is **784 Thurlow Street** at Robson Street. Mikey braves the traffic to bring Travolta and Alley together by an English theme-pub, the **Jolly Taxpayer, 828 West Hastings Street** at Howes Street.

Look Who's Talking Too was also made in Vancouver, though there's a little more New York on view in that movie.

LOOT

(1970, dir: Silvio Narizzano)
Hywel Bennett, Lee Remick, Richard Attenborough.
● SUSSEX

The entrance to McLeavy's Hotel: Bear Road, Brighton

Joe Orton's stage farce is transmuted into a gaudy, frenetic black comedy, now set in a **Brighton** boarding house. The cemetery, where Mrs McLeavy doesn't get buried, is **Lewes Road Cemetery**, east of the town centre. The out-of-control funeral careers down **Bear Road**. The entrance to McLeavy's Hotel can be seen at the top of Bear Road, at Warren Road opposite Brighton Racecourse.

LORD OF THE FLIES

(1963, dir: Peter Brook)
James Aubrey, Tom Chapin, Hugh Edwards.
● PUERTO RICO

Brook's attempt to film William Golding's novel, about a party of English schoolboys reverting to savagery after a plane crash leaves them stranded on a deserted island, filmed at **Frenchman's Cove**, east of Port Antonio, Puerto Rico.

The 1990 American remake, changing the English schoolboys for US military cadets, was shot on the Garden Isle of **Kauai**, Hawaii.

LORD OF THE RINGS: THE FELLOWSHIP OF THE RING, THE

(2001, dir: Peter Jackson)
Elijah Wood, Ian McKellen, Sean Astin.
● NEW ZEALAND

An amazing achievement, three films in *The Lord of the Rings* trilogy filmed simultaneously, against the varied backdrops of director Jackson's native New Zealand, standing in for Tolkien's Middle Earth. Be aware, though, that the locations are spread over both of New Zealand's islands, and some are pretty inaccessible.

The private **Alexander Farm**, near **Matamata**, toward Karapiro in the Waikato area, represented the rolling, bucolic greenery of the Shire, home of Bilbo (Ian Holm) and Frodo Baggins (Wood). In order for Hobbiton to blend naturally into the landscape, the extensive set was planted with crops and flowers a year before the cameras rolled. Matamata, which now proudly advertises itself as Hobbiton, has a Tourist Information Centre at 45 Broadway. You can visit what remains of the Hobbiton set (on guided tours only) with Rings Scenic Tours Ltd (© 7888.6838, *www.hobbitontours.com*).

Tongariro National Park is home to three volcanoes: **Mount Ruapehu** (which is still active), Mount Tongariro and Mount Ngauruhoe, which proved ideal as the dark and savage realm of Mordor and Mount Doom, where the ring is forged. **Whakapapa Ski Field**, on the slopes of Ruapehu (*www.whakapapa.co.nz*), supplied Middle Earth's snowy slopes and the opening battlefield on the slopes of Mount Doom, where an alliance of men and elves defeats the armies of Mordor, and the ring is taken from Sauron.

A quick detour to the South Island: the **Southern Alps** and the extensive glaciers of South Island became the Misty Mountains, in which the wretched Gollum (Andy Serkis) hid away in his cave for 500 years with the ring.

Back to the North Island. **Otaki Gorge Road**, in **Otaki Totara Forest** in the **Manuwatu** region, about 45 miles north of Wellington, was used for the Outer Shire woods and roads surrounding Hobbiton.

Surprisingly, it's in the centre of the city of **Wellington** (*www.wellingtonnz.com*) that the four Hobbits, Frodo, Sam (Astin), Merry (Billy Boyd) and Pippin (Dominic Monaghan), are forced to hide under tree roots to evade the Black Rider after escaping with Farmer Maggot's vegetables. The site was the **Town Belt** of **Mount Victoria**, a peaceful park overlooking the city centre and, incidentally, it was the first day of filming.

Also in Wellington was the town of Bree, where the Hobbits are supposed to meet Gandalf (McKellen) at the Inn of the Prancing Pony, but instead meet up with the mysterious Aragorn (Viggo Mortensen). The set was built on the abandoned army camp of **Fort Dorset** at **Seatoun**, in Wellington's Port Nicholson harbour. There's nothing left of Bree, but you can see the site from the beach at the end of Burnham Street.

Back north of Otaki, to **Keeling Farm** in the tiny country village of **Manakau**, where the Hobbits narrowly escape the ring wraiths by jumping onto the Bucklebury Ferry on the Brandywine River.

South of Wellington is **Waiterere Forest**, which became Trollshaw Forest and the woodlands of Osgiliath.

Harcourt Park, Akatarawa Road, Upper Hutt, 20 miles north of Wellington, became Isengard, the realm of the evil Saruman (Christopher Lee), who has an army of Orcs use ropes to pull down trees to fuel his forge (don't worry, they were old trees shipped in and erected for the movie). In June 2002, the remains of the tree, with bolts still embedded, could still be seen (*www.upperhuttcity.com/city_guide/parks/parks_harcourt.asp; rail: Upper Hutt, bus to Brown Owl shops*).

In **Kaitoke Regional Park** (*www.wrc.govt.nz/rp/kaitoke.htm*), about eight miles from Upper Hutt City, the elvish realm of Rivendell was built. This is where Frodo recovers from his wound and the Fellowship is formed. The Silverlode River and Galadriel's swan-boat were also filmed here. The Great River Anduin is the **Hutt River** between **Moonshine Bridge** and **Poets Park** (*Rail: Wallaceville*).

The woods of Lothlorien, where Frodo gets help and advice from elf queen Galadriel (Cate Blanchett), are the gardens of **Fernside Lodge**, a homestead inn about two miles from **Featherston, Wairarapa**, about 40 miles east of Wellington. Here you can see the White Bridge. And, yes, you can stay here (© *6308.8265, www.fernside.co.nz*).

On New Zealand's South Island you'll find Chetwood Forest near Bree, where the Hobbits first flee, which was filmed on **Takaka Hill**, between Golden and Tasman Bay near Nelson. **Mount Olympus**, in Golden Bay in **Kahurangi National Park**, provided scenes in the Eregion Hills and the rough country south of Rivendell. **Mount Owen** became the Dimrill Dale hillside and Chetwood Forest.

The spectacular **Fiordland** region (*www.fiordland.org.nz*), on the western coast, supplied several locations: Weathertop camp, where the ring wraiths catch up with the Hobbits and Frodo is stabbed in the shoulder, is **Te Anau**.

The **Arrowtown Recreational Reserve**, 15 miles northeast of Queenstown, was used for the West Road, Eregion Hills and the Misty Mountains. The Ford of Bruinen, where Arwen (Liv Tyler) challenges the wraiths – "If you want Frodo, come and claim him!" – before they are washed away in a flash flood, was filmed on the **Shotover River** near **Arrowtown**.

Kawarau Gorge, on the **Kawarau River**, was the site of the Argonath, the gigantic statues of the two kings of Gondor, past which the Fellowship sails (*www.cromwell.org.nz/gorge.htm*).

Wanaka, to the north, on the banks of the **Clutha River** supplied the golden plains, where the Black Riders search for Frodo and Orcs attack the Fellowship.

Closeburn, about ten minutes drive west from Queenstown on **Geary Road**, became the summit of Amon Hen (the actual summit filming site isn't accessible), where Frodo takes his leave of Aragorn and the fellowship after Boromir (Sean Bean) begins to succumb to the ring's power. The **Paradise** area, near the tiny township of

Glenorchy at the head of Lake Wakatipu toward the south of the South Island, became Lothlorien Woods in the elven realm of Lorien, where Boromir is fatally wounded in the battle with the Orcs and Merry and Pippin are captured.

In the Nelson area, **Mavora Lakes Park**, about 30 miles south of Lake Wakatipu in the Green Stone National Park, became Nen Hithoel, where Orcs chase the Hobbits out of the bush and into boats on the lake, and Frodo saves Sam from drowning.

LORD OF THE RINGS: THE TWO TOWERS, THE

(2002, dir: Peter Jackson)
Elijah Wood, Ian McKellen, Liv Tyler.
● NEW ZEALAND

Way east of Queenstown, near **Poolburn Dam** in the Ida Valley about 25 miles east of Alexandra, stood the village on the Plains of Rohan, where the children are sent off to safety before the Orc attack. The village set no longer stands.

For obvious practical reasons, the Dead Marshes had to be created on sets, but the wider landscape shots are the **Kepler Mire**, largest of the wetlands in the Te Anau basin, once again in the Fjordland region and an important nature conservancy area, which gave rise to concern about the effect filming might have on the delicate ecosystem

The huge fortress city of Minas Tirith and Helm's Deep, where the awesome climactic battle takes place, were built at **Dry Creek Quarry**, a vast mining complex surrounded by a chainlink fence at the bottom of **Haywards Hill** in **Wellington** (*rail: Manor Park*). It's a working quarry and the sets have been removed.

LORD OF THE RINGS: THE RETURN OF THE KING, THE

(2003, dir: Peter Jackson)
Elijah Wood, Ian McKellen, Viggo Mortensen.
● NEW ZEALAND

On **Mount Sunday**, on the **Mount Potts Station**, the city of Edoras in the kingdom of Rohan was built. The **Ben Ohau Sheep Station**, near **Twizel** in Canterbury, became the Pelennor Fields, and the foothills of the White Mountains. **Queen Elizabeth Park**, **MacKays Crossing** between Paekakariki and Raumati South, was used to stage the part of the battle of Pelennor Fields with the fallen oliphaunt.

LOST BOYS, THE

(1987, dir: Joel Schumacher)
Jason Patric, Corey Haim, Dianne Wiest.
● CALIFORNIA

A teenage vampire gang in smalltown California. Good ideas – the vampire lair is a Victorian hotel lobby which slipped into a fault in the 1906

The rollercoaster: Santa Cruz Beach Boardwalk

earthquake – and a good cast are squandered. "I sensed that with this picture I could have fun without the result becoming camp," said director Schumacher. Well, there you go. Santa Carla is **Santa Cruz**, an eccentric coastal town between San Mateo and Monterey on the California coast south of San Francisco. The main attraction is the town's lively **Santa Cruz Beach Boardwalk, 400 Beach Street**, California's only surviving traditional seafront funfair, with the wonderful 1911 carousel the boys are barred from at the opening of the movie, and the old wooden rollercoaster.

LOST HIGHWAY
(1996, dir: David Lynch)
Bill Pullman, Patricia Arquette, Balthazar Getty.
● CALIFORNIA

The Lost Highway Hotel exterior: Death Valley Building, Death Valley Junction

The Lost Highway Hotel interiors: Amargoso Hotel, Death Valley Junction

Arnie's, the garage run by Richard Pryor: Firestone Garage, South La Brea Avenue

Lynch's foray into fluid identities is his most disturbing and successful effort since *Blue Velvet*. Bill Pullman's home is Lynch's own – he designed it himself – hidden away in the **Hollywood Hills**. Arnie's, the garage run by Richard Pryor, where Balthazar Getty works, is the 1937 deco **Firestone Garage, 800 South La Brea Avenue** at Eighth Street, midtown LA.

The desert locale is **Silurian Dry Lake**, east of Route 127, between Baker and Shoshone in the Mojave Desert.

The Lost Highway Hotel is a conflation of two buildings. The corridors are the **Amargoso Hotel, Death Valley Junction**, a tiny, one-street town on Route 127, north of Shoshone near the Nevada border. The exterior is the more photogenic **Death Valley Building**, directly opposite (seen also in *The Hitcher*).

LOST HORIZON
(1937, dir: Frank Capra)
Ronald Colman, Jane Wyatt, John Howard.
● CALIFORNIA

The opening airlift of Capra's classic fantasy was filmed at the old Los Angeles Metropolitan Airport, now incorporated into **Van Nuys Airport, 6590 Hayvenhurst Avenue, Van Nuys**, with the San Bernardino Mountains standing in for the mountains of Baskul. The Metropolitan Airport also featured as Casablanca Airport in *Casablanca*. The plane refuels at **Lucerne Dry Lake**, east of Victorville in the Mojave Desert. The aerial shots of the Himalayas are actually the High Sierras northwest of **Lone Pine**, central California. The Lamasery of Shangri-La was built on the Columbia Ranch at 4000 Warner Boulevard, Burbank, and the Valley of the Blue Moon, with its Tibetan village, is in **Sherwood Forest** beyond the San Fernando Valley.

The waterfall scene used **Tahquitz Canyon** (it's closed to the public, and you need a special permit to visit it). Tahquitz Canyon is part of Palm Canyon, stretching for some 15 miles in the Low Desert close to Palm Springs, 107 miles east of LA. You can find the spot from which Ronald Colman looked down onto the valley of Shangri-La northwest of Los Angeles, near Ventura. About ten miles north of Ventura is Ojai. From Ojai, follow Route 150, **East End Drive**, for about three miles to the spot, a promontory with a stone bench, inscribed 'The Ojai Valley'.

The clunky musical remake in 1973 used old sets from *Camelot* at Warner's Burbank Studio, perked up with a bit of Oriental tat, and LA gardens with white sheeting laid down for snow. The snowbound opening scenes are at **Mount Hood, Oregon**, home of the Overlook Hotel in Stanley Kubrick's *The Shining*.

LOST IN TRANSLATION
(2003, dir: Sofia Coppola)
Scarlett Johansson, Bill Murray, Giovanni Ribisi.
● JAPAN

The neon signs, which dazzle Bob (Murray) on his arrival in the city, are along **Yasukuni Don** (Yasukuni Avenue), around the entrance to Shinjuku's **Kabukico** entertainment district, northeast of Shinjuku Station. You can see the huge animated sign with a brontosaurus walking across, the Q-Eye sign, at the phenomenally busy **Shibuya Crossing** (a shot grabbed, guerilla filming-style, from the second floor of Starbucks).

Bob and Charlotte (Johansson) stay in the (not inexpensive) **Park Hyatt Tokyo, 3-7-1-2 Nishi-Shinjuku, Shinjuku-Ku** (© *03.5322.1234, www.tokyo.park. hyatt.com*). The hotel occupies the top 14 floors of a 52-storey office building in Shinjuku. The bar where Bob tries to unwind is the hotel's top-floor **New York Bar**. The temple (she calls it a shrine) visited by Charlotte is **Jugan-ji Temple** in Shinjuku, near to Nakano-Sakaue Station on the Marunouchi Line. There was also filming around Tokyo's **Shinjuku** entertainment district, and **Shibuya**, three stations south on the Yamanote Line. The karaoke bar, where she and Bob savage The Pretenders and Roxy Music, is one of the ubiquitous Karaoke-Kan chain, **Karaoke-Kan, 30-8 Utagawacho**, Shibuya (© *03.3462.0785*).

Charlotte takes the shinkansen (bullet train) to **Kyoto**, where she visits the **Heian Shrine** (subway from Kyoto to Higashiyama Station) and the Zen temple, **Nanzenji Temple** (Keage Station). Bob and Charlotte dine at sushi restaurant **Daikanyama Ikkan Sushi, 9-5 Daikanyama**,

Shibuya-ku (© *03.3464.5559*). The nightclub is hip hangout **Air, Nakagawa Building, Sarugaku-cho 2-11**, Shibuya-ku (© *03.5784.3386*). The strip club is actually ultra-stylish boutique **APC Underground, Jingumae 4-27-6-B1**, Shibuya-ku (*www.apcjp.com*). The minimal warped-timber interior is by French architect Laurent Derco. The restaurant is **Shabu-Zen**, in the basement of the **Shibuya Creston Hotel, 10-8 Kamiyama cho**, Shibuya-ku (© *03.3481.5800*).

LOST PATROL, THE

(1934, dir: John Ford)
Victor McLaglen, Boris Karloff, Wallace Ford.
● ARIZONA

A British army patrol in the Mesopotamian desert during WWI are picked off by Arabs. The desert scenes were filmed around **Yuma**, southwest Arizona.

LOST WEEKEND, THE

(1945, dir: Billy Wilder)
Ray Milland, Jane Wyman, Philip Terry.
● NEW YORK CITY

Milland destroys his liver: PJ Clarke's Saloon, Third Avenue

Grim, realistic study of alcoholism, made on location in New York. The bar is **PJ Clarke's Saloon, 915 Third Avenue** at East 55th Street. This wonderful institution is, amazingly, still open for business, a tiny oasis among the highrise real estate of the East Side. The rumble of the old 'Third Avenue el' – the elevated railway which ran past the bar – meant that many of the scenes had to be re-shot in the studio. Milland dries out at **Bellevue Hospital, First Avenue** at East 29th Street. Milland's painful trek along **Third Avenue**, north from 55th Street to 110th Street in search of a pawnbroker, was shot by a hidden camera inside a bakery truck one quiet Sunday.

LOST WORLD: JURASSIC PARK, THE

(1997, dir: Steven Spielberg)
Jeff Goldblum, Julianne Moore, Pete Postlethwaite.
● CALIFORNIA; HAWAII

Richard Attenborough's house, where Jeff Goldblum has his arm twisted to travel out to the previously unmentioned Isla Sorna, is actually a Catholic girls' school in Pasadena, **Mayfield Senior School, 500 Bellefontaine Street** (seen also in *Devil in a Blue Dress*). And while Site B again used *Jurassic Park*'s main location on the island of **Kauai**, Hawaii, for scene setting, much of

T-rex on the loose in San Diego: Golden Mall, Burbank

John Hammond's house: Mayfield Senior School, Pasadena

the action was filmed on mainland USA, in northern California near to Eureka, at **Patrick's Point**.

The T-rex wreaks havoc on landing at **San Diego**, supposedly in the city's Gaslamp district. But once again, there's a bit of sleight of hand. San Diego only features in a bit of second unit footage to establish the locale. Most of the filming was much closer to the studio in **Burbank**, at **Golden Mall** on **San Fernando Boulevard** between **Palm Grove** and **Orange Grove**, which were renamed with San Diego street signs. The Starbucks coffee shop is at **300 San Fernando Boulevard**. The bookshop where the screenwriter David Koepp, in a cameo as 'Unlucky Bastard', gets chomped by the T-rex, is **Crown Books, 301 San Fernando Boulevard**. The InGen dock where the T-rex boat crashes ashore is actually **San Pedro** harbour in LA. The house where T-rex takes a drink from the swimming pool and snacks on a dog is in **Granada Hills**, a Valley suburb of LA, and here too is the gas station, where the trademark '76' ball rolls down the street. It's the **Chevron Filling Station, Balboa Boulevard** at the corner of **Rinaldi**.

LOVE ACTUALLY

(2003, dir: Richard Curtis)
Hugh Grant, Martine McCutcheon, Bill Nighy.
● LONDON

If you thought *Notting Hill* was cynically contrived, *Love Actually* seems to have been churned out by a software program. Richard Curtis makes a grievous bodily assault on the tear ducts, while letting you feel nothing; the fast food of emotion. There are establishing shots of the **Oxo Tower, Tate Modern** and the **Millennium Bridge**. Harry (Alan Rickman) buys a necklace for his secretary at **Selfridge's, Oxford Street**. The central court of **Somerset House** saw sterling service as a movie location over the years (*GoldenEye*, *Sleepy Hollow* etc) when it was a rather dull parking lot. Since the building's renovation, it has been transformed into a pleasant fountain court and, in winter, a **skating rink**, which is how it appears here. The recording studio, where Billy Mack (Nighy) records his cheesy Christmas record, is **Westway Studios, Ladbroke Grove** in Notting Hill. His record company office is unmistakably the **London Assembly Building** on the South Bank alongside Tower Bridge. The South Bank gallery run by Mark (Andrew Lincoln) was an empty office on **Great Sutton Street, Clerkenwell**. The Prime Minister (Grant) and Natalie (McCutcheon) attend a school concert at **Elliott School, Pullman Gardens, Putney**. Peter (Chiwetel Ejiofor) marries Juliet (Keira Knightley) in the **Grosvenor Chapel, South Audley Street**. Daniel (Liam Neeson) buries his wife at **St Paul's, Clapham**. The PM searches for Natalie in Wandsworth, actually **Poplar Road, Herne Hill**. The movie opens and closes at **Heathrow**. In these days of strict security, 10 Downing Street was a set built in the studio at Shepperton.

The airport from which Colin (Kris Marshall) departs to find fulfillment in Wisconsin is **Sandown Racecourse**. The Wisconsin bar was built on the Shepperton backlot. The radio studio, where Billy Mack reveals that his record is crap and Britney Spears was a lousy shag, is **Heat Radio, Mappin House, 4 Winsley Street**, London W1. The mews where Juliet lives and Mark reveals his unrequited love, is off All Saint's Road, Notting Hill.

The Portuguese restaurant, where Jamie (Colin Firth) finally declares his love for Aurelia (Lúcia Moniz), is **Le Bar de la Marine, 15 quai de Rive Neuve**, the Old Port in Marseille (℡ *91.54.95.42*), which was also the setting for Marcel Pagnol's *Marius*.

LOVE AFFAIR

(1939, dir: Leo McCarey)
Irene Dunne, Charles Boyer, Maria Ouspenskaya.
● **NEW YORK CITY**

First of three versions of the classic tearjerker, with Dunne and Boyer meeting aboard ship, and pledging to reunite at the **Empire State Building, 350 Fifth Avenue**. Dunne misses the appointment when she's hit and crippled by a cab.

LOVE AND DEATH

(1975, dir: Woody Allen)
Woody Allen, Diane Keaton, Harold Gould.
● **PARIS, FRANCE; HUNGARY**

Back in the days when Woody Allen strayed, occasionally, outside Manhattan, he went to Europe to make this funny Bergmanesque version of *War and Peace*, filmed on real locations in **Budapest** and Paris.

LOVE BUG, THE

(1969, dir: Robert Stevenson)
Dean Jones, Michele Lee, David Tomlinson.
● **CALIFORNIA**

The 'Crookedest Street in the World': Lombard Street, San Francisco

Disney fun, with the anthropomorphic VW's first outing, set in San Francisco. And, of course, any comedy car chase set in the Bay City has to take in the self-proclaimed 'Crookedest Street in the World', the **1000 block of Lombard Street**, between Hyde and Leavenworth. The eight switchbacks were introduced in 1922, not by a movie company, but as a practical way of rendering the street accessible to cars. If you want to see it, go on foot or take the Hyde-Powell cable car which runs along the top of the street, as it can get seriously clogged with sightseers. Filming also took place on **Monterey Peninsula**, on the coast south of the city.

LOVE STORY

(1970, dir: Arthur Hiller)

Ryan O'Neal, Ali MacGraw, Ray Milland.
● **MASSACHU-SETTS; NEW YORK CITY**

The college campus: Harvard Yard

Rich kid O'Neal gives up the family fortune to marry working class student McGraw, but it's a bad deal as she's dying from one of those mysterious Hollywood diseases devoid of visible symptoms. O'Neal and McGraw meet at **Harvard**. Along with the sequel, *Oliver's Story*, legal drama *The Paper Chase* and misfiring comedy *Soul Man*, it's one of the few features actually filmed on the hallowed campus. Filming took place at **Harvard Yard** and **Ter-**

Love means...: Oxford Street, Cambridge

centuary Theatre. The intimidatingly grand mansion belonging to Ray Milland, O'Neal's unbending father, is the **Phipps Estate House, Old Westbury Gardens, 71 Old Westbury Road** on Long Island (see *North by Northwest* for details), though the gate leading to it is that of **Planting Fields**, on Long Island.

After their DIY marriage, O'Neal and McGraw set up home in a modest woodframe house at **119 Oxford Street, Cambridge**. It's on the doorstep here that McGraw gets to utter the immortal "Love means never having to say you're sorry". After graduation, the couple move to New York City. The skating scene is at the **Wollman Skating Rink** in Central Park. When McGraw is taken ill, they catch a cab by Central Park opposite the **Hotel Pierre**.

LOVED ONE, THE

(1965, dir: Tony Richardson)
Robert Morse, John Gielgud, Rod Steiger.
● **LOS ANGELES, CALIFORNIA**

Tony Richardson's satire on the movie business and the American funeral industry, based on the Evelyn Waugh novel, is a bit hit and miss, but the hits are priceless, including Liberace as an oleaginous coffin salesman. Robert Morse arrives at **Los Angeles International Airport (LAX)**. Megalopolitan Studios, where he goes to work, is the MGM lot. Behind the Megalopolitan logo is the Metro-Goldwyn-Mayer sign of the Irving Thalberg Building. Whispering Glades is the 16-acre **Greystone Park**, the grounds of **Greystone Mansion, 905 Loma Vista Drive, Beverly Hills**. The park, open daily to the public, disguises a massive underground reservoir. By the way, it's often said in guidebooks that

Whispering Glades: Greystone Park, Loma Vista Drive, Beverly Hills

John Gielgud's home in the movie is the Spadena House,
Beverly Hills' quirky Witch's House – seen in Roger Corman's 1957 *The Undead* – but it ain't.

LUST FOR LIFE
(1956, dir: Vincente Minnelli)
Kirk Douglas, Anthony Quinn, James Donald.
● HOLLAND; FRANCE; BELGIUM

Minnelli's biopic of Van Gogh was shot in Europe on
many of the real locations. Including **Vught** and **Bois-la-
Duc** in Holland, **Paris**, and **St Remy** and **Arles** in
Provence. The Petit Wasmes mine disaster was staged at
Le Borinage in south Belgium, using 200 unemployed
miners as extras. The final wheatfield scenes, of Van
Gogh's suicide, are at **Auvers-sur-Oises**.

M

MA NUIT CHEZ MAUD (aka *My Night at Maud's*)
(1969, dir: Eric Rohmer)
Jean-Louis Trintignant, Marie-Christine Barrault.
● **FRANCE**

Trintignant is obliged to crash down with his mate's girl-friend during a snowstorm. Naturally, they flirt, discuss Jansenism, consider marriage and don't have sex. Trintignant, however, eventually realises he really loves a blonde he's seen on a bicycle. The town is **Clermont-Ferrand**, though the interior of Maud's apartment was recreated in a small studio on the rue Mouffetard in Paris. The epilogue is on the island of **Belle Ile** off St Nazaire, and in **Paris**.

MACBETH

(1971, dir: Roman Polanski)
Jon Finch, Francesca Annis, Martin Shaw.
● **NORTHUMBERLAND; WALES**

Misguided attempt to film Shakespeare's dark nightmare as a too-naturalistic historical bloodbath. Some nice visuals though. Dunsinane is **Bamburgh Castle** in Northumberland (see *The Devils* for details). Inverness is **Lindisfarne Castle** on Holy Island (see Polanski's earlier film, *Cul-De-Sac*, for details). The movie also uses locations in Wales – the opening beach scenes are **Morfa Bychan**, near Portmadoc.

MAD MAX

(1979, dir: George Miller)
Mel Gibson, Joanne Samuel, Hugh Keays-Byrne.
● **VICTORIA, AUSTRALIA**

Mel Gibson shot to fame as futuristic, leather-clad cop Max Rockatansky, unhinged by the murder of his wife and child, in George Miller's low budget actioner, which spawned increasingly spectacular sequels. Filmed on the roads around Melbourne. The Halls of Justice cop station/garage, where Max is seduced by the souped-up motor, is the **Southern Car Park** of **Melbourne University**.

MAD MAX 2 (aka *The Road Warrior*)

(1981, dir: George Miller)
Mel Gibson, Bruce Spence, Vernon Wells.

The final smash-up: Silverton

● **NEW SOUTH WALES, AUSTRALIA**

Sequel takes on an epic sweep, and the visual style launched a slew of rip-offs. It was made at the deserted (except for film crews, that is) ghost town of **Silverton**, about 14 miles northwest of Broken Hill. Once a booming silver town – producing one third of the world's silver – Silverton is now a frequent location, seen in films such as *Razorback* and the TV remake of *A Town Like Alice*. Memorabilia from the various movies shot here is on display. The stretch of road used for the climactic smash-up can be seen just outside town.

MAD MAX BEYOND THUNDERDOME

(1985, dir: George Miller)
Mel Gibson, Tina Turner, Frank Thring.
● **SOUTH AUSTRALIA; NEW SOUTH WALES, AUSTRALIA**

The main location for the third part of the trilogy is the strange, moonlike landscape, scarred by opal mining, around **Coober Pedy** in South Australia. The name means 'White Man's Burrow' – most of the homes here, even the church and the rooms of two of the five motels, are dug out of the ground. You can visit the underground dwelling seen at the end of the movie. It's **Harry's Crocodile Nest**, three miles outside Coober Pedy itself (*admission charge*).

Also featured is **The Castle**, part of the Breakaways, the end of a mountain chain around 20 miles from town. You can fly out to Coober Pedy, or take a daily bus from Adelaide or Alice Springs (expect a lengthy journey, 530 miles from Adelaide, 455 from Alice). To drive there, take National Route 1 from Adelaide to Port Augusta, then continue on Route 87, Stuart Highway. The town is seen also in *The Adventures of Priscilla, Queen of the Desert*. There was more filming at a vast, empty brick pit in the **Blue Mountains**, 50 miles west of Sydney.

MADIGAN

(1968, dir: Donald Siegel)
Richard Widmark, Henry Fonda, Harry Guardino.
● **NEW YORK CITY; LOS ANGELES, CALIFORNIA**

Cop-with-a-grudge movie, which Siegel later recycled as *Dirty Harry*. This time round it's Richard Widmark and the setting is New York, with plenty of sleazy Brooklyn locations. Henry Fonda's apartment is on **57th Street**, Manhattan. The final shoot-out in Harlem was actually shot in downtown LA, with a bit of clever effects work taking out the LA Civic Center and replacing it with a New York skyscraper.

MADNESS OF KING GEORGE, THE

(1994, dir: Nicholas Hytner)
Nigel Hawthorne, Helen Mirren, Rupert Everett.
● **OXFORDSHIRE; LONDON; SUSSEX; BERKSHIRE; WILTSHIRE; MIDDLESEX**

Stage director Nicholas Hytner's film adaptation of Alan

The Palace of Westminster, exterior: School Yard, Eton College

The Palace of Westminster interior: Convocation, Oxford

Bennett's play, *The Madness of George III*, uses a slew of real locations. The opening concert is the sumptuous 17th century Double Cube Room of **Wilton House**, in the town of **Wilton**, two-and-a-half miles west of Salisbury on the A30, Wiltshire. The house and grounds are open in summer (*© 01722. 746720; admission charge*). Another popular location, Wilton House can be seen in *Barry Lyndon*, *The Bounty* and *Mrs Brown* among many others. See *The Music Lovers* for details.

Windsor Castle has been extensively remodelled since George III's reign, so the film uses the exterior of **Arundel Castle, Arundel**, in West Sussex (*rail: Arundel*), the 12th century home of the Duke of Norfolk. The castle is open Sunday to Friday in summer (*© 01903.883136; admission charge*). The entrance is on Lower Lodge Mill Road, Arundel, just north of the A27 between Worthing and Chichester. The Palace of Westminster, too, has changed beyond recognition. The exterior is the **School Yard** of **Eton College**, north of Windsor, Berkshire. The steps lead up to the north porch of **College Chapel**. Between the buttresses at the foot of the steps, the game of Eton Fives originated. You can see the same yard in stacks of other films, including *Chariots of Fire*, *Young Sherlock Holmes*, *The Fourth Protocol* and *Henry VIII and His Six Wives*. The public entrance to the school (it's generally open from April to mid-October) is on Slough Road (*admission charge*). The House of Commons interior, with Bennett himself as an MP, used **Convocation** in Oxford, with the adjoining **Divinity School** standing in for the lobby. Both are part of the Bodleian Library complex, **Catte Street**, and are open to the public. About ten miles east of Oxford is the location used for Kew Gardens, where the King is sent to be cured by strict doctor Ian Holm. It's a private residence, **Thame Park,**

Windsor Castle: Arundel Castle

The music recital: Royal Naval College, Greenwich

Thame Park Road, just southeast of the village of Thame. The grounds of Thame Park were used in *Saving Private Ryan*.

George III is sent to be cured: Thame Park, Thame Park Road

The Queen's royal apartments are **Broughton Castle**, a moated 14th century Medieval castle which was much enlarged in 1550. The home of Lord and Lady Saye and Sele, it's two miles southwest of Banbury, Oxfordshire, on the B40355 Shipston-on-Stour road. It's open to the public Wednesdays and Sundays in summer (*© 0 1 2 9 5 . 2 6 2 6 2 4 , www.broughtoncastle.demon. co.uk*). You can also see the castle in *Shakespeare in Love* and *Three Men and a Little Lady*.

The House of Commons' lobby: Divinity School, Oxford

The Prince of Wales' lodgings also used Wilton House, as well as at the **Royal Naval College, Greenwich**, London SE10 (*rail: Greenwich*). It's in the lavish **Painted Hall** of the Royal Naval College that the royal family suffers through the handbell concert. In Wren's building, until recently used as the dining room of the naval hospital, painter James Thornhill collaborated with architect Nicholas Hawksmoor for nineteen years on this *trompe l'oeil* extravaganza. It was here that the body of Lord Nelson lay in state, and the Painted Hall is open to the public. The Long Gallery, in which the King sees Pitt, is at **Syon House** (*rail: Brentford or Syon Lane*), on the north bank of the Thames between Brentford and Isleworth. The Prince of Wales' breakfast room is also Syon House (*© 020.8560.0881; admission charge*). See *Accident* for details.

MAGNIFICENT OBSESSION

(1954, dir: Douglas Sirk)
Jane Wyman, Rock Hudson, Agnes Moorehead.
● **CALIFORNIA**

Remake of a 1935 movie, with Sirk's customary Technicolor gloss. Rock Hudson is responsible for the death of Jane Wyman's husband, and for blinding her. To atone he becomes a surgeon. Filming took place at **Lake Arrowhead**, an upscale resort in the San Bernardino Mountains, off I-15 east of LA.

MAGNIFICENT SEVEN, THE

(1960, dir: John Sturges)
Yul Brynner, Steve McQueen, James Coburn.
● **MEXICO**

Seven hired guns fight off bandits in this remake of Kurosawa's *The Seven Samurai*, made on sets constructed in the desert at **Cuernavaca** near Mexico City.

MAGNOLIA

(2000, dir: Paul Thomas Anderson)

William H Macy, Julianne Moore, Tom Cruise.

● CALIFORNIA; NEVADA

Donnie declares his love for Brad: Foxfire Room, Magnolia Boulevard, Valley Village

Donnie tries to climb a telegraph pole: LA Popular Alliances, Reseda.

"*Magnolia* fan" may be the ulti-mate put-down for Kevin Smith affi-cionados, but Val-ley boy Ander-son's daring, multi-centred drama barrels through its three-hour running time with blistering energy, carrying a clutch of career-best performances on board. Like *Boogie Nights*, it's set in the direc-tor's own neigh-bourhood, the San Fernando Valley, of Burbank, North Hollywood and Van Nuys, north of LA.

The film is named for Magnolia Boulevard, one of the Valley's main east-west thoroughfares, on which you'll find the bar in which Quiz Kid Donnie (Macy) declares his love for Brad the Bartender (Craig Kvinsland). The **Foxfire Room, 12516 Magnolia Boulevard** at Whitsett Avenue (*© 818.766.1344*) is in Valley Village, north of Studio City. Good-natured cop Jim (John C Reilly) is caught by the unexpected frog deluge as he drives along **Reseda Boulevard**. The Solomon & Solomon store, where he spots Donnie trying to climb a telegraph pole after the clumsy robbery, is **LA Popular Alliances, 7222 Reseda Boulevard** at Sherman Way in Reseda.

The suicide leap: Bryson, Wilshire Boulevard

It's in down-town LA itself that you'll find the nine-story build-ing where the unsuccessful sui-cide of the pro-logue becomes a successful homi-cide. The **Bryson, 2701 Wilshire Boulevard** was seen also in Stephen Frears' excellent *The Grifters*.

MAHLER

(1974, dir: Ken Russell)

Robert Powell, Georgina Hale, David Collings.

● CUMBRIA; HERTFORDSHIRE

Russell's fantasia on the music of composer Gustav Mahler, limited by the budget, was shot mainly in the Lake District, where the composer's waterside cabin was constructed on **Lake Derwentwater**. Other locations include **Borrowdale** and **Keswick**, with the woodland scenes shot close to Pinewood Studios at **Black Park**

Country Park.

MAJOR DUNDEE

(1965, dir: Sam Peckinpah)

Charlton Heston, Richard Harris, James Coburn.

● MEXICO

Violent Western set, and filmed, in Mexico, mainly at that old standby Western town **Durango**, with interiors shot at Churubuscu Studios in Mexico City. For the opening massacre, the Rostes ranch was built at **La Marquesa**, 25 miles southwest of Mexico City. Other exteriors are various Mexican towns, including **Cuautla**; **Teques-quitengo**; **Tehuixtla**; and **Vistahermosa** – all south of Mexico City on the route to Acapulco, as is the setting for the final battle sequence on the Rio Balsas near **Chilpancingo**.

MALCOLM X

(1992, dir: Spike Lee)

Denzel Washington, Angela Bassett, Theresa Randle.

● NEW YORK CITY; NEW YORK STATE; CAIRO, EGYPT; MECCA, SAUDI ARABIA; SOUTH AFRICA

Welcoming Joe Louis: Apollo, West 125th Street, Harlem

Spike Lee's epic biopic of the black leader and activist was filmed (and not without a strug-gle: see *By Any Means Neces-sary* – Lee's book on the mak-ing of the film) largely around New York.

The grand opening shot is supposed to be Dudley Street Station, Roxbury, a black area of Boston, but is actually Brooklyn, with New York City transit trains painted as Boston trains of the forties. The childhood home of Mal-colm Little, the name he later rejected, in Omaha, Nebras-ka, was filmed in **Peekskill**, on Route 9, New York State. The bravura dance sequence in Boston's Roseland is the ballroom of the since-demolished Diplomat Hotel, 108 West 43rd Street. The New England shoreline is at **Hemp-stead House, Sands Point Preserve, Port Washington**. When Malcolm X returns to Boston after falling foul of a Harlem numbers boss, the burglary at Beacon Hill was shot at a classy apartment on Manhattan's **Park Avenue**.

In New York, X gravitates to Harlem. The Paradise Bar, where he hangs out and begins running numbers, is the **Lenox Lounge, 288 Lenox Avenue**, Harlem's recently-restored thirties gem, also seen in John Single-ton's update of *Shaft*. Charleston State Prison, where X converts to Islam, is **Rahway State Penitentiary, Rah-way**, on Route 1, New Jersey, on the River Rahway. The reborn Malcolm X lectures at **Columbia University, 114th-120th Streets**, between Broadway and Amster-dam Avenue (see *Ghostbusters* for details), and tenta-tively enjoys a first date with Betty Shabazz at the **Amer-ican Museum of Natural History, Central Park West** at West 79th Street. The ecstatic welcome for Joe Louis, and the march from the police station to the hospital after the release of brother Johnson, were filmed on 125th Street by the legendary **Apollo Theater, 253 West 125th Street**. The Apollo's famous Amateur Nights, begun in 1934, launched the careers of artists such as Ella Fitzgerald and James Brown. More recently, the likes of Michael Jackson, Stevie Wonder, Tony Bennett and The Strokes have appeared (© *212.531.5300, events hotline: 212.531.5301, www.apollotheater.com*).

The **Audobon Ballroom, 3940 Broadway** at West 166th Street in Washington Heights, scene of Malcolm X's assassination, was actually used for exterior shots. The Audobon was acquired by the city in the mid-seventies, and Columbia University currently has plans to develop the site as a research complex. The Audobon interiors used the Diplomat Ballroom again.

The real Mecca scenes were filmed by a second unit, as only a totally Islamic crew was allowed into the country. The Mecca scenes filmed in Cairo feature the **Mohammed Ali Mosque**. The epilogue was shot at **Phakamani Combined School, Soweto** in South Africa, where Nelson Mandela speaks the film's closing lines, and in the **Alexander** township.

MALLRATS
(1995, dir: Kevin Smith)
Shannen Doherty, Jeremy London, Jason Lee.
MINNEAPOLIS; NEW JERSEY

Smith's follow-up to *Clerks*, with a bunch of bickering teens hanging out in the local shopping mall, the **Eden Prairie Center Mall, Prairie Center Drive** off I-212 in Minneapolis, with more filming, naturally, in New Jersey.

MALTESE FALCON, THE
(1941, dir: John Huston)
Humphrey Bogart, Mary Astor, Sydney Greenstreet.
● **CALIFORNIA**

Huston's directorial début, the classic private detective story, set in San Francisco but filmed almost entirely at Warner Bros studios in Burbank. The only shots of the real San Francisco are a glimpse of the **Golden Gate Bridge**, a few atmospheric night shots and the murder of Spade's partner, Archer, on **Bush Street**. Not featured in the film, but in the book, is John's Grill, 63 Ellis Street. Sam Spade eats here, and the still-extant joint features a collection of memorabilia.

MAN CALLED HORSE, A
(1970, dir: Elliot Silverstein)
Richard Harris, Judith Anderson, Jean Gascon.
● **MEXICO**

English aristocrat Harris is captured by Indians, and endures all kinds of hardships, including the stomach-churning Sun Vow Ceremony, to become a Sioux. Set in 1820's Dakota, it was shot in the standard Western location of **Durango**, Mexico.

MAN FOR ALL SEASONS, A
(1966, dir: Fred Zinnemann)
Paul Scofield, Wendy Hiller, Robert Shaw.
● **OXFORDSHIRE; HAMPSHIRE**

Worthy, well-acted version of Robert Bolt's play about Thomas More's crisis of conscience over Henry VIII's divorce. Despite what guide books say, there was no

Thomas More's Chelsea home: Studley Priory, Horton-Cum-Studley

filming at Hampton Court Palace – Cardinal Wolsey's palace is no more than a movie set. Thomas More's house on the Thames at Chelsea, however, is real. It's **Studley Priory, Horton Hill, Horton-Cum-Studley** (© *01865.351203*), a one-time Benedictine monastery, now a hotel, about seven miles northeast of Oxford. The Thames is the **River Beaulieu**, flowing through the estate of **Beaulieu Abbey**, on the B3504, south of Southampton in Hampshire. The river wall built alongside was reproduced at Studley Priory, allowing characters to leap across counties in one bound!

MAN FROM LARAMIE, THE
(1955, dir: Anthony Mann)
James Stewart, Arthur Kennedy, Donald Crisp.
● **NEW MEXICO**

Another terrific Mann-Stewart collaboration, with Stewart tracking down the bad guys who caused his younger brother's death. It was shot around **Santa Fe** and **Taos**, New Mexico, largely at **Bonanza Creek Movie Ranch**, Tesuque Pueblo, about eight miles south of Santa Fe (*www.bonanzacreekranch.com*), which also hosted filming for *The Cowboys, Easy Rider, Butch Cassidy and the Sundance Kid* and *Young Guns*.

MAN IN THE IRON MASK, THE
(1939, dir: James Whale)
Louis Hayward, Warren William, Alan Hale.
● **LOS ANGELES**

Costume fun, with Dumas' tale of Louis XIV's imprisoned twin brother and the Three Musketeers. The forest scenes are in the **Los Angeles State and County Arboretum, 301 North Baldwin Avenue, Arcadia** (© *818.821.3222, www.arboretum.org*), east of LA. A 127-acre botanical garden, it must be one of the most filmed locations in the world. Its tropical foliage has been seen in *Tarzan* movies, *Road* movies, TV's *Fantasy Island* (the kitschy little Queen Anne cottage is here), classics such as *The Women* and *The Best Years of Our Lives*, a couple of Hitchcock's (*Notorious* and *Under Capricorn*), *Marathon Man* and literally hundreds of others.

MAN ON THE MOON
(1999, dir: Milos Forman)
Jim Carrey, Paul Giamatti, Courtney Love.
● **CALIFORNIA; NEW YORK STATE**

Milos Forman's fantasia on the life of the legendary media guerilla Andy Kaufman, fated to be best remembered as a loveable sitcom character. Its many locations are found around LA and in New York.

The eaterie where Kaufman works:
Jerry's Deli, Studio City

Scenes of Kaufman's childhood home were filmed in his actual neighbourhood of **Great Neck**, northeastern Long Island, New York, though not at the real house. The Carnegie Hall show, transposed to the end of Kaufman's life, uses the real **Carnegie Hall, 154 West 57th Street** (*www.carnegiehall.org*) at Seventh Avenue, for exteriors. The famous concert hall starred in its own movie, *Carnegie Hall*, back in 1947. The interior, with the Mormon Tabernacle Choir, the Rockettes and Santa Claus, is across the States, in the **Los Angeles Theatre, 615 South Broadway**, downtown LA (see *Chaplin* for details of this fave location). Also in LA are the Memphis wrestling scenes, which use the **Olympic Grand Auditorium**, downtown LA. The eaterie, where Kaufman works, is the real thing, still very much in operation: **Jerry's Deli, 12655 Ventura Boulevard, Studio City**. Street scenes are on **Main Street, La Puente**, which also featured as the town in *Halloween H20*.

MAN WHO FELL TO EARTH, THE

(1976, dir: Nicolas Roeg)
David Bowie, Candy Clark, Rip Torn.
● **NEW MEXICO; NEW YORK CITY**

For once, Bowie is perfectly cast as the unearthly Thomas Jerome Newton in Roeg's anti-naturalistic mosaic – although, bizarrely, *Jurassic Park* author Michael Crichton was the director's first choice for the role. The dry, desert locale is New Mexico, though Newton first plummets into the waters of **Fenton Lake, Jemez Springs**, 33 miles northeast of San Ysidro. The small desert town, where innocent alien Newton takes up with Candy Clark, is **Artesia**, down in the southeast corner of the state, 30 miles north of Carlsbad on I-285. The church, where Bowie proves he can't sing, is the **Presbyterian Church of Artesia**. The rocket scenes used the **White Sands Missile Range, Alamogordo**, off I-70 in southern New Mexico. Other New Mexico locations include the old mining town of **Madrid** and the **Civic Plaza, Albuquerque**. Trapped on Earth, Bowie finally ends up in New York.

MAN WHO KNEW TOO MUCH, THE

(1934, dir: Alfred Hitchcock)
Leslie Banks, Edna Best, Peter Lorre.
● **LONDON**

Leslie Banks and Edna Best track down their kidnapped child in this early Hitchcock thriller. The opening scenes are set in a very stagey *faux* St Moritz, with a few stock shots of Alpine skiers, but the action soon moves to London. The atmospheric Wapping scenes were filmed on a huge set, though there's a shot of the real **Tower Bridge**, when it was still surrounded by working docks and cranes. The attempt to assassinate the European diplomat was filmed, like the more famous remake, in the **Royal Albert Hall, South Kensington**.

MAN WHO KNEW TOO MUCH, THE

(1956, dir: Alfred Hitchcock)
James Stewart, Doris Day, Bernard Miles.
● **MOROCCO; LONDON**

Hitch's big-budget, colour remake of his own modest 1934 spy thriller utilised lots of real locations. Stewart and Day are dragged into the plot to assassinate an ambassador after their son is kidnapped in Morocco. The opening scenes were filmed in the souks and **Jemaâ el Fna**, the amazing main square of **Marrakech** with its dizzying array of food stalls, storytellers and snake-charmers. The couple stay in the famous, and phenomenally expensive, **La Mamounia Hotel, Avenue Bab Jdid**

Stewart and Day are drawn into the plot: Jemaâ el Fna, Marrakech

The Marrakech Hotel today: La Mamounia, Avenue Bab Jdid

Stewart looks for Ambrose Chapel: Plender Street, Camden Town

(℡ 44.38.86.00), set in seven acres of garden (used for Oliver Stone's epic *Alexander*) within the old city walls.

Back in london, Stewart follows a red herring to Ambrose Chapel, which turns out to be a taxidermist's. Hitchcock meant to film the scene on a set in Hollywood, but eventually plumped for the real premises of Gerrard Family Taxidermists, who specialised in supplying stuffed animals to Hollywood studios. They were used for both the exterior and interior shots. The company has gone, and the street has been redeveloped, but you can still see **Plender Street** and **Royal College Street**, NW1, where Stewart arrives by taxi, in **Camden Town**. The real Ambrose Chapel, where Doris Day is imprisoned, was St Saviour's church hall in **Brixton**. St Saviour's church is still there, but the church hall has gone. The Embassy, too, has gone. It was Park Lane House, demolished to make way for the Hilton Hotel on Park Lane. The extended, wordless climax, with Hitchcock regular collaborator Bernard Hermann conducting the orchestra, was shot in the **Royal Albert Hall, South Kensington**.

MAN WHO WOULD BE KING, THE

(1975, dir: John Huston)
Sean Connery, Michael Caine, Christopher Plummer.
● **MOROCCO**

Huston's film of Rudyard Kipling's Northwest Frontier fable is set in India, Afghanistan and Kafiristan, but was shot entirely on location in the Atlas Mountains near **Ouarzazate**, Morocco.

MAN WITH THE GOLDEN GUN, THE

(1974, dir: Guy Hamilton)
Roger Moore, Christopher Lee, Britt Ekland.
● **HONG KONG, CHINA; MACAU; THAILAND**

The golden bullet of ace hitman Scaramanga (Lee) has Bond's name on it, literally. 007 traces its manufacture to gun expert Lazar in Macau, the former Portuguese

Following the bullet: Floating Macau Palace

Bond arrives in Kowloon: Peninsula Hotel

enclave west of Hong Kong, where he inevitably gravitates toward the casino, the **Floating Macau Palace, Inner Harbour, Rua das Lorchas**. As its name suggests, the casino is a converted vessel moored on the peninsula's western shore. He takes the ferry across the bay to **Kowloon**, the mainland suburb of Hong Kong, where he follows Andrea Anders (Maud Adams) to the **Peninsula Hotel, Salisbury Road** at Nathan Road (© 852.2920. 2888, www.peninsula.com) which does indeed run a fleet of green Rolls Royces (how did the globe-trotting *bon viveur* not know this?), and was also seen in the 1955 anti-Commie adventure *Soldier of Fortune*, with Clark Gable and Susan Hayward.

Also in Kowloon are the fictitious Bottoms Up club, which was situated amid the neon dazzle of the **Tsim Sha Tsui** shopping district, and Hai Fat's estate, the **Dragon Garden** on **Castle Peak Road, Castle Peak**. MI6 field HQ is deep inside the tilted, rusting hulk of the Queen Elizabeth, which was grounded in Hong Kong harbour.

The trail of Scaramanga leads to Bangkok, and a boat chase through the klongs, the network of canals crisscrossing the city. The karate school is the **Ancient City**, the world's largest outdoor museum, with its scaled-down versions of the famous buildings and temples of Bangkok. It's about 20 miles east of town on **Sukhumvit Highway** in Changwat Samut Prakan (© 226.1936; admission charge). The kickboxing match, at which Bond first meets Scaramanga, was filmed in Bangkok's **Ratchadamnoen Stadium, Ratchadamnoen Nok Road** (© 281.4205).

But, most famously, Scaramanga's island hideout is **Khow-Ping-Kan**, one of a chain of tiny jungle-covered limestone pillars in **Phang Nga Bay** at Phuket, on the tip of the Malay peninsula. At the time of filming it was a remote and undiscovered paradise. Now, it's overrun by tourists, taking the 54 mile bus journey north from

Phuket Town, and the boat trip out to see 'James Bond Island'.

MAN WITH TWO BRAINS, THE

(1983, dir: Carl Reiner)
Steve Martin, Kathleen Turner, David Warner.
● **LOS ANGELES**

Wildly silly comedy, played to the hilt by a game cast, with Sissy Spacek voicing the disembodied brain Steve Martin falls in love with. The Austrian hotel, where Martin honeymoons, is the **Castle Green Apartments, 99 South Raymond Avenue, Pasadena**. For details, see *The Sting* which also used this fabulously bizarre Moorish fantasy.

MANCHURIAN CANDIDATE, THE

(1962, dir: John Frankenheimer)
Frank Sinatra, Laurence Harvey, Angela Lansbury.
● **LOS ANGELES; NEW YORK CITY**

Raymond Shaw (Harvey) is programmed to carry out a political assassination in New York, where most of the story is set. But there was little filming on the East Coast. Yes, it's Los Angeles. The opening scene, the capture of Shaw's company in Korea, was shot in **Franklin Canyon**, in the Santa Monica Mountains north of Beverly Hills. It's at **Santa Monica Airport** that his monstrously overbearing, Commiebaiting mother (Lansbury) hijacks his arrival in Washington DC to be awarded the Congressional Medal of Honor.

"Go jump in the lake...": The steps of Bethesda Terrace in Central Park

Laurence Harvey's apartment: Riverside Drive

Moving to New York, Shaw lives at **67 Riverside Drive** at 79th Street, on the West Side. Marco (Sinatra) catches up with him at Jilly's Bar, on 52nd Street at Eighth Avenue. It was a real New York hangout of the Rat Pack, owned by Sinatra's pal and bodyguard Jilly Rizzo. The highly suggestible Shaw responds literally to a chance aside by Rizzo ("Go up to Central Park and go jump in the lake..."), tripping down the steps of **Bethesda Terrace** in **Central Park** and plopping into the **Lake** between the **Ramble** and **Cherry Hill**.

The climactic political rally is at New York's **Madison Square Gardens**, where the exterior shots, and even the deserted interior, are the real thing. But, once the garden becomes full of (expensive) extras, it's downtown LA's **Olympic Auditorium, 1801 South Grand Avenue** at Olympic Boulevard (see *Rocky* for details).

MANHATTAN

(1979, dir: Woody Allen)
Woody Allen, Diane Keaton, Mariel Hemingway.

Allen and Keaton watch dawn break: Riverview Terrace, Sutton Square

● NEW YORK CITY; NEW JERSEY

The prologue to Woody Allen's stylish monochrome hymn to New York is a montage of the city's iconic images including the thirties-style, stainless steel **Empire Diner, 210 Tenth Avenue** between West 22nd and West 23rd Streets (also seen in *Men In Black II*); the **Staten Island ferry**; the **Lincoln Center**; and the **Temple of Dendur**, an Egyptian complex rebuilt in the **Metropolitan Museum of Art** on Fifth Avenue, illuminated within its purpose-built, glass-walled gallery.

The film is burdened with the line destined to haunt Allen forever ("I'm dating a girl who does homework") during the opening foursome at **Elaine's, 1703 Second Avenue** between 88th and 89th Streets on the East Side – a restaurant to be seen in rather than eat in (*©212.534.8103*). He has an inauspicious meeting with neurotic poseur Diane Keaton at an exhibition in Frank Lloyd Wright's white spiral **Guggenheim Museum, 1071 Fifth Avenue** at 89th Street, but begins a guarded flirtation after a second meeting in the Sculpture Gallery of **MOMA (the Museum of Modern Art), 11 West 53rd Street**. It's afterwards that the pair famously watch dawn breaking from a bench on **Riverview Terrace** on **Sutton Square**, beneath the **Queensboro Bridge**. The stunning image inspired the movie's poster, but there's no bench here and the view is now disfigured by a series of bollards.

The speciality food store, where Allen and Mariel Hemingway diss Keaton, is **Dean & DeLuca Inc, 560 Broadway** between Prince and Spring Streets in SoHo. Allen kvetches to Michael Murphy in **Rizzoli's Bookstore, 31 West 57th Street** between Fifth and Sixth Avenues (where De Niro and Streep meet in *Falling in Love*), after throwing in his TV job. Keaton and Murphy meet furtively at the perfume counter of **Bloomingdale's, 59th Street** between Lexington Avenue and Third Avenue, while Allen collects his kid from ex-wife Meryl Streep for a meal and some guy stuff, at the (since closed, but now newly-renovated) **Russian Tea Room, 150 West 57th Street** between Sixth and Seventh Avenues, the showbiz hangout seen also in *Tootsie*.

An electrical storm in Central Park causes an increasingly friendly Allen and Keaton to duck into the **Hayden Planetarium**, part of the **American Museum of Natural History** at **Central Park West** on 81st Street. Mariel Hemingway's school is the progressive **Dalton School, 61 East 91st Street** on the Upper East Side. The pizza place, where she tells Allen she's off to London, is **John's Pizza, 278 Bleecker Street** at

Allen collects his son: Russian Tea Room, West 57th Street

Morton Street and Seventh Avenue in Greenwich Village. It's small and usually packed, unsurprising since it was recommended by the director as the best pizza in New York.

Allen plays squash with Murphy at the **Uptown Racquet Club, Park Avenue** between 52nd and 53rd Streets; visits the **Whitney Museum of American Art, 945 Madison Avenue** at 75th Street, with Keaton; and watches art movies with her at the now gone Cinema Studio, 1966 Broadway. Still there, though, is **Zabar's, 2245 Broadway** at 80th Street, where Allen and Keaton gaze at the gourmet delights on display.

It's on an outing to the **Palisades** at **Englewood Cliffs**, across the Hudson River in New Jersey, where Allen gets to see Meryl Streep's published account of their marital break-up.

MANHATTAN MURDER MYSTERY
(1993, dir: Woody Allen)
Woody Allen, Diane Keaton, Alan Alda.
● NEW YORK CITY

Minor Allen comedy, grown out of ideas rejected from *Annie Hall*, which began life as a murder mystery. Allen and Keaton are an East Side married couple who begin to suspect their kindly old neighbour may have bumped off his wife. The couple stake out their cultural parameters by watching a New York Rangers hockey game at **Madison Square Garden, Seventh Avenue** between West 31st and West 33rd Streets, Chelsea, and taking in Wagner at the **Lincoln Center** on the West Side.

Keaton voices her first suspicions over a meal at fave Allen hangout **Elaine's, 1703 Second Avenue** between East 88th and East 89th Streets on the Upper East Side (see *Manhattan* for details). Allen and Keaton take their son (*Scrubs*' Zach Braff, director of *Garden State*) to the **21 Club, 21 West 52nd Street** between Fifth and Sixth Avenues, midtown, where you can see its cheery frontage of tiny jockeys. The grand, olde worlde establishment, where Keaton attends a wine tasting and sees the supposedly-dead neighbour on a bus, is the **National Arts Club, 15 Gramercy Park South** at Irving Place (see Martin Scorsese's *The Age of Innocence* for details). Anjelica Huston gives Allen a poker lesson at the **Café des Artistes**, in the **Hotel des Artistes, 1 West 67th Street** at Central Park West, Manhattan (*©212.877.3500; jacket and tie required*). The hotel was once home to the likes of Isadora Duncan, Alexander Woollcott, Noël Coward and Norman Rockwell. The fictitious Hotel Waldron, where a body is discovered, is **Hotel 17, 225 East 17th Street** in the East Village, though the interior is the venerable **Chelsea Hotel, 222 West 23rd Street**, between Seventh and Eighth Avenues, Chelsea (see *Sid and Nancy* for details).

MANHUNTER
(1986, dir: Michael Mann)
William L Petersen, Brian Cox, Tom Noonan.
● GEORGIA; NORTH CAROLINA; WASHINGTON DC; MISSOURI

From the novel preceding *Silence of the Lambs*, and filmed

by visual stylist Michael Mann four years before that film. This time, Hannibal Lecter (Cox, more chillingly psychopathic than Hopkins' *grand guignol* monster) is incarcerated, not in an underground dungeon from a Universal horror movie, but in a glossy, white, hi-tech facility. It's **Atlanta High Museum of Art, 1280 Peachtree Street** (© *404.892.3600; admission charge*), in the Ansley Park Area of Atlanta, Georgia. In Atlanta, investigator Will Graham (Petersen) stays at the luxury, 50-storey **Atlanta Marriot Marquis, 265 Peachtree Center Avenue** (© *404.521.0000*). The FBI works out of the **District Building, 1350 Pennsylvania Avenue NW** at 14th Street, Washington DC. And it's in front of here, on **Freedom Plaza** by the National Theater, that the innocent jogger gets busted. The airport where the Lear jet touches down is **Lambert International Airport, St Louis**, Missouri.

Wilmington in North Carolina, the self-styled 'East Coast Hollywood', with its slew of studio facilities, hosted more of the filming. The hospital was Wilmington's New Hanover Memorial Hospital, now expanded to become part of the **New Hanover Regional Medical Center, 2131 South 17th Street**, and Will Graham's Florida beach house (supposedly at DeSoto Avenue, Captiva) is on nearby **Mansonboro Island**, North Carolina.

MARATHON MAN

(1976, dir: John Schlesinger)
Dustin Hoffman, Laurence Olivier, Roy Scheider.
● **NEW YORK CITY; NEW YORK STATE; PARIS, FRANCE; LOS ANGELES, CALIFORNIA**

Hoffman jogs: Central Park Reservoir jogging path

Schlesinger's beautifully-crafted but confusing thriller is set in Paris and New York, though a little Los Angeles is sneaked in. Student 'Babe' Levy (Hoffman) runs on the 1.6 mile jogging path surrounding the **Central Park Reservoir**, between 86th and 96th Streets.

The brother of Nazi-in-hiding Dr Szell is killed in a tanker conflagration outside the **Carnegie Mansion, 22 East 91st Street** at Fifth Avenue on the Upper East Side (seen in *Arthur* and *Working Girl* among others), though the accident is witnessed by worshippers at the **Park Avenue Synagogue**, which stands a few blocks away at **50 East 87th Street**.

Babe's shady brother, Doc (Scheider), is up to something suspicious in Paris, where he arrives at **Place Vendôme**. He visits dodgy dealer LeClerc (Jacques Marin) in his shop in the old flea-market in **Saint**

The car chase after the escape from Szell: Carmine's Bar, Beekman Street

Olivier in the Diamond District: 47th Street

Ouen, where he narrowly escapes the bomb in the pram. Doc meets Janeway (William Devane) at one of Paris's best seafood restaurants, **Le Dome, 108 boulevard du Montparnasse** (© *43.35.34.82*), in the 14th arrondissement. (Did you spot the gay subplot? Listen to Doc's phone call from his Paris hotel.) He has an

The bank where Szell is entranced by his diamond cache: Spring Street

assignation with LeClerc at the spectacular, if rather kitsch, **Paris Opéra, Place de l'Opéra**, but finds him bloodily murdered. Spooked, he warns off his next contact in the gardens of the **Palais Royale**.

The Uruguayan jungle retreat of Szell (Olivier) is the **Los Angeles State and County Arboretum, 301 North Baldwin Avenue** (see *The Man in the Iron Mask* for details).

Babe studies at New York's **Columbia University** (see *Ghostbusters* for details), though the library where he gets to meet Elsa (Marthe Keller) is the **Doheny Library**, on the campus of the **University of Southern California** (which stood in for Berkeley in Hoffman's début, *The Graduate*). Elsa's apartment is on New York's **94th Street**. Babe and Elsa get robbed by suspiciously well-heeled muggers in Central Park and get cleaned up at the **Bethesda Fountain**.

When Doc gets knifed, he manages to stagger to Babe's Manhattan apartment. No mean feat. The illuminated 'red steps' fountain in front of which he's stabbed by Szell is one of the movie's West Coast locations, the **Arco Plaza, 505 South Flower Street** at West 5th Street in downtown LA.

The warehouse where dentist Szell excruciatingly tortures Babe is on New York's Lower East Side. The car chase roars around the corner of **Carmine's Bar, 140 Beekman Street** at Front Street. Babe manages to escape onto the north ramp of the **Brooklyn Bridge** before leaping down onto the road to Federal Plaza (a sequence which took nine nights to film).

The, apparently, safe house in the country, which turns out to belong to Szell's brother, is on **Ward Pound Ridge Reservation, Cross River**, a 4,700-acre park and wildlife sanctuary in Westchester County, New York State.

Szell gets an understandable

Szell is marched to the gates of Central Park Zoo

Final confrontation: North Gate House, Central Park Reservoir

panic attack in the overwhelmingly Jewish Diamond District, **47th Street** between Fifth and Sixth Avenues. The trade here grew up in the thirties when dealers fleeing Nazi persecution in European diamond centres, such as Amsterdam and Antwerp, took advantage of an area that provided both low rent and proximity to the monied customers of Fifth Avenue. Szell loses his rag at the shop at **32-34**, before being recognised by the shop assistant in **26**, who gets savagely despatched outside the **47th Street Subway Station**. The bank, supposedly at 58th and Madison, where Szell is entranced by his diamond cache, is **650 Spring Street**, downtown Los Angeles (see *Se7en* for details). Outside the bank, on Spring Street, Szell is confronted by Babe, who smartly marches him off to New York, to the gates of **Central Park Zoo**, before the final confrontation, staged at the **North Gate House** of the **Reservoir** in Central Park, though the ironwork grid interior is a studio set, built by designer Richard MacDonald to resemble the layout of an Elizabethan stage.

MARIACHI, EL

(1992, dir: Robert Rodriguez)
Carlos Gallardo, Consuelo Gómez, Jaime de Hoyos.
● **MEXICO**

Rodriguez's masterclass in ultra low-budget filmmaking was shot around **Ciudad Acuna**, a Mexican border town over the Rio Grande from Del Rio, Texas.

MARNIE

(1964, dir: Alfred Hitchcock)
Tippi Hedren, Sean Connery, Diane Baker.
● **PENNSYLVANIA; NEW JERSEY**

Strange psychodrama with Connery titillated by the sexually frigid kleptomaniac Tippi Hedren. Obviously very studio-bound, leaving acres of room for film students to debate whether Hitchcock was deliberately concocting a disquietingly unreal atmosphere, or had simply lost interest after star Hedren allegedly rebuffed a clumsy sexual advance from the director.

Marnie arrives in Philadelphia at **30th Street Station**. She's spotted by a man from her shady past at the

Marnie arrives in Philadelphia: 30th Street Station

Marnie's Virginia hotel: The Red Fox Inn, Middleburg

PHOTOGRAPH COURTESY RED FOX INN, MIDDLEBURG

Atlantic City Racetrack, New Jersey. The horse-riding scenes use the 'Horse and Hunt Capital' of the US, **Middleburg**, a small town in the shadow of the Blue Ridge Mountains, northwestern Virginia, about 35 miles west of Washington DC. Marnie's hotel is the historic **Red Fox Inn, 2 East Washington Street** (© 540.687.6301). Dating from 1728, the Red Fox is one of the oldest inns in the US and still in business.

MARS ATTACKS!

(1996, dir: Tim Burton)
Jack Nicholson, Glenn Close, Pierce Brosnan.
● **LAS VEGAS, NEVADA; ARIZONA; WASHINGTON DC**

Burton's homage to fifties sci-fi is based on a series of notorious sixties bubble gum cards. The fictitious Perkinsville, Texas, is **Burns**, Kansas, 40 miles northeast of

Tom Jones performs at the Luxor Hotel, Las Vegas Boulevard South

Wichita – this is where the donut shop inspired by LA's wacky original was built. The opening scene of burning cattle, taken directly from the gum cards, is in **Lawrence**, Kansas.

The Martian landing site, Pahrump, Nevada, is **Red Lake**, a dust bowl 20 miles from Kingman, Arizona. But it's not long before the little green folk have set their sights on the nation's capital and, naturally, the glitz of Las Vegas. Washington exteriors include the **Washington Monument** and the **Mall**. Pam Grier's neighbourhood is a row of houses in the NW region of DC. The burned out house stood at the corner of **4th and Massachusetts**.

In Vegas, Tom Jones performs at the **Luxor Hotel, 3900 Las Vegas Boulevard South** (© 702.262.4000, www.luxor.com) the giant (30 storey, 2,520 rooms) and, of course, absolutely authentic Egyptian pyramid on the southern reaches of the Strip (the aerial tramway connects it with the Excalibur to the north and Mandalay Bay to the south). Jack Nicholson's Galaxy Hotel is – was – Howard Hughes' Landmark Hotel, a 356-foot tower opened in 1969 near the Hilton, which was actually demolished during the making of the movie (not *for* the making of the movie, of course). At 31 storeys, it was once the tallest building in Nevada but was constantly plagued by financial problems and finally closed in 1990. The neon graveyard is the old sign yard of **Yesco**, the Young Electric Sign Company, which has been making glitter city's twinkling signs for years.

MASK, THE

(1994, dir: Charles Russell)
Jim Carrey, Cameron Diaz, Peter Riegert.
● **LOS ANGELES, CALIFORNIA**

Carrey is ideal casting, if you can stand him, in this live action cartoon. Edge City is, of course, LA. The Edge City Bank, where nerdy Stanley Ipkiss (Carrey) works,

Entrance to the Coco Bongo Club:
Ambassador Hotel

The Coco Bongo Club: Terrace Room,
Park Plaza Hotel

is the old Bank of America building, **650 South Spring Street**, downtown LA (see *Se7en* for details). The Coco Bongo Nightclub is a combination of two LA hotels: the exterior is the entrance to the **Cocoanut Grove** of the **Ambassador Hotel, 3400 Wilshire Boulevard**, midtown (see the 1954 film *A Star Is Born* for details). The interior, though, beneath the dressing of palm trees, deco light fittings and the violet waterfall, is the **Terrace Room** of the **Park Plaza Hotel, 607 South Park View Street**, downtown LA. The garage, where Ipkiss picks up his loan car, is the disused **Firestation No. 23, 225 East Fifth Street**, downtown LA (and not in the most comfortable of areas), also seen as the interior of the New York HQ of the Ghostbusters. The mask is finally returned to the river from the **Sixth Street Viaduct** over the Los Angeles River, south of downtown, a popular filming site seen in *Repo Man* and *S.W.A.T.*.

MASTER AND COMMANDER: THE FAR SIDE OF THE WORLD

(2003, dir: Peter Weir)
Russell Crowe, Paul Bettany, James D'Arcy.
● **GALAPAGOS ISLANDS; MEXICO**

The famous **Galapagos Islands** (*www.gct.org*), with their unique fauna, couldn't be faked, and *Master and Commander* is the first feature film to be shot on the islands. The young Charles Darwin visited the islands aboard HMS Beagle, and the unique ecology contributed to the biologist's understanding of evolution. There are 13 larger islands and six smaller ones, on the equator about 1,000km from the coast of South America. The islands are a national park and can be visited accompanied by a qualified naturalist guide but, be warned, controls are strict, to prevent contamination of the precious environment. Package tours will take you to Ecuador, from where the islands can be visited by boat. Maturin (Bettany) seeing the *Acheron* was filmed on the island of **Pinta**. **Pinnacle Rock** is on the island of **Bartolome**. The Galapagos Conservation Trust assures us that there was no damage to the islands' infrastructure.

Scenes which were more intrusive – the landing, rescuing the whalers, the cricket game and the operation – were filmed at **Todos Santos**, Baja California, Mexico. The seagoing scenes were filmed at **Rosarito Beach**, also in Baja California, in the giant tank built for *Titanic* (ousting *Pirates of the Caribbean*, which had to move to San Pedro Harbor in LA).

MATINEE

(1993, dir: Joe Dante)
John Goodman, Simon Fenton, Omri Katz.
● **FLORIDA**

Goodman is a fifties exploitation producer, not a million miles away from William Castle, previewing his sci-fi schlocker *Mant* ('Half man, half ant!') in a Florida cinema during the real horror of the Bay of Pigs crisis. Set down at the tip of the Florida Keys in Key West, the town is actually **Cocoa**, I-95, on the Florida coast east of Orlando. The Key West Strand Theater is the **Cocoa Village Playhouse, 3000 Brevard Avenue**, Cocoa (© *321.636.5050*). Built in 1924 as the Aladdin Theater, a movie palace, it's been taken over by Brevard Community College and now presents live theatre. The real pink deco Key West Strand Theater can be seen at 527 Duval Street between Petronia and Olivia Streets. The one-time movie palace, built by Cuban craftsmen in 1918, now lives on as a rock and reggae music venue.

MATRIX, THE

(1999, dir: Andy Wachowski; Larry Wachowski)
Keanu Reeves, Laurence Fishburne, Carrie-Anne Moss.
● **NEW SOUTH WALES, AUSTRALIA**

Although the city where Neo lives in the Matrix is never specified, the street names of this hi-hi-hi-tech thriller imply that it's set, like the Wachowski brothers' previous movie, *Bound*, in their hometown of Chicago. Hence the references to the Loop, the Windy City's downtown district. But, also like *Bound*, it wasn't filmed there. Interiors were shot in the Fox Studio at **Moore Park, Lang Road** at Driver Avenue, Sydney, where *Star Wars: Episode II* and Baz Luhrmann's *Moulin Rouge* were shot (*www.foxstudios.com.au*).

The futuristic metropolis is the city of **Sydney** itself, mainly around the central business district. It's a little to the northwest, at **Miller's Point**, west of the southern entrance to Sydney Harbour Bridge, that you'll find the site of the phone box at Wells and Lake, where Trinity (Moss) narrowly escapes being crushed by the truck, beneath the overpass on **Hickson Road** (though there's been some redevelopment in the area).

The Training Programme area, where Neo (Reeves) gets distracted by the woman in red as Morpheus (Fishburne) attempts to explain the complexities of the Matrix, is by the circular fountain on **Martin Place**, in the heart of the business district.

"I know this steak doesn't exist.," muses Cypher (Joe Pantoliano) as he cuts a deal with Agent Smith (Hugo Weaving). But it does, and you can verify that at their meeting place, **Forty One Restaurant, Level 41, Chifley Tower, 2 Chifley Square** (© *02.9221.2500*). the restaurant slowly revolves – it's expensive, but the views are terrific and the food is, well, out of this world.

Morpheus's crew is ambushed by agents in the old General Post Office in Railway Square (with a few storeys digitally added), where the 'deja vu' cat points up a glitch in the Matrix. Want to stay there? The building has been spruced up and is now the **Westin Hotel, 1 Martin Place**

(© *02.8223.1111, www.westin.com.au/s_index.html*).

The government building where Morpheus is held captive by Smith is the **Colonial State Bank Centre, 52 Martin Place** at Elizabeth Street. Trinity is programmed to fly a helicopter and takes off from a rooftop in front of the **Aon Tower, 201 Kent Street**, south of Observatory Park, also at Miller's Point. She flies over the **AWA Building** (the white radio mast, once the tallest building in Australia) at **47 York Street**. Morpheus and Neo land on the roof of the **Allianz Building** (which was then the MMI Centre), **2 Market Street**, between Sussex and Kent Streets, while Trinity's chopper carries on across Market to crash into the **BT Tower, 1 Market Street**.

The underground train station, where Neo battles Agent Smith, was filmed on a section of railtrack which used to serve the **Glebe Island Silos**, now-disused wheat storage facilities built in the '20s at **White Bay** on the Balmain side of the Anzac Bridge.

The phone box, where Neo makes a final call to the machines, was on the southeast corner of **Pitt** and **Hunter Streets** at **O'Connell Street**.

MATRIX RELOADED, THE

(2003, dir: Andy Wachowski; Larry Wachowski)
Keanu Reeves, Laurence Fishburne, Hugo Weaving.
● **NEW SOUTH WALES, AUSTRALIA; CALIFORNIA**

Despite upping the ante in the FX department, the novelty of the original is lost. It's **Sydney** again, but also **Oakland**, across the Oakland Bay Bridge from San Francisco. Oakland is where the spectacular freeway chase takes place, beginning at the parking garage underneath the **16th Street** entrance to the **Latham Square Building, 1611 Telegraph Avenue**, downtown, not far from City Hall. The bizarre twins chase Trinity and Morpheus west on **16th Street**, between Telegraph and Clay Streets (though there's a bit of sneaking back and forth to eke out the relatively short stretch of road available). Link directs them to the Winslow Overpass, which is the **Nimitz Freeway (I-880)**, over **Fifth Street and Broadway**, where the car drops into the **Webster Tube**, an underwater tunnel running beneath Oakland Inner Harbour Channel to **Alameda**.

It would have been impossible to shut down a road long enough for the complex stunts needed for the movie's big set piece, so the 101 Freeway was built on an abandoned airstrip at **Alameda Naval Air Station** (you can glimpse the Oakland Bay Bridge briefly, behind Morpheus). Interior sets were also built at Alameda, in the aircraft hangar, including the huge Zion rave.

The power station which has to be destroyed to avoid triggering the bomb – "No electricity. No alarms." – is the old **White Bay Power Station, Rozelle**, back in Sydney.

MATRIX REVOLUTIONS, THE

(2003, dir: Andy Wachowski; Larry Wachowski)
Keanu Reeves, Laurence Fishburne, Carrie-Anne Moss.
● **NEW SOUTH WALES, AUSTRALIA; CALIFORNIA**

As the trilogy winds up, some pretty impressive spectacle compensates for the dwindling logic. The (somewhat changed) Oracle and the Architect meet up in the **Royal Botanic Gardens, Mrs Macquaries Road** (© *61.2.9231.8111, www.rbgsyd.gov.au*) on Sydney Harbour, **Sydney**.

MATTER OF LIFE AND DEATH, A (aka *Stairway to Heaven*)

(1946, dir: Michael Powell; Emeric Pressburger)
David Niven, Kim Hunter, Marius Goring.
● **DEVON**

Powell and Pressburger's elaborate fantasy stars Niven as a WWII fighter pilot trapped in a surreal limbo after his plane crashes. The giant moving staircase to heaven is an escalator, specially built by the London Transport Passenger Board and Rowson, Drew and Clydesdale. The two-gear, twelve-horsepower engine could run at speeds of 30 and 60 feet per minute. The film's mostly studiobound, but The Burrows, the deserted beach Niven mistakes for heaven, where he encounters the strange goatherd, is **Saunton Sands**, on the B3231, on the north Devon coast south of Ilfracombe and west of Barnstaple.

MAURICE

(1987, dir: James Ivory)
James Wilby, Rupert Graves, Hugh Grant.
● **LONDON; CAMBRIDGESHIRE; WILTSHIRE; GLOUCESTERSHIRE; SICILY, ITALY**

Picking up the guardsman: Black Friar, Blackfriars

After their success with *A Room With a View*, the Merchant-Ivory team turned EM Forster's posthumously published gay novel *Maurice* into a lush Mills and Boon romancer. The Cambridge scenes were actually filmed at Forster's old university. Exterior shots are of **Trinity College, Cambridge**, at the **Quad** and under the **Wren Library**. The gothic William IV Porter's Lodge is **King's College**, and the Latin grace was also shot there, in the Dining Hall. The punt trip is on the River Cam at **Clare Bridge**, and the romantic scene between Wilby and Grant in the field is near **Ely** in Cambridgeshire.

In London, Maurice (Wilby) bumps into his old schoolmaster by the Assyrian statues in the **British Museum, Bloomsbury**, while the marvellous art-nouveau pub where his pal with a taste for the military runs into problems is the **Black Friar, 174 Queen Victoria Street**, EC4, over the road from Blackfriars railway station. The subsequent trial for indecency was staged in **Salisbury Town Hall**, Salisbury, Wiltshire, which also served as Wilby's London office. Wilby and Grant take their minds off the proceedings by attending a concert at the **Wigmore Hall, 36 Wigmore Street** (© *box office: 020.7935.2141, www.wigmore-hall.org.uk*).

Hugh Grant's country house, where Wilby is noticed by groundsman Rupert Graves, is **Wilbury Park, Newton Toney**, a private house owned by actress Maria St

Juste, on the A338 halfway between Andover and Salisbury, Wiltshire. The boathouse in the grounds where they meet up is, however, in the grounds of **Crichel** in Dorset. Hugh Grant's London home is the **Linley-Sambourne House, 18 Stafford Terrace**, just off High Street Kensington, W8 (see *A Room With a View* for details).

The family meal, before Hugh Grant sets off for the Continent, is in the **Café Royal, Regent Street**, W1. His European travels take him to a Grecian amphi-theatre, actually at **Segesta**, near Castellammare in northwest Sicily. The docks, where Wilby goes to say goodbye to Graves before he emigrates, are **Gloucester Docks** on the Severn.

MEAN STREETS

(1973, dir: Martin Scorsese)
Harvey Keitel, Robert De Niro, David Proval.
● **LOS ANGELES, CALIFORNIA; NEW YORK CITY**

The Volpe bar: Via Tutto, Cleveland Plaza

Scorsese's archetypal picture of Italian-Americans in Little Italy, New York, had only eight days filming in the Big Apple (and that stretched from a planned four). And it filmed in Belmont, too, the Italian community in the Bronx, standing in for the much-changed Manhattan locale. But all the interiors, and plenty of

De Niro and Keitel's heart to heart: Mulberry Street, Little Italy

the exteriors too, are in LA, including the final shooting and car crash. Tony's Bar is a soundstage set in Hollywood. The apartment of Charlie (Keitel) is an office building on Hollywood Boulevard near Vine Street. The churchyard where Keitel and De Niro have a heart to heart is real New York though, the **Old St Patrick's**

The neighbourhood: Cleveland Plaza, Little Italy

Cathedral, 264 Mulberry Street between East Houston and Prince Streets in Little Italy (seen also in *The Godfather*). The Vulpe bar stood at **23 Cleveland Plaza**, just north of Broome Street and the Police Building, but it's now **Via Tutto** (*© 212.841.0286*), a small Tuscan restaurant.

MEDITERRANEO

(1991, dir: Gabriele Salvatores)
Diego Abatantuono, Claudio Bigagli, Giuseppe Cederna.
● **DODECANESE**

The island setting for 1993's Best Foreign Language Oscar winner is **Kastellorizo**, a tiny Greek island with one hotel and no restaurant, in the Aegean off the coast of Turkey.

MEET THE PARENTS

(2000, dir: Jay Roach)
Robert De Niro, Ben Stiller, Blythe Danner.
● **NEW YORK; LONG ISLAND, NEW YORK; ILLINOIS**

The Surf and Turf is **Louie's Oyster Bar and Grill, 395 Main Street, Port Washington** (*© 516.883.4242*), on Long Island. Stiller and De Niro are seen in downtown Port Washington. Both Chicago's O'Hare and New York's La Guardia are **Westchester County Airport, 240 Airport Road, White Plains**, New York. The tuxedo shop is **Victor Talbot, Greenvale Plaza, 47 Glen Cove Road, Greenvale**, Long Island. The Byrnes home, in Oyster Bay, is a private Colonial revival house in **Old Brookeville**, New York. Kevin's house is in **Harrison**, New York. The Chicago school was an empty storefront in Manhattan. Interiors were filmed in a New York State armory in Brooklyn. There was also filming at **Trunz Food Center, 364 Port Washington Boulevard**, Port Washington; and **Oyster Bay Animal Shelter, 150 Miller Place, Syosset**.

MEMENTO

(2000, dir: Christopher Nolan)
Guy Pearce, Carrie-Anne Moss, Joe Pantoliano.
● **LOS ANGELES, CALIFORNIA**

Like *The Usual Suspects*, Nolan's ingeniously-plotted, reverse-timescale mystery requires multiple viewings. The Discount Inn, where amnesiac Leonard Shelby (Pearce) holes up, is the **Travel Inn, 7254 Foothill Boulevard, Tujunga** (*© 818.352. 5951*) at Hillhaven Avenue, near to the animal sanctuary location of *Terminator 3*. As he drives to meet Natalie (Moss) he passes **510 North Victory Boulevard**, directly opposite the Burger King behind which Doc Emmett lived in *Back to the Future*).

"OK. So what am I doing? I'm chasing this guy. No. He's chasing

Leonard holes up: in the Discount Inn: Travel Inn, Foothill Boulevard, Tujunga

Leonard drives to meet Natalie: North Victory Boulevard

Shelby plays cat-and-mouse with Dodd: Monte Vista Mobile Estates, Sunland

Fact No. 6 at Emma's Tattoo: Hatti-Kay Coiffures, Edward I Zwern Building, Sunland

Ferdy's Bar: Blue Room, South San Fernando Road, Burbank

me...": Shelby plays cat-and-mouse, or mouse-and-cat, with Dodd (Callum Keith Rennie) around the motor homes of **Monte Vista Mobile Estates, 8100 Foothill Boulevard, Sunland**. Directly across the boulevard, **Hatti-Kay Coiffures**, in the **Edward I Zwern Building, 8119 Foothill Boulevard** at Mather, became Emma's Tattoo, where 'Fact No. 6: car license SG13 7IU' is inked onto Leonard's body.

Natalie puts Leonard's short-term memory loss to the test by serving up disgustingly contaminated beer. Ferdy's Bar is the **Blue Room, 916 South San Fernando Road** at Alameda Avenue, **Burbank** (℗ *323.849.2779*), which can also be seen in *Heat, Touch* and *Change of Heart*. Behind the corrugated front is a stylish neighbourhood bar, good for after-work drinks and with a rep for attracting studio execs.

MEN IN BLACK
(1997, dir: Barry Sonnenfeld)
Tommy Lee Jones, Will Smith, Rip Torn.
● **NEW YORK CITY; NEW JERSEY; LOS ANGELES, CALIFORNIA**

The forbidding MIB HQ is actually the **Holland Tunnel Ventilator Shaft** on **Battery Place**, north of Battery Park. The alien landing site is the home of the 1964-65 New York Worlds Fair in **Flushing Meadow**, Union Turnpike-44th Avenue, Queens. Here you'll find the two towers and the **Unisphere**, the giant hollow globe trashed by the

The alien site: Flushing Meadow, Queens

The jewellery store: MacDougal Street, Greenwich Village

flying saucer (reconstructed in the studio in Hollywood). Will Smith encounters his first alien by **Grand Central Station**. A short chase later and they're climbing up the **Guggenheim Museum, Fifth Avenue** at East 89th Street. The Rosenberg Jewellery store, which gets blown up, is

at **54 MacDougal Street**, Greenwich Village, while the 'squid birth' is at **Liberty Park, Jersey City**, the tip of New Jersey opposite the Statue of Liberty.

In *Men In Black II*, Rosario Dawson works at **Ben's Pizza, 177 Spring Street** in SoHo (℗ *212.966.4494*). Will Smith takes her to the wonderful **Empire Diner, 210 Tenth Avenue** at 23rd Street (℗ *212.924.0011*), briefly seen in

Men in Black HQ: Holland Tunnel Ventilator Shaft, Battery Place

Manhattan. The Massachusetts lighthouse post office where Tommy Lee Jones is discovered, is on **Fire Island**.

MEPRIS, LE (aka *Contempt*)
(1963, dir: Jean-Luc Godard)
Brigitte Bardot, Michel Piccoli, Jack Palance.
● **ROME, ITALY; CAPRI, ITALY**

Piccoli is a screenwriter on a film of *The Odyssey*, whose marriage to Bardot is falling apart. Palance is the producer, veteran Fritz Lang (as himself) is the director. The extraordinary modernistic building is the **Casa Malaporte**, on the south of Capri, designed in 1942 by Curxio Malaporte and Adalberto Libera, with its funnelled staircase and curving white wall on the roof.

METROPOLIS
(1927, dir: Fritz Lang)
Brigitte Helm, Alfred Abel, Gustav Froelich.
● **BERLIN, GERMANY**

This spectacular, futuristic fantasy was filmed largely on sets built in the Neubabelsberg Studios near Potsdam, and in an old Zeppelin hangar at Staaken on the outskirts of Berlin (also where the sets for *M*, Lang's classic with Peter Lorre as the child-murderer stalking the streets, were constructed) . The Paternoster scenes were shot in **Potsdamer Platz**, Berlin.

MICHAEL COLLINS
(1996, dir: Neil Jordan)
Liam Neeson, Julia Roberts, Alan Rickman.
● **IRELAND**

In Neil Jordan's bio-epic, Irish nationalist Collins (Neeson) paves the way for independence, but is set up to take the fall for the compromise of the

The barge: Ha'penny Bridge, Dublin

Irish Free State and finally assassinated. Although the real Dublin – including **Dame Street, Grafton Street, Fitzwilliam Square**, the Dining Room of **Mansion House** and the Members' Room of **City Hall** – forms a backdrop to most of the film, a huge set was built for the assault on the GPO Building during the 1916 Easter Uprising, which opens the movie. It took four months, and £1.5 million, to construct a stretch of O'Connell Street at **Broadstone** in Dublin. The biggest set ever built in Ireland, it was briefly opened to the public for a weekend after filming was completed. The pillars of the real Dublin Post Office on O'Connell Street still bear bullet holes from the abortive battle.

After the failed rising, Collins was interned by the British at Frongoch prison camp, north Wales, though the film uses **Kilmainham Gaol, Inchicore Road, Kilmainham** (© 353.1.453.5984), now open as a museum (seen in *In the Name of the Father* and, on a lighter note, the original *The Italian Job*). The village, where Collins' oratory stirs up the crowd and the intervention of the Royal Irish Constabulary leads to a riot, is **Rathdrum**, about 30 miles south of the city. Collins meets up with subversive double agent Ned Broy (Stephen Rea) in the **Marshes Library, St Patrick's Crescent**, the oldest public library in Ireland, and is given clandestine access to the centre of British rule, **Dublin Castle** (*www.dublincastle.ie*), where he realises the full extent of British intelligence. In the morning, he cycles back across the famous **Ha'penny Bridge** over the Liffey (the first iron bridge in Ireland, there was, as the name suggests, once a toll to cross it).

Shaken by the discovery, the decision is made to take the drastic action of shooting British agents at a meeting held in the famous **Olympia Theatre, 72 Dame Street** (© 353.1677.7744), which can also be seen in *An Awfully Big Adventure*. Kitty (Roberts) accompanies Collins as he sees off his companion Harry Boland (Aidan Quinn), as he leaves from Dublin's **Pearse Railway Station** to drum up suport in the US.

Hostilities escalate as British tanks, after being pelted with rubbish, open fire on residents of **Iveagh Buildings, St Stephen's Green**. Soames (Charles Dance) is drafted in, determined to end the mayhem once and for all. His stay at prestigious **The Shelbourne Hotel, 27 St Stephen's Green** (© 353.1663.4500, www.shelbourne.ie), turns out to be a brief one. It was in Room 112 of the Shelbourne (now the hotel's Constitution Suite) that the real Collins drafted the constitution of the Irish Free State in 1922. Kitty is taken to stay in safety at another Dublin institution, the **Gresham Hotel, 23 Upper O'Connell Street** (© 353.1874.6881, www.gresham-hotels.com/htm/dublin_i.htm).

The British take a terrible retribution for the wave of killings with the 'Bloody Sunday' attack at a Gaelic football match at Croke Park. The notorious massacre of players and spectators by the Black and Tans was filmed in **Carlisle Grounds, Quinnsboro Road, Bray** (the oldest sports ground in the Eircom League, home of Bray Wanderers).

Eamon de Valera (Rickman) orders the disastrous attack on Dublin's Georgian **Custom House, Custom House Quay** (© 353.1.888.2000). Burned to a shell in the attack, the building has been completely restored. Collins, Kitty and Harry enjoy a brief respite at Kingstown, now **Dun Laoghaire**, where they walk on the **South Pier** before hearing the news that the British Government has called a truce.

The '1922 Dail' (the Irish Parliament), at which Collins is demonised for agreeing to the Free State and the partition of the north, meets in the Reading Room of **Trinity College**. The Treaty is, nevertheless, carried by popular vote, provoking de Valera's followers take over the **Four Courts, Inns Quay** (© 353.1.872.5555; admission free when court is in session), home of the Irish judiciary. Like the Custom House, the courts have been fully restored from the damage sustained during the Civil War. The exact circumstances of Collins' death remain a mystery. Beal na Bláth, in County Cork, where Collins is ambushed and gunned down by the nameless gunman (Jonathan Rhys Meyers) is **Hollywood Glen** near Donard.

MIDNIGHT COWBOY

(1969, dir: John Schlesinger)
Jon Voight, Dustin Hoffman,
Sylvia Miles.
● **NEW YORK CITY; TEXAS; FLORIDA**

Sylvia Miles' apartment: East 72nd Street

Joe Buck (Voight) turns himself into a cowboy stud to escape his dreary life washing dishes at **Miller's Restaurant, Big Spring**, Highway 80 between Midland and Abilene, west Texas. The Big Tex drive-in of the opening shot was the **Sahara Drive-in** on Interstate 20. The old house, where Joe makes out with Annie (Jennifer Salt), is **Millhollon House,**

Hoffman improvises "I'm walkin' here...": 58th Street at Sixth Avenue.

Stanton, west Texas. The nightmare baptism flashback was filmed at **Moss Creek Lake**. Moving to New York, he stays at the now-gone Claridge Hotel, which overlooked Times Square. Also gone is the department store he walks past on his arrival in the hostile metropolis. It was Best & Co, Fifth Avenue between 51st and 52nd Streets (used also in *The Godfather*), shortly before demolition. Still there, though, is **Tiffany & Co, 727 Fifth Avenue** at 57th Street. No breakfast here for Joe Buck, but an inert and ignored body lying face down on the sidewalk. It gets no better at the "real damn penthouse" of gorgeous chick Cass (Miles), **114 East 72nd Street** on the East Side, where it all ends in tears when he asks her for money.

One of the movie's most famous moments – parodied in films as diverse as Spike Lee's *Mo' Better Blues* and *Forrest Gump* – has Hoffman famously improvising "I'm walkin' here..." to an intrusive yellow

Berkeley Hotel for Women: Peninsula Hotel, Fifth Avenue

cab as he and Voight cross **58th Street at Sixth Avenue**.

The fictitious Berkeley Hotel for Women, where Buck's enthusiastic 'manager' 'Ratso' Rizzo (Hoffman) fantasises that his property's studly prowess is the key to luxury, was the Gotham Hotel. Gutted and refurbished in the eighties, but still recognisable, it's now the **Peninsula Hotel, 700 Fifth Avenue**. The final bus journey was shot on the **Miracle Mile** stretch of **Coral Gables**, Florida.

MIDNIGHT EXPRESS

(1978, dir: Alan Parker)
Brad Davis, Randy Quaid, John Hurt.
● **MALTA; TURKEY**

Billy Hayes, the young, gay American student imprisoned for smuggling dope, is heterosexualised in this version of his ordeal in the Turkish prison system. The real location of the story, Sagamilcar Prison, Istanbul, was obviously out of the question. The prison set was constructed in **Fort St Elmo**, an old British army barracks in Malta. Built in 1850 on the site of the legendary great Siege of Malta in 1565, it's at the top of the Valetta Peninsula. The exterior balconies and courtyards are real. Filming also took place in the historic **Knight's Hall**, dating from 1574; and at the **Dominican Church, Rabat**.

MIDNIGHT RUN

(1988, dir: Martin Brest)
Robert De Niro, Charles Grodin, Yaphet Kotto.
● **NEW YORK CITY; LOS ANGELES, CALIFORNIA; CHICAGO, ILLINOIS; ARIZONA; NEVADA; MICHIGAN; NEW ZEALAND**

Cross-continental chase movie that calls in just about everywhere, starting from LA, where De Niro gets his mission (to retrieve mob accountant Grodin from New York) at the bail bonds office in the scruffy downtown area. Catching up with Grodin, that old standby plot device, fear of flying, kicks in and the pair leave for LA from New York's **Grand Central Station**.

The little local station where FBI agent Yaphet Kotto boards the train only to find that De Niro and Grodin have already slipped off to take the bus, is **Niles Station, 598 Dey Street, Niles**, on I-33 down in the southwest corner of Michigan toward the Indiana border (seen also in *Only the Lonely*). The bus ride ends in Chicago, where marksmen are waiting at **Chicago Bus Terminal**, on **North State Street** at Lake Street.

The smalltown diner, where De Niro and Grodin can't even afford breakfast, is in **Globe**, Arizona. The helicopter attack is at **Salt River Canyon Bridge**, on I-60 about 35 miles north of Globe, where the pair end up in the Salt River, although the rapids were filmed in warmer water in New Zealand. Grodin attempts to steal a plane at the **Cameron Indian Reservation**. Other Arizona locations include **Flagstaff Train Station**; **Williams**; **Cottonwood**; and **Sedona**. Bad guy Dennis Farina operates out of **Las Vegas**, and it's at **McCarran International Airport** that De Niro exchanges Grodin for that Macguffin of the eighties, computer discs.

MIDSUMMER NIGHT'S DREAM, A

(1999, dir: Michael Hoffman)

Kevin Kline, Rupert Everett, Michelle Pfeiffer.
● **ITALY**

A lush adaptation, shot in Italy. The bustling town square and the theatre are in **Montepulciano**, Tuscany. Theseus' palace consists of two separate locations. The interior was filmed at **Villa d'Este**. The exterior, and the wedding feast, were at **Palazzo Farnese** in **Caprarola**. The magic forest is a studio set, constructed at Cinecittà in Rome. Filming also took place at **Sutri**, near to Caprarola.

MIGHTY APHRODITE

(1995, dir: Woody Allen)
Woody Allen, Mira Sorvino, F Murray Abraham.
● **NEW YORK; ITALY**

Sorvino warns Allen that her pimp is turning nasty: Fifth Avenue

Ignoring the dire warnings of a classical Greek chorus, Lenny (Allen) goes off to track down the biological mother of his adopted child, Max, only to find she's a hooker, Linda (Sorvino), who has graced films such as *The Enchanted Pussy*. The chorus comments on the action from the **Teatro Greco, Taormina** on Sicily.

Allen and partner Helena Bonham Carter discuss adoption in the classy, zebra-patterned Italian restaurant **Gino, 780 Lexington Avenue** at East 61st Street (*©* 212.223.9658). If you think you've seen the distinctive wallpaper in another movie, that's because the design was copied for Wes Anderson's *The Royal Tenenbaums*. Sorvino visits Allen at **85 Fifth Avenue**, to warn him that her pimp is turning nasty.

Sorvino's blandly modern apartment block is **The Eastbrook, 333 East 75th Street**, between First and Second Avenues. Allen takes Sorvino to **Belmont Racetrack**, Nassau County, Long Island, where she loses her money on Eager Beaver. He meets up with her as she leaves the **David Barton Gym, 552 Sixth Avenue** at 15th Street.

The blind Tiresias passes on a warning to Lenny at the Acropolis – that's Manhattan's **New Acropolis Restaurant, 767 Eighth Avenue** at 47th Street (*©* 212.581.2733).

Sorvino's blandly modern apartment block: The Eastbrook, East 75th Street

Linda is fixed up with Kevin in front of the **Naumberg Bandshell** at 72nd Street Drive in Central Park, where the chorus slips into Cole

The amphitheatre: Teatro Greco, Taormina

The chorus slips into 'You Do Something To Me': Naumberg Bandshell, Central Park

Porter's 'You Do Something To Me'. This is also where the band of hippies hung out in Milos Forman's film of *Hair*. At the end of the movie, Allen and Sorvino admire, unwittingly, each other's kids at toystore **FAO Schwarz, 745 Fifth Avenue** at 58th Street (see *Big* for details). There was more filming at **North Tarrytown** and the village of **Quogue**, New York.

MILDRED PIERCE

(1945, dir: Michael Curtiz)
Joan Crawford, Ann Blyth, Zachary Scott.
● **LOS ANGELES, CALIFORNIA**

Darkly glittering deco *noir*, with Joan Crawford clawing her way up in the restaurant business, only to be snubbed by her ungrateful daughter, creepily prefiguring *Mommie Dearest*. Crawford is seduced by smooth-talking Zachary Scott in the stylish Malibu beach house of *Snake Pit* director Anatole Litvak. After the shooting of Scott, Joan is hauled off to **Los Angeles City Hall, 200 North Spring Street**, downtown LA.

MILLER'S CROSSING

(1990, dir: Joel Coen)
Gabriel Byrne, Albert Finney, John Turturro.
● **LOUISIANA**

More wonderful weirdness from the Coens, this time set in the twenties. The anonymous, Prohibition-era city is an unrecognisable, non-touristy New Orleans. Leo's club is the olde worlde-style downstairs dining room of New Orleans' staid **International House**. The gigantic panelled room, where Tom confronts Johnny Caspar, is **Gallier Hall, 545 St Charles Avenue**, formerly City Hall. The Greek revival-style building, designed in 1845 by James Gallier Sr, stands opposite Lafayette Square. Another of its large rooms was used as the Mayor's office. The exterior and the foyer of Caspar's house were filmed at the exclusive **Louis S McGehee School, 2343 Prytania Street**. Leo's home is actually four separate locations: **Northline**; a street in the **Old Metarie** section of town (where the car is blown up); and two purpose-built sets. The sets were built in the huge garage belonging to the estate agents Toye Brothers on **Annunciation Street**.

Unchanged period exteriors were shot on **Magazine Street**, downtown, and on **Picayune Street** (the nighttime scene between Tom and Verna). The shoot-out between the police and members of Leo's social club, the Sons of Erin, was staged on **Church Street**.

Miller's Crossing itself, the wood where Tom has to carry out the killings, is a forest plantation about 30 miles east of Baton Rouge, near Hammond, on Route 190.

MILLION DOLLAR BABY

(2004, dir: Clint Eastwood)
Hilary Swank, Clint Eastwood, Morgan Freeman.
● **LOS ANGELES, CALIFORNIA**

What begins as a female *Rocky* develops into something deeper. Eastwood's Oscar magnet was filmed almost entirely around LA, where aspiring boxer Maggie Fitzgerald

The River Thames Boxing Association: Hollywood Athletic Club, Hollywood Boulevard

(Swank) works in the **On the Waterfront Cafe, 205 Ocean Front Walk** at Ozone Avenue, **Venice Beach** (© *310.392.0322*).

Also in Venice is the **Church of St Mark, 940 Coeur d'Alene Avenue**, where Frankie Dunn (Eastwood) enjoys winding up the priest but ultimately goes for guidance. The Hit Pit, the gym of grizzled veteran Frankie, was constructed by 89 year-old veteran production designer Henry Bumstead in a warehouse in downtown LA. Over in Hollywood, the Broadway Diner is **Shelly Cafe, 7013 Hollywood Boulevard** at North Orange Drive (© *323.467.2233*).

Fight scenes were filmed, naturally, in the **Grand Olympic Auditorium, 1801 South Grand Avenue** at Olympic Boulevard (© *213.749.5171, www.grand-oly.com*), downtown LA, which has hosted countless boxing pictures, including *Raging Bull* and *Rocky*. Even the English bout at the River Thames Boxing Association is LA, in the **Hollywood Athletic Club, 6525 Hollywood Boulevard** (© *323.462.6262*), see *The Usual Suspects* for details; and the Las Vegas Arena is the **Hollywood Palladium, 6215 Sunset Boulevard** (© *323.962.7600*), see *Day of the Locust*.

MILLION DOLLAR HOTEL

(2000, dir: Wim Wenders)
Jeremy Davies, Milla Jovovich, Mel Gibson.
● **LOS ANGELES, CALIFORNIA**

This must be the first movie inspired by a rooftop. If you saw U2's video for 'Where the Streets Have No Name', you'll have seen the huge rooftop sign for the Million Dollar Hotel. Well, actually, it was a recreation built on top of a liquor store. This is the real thing, atop what is now the **Frontier Hotel, 111 West Fifth Street** at Main Street, in one of the scuzzier sections of downtown LA.

MINORITY REPORT

(2002, dir: Steven Spielberg)
Tom Cruise, Colin Farrell, Samantha Morton.
● **WASHINGTON DC; LOS ANGELES, CALIFORNIA; VIRGINIA**

A terrific return to form for Spielberg after the dismal *A.I.*, set in a futuristic department of 'pre-crime'. The setting is Washington DC, where there was some filming around the historic Georgetown district. The Department

Anderton takes precog Agatha to the shopping mall: Hawthorne Plaza Mall, Hawthorne

Where, the precogs predict, Anderton will shoot Leo Crow: Angelus Plaza, South Hill Street

of Precrime exterior is the **Reagan Trade Center, 13th and Pennsylvania Avenue NW**. The fugitive John Anderton (Cruise) is recognised by his new eyes as 'Mr Yakamoto' in the **GAP** store at **1258 Wisconsin Avenue** near M Street, Georgetown.

The waterside home of Anderton's estranged wife is on **Ware Point Road**, near Beulah, Gloucester, on Virginia's east coast. After escaping via a car production line (a sequence dreamed up but never filmed by Hitchcock), Anderton drives the red Lexus through **Beaverdam Park, 8687 Roaring Springs Road, Gloucester**, on the way to see Iris Hineman (Lois Smith).

Most of the movie, however, was filmed in LA, and the home of Hineman, the reluctant inventor of Precrime, where Anderton is attacked by poisonous plants, is **Descanso Gardens, 1418 Descanso Drive** (© *818.949.4200, www.descanso.com; admission charge*), in La Cañada-Flintridge. It can also be seen in *Congo* and *The Jungle Book*. The scuzzy apartment block where Anderton hides from the spyders is the, currently defunct, **El Dorado Hotel, 416 South Spring Street**, downtown LA. The shopping mall, to which Anderton takes precog Agatha (Morton) is the **Hawthorne Plaza Mall, Hawthorne**

Anderton hides from the spyders: El Dorado Hotel, South Spring Street

Boulevard at 120th Street, Hawthorne. The mall had been closed and shuttered for some time. The mall also featured in *Evolution*.

The highrise where, the precogs predict, Anderton will shoot Leo Crow is **Angelus Plaza, 255 South Hill Street**, downtown. It's a subsidised condominium of five highrises built for the elderly in 1980 in Bunker Hill, alongside the Second Street Tunnel (itself a frequent filming location seen in *Con-Air*, *Independence Day*, *The Terminator* and *The X-Files*). It's the **Noontide North** building (the blocks have

The Department of Precrime exterior: Reagan Trade Center, 13th Avenue NW

wonderfully kitschy names – Dawn, Evensong and Jubilate).

It's back to DC for the premature celebration, as Precrime goes national, in the **Willard Room** of the **Willard Intercontinental Washington, 1401 Pennsylvania Avenue** (© *202.637.7440*).

MIRACLE ON 34th STREET (aka *The Big Heart*)
(1947, dir: George Seaton)
Edmund Gwenn, Maureen O'Hara, Natalie Wood.
● NEW YORK CITY

Edmund Gwenn pretends to be the real Santa at **Macy's Department Store**, the biggest in the world, **Herald Square, Broadway** at 34th Street. He's sent for observation to **Bellevue Hospital Center, First Avenue** between 25th and 30th Streets on the Lower East Side. Santa stands trial at **New York County Courthouse, 60 Centre Street** in the Civic Centre district.

MIRACLE ON 34th STREET
(1994, dir: Les Mayfield)
Richard Attenborough, Elizabeth Perkins, Mara Wilson.
● NEW YORK CITY; CHICAGO, ILLINOIS

Mawkish remake of a story long past its sell-by date. This time around, Macy's wanted nothing to do with the production, so the department store becomes the fictitious CF Cole's. It's still set in New York, but that's not where you'll find most of the film's locations. There were only five days filming in the Big Apple. Apart from a couple of establishing shots, New York is restricted to the opening Thanksgiving Day Parade on **Central Park West** between 72nd and 78th Streets, and Perkins and Dylan McDermott's night out at the **Wollman Skating Rink** in Central Park. The clue to the film's real location comes in the opening credits. Like most John Hughes productions, *Miracle* was filmed in Chicago. The exterior of CF Cole's is the **Art Institute of Chicago, South Michigan Avenue** at East Adams Street in the Loop. Central Park Zoo, where Santa gets propositioned by the rival superstore, is actually **Lincoln Park Zoo, 2200 North Cannon Drive** at West Webster Avenue in Lincoln Park, north of the city centre. St Francis' church, where Perkins and McDermott finally submit to an arranged marriage, is **Holy Name Cathedral, 735 North State Street** at East Chicago Avenue.

MISERY
(1990, dir: Rob Reiner)
Kathy Bates, James Caan, Richard Farnsworth.
● NEVADA

Bates picked up an Oscar as the demented fan, nurse and jailer of injured writer Caan in a Stephen King story of a beleaguered scribbler. Set in the fictitious Silver Creek, Colorado, it was shot

The country store: Main Street, Genoa

near Reno, Nevada. The Silver Creek Lodge is an innaccessible Forest Service lodge. The country store and post office are **2299 Main Street**, in **Genoa**, a beautiful little town just west of I-395, south of Reno, also seen in Don Siegel's *Charley Varrick*. The road where Caan crashes his car is the **Old Donner Pass**, on I-80, west of Reno on the Nevada-California border, where the Donner party, heading west, survived the disastrous winter of 1846 by resorting to cannibalism.

Monroe's divorce: Washoe County Courthouse, Reno

Monroe loses her wedding band: Truckee River Bridge, Reno

The bar in the rodeo town: Mia's Restaurant, Odeon Hall, Dayton

MISFITS, THE
(1961, dir: John Huston)
Marilyn Monroe, Clark Gable, Montgomery Clift.

● NEVADA

Mournfully atmospheric movie, overshadowed by the untimely deaths of the three principals. Gable's heart gave out a few weeks after the arduous shoot was over, Clift's system finally caved in after years of pills and booze in 1966, and what actually happened to Monroe in 1962 is anybody's guess.

Centring around the roping of wild mustangs in the desert, the film starts around **Reno**, Nevada, where Monroe is getting a divorce at the **Washoe County Courthouse, 5 Virginia Street** between Mill and Court Streets, before following tradition by tossing her wedding band into the Truckee River. The casino where Gable and Monroe gamble was the now-gone Mapes Casino, in the Mapes Hotel, 30 North Virginia Street, Reno. Most of the company stayed in the hotel. Marilyn and Arthur Miller occupied room 614, while Monty was discovered naked in the lift after one of his notorious barbiturate and alcohol cocktails.

The rodeo town is **Dayton**. Don't expect this tiny, one-street town to be bustling, but you can still eat at **Mia's Restaurant**, the bustling bar in the movie, in the Odeon Hall building, **Pike Street**. The roping of the stallions was filmed on the white salt flats of **Pyramid Lake**, about 30 miles north of Reno. Eli Wallach's ranch is **Quail Canyon Ranch**, off Pyramid Highway.

MISSION, THE
(1986, dir: Roland Joffé)
Robert De Niro, Jeremy Irons, Ray McAnally.

● COLOMBIA; ARGENTINA

Big themes, big vistas, big music. Irons and De Niro bring Jesus to the natives in their different ways. This was the worthy project that the profit from Hugh Hudson's ghastly *Revolution* was supposed to finance.

Location filming took place in Colombia and Argentina. The falls over which the crucified priest plunges are the **Iguazu Falls**, at the junction of the Parana and Iguazu Rivers on the borders of Brazil, Paraguay and Argentina. 350 of the Wuanana tribe played the dooomed Guaranis.

Father Gabriel's San Carlos Mission was built in the jungle around **Santa Marta**, Colombia, on land owned by the brewery producing the country's most popular beer. Being Colombia, it also happened to be on an extremely popular drug route, which necessitated the posting of armed guards on the set, night and day.

The city of Ascension is the walled 16th century **Old Town** area of **Cartagena**, on the northeast coast of Colombia. Another mission was constructed here. Although only a temporary structure, built of plaster, the owner of the land asked for it to be left as a tourist attraction.

MISSION: IMPOSSIBLE
(1996, dir: Brian De Palma)
Tom Cruise, Jon Voight, Vanessa Redgrave.

● LONDON; CZECH REPUBLIC; SCOTLAND; VIRGINIA

It doesn't matter that this breathless adventure hardly pauses to make sense, with kinetic director De Palma pulling out all the stops, and then some. The embassy, where the doomed mission begins, is the rather rundown **Natural History Museum, Václavské nám 68** in Prague. As the mission falls apart, Voight falls into the Vltava River from the famous **Charles Bridge**. Other Prague locations include **Wenceslas Square** at the centre of the old town and the **Lichtenstein Palace, Malostranské nám 13** on Kampa Island. Redgrave's art deco HQ is the **Europa Hotel, Václavské nám 25**, also on Wenceslas Square (℃ *42.2.2365274*).

The exterior of the CIA Building in **Langley**, Virginia, is the real thing, but the interior is London's old **County Hall**, on the South Bank. The London

Max's HQ: Europa Hotel, Prague

The American embassy: Natural History Museum, Prague

Relaxing: Anchor Tavern, Bankside

Jon Voight is shot: Charles Bridge, Prague

safe house is above Liverpool Street Underground Station, **Liverpool Street** at **Broad Street**, EC2, and Cruise meets up with Voight on **Liverpool Street Station**, mightily revamped since its dilapidated appearance in *The Elephant Man*. The supposedly cross-channel railway climax, which so infuriated train buffs, was filmed in Scotland, on stretches of line between **Annan** and **Dumfries**, and **Dumfries** and **New Cumnock**. The terrace pub, where Cruise finally unwinds, is the **Anchor Tavern, Bankside**, on London's South Bank by Southwark Bridge.

MISSION: IMPOSSIBLE 2

(1999, dir: John Woo)
Tom Cruise, Thandie Newton, Anthony Hopkins.
● **NEW SOUTH WALES, AUSTRALIA; UTAH**

John Woo's stylish but empty sequel was made almost entirely in Australia, around Sydney, New South Wales, except for the dizzying rock climbing scene (it really is Tom Cruise in all but one shot, though supporting cables were removed digitally), which was shot at **Dead Horse Point State Park**, about 15 miles southwest of Moab, near the location of the final scene of *Thelma and Louise*, in southeast Utah.

Villain Dougray Scott's island hideout is **Bare Island Fort**, at the entrance to Botany Bay, south of Sydney. His other waterside retreat was built at **Ashton Park**, on the **Mosman** waterfront. The racecourse, where Thandie Newton steals the images from the digital camera, is **Royal Randwick Racecourse** in Sydney's suburb of Randwick. The motorbike chase was filmed at **Boora Point** near Malabar. More action scenes took in the area around **Governor Macquarie Tower** and **Governor Phillip Tower**, modern twin buildings near **Circular Quay**, Sydney.

The Seville scenes were also shot in Australia, at **Argyle Place** in **The Rocks**, Sydney's revived historic core on the western shore of Sydney Cove, and at Sydney's most expensive mansion, **Boomerang**, on the waterfront at **Elizabeth Bay**.

MISSISSIPPI BURNING

(1988, dir: Alan Parker)
Gene Hackman, Willem Dafoe, Frances McDormand.
● **MISSISSIPPI; ALABAMA**

Fictionalised account of the investigation into the deaths of three Civil Rights workers in the sixties, causing much controversy by placing white – and fictitious – FBI agents at the centre of the story. Based on the murder of Andrew Goodman, Michael Schwerner and James Chaney in Philadelphia, East Mississippi, in 1964, the film was shot in Mississippi and Alabama. Chaney's funeral was filmed in **Cedar Hill Cemetery, Vicksburg**, Mississippi. Also in Mississippi is the Jessup County sherriff's office, which is **Vaiden Courthouse**. The town square of 1964 Philadel-

phia is **Lafayette**, Alabama. The movie theatre was given a $25,000 makeover – it's been closed since the sixties and is now actually an auto supply store. Much of the film was shot in small towns around Jackson, Mississippi. Filming also took place at the **Ross Barnett Reservoir**, to the northeast of Jackson, Mississippi; and at **Bovina**, Mississippi.

MRS BROWN (aka *Her Majesty, Mrs Brown*)

(1997, dir: John Madden)
Judi Dench, Billy Connolly, Antony Sher.
● **ISLE OF WIGHT; SCOTLAND; WILTSHIRE**

An Oscar nomination for Judi Dench as Queen Victoria in this account of her friendship with Scots ghillie John Brown. Windsor Castle is played by **Wilton House, Wilton** near Salisbury (see *The Music Lovers* for details). The Scottish scenes are at **Duns Castle**, about 16 miles from Berwick. The 1320 private home is not generally open to the public, except by prior arrangement (℃ *01361. 883211*). And it is, famously, the real **Osborne House**, on the Isle of Wight, to which the Queen retreats. The house, just outside East Cowes on the isle's north shore, is open to the public from March to October (℃ *01983.200022; admission charge*).

MRS DOUBTFIRE

(1993, dir: Chris Columbus)
Robin Williams, Sally Field, Pierce Brosnan.
● **CALIFORNIA**

This coarse, sentimental comedy, which really took off at the box office, is set around San Francisco. The TV studio, where Robin Williams gets a

The Doubtfire house: Steiner Street

job boxing and shipping cans, is **KTVU 2** over on the East Bay. In East Bay, too, you'll find the restaurant where Williams performs his quick-change routine during two fraught meals. It's **Bridges Restaurant, 44 Church Street, Danville**, east of Oakland. Also in the area is the **Claremont Resort Hotel, Claremont Avenue** at Ashby Avenue in the Tilden Regional Park area north of Berkeley. Built in 1915, the Victorian-style resort is where Mrs Doubtfire sabotages Sally Field's flirtation with charmer Pierce Brosnan. Mrs Doubtfire takes the kids to cycle and play soccer at **Crissy Field**, the green area on the bay just east of the Golden Gate Bridge. She fends off a mugger on **Columbus Avenue** (the elegant, pale green Flatiron Building in the background is the HQ of Francis Coppola's movie empire). The family home of Williams and Field is **2640 Steiner Street** at Broadway in Pacific Heights.

MR BLANDINGS BUILDS HIS DREAM HOUSE

(1948, dir: H C Potter)
Cary Grant, Myrna Loy, Melvyn Douglas.
● **LOS ANGELES, CALIFORNIA**

Grant and Loy are New Yorkers doing up their ideal Connecticut country home (an idea rejigged in 1986 as *The Money Pit*, with Tom Hanks). The dream house was built on the Fox Ranch, now the 4,000-acre **Malibu Creek State Park**. The land was owned by film producer George Hunter, who subsequently converted the house into a ranch home. And it's still there, housing the offices of the Santa Monica Mountains Conservancy Foundation, at **3800 Solstice Canyon Road**, Malibu Canyon Road between Mulholland Highway and Cold Canyon Road, in the Santa Monica Mountains above Malibu.

MISTER ROBERTS
(1955, dir: John Ford, Mervyn LeRoy)
Henry Fonda, James Cagney, Jack Lemmon.
● **MIDWAY; HAWAII**

Ford and Fonda, in their eighth film together, fell out over the filming of Thomas Heggen and Joshua Logan's comic-sentimental tale about WWII shipboard life. Fonda, who played the role on stage, objected to the Fordian knock-about coarsening. Ford was eventually hospitalised, to be replaced by veteran Warner Bros director LeRoy. The film was made at **Midway Island** in the Pacific and at the **Kanoehoe Marine Corps Air Station** in Hawaii.

MR SMITH GOES TO WASHINGTON
(1939, dir: Frank Capra)
James Stewart, Claude Rains, Jean Arthur.
● **LOS ANGELES, CALIFORNIA; WASHINGTON DC**

Archetypal Capra little-man-against-bureaucracy fable. Mr Smith does indeed go to Washington, but only just. Most of the movie was made in LA, with some background filming in the nation's capital. James Stewart disembarks at DC's (recently restored) **Union Station, Massachusetts Avenue NE**, where the first building he sees is the reassuring dome of the **US Capitol**.

MO' BETTER BLUES
(1990, dir: Spike Lee)
Denzel Washington, Joie Lee, Wesley Snipes.
● **NEW YORK CITY**

Lee's New York-set film about the confused life of jazz trumpeter Bleek (Washington) looks stunning. The opening shot of 'Brooklyn, 1969' was filmed on the west side of **Prospect Park** in the classy **Park Slope** area of the borough. Bleek's loft was shot on **Brooklyn Heights** near the waterfront, in the shadow of the Brooklyn Bridge, while Clarke's apartment is in a landmark building in the **Fort Greene** neighbourhood.

The Beneath the Underdog club is a composite. The interior is a studio set, but the exterior is Greenwich Village's **Cherry Lane Theater, 38 Commerce Street**, between Bedford and Barrow Streets, dressed as West 52nd Street in the fifties. You can also see the Cherry Lane in Woody Allen's *Another Woman*, Warren Beatty's *Reds* and Cold War thriller *The House on Carroll Street*.

Clarke works as a cashier in the jazz section of **Tower Records, 692 Broadway** at East Fourth Street in the Village. The birth of Bleek's son is at **Harlem Hospital, 135th Street** at Lenox Avenue. The brownstone stoop,

where Indigo waits for Bleek, is on **141st Street** between Convent Avenue and Hamilton Place, Harlem.

The Dizzy Club is the 350-seat **America Restaurant, 9 East 18th Street** between Broadway and Fifth Avenue, northwest of Union Square – once the ultimate trendy restaurant. The alleyway where Giant and Bleek are bloodily beaten up is **Shinbone Alley**, off Bond Street between Broadway and Lafayette Street in the East Village.

MOBY DICK
(1956, dir: John Huston)
Gregory Peck, Richard Basehart, Friedrich Ledebur.
● **IRELAND; WALES; CANARY ISLANDS**

Orson Welles staged Herman Melville's tale on stage in London's West End and desperately wanted to direct the movie, but ultimately the job went to Huston, and Welles was compensated with the small role of Father Mapple. The New Bedford harbour the *Pequod* sails from is **Youghal**, about 25 miles east of Cork, in **County Cork** on the southern coast of the Republic of Ireland. Scenes at sea were filmed in **St George's Channel** off the coast of Fishguard, south Wales.

Filming dragged on, partly due to visa difficulties with Huston and Peck, who could only work 90 days in England, which meant they had to hotfoot it out of Britain every Friday, spend the weekend in Paris, and commute back for work on Monday. When the waters became too cold for filming, the crew upped and moved to **Las Palmas** in the Canaries, where the ending, with Richard Basehart floating on the coffin, was shot. The scene in which Peck, lashed to a rotating, 20-foot section of rubber whale, is finally dragged under, was saved until last. Just in case...

MODESTY BLAISE
(1966, dir: Joseph Losey)
Monica Vitti, Terence Stamp, Dirk Bogarde.
● **NETHERLANDS; ITALY; LONDON; HAMPSHIRE**

Losey's too self-consciously camp spy spoof uses locations in London, **Amsterdam**, the **Bay of Naples** and the slopes of **Mount Vesuvius**. Modesty is lured out of retirement at the crush bar of the **Opera House, Covent Garden**, though the lobby of the Ritz Hotel is a set at Shepperton. Her private plane takes off from the security airfield at **Farnborough** in Hampshire. Filming in Amsterdam includes the notorious **Walletjes**, the Red Light District between Centraal Station, the Dam and the Nieuwmarkt, and the **Old Square**, with its House of Dolls, which is also the setting for the rally of barrel organs. Fluttery villain Bogarde's hideout is the castle and chapel of **St Alessio**, near Messina on the northeast coast of Sicily. The cliffs below are at **Tindari**, on Sicily's northwest coast, which also supplied the stretch of desert sand and volcanic rock, as well as the beach finale. The freighter is in the Bay of Naples, and the car chase along the top of Vesuvius.

MOGAMBO
(1953, dir: John Ford)
Clark Gable, Ava Gardner, Grace Kelly.
● **TANGANYIKA; UGANDA**

Remake of Victor Fleming's 1932 movie *Red Dust*, transposed from an Indo-China rubber plantation to Africa, but with Gable reprising his role as the man torn between brassy showgirl Gardner and prim-but-married Kelly, during a gorilla hunt. Notching up 67 location days, it was the biggest film to have been made in Africa at the time, and one of the biggest headaches, being hampered by temperamental stars, outbreaks of amoebic dysentry and the chorus of animal noises, not to mention the Mau Mau rebellion. The locations were Tanganyika's **Serengeti Plain** and Uganda's **Kagera River**, with its spectacular rapids and falls.

MOMMIE DEAREST

(1981, dir: Frank Perry)
Faye Dunaway, Diana Scarwid, Steve Forrest.
● LOS ANGELES, CALIFORNIA

Hilariously kitsch classic biopic of Joan Crawford, based on daughter C h r i s t i n a ' s 'revenge' autobiography, filmed as an old-fashioned Crawford melodrama. The real

Crawford dines out: Perino's, Wilshire Boulevard

Crawford house, not available for filming, can still be seen at 426 North Bristol Avenue, north from Sunset Boulevard in Brentwood. When Crawford married Douglas Fairbanks Jr, the house was named 'El Jodo' (à la 'Pickfair'). The movie house was a mansion just off the western reach of Sunset Boulevard. MGM Studios, where La Crawford makes her movies, is at **10202 West Washington Boulevard** in Culver City. The wonderful art deco frontage seen in the movie, however, can no longer be seen from the street: it's the eastern entrance at the end of Grant Avenue off Madison or Clarington Avenues, now part of the MGM lot. Crawford dines at **Perino's, 4101 Wilshire Boulevard** at Norton Avenue. The classic restaurant, seen also in *Dead Again* and *Mulholland Falls*, which numbered gangster Bugsy Siegel and Cole Porter among its regulars, closed in 1983 and is up for redevelopment as an apartment complex. It's promised that the deco pink canopy will be preserved. Originally called the Hi-Hat, Perino's in its heyday stood at 3929 Wilshire Boulevard, near Western Avenue. See it in *Sunset Blvd.*, opposite the shop where William Holden gets kitted out by Gloria Swanson. Young Christina is bundled off to **Chadwick School, 26800 South Academy Drive** on the Palos Verdes Peninsula, south of LA.

MON ONCLE (aka *My Uncle*)

(1956, dir: Jacques Tati)
Jacques Tati, Jean-Pierre Zola, Adrienne Servantie.
● FRANCE

Tati's comedy, pitting the eccentric uncle, M Hulot, against a soulless modern world, took the Oscar for Best Foreign Language Film. Hulot's old neighbourhood is **Saint-Maur-des-Fossés**, Paris.

MONA LISA

(1986, dir: Neil Jordan)
Bob Hoskins, Cathy Tyson, Michael Caine.
● LONDON; SUSSEX

Cabdriver Bob Hoskins is hired to ferry high-class hooker Tyson between assignations in a sleazy-looking London. Tyson's regular haunts include the

Cathy Tyson services a rich client: Vanbrugh Castle, Maze Hill, Greenwich

Ritz in Piccadilly, and the florid pink **Hilton St Ermin's Hotel, Caxton Street,** SW1, where Hoskins turns up in his splendid new gear. Tyson is dumped by Hoskins in the traffic at **Hyde Park Corner,** but he relents and gets kitted out in style at **Tommy Nutter's.** The search for Tyson's friend takes in the **King's Cross** area, and the strip- and peep-joints of **Soho.** Whenever the social problems of the King's Cross area are discussed, there's an

Hoskins turns up in his new gear: Hilton St Ermin's Hotel, Caxton Street

inevitable reference to *Mona Lisa* and the hellish bridge where prostitutes ply their trade. In fact, the scene wasn't filmed near King's Cross at all, but on Pindar Street, a roadbridge which once spanned the railway lines at the rear of Liverpool Street Station, demolished during the area's substantial renovation.

Vanbrugh Castle, 121 Maze Hill, the house of architect and dramatist Sir John Vanbrugh, became the grand Highgate house, where Cathy Tyson sends out a tray of refreshments to Bob Hoskins while she services a rich client. Michael Caine issues his orders from what was old strip club Raymond Revuebar, now gay club **Too 2 Much, Walker's Court** at Brewer Street, Soho. There's trouble from the heavies on **Brighton Pier**, and a bloody shoot-out in the **Royal Albion Hotel, 35 Old Steine,** Brighton.

MONSOON WEDDING

(2001, dir: Mira Nair)
Naseeruddin Shah, Lillete Dubey, Vijay Raaz.
● INDIA

Culture clash as a Punjabi wedding in Delhi brings together the old traditions and dot.com modernity. Filmed, on a tight 30-day schedule, mostly at an affluent villa on the outskirts of Delhi, but also at **Mughal Delhi** (the exteriors); and among the gaudy charm of the wedding sari shops of **Karol Bagh** juxtaposed with the city's chic ateliers. The residence of PK Dubey (Raaz) is in **Chandni Chowk**, the main bazaar of Old Delh (seen also in *Kabhi Khushi Kabhie Gham…*).

MONSTER'S BALL

(2001, dir: Marc Forster)

Halle Berry, Billy Bob Thornton, Heath Ledger.

● **LOUISIANA**

Grotowski works on Death Row: Louisiana State Prison, Angola

Leticia ends up working at Airline Motors Restaurant, LaPlace

Redneck prison guard Hank Grotowski (Thornton) finds redemption with Leticia (Oscar-winning Berry) after they both have to deal with sudden bereavement. It's set in Jackson, Georgia, but was filmed in Louisiana, around **LaPlace**. Grotowski works on Death Row in **Louisiana State Prison, Angola** (which was also featured in *Dead Man Walking*). It's the prison's real Death Row and, although Angola now uses lethal injection, the original electric chair was brought from the prison museum for filming.

Leticia is fired from her job at **Bud's Broiler, 500 City Park Avenue, New Orleans** (part of a burger chain in the city), and ends up working at **Airline Motors Restaurant, LaPlace**, exit 209 off I-10 between Baton Rouge and New Orleans (*www.stjohnparish.com/airlinemotors*). Built in 1937, remodelled in 1948 and virtually unchanged since. The motel where Hank and Sonny (Ledger) both relieve sexual tension, is a real no-tell motel ('$17 for three hours; condoms $1'), the **Sugar Bowl Court Motel, 4303 Airline Drive**, at Central Avenue, **Metairie** outside New Orleans.

MONTY PYTHON AND THE HOLY GRAIL

(1975, dir: Terry Gilliam; Terry Jones)

Graham Chapman, John Cleese, Michael Palin.

● **SCOTLAND**

King Arthur and his men, accompanied by their trusty coconut shells, approach **Doune Castle**, a 14th century fortification on the A84 a few miles northwest of Stirling (*© 01786.841742, admission charge*). The Bridge of Death is at the **Meeting of the Three Waters**, where the mountain waterfalls become the River Cae in Glen Coe. The island castle where the Grail resides turns out to be **Castle Stalker**, 20 miles north of Oban. The 15th century stronghold is a quarter of a mile from the shore of Loch Linhe and occasionally open to the public subject to tides and weather (*© 01883.622768; admission charge*).

MONTY PYTHON'S LIFE OF BRIAN

(1979, dir: Terry Jones)

Graham Chapman, John Cleese, Eric Idle.

● **TUNISIA**

Graham Chapman gets mistaken for the Messiah and makes a pretty good job of the position in this brilliant satire. The Holy Land is Tunisia, where most of the film was shot in the **Ribat**, the fortified monastery at **Monastir**, previously the setting for Zeffirelli's terminally pious TV production *Jesus of Nazareth*. Monastir, with its airport, is the centre of the Gulf of Hammamet's tourist coast, though the town itself is small and away from the hotel complexes. The Ribat, with its maze of walls and passages, is open to the public (*admission charge*). The city walls are the **Kasbah** of **Sousse**, the major city about 25 miles west of Monastir. The Kasbah is now a museum, containing a collection of Roman mosaics. The final crucifixion scene uses the landscape around **Tataouine**, the town that gave its name to Luke Skywalker's home planet in the Tunisia-shot *Star Wars*, toward the south of the country.

The city walls: The Kasbah, Sousse

"Welease Woger": Ribat, Monastir

Brian falls from the tower: Ribat, Monastir

MONTY PYTHON'S THE MEANING OF LIFE

(1983, dir: Terry Jones)

Graham Chapman, John Cleese, Eric Idle.

● **LONDON; BUCKINGHAMSHIRE; LANCASHIRE**

More sketches, varying wildly in quality. The 'Find the Fish' interlude was filmed at **Chicheley Hall, Newport Pagnell** in Buckinghamshire (*© 01234.391252; admission charge*). The restaurant, where the disgustingly obese Mr Creosote explodes, is **Porchester Hall, Porchester Centre, Queensway**, London W2. The 'Every Sperm Is Sacred' production number was filmed on the backstreet between **Bankfield Street** and Hargreaves Street in **Colne**, Lan-

Mr Creosote: Porchester Hall, Queensway

Every sperm is sacred...: Bankfield Street, Colne

cashire. Terry Jones' house was **17 Bankfield Street**.

The public school where Cleese gives excruciatingly formal sex instruction is the **International University, The Avenue, Bushey**, until 1977 the Royal Masonic School for Boys. It had previously been seen as the barracks to which innocent graduate Ian Carmichael reports for military duty in the Boulting brothers' 1956 *Private's Progress* and, in 1957, as the red-brick university in *Lucky Jim*.

MOONRAKER
(1979, dir: Lewis Gilbert)
Roger Moore, Lois Chiles, Michael Lonsdale.
● **RIO DE JANEIRO; VENICE, ITALY; NEVADA; CALIFORNIA; FLORIDA; FRANCE; GUATEMALA**

After the terrifically vertiginous opening sequence, *Moonraker* turns out to be just about the klutziest of the Bond movies. Bond arrives at **LA International Airport**, to investigate the disappearance of a space shuttle, and takes a helicopter ride over the city to visit the estate of sauve villain Drax. Drax's lavish mansion was "brought stone by stone from France". Not quite. It is a French chateau, but it stayed firmly on the other side of the Atlantic. It's the 17th century chateau **Vaux-le-Vicomte**, 20 miles southeast of Paris. Built for Fouquet, Louis XIV's finance minister, its grandeur provoked a fit of envy in the king. With the hubris of a Bond villain, Louis had Fouquet thrown into prison and began planning the even more sumptuous Versailles.

Bond follows a lead to Venice, where Drax has his glassworks and museum off St Mark's Square. The glassworks' entrance is **Venini, 314 Piazzetta dei Leoni**, northeast of St Mark's. The cheesy boat chase (a motorised gondola which turns into a hovercraft for no discernible reason) ends with Bond hovering across **St Mark's Square**, to some of the most ridiculous reaction shots in movie history. The clock, behind which Bond slugs it out with the baddies, is the face of the **Torre dell'Orologio**, the clock tower at the north of St Mark's Square. Of course, the villain crashes through a fake. The clock's workings, if you want to check out what they really look like, can be visited. The training camp is **San Nicolo al Lido, Riviera San Nicolo**, a monastery on the northwest coast Venice's Lido.

It's on to Rio de Janeiro for a fight with Jaws on the cable car lift to **Sugarloaf Mountain** (only in longshot – the fight itself filmed on a Pinewood mock-up) and to Guatemala for yet another motorboat chase, leading to Drax's jungle hideout. A US shuttle is sent up to battle Drax's forces from the **Vandenberg Airforce Base**, between San Luis Obispo and Santa Barbara on Coastal Highway 1, southern California (also where Blofeld launched his satellite in *Diamonds Are Forever*).

MOONSTRUCK
(1987, dir: Norman Jewison)
Cher, Nicolas Cage, Danny Aiello.
● **NEW YORK CITY; TORONTO, ONTARIO, CANADA**

Cher has to choose between safe, homely Aiello and his dangerous brother Cage in this enjoyable tale of mix'n'match relationships among Italian-Americans in Brooklyn Heights. Set in New York, of course, but filming took place in Toronto too.

Cher lives in the up-market brownstone Italian neighbourhood just over the Brooklyn Bridge from Manhattan's southern tip, at **19 Cranberry Street** on the corner of Willow Street, overlooking the East River. Nicolas Cage lost his hand and his fiancée, but still works, at **Cammareri Bros Bakery, 502 Henry Street**, a few blocks south. The restaurant where Danny Aiello proposes to Cher is supposedly Greenwich Village's Grand Ticino Restaurant, 228 Thompson Street between Bleecker and West Third Streets, but it's actually one of the scenes shot in Ontario. Cage takes Cher to the **Metropolitan Opera House** in the **Lincoln Centre, Broadway** at 64th Street. Other Toronto locations include **Colborne Street, Victoria Street, Dufferin Street, St Claire Avenue** and the **Keg Mansion Restaurant, 515 Jarvis Street**.

Cher's house: Cranberry Street, Brooklyn Heights

The Cammareri Bros Bakery, Henry Street, Brooklyn

New York interiors: Keg Mansion Restaurant, Jarvis Street, Toronto

MORGAN – A SUITABLE CASE FOR TREATMENT (aka *Morgan!*)
(1966, dir: Karel Reisz)
David Warner, Vanessa Redgrave, Robert Stephens.
● **LONDON**

Could there be a more archetypal sixties movie, as gorilla-fixated, anarcho-Trotskyite Morgan Delt (Warner) baits and hounds his upper-class ex-wife Leonie (Redgrave) and her ghastly new boyfriend (Stephens)? Their boisterous relationship implodes at **13 Campden Hill Square** in Holland Park, west London. Determinedly perverse, Morgan attempts to break *into* **Wormwood Scrubs Prison, Ducane Road** off Scrubs Lane, west London

Morgan's house: Campden Hill Square, Holland Park

(seen in loads of films, including the original *The Italian Job* and *Frenzy*), and disrupts Leonie's wedding reception on the roof terrace of the swanky **Dorchester Hotel, 54 Park Lane** (© *020.7629.8888*, *www.dorchester hotel.com*), before tootling off down Park Lane on his scooter. The Dorchester is also featured in *Brannigan* and in the 1959 music biz satire *Expresso Bongo*.

MOST DANGEROUS GAME, THE (aka *The Hounds of Zaroff*)
(1932, dir: Ernest B Schoedsack; Irving Pichel)
Leslie Banks, Joel McCrea, Fay Wray.
● CALIFORNIA

Excellent, much-imitated horror thriller with Banks as the villainous hunter of human prey. Joel McCrea – or, rather, stuntman Wes Hopper who filmed the scene – swims ashore on the rocky beach near **San Pedro**, south LA. The clifftop scenes were filmed at **Redondo**, while the views of the cove from Banks' studio-bound chateau are the cliffs at **Marineland**, the southwestern tip of the Palos Verdes Peninsula.

MOULIN ROUGE
(1952, dir: John Huston)
Jose Ferrer, Zsa Zsa Gabor, Suzanne Flon.
● PARIS, FRANCE; SUSSEX

The real Moulin Rouge, Montmartre

Lautrec in Paris: Pont Alexandre III

Unlike the 2001 fantasia, Huston's biopic of painter Toulouse Lautrec was made almost entirely on location in Paris, with a complex system of gels and filters to produce a wonderful cinematic equivalent of the artist's style. Real locations include **Maxim's, 3 rue Royale**, and the wildly elaborate **Pont Alexandre III**, seen also in *A View to a Kill*. If you want a tacky, Vegas-style night out, the real **Moulin Rouge** can still be visited, **82 boulevard de Clichy, Montmartre** (© *01.53.09.82.82*, *www.moulin-rouge.com*). The racecourse, though, is **Kempton Park** in Sussex.

MOVE OVER, DARLING
(1963, dir: Michael Gordon)
Doris Day, James Garner, Thelma Ritter.
● LOS ANGELES, CALIFORNIA

James Garner sees his macho rival, Chuck Connors, showing off on the trampoline by the pool at the **Beverly Hills Hotel, 9641 Sunset Boulevard**. Doris Day's home is on the corner of **Wyton Drive** in Beverly Hills.

MUCH ADO ABOUT NOTHING
(1993, dir: Kenneth Branagh)

Kenneth Branagh, Emma Thompson, Keanu Reeves.
● ITALY

Branagh's sunny Shakespearian romp, shot in the 15th century **Villa Vignamaggio**, home of the Gheradini family, reputedly the family of the model for the Mona Lisa. Built after the Florentines destroyed their place in Montagliari, the villa is near **Greve**, in Chianti, on a side road off the SS222 to Lamole. If you want a souvenir, the vineyard in the surrounding park has its own label.

MULHOLLAND DR
(2001, dir: David Lynch)
Naomi Watts, Laura Elena Harring, Justin Theroux.
● LOS ANGELES, CALIFORNIA

The office of Ryan Entertainment: Banks Huntley Building, Spring Street

Intended as the pilot for a TV series, a la *Twin Peaks*, and hurriedly wrapped up to become a feature film, this is still Lynch at his nightmarish best. Filmed around LA, Betty (Watts) arrives, with that charming old couple, at **LAX**. The courtyard apartment complex, presided over by Coco Lenoix, in which Betty stays, is supposedly 1612 Havenhurst Drive in West Hollywood. You can see the apartment at **490 North Sycamore Avenue** at Rosewood Avenue, south of Hollywood toward Hancock Park.

The motor accident, which causes Rita (Harring) to lose her memory, occurs on **Mulholland Drive** itself. The hitman is seen at **Pink's, 709 North La Brea Avenue** at Melrose Avenue, Hollywood (© *323.931.4223*, *www.pinkshollywood.com*), the coolest hot dog stand in the universe, since 1939. You may have to stand in line for upwards of half an hour to sample the legendary chili dogs, but there's always a chance you'll get to see one of the many Hollywood names who bolster their cred by turning up here. I found myself waiting behind Chris 'Nice Guy Eddie' Penn. The exterior of Club Silencio is the rear of the **Palace Theatre, 630 South Broadway**, downtown. The interior is the **Tower Theatre, 802 South Broadway**. The office of Ryan Entertainment, where director Adam Kersher is instructed who must star in his film at a meeting with the espresso-obsessed Castigliani brothers, is the **Banks Hunt-**

The Sierra Bonita apartment: Griffith Park Boulevard, Silverlake

Winkie's Diner: Caesar's, West El Segundo Boulevard, Gardena

The steps down: Caesar's, West El Segundo Boulevard, Gardena

The scary man behind the wall: Caesar's, West El Segundo Boulevard, Gardena

ley Building, 634 Spring Street. The silent brother is Angelo Badalmenti, the composer of the haunting jazzy scores of many of Lynch's movies.

The fictitious Sierra Bonita apartment is 2900 Griffith Park Boulevard off St George Street, part of a cutesy cottage complex behind the ever-popular John Marshal High School, Silverlake.

Winkie's Diner, where Dan dreams he sees the scary face behind the wall, isn't on Sunset at all. You'll find it south of the city in Gardena. It's **Caesar's, 1016 West El Segundo Boulevard** at Vermont. If you want a coffee here, make it early; Caesar's closes at 2pm. Behind the restaurant, if you dare, are the steps and the wall. There was no-one behind it when I checked but, who knows, you might get lucky.

MUMMY, THE
(1999, dir: Stephen Sommers)
Brendan Fraser, Rachel Weisz, Arnold Vosloo.
● MOROCCO; BUCKINGHAMSHIRE; KENT; SURREY

Splurgy horror comedy, a little too knee-deep in CGI effects. Set in Egypt, of course, but filmed mainly in Morocco. Cairo of 1925 was filmed at **Marrakech**, and the lost city of Hamunaptra was a set built at an old fort inside a dormant volcano near **Erfoud**, in the southeast of the country. It's not all quite so exotic, though.

The port of Giza, where the party boards the Nile ship, is actually **Chatham Docks** in Kent, and after the ship goes down in flames, they come ashore at **Frensham Ponds**, on the A287 about five miles south of Farnham in Surrey. The interior of the Museum of Antiquities in Cairo is **Mentmore Towers** at Mentmore, Buckinghamshire (see *Brazil* for details).

MUMMY RETURNS, THE
(2001, dir: Stephen Sommers)
Brendan Fraser, Rachel Weisz, Arnold Vosloo.
● LONDON; BEDFORDSHIRE; BUCKINGHAMSHIRE; MOROCCO; JORDAN

More of the same, a little stale with familiarity. **Mentmore Towers** returns as the exterior of the O'Connells' house. The interior is Ridley Scott's office in the old building on the Shepperton lot. Likewise, the British Museum is two separate locations. The pillared frontage is **University College, Gower Street**, which previously stood in for the same museum in a previous mummyfest – Mike

Newell's sluggish *The Awakening*. The interior, where Mr Hafez (Alun Armstrong) resurrects the Mummy, is the **Dimco Building, Wood Lane**, opposite Macfar-

The British Museum: University College, Gower Street

lane Road in **Shepherds Bush** (behind the set dressing, you might recognise it as the Acme warehouse from *Who Framed Roger Rabbit*). The subsequent bus chase is a dizzying mix of locations: the soldier mummies scuttle along the walls of **Greenwich Naval College**, southeast London; the double decker careers along **Lambeth Palace Road**, on the Thames Embankment by Lambeth Bridge; and past the Georgian houses of **Endsleigh Place**, Bloomsbury; before coming to a halt on **Tower Bridge**.

The Egyptian desert was shot at the spectacular **Erg Chebbi Dunes** at **Merzouga**, about 30 miles south of Erfoud in Morocco.

The train was filmed on the **Hijaz Railway** on the outskirts of **Amman** in Jordan, the railway line repeatedly attacked by the real Lawrence of Arabia. Also in Jordan is the canyon with the giant water head, which is at **Petra**, seen in *Indiana Jones and the Last Crusade*.

Back in the UK, the archaeological dig at 'Hamunaptra, City of the Dead', where Imhotep is exhumed, is **Bryant's Lane Quarry, Heath and Reach**, near Leighton Buzzard in Bedfordshire. And the jungle (with the pygmy mummies) is familar old **Black Park Country Park**, alongside Pinewood Studios in Buckinghamshire.

MURDER BY DEATH
(1976, dir: Robert Moore)
Alec Guinness, Peter Sellers, Maggie Smith.
● BERKSHIRE

Enjoyably broad detective spoof, written, amazingly, by Neil Simon. The gothic home of prissy writer Truman Capote, where the world's top detectives are gathered, is Oakley Court, now the **Oakley Court Hotel, Windsor Road** between Maidenhead and Windsor (see *The Rocky Horror Picture Show* for details of this much-used location).

MURDER ON THE ORIENT EXPRESS
(1974, dir: Sidney Lumet)
Albert Finney, Ingrid Bergman, Lauren Bacall.
● PARIS, FRANCE; TURKEY; YUGOSLAVIA; LONDON; HERTFORDSHIRE

First, and best, of the star-studded, immaculately period Agatha Christie adaptations that have blossomed into a genre of their own. Finney's enjoyably hammy Poirot solves a murder on the snowbound Orient Express. The movie was made mainly at Elstree Studios, with a wonderfully old-fashioned revolving drum passing painted scenery past the windows. The Express departs with style from the shabby **Landy Train Repair Depot** in St Denis, Paris, expertly dressed by veteran set designer Tony Walton. And look out for the fluffy foam posing as snow, wafting about in the breeze as the train is finally dug out by the snowplough.

The snowbound scenes were shot in the **Jura Mountains** of the former Yugoslavia. The arrival of the passengers by ferry was shot in Turkey on the Bosphorus. The Istanbul restaurant of the opening is the Moorish foyer of the old **Finsbury Park Astoria**, now a church, on **Seven Sisters Road**, north London. The Armstrong home on Long Island, New York, scene of the flashback kidnapping, is **High Canons, Buckettsland Lane** in Hertfordshire (see *The Devil Rides Out* for details).

MURDER, SHE SAID

(1961, dir: George Pollock)
Margaret Rutherford, Charles Tingwell, Muriel Pavlow.
● **LONDON; BUCKINGHAMSHIRE**

First of the cosy sixties Miss Marple mysteries with the priceless, though miscast, Margaret Rutherford (Christie herself loathed the casting). Adapted from *4.50 From Paddington*, the opening did indeed film on **Paddington Station**. The railway embankment is at **Gerrards Cross**, southeast of Beaconsfield, Buckinghamshire, convenient for Rutherford's home on nearby Elm Close.

MURIEL'S WEDDING

(1994, dir: P J Hogan)
Toni Collette, Bill Hunter, Rachel Griffiths.
● **AUSTRALIA**

Dumpy fantasist Muriel Heslop (Collette) escapes her ghastly family in dreams of marriage in this broad Aussie satire, set in the gorgeous, but sadly fictitious, beachside community of Porpoise Spit, actually **Coolangatta**, at the southern end of Queensland's Gold Coast. Also on the Gold Coast is **Sea World Nara Resort, Sea World Drive, Main Beach**, which became the tropical Hibiscus Island, where Muriel is dumped by her snotty schoolfriends.

Moving to Sydney, New South Wales, she works (or watches Charles and Di's wedding on TV) at the Dramarama video store. In reality, the store is the exotic fetish outlet **Mephisto Leather, 135 Oxford Street, Darlinghurst**, Sydney.

Muriel covets bridal gowns at **House of Jean Fox** and **Park Avenue Bridal**, in **Parramatta**, finally getting to walk down the aisle (albeit in a marriage of convenience) with hunky swimmer David Van Arckle at **St Mark's Anglican Church, 53 Darling Point Road, Darling Point**.

MUSIC BOX, THE

(1932, dir: James Parrott)
Stan Laurel, Oliver Hardy, Billy Gilbert.
● **LOS ANGELES, CALIFORNIA**

Laurel and Hardy, on peak form, won an Oscar for Best

The Music Box steps: Vendome Street

Short Feature as two delivery men attempting to heave a piano up an endless flight of steps. The steps are still there, though the wide open lawns either side are now built up, and you'll have a job spotting the tiny opening. A plaque marks the location. It's between the buildings at **923-927 Vendome Street**, south of Sunset Boulevard in Silverlake, north of downtown LA. Be aware that some people have expressed concerns about the area, though I have to say, I've never encountered any problems here.

MUSIC LOVERS, THE

(1970, dir: Ken Russell)
Richard Chamberlain, Glenda Jackson, Christopher Gable.
● **LONDON; BERKSHIRE; HAMPSHIRE; WILTSHIRE; BUCKINGHAMSHIRE; AVON**

Much of Russell's overheated, overpowering black comedy fantasia on the life of florid composer Tchaikovsky was shot at Bray Studios, near Windsor, where a huge section of 19th century Moscow, including the opening fairground and the glittering domes of the Kremlin, was built on the backlot.

The firework party at Brailov: West Wycombe House

Madame von Meck at Brailov: The lake, West Wycombe House

The deliberately kitsch country idylls around the Davidov house, the Moscow Public Gardens and the fields and forests for the First Piano Concerto sequence, were filmed in **Milford-on-Sea**, just east of Christchurch on the Hampshire coast, in **Salisbury** and Russell's native **Southampton**. The lavish interior of Brailov, Madame von Meck's house, is **Wilton House**, in the village of Wilton, two-and-a-half miles west of Salisbury on the A30, Wiltshire. A veteran of many movies, including *Barry Lyndon*, *The Bounty*, *The Madness of King George* and *The Return of a Man Called Horse*, it was originally a Tudor manor house, remodelled in the 17th century by Inigo Jones. The lavish interior includes the famous Single Cube and Double Cube rooms. Wilton is open in summer (© *01722.746.729; admission charge*). The exterior of the estate, however, is **West Wycombe House**.

Madame von Meck sits writing in one of the gardens' faux-classical temples. The entrance, where Tchaikovsky delivers his scores, and the scene of

Tchaikovsky's wedding: St Sofia's Cathedral, Bayswater

The suicide attempt: Grand Union Canal, Camden

the disastrous fireworks party at which he is outed by the vengeful Count Chiluvsky, is the house's two-storey colonnaded south front. The alfresco performance of *Swan Lake* is performed on the lawns before the north front, with the great lake as backdrop. West Wycombe Park is south of the Oxford Road (A40), two-and-a-half miles west of High Wycombe, Buckinghamshire. The park is open April to August, the house from June (*© 01494.524411; admission charge*). You can see the house in many other films, including *Agatha Christie's Dead Man's Folly* and Clint Eastwood's *White Hunter, Black Heart*.

Tchaikovsky and Nina are married in **St Sofia's Cathedral**, a Greek orthodox church, appropriately enough in **Moscow Road, Bayswater** (it's also the Russian church seen in *GoldenEye*). The composer's tragi-comic suicide attempt was staged on the **Grand Union Canal**, where the composer jumps into the murky water beneath the Euston railway line alongside **Gloucester Avenue Bridge** between Camden Lock and Regent's Park, NW1. The asylum, where Nina is ultimately confined, is the disused **Royal Artillery Barracks, Artillery Place, Woolwich**, SE18.

MUTINY ON THE BOUNTY

(1935, dir: Frank Lloyd)
Charles Laughton, Clark Gable, Franchot Tone.
● CALIFORNIA; TAHITI

Macho man Gable leads the revolt against sadistic Laughton in this classic version of the familiar story, filmed at all-purpose nautical location **Catalina Island**, 22 miles off the coast of LA, and on location in Tahiti. It's claimed that the *Balclutha*, now berthed at San Francisco's Maritime Museum on Hyde Street Pier, can be seen in the movie, but the real star, the *Bounty* itself, was played by the *Ellen*. The ship also starred in *Hawaii* before being sold by Columbia Studios. She's now safely berthed in an earthquake-proof concrete cradle, also in San Francisco, where she's been transformed into a restaurant. The **Sailing Ship Restaurant** is at **Pier 42, the Embarcadero** by the South Beach Yacht Harbor, South of Market. Further scenes were shot in **Monterey Harbour**, south of San Francisco.

MUTINY ON THE BOUNTY

(1962, dir: Lewis Milestone; Carol Reed; George Seaton)
Trevor Howard, Marlon Brando, Richard Harris.
● TAHITI; BORA BORA; HAWAII

The number of directors attests to the nightmare of the production, as Brando plays Fletcher Christian as a prissy British fop with, for reasons best known to himself, his ears plugged. The *Bounty* was built specially for the

movie in Nova Scotia, and sailed through the Panama Canal to Tahiti at a cost of $750,000. It was diesel powered, and actually a third larger than the original – which didn't need to accommodate movie cameras.

Carol Reed was replaced as director by veteran Lewis Milestone, after the stone fishing scene and Howard's awkward dance filmed in **Bora Bora**. Location filming continued in Tahiti (apart from some early scenes shot in **Honolulu**, Hawaii). Then it was back to Culver City for studio filming, and back again to Tahiti for retakes as George Seaton finally took over from Lewis Milestone.

MY BEAUTIFUL LAUNDRETTE

(1985, dir: Stephen Frears)
Daniel Day-Lewis, Gordon Warnecke, Saeed Jaffrey.
● LONDON

Young Asian entrepreneur Warnecke employs one-time racist Day-Lewis to make sock-washing a feelgood experience in this little gem of a movie. The news-

The launderette: Wilcox Road, Wandsworth

agent's shop is **News Point, 169-171 Wandsworth Road** at Albion Avenue, Stockwell, SW8. The railway bridge, under which Warnecke gets attacked, is over **Stewarts Road**, near Ascalon Street, Wandsworth, SW8. The launderette itself is now a secondhand shop, **Low Gear, 11 Wilcox Road**, SW8, off Wandsworth Road, two doors away from… a launderette.

MY BEST FRIEND'S WEDDING

(1997, dir: P J Hogan)
Julia Roberts, Rupert Everett, Dermot Mulroney.
● CHICAGO, ILLINOIS

Julia Roberts arrives at America's busiest air terminal, the vast **O'Hare Airport**, 17 miles northwest of the city, to move in on Chicago's high society. The prospective bride's father owns the Chicago White Sox baseball team, who play at **Comiskey Park, 333 West 35th Street** at Shields Street. Other upscale Chicago locales include the exclusive **Union League Club, 65 West Jackson Boulevard**; the Conrad Hilton Suite at the **Hilton Hotel and Towers, 730 South Michigan Avenue** (*© 312.922.4400*); the Gold Coast Room of the **Drake Hotel, 140 East Walton Place** at Michigan Avenue (*© 312.787.2200*); **Union Station**; and the office tower at **77 West Wacker Drive**. The swanky restaurant is the expensive and exclusive (for weekends you'll need to book a month ahead) **Charlie Trotter's, 816 West Armitage Avenue** at North Halsted Street, south of DePaul University (*© 773.362.6228, www.charlietrotters.com*). The bride's parents' intimidating estate is the **Cuneo Museum and Gardens, 1350 North Milwaukee Avenue, Vernon Hills**, on Route 60 about 35 miles northwest of Chicago itself, (*© 847.362.3042, www.lake-online.com/cuneo*). A mansion built in 1914 for Thomas Edison's partner, Samuel Insull, it was bought by Chicago businessman John Cuneo in 1937 and remained the family home until 1990. It's now open to the public. The wedding is scheduled to take place on Chicago's Magnificent Mile, at the **Fourth Presbyterian Church, 125 East Chestnut Street** at Michigan Avenue.

MY BIG FAT GREEK WEDDING

(2002, dir: Joel Zwick)
Nia Vardalos, John Corbett, Michael Constantine.
● **TORONTO, ONTARIO, CANADA; CHICAGO, ILLINOIS**

Nia Vardalos' one-woman show is opened up into a feel-good romantic comedy, set in Chicago, but largely filmed around Toronto's Greektown district along Danforth Avenue.

Harry S Truman College, where frumpy Toula (Vardalos) perks up and enrolls in a computer course, is the **Rogers Communication Building** of **Ryerson Polytechnic University**. The interior of Lincoln Park High School, the school where non-Greek fiancé Ian Miller (Corbett) teaches, is **East Kerr Hall** of the same facility, though the exterior is **Jarvis Collegiate Institute, Jarvis Street** at Wellesley. Miller's apartment is **5 Lonsdale Road**, off Yonge Street. As in the similar *Muriel's Wedding*, the dumpy heroine blossoms once she gets a job, this time in a travel agency. But in reality, both establishments are, erm, erotic emporia. What gives? Mount Olympus Travel, where Toula handles online bookings, is a toy store for adults: **Party For Two, 439 Danforth Avenue** (℗ *416.907.5378*), Simcoe Street at Pearl Street.

Toula's family's fabulously Greek house is on **St Clair Avenue East**, east of O'Connor. The driveway was sodded over and a new one built to the (fake) garage with the Greek flag door but, yes, that's how the house is. There's romance for Toula and Ian on the illuminated Chicago bridge, which is **Pier 4** between Rees and Lower Simcoe Streets at Toronto's harbourfront. Dancing Zorbas, the family restaurant, is a branch of the English pub chain, the **Elephant and Castle, 212 King Street West** at Simcoe Street (℗ *416.598.4455*). Despite what you might assume, the nearby neighbourhood establishments **Pappas Grill, 440 Danforth Avenue** (you might be forgiven for taking Pappas as an homage to legendary Greek actress Irene Pappas), and **Louis Meat Market, 449 Danforth Avenue**, weren't dreamed up by the art department. They're real Greektown businesses.

The exterior of the church where Toula and Ian finally get hitched is **Holy Trinity Russian Orthodox Church, 23 Henry Street**, while the interior is **St Nicholas Ukrainian Catholic Church, 770 Queen Street West**. Aphrodite's Palace, the site of the reception, is **Ellas Restaurant and Banquet Hall** (that's Ellas as in the Greek word for Greece, not Ella's), **35 Danforth Road** (℗ *416.694.1194*), seen also in *Sea of Love*.

MY BRILLIANT CAREER

(1979, dir: Gillian Armstrong)
Judy Davis, Sam Neill, Wendy Hughes.
● **NEW SOUTH WALES, AUSTRALIA**

Davis is the 19th century proto-feminist heroine who resists a life of wifely duties to become an independent writer. Filming took place at **Hay**; Macarthur homestead at **Camden Park**; and **Captain's Flat, Micalago**.

MY LEFT FOOT

(1989, dir: Jim Sheridan)
Daniel Day-Lewis, Brenda Fricker, Ray McAnally.
● **IRELAND**

Oscars for both Day-Lewis, as Christy Brown, and Fricker, as his mother, in the story of the writer's achievements using only the toes of his left foot. It was filmed on location around Dublin and Wicklow and at MTM Ardmore Studios. The opening charity gala was staged in **Kilruddery House** (the manor house that 'burned down' in *Far and Away*), just south of Bray, near Dublin. Christy Brown's house is on **St Kevin's Square, Bray**. The art exhibition used film producer Noel Pearson's home in **Old Conna**, near Bray. Christy Brown learns that Dr Cole is to marry at **Locks Restaurant, 1 Windsor Terrace, Portobello** (℗ *4538352*), on the bank of the Grand Canal in Dublin. The ending was shot at the stone monument atop **Victoria Hill, Killiney**, on the coast near Dublin.

MY LITTLE EYE

(2002, dir: Marc Evans)
Sean CW Johnson, Jennifer Sky, Kris Lemche.
● **NOVA SCOTIA, CANADA; LOS ANGELES, CALIFORNIA**

Reality TV gone bad as *Blair Witch* meets *Big Brother*. The house was at **Clementsport**, near the Bay of Fundy, Nova Scotia, though all the interiors were filmed in a set built on tennis courts at **Halifax**. The character intros that kick off the movie were shot later at the Handmade Films offices in Los Angeles.

MY OWN PRIVATE IDAHO

(1991, dir: Gus Van Sant)
River Phoenix, Keanu Reeves, William Richert.
● **OREGON; WASHINGTON; ITALY**

Phoenix and Reeves are hustlers, film director Richert (who made the underrated River Phoenix movie *Jimmy Reardon*) a Falstaff figure in Van Sant's quirky update of Shakespeare's *Henry IV*, or, more accurately, of Welles' *Chimes at Midnight*. Shot in **Portland** and **Maupin**, Oregon; in **Seattle**, Washington State; and in Italy.

MYRA BRECKINRIDGE

(1970, dir: Michael Sarne)
Mae West, John Huston, Raquel Welch.
● **LOS ANGELES, CALIFORNIA**

Fantastic car-wreck of a movie, with 20th Century Fox trying to loosen up and capture the sixties zeitgeist (they also bankrolled Russ Meyer's *Beyond*

Myra stays at the Chateau Marmont, Sunset Boulevard, West Hollywood the Valley of the Dolls, which made up a gloriously demented double bill). Sarne had been a pop singer who scored a hit in 1961 with the novelty record 'Come Outside' (featuring Wendy Richard, now a staple of UK TV soap EastEnders). Author Gore Vidal disassociated himself from the film of his book. Raquel Welch took on the role of post-op transsexual Myra, but refused to act with million-year-old Mae West. Old-school Hollywood stars sued to have clips of their movies removed from the release print. And, with a delicious sense of justice, film critic Rex Reed featured as the pre-op Myron in a movie regarded as one of the greatest turkeys of all time.

The opening sequence sees Myron and Myra dancing along **Hollywood Boulevard** (where else?), opposite Grauman's Chinese Theatre (apart from the venerable Roosevelt Hotel in the background, this stretch of the Boulevard has since been redeveloped). Myra stays at the **Chateau Marmont, 8221 Sunset Boulevard** (see The Doors for details), in the days when the giant blue and red cowgirl dominated the stretch of Sunset. Myra is finally killed off by Myron while she's jaywalking on **Avenue of the Stars** in **Century City**.

MYSTERY TRAIN
(1989, dir: Jim Jarmusch)
Youki Kudoh, Masatoshi Nagase, Joe Strummer.
● **MEMPHIS, TENNESSEE**

More oddball minimalism from Jarmusch: three tales centering on a sleazy hotel, filmed around a very decrepit-looking Memphis, particulary the **Chaucer Street**

Memphis landmark, home of the Blues: Beale Street

area. The hotel itself, the Arcade Hotel, has since been demolished, though the featured **Arcade Café, 540 South Main Street**, can still be seen. Among the sites featured are the legendary **Sun Studios, 706 Union Avenue**, and **Schwab's Dry Goods Store, 163 Beale Street**. Beale Street, once the throbbing heart of Memphis' blues scene, has had a major makeover and is now clean and safe, but bland and featureless as a movie set.

MYSTIC RIVER
(2003, dir: Clint Eastwood)
Sean Penn, Tim Robbins, Kevin Bacon.
● **MASSACHUSETTS**

Set in the blue-collar neighbourhood of East Buckingham, with a screenplay by Brian Helgeland, who wrote L.A. Confidential. It was filmed in **Charlestown**, Boston, with sets built in a warehouse in Canton, a suburb just to the south. The road rage incident was shot on the **Tobin/Mystic Bridge**. Linney and Penn's house is in East Boston.

Jimmy's (Penn) grocery store, Cottage Market, is **Miller's Market, 336 K Street**, South Boston (close to the L Street Tavern, seen in Good Will Hunting). McGill's,

where Dave (Robbins) sees Jimmy's daughter Katie dancing on the bartop, is **Doyle's Braddock Cafe, 3484 Washington Street, Jamaica Plain** (② 617.524.2345, www.doylescafe.com), south of the city. Katie's body is found nearby, in the **Bear Dens** in **Long Crouch Woods** (they're real, but were never used), near the Seaver Street entrance to **Franklin Park**.

Dave's childhood home is a three-storey house on **Falcon Street, Eagle Hill** in East Boston, across Boston Inner Harbor. The young Dave is abducted by the fake cops on **Condor Street**, a block north.

The Black Emerald Bar, where the Savage brothers take Dave and get him drunk ready for the final confrontation with Jimmy, isn't real. It was built from scratch on an empty industrial lot at the water's edge near the Mystic River Bridge in the Chelsea district.

N

NAKED

(1993, dir: Mike Leigh)
David Thewlis, Katrin Cartlidge, Lesley Sharp.

● **LONDON**

The Scots drifter: Lina Stores, Brewer Street

Mike Leigh's bitter comedy took Best Director and Best Actor (for Thewlis) at Cannes in 1993. You can see the house where Mancunian Johnny (Thewlis) holes up at **33 St**

Thewlis' London home: St Mark's Rise, Dalston

Mark's Rise, off Downs Park Road, E8 (*rail: Dalston Kingsland*). The Soho shop doorway where Thewlis meets manic Scots drifter Archie (Ewen Bremner) is **Lina Stores Ltd, 18 Brewer Street** at Greens Court, W1.

The café, ostensibly in the West End, where Johnny meets waitress Gina McKee, is down south of the river. It's the **Jubilee Café, 14a Winchester Walk**, in a car park on the south side of the street. Winchester Walk also became the West End for *An American Werewolf in London*. The "post-modernist gas-chamber" where Johnny speculates on increasingly paranoid philosophical concepts with obsessive nightwatchman Brian (Peter Wight) is **Ariel House, 74a Charlotte Street** in Fitzrovia. The corner of **Caledonian Road** and **Twyford Street**, northeast of King's Cross Station, is where Johnny gets a kicking from the bill-poster at the end.

The "post-modernist gas-chamber": Ariel House, Charlotte Street, Fitzrovia

NAKED CITY, THE

(1948, dir: Jules Dassin)
Barry Fitzgerald, Don Taylor, Howard Duff

● **NEW YORK CITY**

The first of the eight million stories, this police proce-

dure thriller was shot, influentially, on the streets of New York – a real change from the studio-bound productions out of Hollywood. (The title, bought up by Universal, came from a book of photographs by famed shutterbug Weegee, portrayed by Joe Pesci in *The Public Eye*, who advised on the picture and helped find locations.) The cop station, used both for interiors and exteriors, is the **10th Precinct, 230 West 20th Street** in Chelsea. Why this precinct is investigating a murder committed at **52 West 83rd Street**, way up on the Upper West Side, is a mystery left unexplained. Other New York locations include **Wall Street** in the Financial District; and the foyer of the old Roxy Theater, which stood on the northeast corner of 50th Street and Seventh Avenue, demolished in 1960. The final cop vs killer confrontation was shot at the **Williamsburg Bridge**, where the villain takes a nosedive into the East River. The entrance to the bridge, which leads to Washington Plaza, Brooklyn, is at Delancey and Clinton Streets in Chinatown.

NAKED GUN: FROM THE FILES OF POLICE SQUAD!, THE

(1988, dir: David Zucker)
Leslie Nielsen, Priscilla Presley, Ricardo Montalban.

● **LOS ANGELES, CALIFORNIA**

The big screen spin-off from *Police Squad*, the inexplicably shortlived TV series by the makers of *Airplane!*, was filmed around LA. The press conference, to announce the

The royal reception: Ambassador Hotel, Wilshire Boulevard

arrival of Queen Elizabeth II, is held at LA's **City Hall, 200 North Spring Street**, downtown, and Her Majesty's reception is at the **Ambassador Hotel, 3400 Wilshire Boulevard** (see the 1954 *A Star Is Born* for details). The office of villain Vincent Ludwig (Montalban) is the **Park Plaza Hotel, 607 South Park View Street**, overlooking MacArthur Park (see *New York New York*). Just across the park is the **Vagabond Cinema, 2509 Wilshire Boulevard**, where Lt Drebin (Nielsen) and Jane Spencer (Presley) have a good laugh over Oliver Stone's *Platoon*. Harbour scenes are **Los Angeles Harbor, San Pedro**, south of the city, and the car chase is on **Santa Fe Avenue** and the **Fourth Street Viaduct**, downtown. The baseball ground climax uses two different grounds: the exterior and the longshots are the **Anaheim Stadium, 2000 Gene Autrey Way**, Anaheim in Orange County, home to the California Angels and the LA Rams; while the interiors are the **Dodger Stadium, 1000 Elysian Park Avenue**, north central LA.

For the first sequel, *The Naked Gun 2 1/2: The Smell of Fear*, Nielsen struggles with his wetsuit on the pier in **San Pedro Harbor**, south LA.

NAKED GUN 33 1/3: THE FINAL INSULT, THE
(1994, dir: Peter Segal)
Leslie Nielsen, Priscilla Presley, George Kennedy.
● LOS ANGELES, CALIFORNIA

It's a return to the villain's hideout from the first *Naked Gun* movie for Nielsen's dream, a parody of *The Untouchables*' shootout, which turns the cavernous lobby of the **Park Plaza Hotel, 607 South Park View Street**, into a railway station. The station bookstore is the hotel's reception desk. The courtroom is **LA County Municipal Courts Building, 110 North Grand Avenue**, and the Academy Awards are presented at the **Shrine Auditorium, 649 West Jefferson Boulevard** (see the 1954 *A Star Is Born* for details), south of downtown LA.

NAKED LUNCH, THE
(1991, dir: David Cronenberg)
Peter Weller, Judy Davis, Ian Holm.
● ONTARIO, CANADA

A remaining location: Backstage Cinema, Balmuto Street, Toronto

William Burroughs' unfilmable book – written in Room 9, Hotel el Muniria, 1 rue Magellan in Tangier, Morocco – is heterosexualised and hybridised with a Burroughs-bio by squelchmeister Cronenberg. Largely studio-bound, much of the movie was shot inside a General Electric plant in Toronto. Many of the film's real locations are now gone, including Maple Green Landscaping, the Norman Elder Gallery and the El Toro Restaurant; but you can still find the **Backstage Cinema, 31 Balmuto Street** at Bloor Street West, behind the larger first-run Uptown Cinema; and the **Dunlan Restaurant, 1745 Dundas Street West**. The pawn shop, where Burroughs stand-in Weller gets the gun for the fatal William Tell game, is **Youri's Jewellery, 702 Queen Street West**.

Weller gets his gun: Youri's Jewellery, Queen Street West, Toronto

NAME OF THE ROSE, THE
(1986, dir: Jean-Jacques Annaud)
Sean Connery, Christian Slater, F Murray Abraham.
● GERMANY

Medieval whodunnit, which potters through Umberto Eco's plot while jettisoning the novel's philosophical *raison d'être*. Reversing the usual procedure, the Italian monastery, where monk Connery and sidekick Slater investigate, is an enormous set on the outside, but real inside. The interior is **Koster Eberbach**, a 12th and 14th century Cistercian monastery surviving in the Taunus

Mountains in the heart of the Rheingau district which, after secularisation in 1803, became a prison and then a lunatic asylum. During WWI it was a military rehabilitation centre, and is now maintained by the state wine authorities of the Rheingau. Situated 20 miles southwest of Frankfurt, you can visit the monastery and, if arranged in advance, take a guided tour at weekends.

NAPOLEON DYNAMITE
(2004, dir: Jared Hess)
Jon Heder, Efren Ramirez, Aaron Ruell.
● IDAHO; UTAH

Pedro Sanchez's house: South 2nd East, Preston

The geeks inherit the earth in Hess' wryly deadpan one-off, which put **Preston**, Idaho, on the map. Literally. The town, on Highway 91, at the Utah border, 100 miles north of Salt Lake City, has produced a Sweet Map to *Napoleon*'s Preston.

Napoleon (Heder) lives with brother Kip (Ruell) and his Grandma at **1447 East 800 North Road**, a bit to the northeast of town. He attends **Preston High School, 151 East 200 South**; playing tetherball in the playground at **525 South 400 East Street**. It's in front of new boy Pedro Sanchez's house, **59 South 2nd East**, that Napoleon tries a sweet jump on Pedro's Sledgehammer bike.

Pedro (Ramirez) – maybe optimistically – leaves a homemade cake outside the house of Summer Wheatley, his competition for class president, at **3384 South Parkinson Road**; while Napoleon tempts Trisha to the prom by delivering a portrait ("I spent, like, three hours doing shading on the upper lip") to her home at **253 South 2600 East**. He buys his awesome suit at **Deseret Industries Thrift Shop, 36 South State Street** (the store furnished most of the film's wardrobe). The chicken farm, where Napoleon and friends earn six dollars (plus all the eggs they can eat – and drink) moving around chickens with large talons, is **Ritewood Egg Co, 3643 South 4000 East, Franklin**.

Napoleon buys his awesome suit: Deseret Industries Thrift Shop, South State Street, Preston

Kip and Napoleon learn self-respect studying the 'Rex Kwon Do' self-defence system at **12 ½ North State Street**. They're left in the care of Uncle Rico after Grandma

The chicken farm: Ritewood Egg Co, South 4000 East, Franklin

Napoleon's house: East 800 North Road, Preston

Napoleon's school: Preston High School, East 200 South, Preston

breaks her coccyx bike-riding at **St Anthony Sand Dunes**, 11,000 acres of white sand, about eight miles west of **St Anthony**, on Highway 20, north of Idaho Falls. It's a wilderness study area, and consequently a great favourite for dune buggy enthusiasts.

Also out of town – and out of the state – Kip confides in Uncle Rico about his on-line girlfriend, LaFawnduh, at **Big J's Drive-in, 190 South 200 East, Richmond**, Utah, opened in 1959 (as Jed's) and about to be demolished. The bowling alley, in which Kip and Rico plan their sure-fire business venture, is back in Preston: **Pop'n Pin Lanes, 411 South Highway 91**.

Finally, the wedding of Kip and LaFawnduh (shot months after completion of the film) is at **Lamont Reservoir**, a couple of miles east of Preston.

The climactic political rally: Parthenon, Centennial Park, Nashville

NASHVILLE
(1975, dir: Robert Altman)
Geraldine Chaplin, Keith Carradine, Ronee Blakley.
● **TENNESSEE**

Altman's brilliant multi-focused satire on the US via the Nashville country music industry filmed, of course, in **Nashville**, Tennessee. The climactic Replacement Party political rally was filmed at the city's replica of Athens' **Parthenon**, complete with Elgin marbles, in **Centennial Park**. Find it west of the city (© *615.259.6358; admission fee*).

NATIONAL LAMPOON'S ANIMAL HOUSE
(1978, dir: John Landis)
John Belushi, Tim Matheson, Donald Sutherland.
● **OREGON**

Start of the bozo campus comedy genre, shot at the **University of Oregon, Eugene**, on highways 99 and 126 (the university that turned down filming of *The Graduate*). Oregon weather being what it is, the snow had to be swept away before shooting, and the lawns painted green. The homecoming parade was filmed on the Main Street of **Cottage Grove**, 20 miles south of Eugene. Delta House stood at 751 East 11th Street, Eugene, but has since been demolished.

NATIONAL VELVET
(1944, dir: Clarence Brown)

Elizabeth Taylor, Mickey Rooney, Anne Revere.
● **CALIFORNIA**

Rooney and Taylor train a horse which goes on to win the Grand National. The old Warner Bros Ranch, where much of the movie was shot, is now the **Calabasas Golf Club, 4515 Park Entrada**, Calabasas, off Highway 101 northwest of LA in the Santa Monica Mountains. On the edge of the golf course you can still see some of the old barn buildings from the movie. More scenes were filmed at the **Polo Field, Pebble Beach**, south of Monterey, on the central California coast.

NATURAL, THE
(1984, dir: Barry Levinson)
Robert Redford, Robert Duvall, Glenn Close.
● **NEW YORK**

Hollywood bought Bernard Malamud's odd Arthurian-baseball novel and totally reversed the ending to make an entirely different point. Set in the twenties and thirties, the movie was shot entirely within the environs of **Buffalo**, upstate New York, which was fairly unmodernised, and happened to have a period baseball stadium, the 40,000-seater **War Memorial Stadium, Jefferson and Best Streets**, home of the Buffalo Bisons. Much of the stadium has since been dismantled to form a sports complex. Filming also took place at the **Buffalo Psychiatric Center, 400 Forest Avenue**. The farmhouse is in **South Dayton**, about 40 miles southwest of Buffalo, where the the railway station is **South Dayton Station**. Chicago's Wrigley Field is actually the playing field of **Bennett High School, 2895 Main Street**, close to the ice cream parlor where Redford meets Glenn Close, **Parkside Candy Store, 3208 Main Street**.

NATURAL BORN KILLERS
(1994, dir: Oliver Stone)
Woody Harrelson, Juliette Lewis, Robert Downey Jr.
● **NEW MEXICO; ARIZONA; ILLINOIS; INDIANA**

Stone's adaptation of Tarantino's script was filmed all over the US, in New Mexico at **Albuquerque; Taos; Gallup; Redrock; San Jose; Farmington**; and **Shiprock**. The bridge, where Mickey and Mallory marry, is the **Taos Gorge Bridge** over the Rio Grande, seven miles north of Taos itself. M&M's trail of mayhem passes through Arizona, at **Winslow** and **Holbrook**.

The media scrum outside the courthouse, following the arrest of Mickey and Mallory, is at the **Chicago Cultural Center, 78 East Washington Street** at Randolph Street, Chicago, though the trial was shot in **Hammond City Court, 5925 Calumet Avenue, Hammond**, south of the city, just over the state border in Indiana. The prison is **Stateville Correctional Facility** at **Joliet**, highway 53, south of Chicago (where John Belushi was

The media scrum at Mickey's trial: Chicago Cultural Center, East Washington Street, Chicago

incarcerated at the beginning of *The Blues Brothers*).

NETWORK
(1976, dir: Sidney Lumet)
Peter Finch, Faye Dunaway, William Holden.
● NEW YORK CITY; ONTARIO, CANADA

Holden's office: MGM Building, Avenue of the Americas

Paddy Chayevsky's blackly satirical satire on US TV gets a great Lumet treatment, and a posthumous Oscar for Peter Finch as the Mad Prophet of the Airwaves. Set in New York, much of the movie was made in **Toronto**, but there are some real New York locations. Holden's office is the **MGM Building, 1350 Avenue of the Americas** at 55th Street. He shares a lovenest with ambitious TV exec Faye Dunaway at the **Apthorp Apartments, 2211 Broadway** between West 78th and West 79th Streets on the West Side. The pair meet up at showbizzy hangout **Elaine's Restaurant, 1703 Second Avenue** between East 88th and East 89th Streets on the East Side (see Woody Allen's *Manhattan* for details). The boardroom, where Finch gets a lecture from wacko businessman Ned Beatty after putting the station's financial security in jeopardy, is the **New York Public Library, Fifth Avenue** between 40th and 42nd Streets.

NEVER ON SUNDAY
(1960, dir: Jules Dassin)
Melina Mercouri, Jules Dassin, Georges Foundas.
● GREECE

An American in Greece falls for prostitute Mercouri and tries to reform her. Filmed at **Piraeus**, about 30 miles west of Athens, where the leads take in a performance of *Medea* in the amphitheatre.

NEVER SAY NEVER AGAIN
(1983, dir: Irvin Kershner)
Sean Connery, Klaus Maria Brandauer, Kim Basinger.
● BAHAMAS; FRANCE; SPAIN; BEDFORDSHIRE; BUCKINGHAMSHIRE

Remake of *Thunderball*, by a different production company, but with Connery and an excellent supporting cast. Shrublands, the health club where Bond is sent by M to eliminate 'free radicals', is **Luton Hoo**, Luton, open to the public until recently. You can see the house in loads of films, including *Eyes Wide Shut*, *A Shot in the Dark* and *Wilde*. See *Four Weddings and a Funeral* for details.

Shrublands: Luton Hoo

Largo's yacht, the *Flying Saucer*, is the 300-foot *Nabila*, which belonged to Adnan Khashoggi but is now the property of Don-

ald Trump and has been renamed the *Trump Princess*. The motorbike chase was shot in the narrow streets of **Villefranche-sur-Mer**, a picturesque old fishing port east of Nice on the Côte d'Azur.

The end of the motorbike chase: Villefranche-sur-Mer

The 3-D Domination game between Bond and villain Largo was filmed in the French Rococo room of **Waddesdon Manor**, English home of the Rothschild family, seen

Bond plays wargames with Largo: Waddesdon Manor

also in *Carry On – Don't Lose Your Head* and *Isadora*. It's at the west end of Waddesdon village (*rail: Aylesbury*), six miles northwest of Aylesbury on the A41, and open to the public (*© 01296.653226, www.waddesdon.org.uk; admission charge*).

A 110-foot freighter was scuppered for the movie on New Providence Island in the Bahamas, at **Clifton Wall** on the south side. The hotel where Fatima Blush attempts to blow up Bond is the expensive, and revamped, **Best Western British Colonial Beach Resort, 1 Bay Street** at Marlborough Street west of Nassau Harbour (*© 242.322.3301*), a 1923 Spanish-American style affair built on the site of the 17th century Fort Nassau. Bond walks through the **Straw Market** in Nassau, and the outdoor bar is on **Nassau dock**.

Largo's Palmyra fortress (in *Thunderball*, it was on New Providence Island in the Bahamas) is the disused **Fort Carré d'Antibes, Route du Bord du Mer**, north of the

Largo's Palmyra estate: Fort Carré d'Antibes

harbour at Antibes on the Côte d'Azur.

NEVERENDING STORY, THE
(1984, dir: Wolfgang Petersen)
Barret Oliver, Gerald McRaney, Noah Hathaway.
● BRITISH COLUMBIA, CANADA

Munich is actually the old **Gastown** district, just east of downtown, Vancouver, British Columbia.

NEW JACK CITY
(1991, dir: Mario Van Peebles)
Wesley Snipes, Ice T, Chris Rock.
● NEW YORK CITY; NEW YORK

Cops versus drug dealers, filmed on the streets of New York City, and in Nassau County, Long Island. The mansion is **Hempstead House**, on **Sands Point Preserve, 95 Middleneck Road, Port Washington**, Long Island, seen also in *Scent of a Woman* and the 1998 *Great Expectations*. See *The Godfather*, which shot scenes at another mansion on the Preserve, for details.

NEW YORK NEW YORK

(1977, dir: Martin Scorsese)

Liza Minnelli, Robert De Niro, Lionel Stander.

● **LOS ANGELES, CALIFORNIA**

De Niro plays the Sullivan House: The Ballroom, Park Plaza Hotel

The nightclub: Grand Avenue, South Grand Avenue

Scorsese's brave attempt to put real characters into an old-style glossy musical wasn't made in New York at all, but in LA, largely on soundstages at MGM. Creepily, Liza Minnelli was assigned her mum's old dressing room. De Niro had Garbo's. Real locations can all be found in downtown LA, including the **Biltmore Hotel, 506 South Grand Avenue** on Pershing Square. The Sullivan House, where De Niro stands in when bandleader Frankie Harte has to bail out Fowler, is the Ballroom of the **Park Plaza Hotel, 607 South Park View Street** overlooking MacArthur Park. One of the most-used locations in LA, if not the world, you can see its wood-panelled Ballroom in *Barton Fink*, *The Big Picture*, *Chaplin*, *Hocus Pocus*, *Hook*, *Mr Saturday Night*, *Mobsters*, *Primal Fear*, *Stargate*, *What's Love Got to Do With It?* and *Not Another Teen Movie*, among many others, as well as in countless TV series and music videos. Its Terrace Room was featured in *The Mask*; its lobby in *Naked Gun 33 1/3* and *Wild at Heart*; its exterior in *The Naked Gun*, *Tango and Cash* and *The Phantom*; its bathrooms in *Reservoir Dogs*; and even its boiler room in *The Fisher King*. The towering structure, with its spectacular vaulted lobby, was built in the twenties as the Elks Building and long served as a hotel, but as the area around it, particularly Macarthur Park, became associated with drug related violence, it became increasingly deserted and finally closed its doors in 1998. It's now exclusively used for movie shoots and private functions. Other period-style nightspots include the old Myron's Ballroom, now renamed **Grand Avenue, 1024 South Grand Avenue**, and the lobby of the splendid **Los Angeles Theater, 615 South Broadway**.

NEW YORK STORIES

(1989, dir: Martin Scorsese; Francis Coppola; Woody Allen)

Nick Nolte, Rosanna Arquette, Woody Allen.

● **NEW YORK CITY**

Life Lessons: Nick Nolte is a painter in Martin Scorsese's section, filmed in a loft in **SoHo/Tribeca**.

Life Without Zoe: Coppola's mawkish story, written by his daughter, is

Zoe lives in the deluxe Sherry-Netherlands Hotel, Fifth Avenue

the weakest of the three. Zoe lives in the deluxe, showbizzy **Sherry-Netherlands Hotel, 781 Fifth Avenue** at East 59th Street. The party scene was shot, imaginatively, in the arched underpass at **Bethesda Fountain** in Central Park, where the usual bums were moved out, and the space decorated to look like a mansion interior.

Oedipus Wrecks: Woody Allen's section is by far the best, with domineering mother Mae Questel (the voice of cartoon character Betty Boop) disappearing, only to materialise in the sky above Manhattan to discuss her son's shortcomings. The restaurant is the **Tavern on the Green**, in Central Park at Central Park West and 67th Street (see *Ghostbusters* for details).

NIAGARA

(1953, dir: Henry Hathaway)

Marilyn Monroe, Joseph Cotten, Jean Peters.

● **ONTARIO, CANADA**

Monroe is the femme fatale planning to bump off hubby Cotten (in a role meant for James Mason) at the eponymous falls. The movie was shot on location on the Canadian side of the **Horseshoe Falls** before the massive commercialisation of the area, and the cute cabins where the couple stay have gone to make way for the main road overlooking the falls. Some of the locations remain unchanged. you can still visit **Table Rock House** alongside the Horseshoe Falls, and see the rickety-looking wooden walkways alongside the

The bell tower: Falls Museum

Double crossing at the Falls: Table Rock House

American Falls from the Maid of the Mist boat tour, which will take you to the foot of the falls. You can't request your favourite tune to be played on the bells, though. The bell tower, through which Monroe communicates to her lover, is the **Falls Museum**.

NIGHT OF THE DEMON (aka *Curse of the Demon*)

(1958, dir: Jacques Tourneur)

Dana Andrews, Niall MacGinnis, Peggy Cummins.

Lufford Hall: Brocket Hall, Welwyn Garden City

Brilliant and genuinely scary filming of MR James' classic horror story 'Casting the Runes', slightly let down by the studio's insistence on giving the ambiguous demon thumping great close-ups at the beginning of the movie. The opening scenes are at **Stonehenge** on Salisbury Plain, Wiltshire. Demon raiser MacGinnis follows Andrews to the huge circular **Reading Room** of the **British Museum**, where the fatal runes are handed over. MacGinnis' mansion, Lufford Hall, Warwickshire, is **Brocket Hall** just west of Welwyn Garden City in Herfordshire. The mansion, also seen in TV movie *Murder With Mirrors* and the 1991 remake of *A Kiss Before Dying*, was home to the disgraced Lord Brocket, jailed for insurance fraud. It's now a conference, dining and golf centre (✆ *01707.335241*, *www.brockethall.co.uk*). The demon finally materialises on the railway line at **Bricket Wood**, between St Albans and Watford.

NIGHT OF THE IGUANA, THE

(1964, dir: John Huston)
Richard Burton, Ava Gardner, Deborah Kerr.
● MEXICO

Burton is the ex-priest turned tour guide having problems with Gardner, Kerr and nymphet Sue Lyon in this comparatively lightweight Tennessee Williams play, filmed on location on the west coast of Mexico at **Puerto Vallarta**. Although tourists have been visiting the town since the thirties, it was Huston's film that put Puerta Vallarta on the map. There's actually a statue of the director in the park on Isla Río Cuale, the quiet island in the middle of Río Cuale, the river flowing through town. Much of the publicity centred around the Burton-Taylor romance, then at its height, and Burton, Taylor and Huston all stayed at La Jolla de Mismaloya Resort and Spa (✆ *322.3.0660*), **Mismaloya Beach**, six miles south of town, where the movie was shot. The movie is shown nightly at Iggy's, the hotel's nightclub. You can still visit the stone buildings constructed for the movie, on the southern point above the beach.

Burton and Taylor actually bought houses in Puerto Vallarta on 'Gringo Gulch', the hilly neighbourhood of American expats on the north bank of Rio Cuale. Joined by a bridge, the two properties are now a guest house, Casa Kimberley, Zaragosa 445 (✆ *322.2.1336*).

NIGHT OF THE LIVING DEAD

(1968, dir: George A Romero)
Judith O'Dea, Duane Jones, Karl Hardman.
● PITTSBURGH, PENNSYLVANIA

First of the US zombie movies to move into hitherto unexplored areas of grossness, with the low-budget, black and white look adding to the grungy atmosphere. Made, like most of Romero's output, around his native Pittsburgh, this one features **Evans City**, to the north of Pittsburgh itself, where the cemetery at the opening of the movie is situated. The farmhouse, which has since been demolished, stood on the banks of the Monongahela River. The farmhouse cellar was the basement of production company Latent Image, Carson Street, on Pittsburgh's South Side, and the TV studio was Karl Hardman's Studio in Pittsburgh.

For the 1990 colour remake, directed by Romero's make-up wiz Tom Savini, Pittsburgh was once again the setting. The farmhouse is in **East Buffalo**, Pennsylvania.

NIGHT PORTER, THE

(1974, dir: Liliana Cavani)
Dirk Bogarde, Charlotte Rampling, Philippe Leroy.
● ROME, ITALY; VIENNA

When concentration camp survivor Rampling recognises the night porter of her hotel as a sadistic SS commandant, she embarks on a bizarre sado-masochistic relationship with him, in Cavani's queasily exploitative melodrama. The concentration camp scenes used a condemned TB sanatorium on the via Tuscolona in Rome. The present-day setting is Vienna, where Rampling attends performances by her conductor husband at the home of light opera, the **Volksoper, Währingerstrasse** at Währinger Gürtel.

NIGHT TO REMEMBER, A

(1958, dir: Roy Baker)
Kenneth More, Honor Blackman, John Cairney.
● BUCKINGHAMSHIRE; MIDDLESEX; SURREY

Before *Titanic*, there was this multi-focused account of the sinking of the unsinkable, packed with moving cameos and social observation. A 300-

The home of the upper-crust couple: Great Fosters Hotel, Stroude Road, Egham

foot section of the doomed ship was built in a field near the Pinewood Studios, Iver Heath in Buckinghamshire. Some seagoing scenes were actually filmed at **Ruislip Lido** in Middlesex.

The home of Sir Richard and her Ladyship, the upper-crust couple who set out for the doomed liner at the opening of the movie, is the **Great Fosters Hotel, Stroude Road, Egham** in Surrey (✆ *01784.433822*, *www.greatfosters.co.uk*), a 15 minute walk from the railway station (*rail: Egham*).

NIGHTCOMERS, THE

(1971, dir: Michael Winner)
Marlon Brando, Stephanie Beacham, Thora Hird.
● CAMBRIDGESHIRE

A gift to pub trivia quizzes – 'Which film featured both Marlon Brando and Thora Hird?' – this tacky prequel to the excellent *The Innocents* explains how gardener Quint's

SM relationship with governess Miss Jessel gives the children Miles and Flora ideas beyond their years. Bly House (which was Sheffield Park, Sussex, in the 1961 movie) is **Sawston Hall**, a stone-built Tudor manor house five miles south of Cambridge on the A130. It's now a private school, the Cambridge Centre for Languages.

NIGHTMARE ON ELM STREET, A

(1984, dir: Wes Craven)
John Saxon, Ronee Blakely, Heather Langenkamp.
● LOS ANGELES, CALIFORNIA

Freddie terrorises the teens: North Genessee Avenue, Hollywood

Johnny Depp's house: North Genessee Avenue, Hollywood

Wild, surreal, reality-shifting movie, elmstreets ahead of the stalk'n' slashers it's usually bracketted with. Many of the interiors were shot inside the old **Lincoln Heights Jail, 421 North Avenue 19, Lincoln Heights**, near downtown LA, a frequent movie location (see the 1954 *A Star Is Born*). Heather Langenkamp's house, where Freddy Krueger stalks her, is **1428 North Genessee Avenue**, between Fountain Avenue and Sunset Boulevard, west Hollywood. And just over the road at **1419 North Genessee Avenue**, is the house where boyfriend Johnny Depp (in his movie début) gets liquidised.

NINE 1/2 WEEKS

(1986, dir: Adrian Lyne)
Mickey Rourke, Kim Basinger, Margaret Whitton.
● NEW YORK CITY

Flash-trash ads director Lyne films a softcore promo for SM lite in New York. Shooting took place at literary hangout the **Algonquin Hotel, 59 West 44th Street** between Fifth and Sixth Avenues, midtown; funky Italian bar **Mare Chiaro, 176 Mulberry Street**, Little Italy (seen in *Donnie Brasco* among many other films); and at the **Hotel Chelsea, 222 West 23rd Street** (see *Sid and Nancy* for details).

NINETEEN EIGHTY-FOUR

Victory Square: Alexandra Palace, Muswell Hill

(1984, dir: Michael Radford)
John Hurt, Richard Burton, Cyril Cusack.
● LONDON; WILTSHIRE

Designed like a forties dystopian nightmare, and made during the period in which the original story was set (April-May 1984) at Twickenham Studios and on location around London, including the disused **Battersea Power Station**, off Battersea Park Road, and the old railway station which used to serve it (used also in Ian McKellen's *Richard III*). Victory Square is the shell of **Alexandra Palace**, Muswell Hill, N22, after it had been gutted by fire. It has since been completely renovated. The Golden Country is the Wiltshire countryside.

NIXON

(1995, dir: Oliver Stone)
Anthony Hopkins, Joan Allen, James Woods.
● WASHINGTON DC; CALIFORNIA

Nixon meets Mao: Plaza Room, Park Plaza Hotel, South Park View Street

Long, impressionistic and surprisingly sympathetic, Oliver Stone's account of the rise and fall of the conflicted president is set largely in Washington DC, but was filmed almost entirely in LA and its surrounds. The White House is the Sony Studios set built for *The American President*, and the White House gates were built at **El Dorado Park** near Studebaker Road and East Los Arcos Street in Long Beach, south LA. The **Greystone Mansion, 905 Loma Vista Drive**, Beverly Hills (see *The Loved One*) stood in for the corridors and lobbies of the White House.

Although Tricky Dicky (Hopkins) ascends the steps of the real **Lincoln Memorial** in Washington DC, a full-scale recreation of its interior was built on Stage 30 at Sony Studios in Culver City for his confrontation with the anti-war protesters (a seemingly unlikely scene, but one based on fact).

The Del Mar Racetrack, San Diego, south of LA, where Nixon wheels and deals with FBI chief J Edgar Hoover (Bob Hoskins), is the **Santa Anita Racetrack, 285 West Huntington Boulevard, Pasadena**, east of LA (for details see the 1954 *A Star Is Born*, which also filmed at this landmark track). See the same film for details of the old **Ambassador Hotel, 3400 Wilshire Boulevard**, where Nixon's team watches the infamous television debate with JFK. It was in the kitchen of the Ambassador that Robert Kennedy was assassinated in 1968. The press conference, at which Nixon delivers his triumphant speech after being named as the Republican party's candidate for the 1968 election, uses the same hotel.

Another of LA's frequently-used hotel locations doubles as Chairman Mao's study for Nixon's famous initial meeting with Mao in China. It's the **Plaza Room** of the **Park Plaza Hotel, 607 South Park View Street**, midtown LA (see *New York New York* for details of the hotel).

The estate (supposedly outside Dallas, Texas), where Nixon hobnobs with some very shady right-wingers, is the **Circle K Ranch** in the Santa Ynez mountains, near Santa Barbara.

Nixon's childhood home ("The poorest lemon ranch in California.") was in East Whittier, southeast of LA. For the movie, the house and grocery store were built among the citrus groves of **Redlands**, further east on I-10. Nearby is Riverside, where you'll find the site of the brief flashback of the Nixon wedding. He marries Pat Ryan (Allen) at the wildly kitsch **Mission Inn, 3469 Mission Inn Avenue, Riverside** (© 909.784.0300, *www.missioninn.com*), actually the site of the real Nixon 1940 wedding. The inn was also the location for a little-seen 1975 Merchant-Ivory film, *The Wild Party*, loosely based on the Fatty Arbuckle tragedy. The dinner aboard the Presidential yacht, *Sequioa*, on the Potomac, DC, where Nixon comtemplates dropping 'the big one', was filmed on board 1930s yacht *Electra* off the coast of **San Pedro**, LA's harbour.

Apart from the Lincoln Memorial and brief glimpses of the White House frontage, one of the few real DC shots is the clandestine night time meeting between John Dean (David Hyde Pierce) and Watergate conspirator E Howard Hunt (Ed Harris), on DC's **Inlet Bridge**, at Tidal Basin, with the Jefferson and Washington Memorials illuminated in the background.

NORTH BY NORTHWEST

(1959, dir: Alfred Hitchcock)
Cary Grant, Eva Marie Saint, James Mason.
● **NEW YORK CITY; NEW YORK; ILLINOIS; SOUTH DAKOTA; CALIFORNIA**

Cary Grant gets abducted: Plaza Hotel, Fifth Avenue

Hitchcock in peak lightweight form with the greatest of all comedy thrillers. Grant is an advertising exec working in the now demolished CIT Building, which stood at 650 Madison Avenue (Hitch makes his cameo appearance under the credits here, just missing the bus). Grant is mistakenly abducted, in place of the mysterious Mr Kaplan, from the **Plaza Hotel, Fifth Avenue** at 59th Street (© 212.759.3000, *www.fairmont.com/theplaza*). The 19-story landmark was built in 1907 and the list of jaw-dropping features begins with the 1,650 crystal chandeliers. The first nightly rate when the hotel opened? $2.50. Today it's a little more. Other movies featuring the Plaza include *Arthur*, *Barefoot in the Park*, *The Cotton Club*, *"Crocodile" Dundee*, *Funny Girl*, *The Great Gatsby*, *Home Alone II*, *Plaza Suite* (naturally) and *The Way We Were*.

The murder frame-up: United Nations Headquarters, First Avenue

James Mason's house, supposedly 169 Baywood, Glen Cove, where Grant is force-fed bourbon by creepy Martin Landau, is the redbrick man-

Grant is held in Glen Cove: Old Westbury Gardens, Long Island

sion at **Old Westbury Gardens, 71 Old Westbury Road**, the Phipps Estate, a few miles south of the real Glen Cove, Long Island. The estate, north of Westbury on the Long Island Railroad from New York's Pennsylvania Station, is open to the public between May and December (© 516.333.0048, *www.oldwestburygardens.org*; admission charge).

Grant follows a lead to the **United Nations Headquarters, First Avenue** between 42nd and 48th Streets, where he's framed for murder. You can tour the General Assembly Building, quite safely, from the entrance at 46th Street (© 212.963.7113). Grant escapes on the 20th Century from **Grand Central Station, East 42nd Street** at Park Avenue, and meets the compliant Eva Marie Saint, who helps him evade redcaps when they arrive at Chicago's **LaSalle Street Station, 414 South LaSalle Street** between West Van Buren Street and West Harrison Street.

In one of cinema's most famous scenes, Grant goes to meet the strange Mr Kaplan by taking the Greyhound bus to Indianapolis and getting off at the Prairie Stop on Route 41, where he's attacked by the crop-dusting plane. Far from Indiana, the crop fields are actually at **Wasco**, near Bakersfield on Route 99, in the desert 80 miles north of LA. A favourite road of Hitchcock's – it links Hollywood to the vineyards of Northern California – it's the same stretch of road on which James Dean met his fate.

Grant, though, survives and continues his dogged pursuit of Kaplan to the **Omni Ambassador East Hotel, 1301 North State Parkway** at East Goethe Street, Chicago (© 312.787.7200). Built in 1926, to mirror the 1919 Ambassador West over North State Street at 1300, the Ambassador East, and its luxurious Pump Room restaurant, was another favourite of Hitchcock's.

The futuristic home of villain James Mason is a studio mock-up of a Frank Lloyd Wright house. The climax on Mount Rushmore was shot mainly in the studio – the authorities weren't going to allow any disrespect to the dead presidents (at one point, Hitchcock wanted Grant to be given away by a sneeze while hidden inside a huge presidential nostril). The real **Mount Rushmore** can be visited in the Black Hills National Forest, Route 385 southeast of Rapid City, South Dakota.

NORTHWEST PASSAGE

(1940, dir: King Vidor)
Spencer Tracy, Robert Young, Walter Brennan.
● **OREGON**

Tracy hunts for the eponymous passage. Filmed in the **Cascade Mountains** of Oregon.

NOSFERATU

(1922, dir: F W Murnau)
Max Schreck, Alexander Granach, Gustav von Wangenheim.

● GERMANY

Imaginative horror, actually Bram Stoker's *Dracula* under a pseudonym to avoid copyright, with location filming in **Westphalia** and on the **Baltic Coast**.

NOSFERATU, PHANTOM DER NACHT (aka *Nosferatu the Vampyre*)
(1979, dir: Werner Herzog)
Klaus Kinski, Isabelle Adjani, Bruno Ganz.

● GERMANY; NETHERLANDS; CZECHOSLOVAKIA

Remake of the 1921 silent classic, with Kinski copying Max Schreck's original appearance. The Carpathian Mountains are actually the **High Tatra** mountainous region on Czechoslovakia's border with Poland. Period locations include the towns of **Pernstein** and **Telc** in Czechoslovakia; and **Lubeck**, West Germany. The plague of rats is at **Delft** in the Netherlands, and features the 17th century town square. To the alarm of the authorities, not to mention local residents, 11,000 laboratory rats were released, without permission. Well, this is a Herzog movie.

NOT ANOTHER TEEN MOVIE
(2001, dir: Joel Gallen)
Chyler Leigh, Cris Evans, Jaime Pressly.

● LOS ANGELES, CALIFORNIA

John Hughes High: Monrovia High School, West Colorado Boulevard, Monrovia

The first feature from music director Gallen references just about every youth movie from the last twenty years, but it's not as smart or funny as it thinks it is. The exterior of 'John Hughes High is **Monrovia High School, 845 West Colorado Boulevard** at the northeast corner of Madison Avenue, Monrovia, east of Pasadena, itself east of LA. There are plenty of familiar locations. The courtyard is **Torrance High School, 2200 West Carson Street** at El Prado Avenue, **Torrance**, south LA (see also *She's All That*). More of the school was filmed at **Verdugo Hills High School, Tujunga** (see also *Heathers*). The home of 'popular jock' Jake Wyler (Evans) is the mock-Tudor mansion at **4252 Country Club Drive**, down in Long Beach, south LA (which was also Patrick Swayze's mansion in *Donnie Darko*). The home of Preston Wasserstein (Robert Patrick Benedict) in the movie's *Risky Business* parody – **4160 Country Club Drive**, also in Long Beach – was Ferris Bueller's Chicago home and is also seen in *Red Dragon*.

The 'Prom Tonight' number begins with Jake mooching about alongside **Santa Monica Pier**, climaxing with the production number in front of the **Park Plaza Hotel, 607 South Park View Street** (see *New York New York*). The prom, with Good Charlotte covering 'I Want Candy', is held in the Park Plaza's ballroom. Look out for Spicoli's television repair shop on the corner of Sixth Street and South Park View, referencing *Fast Times at Ridgemont High*. The finale (featuring a cameo by John Hughes regular Molly Ringwald) is, of course, at **LAX (Los Angeles International Airport)**.

NOTHING SACRED
(1937, dir: William Wellman)
Carole Lombard, Fredric March, Walter Connolly.

● NEW YORK CITY; CALIFORNIA

The press builds Lombard into a national celeb when it's believed she's dying from a rare disease. March is the cynical hack who brings her to New York. Filming took place at the **Rockefeller Center**, which was then only just beginning to be built. It now occupies 22 acres from West 48th Street to West 51st Street between Fifth and Sixth Avenues. March and Lombard sail the East River, beneath the **Brooklyn Bridge**. Scenes were also shot at **Agoura Hills**, north of Los Angeles, and **San Pedro**, the harbour to the south.

NOTTING HILL
(1999, dir: Roger Michell)
Hugh Grant, Julia Roberts, Rhys Ifans.

● LONDON

The failed restaurant: Portfolio, Golborne Road

The team behind *Four Weddings and a Funeral* follows up with another Transatlantic romance as mega-movie star Roberts falls for mild-mannered English bookseller Grant. The title is the setting, though the famously cosmopolitan locale – site of race riots in the fifties – seems to have been ethnically cleansed: this is the whitest Notting Hill you'll ever see. First off, there is no Travel Book Company, the down-at-heel shop owned by Grant. The store was Nicholls Antique Arcade, now furniture store **Gong, 142 Portobello Road**. The real Travel Bookshop, on which Grant's establishment was based, can be seen around the corner in Blenheim Crescent. Grant's flat, with its heavily-featured shabby blue door, was, in fact, the home of screenwriter Richard Curtis, **280 Westbourne Park Road**, just off Portobello Road, put on the market for a cool £1.3 million just before the film's release. As you can imagine, it's a tad more impressive inside than the film version, which was recreated in the studio. The real flat, a converted chapel, has a courtyard garden, a 1,000 square foot

Hugh Grant's flat: Westbourne Park Road, Notting Hill

The Travel Book Company: Gong, Portobello Road

Grant takes a surprise date to the birthday party: Lansdowne Road, Notting Hill

Roberts stays at the Ritz Hotel, Piccadilly

The wedding reception: Zen Garden, Hempel Hotel, Craven Hill

reception room and a galleried mezzanine. The famous scuffed blue door was sold.

The disused shop where Grant first bumps into Roberts is now **Coffee Republic**. Roberts and Grant see a movie at Notting Hill's **Coronet Cinema**, and afterwards enjoy a meal at **Nobu**, the dizzyingly expensive Japanese restaurant of the **Metropolitan Hotel, Park Lane** (*© 020.7447.4747*). At the other end of the scale, the failed restaurant of Grant's friend is **Portfolio**, an art store on the corner of **Golborne Road and Bevington Road**, W10, at the northern reach of Portobello Road market. Previously an art gallery, it also became an eaterie – Brad Dourif's diner – in a film which took a totally different look at the area, Hanif Kureishi's *London Kills Me*. The private communal garden Grant and Roberts break into at night is **Rosmead Gardens, Rosmead Road**, W11. The party, at which Grant arrives with his surprise date, is **91 Lansdowne Road**.

And outside Notting Hill, there's no shortage of London landmarks to seduce the US tourist dollar. Roberts stays at the **Ritz, Piccadilly**, which rarely permits filming inside, but on this occasion gave unprecedented co-operation to the film company. The site of Julia Roberts' Henry James movie is **Kenwood, Hampstead Lane**, NW3, on Hampstead Heath. The Adam mansion, once home to Lord Mansfield, holds the Iveagh Bequest of old master paintings, and, amazingly, entry is free. Roberts' press conference, at which Grant proposes, is held in the **Lancaster Room** of the **Savoy Hotel, the Strand**. The wedding reception uses the Zen Garden, opposite the hotel entrance, of designer Anouska Hempel's minimalist **Hempel Hotel, Craven Hill**, W2 (*www.the-hempel.co.uk*). The movie première at the end is the **Empire, Leicester Square**.

NOVECENTO (aka *Nineteenhundred*)
(1976, dir: Bernardo Bertolucci)
Robert De Niro, Gerard Depardieu, Burt Lancaster.
● **ITALY**

Bertolucci's examination of Italian fascism, in a family saga spanning 45 years, was beset by problems. Maria Schneider left the production, and Orson Welles was replaced by Burt Lancaster. Like the director's earlier *Before the Revolution*, the movie was shot around **Parma** in the province of Emilia, northern Italy.

NOW, VOYAGER
(1942, dir: Irving Rapper)
Bette Davis, Paul Henreid, Claude Rains.
● **LOS ANGELES, CALIFORNIA**

Davis is the mother-dominated spinster given a new lease of life by psychiatrist Rains, only to fall for married Henreid in this classic tearjerker. Filming allegedly took place at **Whitley Terrace** in the Italianate-style hilltop village of Whitley Heights, reached by Milner Road, east of Highland Avenue and north of Hollywood Boulevard. The terrace is actually seen in *Day of the Locust*, where Burgess Meredith peddles his quack medicine.

NUIT AMERICAINE, LA (aka *Day For Night*)
(1973, dir: François Truffaut)
Jacqueline Bisset, Jean-Pierre Aumont, Valentina Cortese.
● **NICE, FRANCE**

Truffaut puts his love affair with the cinema centre-screen with this backstage movie about the making of a romantic melodrama (dedicated to Dorothy and Lilian Gish).

The film studio: Studios la Victorine, avenue Edoard Grinda

The film-within-the-film, *Je Vous Presente Pamela*, is being made at the famed **Studios la Victorine, 16 avenue Edoard Grinda**, in Nice, where, almost 30 years earlier, Marcel Carné filmed the classic *Les Enfants du Paradis*.

Jacqueline Bisset arrives, and holds a press conference, at **Nice-Côte d'Azur Airport**. The Atlantic Hotel, where the cast act out more dramas than before the camera, is Nice's **Hotel Windsor, 11 rue Dalpozzo**. The man from the British insurance company, who deals with a claim on the death of the leading man, might look familiar. It's writer Graham Greene, in an uncredited cameo.

NUTTY PROFESSOR, THE
(1963, dir: Jerry Lewis)
Jerry Lewis, Stella Stevens, Del Moore.
● **ARIZONA**

One for French cineastes, as nerdy chemistry prof Lewis metamorphoses into lounge lizard Buddy Love. The campus is **Arizona State University, Tempe**.

O

O BROTHER, WHERE ART THOU?

(2000, dir: Joel Coen; Ethan Coen)
George Clooney, John Turturro, Tim Blake Nelson.
● MISSISSIPPI; CALIFORNIA

Homer's *Odyssey* set in Depression-era Deep South, with a title taken from the socially-conscious movie Joel McCrea intends to make in Preston Sturges' 1942 *Sullivan's Travels*. It could only be the Coen brothers. Using a revolutionary digital colour manipulation process, their hayseed epic was shot in Mississippi, around the Jackson area, at **Yazoo City, Valley Park, Church Hill, Hazelhurst, Bolton** and at **D'Lo**, a country park on I-49 south of Jackson.

Escaping a chain gang, Everett (Clooney), Pete (Turturro) and Delmar (Nelson) fail to clamber aboard the **Columbus and Greenville Railway**, at **Leland**, east of Greenville. North of Jackson, you'll find the town where Homer Stokes campaigns and Everett is barred from Woolworth, which is **Canton**, where both *A Time to Kill* and *My Dog Skip* were shot. West, toward the Louisiana border, is Vicksburgh. The Homer Stokes Hoedown, where the Soggy Bottom Boys prove a mighty hit, was filmed in the auditorium of the **Southern Cultural Heritage Foundation, 1302 Adams Street, Vicksburg** (*www.southernculture.org*). Scenes for *Mississippi Burning* were also shot here. The final scene, as the family crosses the railway line and the blind hand-car driver reappears, was filmed on the Kansas City Southern's Shreveport to Jackson line at **Edwards**, about 20 miles east of Vicksburg.

There was at least one scene, though, shot in California: the Ku Klux Klan rally. "I didn't want to shoot a Klan rally in Mississippi," said Joel Coen.

OCEAN'S ELEVEN

(1960, dir: Lewis Milestone)
Frank Sinatra, Sammy Davis Jr, Dean Martin.
● LAS VEGAS, NEVADA; LOS ANGELES, CALIFORNIA

In a plot very similar to *The League of Gentlemen* – ex-army buddies team up to channel their skills into robbery – Sinatra and the Rat Pack plan to rob five Vegas casinos on New Year's Eve, offering a fascinating glimpse of 1960 Vegas, before the age of the mega-corporation and the theme casino

The era of showrooms and lounge acts is a distant memory. Many of the old legends of the Vegas Strip have gone, and the survivors have changed beyond recognition. Of the five establishments targetted, you can still lose a bob or two at three. **The Sahara, 2535 Las Vegas Boulevard South** (© *702.737.2111, www.saharavegas.com*) opened in 1952 and boasts a Moroccan theme. The Flamingo, now the **Flamingo Hilton** (owned by the same corporation as Caesar's Palace), **3555 Las Vegas Boulevard South** (© *702.733.3100, www.caesars.com/flamingo/lasvegas*) dates from 1946 and is, of course, the

brainchild of mobster Bugsy, sorry, Benny Siegel. Although El Rancho, built in 1941, was the first hotel-casino, the success of Vegas is usually dated from the opening of the Flamingo. **The Riviera, 2901 Las Vegas Boulevard South** at Riviera Boulevard (© *702.734.5110, www.rivierahotel.com*), built in 1955, was the first high-rise hotel on the Strip (at a staggering *nine* stories). To see the Riviera as it is now, check out Doug Liman's *Go*.

The Sands opened the same year as The Sahara and stood at 3355 Las Vegas Boulevard South (the Venetian now stands on the site). It hung on as the last of the old-style casinos (Sinatra and Martin not only performed regularly in the Copa Room but had shares in the business), but was demolished in 1996. The Desert Inn (aka Wilbur Clark's Desert Inn), built in 1950, another old-timer, was imploded in October 2001. The Wynn Las Vegas (Steve Wynn is the mastermind behind themed extravaganzas such as Treasure Island, Mirage and Bellagio) now stands in its place at 3145 Las Vegas Boulevard South.

Still going strong is one non-Vegas location: the upmarket barbershop patronised by Akim Tamiroff at the picture's opening. It's **Gornick and Drucker's, 9740 Wilshire Boulevard**, Beverly Hills (© *310.274.7131*). Go for an old-style experience: mahogany and leather furnishings, and a shave with a real razor. Past customers included mobsters Mickey Cohen and Siegel himself.

OCEAN'S ELEVEN

(2001, dir: Steven Soderbergh)
George Clooney, Brad Pitt, Julia Roberts.
● LAS VEGAS, NEVADA; LOS ANGELES, CALIFORNIA; NEW JERSEY; CHICAGO, ILLINOIS; FLORIDA

Soderbergh wisely obeys the golden rule of remakes – choose a film that wasn't perfect in the first place – and whips up first-class lightweight entertainment. Only one casino is

The robbed casino: Bellagio Casino and Hotel, Las Vegas Boulevard South

robbed: the Italianate **Bellagio Casino and Hotel, 3600 Las Vegas Boulevard South** (© *702.693.7111, www.bellagio.com*), with its eight-acre lake and fountains, standing on the site of the legendary Dunes.

Released from **East Jersey State Prison, Route 1, Avenel**, New Jersey, formerly known as Rahway State Penitentiary (seen also in Spike Lee's *Malcolm X*), Danny Ocean (Clooney) is soon violating parole and recruiting a team. Frank Catton (Bernie Mac) at the baccarat pit of the **Trump Plaza Hotel and Casino, The Boardwalk** at Mississippi Avenue, Atlantic City (*www.trumpplaza.com*). Linus Caldwell (Matt Damon) in Chicago, at Irish pub **Emmit's, 495 North Milwaukee Avenue** (© *312.563.9631, www.emmits.com*). And Rusty Ryan (Pitt), who's teaching TV stars poker in the back room (though it doesn't really have a back room) of Hollywood nightclub **Deep, 1707 North Vine Street** at Hollywood Boulevard (*© 323.938.1656*). Conveniently, it's part-owned by director Soderbergh. Ryan, in turn, approaches old hand Saul Bloom (Carl Reiner) at **Derby Lane Dog Track, 10490 Gandy Boulevard, St Petersburg** (*© 727.812.3339, www.derbylane.com*), Florida. The San Diego circus, where Yen (Shaobo Qin) impresses with his acrobatic skills, was set up in the grounds of the dog track.

Rusty and Danny drink in the venerable **Musso and Frank's Grill, 6667 Hollywood Boulevard** (*© 323.467.7788*). Seen also in *Ed Wood* and *Charlie's Angels: Full Throttle*, this is pure Hollywood history, the oldest restaurant in Hollywood (it opened in 1919). It was a favoured hangout for writers – F Scott Fitzgerald, William Faulkner, Raymond Chandler (who supposedly wrote *The Big Sleep* here) and Dashiell Hammett (namechecked as one of the three precogs in *Minority Report*) were regulars. Charlie Chaplin and Humphrey Bogart also drank here and it's still a hangout for Hollywood royalty. Try to get seated in the luxurious older section of the restaurant, and sample the legendary martinis.

The Vegas home of Reuben Tishkoff (Elliott Gould) is in the Californian desert resort of **Palm Springs**, at **999 North Patencio**. The "most successful Vegas robbery ever", according to Tishkoff, is the guy scuttling out of **Caesar's Palace, 3570 Las Vegas Boulevard South** (see *Rain Man*), to the strains of 'Take My Breath Away'. The California Institute of Advanced Science, from which the team steals a 'pinch' to create an electromagnetic pulse, is the **Gillespie Neuroscience Research Facility** on the campus of the **University of California** at **Irvine**. While its vaults are being emptied, Bellagio owner Terry Benedict (Andy Garcia) is watching a boxing match at the **MGM Grand Hotel and Casino, 3799 Las Vegas Boulevard South** at Tropicana Avenue (*© 702.891.1111, www.mgmgrand.com*), currently the largest and most ambitious of the Vegas resorts, but these things change fast. And of course, the heist ends in front of the Bellagio's kitschy, but effective, dancing waters.

OCTOPUSSY

(1983, dir: John Glen)
Roger Moore, Maud Adams, Louis Jourdan.
● INDIA; UTAH; MIDDLESEX; LONDON; BERLIN, GERMANY

Beautifully photographed, but one of the least of the series. The South American Air Force Base of the opening scene is **Northolt Aerodrome** in Middlesex, but the spectacular landscapes flown over are **Moab**, southwest Utah. The exterior of **Sotheby's, 34-355 New Bond Street**, London W1 (*© 020.7293.5000, www.sothebys.com*), where the Fabergé egg is put up for auction, is real,

Bond in Berlin: Kurfürstendamm

though the interior was recreated in the studio at Pinewood. MI6 HQ is, as in John Glen's two other Bond films (*Licence to Kill* and *A View to a Kill*), the **Old War Office Building, Whitehall**.

Bond travels to **Udaipur** in India (via the Taj Mahal, naturally, despite its being several hundred miles out of the way in Acra). He stays at the luxurious **Shiv Niwas Hotel**, part of the City Palace, one of three palaces owned by the Mewar royalty. A second, also converted into a hotel, became the floating palace, Octopussy's island home, the **Lake Palace Hotel** in **Lake Pichola**, both now part of the HRH Group of hotels. The third, Summer Palace, overlooking the area, is used for the retreat of Kamal Khan (Jourdan), where Bond is held captive.

In Berlin, Bond is driven down the main shopping drag, **Kurfürstendamm**, to the one-time crossing point into East Germany, **Checkpoint Charlie**. Bond's escape from Karl Marx-Stadt was staged in the **Nene Valley Railway** yard and station in Peterborough (*www.nvr.org.uk*). Feldstadt, the US Air Force Base in Germany, is the RAF base at **Upper Heyford**, Oxfordshire (*www.raf-upper-heyford.org*).

ODD COUPLE, THE

(1968, dir: Gene Saks)
Jack Lemmon, Walter Matthau, John Fiedler.
● NEW YORK CITY

Perfect casting for the film of Neil Simon's classic play, which spawned a long-running TV series. The home shared by slob Oscar and prissy Felix is **131 Riverside Drive** at 85th Street, overlooking Riverside Park on Manhattan's West Side.

Oscar and Felix's place: Riverside Drive, West Side, Manhattan

OF MICE AND MEN

(1939, dir: Lewis Milestone)
Burgess Meredith, Lon Chaney Jr, Betty Field.
● CALIFORNIA

Milestone wanted to film John Steinbeck's Depression-era story at the actual ranch in the Salinas Valley, northern California, that the author had used as a model, but it turned out to be a ruin. Eventually, the film company rented out William Randolph Hearst's ranch at **Agoura**, off Route 101 in the Santa Monica Mountains, northwest of LA, and built the ranch house there. There was more filming on the **Monterey Peninsula** in northern California.

The 1992 remake, with Gary Sinise and John Malkovich, was shot around Santa Barbara.

OFFICER AND A GENTLEMAN, AN

(1982, dir: Taylor Hackford)
Richard Gere, Debra Winger, Louis Gossett Jr.
● WASHINGTON

Richard Gere suffers hell in a pristine white uniform at **Fort Worden State Park, Port Townsend**, a restored former coastal artillery army base on the Olympic Peninsula. The papermill where Debra Winger works was the old Champion International Corporation, bought up in 1985 and now the **Simpson Tacoma Kraft Company, 801 Portland Avenue, Tacoma**, on Commencement Bay. The inn is the **Tides inn, 1807 Water Street, Port Townsend** (© 360.385.0595, www.tides-inn.com).

OH MR PORTER

(1937, dir: Marcel Varnel)
Will Hay, Moore Marriott, Graham Moffatt.
● HAMPSHIRE

Classic comedy with Will Hay and sidekicks Marriott and Moffatt foiling gun-runners and posing as ghosts at a little Irish railway station. Buggleskelly Station was in fact the already near-derelict **Cliddesden Halt**, dressed up by designer Alex Vetchinsky. It's closed now of course, but if you can pick your way through the weeds, you can see the remains just south of Basingstoke on the Basingstoke-Alton line in Hampshire. The old Victorian engine, also near derelict, was the Gladstone. Sadly, the engine was sold for scrap in 1941.

OH! WHAT A LOVELY WAR

(1969, dir: Richard Attenborough)
John Mills, Ralph Richardson, John Gielgud.
● SUSSEX

Joan Littlewood's stage production put the words and songs from WWI into the mouths of a pierrot troupe. Attenborough's opened-up film was never going to capture the poignancy of the stage images, but instead utilises the faded grandeur of Brighton's now-fire-ravaged **West Pier**, the surrounding seafront

Stylized backdrop to WWI: West Pier, Brighton

area and **Brighton Railway Station**. The pier stood closed and decrepit for many years while various restoration projects were considered, then it was almost totally destroyed by fire in 2003 and its future now looks grim (check out updates at www.westpier.co.uk). The church parade filmed in the picturesque ruins of the 13th century **Bayham Abbey**, a mile and three quarters west of Lamberhurst, near Tunbridge Wells, east Sussex.

OKLAHOMA!

(1955, dir: Fred Zinnemann)
Gordon MacRae, Shirley Jones, Rod Steiger.
● ARIZONA

Not the obvious choice to direct a big musical and, true to form, Zinnemann takes the whole shebang out on location. Oklahoma itself was out – the corn may

Oklahoma?: San Rafael Valley

well be as high as an elephant's eye, but the oil rigs are even higher. A suitable landscape was eventually found in Arizona, at **San Rafael Valley**, near to Nogales on the Mexican border. The corn was brought to the required height with the aid of the University of Arizona's Agriculture Department. The railway station, scene of the big musical number, is **Elgin**, 20 miles west of Tombstone.

OLD SCHOOL

(2003, dir: Todd Phillips)
Luke Wilson, Will Ferrell, Vince Vaughn.
● CALIFORNIA; MASSACHUSETTS

Age is no barrier to starring in a frat-house comedy, as Wilson, Ferrell and Vaughn keep the good times rollin' by starting their own fraternity. The overhead shots of the university campus are **Harvard University** (left over from the director's previous outing, *Road Trip*), but the college is **UCLA, Westwood**, on LA's Westside.

The Marriot, outside which Wilson catches a cab to return home early, is the Coconut Grove entrance to the **Ambassador Hotel, 3400 Wilshire Boulevard** at Catalina Street, midtown LA (see *A Star Is Born* for details). He's embarrassed by his Godfather reputation and the arrival of his boss's (under-age) daughter in the **Quality Coffee Shop, 1238 West Seventh Street**, downtown LA (see *Se7en* for details). Ferrell's wedding reception, with the foul-mouthed classics band, is held in the **Ebell of Los Angeles, 4400 West Eighth Street** at Lucerne Boulevard, midtown (see *Forrest Gump* for details). Unfazed by marriage, his wife later finds him streaking along **Honolulu Boulevard, Montrose**.

OMEN, THE

(1976, dir: Richard Donner)
Gregory Peck, Lee Remick, David Warner.
● LONDON; SURREY; ROME; ISRAEL

The seminal horror film that spawned a whole genre of Antichrist movies. Before things start to get nasty, young

The entrance to the home of the US Ambassador: Pyrford Court

The crazy priest gets spiked: All Saints Church, Fulham

spawn-of-Satan Damien and his family enjoy a day out on **Parliament Hill**, north London. US Ambassador Robert Thorn (Peck) is ensconced, naturally, at the **American Embassy** in **Grosvenor Square**, where he is confronted by crazy priest Father Brennan (Patrick Troughton, UK TV's second *Doctor Who*), who spouts passages from Revelations alongside the Thames at Putney. His nearby church, where he gets spiked by the lightning conductor, is **All Saints Church, Fulham**, which is actually on the north side of Putney Bridge. Meanwhile, Damien is beginning to betray his diabolical leanings by throwing a major wobbly arriving at **Guildford Cathedral** and upsetting the monkeys at **Windsor Safari Park**.

The palatial home of the US Ambassador, supposedly on Seven Hills Road, is **Pyrford Court, Pyrford**, a couple of miles east of Woking in Surrey. A private home, it's well hidden behind a thick screen of trees and not visible from the road. You can, though, see the elaborate gatehouse, **The Bothy**, out of which Ambassador Thorn makes his final desperate drive, on the south side of **Pyrwood Common Road** near Upshot Lane. The funeral of the Ambassador is at **Brookwood Cemetery, Brookwood**, Surrey – once the country's largest cemetery.

ON GOLDEN POND
(1981, dir: Mark Rydell)
Henry Fonda, Katharine Hepburn, Jane Fonda.
● **NEW HAMPSHIRE**

Henry Fonda's final film, and the only one with his daughter Jane, is a predictably sugary affair. The titular pond is **Squam Lake**, just off highway 93 between Plymouth and Meredith, southeastern New Hampshire. Boat trips from Holderness will take you past the house used in the movie, which is a private home. The *Thayer IV* can be seen at the Holiday Inn Docks, Key Largo, on Florida's southern tip.

ON HER MAJESTY'S SECRET SERVICE
(1969, dir: Peter Hunt)
George Lazenby, Diana Rigg, Telly Savalas.
● **SWITZERLAND; PORTUGAL; BUCKINGHAMSHIRE**

A bit more story this time around, but a bit less Bond, with the chiselled woodenness of TV adman George Lazenby. The opening sequence, of Bond rescuing Tracy from the sea, was shot on **Guincho Beach** near Cascais, west of Lisbon, Portugal. Draco's home, scene of the

birthday party, is the **Da Vinho Estate** at **Zambujal**. Bond stays at the **Palacio Hotel, Rua Do Parque, Estoril**, near Lisbon (*© 35121.4648000*).

The office of solicitor Gumpold, where Bond demonstrates that exciting new invention the photocopier, is the **Schweizerhof Hotel, Bahnhofplatz 11, Berne**, Switzerland (*© 31.326.8080*).

M's house is **Thames Lawn**, a riverfront mansion at **Marlow**, near the Pinewood Studios in Buckinghamshire. In order to pass himself off as 'Sir Hilary Bray', Bond gets a crash course in heraldry at the **Royal College of Arms, Queen Victoria Street**, EC4, near Blackfriars (*© 020.7248.2762, www.college-of-arms.gov.uk*), where he discovers that the Bond family motto is 'Orbis non sufficit' – the world is not enough. Good title for a film.

The stock-car rally was staged at **Lauterbrunnen**, two miles from Murren in Switzerland, and the skating rink is nearby **Grindelwald**.

Blofeld's mountaintop allergy clinic is **Piz Gloria**, a revolving restaurant at the 10,000-foot peak of **Schilthorn Mountain** (*www.schilthorn.ch*), above Murren. The five-storey complex, with its own cable-car lift, was still under construction when the movie's locations were being scouted. Permission to film was granted on condition that the film company furnish the interior and build a helipad. They forked out to the tune of £60,000. The restaurant is still in business.

ON THE BEACH
(1959, dir: Stanley Kramer)
Gregory Peck, Ava Gardner, Fred Astaire.
● **AUSTRALIA; CALIFORNIA**

Depressing post-nuclear warning, starting from the grim premise that Australia is the only landmass to have survived – for the time being – atomic devastation. Made mostly on location in **Melbourne**, Australia, but including a nightmarish submarine trip to a disturbingly deserted **San Diego**.

ON THE TOWN
(1949, dir: Gene Kelly)
Gene Kelly, Frank Sinatra, Jules Munshin.
● **NEW YORK CITY; LOS ANGELES, CALIFORNIA**

Three sailors enjoy 24 hours of shore leave in New York. Kelly wanted to film entirely on location, but the studio wanted it all shot in Hollywood. The compromise, despite the way it looks in the completed movie, was a mere week's location filming. Nevertheless, New York landmarks include **Liberty Island**; the **Empire State Building** at Fifth Avenue and 34th Street; **Central Park**; **Federal Hall, 26 Wall Street**; **Coney Island**; **Rockefeller Plaza**, between Fifth and Sixth Avenues and 49th and 50th Streets; and the roof of the 70-storey **RCA Building** (now the GE Building), Sixth Avenue. The opening shot of the singing longshoreman, and the closing shots, were filmed in the **Brooklyn Naval Yard**, just across the East River over the Manhattan Bridge, at Flushing Avenue.

ON THE WATERFRONT
(1954, dir: Elia Kazan)
Marlon Brando, Eva Marie Saint, Karl Malden.

Karl Malden's church: Our Lady of Grace Church, Hoboken

Brando and Eva Marie Saint walk in the park: Stevens Park, Hoboken

● NEW JERSEY

Kazan's drama of mob rule among the longshoremen's unions was made on location on the waterfronts of **Hoboken**, New Jersey (the birthplace of Frank Sinatra). The piers and warehouses are long gone, and Hoboken is now a squeaky clean middle class suburb, but some of the movie's locations remain. The church scene was filmed at **Our Lady of Grace Church, 400 Willow Avenue**, though the park in front of the church is **Stevens Park**, four blocks away, in front of **St Peter and St Paul Church, 400 Hudson Street**, which is also the church used for the interior shots.

ONCE UPON A TIME IN AMERICA

(1984, dir: Sergio Leone)
Robert De Niro, James Woods, Elizabeth McGovern.
● ITALY; FRANCE; CANADA; NEW YORK CITY; NEW JERSEY; FLORIDA

Leone's magnificent, sprawling epic, following on from *Once Upon a Time in the West*, traces the growth of the United States from the twenties to the sixties, as the Western becomes the gangster flick. The 1920s Lower East Side neighbourhood, where Noodles and Max first meet, was filmed on the streets below the towering **Williamsburg Bridge** on **8th Avenue South** at Bedford Avenue,

PHOTOGRAPH COURTESY SIMON ROBSON

The iconic poster image: Manhattan Bridge, Brooklyn

Brooklyn. The bridge towering over the warehouses, an image so striking it was used for the poster art, is **Manhattan Bridge, Water Street** at Washington Street.

Hoboken Railway Station in New Jersey and the **Don Cesar Palace, 3400 Gulf Boulevard, St Petersburg Beach** in Florida (© *813.360.1881*) were also used. New York's Grand Central Station in the thirties flashbacks is actually the **Gare du Nord** in Paris.

The lavish Long Island restaurant, where De Niro takes his dream date, is actually the **Hotel Excelsior, Lungo-**

The Long Island restaurant: Hotel Excelsior, Lido, Venice

mare Marconi 41 on the Lido in Venice. Built in the 1900s, the Excelsior was the world's top resort hotel and is a favourite of the film festival crowd.

The Brooklyn neighbourhood: 8th Street South, Brooklyn

ONCE UPON A TIME IN MEXICO

(2003, dir: Robert Rodriguez)
Antonio Banderas, Salma Hayek, Johnny Depp.
● MEXICO

For the third in the *El Mariachi* trilogy, Rodriguez leaves the flyblown border towns for the more grandiose Colonial setting of central Mexico. The film was shot around **San Miguel de Allende** (seen also in TV movie *And Starring Pancho Villa as Himself*, with Banderas, again, as the revolutionary leader). San Miguel, designated a historical landmark since 1930, is about 70 miles from Aeropuerto de Bajo (BJX), or it's a four-hour bus trip from Mexico City. The imposing flight of steps is **La Universidad de Guanajuato** in **Guanajuato**, built in a ravine, and which used to be Mexico's capital. The city was seen also in Ralph Nelson's 1972 *The Wrath of God*, with Robert Mitchum. Filming also occurred at **Queretaro**, an hour's bus ride from San Miguel.

ONE-EYED JACKS

(1961, dir: Marlon Brando)
Marlon Brando, Karl Malden, Pina Pellicer.
● CALIFORNIA

Sam Peckinpah's original script was discarded and Calder Willingham brought in, and Stanley Kubrick was replaced as director by Brando himself for this long, slow Western. The $1.8 million budget ballooned to $6 million, and the film to five hours. Cut down to two hours and twenty minutes, and with a new ending, the film nevertheless managed to recoup $12 million at the box office, which almost redeemed it. Just pray there's not a director's cut lying about. It was filmed on the west coast of California, north of **Cypress Point, Pebble Beach** and at **Pfeiffer Beach** in Big Sur.

ONE FLEW OVER THE CUCKOO'S NEST

(1975, dir: Milos Forman)
Jack Nicholson, Louise Fletcher, Brad Dourif.
● OREGON

This manipulative and contrived allegory was shot in a wing of the **Oregon State Mental Hospital, Center Street** between 24th and 25th Streets, **Salem**, on highway 5 about 50 miles south of Portland, Oregon. A condition of filming at the hospital was that the period not be updated from the original 1963. After all, we don't treat people like that any more. The fishing trip was shot at **Depoe Bay**, on I-101, about 12 miles north of Newport, which claims the smallest harbour in the world. And you can charter a fishing boat.

ONE FROM THE HEART

(1982, dir: Francis Coppola)
Frederic Forrest, Teri Garr, Raul Julia.
● LOS ANGELES, CALIFORNIA

A simple two-hander set in Vegas became a bloated monster when the director decided to rebuild the city elsewhere. That Francis Coppola wanted to explore the possibilities of the medium is admirable, but the extravagant visuals totally overwhelm the modest little story. All the Las Vegas scenes were recreated on soundstages at the **Hollywood Center** (then Zoetrope Studios), **1040 North Las Palmas Avenue**, off Romaine Street in Hollywood.

The House of DeVil: Minster Court, Mincing Lane

Roger marries Anita: Chelsea Parish Church of St Luke, Sydney Street

101 DALMATIANS

(1996, dir: Stephen Herek)
Glenn Close, Jeff Daniels, Joely Richardson.
● LONDON; BUCKINGHAMSHIRE

This live-action version of the Disney classic uses plenty of real London locations. Roger (Daniels) is dragged by Pongo the dog from **Trafalgar Square** to **St James's Park**, by way of the intimidatingly formal **Burlington Arcade** on Piccadilly, though much of the park sequence is actually **Battersea Park**. The House of DeVil, office of Cruella (Close), is **Minster Court, Mincing Lane**, a bizarre gothicky development in the City, inevitably dubbed 'Munster Court'. The country village where, uniquely in the UK, raccoons and skunks can be found running wild, is **Hambleden**, northeast of Henley-on-Thames, Buckinghamshire, in the Chilterns. Roger marries Anita (Richardson) in **Chelsea Parish Church of St Luke, Sydney Street** at Britten Street, off King's Road in Chelsea, as a crowd of doggies waits outside.

For the 2000 sequel, *102 Dalmatians*, the Second Chance animal shelter, run by Kevin (Ioan Gruffudd), is the rear of the **boathouse, Putney Embankment, Ashlone Road, Putney**, southwest London. Kevin is sprung from **Hampstead High Street Police Station, Rosslyn Hill** at Downshire Hill, Hampstead, by Waddlesworth the parrot.

OPPOSITE OF SEX, THE

(1998, dir: Don Roos)
Christina Ricci, Martin Donovan, Lisa Kudrow.
● CALIFORNIA

Cracking comedy drama with a mission to offend, following the emotional fallout after narrator Ricci runs off with her gay step-brother's boyfriend. Set mainly in Indiana, the movie was made in California. The art deco seafront hotel in which Donovan and Kudrow stay when

Donovan and Kudrow stay at the Georgian Hotel, Ocean Avenue, Santa Monica

they follow Ricci to **Santa Monica** is the **Georgian Hotel, 1415 Ocean Avenue**, near the Santa Monica Pier (© 310.395.9945, *www.georgianhotel.com*). The motel where Ricci's monotesticular boyfriend gets shot is the classic sixties-style **Royal Sun Inn, 1700 South Palm Canyon Drive, Palm Springs** (© 760.327.1564, *www.royalsuninn.com*). The peaceful lakeside cabin over the Canadian border is actually on **Big Bear Lake, San Bernardino**, east of LA.

ORDINARY PEOPLE

(1980, dir: Robert Redford)
Timothy Hutton, Donald Sutherland, Mary Tyler Moore.
● ILLINOIS

Ordinary *very rich* people actually. Redford's classy soap is set in the *très* upper middle class suburb of **Lake Forest**, on the Lake Michigan shore north of Chicago. Many of the interiors were filmed in the abandoned laundry room of Fort Sheridan Military Compound, converted into a temporary studio.

The restaurant where Conrad Jarrett (Hutton) reminisces about his time in hospital over a coke with Karen (Dinah Manoff) is **Walker Brothers Original Pancake House, 153 Green Bay Road** at Isabella Street, **Wilmette** (© 847.251.6000). It still retains its wood panelled and Tiffany glass ambiance.

Conrad's school is **Lake Forest High School, 1285 North McKinley Road, Lake Forest**, though the pool, where Conrad conflicts with the swim coach (M Emmet Walsh), is at **Lake Forest College, 555 North Sheridan Road**. The office of obliging shrink Doc Berger (Judd Hirsch) is in **Highland Park**, south of Lake Forest.

ORPHÉE (aka *Orpheus*)

(1949, dir: Jean Cocteau)
Jean Marais, François Périer, Maria Casarès.
● FRANCE

Classic of poetic cinema, with Maria Casarès as Death, and Orpheus entering alternative worlds through liquid mirrors. Eschewing camera tricks, Cocteau used vats of mercury for the dazzling effects. Location filming was at the Medieval ruins of **Les Baux-de-Provence** near Arles in southern France.

OTELLO

(1986, dir: Franco Zeffirelli)
Placido Domingo, Katia Ricciarelli, Justino Diaz.
● ITALY; CRETE, GREECE

Typically lush Zeffirellian filming of Verdi's opera, financed by Cannon's usually downmarket Golan-Globus team as their contribution to Art.

The main garrison setting is the 13th century Swabian **Hohenstaufen Castle** at **Barletta**, on the northern coast of Puglia, Route 16, 40 miles northwest of Bari (it's been undergoing a slow process of restoration since the seventies and is not at present open to the public).

The harbour exteriors are the port of **Heraklion** in Crete, where virtually an entire keep and monumental entrance were added to the existing Venetian buildings.

Otello's galleon, built at a cost of $80,000, was filmed, not on the coast of Crete, but on the Italian coast north of Rome after the rest of filming had been completed. The ship is still in existence, and could recently be seen moored at Marseilles.

OTHELLO

(1951, dir: Orson Welles)
Orson Welles, Suzanne Cloutier, Michael MacLiammoir.
● **ITALY; MOROCCO**

The rear of Brabantio's house: Palazzo Contarini dal Bovolo

After filming *Macbeth* in three weeks on a cardboard set in Hollywood, Welles took a drastically different approach, and made this classic Shakespearian adaptation on location around Europe over a period of years. Michael MacLiammoir (who played Iago) tells the whole story, hilariously, in his memoir, *Put Money in Thy Purse.*

The use of locations is dizzying, as Welles cuts from country to country in mid-scene. Many of the Venice scenes are the real thing. Othello and Desdemona's secret wedding was filmed at **Santa Maria dei Miracoli** (seen also in *Don't Look Now*) alongside the Rialto in Venice. Brabantio's house is the **Palazzo Contarini-Fasan** on the Canal Grande at **Rio delle Ostreghe** near Piazza San Marco. And indeed, it is known as Desdemona's House. The circular tower, supposedly at the rear, down which Brabantio's servants rush, is the **Palazzo Contarini dal Bovolo**, tucked away in a tiny courtyard at **Calle della Vida 4299**, at the corner of Rio dei Fuseri and Rio di San Luca. The unique spiral stair is seen also in the Britfarce *Blame It on the Bellboy*. The midnight council assembles at the pink and white marble **Palazzo Ducale**, the Doge's Palace. The imposing staircase is the **Scala dei Giganti**, the Giant's Staircase, in the palace courtyard. Othello's house is the elaborate gothic palace of the **Ca' d'Oro**, on the Canal Grande.

Othello's house: Ca' d'Oro on the Canal Grande

Most of the Cyprus scenes were filmed in **Essaouria**, on the coast of Morocco, about 40 miles west of Marrakech. The 18th century town, pre-viously known as Mogador, is surrounded by gothic battlements, which are used for the opening funeral procession, the torture of Iago and the jealousy scenes.

Brabantio's house: Palazzo Contarini-Fasan

The famous steam bath scene was filmed in a local hammam (yes, steam bath) at Essaouria. A spot of improvisation was needed here. The costumes hadn't arrived in time for filming so the setting was dictated by the need for the characters to be wearing only towels. **Safi**, about 30 miles to the north, supplies the steps where Cassio regrets his drunken brawl. Though the town

The senate: Scala dei Giganti, Palazzo Ducale

itself is pretty industrialised nowadays, it does still retain its old walled and turretted Medina. The brawl itself was staged in the 15th century **Portuguese Cistern** at **El Jadida**, on the coast a further 30 miles to the north. It's a vaulted underground chamber which dazzlingly mirrors the pillars and roof in the water which covers the floor. Find it in the city's Medina, known as the Cite Portugaise, at the north end of Boulevard de Suez. It's open to the public (*admission charge*). The fight is brought to a halt by the entrance of Othello – in the **Palazzo Papale** in **Viterbo**, Italy.

Brabantio's scenes were shot at **Torcello**, a peaceful green island six miles northeast of Venice, in the church cloisters, along with the scenes of Othello's rage. Othello strikes Desdemona in the 8th century **San Pietro Church**, a former cathedral externally remodelled in the 12th century, at **Tuscania**, ten miles from Viterbo. The senate scenes used the Umbrian town of **Perugia**, between Rome and Florence. Desdemona's bedchamber is the 13th century round church of **Santa Maria della Salute** in Viterbo.

OTHELLO

(1995, dir: Oliver Parker)
Laurence Fishburne, Kenneth Branagh, Irène Jacob.
● **ITALY**

This time, the Medieval battlements are the 16th century **Castello Orsini-Odescalchi, Piazza Mazzini** (*www.odescalchi.it*) at **Bracciano**, on Lake Bracciano, about 25 miles northwest of Rome.

OTTO E MEZZO (aka *8 1/2*; *Eight and a Half*; *Federico Fellini's 8 1/2*; *Huit et demi*)

(1963, dir: Federico Fellini)
Marcello Mastroianni, Claudia Cardinale, Anouk Aimée.
● **ITALY**

Fellini's dazzling fantasia was filmed at **Ostia** and the village of **Filacciano**.

OUT OF AFRICA
(1985, dir: Sydney Pollack)
Meryl Streep, Robert Redford, Klaus Maria Brandauer.
● **KENYA; TANZANIA**

Karen Blixen's book describes her experiences in Africa, attempting to grow coffee in the Ngong Hills outside Nairobi. The film charts a doomed affair with Denys Finch Hatton. Finch Hatton was a bald, six-foot four Old Etonian with a penchant for Latin and Greek poets. Robert Redford plays him. That's Hollywood. The settings are more authentic though. The small town that was Nairobi in 1914 was built from scratch on farmland at **Langata**, about 30 miles from the modern city. The Osgood and Norfolk Hotels, bazaar, church, and even the railway station were reproduced. Karen Blixen's house is now used as a government building, and the surrounding area developed. An existing farmhouse at the **Ngong Dairy** in **Karen** (yes, named for Blixen), not far from Langata and from the real house, was renovated to replicate the original. The Kikuyu village and the façade of the Muthiaga Club – where Karen marries Bror Blixen – were also constructed on the dairy's grounds. The real Muthiaga Club now stands in one of Nairobi's wealthiest suburbs.

African landscapes were supplied by the **Masai Mara**, Kenya's part of the Serengeti Plain and the **Rift Valley**, west of Nairobi. The wildebeest migration was captured by a second unit at the **Ngorongoro Crater** and **Lake Manyara** in Tanzania.

OUT OF SIGHT
(1998, dir: Steven Soderbergh)
George Clooney, Jennifer Lopez, Ving Rhames.
● **FLORIDA; MICHIGAN; LOUISIANA; CALIFORNIA**

Clooney and Rhames' hotel: Tyler Adams Hotel, Park Avenue, Miami

Elmore Leonard adaptation, shot largely around sunny Florida and in gloomy Detroit, Michigan. Belle Glade Correctional Institution is **Louisiana State Prison, Angola** (seen also in *Monster's Ball* and *Dead Man Walking*), with real convicts playing extras. Lompoc Federal Penitentiary is a holding centre for immigration violations in **Palmdale**, California. The prison library is in the familiar old **Lincoln Heights Jail, 421 North Avenue 19, Lincoln Heights**, near downtown LA (see the 1954 *A Star Is Born* for details).

The Florida hotel, where Jack Foley (Clooney) and Buddy Bragg (Rhames) stay, is an old folks favourite, the **Tyler Adams Hotel and Apartments, 2030 Park Avenue, Miami Beach**.

In Detroit, Foley and Bragg confront Snoopy and White Boy Bob in venerable institution **Kronk's Recreation Center, 5555 McGraw Street**, and the boxing scenes were staged in the **State Theater, 2115 Woodward Avenue**. Ripley's mansion is in the **Bloomfield Hills** section of the Motor City.

OUTLAW – JOSEY WALES, THE
(1976, dir: Clint Eastwood)
Clint Eastwood, Chief Dan George, Sondra Locke.
● **UTAH; ARIZONA; CALIFORNIA**

Violent revenge Western, shot in **Kanab**, Utah; **Glen Canyon** and the artificial **Lake Powell** in Arizona; and **Oroville**, Butte County, California.

OUTSIDERS, THE
(1983, dir: Francis Ford Coppola)
Ralph Macchio, C Thomas Howell, Matt Dillon.
● **OKLAHOMA**

SE Hinton's novel, directed by Coppola using a cracking cast of then-unknowns, was made back-to-back with the more arty *Rumble Fish* in **Tulsa**, Oklahoma. The drive-in is the **Admiral Twin Drive-In, 7355 East Easton Street**, Tulsa (*© 918.838.3114*).

OX-BOW INCIDENT, THE
(1943, dir: William A Wellman)
Henry Fonda, Harry Morgan, Dana Andrews.
● **CALIFORNIA**

The ever-upright Fonda stands up against a Nevada lynch-mob in this powerful Western, which makes use of the barren rock formations of the **Alabama Hills**, at **Lone Pine**, I-395 in central California (see *Kim* for details of this popular location).

P

Chez Joey: Spreckels Mansion, Washington Street

PAL JOEY
(1957, dir: George Sidney) Frank Sinatra, Rita Hayworth, Kim Novak.
● SAN FRANCISCO, CALIFORNIA

Rodgers and Hart's musical about shifty nightclub entertainer Joey is set in San Francisco. Rita Hayworth's mansion is actually the **Coit Memorial Tower, Telegraph Hill Park** on Telegraph Hill Boulevard. This landmark was built for Lillie Hitchcock Coit to 'beautify the city'. Did it? See *Vertigo* for details. The Chez Joey nightclub is the grand **Spreckels Mansion, 2080 Washington Street**, overlooking Lafayette Park in Pacific Heights, seen also in the 1969 thriller *Eye of the Cat*. It's a private home, bought by writer Danielle Steele in 1990.

PALE RIDER
(1985, dir: Clint Eastwood)
Clint Eastwood, Michael Moriarty, Carrie Snodgress.
● IDAHO

Clint helps out prospecting families harassed by the big guys in a spectacular Western which was made around **Sun Valley**, in central Idaho, and the nearby **Sawtooth National Recreation Area**, on I-75.

PANDORA AND THE FLYING DUTCHMAN
(1951, dir: Albert Lewin)
Ava Gardner, James Mason, Nigel Patrick.
● SPAIN

Ava Gardner is the heartless tease who falls for the ghostly sea captain in this dour fable from eccentric director Albert Lewin. The little coastal town is **Tossa De Mar**, near Gerona, on Spain's Costa Brava, about 65 miles northeast of Barcelona.

PANIC ROOM
(2002, dir: David Fincher)
Jodie Foster, Kristen Stewart, Forest Whitaker.
● NEW YORK CITY; LOS ANGELES, CALIFORNIA

Foster and Stewart hole up: West 94th Street, Upper West Side

Fincher seems to alternate masterpieces (*Se7en*, *Fight Club*) with seriously flawed clunkers (*The Game*), and this would-be claustrophobic thriller fizzles by making its trio of villains so bumbling and Whitaker so obviously soft that there's never any real danger. The brownstone where Foster and Stewart hole up in the titular strong room is **38 West 94th Street** on New York's Upper West

Side. The interiors were shot in Manhattan – Manhattan Beach, Los Angeles, that is, where production designer Arthur Max built the giant set.

PAPER MOON
(1973, dir: Peter Bogdanovich)
Ryan O'Neal, Tatum O'Neal, Madeline Kahn.
● KANSAS; MISSOURI; LOS ANGELES, CALIFORNIA

Kendall Alley, Pasadena

The O'Neals, real life father and daughter, are Bible-selling con artists in the US midwest of the thirties. The period-looking towns are **Hays**, I-70, central Kansas, which served as the film's base; **Lacrosse**, 30 miles to the south on I-283; and **St George** on I-55 just southwest of St Louis, Missouri. Filming also took place in the historic **Kendall Alley** in LA's eastern suburb, Pasadena (also seen in *Pulp Fiction*).

PAPILLON
(1973, dir: Franklin J Schaffner)
Steve McQueen, Dustin Hoffman, Victor Jory.
● JAMAICA

McQueen and Hoffman suffer the privations of the notorious French Guyana prison colony, in this epic filmed mainly in Jamaica, where the huge Devil's Island prison set was built at **Falmouth** and interiors lensed at **Montego Bay**. The Indian village is at **Ocho Rios** (a major location for the first Bond movie, *Dr No*) and the arrival of the prison ship filmed at **Kingston**. The work camp is **Paradise Jungle Park** at **Savanna-la-Mar**, the western end of Bluefields Bay, a 1,000-acre private estate about 30 miles south of Montego Bay (*© 809.999.5771; admission charge*).

PARADINE CASE, THE
(1947, dir: Alfred Hitchcock)
Gregory Peck, Alida Valli, Charles Laughton.
● LONDON; LAKE DISTRICT, CUMBRIA

Although Hitchcock's courtroom melodrama, his last picture for David O Selznick, was made at the RKO Studio in Hollywood, it's set in the UK, where a second unit captured location shots. In London, the exterior of the **Central Criminal Court, the Old Bailey**, EC4, where Alida Valli is tried for murder, is real, still showing the extensive

The Paradine estate: Langdale Chase Hotel, Cumbria

Gregory Peck stays at the Station Hotel: Drunken Duck Inn, Barngate

Gregory Peck's house: Portland Place

bomb damage sustained during the Blitz, but the courtroom was meticulously recreated in the studio. Similarly, Bow Street Police Station and the old Holloway women's prison were recreated from photographs. Defence lawyer Gregory Peck's house is **60 Portland Place** at Weymouth Street, W1. When he investigates Valli's past in Cumberland, the Station Hotel, where he stays, is the **Drunken Duck Inn, Barngate** (*www.drunkenduckinn.co.uk*), off the B5286 just southwest of Langdale Chase. Hindley Hall, the Paradine estate, is a mock-Elizabethan manor house built in 1891, now the **Langdale Chase Hotel**, on the A591 between Brockhole and Ambleside on the north shore of Lake Windermere, Cumbria (© *015394.32201, www.langdalechase.co.uk*).

The assassination: Space Needle, Seattle

PARALLAX VIEW, THE

(1974, dir: Alan J Pakula)
Warren Beatty, Paula Prentiss, Hume Cronyn.
● **LOS ANGELES, CALIFORNIA; WASHINGTON**

Brilliant conspiracy thriller with echoes of the Kennedy assassination, the centre of Pakula's great paranoia trilogy between *Klute* and *All the President's Men*. The opening political assassination takes place atop Seattle's **Space Needle, 203 Sixth Avenue North**, the familiar landmark erected for the 1962 World's Fair and featured, not surprisingly, in Elvis Presley's 1962 film *It Happened at the World's Fair*. It's open to the public and, for a fee, you can zoom up to the 518-foot high Observation Deck. The children's train, where Beatty meets up with Kenneth Mars, is **Woodland Park Zoo, 5500 Phinney Avenue North**, Seattle. The dam at fictitious Salmontail, where Beatty comes close to being drowned, is the **Lake Chelan Dam, Chelan**, on Route 97 in central Washington State. The final assassination filmed at the **Los Angeles Convention Center**, Figueroa Street, downtown LA – a building that's since been much enlarged and revamped.

PARENT TRAP, THE

(1961, dir: David Swift)
Hayley Mills, Maureen O'Hara, Brian Keith.
● **CALIFORNIA**

Twins (both Mills) try to reconcile their separated parents. Filming took place at **Monterey Peninsula Airport**; the Lodge of **Pebble Beach Golf Course** and **Cypress Point**, Pebble Beach.

For the 1998 remake, mum's London house is **23 Egerton Terrace** at Egerton Place in South Kensington, while dad's Californian vineyard estate is the **Staglin Family Vineyard**, near **Rutherford** in the **Napa Valley** (*www.staglinfamily.com*).

PARIS, TEXAS

(1984, dir: Wim Wenders)
Harry Dean Stanton, Dean Stockwell, Nastassja Kinski.
● **TEXAS**

Paris, Texas, a real enough town, is the Godot of film locations. Lots of waiting, but it doesn't actually turn up.

Harry Dean Stanton is found at the opening of

The Texas motel: Marathon Motel, West Highway 90, Marathon

Wenders' soft-centred road movie in **Marathon**, a tiny town north of the spectacular Big Bend National Park. The motel he stays in is the **Marathon Motel and RV Park, West Highway 90**, a stunningly picturesque jumble of log cabins on the desert highway, alongside the railway, with breathtaking views over the West Texas desert to the Chisos Mountains (© *432.386.4241, www.marathonmotel.com*). The cross-state journey takes Stanton and Stockwell to **Port Arthur** and **Houston**.

Paris itself, on Highway-82, 90 miles northeast of Dallas, is a cutesy little town (with perhaps one exception: it celebrates its exotic European name with a 45-foot replica of the Eiffel Tower, adorned with a red stetson), totally destroyed by fire in 1916 and rebuilt in the twenties, since when it's largely been unchanged.

PASSAGE TO INDIA, A

(1984, dir: David Lean)
Judy Davis, Victor Bannerjee, Peggy Ashcroft.
● **INDIA**

After the critical trouncing of *Ryan's Daughter*, Lean retired, hurt, from the fray until this acclaimed comeback. It has to be said, though, that it's another overblown epic. Set in the fictitious Chandrapore, most of the movie was shot around **Bangalore**, southern India, where sets, including the British quarter, the bazaar and Dr Aziz's house, were built on the grounds of **Bangalore Palace** in the centre of the city. Filming also took place at the **Bangalore Club, FM Cariappa Road**. The pivotal Marabar Caves location, where Judy Davis crucially succumbs to the exotic atmosphere, is the rock formation at **Ramanagaram**, about 30 miles from Bangalore. The ending of the movie is **Srinagar** in Kashmir, northern India, where, forbidden to buy property, the English lived in houseboats on the sytem of canals.

PASSENGER, THE (aka *Profession: Reporter*)

(1975, dir: Michelangelo Antonioni)
Jack Nicholson, Maria Schneider, Jenny Runacre.
● SPAIN; LONDON; NORTH AFRICA; GERMANY

After the success of *Blowup*, Antonioni returned to west London to shoot scenes for this equally inscrutable film, which sees TV reporter David Locke (Nicholson) stealing the passport and assuming the identity of a dead man. Arriving in London to put together the pieces of his new persona, Locke goes to the then-new **Brunswick Centre, Bloomsbury**, where he first sees the mysterious girl (Schneider). Since he's heading to Notting Hill, Locke seems to be here for no other reason than that the intimidating, arena-like construction represents another of the director's favoured austere, brutalist backdrops.

Locke lurks by **St John's Church, Lansdowne Crescent**, opposite his house at **4 Lansdowne Crescent**, before deciding to follow the itinerary of the dead man. Filming also occurred in Chad; Algeciras; Munich; and Barcelona, where Nicholson rides the cable car above the city and wanders the bird markets of Las Ramblas. The ending, at the Hotel de la Gloria, Osuna, was shot in the southern Spanish desert of **Almeria**.

Locke lurks by his house: Lansdowne Crescent, Notting Hill

PASSION OF THE CHRIST, THE

(2004, dir: Mel Gibson)
Jim Caviezel, Monica Bellucci, Maia Morgenstern.
● ITALY

Gibson's account of the last hours of the life of Christ adds little to the Bible-in-pictures genre of the fifties other than emotionally bludgeoning physical detail. Most of the film was shot on the backlot at **Cinecitta** in Rome. Wider vistas, including the crucifixion, used the nearby **Craco** and the deserted city of **Matera**, seen previously in Pasolini's vastly superior *Gospel According to St Matthew* and Bruce Beresford's *King David*, with Richard Gere. Matera is a city of cave-houses, known as *sassi*, dug from the soft volcanic tufa. Writer Carlo Levi was exiled to the bleak area by Mussolini for his anti-fascist views, and wrote *Christ Stopped at Eboli*, which, ironically, implied that not even Christ would venture south into this bleak district. The nearest airport is Bari.

PASSPORT TO PIMLICO

(1949, dir: Henry Cornelius)
Stanley Holloway, Margaret Rutherford, Betty Warren.
● LONDON

When bomb damage uncovers documents revealing that Pimlico belongs to the Duchy of Burgundy, the neighbourhood declares independence from the post-war

Pimlico declares independence: Lambeth Road

Britain of rationing and licensing laws in this archetypal Ealing comedy. It was made, not in Pimlico, but about a mile east, over the Thames, where a huge set was built on a cleared bomb site on the **Lambeth Road**, SE1. Although the bomb-flattened area has been totally redeveloped, if you stand on the Lambeth Road between Hercules Road and Kennington Road and look north toward Lambeth Bridge, you can clearly recognise the railway arches that dominated the set.

PAT GARRETT AND BILLY THE KID

(1973, dir: Sam Peckinpah)
James Coburn, Kris Kristofferson, Bob Dylan.
● MEXICO

Another slow, bloody Peckinpah hymn to dusty, sweaty machismo, which exists in various versions. After all his past treks around Mexico with *Major Dundee* and *The Wild Bunch*, Peckinpah this time stayed firmly in the time-honoured Western location of **Durango**, about 500 miles northwest of Mexico City, an area seen in many, many movies including *Cahill, US Marshal*, *Chisum*, *The Undefeated*, *The Unforgiven* (1960) and *The War Wagon*.

PATHER PANCHALI

(1955, dir: Satyajit Ray)
Subir Banerji, Kanu Banerji, Karuna Banerji.
● INDIA

Family life in a poverty-stricken Indian village, the first of Ray's Apu trilogy. The village of Gopalnagar is the novel's setting but proved to be unsuitable for filming. Ray settled on **Boral**, six miles from Calcutta's city centre, where the ruined house and the pond stand.

PATHS OF GLORY

(1957, dir: Stanley Kubrick)
Kirk Douglas, Adolphe Menjou, Ralph Meeker.
● MUNICH, GERMANY

Kubrick's WWI drama, set in the French trenches, was made in Munich. The grand palace is the **Neues Schloss** of **Schloss Schleissheim**, to the northwest of the city. For full details, see *L'Année Dernière à Marienbad*, for which the Schloss provided exteriors.

PATRIOT, THE

(2000, dir: Roland Emmerich)
Mel Gibson, Heath Ledger, Joely Richardson.
● SOUTH CAROLIINA

Noble, widowed father Benjamin Martin (Gibson), employer of a happy black workers' collective, is pitched against the irredeemably evil, kiddie-shooting, church-burning Colonel Tavington (Jason Isaacs) in this objective view of the American War of Independence. Martin (based on the unmarried and childless slave-owner Francis Marion) has seven children, which by an astonishing coincidence is *exactly* the same number of children Mel Gibson has. Spooky, huh? But when a party of British soldiers is wiped out by half of the Brady Bunch, it's apparent that Emmerich is not going for the documentary approach. Caleb Deschanel's photography is superb, though, and there's a great use of South Carolina locations.

The production demanded acres of rolling hills and trees, without modern crops, which were found at the **Guy Darby Farm**, near **Rock Hill**, east of Lowrys. Martin's farmhouse, the doomed village of Pembroke and the Battle of Camden were all filmed here.

The Camden plantation, and the interiors of both Aunt Charlotte's (Richardson) plantation and the Howard home were filmed at **Historic Brattonsville, 1444 Brattonsville Road, McConnells**, a 775-acre 'living history village' (*www.chmuseums.org/brattonsville*). **Hightower Hall, Colonel Bratton House** and the **Homestead House** (the house Aunt Charlotte moves to after Charlestown falls to the English, which now contains an exhibition with memorabilia from the movie) were all used.

The exterior of Charlotte's plantation is the **Mansfield Plantation, 1776 Mansfield Road, Georgetown** (*© 843.546.6961, www.mansfieldplantation.com*), now a bed and breakfast. Georgetown is on the South Carolina coast about 60 miles northeast of Charleston.

Martin is summoned to the Assembly at **Charleston** (the real thing, though there's an awful lot of CGI added), where he speaks against entry into the war against England, in the **College of Charleston, 66 George Street** (also seen in *Cold Mountain* and *O*, Tim Blake Nelson's high school update of *Othello*).

With his militia, he manfully suffers the deprivations of camp in the Black Swamp, which is **Cypress Gardens, 3030 Cypress Gardens Road, Moncks Corner** (*© 843.553.0515, www.cypressgardens.org*), also hangout of the Swamp Thing, where the ruined church from the production has been kept. Meanwhile, the decadent British bitch over the dreadful state of their uniforms while attending a ball at **Middleton Place, 4300 Ashley River Roa**d, Charleston (*© 843.556.6020, www.middletonplace.org*).

The enlightened Martin is reunited with his deliriously grateful African-American partners on the beach at **Botany Bay Plantation, Edisto Island**, one of the largest sea islands in South Carolina (seen in the equally credible *Ace Ventura: When Nature Call*s).

PATRIOT GAMES

(1992, dir: Phillip Noyce)
Harrison Ford, Sean Bean, Anne Archer.
● LONDON; MARYLAND; VIRGINIA; CALIFORNIA

The CIA is pitted against the Hollywood wing of the IRA in this messy thriller, cynically aimed at US audiences who won't notice the bizarre London geography. US agent Jack Ryan (Ford), leaving a lecture at the Royal Naval Academy in Greenwich, south of the Thames in south-east London, manages to turn a corner and witness a terrorist attack on the Queen Mother's cousin outside an extraordinary version of Buckingham Palace. This 'palace' actually is in Greenwich. It's **Greenwich Naval College** (the film-makers wanted ex-GLC HQ County Hall, but couldn't get permission). See *Four Weddings and a Funeral* for details. The IRA operates out of a dusty old secondhand bookshop in the exclusive and intimidatingly posh **Burlington Arcade, Piccadilly**, to transmit its messages. When rumbled, the villain legs it out of the arcade and down to the nearest tube station. Green Park, maybe, which is conveniently next door? Nope. It's **Aldwych Station**, over a mile away – the station London Transport makes available for filming.

Back in the US of A, Ford visits the **CIA HQ in Langley**, east Virginia, just over the Potomac from Washington DC. And, unlike Buckingham Palace, it's the real thing – the entrance and the lobby, at least. So you can bet that this isn't going to be a CIA dirty tricks movie. *Mission: Impossible* also filmed in the lobby of CIA HQ, but for the corridors managed to use – County Hall in London. The *Patriot Games* interior is a set of course. Just who are those helpful signs, like 'Terrorism Assessments', meant for? Casual visitors?

Ford attends the **US Naval Academy at Annapolis**, I-301 on Chesapeake Bay, Maryland. The car chase is along Highway 301/50, over the Severn River Bridge. The climactic motor boat chase, supposedly in Chesapeake Bay, was shot in the two-million-gallon tank on the lot at Paramount in Hollywood. The North African terrorist camp was at **Brawley**, Route 86, south of Salton Sea in southern California down near the Mexican border.

PATTON (aka *Patton – Lust For Glory*)

(1970, dir: Franklin Schaffner)
George C Scott, Karl Malden, Michael Bates.
● SPAIN; GREECE; SICILY; ITALY; MOROCCO; CHESHIRE

Epic biopic of the WWII general, with an Oscar-winning script co-written by Francis Coppola and a famously declined Best Actor Oscar for Scott, made mostly on location.

The Battle of the Bulge, which took place in the Ardennes in Belgium, was recreated in the **Segovia highlands**, 80 miles northwest of Madrid. Patton's advance across France used the **Pamplona** region of Basque Spain. Spain also supplied the various terrains of North Africa, Sicily, Italy, France and Germany. The scene of amphibious landings is Sicily; while the Roman ruins and the reviewing of Moroccan troops actually filmed in Morocco. More filming took place in Greece.

The Battle of El Guettar is the familiar desert outside **Almeria** in southern Spain. After the battle, Patton meets his new aide de camp in the **Governor's Palace**, Almeria. The long hallway, down which Patton exits from Eisenhower's office after a rebuke, is the **Tapestry Room** at **La Granja** (which you might recognise as the scene of the climactic ball in Richard Lester's *The Three Musketeers*). Patton has his portrait painted at the castle of

Riofrio, outside Segovia (another *Musketeers* location).

Patton's wartime HQ, where he dedicates the service club and offends the Russians, was filmed in the real location, **Peover Hall, Over Peover**, an Elizabethan manor house near **Knutsford**, Cheshire, in the north of England. The house and gardens are open to the public from April to October (© *01743.708100*).

PEARL HARBOR

(2001, dir: Michael Bay)
Ben Affleck, Josh Hartnett, Kate Beckinsale.
● **HAWAII; LOS ANGELES, CALIFORNIA**

A sudsy fictitious romance set against a historic tragedy that cost hundreds of lives. What were they thinking of? Hardly a failure, but with a launch party alone that

The Honolulu movie house: Warner Grand Theater, West Sixth Street, San Pedro

cost $3 million, it wasn't the titanic hit intended. Bay's slam-bang epic is photographed in eye-popping colours that will leave bruises on your retina.

Pearl Harbor, Honolulu, on the Hawaiian island of Oahu, is now a historical site. *US Arizona*, sunk in the raid, still lies at the bottom of the harbour and has been turned into a permanent memorial, open most days of the year, with free admission. It's about 45 minutes west of Waikiki off the Kamehameha Highway, Highway 99 (*www.nps.gov/usar*). The end of the movie features underwater shots of the real *Arizona*. Most of the film was shot around California, including the Tennessee fields of the opening, which are at **Somis**, between Thousand Oaks and Ventura, northwest of LA.

The movie kicks off on the East Coast, in New York. Mitchell Field, where Jimmy Doolittle (Alec Baldwin) indulges the laddish antics of Rafe (Affleck) and Danny (Hartnett), is **Van Nuys Airport** in the San Fernando Valley (just where are those mountains in the background supposed to be?). See *Casablanca* for details.

The steps of the hospital, where Rafe's romantic gesture ends with a champagne cork thwacking his already bruised nose, is the entrance to the old **LA County Historical and Art Museum**, now part of the Natural History Museum in **Exposition Park**, south of downtown LA. The New York nightclub, where the pilots and nurses fraternise, is the **Queen's Salon** (which used to be the First Class Lounge) of the **Queen Mary**, permanently berthed in **Long Beach** (*www.queenmary.com*). The interior of the Queen Mary was also a New York nightclub in Ridley Scott's *Someone to Watch Over Me*, and a Manhattan bar in *Barton Fink*. Ironically, in

The Black Cat Diner: West Sixth Street, San Pedro

the next scene, Evelyn (Beckinsale) is taken for a nightime cruise around the Queen Mary, supposedly in New York harbor, where she dreams of being aboard the luxury ship. Rafe tells of

Evelyn tells Rafe she's pregnant: Luna Park Auto Court, Parkside Avenue, Lincoln Heights

his posting to Eagle Squadron in England, and promises to come back, at Evelyn's elegant Manhattan hotel. And this is LA, too, downtown. The deco entrance and the lobby are the **Los Angeles Design Center, 433 South Spring Street**. Also downtown is the New York railway station where Josh Hartnett waves bye-bye to Ben Affleck: **Union Station, 800 North Alameda Street**. Rafe's UK base, RAF Oakley, really is England though. It's **Badminton House, Tetbury**, Gloucestershire (seen in *Remains of the Day*).

In Hawaii, the hospital exterior is at **Palm Circle, Fort Shafter**, part of the Pearl Harbor complex in Honolulu, but the interior is the familiar **Linda Vista Hospital, 610 South St Louis**, east LA.

Another strange juxtaposition is the circular pool, where the Japanese high command plans the attack on Battleship Row, which is part of the US army post built to guard LA Harbor. It's the gun emplacement, flooded with water for the movie, of the old **Battery Osgood-Farley**, part of Fort Macarthur in Angel's Gate Park, San Pedro (*www.ftmac.org*). Close by, the Hawaiian lighthouse where Rafe suddenly reappears, fulfilling his promise to return, is the **Point Vicente Lighthouse, Point Vicente Drive South**, on the most southwest point of the Palos Verdes Peninsula (*www.palosverdes.com/pvlight*).

The Honolulu movie house, where Danny and Evelyn go to see Chaplin's *The Great Dictator*, is the **Warner Grand Theater, 478 West Sixth Street** in San Pedro, south LA. And, yes indeed, it is as gloriously deco as it is in the movie. Next door but one, an empty store was transformed into the Black Cat Diner, where they reminisce about Rafe after the movie. Kai Kai Korner, 'crossroads of the Pacific', where Red Winkle (Ewen Bremner) proposes to Betty (Jaime King), was created on **Sixth Street**, a few yards east.

The training scenes with Doolittle were filmed in the enormous Blimp hangars at **Tustin**, California, but the raid on Japan does get a little further afield. The industrial section of Tokyo is the 4,000-acre **US Steel Gary Works** at **Gary**, Indiana, on the shore of Lake Michigan (standing in for the Pacific). The bombers were digitally added to shots taken from the ground, while the reverse aerial shots were taken from a helicopter, with B-25s added later. The peaceful Japanese temple seen as the planes retreat, is the **Byodo-in Temple, 47-200 Kahekili Highway** in the Valley of the Temples, outside Honolulu. It's a replica of the original Byodo-in in Uji, Japan.

The White House rose garden, where President Roosevelt (Jon Voight) is informed that the returning mission has no homing beacons, is the Rose Garden of **Los Angeles County Museum of Natural History, 900 Exposition Boulevard**.

Luna Park Auto Court, 2101 Parkside Avenue, Lincoln Heights, east LA, became the Haleiwi Motor Court, where Evelyn tells Rafe she's pregnant. There was also filming at Camarillo State Hospital, which closed in July 1997 and is now the **California State University: Channel Islands, 1878 South Lewis Road, Camarillo**, in the Santa Monica Mountains; and at **Westward Beach**, Point Dume (the location of the ending of the original *Planet of the Apes*).

PEE-WEE'S BIG ADVENTURE
(1985, dir: Tim Burton)
Pee-Wee Herman, Jan Hooks, Elizabeth Daily.
● **LOS ANGELES, CALIFORNIA; TEXAS**

Fun first feature-film outing for Tim Burton. The shopping mall, where Pee-Wee shops for magic stuff and gets his bicycle stolen, is the **Santa Monica Place Shopping Mall, Fourth Street** at Broadway, Santa Monica, LA. The search for his bike takes him to the giant dinosaur, which you can seen at **Cabazon**, on I-10 near Palm Springs. The 150-foot-long concrete apatosaurus (the trendy new name for the brontosaurus) was built by Claude Bell, who ran the **Wheel Inn Restaurant, 50900 Seminole Drive**. He also started a T-rex, which was left uncompleted on his death in 1988. The apatosaurus has a souvenir stall in its belly.

Pee Wee follows the trail to the **Alamo, Alamo Plaza, San Antonio**, Texas. The Pee-Wee Herman version of the Alamo tour is loads more fun than the dull solemnity of the real thing, basement or no basement (for full details see *The Alamo*). The film studio is, of course, **Warner Bros, 4000 Warner Boulevard, Burbank**. You can tour the studio, too. Unlike the Universal Studios theme park approach, WB has a small tour (see *Casablanca* for details).

PEEPING TOM
(1960, dir: Michael Powell)
Carl Boehm, Anna Massey, Moira Shearer.
● **LONDON**

The newsagent: Percy Street

Reviled on release, but now lauded as one of the great British movies. Boehm (real name Karlheinz Böhm), the disturbed son of a sadistic film-maker, has a fear fixation and a lethal movie camera. Boehm's house stood at 5 Melbury Road, off High Street Kensington near Holland Park. Although number 7 still stands, its neighbour was demolished to make way for a block of flats. Director Powell not only plays the obsessed father, but lived over the road at 8 Melbury Road, which *is* still there. An impressive Norman Shaw Victorian artist's property with enormous windows, the house's garden was

used for home movie footage.

Boehm's first victim, Brenda Bruce, is picked up in **Newman's Court**, just off Oxford Street, and takes the killer up to her room above

Carl Boehm's first murder: Newman Arms, Newman's Court

the **Newman Arms** alongside. The newsagent's, where furtive businessmen buy their adult magazines, is on the corner of **Percy Street** at Rathbone Place, just behind Tottenham Court Road.

PEGGY SUE GOT MARRIED
(1986, dir: Francis Coppola)
Kathleen Turner, Nicolas Cage, Barry Miller.
● **CALIFORNIA**

An Oscar-nominated star turn from Kathleen Turner, regressing to her seventeen year-old self at a school reunion and rekindling romance with her cheesy husband. Look out for an early appearance by Jim Carrey, as a member of Nic Cage's vocal group. The movie was filmed in the towns of **Petaluma** and **Santa Rosa** in northern California. Petaluma, a small, unchanged town, is a frequently used period backdrop, most famously for *American Graffiti*. Peggy Sue's six-

The Donut Hole Café: Millie's Chili Bar, Petaluma

ties home is **226 Liberty Street**, between Prospect and Washington Streets, Petaluma. Her boyfriend Charlie (Cage), lives at **1006 D Street**. The Donut

Boyfriend Charlie's house: D Street

Hole Café, where the young Peggy Sue enjoys a flirtation with mean'n'moody poet Kevin J O'Connor is **Millie's Chili Bar, 600 Petaluma Boulevard** at H

Peggy Sue's house: Liberty Street

Street. Filming also took place on **H Street** at the Petaluma River. The high school is **Santa Rosa High School, 1235**

Peggy Sue's high school: Santa Rosa High School

Mendocino Avenue at Pacific. Santa Rosa was also the high school in *Inventing the Abbotts*.

PELICAN BRIEF, THE

(1993, dir: Alan J Pakula)
Julia Roberts, Denzel Washington, Sam Shepard.
● **LOUISIANA; NEW YORK CITY; WASHINGTON DC**

Riggs National Bank, Pennsylvania Avenue, Washington DC

Another John Grisham thriller, in the capable hands of paranoia specialist Pakula. The opening scene was filmed in front of the **Supreme Court** in Washington DC. Denzel Washington meets his editor John Lithgow at **Mount Vernon**, the home of George Washington. The offices of White and Blazevich are the law

Julia Roberts meets the fake FBI agent: Riverwalk, New Orleans

offices of Howrey and Simon in the **Warner Building, 1299 Pennsylvania Avenue**. DC filming also took place in the courtyard of the FBI's **Hoover Building, 10th Street** at Pennsylvania Avenue; the **Washington Monument**; **Pershing Park**; **National Cathedral**; **Riggs National Bank, 1503 Pennsylvania Avenue** at 15th Street; **Dulles Airport**; and the library, conference rooms and offices of the **Georgetown University Law Center, 600 New Jersey Avenue NW**. The Oval Office is the set built for the Kevin Kline-Sigourney Weaver movie *Dave*.

Marriott Marquis Hotel, Broadway

In New Orleans, law scenes were shot at **Tulane University, New Orleans**. French Quarter locations include **Bourbon Street** and **Spanish Plaza, Riverwalk**, on the banks of the Mississippi, where Roberts meets the fake FBI agent. Roberts and Shepard dine at **Antoine's Restaurant, 713 St Louis Street** in the French Quarter (though the restaurant's frontage was mocked up in the city's warehouse district for the explosion which kills Shepard).

In New York City, Pakula used the enormous, 50-storey **Marriott Marquis Hotel, 1535 Broadway** at 45th Street (℗ *212.398.1900*) overlooking Times Square. The 1,877 room hotel boasts the world's tallest atrium, New York's largest ballroom, and also incorporates the Broadway Theater.

PEOPLE VS LARRY FLYNT, THE

(1996, dir: Milos Forman)

Woody Harrelson, Courtney Love, Edward Norton.
● **MEMPHIS, TENNESSEE; LOS ANGELES, CALIFORNIA; WASHINGTON DC**

Biopic of the publisher of *Hustler*, reinvented in the person of cute fighter for free speech Woody Harrelson. The real Flynt has a wicked cameo as a judge. Most of

The final victory for free speech: Supreme Court Building

the filming was around Memphis, Tennessee. The scenes of Flynt's childhood home in Kentucky were shot over the Mississippi River from Memphis itself, and his first nightclub (opened in Columbus, Ohio, in the seventies), was filmed in the city's downtown area. Most of the court scenes are Memphis too, where a train terminal served as the US Supreme Court. Flynt's Ohio estate, where he throws his lavish 1976 Bicentennial party, is the same Memphis estate Tom Cruise stayed at during filming of *The Firm*. Other Memphis locations include the famous **Peabody Hotel, 149 Union Avenue** (℗ *901.529.4000*, *www.peabodymemphis.com*); **Memphis State University**; the **Shelby County Arena**; and a couple of correctional facilities.

The first courtroom clash with televangelist Jerry Falwell is at the courthouse of **Oxford**, Mississippi. In LA, real locations used include the **Flynt Publications Building** in Beverly Hills and Flynt's former home, **364 St Cloud Road**, Bel Air, where Harrelson is arrested. The outcome of the final Falwell hearing filmed on the steps of the **Supreme Court Building, First Street NE**, Washington DC.

PERFECT STORM, THE

(2000, dir: Wolfgang Petersen)
George Clooney, Mark Wahlberg, Diane Lane.
● **CALIFORNIA; MASSACHUSETTS**

Petersen's account of the final trip of fishing boat *Andrea Gail*, lost in a freak storm in 1991, uses the actual setting of **Gloucester**, Massachusetts, though much was shot on Warner's Burbank lot. **The Crow's Nest, 334 Main Street, Gloucester** (℗ *978.281.2965*, *www.crowsnest-gloucester.com*), is the real bar featured in Sebastian Junger's book. Inconveniently, it's not actually on the dock. No problem. The film company simply built a false front for the exterior scenes. Additional footage at sea was filmed off **Dana Point**, California. The *Gail* is played by *Lady Grace*, which can be seen at the Gloucester Maritime Heritage Center.

PERFECT WORLD, A

(1993, dir: Clint Eastwood)
Clint Eastwood, Kevin Costner, Laura Dern.
● **TEXAS**

Eastwood and Costner team up for a chase movie made entirely on location in **Huntsville** and around Austin, Texas. Escaped convict Costner goes on the run with a young boy, kidnapping him on **Columbus Street**, off Bouldin Avenue, Austin. The fictitious town of Noodle is **Martindale**, where the shop held up by Costner is on **Main Street**. Filming also took place at the **State Capitol Building** in Austin. The various small Texan towns are **Taylor**, **Wimberley**, **Niederwald**, **Manor**, **Cedar Creek**, **Bastrop**, **Utley**, **Volante** and **Canyon Lake**.

Jagger's druggy flat: Powis Square, Notting Hill

The office of gangster boss Harry Flowers: Mount Street, Mayfair

PERFORMANCE

(1970, dir: Nicolas Roeg; Donald Cammell)
James Fox, Mick Jagger, Anita Pallenberg.
● **LONDON**

That old art movie chestnut, the personality swap, is made over by the dream teaming of Roeg and Cammell with such style and innovation that, alongside *Peeping Tom*, this has to be one of the best British movies ever. The rundown Notting Hill house where on-the-lam gangster Chas (Fox) hides out with burned-out rock star Turner (Jagger), is not 81 Powis Square (the address given in the movie), but **25 Powis Square**, W11, at Talbot Road, a couple of blocks east of Portobello Road. The picturesque squalor of the movie is long gone, and the house is now smartly renovated. The interiors were shot at the much posher **93 Lowndes Square**, SW1, in Knightsbridge.

Queen's Gate Mews, running between Queen's Gate and Gloucester Road, is where the unfortunate chauffeur gets

The interiors of the house: Lowndes Square, Knightsbridge

his head shaved. The buffet of **Kensington Olympia Station** stands in for Paddington, where Chas overhears that there's a basement flat vacant in Powis Square. Directly opposite the new Chelsea Village complex on Fulham Road is salon **Hair Brazil, 469 Fulham Road**, which was the betting office of Joey Maddocks (Anthony Valentine), smashed up by Chas. The office of gangster boss Harry Flowers (Johnny Shannon) was **115 Mount Street**, Mayfair, now the **Goedhuis Art Gallery**.

PERSONA

(1966, dir: Ingmar Bergman)
Liv Ullmann, Bibi Andersson, Gunnar Bjornstrand.
● **SWEDEN**

Yet another personality swap movie, but in Bergman's

hands, an overwhelmingly cinematic experience, complete with Brechtian film break. It was made on the island of **Faro**.

PEYTON PLACE

(1957, dir: Mark Robson)
Lana Turner, Diane Varsi, Hope Lange.
● **MAINE**

Archetypal sex-in-a-small-town melodrama, which spawned the mother of all TV soaps. The house of Constance (Turner) is **77 Chestnut Street** and her shop is now **The Emporium** on **Main Street**. There was also filming at **Belfast**; **Rockland**; **Rockport**; **Lincolnville Beach**; and **Hope**.

PHANTASM

(1979, dir: Don Coscarelli)
Michael Baldwin, Bill Thornbury, Reggie Bannister.
● **CALIFORNIA**

The spooky mausoleum of this bizarre horror-comedy is **Dunsmuir House and Gardens, 2960 Peralta Oaks Court, Oakland**, over the bay from San Francisco, a location familiar from movies such as Mike Myers' *So I Married an Axe Murderer* and *A View to a Kill*. It is open to the public. Filming also took place at **Julian**, a southern California mining town about 40 miles northeast of San Diego.

PHANTOM OF THE PARADISE

(1974, dir: Brian De Palma)
William Finley, Jessica Harper, Paul Williams.
● **LOS ANGELES, CALIFORNIA; NEW YORK CITY; TEXAS**

De Palma's wild rock spin on *The Phantom of the Opera* and *Faust* was shot on sets in LA, while its exteriors are mainly New York, but the Paradise rock palace, haunted by the disfigured composer, is in Dallas, Texas. It's the **Majestic Theater, 1925 Elm Street**, a baroque movie palace built in 1921 as the HQ of the Interstate theater chain. It was donated to the city of Dallas and subsequently restored.

The Paradise: Majestic Theater, Elm Street, Dallas

PHILADELPHIA

(1993, dir: Jonathan Demme)
Tom Hanks, Denzel Washington, Antonio Banderas.
● **PHILADELPHIA, PENNSYLVANIA**

Demme's determinedly mainstream movie about Aids prejudice is calculatedly set in the city of

Denzel Washington's law office: Chestnut Street

Washington gets freaked by the gay student: Pickwick Pharmacy, Market Street

Tom Hanks gets a check-up at the Action Aids office: Arch Street

liberty, independence and brotherly love, kicking off with a montage of such Philadelphian images as the **Benjamin Franklin Bridge** over the Delaware River, the glitzy modernistic skyscrapers of **Liberty Place** and the Liberty Bell itself. Like most of Demme's movies, it was made almost entirely on real locations. The Action Aids office, where Hanks gets a check-up at the opening of the movie, is **1216 Arch Street** just east of City Hall, opposite the Pennsylvania Convention Center. The office of the prestigious law firm, Wyant, Wheeler, Hellerman, Tetlow and Brown, where Hanks is initially a rising star, is that of Philly firm Mesirov, Gelman, Jaffe, Cramer and Jamieson (who donated their location fee to Aids charities), in the **Mellon Bank Building, 1735 Market Street**, west of City Hall. A little to the south is Denzel Washington's law office, **1901 Chestnut Street** on the corner of 19th Street. The pharmacy, where Washington's homophobia is provoked by a gay law student, is the **Pickwick Pharmacy, 1700 Market Street**, directly opposite the Mellon Bank Building. Washington delivers a summons to Jason Robards during a ballgame at the **Spectrum Sports Arena, Broad Street** at Pattison Avenue, home of the Philadelphia Kixx soccer team.

Hanks and Banderas' loft apartment is on **10th Street** at Bainbridge Street, and also on Bainbridge Street is the **Famous Fourth Street Delicatessen**, where Washington shops after the birth of his daughter. Hanks studies case law west of the city in the **University of Pennsylvania Fine Arts Library, Walnut Street**. The sauna, where Tom Hanks' coming out is thwarted by the partners' laddish banter, is in the **Raquet Club, 215 South 16th Street**. The trial scenes were filmed in Courtroom 243 of **Philadelphia City Hall, Penn Square**, at Broad and Market Streets. Hanks

The trial scenes: Philadelphia City Hall

The Wheeler Building: Mellon Bank Building, Market Street

ultimately dies at **Mount Sinai Hospital, Fourth Street** at Reed.

PHONE BOOTH
(2002, dir: Joel Schumacher)
Colin Farrell, Forest Whitaker, Kiefer Sutherland.
● LOS ANGELES, CALIFORNIA; NEW YORK CITY

The New York phone booth at 53rd and Eighth: West Fifth Street

This tight little thriller is set in New York but, although there are a few minutes of **Times Square** to establish the locale, the phone booth, where duplicitous PR man Stu Shepard (Farrell) is pinned down by a sniper, supposedly at 53rd and Eighth, was constructed on **West Fifth Street** at South Spring Street, downtown LA, opposite the Alexandria Hotel (seen in *Se7en*). The **Chester Williams Building, West Fifth Street** (seen in *Blade*), was transformed into a subway entrance.

PIANIST, THE
(2002, dir: Roman Polanski)
Adrien Brody, Thomas Kretschmann, Frank Finlay.
● BERLIN, GERMANY; POLAND

There's an understated authenticity to Polanski's Oscar-winner, charting the miraculous survival of Jewish musician Wladyslaw Szpilman (Brody) through WWII in occupied Warsaw. As much of the Polish capital has been rebuilt, location filming was limited to the old **Praga** district, east of the River Vistula, which remains virtually unchanged, and where **Mila Street** and **Stalowa Street** became the infamous ghetto. Warsaw of the thirties was largely recreated on the backlot of the famous Babelsberg Studios, Berlin. The astonishing shots of the ruined city are not computer-generated, as you might assume these days, but are the east German city of **Jüterbog**, which had served as a Soviet military base. It was about to be demolished, so production designer Allan Starski was allowed to destroy the remaining military buildings and barracks.

The abandoned house, where Szpilman encounters Captain Hosenfeld (Kretschmann), is an old villa in **Potsdam**, southwest of Berlin, and the burnt-out military hospital was a disused Soviet facility in **Belitz**, east Germany.

The final concert scene was filmed in the **Filharmonia Narodowa, Plac Emila Mlynarskiego**, home of the Warsaw Philharmonic, where the film was given its world première.

PIANO, THE
(1993, dir: Jane Campion)
Holly Hunter, Harvey Keitel, Anna Paquin.
● NEW ZEALAND

Oscar-winning period drama, featuring some stunning locations, with Campion editing together several different locales. The exteriors of the Stewart and Baines

The spectacular shipwreck beach: Karekare Beach, Karekare Road

houses are in **Walkworth**, just outside Auckland, North Island. The underwater sequence was staged at the **Bay of Islands**, and there was more filming at **Awakino Beach**. The spectacular beach of the shipwreck is **Karekare Beach, Karekare Road** off Piha Road, near Glen Eden to the west of Auckland.

PICNIC

(1955, dir: Joshua Logan)
Kim Novak, William Holden, Rosalind Russell.
● **KANSAS**

Hunky stranger William Holden arrives in town and causes mayhem among the womenfolk in the Oscar-nominated filming of William Inge's play, which was shot in **Hutchinson**, on I-50 about 40 miles northwest of Wichita, Kansas, and **Halstead**, 25 miles to the east. The waterfall scene was filmed in **Salina**, I-135, about 80 miles north of Wichita.

PICNIC AT HANGING ROCK

(1975, dir: Peter Weir)
Rachel Roberts, Helen Morse, Dominic Guard.
● **VICTORIA, AUSTRALIA; SOUTH AUSTRALIA**

Appleyard Girls' School: Martindale Hall, Mintaro

PHOTOGRAPH COURTESY NIC KLAASSEN/FLINDERS RANGES RESEARCH

Turn-of-the-century Aussie spin on Antonioni's *L'Avventura*, where schoolgirls on a picnic inexplicably disappear. **Hanging Rock** is real, and is where the picture was shot. The weird jumble of stone columns can be found near **Woodend** in Victoria, about 35 miles northwest of Melbourne on the Calder Highway. The nearby extinct 3,320-foot volcano, Mount Macedon, gives excellent views of the rocks. Appleyard Girls' School is **Martindale Hall**, a period mansion in the Clare Valley near **Mintaro**, South Australia. You can visit the mansion (© 08.8843.9088) and maybe pick up a bottle of Martindale Hall Chardonnay, which is produced on the estate.

PINK FLAMINGOS

(1972, dir: John Waters)
Divine, Mink Stole, David Lochary.
● **MARYLAND**

The legendary masterpiece of John Waters' underground period, topped with its unrepeatable coda as Divine, to the tune of 'How Much Is That Doggy in the Window', eats freshly exuded doggy-do. Those who've only seen the video version (where the offending sequence is reduced to a series of stills) probably believe it was faked.

If you've seen the original, you know it wasn't. Filmed, like all Waters' early movies, around **Baltimore**. The Marbles' house is **3900 Greenmount Avenue**. But what you really want to know is where Divine ate that turd, which was outside **894 Tyson Street** at Reed.

PINK FLOYD – THE WALL

(1982, dir: Alan Parker)
Bob Geldof, Christine Hargreaves, James Laurenson.
● **DEVON; LONDON; SURREY; YORKSHIRE**

Pompous visualisation of Pink Floyd's concept album, a loose autobiography of Roger Waters, with hero Pink going through all the standard motions of rock star alienation. The wartime Anzio beach scenes, where young Pink's father is killed, were shot on **Saunton Sands**, south of Ilfracombe on the north Devon coast. Pink's childhood home is in **East Molesey**, Surrey, the playground is in **Bermondsey**, London, and the recurring childhood dream was shot on **Epsom Downs**. The other kids' fathers return from war at **Keighley Station**, on the Keighley-Worth Valley Railway near Bradford in Yorkshire.

The US rock concert which gets out of hand, based on a Floyd concert at the Sports Arena in LA, was shot at **Wembley Arena** (apart from a brief second unit glimpse of LA, all the American scenes were filmed in the UK, on sets at Pinewood). When Pink metamorphoses, for no apparent reason, into a neo-fascist demagogue, he presides over a rally in the **Royal Horticultural Hall, Westminster** (see *Indiana Jones and the Last Crusade* for details). The snippet of football violence is in **Muswell Hill**, near Alexandra Palace. The school riot is at **Beckton Gasworks**, where Stanley Kubrick filmed the Vietnam scenes for *Full Metal Jacket*.

PINK PANTHER, THE

(1963, dir: Blake Edwards)
David Niven, Peter Sellers, Capucine.
● **ITALY**

The film that launched Inspector Clouseau is set mostly in the jet-set ski resort of **Cortina d'Ampezzo** in the Ampezzo Valley of the Italian Dolomites (see *For Your Eyes Only* for details). Filming also took place at the ancient village of **Rocca di Papa**, about 15 miles west of Rome. The opening scene, of Capucine making a getaway, is in **Venice**. The dizzying, mile-high roads of Amalfi, the streets of Rome near the Coliseum and Florence were also used.

PIRATES OF THE CARIBBEAN: THE CURSE OF THE BLACK PEARL

(2003, dir: Gore Verbinski)
Johnny Depp, Geoffrey Rush, Orlando Bloom.
● **GRENADINES; CALIFORNIA**

A movie in a long dead genre, based on a theme park ride. Didn't look too promising, did it? But a good script and a great cast save the day.

Fort Charles, Port Royal, was built on a three-acre bluff on the **Palos Verdes Peninsula**, south of LA, on the site of Marineland, a one-time amusement park (near the Point Vicente Lighthouse seen in *Pearl Harbor*). The

Governor's mansion was also built here. The interior was a set at Raleigh studios in Manhattan Beach, a little further north up the coast.

St Vincent in the Grenadines was the production base in the southern Caribbean. The harbour of Port Royal was built at **Wallilabou Bay** on St Vincent (the dock and a façade have been left), and the small town set (which has now gone) at **Chateaubelair**. The outer Grenadine island of **Petite Tabac** became the deserted isle where Jack Sparrow (Depp) and Elizabeth Swann (Keira Knightley) are abandoned by Captain Barbossa (Rush). If you want the full Depp experience, stay at Young Island, a 35-acre resort, ten minute's boat ride from St Vincent, where the star stayed for part of the filming (*www.youngisland.com*).

PIT AND THE PENDULUM, THE
(1961, dir: Roger Corman)
Vincent Price, John Kerr, Barbara Steele.
● LOS ANGELES, CALIFORNIA

Corman's second Edgar Allen Poe picture (suggested by a short story rather than adapted from one) was, like the first, *The House of Usher*, filmed almost entirely in the studio. The sea-battered coastline of Spain, where Kerr arrives at Price's gloomy castle (a matte painting) is – shiver me timbers – the **Palos Verdes** coast, south of LA.

PLACE IN THE SUN, A
(1951, dir: George Stevens)
Montgomery Clift, Elizabeth Taylor, Shelley Winters.
● NEVADA; CALIFORNIA

Theodore Dreiser's *An American Tragedy* given the worthy Hollywood treatment by Stevens. Taylor is rich, Clift is poor, but Winters is pregnant. The location filming was at **Lake Tahoe** in Nevada; and nearby **Cascade Lake**, on Emerald Bay Road, over the border in California at Tahoe's southern tip. The story was based on the Gillette murder trial, which took place in New York State, at the Herkimer County Courthouse in Little Falls, off I-90, 20 miles east of Utica.

PLAGUE OF THE ZOMBIES, THE
(1966, dir: John Gilling)
Andre Morell, Diane Clare, John Carson.
● BUCKINGHAMSHIRE

Excellent little horror from Hammer's golden age, with a terrific dream sequence. The Cornish village, where wicked squire John Carson raises the dead to work in his tin mine, is a set at Bray Studios near Maidenhead. His house is the Victorian gothic extravagance alongside the studio, now the **Oakley Court Hotel** (see *The Rocky Horror Picture Show*, one of the dozens of movies filmed here, for details).

PLAN 9 FROM OUTER SPACE
(1958, dir: Edward D Wood Jr)
Bela Lugosi, Tor Johnson, Vampira.
● CALIFORNIA

The legendary 'Worst Film of All Time', lovingly recreated in Tim Burton's *Ed Wood*, was made around **San Fernando**, north of LA.

PLANES, TRAINS & AUTOMOBILES
(1987, dir: John Hughes)
Steve Martin, John Candy, William Windom.
● NEW YORK; MISSOURI; ILLINOIS; CALIFORNIA

Exec Neal Page (Martin), trying to make it home from New York to Chicago (well, this is a John Hughes movie) for Thanksgiving, is lumbered with the world's worst travelling companion in Del Griffith (Candy). Their paths first cross when Del nabs Neal's hard-fought-for cab on **Park Avenue at 52nd Street**, Manhattan.

Diverted to Wichita, Kansas, Neal and Del get an attack of homosexual panic sharing a room at the Edelen's Braidwood Inn ("They're *not* pillows!"). This is odd, since Braidwood is on I-55, southwest of Chicago, Illinois. The motel became a Days Inn for a while, but is now the **Sun Motel, 140 South Hickory Street, Braidwood**, Illinois (© *815.458.2812*).

The airport, where Neal is "Fucked", is **St Louis Lambert International Airport, St Louis**, Missouri, though many airline scenes had to be filmed on sets, as no one wanted to be associated with delays and incompetence.

The railway station is the **South Dayton Train Station, Buffalo**, New York. The pair are picked up by the truck at **Woodstock**, Illinois, which you might recognise from *Groundhog Day*.

The El Rancho Motel, 36355 North Highway 41, **Gurnee** (© *847.623.5237*), north of Chicago, toward the Wisconsin border, is where Neal tries to book a room with incinerated credit cards after their hire car burns.

Arriving in the Windy City, the pair finally open up at **La Salle-Van Buren 'el' station**.

PLANET OF THE APES
(1968, dir: Franklin Schaffner)
Charlton Heston, Roddy McDowall, Kim Hunter.
● CALIFORNIA; ARIZONA

The desert planet, run by apes, is the desert around **Page, Glen Canyon** and **Lake Powell**, northern Arizona. The ape village sets were built on the Fox Ranch in **Malibu**

Heston is back to Earth: Westward Beach, Malibu

Creek State Park, Las Virgenes Road off Mulholland Highway, south from Route 101, northwest of LA. The final scene, when Heston realises he's been on Earth all along, was shot at a secluded cove on the far eastern end of **Westward Beach**, between Zuma Beach and Point Dume, Malibu.

PLANET OF THE APES
(2001, dir: Tim Burton)
Mark Wahlberg, Helena Bonham Carter, Tim Roth.
● UTAH; CALIFORNIA

Tim Burton's 're-imagining' of the sixties classic has some good ideas, but is too mainstream to be a real Burton movie, and the cutely Disneyfied Bonham Carter make-up deals a death blow. Exteriors were shot at **Lake Powell**, Utah (where much of the 1968 version was filmed). Calima, where the ape civilisation is born and where Capt Davidson (Wahlberg) discovers the remains of his spaceship, is the spectacular landscape of the **Trona Pinnacles**, near Ridgecrest, California (see *Star Trek V: The Final Frontier* for details).

PLATOON

(1986, dir: Oliver Stone)
Charlie Sheen, Willem Dafoe, Tom Berenger.
● PHILIPPINES

The first of Stone's Vietnam trilogy won the Best Picture Oscar. Powerful stuff, with a little help from Samuel Barber's 'Adagio'. Filmed, like so many other 'Nam movies, in the Philippines, in the jungle about 60 miles from Manila.

PLAY MISTY FOR ME

(1971, dir: Clint Eastwood)
Clint Eastwood, Jessica Walter, Donna Mills.
● CALIFORNIA

The bar: Sardine Factory, Monterey

Clint's first movie as director is the original template for *Fatal Attraction*, with Jessica Walter obsessively stalking radio DJ Eastwood. It was made on the director's home territory of Monterey and Carmel on the Pacific coast south of San Francisco. The radio station is Carmel's own KRML. The pier restaurant, where Walter sabotages Eastwood's job interview, is in Monterey. Eastwood's house is on **Spindrift Road, Carmel Highlands** (the same road as Sharon Stone's Stinson Beach home in *Basic Instinct*). The restaurant, where *Dirty Harry* director Don Siegel tends bar, is still there unchanged: it's the **Sardine Factory, 701 Wave Street** at Prescott, Fisherman's Wharf, Monterey.

PLAYER, THE

(1992, dir: Robert Altman)
Tim Robbins, Greta Scacchi, Whoopi Goldberg.
● CALIFORNIA

Disposing of the writer: Carpark behind the Rialto, Pasadena

Altman bounced back into the limelight with this joyfully scabrous satire on the movie biz after several years of treading water with small-scale theatrical adaptations. The cinema, where paranoid studio exec Tim Robbins meets – and subsequently kills – the writer he thinks is sending death threats, is the **Rialto Theater, 1023 South Fair Oaks Avenue, Pasadena**. It's the same movie house

premièring *Stab* in *Scream 2*. Robbins gets a message to meet 'Joe Gilles' (the name of William Holden's screenwriter character in *Sunset Blvd.*) in the patio of the St James' Club, formerly and now once again, the **Sunset Tower Apartments, 8358 Sunset Boulevard**, west Hollywood. Built in 1931, this luxu-

Robbins meets the writer: Rialto Theater, Pasadena

The clifftop restaurant: Geoffrey's, Malibu

ry block once housed Errol Flynn, Clark Gable, Howard Hughes and the Gabor sisters. Legend has it, John Wayne kept a cow on the balcony. Whatever, it's a stunning zigzag moderne tower, recently restored, and seen in movies as diverse as Jean-Claude Van Damme's *A.W.O.L.*, *Farewell My Lovely*, *Strange Days*, *Get Shorty* and the remake of *The Italian Job*.

Look out for the funeral scene, when the murdered writer is laid to rest. The tomb seen over the shoulder of sinister cop Lyle Lovett bears the family name Douras, the real handle of Marion Davies – born Marion Douras, longtime partner of William Randolph Hearst, the original model for Charles Foster Kane. Also glimpsed is the **Cathedral Mausoleum**, where Rudolph Valentino, Peter Finch and the ashes of Peter Lorre lie. And under the lawn behind the Douras monument lies actress Virginia Rappé, who died at Fatty Arbuckle's notorious sex and booze party at the St Francis Hotel in San Francisco, 1921 (chronicled in detail in the book *Hollywood Babylon*). The cemetery also contains the mortal remains of Tyrone Power, Douglas Fairbanks Sr, Cecil B DeMille, John Huston, Paul Muni and gangster Bugsy Siegel among others. Once a prime spot, adjoining the Paramount lot, the neighbourhood has declined and you'll now find the cemetery tucked away behind a mini-mall. It's the **Hollywood Memorial Cemetery, 6000 Santa Monica Boulevard**, between Gower and Van Ness, Hollywood.

The police station was the old Pasadena Police Station, which stood at Holly and Arroyo Parkway, Pasadena. It has since been demolished, but still extant are the clutch of Tinseltown landmarks Altman uses as backdrops. The star-studded charity ball is held in the **LA County Museum of Art, 5905 Wilshire Boulevard** (see *LA Story* for details). The clifftop terrace restaurant, site of Burt Reynolds' cameo,

Burying the writer: Hollywood Memorial Cemetery, Santa Monica Boulevard

is swanky **Geoffrey's, 27400 Pacific Coast Highway** in Malibu (*© 310.457.1519*). And even more exclusive is the luxurious spa Robbins retreats to with Greta Scacchi: **Two Bunch Palms, 67-425 Two Bunch Palms Trail, Desert Hot Springs**, north of Palm Springs.

PLEIN SOLEIL (aka *Purple Noon/Blazing Sun*)
(1960, dir: René Clément)
Alain Delon, Maurice Ronet, Marie Laforêt.
● **ITALY**

First filming of Patricia Highsmith's *The Talented Mr Ripley*, with Alain Delon as the amoral impostor. Mongebello this time was **Sant' Angelo**, on the southern tip of the island of **Ischia** in the Bay of Naples.

POINT BLANK
(1967, dir: John Boorman)
Lee Marvin, Angie Dickinson, Keenan Wynn.
● **CALIFORNIA**

The opening scene is on **Alcatraz Island** (see *Escape From Alcatraz* for details) in San Francisco Bay. Lee Marvin manages the hitherto impossible feat of swimming the treacherous waters to the city. From here on, the action of the movie is transposed from San Francisco to Los Angeles, for its tougher visual appeal. The penthouse is at Santa Monica, and the ultra-modern ranch house is atop the **Curson Avenue Mall**.

POINT BREAK
(1991, dir: Kathryn Bigelow)
Patrick Swayze, Keanu Reeves, Gary Busey.
● **HAWAII; OREGON**

The California beach: Sunset Beach, Oahu

FBI agent Reeves goes undercover as a surfer to catch The Ex-Presidents, a bunch of bank robbers in rubber masks. Set in LA, the southern California beach scenes are actually in Hawaii, at the surfers' paradise locations of **Pipeline Beach**, **Sunset Beach** and **Waimea Bay**, on Oahu's north shore, Route 83. Lori Petty teaches new boy Reeves to surf at Oahu's Sunset Beach. The stormy finale, set at Bell's Beach, Australia, was filmed on the coast of Oregon at **Wheeler**, Ecola State Park, on coastal highway I-101, about 20 miles south of Cannon Beach and 60 miles west of Portland, though the titanic waves, where Swayze (or his stunt double) finally disappears, were filmed back on Oahu at Waimea.

POLLYANNA
(1960, dir: David Swift)
Hayley Mills, Jane Wyman, Karl Malden.
● **CALIFORNIA**

Gruesomely cheery orphan Hayley Mills brings a ray of sunshine into the lives of grumpy old townsfolk in this long, long version of the kiddie classic. The small town

is **Santa Rosa**, northern California, where Pollyanna's house is the **Mableton Mansion, 1015 McDonald Avenue** at 15th Street.

Pollyanna's house: Mableton Mansion, Santa Rosa

POLTERGEIST
(1982, dir: Tobe Hooper)
JoBeth Williams, Craig T Nelson, Heather O'Rourke.
● **LOS ANGELES, CALIFORNIA**

Producer Spielberg is obviously the driving force, as malign forces enter a suburban household through the television set. The Freeling house is **4267 Roxbury Street** in the small estate of **Forest Hills** in the Simi Valley north of LA.

Poltergeist II was set in Chicago, and featured the **John Hancock Center, North Michigan Avenue** between Chestnut and Delaware Streets.

POPIOL Y DIAMENT (aka *Ashes and Diamonds*)
(1958, dir: Andrzej Wajda)
Zbigniew Cybulski, Ewa Krzyzanowska, Adam Pawlikowski.
● **POLAND**

Cybulski is a James Dean-like partisan caught up in the confusion of post-war Poland in Wajda's classic, which was filmed in **Lodz** and **Wroclaw**.

PORTRAIT OF JENNIE
(1948, dir: William Dieterle)
Joseph Cotten, Jennifer Jones, Ethel Barrymore.
● **MASSACHUSETTS; NEW YORK CITY**

Strange supernatural romance, with artist Joseph Cotten falling for ethereal muse Jennifer Jones. Set in New York, with filming in **Central Park**, and at the **Tavern on the Green**, Central Park West at 67th Street – a chance to see this much-used location before its 1974 revamp. The lighthouse of the stormy climax is **Graves End Light**, off Boston Harbor.

POSEIDON ADVENTURE, THE
(1972, dir: Ronald Neame)
Gene Hackman, Shelley Winters, Ernest Borgnine.
● **CALIFORNIA**

First of the seventies cycle of disaster movies, featuring the spectacular capsizing of a luxury liner. The pre-capsize *Poseidon* is the **Queen Mary**, permanently berthed at **Pier J, Long Beach** at the south end of Long Beach Freeway, south of LA. The art deco treat has a restaurant, shops and accommodation in its tiny but glorious staterooms. See more of its plush interior in Ridley Scott's *Someone to Watch Over Me*, *Barton Fink* or *Pearl Harbor*, all of which use it as a New York nightspot. A myth seems to have grown up that the upside-down ballroom is the Crystal Ballroom of the Biltmore Hotel, downtown LA. In fact, it was a full-size replica of the *Queen*

Mary's ballroom which was built on Stage 6 at the 20th Century Fox studio.

You can see the model liner used for filming among the many model ships in the Los Angeles Maritime Museum, Berth 84 at Los Angeles Harbor in San Pedro, just west of Long Beach.

PREDATOR

(1987, dir: John McTiernan)
Arnold Schwarzenegger, Carl Weathers, Jesse Ventura.
● MEXICO

Arnie meets up with a semi-invisible, near-invincible monster in the jungle. After the exciting build-up and demonstrations of truly scary prowess, the creature inexplicably resorts to fisticuffs. No contest. The movie was filmed in **Puerto Vallarta**, on the west coast of Mexico, 400 miles from Mexico City (see *The Night of the Iguana*, which put Puerto Vallarta on the map, for details). The set has since been turned into a restaurant, **El Edén**, off highway 200, between the Camino Real and La Jolla Mismaloya. It's a difficult place to get to, three miles along a dirt track. And there's no phone. Good luck! The jungle scenes used the lush greenery in the south of the country around **Palenque**.

PREDATOR 2

(1990, dir: Stephen Hopkins)
Danny Glover, Maria Conchita Alonso, Gary Busey.
● CALIFORNIA

The police building: Pacific Coast Stock Exchange, South Spring Street

The dreadlocked, semi-invisible alien now turns up in futuristic downtown LA. The City of LA Police Administration building is actually the **Pacific Coast Stock Exchange, 618 South Spring Street**, downtown LA. The Lloyd Wright-style Mayan penthouse is a set, but the glorious peacock blue art deco building, where the creature materialises, is real. It's the **Eastern Columbia Building, 849 South Broadway**, which you can also see in Antonioni's *Zabriskie Point*. The squeaky clean LA subway – there was no such thing in 1990 – is BART, the Bay Area Rapid Transport system beneath Oakland, across the bay from San Francisco.

The creature materialises: Eastern Columbia Building, South Broadway

PRETTY BABY

(1978, dir: Louis Malle)
Keith Carradine, Susan Sarandon, Brooke Shields.
● NEW ORLEANS, LOUISIANA

Dubious but beautiful (photographed by Bergman collaborator Sven Nykvist) story of Shields' childhood in a turn-of-the-century New Orleans brothel. Bellocq's house is a gothic mansion at **1221 Orange Street**, New Orleans, though the interiors were shot at the **Columns Hotel, 3811 St Charles Street**.

PRETTY IN PINK

(1986, dir: Howard Deutch)
Molly Ringwald, Andrew McCarthy, Jon Cryer.
● LOS ANGELES, CALIFORNIA

This seems such an archetypal John Hughes movie that it's easy to forget it was actually directed by Howard Deutch, until you realise that none of it was filmed in Chicago. Set in Elgin, Illinois, it's all LA. Trax, the record shop where Blane (McCarthy) buys a Steve Lawrence album from Andie (Ringwald), is now the **Broadway Bar and Grill, 1460 Third Street**, on the **Third Street Promenade** at Broadway, Santa Monica (directly opposite the Broadway Deli seen in *Heat*). The house of Steff (James Spader) is the Rothschild home in the posh neighbourhood of **Hancock Park**, midtown. Andie's working class home is on **Hope Street**, south Pasadena. The school exterior is **John Marshall High School, 3939 Tracy Street, Silverlake**, seen also in the original film of *Buffy the Vampire Slayer*, among others. Interiors are **Burroughs Junior High, 600 South McCadden Place, Hancock Park**. Andie and Duckie attend the prom in the often-seen Crystal Ballroom of the **Biltmore Hotel, 506 South Grand Avenue**, downtown (see *Beverly Hills Cop* for details).

PRETTY WOMAN

(1990, dir: Garry Marshall)
Richard Gere, Julia Roberts, Hector Elizondo.
● LOS ANGELES, CALIFORNIA

Fairy tale romance for the eighties, complete with designer labels to die for, as a poverty-row hooker who looks like a movie star crosses the path of a millionaire who also looks like a movie star. Only true love can possibly follow. As all the guide books point out, the intimidatingly luxurious hotel where Vivian (Roberts) gets her first taste of the high-life is the 1928 Beaux Arts-style **Regent Beverly Wilshire, 9500 Wilshire Boulevard** (© *310. 275.5200*) at the foot of Rodeo Drive. So handy for the shops. It's become a mecca for appallingly rich romantics who want to spend a 'Pretty Woman' weekend, but sadly even this amount of money can't buy a night in the suite used by Richard and Julia. Although the exterior and the lobby are the real Beverly Wilshire, the rooms were a set built at the Disney Studio in Burbank, and bear little resemblance to the real thing. The scene where the Hotel Manager (Elizondo) teaches Vivian about place settings was filmed in the ballroom of the now-closed **Ambassador Hotel, 3400 Wilshire**

The Beverly Hills hotel: Regent Beverly Wilshire, Wilshire Boulevard

The snotty clothes shop: Boulemiche Boutique, Santa Monica Boulevard

Julia Roberts' hotel: Las Palmas Hotel, Las Palmas Avenue, Hollywood

Boulevard, midtown (see the 1954 *A Star Is Born* for details).

Back down to earth, Viv plies her trade alongside the tacky souvenir shops of **Hollywood Boulevard**. The Rodeo Drive boutique where she's snubbed by the staff, but gets her revenge bigtime – "Big mistake… huge" – and which goes to great pains to hide its name (come on, we know it's only a movie) is **Boulmiche Boutique**, actually at **9501 Santa Monica Boulevard** (© 310.273.6443), albeit on the corner of Rodeo Drive. The fancy restaurant where she has trouble with snails ("Slippery little suckers…") was the Rex II Ristorante, now **Cicada**, in the **Oviatt Building, 617 South Olive Street**, downtown (see *Indecent Proposal* for details). Don't be fooled by the (bought-in) aerial shot of San Francisco. The exterior of the opera house, where Vivian and Edward Lewis (Gere) watch *La Traviata*, is **The Museum of Natural History** in LA's **Exposition Park**, and the interior is a studio set.

But real romantics, of course, would much rather check out the fire escape Edward climbs to the strains of *Traviata* than the overblown grandiosity of the Beverly Wilshire. It's attached to the **Las Palmas Hotel, 1738 Las Palmas Avenue**, just off Hollywood Boulevard.

PRICK UP YOUR EARS

(1987, dir: Stephen Frears)
Gary Oldman, Alfred Molina, Vanessa Redgrave.
● **LONDON; MOROCCO**

Neat Alan Bennett adaptation of John Lahr's biography of playwright Joe Orton, shot on various locations around London. For Orton and Kenneth Halliwell's flat, which was in Noel Road, Islington, N1, a house south of London in **Croydon** was substituted. Orton's boyhood in Leicester used nearby **Thornton Heath**, just north of Croydon. The exotic holiday is Morocco.

PRIMA DELLA RIVOLUZIONE (aka *Before the Revolution*)

(1964, dir: Bernardo Bertolucci)
Francesco Barilli, Adriana Asti, Morando Morandini.
● **PARMA, ITALY**

Bertolucci's second film is a loose adaptation of Stendhal's *Charterhouse of Parma*, with Francesco Barilli as a young bourgeois who carries on a passionate affair with his Milanese aunt, Asti, while tussling with the complexities of Euro-Communism. The movie was made in **Parma** itself (but don't go searching – there is no Char-

terhouse. It features only at the very end of the novel, when the hero retires to it, "in the woods by the Po, a couple of leagues from Sacca"), where Barilli and Asti hang around the main square, **Piazza Garibaldi**. The Medieval church, where Cristina Pariset is found at the beginning, is the 12th century **Baptistery** of Parma's **Cathedral of St Maria Assunta**, Piazza di Duomo. Barilli mooches around the aftermath of the Communist Summer Rally in the **Park Ducal**, the grounds of a Farnese palace over the Ponte Verdi from the town centre, while Asti and Barelli attend a performance of Verdi's *Macbeth*, at the **Teatro Regio** on the **via Garibaldi**.

PRIME OF MISS JEAN BRODIE, THE

(1969, dir: Ronald Neame)
Maggie Smith, Robert Stephens, Celia Johnson.
● **EDINBURGH; MIDDLESEX**

Miss Brodie's house: Admiral Terrace

Marcia Blaine: Edinburgh Academy, Henderson Row

Maggie Smith takes over from Vanessa Redgrave, who originally played Brodie on stage to great acclaim, in the film of Muriel Spark's thirties-set novel. Rod McKuen growls what must be the least appropriate title song ever. A backdrop of real Edinburgh locations (minus TV aerials) includes the old **Grassmarket**, the **Vennel**, **Greyfriars Kirkyard**, the **Scottish National Museum** and **Edinburgh Castle** itself. Miss Brodie's home is the Victorian house at **5 Admiral Terrace**, opposite Lothian Regional Council Office, southwest of the city centre. Teddy Lloyd's studio is the Mary Tudor house at **1 Candlemaker Row**, on the corner of Merchant Street opposite Greyfriars Kirkyard. Although interiors were built in the studio, Marcia Blaine School was the Donaldson School for Deaf and Dumb Children, now part of **Edinburgh Academy, Henderson Row**. Cramond, the estate to which Miss Brodie retreats at weekends, is **Barnbougle Castle**, just outside Edinburgh by the Firth of Forth. Part of the Dalmeny Estate, it's home to the Earl and Countess of Roseberry. The library of Marcia Blaine was in Grim's Dyke House – now the **Grim's Dyke House Hotel** – former home of WS Gilbert (who drowned in the lake here) at **Old Redding** in Middlesex (see *The Curse of the Crimson Altar* for details).

PRINCE OF DARKNESS

(1987, dir: John Carpenter)
Donald Pleasence, Victor Wong, Lisa Blount.
● **LOS ANGELES, CALIFORNIA**

There's a vat of something nasty in a deserted church vault, which might mean the end of, oh, you know, everything. The church is **St Godard's Church, 120 North San Pedro Street**, downtown LA, which is now an arts centre.

PRIVATE FUNCTION, A
(1984, dir: Malcolm Mowbray)
Michael Palin, Maggie Smith, Richard Griffiths.
● **YORKSHIRE**

The Parade: Albert Road, Barnoldswick

Alan Bennett's wartime comedy, with Maggie Smith turning into a suburban Lady Macbeth, urging her chiropodist husband to evade the rigours of rationing by killing an illegal pig, was made in the village of **Barnoldswick**, about ten miles west of Skipton, Yorkshire, in **Bradford**, and to the east of Skipton on **Ilkley Moor**.

Barnoldswick

The cinema, where Maggie Smith plays the old fashioned organ, is further south. It's the **Regal Cinema, 2 Boroma Way, Henley-on-Thames**, Oxfordshire.

PRIVATE LIFE OF SHERLOCK HOLMES, THE
(1970, dir: Billy Wilder)
Robert Stephens, Colin Blakely, Genevieve Page.
● **LONDON; SCOTLAND; YORKSHIRE**

Hugely underrated, affectionately romantic send-up of the Holmes myth, during which Holmes (Stephens) manages to chase the Loch Ness monster. The mysterious castle really is on Loch Ness. One of Scotland's largest, it's **Castle Urquhart**, a mile-and-a-half southeast of Drumnadrochit on the Loch's west shore, about 13 miles southwest of Inverness. It's open to the public.

The entrance to the Diogenes Club, where Holmes is summoned to meet his smarter older brother Mycroft (Christopher Lee), is **Somerset House**, in the **Strand** (see *Wilde* for details). The convincing-looking Baker Street is a vast and expensive set, 150 yards long, and built in perspective at Pinewood by veteran designer Alexander Trauner. It was subsequently much re-used. The railway scenes were filmed on the **Keighley and Worth Valley Railway** in Yorkshire.

PRIZZI'S HONOR
(1985, dir: John Huston)
Jack Nicholson, Kathleen Turner, Anjelica Huston.
● **NEW YORK CITY; LOS ANGELES, CALIFORNIA; LAS VEGAS, NEVADA**

Nicholson's place: the Breukelen Apartments

Nicholson and Turner are mob hitpersons, falling in love but hired to rub each other out in Huston's wonderful black comedy. The New York City neighbourhood is

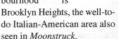

Don Corrado's: Pierrepoint Place, Brooklyn

Brooklyn Heights, the well-to-do Italian-American area also seen in *Moonstruck*.

The opening wedding scene, where Nicholson first lays eyes on Turner, is at the **Church of St Ann and the Holy Trinity**, now a performing arts centre, at the northwest corner of **Montague and Clinton Streets**. The reception, where Nicholson asks Turner to dance, is at **Grand Prospect Hall, 263 Prospect Avenue, Park Slope** in Brooklyn (see *The Cotton Club* for details).

The wedding: Church of St Ann and the Holy Trinity

Mob chief Don Corrado lives at nearby **2 and 3 Pierrepoint Place**, while Jack Nicholson's apartment, with its great view of the Brooklyn Bridge, is the **Breukelen Apartments**, over the road at **57 Montague Street**. He contemplates marriage or murder on the nearby **Brooklyn Heights Promenade**.

PROBLEM CHILD
(1990, dir: Dennis Dugan)
John Ritter, Amy Yasbeck, Jack Warden.
● **TEXAS**

Sub-John Hughes kid-from-hell movie pitched somewhere between *Home Alone* and *The Omen*, made in and around Dallas, Texas. Directed by nerdy comedy actor Dennis Dugan (*The Spaceman and King Arthur*), who plays one of the dads, and with a theme song by the Beach Boys. St Brutus, the orphanage Ritter and Yasbeck collect their bundle of joy from was the Lady of Victory Catholic Boarding School, since closed, **3300 Hemphill Street, Fort Worth**. Junior's penpal is serving time in the **Old City Jail, Main Street** at Harwood, where Lee Harvey Oswald was held after the shooting of JFK.

PRODUCERS, THE
(1967, dir: Mel Brooks)
Zero Mostel, Gene Wilder, Kenneth Mars.
● **NEW YORK CITY**

Brooks' best comedy, set and made in New York at the **Production Center Studios, 221 West 26th Street**. Max Bialystock's (Mostel) seduction of timid accountant Leo Bloom (Wilder) begins with a stolen afternoon in **Central Park**, where the pair ride the old **Carousel, 65th Street Transverse** at Center Drive. Bloom finds happiness boating on the lake, gets tempted atop the **Empire State Building** and finally succumbs as the fountains of

Bialystock and Bloom ride the old Carousel, 65th Street Transverse, Central Park

the **Lincoln Center**, Broadway between 62nd and 66th Streets, burst into life. *Springtime for Hitler* was staged in the Playhouse Theatre on West 48th Street, demolished in 1969. It stood opposite the **Cort Theatre, 138 West 48th Street**, the exterior of which is seen during the attempt to blow up the theatre.

PSYCHO

(1960, dir: Alfred Hitchcock)
Anthony Perkins, Janet Leigh, Martin Balsam.
● **LOS ANGELES, CALIFORNIA; PHOENIX, ARIZONA**

The Bates Motel house: Universal Studio, Hollywood

Filmed at the Revue Studios, the television branch of Universal Studios rented for Hitchcock by Paramount. Filming began on Stage 18-A (which is where the shower murder – arguably the most famous scene in movies – was filmed). Marion Crane's car journey was, of course, done with rear projection. The road shots used were filmed on **I-99** between Fresno and Bakersfield, California. A Second Unit filmed the opening shot of Phoenix, Arizona, where Marion supposedly lives. Notice the Christmas decorations? The shot was filmed at the beginning of December, but Christmas doesn't get mentioned and the weather seems surprisingly hot. To cover this glitch, the time and date are added over the shot ('Friday, December the Eleventh…'), but the season is never referred to again.

The film was shot on a tiny budget, using a TV crew, mostly on the studio lot. The swamp, where Norman disposes of Marion's car, was intended to be filmed on location at Grizzly Island near Fairfield, north of San Francisco, but budget constraints meant that Hitch finally used Falls Lake on the Universal-Revue backlot. The lake is named for the artificial falls built in the studio's early days. The fictitious town of Fairvale was simply the Universal lot's Main Street, and Fairvale Presbyterian Church

The garage: Century West BMW, Lankershim Boulevard

can be seen on Circle Drive here. Fairvale Courthouse was the studio's main executive office, which has since been demolished. And, of course, the

Bates house is now a main attraction on the Universal Studio Tour. The entrance is at **100 Universal City Plaza**, Universal City off the Ventura Freeway north of Hollywood (*C 818.508.9600*).

A couple of real locations were used, however: Marion is stopped by the cop on I-5, the Golden State Freeway at **Gorman**, north of LA. And the used car lot where Marion changes her vehicle is still in operation. It's now **Century West BMW, 4270 Lankershim Boulevard** at Whipple Street and Valley Spring, just north of the studio. In 1960 it was Harry Maher's Used Car Lot, well stocked with Edsels, Fairlanes and Mercury's – one of the sponsors of Hitch's TV show was Ford.

For *Psycho II*, many of the original props and set dressing were hunted down in the studio to furnish the Bates Motel in its original style.

In the Perkins directed *Psycho III*, Norman takes his date to the restaurant of the **Park Plaza Hotel, 607 South Park View Street**, downtown LA.

PULP FICTION

(1994, dir: Quentin Tarantino)
John Travolta, Samuel L Jackson, Bruce Willis.
● **LOS ANGELES, CALIFORNIA**

Tarantino's cool and flashy homage to pop culture was, naturally, filmed around LA. The diner held up by Pumpkin (Tim Roth) and Honey Bunny (Amanda

Butch sees Marcellus outside Foster's Freeze, Fletcher Drive

Plummer) was the Hawthorne Grill, 13763 Hawthorne Boulevard at 137th Street, Hawthorne, south of Los Angeles Airport. The grill stood empty for a while, and has now been demolished. Also vanished without a trace is the motel where Butch (Willis) hides out after unwisely winning the Battle of the Titans. It was the River Glen Motel, which stood at 2934 Riverside Drive off Los Feliz Boulevard, just to the west of the Golden State Freeway southeast of Griffith Park. The site for the match itself, though, is hanging on. Just. There are plans to redevelop the **Raymond Theatre, 129 North Raymond Avenue** in Pasadena, though the Friends of the Raymond Theatre is waging a valiant battle to save the historic venue, where concert scenes for *This Is Spinal Tap* were also filmed. Keep up with the latest developments at *www.raymondtheatre.com*. Butch escapes into an alleyway, which isn't the rear of the Raymond at all, but across the road in **Kendall Alley**. Thinking he's got away, Butch sees Marcellus Wallace (Ving Rhames) crossing **Fletcher Drive**, up toward

Honey-Bunny and Pumpkin: The now-demolished Hawthorne Grill, Hawthorne

Battle of the Giants: Raymond Theatre, Pasadena

Thinking he's got away, Butch sees Marcellus crossing Fletcher Drive

Glendale, alongside the Glendale Freeway (in a sly homage to Marion Crane glimpsing her boss in *Psycho*) outside **Foster's Freeze, 2760 Fletcher Drive** at Atwater Avenue.

The apartment block where Vince (Travolta) and Jules (Jackson) sample Big Kahuna burgers before wiping out the guys who crossed Marcellus, is on **Van Ness Avenue**, just north of Hollywood Boulevard, Hollywood. Marsellus' place is in **Beverly Hills**. The home of druggies Lance (Eric Stoltz) and Jody (Rosanna Arquette) is in **Echo Park**.

There is no Jack Rabbit Slim's, which was no more than a huge set built in the film company's warehouse in Culver City. In case you hadn't noticed, the raised dancefloor in the center of the diner is shaped as a tachometer and, as an homage to Howard Hawks' *Red Line 7000* and Elvis Presley's *Speedway*, the dining areas are six vintage convertibles. The exterior is a disused bowling alley. The idea, though it's a long way away, was supposedly based on either architect John Lautner's diners or Ed Debevic's fifties-themed diner, 134 North La Cienega Boulevard near Beverly Hills.

PUNCH-DRUNK LOVE

(2002, dir: Paul Thomas Anderson)
Adam Sandler, Emily Watson, Philip Seymour Hoffman.

● **LOS ANGELES, CALIFORNIA; HAWAII**

The toilet-plunger business where Sandler works: Eckhart Autobody, Canoga Avenue, Chatsworth

After the multifocus sweep of *Magnolia*, Anderson turned to this strangely quirky romance, which begins like a David Lynch movie, with a shocking car smash and the arrival of a mysterious harmonium, on **Canoga Avenue**, outside the toilet-plunger business where Barry Egan (Sandler) works. In reality, it's a bodyshop, **Eckhart Autobody, 10101 Canoga Avenue** at Mayall Street, **Chatsworth**, in the San Fernando Valley. Lovestruck Barry follows Lena Leonard (Watson) to Hawaii where they stay at the venerable 'Pink Palace of the Pacific', the **Royal Hawaiian Hotel, 2259 Kalakaua Avenue, Honolulu, Oahu** (℗ *808.923.7311, www.royal-hawaiian.com*).

The shady Utah operation of Dean Trumbell (Hoffman) is **Foothill Furniture & Mattresses, 390 West Foothill Boulevard** at Falcon Street, **Pomona**, east of LA.

PURPLE ROSE OF CAIRO, THE

(1985, dir: Woody Allen)
Mia Farrow, Jeff Daniels, Danny Aiello.
● **NEW JERSEY; NEW YORK**

One of Allen's best movies, packing a wealth of ideas into its 82 minutes. Farrow is Aiello's bullied wife, who escapes into the fantasy world of movies at every opportunity, until her screen idol pops out of the silver screen into real life. The small town Allen chose for the thirties setting is **Piermont**, off I-9W, on the west bank of the Hudson River, New York State. The Jewel theater exterior is no more than a façade, masking a parking lot on Piermont's Main Street, but you can find the interior of the Jewel in south Brooklyn, in Woody Allen's home district of Midwood, toward Coney Island. It was the Kent Movie Theater, now the **Kent Triplex, 1168 Coney Island Avenue** (℗ *718.338.3371*). The deserted amusement park, where Daniels takes Farrow, is **Bertrand Island, Mount Arlington**, north of Route 80 near Lake Hopatcong, northern New Jersey. The park closed in 1983 and the area is being redeveloped. The carousel is at **Prospect Park Zoo, Flatbush Avenue** in Brooklyn (℗ *718.330.1234, www.prospectparkzoo.com*). The whorehouse, where Daniels begins to discover the joy of sex, is a shelter for the homeless on **West 71st Street**, belonging to Grace and St Paul's Lutheran Church, used also in *Radio Days*.

Q

Q – THE WINGED SERPENT

(1982, dir: Larry Cohen)
Michael Moriarty, David Carradine, Candy Clark.
● NEW YORK CITY

The serpent's den: Chrysler Building

A neat, satirical little monster movie written and directed by low-budget expert Larry Cohen. Michael Moriarty is splendidly sleazy as the small-time crook who discovers the secret of a creature flying about chomping the heads off New Yorkers. The serpent of the title (which turns out to be an Aztec god, no less) has great taste in art deco architecture, choosing as its lair a cosy loft just beneath the gleaming spire of the **Chrysler Building, 405 Lexington Avenue** at 42nd Street.

QUADROPHENIA

(1979, dir: Franc Roddam)
Phil Daniels, Leslie Ash, Sting.
● LONDON; SUSSEX

The Mods' hangout: S&M Café, Islington

The Who's album is used as a framework for teen angst and a recreation of the early sixties running battles between the supersharp Mods and the leatherclad Rockers. The Who hailed originally from Shepherds Bush in west London, and this is where the London scenes are set. Jimmy rides his scooter along **Goldhawk Road**, and it's from Goldhawk Road tube station that his greaser pal is chased into **Shepherd's Bush Market** and beaten up.

Jimmy's home is **115 Wells House Road**, backing onto the railway line between Willesden Junction and Acton Central, near Old Oak Common. The Rockers attack Spi-

Jimmy's home: Wells House Road, Old Oak Common

der after his scooter breaks down outside the **Bramley Arms**, Notting Hill, a pub seen in movies such as *The Lavender Hill Mob* and *Sid and Nancy*. Opposite the Bramley is the scrapyard where Pete works. During the seventies, much of the area was squatted and, in a gesture inspired by Ealing's *Passport to*

The riot: East Street, Brighton

Bellboy: Grand Hotel, Brighton

Pimlico, seceded from the UK. When threatened with eviction, residents appealed to the UN. The *Quadrophenia* film crew needed to get 'passports' for the 'Kingdom of Frestonia' in order to film there. The Mods' London hangout is the **S&M Café, 4-6 Essex Road, Islington**, just north of Angel tube station. This art deco institution, dating from the twenties, is more famous under its former name, Alfredo's. It also appeared as Luigi's coffee bar in 1997's fifties-set music biz drama *Mojo*.

It's while using the, now closed, public baths of **Porchester Hall, Porchester Centre, Queensway**, that old pals Jimmy and Kevin meet up, only to realise that they've fallen on opposite sides of the Mod/Rocker divide when they come to get dressed. The complex also contains a Turkish bath which is still functioning.

Down in Brighton, the rival gangs congregate by the **Palace Pier**, in front of the now-closed Heart and Hand – then one of Brighton's most famous gay bars. The marquee of the cinema next door is advertising *Heaven Can Wait* – the Warren Beatty movie released in (whoops) 1978. East along the seafront, the Mods meet for breakfast at the **Waterfront Café** at the **Peter Pan Play Area, Madeira Drive**. Opposite the pier entrance you can see the exterior of the ballroom, where Jimmy upstages Ace by leaping from the balcony, which is now the **Brighton Sea Life Centre**. The **LA Fitness, Winchmore Hill Road**, at the end of Dennis

The alleyway: East Street, Brighton

The dance hall: Brighton Sea Life Centre

The café: King's Road at Ship Street

Parade opposite Southgate tube, used to be the old Royalty Ballroom, which stood in for the dance hall interior. Just across Old Steine is **East Street**, where the rioters get hemmed in by the law and Jimmy finally manages a quickie with Steph in the narrow alley by number 11, leading to Little East Street. The wrecked café is a little to the west, on the seafront at the corner of **King's Road** and **Ship Street**.

The hotel where Jimmy is ultimately disillusioned by the sight of Ace working as a bellboy is, of course, the **Grand Hotel, King's Road** (© *01273.224300*, *www.grandbrighton.co.uk*). The spectacular white cliffs, off which Jimmy ultimately takes a dive on Ace's jazzed-up scooter, are almost 20 miles east of Brighton, at **Beachy Head**, southwest of Eastbourne.

QUATERMASS XPERIMENT, THE (aka *The Creeping Unknown*)
(1955, dir: Val Guest)
Brian Donlevy, Jack Warner, Richard Wordsworth.
● **BERKSHIRE; LONDON**

The ambulance races to the crash: Bray High Street

Film of Nigel Kneale's excellent and scary fifties TV series, with astronaut Richard Wordsworth succumbing to an alien fungus. His rocket falls to earth in a field alongside Bray Studios near **Bray**, southeast of Maidenhead in Berkshire. The ambulances race through **Bray High Street** to the A308, past Bray Garage, which is still there, unchanged from its appearance in the film.

The chemist shop, where a slowly mutating Wordsworth steals drugs, is **Woods of Windsor, Queen Charlotte Street** (at 51 feet ten inches, a plaque officially records this as the shortest street in Britain), a perfumery still going strong, just off Windsor High Street. The Frankenstein-like riverside scene with the little girl was filmed at **Deptford Creek**, south London.

But it's back to Windsor for the discovery of the slime trail glooping 30 feet up a sheer wall, which was filmed in the narrow alleyway of **Goswell Hill**, off Peascod Street. There's not a frame of the real Westminster Abbey in the climax of the movie, with the monster

The mutating astronaut steals drugs: Woods of Windsor, Queen Charlotte Street

holed up in the abbey's scaffolding. After permission to film at the real location was, not surprisingly, refused, sections of the interior and exterior were recreated in the studio.

QUATERMASS II (aka *Enemy From Space*)
(1957, dir: Val Guest)
Brian Donlevy, John Longden, William Franklyn.
● **ESSEX; HERTFORDSHIRE.**

The second adaptation of a Nigel Kneale TV series is a genuinely frightening low-budget sci-fi. A hush-hush military research station, supposedly manufacturing artificial food, houses giant blobs from space.

The about-to-be-developed landscape is the under-construction **Hemel Hempstead** new town in Hertfordshire. The military installation itself is Shell's giant Haven Refinery at **Canvey Island**, near to Southend-on-Sea in Essex.

QUATRE CENTS COUPS, LES (aka *The Four Hundred Blows*)
(1959, dir: François Truffaut)
Jean-Pierre Léaud, Patrick Auffay, Claire Maurier.
● **PARIS, FRANCE**

Truffaut's first feature film, introducing the character of Antoine Doinel as an adolescent, is one of the key movies of the French Nouvelle Vague movement, which

Insulting the priest: Sacre Coeur, Montmartre

moved film-making out of the studio and onto the streets of Paris. Doinel's house is on **rue Marcadet**, running from Guy Moquet metro to Marcadet Poissonniers metro in the 16th Arrondissement. The kids insult a priest on the steps of **Sacre Coeur** in Montmartre.

QUIET MAN, THE
(1952, dir: John Ford)
John Wayne, Maureen O'Hara, Barry Fitzgerald.
● **IRELAND**

Ex-boxer Wayne returns to the family roots to claim a wife in this colourful Irish romp, unlikely to appeal to feminists. Hard-man Ford, proud of his Irish ancestry, actually made the movie on location in Ireland around the village of **Cong**, between Lough Mask and Lough Corrib, Connemara; in the **Maam Valley**; and in the grounds of **Ashford Castle**. The railway scene is **Ballyglunin**, on the line between Sligo and Limerick.

The Quiet Man Hostel on Abbey Street, in Cong, shows the movie every night, and also has a *Quiet Man* locations tour.

QUIZ SHOW
(1994, dir: Robert Redford)
Ralph Fiennes, John Turturro, Paul Scofield.
● **NEW YORK CITY; NEW YORK**

The TV studio: NBC Building, Rockefeller Plaza

Redford's recreation of the famous fifties scandal, when TV execs ensured that handsome WASP Charles Van Doren triumphed on top-rating quiz show *Twenty-One* over Jewish Herbie Stempel. *Twenty-One* was recorded at the art deco **NBC Building, Rockefeller Plaza**, though the interiors of the NBC Studios of 1958 were recreated inside the **Red Zone, 440 West 45th Street**, a huge Manhattan disco (previously used for scenes for *The Godfather Part III*).

Herbie Stempel's blue-collar neighbourhood is Astoria, Queens, while the Van Doren patrician family home in Cornwall, Connecticut is actually in Ossining, New York State. Columbia University, itself a familiar film location for such movies as *Ghostbusters*, is here played by **Fordham University**, an 85-acre campus on **Webster Avenue** in the Bronx. As the scandal emerges, the Congressional hearings are held in the **New York Historical Society, 170 Central Park West** at 77th Street. The NBC Executive Offices are **Murdoch Hall**, a thirties art deco building over the Hudson River in Jersey City. Other locations include the lobby of the **Roosevelt Hotel, Madison Avenue** at East 45th Street, midtown New York (see *The French Connection* for details).

R

RABID

(1977, dir: David Cronenberg)
Marilyn Chambers, Frank Moore, Joe Silver.
● QUÉBEC, CANADA

Cronenberg's early visceral horror has Rose (Chambers, star of the hardcore *Behind the Green Door*) developing a bloodsucking growth in her armpit after undergoing experimental surgery. Like his earlier *Shivers*, it's shot around Montreal, where Rose's first victim discharges himself from **Notre Dame Hospital, 1560 Sherbrooke Street East, Montreal**, and begins to spread the rabies-like infection. The shopping mall, where the cop guns down a rabid attacker and also – whoops! – kills Santa Claus, is the **Cavendish Mall, 5800 Boulevard Cavendish** at Côte St Luc. Rose hides out with her friend in the highrise apartment block **2121 St-Mathieu** at Avenue Lincoln.

RADIO DAYS

(1987, dir: Woody Allen)
Woody Allen, Mia Farrow, Seth Green.
● NEW YORK CITY; NEW JERSEY

Little Joe's neighbourhood: Beach 115th Street, Rockaway Park

Allen usually borrows from Ingmar Bergman, but occasionally he takes Fellini as his model. If *Stardust Memories* is his *8 1/2*, then *Radio Days*, in its fragmentary, evocative nostalgia, is a New York *Amarcord*. With his usual uncanny eye for period locations, Woody Allen conjures up both the working class neighbourhood of Queens and the stylish Manhattan of the forties. The neighbourhood of Little Joe (Green, as the young Allen) is Rockaway, the spit of land on the Atlantic coast of south Queens. His house is **180 Beach 115th Street** between Ocean Promenade – the Boardwalk – and **Rockaway Beach Boulevard**, the neighbourhood shopping centre, from the roof of which the schoolkids watch their teacher's naked dance. The radio repair shop, on the way back from which Lit-

Little Joe's childhood home, and the house of his 'Communist' neighbours: Beach 115th Street, Rockaway Park

tle Joe meets his father working as a cab driver, is a few blocks east on **Beach 97th Street**. Rock-away's Playland, the amusement park Joe passes on the way to school

Watching the naked teacher: Rockaway Beach Boulevard at Beach 115th Street

while coveting the Masked Avenger Secret Compartment Ring, stood at 185 Beach 97th Street, until it was torn down in 1987, shortly after *Radio Days* was filmed. Built as Thompson's Amusement Park in 1938, its huge Atom Smasher rollercoaster, seen in the movie, was the one used in the 1952 spectacular, *This Is Cinerama*.

Joe and his friends hang out at **Breezy Point**, on the north shore at the far west end of the Rockaway peninsula, and at **Coney Island Fishing Pier**, on the Boardwalk at 21st Street. Joe's school, where the anatomically explicit snowman is built, is **PS70, 30-45 42nd Street** in Manhattan, and the Hebrew class, where Joe steals the money meant for the Jewish National Fund, is the **Synagogue Congregation Mogen Abraham** on the Lower East Side.

Aunt Bea (Diane Wiest) and her beau Chester take young Joe to see *The Philadelphia Story* at **Radio City Music Hall, 1260 Sixth Avenue** (www.radiocity.com), where he's understandably overwhelmed by the spectacular gold-leaf foyer – it's also where Daddy Warbucks takes Annie to see *Camille* in the film of the stage musical. The fast food establishment they visit was Horn and Hardart, then one of the few remaining automats in the city, which stood at 200 East 42nd Street. The site has since been redeveloped. Still going strong, though, is **Macy's, 34th Street** between Seventh Avenue and Broadway, where Joe gets a chemistry set with Aunt Bea's winnings from the radio quiz. The family bumps into the snotty radio whizz-kid at **Prospect Park Zoo, Flatbush Avenue** in Prospect Park, Brooklyn (© *718.399.7399*).

On the other side of the tracks, the nightclub, frequented by Manhattan sophisticates Roger and Irene, where Sally (Farrow) works as a cigarette girl, is the King Cole Dining Room of the **St Regis-Sheraton Hotel, Fifth Avenue** at East 55th Street (see *The Godfather* for details). In fact, women weren't allowed into the King Cole Room until 1950 – and then only after 4pm. Roger and Irene's chic chrome-and-glass townhouse was one of the city's most famous gay discos, the Paradise Garage, which stood at **84 King Street**. Pumping out garage music from the late seventies through the eighties, its doors finally

Kids on the rooftop: Rockaway Beach Boulevard at Beach 115th Street

Little Joe gets a chemistry set: Macy's art deco entrance, 34th Street

Listening to the radio: Nam Wah Tea Parlor, Doyers Street, Chinatown

closed in 1987, though the building still remains.

Biff Baxter (Jeff Daniels) broadcasts his show from the **RCA Building, 50th Street** between Fifth and Sixth Avenues, while Sally is fired from a studio in the **Metropolitan Life's North Building, Madison Avenue** between 24th and 25th Streets, after failing to give a laxative commercial "inner life". Before finding fame, she hangs around outside famed showbiz restaurant **Sardi's, 234 West 44th Street** at Broadway (seen also in *King of Comedy* and black comedy *No Way To Treat a Lady*).

Among the bars where people gather to follow the tragedy of the little girl trapped down a well is the **Nam Wah Tea Parlor, 13 Doyers Street** at Pell Street, New York's oldest dim sum parlor, situated on an oddly angled street in Chinatown, featured also in *King of New York*. The malt shop counter, where the girls swoon to the radio crooner, is **Brummer's Confectionary** (sic), **Grand Street**, in Jersey City, New Jersey.

Among other New York landmarks used are the **Brill Building, 1619 Broadway** (see *The Sweet Smell of Success* for details), and the **New Yorker Hotel, 481 Eighth Avenue** (© 212.971.0101). The ballroom also appeared, albeit differently decorated, in *Bullets Over Broadway*. Studio sets were built at the Kaufman-Astoria Studios, 34-12 36th Street in Queens.

RAGING BULL
(1980, dir: Martin Scorsese)
Robert De Niro, Cathy Moriarty, Joe Pesci.
● NEW YORK CITY; NEW YORK ; LOS ANGELES, CALIFORNIA

The outdoor pool: Carmine Street Public Pools, Greenwich Village

Four years after *Rocky* scooped the Oscars for Best Picture and Best Director, Scorsese brought out the best boxing movie ever, a biopic of self-destructive bruiser Jake LaMotta. Ironically, it was the success of *Rocky* which gave the long-gestating project the go-ahead.

Most of the film was shot in New York, with just a little Los Angeles. The bravura fight sequences were shot over several weeks in the controlled environment of the

MGM studio, but longshots and crowd scenes (including Scorsese's trademark Steadicam shot) are the **Grand Olympic Auditorium, 1801 South Grand Avenue** at Olympic Boulevard (© 213.749.5171, *www.grandoly.com*), downtown LA. Built for the 1932 Olympics, it was the site of the climactic fights in – yes – *Rocky I, II* and *III* as well as the wrestling matches of films as diverse as *Ed Wood* and *Man On the Moon*. Also in LA is the Florida home of the older LaMotta (De Niro), which was a house in **San Pedro**, Los Angeles Harbor west of Long Beach, kitted out with a couple of palm trees.

In New York, LaMotta's neighbourhood is **Pelham Parkway** in the Bronx, where apartment interiors were shot, although the exterior street scenes are Manhattan's Hell's Kitchen, around West 53rd and 54th Streets. LaMotta works spars with his brother Joey (Pesci) at the famous Gleason's Gym, which used to be at 149th Street at Third Avenue in the Bronx, until 1974, when it moved to 83 Front Street, Brooklyn. It's still used by Hollywood for training: more recently Colin Farrell (for *The Recruit*) and Hilary Swank (for *Million Dollar Baby*) buffed up here. The movie, though, uses the Gramercy Gym, demolished in 1993, which stood at **116 East 14th Street**.

The Chester Palace dance, where LaMotta first sees wife-to-be Vickie (Moriarty), is **Webster Hall, 125 East 11th Street** in Greenwich Village (*www.webster-hall.com*). A music venue since the turn of the century, the hall was the site of the drag competition which opens *To Wong Foo, Thanks For Everything! Julie Newmar*. It's at the old Copacabana Nightclub that LaMotta's obsessive jealousy begins to emerge. The Copa (now closed), which stood at **10 East 60th Street** at Fifth Avenue, was revisited by Scorsese for another famous steadicam shot in *Goodfellas*. LaMotta meets Vickie at the open-air pool of the **Carmine Street Recreation Center, Seventh Avenue South** at Clarkson Street in Greenwich Village. Finding a kind of redemption, LaMotta re-invents himself as a nightclub entertainer, rehearsing Brando's "I coulda been a contender" speech from *On the Waterfont* in the old Barbizon Plaza Theatre, in the Barbizon Plaza Hotel, now transformed into the **Trump Parc, 106 Central Park South**.

RAIDERS OF THE LOST ARK
(1981, dir: Steven Spielberg)
Harrison Ford, Karen Allen, Paul Freeman.
● HAWAII; TUNISIA; FRANCE; CALIFORNIA

The opening South American scenes of Spielberg's glorified Saturday morning feature were actually filmed on the garden isle of **Kauai** in Hawaii, to which the director would return for *Jurassic Park*. The location is the **Huleia River**, leading to Fern Grotto on the east coast, north of Lihue.

The classroom, where Indie (Ford) teaches archaeology, is **Rickmansworth Masonic School, Chorleywood Road** (used again in *Indiana Jones and the Last Crusade*). Studio sets, including the Raven Bar, the Peruvian temple and the Well of Souls, were built at Elstree in Hertfordshire. The German sub (it's the submarine from *Das*

Boot) was shot at a genuine ex-German base at **La Rochelle**, France.

1930s Cairo is the holy city of **Kairouan**, in northern Tunisia, about 35 miles west of Sousse. The Tanis archaeological dig uses the deserts of Tunisia – the vast dry salt lake of **Chott El Jerid** and, east toward the Algerian border, the oasis towns of **Nefta** and **Tozeur**. The film shares locations with *Star Wars*, including **Sidi Bouhel**, now known as Star Wars Canyon, east of Tozeur on the edge of the Chott. The ending was shot on the steps of one of the government buildings in downtown San Francisco.

RAILWAY CHILDREN, THE

The paperchase: Mytholmes Tunnel

(1970, dir: Lionel Jeffries)
Jenny Agutter, Bernard Cribbins, Dinah Sheridan.
● **YORKSHIRE**

Fine filming of E Nesbit's famous book about three Edwardian children and their mother, who have to move to Yorkshire when daddy is wrongly imprisoned. Bradford Recreation Division helpfully produces a guide to *The Railway Children* walk, which covers the main locations: info from the Countryside Warden Service, Third Floor, Provincial House,

The railway station: Oakworth, Keighley and Worth Valley Railway

Bradford BD11 1NP (© *01274.752666 or 01535.423329*).

The railway line used for filming is the **Keighley and Worth Valley Railway**, mainly on the stretch between Keighley and Oxenhope, about five miles to the south. Oakworth Station is, indeed, **Oakworth**, about halfway between the two towns. The house of station-master Perks (Cribbins) is just over the level crossing from the station.

The children's home, Three Chimneys, can be found a couple of miles to the south of Oakworth in the village of **Oxenhope**. It's **Bent's Farm**, a little to the north of Oxenhope Station.

The village seen in the film is **Haworth**, halfway between Oakworth and Oxenhope, famous as home to the Bron-

Perks' house: Oakworth

Three Chimneys: Bent's Farm, Oxenhope

të sisters. You can see the shops, where the children collect presents for Perks' birthday, on **Main Street**, **Lodge Street** (the ironmonger's where the children get a shovel) and

The doctor's house: Brontë Parsonage, Haworth

Church Lane (where the **Tweed Room** shop, with its little flight of stone steps, stood in for the Post Office and General Store). The Doctor's house is in fact the **Brontë Parsonage** itself, south of the village, where Emily, Charlotte and Anne wrote *Wuthering Heights*, *Jane Eyre* and *The Tenant of Wildfell Hall* respectively (© *01535.642323*, *www.bronte.info; open daily, admission charge*). You'll find the tunnel, where schoolboy Jim injures his leg during the paperchase, north of Haworth toward Oakworth. It's the **Mytholmes Tunnel**, **Mytholmes Lane**, while a few yards south on the line is the **Metal Bridge** seen in the 'goodbye' shot.

The Post Office: Tweed Room, Haworth

RAIN MAN

(1988, dir: Barry Levinson)
Dustin Hoffman, Tom Cruise, Valeria Golino.
● **OHIO; KENTUCKY; INDIANA; OKLAHOMA; NEVADA; CALIFORNIA**

On hearing of his father's death, hard-hearted businessman Charlie Babbitt (Cruise) travels from LA, where his business operates out of the docks of **San Pedro**, to Cincinnati. The Oscar-grabbing movie travelled all over the US, but was based in Cincinnati for four weeks, and used Indiana and Kentucky locations.

Charlie's childhood home is the Tudor-style mansion at **2 Beech Crest Lane**, off Madison Road in Cincinnati's East Walnut Hills district, on the Ohio River's northern shore, northeast of downtown. The Cincinnati Trust, where Charlie charms the desk clerk to divulge the whereabouts of the $3 million trust fund, is the lobby of the **Dixie Terminal, 120 East Fourth Street** at Walnut Street, downtown Cincinatti.

If Wallbrook, the home where he finds brother Raymond (Hoffman), looks a bit religiose, with statues of the virgin in the walls, that's because it's **St Anne's Convent, 1000 Saint Anne Drive, Melbourne**, just to the southeast of Cincinnati over the Ohio River on Route 8, Kentucky. Built in 1919 by architect Howard McClorey, it now houses a Montessori school. The bridge Charlie and Raymond cross leaving town is the **John A Roebling Suspension Bridge**, a prototype for the designer's later Brooklyn Bridge in New York (you can see it from the window of the Dixie Terminal building).

It's on to **Newport**, Kentucky, for the first night away

"You... you're the Rain Man": Big 8$ Motel, El Reno

Skill with cards: Caesar's Palace, Las Vegas

from Wallbrook, spent at the **Vernon Manor Hotel, 400 Oak Street** (℗ *513.281.3300, www.vernon-manor.com*), a 1924 landmark in the historic uptown district, loosely modelled on much-used movie location Hatfield House, Hertfordshire, in the UK. Actually, Charlie had already been to Newport. His father's funeral was filmed at **Evergreen Cemetery, 25 Alexandria Pike, Southgate,** south of Newport.

And also in Newport is the café where Raymond reveals his numerical skills by remembering the waitress's phone number and counting scattered toothpicks. It's **Pompilio's Bar and Restaurant, 600 Washington Avenue** (℗ *859.581.3065*). A southern Italian restaurant, built in 1933, Pompilio's was granted one of the US's first post-Prohibition liquor licences.

It's back to Ohio, to **Greater Cincinnati International Airport**, where Raymond quotes a few useful statistics, decides that road travel is preferable and the two take the highway, I-275, which happens to be the ring road around Cincinnati.

The film's crew was based in Oklahoma City for the cross-States journey. The motel in Amarillo, Texas, where Charlie realises that Raymond was his imaginary friend, the 'Rain Man', is the **Big 8$ Motel, 1705 East 66th Highway, El Reno**, on I-40 about 15 miles west of Oklahoma City. The sign, 'Amarillo's Finest', was added for the movie, and, much to the confusion of passing motorists, it's been retained as a feature of the motel. The brothers' room was 117. The gas station, where they stop to make a phone call, is a disused, and now once again dilapidated, stop at **Cogar**, about ten miles south of El Reno over the South Canadian River. 20 miles west of El Reno, south of I-40, is **Hinton**, where Raymond gets to watch Judge Wapner on the farmhouse TV. Way up about 20 miles north of Oklahoma City, on I-35, is the town of **Guthrie**, where Charlie takes Raymond to see the doctor at the Guthrie Clinic, on the corner of **Oklahoma Street** and **Division Street**.

More road filming took place in south Nevada, *en route* to Las Vegas. Raymond demonstrates his skill with cards and Charlie teaches him to dance in **Caesar's Palace, 3570 Las Vegas Boulevard South** (℗ *702.731.7110, www.caesars.com/caesars/lasvegas*). The complex has been enlarged since filming.

Susanna (Golino) is dropped off at her apartment, **Ocean View Apartments, 1435 South Beacon Street** in San Pedro, south LA, and Charlie, reborn as a caring brother, turns

The gas station: Cogar

down a $250,000 offer from Dr Bruner poolside in the **Westin Bonaventure Hotel, 404 South Figueroa Street**, downtown LA (see *In the Line of Fire* for details).

He takes Raymond for pancakes at the Pink Cadillac Cafe (you can't do the same – the pancake house is now **Blue Bamboo, 359 North La Cienega Boulevard** [℗ *310.854.0622*], serving up Asian fusion fare), before battling it out with the medical profession (a cameo from director Levinson) for custody of Raymond at the **Wattles Mansion, 1824 North Curson Avenue** on the south end of Runyon Canyon Park in Hollywood, a 1905 house and gardens built as the winter residence of an Omaha businessman. It's now the HQ of Hollywood Heritage and, though you can't visit, you can hire it for your party, wedding – or as a film location (*www.hollywoodheritage.org*). Charlie finally sees Raymond off back to Wallbrook at **Santa Ana Train Station, 2800 North Main Street, Santa Ana,** southeast of LA.

RAINING STONES

(1993, dir: Ken Loach)
Bruce Jones, Julie Brown, Ricky Tomlinson.
● MANCHESTER

Loach's brand of hyper-realism brought to Jim Allen's story of an unemployed van driver trying to raise the loot for his daughter's confirmation dress. Filmed in **Middleton** near Manchester, on the **Langley Estate**, which writer Allen had helped to build. Jones attempts to sell bits of rustled sheep in the, since demolished, Falcon pub on the estate.

RAINMAKER, THE

(1997, dir: Francis Ford Coppola)
Matt Damon, Danny DeVito, Jon Voight.
● TENNESSEE; CALIFORNIA

Another Grisham legal thriller, with greenhorn Damon fighting the system to get a dying worker compensation from a big, bad company. The movie was shot in **Memphis**, Tennessee, and **San Francisco**.

RAINTREE COUNTY

(1957, dir: Edward Dmytryk)
Elizabeth Taylor, Montgomery Clift, Lee Marvin.
● MISSISSIPPI; KENTUCKY; TENNESSEE

This attempt to out-wind *Gone With the Wind* was hampered by all kinds of problems, not the least of which was the traumatic car smash that ripped up Clift's face. Most of the studio interiors were filmed before the crash, the exteriors afterwards.

Locations were found in **Natchez**, on highway 61, Mississippi; in **Danville**, highway 127, 30 miles south of Lexington, central Kentucky; and **Paducah**, on I-24, McCracken County in far west Kentucky on the Illinois border. The ruined mansion is **Windsor**, near **Port Gibson**, Mississippi. Only 23 columns remain of this vast antebellum mansion, which was destroyed by fire in 1890.

The climax is at **Reelfoot Lake**, Tennessee, a weirdly beautiful place, scattered with cypress trees. The 13,000-acre lake was formed when an earthquake caused the Mississippi to overflow and flood a sunken forest. It's just west of Union City on the Missouri-Kentucky borders. Reelfoot Lake State Resort Park is a sanctuary for the rare American Bald Eagle, and there are eagle spotting tours.

RAISING ARIZONA
(1987, dir: Joel Coen)
Nicolas Cage, Holly Hunter, John Goodman.
● ARIZONA

The funniest, most inventive film of the year, made in, yes, Arizona, in Phoenix and its suburb Scottsdale. The supermarket, where Cage attempts to steal a pack of diapers and sets in motion the great car (and dog) chase, is in **Tempe**, in a long flat stretch of shopping centres outside Phoenix. Filming also took place at one of the **Denny's** restaurants in Scottsdale. The bank robbed by Goodman and William Forsythe is actually a restaurant, the **Reata Pass Steakhouse, 27500 North Alma School Parkway**, south from East Dynamite Boulevard, Scottsdale (© 480.585.7277). The prison is the **Squaw Peak Water Treatment Plant, 20th Street**, Phoenix. Unpainted Arizona is the **Home Depot, 12434 North Cave Creek Road, Cave Creek**, a northern suburb of Phoenix. The film's interiors used the historic 1925 **Jokake Inn**, now incorporated into the lavish **Phoenician Resort, 6000 East Camelback Road**, at the foot of Camelback Mountain, and Phoenix's **Old City Hall, 17th Street** at Second Avenue.

RAMBO: FIRST BLOOD PART II
(1985, dir: George Pan Cosmatos)
Sylvester Stallone, Richard Crenna, Steven Berkoff.
● MEXICO

Rambo returns with bigger guns in this first sequel, shot around Acapulco, Mexico, where the compound, which had to serve as living accommodation for the crew, was built in the nearby jungle. CIA HQ is the **Acapulco Convention Centre, Costera Miguel Alemán**. Rambo kits himself out with knife and bow in the terrible privations of a room in the **Acapulco Plaza Hotel, Costera Miguel Alemán 123** (© 001.5.9050).

RAN
(1985, dir: Akira Kurosawa)
Tatsuya Nakadai, Satoshi Terao, Jinpachi Nezu.
● JAPAN

Kurosawa's epic version of Shakespeare's King Lear was made at various historic locations around Japan, including **Aso National Mountain Park** on the most westerly of Japan's four main islands, Kyushu, and **Kumamoto Castle**, Kumamoto, to the southwest of Aso National Park. The huge castle was entirely rebuilt in 1960, with a reinforced concrete frame, as was another of the film's

locations, **Nagoya Castle**, one of Japan's finest, which had been destroyed by allied bombing in 1945. The castle is one-and-a-half miles northeast of Nagoya, on the south coast of Honshu, about 213 miles west of Tokyo, and **Gotemba**, again on Honshu, at the foot of Mount Fuji, is also seen. **Himeji Castle**, Himeji, west of Osaka (see You Only Live Twice for details), **Kokonoe** and **Shonai** are also featured.

RAY
(2005, dir: Taylor Hackford)
Jamie Foxx, Kerry Washington, Regina King.
● LOUISIANA; LOS ANGELES, CALIFORNIA

Hackford's apparently globetrotting biopic (Seattle, New York, Chicago, Paris, Rome…) was made almost entirely around the production's base of **New Orleans**, thanks to the ingenious use of stock newsreel footage, and the shots of 1950s Los Angeles, borrowed from Carl Franklin's Devil in a Blue Dress.

About 50 miles southwest of the Big Easy is **Thibodaux**, and two miles south of the town you find the **Laurel Valley Village Museum, 595 Highway 308** (© 985.446.8111), see Angel Heart for details. This perfectly preserved sugar plantation, dating from 1832, became Jellyroll, Florida, where the young Ray Charles (Foxx) is traumatised (before losing his sight) by the death of his younger brother.

Both 1940s Seattle, where Charles first meets Quincy Jones, and 1950s Atlanta, are downtown **Hammond**, off I-55, about 50 miles to the northwest of New Orleans.

Hitting the road with the Lowell Fulson Band, Charles plays the round of black nightclubs which came to be dubbed the 'Chitlin Circuit', including the **Half Moon Lounge, 1125 St Mary Street** (© 504.522.0599) – although the interior seen is that of New Orleans' famed **Maple Leaf Bar, 8316 Oak Street** (© 504.866.9359), another location used in Angel Heart; the **Sandpiper Lounge**; and El Matador (owned by the director's son, and now closed). It's in the the eccentric **Saturn Bar, 3067 St Claude Avenue, Bywater** (© 504.949.7532), that Charles attacks his road manager and finally leaves Fulson. The Saturn, a reminder of the days when Saturn V rockets were built at the Lockheed-Michoud facility in New Orleans East, was previously featured in The Pelican Brief.

Houston, Texas, where Charles meets wife-to-be Della Bea (Washington), is the picturesque town of **Algiers**, across the Mississippi from New Orleans' French Quarter. Here you can find the 1930s brick-and-tile **Gulf Gas Station, 446 Pelican Avenue** (which closed in 1990) and **Algiers Point Fire Department, Opelousas Avenue**, past which the couple stroll.

The stylish ABC record office of Sam Clark was found within the the Masons' Scottish Rite Temple, now the **University of New Orleans Downtown Theater, 619 Carondelet Street**. As his backing singer, and mistress, Margie (King) leaves him, Charles performs 'Hit The Road, Jack' in the **Blue Room** of the elegant **Fairmont New Orleans Hotel, 123 Baronne Street** (© 504.529.7111, www.fairmont.com/neworleans). Charles turns and gets back on the bus rather than play to a seg-regated audience in Augusta, Georgia. The demonstrating crowd is actually outside New Orleans' **Morris Municipal Auditorium, 1201 St Peters Avenue**.

As his fame increases, Charles plays bigger venues: Indianapolis, where he performs 'Unchain My Heart' (which was the original title of the film) is the **Orpheum Theater, 129 University Place** (© *504.524.3285, www.orpheumneworleans.com*) in the Central Business District; and he silences a restless audience with 'I Can't Stop Loving You' at the **Saenger Theatre, 143 North Rampart Street** (© *504.525.1052, www.saenger-theatre.com*).

New Orleans' **Louis Armstrong International Airport** stands in for Boston as Charles' career hits low with a drug bust, but he's redeemed as the **Louisiana State Legislature** in the **State Capitol, 900 North Third Street, Baton Rouge**, becomes Georgia State Capital for the singer's induction as Georgia's Favorite Son.

A couple of genuine Los Angeles locations include Ray's one-time home on **Hepburn Avenue, Leimert Park**, near the Coliseum, and his former mansion in **View Park**, Baldwin Hills, northeast of Los Angeles Airport, where the production managed to film just before new owners carried out renovations.

REALITY BITES

(1994, dir: Ben Stiller)
Winona Ryder, Ethan Hawke, Ben Stiller.
● **TEXAS; LOS ANGELES, CALIFORNIA**

Ryder has to choose between yuppie Stiller and slacker Hawke in Stiller's directorial début, set in Houston, Texas. After being fired from her job at the TV studio, Ryder

Ethan Hawke comforts Winona Ryder: Tranquillity Park, Houston

is comforted by Hawke alongside the cylindrical water features of **Tranquillity Park**, Houston. The coffee shop, where Ryder and Janeane Garofalo have a heart to heart, though, is in LA: it's **Johnie's Broiler, 7447 Firestone Boulevard, Downey**, seen also in Tina Turner biopic *What's Love Got to Do With It?* and Michael Mann's *Heat*.

REBECCA

(1940, dir: Alfred Hitchcock)
Laurence Olivier, Joan Fontaine, Judith Anderson.
● **CALIFORNIA**

Hitchcock's first US film, adapted from Daphne du Maurier's novel and set in Monte Carlo and Cornwall, but made entirely in California. Manderley, of course, never existed. The house it was supposedly based on is Menabilly, on the east side of St Austell Bay, close to Fowey, Cornwall. The set for Hitchcock's gothic mansion was built at the old Selznick Studios, on the site of the *Gone With the Wind* sets. The studio still stands, unchanged, but now called **Laird International Studios**, at **9336**

West Washington Boulevard, Culver City. The estate grounds were in the **Del Monte** area of California, while beach exteriors used **Catalina Island**, off the

The Cornish coast: Point Lobos State Reserve

coast of LA. The rugged cliffs, where Fontaine first meets Olivier, were filmed, using stand-ins, by a second unit at **Point Lobos State Reserve**, three miles south of Carmel. The delicate ecology of the area was endangered when the crew entered padlocked areas, bringing imported vines and ivy into contact with the native cypress trees. With poetic justice, most ended up hospitalised with poison ivy. You can visit the wildly beautiful state park, but the ground cover is still a mat of the very nasty weed. To remove it would upset the environmental balance, so warning notices are posted throughout.

REBEL WITHOUT A CAUSE

(1955, dir: Nicholas Ray)
James Dean, Natalie Wood, Sal Mineo.
● **LOS ANGELES, CALIFORNIA**

Dawson High, the new school of the original angst-ridden teen Jim Stark (Dean), at University and 10th is actually **Santa Monica High School, 601 Pico Boulevard** at

Dawson High: Santa Monica High School, Pico Boulevard

4th Street, Santa Monica, though some interiors were shot at **John Marshall High School, 3939 Tracy Street**, Los Feliz. Marshall High, apart from being Leonardo DiCaprio's old school, has featured in lots of movies, including *Buffy the Vampire Slayer*, *Like Father, Like Son* and fifties teen drama *The Young Stranger*.

The mansion, in which Dean, Mineo and Wood play house, was also featured in *Sunset Blvd.*, and it stood at 641 Irving Boulevard at Wilshire Boulevard. Two years after *Rebel* was filmed, it was demolished. The planetarium visited by the schoolkids, and the site of the final shootout, is the **Griffith Observatory, 2800 East Observatory Road** (© *323.664.1181, www.griffithobs.org*), in Griffith Park. The film put the observatory firmly on the map, and there's now a bust of Dean in the grounds (coincidentally, James Dean's first professional acting job was a Coca Cola commercial filmed in Griffith Park). Other films featuring the observatory

"I've got the bullets...": Griffith Observatory, Griffith Park

include *Bowfinger*, *Charlie's Angels: Full Throttle*, *Dragnet* (1987), *The Rocketeer* and *The Terminator*. It even became an LA nightclub in *Earth Girls Are Easy*.

RECRUIT, THE

(2003, dir: Roger Donaldson)
Al Pacino, Colin Farrell, Bridget Moynahan.
● **ONTARIO, CANADA; WASHINGTON DC**

After *Memento* and *The Usual Suspects*, any film using the tag-line "Nothing is what it seems" has a lot to live up to, and if Donaldson's CIA thriller doesn't deliver brain-aching convolutions, it's kept afloat by the onscreen pairing of old guard Pacino and young pretender Farrell.

Originally called The Farm (after the secret CIA training facility), the film is set in Boston and Washington DC but made (apart from a little scene setting in the US capital) around **Toronto**, Ontario.

The Cambridge, Massachusets student lodging of techhead Jim Clayton (Farrell) is the **Alpha Delta Phi Fraternity House** of the University of Toronto at **94 Prince Arthur Avenue**. Marketing a computer-age MacGuffin, Clayton is approached by devious CIA recruiter Walter Burke (Pacino) as he tends bar in Toronto's studenty **Lava Lounge, 507 College Street West** at Palmerston in Queen's Park (© *416.966.5282*). After a furious workout, Clayton meets up with Burke outside **Epic Fitness, 9 St Joseph Street** at Yonge Street (© *416.960.1705*), downtown Toronto, and takes the bait.

He's soon headed for CIA HQ in Langley, Virginia, the interior of which was carefully recreated in the studio, and the gates constructed on the far east parking lot of **Sunnybrook Park**, northeast of Toronto. The grounds of The Farm itself, to which Clayton is sent for training, are **Morningside Park**, off Morningside Avenue south of Ellesmere Road, **Scarborough**. The recruits' target practice is on the firing range of **CO Bick Police College, 4620 Finch Avenue East**, also in Scarborough.

Love interest is supplied by Clayton's pairing with Layla (Moynahan) for a surveillance operation in Williamsburg. The Virginia town, from which Clayton is abducted, is really **Niagara-on-the-Lake** (which also provided the backdrop for Stephen King's *The Dead Zone*).

And it's time for a glimpse of the real DC. Fired from the programme, Clayton is clandestinely reinstated and taken by Burke for a breakfast burrito in front of the **Iwo Jima Memorial** (the sculpture based on the iconic photo of US troops raising the stars'n'stripes on the Pacific island), **Arlington Boulevard** at Meade Street, across the Potomac at Arlington National Cemetery. Layla is thoughtfully provided with a rather classy apartment at **3146 P Street NW**, between 31st and 32nd Streets in the picturesque **Georgetown** district (Regan's neighbourhood in *The Exorcist*), from where Clayton tails her to **Union Station, Massachussets Avenue NE** (this is where Dr Lecter rode the carousel in *Hannibal*). After a chase and a shootout, he escapes on the swishy DC subway to **Dupont Circle Metro**, Seventh Street SW.

Back to Toronto for the climax. The Navy Yards at M Street, where the villain helpfully expounds his plan with

traditional thoroughness, is the old **Gooderham & Worts distillery building, Mill Street** toward the Toronto waterfront. The complex is regularly used as a production centre for films, including *Chicago* and *X-Men*.

RED DRAGON

(2002, dir: Brett Ratner)
Anthony Hopkins, Ralph Fiennes, Ed Norton.
● **MARYLAND; FLORIDA; CALIFORNIA; WASHINGTON DC**

An A-list cast brings a return to form for the third in the Hannibal Lecter movies, following the campy disappointment of *Hannibal*. Based on the same novel as Michael Mann's excellent *Manhunter*, it's also photographed by the same cinematographer, Dante Spinotti.

The Baltimore concert hall, where a bumbling flute player is unfortunate enough to irritate the fastidious Dr Lecter, is **Pasadena Civic Auditorium, 300 East Green Street** (location for the Bette Midler concert movie *Divine Madness*). Veteran composer Lalo Schifrin puts in a cameo appearance as the conductor. Lecter's white-brick home, the fictitious 5 Chandlers Square, really is **Baltimore**, though, on **Mount Vernon Square**. The interior, where there's a bloody confrontation with investigator Will Graham (Norton), is modelled on Sigmund Freud's Viennese office. Surviving his injuries, Graham retires with his family to a quiet life on the coast, at **Marathon**, in the Florida Keys.

The Pittsburgh building used in *The Silence of the Lambs* as the exterior of Baltimore State Forensic Hospital has been partly demolished, so a shot from the Jonathan Demme movie was recycled.

Baltimore supplies two more key locations: the Chicago office of opportunistic hack Freddy Lounds' *National Tattler* magazine is the **Baltimore Sun Building, 501 North Calvert Street** (where Meg Ryan works in *Sleepless In Seattle*); and the Brooklyn Museum, where Tooth Fairy Francis Dolarhyde (Fiennes) attempts to silence the voice in his head by consuming William Blake's Red Dragon picture, is the **Baltimore Museum of Art, Art Museum Drive**, at North Charles and 31st Streets in Wyman Park (*www.artbma.org*).

The entrance to the Dolarhyde mansion, and the actual house on which the set is based, is at **Darlington**, Maryland, but even Hollywood occasionally balks at burning down a historic property. The house itself was duplicated in California, on the Disney Ranch in Santa Clarita, north of Los Angeles.

Several other locations were found around LA: the Chromolux photolab interior is in **Van Nuys**, in the San Fernando Valley; the newsstand, where Dolarhyde gets an early paper, is the rear of the **Los Angeles Theatre, 615 South Broadway**, downtown; and the Atlanta home of the slaughtered Leeds family is **4160 Country Club Drive, Long Beach**, south LA. This house really enjoys being in the movies; it was not only Matthew Broderick's Chicago home in *Ferris Bueller's Day Off*, but also the house of Preston Wasserstein in the *Risky Business* parody in *Not Another Teen Movie*. To the east of LA, the **Central Library, Pasadena** (seen in *Arachnophobia* and

Matilda), became the Library of Congress, where Ken Leung decodes Lecter's message to the Tooth Fairy ("Save yourself. Kill them all").

The safe house, to which the Graham family is optimistically whisked, is at **Westminster**, Maryland.

RED RIVER
(1948, dir: Howard Hawks)
John Wayne, Montgomery Clift, Walter Brennan.
● **ARIZONA**

Wayne and Clift follow Texas's Chisholm Trail, though this classic Western was filmed in southern Arizona at **Rain Valley**, 60 miles east of Tucson. Filming also took place in the **Coronado National Forest**, south of Benson. The river is the **San Pedro**.

RED SHOES, THE
(1948, dir: Michael Powell; Emeric Pressburger)
Moira Shearer, Anton Walbrook, Marius Goring.
● **LONDON; FRANCE; MONACO**

Powell and Pressburger's extravagantly romantic dance drama opens at London's **Royal Opera House, Covent Garden** (more recently seen in Luc Besson's *The Fifth Element*). Boris Lermontov (Walbrook) sees Vicky Page (Shearer) dancing Odette in *Swan Lake* (to gramophone records) at the Mercury Theatre, **2 Ladbroke Road**, W11, a converted chapel in **Notting Hill**. Opened as a theatre in 1933, this tiny 150-seater was indeed the birthplace of the Ballet Rambert. It's now a private residence. A star ballerina, Page is soon touring France, ending up in Monte Carlo. Be warned, the Monte Carlo of today is not the Monte Carlo of 1948. The classy elegance has been wiped away by crass development and the city is now a dump. The flower bedecked railway station, with its wrought iron decoration, has been replaced by a dismal concrete bunker. Page stays at the **Hotel de Paris, Place du Casino**, thankfully still standing and recognisable, tucked away behind the Casino. Also here is the **Monte Carlo Opera House**. The party spends an evening at **Villefranche-sur-Mer**, the beautiful little town on the coast just east of Nice, also seen in Jean-Claude Van Damme actioner *Maximum Risk* and *Never Say Never Again*. The deserted mansion, with its atmospheric staircase, where the dancer visits her mentor Lermontov, is **Villa Leopolda, Avenue Leopold II**, east of Centre Ville, overlooking Villefranche.

The curving art nouveau terrace, from which Page ultimately flings herself, was demolished to make way for an ugly concrete walkway, and was way over the other side of the principality from the railway line onto which she falls.

RÈGLE DU JEU, LA (aka *Rules of the Game*)
(1939, dir: Jean Renoir)
Marcel Dalio, Nora Gregor, Jean Renoir.
● **FRANCE**

Renoir's classic satirical comedy concerning relationships among aristocrats and their servants during a shooting weekend at a French château was believed destroyed in a bombing raid during WWII. Although there was some damage to the film, the full version was eventually restored in 1959. The house used for locations is the 17th century **Château la Ferté-Saint-Aubin**, in the Sologne. The chateau, set in a vast park, is open for tours (*© 02.38.76.52.72; rail: Orleans; admission charge*).

REMAINS OF THE DAY, THE
(1993, dir: James Ivory)
Anthony Hopkins, Emma Thompson, James Fox.
● **DEVON; AVON; WILTSHIRE; SOMERSET**

Exterior of Darlington Hall: Dyrham Park

The Merchant-Ivory team's thirteenth outing is a film of Kazuo Ishiguro's prizewinning novel, with Hopkins as Stevens, the ultimate gentleman's gentleman, putting duty to the pro-Nazi Lord Darlington (Fox) before his buttoned-up feelings for housekeeper Miss Kenton (Thompson).

Darlington Hall is an ingenious conflation of several houses. The exterior is **Dyrham Park**, about six miles north of Bath, Avon, on the A46. It was built between 1692 and 1704 by William III's Secretary of State, William Blathwayt, on the site of a Tudor manor house. It's a National Trust property, open to the public from April through October, except Wednesdays and Thursdays (*© 0117.937.2501; admission charge*). Most of the interior is **Badminton House**, about ten miles north of Bath off the B4040, which provided the entrance hall, Thompson's and Hopkins' parlours, and the conservatory where Hopkins' father collapses (see the house's exteior in *Pearl Harbor*). **Powderham Castle** (*© 01626.890.243/252*), a Medieval pile dating from 1390 set in a deer park, supplied more interiors. It was damaged during the Civil War, then restored and much altered in the 18th and 19th centuries. It's now the home of Lord and Lady Courtenay, and open to the public from May to October. The house is eight miles south of Exeter off the A379, Devon. Here you can see the Blue Staircase to the right of the entrance hall, the library, music room, and the domed ceiling of the final scene with the trapped pigeon. **Corsham Court** (*© 01249.712214*), an Elizabethan and Georgian house, is the site of the conference in the Cabinet Room. Four miles west of Chippenham off the A4 in Wiltshire, it's open from the beginning of January to the end of November. It's also seen in Stanley Kubrick's *Barry Lyndon*.

Tim Pigott-Smith proposes at the historic **George Inn, High Street, Norton St Philip**, six miles southeast of Bath, while Hopkins spends the night at the **Hop Pole Inn, Woods Hill, Lower Limpley Stoke** – a village used for another British classic. Limpley Stoke, a couple of miles south of Bath, appeared as the village of Titfield in the Ealing comedy *The Titfield Thunderbolt*. Stevens eventually travels to meet Miss Kenton in **Weston-Super-Mare** on the Somerset coast about 20 miles west of Bristol. The hotel where he pulls up is the **Royal Pier Hotel,**

Birnbeck Road (*© 01934.626644*), and Miss Kenton's boarding house is the **Highbury Hotel, Atlantic Road** (*© 01934.621585*). They go for tea in the **Pavilion** and sit morosely together on the town's **Grand Pier**.

The cartoon festival: Tower Theater, South Broadway

REPLACEMENT KILLERS, THE

(1998, dir: Antoine Fuqua) Chow Yun-Fat, Mira Sorvino, Michael Rooker.
● CALIFORNIA

Visually lush, violent gunfest filmed around LA. The pre-Columbian fantasy disco of the first of the many shootouts is the **Mayan Theater, 1038 South Hill Street**, downtown LA, a cousin of Mann's Chinese Theatre (see *The Bodyguard* for details). The cinema, where Yun-Fat and Sorvino thwart an attempt on the cop's son at a cartoon festival, is the **Tower Theater, 802 South Broadway**, also downtown.

The film makes use of a clutch of locations previously seen in *Blade Runner*. Mr Wei's stylish home is, almost inevitably, Frank Lloyd Wright's **Ennis Brown House, 2607 Glendower Avenue**, Los Feliz, below Griffith Park. It was Harrison Ford's apartment block in the Ridley Scott film, but has also been used as the villain's lair in *Black Rain* and *The Karate Kid III*. See *The House on Haunted Hill* for details. Sorvino's dismal office was the Hotel Yukon in *Blade Runner*, as well as home to the emaciated Sloth victim in *Se7en*. It's the **Pan Am Building** on **South Broadway** at Third Street, opposite the Bradbury Building. The airport, where the replacement killers arrive and from which Yun-Fat finally departs, is actually the ever-adaptable **Union Station, 800 North Alameda Street**, also downtown LA. It became the police station in *Blade Runner*.

REPO MAN

(1984, dir: Alex Cox) Emilio Estevez, Harry Dean Stanton, Tracey Walter
● LOS ANGELES, CALIFORNIA

"The life of a repo man is always intense," as aimless punk Otto (Estevez) discovers when he's co-opted into the world of car repossession. Cox's post-punk, genre-busting movie preempted much of American cinema for the next two decades, from the post-Roswell paranoia of *The X-Files* and *Men In Black*, to the squalid settings and inconsequentially quotable dialogue of Tarantino. And, with the glowing trunk of the '64 Chevy Malibu (which even contained a nuclear weapon in an early version of the script), he even managed to pre-empt the *Kiss Me Deadly* homage of *Pulp Fiction*. Even the credits run irritatingly from top to bottom as in the Aldrich movie. Set in Edge City, which looks as much like LA as it did in Jim Carrey's *The Mask*, most of the film was shot in the rundown industrial area south of downtown. If you're a fan of the movie, you don't need me to remind you that Beverly Hills this ain't.

The **Sixth Street Bridge** over the Los Angeles River (seen also in the remake of *Gone In 60 Seconds, S.W.A.T.* and *Them!*) features as a backdrop to many of the scenes, and it's beneath the bridge that Otto is first seen. He's conned into the repo man profession by Bud (Stanton) – like most of the characters, named after a US beer – on Tenth Street. The repo office is **2190 Wall Street** at East 21st Street. Otto and Bud race with rivals the Rodrigues brothers along the Los Angeles riverbed between Fourth and Sixth Street. Otto gets mace sprayed into his face, when the rat trick fails, outside **810 East Pico Boulevard** at Stanford Avenue. He meets Leila (Olivia Barash) after crashing into the English lady's trash at **Stanford Avenue and East 23rd Street**. The phone booth is rammed by the men in black on the 800 S block of **Wilson Street**, near Sacramento, where J Frank Parnell (Fox Harris) is using a scrambler. The CIA control centre is the TV Master Control at **UCLA**. The club, where the Circle Jerks play, is Rodney Bingenheimer's English Disco, 7561 Sunset Boulevard, west Hollywood. The steps Otto flies down to reach the Malibu are the **Fourth Street Viaduct**.

REPULSION

(1965, dir: Roman Polanski) Catherine Deneuve, John Fraser, Ian Hendry.
● LONDON

Brilliant, cold and terrifying case history, with sexually repressed and mystifyingly psychotic Deneuve killing off predatory males.

Madame Denise's beauty parlour, where Deneuve works, is still a beauty salon, at **31 Thurloe Place, South Kensington**, SW1. A couple of doors away is the **Hoop and Toy**, the pub where wannabe-boyfriend John Fraser drinks with his appalling cronies. He takes Deneuve for fish and chips at **Dino's**, also still doing good business, alongside South Kensington tube station. It's just opposite the tube station entrance where Deneuve is hassled by workman Mike Pratt. Deneuve's gloomy apartment block (though the incredible expanding interior was reproduced in the studio at Twickenham) is **Kensington Mansions, Trebovir Road**, off Warwick Road

Catherine Deneuve goes mad: Kensington Mansions, Trebovir Road

Madame Denise's beauty salon: Thurloe Place, South Kensington

Fish and chips for Deneuve: Dino's, South Kensington

behind Earls Court tube station, SW5.

REQUIEM FOR A DREAM
(2000, dir: Darren Aronofsky)
Ellen Burstyn, Jared Leto, Jennifer Connelly.
● NEW YORK CITY

Hubert Selby Jr (*Last Exit to Brooklyn*) novel about four people and their addictions. The film was shot in director Aronofsky's neighbourhood of **Coney Island** and **Brighton Beach**, Brooklyn. The apartment of TV obsessed Sara Goldfarb (Oscar-nominated Burstyn) is **3152 Brighton Sixth Street** at Ocean View, Brighton Beach (the block also contains the Winter Garden Russian restaurant, which you can glimpse). Harry Goldfarb (Leto), with his buddy Tyrone (Marlon Wayans), drags his mum's TV set along the **Coney Island Boardwalk**, past the vast hulk of the old Thunderbolt rollercoaster, which has since been demolished. He dreams of seeing Marion (Connelly) at the end of **Steeplechase Pier** on the Boardwalk between West 16th and West 19th Streets. The red tower in the background is the 262-foot **Parachute Jump**, built as a military training aid, and later converted to an amusement park ride in the old Steeplechase Park. Closed in 1968, it's recently been restored as part of a massive regeneration of the area, and is now a protected landmark.

RESERVOIR DOGS
(1992, dir: Quentin Tarantino)
Harvey Keitel, Michael Madsen, Tim Roth.
● LOS ANGELES, CALIFORNIA

Orange retails his story to the other Dogs: The Lodge, Lankershim Boulevard

Forget the ego and the irritating cameos, Tarantino's first movie really delivers. The diner, where the Dogs discuss Madonna lyrics and the ethics of tipping, is **Pat and Lorraine's, 4720 Eagle Rock Boulevard, Eagle Rock**, between Glendale and Pasadena, south of Ventura Freeway to the east of LA. The robbery of Karina's (named after Jean-Luc Godard's muse and one-time wife Anna Karina) filmed a little to the east in the **Highland Park** district. More movie references abound – Mr Blue is "Dead as Dillinger" and Laurence Tierney (gangleader Joe Cabot) played Dillinger in 1945 for Monogram Pictures, the company to whom Jean-Luc Godard dedicated *A Bout de Souffle*. Mr Brown (Tarantino himself) gets

Orange rehearses his druggy cover story: Beverly Boulevard, Second Street and Toluca Street junction

shot, while Mr White kills the cops, in the alleyway between **55th and 56th Avenues** here. Mr Orange receives his bloody gunshot wound by **5518 Marmion**

The Dogs discuss Madonna lyrics: Pat and Lorraine's, Eagle Rock Boulevard

Way, near Avenue 56. Mr Pink shoots his way out and heads down **Figueroa Street** (play spot-the-camera crew in the shop windows in this scene), south of, and parallel to, Marmion Way. He gets hit by a car at the corner of **York Boulevard** and **57th Avenue**, commandeers the motor and makes off on 57th.

Orange meets his contact: Johnie's Coffee Shop, Wilshire Boulevard

The café, where Mr Orange meets up with his superior, is **Johnie's Coffee Shop, 6101 Wilshire Boulevard** at Fairfax Avenue (a familiar location – it's where Anthony Edwards receives news of the impending apocalypse in the underrated thriller *Miracle Mile* and Eds Norton and Furlong stop off in *American History X*).

The graffiti-covered walls, where Orange rehearses his druggy cover story, can be seen at the junction of **Beverly Boulevard**, **Second Street** and **Toluca Street**, just northwest of downtown (take care around here if you're visiting – that graffiti isn't set dressing!).

He retails the story to the other Dogs in **The Lodge, 4923 Lankershim Boulevard** (© *818.769.7722*) between Vineland and Magnolia, which is in reality a north Hollywood gay bar, and flashbacks to the toilets of the **Park Plaza Hotel, 607 South Park View Street**, midtown LA. "The hotel has been featured many times in films," claimed Tarantino, "but I'm the only director that has used only its bathroom." Maybe, but it's a close thing. The Park Plaza also supplied the men's room at Capitol Pictures for the Coens' *Barton Fink*, but it was used for the USO dance scene. See *New York New York* for details.

The Dogs' warehouse has sadly been demolished, but you're sure to recognise the (currently empty) site at **Figueroa Street and 59th Avenue** in Highland Park. Fittingly, it was a former mortuary, and was also used for Mr Orange's scuzzy hotel room.

REVERSAL OF FORTUNE
(1990, dir: Barbet Schroeder)
Jeremy Irons, Glenn Close, Ron Silver.
● NEW YORK CITY; NEW JERSEY; NEW YORK

The true story becomes a jet-black comedy, tiptoeing carefully through a legal minefield, as liberal lawyer Alan Dershowitz (Silver) defends Claus von Bulow (an Oscar-winning Irons) against a charge of murder, after von Bulow's wife, Sunny (Close), is found in a drug-induced coma. The von Bulow's house at the time was Clarendon Court, near Newport, Long Island. Not surprisingly, this is not used in the film, although you can see Clarendon Court on screen as the mansion in *High Society*. Schroeder used the **Knole Mansion, Post Road** in Old Westbury, just south of the Long Island Expressway on Long Island's North Shore (it's a private house, not open to the public). Interiors, though, were filmed at **Lyndhurst**, just south of **Tarrytown**, New York State. The crenellated castle of robber baron Jay Gould was donated to the National Trust for Historic Preservation by Gould's daughter in 1961.

Filming also took place in **Montclair**, New Jersey, and in Manhattan. The hospital, where Sunny lies comatose, is **St John's Hospital, Yonkers**, north of the Bronx. Dershowitz's law classes were filmed on the 34-acre campus of **City College**, between West 130th and West 140th Streets, and St Nicholas Terrace and Amsterdam Avenue in Hamilton Heights. Other locations include the area of **Flatbush**, Brooklyn; the **Carlyle Hotel, 35 East 76th Street** at Madison Avenue on the East Side; **Larchmont Yacht Club, New Rochelle** on Long Island Sound; the **Small Claims Court**; and Jewish dairy restaurant **Ratner's, 138 Delancey Street** between Norfolk and Suffolk Streets on the Lower East Side, Manhattan.

REVOLUTION

(1985, dir: Hugh Hudson)
Al Pacino, Nastassja Kinski, Donald Sutherland.
● **NORFOLK; DEVON; CAMBRIDGESHIRE; NORWAY**

If a local whizz-kid, with a couple of flashy car commercials under his belt, came home to film the village pageant, the result might resemble *Revolution*. Legendary turkeys, like *Heaven's Gate*, are rarely as bad as their reputations. But this is the real thing, an appallingly made mess, loosely following a father and son through an endless American Revolution.

The sole good idea is the inventive use of locations, with **King's Lynn** in Norfolk standing in for 18th-century Manhattan (Wall Street is still no more than an alleyway). The dockside warehouses are **South Quay** grain silos. New York Harbor, where Pacino and son sail into the middle of anti-English riots, is the area around King's Lynn's **Custom House**. Filming also took place in **King's Staithe Square**.

The American camp at Valley Forge is **Thetford**, in Norfolk, while the Brits camped in the **Burrator** area of southwest **Dartmoor**, Devon. More battle scenes used **Kingston** on the south coast. The Second Battle of Upper Manhattan was shot at **Deancombe Valley**, above Burrator reservoir. The Battle of Yorktown filmed at **Scobbiscombe Farm**, Kingston, and there was filming also at **Bigbury Bay**. A camera worth half a million pounds was lost at the Devon location when it tumbled over a cliff during the night. Philadelphia's state buildings are **Melton Constable Hall** in Norfolk (see *The Go-Between* for details), and other Philadelphia scenes were filmed in **Ely**, Cambridgeshire.

RICHARD III

(1995, dir: Richard Loncraine)
Ian McKellen, Nigel Hawthorne, Maggie Smith.
● **LONDON; SUSSEX; MIDDLESEX; LANCASHIRE**

Filming of the Shakespeare history, based on Richard

Eyre's National Theatre production, and making imaginative use of London and Home Counties locations to conjure up an alternative England with the Victorian gothic style of King Edward's old order overtaken by the austere thirties look of Richard's neo-fascist dictatorship.

The new order, Richard's HQ: Senate House, Malet Street

The Tower of London: Bankside Power Station, now Tate Modern

The royal family's London palace is **St Pancras Chambers, Euston Road**, cheekily relocated to the banks of the Thames, though the interior is a crafty combination of **St Cuthbert's Church, Philbeach Gardens, Earl's Court,** SW5 (the opening musical number), and the **Holbein Room** of **Strawberry Hill House, Waldegrave Road, Twickenham** (© 020.8892.0051; visits by appointment), the elaborately gothic home of 18th century

The royal family's London palace: St Pancras Chambers, Euston Road

writer Horace Walpole. The royal breakfast is served in the **Undercroft**, a vaulted pedestrian walkway beneath the chapel of **Lincoln's Inn Fields**, WC2 (used for the duel in *Tom Jones*); and the royal family's seaside retreat is a conflation of two Sussex landmarks, the **Royal Pavilion, Brighton** (© 01273.290900, www.royalpavilion.org.uk), and the seafront terrace is the Grade 1-listed **De La Warr Pavilion**, Bexhill-on-Sea, now an arts centre (© 01424.787900, www.dlwp.com).

The fascist rally, where Richard is offered the crown, is held in the **New Horticultural Hall**, on the corner of **Greycoat** and **Elverton Street** in Westminster, SW1 (seen in *Indiana Jones and the Last Crusade* and *The Saint*), while the backstage preparations are beneath

The old order: Strawberry Hill House, Twickenham

The seaside palace: Brighton Pavilion

"Live with me and be my love...": St Cuthbert's Church, Earl's Court

Earl's Court Exhibition Centre, Warwick Road, SW5. The giant clockface, where Richard refuses to give Buckingham his promised title, is way up on **Shell Mex House**, on the Victoria Embankment.

Richard's cold but stylish bunker is **Senate House, University of London, Malet Street** (which you might have seen as the New York clinic in Tony Scott's *The Hunger* and, more recently, in *Batman Begins*), and his military HQ is **Steam Town**, a rail museum at **Carnforth** in Lancashire. Two of London's famous ex-power stations are also featured: Bankside Power Station, now the **Tate Modern**, is used as the Tower of London, and the deserted bulk of the old **Battersea Power Station** is the site of the climactic Battle of Bosworth.

RIDE THE HIGH COUNTRY (aka *Guns in the Afternoon*)

(1962, dir: Sam Peckinpah)
Joel McCrea, Randolph Scott, Mariette Hartley.
● **CALIFORNIA**

The High Country: Bishop, central California

Randolph Scott came out of, and then went back into, retirement for this excellent early Peckinpah. The setting is the fictional Coarsegold, in Crane Valley, but the chosen location was over the mountains in the **Mammoth Lakes** region of the High Sierras, near Bishop, California. Peckinpah wanted to capture the change in terrain and vegetation as the party climbs and descends, but unseasonal bad weather cut short filming and the crew were forced to head back to LA, to the inevitable all-purpose **Bronson Canyon** in the heart of Griffith Park, where soapsuds were substituted for snow, and the tents were cut from the sails of the *Bounty* built for the 1962 version of *Mutiny on the Bounty*!

Other locations in the area include **Frenchman's Flat**; the **Conejo Valley**; the Fox Ranch in Malibu Canyon; and even the MGM backlot.

RING, THE

(2002, dir: Gore Verbinski)
Naomi Watts, Martin Henderson, David Dorfman.
● **WASHINGTON; OREGON; LOS ANGELES, CALIFORNIA**

A more comprehensible or less mysterious remake of the Japanese *Ringu*? The US location was to have been Boston, but the dank mistiness of the Pacific northwest, in Washington state and Oregon, couldn't have been bet-ter (although interiors were filmed in the studio in sunny old LA).

Rachel Keller (Watts) works for the Seattle Post-Intelligencer, although the newspaper office scenes were shot in LA (supposedly, the real P-I office, with its grand views of Elliott Bay, was just not glum enough for the film's claustrophobic atmosphere).

Rachel picks up the photographs belonging to the dead girl from **1923 Fifth Avenue** at Stewart Street, beneath the monorail, downtown Seattle (the address on the stub is 1925 Fifth Avenue, which is the Gee Whiz coffee shop). Later, a frantic Rachel weaves through traffic beneath the **Alaskan Way Viaduct**, along the waterfront. The Shelter Mountain Inn, to which Rachel traces the sinister videotape, is **Camp Firwood, 4605 Cable Street**, on the Lake Whatcom waterfront, southeast of **Bellingham**, way north toward Vancouver.

A couple of out-of-state locations: the institution where Becca is confined is **Metropolitan State Hospital, 11401 Bloomfield Avenue, Norwalk**, California; and to find the mysterious Moesko Island Lighthouse, you'll need to travel south to the coast of Oregon. It's the **Yaquina Head Lighthouse**, off US101, near **Newport**.

On their way up to Astoria, Rachel and Noah (Henderson) drive across **Deception Pass Bridge**, at the northern tip of Whidbey Island. The Quinault ferryboat, from which the crazed horse (don't fret – it's computer generated) leaps, is the **Whidbey Island Ferry**, between Quincy Street Dock, **Port Townsend** on the mainland, and **Keystone**, north of Seattle.

The Morgan Ranch, where Rachel confronts the secret of the terrifying Samara, is **Emerald Glen Farm, 23200 Yeager Road, Monroe**, Highway 2 northeast of Seattle.

RIO BRAVO

(1959, dir: Howard Hawks)
John Wayne, Dean Martin, Ricky Nelson.
● **ARIZONA**

Wayne and Martin hold out against a band of outlaws in this movie, which was reworked by Hawks as *El Dorado* in 1966, by Hawks again as *Rio Lobo* in 1970, and by John Carpenter in 1976 as *Assault on Precinct 13*. It was shot at **Old Tucson Studios, 201 South Kinney Road** near Tucson, built for the 1940 movie *Arizona*. The studio-cum-tourist attraction, claiming the largest Western street in the movie business, was restored at a cost of $1 million, including the set of *The High Chaparral*, which filmed here.

RIO GRANDE

(1950, dir: John Ford)
John Wayne, Ben Johnson, Maureen O'Hara.
● **UTAH**

More Ford-Wayne Injun-bashing, shot around **Moab**, in southeast Utah, at **White's Ranch, Professor Valley** and **Onion Creek Narrows**.

RISKY BUSINESS

(1983, dir: Paul Brickman)
Tom Cruise, Rebecca De Mornay, Joe Pantoliano.
● **ILLINOIS**

Cruise meets De Mornay: Drake Hotel, East Walton Place, Chicago

Dunking the Porsche: Belmont Harbor, Lake Michigan

It's the go-getting eighties, greed is good, and home-alone teen Cruise sets up a lucrative prostitution business while his parents are away. The movie was made around Chicago, where Cruise meets up with hooker De Mornay in the Palm Court of the **Drake Hotel, 140 East Walton Place** (*© 312.787.2200*), also where faker Andy Garcia lives it up in *Accidental Hero*. Cruise's father's Porsche slips into the water at the marina of **Belmont Harbor** on Lake Michigan. Cruise's school is **Highland Park High School**, and the house, where he shot to fame dancing in his underwear, can be found on **Linden Avenue, Highland Park**.

RIVER OF NO RETURN
(1954, dir: Otto Preminger)
Robert Mitchum, Marilyn Monroe, Rory Calhoun.
● ALBERTA, CANADA

Scenic drama, made at **Banff**, in the Rockies of Alberta, Canada, where the raft scenes were filmed on the **Bow River**. Monroe stayed at the Banff Springs Hotel (where Betty Grable shot *Springtime in the Rockies*). The hotel is now used as the backdrop to a Japanese soap opera and, as a consequence, is full of Asian location hunters.

RIVER'S EDGE
(1986, dir: Tim Hunter)
Crispin Glover, Keanu Reeves, Ione Skye.
● CALIFORNIA

Admirably downbeat drama, based on a true story, with a group of teens facing crisis when one of their number casually murders his girlfriend. Set in California capital Sacramento, the film shot mostly around Sunland and Tujunga in the San Fernando Valley. The school is **Verdugo Hills High School, 10625 Plainview Avenue, Tujunga**, north of LA, also used in *one eight seven*, *The Craft* and *Heathers*.

ROAD TO MOROCCO
(1942, dir: David Butler)
Bob Hope, Bing Crosby, Dorothy Lamour.
● CALIFORNIA

The desert of Morocco is actually the sand dunes of **Imperial County**, way down in southern California toward the Arizona border.

ROAD TO PERDITION
(2002, dir: Sam Mendes)
Tom Hanks, Paul Newman, Jude Law.

● ILLINOIS; MICHIGAN; INDIANA; CALIFORNIA

The real star of Mendes' film of the graphic novel is the sombre cinematography of veteran Conrad L Hall, who died shortly after filming. Most of the film was shot on real locations around Chicago, although the city's Bronzeville Armory was converted into a soundstage for the house interiors of hitman Michael Sullivan (Hanks) and of mob boss John Rooney (Newman). The armory, at 35th Street and Giles Avenue, south of Chicago's Loop, has since been redeveloped as a school.

Rock Island, the town where the Sullivans and Rooneys live, is downtown **West Dundee**, about 30 miles west of Chicago. The opening scenes of Michael Jr (Tyler Hoechlin) shoplifting were filmed on **Main Street**, between First and Second Streets. One LA studio set, though, is the town street, where Sullivan and Rooney drink at O'Neill's, which is on the Warner Bros backlot in Burbank.

About ten miles northeast of Dundee is the town of **Barrington Hills**, where a country house became Michael Sullivan's home. Rooney's grander mansion is the **Charles Dawes House, 225 Greenwood, Evanston**, north of Chicago, now home to the Evanston Historical Society, and open to the public (*© 847.475.3410, www.evanston-historical.org; admission charge*).

On Chicago's far southside is the **Pullman Historic District**, where you'll find the **Florence Hotel, 11111 South Forrestville Avenue** (*© 773.785.8900*), where Rooney's son Connor (Daniel Craig) resides, as well as the warehouse where young Michael discovers his father's line of work.

The Sullivans head off to make a deal with Al Capone's right-hand man, Frank Nitti, arriving in Chicago at the **LaSalle Street Bridge** – where it was necessary to remove modern buildings digitally from the cityscape. Nitti's Hotel Lexington is the **Wrigley Building, 400-410 North Michigan Avenue**. The Eatmore Grill is also in the city. It's the **Salvation Army Clothing Store, 3900 North Lincoln Avenue**.

On the road, Sullivan and his son stop off at a country church in **Beecher**, south of Chicago. Meanwhile, unscrupulous crime-scene photographer Maguire (Law) is dispatched to track down the pair. He catches up with Sullivan at the Englewood Diner, a real diner, originally sited on Peabody Square in the Boston suburb of Dorchester. It was bought on eBay and transported to open land outside Chicago for filming. Fully restored, it was sold back to its original owner and is now the **Downeast Diner, 41 Dow Highway, Eliot**, on the southernmost tip of Maine (*© 207.439.5436*).

With Nitti protecting Connor Rooney, Sullivan decides to hit Capone's organisation where it hurts. Teaching his son the skills to be a getaway driver on the tree-lined road at **Sweet Woods Forest Preserve** in **Glenwood**, south of east Chicago, he embarks on a series of bank robberies. The string of banks, which appear to be all over the place, can be seen in the downtown business district of **Momence**, on Route 1, about 50 miles south of Chicago. When the mob's money is withdrawn, Sullivan tracks down Capone's accountant Rance (Dylan Baker) to the

Geneva Hotel (a real establishment, but long-closed) in the town of **Geneva**, south of Dundee. Home to, not a Swiss, but a large Swedish community, this historic town is the site of the bloody shoot-up in which Maguire suffers a shotgun blast to the face.

The motel, at which Sullivan narrowly evades Maguire, was in **Saugatuck**, Michigan. Previously the 1930s White Dog Inn on Blue Star Highway, it had been damaged by fire in 1998 and was scheduled for demolition after filming. Also gone is the Perdition beach house, where the film ends. It was built for the movie, and then dismantled, at **Port Sheldon Township** on the shore of Lake Michigan.

ROAD TRIP
(2000, dir: Todd Phillips)
Breckin Meyer, Seann William Scott, Paulo Costanzo.
● **GEORGIA; TENNESSEE; CALIFORNIA; MASSACHUSETTS**

Meyer and chums undertake a cross-country dash, from Ithaca, New York State, to Austin, Texas, to retrieve a compromising videotape posted to his girlfriend in this tired and unfunny addition to the college sexcom genre. The film was shot in the South, mainly around **Atlanta**, **Cumming** and **Lawrenceville**, Georgia, and in **Nashville**, Tennessee.

The campus of the fictitious Ithaca University is the **University of Georgia, Athens** (though the opening aerial shot is of **Harvard University, Cambridge**, Massachusetts, later recycled in the same director's *Old School*). The **University of Tennessee, Knoxville**, is the real thing, though the University of Austin is **Emory University, Atlanta**, and Memphis is **Broadway, Nashville**.

The foursome stop for breakfast in the **Gwinnett Diner, Highway 124 at Gwinnett Drive, Lawrenceville**, Georgia. And maybe you'd want to leave the sugar on the French toast.

ROB ROY
(1995, dir: Michael Caton-Jones)
Liam Neeson, Jessica Lange, Tim Roth.
● **SCOTLAND**

Dour version of the historical legend enlivened by Tim Roth's Oscar-nominated villain. The opening shot is of **Kinlochleven**. Rob Roy's cottage was built specially for the movie at **Bracorina**, on Loch Morar, and was dismantled after filming. The home of the Marquis of Montrose, with its elegant 17th century gardens, is **Drummond Castle Gardens**, west of the Muthill Road about two miles south of Crieff. The castle is not open to the public, but you can visit the gardens (*© 01764.681257; admission charge*). The village square is the courtyard of **Megginch Castle Gardens**, on the A90, eight miles east of Perth. Once again, you can visit the gardens, but not the castle (*© 01821.642222; admission charge*). The gambling den, where Rob Roy faces Cunningham, is **Crichton Castle**, two miles south of Pathhead in Midlothian (*© 01875.320017; admission charge*). Filming also took place at **Loch Earn**, **Glencoe** and at **Caig Falls Bridge, Loch Arkaig**.

ROBIN HOOD
(1991, dir: John Irvin)
Patrick Bergin, Uma Thurman, Jurgen Prochnow.
● **CHESHIRE; WALES**

Totally overshadowed by the flashy, attention-grabbing Kevin Costner movie made the same year, this superior version was largely shot around **Peckforton Castle**, on the A49 just south of the A51, between Chester and Nantwich, Cheshire, and also at the caves of nearby **Beeston Castle**. Also seen are **Tatton Park**, Cheshire, and the countryside around **Betwys-y-Coed** in north Wales.

ROBIN HOOD: PRINCE OF THIEVES
(1991, dir: Kevin Reynolds)
Kevin Costner, Alan Rickman, Morgan Freeman.
● **SUSSEX; WILTSHIRE; YORKSHIRE; BUCKINGHAMSHIRE; NORTHUMBERLAND; LONDON; FRANCE**

Costner's hyperactive, one-note extravaganza, famously using locations all over the UK, kicks off with Robin arriving home from the Crusades on a beach overlooked

Nottingham Cathedral: St Bartholomew the Great, Smithfield

by gleaming white cliffs. And where better than the **Seven Sisters**, on the Sussex coast west of Eastbourne toward Cuckmere Haven. You can access the clifftop path from car parks at Exceat Barn and Birling Gap, or view the Sisters from Seaford Head.

From the coast, Robin's trek north to Nottingham overshoots a little, to Northumberland in fact. In no time at all, he's giving directions to Morgan Freeman at **Sycamore Gap**, on **Hadrian's Wall** near to Housesteads Roman Fort. Housesteads is on the B6318 about 25 miles west of Newcastle-on-Tyne (*rail: Bardon Mill*). But it's soon back south, to Wiltshire, for the ruin of Locksley Castle, Robin's family home, which turns out to be **Wardour Castle**, between Salisbury and Shaftesbury, off the A30. Wardour's great advantage for the movie is that it's partly destroyed and, depending on the angle it's seen from, can appear intact or totally wrecked. Then north again, to Yorkshire. The river, where Robin fights with Little John, is **Aysgarth Falls**, a series of broad limestone steps on the River Ure at Aysgarth, on the A684 about 25 miles west of Northallerton in the Pennines.

Robin Hood's Sherwood Forest camp was built near to the film studio at Shepperton, about 50 yards from a public footpath in **Burnham Beeches**, off the A335, north of Slough, Buckinghamshire. Maid Marion keeps her distance, though, at **Hulne Priory**, in Hulne

The walled castle of Nottingham: Carcassonne, southern France

The three films in *The Lord of the Rings* trilogy (*The Fellowship of the Ring*, *The Two Towers* and *The Return of the King*) were filmed simultaneously, against the varied backdrops of director Peter Jackson's native New Zealand, standing in for Tolkien's Middle Earth. Some of the locations will not be seen until the release of the final film in 2003.

NEW ZEALAND IN THE LORD OF THE RINGS

NORTH ISLAND

Private farmland near **MATAMATA** (**1**), toward Karapiro in the Waikato area, represented the rolling, bucolic greenery of the Shire, home of Bilbo Baggins and Frodo. Hobbiton was an elaborate set, with crops and flowers planted a year before filming to give the landscape time to age naturally. There's nothing left of the set, but you can enjoy the lush countryside around Matamata, which now proudly advertises itself as Hobbiton (**1b**).

TONGARIRO NATIONAL PARK (**2**), is home to three volca-

noes. Mt Ruapehu (which is still active), Mt Tongariro and Mt Ngauruhoe proved ideal as the dark and savage realm of Mordor and Mt Doom, where the ring is forged. **Whakapapa Ski Field** (**2a**), on the slopes of Ruapehu, supplied Middle Earth's snowy slopes and the battlefield on the slopes of Mt Doom (at the opening of *Fellowship*), where an alliance of humans and elves defeats the armies of Mordor, and the ring is taken from Sauron.

WELLINGTON AREA (**3**): The **Town Belt** on **Mount**

Victoria (**3a**), a park overlooking central Wellington, is where the four hobbits, Frodo, Sam, Merry and Pippin, are forced to hide under tree roots to evade the black rider after escaping with Farmer Maggot's vegetables.

Harcourt Park (3b), **Akatarawa Road, Upper Hutt**, 20 miles north of Wellington, became Isengard, the realm of the evil Saruman, who has the goblins use ropes to pull down trees (don't worry, they were old trees shipped in and erected for the movie). In June 2002, the remains of the tree, with bolts embedded, could still be seen (**3c**) (*rail: Upper Hutt, bus to Brown Owl shops*).

In **Kaitoke Regional Park (3d)**, about 8 miles from Upper Hutt City, the elvish realm of Rivendell was built. This is where Frodo recovers from his wound and the Fellowship is formed. The Silverlode River and Galadriel's swan-boat were also filmed here (**3e**).

The Great River Anduin is actually the **Hutt River (3f)** between **Moonshine Bridge** and **Poets Park** (*Rail: Wallaceville*).

Queen Elizabeth Park, MacKays Crossing, between Paekakariki and Raumati South, was used to stage the section of the battle of Pelennor Fields with the fallen oliphaunt in *The Return of the King*.

In **Dry Creek Quarry (3g)**, a vast mining complex surrounded by a chainlink fence at the bottom of **Haywards Hill** in Wellington, the huge fortress city of Minas Tirith was built, and the battle of Helm's Deep was staged (*rail: Manor Park*).

Otaki Gorge Road, in **Otaki Totara Forest (4)** in the **Manuwatu** region, north of Wellington, was used for the woods and

roads surrounding Hobbiton.

Near the tiny country village of **Manakau (5)**, north of Otaki, the hobbits narrowly escape the ring wraiths by jumping onto the Brandywine River ferry.

The town of Bree, where the hobbits are supposed to meet Gandalf at the Prancing Pony Inn, but instead meet up with the mysterious Strider, was a set built on the abandoned army camp of **Fort Dorset** at **Seatoun**, in Wellington's Port Nicholson Harbour. You can see the site from the beach at the end of Burnham Street.

The woods of Lothlorien, where Frodo gets help and advice from elf queen Galadriel, are the gardens of **Fernside Lodge (6a)**, a homestead inn about 2 miles from **Featherston, Wairarapa**, about 40 miles east of Wellington. Here you can see the White Bridge (**6b**). And, yes, you can stay here (*✆ 06.308.8265; website: www.fernside.co.nz*).

SOUTH ISLAND
QUEENSTOWN AREA: The **Arrowtown Recreational Reserve**, 15 miles northeast of Queenstown, was used for the West Road, the Eregion Hills and the Misty Mountains.

The Ford of Bruinen, where Arwen challenges the wraiths, "If you want Frodo, come and claim him!" before they are washed away in a flash flood, was filmed on the **Shotover River** near **Arrowtown**.

Closeburn, about ten minutes drive west from Queenstown on Geary Road, became the summit of Amon Hen, where Frodo takes his leave of Strider and the Fellowship after Boromir begins to succumb to the ring's power.

The **Paradise** area, near the tiny township of **Glenorchy** at the head of Lake Wakatipu (**7**), became Lothlorien Woods in the elven realm of Lorien, the site where Boromir is fatally wounded in the battle with the orcs.

Wanaka, to the north, on the banks of the **Clutha River**, stood in for the Golden Plains, where the black riders search for Frodo and orcs attack the Fellowship.

Kawarau Gorge, on the Kawarau River, was the site of the Argonath, the gigantic statues of the two kings of Gondor.

Way east of Queenstown, near **Poolburn Dam** in the Ida Valley about 25 miles east of Alexandra, a village set was built for the Plains of Rohan in *The Two Towers*.

The **Ben Ohau Sheep Station**, near **Twizel** in Canterbury, became the Pelennor Fields in *The Return of the King*, and the foothills of the White Mountains.

On **Mt Sunday** (**8**), on the **Mount Potts Station**, the city of Edoras in the kingdom of Rohan was built for *The Two Towers* and *The Return of the King*.

NELSON AREA: Chetwood Forest near Bree, where the hobbits first flee, was filmed on **Takaka Hill** (**9**), between Golden Bay and Tasman Bay near Nelson. **Mt Olympus**, Golden Bay, in **Kahurangi National Park**, provided scenes in the Eregion Hills and the rough country south of Rivendell. **Mt Owen** (**10**) became the Dimrill Dale hill-side and Chetwood Forest.

FJORDLAND (**11**), the spectacular region, on the western coast, supplied several locations: Weathertop camp, where the ring wraiths catch up with the hobbits and Frodo is stabbed in the shoulder, is **Te Anau**. The **Kepler Mires** became the Dead Marshes and Midgewater Marshes in *The Two Towers*. **Mavora Lakes Park** became Nen Hithoel, where orcs

chase the hobbits out of the bush and into boats on the lake.

The **SOUTHERN ALPS** and the extensive glaciers (**12**) of South Island became the Misty Mountains, where the wretched Gollum hid away in his cave for 500 years with the ring.

STAR WARS EPISODE II: ATTACK OF THE CLONES

TUNISIA: George Lucas returns to some familiar locations. Once again, the **Sidi Driss Hotel** (**1**) in **Matmata** becomes the interior of the Tatooine homestead, made famous by *Episode IV: A New Hope*. The exterior is a set built in the **Chott el Jerid** near **Nefta** (**2**).

ITALY: Palazzo Reale (**3**), **Caserta** near Naples, seen in *Episode I: The Phantom Menace*, is once again used as the interior of the Palace of Naboo. **Villa Balbianello** (**4a**), on a promontory overlooking Lake Como in northern Italy, is the Lake Country retreat. Although the villa is disguised with CGI, you won't fail to recognise the breathtaking loggia wreathed in climbing plants (**4b**). It's open Tuesday and Thursday to Sunday (*☎ 03.445.6110*). On certain days of the week you can walk from **Lenno**, or take a boat from the nearby village of **Sala Comacini** and arrive, like Anakin and Padme, at the villa's landing stage.

SPAIN: The exterior of Naboo's Theed Palace is the huge, mock-Moorish **Plaza de Espana** complex in Seville, southern Spain, built for the 1929 Spanish-American exposition. Anakin and Padme approach over one of the blue and white Venetian-style bridges (**5a**) and walk through the semicircular colonnade (**5b**). It's in the Parque de Maria Luisa, Avenida de Isabel la Catolica. See *Lawrence of Arabia* for details.

BRIDGET JONES'S LONDON

BEDALE STREET, SE1: In Helen Fielding's book, Bridget's London home was in Holland Park, west London, but for the movie she's been relocated south of the river to Borough. Her singleton flat is above **The Globe Pub** (**1**) at Green Dragon Court (where the Victorian prostitutes hung out in *The French Lieutenant's Woman*). Across the street you can see the shop which was transformed into the fictitious Greek restaurant where Daniel Cleaver and Mark Darcy slug it out during a birthday party. Bridget plods glumly through **Borough Market** (**1b**) after discovering caddish Cleaver with "Lara, from the New York office".

BANKSIDE: Grab a bite at the café in **Tate Modern** (**2**), the old Bankside Power Station turned cutting-edge art gallery (✆ *020.7401.5020*),where Bridget and her friends hang out.

WEST END (**3**): Shop at **Dickens & Jones, 224 Regent Street** (**3a**), the venerable department store where Bridget's mum demonstrates the strangely erotic egg peeler. Then splash out on an exotic north African feast at **Momo** (**3b**), **25 Heddon Street** (✆*020.7434 4040*), a fashionable and expensive Maghreb restaurant where Bridget gets advice from her friends before the first date with Daniel. (Heddon Street, tucked away behind Regent Street, by the way, might be familiar to David Bowie fans as the benighted backstreet featured on the 1972 *Ziggy Stardust* album cover.)

THAMESSIDE (**4**): Enjoy a romantic evening at **Cantina** (**4a**), **36 Shad Thames** (✆ *020.7403 5403*), the restaurant where Daniel takes Bridget. The pair get frisky beneath the walkways of the old **Shad Thames** warehouses (**4b**) (see *The Elephant Man* for details), before retiring to Daniel's flat, which is a wharf conversion on nearby **Clink Street**.

ICA (**5**), the **Institute of Contemporary Art** on the **Mall**, is the site of the horribly embarrassing book launch for *Kafka's Motorbike*, attended by Salman Rushdie.

ROYAL COURTS OF JUSTICE (**6**), the **Strand**, is where Bridget bungles her assignment to cover the extradition case for TV show *Sit Up Britain*.

EXCHANGE BUILDINGS (**7**), **Cornhill**, is where Bridget finally gets her long-awaited clinch with Darcy, after apparently having run all the way from Borough in her tiny stripy pants.

STANSTED AIRPORT (**8**), in Essex, had its ultra-modern terminal transformed into New York for the scene of Mark Darcy's arrival at JFK.

MARTINS HERON (1): 12 Picket Post Close, in this picture postcard suburb one rail stop away from Bracknell in Berkshire, became the home of the dreadful Dursley family, 4 Privet Drive, where young Harry lives under the stairs.

LONDON: At the **Reptile House (2a)** of the city's famous **Regents Park Zoo** (*website: www.london-zoo.co.uk*), Harry liberates the boa constrictor (though what kind of life can it expect in Regents Park?) and learns he can speak to snakes.

On **Bull's Head Passage (2b)** in **Leaden Hall Market**, London EC3, you can see the entrance to The Leaky Cauldron which, in turn, contains the magical entrance to Diagon Alley.

The **Ground Floor Exhibition Hall** of the Australian High Commission, **Australia House** in the **Strand**, was transformed into Gringotts, the wizard bank run by goblins. It's not generally open to the public, but there are daily guided tours.

King's Cross Station (2c): Don't go running into brick walls – there is no platform 9³/₄. Hagrid leaves Harry on the station's elevated walkway. The entrance to the magic platform was filmed between platforms 4 and 5 .

GOATHLAND STATION (3): This station, on the North Yorkshire Moors Railway, became Hogsmeade Station (*website: www.nymr.demon.co.uk*).

GLOUCESTER CATHEDRAL (4): The cathedral's richly vaulted cloisters became the corridors leading to Gryffindor House, where the lady in the oil painting asks for the password (*website: www.gloucestercathedral.uk.com*).

DURHAM CATHEDRAL (5): The cloisters of the Cathedral became the snowy quadrangle of Hogwarts School where Harry sets the owl flying.

LACOCK ABBEY (6): The Cloisters of the abbey, in the village of Lacock, Wiltshire, were used for several scenes.

The **Sacristy** (**6a**) became Professor Snape's Potion Class: "How to bottle fame, brew glory and even put a stopper in death." The **Warming Room** (**6b**), which really does contain a genuine cauldron, became Professor Quirrell's Defence Against the Dark Arts classroom, while the

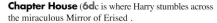

Chapter House (**6d**c is where Harry stumbles across the miraculous Mirror of Erised .

ALNWICK CASTLE (**7**): The **Outer Bailey** of the Northumbrian castle was the site of Madam Hooch's flying lesson (*website: www.alnwickcastle.com*).

HARROW SCHOOL (**8**): **Fourth Form Rooms** in **Harrow Old Schools** became Professor Flitwick's Charms Class, where Hermione manages to levitate a feather: "Wingardium Leviosa!"

BODLEIAN LIBRARY, OXFORD, contains **Duke Humphrey's Library**, where Harry tries to find out about Nicholas Flamel, and the elaborately fan-vaulted **Divinity School** (**9**), which became Hogwart School's hospital.

AMÉLIE'S PARIS

Amelie's world centres around **Montmartre**, where she sets up a complicated assignation with Nino on the steps in front of **SACRE COEUR** (**1**).

At the opening of the film, a bluebottle buzzes along **RUE SAINT VINCENT** (**2**), behind Sacre Coeur.

The double staircase at **LAMARCK-CAULAINCOURT METRO** (**3**), rue Lamarck, is where Amélie describes the sights and sounds of the bustling market to the blind man. This is also the metro station where Amélie first sees Nino groping about under a photobooth (though it's supposed to be Abbesses)

Amélie's apartment is at **56 RUE DES TROIS-FRERES** (**4a**) at Passage des Abbesses. Around the corner is the greengrocer shop, **AU MARCHE DE LA BUTTE** (**4b**), Passage des Abbesses.

The lovely art deco café where Amélie works is **CAFÉ DES 2 MOULINS, 15 RUE LEPIC AT RUE CAUCHOIS** (**5**). It can be a bit tricky to find. Rue Lepic winds down from Place du Tertre then seems to merge into rue des Abbesses. In fact, it turns sharply south and the café is south of rue des Abbesses.

Nino works in **PALACE VIDEO, 37 BOULEVARD DE CLICHY** (**6**), a sex shop in the raunchy Pigalle district (where

you'll find the original Moulin Rouge nightclub).

The stairs where Amélie sees Nino's 'Ou et quand?' posters are those of the overground **LINE 6 STATION OF LA MOTTE-PICQET-GRENELLE** (**7**), south of Champ de Mars. This is also the station Amélie stands beneath when she scratches the name of the first 'Dominique Bredoteau' from her list.

Amélie searches for Bretodeau, to return his box of precious mementoes, in a phone booth at the northern end of rue Mouffetard at rue Clovis. The bar where she overhears the result is to the south, **LE VERRE A PIED, 118 BIS RUE MOUFFETARD** (**8**).

Park, northwest of Alnwick on the A1 in Northumberland. Piggily villainous Harold Innocent is popped out of the window to land in the courtyard of 12th century **Alnwick Castle** itself. Nottingham Castle square sat on the backlot at Shepperton, though the castle itself – in longshot – is the fortified city of **Carcassonne** down in the south of France close to the Spanish border (seen also in *The Bride*, Franc Roddam's 1985 spin on the *Bride of Frankenstein*). The interior of Nottingham Cathedral is the **Church of St Bartholomew the Great**, a tiny church – repository of the bones of St Rahere – tucked away behind Smithfield, London, and seen also in *Four Weddings and a Funeral*.

ROBOCOP
(1987, dir: Paul Verhoeven)
Peter Weller, Nancy Allen, Ronny Cox.
● **DALLAS, TEXAS; NEW YORK; PENNSYLVANIA**

OCP HQ: Dallas City Hall, Marilla Street

PHOTOGRAPH COURTESY DALLAS CONVENTION AND VISITORS BUREAU

Terrific black comedy actioner, with sleazoid techno-freaks incorporating dead cop Weller into a damn near indestructible law'n'order machine. Set in a futuristic New Detroit, the vaguely familiar skyline is eighties Dallas. The sinister OCP HQ is **Dallas City Hall, 1500 Marilla Street**, stretched to 95 storeys with some optical effects, though the dizzying Atrium is that of **Le Meridien** (formerly the Plaza of the Americas Hotel), **650 North Pearl Street** (*℡ 214.979.9000*). The rundown Detroit Police Precinct, Metro West, is the old **Sons of Hermann Hall, 3414 Elm Street** at Exposition, built in 1911 by the Order of the Sons of Hermann, a German emigré's organisation. Other Dallas locations include the **Renaissance Tower, 1201 Elm Street**, and music venue the **Bomb Factory, 2713 Canton Street**. The Detroit factory, in which Weller is shot to bits, was a disused car assembly plant at Long Island. The climax takes place at the **Duquesne Steel Works**, off Route 837, **Duquesne**, Pennsylvania.

ROBOCOP 2
(1990, dir: Irvin Kershner)
Peter Weller, Nancy Allen, Daniel O'Herlihy.
● **TEXAS**

Robocop takes on the newer, bigger version, Robocop 2, in this sequel, which found its futuristic cityscapes in

Civic Centrum, exterior: Wortham Theater Center, Texas Avenue

Houston, Texas. Civic Centrum is a combination of the **Wortham Theater Center, 500 Texas Avenue** (outside) and the **George R Brown Conven-**tion Center, 1001 Avenue of the Americas (inside). The OCP office this time around is the **Cullen Center, 1600 Smith Street**.

Robocop 3's Motor City is **Atlanta**, Georgia, with filming on **Auburn Avenue**.

Civic Centrum, interior: George R Brown Convention Center

ROBOT MONSTER
(1953, dir: Phil Tucker)
George Nader, Claudia Barrett, Selena Royle.
● **LOS ANGELES, CALIFORNIA**

Legendary movie dreck with the last six people on Earth pitted against a fabulously inventive monster – a guy in a gorilla suit wearing a diving helmet. Filmed in the thrilling glory of Tru-Stereo 3D, too. It was shot in the wilds of **Bronson Caverns**, Griffith Park, LA.

OCP HQ: Cullen Center, Smith Street

ROCK, THE
(1996, dir: Michael Bay)
Sean Connery, Nicolas Cage, Ed Harris.
● **CALIFORNIA**

Connery's luxury suite: Fairmont Hotel, Mason Street

High-octane actioner, with embittered major Harris and his crack troops taking over Alcatraz Island and pointing some very nasty chemical warheads at the City by the Bay. Only ex-inmate and political prisoner Connery can sort the problem out, along with nervous scientist Cage. And it is the real **Alcatraz Prison** on Alcatraz Island in San Francisco Bay. It wasn't possible to close down the national monument, so filming had to accommodate tour parties milling around. See *Escape From Alcatraz* for visiting details, if you still want to risk a potential hostage situation. Nicolas Cage's apartment is supposedly in Washington DC, but the view from the window clearly shows the World Interstate Centre in downtown LA, while the sign on the roof, where he cavorts with his girlfriend, identifies it as the **Hotel Rosslyn, 112 West 5th Street** (*℡ 213.624.3311*), downtown LA (also in Sam Raimi's *Darkman*).

While the FBI agents set up a mobile command HQ on **Pier 39** on San Francisco Bay, Cage is summoned to FBI offices in **City Hall, Van Ness Avenue** at McAllister Street in the Civic Center. Connery demands, and gets, a penthouse suite at the **Fairmont Hotel, 950 Mason**

Connery meets up with his daughter: Palace of Fine Arts, Lyon Street

Cage's Washington DC apartment: Hotel Rosslyn, West 5th Street, LA

Street on Nob Hill (*© 415.772.5000*), seen also in Hitchcock's final film, *Family Plot*. It's from here that Connery escapes after leaving the FBI boss dangling from the roof. But look again. The hotel that Cage chases Connery from is the **Biltmore**, on Pershing Square in downtown LA (see *Beverly Hills Cop* for details of this frequent movie location).

The San Francisco ritual of a bouncy car chase down the city's hills is pepped up with a spectacular cable car crash, filmed in **Russian Hill**. Connery is apprehended when he meets up with his estranged daughter at the **Palace of Fine Arts, 3601 Lyon Street** between Jefferson and Bay Streets in the Marina district, a backdrop for both *Vertigo* and inventive time-travel thriller *Time After Time*, which had HG Wells tracking Jack the Ripper through modern-day California. Built in 1915 for the Panama-Pacific Exhibition, the grandiose Romanesque buildings of the Palace were retained and restored, and now house a kids' museum, the Exploratorium.

ROCKY

(1976, dir: John G Avildsen)
Sylvester Stallone, Burgess Meredith, Talia Shire.
● PHILADELPHIA, PENNSYLVANIA; LOS ANGELES, CALIFORNIA

In the year of *Taxi Driver*, *All the President's Men* and *Network*, this old fashioned fairytale of the underdog coming out on top took Oscars for Best Film and Best Director. The main

The end of the run: Philadelphia from the top of the steps

The Rocky steps: Philadelphia Museum of Modern Art, Benjamin Franklin Parkway

location you'll want to see is, of course, the flight of 68 steps up to the **Philadelphia Museum of Modern Art, Benjamin Franklin Parkway** at 26th Street (*© 215.763.8100, www.philamuseum.org*), seen also in *Dressed to Kill*. But although *Rocky* is set in Philadelphia, the film's locations

are split between the City of Brotherly Love and Los Angeles. Rocky's neighbourhood is South Philly. During training for his big break he runs past **Philadelphia City Hall** and through the **Italian Market, Ninth Street** between Federal and Christian Streets. The opening boxing match, though, with the religious mural overlooking the ring, is in LA. It's the **Oscar de la Hoya Boxing Youth Center, 1114 South Lorena Street** in east LA. The press conference is held in the **Ambassador Hotel, 3400 Wilshire Boulevard**. The future of this LA landmark, bought up by Donald Trump, is currently in the balance. Catch it while it's still there, locked up and empty, and now used almost exclusively as a movie set (see the 1954 *A Star Is Born* for details). Rocky works out by pounding sides of beef at **Shamrock Meats Inc, 3461 East Vernon Avenue** at Alcoa Avenue, just south of the Los Angeles River in Vernon, southeast of downtown. The climactic fight itself, against Apollo Creed, is in Los Angeles, at the **Olympic Auditorium, 1801 South Grand Avenue** at Olympic Boulevard, downtown LA. It was built for the 1932 Olympics. The fight scenes for *Raging Bull*, and wrestling matches in *Ed Wood* and *Man on the Moon* were also shot here.

Rocky trains: Italian Market, Ninth Street

The climactic fight: Olympic Auditorium, South Grand Avenue

ROCKY II

(1979, dir: Sylvester Stallone)
Sylvester Stallone, Talia Shire, Carl Weathers.
● PHILADELPHIA, PENNSYLVANIA; LOS ANGELES, CALIFORNIA

Rocky hits the skids, but bounces back to win another fight, in this sequel with a budget eight times that of the original *Rocky*. Once again, Rocky trains in Philadelphia, runs in the **Italian Market**, trots up the steps of the **Museum of Modern Art** and triumphs over adversity in LA's **Olympic Auditorium** (see *Rocky* for details).

ROCKY III

(1982, dir: Sylvester Stallone)
Sylvester Stallone, Talia Shire, Carl Weathers.
● PHILADELPHIA, PENNSYLVANIA; LOS ANGELES, CALIFORNIA

Rocky gets beaten early on, but don't worry – he wins out in the end, in LA's **Olympic Auditorium** again. The fight arena is the Crystal Ballroom of the **Biltmore Hotel, 506 South Grand Avenue**, downtown LA (see *Beverly Hills Cop* for details). Meanwhile, in Philadelphia, Rocky now has a statue atop the steps of the **Museum of Mod-**

Rocky trains: Park Hyatt Philadelphia at the Bellevue, Broad Street

ern **Art**. After filming, Stallone generously donated the statue to the museum. Errrm, thanks, but no thanks, they said, and the statue languished in Stallone's own backyard, until local petitions resulted in its being installed at the Spectrum Stadium, home of the Flyers hockey team and the 76ers basketball team (a location for the movie *Philadelphia*). Rocky trains at the ultra-luxurious **Park Hyatt Philadelphia at the Bellevue, Broad Street** at Walnut Street (© *215.893.1776*), just south of City Hall.

ROCKY IV
(1985, dir: Sylvester Stallone)
Sylvester Stallone, Dolph Lundgren, Carl Weathers.
● **WYOMING; BRITISH COLUMBIA, CANADA**

Rocky takes on Blond Bombshell Lundgren in laboured East-West allegory, filmed in **Jackson**, Wyoming, passing itself off as Siberia. Replacing the Philadelphia steps is **Rendezvous Peak** at Jackson. Filming also in Vancouver, with local extras sweating through a summer heatwave under fur coats and winter wrappings. The fight, supposedly at Caesar's Palace, Las Vegas, was shot in the vast **Pacific National Exhibition Agrodome, Vancouver** (© *604.253.2311*), British Columbia.

In *Rocky V*, Rocky's mansion is **160 San Rafael Avenue**, Pasadena.

ROCKY HORROR PICTURE SHOW, THE
(1975, dir: Jim Sharman)
Tim Curry, Susan Sarandon, Richard O'Brien.
● **BERKSHIRE**

Frankenfurter's: Oakley Court Hotel, Windsor Road

The cult movie to end all cult movies, despite being a bit *too* calculatingly camp and being constricted by its microbudget. Interiors filmed, fittingly, at Hammer Films' old Bray Studio near Maidenhead in Berkshire. Frankenfurter's mansion is, conveniently, alongside the studio, and has naturally figured in a whole slew of horror movies. It was Oakley Court, a Victorian gothic folly that lay for many years in a state of disrepair. It's been seen in dozens of movies, particularly Hammer films such as *The Curse of Frankenstein* and *The Plague of the Zombies*. It has since been renovated and is now the rather swanky **Oakley Court Hotel, Windsor Road, Water Oakley** (© *01753.609988*), on the A308 between Maidenhead and Windsor.

ROLLERBALL
(1975, dir: Norman Jewison)

James Caan, John Houseman, Maud Adams.
● **GERMANY; SWITZERLAND**

Jewison's futuristic sci-fi was made in Europe, at Pinewood and in Munich. The Rollerball stadium is the vast, circular **Olympic Basketball Hall** in Munich. The cylindrical towers of the Energy Corporation HQ are the **BMW Building** in Munich, and the world library, where Jonathan E (Caan) consults the supercomputer Zero, is the **League of Nations Building** in **Geneva**, Switzerland.

ROMAN HOLIDAY
(1953, dir: William Wyler)
Audrey Hepburn, Gregory Peck, Eddie Albert.
● **ROME, ITALY**

The Mouth of Truth: Santa Maria in Cosmedin

American newspaperman Peck romances Euro-princess Hepburn around the touristy sights of Rome, including the **Spanish Steps**. The **Mouth of Truth (Bocca della Verita)**, the carved stone face which supposedly bites the hands off liars, can be found in the church of **Santa Maria in Cosmedin, Piazza Bocca della Verita**. Filming also took place in the 19th century **Palazzo Brancaccio, Viale del Monte Oppio 7**, now a conference centre, between the Colosseum and the Basilica of Santa Maria Maggiore; and one of Rome's largest palaces, **Palazzo Colonna, Piazza Santa Apostoli**. Open only on Saturdays, the entrance is on Via della Pilotta 17.

ROMANCING THE STONE
(1984, dir: Robert Zemeckis)
Kathleen Turner, Michael Douglas, Danny DeVito.
● **NEW YORK CITY; MEXICO; UTAH; NEVADA**

Turner's apartment: West End Avenue

Kathleen Turner is a New York novelist dreaming of a handsome hero who gets into trouble tracing her missing sister in Colombia and finds – go on, guess. Turner's apartment is **495 West End Avenue**, on the Upper West Side of Manhattan. The Colombian scenes were filmed, during a spectacularly wet rainy season, in Mexico – the cliffs at **Xica**; the fortress at **San Juan de Ulua**; the narrow roads of **Barraca Grande**; **Xalapa**; and the jungles of **El Arsenal**. The desert scenes are **Washington County**, southwest Utah; and the **Mojave Desert** near Las Vegas, Nevada.

ROMEO AND JULIET
(1968, dir: Franco Zeffirelli)
Leonard Whiting, Olivia Hussey, Milo O'Shea.
● **ITALY**

Beautiful to look at but slightly schmaltzy version of the Shakespeare play. After filming his *Taming of the Shrew* entirely in the studio, Zeffirelli takes the tearjerker out on location around Italy. Sites include the Tuscan hill town of **Pienza** – whose main square was recreated in the studio at Cinecittà. The fight scenes use the streets of the small Medieval town of **Gubbia**, on the slopes of Mount Ingino in Umbria. More Medieval backdrops were provided by the towns of **Tuscania**, on the River Marta, 50 miles northwest of Rome; and **Serravalle**, a walled village below the Meschio gorge, part of Vittorio Veneto, about 45 miles to the north of Venice.

ROMPER STOMPER
(1992, dir: Geoffrey Wright)
Russell Crowe, Daniel Pollock, Jacqueline McKenzie.
● VICTORIA, AUSTRALIA

A gang of neo-Nazi skinheads (led by a pre-*Gladiator* Crowe) feuds and splinters after terrorising the Vietnamese community in **Melbourne**, in this violent movie, shot around the **Footscray** district. The Vietnamese skateboarders are attacked at **Richmond Station**, standing in for Footscray Station, which is in the heart of the Vietnamese community but doesn't look as threatening as the underpass at Richmond. Hando (Crowe) finally pops his DMs in the surf at **Point Addis** (in reality, a nudist beach) on the **Great Ocean Road**.

RONIN
(1998, dir: John Frankenheimer)
Robert De Niro, Jean Reno, Natascha McElhone.
● FRANCE

The Bar de Montmartre, where the crew meets up: Blue Sky, rue des Trois Freres

Back in the 60s, Frankenheimer was a major player, with films such as *The Manchurian Candidate*, *Seconds* and *The Birdman of Alcatraz* to his credit. Then he seemed to lose his way (even taking over the disastrous *Island of Dr Moreau* in 1996). Before his death in 2002, he enjoyed a brief return to form with this classy thriller, boasting tough, spare dialogue by an uncredited David Mamet.

The opening scene is, of course, **Montmartre**, Paris. The steep flight of steps down which Sam (De Niro) cautiously makes his way is **rue Drevet**. At the foot of the steps, the Bar de Montmartre, where the crew meets up, is TexMex restaurant **Blue Sky, rue des Trois Freres**. If you watch carefully, you'll see a crafty cut (as extras pass in front of the camera) to a studio set of the bar, recreated at the **Studios Éclair** in Epinay. This explains why Sam can walk alongside the steps, but you can't. The warehouse where Deirdre (McElhone) explains the plan is an abandoned workshop in Paris's working-class suburb of **Aubervillers**.

Sam and Vincent (Reno) have reservations as the crew is led into an ambush in the tunnel beneath the elaborate **Pont Alexandre III** after a meeting on **Port du Gros Caillou**. Seamus (Jonathan Pryce) contacts Deirdre on the escalator at **Port de Lilas** metro.

The quest for the mysterious suitcase (it's a MacGuffin, it doesn't need explaining) moves to **Nice**, though the hotel in which Sam and Deirdre check out the prey is the **Majestic Barrière, 10 la Croisette**, along the coast in Cannes (© *04.92.98.77.00, www.lucien-barriere.com/localized/en/hote/maje*), which was conveniently closed for renovation. The villa where the case is held

De Niro cautiously makes his way down the steps: Rue Drevet

is at **La Turbie**, and the subsequent attack on the car and chase are in the beautiful seafront village of **Villefranche-sur-Mer**. The chase continues to Vieux Nice (the Old Town), ending at **Quai des Deux Emmanuel** on the harbour. The church outside which a choir sings carols is the **Cathedral St Reparate** on **Place Rosetti**, and Sam and co retire to **La Claire Fontaine, Place Rosetti**, after Gregor (Stellan Starsgard) pulls a fast one and switches cases. They catch up with him and the Russians (who're now after this case too) in the town of **Arles**, where there's another shoot-out in the **Place du Forum d'Arles**, the huge Roman amphitheatre. The spectacular rocky landscape through which Vincent drives the wounded Sam for help is **Les Baux-de-Provence**, just outside Arles.

It's back to Paris for the thunderous car chase, through streets south of Les Invalides, along **avenue Duquesne**, **avenue de Ségur** and **avenue de Breteuil**; through the **Champerret Tunnel**; toward the great modernistic arch at **La Defense**; driving the wrong way against 300 stunt drivers along the **Périphérique** ring road.

The final showdown is at an ice-show in the 6,000-seat concert hall **Le Zenith, 211 avenue Jean-Jaurès**, on the eastern edge of Paris in the middle of **La Villette** park (© *01.42.08.60.00, www.le-zenith.com/paris*).

ROOM AT THE TOP
(1958, dir: Jack Clayton)
Laurence Harvey, Simone Signoret, Donald Wolfit.
● YORKSHIRE

The screech of a train whistle and Mario Nascimbene's jazzy score heralded the arrival of the New Wave in Britain. And while Home Counties actors struggle embarrassingly with northern accents, this adaptation of John Braine's novel about Joe Lampton (Harvey), a working

The dance: Cartwright Memorial Hall, Lister Park

Joe Lampton arrives at Warnley Town: Halifax Station

Heather Sears' house: Jarvis Bankfield Hotel, Bingley

Joe meets Alice: Boy and Barrel, James Gate, Bradford

Joe Lampton works for the council: Bradford City Hall

The fight in the piazza: Piazza della Signorina

class lad with a whole plate of chips on his shoulder, still packs a punch. Many of the locations are surprisingly unchanged. The opening scene of Lampton arriving at the fictitious setting of Warnley Town Station uses **Halifax Station**. Warnley itself is Bradford, where Lampton works in **Bradford City Hall**. The dance was filmed inside Bradford's art gallery, **Cartwright Memorial Hall** in **Lister Park, Keighley Road**, a couple of miles northwest of the city centre. The posh home of Susan Brown (Heather Sears), to which Joe aspires, has been extended to become the **Jarvis Bankfield Hotel, Bradford Road, Bingley** (© 01274.567123). And you can still sink a pint in the pub where Joe and Alice (Signoret) meet up: the **Boy and Barrel, 60 Westgate** at James Gate.

ROOM WITH A VIEW, A

(1986, dir: James Ivory)
Maggie Smith, Helena Bonham Carter, Julian Sands.
● FLORENCE, ITALY; KENT; LONDON

Perfect Merchant-Ivory drama from EM Forster's novel, blessed with a wonderful camp sensibility – just look at the interspersed captions – and a clutch of priceless cameos.

The Pensione Bertolini in Florence, where English rosebud-abroad Lucy Honeychurch (Bonham Carter) finds herself in a room *without* a view, was the Quisisana e Ponte Vecchio, alongside the Arno in Florence. Damaged in a bomb explosion, it closed in the early 1990s, but has been renovated and reopened as **Hotel degli Orafi, Lungarno Archibusieri 4** (© 39.055.26622, *www.hoteldegliorafi.it*). Flouncy novelist Eleanor Lavish whisks mousy Charlotte Bartlett (Smith) off to see the *real* Florence, starting at the

The hotel: Pensione Quisisana e Ponte Vecchio, now Hotel degli Orafi

statue of Grand Duke Ferdinand in the **Piazza Santissima Annunziata**, while Lucy sets off to explore the sights alone. She's hassled by locals at the monument to Dante in the **Church of Santa Croce, Piazza Santa Croce 16** (unlike Michelangelo, Galileo, Machiavelli and Rossini who are buried in Santa Croce, Dante Alighieri has only a monument – he was exiled to, and died in, Ravenna). The bloody knife fight was filmed in the **Piazza della Signorina** – the site of the original 'Bonfire of the Vanities' when in 1497 followers of religious fanatic Savonarola burned all their worldly possessions. The idea really took off, and a year later they burned Savonarola too. There's a pretty fine selection of Florentine statuary seen here, including Cellini's Perseus Holding the Head of Medusa and a copy of Michelangelo's David. The huge fountain where the crowd try to revive the knife victim is Bartolommeo Ammannati's 1565 **Neptune Fountain**. Judged to be somewhat less successful than its neighbours, it's now known as Il Biancone – roughly, the Big White Lump. The drive out to the picnic was filmed on the road from Florence to Fiesde, and the picnic itself took place at **Villa di Maiano**, on a hillside near **Maiano**.

Back in England, Windy Corner, the home of the Honeychurch family in Summerstreet, is a private home (that of film critic John Pym), **Foxwold, Pipers Lane, Brasted Chart**, south of Brasted and west of Sevenoaks in west Kent – not visible from the road. The lake where George Emerson (Sands) goes skinny-dipping with Freddy and the Reverend Beebe was created in the grounds here. Lucy's engagement party was filmed in the grounds of **Emmett's Garden**, a National Trust property just north of Ide Hill off New Road a couple of miles from Brasted. The five-acre garden, once densely wooded and, in spring, carpeted with bluebells, suffered heavily in the 1987 hurricane and is only slowly being restored to its former state. It's open to the public April to October. The railway station is **Horsted Keynes Station**, the northern terminus of the famous Bluebell Line, a few miles north of Haywards Heath in Sussex.

The 'well appointed home' of Cecil Vyse is the **Linley-Sambourne House, 18 Stafford Terrace**, London W8. Built for *Punch* cartoonist Edward Linley-Sambourne in the 1870s, this unique perfectly preserved late Victorian house is managed by the Victorian Society and open to the public on Wednesdays and Sundays, March to October. You can find it just north of High Street Kensington (© 020.8994.1019; *tube: High Street Kensington*), and see it again, as

Windy Corner: Foxwold, Brasted Chart

The village: Chiddingstone

Hugh Grant's London pad, in *Maurice*. It's in the **National Gallery, Trafalgar Square**, that Cecil invites the Emersons to Summerstreet, which turns out to be **Chiddingstone**, a street of Tudor houses off the Edenbridge-Tonbridge road, B2027, at Bough Beech about 10 miles from Sevenoaks, Tonbridge or Tunbridge Wells in Kent, and about five from Emmett's. Here you can see the Reverend Beebe's church, **St Mary's**, opposite the row of houses. The sitting room, where Mr Emerson persuades Lucy to tell the truth, is a room in St Mary's rectory, and the Emersons' house is **Chiddingstone Village Hall**. Back in London, the home of the two Miss Alans is **167 Queensgate**, South Kensington, SW7. At the time of filming this was the home of the Soviet representative for Estonia, but it's now a private residence.

ROSEMARY'S BABY

(1968, dir: Roman Polanski)
Mia Farrow, John Cassavetes, Ruth Gordon.
● **NEW YORK CITY**

The gloomy Bramford apartment building: Dakota Apartments, West 72nd Street, West Side

The Bramford, the brooding gothic building where newlyweds Farrow and Cassavetes set up home is, of course, the **Dakota Apartments, 1 West 72nd Street** at Central Park West, home to many celebs over the years, including Judy Garland, Lauren Bacall, Boris Karloff and Leonard Bernstein. It is most famously the last home of John Lennon, who was shot outside it in 1980. Over the road, in Central Park, is Lennon's memorial, Strawberry Fields. The Dakota was also home to David Aames (Tom Cruise) in *Vanilla Sky*. Ira Levin's original story was reputedly inspired by the Alwyn Court Apartments, a Renaissance-style block, decorated with terracotta dragons, at 180 West 58th Street.

ROUNDERS

(1998, dir: John Dahl)
Matt Damon, Edward Norton, John Turturro.
● **NEW YORK CITY; NEW JERSEY**

Damon is a gambling addict getting into hot water in John Dahl's poker drama, set in New York and Atlantic City. The City Law School, where Damon studies, is **Rutger's Law School, 123 Washington Street, University Heights, Newark**, New Jersey.

ROXANNE

(1987, dir: Fred Schepisi)
Steve Martin, Daryl Hannah, Rick Rossovich.

● **BRITISH COLUMBIA, CANADA**

Beautifully filmed updating of Rostand's *Cyrano de Bergerac*, which could have been a classic tearjerker without the cop-out ending. Shot on location in British Columbia, the photogenically precipitous streets and pine-clad hills are **Nelson**, in the southeast corner of the state, north of the US border.

ROYAL TENENBAUMS, THE

(2001, dir: Wes Anderson)
Gene Hackman, Anjelica Huston, Gwyneth Paltrow.
● **NEW YORK CITY; NEW JERSEY**

The Tenenbaum house: Convent Avenue, Harlem

Rushmore just about survived its arch whimsicality but, despite a top-drawer cast, the studied eccentricity of Wes Anderson's over-achieving, under-functioning family feels irritatingly contrived. This off-kilter Manhattan seems to exist in a parallel universe. The Tenenbaum house at 111 Archer Avenue is **339 Convent Avenue at 144th Street, Harlem**. The zebra wallpaper in Margot's room is taken from the striking patterns at Gino, 780 Lexington Avenue at East 61st Street (seen in Woody Allen's *Mighty Aphrodite*). The **Waldorf Astoria, 301 Park Avenue** (see *Scent of a Woman* for details) becomes the Lindbergh Palace Hotel, from which Royal (Hackman) is finally evicted after 22 years, and the old **US Customs House, Battery Place**, Battery Park (seen in *Batman Forever* and *Ghostbusters II*) is transformed into the City Public Archives, in which the young Tenenbaums camp out. Richie Tenenbaum's disastrous final tennis match was filmed on the Centre Court of the **West Side Tennis Club, 1 Tennis Place, Forest Hills**, Queens. The restaurant where Royal has an edgy meeting with Margot (Paltrow) is **Grand Prospect Hall, 263 Prospect Avenue, Park Slope** in Brooklyn (see *The Cotton Club* for details).

RULES OF ATTRACTION, THE

(2002, dir: Roger Avary)
James Van Der Beek, Ian Somerhalder, Shannyn Sossamon.
● **CALIFORNIA**

Bret Easton Ellis's novel, brought to the screen by the screenwriter of *Pulp Fiction*, is set in winter-bound Camden College, England, but shot during a sizzling August at the **University of Redlands**, San Bernardino County (seen also in 1981's *Hell Night* and *Slackers*) – with the camera carefully avoiding palm trees.

RULING CLASS, THE

(1971, dir: Peter Medak)
Peter O'Toole, Harry Andrews, Arthur Lowe.
● **LINCOLNSHIRE; SURREY; BUCKINGHAMSHIRE; HAMPSHIRE; LONDON**

Peter Barnes' wild, black satire on the British upper class, with O'Toole as the gentle Jesus freak. His venal family is thrown into confusion when he inherits the earldom of Gurney, after the 13th Earl (Andrews) succumbs to a tutu-clad auto-erotic asphyxiation (a scene filmed in the banqueting hall of the **Worshipful Company of Stationers and Newspaper Makers, Stationers' Hall, Ave Maria Lane**, London EC4). The fantastical exterior of Gurney Manor is **Harlaxton Manor**, an extravagant neo-Elizabethan extravaganza a couple of miles west of **Grantham**, Lincolnshire. Owned by the University of Evansville, the house is open in May and June (*©* *01476.564541*). It's now probably more famous from the trashy remake of *The Haunting*. Interiors were filmed in **Cliveden** near Maidenhead, scene of the sixties sexual frolics portrayed in *Scandal*, and seen in The Beatles' movie *Help!*. The Gurney estate village is **Shere**, on the A25 between Guildford and Dorking in Surrey. There was also filming at **The Elvetham** (formerly Elvetham Hall), now a hotel and conference centre, at **Hartley Wintney** near Fleet in Hampshire (*© 01252.844871, www.elvethamhotel.co.uk*).

RUMBLE FISH

(1983, dir: Francis Ford Coppola)
Matt Dillon, Mickey Rourke, Diane Lane.
● OKLAHOMA

Filmed back-to-back with *The Outsiders*, and from another SE Hinton book, *Rumble Fish* couldn't be more different, with strange, dreamlike, bleached out monochrome photography, time-lapse landscapes and surreal set pieces. It was made on location in **Tulsa**, Oklahoma (where the fish are released into the Arkansas River at the **21st Street Bridge**), and a few miles southwest down I-44 in the town of **Sapulpa**.

RUSH HOUR

(1998, dir: Brett Ratner)
Jackie Chan, Chris Tucker, Tom Wilkinson.
● LOS ANGELES, CALIFORNIA; HONG KONG, CHINA

Hollywood sightseeing: Mann's Chinese Theatre, Hollywood Boulevard

The opening scene is **Hong Kong Harbour**, but Tom Wilkinson's home, despite the view of the city from the windows, is in LA. It's Frank Lloyd Wright's **Ennis Brown House, 2607 Glendower Avenue**, Silverlake, below Griffith Park (see *The House on Haunted Hill* for details). Chris Tucker takes Jackie Chan to see John Wayne's footprints at **Grauman's Chinese Theatre, 6925 Hollywood Boulevard** in Hollywood. The China Exposition is at the **New Los Angeles Convention Center, Figueroa Street** between 11th Street and Venice Boulevard, downtown LA. See it also in *Face/Off* and as the spaceport in *Starship Troopers*.

RUSHMORE

(1998, dir: Wes Anderson)
Jason Schwartzman, Bill Murray, Olivia Williams.
● TEXAS

Max's long-suffering private school: St John's School, Claremont Lane

Made in the director's home town of **Houston**, Texas, Anderson's too-whimsical tale is made bearable by Schwartzman's endearingly geeky enthusiasm as Max Fischer blithely attempting to build a multi-million dollar aquarium or staging *Serpico* as a school play. Rushmore Academy, Max's long-suffering private school, is **St John's School, 2401 Claremont Lane**, north of West-

The chapel: St John's School, Claremont Lane

heimer Road, the director's old school, west of downtown. Across Westheimer is Grover Cleveland High School, the public school to which he's banished: **Lamar High School, 3325 Westheimer Street** at Buffalo Speedway (and not nearly as run-down as it's shown in the film).

Max's house: Emerson Street

Max's house is on **Emerson Street**, east of Montrose Boulevard; Bert's, his dad's haircutting business, is **Doug and Don's Barber Shop, 219 East Eleventh Street** at Harvard Street; and Max visits his mother's grave in **Hollywood Cemetery, 3506 East Main Street**.

Blume International Saw Pipes, the enormous factory of businessman Herman Blume (Murray), is **Saw Pipes USA Inc, 5200 East McKinney Road, Baytown**, east of Houston. After his wife asks for a divorce, Blume is obliged to move into the classy **Warwick Hotel, 5701 Main Street** (*© 713.526.1991, www.warwick-hotelhouston.com*) in Houston's Museum District, south of town.

Max's dad's haircutting business: Doug and Don's Barber Shop, East Eleventh Street

Max flies a kite: the parking lot of Delmar Stadium, Mangum Road

Max flies a kite with Dirk, and meets Margaret with her plane, in the parking lot of **Delmar Stadium, 1900 Mangum Road** at West 18th Street, northwest Houston.

RYAN'S DAUGHTER
(1970, dir: David Lean)
Sarah Miles, Robert Mitchum, Christopher Jones.
● IRELAND; SOUTH AFRICA

The critical mauling of this vastly overblown epic caused David Lean to retire from the screen for fourteen years. Despite the visual splendour and some stunning sequences (the real storm is breathtaking), the small love story is uninvolving. The entire village of Kirrary was a set, now vanished, built near Carhoo on the **Dingle Peninsula**, down at the southwesternmost tip of Ireland. Most of the beach scenes were shot at **Inch Strand**, about 12 miles east of Dingle itself, and at **Coumeenoole Strand** near Dunquin. The beach where Rosie Ryan (Miles) loses her parasol is at the **Cliffs of Moher**, County Clare, while other scenes used **Barrow Strand**, north of Tralee.

The highlight of the movie, the breathtaking storm sequence, uses the rocky coast at **Bridges of Ross**, 30 miles to the south. As the troubled shoot rolled on and winter arrived, a new – and warmer – beach had to be found for the explosive suicide of Major Dorian (Jones). The impenetrable logistics of film-making meant the scene was finally shot in South Africa, where the local white rock was painted to match the Irish locations.

S

S.W.A.T.
(2003, dir: Clark Johnson)
Samuel L Jackson, Colin Farrell, LL Cool J.
● LOS ANGELES, CALIFORNIA

Montel is pulled over by the cops: Key Club, Sunset Boulevard, Hollywood

Actions fortunately speak louder than the rather cheesy words in this energetic actioner, that opens with a bank raid which goes horribly wrong for SWATsters Brian Gamble (Jeremy Renner) and Jim Street (Farrell). The Valley Trust Bank, supposedly in the San Fernando Valley, was in **Lincoln Heights**, northeast of downtown LA, where the building, which was due for demolition, stood on **Workman Street** at North Broadway. After being disciplined, Gamble walks, but Street stays on, demoted to the Armory in the **Parker Center** (the former Police Administration Building), to the southwest of LA City Hall at **150 North Los Angeles Street**. He energetically works out at **Venice Beach**.

Enter veteran Hondo (Jackson), recruiting a crack SWAT team, and two downtown locations familiar to Farrell: he drives Hondo along **West Fifth Street**, past the site of *Phone Booth* (and the Alexandria Hotel from *Se7en*), to interview the veggie cop in front of the **Arcade Building, 542 South Broadway**, between Fifth and Sixth Streets, which was Matt Murdock's apartment in *Daredevil*.

With the team assembled, there's a training raid, to Hendrix's 'Crosstown Traffic', in front of the Cocoanut Grove entry to the old **Ambassador Hotel, 3400 Wilshire Boulevard** (see the 1937 and 1954 *A Star Is Born* for details), and a brief chill-out in the hotel's empty pool, before the simulated hijacking on the plane at the airline graveyard at **Lancaster** in the Mojave Desert.

Lethal kingpin Alex Montel (Olivier Martinez) dispatches a rival in the **Figaro Cafe, 1804 North Vermont Avenue** at Melbourne Avenue in Los Feliz (© 323.662.1587, www.figarorestaurants.com). Montel is pulled over by the cops, for having a dodgy rear light, on **Sunset Boulevard** in west Hollywood, outside the **Key Club, 9029 Sunset Boulevard**. The attempt to spring him from the police bus is on **Wilcox Street at Hollywood Boulevard**, across from Thomas Suriya's famous

Alex Montel dispatches a rival: Figaro Cafe, North Vermont Avenue, Los Feliz

The incendiary attempt to free Montel from the police convoy: Sixth Street at South Main Street

'You Are A Star' mural (which you can glimpse in the background). Montel is pinned to the ground by Jim Street on the Walk of Fame star of Alex Trebek (the gameshow host of *Jeopardy!*), outside **Roma Lingerie Clubwear, 6501 Hollywood Boulevard**.

With a $100 million reward on offer, there's an incendiary attempt to free Montel from the police convoy on **Sixth Street** at **South Main Street**, outside **Cole's** restaurant (housed in the **Pacific Electric Building** used in *Forrest Gump*, *L.A. Confidential*, *Se7en*, *Face/Off* and *Spider-Man*).

"Did they build a new airport downtown?" is the question, as a hijacked Lear jet prepares for landing. It's set down on the 3,446-foot, art deco **Sixth Street Bridge** over the concrete bed of the Los Angeles River toward Boyle Heights, southeast of downtown LA, for the movie's spectacular climax, with Street and Gamble slugging it out on the railway lines below.

SABOTAGE (aka *A Woman Alone*)
(1936, dir: Alfred Hitchcock)
Sylvia Sidney, Oscar Homolka, John Loder.
● LONDON

Foreign agent Oscar Homolka's Bijou cinema, the High Street Station and neighbouring street are a studio set, but Hitchcock's early suspenser contains more real London locations than any other feature film seen at the time. The opening scene sees sabotage at **Battersea Power Station** on the South Bank of the Thames, plunging into darkness central London landmarks like the Palace of Westminster, Trafalgar Square and Piccadilly Circus. It's in **Trafalgar Square** that Sylvia Sidney later meets up with undercover cop John Loder, before going for a meal at Simpson's in the Strand. The restaurant, one of Hitchcock's favourites and where he entertained the press to publicise the movie, was mocked up in the studio, but you can see the real thing in *Howards End*. The Lord

The hijacked Lear jet is set down on the Sixth Street Bridge over the concrete bed of the Los Angeles River

Mayor's Show, where Sidney's young brother waits unknowingly with the bomb, was also faked. Supposedly in the Strand, the parade was shot in front of a giant photograph of the Law Courts.

SABOTEUR
(1942, dir: Alfred Hitchcock)
Robert Cummings, Priscilla Lane, Norman Lloyd.
● CALIFORNIA; NEW YORK CITY; NEVADA

Cummings is the innocent man suspected of being a wartime saboteur. Though made largely at Universal Studios in Hollywood, there are the usual Hitchcockian landmark locations, largely supplied by a second unit. Cummings thumbs across the desert near **Lone Pine**, on Route 395, central California, before arriving at the ghost town which overlooks the saboteurs' next target, **Boulder Dam**, over the Colorado River just outside of Las Vegas, Nevada (see *The Amazing Colossal Man* for details). Arriving in New York, Priscilla Lane is held captive in the Rockefeller Center, and there's a shoot-out at a film screening in **Radio City Music Hall, 1260 Sixth Avenue** (though the deco interior was largely recreated in the studio; see *Radio Days* for details).

A new ending was added, incorporating shots of the SS *Normandie*, supposedly in the Brooklyn Navy Yard. The ship had been renamed USS *Lafayette*, and burned in a suspicious fire at a Manhattan pier in February 1942. Listing under the weight of water used to extinguish the blaze, the ailing ship was inserted into the movie, a supposed victim of the saboteur. The Navy was not best pleased, but the shot remains. The famous climax atop the Statue of Liberty was filmed, of course, mainly in the studio.

SABRINA (aka *Sabrina Fair*)
(1954, dir: Billy Wilder)
Humphrey Bogart, Audrey Hepburn, William Holden.
● NEW YORK

Wealthy brothers Holden and Bogart vie for the affections of chauffeur's daughter Hepburn in Wilder's romantic comedy, which was filmed at the **Welland House, Glen Cove**, on Route 107 on the northeast coast of Long Island, New York.

SAFETY LAST
(1923, dir: Sam Taylor, Fred Newmeyer)
Harold Lloyd, Mildred Davis, Noah Young.
● LOS ANGELES, CALIFORNIA

Silent comedian Harold Lloyd's stock-in-trade was a series of dizzying stunts involving dangling from the outside of tall buildings. In *Safety Last* he's a smalltown boy trying to impress his girlfriend by entering a skyscraper-climbing contest. The De Vore Department Store in the Bolton Building is a combination of two downtown LA structures, only one

The De Vore Department Store: South Broadway

of which still survives. **801 South Broadway** can still be seen, but 908 South Broadway, where he famously hung from a clock face, has been demolished. It's not quite as dangerous as it looked. The clock face was built over a platform, and for the longshots, Lloyd hired 'human fly' Bill Struthers to climb the building. That's the LA Stock Exchange you can see in the background. Lloyd worked over the same ideas later in *Feet First*.

SALAAM BOMBAY!
(1988, dir: Mira Nair)
Shafiq Syed, Raghudir Yadav, Chanda Sharma.
● INDIA

Former documentarist Nair mixes real street kids and seasoned actors in her first fiction film, as village boy Krishna (Syed) tries to make a living on the streets of what is now **Mumbai**. Krishna works as a teaboy around the 'Red Light' neighbourhood of **Grant Road**, and hangs out with drug-dependent Chillum (Yadav) on the **Grant Road Station**.

SALÒ (aka *Salò o Le 120 Giornate Di Sodoma/Salò, or The 120 Days of Sodom*)
(1975, dir: Pier Paolo Pasolini)
Paolo Bonacelli, Giorgio Cataldi, Caterina Boratto.
● ITALY

Pasolini's ice-cold and disturbing final film, banned until recently in the UK, transposes de Sade's *120 Days of Sodom* to the last days of fascist rule in northern Italy during WWII. Four upstanding pillars of the community spirit away a group of local youngsters for a terminally sadistic orgy. The estate was the decayed pre-Umbertine Villa Mirra, with overgrown gazebos and rose bushes choked by wisteria, at **Cavriana**, a few miles from Mantua, northern Italy. It's now the **Archaeological Museum of Alto Mantovano** (✆ *0376.806330*). Another Emilian villa not far from Bologna, and now a public park, was used for the scene in which the choicest local teens are selected. For the final scenes of torture and death, the courtyard of Villa Mirra was recreated in the studio at Cinecittà, Rome.

And, for those foodies who enjoy recreating meals from the movies, the recipe for the coprophagic banquet scene is: Swiss chocolate mixed with broken biscuits, condensed milk and marmalade, extruded through plastic tubing. Enjoy.

SAMOURAÏ, LE (aka *The Samurai/The Godson*)
(1967, dir: Jean-Pierre Melville)
Alain Delon, François Périer, Nathalie Delon.
● PARIS, FRANCE

Director Melville had a cameo in Jean-Luc Godard's groundbreaking *A Bout de Souffle* and his cool, minimalist gangster movie was also made on the streets of Paris. Delon, like Jean-Paul Belmondo before him, dodges the law on the Champs Elysées by ducking through an entrance at **1 rue Lord Byron** (behind the Champs) to pop out at **116 bis**, by the Lido, and duck into the **George V metro station**. He takes the Vincennes line to **Porte d'Ivry** where he's shot and wounded on meeting his contact. There's a convoluted metro chase as the law follows

Delon from the **Telegraphe metro** (near his apartment) to **Place des Fêtes**. He gets off at **Jourdain**. The law despatches cars to Place des Fêtes, **Botzaris** and **Pre Saint Gervais**. Delon finally gives them the slip at the world's largest subway interchange, **Chatelet Les Halles** (the setting for much of *Subway*), where he leaps off the travelator.

SAND PEBBLES, THE
(1966, dir: Robert Wise)
Steve McQueen, Richard Attenborough, Richard Crenna.
● TAIWAN; HONG KONG, CHINA; LOS ANGELES, CALIFORNIA

Vietnam parallels abound as the US gunboat, *San Pablo*, tangles with Chinese warlords on the Yangtse River in 1926. Wise's movie was made at **Taipei**, on the island of Taiwan, on the **Keelung** and **Tam Sui Rivers**. In the Tam Sui district, 900 of the 5,000 locals were recruited as extras to storm across the **Changsha Bund** and hurl lighted torches at the *San Pablo*. The boat itself, at $250,000 the most costly action prop built at the time, was modelled on the *Villa Lobos*, which had been captured from Spain after the Spanish-American War. The climactic fight, with 30 Chinese junks, supposedly on the Chien River, was shot on the **Sai Kung** backwater inlet at Hong Kong.

The interiors were filmed back at 20th Century Fox in LA (you can see some of the sets recycled in Roger Corman's *The St Valentine's Day Massacre*).

SARABAND FOR DEAD LOVERS
(aka *Saraband*)
(1948, dir: Basil Dearden; Michael Relph)
Stewart Granger, Joan Greenwood, Flora Robson.
● OXFORDSHIRE

Tragic historical romance, shot at **Blenheim Palace**, Sir John Vanbrugh's classic house, built for the Duke of Marlborough, and the birthplace of Sir Winston Churchill. It's open to the public from mid-March to the end of October (*© 0870.0080; admission charge*). You can find Blenheim southwest of Woodstock village, on the A44, eight miles north of Oxford.

SATANIC RITES OF DRACULA, THE (aka *Count Dracula and His Vampire Bride*)
(1973, dir: Alan Gibson)
Christopher Lee, Peter Cushing, Freddie Jones.
● LONDON; HERTFORDSHIRE

Another update, following the kitschy *Dracula AD 1972*, with the Count as a vampiric property developer in central London. Pelham House in Croxted Heath –

The Keeley Foundation for Science: Queens Gate Lodge, Elvaston Place, South Kensington

headquarters of the Psychical Examination and Research Group, the front for a vampiric cult – is really **High**

Canons, Buckettsland Lane, Well End, just to the north of Borehamwood in Hertfordshire. No stranger to such goings on, the house can be seen in plenty of other movies, including *The Devil Rides Out*. In London's south Kensington, **Queens Gate Lodge, 23a Elvaston Place** at Elvaston Mews, SW7, became The Keeley Foundation for Science, where Peter Cushing confronts scientist Freddie Jones, who, for some obscure reason, is incubating plague viruses.

SATURDAY NIGHT AND SUNDAY MORNING
(1960, dir: Karel Reisz)
Albert Finney, Shirley Anne Field, Rachel Roberts.
● NOTTINGHAMSHIRE; LONDON

Resentful factory worker Arthur Seaton has a fling with a married woman, but ultimately settles for dull conformity. One of the key British New Wave movies, it

Seaton gets beaten up by squaddies: The British Flag, Culvert Road, Battersea

launched Albert Finney to stardom as Seaton, and was made on location around Nottingham in the Midlands. Seaton works at the **Raleigh Bicycle Factory** in **Radford**, where the story's author, Alan Sillitoe, had actually worked. The factory still survives, though the surrounding streets have been demolished to provide car parking space. The pub, where Arthur gets totally smashed, still exists. It's the **White Horse Inn, 313 Ilkeston Road** in Radford.

Despite claims to background authenticity, not all the locations are in the Midlands. The funfair scenes were shot in London, at **Wimbledon**, and some interiors in the studio at Twickenham. It's outside **The British Flag, 103 Culvert Road**, on the corner of Rowditch Lane, Battersea, that Seaton and his pal witness a drunken old man smash a shop window and, later, that Seaton gets beaten up by squaddies.

SATURDAY NIGHT FEVER
(1977, dir: John Badham)
John Travolta, Karen Lynn Gorney, Barry Miller.
● NEW YORK CITY

Nik Cohn's account of social rituals is transformed into the disco hit of the seventies, with Travolta as the blue-collar kid from Brooklyn whose dancing opens up a new world over the East River. Travolta's neighbourhood is Bay Ridge. The opening scene of Travolta swaggering down the street is at **86th Street**, Brooklyn. The kids display macho bravado on the **Verrazzano Narrows**

Travolta's home: 79th Street, Bay Ridge

The 2001 disco: Spectrum, 64th Street, Bay Ridge

Bridge, where I-278 crosses New York Bay, south of Bay Ridge.

Travolta's home is **221 79th Street, Bay Ridge**, in a smart middle class area of the borough. Not far away is the disco where white-suited Travolta provided the iconic image of seventies dance culture. In '78 it was 2001 Odyssey. It's now **Spectrum**, a gay men's dance club, **802 64th Street** at Eighth Avenue (© 718.238.8213).

SAVING PRIVATE RYAN
(1998, dir: Steven Spielberg)
Tom Hanks, Tom Sizemore, Matt Damon.
● **HERTFORDSHIRE; IRELAND; OXFORDSHIRE; WILTSHIRE**

Omaha Beach, site of the real Normandy landings, is now a historical landmark and the surrounding area has been substantially redeveloped, so the harrowing D-Day scenes were filmed on the southeast coast of the Republic of Ireland, at **Curracloe Beach, Ballinesker**, just north of Wexford, about 70 miles south of Dublin (*rail: Wexford*). The French village was built at the former British Aerospace factory in **Hatfield**, Hertfordshire. The Ryans' midwest farm in Iowa is a field in **Marlborough**, Wiltshire. The skirmish with the German machine-gun nest filmed on the grounds of **Thame Park** in Oxfordshire (see *The Madness of King George*).

SAYONARA
(1957, dir: Joshua Logan)
Marlon Brando, Miyoshi Umeki, Red Buttons.
● **LOS ANGELES, CALIFORNIA**

The American Officers' Club: Yamashiro, North Sycamore Avenue, Hollywood

Parallel romances in post-war Japan. The American Officers Club is **Yamashiro, 1999 North Sycamore Avenue** (© 323.466.5125, www.yamashiro-restaurant.com). A Japanese restaurant, built by hundreds of Oriental craftsmen in 1913-14, the cedar and teak replica of a Japanese palace comes complete with teahouse, gardens and an imported 600-year-old pagoda. It stands in the Hollywood Hills on a single track road, north of the suburb, with spectacular views over Hollywood. Yamashiro can also be seen in the remake of *Gone In 60 Seconds* and Blake Edwards' *Blind Date*.

SCANDAL
(1989, dir: Michael Caton-Jones)
John Hurt, Ian McKellen, Joanne Whalley-Kilmer.
● **LONDON; WILTSHIRE; MERSEYSIDE; NOTTING-**

Stephen Ward's flat: Bathurst Mews, Bayswater

Straightforward account of the Christine Keeler-John Profumo scandal that rocked British politics in the sixties, somewhat upstaged by McKellen's bizarre Samurai topknot, the misjudged result of shaving his hairline for the role of Profumo rather than resorting to a wig.

Stephen Ward (Hurt), the fall guy in the scandal who committed suicide, lived at 17 Wimpole Mews in Marylebone. Too redeveloped for filming, Ward's flat in the movie is **42 Bathurst Mews**, a cobbled mews in Bayswater.

The country house, where a monied elite indulged in poolside frolics, was, notoriously, Cliveden, home of the Astor family, two miles north of Taplow on the Hedsor Road near Maidenhead, Buckinghamshire. It's now a hotel (© 01628.668561, www.clivedenhouse.co.uk). Its connection with the Keeler-Profumo affair was not one the owners wanted to emphasise and permission to film was refused (although Cliveden has been seen in plenty of other movies, including *Help!*, where it stood in for Buckingham Palace). The country estate in the film is the much-used **Wilton House, Wilton**, three miles from Salisbury, Wiltshire, and **Longleat House, Warminster**, also in Wiltshire.

There was additional filming in Liverpool, and the Old Bailey is a conflation of **County Hall**, London (see *Mission: Impossible* for details), and **Shire Hall, High Pavement**, Nottingham.

SCANNERS
(1980, dir: David Cronenberg)
Jennifer O'Neill, Patrick McGoohan, Stephen Lack.
● **TORONTO, ONTARIO, CANADA; QUÉBEC, CANADA**

The railway station: Yorkdale Station

Telepaths with powerful mind-control abilities in Cronenberg's influential sci-fi horror, made largely around **Montréal**. The railway station, though, is **Yorkdale Station** on the Downsview Line in **Toronto**, north of the city centre.

SCARFACE
(1983, dir: Brian De Palma)
Al Pacino, Steven Bauer, Michelle Pfeiffer.
● **CALIFORNIA; FLORIDA; NEW YORK CITY**

When Fidel Castro opened up the harbour at Mariel in May 1980 to allow 125,000 Cubans to join relatives in the US, he took the opportunity to export some of the country's toughest criminals. Smalltime thug Tony Mon-

Chainsaw at the Sun-Ray Apartment: Johnny Rocket's, Ocean Drive

The bomb attempt in New York: Tudor City Place

tana (Pacino) grabs the opportunity to make it as a big-time drug lord in screenwriter Oliver Stone's loose reworking of the thirties gangster classic.

Set in Miami and Bolivia, the movie's locations are mostly divided between Florida and California. The Florida internment camp, where Montana wins his freedom by killing a Castro agent, was constructed under the knot of freeway interchanges at the intersection of I-10, the Santa Monica Freeway, and I-110, the Harbor Freeway, downtown LA behind the New LA Convention Center. Miami's Little Havana district, where Montana starts out working at the El Paraiso lunch stand, was recreated at **Little Tokyo** in downtown LA. Montana's arrival in the art deco district of Miami Beach is impossible to fake, though, and was shot on **Ocean Drive** at 13th Street. The Sun Ray Apartments, where Montana's brother is dismembered by chainsaw, has been revamped to become **Johnny Rocket's, 728 Ocean Drive** between the Beacon and Colony hotels near 7th Street.

The movie's two estates, one supposedly in Bolivia, one in Florida, are both in the town of **Montecito**, on the California coast a few miles east of Santa Barbara. Sosa's South American estate, where Omar is ousted, is a rococo Spanish hacienda designed by architect Addison Mizener. Montana's own Coral Gables estate is **El Fureidis** ('Little Paradise'), a mediterranean villa built for Waldron Gillespie, a wealthy upstate New Yorker, by Bertram Goodhue. Neither estate is open to the public. The luxury hotel grounds, where Montana and pal Manny Ray (Bauer) ogle women, are of the **Fontainebleau Hilton Resort and Spa, 4441 Collins Avenue**, Miami (© 305.538.2000), see *Goldfinger* for details.

In New York, the gothic apartment block of the intended bomb victim is **5 Tudor City Place** at East 41st Street (seen also in *Splash!* and the *Spider-Man* movies).

SCARY MOVIE

(2000, dir: Keenan Ivory Wayans)
Anna Paris, Shawn Wayans, Marlon Wayans.
● BRITISH COLUMBIA, CANADA

Filmed in the picturesque fishing village of **Steveston Harbour**, Richmond and Victoria. BA Corpse High School (ouch!) is **Vancouver Technical Secondary School, 2600 East Broadway**, Vancouver.

SCENT OF A WOMAN

(1992, dir: Martin Brest)
Al Pacino, Chris O'Donnell, Gabrielle Anwar.

● NEW YORK CITY; NEW YORK

College kid Charlie Simms (O'Donnell) accompanies blind, suicidal ex-soldier Lt Col Frank Slade (Pacino) on one last fling in New York. And it's nothing but the best. They stay at the **Waldorf-Astoria Hotel, 301 Park Avenue** (©

Pacino and O'Donnell in New York: Waldorf-Astoria Hotel, Park Avenue

The tango: Pierre Hotel, East 61st Street

212.355.3000) between East 49th and East 50th Streets, midtown Manhattan; and dine out in style in the **Oak Room** of the **Plaza Hotel, West 59th Street** at Fifth Avenue (see *North By Northwest* for details). Slade visits a high-class escort at **817 Fifth Avenue** at 63rd Street; and dances a mean tango in the ballroom of the grand old European-style **Pierre Hotel, 2 East 61st Street** at Fifth Avenue on the East Side (© 212.838.8000, www.four-seasons.com/pierre). Visual impairment doesn't stop Slade driving a Ferrari at speed along the East River front, beneath the **Williamsburg Bridge**.

Simms's snooty Baird School is the **Emma Willard School, 285 Pawlings Avenue, Troy** (the New York State town used as turn-of-the-century Manhattan in *The Age of Innocence*), though the final scene uses **Hempstead House**, one of the four mansions (another was used as the estate where the movie producer gets a horse's head in his bed in *The Godfather*) on **Sands Point Preserve, 95 Middleneck Road, Port Washington** on Long Island.

O'Donnell's School: Hempstead House, Long Island

SCHINDLER'S LIST

(1993, dir: Steven Spielberg)
Liam Neeson, Ben Kingsley, Ralph Fiennes.
● POLAND; ISRAEL

Spielberg finally achieved respectability and got his long-delayed Oscar for this story of Oskar Schindler, the wheeler-dealing Gentile businessman who saved over a thousand Jews from the gas chambers. Initial controversy with the custodians of the Auschwitz Memorial,

Oskar Schindler's factory: Lipowa Street, Krakow

The bridge over the Vistula: Krakowska Street

Clearing the ghetto: Jozefa Street

worried by the prospect of Hollywood schmaltz, was resolved by filming only outside the gatehouse of the Birkenau camp, in the Polish town of **Oswiecim**. Actually, several other Hollywood movies, including *Triumph of the Spirit*, had already filmed inside the camp.

The movie was made in **Krakow**, one of the few Polish cities to escape devastation during WWII, and listed by UNESCO as one of the world's great historic cities. Nothing, though, remains of Plaszów labour camp, which stood on the slope of Krzemionki Hill, to the east of the old town. The only set built for the movie, a replica of Plaszów, consisting of 34 barracks, seven watchtowers and even the road into the camp – paved with Jewish tombstones – was built, from the original plans, in a disused quarry at the foot of Krakus mound close to the actual site. Amon Goeth's villa was reproduced above the camp, less than a mile from the original building, which still stands on Jerozolimska Street. Many of the real locations were used, including Schindler's own elegant apartment, at **7 Straszewskiego Street**, north of Kazimierz district and Wawel Hill.

For the wartime ghetto of Zgoda Square, which has been extensively redeveloped, the film uses **Szeroka Street** in the former Jewish district of Kazimierz. Nearby is **Ciemna Street**, where Poldek Pfefferberg narrowly escapes death after bumping into Amon Goeth by claiming that he had orders to clear the street. The expulsion of the Jews from the ghetto used the picturesque courtyard at **12 Jozefa Street**, linking to Meiselsa Street. The bridge over the Vistula, over which they are herded, is at the end of **Krakowska Street** (for the film, the crossing of the bridge had to be reversed). Schindler's factory is the real thing, virtually unchanged, at **4 Lipowa Street**. It now produces electrical components. The interiors, though, used the enamel factory in **Olkusz**, in the Malopolska province.

The church, where the Jews meet clandestinely, is Krakow's most important church, the 14th century **Church of St Mary's**. The railway station is **Krakow Glowny**. The Brinnlitz scenes used the quaint old town of **Niepolomice**, about 25 miles east of Krakow.

SCHOOL FOR SCOUNDRELS
(1960, dir: Robert Hamer)
Ian Carmichael, Alastair Sim, Terry-Thomas.
● HERTFORDSHIRE

Mild-mannered loser Henry Palfrey (Carmichael) takes lessons in one-upmanship from the cynical Mr Potter (Sim) in this film adaptation of Stephen Potter's books, from the director of *Kind Hearts and Coronets*. The railway station, at Yeovil, Somerset, is actually **Hertford East**, Hertfordshire. The **Edgwarebury Hotel, Edgwarebury Lane** (© *0870.609.6151*), became the tennis club where Palfrey is embarrassed by his clunky Swiftmobile, before turning the tables on caddish Raymond Delauney (Terry-Thomas). A movie favourite, the hotel has been seen in 1939's *Sons of the Sea*, with Leslie Banks, the rather dated 1971 Agatha Christie mystery *Endless Night*, the 1970s black comedy *Hawks* (with *ER*'s Anthony Edwards and Bond-to-be Timothy Dalton), *Hide and Seek* (1963), *Not Now Comrade* and, most memorably, *The Devil Rides Out*.

SCHOOL OF ROCK
(2003, dir: Richard Linklater)
Jack Black, Joan Cusack, Mike White.
● NEW YORK; NEW JERSEY; NEW YORK CITY

Jack Black steals the show as rock-obsessed slacker Dewey Finn, forging a class of aspirational prep school kids into a rock band. Finn is fired from his band, Maggotdeath, after executing a truly tragic stagedive at **Northsix, 66 North 6th Street, Williamsburg**, Brooklyn (© *718.599.5103, www.northsix.com*). The gothic exterior of Horace Green Preparatory School, where he connives to wangle a job as substitute teacher, is **Wagner College, 1 Campus Road, Grymes Hill** on Staten Island; but the interior is over on Long Island: **Buckley Country Day School, I.U. Willets Road, Roslyn**.

Back to Staten Island, where Finn softens up apparently straitlaced Principal Mullins (Cusack) with beer and Stevie Nicks at **Cargo Cafe, 120 Bay Street, St George** (© *718.876.0539*). St George is also the site of the climactic 'Battle of the Bands', staged at the **St George Theatre, 31 Hyatt Street**. The exterior, though, is in Jersey, at the lovingly restored **Union County Arts Center, 1601 Irving Street, Rahway**, New Jersey (© *732.499.8226, www.ucac.org,*), formerly the old Rahway Theatre.

SCOTT OF THE ANTARCTIC
(1948, dir: Charles Frend)
John Mills, Derek Bond, James Robertson Justice.
● NORWAY; ANTARCTICA; CORNWALL

The story of Captain Scott's doomed expedition to the South Pole in 1912, with a score by Vaughan Williams. The location snowscapes are a glacier near **Finse** in Norway (an area which became Hoth in *Star Wars Episode V*), with second unit shots from **Grahamland** in the real Antarctic. The departure of the *Discovery* was filmed at the eastern breakwater of **Falmouth Docks**, down in southwest Cornwall.

SCREAM
(1996, dir: Wes Craven)
Neve Campbell, Courteney Cox, Skeet Ulrich.
● CALIFORNIA

The bloodbath mansion: Tomales

Woodsboro town square: Healdsburg

First of that whole new genre, the post-modern, ironic slasher movie, from the pen of Kevin Williamson. It was made around northern California. Drew Barrymore's isolated house is on **Sonoma Mountain Road, Glen Ellen**, Route 12 southeast of Santa Rosa. Neve Campbell's home is on **Calistoga Road**, north of Santa Rosa toward Calistoga. Woodsboro High was to have been Santa Rosa High School, but the school board pulled out when they read the script – hence the 'No thanks at all to…' credit at the end of the movie. In the end, the school was played by **Sonoma Community Center, 276 East Napa Street, Sonoma**, a few miles south of Glen Ellen. The town square of the fictitious Woodsboro, where the teens gather by the fountain to discuss the grisly details, is the **Town Square, Healdsburg**, and the cop station is **Healdsburg Police Station**. The video store, where film buff Jamie Kennedy works, is **Bradley Video, 3080 Marlow Road, Santa Rosa**. The mansion where the climactic bloodbath takes place is a private house, overlooking **Tomales**, just east of town, south from the **Petaluma Road**.

SCREAM 2

(1997, dir: Wes Craven)
Neve Campbell, Liev Schreiber, David Arquette.
● **GEORGIA; CALIFORNIA**

The première of *Stab*: Vista Theater, Hollywood

Two years after the Woodsboro murders, Neve Campbell attends college, when the fictional version of the killings, *Stab*, is released. Windsor College is **Agnes Scott College, Decatur**, outside Atlanta, Georgia. The movie première of *Stab* was filmed at the little **Vista Theater, 4473 Sunset Drive, Hollywood** (seen as the Detroit movie house at the opening of *True Romance*), though the exterior is the **Rialto Theater, 1023 South Fair Oaks Avenue, Pasadena** (see *The Player* for details). *Stab* itself was shot in **Malibu**.

SCREAM 3

(2000, dir: Wes Craven)
Neve Campbell, David Arquette, Courteney Cox Arquette.
● **CALIFORNIA**

Stab 3 is in production and… well, figure out the convolutions for yourself. Set around Hollywood, the movie producer's office overlooks MacArthur Park, downtown, and the fictitious Sunrise Studios are the **CBS Studio Center, 4024 Radford Avenue**, Studio City. The home of Cotton Weary (Liev Schrieber), where he's killed off at the opening of the movie, is **1336 North Harper Avenue** in west Hollywood. Gale Weathers and Officer Dewey meet up to mull over old times at **Le Pain Quotidien, 8607 Melrose Avenue** (formerley Replay Café), at Westbourne Drive.

Cotton is killed: North Harper Avenue

The house in the hills, where everyone gathers as script developments arrive via fax, is **Runyon Ranch, Runyon Canyon Park** in the Hollywood Hills. The house was seen also in *Crazy In Alabama*. The mansion of the climactic denouement is the **Canfield-Moreno Residence and Complex, 1923 Micheltorena Street, Silverlake**, also seen as the private school in the *Halloween* sequel *H20*.

SEA OF LOVE

(1989, dir: Harold Becker)
Al Pacino, Ellen Barkin, John Goodman.
● **NEW YORK CITY; ONTARIO, CANADA**

The singles set-up: O'Neal's Baloon, West 63rd Street

Engrossing did-she-didn't-she thriller with Ellen Barkin suspected of bumping off lonely hearts. Set in New York, there are plenty of real locations, although much of the movie was made north of the border at the Kleinburg Studios in Toronto. The opening police scam, where Pacino manages to execute a whole roomful of warrants, used the old Savoy Manor Ballroom on **East 149th Street**. It's now part of the Hostos Community College in Hamilton Heights. The first murder takes place at **365 West End Avenue**, near 78th Street on Manhattan's West Side. Pacino lives just to the north on 85th Street, Barkin even further north at **45 88th Street**. The second murder is on **Yellowstone Boulevard**, running north-south between the Long Island Expressway and Queens Boulevard, Queens.

The restaurant, where Pacino and Goodman set up an elaborate scam to check out the suspect singles, is **O'Neal's Baloon, 48 West 63rd**

Jerry's Diner, Dundas Street, Toronto

The first murder: West End Avenue, West Side

Street at Columbus Avenue near the Lincoln Center. Barkin sells swanky slingbacks at **Maud Frizon, 19 East 60th Street** on the East Side. There was more filming on **Broadway**; **Amsterdam Avenue**; **East 57th Street**; **Eighth Avenue**; and the **Taft Houses** on Madison Avenue between 112th and 115th Streets in east Harlem.

Toronto locations passing themselves off as New York include **Jerry's Diner, 132 Dundas Street** (seen also in the New York-set *Cocktail* and the Bette Midler weepie *Stella*); **Metro Hall, St John Street**; **Sutton Place Hotel, 955 Bay Street** (featured in *The January Man* and *Suspect*); the **Horseshoe Tavern, 368 Queen Street West**; and **St Nicholas Ukranian Catholic Church, 4 Bellwoods Avenue**.

SEARCHERS, THE

(1956, dir: John Ford)
John Wayne, Jeffrey Hunter, Natalie Wood.
● **ARIZONA; COLORADO; UTAH; CALIFORNIA**

Finding Scar: Twelve Dancers, Monument Valley

Arguably Wayne's best role, as Ethan Edwards, obsessively tracking down the niece abducted by Indians. The opening title, 'Texas 1868', is blatantly belied by a view of Ford's beloved **Monument Valley**, Arizona, where much of the film was shot, along with Utah, on the San Juan River at **Mexican Hat**, several miles to the north. Second unit filming, capturing snow scenes and buffalo herds, took place all over the West, including **Aspen** and southwestern Colorado. The dusty climax, where Wayne finally meets up with, and accepts, Wood, is actually **Griffith Park**, Los Angeles.

SECONDS

(1966, dir: John Frankenheimer)
Rock Hudson, Richard Anderson, Salome Jens.
● **NEW YORK CITY; CONNECTICUT; CALIFORNIA**

Hudson is the middle-aged businessman offered a new lease of life by a sinister rejuvenation company in John Frankenheimer's classic scarer. Kirk Douglas (then starring in *One Flew Over the Cuckoo's Nest* on Broadway) bought the rights and was to have played the lead, but contractual obligations sent him elsewhere. The opening scene is New York's **Grand Central Station**. Train scenes use the commuter services of New York, **New Haven** and **Hartford**, Connecticut. Hudson's pre-op suburban home is in **Scarsdale**, a suburb of Westchester County. After rejuvenation, Hudson moves to the West Coast. The party scene, with Hudson drunkenly blurting out his secret (and Hudson really was drunk for the scene) was shot in John Frankenheimer's own beachfront house in **Malibu**.

SECRETS & LIES

(1996, dir: Mike Leigh)
Brenda Blethyn, Marianne Jean-Baptiste, Timothy Spall.
● **LONDON**

Timothy Spall's studio: Studio on the Green, Winchmore Hill

Cannes award winner for Mike Leigh, and Brenda Blethyn as Best Actress, is light years away from the bleak pessimism of *Naked*, with Marianne Jean-Baptiste the black daughter tracing her white natural mother. Blethyn's terraced house is **76 Quilter Street, Bethnal Green**, SE17.

Brenda Blethyn's terraced house: Quilter Street, Bethnal Green

Jean-Baptiste gets a copy of her birth certificate from the **Office of Population Censuses and Surveys, St Catherine's House, 10 Kingsway** at Aldwych; and meets up with her mother at **Holborn Underground Station**. Timothy Spall's shop is a real photographer's studio, **Studio on the Green, 34 The Green, Winchmore Hill**; and his house is nearby at **87 Whitehouse Way** at Hampden Way, **Southgate**.

SENSE AND SENSIBILITY

(1995, dir: Ang Lee)
Emma Thompson, Kate Winslet, Alan Rickman.
● **DEVON; WILTSHIRE; SOMERSET; LONDON**

Mrs Jennings' London house: Mompesson House, Cathedral Close, Salisbury

Ang Lee brings a fresh sensibility to the English Heritage genre with his adaptation of the Jane Austen novel. Norland Park, home of the Dashwood family, is **Saltram House**, a George II house set in a landscaped park. It's open to the public from April through October (*℗ 01752.336546*). Find it three-and-a-half miles east of Plymouth between the A38 and the A379, in Devon. The Dashwoods' London home is **Chandos House, 2 Queen Anne Street**, near to Broadcasting House. This Grade I listed building, a Robert Adam mansion built in 1769, was recently compulsorily purchased from an investment company after years of neglect and has been fully restored by the Royal Society of Medicine. Want to hire it for your wedding?

The London street: Queen's House, Greenwich

The Dashwoods' London home: Chandos House, Queen Anne Street

Check out *www.rsm.ac.uk/chandoshouse*.

The front room of Mrs Jennings' London house is the owner's home of the **Flete Estate**, 11 miles east of Plymouth, open Wednesdays and Thursdays, May to September. The rest of the house used **Mompesson House, Cathedral Close** on the north side of Choristers' Green in Salisbury. This furnished Queen Anne townhouse is also open May through October (✆ *01722. 335659*). Cleveland, home to the Palmers (Imelda Staunton and Hugh Laurie), is the striking Elizabethan **Montacute House**, Montacute village, four miles west of Yeovil in Somerset, which you might also have seen in Derek Jarman's *The Angelic Conversation*. You can visit April through October (✆ *01935.823289*). The ballroom scene, where Greg Wise encounters Kate Winslet, uses another familiar old location, **Wilton House, Wilton**, two-and-a-half miles west of Salisbury on the A30 (✆ *01722.743115*), seen also in Ken Russell's *The Music Lovers* and in *The Bounty* amongst many other films.

The bustling London street scenes are the covered walkway at the carefully restored **Queen's House, Greenwich** (✆ *020.8858.4422*), a one-time royal palace, occupied by the dowager Queen Henrietta Maria, wife of Charles I. The final wedding was filmed at the church in the village of **Berry Pomeroy**, between Torbay and Totnes, Devon.

SENSO (aka *The Wanton Countess*)
(1953, dir: Luchino Visconti)
Alida Valli, Farley Granger, Massimo Girotti.
● **VENICE, ITALY**

Sumptuous melodrama from Visconti, with Valli as the Venetian noblewoman falling for an officer of the hated invading Austrian army. The opening scene, with loyal Venetians disrupting an opera performance, is **Teatro La Fenice** (*www.teatrolafenice.it*), Venice's ill-fated opera house. Burned down in 1836, and rebuilt – hence the name 'The Phoenix' – it was gutted by fire once again in 1996, not reopening until December 2003. Originally built in 1792, the lush red and gilt interior saw the premières of many famous works, including *Rigoletto* and *La Traviata*. It was the rallying point for Venetian patriots after the Austrian invasion of 1866. It stands on **Campo San Fantin**, west of the Piazza San Marco.

Meeting up at the well: Campo di Ghetto Nuovo

Granger's barracks are on the **Campo di Ghetto Nuovo**, a tiny island in the Cannareggio district linked by three bridges which was the original Jewish ghetto. The word 'ghetto' was a Venetian term for the iron foundry which once stood on this site. The Jews lived under a curfew – at night, the gates to the island would be padlocked. The uncharacteristic high-rise apartments are a result of this overcrowding. The well where Valli and Granger meet up is one of three in the centre of the campo. As dawn rises, Valli and Granger walk along the nearby **Fondamenta di Cannareggio** on the Canale di Cannareggio. Valli looks for Granger at the **Arsenale, Campo dell'Arsenale**.

Valli and Granger walk at dawn: Fondamenta di Cannareggio

Alida Valli looks for Farley Granger: The Arsenale, Campo dell'Arsenale

SERIAL MOM
(1994, dir: John Waters)
Kathleen Turner, Sam Waterston, Ricki Lake.
● **MARYLAND**

Standing alone in a genre all its own, the serial killer-feelgood movie, John Waters' best film since his underground trash days, was shot, inevitably, around Baltimore, Maryland. The church where Turner eludes the cops is **Church of the Good Shepherd, 1401 Carrolltown Avenue**. The video store, where her son works and where you neglect to rewind at your peril, is **Video America, Cold Springs Lane**. Turner is finally arrested at a Camel Lips gig at Hammerjacks, which stood underneath I-395 at 1101 South Howard Street, before being demolished in 1997 to make way for the Baltimre Ravens football stadium. Her subsequent trial was filmed in **Baltimore County Courthouse, 400 Washington Avenue, Towson**.

SERPICO
(1973, dir: Sidney Lumet)
Al Pacino, John Randolph, Jack Kehoe.
● **NEW YORK CITY**

Lumet's gruelling exposé of police corruption was based on real events and made on real locations around New York. Upright undercover cop Frank Serpico (Pacino) crosses the **Williamsburg Bridge** from Brooklyn to start a new life in Greenwich Village. The apartment he moves into is **5-7 Minetta Street**.

He studies Spanish at **New York University** in

Serpico's Greenwich Village apartment: Minetta Street

Greenwich Village, on the east side of Washington Square Park. Though his classmate says she works in Caffe Reggio, 19 MacDougal Street at West 3rd Street, we don't – as is claimed in many New York guidebooks – actually get to see the famed Village hangout. You can, though, see the café, New York's oldest, in dull Sean Connery thriller *The Next Man* and in the original *Shaft*. Serpico takes in a ballet at the **New York State Theater**, on the south side of **Lincoln Center Plaza, 150 West 65th Street** at Broadway, on the West Side.

The subway station, where Serpico gives chase after seeing a burglary in progress, only to get shot at by the cops for his troubles, is **Ditmars Boulevard**, Astoria, in north Queens, at the end of the Broadway Local line. And, on the same line, he encounters a cop, stoned out of his mind after a drug lesson, at **57th Street Station**.

Serpico masquerades as a porter in the meatpacking district on the West Side, collaring loan shark Casaro at the **Red Triangle Building**, which was home to both Glenn Close in *Fatal Attraction* and Ed Harris in *The Hours*.

SERVANT, THE
(1963, dir: Joseph Losey)
Dirk Bogarde, James Fox, Sarah Miles.
● LONDON

Aristocrat James Fox's house: Royal Avenue, Chelsea

Bogarde is Hugo Barrett, the sinister servant indulging in class-war power games with dissipated aristocrat Tony (Fox), in this classic sixties film of Robin Maugham's novel, by the Losey-Harold Pinter-Bogarde team. Fox's house is situated at **30 Royal Avenue**, Chelsea, SW3, opposite the one-time home of Somerset Maugham, some of whose pictures were borrowed to give James' home a suitably 'homo-centric' atmosphere. The wonderfully named 'Thomas Crapper, Sanitary Engineer', seen in the opening shot, was for a long while the Laura Ashley shop, in the King's Road opposite Royal Avenue, now The Vestry. Barrett meets his slutty 'sister', Vera (Miles) at **St Pancras Station**.

Losey's film drips with baroque embellishment: when Tony meets his fiancée Susan (Wendy Craig) in

The home of Tony's parents, Lord and Lady Mounset: Chiswick House, Burlington Lane, Chiswick

a Knightsbridge restaurant, the camera drifts in and out of surrounding conversations, including a louche Harold Pinter himself as Society Man, and Patrick Magee and

The restaurant: Lowndes Street, Knightsbridge

writer Alun Owen (scripter of the Beatles' *A Hard Day's Night*) as a pair of disturbingly worldly priests. The restaurant stood on **Lowndes Street** at Motcomb Street in Knightsbridge. It's now a shop, but the street itself is pretty much unchanged.

The home of Tony's parents, Lord and Lady Mounset, is **Chiswick House, Burlington Lane** (© *020.8995.0508; admission charge*), Chiswick, west London. Built in 1725 for the Earl of Burlington, the house, modelled after the Villa Rotonda in Vicenza, Italy, it's one of the finest Palladian villas in the country, set in formal gardens populated with classical statuary, obelisks and sphinxes. The rear of the house is seen in *Velvet Goldmine*.

SE7EN
(1995, dir: David Fincher)
Morgan Freeman, Brad Pitt, Kevin Spacey.
● LOS ANGELES, CALIFORNIA

The dismal, rainswept city where Somerset (Freeman) and Mills (Pitt) track down a serial killer, left deliberately vague in the movie, is neither New York nor Philadelphia, as has been claimed. It's downtown Los Angeles, with filming screened from the California sun, and rain machines in overdrive.

The police HQ (a frequent filming site, see *Face/Off* for details) is the third floor of the **Pacific Electric Building, 610 South Main Street** at Sixth Street; and the gloomy library in which ever-diligent Somerset bones up on the Seven Deadly Sins is the old disused Bank of America building at **650 South Spring Street**. It's another really familiar location, seen in films as diverse as *Marathon Man*, *Ghost*, *The Mask*, *Prizzi's Honor*, *St Elmo's Fire* and *Spider-Man 2*, and it's also the law firm office where Lily Tomlin jumps into the body of Steve Martin in *All Of Me*. A way to the west, in midtown, is the 'safe house' in which the widow of the 'Greed' victim is ensconced, which was one of the bungalows of the old **Ambassador Hotel, 3400 Wilshire Boulevard** at Catalina Street (see the

The library: South Spring Street

'Sloth': Pan-Am Building, Third Street

Paltrow confides in Freeman: Quality Coffee Shop, West Seventh Street

John Doe's apartment: Alexandria Hotel, West Fifth Street

1937 and 1954 *A Star Is Born*).

Back in the heart of downtown, John Doe's place, where the killer narrowly escapes, is only a few blocks away, the **Alexandria Hotel, 218 West Fifth Street** at the southwest corner of South Spring Street. Once one of LA's most prestigious hotels, a favourite of movie stars in the twenties and thirties, it has suffered from the general decay of the surrounding area. The subsequent chase was filmed on **West Fifth Street**. Gwyneth Paltrow reveals she's pregnant to Morgan Freeman in the **Quality Coffee Shop, 1238 West Seventh Street**, which you might remember from the remake of *Gone In 60 Seconds*, *Training Day* and *Ghost World*. The apartment of the comatose 'Sloth' victim is in the **Pan-Am Building, Third Street** at South Broadway, seen also in *Blade Runner* and just across from that movie's most famous location, the Bradbury Building. More recently, it became the apartment of John Constantine (Keanu Reeves) in *Constantine*.

SEVEN BRIDES FOR SEVEN BROTHERS
(1954, dir: Stanley Donen)
Howard Keel, Jane Powell, Russ Tamblyn.
● LOS ANGELES, CALIFORNIA; UTAH

It's the age-old story: director Donen wanted to film on real locations but, for financial reasons, the movie ended up being shot on the MGM backlot in Hollywood. The avalanche, though, was filmed at **Corral Creek Canyon, Sun Valley**, Utah.

Marilyn's New York apartment: East 61st Street, East Side

SEVEN YEAR ITCH, THE
(1955, dir: Billy Wilder)
Tom Ewell, Marilyn Monroe, Evelyn Keyes.
● NEW YORK CITY; LOS ANGELES, CALIFORNIA

Wimpy Ewell gets hot and bothered by neighbour Monroe. Though it's set in New York, the movie was shot largely in Hollywood. The apartment, out of which Marilyn dangles Ewell's shoes, actually is in New York. See it on the East Side, unchanged, at **164 East 61st Street**. It was owned by Julian Bach, who received $200 worth of whiskey for the use of it.

At the time of filming, in September 1954, Monroe's

marriage to Joe DiMaggio was falling apart. They were staying at Suites 1105 and 1106 in the St Regis-Sheraton Hotel, 2 East 55th Street at Fifth Avenue. The notorious subway grating scene was largely staged as a publicity stunt. The studio made sure that the press knew exactly when and where the scene was to be shot, and that Marilyn would be wearing an outfit that would 'stop the traffic'. Around 2,000 people turned up to witness the film-

The subway grating: Lexington Avenue at 52nd Street

ing, including an enraged DiMaggio. The crowd roared as Monroe's skirt billowed up, and one of the most enduring Hollywood images was born. The next day, Monroe was sporting bruises and within a few days she and DiMaggio had split. The close-ups of her legs were re-shot in Hollywood. The subway grating was outside the Trans-Lux Theater, where Ewell and Monroe had just watched *The Creature From the Black Lagoon*. The Trans-Lux has since moved to 1221 Avenue of the Americas, but the subway grating can still be seen at the northwest corner of **Lexington Avenue** and **52nd Street**.

SEX, LIES, & VIDEOTAPE
(1989, dir: Steven Soderbergh)
James Spader, Andie MacDowell, Laura San Giacomo.
● LOUISIANA

Relationship problems down south, when Spader brings his video camera to town. Spot-on character piece shot on location in Lousiana state capital Baton Rouge. The bar, where Steven Brill peddles his surreal chat-up lines and Laura San Giacomo serves drinks, was the Bayou, **124 West Chimes Street** between Infirmary Drive and Highland Road, Baton Rouge. It's now Jamaican restaurant **Cafe Reggae**. Not far away, east toward I-10, is the fern restaurant, **Zee Zee Gardens, 2904 Perkins Road** (© *225.346.1291*).

SHADOW OF A DOUBT
(1943, dir: Alfred Hitchcock)
Joseph Cotten, Teresa Wright, Macdonald Carey.
● CALIFORNIA

Charlie's (Wright) favourite uncle, also Charlie (Cotten), is actually the Merry Widow serial killer in Hitchcock's quietly understated thriller, co-scripted by playwright Thornton Wilder. Hitchcock's intention to film the whole movie on location, paying scrupulous attention to the details of small-town Americana, was ultimately compromised, but there's still plenty of filming in northern California, around **Santa Rosa**, on Route

Uncle Charlie arrives in Santa Rosa: Old Railroad Depot, Fourth Street

Teresa Wright's home: McDonald Avenue, Santa Rosa

101 about 50 miles north of San Francisco. Most of the city centre has been redeveloped, but you can still see the old railway station, where Uncle Charlie arrives. The railway itself is unused, but the station is now the tourist office, the **Old Railroad Depot, 9 Fourth Street**. You can buy the video of *Shadow of a Doubt* here. Amazingly, the unchanged family home can still be seen just out of town at **904 McDonald Avenue** at 15th Street.

SHADOWLANDS

(1993, dir: Richard Attenborough)
Anthony Hopkins, Debra Winger, Joseph Mazzello.
● **OXFORDSHIRE; LONDON; HEREFORDSHIRE; LEICESTERSHIRE**

CS Lewis meets Joy Gresham: Randolph Hotel, Beaumont Street

Dry old stick CS Lewis discovers emotional commitment with Joy Gresham just as she discovers she has terminal cancer, in this filming of William Nicholson's play.
Lewis, author of *The Lion, the Witch and the Wardrobe*, is an Oxford don. The college, where he teaches and suffers the cynicism of his fellows, is **Magdalen College**, with its 15th century chapel and carved oak dining hall. Other Oxford locations include **Christ Church Meadow**; **Duke Humphrey's Library**, part of the Bodleian complex; the circular reading room of the **Radcliffe Camera**, where Lewis lectures; and the **Sheldonian Theatre**. The tea room, where he first meets Gresham, is the **Fellows Lounge** of the **Randolph Hotel, Beaumont Street** (℗ *01865.247481*). Hopkins, Winger and director Attenbor-

The choir at dawn: Magdalen College, Oxford

ough all stayed at the Randolph during the Oxford shoot. What higher recommendation could you ask for? Oxford Station has been completely rebuilt, so the railway scenes used Britain's only perfectly preserved mainline steam facility, the **Great Central Railway, Loughborough Station**, Leices-

The wedding: BT Office, Hastings Street, King's Cross

tershire (also used for railway scenes in *Buster*). The hotel Lewis and Gresham stay in, on their way to the Golden Valley, is **Pengethley Manor Hotel, Pengethley Park** (℗ *01989.730211*) off the A49 near Ross-on-Wye. The Golden Valley honeymoon is set in the rolling hills of Herefordshire at the Welsh border, but the real thing turned out to be just not photogenic enough. The stand-in is **Symond's Yat Rock** near Goodrich, about 30 miles away. The wedding is not Camden Town Hall as sometimes claimed, but just around the corner at, bizarrely, the back door of the **BT Office** in **Hastings Street** opposite Thanet Street. The windows opposite are **Salvationist Publishing**, and the period buses trundle up **Judd Street**.

SHAFT

(1971, dir: Gordon Parks)
Richard Roundtree, Moses Gunn, Charles Cioffi.
● **NEW YORK CITY**

The No-Name bar: Piccolo Angelo, Greenwich Village

Who's the black private dick that's a sex machine to all the chicks? Damn right! The 70s blaxploitation genre started here and, though much of the action centres on **125th Street** in Harlem, John Shaft's office was on **Times Square** and his apartment in west Greenwich Village, at **55 Jane Street**. Just across Hudson Street stood the 'No Name Bar', where Shaft turns the tables on a stakeout with a stint behind the bar. It's now an excellent Italian restaurant, **Piccolo Angelo, 621 Hudson Street** (℗ *212.229.9177*).

Shaft's apartment: Jane Street, Greenwich Village

Remaining unchanged is venerable Village hangout **Cafe Reggio, 119 MacDougal Street** at West Third Street (℗ *212.475.9557*). Shaft meets the mafia contact over an espresso here, before walking off down MacDougal Street, past another Village institution, the **Minetta Tavern**, seen in *Sleepers*.

SHAFT

(2000, dir: John Singleton)
Samuel L Jackson, Christian Bale, Busta Rhymes.
● **NEW YORK CITY; NEW JERSEY**

Samuel L Jackson takes on the Shaft mantle for this revisiting of the cult seventies hit. The restaurant, where Shaft punches out racist rich-kid Walter Wade Jr (Bale), was Metronome, now revamped as **Strata, 915 Broadway** at 21st Street (℗ *212.505.7400, www.stratanyc.com*). The man's favourite hangout is now the recently restored Harlem landmark bar the **Lenox Lounge, 288 Lenox Avenue** between 124th and 125th Streets (℗ *212.427.0253*). The cop station exterior is in the Bronx, though the interior is a deserted Beaux Arts building in

Jersey City, New Jersey. Other locales include the Brooklyn neighbourhoods of **Vinegar Hill**, **Red Hook**, **Bedford-Stuyvesant** and **Crown Heights**. Villain Peoples Hernandez (Jeffrey Wright) rules over the Dominican enclave in **Washington Heights**, way to the north of Manhattan.

SHAKESPEARE IN LOVE

(1998, dir: John Madden)
Joseph Fiennes, Gwyneth Paltrow, Judi Dench.
● LONDON; BERKSHIRE; OXFORDSHIRE;
HERTFORDSHIRE; NORFOLK

Fireworks at Greenwich: Hatfield House, Hatfield

Multi-Oscar winner, including Best Picture, with a hunky young Shakespeare (Fiennes) struggling to write *Romeo and Ethel, the Pirate's Daughter* and aristocrat Paltrow (Paltrow) defying convention by wanting to act. The Rose Theatre is a set built for the movie. After filming, it was presented to Dame Judi with an eye to restoring it as a working theatre. The real Rose was actually uncovered during building work in Southwark in the late eighties, and a massive campaign was launched to preserve it. The property developers eventually agreed to preserve the theatre in the basement of the new building, but it sadly remains inaccessible.

Viola's home, the de Lesseps house, is **Broughton Castle**, home of Lord and Lady Saye and Sele, two miles southwest of **Banbury**, Oxfordshire. The dance, where Will first meets Viola, is the house's Great Hall, while it's in the Oak Room that Wessex informs Viola they are to be married. Viola's bedroom is a studio set, but for the exterior, a false wooden balcony was built onto Broughton Castle, overlookiing the formal gardens. The castle was also seen in *Joseph Andrews*, *Tom Jones*, Trevor Nunn's *Lady Jane*, *The Madness of King George* and *Three Men and a Little Lady*. It's open to the public on various days

Shakespeare meets Viola at the dance: The Great Hall, Broughton Castle

between May and September (*©* *01295.276070, www.broughton-castle.demon.co.uk*). The command performance of *Two Gentlemen of Verona* for Queen Elizabeth, in the Banqueting Hall at the Palace of White Hall, is in the **Great Hall** of **Middle Temple** in London. The Greenwich fire-

Shakespeare woos Viola from the garden: Broughton Castle

works scene, where Viola meets the Queen, and Shakespeare accepts a bet in drag, used the rear of **Hatfield House** (see Tim Burton's *Batman* for

Illyria: Holkham Beach

details). The riverside scenes were shot on the Thames at **Barnes**. The interior of the church, where Shakespeare begs forgiveness after hearing about the murder of Kit Marlowe, is **Church of St Bartholomew the Great**, a tiny church – repository of the bones of St Rahere – tucked away behind Smithfield, and seen also in *Robin Hood, Prince of Thieves* and *Four Weddings and a Funeral*. The church exterior, after Viola's wedding to Wessex, is the courtyard of **Eton School**, Berkshire – which also served as the exterior of the Houses of Parliament in *The Madness of King George*. More filming took place in the grounds of **Marble Hill House**, Twickenham.

The spectacular beach of Illyria at the end is **Holkham Beach**, part of the Holkham Hall estate, three miles west of Wells-next-the-Sea on the A149 on the north coast of Norfolk.

SHAKESPEARE WALLAH

(1965, dir: James Ivory)
Shashi Kapoor, Geoffrey Kendal, Felicity Kendal.
● INDIA

Story of a British theatrical troupe crumbling during a tour of India, filmed by the Merchant-Ivory-Jhabvala team on location. The opening is at **La Martiniere College, Dilkusha Road, Lucknow**, an enormous European-style palace. The company performs at the **Gaiety Theatre, Mall Road, Simla**, the spectacular hill station where the British made camp in 1819. The theatre, opened in 1887, still houses performances, though the bar is supposedly a greater attraction than the plays. Other locations include the hill station of **Kasauli; the Punjab; Alwar; Rajasthan**; and **Bombay**.

SHALLOW GRAVE

(1994, dir: Danny Boyle)
Ewan McGregor, Kerry Fox, Christopher Eccleston.
● SCOTLAND

Pitch black comedy thriller, set in Edinburgh but shot for the most part in Glasgow. The real Edinburgh New Town is used to set the scene in the opening car ride, racing down **St Vincent Street**, glimpsing St Stephen's Church before swinging left into North East Circus Place. The flat shared by McGregor, Fox and Eccleston is **6 North East Circus Place** on the corner of Royal Circus. The flat interior, though, was constructed in a

The flat: North East Circus Place, Edinburgh

349

The shallow grave: Rouken Glen Park, Thornliebank

warehouse in the Anniesland district of Glasgow.

McGregor's office is the newsroom of Glasgow's *Evening Times*, while Fox's hospital is the **Royal Alexandra Hospital** off Crow Road, Castlehead, west of Glasgow city centre. This also houses the mortuary where Christopher Eccleston finally ends up.

The flooded quarry where the car is disposed of is **Mugdock Loch**, in **Mugdock Country Park, Mugdock Road** north of Milngavie (*rail: Milngavie*). The charity do, where Eccleston gets to assert his manhood, is in the **Townhouse Hotel, 54 West George Street**, Glasgow (*℡ 0141.332.3320*).

The grave itself, where Keith Allen is planted, is a wooded section of **Rouken Glen Park, Rouken Glen Road, Thornliebank** (*rail: Thornliebank*). The production team returned to Rouken Glen Park for the 'Sean Connery' scene in *Trainspotting*.

SHAMPOO

(1975, dir; Hal Ashby)
Warren Beatty, Julie Christie, Lee Grant.
● **LOS ANGELES, CALIFORNIA**

Christie's offer: Site of Bistro, North Canon Drive, Beverly Hills

Hot stuff in its day, a political satire with Beatty the priapic hairdresser seducing his glamorous female clients on the eve of election night 1968, set, and filmed, in Beverly Hills. Jack Warden's mansion – which was in real life Warren Beatty's former home – is **1120 Wallace Ridge**, off Loma Vista Drive north of Sunset Boulevard. Sloshed Julie Christie offers Beatty a blow-job in the now-gone Beverly Hills eaterie, Bistro, **240 North Canon Drive**, between Sunset and Santa Monica Boulevards. Also featured is the exclusive **Beverly Hills Hotel, 9641 Sunset Boulevard**.

SHANE

(1953, dir: George Stevens)
Alan Ladd, Jean Arthur, Brandon de Wilde.
● **WYOMING**

A mysterious stranger turns up to help a family of homesteaders in this epic Western. The luscious, Oscar-winning photography, by Loyal Griggs, makes full use of the location filming around **Jackson Hole**, Wyoming, at the southern end of the Grand Teton National Park. This has to be another of the great, all-time movie locations, regularly seen since silent movie days. Jackson Hole is a 50-mile-long, mile-high mountain valley over-

looked by the Grand Tetons – the Big Breasts – a name bestowed by French trappers. To the original people of the land they were Teewinot – Many Pinnacles. Route 191 runs through the valley, alongside the Snake River, from Jackson north to Yellowstone National Park. The cabin itself stood on **Gros Ventre Road**, just west of Kelly, but has since burned down.

SHAUN OF THE DEAD

(2004, dir: Edgar Wright)
Simon Pegg, Kate Ashfield, Nick Frost.
● **LONDON**

Celebrate! A British comedy that (a) isn't written by Richard Curtis and (b) is funny. The neighbourhood of Shaun (Pegg) is Crouch End, north London, where his

The Winchester Arms: Duke of Albany, Monson Road, New Cross

flat is **83 Nelson Road** at Weston Park, N8. Across the road, the local grocery store is **Weston Park Grocery, 96 Weston Park**. Shaun works in an electronics store on High Road, North Finchley, and his parents live at **37 Abbots Gardens, East Finchley**. The Winchester Arms,

Shaun's flat: Nelson Road, Crouch End

The local grocery store: Weston Park Grocery, Weston Park, Crouch End

though, can hardly be his local. It's way across London, south of the river. It's the **Duke of Albany, 39 Monson Road, New Cross**, SE14.

SHAWSHANK REDEMPTION, THE

(1994, dir: Frank Darabont)
Tim Robbins, Morgan Freeman, Bob Gunton.
● **OHIO**

Shawshank State Prison, Maine, is the **Ohio State Reformatory, 100 Reformatory Road, Mansfield**, on I-30, 65 miles southwest of Akron, Ohio. The facility had lain dormant for four years and was scheduled for demolition, but it's now a museum (*℡ 419.522.2644, www.mrps.org*). The website has a detailed break-

Shawshank State Prison: Ohio State Reformatory, Mansfield

down of scenes filmed around Mansfield.

SHELTERING SKY, THE

(1990, dir: Bernardo Bertolucci)
Debra Winger, John Malkovich, Campbell Scott.

● MOROCCO; ALGERIA; NIGER

The brothel: Kasbah, Ouarzazate

Long and meandering – but beautiful to look at – adaptation of Paul Bowles' novel, shot on location in Africa. Oran, the port of arrival, is **Tangier** in Morocco, where filming was held up for the arrival of King Hussein II's yacht. The movie begins and ends here, among the old colonial boulevards and the labyrinth of the Medina. The hotel is the **Pension Palace, 2 Rue des Postes** (℅ *039.93.61.28*), in the Medina. There was also filming at the **Hotel Continental, 36 Rue Dar el Baroud** (℅ *039.931024*), also in the Medina.

The southern oasis area of Morocco, southeast of Ouarzazate toward the High Atlas mountains, hosted most of the shoot. The Hotel Majestic, Ain Krofa, is actually near Efroud, south of Er Rachidia, in the small town of **Rissani** close to the Algerian border. The arrival at the gates of El Gala used the market of **Gla Gla**. Debra Winger and the guide are followed by the ubiquitous Steadicam through the dry mud passageways of **Maadid**. The bicycle ride ends in the little town of **Zagora**, to the west, at the end of the spectacular Draa Valley. The love scene was filmed at the top of the strange, rather unreal, mountain overlooking the town and the surrounding desert.

The narrow streets of the historic core of Ouarzazate (in an area used for *Gladiator*, *Lawrence of Arabia* and *The Man Who Would Be King*, among others) leads to the movie's Hotel Transatlantique in Bou Noura, though the terrace of the hotel in Boussif is actually a replica in the hamlet of **Ait Saoun** and the exteriors of Bou Noura were filmed in the mud brick village of **Tamnougalt**, halfway between Ouarzazate and Zagora. The brothel is the **Kasbah** (the fortified palace) of Ouarzazate.

Algerian locations include the oasis **Beni Abbes**, where the fort of Sba, sheltered by the great dune, was built. Here also is the white room in which John Malkovich expires and the Grand Erg Occidental mineral landscape.

The Sheltering Sky was the first movie to film in Niger, one of the world's poorest countries, where the scene of Winger and Eric Vu-An in the mud room was shot in **Agadez**.

SHE'S ALL THAT

(1999, dir: Robert Iscove)
Freddie Prinze Jr, Rachael Leigh Cook, Matthew Lillard.

● LOS ANGELES, CALIFORNIA

Nineties teen spin on *Pygmalion*, with Freddie Prinze Jr turning Rachel Leigh Cook into a Prom Queen. William

Henry Harrison High is **Torrance High School, 2200 West Carson Street** at El Prado Avenue, **Torrance**. The school is also Sunnydale High in the TV series of *Buffy*

William Henry Harrison High: Torrance High School, West Carson Street, Torrance

the Vampire Slayer, West Beverly High in *Beverly Hills 90210*, Gilmore High in *Whatever It Takes* and John Hughes High in *Not Another Teen Movie*.

SHE'S GOTTA HAVE IT

(1986, dir: Spike Lee)
Tracy Camilla Johns, Tommy Redmond Hicks, John Canada Terrell.

● NEW YORK CITY

Spike Lee's first feature, a low-budget black-and-white comedy about Johns' multiple entanglements, made in a mere twelve days in July 1985 on location in New York. Johns' loft is **1 Front Street**, Brooklyn, over what used to be the Ferry Bank Restaurant, now the Hot Spot – Brooklyn's only gay bar. The park is Brooklyn's **Fort Greene Park**, with its views across to Manhattan. It's southeast of Brooklyn Heights, bounded by De Kalb and Myrtle Avenues, St Edwards Street and Washington Park. A crypt below the park (not open to the public) holds the remains of some of the 12,000 American soldiers who died on British prison ships in Wallabout Bay between 1780 and 1783.

SHI MIAN MAI FU (aka *House of Flying Daggers*)

(2004, dir: Yimou Zhang)
Takeshi Kaneshiro, Andy Lau, Ziyi Zhang.

● CHINA; UKRAINE

The literal translation of the title is 'Ambush From Ten Directions', for a while it was retitled *Lovers*, but it was eventually marketed to sound like an old Hong Kong kung-fu picture.

Most of the film was shot near **Lviv**, western Ukraine, a location previously used for Jackie Chan's *First Strike*.

Sets were built at **Yongchuan**, Sichun Province, in the bamboo forests of **Tea Mountain and Bamboo Sea Scenery Park**, near the city of Chongqing. To visit China's 120-km² park, the largest primaeval bamboo park in the country, you take a two-hour flight from Shanghai to Chengdu, from where there's a bus trip (approximately five hours) to the Bamboo Sea. There's the unique Bamboo Museum and a bamboo restaurant featuring dishes based on the local speciality.

Interiors, including the Peony Pavilion brothel and the abandoned Buddhist temple in the bamboo forest, lensed in Beijing Film Studio (where films such as *Crouching Tiger, Hidden Dragon* and *Kill Bill* were shot).

SHINE

(1996, dir: Scott Hicks)
Geoffrey Rush, Armin Mueller-Stahl, Lynn Redgrave.

● SOUTH AUSTRALIA; LONDON

Helfgott studies in London: Royal College of Music, Prince Consort Road

Scott Hicks' Oscar-winning biopic of troubled pianist David Helfgott was made in South Australia, on 40 separate locations around Adelaide, including **Carrick Hill** and the **Adelaide Botanic Garden, North Terrace**. Helfgott performs at **Adelaide Town Hall, 126 King William Street**. The psychiatric hospital is **Glenside Hospital, 226 Fullarton Road, Eastwood**. In London, young Helfgott studies at the **Royal College of Music, Prince Consort Road, South Kensington**, SW7, opposite the Royal Albert Hall.

SHINING, THE
(1980, dir: Stanley Kubrick)
Jack Nicholson, Shelley Duvall, Danny Lloyd.
● OREGON

Nicholson is the blocked writer going barmy in a creepy snowbound hotel in Kubrick's very free adaptation of the Stephen King novel. The movie was shot almost entirely in the studio at Elstree in England, where the hotel interior was constructed. The exterior of the Overlook Hotel is the **Timberline Lodge, Mount Hood** in the Hood River area of northern Oregon. Built during the Depression, it's 45 miles east of Portland, just east of Zig Zag on Route 26 (*© 503.272.3311, www.timberlinelodge.com*). The interior sets were partly based on the Ahwanne Hotel, Yosemite, California.

The hotel which inspired the original story is the Stanley Hotel in Colorado, where King had stayed in 1973. The writer hated the Kubrick adaptation, which junked most of his plot in favour of atmosphere, and sanctioned a TV movie remake, which did indeed use the Stanley. For details of the hotel see *Dumb and Dumber*, which also filmed there.

SHIRLEY VALENTINE
(1989, dir: Lewis Gilbert)
Pauline Collins, Tom Conti, Joanna Lumley.
● LONDON; MERSEYSIDE; GREECE

Shirley's school: Waldegrave School for Girls, Twickenham

Opening-up of Willy Russell's one-woman play about a Merseyside housewife who takes off for the Greek islands. Although it's set in Russell's native Merseyside, there's nothing more than a few establishing shots of Liverpool. Shirley Valentine's house is in Twickenham, not far from the film studios. Shirley's school is **Waldegrave School for Girls, Fifth Cross Road** in Twickenham. She buys exotic undies in **Littlewoods, Oxford Circus**, and

gets her passport picture taken on **Marylebone Station**. The hotel, where she meets old school friend Joanna Lumley, is the luxurious **Marlborough Hotel, Bloomsbury Street**, WC1 (*© 020.7636. 5601*). The Greek island holiday destination where she finds liberation is the beach of **Aghios Ioannis**, southwest Mykonos, a couple of miles from Mykonos town, where she stays at the **Manoulas Beach Hotel** (*© 30.22890, www.hotelmanoulas.gr*).

Shirley meets her schoolfriend: Marlborough Hotel, Bloomsbury

SHIVERS (aka *They Came From Within*)
(1975, dir: David Cronenberg)
Paul Hampton, Joe Silver, Barbara Steele.
● QUÉBEC, CANADA

Early Cronenberg shocker, with gross sexually-transmitted parasites turning apartment dwellers into raving sex maniacs. The Starliner Towers high-rise block is a de luxe condo on **Nun's Island**, over the Pont Champlain in the St Lawrence river, southwest Montréal.

SHOOTING FISH
(1997, dir: Stefan Schwartz)
Stuart Townsend, Dan Futterman, Kate Beckinsale.
● LONDON

Townsend and Futterman are two orphans getting by as scam artists in this excellent caper comedy, which falls into sentimentality only toward the end. The gasometer, in which the boys live, can be seen at Mill Hill East, towering over the station at the terminus of the Northern Line. The entrance to their home is between **12** and **13 Lee Road**, NW7. They rummage in a rubbish skip in front of **Alexandra Palace**. The country home, which Kate Beckinsale saves, is **Poleseden Lacey**, a Regency villa near **Dorking**, Surrey (*© 01372.452023; admission charge*).

Entrance to the gasometer home: Lee Road, Mill Hill East

SHOOTIST, THE
(1976, dir: Don Siegel)
John Wayne, Lauren Bacall, James Stewart.
● NEVADA

Wayne's elegiac last turn as a gunfighter dying of prostate cancer (Wayne refused to succumb to the bladder cancer of the source novel). Although it's a Paramount movie, the street scenes were filmed on the Western Street of Warner Bros' Burbank lot. The sparkling location filming is **Carson City**, east of Lake Tahoe on I-395, Nevada. The buggy ride was filmed in **Washoe Lake State**

Lauren Bacall's boarding house: Krebs-Paterson House, Carson City

Park. Lauren Bacall's boarding house, where Wayne sees out his final days, is the 1914 **Krebs-Paterson House, 500 Mountain Street**, Carson City. The house is one of the historic sites on the Kit Carson Trail, a two-and-a-half mile path through Carson City's historic district. Sound effects and recorded messages can be found on a special AM frequency at 24 of the houses – the Krebs-Paterson, of course, features the voice of John Wayne. Details from Carson City Chamber of Commerce, 1900 South Carson Street (*© 775.882.1565*).

SHORT CIRCUIT
(1986, dir: John Badham)
Steve Guttenberg, Ally Sheedy, Fisher Stevens.
● OREGON

Cutesy sub-*E.T.* fluff with a 'lovable' robot coming to life, marred by Fisher Stevens blacked up as a crass 'Goodness gracious me' Asian. It was made in **Astoria**, northeast Oregon. Ally Sheedy's house is **197 Hume Street**, Astoria. Filming also took place at **Bonneville Dam** on the Columbia River, Route 84, 30 miles east of Astoria and at **Cascade Locks**, a further ten miles east.

For the limp sequel, *Short Circuit 2*, Sheedy and Guttenberg are gone, and Stevens' ridiculous racial stereotype takes centre stage. The would-be cute robot makes it to the big city, but if New York looks a tad squeaky clean and airy, that's because it's actually **Toronto**.

SHORT CUTS
(1993, dir: Robert Altman)
Anne Archer, Lily Tomlin, Tim Robbins.
● CALIFORNIA

Lily Tomlin's coffee shop: Johnie's Broiler, Downey

Altman weaves together a collection of Raymond Carver short stories, transplanting the locale from the Pacific northwest to LA. The hospital is **Panorama Community Hospital, Panorama City** in the San Fernando Valley, north of LA. The coffee shop, where Lily Tomlin works as a waitress, is **Johnie's Broiler, 7447 Firestone Boulevard, Downey** (see *Heat* for details). The fishing trip is on the Kern River, and the final tragic outing, cut short by the earthquake, is **Bronson Canyon** in Griffith Park.

SHOT IN THE DARK, A
(1964, dir: Blake Edwards)
Peter Sellers, Herbert Lom, Elke Sommer.
● HERTFORDSHIRE

The French chateau: Luton Hoo, Luton

The French mansion of this follow-up to *The Pink Panther* is solidly Home Counties. It's **Luton Hoo, Luton**, in Hertfordshire. Until recently open to the public, it has since been put up for sale. See *Four Weddings and a Funeral* for details.

SHOWGIRLS
(1995, dir: Paul Verhoeven)
Elizabeth Berkley, Kyle MacLachlan, Gina Gershon.
● NEVADA

Paul Verhoeven's wildly trashy wallow in Vegas sleaze is set in Nevada's glitzy city of slot machines, but the musical numbers were staged at the **Horizon Casino Resort** (*© 775.588.6211*) on I-50, Stateline, Lake Tahoe at the California border.

SID AND NANCY
(1986, dir: Alex Cox)
Gary Oldman, Chloe Webb, Drew Schofield.
● LONDON; NEW YORK CITY; LOS ANGELES, CALIFORNIA

Sid and Nancy check out: The Hotel Chelsea, West 23rd Street

Oldman and Webb are Sex Pistols 'bassist' Sid Vicious and girlfriend Nancy Spungen in this bleak fantasia on their doomed relationship (Sid OD'd while awaiting trial for Nancy's murder). Filming took place in London and New York, where the couple stay at, and Nancy dies in, the **Hotel Chelsea, 222 West 23rd Street**, between Seventh and Eighth Avenues (*© 212.243.3700*). The landmark hotel, where you pay for the ambience more than for amenities, has been home to countless arty celebs over the years (as witnessed by the clutter of plaques around the entrance) including O Henry, Thomas Wolfe, Arthur Miller, Brendan Behan, Mary McCarthy, Vladimir Nabokov, Sarah Bernhardt and Dylan Thomas. The lobby and stairwells are decorated with works of art, of varying quality, donated by past residents. See the hotel's stairwell and corridors also in *Leon*.

The legendary Q Club, a soul/reggae dive presided over by Count Suckle since the sixties, at 5 Praed Street near Harbet Road, was transformed into Malcolm Maclaren's club, where a strangely

The gaff of Wally, the crimson-haired punk: Pennard Road, Shepherd's Bush

The hotel of rock star Rock Head: Inverness Court Hotel, Inverness Terrace, Bayswater

glamorous Poly Styrene performs with seminal punk band X-Ray Specs. The club closed and Mimet House now stands on the site.

The hotel of cleaned-up American rock star Rock Head (a character not a million miles from Iggy Pop, or perhaps Johnny Thunder of the New York Dolls), where he's visited by the definitely not cleaned-up Sid and Johnny Rotten, is the **Inverness Court Hotel, 1 Inverness Terrace** (*020.7229.1444*) at Fosbury Mews, Bayswater. "This is a respectable hotel," announces pompous manager Eddie Tudor-Pole, "Lillie Langtry stayed here." And it's true. The hotel was built as a private home for the actress by Edward VII, during his affair with her. See it again in Ken Russell's biopic *Valentino* and, also in 1977, as The Dunchester Club, hangout of slippery PR man Barry Foster, quizzed by disgraced cop Regan (John Thaw) in *Sweeney!*. The hotel rooftop, though, where Sid and Nancy enjoy a spot of gunplay, is that of the **Jolly St Ermin's, 2 Caxton Street** (*020.7222.7888*). A risky scene to shoot atop a building which overlooks – erm – New Scotland Yard. "All of a sudden, about twenty armed police appeared on the roof," says the film's location manager, Paul Raphael – the anti-terrorist squad taking a keen interest in weapons brandished on central London rooftops.

The Bramley Arms, Freston Road at Bramley Road, became not only The Old Mahon, where Sid boozes, but the office of MacLaren (David Hayman), which was filmed in rooms above the bar. The pub has a long history as a film location, since its appearance in Ealing's *The Lavender Hill Mob*. Jeremy Irons drinks here in the film of Harold Pinter's reverse-timescale drama *Betrayal*; the pub was seen in John Boorman's offbeat drama of west London life *Leo the Last*; and is also featured in *Quadrophenia*.

Oakwood Court, Abbottsbury Road, is the luxury Victoria pad of the hooker, where Sid and Johnny terrorise the poor doggy in the car and feast on baked beans and fag-ends.

In Shepherds Bush, west London, **17 Pennard Road** is the gaff of Wally, the crimson-haired punk (a character loosely based on Billy Idol). Nearby, alongside Goldhawk Road tube station, on the south side of the road, is the tiny **Metro Café**, where Nancy is told she's not wanted on the tour by the rest of the shade-wearing entourage.

Sid and Nancy live in less-than-perfect harmony in **Bermondsey**, at the jolly red-and-green pop-arty

Nancy is told she's not wanted on the tour: Metro Café, Shepherd's Bush

apartment block **37-77 West Lane**. 35 West Lane, now a smart office building, used to be the Two Brewers pub, outside which the fun couple have a blazing row.

All the US concert scenes (including CBGB in New York) were filmed in LA, in the Starwood, Hollywood. This legendary 70s club, which stood on the northwest corner of **Santa Monica Boulevard** and **Crescent Heights**, was one of the first clubs to book LA punk bands, but neighbourhood pressure eventually closed it down. The site is now a mall.

SIDEWAYS
(2004, dir: Alexander Payne)
Paul Giamatti, Thomas Haden Church, Virginia Madsen.

● **CALIFORNIA**

Wine Country, Santa Barbara County

Bit of a dark horse from Payne (*Election*), with a handful of Oscar nominations and Church walking off with one of the little gold chaps.

Before committing to married middle-age, Jack (Church), with old college pal Miles (Giamatti), takes to the road for a weekend of winetasting (depressed Miles) and casual sex (reckless Jack). Most of the film was shot north of LA, around the Santa Barbara area, and you can get a free map of their tour from the **Santa Barbara Conference & Visitors Bureau** (*© 805.966.9222, www.santabar-baraca.com*). In fact, the opening, supposedly San Diego, is **Santa Barbara** itself; and Miles' mother's home in Oxnard is **Santa Maria**, north toward San Luis Obispo (we'll be back to Santa Maria later).

As Miles heads into LA to collect Jack, he drives past the towering, circular **Holiday Inn, 170 North Church Lane**, in **Brentwood** (Al Pacino's hotel in *Heat*), but once on the road, the pair travel around the California coastal area, between San Luis Obispo and Santa Barbara.

Miles teaches Jack the finer points of wine tasting – "the faintest soupcon of asparagus, and just a flutter of nutty Edam cheese" – at **Sanford Winery, 7250 Santa Rosa Road, Buellton** (*© 805.688.3300, www.sanford-winery.com*), before travelling on to **Solvang**, built to look like a Scandinavian village, and then **Buellton** (it doesn't always make a lot of sense, geographically).

The 'windmill' motel at which Miles and Jack stay is **Days Inn Buellton, 114 East Highway 246** (*© 805.688.8448, www.daysinn-solvang.com*), Buellton. They walk down to Buellton's **Hitching Post II, 406 East Highway 246** (*© 805.688.0676, www.hitchingpostwines.com*), where Maya (Madsen) waits tables, and where Miles recommends the ostrich steak. Cracks in the odd couple relationship start to appear over breakfast at the **Solvang Restaurant, 1672**

Wine country: Santa Ynez

Wine country: Santa Maria

Copenhagen Drive (℗ *805.688.4645, www.solvangrestaurant.com*). Moving on, Miles and Jack cheekily help themselves to full glasses at **Foxen Winery, 7200 Foxen Canyon Road** (℗ *805.937.4251, www.santamaria.com*), Santa Maria – we'll be back there yet again. The next stop, where Jack meets the flirtatious Stephanie (Sandra Oh), is **Kalyra Winery, 343 North Refugio Road, Santa Ynez** (℗ *805.693.8864, wwwkalyrawinery.com*).

Three of the foursome enjoy dinner at **Los Olivos Cafe and Wine Merchant, 2879 Grand Avenue** (℗ *888.946.3748, www.losolivoscafe.com*), **Los Olivos**, while Miles ("I am not drinking any fucking Merlot!") phones his ex.

An awkward romance blooming, Jack goes bowling with Steph and her daughter at **Ocean Lanes, 1420 East Ocean Avenue** (℗ *805.736.4541*), **Lompoc**; and plays golf with Miles at **River Course at the Alisal, Alisal Guest Ranch, 150 Alisal Road** (℗ *805.688.6042, www.rivercourse.com*), Solvang.

The barrel room, into which Jack, Miles and Maya sneak from a particularly boring lecture, is **Firestone Winery, 5000 Zaca Station Road** (℗ *805.688.3940, www.firestonewine.com*), Los Olivos. Things are starting to look up for Miles as he and Maya enjoy a stroll through **Lompoc Farmers' Market, Ocean Avenue and I** (℗ *805.459.6050, www.lompoc.com*), **Lompoc**.

The much-derided winery lurking behind the name Frass Canyon ("frass' is fly shit, and no, of course the winery isn't that bad), where Miles discovers his novel isn't going to be published and attempts to drink the spit-bucket, is the **Fess Parker Winery and Vineyard, 6200 Foxen Canyon Road** (Fess Parker played Davy Crock-ett in a couple of Disney films in the '50s), Los Olivos. Oh, and Michael Jackson's Neverland Ranch is in Los Olivos, too, if you want to drop in and try your wine from a Coke can.

There's consolation for Miles at **Gaviota State Beach** (℗ *805.968.1033, www.parks.ca.gov*), Highway 101, 33 miles west of Santa Barbara, but more problems for Jack when he gets involved with married waitress Carri who works at **AJ Spurs, 350 Easy Highway 246** (℗ *805.686.1655, wwwajspurs.com*), Buellton.

Back home, and spiralling into deeper depression after meeting his (happily pregnant by another man) ex at Jack's wedding, Miles surreptitiously downs his precious 1961 Cheval Blanc from a plastic cup, with a burger and onion rings, not in San Diego at all, but

The 'windmill' motel: Days Inn Buellton, East Highway 246, Buellton

back in Santa Maria, at **Orcutt Burger, 1785 South Broadway** (℗ *805.928.0811*). Maybe it's not as bad as it seems. Orcutt has a reputation as the best burger joint in the area.

And those ostriches? You can see them at **Ostrich Land, 610 East Highway 246** between Buellton and Solvang (℗ *805.686.9696, www.ostrichland.com*).

SIGNS
(2002, dir: M Night Shyamalan)
Mel Gibson, Joaquin Phoenix, Cherry Jones.
● **PENNSYLVANIA**

Shyamalan's speciality is the surprise twist, but with Gibson playing an ex-priest who's lost his faith, we can pretty much guess his family is not going to die in an alien bloodbath. The Hess family farmhouse was built (and torn down after filming) on the grounds of an agricultural college (so they knew how to grow corn), **Delaware Valley College, Doylestown**, Bucks County, about 20 miles north of Philadelphia. The local main street is **South State Street, Newtown**, to the east. Here you'll find the bookstore (**Newtown Book and Record Exchange, 102 South State Street**); the military recruiting office (the old billiard hall at **201 South State Street**); and the pizza house, where the family glimpses director Shyamalan (**Mom's Bake at Home Pizza, 19 South State Street**). Further east, the pharmacy, where Graham (Gibson) picks up his son's asthma remedy, is **Burns Pharmacy, 82 North Pennsylvania Avenue, Morrisville**.

SILENCE OF THE LAMBS, THE
(1991, dir: Jonathan Demme)
Jodie Foster, Anthony Hopkins, Scott Glenn.
● **PITTSBURGH, PENNSYLVANIA; VIRGINIA; BAHAMAS**

Although set in such wide-ranging locales as Ohio, west Virginia and Tennessee, Demme's superior thriller was made largely around Pittsburgh, western Pennsylvania.

Clarice Starling meets the entomologist at the **Carnegie Museum of Natural History** in the **Carnegie Institute, 4400 Forbes Avenue, Oakland** (it's where Jennifer Beals gets snubbed in *Flashdance*). The exterior of Lecter's place of internment, the Baltimore Hospital, was the Western Center, an old mental hospital in Canonsburg, on I-79 about 15 miles south of Pittsburgh. It's since been demolished. Memphis Town Hall, where Lecter escapes from the holding cell and borrows the face of his guard, is the **Allegheny County Soldiers and Sailors Memorial Hall, 4141 Fifth Avenue**, a Civil War museum, part of the University of Pittsburgh. Many of the film's interiors were shot in the abandoned Westinghouse turbine factory (now known as **Keystone Commons**). The Grieg Funeral Home, where Clarice views the body of the murder victim and has a flashback to her own father's funeral, was an empty house, formerly a real funeral parlor, on **Main Street, Rural Valley**, about 40 miles east of Pittsburgh. Filming also took place at **Allegheny County Jail, 950 Second Avenue**, Pittsburgh, and at the **Greater Pittsburgh National Airport**, to the west of the city.

Clarice Starling works out of the real **FBI Training HQ, Quantico**, Virginia, on the US Marine Corps Base about 40 miles southwest of Washington DC.

Dr Lecter's tropical retirement home at the end of the movie is **Alice Town**, on the island of **North Bimini** in the Bahamas. The Bimini Islands, 50 miles off the coast of Florida, are the closest of the Bahamas to the USA. Famed for big game fishing and celebrated by Ernest Hemingway, who also took up residence here and wrote of the islands in *Islands in the Stream* (filmed by Franklin Schaffner with George C Scott, in 1977). The Biminis, like many islands in the Atlantic, were believed to have been the site of Atlantis, and are claimed to be home to the 'Fountain of Youth', the Healing Hole, which you can find on South Bimini.

SIMPLE PLAN, A

(1998, dir: Sam Raimi)
Bill Paxton, Billy Bob Thornton, Bridget Fonda.
● MINNESOTA; WISCONSIN

In a winterbound small town, two brothers stumble upon a huge amount of money, which brings inevitable complications. The little town location is **Delano**, on I-12, about 25 miles west of Minneapolis, Minnesota. As unseasonably warm weather caused the snow to melt, the unit had to move north to Wisconsin to film snowscapes.

SINGLE WHITE FEMALE

(1992, dir: Barbet Schroeder)
Bridget Fonda, Jennifer Jason Leigh, Steven Weber.
● NEW YORK CITY

Bridget Fonda's apartment: Ansonia Hotel, Broadway

Bridget Fonda invites mousy little Jennifer Jason Leigh to share her New York apartment, only to find she's living with a Bitch From Hell. Leigh works in **Rizzoli's Bookstore, 31 West 57th Street** between Fifth and Sixth Avenues, midtown. Fonda's Victorian apartment is supposedly 768 West 74th Street. Close, but not quite. It is, in fact, the gloriously embellished turn-of-the-century **Ansonia Hotel, 2109 Broadway**, between West 73rd and West 74th Streets. Not actually a hotel, the Ansonia is, as in the movie, a private apartment block. Its heavily soundproofed walls have made it an ideal home for musicians, and artists such as Caruso, Toscanini, Pinza and Stravinsky have stayed here. See it also as George Burns' home in Neil Simon's *The Sunshine Boys* and as Robert Redford's office in *Three Days of the Condor*.

SINGLES

(1992, dir: Cameron Crowe)
Campbell Scott, Kyra Sedgwick, Matt Dillon.
● SEATTLE, WASHINGTON

Seattle's grunge scene is the backdrop for Cameron Crowe's quirky look at relationships. Rock venues fea-

tured include the Off-Ramp, now **Graceland, 109 Eastlake Street** at Denny Way and Stewart Street, and the **Re-Bar, 1114 East Howell Street** off Boren Avenue – a mixed

The grunge club: Off-ramp, now Graceland, Eastlake Street

straight-gay club. Kyra Sedgwick says "yes" to Campbell Scott in the romantically-named **Gasworks Park, North Northlake** at Meridian North. Matt Dillon plays guitar on the grave of Jimi Hendrix in **Evergreen Memorial Cemetery** in **Renton**, east of Seattle.

Scott and Sedgwick meet up at **Virginia Inn Tavern, 1937 First Avenue** at Virginia Street (© *206.728.1937*). Opposite, at **1936 First Avenue**, is Expect the Best dating agency, where director Tim Burton cameos as a video director.

SISTER ACT

(1992, dir: Emile Ardolino)
Whoopi Goldberg, Maggie Smith, Kathy Najimy.
● CALIFORNIA; NEVADA

Goldberg performs in Reno: Fitzgerald's Casino, North Virginia Street

Nightclub singer Whoopi Goldberg, obliged to pose as a nun after witnessing a murder, leads the convent to success in a choir competition. Harvey Keitel's casino, where Goldberg performs old Motown numbers, is the **Nevada Club, Commercial Street, Reno**, on the outside, but the interior is over the road. It's **Fitzgerald's Casino, 255 North Virginia Street**, next to the famous 'Biggest Little City in the World' illuminated sign. Also in Reno, you can find the police station, which is actually **Reno Post Office, 50 South Virginia Street**, and the school that the young Goldberg attends: **St Thomas Aquinas Church, 310 West Second Street**. St Katherine's, the convent where Goldberg hides out, is actually **St Paul's Church, 221 Valley Street** at Church, in San Francisco's quaint Victorian Noe Valley neighbourhood, just below the eastern slopes of Twin Peaks. Some interiors were shot in the **First United Methodist Church, 6817**

Goldberg hides out: St Paul's Church, Valley Street, Noe Valley

Young Goldberg's school: St Thomas Aquinas Church, West Second Street

Franklin Avenue, Hollywood.

SIX DEGREES OF SEPARATION

(1993, dir: Fred Schepisi)
Will Smith, Donald Sutherland, Stockard Channing.
● NEW YORK CITY

Sutherland's apartment: Fifth Avenue

A group of disparate New Yorkers find themselves linked by a conman claiming to be Sidney Poitier's son (and Kevin Bacon becomes the subject of a movie buff party game). Adapted from John Guare's stage play, there's still a theatrical feel despite the frantic location-hopping around upscale Manhattan. The exterior of the swish Kittredge apartment is **860 Fifth Avenue**, at the southeast corner of 68th Street, though the overwhelming red interior, with fabulous views over Central Park, is that of **1049 Fifth Avenue** (which, bizarrely, stands on 86th Street). The apartment overlooks the statue of **Balto the Husky**, in Central Park at 67th Street, which crops up at key points in the story. If you want the full story (well, the Hollywood version) of this "indomitable sled dog", check out the 1995 animated film *Balto* (voiced by, who else? Kevin Bacon).

The restaurant, in which rich liberals Flan and Ouisa Kittredge (Sutherland and Channing) meet up with another couple taken in by the charming Paul (Smith), was Mortimer's, closed in 1999, which stood at 1057 Lexington Avenue. There's small talk at a party held in the vast, glass-walled gallery housing the Egyptian **Temple of Dendur** in the **Metropolitan Museum of Art, Fifth Avenue** at East 82nd Street on the East Side (℃ *212.535.7710, www.metmuseum.org*). The museum also appears in *A Perfect Murder* (the remake of Hitchcock's *Dial M For Murder*), Michael Winner's schlocker *The Sentinel* and *When Harry Met Sally...*. The exterior is seen in *Dressed to Kill* and the update of *The Thomas Crown Affair*.

The conned couples check for a copy of Poitier's autobiography at the **Strand Bookstore, 828 Broadway** at 12th Street, Greenwich Village (℃ *212.473.1452, www.strandbooks.com*). As the store boasts 18 miles of books, it's not surprising that they find a copy. Incidentally, if you're a set designer, the Strand will happily sell or rent books by the foot. The Strand was seen in Peter Yates' 1950s-set thriller *The House on Carroll Street*.

Paul, meanwhile, takes hippy boy Rick (Eric Thal) for a wildly expensive dinner at the **Rainbow Room, 65th Floor, 30 Rockefeller Plaza** (*www.rainbowroom.com*). Their tango is less well-received than Al Pacino's at the Pierre in *Scent of a Woman* and they're soon shown the door. Feeling flush? Book a table on ℃ *212.632.5100*.

A couple of locations outside Manhattan: the college scenes use **Manhattan College, Manhattan College Parkway, Riverdale** in the Bronx (which also hosted *A Beautiful Mind* and *The Object of My Affection*), and the

church where the Kittredges attend a wedding is in **West Orange**, northwest of Newark, New Jersey.

Paul is arrested in front of Greenwich Village's famous **Waverly Theater, 323 Sixth Avenue** at Third Street, which closed in 2001 and is being renovated as **IFC (Independent Film Channel) Center**. But Ouisa is liberated, finally walking out on Flan at a dinner party in the impossibly grand apartment at **1088 Park Lane** at 88th Street, and swanning happily off down Park Avenue.

SIXTH SENSE, THE

(1999, dir: M Night Shyamalan)
Bruce Willis, Haley Joel Osment, Toni Collette.
● PHILADELPHIA, PENNSYLVANIA

The church: St Augustine's Church, 4th Street

M Night Shyamalan's tricksy supernatural thriller, which turned out to be one of the year's unexpected smash hits, was shot around Philadelphia. You can find the garden street where young Cole Sear (Osment) and his mother live southwest of the city at **2302 St Alban's Place**, St Alban's Street at 23rd Street. The more upmarket Locust Street home of Malcolm Crowe (Willis) is really on **Delancy Street** in the solidly respectable, Society Hill district.

Cole's house: St Alban's Place

The church to which haunted Cole retreats is **St Augustine's Roman Catholic Church, 4th Street** at New Street, near the entrance to the Benjamin Franklin Bridge. The restaurant, where Crowe keeps an appointment with his wife, is the classy

Willis keeps the appointment: Striped Bass, Walnut Street

Striped Bass, 1500 Walnut Street (℃ *215.732.4444*), occupying the marble grandeur of a former brokerage house in the centre of town.

SJUNDE INSEGLET, DET (aka *The Seventh Seal*)

(1957, dir: Ingmar Bergman)
Max von Sydow, Gunnar Bjornstrand, Bibi Andersson.
● SWEDEN

One of the most enduring icons of Euro art cinema is that of Antonius Block (von Sydow) playing chess with Death, in Bergman's bleak period fable questioning religious faith, mostly filmed in the studios at **Rasunda**, Sweden. The opening scenes, of Medieval knight Block arriving at the rocky beach and confronting Death, are **Hovs**

Hallar in Skane Province, southwest Sweden. The site was used for the wider landscapes, too, including the stunning Dance of Death ending.

SLACKER
(1991, dir: Richard Linklater)
Richard Linklater, Rudy Basquez, Jean Caffeine.
● **TEXAS**

Indie production, featuring a series of character encounters, shot around **Austin**, Texas. Quackenbush's, the café featured, stood at **2121 Guadalupe Street**, but has since closed. The ending is **Mount Bonnell Overlook**, above Lake Austin, which you might recognise from the Coen brothers' *Blood Simple*.

SLEEPER
(1973, dir: Woody Allen)
Woody Allen, Diane Keaton, John Beck.
● **COLORADO; CALIFORNIA**

This untypical futuristic satire, with Allen as a Greenwich Village health food store owner waking up after 200 years of cryogenic storage, uses an impressive array of sixties and seventies modernistic architecture. The 'clamshell' house of Dr Melik in the Central Parallel of the American Federation, where the newly-defrosted Allen is hidden from government agents, is architect Charles Deaton's **Sculpture House**, overlooking I-70 at **Genessee**, west of Denver, Colorado. The ovoid pod, perched on a stalk, was begun in 1963 by the architect, for himself, but never finished. It lay derelict for many years but has recently been purchased and renovated as a private home. More futurescapes were provided by the **Conservatory Building** of **Denver Botanical Garden, 1005 York Street** (© *303.331.4000*), Denver. The countryside hideout is **Rancho San Carlos** in **Carmel Valley**, northern California.

The sinister government complex, in which Allen and Diane Keaton foil Project Aries, the plan to clone the quasi-fascist leader, is IM Pei's chunky, concrete **Mesa Lab** at the **National Center for Atmospheric Research, 1850 Table Mesa Drive, Boulder**, Colorado. Allen's living accommodation here, though, is actually in LA. It's the curvilinear **Robert Lee Frost Auditorium** of **Culver City High School, Elenda Street** at Franklin Avenue, Culver City in LA.

SLEEPERS
(1996, dir: Barry Levinson)
Brad Pitt, Kevin Bacon, Robert De Niro.
● **NEW YORK CITY; NEW YORK; CONNECTICUT**

Levinson's film of Lorenzo Carcatera's revenge melodrama should have been harrowing but, despite a top-

The disaster at the subway station: Astor Place, Fourth Avenue, East Village

drawer cast, comes across as glibly contrived. Supposedly based on a true story, no one seems able to find any record of the events. **Greenpoint**, Brooklyn, stands in for New York's Hell's Kitchen neighbourhood, which has been radically redeveloped since the sixties, when the film begins. De Niro's Church of the Holy Angels is **Most Holy Trinity, 138 Montrose Avenue** at Ewen. The canopied subway station, where a reckless jape goes so horribly wrong, is **Astor Place**, Fourth Avenue at

John and Tommy take revenge: McHale's, Eighth Avenue

The four friends meet up for a final celebration: Minetta Tavern, MacDougal Street, Greenwich Village

Stuyvesant Street, over in the East Village. The grim Wilkinson Home for Boys, Breckenridge, to which the four boys are sent, is **Fairfield Hills Hospital, Mile Hill Road**, a facility for the mentally disabled near **Newtown**, Connecticut.

Years later, the adult John and Tommy take revenge on sadistic guard Sean Nokes (Bacon) in **McHale's, 750 Eighth Avenue** at 46th Street (© *212.997.8885*). You might remember the bar as the hangout of Woody Harrelson and Wesley Snipes in 1995's *Money Train*. King Benny (Vittorio Gassman, who played the Pacino role in the original Italian *Scent of a Woman*), has a quiet word at the **Market Diner, 572 11th Avenue** (© *212.695.0415*). The grand but faded HQ of Little Caesar, the older brother of Rizzo who died in the Wilkinson home, is **Loew's King's Theater, 1049 Flatbush Avenue**, Brooklyn, closed since 1977 (seen also in Jim Jarmusch's *Night on Earth*).

The murder trial seems to be taking place in the **Municipal Building, 1 Centre Street** at Chambers Street (though a quick insert shot tries to sell the location as the United States Courthouse), but the interior was actually filmed at **Yonkers**, in the **County Courthouse, 100 South Broadway**, New York State. Michael Sullivan (Pitt) and 'Shakes' (Jason Patric) discuss the future in the Municipal Building's colonnaded entrance, before Sullivan disappears into the **Chambers Street** subway station.

The four friends meet up for a final celebration in the **Minetta Tavern, 113 MacDougal Street** at Minetta Lane, Greenwich Village (© *212.475.3850*). A speakeasy called The Black Rabbit during Prohibition, the tavern was something of a literary hangout for the likes of Ezra Pound, e e cummings, Ernest Hemingway and Eugene O'Neill. *Reader's Digest* was founded in the tavern's basement in 1923. You can glimpse the Minetta in the original *Shaft*.

SLEEPLESS IN SEATTLE
(1993, dir: Nora Ephron)
Tom Hanks, Meg Ryan, Bill Pullman.
● **SEATTLE, WASHINGTON; CHICAGO, ILLINOIS; MARYLAND; NEW YORK CITY**

Nora Ephron's cutesy romance, sparklingly photographed by longtime Bergman collaborator Sven Nykvist, was the sleeper of '93, and although Vancouver was considered as a location, the real Seattle finally won out. Most of the Chicago, Baltimore and New York interiors are Seattle, too, plus some of the Baltimore exteriors. Tom Hanks leaves Chicago, and his unhappy memories, from the city's vast and modern **O'Hare International Airport**.

Moving to Seattle, he sets up home with his young son in a houseboat on **Westlake Avenue North**, on the west shore of Lake Union in the Queen Anne Hill district. The upscale neighbourhood also supplied other characters' classy homes. Hanks' pal, director Rob Reiner, gives him some man-to-man advice about tiramisu – among other mysteries – in the **Athenian Inn, 1517 Pike Place** (© *206.624.7166*), a breakfast and lunch eaterie in the Main Arcade of Seattle's landmark Pike Place Market. It's in the market that Hanks shops with his prospective date, Victoria. He takes her for a meal at the **Dahlia Lounge**, one of Seattle's top restaurants, where Meg Ryan's detective surreptitiously photographs the couple. The restaurant, which stood at 1904 Fourth Avenue, has since moved premises, though not too far, to **2001 Fourth Avenue** at Virginia Street (© *206.682.4142*).

Ryan spies on Hanks playing with his son at **Alki Beach Park, Alki Avenue SW**, on the northwest shore of west Seattle. Supposedly in Baltimore, the New Year party, where Meg Ryan and Bill Pullman make plans for the future, is the **Dome Room** of the **Arctic Building, 700 Third Avenue** at Cherry Street, in Seattle's Business District. The 9-storey building was built in 1916 as a private club by men returning rich from the Klondike gold rush in the Yukon, hence the terracotta walrus heads decorating the façade. Supposedly in Washington DC, but actually in Baltimore, is the Capitol Diner, apparently in the shadow of the Capitol Building. It's the **Hollywood Diner, 400 East Saratoga Street** (© *410.962.5379*) – the original setting of Barry Levinson's *Diner*. Also in Baltimore are Ryan's apartment, at **904 South Broadway**, east of downtown, and the **Sun Newspaper Building** where she works (as does Freddy Lounds in *Red Dragon*).

In New York, Ryan and Pullman tentatively settle for unadventurous domesticity at **Tiffany and Co, 727 Fifth Avenue** at 57th Street, but in no time are splitting up in the **Rainbow Room, 30 Rockefeller Plaza** (© *212.632.5115*), the Rockefeller Center's pricy, highrise restaurant with its fabulous views over Manhattan.

The **Empire State Building, 350 Fifth Avenue** at West 34th Street, is only partly the real thing. The exterior and lobby are genuine enough, but for ease of filming, a slightly larger replica of the Observation Deck was built in a hangar at Sands Point Naval Base on Puget Sound.

SLEEPY HOLLOW

(1999, dir: Tim Burton)
Johnny Depp, Christina Ricci, Christopher Walken.
● **HERTFORDSHIRE; BUCKINGHAMSHIRE; LONDON**

Burton's film, inspired by the Washington Irving story, shot largely on sets built at the Leavesden studios in Hert-fordshire where the Western Woods were created on the soundstage. The village of Sleepy Hollow was built from scratch on the **Hambledon Estate**, near Marlow in Buckinghamshire. Turn-of-the-century New York is the central courtyard of **Somerset House**, the **Strand** in London. Christopher Walken rides the mechanical horse built for Elizabeth Taylor in *National Velvet*. The real US setting of Sleepy Hollow is now part of Tarrytown, New York State.

SLEUTH

(1972, dir: Joseph L Mankiewicz)
Laurence Olivier, Michael Caine, Alec Cawthorne.
● **DORSET**

Laurence Olivier's stately home, in this rather stagey adaptation of Anthony Shaffer's tricksy play, is **Athelhampton** (although the interior was recreated at Pinewood). One

Laurence Olivier's country seat: Athelhampton

of England's finest Medieval houses, Athelhampton was built in 1485 on the site of King Athelstan's palace, and encircled by the River Piddle. It's about a mile east of Puddletown on the A35 Dorchester-Bournemouth road, and is open to the general public from Easter to the end of October (© *01305.848135, www.athelhampton.co.uk*).

SLIDING DOORS

(1998, dir: Peter Howitt)
Gwyneth Paltrow, John Hannah, John Lynch.
● **LONDON**

Helen Quilley's life takes off in two separate directions, depending on whether or not she catches a tube train, in Peter Howitt's imaginative

Paltrow's flat: Princes Square, Notting Hill

romance. The use of London locations is equally tricksy. Although the station Helen (Paltrow) appears to exit and enter is **Embankment**, the spot where she actually misses/catches the train is the Waterloo and City Line platform of **Waterloo Underground Station**. The attempted mugging, after Helen misses the train, takes place, strangely, outside the **Landmark Hotel, Melcombe Place**, opposite Marylebone Station. Paltrow lives with John Lynch at **62 Princes Square, Notting Hill**, W8.

Helen organises the grand opening party: Manor, All Saints Road, Notting Hill

Paltrow works or drinks: Bertorelli's, Charlotte Street

Rowing on the Thames: Lower Mall, Hammersmith

The restaurant where she either drinks with James (Hannah) or works to support Gerry (Lynch), is **Bertorelli's, 19 Charlotte Street** (© 020.7636.4174), behind Tottenham Court Road, W1. Helen and James hang out and eventually reconcile at **Albert Bridge**, Chelsea, SW3. They enjoy a post-rowing "sponsored epileptic fit" at **The Blue Anchor, 13 Lower Mall, Hammersmith**, W6, alongside the Auriol Kensington Rowing Club. Clive's restaurant, where Helen organises the grand opening party, was the West Indian Mas Cafe, now reinvented in cool, classic shades as **Manor, 6-8 All Saints Road**, Notting Hill (© 020.7243.0969), serving up modern Euro cuisine.

Bitch From Hell Jeanne Tripplehorn works at **66 Chiltern Street**, though the entrance is actually on **Paddington Street**, W1. Her apartment is **G4 Pattern House, 223-227 St John Street**, between Sekforde and Skinner Streeets, Clerkenwell, EC1, where Helen falls downstairs in the rather contrived ending.

SMALLEST SHOW ON EARTH, THE (aka *Big Time Operators*)
(1957, dir: Basil Dearden)
Bill Travers, Virginia McKenna, Margaret Rutherford.
● LONDON

Site of the Bijou: Kilburn

Travers and McKenna inherit a fleapit cinema. Sadly, there is no Bijou, and never was, but you can still see the site where the frontage was erected. The old picture house was squeezed into the tiny gap between two railway bridges and rattled as trains thundered overhead. The two bridges can be seen just to the left of the entrance to **Kilburn Underground Station**, NW6.

SMILES OF A SUMMER NIGHT
(1955, dir: Ingmar Bergman)
Gunnar Bjornstrand, Eva Dahlbeck, Harriet Andersson.
● SWEDEN

Ageing lawyer meets up with old flame ageing actress at an elegant country house, in this turn-of-the-century comedy of sexual manners, which provided the basis for the Stephen Sondheim musical *A Little Night Music*. The country house is **Jordeberga Castle**, three miles south of Malmo, Sweden. The theatre, at which Desiree appears, is based on a rococo gem in the town of Ystad.

SMOKEY AND THE BANDIT
(1977, dir: Hal Needham)
Burt Reynolds, Sally Field, Jackie Gleason.
● GEORGIA

Reynolds is a bootlegger who picks up disgruntled bride-not-to-be Field, sparking off a long and noisy chase by prospective father-in-law and sherriff Gleason. Filmed, like many of Reynolds' movies, in his home state of Georgia at **Riverdale** and **Jonesboro**. The house of Cledus 'Snowman' Snow (Jerry Reed) stood on **North Avenue, Jonesboro**, but has since been demolished. Texarkana is downtown Jonesboro. The racetrack at the end was at the **Lakewood Fairgrounds, 2000 Lakewood Avenue, Atlanta** (© 404.622.4488). You can see memorabilia from the movie at the Burt Reynolds Museum, 100 North US Highway 1, Jupiter (© 561.743.9955, www.burt-reynoldsmuseum.org).

SNATCH
(2000, dir: Guy Ritchie)
Jason Statham, Brad Pitt, Lennie James.
● LONDON

Doug's local: Ye Olde Mitre Tavern, Hatton Gardens

Snappy and inventive, but Ritchie's compulsive laddishness is starting to outstay its welcome. Naturally, the setting is London, where the diamond store of Doug 'The Head' (Mike Reid) is **Premier House, 12-13 Hatton Gardens**, EC1, near Holborn. His nearby local (where director Ritchie puts in a microcameo as Man Reading Newspaper) is **Ye Olde Mitre Tavern**, between 8 and 9 Hatton Gardens. For once the 'Ye Olde' isn't a faux addition from the seventies, but the real deal (© 020.7405.4751). Tucked away in a narrow alley marked by an old crooked street lamp and a small sign in the shape of a bishop's mitre, this tiny pub with wood-panelled bars can get pretty busy at lunchtimes. It was built in 1547 for servants of the palace of the Bishops of Ely, Cambridgeshire (and is technically still part of Cambridgeshire), but after the reformation, Queen Elizabeth obliged the bishops to rent land to one of her courtiers, Sir Christopher Hatton, hence the name of the area. Shades of *Passport to Pimlico* – since the bar is technically not part of London, legend has it that police must ask permission to enter, which is quite possibly why it's Doug's local.

To the East End, and Bethnal

The diamond store of Doug the Head: Premier House, Hatton Gardens

The office of wide-boy Turkish: Jesters Amusements, Broadway, West Ealing

Brad Pitt's unlicensed boxing match: Caesars Nightclub, Streatham Hill

Green. **88 Teesdale Street**, E2, became Sol's (James) pawn shop. **Bethnal Green Town Hall, Cambridge Heath Road** at Patriot Square (also used in *Lock, Stock and Two Smoking Barrels*), became Franky Four Fingers' (Benicio Del Toro) tailor's. On the **Park Royal Industrial Estate** just behind Central Middlesex Hospital, west London, a casually tossed carton of milk precipitates the motor smash. Even further west, in west Ealing, **Jesters Amusements, 127 Broadway** at Coldershaw Road, is the games arcade and the office of wide-boy Turkish (Statham) that gets smashed up. **14 Tees Avenue, Perivale**, was home to Boris 'The Blade' (Rade Serbedzija).

Way south of the river, **Caesars Nightclub, 156-160 Streatham Hill** (℃ 020.8671.3000), is the site of Mickey's (Pitt) unlicensed boxing match. Seventies and eighties music is the more usual fare. Cheap and cheerful or huge and cheesy? It probably amounts to the same thing.

The Drowning Trout, the big old pub where Bullet Tooth Tony (Vinnie Jones) is confronted by Sol and co before the bloody shoot up, is **The Jolly Gardeners, 49 Black Prince Road** at Tyers Street, SE11. Despite its proximity to Westminster, do remember that this is a local boozer, not a Mayfair winebar. Nearby, **Salamanca Place** is where Brick-Top's heavies catch up with Tyrone (Ade), but it has since been completely redeveloped.

SOCIETY
(1989, dir: Brian Yuzna)
Billy Warlock, Devin DeVasquez, Evan Richards.
● **LOS ANGELES, CALIFORNIA**

Imaginative script by Woody Keith and Rick Fry, about upper class slimesters literally feeding off the lower orders, is near scuppered by the ham-fisted direction of former producer Yuzna, though Screaming Mad George's FX are, erm, eye-popping. It was made around LA at mansions in **Pasadena** and **Malibu**; and in **Griffith Park**. The hospital is the **Veteran's Administration Medical Center** between Lassen and Plummer Streets in Northridge, northern LA. The school is **Birmingham High School, 17000 Haynes Street, Van Nuys** (seen also in *Charlie's Angels: Full Throttle*), which includes Sally Field among its past students. No, don't even think about it...

SOME CAME RUNNING
(1959, dir: Vincente Minnelli)
Frank Sinatra, Shirley MacLaine, Dean Martin.
● **INDIANA**

Minnelli's colourfully soapy melodrama, from James Jones' novel of smalltown life after WWII, is set in Parkman, Illinois, but was made in **Madison**, on I-421, southwest Indiana by the Kentucky border. Arthur Kennedy's Hirsh Jewelry Store is actually **Stanton's Shoe Store, 110 East Main Street**. Smitty's Bar was a vacant store nearby. Other genuine locations used include the local hotel, bank, and **Hanover College**.

SOME LIKE IT HOT
(1959, dir: Billy Wilder)
Marilyn Monroe, Jack Lemmon, Tony Curtis.
● **SAN DIEGO, CALIFORNIA**

The Miami hotel: Hotel del Coronado

The exteriors for this classic comedy were filmed in a mere seven days at **Coronado Beach** near San Diego, standing in for 1920s Miami. The hotel, where Lemmon and Curtis hide out in drag with Monroe, is the **Hotel del Coronado, 1500 Orange Avenue** (℃ 619.435.6611, www.hoteldel.com). This 700-room Victorian fantasy, built in 1888, has long been frequented by the rich and famous, including no less than eight US presidents, Sarah Bernhardt, Charlie Chaplin, and – according to legend – it's where Edward met Wallis Simpson. Its other connection with movie history is that this is where Frank L Baum wrote much of *The Wizard of Oz*, and its fussy gingerbread appearance is said to have inspired the description of Oz. So, fittingly, Buddy Ebsen spent a month recuperating here from the effect of breathing in aluminium dust – and considering whether to sue MGM – after starting work as the original Tin Man. The Coronado is also the setting for Richard Rush's brilliant, Oscar-nominated 1980 one-off, *The Stunt Man* with Steve Railsback and Peter O'Toole.

SOMMAREN MED MONIKA (aka *Summer With Monika*)
(1952, dir: Ingmar Bergman)
Harriet Andersson, Lars Ekborg, John Harryson.
● **SWEDEN**

Early Bergman, a doomed summer romance, made on **Orno**, a large island in the south of the Stockholm archipelago.

SOMMERSBY
(1993, dir: Jon Amiel)
Richard Gere, Jodie Foster, Bill Pullman.
● **VIRGINIA**

US remake of France's *The Return of Martin Guerre*, set in Tennessee during the Civil War. The brick mansion is now a hotel, the **Hidden Valley Bed and Breakfast, Hidden Valley Road, Warm Springs** (℃ 540.839.3178) in the George Washington National Forest, west Virginia. Originally Warwickton Mansion, it was built by slaves for Judge John Woods Warwick between 1848 and 1851.

The town is **Lexington**, with filming on **Main Street** and **Washington Street**. The courtroom scenes were shot in **Charlotte**.

SONS AND LOVERS

(1960, dir: Jack Cardiff)
Dean Stockwell, Trevor Howard, Wendy Hiller.
● NOTTINGHAMSHIRE

DH Lawrence's semi-autobiographical novel, filmed by former cinematographer Jack Cardiff, and winning an Oscar for its cinematography by veteran Freddie Francis. Shot largely on location in Lawrence country around Nottinghamshire. The house is Lawrence's real childhood home in **Eastwood**, about eight miles west of Nottingham, and the mine is the local **Brinsley Colliery**, where Lawrence's father actually worked. The colliery closed in 1970, but the wooden headstocks, which were removed, have been returned and reassembled.

SOPHIE'S CHOICE

(1982, dir: Alan J Pakula)
Meryl Streep, Kevin Kline, Peter MacNicol.
● NEW YORK CITY; YUGOSLAVIA

Streep is a Polish concentration camp survivor plagued by guilt. The Pink Palace (which is in reality dull grey) is **101 Rugby Road, Flatbush** in Brooklyn. Meryl quaffs champagne on the **Brooklyn Bridge** and frolics with Kevin Kline at **Coney Island Amusement Park**. The Polish scenes were filmed in **Zagreb**, Yugoslavia, at the Jadvan Studios.

SORCERERS, THE

(1967, dir: Michael Reeves)
Ian Ogily, Boris Karloff, Catherine Lacey.
● LONDON

The Glory Hole, Roscoe's antique shop: Lisson Grove, Marylebone

Reeves made only three films before succumbing to a drugs overdose at the age of twenty-four: the microbudget *Revenge of the Blood Beast* (a campy horror flick made in Italy), the awesome *Witchfinder General* and, between those two, *The Sorcerers*. Karloff (in one of his last roles) and Lacey are an elderly couple anticipating virtual reality with a hypnotic device (operating on the same sixties disco light-show principle as the Ipcress device). Ogilvy is Mike Roscoe, the hip, young antique dealer through whom they experience the vicarious pleasures of biking, stealing and, um, serial killing.

There's nothing to see now at 121 Queen's Gate, South Kensington, but this was the site of legendary 60s club Blaises (named after cartoon character Modesty Blaise, incarnated by Monica Vitti in Joseph Losey's leaden fantasy). The basement venue, which hosted performances from the likes of Jimi Hendrix, is Roscoe's hangout. The **Dolphin Square** complex in Pimlico houses the swimming pool to which Roscoe is sent for a midnight dip by the creepy oldsters. The Glory Hole, Roscoe's antique shop, was **95 Lisson Grove**, at Broadley Street, Marylebone, still astonishingly unchanged amid the wholesale renovation of the district.

SOTTO GLI OCCHI DELL'ASSASSINO (aka *Tenebrae/Unsane*)

(1982, dir: Dario Argento)
Anthony Franciosa, Veronica Lario, John Saxon.
● ROME, ITALY; NEW YORK CITY

Another of Argento's triumphs of style over content, with a superb shock effect cheekily lifted by Brian De Palma for the ending of *Raising Cain*. Apart from a brief opening sequence of author Franciosa cycling to **JFK Airport** in New York, the film was shot in Rome. Argento, unusually, chose to film in dazzling sunlight (the ironic title means 'darkness') around the near-deserted, antiseptic suburb of **EUR (Esposizione Universale Romana)**, a grandiose project planned by Mussolini but not completed until the fifties, about four miles south of Rome on Via Cristoforo Colombo. You can see more of the area's fascist architecture in *Titus*.

SOUND OF MUSIC, THE

(1965, dir: Robert Wise)
Julie Andrews, Christopher Plummer, Peggy Wood.
● AUSTRIA

This phenomenally successful musical, based on a true story, was shot on lots of real locations around **Salzburg**, Austria (though plenty more were recreated in the 20th

Maria leaving: The entrance to Nonnberg Abbey...

Century-Fox studios in Hollywood). The opening aerial shots are Salzburg's glorious Lake District, the **Salzkammergut**. The castles are **Fuchsl**, 12 miles east of Salzburg on the **Fuchslee**, clearest of the Salzkammergut lakes, and **Schloss Anif**, off E55 a few miles south of Salzburg. Maria's mountain is **Mellweg**, near the Bavarian village of Schellenberg, about six miles from Salzburg. The birch trees were added for the movie and the babbling brook specially dug.

Convent interiors were recreated in the studio, but the exterior really is Maria's abbey. It's **Nonnberg Abbey, Nonnberg Gasse**, where you can visit the courtyard and peek into the chapel. The film cheats a little. The abbey looks out not to the picturesque old town of Salzburg, but to the nondescript southern suburbs. The reverse shot, of Maria leaving the abbey, was

...and the view from Winkler Terrace, across the city

Arriving at the Von Trapp mansion:
Hellbrunner Allee

filmed across the city on the **Winkler Terrace**. As Maria leaves to take up her post with the Von Trapps, 'I Have Confidence in Me' was filmed in Salzburg's Old Town, in the **Residenzplatz**, where you'll see the **Domplatz** arches, through which Maria enters, and the **Residenz Fountain**.

The Villa Von Trapp is a combination of two Salzburg locations. The tree-shaded lane, where Maria alights from the bus, is **Hellbrunner Allee**, running south from the old town. Here you'll recognise **Schloss Frohnburg**, a 17th century country house, now the Mozarteum Music Academy, which was used for the intimidating gates and front entrance of the villa. The lakeside terrace was filmed at **Schloss Leopoldskron**, a rococo castle on **Leopoldskroner Teich**, a small artificial lake on the southwest of the town. Now a private college, you can see Leopoldskron across the lake from **König Ludwig Strasse**. The real Villa Trapp, by the way, is in Aigen, 30 miles northwest of Linz in the very north of Austria near the German and Czech borders. The 'Do-Re-Mi' number begins atop the **Monchsberg Cliffs** on Winkler Terrace, which you can reach from the Monchsberg elevator in Anton Neumayrplatz, at the end of the Gstattengasse shopping street. The picnic is at the village of **Werfen**, 25 miles south of Salzburg in the Salzach River valley (the location for wartime action movie *Where Eagles Dare*). The number continues at **Mirabell Gardens**, on **Schwarzstrasse**, over the Salzach River behind Schloss Mirabell, where you'll find the fountains, statues and, famously, the flight of steps the children hop on. The little footbridge is **Mozart Steg**, north of Mozart Platz.

The Von Trapp gazebo, used for 'Sixteen Going on Seventeen', once stood in the grounds of Leopoldskron, but constant trespassing resulted in it being moved and reconstructed in the ornamental gardens of **Schloss Hellbrunn**, **Morzger Strasse**, south of the city.

Maria's wedding, which took place in Nonnberg Abbey, was shot in the baroque, twin-towered cathedral of **Mondsee**, about 15 miles east of Salzburg on the E55/E60.

Maria's wedding:
Mondsee Cathedral

The Anschluss scene, showing Austria's enforced unity with Nazi Germany, was staged back in the centre of town in **Residenzplatz**. The music festival, where the family perform their disappearing act, is at the **Felsenreitschule** ('Rock Riding School') on **Toscaninihof**, a massive rock arena built by the Romans for tournaments and part of the Festspielhaus. The cemetery, where the Von

Trapps hide from the Nazis, is loosely based on St Peter's Graveyard just off Kapitelplatz, but was built in Hollywood. The mountain over which the family finally escapes to freedom is **Mount Obersalzburg** (once proposed as the site for Hitler's Eagle's Nest hideaway), near the village of Rossfeld, on the 319, 12 miles south of Salzburg.

Several companies offer *Sound of Music* tours which visit the locations: try Bob's Special Tours (℗ *0662.872484*) or Panorama Tours, Mirabell Square (℗ *0662.871618, www.panoramatours.at*).

SOUTH PACIFIC

(1958, dir: Joshua Logan)
Mitzi Gaynor, Rossano Brazzi, Juanita Hall.
● HAWAII; SPAIN

There are some great Hawaiian locations for this musical, which suffers from Logan's over-enthusiastic use of lurid colour filters. Mitzi Gaynor washes her hair on

Mitzi washes her hair: Lumahai Beach, Kauai

Lumahai Beach, on **Kauai**. And just to the north, on the island's spectacular Na Pali Coast, is **Makahoa Point**, which stood in for the magic island of Bali Hai.

SOUTHERN COMFORT

(1981, dir: Walter Hill)
Keith Carradine, Powers Boothe, Fred Ward.
● LOUISIANA; TEXAS

Hill's tough Vietnam allegory, with National Guardsmen on an exercise in the Louisiana swamps caught in a cat-and-mouse game of death with local inhabitants, was shot on location in the swamps of Louisiana and at **Caddo Lake**, Texas.

SOUTHERNER, THE

(1945, dir: Jean Renoir)
Zachary Scott, Betty Field, Beulah Bondi.
● CALIFORNIA

Scott battles to save his cotton farm in Renoir's beautiful-looking film about the hardships of tenant farmers in Texas. The ramshackle farmhouse was built on the bank of the San Joaquin River near **Madera** on Route 99, north of Fresno.

SPANKING THE MONKEY

(1994, dir: David O Russell)
Jeremy Davies, Alberta Watson, Carla Gallo.
● NEW YORK

Russell's taboo-breaking family melodrama, in low key style, was made on a shoestring and trailed awards from the Sundance Institute. At one point it attracted Faye Dunaway, who eventually dropped out. It was shot entirely in **Pawling**, a town of around 2,000 on Route 22, about 70 miles north of New York City near to the Connecticut border.

SPARTACUS

(1960, dir: Stanley Kubrick)
Kirk Douglas, Jean Simmons, Tony Curtis.
● CALIFORNIA; SPAIN

Crassus' villa: Hearst Castle, San Simeon

One of the best, if not the best, of the great epics, begun by Anthony Mann. Mann is responsible for the opening sequence, of a wickedly scene-stealing Peter Ustinov picking Spartacus from the Sicilian mines (actually the parched landscape of **Death Valley**, California) for his gladiator school. After two weeks of work, Mann was fired and the frantic search for a new director eventually turned up trumps with Stanley Kubrick.

Most of the film was shot on the Universal lot in Hollywood, although the spectacular battle sequences were filmed in Spain, with the Spanish army brilliantly executing the complex manoeuvres of the ancient Romans. The sound was something else. The roar of battle was the sound of 76,000 football fans attending a game between Michigan State and Notre Dame.

The exterior of Crassus' villa is the white marble swimming pool of newspaper magnate William Randolph Hearst at **Hearst Castle, 750 Hearst Castle Road, San Simeon**, on California's Pacific coast, halfway between Los Angeles and San Francisco. The model for Charles Foster Kane's Xanadu in *Citizen Kane*, the monument is now open to the public (© *805.927.2020, www.hearst-castle.com*).

SPECIES

(1995, dir: Roger Donaldson)
Natasha Henstridge, Ben Kingsley, Michael Madsen.
● CALIFORNIA; UTAH; PUERTO RICO

Sil's hideout: Saharan Motor Hotel, Sunset Boulevard

Scientist Kingsley combines alien and human DNA to produce a speed-growing supermodel who, in the space of a few days, learns language, reading, dress sense and how to follow the instructions on a bottle of hair dye. Alien messages are first received at the **Arecibo Observatory**, about ten miles south of **Arecibo** in **Puerto Rico**, a familiar movie star seen in *GoldenEye* and *Contact*. You can visit the obervatory's Angel Ramos Visitor Center, Wednesday to Sunday (*www.naic.edu*).

The escape of young alien Sil (Michelle Williams) filmed at the **Tooele Army Depot**, Tooele, about 30 miles southwest of Salt Lake City, northern Utah. The Victorian railway station is **Brigham City**, also Utah. She arrives, grown up (into Henstridge) and with an urge to mate, conveniently in LA, at **Union Station, 800 North Alameda Street**, downtown. The wedding dress shop where Sil

picks up a little something to wear is at the intersection of Fifth Street and Broadway, downtown LA. The motel she checks into is the **Saharan Motor Hotel, 7212 Sunset Boulevard** at Alta Vista Boulevard in Hollywood

The entrance to the Id club: Yucca Street, Hollywood

(where the body of the murdered prostitute is discovered in Michael Mann's *LA Takedown*, his dry-run for *Heat*). You won't be able to pick up at the Id Club, to which Sil is directed in search of a man, as it's a fictional venue. You can see the elaborately decorated location though, which is the foyer of the **Pantages Theater, 6233 Hollywood Boulevard**, a movie palace now turned musical showcase (© *310.410.1062*). The entrance to the Id uses the building's rear entrance on **Yucca Street** – that's the striking blue-and-white frontage of the Hollywood Palace Theater and the base of the Capitol Records Tower in the background. The team of oddball specialists on Sil's tail, almost literally, are based in the **Biltmore Hotel, 506 South Grand Avenue**, downtown LA – a frequent location, see *Beverly Hills Cop* for details. The car park where Sil is knocked down, and picked up by her next victim, is on **Appia Avenue** at Seaview Terrace, in Santa Monica alongside the Santa Monica Pier. The lavish house he takes her to is just to the north in Pacific Palisades. The car and helicopter chase was shot in the hills near Elysian Park just above the Dodger Stadium and alongside railroad yards at Union Station.

SPEED

(1994, dir: Jan De Bont)
Keanu Reeves, Sandra Bullock, Dennis Hopper.
● CALIFORNIA

Simple plot turned into mega-blockbuster by cinematographer-turned-director De Bont's high-octane direction. The office block where the embit-

The bus blows up: Main Street, Venice

tered Howard Payne (Hopper) is foiled in his attempt to bomb the elevator is the 52-storey **Gas Company Towers, 555 West Fifth Street** at the northwest corner of Olive Street, downtown LA (see it again in *Charlie's Angels*). Jack Traven (Reeves) celebrates his award at **The Derby, 4500 Los Feliz Boulevard** (© *323.663.8979*). The old Brown Derby Restaurant, it was renovated and reinvented as a swing venue in 1993 (see *Swingers* for details).

Traven chats to the bus driver at the **Firehouse Restaurant, 213 Rose Avenue** at Main Street, Venice (© *310.392.4275*), opposite the Koo Koo Roo Californian Kitchen with its landmark ballerina/clown sculpture

Foiling the bomber: Gas Company Towers, West Fifth Street

Reeves chats to the bus driver: Firehouse Restaurant, Venice

hanging on the corner. The bus blows up on **Main Street**, just south of Rose Avenue, and this is where Traven receives the phone call from Payne. Spunky Annie Porter (Bullock) boards the bus at **Ocean Park Boulevard and Main Street**. Much of the bus ride was filmed on the I-105 in south-central LA around Watts. The spectacular bus jump on the unfinished freeway used the recently completed Glenn Anderson Freeway (Century Freeway). The yawning gap was added later with computer-generated imagery. The bus is finally diverted to the airstrips of Los Angeles International Airport. Kind of. The airport actually used for the filming is **Mojave Airport**, at Mojave in Kern County.

The money drop: Pershing Square

The money drop is at Fifth and Hill Streets, by the steps at the northeast corner of recently renovated **Pershing Square**, downtown Los Angeles. Here too is the station of the recently completed first section of the long-awaited LA subway, Metrorail Red Line at Pershing Square Station. Most of the underground sequences were filmed on studio mock-ups, but it's on the real Hollywood Boulevard, at the near-completed **Hollywood Metrorail Station** just outside Grauman's Chinese Theatre between Highland and La Brea Avenues, that the train finally explodes into daylight.

SPIDER, THE (aka *Earth Versus the Spider*)
(1958, dir: Bert I Gordon)
Ed Kemmer, June Kenny, Geene Persson.
● NEW MEXICO

Spider's lair: entrance to Carlsbad Caverns

A high school rock band revives an apparently dead giant spider, found in the spectacular **Carlsbad Caverns, Whites City**, on Route 180/62, south of Carlsbad, in the southeastern corner of New Mexico. The caverns, 83 separate caves forming one of the world's largest underground chambers, can be visited on tours of varying strenuousness (*©*

505.7852232, www.carlsbad.caverns.national-park.com; admission charge).

SPIDER-MAN
(2002, dir: Sam Raimi)
Tobey Maguire, Willem Dafoe, Kirsten Dunst.
● NEW YORK CITY; CALIFORNIA

The school field-trip: Columbia University, Morningside Heights

Like *Ghostbusters*, with which it shares a good few locations, Raimi's film of the Stan Lee comic is set in New York, but mostly shot around LA. The neighbourhood of Peter Parker (Maguire) is **Woodhaven**, central Queens, among streets of near-identical houses. It's a way to the northwest, in **Woodside**, that he runs for the school bus, along **44th Street** at Queens Boulevard. The school field-trip is to **Columbia University**, up in Manhattan's Morningside Heights (see *Ghostbusters* for details). It's at the steps of the **Low Memorial Library** that Norman Osborn (Dafoe) drops off young Harry (James Franco), but the university interior, where Parker gets the fateful spider bite, is over on the west coast. It's the **Los Angeles County Museum of Natural History, 900 Exposition Boulevard**, downtown LA (*© 213.763.DINO, www.nhm.org*), which masquerades as New York in *Bonfire of the Vanities* and is also seen in *Spawn*.

It's outside another *Ghostbusters* location, the **New York Public Library, Fifth Avenue**, that Uncle Ben (Cliff Robertson) leaves Parker, warning him, "With great power comes great responsibility." Down in SoHo, Mary Jane (Dunst) works in the **Moondance Diner, 80 Sixth Avenue** at Grand Street (*© 212.226.1191*). A genuine thirties diner, and good value, too, the Moondance was featured in Martin Scorsese's *After Hours*.

Midtown High School is, yes, in LA. The interiors were filmed in **Dorsey High School, 3575 Farmdale Avenue**, at Rodeo Road, West Adams, midtown. The graduation ceremony was filmed in front of the **Thalberg Building** on the Sony lot in **Culver City**. You can see the site, along with plenty of other goodies (it's your chance to see a clutch of Oscars

The university interior: Los Angeles County Museum of Natural History, Exposition Boulevard

Peter Parker runs for the school bus: 44th Street, Woodside

Midtown High School interiors: Dorsey High School, West Adams

The 'upside-down' kiss: Warner Bros backlot, Burbank

up close), on the **Sony Pictures Studio Tour**. The tour takes in what is left from the old MGM backlot, most of which was sold off (© *323.520.TOUR, www.sonypictures studios.com/ tours.html*).

Back to Queens, as Parker runs off down **Austin Street** at the junction with Ascan Avenue in **Forest Hills**, after discovering his secret powers.

Norman Osborn's gothic Manhattan mansion is the **Tudor City** complex, **East 40th** to **East 43rd Street** between First and Second Avenues, overlooking the East River, midtown (seen also in *Scarface* and *Splash!*). The interior, once again, is in Los Angeles. This time it's the **Greystone Mansion, 905 Loma Vista Drive** in Beverly Hills (see *The Loved One* for details). Likewise, although the *Daily Bugle* building is the famous **Flatiron Building, 175 Fifth Avenue**, seen in *Bell, Book and Candle*, *Godzilla* and Warren Beatty's *Reds*, the newspaper office interior is the **Pacific Electric Building, 610 South Main Street**, downtown LA, familiar from *LA Confidential*, *Se7en* and *Face/Off*.

Spidey swinging through the Manhattan streets was filmed around downtown LA, at **Fourth Street** between Beaudry Avenue and Hill Street; **Grand Avenue** between Third Street and Hope Place; **Fifth Street** between Los Angeles Street and Hill Street; **Spring Street** between Fourth and Fifth Street. Wide shots show Manhattan's real **Times Square**, but most of the Green Goblin's deadly attack on the World Unity parade was filmed on a set built at the Rockwell Defense Plant, Bellflower and Imperial Highway in Downey, California. And you can see the site of the 'upside down kiss' on the New York Street on the Warner Bros Studios VIP Tour (see the 1954 *A Star Is Born* for details).

Mary Jane works in the Moondance Diner, Sixth Avenue, SoHo

The Osborn mansion interior: Greystone Mansion, Loma Vista Drive, Beverly Hills

The Goblin's attack on the aerial tramway was mostly mocked up in the studio. The **East River Tram** runs from **Second Avenue**, between East 59th and East 60th Streets, alongside the Queensborough Bridge, to Roosevelt Island (where parts of the first two *Exorcist* movies were shot). The tramway can be seen in *City Slickers* and gets hijacked by terrorists in the 1981 Sly Stallone actioner *Nighthawks*.

SPIDER-MAN 2

(2004, dir: Sam Raimi)
Tobey Maguire, Kirsten Dunst, Alfred Molina.
● **NEW YORK CITY; CALIFORNIA; CHICAGO, ILLINOIS**

Once again, there's a mix of Los Angeles and the real New York – and even a bit of Chicago. After the success of the first film, the budget allowed for a little more filming in the real Big Apple. There's **Columbia University** again (where Peter Parker bumps into Dr Connors), and Aunt May's house in **Woodhaven**, Queens. Harry Osborn's place is still a mix of **Tudor Place**, Manhattan, and the **Greystone Mansion**, Beverly Hills (and studio sets).

Peter Parker delivers pizzas: Joe's Pizza, Bleecker Street, West Village

Dr Octavius' laboratory: Anthology Film Archive, Second Avenue, East Village

Parker is sacked from his job delivering pizzas for **Joe's Pizza, 233 Bleecker Street** at Carmine Street in the West Village.

The laboratory, where Dr Octavius (Molina) disastrously demonstrates his fusion project and ends up with a permanent set of tentacles, is the old Second Avenue Courthouse building, now the **Anthology Film Archive, 32 Second Avenue** at Second Street in the East Village. Fittingly, it's a centre for the preservation and exhibition of film and video (*www.anthologyfilmarchives.org*). The Science Library benefit, at which everything seems to go pear-shaped for Peter as MJ announces her engagement and Harry turns ugly, is held at the **Rose Center for Earth and Space, 81st Street** at Central Park West (*www.amnh.org/rose*), part of the **American Museum of Natural History**, housing the Hayden Planetarium (seen in *Manhattan*).

In LA, the interior of the theatre where Parker tries unsuccessfully to catch Mary Jane's performance in *The Importance of Being Earnest* (the elaborate exterior is a set) is the somewhat plainer **Ivar Theatre**,

The interior of the theatre: Ivar Theatre, North Ivar Avenue, Hollywood

PHOTOGRAPH COURTESY MALCOLM DAVIS

PHOTOGRAPH COURTESY NILS REUCKER

The Science Library benefit: Rose Center for Earth and Space, 81st Street

PHOTOGRAPH COURTESY NILS REUCKER

Mary Jane doesn't get married: Riverside Church, Morningside Heights

1605 North Ivar Avenue in Hollywood. The bank Doc Oc robs, as Aunt May tries to get a loan, is **650 Spring Street** (see *Se7en* for details). But when Spidey rescues May from Oc's clutches, he gently deposits her in front of **City Hall, City Hall Park, Broadway** at Park Row in Lower Manhattan.

The New York 'el' (the elevated railway) no longer runs through Manhattan, and had to be filmed on the **Chicago Loop**.

Doc Oc hurls a car through the restaurant window at **Astor Place** at Lafayette Street, East Village (site of the horrible mishap in *Sleepers*). The church where Mary Jane is due to get married is **Riverside Church, 490 Riverside Drive** between 120th and 122nd Streets, up in Morningside Heights, north of Columbia University.

SPLASH
(1984, dir: Ron Howard)
Tom Hanks, Daryl Hannah, John Candy.
● **NEW YORK CITY; LOS ANGELES, CALIFORNIA**

The little park: Sutton Place Park

Mermaid Daryl Hannah follows Tom Hanks to New York, and turns up on **Liberty Island**, at the foot of the Statue of Liberty. Hanks works at **Fulton Fish Market, South Street** at Fulton Street. He lives at **25 Tudor City Place**, part of the kitschily gothic Tudor City development, East 40th to East 43rd Streets between First and Second Avenues (also home to the Osbornes in the *Spider-Man* movies). Hannah learns English in an afternoon at the electrical department of **Bloomingdale's, 1000 Third Avenue** at East 59th Street. The fishy fountain she admires (don't go looking – it was just put there for the movie) is in the tiny park at **Sutton Place**, at the end of 57th Street, beneath the Queensboro Bridge (it's near to the same stunning view used for the poster of Woody Allen's *Manhattan*). Hannah and Hanks fall out at the **Wollman Memorial**

Tom Hanks' apartment: Tudor City Place

Rink, 59th Street at Sixth Avenue in Central Park. It's not all kosher New York, though. The Presidential dinner, where Eugene Levy is mistaken for an assassin, filmed in the Crystal Ballroom of LA's **Biltmore Hotel**, a familiar location seen in *The Bodyguard* and *The Fabulous Baker Boys* among many others. And it's by the hotel's entrance, **506 South Grand Avenue** on Pershing Square, that Hannah gets drenched and comes out as a mermaid. Then it's back to New York, where she's incarcerated in the **American Museum of Natural History, Central Park West** at 79th Street.

Daryl Hannah learns to speak: Bloomingdale's, Third Avenue

Hannah incarcerated: American Museum of Natural History

SPLENDOR IN THE GRASS
(1961, dir: Elia Kazan)
Natalie Wood, Warren Beatty, Pat Hingle.
● **NEW YORK**

Racy sounding title actually comes from a Wordsworth poem, though I bet he didn't spell it like that. And the following line, 'Glory in the flower', doesn't sound half so raunchy. Supposedly set in smalltown Kansas during the twenties, the film was actually made in New York, on **Staten Island**; and in upstate New York, at **High Falls**, northwest of Poughkeepsie. Natalie Wood's house, with the addition of a little dressing, is the corner house at **4144 Victory Boulevard, Travis**, west Staten Island.

SPY GAME
(2001, dir: Tony Scott)
Robert Redford, Brad Pitt, Catherine McCormack.
● **LONDON; OXFORDSHIRE; HERTFORDSHIRE; WASHINGTON DC; VIRGINIA; HUNGARY; MOROCCO; HONG KONG, CHINA**

Scott's flashy thriller seems to bounce around the globe, but an awful lot of it is simply an imaginative use of London and its environs. Take the Chinese prison at Su Chou where agent Tom Bishop (Pitt) is held. It's **Oxford Gaol**, previously seen in *A Fish Called Wanda* and *Wilde*. The US Embassy in Hong Kong is the HQ of the **Hong Kong and Shanghai Banking Corporation**, but after a quick establishing shot, it quickly morphs into the **Lloyd's Building**, Leadenhall in London. After receiving a phone call, Nathan Muir (Redford) is soon roaring through Washington DC. There's a quick glimpse of the US capital, to sell us the location, but the street Muir drives along is **Nash Terrace**, NW1, along the east side of Regent's Park, where traffic lanes were temporarily reversed for filming.

The first view of CIA HQ in Langley, Virginia, is the

real thing, but as Muir arrives, it's the gates of the **Glaxo Smith Klein** factory in **Stevenage**, Hertfordshire, he enters. The lobby is the severe deco interior of **Senate House, the University of London Union, Malet Street** (which also became the US in Tony Scott's earlier *The Hunger*, and the king's HQ in *Richard III*). The CIA offices were built in the studio at Shepperton.

Morocco provided two rather more exotic locations, which just couldn't be faked in London. The seemingly lush jungle of Vietnam is the oasis at **Fint**, west of Ouarzazate; and Beirut is **Casablanca**.

Budapest stands in for Berlin, though it's back to the UK for the Eck Bar, where Bishop stops to contact Muir, which is the bar of the **Rivoli Ballroom, 350 Brockley Road**, opposite Crofton Park Railway Station, south London. The ballroom itself can be seen in David Kane's underrated rom-com *This Year's Love* and in the David A Stewart turkey *Honest*.

PHOTOGRAPH COURTESY TROIS ESTATE, AUSTIN
The Cortez house: Trois Estate, Pearce Road, Austin

SPY KIDS
(2001, dir: Robert Rodriguez) Antonio Banderas, Alexa Vega, Daryl Sabara.
● **TEXAS; CHILE**

Rodriguez's inventive romp was filmed almost entirely in the Texas state capital, **Austin**, apart from a glimpse of Chile and a little of the director's home town, **San Antonio**.

You probably won't get the chance to visit the breathtaking location for the wedding of agents Gregario Cortez (Banderas) and Ingrid (Carla Gugino) in South America unless you're extremely well-connected in Austin. It's **Villa del Sol**, the private home of Beau Theriot, owner of the nearby Oasis restaurant, 300 feet above **Lake Travis**, (formed when the Colorado River was blocked by Mansfield Dam in the late '30s), 12 miles west of the capital. By way of compensation, you might want to stay at (or celebrate your wedding at) the seductively picturesque, stone-walled home of the Cortez family. Amazingly, the location is real, it's the **Trois Estate, 3612 Pearce Road** (© *512.345.1772, www.thetroisestate.com*), Austin, west of town near Emma Long Metropolitan Park. The stone castle dates back to, erm, 1989. In Austin itself, hangars at the old Robert Mueller Airport, Austin, were turned into soundstages; and Machete's Spy Store is the **Millennium Center** on **West 4th Street** at Lavaca, directly across from Ruta Maya coffeehouse, 218 West 4th Street.

The aerial view of San Diablo is **Santiago de Chile**, but as the camera zooms in, the empty grass square mysteriously becomes the busy **Travis Park, 301 East Travis, San Antonio**, where the kids fight with their robot doubles.

SPY KIDS 2: ISLAND OF LOST DREAMS
(2002, dir: Robert Rodriguez)
Antonio Banderas, Alexa Vega, Daryl Sabara.
● **TEXAS; COSTA RICA**

Wildly imaginative sequel, an homage to animator Ray Harryhausen (reprising the sword-swinging skeletons from *Jason and the Argonauts*). The Troublemaker Theme Park (named after Rodriguez's studio, and invented when Disneyland refused permission to film in their park), where Juni rescues the President's daugh-

The kids meet the President: State Capitol Building, Congress Avenue, Austin

PHOTOGRAPH COURTESY BETH GRAHAM, SAN ANTONIO PUBLIC LIBRARY
The OSS Junior Building: San Antonio Central Library, Soledad Street, San Antonio

ter from the Juggler, is **Six Flags Over Texas, Arlington** (© *817.530.6000, www.sixflags.com/parks/overtexas*), at the intersection of I-30 and highway 360 between Dallas and Fort Worth. Disappointingly – but perhaps not surprisingly – you won't find the Whippersnapper, the Vomiter or the Juggler, which were CGI creations.

The capitol building, where the kids meet the President, is, naturally, the **State Capitol Building, Congress Avenue** between 11th and 14th Streets, Austin (previously featured in *The Best Little Whorehouse in Texas* and the 1988 remake of *D.O.A.*). Its design is based on that of the US State Capitol in Washington DC, but being Texas, of course, it's bigger. When I visited in the '90s it was taller than DC's by seven feet but, according to the Senate of Texas website (*www.senate.state.tx.us*), it's now fourteen feet taller…

The brightly coloured OSS Junior Building, which you might assume is a set, is actually **San Antonio Central Library, 600 Soledad Street**, downtown San Antonio. Opened in 1995, the striking design is by Mexican architect Ricardo Legorreta.

Once again, the 'ocean' is **Lake Travis**, Austin, with the shoreline digitally removed. The beach of Romero's island is, briefly, **Costa Rica**, but quickly reverts to the shore of Lake Travis for the rest of the action. The island itself is partly Costa Rica (**Manuel Antonio National Park**, with the conical **Arenal Volcano** rising above the trees), but the 'hotdog' rock formation and the barren landscape is the wild and spectacular **Big Bend National Park** (*www.nps.gov/bibe*), seen in *Barbarosa, Paris, Texas* and *All the Pretty Horses*. Big Bend, the least visited of the USA's national parks, is a great chunk bitten out of Mexico, where the Rio Grande is diverted around the Chisos Mountains in west Texas.

The island: Santa Elena Canyon, Big Bend National Park

The end credits rock concert is in the **Paramount Theatre, 713 Congress Avenue** (© *512.472.2901*), between 7th and 8th Streets, Austin.

SPY KIDS 3-D: GAME OVER

(2003, dir: Robert Rodriguez)
Antonio Banderas, Alexa Vega, Daryl Sabara.
● **TEXAS**

The wit and invention of the first two movies is replaced by endless slam-bang cartoon graphics, a 3-D *Tron* for the 21st century. The deserted Agua Park water park in the *Chinatown* spoof opening is **Schlitterbahn Waterpark Resort, Common Street, New Braunfels** (*www.schlitterbahn.com*). The final battle, in the real world, is fought on **Congress Avenue**, in front of the **State Capitol Building**, alongside the Paramount, seen in *SK2*.

SPY WHO LOVED ME, THE

(1977, dir: Lewis Gilbert)
Roger Moore, Barbara Bach, Curt Jurgens.
● **CANADA; SCOTLAND; SARDINIA; EGYPT; BAHAMAS**

The tenth Bond saga retains no more than the title from Ian Fleming (the author had refused permission to use the story, which he wasn't pleased with), in a lavish megaproduction, with Jurgens planning to rule an undersea kingdom after destroying terrestrial civilisation. The spectacular opening ski jump, supposedly at Berngarten, Austria, was filmed on the 3,000-feet **Asgard Peak**, 50 miles from the town of Pangnirtung, Auquittuq National Park on the east coast of Baffin Island, Canada.

The naval establishment, where Bond is briefed about submarines, is **Faslane Submarine Base** on the Clyde near Glasgow. The Egyptian black-marketeer, Fekkesh, is killed during the spectacular lightshow shot at the **Pyramid of Cheops, Gaza**, near Cairo, Egypt. Before heading off to Jurgens' underwater hideout, Bond and KGB Major Amasova (Bach) stay at the huge **Hotel Cala de Volpe, Costa Smeralda**, perched, like a faux-Mediterranean village, atop the cliffs on the north coast of Sardinia (© *39.0789.976.111*).

It was to film the interior of Jurgens' *Liparus* super-super-tanker, large enough to swallow up nuclear subs, that the vast 007 Soundstage was constructed at Pinewood. At 374 feet by 160 feet, and 53 feet high, it was the biggest in the world. It was badly damaged in a fire during the filming of Ridley Scott's *Legend* in 1985. The aerial shots of the super-tanker swallowing a sub were achieved with models, filmed at **Coral Harbor, Nassau**, in the Bahamas.

STAGE FRIGHT

(1950, dir: Alfred Hitchcock)
Richard Todd, Marlene Dietrich, Jane Wyman.
● **LONDON**

Minor Hitchcock, with Jane Wyman (refusing to look too plain alongside the ineffably glam Marlene Dietrich) taking a maid's job to investigate the murder Richard Todd is accused of. Hitchcock returned to London to film this backstage murder mystery, which infuriated critics no end by breaking the rules and cheating in a flashback sequence, and opens with a safety curtain rising on a view of St Paul's Cathedral towering above the

Wyman meets the detective: Shepherd's Tavern, Shepherd Street, Mayfair

post-war rubble. Todd eludes the police by crashing Jane Wyman's acting class at the **Royal Academy of Dramatic Art (RADA), 62-64 Gower Street**, WC1.

The house of Charlotte Inwood (Dietrich), scene of the murder, has sadly now been demolished. Although you may be able to recognise Hertford Street near the corner of Stanhope Row, W1, the block containing number 78 has gone to make way for the Hilton Hotel on Park Lane. A surviving location is the **Shepherd's Tavern, 50 Shepherd Street** at the corner of Hertford Street, where Wyman meets detective Michael Wilding over a brandy after her first visit to the Inwood house.

Jane Wyman's class: RADA, Gower Street

STAGECOACH

(1939, dir: John Ford)
John Wayne, Claire Trevor, Thomas Mitchell.
● **CALIFORNIA; UTAH**

John Ford's Western classic is based on a short story, 'Stage to Lordsburg', by Ernest Haycox, published in *Collier's Magazine* in 1937, which was in turn based on Guy de Maupassant's *Boule de Suif*, set during the 1870 Franco-Prussian War. Wisely, John Wayne's character name was changed from Malpais Bill to the Ringo Kid.

The film established **Monument Valley**, on the Arizona-Utah border, as an icon of the American West, although, of the passengers, only John Wayne actually trekked out to Utah. None of the principals made it past California's San Fernando Valley.

Monument Valley, an area of striking, flat-topped mesas and buttes, was a tough location in 1938, at the end of a 200-mile dirt road from Flagstaff. The Navajo, already troubled by disease and unemployment, were employed to play Apaches – one of the many nations they were to play over the years. The Valley is not a National Park, but a Tribal Park still belonging to, and managed by, the Navajo nation. It can be reached on Route 163, 24 miles north from the town of Kayenta, Route 160. There's a visitor centre (© *435.727.3353; admission charge*). A 14-mile loop snakes through the valley, but not all roads are open to the public. You can see more of the park on a guided tour, from the parking lot at the visitor centre.

But the Valley is only a part of *Stagecoach*. The river crossing is the Kern River, near to **Kernville**, 40 miles

Iconic image: Monument Valley

east of Bakersfield, California. The old wagon cut at **Newhall**, on I-5 – also called **Fremont Pass** – is the entrance to the dry lake. Nearby **Chatsworth** and **Calabasas** also provided locations. The chase by Indians was staged at the **Muroc Dry Lake** salt flats near Victorville, California, recreated by stunt artist Yakima Canutt from the 1937 Monogram movie *Riders of the Dawn*, which was filmed at the same location. To soften the ground for filming, 20 acres of ground had to be dug up by tractor. The real journey of the movie, though, is from the Western Street at Republic Studios (the town of Tonto) to the Goldwyn Studios (Lordsburg), where the interiors were shot.

STAND BY ME
(1986, dir: Rob Reiner)
River Phoenix, Wil Wheaton, Corey Feldman.
● OREGON; CALIFORNIA

Stephen King's untypical coming-of-age story, 'The Body', was shot at **Eugene**, on Highway 5, eastern Oregon, about 100 miles south of Portland. The fictional New England town of Castle Rock, after which King named his production company, is **Brownsville**, a couple of miles west of I-5 to the north of Eugene. The railway viaduct is over the McCloud River in the **Mount Shasta** area of northern California.

STAR IS BORN, A
(1937, dir: William Wellman)
Fredric March, Janet Gaynor, Adolphe Menjou.
● LOS ANGELES, CALIFORNIA

Classic Hollywood: Hollywood Bowl, North Highland Avenue

Second version (*What Price Hollywood?* was the first) of the classic Hollywood see-saw story, filmed in luscious Technicolor. Scenes were filmed at the **Hollywood Bowl, 2301 North Highland Avenue**, LA. The Oscar ceremony was staged at the actual location used in the 1930s, the ballroom and nightclub of the **Ambassador Hotel, 3400 Wilshire Boulevard** (see the 1954 version for details). More scenes were shot at the pool patio of the plush **Beverly Hills Hotel, 9641 Sunset Boulevard**, Beverly Hills, and the long-gone Tro-

The Academy Awards: Ambassador Hotel, Wilshire Boulevard

cadero Nightclub, which stood at 8610 Sunset Boulevard. The racetrack scenes are at the **Santa Anita Racetrack, 285 West Huntington Boulevard, Arcadia**, between LA and Pasadena (also used for the 1954 remake and for the Marx Brothers' *A Day at the Races*). The tear-jerky ending is in front of **Grauman's Chinese Theatre, 6925 Hollywood Boulevard**.

STAR IS BORN, A
(1954, dir: George Cukor)
Judy Garland, James Mason, Charles Bickford.
● CALIFORNIA

Norman Maine in the drunk tank: Lincoln Heights Jail, North Avenue 19, Lincoln Heights

Expanded, musicalised, widescreen remake of the 1937 movie, charting the rise of singer Esther Blodgett (Garland) and the fall of matinee idol Norman Maine (Mason). One of the most expensive movies of its time (pipped by *Duel in the Sun*), and Warner's costliest, it spanned a massive ten-month shoot, but was subsequently butchered by the studio. Shockingly, every copy, including the original negative, was cut – the ever-penny pinching Jack Warner wanting to retrieve each last grain of silver.

Production began during the hysterical flap caused by the arrival of television, with film companies desperately experimenting with every gimmick available. *Star* was thus filmed in Technicolor and Cinemascope. It was beaten by 20th Century Fox's *The Robe*, the first film released in the new widescreen format, but Warner cheekily managed to incorporate into the opening scene shots of the Fox epic's old-style searchlight première, at **Grauman's Chinese Theatre, 6925 Hollywood Boulevard**. The event is supposedly the 'Night of the Stars' benefit at LA's **Shrine Auditorium, 655 West Jefferson Boulevard**(© 213.748.5116, www.shrineauditorium.com), south of downtown in the Exposition Park district. The bright, clear shots were specially filmed, in Cinemascope, at the Shrine, and the grainier, newsreel footage is the Grauman's première. The Shrine, a massive 6,700-seat Moorish fantasy built in 1926, occasionally hosts the Oscars (the usual Dorothy Chandler pavilion isn't large enough to accommodate all the Academy members) – it was here that James Cameron became King of the World in 1998. Another king, *King Kong*, was exhibited here in 1933 (it was supposed to be New York), and one more lumbering colossus of the cinema, Arnold Schwarzenegger, was similarly exhibited here 50 years later, clad in red, white and blue, when he and 2,000 other worthies became citizens of the USA.

The real Shrine stage and backstage areas were used for Blodgett's first encounter with wobbling star Norman Maine. The boorishly drunken Maine lurches on to the Cocoanut Grove at the **Ambassador Hotel, 3400 Wilshire Boulevard** at Catalina Street, midtown. The exterior is real, though the Grove's campy, palmy interior was recreated in the studio at Warner's. The Ambassador – site of Oscar ceremonies in the thirties and of Bobby Kennedy's assassination in 1968 – has stood empty for many years, used only as a movie location. The threat of demolition currently hangs over the building (keep up with events at www.cocoanutgrove.org). Catch it while – and if – you can. Among the hundreds of films shot here are The Graduate, Se7en, Rocky, S.W.A.T. and Old School.

The Oleander Arms, where Blodgett stays, was an apartment complex at the corner of Crescent Heights Boulevard and Fountain Avenue, west Hollywood. In 1983, when still photographs were taken for the film's restoration, the building was unchanged, but by 1984 it had been dismantled and carted away. Also gone is Robert's Drive-in Restaurant, where Blodgett works as a car-hop. It stood at Sunset Boulevard and Cahuenga. The Bomba Club, where the desperate Esther tries out, unsuccessfully, for a singing job, was downtown at 626 Spring Street but has also now gone.

The Oliver Niles Studio is, obviously, the Warner's lot itself, at **4000 Warner Boulevard, Burbank**. Cukor, though, reassigns buildings for visual effect: Norman Maine's lavish dressing room, where he gets rid of the blond wig and false nose foisted onto Esther, is one of WB's Executive Offices; the Publicity Department is actually the Wardrobe Building; the screening room, where studio head Niles watches a deafening Western, is the Sound Building. At the payroll window, a warehouse opposite the studio's Commissary, Blodgett finds out her new name is Vicki Lester, and a star is born. You can view the lot on a VIP Studio Tour (© *818.846.1403, wbsf.warnerbros.com*). Unlike the huge Universal theme park approach, the WB tour is a small, low-key affair which will take you around the venerable soundstages where classics such as *42nd Street*, *The Maltese Falcon*, *Now, Voyager*, *Casablanca* and *Rebel Without a Cause* were shot.

Maine and Lester sneak off to San Verdo for a quiet wedding. The tiny town used for the wedding scene is **Piru**, a main street and a railway line off I-126, north of LA.

At the studio, Vicki goes from bright and fresh-faced to exhausted and drained in one cut. A whole musical number, 'Lose That Long Face', was cut (but has since been restored). The New Orleans backdrop is the old Elysian Fields set from Elia Kazan's *A Streetcar Named Desire*, prettied up with a lick of white paint.

Cleaned-up and dried-out, Norman Maine turns up at the **Santa Anita Racetrack, 285 West Huntington Boulevard, Arcadia**, between LA and Pasadena. With its towering palms and distinctive green and yellow wrought ironwork, the Santa Anita has long been a favourite with Hollywood punters since 1934 (it's where the

Norman Maine's memorial: Church of the Good Shepherd, Beverly Hills

Marx Brothers spent *A Day at the Races* in 1937) and is still going strong. Fredric March ran into trouble here in the 1937 movie, and James Mason follows suit, falling off the wagon in spectacular fashion. Before you can say "large scotch", Vicki Lester is racing along Sunset Boulevard (yes, that's the legendary but long-gone Schwab's Drugstore zooming by) to bail Norman out of the drunk tank at frequent movie location **Lincoln Heights Jail, 421 North Avenue 19, Lincoln Heights**, near downtown LA.

At their Malibu beach house, Norman makes the ultimate Hollywood gesture of self-sacrifice for Vicki's career. It's not Malibu, though, but **Laguna Beach**, on I-1 south of LA, where he walks into the sea.

His memorial service is held at the **Church of the Good Shepherd, 505 North Bedford Drive, Beverly Hills** (affectionately known as Our Lady of the Cadillacs). Forbidden to use lighting within the church, Cukor silhouettes the emerging figures in sepulchral gloom against the stained glass windows before letting rip with a barrage of flashbulbs outside the church, where screeching fans rip off grieving Vicki's veil.

And the final shot is, once more, the Shrine Auditorium: "Hello everybody, this is Mrs Norman Maine…" ●

STAR IS BORN, A
(1976, dir: Frank Pierson)
Barbra Streisand, Kris Kristofferson, Gary Busey.
ARIZONA; LOS ANGELES, CALIFORNIA

Another star, another birth, but no Oscars this time, and no Ambassador. It's the **Arizona State University, Tempe**, Arizona. Filming also took place at that much-used location, LA's **Biltmore Hotel, 506 South Grand Avenue** on Pershing Square, downtown.

STAR TREK – THE MOTION PICTURE
(1979, dir: Robert Wise)
William Shatner, Leonard Nimoy, DeForest Kelley.
● CALIFORNIA

Studio-bound, determinedly epic, first big-screen spin-off from the TV series. The glimpse of Earth locates the Starfleet Academy north of San Francisco, in the Presidio area alongside the **Golden Gate Bridge**.

STAR TREK IV: THE VOYAGE HOME
(1986, dir: Leonard Nimoy)
William Shatner, Leonard Nimoy, DeForest Kelley.
● CALIFORNIA

After a couple of totally studio-bound sequels, the series begins to use real locations with this eco-conscious adventure, as the crew of the *Enterprise* zooms back to 1986 San Francisco in time to save the whale. They split up at the junction of **Columbus, Kearny** and **Pacific Avenues**. The crew's purloined Klingon ship flies under the **Golden Gate Bridge**. Golden Gate Park, where the crew parks the Bird of Prey, is actually **Will Rogers State Park, 14253 Sunset Boulevard**, Pacific Palisades in LA. More filming took place at Vasquez Rocks State Park (see *Apache* for details).

The Sausalito Cetacean Institute, where the *Enterprise* crew find the two humpback whales, was supposedly over the bay, just north of San Francisco. You can actually find it on the coast south of the city. It's the **Monterey Bay Aquarium, 886 Cannery Row, Monterey** (*www.mbayaq.org*). The aquarium, by the way, does not contain any whales, but does have loads of other fascinating stuff.

STAR TREK V: THE FINAL FRONTIER

(1989, dir: William Shatner)
William Shatner, Leonard Nimoy, DeForest Kelley.

● CALIFORNIA; WYOMING

Captain Kirk spends his shore leave climbing on **El Capitan** and **Inspiration Point, Yosemite National Park**, Wyoming (and ends up on the Paramount lot in Hollywood). 'Nimbus III in the Neutral Zone, the Planet of Galactic Peace' is **Owens Dry Lake** in the Mojave Desert, south of Lone Pine, central California, between Routes 395 and 136. The planet Shakari, where Kirk gets a wee bit suspicious at the appearance of 'God', is the **Trona Pinnacles**, an area of tufa spires rising up from Searles Dry Lake Bed, Trona, near Ridgecrest, Kern County, central California. The strange columns, up to 140 feet tall and covering 15 square-miles, were formed by algae 10,000 years ago when the area lay underwater. The area is reached by a bumpy, seven-mile dirt road (it is accessible to 2-wheel-drive vehicles) off Route 78, about eight miles south of the town of Trona. You can see the otherworldly landscape again in Tim Burton's *Planet of the Apes*.

STAR TREK VI: THE UNDISCOVERED COUNTRY

(1991, dir: Nicholas Meyer)
William Shatner, Leonard Nimoy, DeForest Kelley.

● ALASKA; CALIFORNIA

"Definitely the very last", they said. The penal asteroid of Rura Penthe, where Kirk and McCoy are condemned to work in the dilithium mines for the assassination of the Klingon chancellor, is the **Knik Glacier, Chugach State Park**, north of Anchorage, Alaska, though the penal colony set was built back in LA, in **Bronson Canyon**, Griffith Park. Camp Khitomer, site of the peace conference, is a conflation of the **Firemen's Fund Building, 777 San Marin Drive**, off I-101 in Novato, Marin County, northern California (the live-action foreground and lake), and the **Brandeis-Bardin Institute, 1101 Peppertree Lane, Brandeis**, in the Simi Valley north of LA (the cylindrical building beyond the lake).

STAR TREK GENERATIONS

(1994, dir: David Carson)
Patrick Stewart, William Shatner, Malcolm McDowell.

● NEVADA; CALIFORNIA

A shot in the arm for the series as the *Enterprise*'s original captain hands over the baton to the Next Generation. Viridian 3, where Malcolm McDowell tries to return to the total joy of the Nexus, and where Kirk finally drops off the intergalactic perch, is **Silica Dome** in the **Valley of Fire State Park**, northwest of Las Vegas, Nevada. To reach the valley, take I-15 north from Vegas for 33 miles.

Captain Picard's Dickensian Christmas fantasy: South Grand Avenue, Pasadena.

A signposted turnoff, Route 169, winds for another 18 miles to the park entrance, and on to the Visitor Center (© 702.397. 2088, www.desert-usa.com/nvval; admission charge). Silica Dome, a dazzling white rounded peak among the fiery red sandstone outcrop, is off Fire Creek Road. Captains Kirk and Picard meet up near **Hart Flat**, Kern County, central California. The scenes of Captain Kirk riding his horse were filmed, with Shatner's own horse, on his own farm.

Picard's oddly Dickensian Christmas fantasy in the Nexus was filmed in the elegant mansion (recently put up for sale at $4,250,000) at **465 South Grand Avenue, Pasadena**.

STAR TREK: FIRST CONTACT

(1996, dir: Jonathan Frakes)
Patrick Stewart, Jonathan Frakes, Brent Spiner.

● CALIFORNIA; ARIZONA

The crew battle the Borg in this action-packed entry in the series. The film noir holodeck sequence was filmed in LA's stunning **Union Station, 800 North Alameda Street**, downtown (seen in lots of films, it was used as the police station in *Blade Runner*). Filming also took place in the **Angeles National Forest**, north of LA, and at the **Titan Missile Museum, 1580 West Duval Mine Road, Sahuarita, Green Valley**, Arizona (© 520.625.7736, *www.pimaair.org/titan_01.html; admission charge*). Home of the Titan II intercontinental ballistic missile, it's the only one of the 54 bases still in existence, now turned into a museum, after the programme was phased out in the eighties.

STAR TREK: INSURRECTION

(1998, dir: Jonathan Frakes)
Patrick Stewart, Jonathan Frakes, Brent Spiner.

● CALIFORNIA

Will Captain Picard actually defy the Federation to prevent the lo-tech, hippy Ba'ku being forcibly ejected from their paradise by the nasty Son'a? The idyllic Ba'ku colony was built at **Lake Sherwood, Thousand Oaks**, north of LA. The lake scenes used the **San Gabriel River** at the **San Gabriel Dam**, seven miles north of Azusa, Los Angeles. The Ba'ku mountain refuge filmed on an inaccessible (unless, like the cast and crew, you have access to a helicopter) mountaintop above the beautiful Alpine reservoir, **Lake Sabrina**, 19 miles west of Bishop, Route 395, in the Inyo National Forest.

STAR TREK: NEMESIS

(2002, dir: Stuart Baird)
Patrick Stuart, Jonathan Frakes, Brent Spiner.

● CALIFORNIA

The gap since the last *Trek* movie (*Insurrection* in 1998) was an indication that the franchise was running out of steam. Pieces of Data's prototype, B-4, are discovered on Kolarus III which, from the presence of Joshua Trees, can only be California's **Mojave Desert**, actually not far from Edwards Air Force Base. Picard drives an Argo, a 24th century off-roader.

STAR WARS EPISODE I: THE PHANTOM MENACE

(1999, dir: George Lucas)

Ewan McGregor, Liam Neeson, Natalie Portman.

● **ITALY; TUNISIA**

The fight with Darth Maul: Chott el Gharsa

It's back to Tunisia (after *Episode IV*) for the Tatooine scenes, this time at **Tozeur** – also a location for *The English Patient.* Young Anakin's slave-quarter home is a ksar (originally a grain store) in **Medenine**, about 35 miles southeast of Matmata in southern Tunisia. The last remaining square of this once-vast complex has been turned into a bustling bazaar at **avenue 7 Novembre** in the centre of the town. The narrow street, where Anakin says goodbye to his mother, runs behind the square. The rear of the slave-quarters, where Anakin works on the pod racer, and where his mother reveals portentous hints about a virgin birth to Qui-Gon Jinn, is the **Hotel Ksar Hadada, Ksar Hadada** near Ghomrassen, south of Medenine toward Tataouine. No longer used as a hotel, this complex maze of crazily-angled ksar still bears traces of the plastic tiled set-dressing.

Mos Espa: Watto's workshop, Chott el Gharsa

You'll need a four-wheel-drive vehicle, and probably a guide, to visit the sets of Mos Espa crumbling away among the dunes of **Chott el Gharsa**. The Chott is north of Nefta, an oasis town across the dry salt lake of Chott el Jerid in western Tunisia, near the Algerian border. The remains of two sets can be seen here, along with the strange, windblown, angular rock formations seen in the desert fight with Darth Maul. The site is near to the location of the desert camp in *The English Patient.*

The staterooms and staircases of Queen Amidala's Theed Palace on Naboo are the overwhelming marble interior of **Palazzo Reale**, the Royal Palace, **Piazza Carlo III, Caserta**, about 15 miles north of Naples in Italy. The baroque palace, built in 1752 for King Charles III of Naples to rival France's Versailles, is open to visitors. A regular rail service runs from Naples, and the palace is directly opposite the station at Caserta.

STAR WARS EPISODE II: ATTACK OF THE CLONES

(2002, dir: George Lucas)

Hayden Christensen, Ewan McGregor, Natalie Portman.

● **ITALY; SPAIN; TUNISIA; NEW SOUTH WALES, AUSTRALIA**

Theed Palace interior: Palazzo Reale, Caserta

Studio interiors were filmed in Australia. The production returned, once again, to Tunisia, where the original *Star Wars* (now *Episode IV: A New Hope*) and *Episode I: The Phantom Menace* used the desert landscapes and native architecture. Another revisited location is the **Palazzo Reale** in **Caserta**, near Naples, which again is used to represent Theed Palace on Naboo. This time around, though, the exterior (which was entirely computer-generated in *Episode I*) is the **Palácio Español**, a semi-circular arcaded building in the **Plaza de España**, **Seville**, built for the 1929 Spanish-American exhibition. You may remember the pillared colonnade as the Cairo hotel, where TE Lawrence ruffles the feathers of the British officers by demanding lemonade for his Arab companion, in David Lean's *Lawrence of Arabia.*

The stunning lake retreat is on **Lake Como** in northern Italy near the Swiss border. The summer palace is **Villa del Balbionello**, near the village of **Lenno**, about 27km north of Como on the lake's western shore. The villa, with its unique loggia commanding views north and south, stands on the tip of a steep, wooded promontory. It is open to the public (gardens admission €5) Tuesdays and Thursdays to Saturdays. The villa itself can be toured by prior arrangement (℃ *034456110*). You reach the villa by boat from Lenno or nearby Sala Comacina. On Tuesdays, Saturdays and Sundays it's possible to walk from Lenno. It's about 15 minutes, and quite steep, from the southern end of the bay or from the wooded path leading up from Via Degli Artigiani, at the southern end of Lenno.

STAR WARS EPISODE III: REVENGE OF THE SITH

(2005, dir: George Lucas)

Hayden Christensen, Ewan McGregor, Natalie Portman.

● **NEW SOUTH WALES, AUSTRALIA; SWIZERLAND; THAILAND; TUNISIA; SICILY, ITALY**

Lucas retreats to the Fox Studios, **Sydney**, New South Wales, for the last of the trilogy. Background landscapes for the Wookiee planet of Kashyyyk were filmed at the awesome limestone towers of **Guilin**, in the northeast corner of the Guangxi Zhuang region, and the the islands of **Phang Nga Bay** in Thailand (previously seen in *The Man With the Golden Gun*). The mountains of **Grindelwald** in Switzerland are also featured. The Mustafar lava flow was the real thing, filmed on **Mount Etna** in Sicily. And, of course, there's a glimpse of Tunisia for the final shot of Tatooine, filmed at **Tozeur**.

STAR WARS EPISODE IV: A NEW HOPE (aka *Star Wars*)
(1977, dir: George Lucas)
Mark Hamill, Carrie Fisher, Harrison Ford.
● **CALIFORNIA; TUNISIA; GUATEMALA**

It may have been set in 'a galaxy far, far away', but you can visit some of it. For Luke Skywalker's home, the desert planet of Tatooine, George Lucas used the landscapes and native architecture of Tunisia (Tataouine is a real Tunisian town, some miles south of the movie location).

Luke's sunken home was in the troglodyte town of **Matmata**, where homes are burrowed into the soft local sandstone from the sides of circular pits. The interior is one of the inner courtyards of the **Sidi Driss Hotel** (© *216.230.066*), where you can still see the murals and some of the set dressing from the movie. Disturbed by the tourist influx, or just tired of living in the traditional pit homes, many of the residents have moved to the recent development of Nouvelle Matmata a few miles to the north. The exterior of the homestead, where Luke contemplates the two suns, is part of the vast **Chott el Jerid**, the dry, white salt flat stretching across central Tunisia to the oases of Tozeur and Nefta. The site of Luke's home, now a couple of filled-in circular pits, can be found a few miles south from Highway 3 on a turnoff just west of Nefta. The same turnoff, followed six miles north, leads to **La Grande Dune**, used for the Dune Sea, where C3P0 and R2D2 wander aimlessly. Take care on Highway 3, which leads into Algeria – if you inadvertently cross the border, you can end up in all kinds of trouble. The gully, where R2D2 is captured by the Jawas, now known locally as 'Star Wars Canyon' (you can see it again in *Raiders of the Lost Ark*), is **Sidi Bouhel**, east of Tozeur on the edge of the Chott el Jerid.

Mos Eisley, the sleazy spaceport where Luke and Obi-Wan meet Han Solo, is **Ajim**, a sponge fishing town near the Ile de Jerba. You can see the exterior of the Cantina here. A little to the north, overlooking the Gulf of Gabes, is Obi-Wan's remote home, and a mosque used as the entrance to Mos Eisley. Extra desert scenes, featuring R2D2, Luke's landspeeder and the banthas (underneath the bantha costume is an elephant hired from Marine World), were shot in **Death Valley**, California, and cut in to match existing Tunisian footage.

The rebel base, 'the Massassi Outpost on the fourth moon of Yavin', seen toward the end of the movie, is the giant Mayan temple complex at **Tikal**, Guatemala. The spectacular ruins, 2,500 years old and set in the 222-square-mile rainforest of the **Parque Nacional Tikal**, are in northern Guatemala, about 40 miles from Flores (there's a two-lane road, or you can travel by air from nearby Santa Elena Airport) and can be visited from the Tikal Visitor Centre.

STAR WARS EPISODE V: THE EMPIRE STRIKES BACK (aka *The Empire Strikes Back*)
(1980, dir: Irvin Kershner)

Mark Hamill, Carrie Fisher, Harrison Ford.
● **NORWAY**

The script for part V of the *Star Wars* saga was the last work of Leigh Brackett, veteran screenwriter of *The Big Sleep* and *Rio Bravo*.

The Millennium Falcon was built on a huge soundstage at Elstree, where most of the filming took place – 64 sets and 250 scenes over a four month shoot. The ice planet Hoth was the **Hardanger Jøkulen Glacier**, at **Finse**, the highest railway station in Norway.

STAR WARS EPISODE VI: RETURN OF THE JEDI (aka *Return of the Jedi*)
(1983, dir: Richard Marquand)
Mark Hamill, Carrie Fisher, Harrison Ford.
● **ARIZONA; CALIFORNIA**

Studio filming for this, the third in the original trilogy, was again in England, but exteriors were further afield. Tatooine, which was found in Tunisia for *Episode IV*, is now **Buttercup Valley**, near Yuma in the Arizona desert (*Raiders of the Lost Ark* had run into problems filming in Tunisia, though Lucas returned to the country for *The Phantom Menace*). Jabba the Hutt's huge (80 feet high, 212 feet long) hover barge was built in Yuma. More otherworldly landscapes were found in **Death Valley** and at **Smith River**, California. The monster trees on the Moon of Endor, up to 300 feet tall and twenty feet in diameter, are the giant Redwood groves of the **Jedediah Smith Redwood State Park, 4241 Kings Valley Road, Crescent City**, northern California. *Jedi* was shot in strict secrecy, masquerading on location under the title *Blue Harvest – Horror Beyond Imagination*.

STARDUST MEMORIES
(1980, dir: Woody Allen)
Woody Allen, Charlotte Rampling, Jessica Harper.
● **NEW JERSEY**

Woody Allen's sour retread of Fellini's *8 1/2* was shot around New Jersey. Locations include the **Boardwalk** at **Asbury Park**, a rather faded resort on the north Jersey shore; **Ocean Avenue** in adjoining **Ocean Grove** to the south; and at **Planting Fields Arboretum, Planting Fields Road, Oyster Bay** on Long Island (© *516.922.9206*), 400 acres of gardens and woodland.

STARGATE
(1994, dir: Roland Emmerich)
James Spader, Kurt Russell, Jaye Davidson.
● **CALIFORNIA; ARIZONA**

School-of-Spielberg sci-fi spectacle, from the director who went on to make blockbuster *Independence Day*. The desertscapes are at **Yuma**, Arizona. Viveca Lindfors arrives at the cavernous lobby of the **Park Plaza Hotel, 607 South Park View Street**, downtown LA, where James Spader lectures in the Ballroom (see *New York New York* for details of the Park Plaza).

STARMAN
(1984, dir: John Carpenter)
Jeff Bridges, Karen Allen, Charles Martin Smith.

● TENNESSEE; NEVADA; ARIZONA; IOWA; COLORADO; NORTH CAROLINA

Sci-fi fantasy road movie, with alien Bridges taking the form of widow Allen's recently deceased husband. This was filmed all over the US, in Tennessee; Iowa; Colorado; **Las Vegas**, Nevada; and at the **University of North Carolina**. The diner where Jeff Bridges brings the deer back to life is the now closed Bus Stop Restaurant on I-24 near Kimball, Tennessee. You can visit the meteor crater, at which Bridges has his final rendezvous with his ship, about 15 miles west of **Winslow**, Arizona, just to the south of I-40 (*www.meteorcrater.com; admission charge*).

STARS LOOK DOWN, THE

(1939, dir: Carol Reed)
Michael Redgrave, Margaret Lockwood, Edward Rigby.
● CUMBERLAND

After the success of the 1938 adaptation of *The Citadel*, a version of AJ Cronin's coal mining novel was next. Carol Reed wanted to make as much of the movie as possible on location, but sound recording problems necessitated some studio work, with one of the biggest sets ever built at Twickenham constructed to match up with the real location of miners' cottages at **Great Clifton**, outside Workington. The colliery was the St Helen's Siddick Colliery at **Workington**, and the football match was shot at the Borough Park ground of **Workington FC**.

STARSHIP TROOPERS

(1997, dir: Paul Verhoeven)
Casper Van Dien, Dina Meyer, Neil Patrick Harris.
● WYOMING; SOUTH DAKOTA; LOS ANGELES, CALIFORNIA

The spaceport: New Los Angeles Convention Center

Compulsive controversialist Verhoeven follows up the disappointment of his would-be sex-ploitation shocker *Showgirls* with a violent and FX-laden monster movie set in a neo-fascist future. The bizarre rock formations of Tango Urilla, the alien world of sci-fi writer Robert Henlein's novel (most of which is dumped to leave more room for man-eating bugs) can be found in **Hell's Half Acre**, a county park west of Casper, Wyoming. A vast set was built here for the humans' command centre. More landscapes were shot at **Kadoka**, on highway 90, about 100 miles east of Rapid City in the badlands of South Dakota. Van Dien's parents' home is a 1993 house designed by architect Ed Niles in the **Agoura Hills**, north of Malibu. It also features as the lab in John Woo's *Face/Off* and in *Mr Wrong*.

More futuristic locations around LA include the **California Institute of Technology (Caltech), 1201 East California Boulevard**, between Hill and Wilson Avenues, Pasadena (seen also in *Beverly Hills Cop*, *Real Genius*

and *The Witches of Eastwick* among many others), and **The Pyramid, 1250 Bellflower Boulevard** at **California State University, Long Beach**. The spaceport is the concourse of the **New Los Angeles Convention Center, 1202 South Figueroa Street**, between Pico Boulevard and 11th Street, downtown LA – seen also in *Demolition Man* and *Face/Off*.

STAZIONE TERMINI (aka *Terminal Station/ Indiscretion of an American Wife*)

(1953, dir: Vittorio De Sica)
Montgomery Clift, Jennifer Jones, Gino Cervi.
● ROME, ITALY

All kinds of problems lie behind the array of titles. Originally *Terminal Station*, the title was changed in the US to *Indiscretion of an American Wife* by hands-on produc-

The railway station: Stazione Termini, Rome

er David O Selznick, who was using the vehicle to showcase his then-wife Jennifer Jones, much to the annoyance of star Clift and writer Truman Capote. The final movie checks in at a savagely hacked 75 minutes. It was made almost entirely on location on Rome's central train station, **Stazione Termini, Piazza dei Cinquecento**.

STEEL MAGNOLIAS

(1989, dir: Herbert Ross)
Shirley MacLaine, Sally Field, Dolly Parton.
● LOUISIANA

Robert Harling's terminally sentimental stageplay was filmed in **Natchitoches**, on I-1 between Shreveport and Alexandria, Louisiana. Dolly Parton's beauty parlor (based on that of Liz Landrum, who was allegedly appalled at the movie version, at 316 Sirod Street, Natchitoches) was a private house on **Henry Street**, with the addition of a fake bay window. The Easter egg hunt takes place on a levee behind Natchitoches Chamber of Commerce, tricked out with 200 silk crocuses, tulips, irises and daisies. More stats – the production used thirteen three-tiered wedding cakes, 9,000 dyed Easter eggs and 600 roses. And if the crapping 'blackbirds' look a mite hefty, well, that's because they're actually pigeons, dyed with shoe polish.

STEPFORD WIVES, THE

(1975, dir: Bryan Forbes)
Katharine Ross, Paula Prentiss, Nanette Newman.
● CONNECTICUT

Ira Levin's wickedly dark allegory just about survives a monumental piece of miscasting which throws the whole

Stepford Men's Organization HQ: Lockwood-Mathews Mansion Museum, West Avenue, Norwalk

concept out of whack (see screenwriter William Gold-man's book *Adventures in the Screen Trade* for the full story). A leafy US suburb is a perfect heaven for the men, a town where beautiful, compliant women are just *thrilled* to do housework. Ross and the wonderful Prentiss get the creeps. Stepford is **Westport**, Route 95 northeast of Stam-ford, on the south coast of Connecticut. The HQ of the Stepford Men's Organization is the Second Empire-style, 62-room **Lockwood-Mathews Mansion Museum, 295 West Avenue, Norwalk** (© *203.838.9799, www.lock-woodmathewsmansion.org*), between Westport and Stam-ford. The same location is used in Frank Oz's misfiring 2004 remake, with Nicole Kidman, which also filmed in nearby **Darien** and **New Canaan** (a location for Ang Lee's *The Ice Storm*).

STING, THE

(1973, dir: George Roy Hill)
Paul Newman, Robert Redford, Robert Shaw.
● **CHICAGO, ILLINOIS; LOS ANGELES, CALIFORNIA**

This phenomenal-ly successful con movie is set in thirties Chicago, but many of the period locations were found around LA. In

The Chicago carousel: Santa Monica Pier, Santa Monica

fact, much of the film was shot at Universal in Hollywood, on the backlot's all-purpose Main Street. Paul Newman's carousel, the 1916 **Looff Carousel**, can be seen, still in action, on the **Santa Mon-ica Pier**, at the end of Colorado Avenue, Santa Monica (*www.santamonicapier.org*). Some tricky artwork turns the pier itself into Chicago's 'el', the elevated railway. The Chicago 'el' seen in the movie is on the Universal backlot, where it was built for Norman Jewison's period comedy *Gaily Gaily*. Several real bars served as sets: the plush New York gambling casino is a lounge of the **Cas-tle Green Apartments, 99 South Raymond Avenue, Pasadena** (*www.castlegreen.com*). A venerable old LA hotel, the Castle Green was drafted into service when the set-building budget began to run low. It was also used for corridors of the Chicago hotel. You can also see the apart-ments in *The Man With Two Brains*, as the piano teacher's studio in the Coens' *The Man Who Wasn't There*, *The Last Samurai*, and the building's bizarre Moorish exterior in *Bugsy*. The bank is the Italian marble lobby of the 1912, seven-storey **Commercial and Savings Bank, Pasade-na**. Nearby is the Chicago alleyway. The FBI hideout is the old **Koppel Plant**, a storage building for grain ship-ments in the San Pedro harbor district. The burlesque the-atre is the old *The Phantom of the Opera* set at Univer-sal Studios, in Hollywood.

The railway terminals of Joliet, Chicago and New York are all Chicago, though. Two of the railway terminals were no longer in use and had been converted into office space, which meant that renovations had to be stripped

away and old ticket offices restored. The termini are **Union Station** (still in use); **La Salle Street Station** (still in use, but the period exterior seen in the movie has since gone); **Penn Central Freight Yards**; and **Illinois Central Station**.

The limp 1983 sequel, imaginatively titled *The Sting II*, used the **Santa Cruz Boardwalk, 400 Beach Street, Santa Cruz**, on the coast south of San Francisco (see *The Lost Boys* for details).

STIR CRAZY

(1980, dir: Sidney Poitier)
Richard Pryor, Gene Wilder, Georg Stanford Brown.
● **NEW YORK CITY; ARIZONA; NEVADA**

Over-mugged farce with Pryor and Wilder wrongly banged up for a bank robbery after they move west from New York. The penitentiary is **Arizona State Prison, 1305 East Butte Avenue, Florence**, Arizona. More film-ing took place in the **Valley of Fire State Park**, Nevada.

STRADA, LA (aka *The Road*)

(1954, dir: Federico Fellini)
Giulietta Masina, Anthony Quinn, Richard Basehart.
● **ITALY**

Masina is the maltreated, waif-like sidekick of macho travelling showman Quinn in Fellini's hauntingly magi-cal fable, made on location around central and southern Italy, largely in **Viterbo**, **Ovindoli** and **Bagnoregio**.

STRAIGHT STORY, THE

(1999, dir: David Lynch)
Richard Farnsworth, Sissy Spacek, Harry Dean Stanton.
● **WISCONSIN; IOWA**

Exactly what it says. The Wizard of Weird produces a perfectly straightforward, low-key but affecting account of Alvin Straight's cross-country journey on his lawn-mower to find his estranged brother. The film, shot chrono-logically, follows the real Alvin's route from **Laurens**, northwest Iowa, east across almost the entire width of the state, to **Mount Zion**, Wisconsin. He calls in at **New Hampton**, **West Bend**, **West Union** and **Clermont** in Iowa; then crosses the Mississippi into Wisconsin at **Prairie du Chien**, finally reaching Mount Zion.

STRANGERS ON A TRAIN

(1951, dir: Alfred Hitchcock)
Robert Walker, Farley Granger, Ruth Roman.
● **NEW YORK CITY; NEW YORK; LOS ANGELES, CALIFORNIA; WASHINGTON DC; CONNECTICUT**

Hitchcock sneakily managed to acquire the rights to Patri-cia Highsmith's novel for peanuts. Creepily camp Walk-er offers to swap murders with manly, strapping tennis player Granger, and before you can say 'criss-cross', he's carried out his half of the bargain. Set largely in Wash-ington DC and the fictitious town of Metcalf. The open-ing scene, of Granger and Walker boarding the train, is DC's **Union Station, Massachusetts Avenue NE**, between First and Second Streets. After years of neglect, the grandiose Beaux Arts building was beautifully restored in 1988 and has since appeared on screen in *Hannibal* and *The Recruit*. Granger's hometown of Metcalf, where he rows with his wife, is the **Danbury** railroad stop, Connecticut, on I-84, 50 miles or so north of New York on the New York State border. This is where Hitch makes his trademark cameo appearance, humping a double bass onto the train as Granger alights.

The amusement park, where Walker commits Granger's murder, and the site of the climactic carousel crash, is a conflation of a set constructed on the ranch of movie director Roland V Lee (*Son of Frankenstein*) in the LA suburb of Chatsworth, and the real **Canoga Park Fairground**, which supplied the Tunnel of Love, into which Walker follows his victim. Walker haunts Granger by hanging about on the steps of the **Jefferson Memorial, East Potomac Park**, 14th Street at East Basin Drive SW, Washington DC. After the suspenseful tennis match, suspicious cops tail Granger to New York's **Pennsylvania Station**, 31st-33rd Streets between Seventh and Eighth Avenues.

Long shots for the climactic tennis game were taken at the Davis Cup match between America and Australia at the famous **West Side Tennis Club, 1 Tennis Place, Forest Hills** (© *718.268.2300*), while more tennis scenes used the **South Gate Tennis Courts**, southeast LA.

STRATEGIA DEL RAGNO (aka *The Spider's Stratagem*)
(1970, dir: Bernardo Bertolucci)
Giulio Brogi, Alida Valli, Tino Scotti.
● **ITALY**

Brogi revisits the town where his father was murdered by fascists in the thirties, only to find that the truth is not so simple. Story by Jorge Luis Borges, photography by Vittorio Storaro. The strange setting is the town of **Sabbionetta**, a way outside Mantua. Built by a member of a wealthy Mantua family as the 'Ideal City', it never took off and now lies crumbling, dusty, and looking fabulous as a movie backdrop.

STRAW DOGS
(1971, dir: Sam Peckinpah)
Dustin Hoffman, Susan George, David Warner.
● **CORNWALL**

Down in deepest Cornwall, pacifist Hoffman turns to ultraviolence when local heavies lay siege to his farmhouse. The violence is all very jolly, but the rape scene is seriously leery. What might have worked in dusty Mexico seems wildly contrived in the West Country. The village is **St Buryan**, on the B3283 a few miles west of Penzance, toward Lands End.

STREETCAR NAMED DESIRE, A
(1951, dir: Elia Kazan)
Vivien Leigh, Marlon Brando, Kim Hunter.
● **LOS ANGELES, CALIFORNIA; NEW ORLEANS, LOUISIANA**

The rather stagey adaptation of Tennessee Williams' play is set in steamy New Orleans, but was shot almost entirely at Warner Bros' Burbank Studio. Stanley Kowalski's bowling alley is one of the real locations, though not in

the Deep South: it stood on Pico Boulevard in LA. There was some location work on the Big Easy, though. The railway station is the **L&N Train Station** at the foot of Canal Street, the wide north-south roadway bordering the French Quarter. By 1951, the streetcars had been replaced by buses, but an old Desire streetcar

The real Desire Streetcar: Esplanade Avenue

The real Elysian Fields

was trundled out of retirement for the shot. Sadly, almost all of the location filming was eventually cut from the movie. You can see a streetcar from the Desire line on display behind the Mint at 400 Esplanade Avenue, New Orleans. Elysian Fields, far from being a poetic invention of the playwright, is a real thoroughfare, a street of wooden shacks in a fairly poor neighbourhood.

STRICTLY BALLROOM
(1992, dir: Baz Luhrmann)
Paul Mercurio, Tara Morice, Gia Carides.
● **NEW SOUTH WALES, AUSTRALIA; VICTORIA, AUSTRALIA**

Winning, primary-coloured fantasy with drop-dead gorgeous Mercurio and plain-Jane Morice defying the carved-in-stone rules of ballroom dancing and, wouldn't you know, triumphing in style. Filming took place at the **Signal Room** near Pier 13, **Pyrmont**. The rooftop where Mercurio and Morice dance is estate agent **LJ Hooker's, 322 Victoria Road** at Marrickville Road, **Marrickville**, Sydney. The joyous climax is at the **Melbourne Sports and Entertainment Centre, Swan Street**, Melbourne, Victoria.

STROMBOLI
(1949, dir: Roberto Rossellini)
Ingrid Bergman, Mario Vitale, Renzo Cesana.
● **ITALY**

This melodrama, made at the height of Bergman's scandalous affair with Rossellini, was shot, naturally enough, around the volcano of **Stromboli**.

SUBWAY
(1985, dir: Luc Besson)
Christophe Lambert, Isabelle Adjani, Jean-Hugues Anglade.
● **PARIS, FRANCE**

Style, style, style is all in this designer thriller filmed almost entirely within the Paris Métro system, so it's play 'spot the station'. The station where Lambert, escaping the hitmen, first catches a train is **Dupleix** on Boulevard Grenelle just south of the Pont de Bir-Hakeim. The inspector meets up with flower-seller Bohringer at **Porte de Versailles**, south toward Mairie d'Issy. Lambert listens to the sax player at eastern terminus **Gallieni**. Rollerskater Anglade is followed onto the train at **Concorde**, before being handcuffed to the carriage pole at **La Motte-Picqet-Grenelle** – back toward Dupleix again. Most of the action centres around the vast interchange of the world's largest underground station, **Chatelet-Les Halles** beneath the Forum des Halles.

SUDDEN IMPACT

(1983, dir: Clint Eastwood)
Clint Eastwood, Sondra Locke, Pat Hingle.
● **CALIFORNIA**

"Go ahead, make my day…": Burger Island, Third Street, San Francisco

Fourth outing for Dirty Harry Callahan. Reputedly no longer welcome in cute, touristy and liberal San Francisco, most of the action takes place in the fictitious San Paula, which is in fact **Santa Cruz**, just down the coast on highway 1 (see *The Lost Boys* for details). The wedding party, where Harry provokes a suspect into a heart attack, filmed in the **Cocoanut Grove Ballroom** on the **Santa Cruz Boardwalk**. A pretty klutzy movie, but Eastwood's line as he deals with the robbery at a restaurant has passed into the language: "Go ahead, make my day." The restaurant, still there, is **Burger Island, 901 Third Street** at Townsend, San Francisco.

SUGARLAND EXPRESS, THE

(1974, dir: Steven Spielberg)
Goldie Hawn, William Atherton, Michael Sacks.
● **TEXAS**

Spielberg's first made-for-cinema movie (although *Duel* played cinemas in the UK, it was made for US TV) is a dazzlingly-directed comedy car chase which plunges into tragedy as the naïve Lou Jean Poplin (Hawn) springs husband Clovis (Atherton) from Pre-Release Center to retrieve Baby Langston, who's been taken into care in the fictitious Sugarland. The title was obviously inspired by the location of the prison facility, which is **Jester State Prison, Sugar Land** (the town was once HQ of the Imperial Sugar Company), southwest of Houston. The movie opens at **Rosenberg**, on I-59, 30 miles southwest of Houston and about 20 miles west of the real Sugar Land. The fugitives stop for gas at **Humble**, Route 90, I-59, just north of Houston. As the media circus surrounding their flight begins to grow, they call in at **San Antonio**; at **Pleasanton**, 30 miles south, where Captain Tanner (Ben Johnson) has second thoughts about using snipers to pick the couple off; and at nearby **Floresville**; ending up over in west Texas near the Mexico border, at **Del Rio**. Cap'n Tanner finally resorts to the ultimate deterrent and the chase grinds to a halt in the Rio Grande.

SUMMER MADNESS

(aka *Summertime*)
(1955, dir: David Lean)
Katharine Hepburn, Rossano Brazzi, Isa Miranda.
● **VENICE, ITALY**

Hepburn's alfresco drink: Cafe Chioggia, Piazzetta San Marco

Starchy 'spinster' Hepburn falls for married Rossano Brazzi on a European vacation. David Lean's lightweight travelogue-romance was made on location in Venice, in the days before mass tourism, though the film's release doubled the city's tourist trade overnight. Lean takes advantage of the audience's presumed unfamiliarity with the city by playing fast and loose with the geography.

Hepburn's hotel: Pensione Accademia, Fondamenta Bollani

Movie camera-toting Hepburn arrives by train at **Stazione Ferroviaria Santa Lucia**, the then-spanking new railway station, one of Venice's few unapologetically modern buildings, on **Fondamenta di Santa Lucia** at the northern end of Canal Grande. In order to conjure up an instant flavour of Venice, Lean has Hepburn's vaporetto trip to the hotel take a bizarrely circuitous route, taking in the church of **Santa Maria della Salute**, which stands at the canal's southern entrance. Likewise, the Pensioni Fiorini, where she stays, has windows which look out on totally different areas of the city. The actual hotel itself, a detached villa with canalside terrace, is **Pensione Accademia, Fondamenta Bollani 1058**, in the Dorsoduro district (© 523.7846) just to the west of the Galleria dell'Accademia (*vaporetto: Accademia*).

Hepburn, inevitably for a Venice-set movie, enjoys a drink alfresco at **Cafe Chioggia**, opposite the Basilica San Marco in the **Piazzetta San Marco**, where she first meets Brazzi. Northwest of the Pensione Accademia is the site of the film's most famous scene, Hepburn falling into the canal. The canal is the Canal San Barnaba, at **Campo San Barnaba** in the Dorsoduro district. At the foot of the sweet little Ponte San Barnaba on

Hepburn falls into the canal: Campo San Barnaba

Rossano Brazzi's antique shop: Dorsoduro

the campo is Brazzi's antique shop, **2808 Dorsoduro**. The church dominating the campo, by the way, is the major Venice location for *Indiana Jones and the Last Crusade*.

SUMMER OF '42

(1971, dir: Robert Mulligan)
Gary Grimes, Jennifer O'Neill, Jerry Houser.
● **CALIFORNIA**

Soft-focus, sentimental nostalgia, with schoolboy Grimes enjoying his first sexual experience with recently widowed O'Neill. Set in New England, the real location is over on the west coast, in the seaport of **Mendocino**, originally a Gold Rush town, then a mill town, now reinvented as an upmarket artists' colony, with filming at **Ten Mile Beach**.

SUMMER OF SAM

(1999, dir: Spike Lee)
John Leguizamo, Adrien Brody, Mira Sorvino.
● **NEW YORK CITY**

Spike Lee's evocation of the blistering summer of 1977 and the effect on the inhabitants of New York of serial killer the Son of Sam. The 'dead end street' neighbourhood is **Layton Avenue** in the **Country Club** district, on Eastchester Bay in the Bronx. Leguizamo and Sorvino chicken out of joining the, rather anachronistic, punk crowd at **CBGB's, 315 Bowery** between First and Second Streets (℡ *212.982.4052*), and join the hopefuls lined up outside **Studio 54, 254 West 54th Street** between Broadway and Eighth Avenue, Manhattan. After the club's owners were jailed for tax evasion and drug offences, the celebs drifted away, and the emergence of Aids finally killed off the hedonistic, anything-goes scene. In 1986 the club closed. It came close to demolition, but has survived as a performance space. Fittingly, it became home to Sam Mendes' production of *Cabaret*.

SUNDAY, BLOODY SUNDAY

(1971, dir: John Schlesinger)
Peter Finch, Glenda Jackson, Murray Head.
● **LONDON**

Dr Finch's surgery: Pembroke Square, Kensington

Both Dr Daniel Hirsh (Finch) and Alex Greville (Jackson) are besotted with artist Bob Elkin (Head) in this immaculately written, acted and directed slice of London life in the seventies. But the icing on the cake comes in the collection of priceless cameos and caricatures surrounding the central relationships. Alex and Bob take the precocious kids for a scamper around **Greenwich Park**, SE10, which is quite a walk from the family house. The passageway lined with gravestones is alongside **St Alphege**, in Greenwich. One of the kids vandalising cars here is Daniel Day-Lewis, in his first screen appearance.

Although the appalling Hodson family is quintessentially 'Hampstead', the house is actually in south London, about 12 miles from Greenwich, on the north side of Wands-

Home of the Hodson family: Spencer Park, Wandsworth

worth Common: **5 Spencer Park**, SW18. Dr Hirsh's surgery, where he and Bob raised a few eyebrows back in 1971 with a passionate screen kiss, is **37 Pembroke Square**, W8, just off Earls Court Road. The scene took the film crew by surprise, too. Until that point, they'd been led to believe the couple were uncle and nephew.

SUNSET BLVD.

(1950, dir: Billy Wilder)
Gloria Swanson, William Holden, Erich Von Stroheim.
● **LOS ANGELES, CALIFORNIA**

Forget the musical, this is the real thing. Ageing silent movie star Swanson takes in flat-broke screenwriter Holden in Wilder's brilliant satire noir. The

The Paramount Gate, Hollywood

glorious old Renaissance-style mansion, which stood at 641 Irving on the corner of Wilshire and Crenshaw Boulevards, midtown LA, was demolished in 1957 to make way for the Getty headquarters, now the glumly nondescript Harbor Building. The mansion, seen also in *Rebel Without a Cause*, was built in the twenties for a former US Consul in Mexico, who abandoned the building, which stood vacant for over ten years until bought by J Paul Getty. At the time of filming *Sunset Blvd.*, the mansion had passed to Mrs J Paul Getty in a divorce settlement and she, in turn, rented the property out to Paramount on condition the film company built her a swimming pool. And if Mrs Getty didn't like the pool, the studio would have to remove it. Paramount built it, Mrs Getty liked it, and it stayed, which is just as well…

You can still, however, see the digs of scriptwriter Holden, the Mediterranean-style **Alto Nido Apartments, 1851 North Ivar Street**, Hollywood. Just down the road a bit, in the mock-Tudor Para Sed Apartments at 1817 North Ivar, lived real-life writer Nathanael West who began penning the classic Hollywood satire *Day of the Locust* here in 1935.

Gloria Swanson visits Cecil B DeMille on set at **Paramount Studios, 5555 Melrose Avenue** in Hollywood. The

William Holden's digs: Alto Nido Apartments, North Ivar Street

studio, built in 1917 as the Peralta Studios, became Brunton Studios in 1920, then United Studios in 1921, before being bought by Paramount in 1926. The studio has since expanded and swallowed up surrounding streets, which means that the main entrance is no longer the famous Paramount gate seen in the movie. The arch can now only be glimpsed from a distance across the lot, unless you can manage the under-publicised walking tour of the lot (three times a day, Monday to Friday, $15).

Disastrous previews (one in Evanston, Illinois, home to the Women's Christian Temperance Union – Wilder had earlier made *The Lost Weekend*) led to Wilder junking the original opening scene (the corpse of Holden and a bunch of other stiffs in the morgue discuss how they ended up dead) and trying something with the swimming pool. The rest is history.

SUNSHINE BOYS, THE

(1975, dir: Herbert Ross)
George Burns, Walter Matthau, Richard Benjamin.
● **NEW YORK CITY**

Burns and Matthau, two old vaudevillians who can't stand the sight of each other, are brought together for a TV reunion in this filming of Neil Simon's stage play. Matthau's New York apartment block is the **Ansonia Hotel, 2107-2109 Broadway** between West 73rd and West 74th Streets on the West Side. The Belle-Epoque block has never been a hotel, but private apartments whose thick, soundproofed walls have made it popular with musicians such as Caruso, Toscanini, Stravinsky and Lily Pons. The Ansonia basement, incidentally, was home to the Continental Baths, the gay bathhouse and cabaret where Bette Midler, accompanied by pianist Barry Manilow, began her career. Also featured is the **Friars Club, 57 East 55th Street**, the private actors' club famous for celebrity roasts, between Park and Madison Avenues, midtown New York.

The *Daily Planet* building: News Building, East 42nd Street

SUPERMAN

(1978, dir: Richard Donner)
Christopher Reeve, Margot Kidder, Gene Hackman.
● **NEW YORK CITY; ALBERTA, CANADA; CALIFORNIA; NEW MEXICO; ST LUCIA**

Clark Kent's *Daily Planet* building really is a newspaper office. It's the **News Building, 220 East 42nd Street** between Second and Third Avenues, New York. A splendid art deco skyscraper, it was formerly the New York *Daily News* Building (the fifties TV series of *Superman* famously used Los Angeles City Hall, 200 North Spring Street, downtown). Lois Lane's apartment is **240 Central Park South**. Lois and Supes go for a nighttime spin around the **Statue of Liberty**. Another New York landmark featured is the **Brooklyn Bridge**. More filming took place at **Calgary** and **Drumheller** in Alberta, Canada; and at **Red Rock State Park** near Gallup, New

Mexico (the area has been renamed Superman Canyon). Superman saves the school bus on San Francisco's **Golden Gate Bridge**, and steps in again at **Niagara Falls**. The studio work for the film, including Lex Luthor's Grand Central Station hideout, was in the UK, at Pinewood Studios. The Boulder dam sequence features the Pinewood tank, the biggest cinema water tank in Europe.

Superman picks the red immortal flower for Lois at **Dasheene Resort, St Lucia**. Dasheene is on a ridge looking out over the Pitons. Christopher Reeve stayed at the Anse Chastanet Hotel, Dasheene.

SUPERMAN II

(1980, dir: Richard Lester)
Christopher Reeve, Valerie Perrine, Terence Stamp.
● **NEW YORK; ONTARIO, CANADA; BUCKINGHAMSHIRE**

The three supervillains arrive on Earth at that old favourite location, **Black Park Lake, Black Park** behind Pinewood Studios at Iver Heath,

Superman to the rescue: Niagara Falls

Buckinghamshire. The small Western town was built at Chobham Common, Surrey. The Metropolis set was, at the time, the largest ever constructed at Pinewood. Superman rescues a little boy plummeting into **Niagara Falls**. The Honeymoon Haven Hotel is **Table Rock House**, alongside the Canadian side of Horseshoe Falls.

SUPERMAN III

(1983, dir: Richard Lester)
Christopher Reeve, Richard Pryor, Jackie Cooper.
● **ARIZONA; ALBERTA, CANADA**

Superman is corrupted by synthetic Kryptonite, while villains Pryor and Robert Vaughn beaver away at a supercomputer. Filming took place at the **Glen Canyon Dam**, near Page, northern Arizona. The fallen chimney is **Turbo Resources Ltd Oil Refinery** in Alberta, Canada. There was more filming at **Calgary**; **Drumheller**; and **High River** in Alberta.

For *Superman IV: The Quest For Peace*, Metropolis is played by **Milton Keynes** in Buckinghamshire, England.

SUPERVIXENS

(1975, dir: Russ Meyer)
Shari Eubank, Charles Pitts, Charles Napier.
● **ARIZONA**

Another bizarre confection from breast-obsessed Meyer, though more bloody than usual, with Charles Pitts getting involved with a succession of Amazonian females after fleeing his job at Martin Bormann's gas station when he's accused of... well, you get the picture. It was shot in **Quartzsite**, Arizona.

SUSPICION

(1941, dir: Alfred Hitchcock)

Cary Grant, Joan Fontaine, Nigel Bruce.

● CALIFORNIA

Is playboy Cary Grant scheming to kill his poor, naïve, young wife Joan Fontaine? You bet. Until Hitch played safe to please the studio execs and refilmed a happy ending with Grant totally exonerated. Set in England, the coastscapes are the rugged seafront of northern California, between **Carmel** and **Big Sur**.

SWAMP THING

(1982, dir: Wes Craven)
Ray Wise, Adrienne Barbeau, Louis Jourdan.

● SOUTH CAROLINA

Ray Wise turns into a lumbering green eco-warrior in this comic book adaptation from a pre-*Nightmare* Craven. The fearful, impenetrable swamplands are the Cypress Gardens and the Magnolia Plantations of **Charleston**, down on the southeast coast of South Carolina.

SWAMP WATER

(1941, dir: Jean Renoir)
Walter Huston, Walter Brennan, Anne Baxter.

● GEORGIA

A fugitive hides out in the **Okeefenokee Swamp**, where this was actually filmed, down in southwest Georgia.

SWEET AND LOWDOWN

(1999, dir: Woody Allen)
Sean Penn, Samantha Morton, Uma Thurman.

● NEW YORK; NEW JERSEY

Although Allen's biopic of a fictitious jazz musician used the Teaneck Armory in New Jersey as a soundstage, plenty of thirties-style locations were found around the state, as well as in upstate New York and New York City. The amateur talent contest won by Penn is at the **Eagles' Club, 7 Old Albany Post Road, Ossining**. The railroad yards are the **Sunnyside Railyards** in Queens, while the Chicago stockyards were found in **Patterson**, New Jersey.

The nightclub, where a drunken Sean Penn drags his companion off into the night to watch trains, is **Chumley's, 86 Bedford Street**, between Grove and Barrow Streets, Greenwich Village. This atmospheric little bar was once a speakeasy and still has no sign outside to indicate its presence. The unmodernised interior can also be seen in *Bright Lights, Big City*, Warren Beatty's epic *Reds* and Mike Wadleigh's eco-horror *Wolfen*. Another venue is the old **Gage and Tollner** restaurant in Brooklyn. The gas station is on Highway 9W, upstate New York, and the park is **Rockland Lake State Park**, Route 9W in **Congers**.

SWEET DREAMS

(1985, dir: Karel Reisz)
Jessica Lange, Ed Harris, Ann Wedgeworth.

● WEST VIRGINIA; TENNESSEE; CALIFORNIA

Biopic of country singer Patsy Cline, shot partly in Cline's hometown of **Martinsburg**, off I-81 way over in the northeastern corner of West Virginia. Locations here include the **Rainbow Road Club**, Route 340, and **Green Hill Cemetery, East Burke Street**. Filming also took place at the inevitable Grand Ol' Opry in the **Ryman Auditori-**

um, **116 Opry Place, Nashville**; and in LA.

SWEET HEREAFTER, THE

(1997, dir: Atom Egoyan)
Ian Holm, Sarah Polley, Bruce Greenwood.

● ONTARIO, CANADA

An adaptation of Russell Banks' novel. Filmed around Ontario: at **Barrie**, on the west shore of Lake Simcoe, I-400; **Caledon**, northwest of Toronto; **Stouffvill**e, 20 miles north of east Toronto; **Goodwood**, just to the northeast of Stouffville; **Whitevale**; and **Lake Musselman**.

SWEET SMELL OF SUCCESS

(1957, dir: Alexander Mackendrick)
Tony Curtis, Burt Lancaster, Marty Milner.

● NEW YORK CITY

"I love this dirty town," beams control-freak showbiz columnist JJ Hunsecker (Lancaster), aka 'The Eyes of Broadway', surveying the gleaming nightscapes of Manhattan in this brilliantly cynical melodrama from one-time Ealing director Mackendrick (*The Ladykillers*, *The Man In the White Suit*).

Hunsecker's apartment is in the art deco **Brill Building, 1619 Broadway** between 49th

Burt Lancaster's place: Brill Building, Broadway

and 50th Streets. The Brill was the original heart of Tin Pan Alley. During the sixties, when it housed 165 music biz companies, its roster of songwriting teams included Goffin-King, Greenwich-Barry, Mann-Weil and Leiber-Stoller. For 1997's *Grace of My Heart*, the Brill was faked in downtown LA.

Devious press agent Sidney Falco (Curtis) tries to plant a smear in a rival column at the now-gone celeb hangout of the forties and fifties, Toots Shor Restaurant and Lounge, which stood at 51 West 51st Street (it closed in 1971). He meets up with JJ at the **21 Club, 21 West 52nd Street** near Fifth Avenue (© *212.582.7200, www.21club.com*). This classy restaurant is also featured in *All About Eve*, *Manhattan Murder Mystery*, *Wall Street* and *Written on the Wind*. The office of *The New York Globe*, where Falco manages a sneak peek at Hunsecker's upcoming column, is **200 Fifth Avenue** at 23rd Street, alongside the Flatiron Building.

SWINGERS

(1996, dir: Doug Liman)
Jon Favreau, Vince Vaughn, Ron Livingston.

● LOS ANGELES, CALIFORNIA; NEVADA

Liman's excruciatingly spot-on

The coffee shop, where the swingers meet up: 101 Coffee Shop, Best Western, Hollywood

"Vegas, Bob, Vegas.": Stardust Hotel and Casino, Las Vegas Boulevard

The club where Liman parodies *Goodfellas*: The Derby, Los Feliz Boulevard

comedy of LA-scene manners is set against the retro-swing dance movement. The coffee shop, where the swingers meet up for their heart-to-hearts, is the **101 Coffee Shop**, within the **Best Western, 6145 Franklin Avenue**, east Hollywood – this is where much of the script was actually concoct-ed. The Vegas trip takes Vaughn and Favreau to the **Fremont Hotel and Casino, 200 East Fremont Street** (© *702.385.3232*) in the old downtown district, though the exterior is the **Stardust Hotel and Casino, 3000 Las Vegas Boulevard** (© *702.732.6111*) on the Strip.

Back in LA, Favreau plays a round at the **Los Feliz Golf Club, 3207 Los Feliz Boulevard**. The convoy of cars from the Hollywood Hills party passes a couple of familiar locations – **Canter's** on Fairfax, as seen in *Enemy of the State*, and the now-demolished Hollywood Star Lanes Bowling Alley on Hollywood Boulevard, from *The Big Lebowski*. Their destination is the **Dresden Room Restaurant, 1760 North Vermont Avenue**, just north of Barnsdall Park in Los Feliz (© *323.665.4294*), one of the top swing venues, where Favreau meets the Starbucks waitress. The club where Liman parodies Scorsese's famous tracking shot from *Goodfellas* is **The Derby, 4500 Los Feliz Boulevard** at Hillhurst (© *323.663.8979*). The old Brown Derby (though not the famed hat-shaped restau-rant, which stood on Wilshire Boulevard) was reinvent-ed in 1993 as a swing bar and restored to its Hollywood glory (*www.the-derby.com*). And to top it all, the oval bar was used in the Joan Crawford noir *Mildred Pierce*.

T

TAKING OF PELHAM ONE TWO THREE, THE
(1974, dir: Joseph Sargent)
Walter Matthau, Robert Shaw, Martin Balsam.
● NEW YORK CITY

The ransom delivery: 28th Street Station

This laconic, laid-back thriller invented colour-coded villains, later picked up by Tarantino for *Reservoir Dogs*, while providing more-than-usually serious roles for Walter Matthau and Jerry Stiller as New York transit cops. The subway scenes were shot on the **Pelham Bay Line**. Mr Green boards the train at **59th Street Station**, but most of the interiors used the disused **Court Street Station** in Brooklyn Heights, on a forked section of track which looks different enough from various angles to stand in for both Grand Central and 28th Street. In 1976, the station became the New York Transit Museum (© *212.878.0106, www.mta.nyc.ny.us/mta/museum*). The flu-ridden mayor, who bears an uncanny resemblance to Ed Koch, is laid up in bed in his official residence at the **Gracie Mansion, 590 East 89th Street** at East End Avenue (*www.ci.nyc.ny.us/html/om/html/gracie.html*). He OKs the ransom delivery, which comes to grief in a crash at **Astor Place**, but is ultimately delivered to **28th Street Station**, at 28th Street and Park Avenue South. In the background you can see the Belmore Cafeteria, the cabbies' hangout from *Taxi Driver*.

TALENTED MR RIPLEY, THE
(1999 , dir: Anthony Minghella)
Matt Damon, Jude Law, Gwyneth Paltrow.
● ITALY; NEW YORK CITY

The second filming of Patricia Highsmith's novel (the first was *Plein Soleil*, which cast Alain Delon as the sexually ambiguous anti-hero) conjures up Italy of the 1960s from a patchwork of niftily chosen locations, not all of them what they seem.

The theatre where Ripley works: Lyceum, West 45th Street

The opening, though, is New York, where Tom Ripley (Damon) works at the **Lyceum Theater, 149 West 45th**

Ripley's basement apartment: Franklin Place, Tribeca

Tom Ripley arrives in Mongibello: Ischia Ponte, Ischia

Street between Sixth and Seventh Avenues (used in the 1947 George Cukor backstage melodrama *A Double Life*, starring Ronald Colman). The interior of Ripley's dismal basement apartment was actually the ground floor of a tenement on Second Avenue at 26th Street in the Gramercy district, but you'll find the exterior, with the steep flight of iron steps, in the tiny passageway of **Franklin Place**, between White Street and Franklin Street in Tribeca.

Taking the job of tracking down spoiled rich kid Dickie Greenleaf (Law), Ripley arrives in Italy at the art deco terminal of **Palermo**, on the northwest coast of Sicily.

To represent the fictitious resort of Mongibello, where Dickie idles away his time with girlfriend Marge (Paltrow), the movie uses the island of **Ischia** in the Bay of Naples. The cobbled square where Ripley gets off the bus is **Ischia Ponte**, below the towering 12th century Castello Aragonese which dominates the island's northeast coast. The best way to reach Ischia Ponte is by catching a bus, about a mile east of the ferry landing at Ischia Porto. Between Ischia Ponte and Ischia Porte you'll find **Bagno Antonio**, the private beach where Ripley first discovers Dickie and Marge. Close by are Dickie's house and the small harbour where the body of Dickie's girlfriend Silvana turns up during the ceremony of the Madonna. The main shopping street and town square of Mongibello, however, can be found on **Procida**, a neighbouring island, 20 minutes away by ferry.

The Vesuvio nightclub, supposedly in Naples, where Dickie and Ripley perform 'Tu Vuo Fa L'Americano' is the **Caffè Latino, Via Monte Testaccio 96** (© *06.5728.8384*) in Rome, whereas the Rome opera house, where

Ripley meets Dickie Greenleaf: Bagno Antonio, Ischia

The Rome opera house: Teatro San Carlo, Naples

Freddie turns up at the café: Piazza Navona, Rome

Marge has suspicions at the Venice café: Cafe Florian, Piazza San Marco

Smith-Kingsley rehearses the choir: Chiesa Martorana, Palermo

Ripley poses as Dickie, is the **Teatro San Carlo, Via San Carlo** in Naples. And also in Naples is the imposing vaulted Galleria where Dickie draws his allowance. The San Remo jazz festival, where Ripley begins to realise that the idyll is coming to an end, is the seafront at **Anzio**, on the coast about 30 miles south of Rome (the real San Remo is up at the French border).

Ripley's Roman hotel, the sumptuous **Grand Hotel, Via Vittorio Emanuele Orlando 3** (© 06.47091), off Piazza della Republica, really is in the Eternal City, as is the café where Dickie's obnoxious chum, Freddie Miles (Philip Seymour Hoffman), turns up, on **Piazza Navona** opposite Bernini's Fountain of the Four Rivers. When he returns to Rome after Dickie's murder, surveying the ruins of the **Forum** from **Capitoline Hill** and viewing the monumental sculptures of the **Capitoline Museum**, Ripley stays in an apartment on the fictitious Piazza Gioia, which is actually near the old Jewish Ghetto, on **Piazza Mattei**. The interior of the apartment – which also functioned as the Grand Hotel suite – is the 14th century **Palazzo Taverna, Via di Monte Giordano 36**. The terrace café, where Ripley arranges for Meredith, Marge and Peter Smith-Kingsley to meet up, is **Cafe Dinelli, Piazza di Spagna**, at the foot of the Spanish Steps.

Moving on to Venice, Ripley stays in an apartment which is an amalgam of the abandoned **Ca' Sagredo** and the **Palazzo Mosto**. Marge, having arrived at the streamlined, fifties-style **Santa Lucia Railway Station**, at the northern end of Canal Grande, finally voices her suspicions about Dickie's disappearance at Venetian landmark **Cafe Florian, Piazza San Marco 56-59**. The hotel where Ripley meets Dickie's father is the **Europa e Regina, Calle Larga 22 Marzo, San Marco 2159** (© 520.0477), on the Canal Grande, facing the Chiesa della Salute.

The Venetian church, though, where Smith-Kingsley rehearses the 'Stabat Mater', is in fact the 14th century **Chiesa Martorana, Piazza Bellini** in Palermo, Sicily.

TARGETS
(1968, dir: Peter Bogdanovich)

Boris Karloff, Tim O'Kelly, James Brown.
● **CALIFORNIA**

Another directorial career is launched by Roger Corman, as Bogdanovich rises to the challenge of assembling a film from two days work owed to the producer by veteran Boris Karloff, and 20 minutes of footage from *The Terror*, one of Corman's own Poe-inspired pictures (starring a very young Jack Nicholson).

The inventive script contrasts the old-style gothic embodied by actor Byron Orlok (Karloff, virtually playing himself), with the banality of modern horrors. The parallel story was inspired by sniper Charles Whitman, who randomly picked off victims from the the tower of Austin University, but the film doesn't stray far from LA. The Brass Rail gunshop, where all-American boy Bobby Thompson (O'Kelly) shops, stood on Sunset Boulevard in Hollywood. It's now gone, but still standing are the gas tanks overlooking the I-405, San Diego Freeway at **Oxnard Street, Van Nuys**, in the San Fernando Valley, from the top of which Bobby casually takes out passing motorists.

Bogdanovich's ingenious climax brings the two worlds together as Thompson takes pot-shots at a cinema audience from behind the screen of a drive-in showing a 'Byron Orlok' movie (*The Terror* – what else?). The outdoor picture house was the Reseda Drive-in Theater on **Reseda Boulevard** at Vanowen Street, Reseda. It closed in 1985 and has since been demolished.

TARZAN AND HIS MATE
(1934, dir: Cedric Gibbons)
Johnny Weissmuller, Maureen O'Sullivan, Neil Hamilton.
● **CALIFORNIA**

The jungle is **Sherwood Forest** and **Sherwood Lake**. The swamp is **Woodland Park**, near Pico-Rivera in Whittier. More CA locations include **Big Tujunga** and **China Flats** (now a restricted Naval Weapons Center, north of Ridgecrest in the Mojave Desert).

TASTE OF HONEY, A
(1961, dir: Tony Richardson)
Rita Tushingham, Dora Bryan, Murray Melvin.
● **MANCHESTER; LANCASHIRE; LONDON**

A compendium of sixties hot potatoes – unmarried motherhood, race, homosexuality – baked in a cracking script from Shelagh Delaney's stage play. It was the first British feature film to be made entirely on location, around the streets and canals of **Manchester** and **Salford**.

Jo (Tushingham) tags along for a seriously glum day out at **Blackpool**, the traditional rainswept resort of the working class north, with its Tower based on the original in Paris. The eagle-eyed might spot director Richardson (in the anorak) strolling immediately behind Helen (the priceless Bryan). See the resorts blowsy splendour in *Bhaji on the Beach* and *Funny Bones*, and the Tower's extravagant ballroom in Ken Russell's Hollywood biopic *Valentino*.

Much of the terraced housing has gone, but you can still see the **Stockport Viaduct** where Jo and Geoffrey

(Melvin) cut loose. Claimed to be western Europe's biggest brick structure, it was opened in 1842, and restored in 1989. Helen and fancy man Peter dance at the **Ritz Ballroom, Whitworth Street West** (*© 0161.236.4355*), Manchester.

The neighbourhood's not entirely Salford, though. It's partly, um, Chelsea. It might be difficult to envisage, but SW10 was not always as expensively 'chichi' as it is today. The production base, which was used for the rickety flat Jo shares with Geoffrey, was the scenic workshop of the English Stage Company (based at the opposite end of the King's Road, in Sloane Square's Royal Court Theatre). The workshop and yard (where the film ends with a firework display) have since been demolished, but **74 Elm Park Road**, just around the corner, is the house – then in a state of disrepair – used for the interior of Helen's Salford home.

TASTE THE BLOOD OF DRACULA
(1969, dir: Peter Sasdy)
Christopher Lee, Geoffrey Keen, Peter Sallis.
● **HERTFORDSHIRE**

One of Hammer's better sequels, with three jaded Victorian businessmen conjuring up Dracula for kicks, and in turn being destroyed by their own children. Mostly set-bound, with exteriors at **Tykes Water Lake, Aldenham Country Park**, off the A411 west of **Elstree, Hertfordshire**.

TAXI DRIVER
(1976, dir: Martin Scorsese)
Robert De Niro, Jodie Foster, Harvey Keitel.
● **NEW YORK CITY**

The cab office: 57th Street

De Niro is so identified with the role of unhinged loner Travis Bickle, it's difficult to believe the first choice for the role was crooner Neil Diamond. Second up was Jeff Bridges, under the direction of Robert Mulligan. Thankfully, the script finally passed to the dream team of Scorsese and De Niro, who produced arguably the greatest movie of the seventies.

Scorsese, naturally, uses real New York locations. The cab office Bickle works out of was at the western end of **57th Street**, at 11th Avenue. The building is still there, but the photogenic backdrop has been bulldozed to make way for the West Side Highway. Gone too is the café where Bickle meets with Wizard (Peter Boyle) and the other drivers. It was a real cabbies' hangout, the Belmore Cafeteria, which stood on Park Avenue

The final bloody shootout: 13th Street, East Village

South at 28th Street. The porno theatres, where Bickle spends his days, are along the 48th Street block of Eighth Avenue. The political rally is on Seventh Avenue at 38th Street. Bickle sports a mohican to shoot the senator at **Columbus Circle**. He's finally picked up by Betsy (Cybill Shepherd) outside the **St Regis-Sheraton Hotel, 2 East 55th Street** at Fifth Avenue.

The scuzzy hotel, to which Bickle takes underage hooker Iris (Foster), and the site of the climactic bloodbath, is **226 13th Street**, between Second and Third Avenues in the East Village.

TEEN WOLF
(1985, dir: Rod Daniel)
Michael J Fox, James Hampton, Scott Paulin.
● **CALIFORNIA**

Highschool basketball player Scott Howard (Fox) turns hairy in this amiable comedy, set in Nebraska but filmed around LA. Scott's home is **1727 Bushnell**

The hardware store: Mission Street, South Pasadena

Avenue, off West Huntington Drive, **South Pasadena** (the same house Fox was taken into in *Back to the Future*). Also in South Pasadena was the hardware store he works in, which was Balk's, at **1518 Mission Street** in **South Pasadena**, which closed down in 2000. Up in the Valley, Scott attends **John Burroughs High School, 1920 West Clark Avenue**, at North Parish Place, **Burbank**; and Tony's Liquor, where he uses his werewolf stare to buy beer, is now **Quick Stop Liquor, 6670 Foothill Boulevard** near Tujunga Canyon Boulevard, **Tujunga** (not far from locations used for *Memento* and *Terminator 3*).

10
(1979, dir: Blake Edwards)
Dudley Moore, Julie Andrews, Bo Derek.
LOS ANGELES, CALIFORNIA; MEXICO

Crude sex farce that briefly turned Moore into a diminutive sex symbol and Ravel's *Bolero* into the soundtrack for sex. Lustful Moore first spies buxom

Moore's first glimpse of Bo Derek: All Saints Episcopal Church, Beverly Hills

Derek in the **All Saints Episcopal Church, 504 Camden Drive** at Santa Monica Boulevard in Beverly Hills. Filming also took place at the **Pasadena Civic Auditorium, 300 East Green Street, Pasadena** (also seen as the concert venue for Bette Midler's *Divine Madness* and in *Red Dragon*). The Mexican scenes were filmed at the luxury resort of **Puerto Las Hadas**, on the Bay of Manzanillo, Mexico (*© 52.333.400.00*). The beach scenes are the nearby cove of **Playa Audiencia**.

TEN COMMANDMENTS, THE
(1923, dir: Cecil B DeMille)
Theodore Roberts, Richard Dix, Charles de Roche.
● CALIFORNIA

DeMille's early silent version of the Biblical story of Moses and the Israelites bizarrely grafts on a modern morality fable. Plans to film in Egypt were rejected by producer Adolph Zukor as too expensive, so the epic sets were finally built on the **Nipomo Sand Dunes**, which extend from Point Sal to Pismo Beach, north of LA, around Guadalupe. The huge mountains of sand, up to 450 feet high, are held together by a network of grasses, ice plant, verbena and silver lupine. The city of Per Rameses, its grand boulevard lined with an avenue of sphinxes and pharaohs, was subsequently buried beneath the shifting sands, and is now being uncovered as a genuine archaeological relic.

The Israelites were chased by 250 Egyptian chariots across the famous **Muroc Dry Lake Bed** in the Mojave Desert. After the parting of the Red Sea, the Israelites journey across **Balboa Beach**, between Newport and Laguna Beaches, south of LA. Pharaoh's chariot host is stopped by the Pillar of Fire at **Anaheim Landing**.

The modern day sequences feature the **Cathedral of St Peter and St Paul, 666 Filbert Street** in San Francisco, which was still under construction (see *Dirty Harry* for details). Gutsy Leatrice Joy ascended 200 feet on the workmen's elevator, to cheers from an appreciative crowd below.

TEN COMMANDMENTS, THE
(1956, dir: Cecil B DeMille)
Charlton Heston, Anne Baxter, Yul Brynner.
● LOS ANGELES, CALIFORNIA; EGYPT

Over 30 years later, DeMille returned to the subject, ditching the modern day moralities to produce the peak of Hollywood mega-kitsch, which lurches wildly from hysterical camp to heart-in-mouth drama. The epic was shot largely on the Paramount lot in Hollywood, though this time there was some genuine location filming in Egypt.

First off, where's Mount Sinai? Not on any map. There is, however, in the Sinai massif, a cluster of peaks among which **Jebel Musa** – the Mount of Moses – is the most popular candidate. And that's where CB and crew turned up in October 1954. The crew stayed at St Catherine's Monastery at the foot of the range. Footage was shot for the Burning Bush scene, though the bush itself, with risible cartoon flames, was obviously filmed in the studio. Pharaoh Cedric Hardwick's Treasure City was built at **Beni Youssef**, near Cairo, which is also where the moving Exodus scene was staged. 10,000 Arabs, playing the Children of Israel, were drafted in,

St Catharine's Monastery: Base camp for the Egyptian location

along with 15,000 camels, water buffaloes, sheep, horses, oxen, goats, ducks, geese, pigeons, dogs, donkeys and, of course, many cattle.

Yul Brynner also shot some scenes on location, chasing the Children of Israel to the Red Sea. But clearly not the banishment of Moses into the wilderness, which crosscuts between Chuck Heston, very obviously alone and on location, and Yul Brynner, very obviously in a studio.

10 RILLINGTON PLACE
(1971, dir: Richard Fleischer)
Richard Attenborough, John Hurt, Pat Heywood.
● LONDON

Grim and sober account of mass-murderer John Christie, and the wrongful hanging of Timothy Evans, with exteriors filmed in Rillington Place itself (though not at the actual house), before the notorious street was demolished and renamed. The cul-de-sac became Ruston Close, now Ruston Mews, W11. It's on the west side of St Mark's Road just before Lancaster Road, overshadowed by the Westway. Number ten was the last house on the left.

10 THINGS I HATE ABOUT YOU
(1999, dir: Gil Junger)
Heath Ledger, Julia Stiles, Joseph Gordon-Levitt.
● WASHINGTON

Smart high school reworking of Shakespeare's *The Taming of the Shrew*. Padua High is **Stadium High School, 111 North E Street, Tacoma**, in Washington State. The striking building, on a bluff overlooking Commencement Bay, was built as a luxury hotel at the turn of the century. It is named for the school's huge athletic stadium, constructed in a ravine known as Old Woman's Gulch, after the widows of local fishermen who once squatted in little shacks here. The theatre is the **Paramount Theatre, 901 Pine Street** at Ninth Avenue, downtown Seattle.

TEOREMA (aka *Theorem*)
(1968, dir: Pier Paolo Pasolini)
Terence Stamp, Silvana Mangano, Massimo Girotti.
● MILAN, ITALY

Allegorical fable, shot in Milan, with handsome stranger Stamp seducing all the members of a bourgeois family, and the maid. The family react in different ways: mother Silvana Mangano goes cruising the streets of Milan for men; father strips naked on the platform of **Milan Central Railroad Station**.

TERMINAL, THE
(2004, dir: Steven Spielberg)
Tom Hanks, Catherine Zeta-Jones, Stanley Tucci.
● CALIFORNIA; QUÉBEC, CANADA

The airport terminal is a vast and complex set built in **Air Force Plant 42**, a hangar at **Palmdale**, 80 miles north of LA, where getting on for 40 national chains volunteered to build replicas of their outlets. External shots are of **Mirabel International Airport, 12300 Service A-4 Street, Montréal** (© *514.394.7377*). Although Viktor (Hanks) hails from the fictitious Krakhozia, the story is based on Iranian Merhan Karimi Nasseri, who has been trapped in Terminal 1 of Charles De Gaulle Airport, Paris, since 1988.

TERMINATOR, THE
(1984, dir: James Cameron)
Linda Hamilton, Michael Biehn, Arnold Schwarzenegger.

● LOS ANGELES, CALIFORNIA

The Terminator materialises above LA: Griffith Observatory

Schwarzenegger, the cyborg sent back from 2029AD to terminate future heroine Sarah Connor (Hamilton), first materialises in a flurry of animated lightning at the **Griffith Park Observatory, Observatory Drive** in Griffith Park, where he rips the hearts out of a couple of punks and takes their clothes (while thanking God he didn't land in a convent). See *Rebel Without a Cause* for details of the Observatory. The scene features some stunning nighttime views over the great flat expanse of LA. The human resistance is not far behind, in the form of Kyle Reese (Biehn), travelling economy class and landing in a back-alley of LA's grubby downtown area, near Seventh and Broadway. Connor (Hamilton) is working as a waitress in Big Buns café, which is actually **Carrows Restaurant, 815 South Fremont Avenue** at Mission Street, South Pasadena.

Newly kitted out, the Terminator gets tooled up at the Alamo Gun Shop, which is now, and has been for the last ten years, **Mexico Auto Sales, 14329 Victory Boulevard** at Tyrone Avenue, Van Nuys in the San Fernando Valley. The motel, where Reese teaches Connor survival skills and where, presumably, John Connor is conceived, is the **Tiki Motel, 7301 Santa Fe Avenue, Huntington Park** (© 323.582.5261). Be aware that this is not five-star accommodation.

The Terminator gets tooled up at the Alamo Gun Shop: Mexico Auto Sales, Victory Boulevard, Van Nuys

Big Buns, where Linda Hamilton works: Carrows Restaurant, South Fremont Avenue, South Pasadena

The car chase is around downtown LA, on **Sixth** and **Seventh Streets** and **Broadway**, leading to a shootout in the huge indoor parking lot of the **Department of Power and Water, 111 North Hope Street**. The tunnel chase, with Arnie's bike dodging home-made bombs, was filmed in the **Second Street Tunnel**,

which dives underground between Hill Street and Figueroa Street, also downtown.

The final confrontation, with the Terminator reduced to a metal skeleton before being crushed in the jaws of a metal press, was filmed at **Kern's of California, 13010 East Temple Avenue**, down in City of Industry, southeast LA.

The motel, where John Connor is conceived: Tiki Motel, Santa Fe Avenue

Before disappearing into the Mexican desert, Connor gets her picture taken at the remote gas station in **Sun Valley** in the Mojave (Joshua Trees are a dead giveaway), on the outskirts of Palmdale, north of LA.

TERMINATOR 2: JUDGEMENT DAY
(1991, dir: James Cameron)
Arnold Schwarzenegger, Linda Hamilton, Robert Patrick.

● CALIFORNIA

The Pescadero State Hospital for the Criminally Insane: Phoenix Academy, Lake View

Some years on from *The Terminator*, and future resistance hero John Connor (Edward Furlong) is an eleven-year-old, farmed out to foster parents in the northern LA suburb of Reseda (don't go looking for South Almond Avenue – it's fictitious), while mom Sarah is banged up in a maximum security asylum.

At $94 million, *T2* was the most expensive movie ever (the original *Terminator* came in at a neat $6 million). But that was before *Titanic*. Cameron took the opportunity to revisit ideas from the first *Terminator* movie on a grander scale. The opening 'future war' is reprised, using the ruins of a demolished steel plant at **Fontana**, on the outskirts of San Bernardino, Route 10 east of LA. With a sense of thrift that would gladden his old mentor (Cameron is a graduate of the Roger Corman school of moviemaking – at age 26 he handled the special effects on the Corman-produced *Battle Beyond the Stars*), the twisted bikes, burned-out cars and blackened cinders used as dressing are charred debris from the Universal Studio fire of 1989, when a disgruntled security guard torched the famous backlot.

The Pescadero State Hospital for the Criminally Insane, where Sarah Connor is incarcerated, has nothing to do with Pescadero, which is a small California fishing town between San Francisco and Santa Cruz. The institution of the movie is closer to LA. It's the **Phoenix Academy** (previously the Lake View Medical Center), **11600 Eldridge** at Kagel Canyon, off Foothill Boulevard to the north of Hansen Dam Park in the San Fernando Valley. Built as a medical facility in the early seventies, it was closed, either due to earthquake damage or lack of funding, according to which story you buy, and started a new

The truck dives into the flood-control channel: Bull Creek at Plummer and Hayvenhurst

career as a movie location, but now seems to be back on course.

The new user-friendly T-800 Terminator, by another stroke of luck, finds himself naked in the San Fernando Valley at biker hangout **The Corral Bar, 12002 Osborne Street, Lakeview Terrace** (© *818.899.9944*), where he gets himself not only a leather jacket, but a cool bike, shades and a large gun as well. Meanwhile, the upgrade liquid-metal T-1000 Terminator fetches up beneath the **Sixth Street Bridge**, and has soon tracked young Connor down to Reseda. The shopping mall chase and confrontation between the two Terminators wasn't filmed in Reseda, though. The exterior is nearby, the **Northridge Mall, 9301 Tampa Avenue, Northridge**; though the interior is on the coast at Santa Monica, in the 162-store **Santa Monica Place Mall, Broadway** at Third Street (which became Ridgemont Mall in *Fast Times at Ridgemont High*). Escaping on his dirt bike, Connor tears into one of LA's concrete flood control channels, back in the San Fernando Valley. The spillway used is **Bull Creek**, which leads down to the Sepulveda Flood Control Area (in drier times, the Balboa and the Encino Golf Courses). The T-1000 gives chase in an eighteen-wheel truck, and, at the junction of **Plummer and Hayvenhurst**, makes the spectacular leap down into Bull Creek, tearing through the 40-foot wide spillway.

Having sprung mom from Pescadero, Connor and the good Terminator head out to a desert compound on the western rim of the Mojave Desert, at **Lancaster** in Antelope Valley. Mom Connor, spurred on by visions of LA engulfed in a nuclear firestorm, takes off to kill scientist Dr Dyson (Joe Morton), whose research is destined to lead to the Skynet System and hence the future war. Dyson's house, where the Terminator stomach-churningly demonstrates his non-human status, is a private home on **Pacific Coast Highway**, just west of South Malibu Canyon Road, west of Malibu (though it's not visible from the road).

The Cyberdyne HQ, high security home of the lethal cyborg chip, really is situated in California's Silicon Valley, the heart of the computer industry. The building is the **Renco Investment Company, 47131 Bayside Park**, at Gateway Boulevard, Fremont, a suburb of San Jose. A glass façade added a third storey to the building, and the

The Cyberdyne HQ: Bayside Park, Fremont

(real glass) windows were wired to blow out simultaneously with a gasoline fireball. The commandeered SWAT truck crashes through a special-

ly added lobby. Fremont is east of San Francisco Bay over the Dunbar Bridge where Route 17 intersects with Route 84.

The T-1000 oozes into the helicopter for the climactic chase sequence. LA's constantly packed freeways are vital arteries constantly teetering on the verge of terminal gridlock. Closing a section down is risking fatal thrombosis, but LA is also movie city, and there's always a way. A four-lane section of freeway was discovered down toward San Pedro. In this scruffy industrial hinterland of the port is a three-mile north-south stretch of roadway linking Sepulveda Boulevard with the naval base on Terminal Island. The **Terminal Island Freeway** could be closed for the night without major disruption to the city's traffic flow. For most of the chase, the helicopter was suspended from a crane mounted on a flatbed truck which drove along the adjacent lane, but for one hair-raising stunt, a real helicopter flew under the twenty-foot overpass of the **Pacific Coast Highway**.

The end of the chase brings the movie full circle. The steelworks, supposedly at the end of the freeway, is adjacent to the ruins at Fontana used for the opening sequence. Here a steel mill, abandoned for seventeen years, was brought to life with a battery of trick effects. Molten metal gives insurance companies panic attacks – see *The Deer Hunter* – so the film uses rivers of white paint and illuminated plastic panels amid showers of sparks.

TERMINATOR 3: RISE OF THE MACHINES
(2003, dir: Jonathan Mostow)
Arnold Schwarzenegger, Nick Stahl, Claire Danes.
● **LOS ANGELES, CALIFORNIA**

Just as *Jurassic Park III* sagged without Spielberg, so the third *Terminator* movie lacks the Cameron touch. Whereas male Terminators appeared in tough

The United Rentals branch: Built on the 7500 block of Foothill Boulevard, Sunland

areas such as LA's scuzzy downtown or the California desert, the T-X Terminatrix (Kristanna Loken) goes all girlie, and materialises in a Rodeo Drive shop window, at the glitzy complex, **Two Rodeo Drive**, Beverly Hills. But it's downhill all the way. It's in Culver City that she takes the cop's gun, and her mission to wipe out John Connor's future lieutenants takes her across downtown to the somewhat less glitzy Boyle Heights. The burger bar where she shoots the burger boy is **Jim's, 1901 East First Street** at State Street, Boyle Heights, east of downtown LA (© *323.266.3886*).

The clunky old T-800 (Schwarzenegger) materialises in the Valley again, conveniently close to Ladies' Night at the Desert Star. In reality, the raucous bar where the Terminator takes the leathers of the male stripper is **Cowboy Palace, 21635 Devonshire Street** at Owensmouth Avenue, **Chatsworth** (© *818.341.0166, www.cowboypalace.com*). The bar has also been seen in *Deep Impact*,

The Emery Animal Hospital: Built on the 7500 block of Foothill Boulevard, Sunland

Twins and *La Bamba*. This is the place, so it's claimed, you might find William Shatner line-dancing. Steady on, there. Connor himself (Stahl) is working on a building site alongside the Harbor Freeway at Wilshire Boulevard, downtown, and moping about on the **First Street Bridge** over the LA River, to the east. But when he feels the need for drugs, he's way north, in the San Fernando Valley. The Emery Animal Hospital, and the adjoining United Rentals branch, were sets built on the **7500 block of Foothill Boulevard, Sunland** (close to *Memento*'s filming locations). The road chase with the giant crane, though, is back downtown, roaring north from Boyle Heights, across the **Sixth Street Bridge** (seen in *S.W.A.T.* and beneath which the T-1000 appeared in *T2*). The spectacular destruction is a dizzying mix of CGI, real streets in the industrial area east of downtown, and a street set built at Downey.

The stash of guns is discovered in Sarah Connor's coffin at the mausoleum in **Rose Hills Cemetery, 3888 Workman Mill Road, Whittier**, southeast of LA, but the subsequent hearse chase was filmed in that reliable standby, LA's **Griffith Park**, before moving on to **Antelope Valley**, north of the city. The Skynet complex was built on the site of the old **Rockwell Defense Plant, Bellflower and Imperial Highway** in **Downey**, where sets for *Spider-Man* were constructed.

TERMS OF ENDEARMENT

(1983, dir: James L Brooks)
Shirley MacLaine, Debra Winger, Jack Nicholson.

● **TEXAS; NEBRASKA**

Oscar-laden and well acted, but soapy, tearjerker, set in **Houston**, Texas (well, where else would you be living next door to an astronaut?).

In Houston, Jack Nicholson lives at **3068 Locke Lane**, in the smart **Avalon** district. Although the house has been completely renovated, you will recognise the home of Shirley MacLaine next door. The couple's lunch date is at **Brennan's Restaurant, 3300 Smith Street**, downtown Houston (© *713.522. 9711*) – originally a branch of the

MacLaine and Nicholson's lunch date: Brennan's, Smith Street, Houston

Shirley MacLaine's house: Locke Lane, Avalon, Houston

famous New Orleans eaterie, it's since severed connections. Nicholson and MacLaine drive onto **East Beach, Galveston**. There was more filming at **River Oaks**, the posh area to the northwest of Houston.

The town Debra Winger and Jeff Daniels move to is **Lincoln**, Nebraska, where their home is at **847 14th Street**. Winger meets John Lithgow at **Leon's Food Mart, North 32nd Street** at South Street, Lincoln, and confronts the errant Daniels at the **University of Nebraska, 14th Street** at R Street. Winger tearily expires at **Lincoln General Hospital, Van Dorn Street**, while MacLaine and Nicholson finally get to mumble "I lurve you" at **Lincoln Municipal Airport, 2400 West Adams**.

TERROR, THE

(1963, dir: Roger Corman)
Boris Karloff, Jack Nicholson, Sandra Knight.

● **CALIFORNIA**

'Mr Thrift' Corman finished *The Raven* a couple of days ahead of schedule. He still had the sets and the cast, so he quickly cobbled together this little number, complete with vaguely generic title. The shots of the Baltic Coast are California's **Big Sur** coastline, south of San Francisco, photographed by second unit director Francis Ford Coppola. As if that weren't enough, Corman recycled footage from the film to pad out Peter Bogdanovich's début movie, *Target*. Why isn't this man running the economy?

TESS

(1979, dir: Roman Polanski)
Nastassja Kinski, Leigh Lawson, Peter Firth.

● **FRANCE**

Thomas Hardy's *Tess of the D'Urbervilles* filmed, not in the West Country of England, but in Brittany, northern France, around the old town of **Morlaix**, towards the northern coast.

TESTAMENT D'ORPHÉE, LE (aka *The Testament of Orpheus*)

(1960, dir: Jean Cocteau)
Jean Cocteau, Edouard Dermithe, Maria Casares.

● **FRANCE**

Cocteau's final film is a rambling, imaginative rumination on the nature of his art, with contributions from Yul Brynner and Picasso. The strange underground street is

The underground street: Rue Obscure, Villefranche-sur-Mer

rue Obscure in the old town of **Villefranche-sur-Mer**, the beautiful little fishing port just east of Nice on the French Riviera (a favourite for car-chase sequences, in *Maximum Risk*, *Never Say Never Again* and *Ronin*). It was in the subterranean warren that the French Resistance was able to evade the German army during WWII.

389

TEXAS CHAIN SAW MASSACRE, THE
(1974, dir: Tobe Hooper)
Marilyn Burns, Gunnar Hansen, Jim Siedow.
● TEXAS

Not as explicitly gory as its reputation, Hooper's grisly classic gets its nasty atmosphere across largely by suggestion. It was filmed in 16mm, with a largely amateur cast recruited from the drama department of the University of Texas in Austin, and the movie was shot in the area. The desecrated cemetery is **Bagdad Cemetery, Bagdad Road, Leander**, on Route 183, about 25 miles northwest of the city. The gas station was Ryan's Hills Prairie Grocery, which recently became **Bilbo's Texas Landmark, 1073 State Highway 304, Bastrop** (© *512.321.2049*), east of Austin.

The chicken-infested Sawyer family home stood on **Quick Hill Road, Round Rock**, I-35, about ten miles north of Austin, Texas. In 1998, after falling into disrepair, it was dismantled and transported to the grounds of the Antlers hotel in Kingsland, way to the northwest of Austin. And now? It's a restaurant. **The Four Bears, 1010 King Street, Kingsland** (© *325.388.4411, www.theantlers.com/ grill*). Best stick to the vegetarian special.

THAT'LL BE THE DAY
(1973, dir: Claude Whatham)
David Essex, Ringo Starr, Rosemary Leach.
● HAMPSHIRE

Essex plays a 1950s working class drifter, then fairground worker, who finally makes it as a pop star. The title comes from the Buddy Holly song, which in turn came from John Wayne's line in *The Searchers*. It was made on the **Isle of Wight**. The sequel, following the rise and fall of Essex's character, is *Stardust*.

THEATRE OF BLOOD
(1973, dir: Douglas Hickox)
Vincent Price, Diana Rigg, Ian Hendry.
● LONDON; BERKSHIRE

Price is the barnstorming Shakespearian ham Edward Lionheart, believed dead, who returns to kill off members of the despised Critics' Circle, using appropriately Shakespearian murders, in this gloriously tasteless black comedy, filmed entirely on location around London.

Michael Hordern's flat is in **Digby Mansions, Hammersmith Bridge Road** at Lower Mall overlooking Hammersmith Bridge (just along-

Home of the the first victim: Digby Mansions, Hammersmith

side the rowing club and pub seen in *Sliding Doors*). The mansion block was previously home to Gloria Grahame, where she's visited by German spy Stephen Boyd, in 1955 wartime drama *The Man Who Never Was*.

Jack Hawkins, who must be an *extremely* successful critic, strangles Diana Dors at his swanky Chelsea Embankment house, **8 Cheyne Walk** at

Royal Hospital Road, SW3, overlooking Albert Bridge (another location for *Sliding Doors*). Blue Plaque spotters might notice that the house is sandwiched between the former homes of poet Dante Gabriel Rossetti and George Eliot. Coral Browne gets her ash highlights well and truly lit at (now gone) Robert Fielding, Knightsbridge, SW7, opposite Harrods. Lionheart's actress daughter Edwina (Rigg) works

Lionheart's suicide: Thames embankment

on a movie filming at the **Long Walk** by Windsor Castle. Ian Hendry's apartment, and the meeting place of the Critics' Circle, from which Price plunges into the Thames, is **Peninsula Heights** (formerly Alembic House), on the Albert Embankment between Lambeth and Vauxhall Bridges. Home of disgraced peer Lord Archer, the tower's unparalleled views over the Thames and the Houses of Parliament make it irresistible to film-makers (the original *The Italian Job*, *A Touch of Class* and *Sweeney!* all filmed here).

Edwina tends her father's monument, and Dennis Price's body appears, dragged behind a horse, at **Kensal Green Cemetery, Harrow Road**, Kensal Green, NW10. Along with Highgate and Brompton, this is one of the city's great 19th-century necropolises. Among the elaborate grave monuments are the last resting places of such Victorian luminaries as engineer Isambard Kingdom Brunel, writer Anthony Trollope, Lady 'Speranza' Wilde, the mother of Oscar. Playwright and screenwriter Terence Rattigan also rests here, unmarked, in the family memorial. On screen, the cemetery was also seen in Cliff Owen's 1972 film of the British TV sitcom *Steptoe and Son*; Neil Jordan's 1999 *The End of the Affair* and *Look Back in Anger*.

The bloody theatre itself was Putney Hippodrome, on the corner of Putney High Street and Felsham Road, SW15, since demolished. Built in 1906 as a vaudeville variety house, it was converted into a cinema in the thirties but had been closed for fourteen years when it was chosen as Lionheart's hideout. The proscenium was specially built for the film, a chandelier added and 500 seats (at 50p each) were bought from the Croydon Odeon to fill the decrepit stalls.

THELMA & LOUISE
(1991, dir: Ridley Scott)
Susan Sarandon, Geena Davis, Brad Pitt.
● CALIFORNIA; UTAH; COLORADO

Feminist road movie or male fantasies in drag? You takes your choice. The movie's journey is from Arkansas through Oklahoma and Col-

The mid-west C&W bar: Cowboy Country, South Street, Long Beach

The mid-west motel: Vagabond Inn, South Figueroa Street

orado to Arizona, but the master of deceptive locations, Scott, filmed only the last third of the movie in the desert, outside greater LA and Bakersfield. And that was mainly in Utah.

The green, wet landscape of Arkansas is actually an area around **Gorman**, north of LA, and the **Lockwood Valley**, dressed with appropriate cattle. The gradual descent into the central valley of California at **Bakersfield** is used for the transition from the crowded, narrow mountains of Arkansas to the open plains of Oklahoma. It's north to **Shafter** for the train sequence, then to the dust fields and oil rigs of **Taft** in the west central valley.

The mid-west C&W bar, where the attempted rape that turns the adventure sour takes place, is in southern LA. It was the Silver Bullet, now **Cowboy Country, 3321 South Street** (© *562.630.3007*), between Obispo and Downey Avenues, Long Beach. The motel, where the pair meet up with studly JD (Pitt), can also be found in LA. It's the **Vagabond Inn, 3101 South Figueroa Street** (© *213.746.1531*), south of downtown LA.

There's some filming in the real Colorado, at **Unaweep Canyon, Grand Junction** on I-70 in the west of the state. Sarandon phones the FBI agent from **Bedrock General Store, Bedrock**, Colorado. The desert scenes, while pretending to be the rather flat New Mexico, are the spectacular sandstone landscapes of the **La Sal Mountains**, Route 46, southeast of Moab in eastern Utah; **Arches National Park**, to the north of Moab; and **Canyonlands** to the southwest. The police chase is at **Cisco**, Utah. Filming also took place at **Thompson Springs** and **Valley City**. And the Grand Canyon? Nope. The spectacular gorge of the final scene is not the Grand Canyon, but **Shafer Overlook**, at **Gooseneck State Park**, the snaking s-bends of the San Juan River near the bizarre rock formation of Mexican Hat, Route 163 down in the southeast corner of Utah.

THEM!

(1954, dir: Gordon Douglas)
Edmund Gwenn, James Whitmore, Joan Weldon.
● **CALIFORNIA**

Classic fifties sci-fi, with atomic tests giving rise to giant mutated ants. The ants appear initially in the New Mexico desert – actually the Mojave Desert around **Palmdale**, California – but soon they're headed for the concrete spillways of LA, popping out at the **Sixth Street Viaduct**, downtown, seen also in *Repo Man*, *Terminator 3* and *S.W.A.T.*.

THERE'S SOMETHING ABOUT MARY

(1998, dir: Bobby Farrell; Peter Farrelly)
Cameron Diaz, Ben Stiller, Matt Dillon.
● **MIAMI, FLORIDA; RHODE ISLAND**

The high school, where nerdy Ben Stiller doesn't quite make it to the prom with Cameron Diaz, is **Plantation City Hall, Plantation**, down on highway 1 in the Florida Keys. Most of the film is shot around Miami. The café where Matt Dillon meets Jeffrey Tambor is the **Big Pink Restaurant, 157 Collins Avenue**, south of South Beach's art deco district. Diaz takes faker Dillon to an architecture exhibition at the **Center for the Fine Arts**, in the **Miami Dade Cultural Center, 101 West Flagler Street**, downtown Miami. Cameron Diaz's office, where Stiller meets up with her after 13 years, is on the downtown Miami waterfront at **Brickell Park**, overlooking the Brickell Key Causeway. Stiller's Miami hotel, site of the movie's most infamous 'pipe cleaning' scene, is the **Cardozo Hotel, 1300 Ocean Drive** at 14th Street (© *305.535.6500* ,*www.cardozohotel.com*). This art deco gem can also be seen in *A Hole in the Head*.

The waterside bar, where Dillon reports back to Ben Stiller, though, can be found in Rhode island. It's **The Hot Club, 575 South Water Street** off Bridge Street (© *401.861.9007*), **Providence**, Rhode Island.

THEY DIED WITH THEIR BOOTS ON

(1941, dir: Raoul Walsh)
Errol Flynn, Olivia de Havilland, Arthur Kennedy.
● **NEW YORK**

This highly fictionalised account of Custer's Last Stand was shot partly at **West Point Military Academy**, as a thinly disguised recruiting drive. Director Walsh was made a brother of the Sioux Nation in a publicity stunt toward the end of the shoot. Only the ninth white person to receive such an honour, he was named Thunder Hawk. The Academy is on the Hudson River, Route 9W, north of New York City.

Matt Dillon meets Jeffrey Tambor: Big Pink Restaurant, Collins Avenue, Miami Beach

Cleaning the pipes: Cardozo Hotel, Ocean Drive, Miami Beach

The architecture exhibition: Dade Cultural Center

Cameron Diaz's office: Brickell Park

THEY DRIVE BY NIGHT
(1940, dir: Raoul Walsh)
George Raft, Humphrey Bogart, Ann Sheridan.
● CALIFORNIA

Tough, pacy trucking drama, using locations around **Wharf No2, Monterey**, northern California.

THEY LIVE BY NIGHT
(1948, dir: Nicholas Ray)
Farley Granger, Cathy O'Donnell, Howard da Silva.
● LOS ANGELES, CALIFORNIA

Ray's stylish melodrama, remade by Robert Altman in 1974 as *Thieves Like Us*, has Granger as a young con escaping with a couple of hardened criminals and enjoying a doomed romance with O'Donnell while on the run. Made in the RKO Studios and around LA. The opening helicopter shot is **Canoga Park**, northwest LA.

Altman's 1974 remake, *Thieves Like Us*, filmed in Jackson and Canton, Mississippi.

THEY SHOOT HORSES, DON'T THEY?
(1969, dir: Sydney Pollack)
Jane Fonda, Michael Sarrazin, Gig Young.
● LOS ANGELES, CALIFORNIA

A clutch of great performances, as desperate couples struggle to survive a dance marathon during the thirties Depression, with Gig Young's cynical compere scooping a Best Actor Oscar. The dance hall is on the **Santa Monica Pier, Colorado Avenue**, Santa Monica, LA. Additional filming took place at Myron's Ballroom, now dance club **Grand Avenue, 1024 South Grand Avenue**, downtown LA (seen in *New York New York*).

THIEF OF BAGDAD, THE
(1940, dir: Ludwig Berger; Michael Powell; Tim Whelan)
Sabu, Conrad Veidt, John Justin.
● CORNWALL; ARIZONA

Alexander Korda's lavish Arabian Nights fantasy began filming in the UK, but ultimately shifted to the US as WWII threatened production. It had been intended to film in the Middle East but this obviously became impossible. The beach, where Sabu unleashes the Genie of the Bottle, is **Sennen Cove**, about a mile north of Land's End on the western tip of Cornwall. The other spectacular locations were found in the US, at the **Grand Canyon** and in the **Painted Desert**, at the multicoloured plateau of the Little Colorado River to the southeast.

THIN RED LINE, THE
(1998, dir: Terrence Malick)
Sean Penn, Jim Caviezel, Ben Chaplin.
● QUEENSLAND, AUSTRALIA; SOLOMON ISLANDS

The eagerly-awaited return to film from reclusive director Malick (*Badlands* and *Days of Heaven*) is a war drama set during the crucial 1942-43 Guadalcanal campaign of WWII, and indeed part of the movie was shot near **Honiara**, the capital of Guadalcanal, largest of the Solomon Islands in the Pacific. For the most part, however, the lush jungle is the **Daintree Rainforest**, about 50 miles north of Cairns, Queensland, on the northeastern coast of Australia.

THING, THE (aka *The Thing From Another World*)
(1951, dir: Christian Nyby; and possibly Howard Hawks)
James Arness, Robert Cornthwaite, Kenneth Tobey.
● LOS ANGELES, CALIFORNIA; MONTANA

The RKO original, with James Arness (Matt Dillon in TV's *Gunsmoke*) as a human vegetable from space. The Arctic location, where the creature is discovered (a scene being shown on TV in John Carpenter's original *Halloween*) is Montana. The first choice had been Fairbanks or Nome in Alaska, but the presence of sensitive USAF bases saw the Pentagon stepping in to nix that idea. The final choice was **Cut Bank**, in Glacier National Park about 100 miles northwest of Great Falls on I-2, northern Montana, where the cast stayed at the Glacier Hotel. The fire and explosion were filmed out on the **Iverson Movie Ranch**, Chatsworth, 30 miles north of LA. Arctic scenes were also shot in the ice-house of a meat packing company on Mesquit Street, alongside the Los Angeles River, southeast of downtown, also used for filming snow scenes in Frank Capra's *Lost Horizon*.

THING, THE
(1982, dir: John Carpenter)
Kurt Russell, A Wilford Brimley, Richard Dysart.
● BRITISH COLUMBIA, CANADA; ALASKA

John Carpenter's FX-heavy remake bombed at the box-office but has since acquired a heavy reputation. The snowbound locations were found in British Columbia. The opening icescapes are icefields above **Juneau**, Alaska.

THIRD MAN, THE
(1949, dir: Carol Reed)
Joseph Cotten, Orson Welles, Alida Valli.
● AUSTRIA; LONDON

Naïve Western writer Holly Martins (Cotten) arrives in war-ravaged **Vienna** on the promise of a job from his friend, the shady Harry Lime (Welles). Graham Greene's story is given heavy impressionist treatment with wildly tilting camera angles. After seeing the film,

Harry Lime's first appearance: Schreyvogelgasse, Vienna

veteran director William Wyler sent Reed a spirit level.

The movie makes great use of the rubble-strewn city, though some interiors were reconstructed at Shepperton Studios in London. Arriving at **Westbahnbof, Europaplatz** (Vienna's West Railway Station, where he later goes to watch Anna Schmidt [Valli] depart), Martins is taken to Harry Lime's apartment building, which is supposedly 15 Stiftgasse. The palatial building, though, with its statuesque entrance, is **Palais Pallavicini, Josefsplatz 5**, which is where Martins learns his pal died after being hit

Harry Lime's 'cuckoo clock' speech: Prater

by a truck. Lime is – apparently – being buried with the great and the good in Vienna's Central Cemetery, the **Zentral-Friedhof, Simmeringen Hauptstrasse** in District 11. A deleted shot, intended to establish the locale, panned across the memorials of celeb internees Brahms and Beethoven. Music lovers can also pay homage at the graves of Schubert and the Strausses.

At the funeral, Martins meets English intelligence officer Major Calloway, who arranges for him to stay at the venerable **Hotel Sacher Wien, Philharmonikerstrasse 4** (© *0222.514560*, *wien.sacher.com*), behind the Opera House. At today's top-of-the-range rates, that's a pretty generous offer.

Martins meets Lime's sinisterly camp friend, Kurtz, at another Viennese institution, the Cafe Mozart. Although the scene was not actually filmed at the café, but nearby, on **Tegetthofstrasse** at Neuer Markt, you'll probably want to visit anyway: Cafe Mozart, Albertinaplatz 2.

And, like Holly Martins, going to see Anna, you can still attend performances at the **Theater in der Josefstadt Theatre, Josefstadterstrasse 26** (© *0222.4025127*); or spend some time at the **Casanova Club, Dorotheergasse 6**, where Martins meets Kurtz and the second man to witness Lime's 'accident', Popescu. You can take a stroll on the **Reichsbrucke**, over the Danube, but it's not the same bridge on which Dr Winkel meets up with Kurtz, Popescu and the mysterious third man. A sleek, modern structure has replaced the original suspension bridge, which collapsed in the 1970s.

Harry Lime finally makes his long-awaited entrance, a kitten nibbling the laces of his shoes (the laces having been coated with pilchard) in the ornate doorway at **8 Schreyvogelgasse**. The unpredictable Welles proved to be almost as elusive as Lime himself, and wasn't always available for filming. As the sly racketeer scoots off into the night, the shadow on the wall is actually that of assistant director Guy Hamilton, director of several Bond movies, including *Goldfinger* and *The Man With the Golden Gun*. The vast, cobbled square, in which Lime disappears, is **Am Hof**. Disappointingly, you won't see the central kiosk that hides the entrance to the sewers in the movie – it was no more than a prop erected for the film.

Lime comes to meet Martins at the big wheel (where Welles gives his, allegedly, self-penned 'cuckoo clock' speech). The **Riesenrad**, the Grand Ferris Wheel, erected in 1896 and restored in 1948 after war damage, still stands in the **Prater**, Vienna's huge park in District 2, between the Danube and the Danube Canal (*subway: Praterstern*). Finally convinced of Lime's villainy, Martins colludes with the trap, set at **Hoher Markt**, the oldest square in Vienna, with its elaborate 17th-century nuptial fountain. Lime retreats into the sewers beneath the city, where his career is cut short. You can tour the sewer system, if you like. For latest details, consult the Vienna

tourist board site: *wien.info*. You can also take guided *Third Man* walking tours of the city, *www.viennawalks.tix.at*.

39 STEPS, THE
(1935, dir: Alfred Hitchcock)
Robert Donat, Madeleine Carroll, Godfrey Tearle.
● **LONDON; SCOTLAND**

Hannay leaves the milkman's horse and cart: Park Crescent East

This Hitchcock classic was shot almost entirely in the studio, at the old Lime Grove Studios, Shepherds Bush, demolished in the nineties. Richard Hannay (Donat) supposedly lives at 122 Portland Place, but the exterior was recreated in the studio, and the grand six-lane road is reduced to the width of a minor sidestreet. Around the corner from Portland Place is **Park Crescent East**, the pillared semicircle south of Marylebone Road. The eastern curve is where Hannay leaves the milkman's horse and cart, borrowed after the murder of the mysterious woman.

Hannay's train journey to Scotland takes him over the **Forth Bridge**, spanning the Firth of Forth, between Edinburgh and Dunfermline. The climax leads back to London, with the unfortunate Mr Memory getting a bullet at the **London Palladium, Argyll Street**, W1 (© *020.7494.5020*). This 2,286-seat theatre became something of a national institution during the fifties and sixties, when the entire nation would round off the weekend huddled in front of their black and white TV sets to watch variety show *Sunday Night at the London Palladium*. In 1963, a coolly professional Dirk Bogarde persuades a quiveringly neurotic, and very drunk, Judy Garland to brave the Palladium's stage and belt out the title number of her final film, *I Could Go on Singing*.

The bland and boring 1959 remake of *The 39 Steps* (filmed virtually shot for shot, but for a prologue in **Regent's Park**, north London) also features the Forth Bridge.

37°2 LE MATIN (aka *Betty Blue/37°2 in the Morning*)
(1986, dir: Jean-Jacques Beineix)
Jean-Hugues Anglade, Beatrice Dalle, Gerard Darmon.
● **FRANCE**

Anglade is the indolent under-achiever who realises his potential as a writer after an affair with irritatingly intolerable wacko Dalle. In the Director's Cut, there are an extra 60 minutes of stylishly photographed pouting and tantrums until the most welcome pillow job since *One Flew Over the Cuckoo's Nest*. The coastal village of the opening scenes, with its stilt houses, is **Gruissan**, ten miles southeast of Narbonne in the Languedoc-Rousillon area toward the Spanish border. The other French villages used are **Marvejois**, a tiny market town in the

Colagne Valley about 100 miles north of Narbonne on E9/N9, and **Nogent-sur-Marne**, east of Paris.

THIS IS SPINAL TAP
(1984, dir: Rob Reiner)
Christopher Guest, Michael McKean, Harry Shearer.
● LOS ANGELES, CALIFORNIA; TENNESSEE

Tap's version of 'Heartbreak Hotel' at the King's grave: Graceland, Memphis

Spot-on mockumentary, well-deserving its regular place in lists of the funniest movies of all time, following the rock group of the title. The Atlanta record office is the futuristic **Westin Bonaventure Hotel, 404 South Figueroa Street**, downtown LA. The group pays tribute to the King with a moving version of 'Heartbreak Hotel' at his tastefully restrained graveside in the grounds of **Graceland, 3717 Elvis Presley Boulevard, Memphis**, Tennessee (*©* *901.332.3322*). Spot how the necessarily reverential longshots, on location, are craftily spliced into wicked close-ups, which were filmed separately. Concert scenes were shot in the

The concert scenes: Raymond Theatre, Pasadena

The Atlanta record office: Westin Bonaventure Hotel

Raymond Theatre, 129 North Raymond Avenue, Pasadena, seen also in *Pulp Fiction*. The future of the, currently closed, historic gem is uncertain. You can join the Friends of the Raymond Theatre campaign to save it from redevelopment at *www.raymondtheatre.com*.

The rooftop pool is atop the **Continental Hyatt, 8401 Sunset Boulevard**, on the Strip in west Hollywood, the infamous Riot House (see Cameron Crowe's *Almost Famous* for details).

THIS SPORTING LIFE
(1963, dir: Lindsay Anderson)
Richard Harris, Rachel Roberts, William Hartnell.
● YORKSHIRE

Harris sprang to fame as the tough but sensitive rugby player Frank Machin in Anderson's grim tale of the dour monochrome north. Machin's rugby club is Wakefield Trinity Rugby League Club, now **Wakefield Wildcats, Doncaster Road, Belle Vue, Wakefield**, in West Yorkshire (*www.trinitywildcats.co.uk*). Frank takes his widowed landlady Margaret (Roberts) and her kids for a dayout at **Bolton Abbey, Skipton**, northwest of Bradford (*©*

01756.718009, www.boltonabbey.com).

THOMAS CROWN AFFAIR, THE
(1968, dir: Norman Jewison)
Steve McQueen, Faye Dunaway, Paul Burke.
● MASSACHUSETTS

The bank robbery: Congress Street, Boston

Unlikely insurance investigator Dunaway on the trail of bored tycoon McQueen, who's pulled off a bank heist, in Jewison's glossy, romantic thriller, set around the wealthier areas of **Boston**. The opening bank robbery used a real bank (even grabbing authentic reaction shots with a hidden camera), at **55 Congress Street** in the Financial district. The polo match, where Faye Dunaway first sees Steve McQueen, is at the **Myopia Hunt Club, Hamilton**, on Route 1A, 20 miles northeast of Boston.

THOMAS CROWN AFFAIR, THE
(1999, dir: John McTiernan)
Pierce Brosnan, Rene Russo, Denis Leary.
● NEW YORK CITY; NEW YORK; MARTINIQUE

Crown's posh townhouse: Bell Residence, East 68th Street

For McTiernan's witty and stylish update, Thomas Crown (Brosnan) now robs an art gallery. The exterior of the gallery is, quite obviously, New York's **Metropolitan Museum of Art, Fifth Avenue** at 82nd Street (*©* *212.535.7710, www.metmuseum.org*), though it is never identified as such in the movie. The gallery had a problem admitting the possibility of such a robbery and refused cooperation. They couldn't, however, prevent filming of the exterior, which belongs to the city of New York, which is why the exhibition banners change from shot to shot. The interior galleries are impressive studio sets, but the entrance concourse is the **New York Public Library, Fifth Avenue** at 42nd Street (*©* *212.869.8089; www.nypl.org*) – the exterior of which was the haunted library in *Ghostbusters*.

Crown's suitably posh townhouse is the 1925 **Bell Residence, 16 East 68th Street**, though the lavish interior was created in a warehouse in Yonkers.

The restaurant, where insurance investigator Catherine Banning (Russo) borrows Crown's keys, is

The art gallery, interior: New York Library, Fifth Avenue

The art gallery, exterior: Metropolitan Museum of Art, Fifth Avenue

the **Harry Cipriani Restaurant** in the **Sherry-Netherland Hotel, 781 Fifth Avenue** (© *212.355.2800, www.sherry-netherland.com*). The entrance to Crown Towers, Thomas Crown's luxury office building, was an unoccupied office near New York's Stock Exchange, but the terrific view over the East River is from the window of Lucent Technologies. The National Arts Club (you can see the real thing in Martin Scorsese's *The Age of Innocence* and Woody Allen's *Manhattan Murder Mystery*) is the 1850 Italianate mansion which houses **Bayard's, 1 Hanover Square**, in between Pearl and Stone Streets (© *212.514.9454*) in the Financial District, on the outside, while inside, it's **Manhattanville College, Purchase**, New York. The ballroom of the Pierre Hotel (the real thing is seen in *Scent of a Woman*), where Banning comes on strong to Crown, is the old library of **Bronx College, University Avenue** at West 181st Street. Thomas Crown's exotic getaway is the island of **Martinique**.

THREE DAYS OF THE CONDOR
(1975, dir: Sydney Pollack)
Robert Redford, Max von Sydow, Faye Dunaway.
● NEW YORK CITY

New York-set conspiracy thriller, with Redford on the run from assassins after escaping a massacre in the office where he works. The office is the 1902 Beaux Arts house at **55 East 77th Street** at Madison Avenue on the East Side. He's set up and narrowly escapes death in the alleyway behind the **Ansonia Hotel, 2109 Broadway**, between West 73rd and West 74th Streets. Villainous Cliff Robertson's office was in the World Trade Center, Lower Manhattan. Dunaway lives in Brooklyn Heights, and Redford has a confrontation with Robertson on **Brooklyn Heights Promenade**, over the East River from Lower Manhattan.

THREE KINGS
(1999, dir: David O Russell)
George Clooney, Mark Wahlberg, Ice Cube.
● ARIZONA; MEXICO

Russell's intelligent, cinematically thrilling adventure, set in the aftermath of the Gulf War, needed a flat, blasted landscape to represent the featureless wastes of Iraq. The opening scene is a dry lake bed outside **Mexicali**, Mexico. Most of the film was shot at the abandoned **Sacaton Copper Mine** at **Casa Grande**, between Tucson and Phoenix, Arizona, where chemical poisoning had wiped out any vegetation. The Iraqi villages were constructed on various plateaux left after the extraction of the mineral ore.

3 MEN AND A BABY
(1987, dir: Leonard Nimoy)
Ted Danson, Tom Selleck, Steve Guttenberg.

● **NEW YORK CITY; ONTARIO, CANADA**

This remake of the 1985 French film *Three Men and a Cradle* is set in New York, but is one of the increasing number of films shot, for financial reasons, largely in Toronto. Real New York locations include the bachelor apartment, **50 Central Park West** – next to Sigourney Weaver's haunted block from *Ghostbusters*.

The three men's apartment: Central Park West

Much of the movie shot in Toronto: Royal Alex Theatre, King Street West

The Toronto locations include the **Royal Alex Theatre, 260 King Street West**; the **John Innes Community Centre**; **Scotia Plaza**; and **Duncan Street** at Pearl Street. As with many Toronto-based films (*Chicago*, *X-Men*), sets were built in the old **Gooderham & Worts distillery building**.

THREE MUSKETEERS: THE QUEEN'S DIAMONDS, THE
(1973, dir: Richard Lester)
Michael York, Oliver Reed, Richard Chamberlain.
● SPAIN

Quirkily off-centre version of the Dumas classic. Set, naturally, in France, it was filmed back to back with the sequel, *The Four Musketeers: The Revenge of Milady*, around Spain. The decadent court of Versailles, where Anna of Austria (Geraldine Chaplin) rides a human-powered roundabout, King Louis XIII (Jean-Pierre Cassel) plays living chess and d'Artagnan (York) finally becomes a musketeer, is the **Palacio Real, Aranjuez**. The Royal Palace, dating from 1722, was built in the classical style after fire destroyed Charles V's extension to Philip II's original hunting lodge.

The Bastille, where Bonancieux (Spike Milligan) is questioned by Cardinal Richelieu (Charlton Heston), is the **Alcazar, Segovia**, a mid-14th-century building remodelled in the 15th century. A royal residence until 1570, it subsequently became a state prison. The Hotel de Ville, scene of the climactic ball, where the queen reveals her jewels, is **La Granja de San Ildefonso**, a mini-Versailles 30 miles northwest of Madrid, built in the 1720s as a summer lodge for Philip V. The firework display is by the **Gran Cascada** here. More French locations were found at the palace of **Riofrío**, about 40 miles northwest of Madrid.

THREE MUSKETEERS, THE
(1993, dir: Stephen Herek)
Kiefer Sutherland, Charlie Sheen, Chris O'Donnell.
● AUSTRIA; CORNWALL

The bratpacky remake, from the director of the first *Bill and Ted* movie, was shot on location in Austria, where the town square was built next to the village church of **Perchtoldsdorf**, just southwest of Vienna. There was more filming in Cornwall (where Milady plummets to her death from the cliffs), at **Charlestown Harbour**, on the south coast by St Austell.

THROUGH A GLASS, DARKLY
(1961, dir: Ingmar Bergman)
Harriet Andersson, Gunnar Bjornstrand, Max von Sydow.
● SWEDEN

One of Bergman's bleakest dramas of non-communication, with Harriet Andersson suffering a breakdown, culminating in a disturbing vision of God as a malign spider. The first of many of the director's movies to be filmed in the barren landscape of the private island of **Faro**.

THROW MOMMA FROM THE TRAIN
(1987, dir: Danny DeVito)
Billy Crystal, Danny DeVito, Anne Ramsey.
● LOS ANGELES, CALIFORNIA; HAWAII

Blackish (though not quite as dark as it promises) comedy, with mother-ridden DeVito inspired by Hitchcock's *Strangers on a Train* to swap murders with Billy Crystal. The college, where Billy Crystal teaches creative writing, is **Los Angeles Valley College, 5800 Fulton Avenue** at Burbank Boulevard, North Hollywood in the San Fernando Valley. DeVito sneaks off to Hawaii to bump off Crystal's wife, who stays at the **Sheraton Princeville Hotel, 5520 Ka Haku Road** overlooking Hanalei Bay on Kauai's spectacular north shore. It all ends (sort of) happily on nearby **Ke'e Beach**.

THUNDERBALL
(1965, dir: Terence Young)
Sean Connery, Claudine Auger, Adolfo Celi.
● BAHAMAS; FRANCE; FLORIDA; NORTHAMPTONSHIRE; BUCKINGHAMSHIRE

The fourth Bond, eagerly awaited after *Goldfinger*, had the biggest budget of the series so far and was the first shot in full Panavision widescreen. It turned out to be phenomenally successful, despite a protracted underwater battle that just drags on forever. The opening teaser, with Bond (Connery) beating the life out of the rather butch widow at the funeral and the jetpack escape, is at the **Château d'Anet** (© *33.2.37.41.90.07*, *www.chateaux-france.com/anet.e*n), a partly-destroyed palace built for Diane de Poitiers at Anet, about 50 miles west of Paris.

Largo (Celi) arrives at the Centre International d'Assistance Aux Personnes Déplacées, which is a front for the SPECTRE HQ, on **Avenue d'Eylau**, in the 16th arrondissement, northwest of the Palais de Chaillot, Paris. Shrublands, the health farm where Bond roasts Count Lippe in the Sitz bath, was **Chalfont Park House, Chalfont St Peter, Gerrards Cross**, a converted hotel in Buckinghamshire, near to the Pinewood studios. The incineration of Count Lippe, blown up in his car, uses **Silverstone** racetrack in Northamptonshire.

Most of the other locations are – surprise! – at Nassau, in the Bahamas. The swish nightspot, where Bond gambles with Largo and dances with Domino (Auger), is the **Cafe Martinique** on **Paradise Island**, a two-mile strip of sand and rock at the outer edge of Nassau harbour. The dressed-up-to-the-eyeballs extras are locals, tempted out in their poshest frocks, with the promise of free caviar and champers – very much director Terence Young's style. At the time, the island could be reached only by boat (there's now a bridge) and was called by its pre-tourism name of Hog Island.

Largo's Palmyra estate, with its shark-infested swimming pool, was the summer home of the Nicholas Sullivans of Philadelphia (no, I don't know who they are, either), **Rock Point, West Bay Street**, east of Compass Point on **New Providence Island**. The Junkanoo, Nassau's Boxing Day parade, used **Parade Street** in downtown Nassau.

The stolen Vulcan bomber crash-lands in the sea off **Rose Island**, on the northeastern coast of New Providence Island. It is hidden alongside **Clifton Wall**, part of Nassau Harbour, where the framework of the purpose-built prop (despite being blown up after filming) can still be seen, almost alongside the sunken freighter from the *Thunderball* remake, *Never Say Never Again*. The speargun sequence uses the Golden Grotto, now known as **Thunderball Reef**.

Clifton Pier in Nassau Harbour is the site of Bond and Domino's underwater tryst, though the beach where they come ashore is the aptly-named **Love Beach** (it's actually named for the Love family), west of Gambier Village on the northwest shore of New Providence. The climactic, and tiresomely protracted, underwater battle is also alongside Clifton Pier. The underwater scenes were staged by Ricou Browning, the veteran diver inside the rubber suit as the original *Creature From the Black Lagoon*, and a few close-up shots were recreated at the all-purpose underwater location of **Silver Springs** in Florida, where much of the *Creature* movie was shot. Silver Springs is a tourist attraction just east of Ocala, Route 40, central Florida. Also in Florida are the skydiving frogmen – that's clearly the city of Miami in the background.

Bond's Aston Martin, which appears in both *Thunderball* and *Goldfinger*, can be seen in Carbo's Smoky Mountain Car Museum, Pigeon Forge, Route 66, southeast of Knoxville in eastern Tennessee.

THX 1138
(1970, dir: George Lucas)
Robert Duvall, Donald Pleasence, Maggie McOmie.
● CALIFORNIA

George Lucas' first feature film, before he went on to *American Graffiti* and the phenomenally successful *Star Wars* films, is a self-consciously film-student art movie. Set in a clinically dystopian future, the film utilised a number of real Cali-

The clinical future: Marin County Civic Center, San Rafael

fornian locations. The claustrophobic underground environment is the (uncompleted) tunnel system of the **San Francisco Bay Area Rapid Transit** system (BART). Other locations include the **Lawrence Hall of Science, 1 Centennial Drive**, in the hills above the main University of California campus at Berkeley, and Frank Lloyd Wright's magnificent fifties extravaganza, the **Marin County Civic Center, Civic Center Drive, San Rafael**, northern California (seen also in *Gattaca*).

TIGER BAY
(1959, dir: J Lee Thompson)
Hayley Mills, John Mills, Horst Buchholz.
● WALES

Hayley Mills is kidnapped by, but ends up protecting, Polish sailor Horst Buchholz, who is wanted by the police for the murder of his girlfriend. Made around **Cardiff**, and at sea in the Bristol Channel.

TIGERLAND
(2000, dir: Joel Schumacher)
Colin Farrell, Matthew Davis, Clifton Collins Jr.
● FLORIDA

Joel Schumacher continued his self-imposed exile to Indieland penitence after the overblown disaster of *Batman and Robin*, though this softer cousin of *Full Metal Jacket* isn't the Dogme-style experience promised. This love-letter to the bad boy with a heart of gold never found an audience, though it launched the career of professional hellraiser Farrell. Set in 1971, in the Fort Polk boot camp, Louisiana, the movie was shot, in 28 days, without the luxury of trailers or hairdressers or any of the usual paraphernalia of Hollywood, at **Fort Blanding**, on the shore of Kingsley Lake, a few miles east of **Starke**, north Florida (where parts of *GI Jane* were shot). Dating from 1939, the camp is the Florida Army National Guard's primary training area. A large area of the base is now a state park. You can visit the Camp Blanding Museum, Building 3040, Tallahassee Street, Starke (*© 904.682.3196*).

TIME BANDITS
(1981, dir: Terry Gilliam)
Craig Warnock, David Rappaport, John Cleese.
● MOROCCO; WALES; BERKSHIRE

The home of young time-traveller Kevin (Warnock) is at **Haywood, Birch Hill** in **Bracknell**, Berkshire. The ruined castle, where Napoleon (Ian Holm) enjoys watching little people hit each other, is **Raglan Castle** in Wales. Ancient Greece, where Kevin meets Agamemnon (Sean Connery), is **Aït Ben Haddou** near Ourzazate in southern Morocco (conveniently close to the Aloha Golf Course for Sean Connery), a familiar location from films like *The Jewel of the Nile* and *Gladiator*. The sinking of the Titanic is colourised footage from the British account of the disaster, *A Night to Remember*.

TIN MEN
(1987, dir: Barry Levinson)
Richard Dreyfuss, Danny DeVito, Barbara Hershey.
● MARYLAND

Dreyfuss and DeVito are feuding aluminium salesmen in sixties Baltimore. The house, where the *Life* magazine scam – "a monument to your good taste" – is foisted on a gullible housewife, is director Berry Levinson's old home, at **4211 Springdale Avenue, Forest Park**, south of Liberty Heights Avenue. The Cadillac showroom, outside which Dreyfuss gets his new motor dented, is **242 West 29th Street**, near Remington Avenue, south of Johns Hopkins University campus. DeVito lives, not on Pimlico Road, but at **3107 Cliftmount**. The restaurant/piano lounge, where DeVito and pals hang out, is elegant dining room the **John Eager Howard Room** of the **Belvedere Hotel, 1 East Chase Street**. The Belvedere, now a restaurant and residential condominiums, can be found in the Mount Vernon district. Outside, Dreyfuss kicks in headlights and zooms off down **East Chase Street**. The diner, where DeVito and Dreyfuss eat, is a nod to an earlier Levinson film. It's the **Hollywood Diner, 400 East Saratoga Street**, the main setting for *Diner*.

TIREZ SUR LE PIANISTE (aka *Shoot the Pianist*)
(1960, dir: François Truffaut)
Charles Aznavour, Marie Dubois, Nicole Berger.
● FRANCE

Truffaut's second full-length feature, from the novel *Down There* by David Goodis. Filmed at a café, **A la Bonne Franquette, rue Mussard, Levallois** near Paris, and at **Le Sappey**, 15 miles from Grenoble.

TITANIC
(1997, dir: James Cameron)
Leonardo DiCaprio, Kate Winslet, Gloria Stuart.
● MEXICO; NORTH ATLANTIC; SAN FRANCISCO, CALIFORNIA

Fourteen Academy Award nominations, eleven wins – tying with *Ben-Hur* for top Oscar winner of all time. The vast *Titanic* set was constructed, in 100 days, as a fully-functioning studio at **Rosarito Beach**, 18 miles south of Tijuana on the Mexican coast, though not without a wave of protest from local residents. Footage of the real *Titanic* wreck on the floor of the North Atlantic is used in the opening scenes. Twelve dives were made down to the hulk of the ship, and on the last two the remotely operated camera, intended only as a prop, went deeper into the ship than any other previous dive.

The engine room is the Triple Expansion Engine of the **SS Jeremiah O'Brien**, the **National Liberty Ship Memorial**, which you can visit at **Pier 45, Fisherman's Wharf**, San Francisco (used also in sci-fi epic *Sphere*).

TITFIELD THUNDERBOLT, THE
(1952, dir: Charles Crichton)
Stanley Holloway, George Relph, Naunton Wayne.
● AVON; OXFORDSHIRE; LONDON

The scheming

The commuters off to work: Mill Lane

397

Site of the old station: Monckton Coombe

The farm: Mott Farm

owner of a coach service attempts to close down an old steam train service. Just when all seems lost, the locals rally round to save the day, in this archetypal people-versus-business Ealing comedy. Filmed, in luscious colour, on the now-defunct railway line at Limpley Stoke, near Bath. The fictitious Titfield-Mallingford branch line is a seven mile stretch of track between **Limpley Stoke** and **Camerton**, just south of Bath. Junction Point is actually Bristol. The station was a derelict stop at **Monckton Coombe**, just a couple of miles south of Bath. The village, with its distinctive mill chimney, is still recognisable. The road down which the commuters march to catch the Thunderbolt is **Mill Lane**, which has changed only slightly over the years. The turning into the station entrance is now a sadly overgrown mess, and the site of Titfield Station is now buried under tennis courts, though you can still clearly make out the site, and the route of the old line along the valley of the River Misbourne. Across the valley, you can see **Mott Farm**, the farmhouse pillaged for pots and pans after the water tank is sabotaged. Stanley Holloway's house is in the village of **Freshford**.

There was one day's filming with the locomotive *The Lion* at Bristol's **Temple Meads Station**, standing in for Mallingford. The derailed train, which takes to the road, isn't a train at all, but a shell built onto a lorry chassis. Its night-time journey filmed in the village of **Woodstock**, Oxfordshire. The railway museum, from which the locals steal a steam engine and manhandle it down a flight of steps, was the old Imperial Institute, since demolished, which stood on Exhibition Road, Kensington.

TO CATCH A THIEF
(1955, dir: Alfred Hitchcock)
Cary Grant, Grace Kelly, Jessie Royce Landis.
● **FRANCE; MONACO**

Minor Hitchcock, kept afloat by the sparkling interplay between Grant and Kelly, set against the glitzy background of the French Riviera, where Grant, suspected of being a cat burglar, sets out to unmask the real culprit. Kelly stays at the Carlton Hotel, now the **Carlton Inter-Continental, 58 la Croisette, Cannes** (℃

The flower market: Cours Saleya, Nice

04.93.06.40.06, cannes.intercontinental.com). Monte Carlo has been drastically, and grossly, redeveloped, and the terrace restaurant on the bay is long gone. Cary Grant's villa is just below the huge rocky outcrop of **Baou de St Jeannet**. The flower market is on **Cours Saleya**, in the old town of **Nice**. The bridge is at **Éze**. The chase was shot on the **Grande Corniche**, above Monte Carlo.

Grace Kelly's hotel: Carlton Hotel, Cannes

TO DIE FOR
(1995, dir: Gus Van Sant)
Nicole Kidman, Joaquin Phoenix, Matt Dillon.
● **ONTARIO, CANADA; FLORIDA**

Black comedy from indie director Van Sant, shot around Toronto. The high school is **King City**, about 15 miles north of Toronto. The movie was shot at **Jackson's Point,**

The observatory: McLaughlin Planetarium, Toronto

Lake Simcoe; **Brampton**, a western suburb of Toronto; **Georgetown**, just west of Toronto; **Hamilton**, a southern suburb on the south shore of Lake Ontario; **Mississauga**, to the southwest; **Oakville**, southwest Mississauga; **Schomberg**, north toward Lake Simcoe; **Whitby**, about 20 miles east of Toronto; and **Port Hope**, on the shore of Lake Ontario a further 60 miles east. The observatory is the **McLaughlin Planetarium**. Suzanne and Larry's honeymoon, however, did film in Florida.

TO KILL A MOCKINGBIRD
(1962, dir: Robert Mulligan)
Gregory Peck, Mary Badham, Philip Alford.
● **LOS ANGELES, CALIFORNIA**

Peck takes home the Best Actor Oscar as Atticus Finch, the lawyer in the Deep South who has his work cut out defending a black man accused of rape. Harper Lee, author of the original novel, based the fictitious setting of Maycomb on hometown Monroeville in Alabama, which seemed the obvious place to film. But the town had undergone too many changes and the movie ended up being shot on the Universal backlot in Hollywood. Monroeville is on Route 21, between Mobile and Montgomery, Alabama.

TO THE DEVIL A DAUGHTER
(1975, dir: Peter Sykes)
Richard Widmark, Christopher Lee, Denholm Elliott.
● **BUCKINGHAMSHIRE**

When Satanists promise Natassja Kinski to the Devil, her father, Denholm Elliott, appeals to occult novelist Widmark for help, in this adaptation of a Dennis Wheatley

Satanic goings-on at the home of the Hellfire club: West Wycombe Caves

novel. Filming took place at **West Wycombe Caves**, legendary haunt of the notorious Hellfire Club, off the A40 at West Wycombe, northwest of High Wycombe in Buckinghamshire. The caves, nondescript mining tunnels hewn out of the rock, are open to the public (*admission charge*), but they're a truly underwhelming experience.

TOM JONES

(1963, dir: Tony Richardson)
Albert Finney, Susannah York, Hugh Griffith.
● **DORSET; SOMERSET; LONDON**

Squire Allworthy's estate: Minterne

Richardson pulls out all the cinematic stops for this picaresque sex adventure, made mainly in the West Country. One of the key locations is **Cranborne Manor**, on the B3078, about 18 miles north of Bournemouth, Dorset. The 17th century gardens here are open to the public March to September (*admission charge*). The famous eating scene, with Tom (Finney) and the lusty Mrs Waters (Joyce Redman), uses the stables of **Nettlecombe Court**, which in 1963 was a girls' boarding school, near **Williton** on the A39, eight miles east of Minehead, north Somerset. Newgate Jail is Nettlecombe's courtyard. The estate of Squire Allworthy (George Devine) is **Minterne**, on the A352, two miles from Cerne Abbas and ten miles north of Dorchester in Dorset. The 18th century rhododendron and shrub garden is open April to October (© *01300.341370, www.aboutbritain.com/minterne-gardens.htm; admission charge*). **Castle Street, Bridgwater**, in Somerset, provided more picturesque backdrops.

Tom duels with Fitzpatrick: The undercroft beneath Lincoln's Inn Chapel, Old Square

Tom contemplates marriage: Lincoln's Inn Fields

The London home of Lady Bellaston (Joan Greenwood) was Londonderry House, since demolished, which stood at Hyde Park Corner, while more period London street scenes used the old warehouses along **Shad Thames, Southwark**.

Cynical servant Partridge (Jack MacGowran) suggests that the penniless Tom get out of his entanglement with Lady Bellaston by proposing to her, as they walk along the west side of **New Square, Lincoln's Inn**, WC2, off Holborn. Just to the north, beneath **Lincoln's Inn Chapel, Old Square** is the elaborately vaulted undercroft, where Tom duels with Fitzpatrick and, for his pains, ends up arrested for armed robbery. The undercroft was ingeniously glazed and furnished to provide the queen's lodgings in Richard Loncraine's *Richard III*.

TOMB OF LIGEIA, THE

(1964, dir: Roger Corman)
Vincent Price, Elizabeth Shepherd, John Westbrook
● **NORFOLK**

Price's dead wife becomes a cat, and thence the Lady Rowena, in this adaptation of an Edgar Allen Poe story by Robert Towne, the writer of *Chinatown*. Roger Corman left the AIP studios in LA, where he had filmed his series of atmospheric Poe/Price movies, to take advantage of the British studios' practice of reusing old sets for gratis. Unusually, Corman ventured out to a real location. The ruined abbey is **Castle Acre**, a 900-year-old priory four miles north of Swaffham in Norfolk. The graveyard is in **Swaffham** itself.

TOMBSTONE

(1993, dir: George P Cosmatos)
Kurt Russell, Val Kilmer, Michael Biehn.
● **ARIZONA**

Epic Western, filmed at the **Old Tucson** movie set-cum-tourist attraction, **201 South Kinney Road, Tucson** (*www.old-tucson.com*). The real Tombstone, where you can see

The *Tombstone* set at Old Tucson studios, Arizona.

the OK Corral and Boot Hill Cemetery, is about 50 miles southeast of Tucson.

TOMMY

(1975, dir: Ken Russell)
Roger Daltrey, Ann-Margret, Oliver Reed.
● **HAMPSHIRE; LAKE DISTRICT, CUMBRIA; LONDON; HERTFORDSHIRE**

The film adaptation of The Who's rock opera has a great first half – virtually inventing the music video – as Russell gives full rein to his imagination, but then trips up on the obvious budgetary restrictions as the lumpen allegory takes over. The opening and closing countryside idylls are the Lake District.

Apart from

The 'Pinball Wizard' theatre: King's Theatre, Southsea

The Marilyn Monroe Church: Henderson Road, Eastney

The fifties holiday camp chalets: Eastney Esplanade

Tommy's birth, a scene shot in **Harefield**, Hertfordshire, the movie was shot a r o u n d **Portsmouth** and nearby **Hayling Island**, Hampshire.

The opening Blitz scene was **C u m b e r l a n d Road**, near Fratton Station, as the street was being demolished. It's now a smart new housing estate.

The subterranean tunnel, through which Uncle Frank (Reed) and his Mum (Ann-Margret) take the young Tommy to the funfair, is at **Southsea Castle**, south of Southsea Common. The fair itself is at the northwestern end of the common.

You won't find Uncle Frank's campy fifties holiday camp. It's a composite of several different locations. The row of chalets, actually tiny sun huts, can be seen along **Eastney Esplanade** at St George's Road, east of Southsea. The swimming pool is **Hilsea Lido**, off London Road at the roundabout by Port Creek, Hilsea, north of Portsmouth. The ballroom was the theatre on the old **South Parade Pier**, Southsea. The pier caught fire and burned down during filming. But waste not, want not – film of the pier burning is incorporated into the conflagration at the movie's climax. The replacement is a sad, bland reconstruction of the original. Elton John's 'Pinball Wizard' number is staged in the **King's Theatre, Albert Road**, Southsea (© 023.9282.8282, www.kings southsea.com). The Church of Marilyn Monroe, where Eric Clapton performs 'Eyesight to the Blind', was St Andrew's Garrison Church, now imaginatively converted to luxury housing, on **Henderson Road, Eastney**, east of Southsea.

Tommy's holiday camp: Fort Purbrook, Portsmouth

The holiday camp pool: Hilsea Lido

Hang-gliding Tommy (and what seventies movie would be complete without its h a n g - g l i d i n g sequence?) perches atop the remaining tower of **Warblington Castle**, the rest of which was largely destroyed during the Civil War. It's on private land just east of the B2149 by the bridge to Hayling Island, south of Havant.

Tommy's Holiday Camp, where a manic Uncle Ernie flogs trinkets to the converts, is **Fort Purbrook**, one of five

Going up in flames: South Parade Pier, Southsea

Victorian forts overlooking Portsmouth. Known collectively as Palmerston's Folly, after the Prime Minister who oversaw their construction, they were meant to defend the south coast against a French invasion, which never materialised. Purbrook, most easterly of the five, is on **Portsdown Hill Road**, off London Road, northwest of Cosham. The entrance to Tommy's camp is the fort's westerly gate. The interior of the camp used piles of buoys, painted silver in an imaginative, if unsuccessful, attempt to resemble giant pinballs. The buoys were stacked at the now-gone Pound's Scrapyard, Twyford Avenue, by Alexandra Park.

TOMORROW NEVER DIES

(1997, dir: Roger Spottiswoode)
Pierce Brosnan, Jonathan Pryce, Michelle Yeoh.
● **LONDON; SUFFOLK; OXFORDSHIRE; HERTFORDSHIRE; MIDDLESEX; BUCKINGHAM-SHIRE; GERMANY; THAILAND; FRANCE; MEXICO**

Media mogul Elliot Carver (Pryce) is bent on engineering a conflict between Britain and China. The opening teaser sees Bond (Brosnan) single-handedly blitzing a terrorist arms bazaar on the Russian border. The remote location is one of the world's few high-altitude airfields, **Peyresourde**, in the central French Pyrenees.

After the unfeasibly narrow escape, Bond unwinds by learning a new tongue, at **New College, Oxford**, when he receives the inevitable call from M (Judi Dench). Although the real MI6 HQ at Vauxhall was seen in *GoldenEye*, Bond is now driven into the courtyard of **Somerset House** in the **Strand** (which, to confuse matters, served as the St Petersburg square in the previous film).

He's despatched to Germany, and meets up with Q (Desmond Llewelyn) at **Hamburg International Airport**. Although this is real enough, the extravagant bash, where Bond meets old flame Paris Carver (Teri Hatcher), is closer to the studio. The Hamburg centre of Carver's media empire is the **IBM Building, New Square, Bedfont Lakes, Feltham**, south of Heathrow Airport. And *Tomorrow*'s print works is an amalgamation of two London printers: **Harmsworth Quays Printers Ltd, Surrey Quays Road**, SE16, and **Westferry Printers, 235 Westferry Road**, E14, at Millwall Dock (printers of the London *Evening Standard* and the *Daily Telegraph*).

The exterior of Bond's hotel is the **Hotel Atlantic Kempinski, An der Alster 72-79** (© 40.288.80) on the banks of the Aussenalster Lake in central Hamburg. But the interior, where he finds Paris Carver dead and faces off against hitman Dr Kaufman (Vincent Schiavelli), is **Stoke Park Club, Stoke Road, Stoke Poges** in Buck-

The Atlantic garage: Brent Cross Shopping Centre carpark Level Four, Golders Green

inghamshire (℃ *01753.717171, www.stokepark-club.com*). Other films shot here include *Bridget Jones's Diary, Bride and Prejudice, Layer Cake, Wimbledon* and, of course, a previous classic Bond, *Goldfinger*.

The Atlantic garage, from which Bond escapes in the remote-controlled BMW750, is, famously, Level Four of the multi-storey carpark of **Brent Cross Shopping Centre** in Golders Green, north London. The fire brigade was called out after the stunts produced a little more smoke than anticipated. The final leap into the fake Avis office, though, is the real Hamburg.

Despite Jack Wade (Joe Don Baker) sporting a floral shirt, the US airbase at Okinawa, in the South China Sea, is really **RAF Lakenheath** in Suffolk. The sea landing uses the vast tank built for *Titanic* at **Rosarito** in Baja California, Mexico.

Negotiations to film in Vietnam fell through, and the Saigon scenes are actually **Bangkok**, Thailand. The skyscraper down which Bond and Wai Lin (Yeoh) descend on a banner is the **Banyan Tree Hotel, 21/100 South Sathorn Road, Sathorn** (℃ *2.679.1200, www.westin-bangkok.com*). The motorbike chase roars along **Tannery Row** and **Mahogany Wharf**, Bangkok, before climaxing on a set built at the old Radlett Aerodrome site in **Frogmore**, Hertfordshire, which had been converted into **Eon Studios**. Ha Long Bay, where Bond and Wai Lin search for Carver's stealth boat, is **Phuket Bay**, Thailand, among the limestone towers familiar from *The Man With the Golden Gun*.

TOOTSIE
(1982, dir: Sydney Pollack)
Dustin Hoffman, Jessica Lange, Teri Garr.
● **NEW YORK CITY; NEW YORK**

Hoffman cheekily guys his own reputation as notoriously 'difficult' thesp Michael Dorsey, who transforms himself into Dorothy Michaels to get work. As everyone knows, there are so many more opportunities for middle-aged women in the acting profession.

Michael's apartment is **15-17 West 18th Street** at Fifth Avenue. Unemployable in the acting profession, Michael and his playwright friend Jeff Slater (Bill Murray) are reduced to working in the kitchen at Jim McMullen, now the **Atlantic Grill, 1341 Third Avenue** between 76th and 77th streets on the East Side.

Dressed to impress, 'Dorothy' checks out 'her' credibility by contriving to bump into her agent George Fields (director Pollack) at the **Russian Tea Room, 150 West 57th Street** – seen also in Woody Allen's *Manhattan*. Laden with shopping, she gets into a fracas over a yellow cab outside **Bloomingdale's, 1000 Third Avenue** at East 59th Street on the East Side.

The hospital sudser *Southwest General*, in which

Dorothy finds a little too much fame, is recorded at the National Video Centre, now the **National Studios, 460 West 42nd Street**, between Ninth and Tenth Avenues.

And life gets more complicated as fellow cast member Julie Nichols (Lange) invites Dorothy to her upstate farmhouse, the 1690s **Wynkoop House**, homestead of Cornelius Wynkoop on **Wynkoop Road, Hurley**, just outside Kingston, New York State. Julie's father, Leo (Charles Durning), is so smitten, he proposes to Dorothy at the (now closed) Copacabana Nightclub, 10 East 60th Street at Madison Avenue (seen in *Carlito's Way* and *Goodfellas*).

The upstate bar, where Dorsey makes up with Leo after revealing himself as a man, is **Hurley Mountain Inn, Old Route 209** (℃ *845.331.1780, www.hurley-mountaininn.com*), west of Route 209, between Esopus Creek and Brinks Lane, **Hurley**, New York State.

TOP GUN
(1986, dir: Tony Scott)
Tom Cruise, Kelly McGillis, Val Kilmer.
● **CALIFORNIA; NEVADA**

Rose-tinted (literally) Navy recruiting movie from a director grounded in advertising: the hardware looks good enough to eat and there's a choice of love interest – Kilmer or McGillis according to orientation. The movie is set in San Diego, home of the 11th Naval District HQ, one of the world's largest navy bases, Route 5, 120 miles south of LA. The 'TOPGUN' base (it's actually one word) is **Marine Corps Air Station Miramar** in San Diego. You can tour the facility (*www.mccsmiramar.com/sfse.htm*). Maverick (Cruise) and Goose (Anthony Edwards) serenade instructor Charlie Blackwood (McGillis) with 'You've Lost That Lovin' Feelin'' in the **Miramar Officers' Club**. In 1996, the Navy Fighter Weapons School relocated to the **US Naval Air Station Fallon** (*www.fallon.navy.mil*), east of the town of Fallon, on I-50, Nevada. The control tower buzzed by Maverick is at Fallon, and much of the aerial footage of the film was shot here. The flyers' hangout, where Goose hammers out 'Great Balls of Fire' on the piano, and Maverick finally hooks up with Charlie, is the **Kansas City Barbeque Restaurant, 610 West Market Street** at Kettner Boulevard (℃ *619.231.9680*), by the railroad tracks in downtown San Diego. Charlie's beachfront home is **102 South Pacific Street** at First Street, **Oceanside**, on I-5 between LA and San Diego. The bar with the great view of the airport runway, where Charlie finds a morose Maverick after the death of Goose, was the Windsock Bar and Grill, 2904 Pacific Highway. It was the upstairs bar of Jimsair Aviation, the private jet terminal alongside Lindbergh Field (San Diego International Airport) but, sadly, was torn down in 2002.

TOPAZ
(1969, dir: Alfred Hitchcock)
Frederick Stafford, John Forsythe, Roscoe Lee Browne.
● **DENMARK; FRANCE; NEW YORK CITY; WASHINGTON DC; CALIFORNIA**

Far and away the worst Hitchcock, a confused, uninteresting, unfocused international spy thriller with a truncated ending that has to be seen to be believed (check out Hitch's original ending, plus yet another version, on the DVD release). Hitch, feeling that his precise, storyboarded style was dated for the freewheeling sixties, unwisely attempted to wing it with an unfinished script and poor preparation.

The movie shot all over, in Paris; New York; Washington DC; and California; kicking off in the Danish capital, Copenhagen, where suspicious agents follow defector Boris Kusenov and his family as they leave the Russian embassy. Passing the **Bull and Dragon Fountain, Radhuspladsen** (Town Hall Square), the Kusenovs duck into the **Royal Copenhagen Porcelain Manufactory, Sondre Fasanvej 5** at Smallegade, 2000 Frederiksburg. You can take a tour of the factory, too (© *38.14.92.97, www.royalcopenhagen.com*). The family is spirited away by US agents at **Den Permanente Department Store**, on **Stroget**, the city's main shopping street.

In Washington DC, they're whizzed past those symbols of western democracy, the **Capitol Building** and the **White House** – "It's nice." – before being taken over the Potomac to a safe house for debriefing.

As rumours of Russian involvement in Cuba surface, French agent André Devereaux (Stafford) and wife Nicole (Dany Robin) leave their Georgetown house for a trip to New York, staying at the **St Regis-Sheraton, 2 East 55th Street** (© *212.767.0525*). Devereaux approaches Dubois (Lee Browne) to bribe one of the raucous Cuban delegation staying at the Hotel Theresa, **125th Street at Seventh Avenue** (Adam Clayton Powell Jr Boulevard) in Harlem. Indeed, Fidel Castro did stay at the Theresa in 1960 on his first visit to the US after coming to power. For the complex scene, one of Hitchcock's impressive wordless set-pieces, the Theresa was recreated on the studio backlot. Although it ceased to be a hotel in 1970, the monumental block still towers over Harlem.

Salinas, on I-101 south of San Jose, California, stands in for Revolutionary Cuba, where Devereaux gets the dirt on Soviet involvement in the missile programme. The political rally cheekily includes footage of the real Fidel Castro and even Che Guevara.

The trail leads back to a mole in the French secret service. The home of traitorous Granville (Michel Piccoli), who is either killed in a duel or escapes to Moscow, according to which ending you see, is on **Place de la Visitation**, off boulevard Saint Germain on the Left Bank.

TOPKAPI

(1964, dir: Jules Dassin)
Melina Mercouri, Maximilian Schell, Peter Ustinov.
● **TURKEY**

Classic caper movie, with Schell stealing a dagger from the **Topkapi Palace Museum**, on Seraglio Point overlooking the Marmora and Bosphorus, Istanbul (© *90.212.5120480, www.ee.bilkent.edu.tr/~history/topkapi*). The interior of the museum is a set, which bears no resemblance to the real thing.

TOPPER

(1937, dir: Norman Z McLeod)
Cary Grant, Constance Bennett, Roland Young.
● **LOS ANGELES, CALIFORNIA**

Cary Grant and Constance Bennett are the Kirbys, a smart – but dead – couple who haunt stuffy banker Roland Young's Connecticut estate is the gothic man-

The Sea Breeze Hotel: Southwestern Law School, Wilshire Boulevard

sion at **380 San Rafael Avenue, Pasadena** (a private home, not visible from the road). The entrance to the Sea Breeze Hotel, supposedly also in Connecticut, is the rear porte cochere of the striking Bullock's Department Store building. Long closed, the towering landmark has been restored as home to the **Southwestern Law School, 3050 Wilshire Boulevard**, midtown LA. The store was seen in Hitchcock's *Family Plot*, and more recently, it was featured in *The Aviator*.

TOPSY-TURVY

(1999, dir: Mike Leigh)
Jim Broadbent, Allan Corduner, Timothy Spall.
● **SURREY; HERTFORDSHIRE**

Mike Leigh springs a surprise with this genial, episodic analysis of the creative process, as Gilbert and Sullivan, stuck in a rut and about to go their separate ways,

The Savoy Theatre interiors: Richmond Theatre, Richmond

come up with *The Mikado*. The Savoy Theatre has changed beyond all recognition since the days of D'Oyly Carte, revamped in a twenties deco style. The theatre scenes filmed in **Richmond Theatre, The Green, Richmond** in Surrey (© *020.8940.0088*), see *Evita* for details. Budgetary constraints meant that there are no exterior 'money shots'; in fact, most of the film was shot inside **Langleybury Mansion**, an abandoned Victorian school in King's Langley, Hertfordshire.

TORN CURTAIN

(1966, dir: Alfred Hitchcock)
Paul Newman, Julie Andrews, Lila Kedrova.
● **CALIFORNIA; GERMANY**

This second division Hitchcock is miscast, but has some great sequences. Paul Newman, whose methody style was anathema to Hitch, poses as a defector in order to get some Macguffins from behind the Iron Curtain, but girlfriend Andrews almost scuppers the plan by doggedly tailing him. The story grew out of the Burgess-Maclean spying episode (a treatment of which Hitchcock was still working on at the time of his death), looking at political and sexual betrayal from the wife's point of view.

By the time Universal had junked the homosexual element of the story and lumbered Hitchcock with two unsuitable leads, the project was sinking fast. The film also marked the director's final rift with brilliant but temperamental composer Bernard Herrmann. In 1966, the studio felt him 'too old fashioned'. He went on to score *Obsession* for Brian De Palma, *Taxi Driver* for Martin Scorsese, and when *Cape Fear* and *Psycho* were remade, both films retained the original Herrmann scores.

The movie was made largely on the Universal backlot, and on the campus of the **University of Southern California**, in LA's Exposition Park area, south of downtown. The remote farm, where the gruesomely protracted killing of the East German agent takes place, was at **Camarillo**, on Route 101 between LA and Ventura. The airport is in San Fernando Valley. The port is **Long Beach**, southern LA. Surprisingly, there are a few shots of the real **East Berlin**, snatched surreptitiously by a second unit ostensibly filming a travelogue. When Newman leaves the hotel, looks up the street and sees the yellow bus, it really is in East Berlin. The bus he gets on board is a duplicate at Universal. The museum chase was tricked up with matte shots.

TOTO LE HEROS (aka *Toto the Hero*)
(1991, dir: Jaco van Dormael)
Michel Bouquet, Jo De Backer, Thomas Godet.
● BRUSSELS

Van Dormael's dazzling, off-centre black comedy has Bouquet, convinced that a mix-up at birth robbed him of his life, out to settle the score. The film is set in Brussels, mainly in the southeastern suburb of **Watermael-Boitsford**: in **rue Friquet**; **rue de la Hulotte**, **rue de Loriot** and **rue du Troglodyte**. Also seen are the suburbs of **Uccle**; **Lxelles**; **Saint-Josse-ten-Noode**; and **Schaerbeek**.

TOUCH OF EVIL
(1958, dir: Orson Welles)
Charlton Heston, Janet Leigh, Orson Welles.
● LOS ANGELES, CALIFORNIA

The Mexican border town: Windward Avenue, Venice

Welles tiptoed back to Hollywood to film Whit Masterson's novel *Badge of Evil*, and adapted the book himself. He wanted to film the corrupt and decaying labyrinth of a Mexican border town in Tijuana or Juarez, but the Mexican authorities objected to the sleaziness in the script. Universal wanted Welles to film in the studio. In the end, it was writer Aldous Huxley who came up with the inspired choice of **Venice**.

The once-elegant recreation of the Italian city, with canals and arched walkways, had degenerated into a decrepit backwater, the buildings crumbling, the stagnant canals stinking and oil derricks disfiguring the landscape.

The ending of the screenplay was rewritten to accommodate the locale. The area has been spruced up no end since the fifties, and is now a lively, old-hippyish neighbourhood. The remaining arcades can be seen on **Windward Avenue**, between Pacific Avenue and Speedway; the canals are southeast of Pacific Avenue and Venice Boulevard.

TOWERING INFERNO, THE
(1974, dir: John Guillermin)
Paul Newman, Steve McQueen, William Holden.
● CALIFORNIA

Fox and Warners both planned highrise conflagration movies, based on books *The Tower* and *The Glass Inferno*. They decided to pool their resources and produce *The Towering Inferno*. Five storeys of the doomed building were built at Fox's Malibu Ranch. Set in San Francisco, the opening matte shot places the tower just about on the site of the Transamerica Pyramid. The entrance is actually the plaza entrance to the **Bank of America World Headquarters, California Street** at Kearney Street. The lobby, with its glass elevators, is the **Hyatt Regency Hotel, 5 Embarcadero Center** (© *415.788.1234, sanfranciscoregency.hyatt.com*), a dizzying location seen also in Mel Brooks' *High Anxiety* and sci-fi adventure *Time After Time*. This being, in part, a 20th Century Fox movie, the computer controlled building surveillance centre was shot in the basement of a Century City office building.

The entrance to the glass tower: Bank of America World HQ, California Street

The tower's lobby: Embarcadero Center

TRADING PLACES
(1983, dir: John Landis)
Eddie Murphy, Dan Aykroyd, Ralph Bellamy.
● PENNSYLVANIA; NEW YORK CITY; NEW YORK; VIRGIN ISLANDS

Rich old men Randolph and Mortimer Duke (Bellamy and Don Ameche) get their comeuppance after swapping the lifestyles of beggar Billy Ray Valentine (Murphy) and stockbroker Louis Winthorpe III (Aykroyd) for a bet. It's set mainly in Philadelphia, where 'legless' Billy Ray begs in a wintry **Rittenhouse Square**, at 18th and Walnut Streets, to the southwest of the city centre. In

Dan Aykroyd's house: Delancey Street

'Legless' Murphy begs in Rittenhouse Square

The Duke and Duke Bank: Fidelity Bank, South Broad Street, Philadelphia

Aykroyd is saved by Jamie Lee Curtis: The Clothespeg, 15th Street

the classy district a little further southwest is Winthorpe's house, taken over by Valentine, at **2014 Delancey Street** near 21st Street. Randolph and Mortimer's Duke and Duke bank is the **Fidelity Bank, 135 South Broad Street**, just south of City Hall. After he's had his credit cards confiscated, the destitute Winthorpe is offered help by hooker Ophelia (Jamie Lee Curtis) on **15th Street** in front of Claes Oldenburg's giant, 45-foot steel Clothespeg statue, Market Street west of City Hall. Billy Ray and Winthorpe set out for New York from the elegant deco concourse of **Thirtieth Street Station, 30th Street**, Philadelphia (seen also in *Blow Out, Marnie* and *Witness*). The Dukes' mansion isn't Pennsylvania at all, but **Mill Neck Manor for the Deaf, Frost Mill Road, Mill Neck**, Nassau County, Long Island. The frantic climax, with Billy Ray and Winthorpe joining forces to bankrupt their tormentors, is in the Comex Commodities Exchange Center, of the World Trade Center in New York. The good guys end up on the tropical beaches of **St Croix** in the Virgin Islands.

TRAFFIC

(2000, dir: Steven Soderbergh)
Michael Douglas, Catherine Zeta-Jones, Benicio Del Toro.

● **CALIFORNIA; NEW MEXICO; OHIO; TEXAS; MEXICO; WASHINGTON DC**

The director's decision to operate his own (mainly hand-held) camera gives Soderbergh's take on the UK TV miniseries, *Traffik*, a feeling of documentary immediacy.

The production uses over 100 separate locations to chart the complexities of the international drug trade. Three separate story strands centre on cop Javier (Del Toro) in Mexico, Helena Ayala (Zeta-Jones), the wife of a wealthy drug lord in San Diego; and anti-drug czar Robert Wakefield (Douglas) in Cincinnnati and Washington DC.

The Mexican desert, where Javier is relieved of confiscated drugs by the dubious General Salazar, is **Box Canyon, Las Cruces**, New Mexico. And though there are

a couple of establishing shots of **Tijuana**, the bordertown scenes were actually shot about 500 miles east, on the streets of **Nogales**. General Salazar's HQ, where contract killer Frankie Flowers is tortured, is **Rio Vista Farm Historic District, 800-801 Rio Vista Road** in Socorro on the outskirts of El Paso, Texas. In the San Diego section, Helen and her society friends twitter over the duck salad at **Rancho Bernardo Inn, 17550 Bernardo Oaks Drive, San Diego** (© 877.517.9342, *www.ranchobernardoinn.com*). The Ayala house is north of San Diego, on **Whitefield Place**, a short cul-de-sac off Soledad Avenue on the coast at **La Jolla**, where an otherwise perfect house, which fronted directly onto the street, was given a false front yard. Husband Carlos Ayala is standing trial at the **Hall of Justice, 330 West Broadway**, downtown San Diego, while crucial witness Ruiz is kept secure, across the street, in the Hotel San Diego, **339 West Broadway**. The 1914 hotel closed in 2002 and was scheduled for demolition to make way for a courthouse extension. With her comfortable world threatened, Helen hires Frankie Flowers to remove Ruiz. She meets up with him in the innocuous surroundings of the **Botanical Building** in the Botanical Garden of **Balboa Park, 1549 El Prado** (© 619.239.0512, *www.balboapark.org*). As the strands of the storylines weave together, Javier meets with FBI agents at the **San Diego Marriott Hotel and Mariona, 333 West Harbor Drive** (© 619.234.1500, *www.sdmarriott.com*).

The Cincinnati home of Judge Wakefield is supposedly on Indian Hill, but was filmed in the city's **Hyde Park** district. Discovering his own daughter is dabbling in illegal substances, Wakefield cruises the troubled **Vine Street** neighbourhood, downtown, where rich white kids provide the end-users in the chain of supply and demand.

In Washington DC, Wakefield is interviewed by the Chief of Staff, apparently at the **Old Executive Building, 17th Street** at Pennsylvania Avenue. A bit of photogenic licence, presumably, since the Chief of Staff's office is in the White House. And anyway, the scene was filmed in LA, at the familiar **Craven Estate, 430 Madeline Avenue, Pasadena** (seen in *Being There* and *Enemy of the State)*. Wakefield is later seen leaving the **White House** gate (a craftily sneaked shot, which is what you can get when you have the clout of Michael Douglas). But not even Douglas could get a camera crew inside the White House, so the interior is the set of TV's *The West Wing* on the Warner Brothers' Burbank lot. The cocktail party, where Wakefield meets a clutch of (real) senators, is held in the mansion at the corner of **O Street NW at 26th Street NW**, in **Georgetown**.

Fact-finding takes the newly-appointed supremo down Mexico way. Although the aerial shots of **Mexico City**'s vast **Zócalo** (the second largest square in the world, after Moscow's Red Square) and the **National Palace** are real enough, the meeting with Salazar filmed in a bank building in downtown LA.

As Wakefield mingles with real-life officials at two genuine locations, Soderbergh blurs the line between fact and fiction. At the **San Ysidro/ Tijuana** border crossing, south of San Diego, Wakefield glimpses the sheer scale of the customs' problem – 28 lanes of traffic make up the world's busiest international crossing. And in the real **El Paso Intelligence Center Headquarters (EPIC), 11339 SSG Sims Street, El Paso**, Texas, he's briefed by Craig Chretien, the official who acted as technical consultant on the film.

TRAINING DAY

(2001, dir: Antoine Fuqua)
Denzel Washington, Ethan Hawke, Scott Glenn.
● **LOS ANGELES, CALIFORNIA**

Alonzo meets up with the 'three wise men': Pacific Dining Car, West Sixth Street

All-round good guy Washington takes on the role of irredeemably corrupt cop Alonzo Harris (originally written as Latino), and is rewarded with an Oscar. The drama of cynicism and street-level *realpolitik* is set over 24 hours in a scruffy, urban LA. "All the locations are real," says production designer Naomi Shohan. "All the interiors done on stage were taken from the locations and researched in the neighbourhoods with the help of the residents. We sort of became urban anthropologists."

Seasoned veteran Alonzo toys with rookie Jake Hoyt (Hawke) in the familiar **Quality Coffee Shop, 1238 West Seventh Street**, downtown LA, seen also in *Se7en*, *Ghost World* and *Gone in 60 Seconds*. The pair head out to Alonzo's snazzy customised 1978 Chevy Monte Carlo, parked in the lot across West Seventh, and are soon having fun scaring the bejasus out of a VW full of college kids at the graffiti-emblazoned junction of **Beverly Boulevard**, **Second Street** and **Toluca Street**, just northwest of downtown (alongside the spot where Mr Orange rehearses his cover story in *Reservoir Dogs*). Jake unwittingly starts to get sucked into Alonzo's plan with a powerful hit of PCP as they drive north on **Glendale Boulevard**, past **Echo Park**.

Jake gets a taste of work on the streets, cruising Crenshaw Boulevard, chasing Blue (Snoop Dogg) into **Parisian Wigs, 4102 Crenshaw Boulevard** at Martin Luther King Jr Boulevard, **Leimert Park**. He gets sidelined, though, as Alonzo meets up with the 'three wise men' in the **Pacific Dining Car, 1310 West Sixth Street**, at Witmer Street just west of downtown (© *213.483.6000, www.pacific-diningcar.com*). Pretty unprepossessing from the outside, the restaurant has been serving up steaks since 1921. Don't confuse it with the newer branch in Santa Monica.

The house of drug dealer Roger (Glenn), where Jake finds himself set up as the fall guy, is **1031 Everett Street**, on the tiny green patch of **Everett**

Jake is set up at the house of drug dealer Roger: Everett Street, Everett Park

Park, off Sunset Boulevard, southwest of Elysian Park.

The drive for authenticity led to some pretty dodgy areas of south-central LA. With the support of the local community, the production got unprecedented cooperation from local gangs, allowing filming for the first time in areas of Crenshaw; Hawthorne; and Rampart (home of the infamous LA police corruption scandal which inspired the movie). The Sandman's apartment, where Alonzo serves a fake warrant on Sandman's wife (Macy Gray), is in the **Imperial Courts Housing Project, Croesus Avenue** at Imperial Highway, **Watts**.

The Jungle – "You don't come in here with anything less than a platoon" – got its nickname, despite what you might assume, from the lush plantings of early developers. Officially Baldwin Village, it's the area south of Coliseum Street between South La Brea Avenue and Crenshaw Boulevard. The dead-end street on which Alonzo finally finds himself without friends is **Palmwood Drive**, off Martin Luther King Jr Boulevard.

TRAINSPOTTING

(1996, dir: Danny Boyle)
Ewan McGregor, Ewen Bremner, Jonny Lee Miller.
● **SCOTLAND; LONDON**

Irvine Welsh's druggy novel, filmed by the *Shallow Grave* team with manic energy and a vow to keep the running time down to 90 minutes, de-

Shoplifting: Princes Street, Edinburgh

servedly turned out to be one of the UK's most profitable movies. Set in Edinburgh but, as with *Shallow Grave*, most of the filming took place in Glasgow.

The opening scene is the only real glimpse of Edinburgh, with Renton (McGregor) and co raiding **John Menzies Bookstore** and sprinting off down **Princes Street** to the **Calton Street Bridge**, where Renton is hit by the car. From here on it's Glasgow. The studio filming utilised a disused cigarette factory (it provides 30 of the film's 50

locations). The down-at-heel pub where the American tourist gets done over, and everyone gathers after the trial, is the old Social Club of the factory.

Renton and the car: Calton Street Bridge, Edinburgh

The football match filmed at the **Firhill Health Complex, Hopehill Road**, north from Maryhill Road, North Kelvin (*under-*

Shooting the dog: Rouken Glen Park, Thornliebank, Glasgow

Gearing up for the job interview: Cafe d'Jaconelli, Maryhill Road, Glasgow

Begbie and the beermug: Crosslands, Queen Margaret Drive, Glasgow

The hotel interior: George Hotel, Buchanan Street, Glasgow

The drug deal hotel, exterior: Royal Eagle Hotel, Craven Road, Bayswater

Renton's London flat: Talgarth Road, west Kensington

ground: *St Georges Cross*). The park where Renton and Sick Boy (Miller) discuss the career of Sean Connery and shoot the dog's behind is **Rouken Glen Park, Rouken Glen Park Road, Thornliebank**, south of the city centre on the line from Central Station. The park was also the site of the grave in *Shallow Grave*.

The café where Renton and Spud (Bremner) share a milkshake before speeding is **Cafe d'Jaconelli, 570 Maryhill Road**, in North Kelvin not far from the Firhill Health Complex. A little further up the road on the left is Queen Margaret Drive. A few minutes down the road you can find the galleried bar where Begbie entertains the crowd with his pool story and demonstrates how not to dispose of a beermug. It's **Crosslands, 182 Queen Margaret Drive**.

The nightclub where Renton meets the schoolgirl was Volcano, **15 Benalder Street**, close to Kelvinhall Station. You won't be so lucky, the nightclub has since been demolished. The rear of the club is the grey building facing Dumbarton Road. The railway station where Tommy tries vainly to whip up some enthusiasm for the Scottish countryside is **Rannoch Moor**, on the West Highland line up toward Fort William.

Renton's west London flat is **78A Talgarth Road** at North End Road, opposite West Kensington tube station. The London hotel, scene of the drug deal, is the **Royal Eagle Hotel, 26-30 Craven Road**, Bayswater (*©* *020.7706.0700*, *w w w . r o y a l -*

eagle.com), though the interior is still in Glasgow. It's the **George Hotel, 235 Buchanan Street** not far from Central Station.

TRAMP, THE (aka *Charlie the Tramp*)
(1915, dir: Charles Chaplin)
Charles Chaplin, Edna Purviance, Bud Jamison.
● CALIFORNIA

The tramp rescues Purviance from crooks. He's given a job on her parents' farm and gets looked after by her, until her lover turns up, and we get the original walk off into the sunset. The final shot filmed at **Niles**, California, which was the site of hundreds of old silent Westerns.

TRAPEZE
(1956, dir: Carol Reed)
Burt Lancaster, Tony Curtis, Gina Lollobrigida.
● PARIS, FRANCE

Lollobrigida comes between acrobats Burt and Tony in this sawdust melodrama. Much of the atmosphere comes from the location

The circus: Cirque d'Hiver, rue Amelot

filming. Almost all of the movie was shot in, or around, the domed, 5,000 seat **Cirque d'Hiver, 110 rue Amelot** (*www.cirqued-hiver.com*). Built as the Cirque Napoleon by Louis Dejean, one of the most acclaimed circus managers of the 1850s, and opened in the presence of Napoleon III, it was here that the flying trapeze was invented by M. Leotard. A parade along the Grand Boulevard and the Champs Elysées filmed before a crowd of 9,000 Parisians.

TREASURE ISLAND
(1934, dir: Victor Fleming)
Wallace Beery, Jackie Cooper, Lionel Barrymore.
● CALIFORNIA

Treasure Island: Point Lobos State Reserve

The seafront location is **Point Lobos State Reserve**, northern California – a site credited as being the inspiration for Robert Louis Stevenson's story.

TREASURE ISLAND
(1950, dir: Byron Haskin)
Robert Newton, Bobby Driscoll, Walter Fitzgerald.
● CORNWALL

Colourful Disney version of the classic yarn, filmed in **Falmouth** in Cornwall. Filming took place at **Carrick Roads** and **River Fal**. The *Hispaniola* is the Ryland Training Schooner, converted at Bideford. There was a little filming up the **Helford River**, but most of the shooting was at the entrance to the River Fal at **Turnaware Bar**, opposite Feock, and further upriver near to **King**

Harry Ferry. For the Treasure Island itself, painted palm trees were matted in.

TREASURE OF THE SIERRA MADRE, THE
(1948, dir: John Huston)
Humphrey Bogart, Walter Huston, Tim Holt.
● **MEXICO; LOS ANGELES, CALIFORNIA**

The somewhat obvious studio sets were at Warner Bros in Burbank, but there is real location filming in the mountains surrounding the village of **Jungapeo**, near San Jose Purua, Mexico, west from Mexico City, in the district of Michoacan; at **Tampico**, and a few shots in **Durango**.

TREMORS
(1990, dir: Ron Underwood)
Kevin Bacon, Fred Ward, Finn Carter.
● **CALIFORNIA**

Horror comedy, with giant carnivorous worms popping up in the desert around the **Alabama Hills** of Lone Pine, Route 395 in central California, and at nearby **Olancha**.

TRIAL, THE
(1962, dir: Orson Welles)
Anthony Perkins, Orson Welles, Jeanne Moreau.
● **YUGOSALVIA; PARIS, FRANCE; ROME, ITALY; MILAN, ITALY**

Part Kafka, part Welles, all brilliant. The grand, impressive locations, dotted all over Europe, are stitched together to

Musée d'Orsay, Paris

form a nightmarish landscape. The office of protagonist Joseph K (Perkins) is a huge exhibition hall outside **Zagreb**, in the former Yugoslavia, now Croatia, with 850 desks, typewriters and secretaries. Other locations include: **Dubrovnik**; Rome; Milan; and Paris. A typical sequence has Perkins at the old Gare d'Orsay, **1 rue de Bellechasse**, Paris (now the **Musée d'Orsay**; *www.musee-orsay.fr*), then walking down the steps of the **Palazzo di Giustizia**, Rome, to meet his cousin, strolling to a factory entrance in Milan, and returning to a council house in Zagreb.

TRIP, THE
(1967, dir: Roger Corman)
Peter Fonda, Susan Strasberg, Bruce Dern.
● **CALIFORNIA**

Jack Nicholson-scripted sixties acid movie, with Fonda tripping out of his brain. The low dives are on the Strip, the stretch of **Sunset Boulevard** running through West Hollywood. The Medieval flashbacks are the Californian coast at **Big Sur**, I-1; the deserts are at **Big Dune**, Yuma, Route 8 down in southeast California at the Arizona border.

TRIP TO BOUNTIFUL, THE
(1985, dir: Peter Masterson)
Geraldine Page, John Heard, Carlin Glynn.
● **TEXAS**

Near-senile Geraldine Page is obsessed with making one last trip, away from her ghastly family in Houston, to see the old family home, in this predictable tearjerker just about rescued from sentimentality-hell by the wonderful Page's Oscar-grabbing performance. It was shot in **Waxahachie**, that favourite Texas location, south of Dallas; in **Venus**, some 15 miles to the west; and **Five Points**. The Houston Bus Terminal is the old **Dallas Railroad Terminal**.

TRISTANA
(1970, dir: Luis Buñuel)
Catherine Deneuve, Fernando Rey, Franco Nero.
● **SPAIN**

Another surreal psychosexual puzzle from Buñuel, with Deneuve as a young woman given into the charge of ageing Spanish liberal Rey. The film is set in one of Spain's oldest cities, **Toledo**. The alabaster tomb, which so fascinates Deneuve, is modelled on the tomb of Cardinal Tavera, by Alonson Berruguete, in the Church of the Hospital Tavera, north of the Puerta de Bisagra, outside Toledo's city walls.

TROIS COULEURS: BLEU (aka *Three Colours: Blue*)
(1993, dir: Krzysztof Kieslowski)
Juliette Binoche, Benoît Régent, Florence Pernel.
● **FRANCE; POLAND**

First of Kieslowski's trilogy based on the colours of the French flag, symbolising Liberty (Blue), Equality (White) and Fraternity (Red).
Julie (Binoche) gains a kind of

The law court, where Binoche goes to meet her husband's mistress: Palais de Justice

empty freedom, trying to bury her past existence after the loss of her composer husband and her daughter in a car crash. She begins a new life in an apartment off **rue Mouffetard** in the bustling 5th arrondissement. A frantic phone call from her neighbour Lucille takes her to a sex club in the neon-lit neighbourhood of **Pigalle**. Julie visits the copyist to find out about her late husband's mistress, at **rue Schubert**, and confronts Olivier about finishing his score beneath the **Pont Bir Hakeim** in **Passy** (seen also in Bertolucci's *Last Tango in Paris*). The law court, where Binoche goes to meet her husband's mistress, is the **Palais de Justice** (see *Trzy Kolory: Bialy*, which overlaps with this film here).

TROIS COULEURS: ROUGE (aka *Three Colours: Red*)
(1994, dir: Krzysztof Kieslowski)
Irène Jacob, Jean-Louis Trintignant, Frédérique Feder.
● **SWITZERLAND**

The final part of Kieslowski's *Three Colours* trilogy – and the director's final film – was made in **Geneva**, Switzerland, and its southern suburb, **Carouge** –

dubbed the 'Greenwich Village of Geneva' (no, I can't picture that either). Kieslowski chose Switzerland, "an island in the middle of Europe", to mirror one of the film's themes of social isolation.

When the perfect apartment for Valentine (Jacob) was found in Geneva, the canny owner agreed to move out for two months, provided she could stay – all expenses paid – at the Hotel des Bergues, Geneva's finest, and most expensive. Valentine's apartment, above the (fake) Café Joseph is at the corner of rue **Micheli du Crest and rue des Sources**.

The overwhelmingly red theatre interior, in which the judge (Trintignant) finally opens up and reveals his humanity to Valentine after the fashion show, is Le Théâtre Municipal de Lausanne, now the **Lausanne Opera, Avenue du Théâtre 12, Lausanne**, around 40 miles northeast of Geneva (© *41.21.310.16.00*).

TROUBLE WITH HARRY, THE
(1955, dir: Alfred Hitchcock)
Edmund Gwenn, Mildred Natwick, Shirley MacLaine.
● **VERMONT**

One of Hitchcock's own favourites, this amiable, gently black comedy centres around the attempted disposal of a dead body. It's also Shirley MacLaine's screen début, and looks a treat thanks to Robert Burks' photography of the autumnal New England location of **East Craftsbury**, 30 miles north of Montpelier, northern Vermont. Much of the planned shooting had to be rearranged because of unexpected rainstorms. Interior sets were built inside a school gym in Morrisville, some 15 miles away.

TROY
(2004, dir: Wolfgang Petersen)
Brad Pitt, Orlando Bloom, Diane Kruger.
● **MALTA; MEXICO; LONDON**

Brad Pitt was heavily marketed as Achilles, poster boy for the Greeks, as Petersen disappointingly compresses the ten-year Trojan siege into a fortnight of set-piece battles. Originally scheduled to be filmed in Morocco, the production decamped to Baja California and Malta after the terrorist bomb attack in Casablanca. Interiors, including the Palace of Troy, were filmed on sets built at Shepperton Studios, London.

Exteriors of Troy were built on a ten-acre site within the 17th century military compund **Fort Ricasoli**, on the south entrance to the Grand Harbour on Malta (where the sets for *Gladiator* stood, and opposite Fort St Elmo, the Turkish prison location for *Midnight Express*). Ricasoli is managed by the Malta Film Commission, open to visit, and entrance is free. The wooden horse (actually steel and fibreglass), standing 38 feet high, was made at Shepperton and shipped out to Malta in sections. Brad and the Greeks storm ashore at **Ghajn Tuffieha Bay** (Golden Bay), seen also in *A Different Loyalty*. More sets were built at a hangar in **Hal Far**, and on the cliffside at **Mellieha**, a 15th century town between St Paul's Bay and Mellieha Bay. There was filming at **Mtahleb**, **Cirkewwa** (where you can catch the ferry to Gozo) and the natural arch at **Dwejra**, on the west coast of Gozo (seen also in

the Guy Ritchie-Madonna masterpiece *Swept Away*), Malta.

Coincidentally, two other TV productions based on Greek legends, *The Odyssey* (1997) directed by Andrei Konchalovsky (with Isabella Rossellini and Christopher Lee), and *Helen of Troy* (2003), filmed on many of the same locations.

Battle scenes were filmed in Mexico, on the coast at **Cabo San Lucas** (Las Dunas and El Faro Viejo) on the southern tip of Baja California. With a mere two weeks of filming left to complete, the walls of Troy were substantially damaged by Hurricane Marty in September 2003.

TRUE GRIT
(1969, dir: Henry Hathaway)
John Wayne, Glen Campbell, Kim Darby.
● **COLORADO; CALIFORNIA**

Wayne dons an eyepatch as crotchety marshall Rooster Cogburn in this likeable Western, made in the **Gunnison** area south of Montrose, in southwest Colorado. The opening shots are the **Wilson Peaks** in the San Juan national Forest. The frontier town is the main square of **Ridgway**, on I-550, about 30 miles to the south. Scenes were also shot at **Mammoth Lakes**, Route 395, east of Yosemite National Park in central California.

TRUE LIES
(1994, dir: James Cameron)
Arnold Schwarzenegger, Jamie Lee Curtis, Tia Carrere.
● **CALIFORNIA; WASHINGTON DC; FLORIDA; RHODE ISLAND**

Dull family man Harry Tasker (Schwarznegger) moonlights as a Bondian special agent in Cameron's tongue-in-cheek thriller, set around Washington DC, which took some flak for its casual racial stereotyping.

The lakeside Swiss chateau, infiltrated by Harry during the opening caper, is a mix of locations – both in Rhode Island. The exterior is Ochre Court – now the **Salve Regina University, 100 Ochre Point Avenue, Newport** (Lake Chapeau itself was nothing more than a canal, dug alongside the mansion). The interior, where Harry indulges in a tango with Juno (Carrere) while downloading something or other, is **Rosecliff, Bellevue Avenue** (see *The Great Gatsby* for details) near Newport, another of the grand Rhode Island mansions. The snowy ski getaway is at Lake Tahoe, near **Truckee**, a few miles north of Squaw Valley in the High Sierra Mountains of central California.

Back home in DC, Harry is tailed by Middle Eastern fanatic Salim (Art Malik) to the **Georgetown Park Mall, 3222 M Street NW** at Wisconsin Avenue (seen in *No Way Out*), where there's a spectacular shoot-out in the men's bathroom (OK, that's a studio set). Crashing through the window onto **M Street**, Harry com-

The horse leap at the DC hotel: Westin Bonaventure Hotel

The chase and shootout: Georgetown Mall

The Harrier jet climax: Colonial Bank Center, Brickell Avenue, Miami

mandeers a police horse in **Franklin Park** – but the DC hotel lobby, into which he gallops is the old **Ambassador Hotel, 3400 Wilshire Boulevard**, midtown LA (see the 1937 and 1954 *A Star Is Born* for details). The traditional twenties decor mysteriously metamorphoses into futuristic chrome and glass as Harry is chased into the scenic elevators of the **Westin Bonaventure Hotel, 404 South Figueroa Street**, in downtown LA (see *In the Line of Fire* for details).

Meanwhile, Harry's wife, Helen (Curtis), is off on her own adventure, meeting sad-wannabe spy Simon (Bill Paxton) beneath DC's Key Bridge – really the **Sixth Street Bridge**, downtown LA (where the T-1000 materialised in Cameron's *Terminator 2*). The Hotel Marquis, where Helen is obliged to pose as Doris the Prostitute, is the third famous LA hotel passed off as Washington; this time, downtown's **Millennium Biltmore Hotel, 506 South Grand Avenue** (see *Beverly Hills Cop* for details).

Abducted by Crimson Jihad to the **Florida Keys**, Harry and Helen escape, with a marathon helicopter/limo chase across the **Old Seven Mile Bridge** joining Key Vaca and Bahia Honda Key. Originally a railway bridge built in 1910, it once carried Overseas Highway, US1, but was replaced by a new bridge in 1982.

The gleaming black highrise where the terrorists hole up, and which Harry trashes with a Harrier jump jet, is the **Colonial Bank Center, 1200 Brickell Avenue** at SE 13th Street, downtown **Miami**. Harry and Helen's final tango is in the **Crystal Ballroom**, back in the **Millennium Biltmore**.

TRUE ROMANCE
(1993, dir: Tony Scott)
Christian Slater, Patricia Arquette, Gary Oldman.
● **LOS ANGELES, CALIFORNIA; DETROIT, MICHIGAN**

Tony Scott's film of Tarantino's script shamelessly rips off the musical style and flat narrative voiceover of Terrence Malick's *Badlands*. But if you're going to borrow, borrow from the best. The movie opens in Detroit, and indeed this is where you'll find Clifford Worley's trailer park, on the Detroit River. He works at the **Packard Plant, East Grand Boulevard** at Mount Elliott. The cop station is at **1300 Beaubien**, and Clarence Worley (Slater) and Alabama Whitman (Arquette) marry at the **Wayne County Building, 600 Randolph**. But the Sonny Chiba *Street Fighter* triple bill, where Clarence and Alabama first meet,

The hideout: Safari Inn, Olive Boulevard, Burbank

is in LA, at the beautifully-restored **Vista Theater, 4473 Sunset Drive**, Los Feliz (℃ 323.660.6639), which was also seen in Christopher Guest's underrated *The Big Picture* (1989), and was used for the première of *Stab* in *Scream 2*. The exterior of the theatre is Spanish Revival, but its 1922 construction coincided with the hysteria surrounding the discovery of Tutankhamun's tomb, and the interior is wonderfully kitschy Egyptian. Also in LA is the diner, where the couple eat pie afterwards: the fifties-style **Rae's Restaurant, 2901 Pico Boulevard**, at the corner of 29th Street in **Santa Monica** (℃ *310.828.7937*), seen also in the Eddie Murphy-Steve Martin satire *Bowfinger* and in 2004's *Win a Date With Tad Hamilton!*.

Other locations include the mansions of **Pasadena**; **Hollywood** bungalows; downtown LA; the beach at **Malibu**; and the desert at **Palmdale**. The construction site is alongside the landing strips of **Los Angeles International Airport**. The roller-coaster is the **Viper**, at **Six Flags Magic Mountain, Magic Mountain Parkway**, off I-5, Valencia, north of LA. Movie producer Lee Donowitz's lavish Beverly Ambassador suite filmed in the **Ambassador Hotel, 3400 Wilshire Boulevard**, midtown LA (see the 1937 and 1954 *A Star Is Born* for details). The fabulously kitsch motel, where Clarence and Alabama hide out, is the **Safari Inn, 1911 Olive Boulevard** (℃ *818.845.8586*), near Buena Vista, just north of the Disney Studios in Burbank – though the leopardskin interior isn't for real. You can also see the Safari in Ron Howard's *Apollo 13*.

Filming also took place at the **Athenaeum**, the dining club of the California Institute of Technology, at **551 South Hill Avenue** in Pasadena (see *Beverly Hills Cop* for details).

TRUMAN SHOW, THE
(1998, dir: Peter Weir)
Jim Carrey, Laura Linney, Ed Harris.
● **FLORIDA**

Weir's surprise sleeper, with Carrey as Truman Burbank – unwitting star of a 24-hour soap since his birth – needed a slightly stagey location. The fictitious town of Seahaven is in actuality a planned resort, called, generically, **Seaside**, this pastel newtown fantasy of a traditional resort can be found on the Gulf coast of Florida, on I-98 about 30 miles east of Panama City toward Fort Walton Beach.

TRZY KOLORY: BIALY (aka *Trois Couleurs: Blanc/Three Colours: White*)
(1994, dir: Krzysztof Kieslowski)
Julie Delpy, Zbigniew Zamachowski, Janusz Gajos.
● **FRANCE; POLAND**

The centre section of Kieslowski's trilogy was filmed in **Paris**, France, and in **Warsaw**, Poland. The opening scene overlaps with *Trois Couleurs: Bleu*, as Karol Karol (Zamachowski) arrives at the divorce court. This is the **Palais de Justice, 2 boulevard du Palais** (metro: Cité). Juliette Binoche, from the earlier movie, can be glimpsed wandering into the wrong court. It's from the courtyard, the **Cour du Mai**, that the tumbrils once rolled to the guillotine on the Place de la Concorde. The metro station, where Karol plays comb and paper, and gets a chance to return to Poland, is **Place de Clichy**.

TWELFTH NIGHT

(1996, dir: Trevor Nunn)
Imogen Stubbs, Helena Bonham Carter, Toby Stephens.
● **CORNWALL**

Shakespeare's romantic comedy, set in Illyria on Italy's sun-kissed Adriatic coast, is transposed to Cornwall. The two locations are **Lanhydrock**, a 17th century house two-and-a-half miles southeast of Bodmin (rail: Bodmin Parkway) on the B3268 Lostwithiel Road. The great house, set in extensive formal gardens, is open from the beginning of April to the end of October (except Mondays), the gardens and grounds all year (© 01208.73320).

The other location is **Prideaux Place**, an Elizabethan mansion set in extensive grounds above the little port of Padstow, about seven miles from Wadebridge (rail: Wadebridge). The house is open to the public for two weeks from Easter Saturday, and then from the Spring Bank Holiday to the end of September (© 0841.532411 or 0841.532945).

12 ANGRY MEN

(1957, dir: Sidney Lumet)
Henry Fonda, Lee J Cobb, EG Marshall.
● **NEW YORK CITY**

Lumet's classic, claustrophobic jury room drama was filmed in **New York County Courthouse, 60 Center Street** on the northeast corner of Pearl Street and Foley Square, and inside the building's rotunda.

New York County Courthouse, Center Street

TWELVE MONKEYS

(1995, dir: Terry Gilliam)
Bruce Willis, Brad Pitt, Madeleine Stowe.
● **PENNSYLVANIA; MARYLAND**

Gilliam's dizzyingly time-shifting, Philadelphia-set sci-fi, based on Chris Marker's experimental film, *La Jetée*, has James Cole (Willis), sent back in time, first appear outside a wintery **City Hall, Penn Square** between Broad and Market Streets, Philadelphia. The WWI battlefield is Baltimore. The asylum where he's subsequently incarcerated is Philadelphia's **Eastern State Penitentiary,**

22nd Street at Fairmount Avenue (© 215.236.3300, *www.easternstate.org*). When Charles Dickens visited the US, there were two things he wanted to see: Niagara

The vagrants: Met Theatre, Broad Street, Philadelphia

Falls and the Eastern State Pen. This architectural wonder, a central hub with seven 'spokes' radiating outwards, was the brainchild of the Quaker movement, a humane alternative to the corrupt, disease-ridden dumping grounds that served as prisons in the 19th century. The guiding principal was solitary confinement. With only the Bible, a little daily work and no human contact whatsoever (meals were served through holes in the wall so the prisoner could have no contact with the warder), the inmate, freed from temptation, would revert to a natural state of innocence. In fact, they mostly went mad. One who didn't was Al Capone, who resided here for eight months in 1929, in a tastefully decorated cell, with a desk, music and all the luxuries a crime boss could afford. You can see his restored cell on the prison tour. The Eastern State can also be seen in *Return to Paradise* (1998).

The homeless enclave where Cole battles with vicious vagrants is the old, abandoned **Met Theatre, Broad Street** at Poplar, in a poor area north of Philadelphia city centre. Also used is the once-majestic, now graffiti-covered Greek Revival **Ridgway Library, 901 South Broad Street** at Carpenter Street, also Philadelphia. The library, which had been abandoned for 30 years when the film was made, has since won several awards for adaptive re-use since being renovated to house the Philadelphia High School for Creative and Performing Arts. The vast underground chamber is Philadelphia's abandoned **Delaware Power Station**, where the floodgates were opened for the first time in years.

The elegant home of Dr Goines, the scientist father of Jeffrey Goines (Pitt), is the **Garrett-Jacobs Mansion, 11 West Vernon Place**, Baltimore (© 410.539.6914), home to the Engineers Club.

The future prison is Philadelphia's **Richmond Power Station**. The Engineering Room where Cole is interrogated is the No.4 Turbine Basement of the **Westport Power Plant** on the shores of the Patapsco River in Baltimore. The University lecture

Bruce Willis travels back to the 20th century: Philadelphia City Hall

The airport: Philadelphia Convention Center

Madeleine Stowe gets the blond wig: Wanamaker's Department Store, Philadelphia

The asylum: Eastern State Penitentiary, 22nd Street, Philadelphia

hall is the **Memorial Hall, North Concourse Drive**, in West Fairmount Park, part of the Centennial Exhibition of 1876 on Benjamin Franklin Parkway towards the Schuylkill River Philadelphia. The airport, seen in the recurring dream, is actually Philadelphia's spanking new **Convention Center** between 11th and 13th at Market Street. There are daily tours. The vast department store where Kathryn Railly (Stowe) buys wigs is **Wanamaker's Department Store, Market Street** at 13th Street (see *Mannequin* for details). The deco cinema where Cole and Railly sit through a 24-hour Hitchcock Fest is the **Senator Theater, 5904 York Road**, in Baltimore. You might recognise it from Barry Levinson's *Avalon*.

28 DAYS LATER

(2002, dir: Danny Boyle)
Cillian Murphy, Naomie Harris, Christopher Ecclestone.
● **LONDON; HAMPSHIRE; WILTSHIRE; CUMBRIA; GERMANY**

Raging speedfreaks prove far more terrifying than the usual clumsy lumberers, but Boyle's apocalyptic zombie movie tails off to an unsatisfyingly peremptory conclusion (alternative endings are always a bad sign). The Cambridge Primate Reseach Centre, where activists release monkeys infected with Rage, had to be filmed in **Stuttgart**, Germany, where one of only two troupes of suitable chimps was found.

The movie proper kicks off in London, where Jim (Murphy) wakes from a coma to discover himself seemingly the sole inhabitant of the capital. The deserted hospital, clearly intended to be St Thomas', across the Thames from Westminster, is a combination of **Central Middlesex Hospital, Acton Lane**, NW10, and the closed **Greenwich District Hospital, Woolwich Road**. In an amazing feat of location shooting, early morning traffic was held up for brief moments to capture awesome shots of an eerily empty city. Jim crosses **Westminster Bridge**; passes an overturned bus (positioned and removed in 15 minutes) in **Whitehall**; trudges through **Horse-**

The Dockland Light Railway escalators at Canary Wharf tube station

guards Parade; and up the **Duke of York's Steps**. There's an odd detour into the City, the **Bank of England** and the old **Royal Exchange**, before Jim sets off a car alarm beneath **Centre Point**, at **St Giles Circus**. He begins to get an inkling of the catastrophe at the boarded-up Eros fountain in **Piccadilly Circus**. The graffiti-scrawled church entrance – "The end is extremely fucking nigh" – is Nicholas Hawksmoor's **St Anne's Church, Commercial Road** at Newell Street, **Limehouse**, but the body-strewn interior, where Jim is attacked by the raging priest, is another Hawksmoor masterpiece: **Christ Church, Commercial Street** at Fournier Street, **Spitalfields**. Its exterior looms over the historic Ten Bells pub (recreated in Prague for *From Hell*) and Dil's hairdressing salon from *The Crying Game*.

Jim narrowly escapes a mob of the infected after a handful of survivors blow up a petrol station on the **Isle of Dogs**, the loop in the Thames north of Greenwich, and the rest of the London filming is down in the southeast. The vast steel escalators at **Canary Wharf tube station** lead down to the tracks of the **Dockland Light Railway**, and a trek to **Deptford** and the house of Jim's parents. The tower block, which provides a temporary haven, was River Heights, **Glyndon Road, Plumstead**, SE18, demolished shortly after filming.

The band stocks up on food at the (now gone) Budgens supermarket, **145 Tottenham Court Road** in the West End, before driving through the **Blackwall Tunnel** (under the Thames) in order to reach Manchester, in the north. The Blackwall entrance is real, but you can't close down this main artery for long, and the rat pack fleeing the zombie horde was filmed in the much-newer **Limehouse Link Tunnel**, linking the City with Docklands.

Supposedly heading up the M1 to Manchester, the fugitives enjoy a brief countryside idyll down in the southwest, at **Waverley Abbey**, Hampshire (*www.waverley.gov.uk/abbey*); and the army HQ is **Trafalgar Park** (*www.trafalgarpark.com*), about five miles south of Salisbury, Wiltshire. But it's on to the real north of England for the ending, which was shot on Forestry Commission land at **Ennerdale Water**, between Cockermouth and Egremont in Cumbria's beautiful Lake District.

21 GRAMS

(2003, dir: Alejandro González Iñárritu)
Sean Penn, Naomi Watts, Benicio Del Toro.
● **TENNESSEE; NEW MEXICO**

A traumatic road accident knots together three strangers, but despite powerhouse acting from the leads, Iñárritu's fragmented style makes heavy going of the melodramatic story. The unspecified setting is a strange hybrid of **Memphis**, Tennessee, and **Albuquerque**, New Mexico. In Memphis, Cristina Peck (Watts) lives in the upscale **Chickasaw Gardens** neighbourhood, and the hospital in which Paul Rivers (Penn) recovers after transplant surgery was a disused Baptist Hospital. The golf club, from which born-again ex-con Jack Jordan (Del Toro) is sacked, is **Windyke Country Club, 8535 Winchester Road**; and the apartment block is the historic **William Len Building, 110 Monroe Avenue** at South Main Street (which opened in June 2004 as the **Residence Inn**).

Feeling compelled to discover the origin of his new heart, Paul meets up with a private investigator at **Winchester Bowl, 3703 South Mendenhall Road** (© *901.362.1620*). It's in **Anderton's East Restaurant, 1901 Madison Avenue** (© *901.726.4010*) that he learns the donor's identity, and goes on to contrive a meeting with Cristina at the swimming baths in the gymnasium of **Grace-St Luke's Episcopal School, 246 South Belvedere Boulevard**. More Memphis scenes were filmed at the North End Restaurant, now **Westy's, 346 North Main Street** (© *901.543.3278*), between North Front and North Third Streets in the Pinch District.

The rest of the filming was around **Albuquerque**, New Mexico. Earnestine's (based on a real hangout, in Memphis), outside which a drug-addled Cristina shunts her car, was a façade erected on the **600 block of Central NW**, downtown Albuquerque.

The police station is way west of Albuquerque, at **619 Uranium Street** in the tiny town of **Milan**, near Grants, and the scrubby wasteland is **Zia Pueblo territory**, which was seen also in *Ghosts of Mars*. Seeking some form of retribution, Paul and Cristina track down the tormented Jack to the **Leisure Lodge, 1204 East Santa Fe Avenue, Grants** (© *505.287.2991*) itself, on the old Route 66.

20,000 LEAGUES UNDER THE SEA
(1954, dir: Richard Fleischer)
Kirk Douglas, James Mason, Peter Lorre.
● JAMAICA

Jules Verne's fantasy about a group of Victorian scientists wrecked at sea and held captive by submariner Captain Nemo, with exotic location scenes filmed in Jamaica.

20,000 YEARS IN SING SING
(1932, dir: Michael Curtiz)
Spencer Tracy, Bette Davis, Arthur Byron.
● NEW YORK

Cracking prison melodrama with, unusually for the period, filming at the notorious prison, **Sing Sing Penitentiary, Ossining**, on the Hudson River, 30 miles north of New York, also the backdrop for crime dramas including *The Big House* (1930), *Angels With Dirty Faces* (1938) and *Analyze This*. Still in operation, there's talk of converting part of the facility into a museum, in the meantime, you can visit the Sing Sing Museum, which contains memorabilia, a replica of 'Old Sparky', Sing Sing's electric chair, and mock-up cells, in the Caputo Community Center, 95 Broadway, Ossining (© *914.941.3189*). The real Old Sparky – which saw off 614 people – can be seen at the Newseum, Arlington, Virginia.

TWIN PEAKS: FIRE WALK WITH ME
(1992, dir: David Lynch)
Sheryl Lee, Kyle MacLachlan, David Bowie.
● WASHINGTON

Disappointing prequel to the weird'n'wonderful TV series. The Double R Diner, home of the legendary cherry pie, was the Mar T Cafe, but it's changed hands and is now **Twede's Cafe, 137 West North Bend Way** at North

Bend Boulevard in, yes, **North Bend** (© *425.831.5511, twedescafe.com*), on I-90, about 20 miles east of Seattle, Washington State.

The Great Northern Hotel, sadly missing from the movie but heavily featured in the TV show, is the Salish Lodge, 37807 SE Snoqualmie Falls Road, Snoqualmie, Route 202 just north of North Bend. The Roadhouse bar is the **Colonial Inn, 4200 Preston Fall City Highway, Fall City** (© *425.222.5191*), northwest of Snoqualmie.

TWISTER
(1996, dir: Jan De Bont)
Bill Paxton, Cary Elwes, Helen Hunt.
● OKLAHOMA; TEXAS

Flimsy actioner with Paxton and Hunt chasing computer generated tornados across the American midwest. In an odd turnaround, the production was hampered by good weather. In order to make the skies look dark, the car interiors had to be compensatingly overlit, leading to temporary eye problems for Paxton (shades of the industry's old Klieg Light problem from the early days of motion pictures). The stop-off is the **Hot Pit Bar-B-Q, 309 Avenue F, Del Rio**, southern Texas on the Rio Grande. The drive-in is the **Beacon Drive-in, 2404 South Division Street, Guthrie** (© *405.282.4512, www.beacondi.homestead.com*), on I-35 about 30 miles north of Oklahoma City, Oklahoma. A section of the town of **Wakita**, northern Oklahoma near the Kansas border, scheduled for demolition, was 'blown down' for the movie. Warner Bros then spent $250,000 replacing the area with a park, the bricks of which are emblazoned with the legend 'Twister '95'.

TWO MULES FOR SISTER SARA
(1969, dir: Don Siegel)
Clint Eastwood, Shirley MacLaine, Manolo Fabregas.
● MEXICO

Come on, did you really believe Shirley was a nun? Siegel's comedy Western was made on location out in **Cocoyoc**, a small town in the tiny state of Morelos, south of Mexico City. Clint and Shirl hide from the troops, and are threatened by a rattler, in the ruins of a sugarcane plantation, bombed by Zapata during the Revolution.

2001: A SPACE ODYSSEY
(1968, dir: Stanley Kubrick)
Keir Dullea, Gary Lockwood, Leonard Rossiter.
● HERTFORDSHIRE; SCOTLAND; ARIZONA

A giant step forward in the way space movies looked, made mostly in the studio at Borehamwood, Hertfordshire. The first scenes to be filmed, the discovery of the giant monolith on the moon, had to be shot at Shepperton, where there was a soundstage large enough. 90 tons of dyed (that is, moon-coloured) sand had to be shipped in. The African landscapes, for the ape scenes, were achieved with a complex system of front projection. The alien landscapes, seen during the trippy ending through the Stargate, are optically distorted shots of the **Hebrides** and of **Monument Valley**, Arizona.

U

U TURN
(1997, dir: Oliver Stone)
Sean Penn, Jennifer Lopez, Nick Nolte.
● ARIZONA

When bigger projects fell through, Oliver Stone filmed this small, Western-noir. The location is the abandoned mining town of **Superior**, 60 miles from Phoenix, Arizona, which was dressed to look like a town decaying since the sixties. The Waldorf Café, where Penn meets a bizarre assortment of local characters, was a derelict café restored for the movie, though retaining its original name. The climax is at nearby **Apache Leap**, a rock bluff named for an incident in the 1800s when Apache tribesmen leapt to their deaths rather than face capture by the US Cavalry.

UNBREAKABLE
(2000, dir: M Night Shyamalan)
Bruce Willis, Samuel L Jackson, Robin Wright Penn.
● PENNSYLVANIA

"They say this one has a surprise ending", says young Elijah Price's mother, handing her son a comic book. We're back in Shyamalanland, as security guard David Dunn (Willis), the sole – and unharmed – survivor of a train wreck, is contacted by the adult Price (Jackson), his seeming opposite, afflicted with painfully fragile bones.

Dunn works – without ever having taken a day's sick leave – at the stadium of the University of Pennsylvania, **Franklin Field, 235 South 33rd Street** at Spruce Street, Philadelphia. The church at which he attends a memorial service for the victims of the crash is **Immaculate Conception Church, 1020 East Price Street** at Ardleigh Street, **Germantown**, northern Philadelphia. And it's outside the church that Price leaves a message on his windscreen.

Sets were built at the Philadelphia Civic Center, Convention Avenue at 34th Street, which, since 1995 has been used as a soundstage facility (*The Sixth Sense* also filmed here, as did *Beloved*), but there are plenty of real Philly locations, though not always what they seem. You can't pick up a piece of classic artwork from Limited Editions, Elijah Price's comic book art gallery, which was nothing more than an empty restaurant building at **1620 Locust Street**, central Philadelphia. And, unlike David and Audrey (Wright Penn), you won't be able to enjoy a romantic cocktail at the rather enticing restaurant with the giant mural. It's not a bar at all, but the lobby of the **Curtis Center, 601-645 Walnut Street** at Sixth Street (HQ of Curtis Publishing), on the northeast corner of Washington Square. The huge, gleaming 1916 'mural' is The Dream Garden, a Tiffany glass mosaic, based on a Maxfield Parrish painting. (In 1998, it narrowly avoided being shipped off to grace a Vegas casino, before it was purchased by the Pennsylvania Academy of Fine Arts.) You can take a peek. The lobby is open to the public. And don't plan to catch a train from the cavernous railway station in which

Dunn explores his colour-coded supersenses. It's another Philly lobby, that of the **Packard Building, 111 South 15th Street** at Chestnut Street. Built as the showroom and assembly plant for Packard cars, it became the publishing plant for the *Philadelphia Record*, before lying abandoned. It's now luxury apartments.

Dunn meets his son at the quaintly-named **Pretzel Park, 4300 Silverwood Street, Manayunk**, just west of city centre Philadelphia, on the banks of the Schuylkill River. The bar where a slightly too-talkative security guy lets the wrong guy know his hotel's vulnerable spots, is **United States Hotel Bar & Grill, 4439 Main Street** (© *215.483.9222, www.ushotelbargrill.com*), Manayunk.

UNDER CAPRICORN
(1949, dir: Alfred Hitchcock)
Ingrid Bergman, Joseph Cotten, Michael Wilding.
● CALIFORNIA

Underrated Hitchcock costume melodrama, in lush colour. Set in Australia, the elaborate flyaway sets – Hitchcock was still experimenting with long unbroken takes after *Rope* – were constructed at MGM Studios in Elstree. The Australian village was on the backlot at the Warner's Ranch in LA. Government House, Sydney, is the pillared frontage of the old Canoga Park High School, since demolished. Filming also occurred at **Los Angeles State and County Arboretum, 301 North Baldwin Avenue**, Arcadia, east of Pasadena (© *818.821.3222*). See *The Man In the Iron Mask* for details.

UNDER SIEGE
(1992, dir: Andrew Davis)
Steven Seagal, Tommy Lee Jones, Gary Busey.
● ALABAMA

Seagal is the ship's cook who saves the battleship from Jones and Busey in this actioner made aboard the **USS Alabama, Battleship Memorial Park, Mobile Bay, Mobile**, Alabama.

UNDER THE CLOCK (aka *The Clock*)
(1945, dir: Vincente Minnelli)
Judy Garland, Robert Walker, James Gleason.
● NEW YORK CITY

Judy Garland meets GI Robert Walker under the clock in the concourse of New York's **Grand Central Station**, and marries him during his 24-hour leave. With the help of a little back-projection, the couple walk in the Egyptian Gallery of the **Metropolitan Museum of Art, Fifth Avenue** at East 82nd Street.

UNFORGIVEN
(1992, dir: Clint Eastwood)
Clint Eastwood, Gene Hackman, Morgan Freeman.
● ALBERTA, CANADA; CALIFORNIA

After a series of forgettable lightweight knockabouts, Eastwood's dark, introspective Western proved to be an unexpected box-office smash and an Oscar grabber. It was shot in various towns around Calgary, Alberta, Canada: **Brooks**, **Drumheller**, **Stettler** and **Longview**.

Railroad scenes filmed on the dependable old **Sierra Railroad, Jamestown**, northern California (see the Marx Brothers' *Go West* for details).

UNION STATION
(1950, dir: Rudolph Maté)
William Holden, Barry Fitzgerald, Nancy Olson.
● **CHICAGO, ILLINOIS; LOS ANGELES, CALIFORNIA**

Kidnappers use Chicago's famous railway station as the ransom drop. Part of the fifties trend for getting out of the studio and into real locations. Well, almost. Although there is some filming at **Union Station, 210 South Canal Street**, Chicago, most of the time it's **Union Station, 800 North Alameda Street**, downtown Los Angeles.

UNIVERSAL SOLDIER
(1992, dir: Roland Emmerich)
Dolph Lundgren, Jean-Claude Van Damme, Ally Walker.
● **MEXICO; ARIZONA**

Sci-fi, with dead soldiers revived for more active service, made in Mexico; and in Arizona, at **Clarkdale**, **Verde Valley**, **Kingman** and **Prescott**.

UNTOUCHABLES, THE
(1987, dir: Brian De Palma)
Kevin Costner, Sean Connery, Robert De Niro.
● **CHICAGO, ILLINOIS; MONTANA**

Terrific return to form for De Palma, and deserved Oscar nominations for production design and costumes as the film recreates Prohibition era Chicago on location.

The café blown up by the protection racketeers' bomb at the opening was under the 'el' (elevated train) in Wrigleyville, north of town at the junction of **West Roscoe and North Clark Streets**. Just a couple of blocks south of Wrigley Field, the same location can be seen as John Candy's home in the John Hughes-Chris Columbus comedy *Only the Lonely*.

Eliot Ness' police HQ is the **Rookery Building, 202 South La Salle Street**. Built in 1886, its lobby was remodelled in 1907 by Frank Lloyd Wright. It's recently been renovated. South La Salle Street, with its vista leading down to the Chicago Board of Trade Building, is prominently featured, and is the image used on the movie poster. The liquor raid on the US Post Office is here, opposite the Rookery, at the **Continental Illinois Bank and Trust Company, 231 South La Salle Street**.

Ness meets up with incorruptible Irish cop Malone (Connery) on the lower pedestrian deck of the **Michigan Avenue Bridge**, another familiar location you can see in *Rent-a-Cop* and *The Package*. Malone's apartment is in an unchanged block of terraced houses on **South Racine Avenue** at West Harrison Street.

The Lexington Hotel, where Al Capone kept a suite, is no longer in its original state. For the movie, the interior is a conflation of two different locations. The first view of the Lexington, with the newspaper being delivered to Capone (De Niro) in bed, is the upper foyer of the **Chicago Theater, 175 North State Street** at East Lake Street. The exterior of this movie house, with its convenient

The Untouchables' HQ: Rookery Building, South La Salle Street

Capone toasts Pagliacci: Preston Bradley Hall

Capone's Lexington Hotel exterior: Roosevelt University

Ness wises up to Frank Nitti: The Grand Army of the Republic Rotunda

Blowing up the café: West Roscoe and North Clark Streets

The poster image: South La Salle Street

The station shoot-out: Union Station

The bloody banquet: Blackstone Hotel, South Michigan Avenue

'Chicago' sign, is the ubiquitous scene-setting shot for countless Windy City movies (it's briefly glimpsed in *Chicago*), but *The Untouchables* utilises its lavish Baroque interior. The Lexington's lower lobby is the foyer of **Roosevelt University, 430 South Michigan Avenue** – you can peek inside at the Grand Staircase, where Ness confronts Capone after the murder of his fellow Untouchables.

The banquet scene, where Capone gives a pep talk on teamwork before braining a freelancer with a baseball bat, was filmed in the ballroom of the 1910 **Blackstone Hotel, 636 South Michigan Avenue** at East Balbo Drive (© *312.427.4300*) overlooking Grant Park.

The opera house lobby, in which Capone pleads his innocence to the press, is the Grand Staircase of the **Chicago Public Library Cultural Center, 78 East Washington Street**. The staircase, of white Carrara marble inlaid with multi-coloured glass mosaic work, can be seen inside the main southern entrance on Washington Street (© *312.269.2900; free admission to the public daily except Sundays*). It leads up to the **Preston Bradley Hall** on the third floor, with its spectacular 38-foot glass dome – supposedly the largest Tiffany dome in the world, renovated in the 1970s and worth an estimated $35 million. This is the spot where Capone tearfully toasts Pagliacci after the murder of Malone. The center houses another grand glass dome, in the **Grand Army of the Republic Rotunda**, located on the second floor of the

The exterior of the much-used Chicago Theater, North State Street

The lobby of Capone's hotel: Roosevelt University

Capone's hotel: Chicago Theater, North State Street

Ness meets Irish cop Malone: Michigan Avenue Bridge

northern entrance on Randolph Street. The rotunda walls are of Knoxville Pink Marble from Tennessee, the dome Renaissance-style stained glass. This is the courtroom lobby where Ness finds Malone's address in Frank Nitti's matchbook. The subsequent chase leads up to the Cultural Center's roof, from which Nitti is finally thrown.

The set-piece shootout, with De Palma paying homage to the Odessa Steps sequence from *Battleship Potemkin*, was staged in Chicago's imposing **Union Station, 210 South Canal Street**.

A non-Chicago location is the shootout with the rumrunners at the bridge, which uses **Hardy Bridge**, near **Great Falls** on the Missouri in Montana.

The real Eliot Ness operated out of Room 308 in the Transportation Building, 608 South Dearborn Street, still standing but now converted into stores and apartments.

URBAN LEGEND

(1998, dir: Jamie Blanks)
Jared Leto, Alicia Witt, Rebecca Gayheart.
● ONTARIO, CANADA

College kids are offed in the style of various urban myths in this addition to the ironic-slasher genre. The New England college, Stanley Hall, Melbourne, New Hampshire, is the **University of Toronto** campus, smack in the middle of the city of Toronto, Ontario. The Frat house is **Lakeshore Psychiatric Hospital**.

Stanley Hall, New Hampshire: University of Toronto

USUAL SUSPECTS, THE

(1995, dir: Bryan Singer)
Gabriel Byrne, Chazz Palminteri, Kevin Spacey.
● LOS ANGELES, CALIFORNIA; NEW YORK

Set in New York and Los Angeles, Bryan Singer's dazzling, convoluted who-dun-what was made almost entirely on the west coast.

The exterior of Suzy Amis's law office is indeed Manhattan's **Flatiron Building, 175 Fifth Avenue** (the *Daily Bugle* office in *Spider-Man*); the NYPD taxi service drives high-ranking smuggler (Paul Bartel, director of cult favourite *Death Race 2000*) across the **Verrazano Narrows Bridge** (famous from *Saturday Night Fever*), linking Brooklyn to Staten Island; and a few shots of the raid on the New York police car were shot in New York, but the rest is LA. Even the entrance to the New York police station, where the suspects are lined up, is LA's downtown **City Hall, 200 North Spring Street** (the New York subway entrance was built for the film).

The New York restaurant, from which Dean Keaton

Interior filming: Herald Examiner
Building, South Broadway

(Byrne) is unceremoniously hauled off, is the lobby of the old **Herald Examiner Building, 1111 South Broadway**, downtown Los Angeles. In fact, much of the film was shot in this abandoned newspaper office, including the San Pedro police station in which 'Verbal' Kint (Spacey) weaves his dubious tale. Designed, in 1912, by Julia Morgan, the architect of William Randolph Hearst's San Simeon estate (see *Citizen Kane* for details of Hearst's folly), the building was inspired by the California Building from the 1893 Chicago World's Fair, and was home to the *Herald Examiner* newspaper. It has been empty, used only as an occasional movie location, since the paper closed, hosting productions including *Strange Days*, *The Cable Guy* and *End of Days*.

The shipboard conflagration, which wipes out most of the gang, is in LA's harbour, at **San Pedro** (in the background, you can see the Southwest Marine building familiar from *The Lost World: Jurassic Park*).

The mysterious Mr Kobayashi approaches the five on behalf of Keyser Soze in the pool room of the **Hollywood Athletic Club, 6525 Sunset Boulevard** (*www.hollywoodathleticclub.com*). Charlie Chaplin and Rudolph Valentino both kept suites here in the club's heyday as a, somewhat notorious, gentlemen's club. It also houses the London boxing venue where Hilary Swank triumphs in the Oscar-laden *Million Dollar Baby*.

The meeting with Redfoot: Korean Bell
of Friendship, Angels Gate Park

A spectacular location is the huge bell, alongside which the suspects meet up with Redfoot. It's the **Korean Bell of Friendship, Angels Gate Park, 3601 South Gaffey Street** in San Pedro, presented by Korea during the US bicentennial celebrations in 1976. You can find it on the breathtaking wild bluff which overlooks the harbour of San Pedro to the east and the Palos Verdes Peninsula to the west.

V

VACANCES DE MONSIEUR HULOT, LES
(aka *Monsieur Hulot's Holiday*)
(1953, dir: Jacques Tati)
Jacques Tati, Nathalie Pascaud, Michèle Rolla.
● FRANCE

The hotel, where M Hulot causes unintentional havoc, can still be seen, though it's changed a lot since the movie was made in the fifties. It's the **Hotel de la Plage, 37 rue Commandant Charcot, St Marc-sur-Mer** (*©* *02.40.91.9901, www.hotel-de-la-plage-44.com/htgb/ home.htm*) on the mouth of the Loire, between swanky resort La Baule and naval base St Lazaire, about 45 miles west of Nantes, Loire Valley West.

VALLEY OF THE DOLLS
(1967, dir: Mark Robson)
Barbara Parkins, Patty Duke, Susan Hayward.
● LOS ANGELES, CALIFORNIA; NEW YORK CITY; CONNECTICUT

Jacqueline Susann's soapy melodrama about an innocent actress heading down the path of drink and drugs is set in New York and LA. When smalltown girl Barbara Parkins leaves home to find work in the big city, she wisely stays at the Martha Washington Hotel for Women. This New York institution opened in 1903 to provide reputable accommodation for single women travellers in the city. It closed down, only to be reopened as the (mixed) **Thirty Thirty Hotel, 30 East 30th Street** between Madison and Fifth Avenues, Murray Hill.

The sweet little New England town from which Anne Welles (Parkins) hails, and to which she finally returns, suitably chastened, is **Redding Center**, Connecticut.

VAMPIRE LOVERS, THE
(1970, dir: Roy Ward Baker)
Ingrid Pitt, Peter Cushing, Pippa Steele.
● HERTFORDSHIRE

George Cole's mansion: Wall Hall College, Aldenham

Softcore vamping in a late-period Hammer filming of J Sheridan Le Fanu's lesbian vampire novella *Carmilla*. The palatial home of von Spielsdorf (Cushing), where Marcilla (Pitt) first stays, is **Moor Park Golf Club, Anson Walk**, on the A404, northwest of Northwood (seen also in the colourful period romance *Jassy*). The rather more modest mansion of Roger Morton (George Cole) is **Wall Hall College** (now the University of Hertfordshire), north of Aldenham, to the northeast of Watford – seen as the psychiatric clinic in Hammer's Bette Davis shocker *The Nanny*.

VAMPIRES (aka *John Carpenter's Vampires*)
(1998, dir: John Carpenter)
James Woods, Daniel Baldwin, Sheryl Lee.
● NEW MEXICO

John Carpenter's southwest vampires are closer to the bloodsucking family of Kathryn Bigelow's *Near Dark* than the mittel-European nobility of Hammer films. The movie is shot around the red deserts of **Santa Fe**, New Mexico. The Sun God Motel is a set built around the existing sign of a motel that burned down several years ago. Slayer Daniel Baldwin and on-the-change vamp victim Sheryl Lee hole up at the **Plaza Hotel, 230 Plaza, Las Vegas** (*© 505.425.3591*), east of Santa Fe. The hotel already has a footnote in film history. In 1913 it became the HQ of Romaine Fielding's Lubin Film Company, and later became home to silent Western star Tom Mix, who made many of his movies in the Las Vegas area, occasionally using the Plaza as a location. The fictitious town of Santiago is **Cerrillos**, a small desert town on I-14 between Santa Fe and Albuquerque, previously used in *Young Guns*.

VAN HELSING
(2004, dir: Stephen Sommers)
Hugh Jackman, Kate Beckinsale, Richard Roxburgh.
● CZECH REPUBLIC; LOS ANGELES, CALIFORNIA

Having revived the mummy, Sommers exhumes the rest of the old Universal back-catalogue of monsters – as well as Mr Hyde – though, with admirable restraint, he leaves out Abbott and Costello. For copyright reasons, this is not crusty old vampire-chaser Abraham Van Helsing (as previously portrayed by Edward Van Sloan, Peter Cushing and Anthony Hopkins), but proto-Goth rocker *Gabriel Van Helsing* (Jackman), first encountered dealing with Mr Hyde atop Notre Dame Cathedral. The Parisian street into which the crudely cartoonish Hyde plunges is the **Old Town Square of Prague**. Most of the elaborate sets were built in LA, but location filming was around the Czech capital, standing in, not only for Paris, but for Budapest and, of course, Transylvania – the country to which Van Helsing is despatched by the Vatican.

The Transylvanian village, in which Van Helsing encounters Anna Valerious (Beckinsale), was built at **Kunratice U Prahy**, on the outskirts of southern Prague. The forest clearing, in which Anna and Velkan Valerious unsuccessfully attempt to trap a werewolf, is **Pruhonice Park**, the grounds of the **Botanical Institute of the Czech Academy of Sciences**, housed in the restored 13th century chateau of **Pruhonice**. The park (but not the castle), at the southeastern edge of Prague, is open to the public. Further out is the interior of the Valerious family home, which is the castle in the Medieval town of **Tabor**, 55 miles south of Prague.

To the east, toward Brno, is Castle Frankenstein. Embellished with maybe just a little CGI, it's **Pernstejn Castle** (*© 0505.96101; admission charge*), about 20 miles northwest of Brno in the Moravian highlands. The castle was damaged by fire in April 2005, and is currently being restored. The werewolf attack on the improbably inflammable coach was filmed in the forest at **Alkazar**, in the Berounka River valley, near Srbsko, between Karlstein and Beroun, southwest of Prague. There was more filming at the picturesque town of **Cesky Krumlov**.

In Prague itself, the Budapest street, where Van Helsing agrees to trade Frankenstein's monster for Anna and receives an invite to the Count's ball, is beneath **Karluv Most** (the Charles Bridge; seen also in *Mission: Impossible* and *XXX*). Dracula's summer palace, site of the lavish masquerade, is the extravagantly baroque interior of the 1761 **St Nicholas Church, Malostanske namesti**, Mala Strana. The palace graveyard, where Frankenstein's monster is hidden, is the **Olsanske hrbitovy** (the Olsanske Cemetery), **Vinohradska trida**, seen also in *The League of Extraordinary Gentlemen* and *Dungeons & Dragons*.

Back to California for the ending. Anna's funeral pyre is on the bluffs overlooking the Pacific at – where else? – **Palos Verdes**, south LA; and the final shot of Van riding off into the sunset is **Piru**, north of LA.

VANGELO SECONDO MATTEO, IL (aka *The Gospel According To St. Matthew*)
(1964, dir: Pier Paolo Pasolini)
Enrique Irazoqui, Margherita Caruso, Susanna Pasolini.
● **ITALY**

Non-professional actors, world music and stark monochrome cinematography – Pasolini's Marxist-Humanist version of the gospel story is a long, long way from Cecil B DeMille. Filmed around **Calabria** and **Lucania** in southern Italy, and the plains of **Massafra** in **Puglia**. The temptation by Satan was filmed on the slopes of **Mount Etna**. Scenes were also shot at **Matera**, used in Mel Gibson's *The Passion of the Christ*.

VANILLA SKY
(2001, dir: Cameron Crowe)
Tom Cruise, Penelope Cruz, Cameron Diaz.
● **NEW YORK CITY; LOS ANGELES, CALIFORNIA**

Crowe's retelling of the Spanish film *Abre Los Ojos* relocates the story from Madrid to New York, where the apartment of wealthy publisher David Aames (Cruise) is the **Dakota Building, 1 West 72nd Street** at Central Park West (see *Rosemary's Baby* for details). Since filming is no longer permitted at the Dakota, only the exterior is

The fashionably Bohemian apartment of Penelope Cruz, Jay Street, Dumbo

seen. Aames drives along a traffic-free **Central Park West** to an eerily deserted **Times Square** (no CGI here – the normally packed square was emptied for three hours one Sunday morning).

Unhinged Julie Gianni confronts Aames on Water Street

Likewise, the Aames Building, in reality the **Condé Nast Building, 4 Times Square**, the offices of *Vanity Fair*, was temporarily empty during the Christmas period.

Julie swerves out of control on Riverside Drive

There are few areas in Manhattan which don't have a cute acronym, and the fashionably

The crash onto 95th Street

Bohemian apartment of Sofia Serrano (Cruz) is in **Dumbo** (down under the **Manhattan Bridge Overpass**), **57 Jay Street** at Water Street, on the Brooklyn side of the East River. The rather unhinged Julie Gianni (Diaz) confronts Aames on **Water Street**, before taking him on a nervewracking drive up to the West Side. It's on **Riverside Drive** that Julie swerves out of control, careering off the overpass to crash sickeningly onto **95th Street**.

Although a sequence filmed at the Edison Electric Building, Main Street, downtown Los Angeles, was cut from the movie, LA does make an appearance. The bar, where Aames removes his mask, is **The Brewery**, a huge arts complex (which was formerly the Pabst Blue Ribbon factory), **620 Moulton Avenue** at North Main Street, downtown LA. It houses Barbara's at the Brewery, a restaurant and bar.

VANISHING, THE
(1993, dir: George Sluizer)
Jeff Bridges, Kiefer Sutherland, Sandra Bullock.
● **WASHINGTON; WYOMING; CALIFORNIA**

What's surprising is that this Hollywood remake of *Spoorloos*, which throws out the elements that made the original so great, was made by the same director. The locale is changed to *Twin Peaks* territory, around the Seattle area of the Pacific northwest. Kiefer Sutherland and Sandra Bullock drive through the blasted landscape of **Mount St Helens**, Washington State, but the tunnel, where they run out of gas, on on I-14/16/20, six miles west of **Cody**, leading to Yellowstone National Park, Wyoming. The gas station, where Bullock disappears, is the **Texaco Station, 742 SW Mount Si Boulevard, North Bend**, off I-90.

Jeff Bridges' lakeside cabin is at **Camp Omache, 24225 Woods Creek Road, Snohomish**, on Lake Hughes near **Monroe** in the Cascade Mountains, Washington State. He accosts women at Seattle's famous **Pike Place Market**. There was filming also in California, at **234 North Canyon Boulevard, Monrovia**, east of Pasadena.

VANISHING POINT
(1971, dir: Richard C Sarafian)
Barry Newman, Cleavon Little, Dean Jagger
● UTAH; NEVADA; COLORADO

If the studio suits sat down to assemble a post-*Easy Rider* cliché compendium, this is the market-led package they would have put together. Ex-cop, ex-racing driver, ex-surfer, turned drugs courier, Kowalski (Newman), races across the desert, establishing a psychic link with blind soul DJ Super Soul (Little), while flashbacks crop up with the regularity of ad breaks, though the movie's acquired enough cultish clout to have inspired an album by Primal Scream. The real pleasure comes in the form of the fabulous dusty wastes of the Nevada and Utah deserts. Kowalski's journey begins in Denver, Colorado; and crosses three central counties of Utah: Lander, Nye and Esmeralda. Super Soul broadcasts from the now-abandoned **Goldfield Hotel, Goldfield**, a near-ghost town in Utah. The small town where the cop car overturns is **Salina**, Utah. The towns Kowalski whizzes through are **Thompson Springs**, **Green River** and **Wendover**, Utah; **Glenwood Spring** and **Grand Junction**, Colorado; and **Tonopah, Elko** and **Austin**, Nevada. The climactic smash-up is at **Cisco**, on I-70, near Moab, Utah.

VARGTIMMEN (aka *Hour of the Wolf*)
(1967, dir: Ingmar Bergman)
Max von Sydow, Liv Ullmann, Ingrid Thulin.
● SWEDEN

Bleak, powerful Bergman, from his peak period. Artist alter-ego von Sydow suffers nightmares straight out of thirties Universal horror movies on a bleached out Frisian island. The island is a composite of the rocky headland at **Hovs Hallar** in southwest Sweden (where von Sydow memorably met Death in *The Seventh Seal*) and the island of **Faro**, off the island of Gotland in the Baltic Faro. The setting of many later Bergman films, it is a very private island, off limits to foreigners.

VELVET GOLDMINE

Oscar Wilde deposited on the Dublin doorstep: Elder Street, Spitalfields

(1998, dir: Todd Haynes)
Jonathan Rhys Meyers, Ewan McGregor, Christian Bale.
● LONDON

Brave, but ultimately botched, fantasia on the seventies glam-rock phenomenon, from the maverick director who went on to make the Sirkian melodrama *Far From Heaven*. It's structured as a pastiche of *Citizen Kane*, with Rhys Meyers as Brian Slade, aka Maxwell

The glitter kids first glimpse Jack Fairy: Hanway Place

Maxwell Demon's final concert: Brixton Academy

Demon, a pouting Bowie-figure, and McGregor an amalgam of Iggy Pop and Kurt Cobain. It's all filmed around London, including the bizarre opening, in Dublin, 1854. The doorway at which the baby Oscar Wilde is deposited by aliens, is **15 Elder Street**, a tiny cobbled lane off Folgate Street, **Spitalfields**, E1. Still in the East End, star-to-be Slade learns a bit about theatre – and life – watching panto dame Lindsay Kemp perform (on- and off-stage) at the famous **Hackney Empire, 291 Mare Lane** (*© 020.8510.4500, www.hackney-empire.co.uk*). See *Chaplin* for details.

The small angled backstreet of **Hanway Place**, behind Hanway Street off Tottenham Court Road in the West End, is where the glitter kids first glimpse Jack Fairy, on their way to the concert at which Demon fakes his onstage assassination. The venue, though, is way, way south, across the Thames at the famous **Brixton Academy, 211 Stockwell Road**, SW9 (*© 020.7771.3000, www.brixton-academy.co.uk*).

Fast-forward to 1984 and the assignation of journalist Arthur Stuart (Bale) to trace the disappeared rock star in New York. The quest takes him no further than the sixties concrete canyons of central **Croydon**. And the Midtown dive is the bar of the **Railway Social Club, 78 Goodhall Street**, off Old Oak Lane, near glamorous **Willesden Junction**, while the club's Upper Hall became the Last Resort club, where he interviews washed-up Mandy Slade (Toni Collette). The social club had previously been seen as Hamburg in *Backbeat* but, for *Goldmine*, the immediate area soon reverts to being London when Slade, as a young Mod, picks up a schoolboy nearby, on **Stephenson Street**. It's a popular area for filming – 29 Goodhall Street was home to the titular Spider (Ralph Fiennes) in the David Cronenberg movie.

The obligatory rock'n'roll orgy is at **Mentmore Towers**, the gothic pile at the village of **Mentmore** in Buckinghamshire (the exterior of the Long Island mansion where Tom Cruise attends the bizarre orgy in Kubrick's *Eyes Wide Shut* – see Terry Gilliam's *Brazil* for details).

The Sombrero Club, where Slade is discovered playing guitar, *Man Who Sold the*

The Sombrero Club, Kensington: Brigade Street, Blackheath

Devine directs the glitzy promo: Rear of Chiswick House, Burlington Lane

World-style, in a frock, is somewhat glamorised. The famous gay hangout lay behind an unremarkable doorway at 142-144 High Street Kensington, but the film uses **17 Brigade Street**, a tiny cobbled passageway between Tranquil Passage and Royal Parade, **Blackheath**, south London, where Haynes takes a break from *Kane* to pastiche the party scene from Welles's *The Magnificent Ambersons*. The Sombrero interior, where the denizens speak entirely in subtitled polari (gay slang), is the upstairs pub theatre at **The Bedford, 77 Bedford Hill** at Fernlea Road, **Balham** (*© 020.8673.1756, www.thebedford.co.uk*).

Stuart and polysexual Curt Wild (McGregor) get it together on the roof of **Stanley Buildings, Stanley Passage**, behind King's Cross Station, between Pancras Road and the famous stretch of Cheney Road, by the now-gone gasometers – gamely humping away, unaware that the cameras, sited on a nearby rooftop, had long since stopped turning. The block, now half-demolished to be redeveloped as luxury apartments – seen in Mike Leigh's *High Hopes* and the Ian McKellen version of *Richard III* – was Michael Palin's dockland mission to fallen women in *The Missionary* and home to Kathy Burke in Camden-set romcom *This Year's Love*.

The wood-panelled deco office of Bijou Records supremo Jerry Devine (Eddie Izzard) is in **Bethnal Green Town Hall, Cambridge Heath Road** at Patriot Square (see *Lock, Stock and Two Smoking Barrels* for details), and the formal garden, in which Devine directs the glitzy promo, can be found at the rear of **Chiswick House, Burlington Lane, Chiswick** (see *The Servant* for details).

VERA DRAKE

(2004, dir: Mike Leigh)
Imelda Staunton, Philip Davis, Eddie Marsan.
● **LONDON; SURREY**

Deals in the local boozer: The Mitre, Copenhagen Street, King's Cross

Mike Leigh's affecting and Oscar-nominated drama mixes beautifully observed performances with some clunky cliches and plot contrivances. The 1950 period is conveyed by perfectly chosen locations around London. Interior sets were built at Hornsey Central Hospital, Park Road, Hornsey, N8, which was also used as a rehearsal space. Director Leigh envisioned Vera (Staunton) as a north Londoner, living in Copenhagen Street, the *Ladykillers* neighbourhood near King's Cross (she gives her address as 82 Essex Buildings, Oslo Street). The ideal housing block was found in the East End, **Cressy Hous-**

Vera's apartment block: Cressy Houses, Hannibal Road

The home of Frank, and his upwardly-mobile wife Joyce: Wood Vale, Hornsey

es, at the south end of **Hannibal Road**, off Mile End Road, near Stepney Green tube, E1.

The local boozer, though, where Vera's son, Sidney, and his pals keep the wheels of the alternative economy turning, *is* in Copenhagen Street. It's **The Mitre, 181 Copenhagen Street**, N1. Vera's husband, Stan (Davis) works for his brother at Frank Drake's Garage, which is the nearby **North London Freight Depot, York Way** at King's Cross. Frank, and his upwardly-mobile wife Joyce, live further north, at **4 Wood Vale, Hornsey**, N10, alongside Queen's Wood, near Highgate tube.

Getting away from the Mitre, Sidney and his mates let rip, pre-rock'n'roll style, with the local girls at the **Mildmay Club, 34 Newington Green**, N16; while Vera's daughter Ethel walks in the park with good-natured neighbour Reg (Marsan) in **St Dunstan's Cemetery, Whitehorse Road, Stepney**, E1.

On to Leigh's weaker spot, the ghastly middle classes. Mabel Fowler's basement, where Vera polishes the brass, David's flat and the private clinic to which Susan is sent for her termination, were all in **Portland Place, Fitzrovia**, W1. Fitzrovia is named for Fitzroy Square, and it's **6 Fitzroy Square** which became the house of Susan Wells and her family.

This was the benighted fifties, and when one of the girls Vera tries to help gets sick, the law descends on the Drake household. The police station to which Vera is taken, and the magistrate's court in which she's charged, are the **Old Thames Magistrates Court, Arbour Square**, off Commercial Road, **Stepney**, E1. The Central Criminal Court, the 'Old Bailey', in which Vera is sentenced to prison, is **County Hall Kingston, Penrhyn Road, Kingston-upon-Thames** in Surrey.

VERTIGO

(1958, dir: Alfred Hitchcock)
James Stewart, Kim Novak, Barbara Bel Geddes.
● **CALIFORNIA**

The portrait of Carlotta: Palace of the Legion of Honor, Lincoln Park

Starting out as a conventional enough thriller, with ex-cop Scottie (Stewart) hired by worried husband Gavin Elster to keep an eye on

Scottie and Madeleine at the seashore: Seventeen-Mile Drive

The giant redwood trees: Big Basin Redwoods State Park

the bizarre behaviour of his wife, Madeleine (Novak), acrophobia segues imperceptibly into the fear of sex and of death as Scottie becomes Hitchcock-by-proxy, recreating and controlling his unattainable object of desire.

Hitchcock signals the sudden flare-up of irrational passion by disrupting the pastel colour scheme and setting Scottie's first glimpse of Madeleine against the rich red silk interior of Ernie's Restaurant, near Washington Street in the Jackson Square Historic District. One of Hitch's own favourite San Francisco hangouts, Ernie's had been serving up *haute cuisine* to the well-heeled since 1934, but finally closed its doors only to reopen as the Essex Supper Club. Sadly, this too has since closed. The restaurant stood at **847 Montgomery Street**.

A few blocks southwest, on the summit of the appropriately named Nob Hill, is Elster's imposing apartment block, from which the smitten Scottie tails Madeleine Elster. Its unmistakable entrance court guarded by elaborate lamps, the 277-room **Brocklebank Apartments, 1000 Mason Street** at Sacramento Street, is a major location for Gene Wilder's 1984 *The Woman in Red*, and also features in the TV adaptation of Armistead Maupin's *Tales of the City*.

There's nothing left to see on the northwest corner of Gough and Eddy Streets, where Scottie trails Mrs Elster to McKittrick's Hotel, the old house of long-dead Carlotta Valdes (the area, north of the Civic Center district, has been redeveloped, and the elaborate gothic St Paul's Lutheran Church dating from 1872, which you can see behind James Stewart, has since been destroyed by fire). You can, though, visit the gleaming white-pillared palace in which Madeleine sits spellbound by Carlotta's portrait. Situated between China and Ocean Beaches on San Francisco's northwesterly tip, it's the **Palace of the Legion of Honor, Legion of Honor Drive** in Lincoln Park (*© 415.750.3659; admission charge*). A twin of the Legion d'Honneur in Paris, the gallery houses a rather more impressive collection of paintings than Carlotta Valdes'

The mission: San Juan Bautista

kitschy portrait, including works by Rembrandt, Titian, Monet, Renoir and Degas along with one of the world's finest collections of

The interior of the mission: San Juan Bautista

Rodin sculptures.

Madeleine continues to sign-post her obsession by visiting the grave of Valdes. The tiny cemetery, in which the suicidal Carlotta supposedly rests – every bit as atmospheric as it appears in the movie – has its own share of buried secrets. You can find it behind the **Mission Dolores, 320 Dolores Street** at Sixteenth Street in the Mission District (*BART metro: 16th Street-Mission*). Once you've seen the ornate exterior, you can forget the pompous basilica which was grafted on next door in 1913, the real interest here is the Misión San Francisco De Asis, completed in 1791. One of the 21 California missions established by the Spanish in the 18th century and the oldest intact survivor, its four-foot thick adobe walls having withstood the worst assaults of San Andreas, the mission of St Francis of Assisi is not only the oldest building in San Francisco but gives the city its name. Visit the cool, dark chapel interior with its unique Spanish-Mexican decoration and ceiling painting based on the designs of the Ramaytush people – dubbed Costanoans ('coast dwellers') by the 'kindly' Spanish Franciscans who occupied their land, resettled them and oversaw their complete extinction. By 1850 there was only one Ramaytush left alive. A small museum records sanitised highlights of the mission's history – for a while in the 1840s and 1850s under Mexican rule it became a hotel and a gambling den, and bullfights were held on the plaza where Dolores Street now stands. The museum exits into the cemetery itself. Don't be fooled by the size. Over 5,500 of the native people are buried here in a common grave, commemorated by a single stone shrine. The grander monuments record the founding Father Palou, the city's bigwigs and the, mainly Irish, immigrants who poured into the area after the Gold Rush.

Back northwest of the city is the granite sea wall beneath the southern anchoring of the Golden Gate Bridge at **Fort Point, Marine Drive** off Long Avenue, the spot where Madeleine takes a reckless plunge into the notoriously treacherous waters of the bay. The site is named for the brick fort, built in the 1850s to defend the city from sea attack long before the bridge was conceived. It now houses a museum of militaria (*© 415.556.1693*).

Falling for the possessed woman act, Scottie rescues Madeleine and takes her back to his apartment. Scottie's home stands, virtually unchanged, at **900 Lombard Street** on the corner of Jones Street, just at the foot of the series of famous hairpin bends on the 'Crookedest Street in the World'. Looking east along Lombard Street you can't miss Telegraph

The stables: San Juan Bautista

The inquest: Plaza Hall, San Juan Bautista

Scottie thwarts Madeleine's suicide attempt: Fort Point, Marine Drive

Hill, and crowning it, the **Coit Memorial Tower, Telegraph Hill Boulevard**, the landmark Madeleine later uses to find her way back to Scottie's apartment. The tower was built 'to beautify San Francisco' with a bequest left to the city by Lillie Hitchcock Coit (no relation), a Bay City pioneer woman apparently fascinated by firemen (as a girl she was made an honorary member of the Knickerbocker No.5 Fire Company). It's claimed, presumably by people unfamiliar with the works of Freud, that the monument is intended to resemble a firehose nozzle. If your ambition is to visit the top of a reinforced concrete tower perched on the summit of a steep hill in a notorious earthquake zone, you can take the elevator to a 210-foot observation deck, which does actually give wonderful views of the bay (*admission charge*).

Over the Golden Gate Bridge, about 15 miles north on Shoreline Drive, Mill Valley, off Route 1, are Muir Woods (© *415.388.2595; open 8am-sunset*), the Giant Redwood grove, home to some of the largest and oldest living creatures on the earth, *Sequoia Sempervirens* – "Always green, ever living" – supposedly where Madeleine gets the heebie-jeebies contemplating the past. Although it's here, near the visitor centre, that you can find a section of tree trunk on which significant dates in history are recorded, the actual filming location was **Big Basin Redwoods State Park, 21600 Big Basin Way** – Route 236 – at Boulder Creek (© *408.338.6132*) off Pacific Coast Highway 1 south of San Francisco toward Santa Cruz. (I don't have a photograph as the tree is, unbelievably, copyrighted. Only, as they say, in America.) The seashore, where Scottie follows the apparently distraught Madeleine, is **Cypress Point** on **Seventeen-Mile Drive**, on the wild Monterey Peninsula.

When Madeleine finally succumbs to her suicidal impulse, Scottie suffers a nervous breakdown, recuperating in a sanitarium at **351 Buena Vista Avenue East**. Overwhelmed by his own obsession, he refashions lookalike actress Judy Barton into Madeleine's dead image.

Scottie's apartment: Lombard Street

For the transformation of Judy back into Madeleine, Hitchcock pulls off one of his dazzling visual coups, filling the seedy hotel

room with an unearthly green neon glow. Although the film's Hotel Empire has undergone a name change and a major facelift, you'll still recognise Judy's lodging. Not only is it now quite posh, it also houses one of the city's top cabaret spots, the Plush Room. You can see the **York Hotel** at **940 Sutter Street** (© *415.885.6800, www.yorkhotel.com*) between Hyde and Leavenworth Streets just west of the downtown area.

Elster's luxury apartment block: Brocklebank Apartments, Mason Street

Judy's Lodging: York Hotel, Sutter Street

The movie's climax returns to the scene of Madeleine's suicide/murder. About 90 miles south of San Francisco, just east from Route 101, is the quiet little town of San Juan Bautista, home to a clutch of beautifully restored period buildings preserved as a State Historic Park. On the town's central plaza you'll find not only the mission, but the **Plaza Stables** Madeleine claims to remember from a previous existence, and **Plaza Hall**, the courtroom where the inquest is held (though, once again, the interior was recreated in the studio). The 19th century **Mission San Juan Bautista** is the largest of the Spanish missions and houses a small museum, open daily from 10am to 4pm. Don't expect to see the belltower, from which Judy finally plunges to her death. The church's tower had collapsed many years before and the movie's climax makes use of a superimposed painting.

VICTIM

(1961, dir: Basil Dearden)
Dirk Bogarde, Sylvia Syms, Peter McEnery.
● **LONDON**

For its time, this was an extraordinarily brave attempt to encourage reform of the UK's anti-homosexual laws, with this melodrama about the blackmail of bisexual barrister Melville Farr (Bogarde). Many of the locations are around London's

Melville Farr's riverside home: Morton House

West End, including the gleaming glass-and-brass pub, **Salisbury, 90 St Martin's Lane** (where Maggie Smith stays in *Travels With My Aunt*), which at the time was indeed one of the capital's most famous theatrical gay bars (© *020.7836.5863*). The barber shop, where fluttery hairdresser Henry (Charles Lloyd Pack) keels over from a heart attack after being threatened by sinister Derren Nesbitt, was **2 Earlham Street**, alongside the Marquis of Granby pub, just off Cambridge Circus. It's now a

The West End gay bar: Salisbury, St Martin's Lane

newsagent. Farr meets up with blackmailer Nesbitt on the **Embankment** south of **Dolphin Square** in **Pimlico**. The barrister's riverside home is **Morton House, Chiswick Mall**, next door to Strawberry House, seen in two Merchant-Ivory productions, *Howards End* and *The Golden Bowl*.

VIDEODROME

(1982, dir: David Cronenberg)
James Woods, Deborah Harry, Sonja Smits.

● ONTARIO, CANADA

A TV signal induces the growth of a new organ within the brain in another of the director's explorations of the blurring borderline between the human body and new technology. If it's Cronenberg, chances are it's Toronto. And it is. The 'Spectacular Optical' presentation, where James Woods rebels and blows away the Videodrome chief, is at the **Westin Harbour Castle, 1 Harbour Square**, Toronto (*© 416.869.1600*).

VIEW TO A KILL, A

(1985, dir: John Glen)
Roger Moore, Christopher Walken, Grace Jones.

● CALIFORNIA; FRANCE; BERKSHIRE; SUSSEX; ICELAND; SWITZERLAND; LONDON

Bond's leap onto the pleasure boat: Pont Alexandre III

Fourteenth in the mainstream Bond series uses much the same plot as the 1978 *Superman*, with electronics wiz Zorin (Walken) attempting to trigger the San Andreas fault into action and flood California's Silicon Valley… or something.

The pre-credits Siberia teaser is actually **Glacier Lake**, on the southeast tip of the huge **Vatnajökull Glacier** and the tiny hamlet of **Höfn** on the southeast coast of Iceland. You can visit the glacier on a trip from the Hotel Höfn, 781 Hornefjöur (*© 478.1240*), though be warned, the Vatnajökull volcano erupted under the ice-sheet in 1996. The chase continues at a larger glacier, the **Vadretta di Scerscen Inferiore** on the Swiss/Italian border.

M's London HQ is now in **Whitehall**. Bond (Moore) first checks out Zorin at **Ascot Race-**

Bond meets CIA agent Jack Lee: Fisherman's Wharf, San Francisco

course, on the A330 five miles south of Windsor, Berkshire.

In Paris, Bond meets up with the unlikely French detective M Aubergine, who's killed by a butterfly in the **Restaurant Jules Verne**, the pricey eaterie on the second floor of the Eiffel Tower (*© 01.45.55.61.44*). After Zorin's henchwoman, May Day (Jones) makes a spectacular leap from the Tower, there's a car chase culminating in Bond's leap into the Seine pleasure boat from the **Pont Alexandre III** (a wonderfully over-the-top confection also used in *Anastasia*, John Huston's 1952 Toulouse Lautrec biopic *Moulin Rouge* and John Frankenheimer's *Ronin*).

Zorin's Silicon Valley mine: Amberley Chalk Pits Museum

Zorin's estate is the 18th century (he says it's 16th century, but that's a Bond villain for you) **Chateau Chantilly**, 20 miles north of Paris on the N16 in the Picardy region. The dazzling chateau, open to the public (*© 01.44.57.08.00; admission charge*), is set among gardens and lakes to the west of the town of Chantilly. It's a 30-minute walk from Chantilly-Gouvieux station, reached from the Gare du Nord. The chateau also appears in *The Longest Day*, *Valmont* and 1958's *The Young Lions*, with Marlon Brando and Montgomery Clift. The racecourse here is the spectacular **Piste d'Avilly**. Bond pits himself against Zorin in a steeplechase in the Forest of Chantilly, while Sir Godfrey gets garotted in a carwash in the city of Chantilly itself.

Bond follows Zorin to San Francisco, where he meets CIA agent Jack Lee at bright but touristy **Fisherman's Wharf** on the bay. The State Office Building, where Zorin's corrupt official, Howe, has his Divisions of Oil and Mines office, is **San Francisco City Hall, Van Ness Avenue** at McAllister Street. This 1915 domed building, modelled on St Peter's in Rome, is no stranger to movies – *Dirty Harry* seems to spend an inordinate amount of time being insubordinate to city officials here. The moviemakers were allowed plenty of licence to simulate Zorin's burning down of the building, including fitting out the balconies with gas jets. The fire-truck chase hares off down **Market Street** to the **Lefty O'Doul Drawbridge** on Third Street at China Basin (just past the Burger Island where Clint uttered the immortal line "Go ahead, make my day" in *Sudden Impact*). Lefty O'Doul, if you're wondering, was an old-time ball-player. The home of oil heiress Stacey Sutton is **Dunsmuir House and Gardens, 2960 Peralta Oaks Court, Oakland**, (*© 510.615.5555; guided tours April to September*) over the bay from San Francisco. Zorin's Main Strike, the abandoned silver mine in Silicon Valley, isn't in California

Stacey's mansion: Dunsmuir House and Gardens

at all, or even in the US. You can see the entrance to the mine at the 36-acre, open-air **Amberley Chalk Pits Museum** (© *01798.831370, www.amberleymuseum.co.uk; admission charge*), opposite Amberley Station in west Sussex.

VIKINGS, THE
(1958, dir: Richard Fleischer)
Kirk Douglas, Tony Curtis, Janet Leigh.
● **NORWAY; FRANCE**

Douglas and Curtis slug it out in this enjoyably butch Norse saga, shot on location in Norway, near to **Bergen**. Sea battles were filmed in the **Hardanger Fjord**. The castle is the 14th century **Fort Lalatte**, on the north Brittany coast between St Brieuc and St Malo.

VILLAGE, THE (aka *M Night Shyamalan's The Village*)
(2004, dir: M Night Shyamalan)
Bryce Dallas Howard, Joaquin Phoenix, Adrien Brody.
● **PENNSYLVANIA; NEW JERSEY**

Having made his reputation with the tricksy *Sixth Sense*, Shyamalan's films are now hampered by the anticipation of a fiendish twist. The 19th century town of Covington in this disappointingly contrived drama was built from scratch in a field off **Cossarts Road, Chadds Ford**, in the Brandywine Valley, I-1 about 30 miles southwest of Philadelphia. The set was due to be dismantled after filming. Chadds Ford is a Revolutionary War battlefield park.

Without giving too much away, the ending was filmed on **Straughns Mill Road**, off I-295, **Pedricktown**, just across the Delaware River in New Jersey.

VILLAGE OF THE DAMNED
(1960, dir: Wolf Rilla)
George Sanders, Barbara Shelley, Michael Gwynn.
● **HERTFORDSHIRE**

The 'village of the damned': Letchmore Heath, Hertfordshire

Creepy sci-fi horror, adapted from John Wyndham's *The Midwich Cuckoos*, with a clutch of unemotional, super-intelligent kids born simultaneously in a small English village. The damned village of Midwich is **Letchmore Heath**, just east of Watford and, conveniently, within four miles of MGM's Borehamwood Studios.

VIRGIN SPRING, THE
(1959, dir: Ingmar Bergman)
Max von Sydow, Gunnel Lindblom, Brigitta Valberg.
● **SWEDEN**

Von Sydow kills the three men who raped and murdered his daughter, at which point a spring bubbles up from the spot on which she died, in this odd Medieval fable. It was loosely remade by Wes Craven, in 1972, as the notorious *Last House on the Left*. Bergman's original was shot in the forest around **Styggforsen**, in Dalarna, not far from Rattvik, central Sweden.

VISKNINGAR OCH ROP (aka *Cries and Whispers*)
(1972, dir: Ingmar Bergman)
Harriet Andersson, Ingrid Thulin, Liv Ullmann.
● **STOCKHOLM**

Harriet Andersson dies slowly of cancer, tended by sisters Ingrid and Liv, and earthmother Kari Sylwan in Bergman's beautiful, elegaic movie. The mansion setting is the **Taxinge-Nasby estate**, a decayed old manor house which was in such a dilapidated state that the film crew were allowed to do what they liked, which included painting the interior walls of the house blood-red (a favourite Bergman device). The mansion is outside Mariefried in the Malar district west of Stockholm.

VITA E BELLA, LA (aka *Life Is Beautiful*)
(1997, dir: Roberto Benigni)
Roberto Benigni, Nicoletta Braschi, Giustino Durano.
● **ITALY**

"The indomitability of the human spirit" is always a winner with Oscar voters and, yes, Benigni's Chaplinesque fable picked up three of the little gold chaps. The town in which zanily romantic Guido Orefice (Benigni himself) has ambitions to open a bookshop is **Arezzo**, southeast of Florence in Tuscany (information boards pointing out the film's locations are helpfully dotted about). The opera house, in which Guido shows more interest in his 'principessa' than in *The Tales of Hoffman*, is the 19th century **Teatro Signorelli, Piazza Signorelli** in **Cortona** (© *0575.601882, www.teatrosignorelli.com*).

The mood turns darker as Guido and his son are transported to Germany. The forbidding concentration camp (designed by longtime Fellini collaborator Danilo Donati) was built on the remains of an abandoned chemical factory near the Marmore Falls in **Terni**. The complex has since been developed by Benigni into the Papigno film studio, where his live-action film of *Pinocchio* was shot.

VITELLONI, I
(1953, dir: Federico Fellini)
Franco Interlenghi, Alberto Sordi, Franco Fabrizi.
● **ITALY**

The title translates – awkwardly – as 'the overgrown calves', twentysomething mama's boys lounging and scrounging aimlessly between school and marriage in, essentially, the original slacker movie. Although it's never overtly stated, the setting for Fellini's first major success (and his personal favourite) is Rimini. Fellini always shied away from filming in his hometown – when he made *Amarcord* in 1974 he recreated the town at Cinecitta studios. The town exteriors are **Viterbo**, about 40 miles northwest of Rome, where the *vitelloni* hang out in **Piazza della Rocca**. Viterbo is landlocked, and the forlorn beach is Rome's nearest seaside resort, **Ostia**.

Interiors were filmed much further north, in **Florence**. The carnival dance is celebrated in the **Goldoni Theatre, via Santa Maria, Florence**. which is also where wannabe playwright Leopoldo goes to meet grand actor Sergio Natali. Achille Majeroni, who played the ageing ham (replacing Fellini's first choice, the neo-realist director Vittori de Sica), was clearly not too hot on subtext. Only after the film was completed did he discover, to his horror, that his character was gay.

VIVA LAS VEGAS (aka *Love in Las Vegas*)
(1964, dir: George Sidney)
Elvis Presley, Ann-Margret, Cesare Danova.
● LOS ANGELES, CALIFORNIA; NEVADA

The 'Folies Bergere' number: Hotel Tropicana, Las Vegas Boulevard South, Las Vegas

Presley (apparently unknown in Vegas) enters a talent contest to pay for his racing car. The film was, as usual for Presley pictures, mostly shot in Hollywood, though there is some real Vegas. The 'Folies Bergere' number filmed at the **Hotel Tropicana, 3801 Las Vegas Boulevard South** at Tropicana Avenue (*www.tropicanalv.com*). Last, fanciest and most expensive of the Strip hotels to be built in the fifties, the Tropicana houses the Strip's longest-running revue, *Les Folies Bergere*, which opened in 1959.

W

WAIT UNTIL DARK

(1967, dir: Terence Young)
Audrey Hepburn, Alan Arkin, Richard Crenna.
● **NEW YORK CITY**

Audrey Hepburn is tormented: St Luke's Place, Greenwich Village

It's bad news for blind Audrey Hepburn when ruthless psychos discover that a cache of drugs is hidden in her New York apartment. This little suspenser, prefiguring David Fincher's *The Panic Room*, contains one of the all-time great seat-jumping moments. Hepburn's basement is the classic 1860s townhouse at **4 St Luke's Place**, off Hudson Street in a classy part of Greenwich Village. Incidentally, her neighbours include, at number 12, that nice family the Huxtables, from TV's *The Cosby Show*.

WAKING NED (aka *Waking Ned Devine*)

(1998, dir: Kirk Jones)
Ian Bannen, David Kelly, Fionnula Flanagan.
● **ISLE OF MAN**

A lottery win for a dead man in a tiny Irish village has oldsters Bannen and Kelly working a scam to get the money. The fictitious Irish village of Tullymore is **Cregneish**, on the A31 at the southwest tip of the Isle of Man.

WALL STREET

(1987, dir: Oliver Stone)
Michael Douglas, Charlie Sheen, Daryl Hannah.
● **NEW YORK CITY**

The defining eighties movie, with Douglas' reptilian Gordon Gekko providing a yuppie role model for the ambitious Bud Fox (Sheen). Both Jackson Steinem, the office in which broker Fox dreams of being on the other end of the phone, and Gekko's own company were filmed at **222 Broadway**, downtown Manhattan. As Fox "bags the elephant", insinuating himself into Gekko's exclusive circle, he's invited to sample steak tartare at exclusive hangout **The 21 Club, 21 West 52nd Street** (*© 212.582.7200, www.21club.com*) between Fifth and Sixth Avenues (seen also in *All About Eve*, *Manhattan Murder Mystery* and *The Sweet Smell of Success*). Rock Hudson takes Lauren Bacall to the 21 (which was recreated in the studio) for "the best steak sandwich in the world" in Douglas Sirk's 1956 melodrama *Written On the Wind*.

Exclusive hangout: The 21 Club, West 52nd Street

Given the task of tailing Gekko's rival, Fox follows Sir Larry Wildman (Terence Stamp) to **26 Broadway**, and on to the exclusive Le Cirque Restaurant in the old Mayfair Regent Hotel. The hotel at **610 Park Avenue** at the southwest corner of 65th Street on the prestigious East Side, outside which Fox waits, has been redeveloped by Donald Trump as a condominium. Le Cirque itself moved to the New York Palace Hotel, 451 Madison Avenue, in 1997, and the restaurant is now Daniel, 60 East 65th Street (*© 212.288.0033, www.daniel-nyc.com*).

Gekko provides one of the iconic images of the decade, delivering his "Greed is good" speech at the Teldar Stockholders Meeting in the **Grand Ballroom** of the **Roosevelt Hotel, 45 East 45th Street** at Madisdon Avenue, midtown (*© 212.661.9600, www.theroosevelthotel.com*).

After being coerced into entrapping his former mentor, Fox meets up with Gekko in Central Park. The restaurant where it's revealed that Fox has been wearing a wire is the **Tavern on the Green, Central Park** at West 67th Street (see *Ghostbusters* for details). Fox is finally dropped off by his dad to face the music at the **New York Supreme Court Building, 60 Centre Street**.

WAR GAMES

(1983, dir: John Badham)
Matthew Broderick, Ally Sheedy, John Wood.
● **WASHINGTON; CALIFORNIA**

Schoolkid David Lightman (Broderick, still playing teens at 22) hacks into the US defence system for a quick game of Global Thermonuclear War. Set in the Pacific North-

The Goose Island ferry: Steilacoom Ferry, Tacoma

west, most of the filming was closer to Hollywood. Lightman's school is **El Segundo High School, 640 Main Street, El Segundo**, seen also in *Sleepover* and the 2004 Lindsay Lohan remake of *Freaky Friday*, as well as TV shows such as *The OC*, *Ally McBeal* and *Joan of Arcadia*, while his house is smack in the centre of LA itself, in the exclusive neighbourhood of **Hancock Park.**

NORAD, the North American Aerospace Defense Command, is real (it's beneath the Cheyenne Mountains, near Colorado Springs, Colorado), but the HQ seen in the movie is a set built at **Newhalem**, Route 20, in the North Cascade Mountains, Washington State. The tunnel which leads to the facility, though, is the **Griffith Park Tunnel**, LA, seen in *Back to the Future II* and *Who Framed Roger Rabbit*. The 7-11 Store, where Lightman is picked up by the FBI, is at **Big Bear**, the lakeside resort north of LA.

David and Jennifer (Sheedy) track down the elusive Falken (Wood, playing a character inspired by Stephen Hawking and written, strangely, for John Lennon) to the fictitious Goose Island. The ferry they catch is the **Steilacoom Ferry**, in a suburb of **Tacoma**, south of Seattle, and Goose Island itself is **Anderson Island**, in Puget Sound.

WAR OF THE ROSES, THE
(1989, dir: Danny DeVito)
Michael Douglas, Kathleen Turner, Danny DeVito.
● LOS ANGELES, CALIFORNIA; WASHINGTON

DeVito's gleefully pitch-black comedy sees high-flying professionals Michael Douglas and Kathleen Turner turning divorce into a fight to the death. Nantucket, where Douglas and Turner first meet up, is not the classy New England resort at all, but **Coupeville**, Route 20, on **Whidbey Island**, 40 miles north of Seattle, Washington State, over on the Pacific Northwest coast. And the cutesy, snow-covered street, in Cambridge, Massachusetts, where Turner presents Douglas with a Morgan, is no more than the Universal backlot in LA.

The movie was shot largely, though, on stages at 20th Century-Fox in LA, where the huge, three-storey set was built, to match up with a real house at **119 Fremont Place**, a private road in LA's posh Hancock Park district. The senate hearing is in LA's **City Hall, 200 North Spring Street**, downtown LA. There was also filming at the **California Institute of Technology (Caltech), 1201 East California Boulevard** between Hill and Wilson Avenues, Pasadena.

WAR OF THE WORLDS, THE
(1953, dir: Byron Haskin)
Gene Barry, Ann Robinson, Les Tremayne.
● LOS ANGELES, CALIFORNIA

The troops are called out: US Government District Court Building, Spring Street

Byron Haskin's cheerfully colourful adaptation transposes the HG Wells story from village England to California, and replaces the lumbering tripods of the book with sleek, copper-coloured flying machines. As the alien invasion hits the headlines, the military convoy speeds past the **United States Government District Court Building, 312 North Spring Street** at Aliso Street, toward **City Hall, 200 North Spring Street**, downtown LA. City Hall itself (OK, a miniature), is later blown to smithereens during the Martian attack. As LA is evacuated, Dr Forrester (Barry) drives down a deserted **Eighth Street** (past the Olympic, seen in *Daredevil*, and the Clifton Cafeteria exterior from *Fight Club*) before turning right into **Hill Street**. The film makes the most of its downtown location: after escaping looters, Forrester runs past the Eighth-Hill Street intersection several times. The church, where

The ending: St Brendan's Church, Third Street

he searches for Sylvia (Robinson) as time runs out for the human race, is **St Brendan's, Third Street** at Van Ness Avenue, Hollywood.

WAR OF THE WORLDS, THE
(2005, dir: Steven Spielberg)
Tom Cruise, Dakota Fanning, Tim Robbins.
● NEW YORK; NEW JERSEY; VIRGINIA; CONNECTICUT; CALIFORNIA

No Martians this time – we're all too savvy for that now – but Spielberg's updating of the story still relocates the invasion of non-specific aliens to the US, beginning in the downtown, blue-collar **Ironbound** area of **Newark**, New Jersey. The neighbourhood of Ray Ferrier (Cruise), though, is **Bayonne**, on the southern tip of the spit of land below Jersey City (given a dowdy makeover to take it down a few social notches). Ferrier's house is **11 Kennedy Boulevard**, at West First Street, by Kill Van Kull Park. The vast bridge overshadowing the house is the **Bayonne Bridge**, which connects New Jersey with Staten Island (the major traffic snarl-up was staged over on Staten Island, on the **West Shore Expressway**). An understandable nervousness about detonating explosions close to the world's second-largest steel arch bridge meant duplicating Harrington's gas station, on Kennedy Boulevard, a few blocks away on **Klumpp Field, 210 West First Street**, a Little League baseball stadium. The deal was that the stadium (previously Bridge Field) would benefit from a major renovation after filming. Sets were constructed in Bayonne, too, in the decommissioned Military Ocean Terminal (which previously hosted filming for both Ron Howard's *A Beautiful Mind* and Todd Haynes' Sirkian melodrama *Far From Heaven*).

Ferrier visits his ex-wife at her house on **Canterbury Way, Howell**, I-95 down near Asbury Park, New Jersey, before fleeing upstate New York. The landing stage, where panicked crowds attempt to board the last Hudson ferry, is at **Second Street, Athens**, off I-87 towards Albany. The town was previously seen in Hector Babenco's boozily downbeat 1987 *Ironweed*, with Jack Nicholson and Meryl Streep.

Fleeing crowds mob Ferrier's car, not in New York, but over in California. The scene was shot on **Main Street, Piru**, on the northwest fringes of LA. Major battle scenes were also filmed in California, at **Mystery Mesa**, south of **Vasquez Canyon Road** between Sierra Highway and Bouquet Canyon Road in Canyon Country.

The valley farm is in Virginia, where the 19th century farmhouse is on **Pisgah Road, Raphine**, off I-81 southwest of Staunton. National Guard tanks bump along **Decatur Road**, near **Bustleburg**, between Hyde Road and the Brownsburg Turnpike, which had been deliberately pitted with potholes.

And to Connecticut, where a Wellesian panic was narrowly avoided after a couple of dummy bodies broke loose and drifted off down the **Farmington River** during filming in **Windsor**, north of Hartford. The factory of the climax is the old **Uniroyal Chemical Plant, Elm Street** in **Naugatuck**, to the southwest, south of Waterbury.

If you want to see a gleaming silver, three-legged Martian war machine, as described by HG Wells, you need to visit the UK. Head down to the town centre of Woking, Surrey, where you'll find one striding across the pavement (sidewalk) at Crown Passage. In the original story, the Martian cylinders landed on Horsell Common, Woking, and the seven-metre-tall sculpture, by Michael Condron, celebrates the local author.

WARRIORS, THE
(1979, dir: Walter Hill)
Michael Beck, James Remar, Thomas Waites.
● NEW YORK CITY

Early, culty Walter Hill movie, with a New York street gang away from their territory trying to make it home to **Coney Island**. The opening scene, with thousands of extras, including real gang members and all the problems that entails, is in the **Riverside Park Playground, 96th Street** at Riverside Drive. Also filmed at **The Bathhouse**, Coney Island.

Louis XVIII flees the Tuileries: Palazzo Reale, Caserta

WATERLOO
(1970, dir: Sergei Bondarchuk)
Rod Steiger, Christopher Plummer, Orson Welles.
● UKRAINE; ITALY

A sumptuous Italian-Russian co-production, with Steiger as a wracked Napoleon and Plummer as an arrogant Duke of Wellington, about the events leading up to, and the battle of, Waterloo in 1815. The gigantic battle scenes were shot in the Ukraine. Louis XVIII's Paris court, the Tuileries, is the **Palazzo Reale, Caserta**, about 15 miles from Naples, which you might recognise as

Napoleon's triumphal return to Paris: The Palazzo Reale grand staircase, Caserta

Queen Amidala's palace (see *Star Wars Episode I: The Phantom Menace* for details).

WATERLOO ROAD
(1944, dir: Sidney Gilliat)
John Mills, Stewart Granger, Alastair Sim.
● LONDON

A soldier goes AWOL to sort out his family life, in this London-set pre-kitchen sink piece of social realism, which includes a chase across the tracks at **Waterloo Station**.

WAY DOWN EAST
(1920, dir: DW Griffith)
Lillian Gish, Richard Barthelmess, Lowell Sherman.
● NEW YORK; VERMONT

Old fashioned melodrama, saved by Griffith's bravura direction and Gish's performance as the naïve country girl seduced, abandoned, shamed and packed off to the icy wastes, where Barthelmess rescues her. Griffith's studio was at **Orienta Point, Mamaroneck**, New York State.

The blizzard scenes were also filmed at Orienta Point, but outside on Long Island Sound, during a spell of genuine bad weather. Several crew members suffered exposure and were lost to pneumonia. For the rightly famous ice-floe climax, shot without stunt doubles at **White River Junction**, up in Vermont where the White River and the Connecticut River flow alongside each other, solid ice was dynamited to provide individual floes.

WAY WE WERE, THE
(1973, dir: Sydney Pollack)
Barbra Streisand, Robert Redford, James Woods.
● LOS ANGELES, CALIFORNIA; NEW YORK CITY; NEW YORK

Leftish firebrand Streisand endures a mismatched relationship with rich-kid writer Redford in Pollack's nostalgia-drenched star vehicle. The fictitious Wentworth

Streisand and Redford escape the red-baiters: Union Station

College, where the mismatched pair first meet up, is **Union College, Schenectady**, New York State. Streisand harangues the student activists in front of the domed, 16-sided **Nott Memorial**. Also featured is the **Chester Arthur statue**, and the prom scene is **Memorial Field House**. LA locations include the **Beverly Hills Hotel, 96641 Sunset Boulevard**, Beverly Hills. Streisand endures a demo of hysterical red-baiters at **Union Station, 800 North Alameda Street**, downtown. The final meeting of Streisand and Redford takes place in New York City, outside the Fifth Avenue entrance of the **Plaza Hotel, 59th Street**.

WAYNE'S WORLD
(1992, dir: Penelope Spheeris)
Mike Myers, Dana Carvey, Rob Lowe.
● LOS ANGELES, CALIFORNIA; CHICAGO, ILLINOIS

Saturday Night Live spinoff, getting the big screen treatment from one-time youth scene observer Spheeris. Set in Aurora, Illinois, 30 miles west of Chicago, the low-budget movie was shot mainly around LA, and often on the Paramount lot. The nightclub, where Garth seeks revenge on a bully, is the très chic gay club **Arena, 6655 Santa Monica Boulevard**, at North Las Palmas Avenue, Hollywood (© 323.462.1291).

The sequel was shot in the LA suburb of Monrovia, on **Huntington Avenue** and **Lemon Avenue**.

WE FAW DOWN
(1928, dir: Leo McCarey)
Stan Laurel, Oliver Hardy, Bess Flowers.

On the town: Hotel Adams, Main Street, Culver City

● **LOS ANGELES, CALIFORNIA**

Stan and Ollie fib to their wives when planning an evening out on the town. Filmed at the **Hotel Adams, 3896 Main Street**, Culver City, LA.

WE WERE SOLDIERS
(2002, dir: Randall Wallace)
Mel Gibson, Chris Klein, Madeleine Stowe.
● **CALIFORNIA; GEORGIA**

Forget everything you've seen before. This, claims the film's publicity, is the way Vietnam really was. And, from the team who brought such painstaking historical accuracy to *Braveheart*, who am I to doubt it? The military base, where saintly GIs live in marital bliss with wives who make Stepford women look like radical feminists, is the real **Fort Benning**, Georgia.

Forget, too, the Far East nonsense of such Hollywood frippery as *Apocalypse Now* or *Platoon*. Director Wallace found that the grounds of **Fort Hunter Liggett Military Reservation**, in Monterey, California, were a dead ringer for central Vietnam's Ia Drang Valley.

WEDDING, A
(1978, dir: Robert Altman)
Carol Burnett, Paul Dooley, Desi Arnaz.
● **CHICAGO, ILLINOIS**

Great ensemble cast of 48 (thus doubling *Nashville*'s cast of 24), and Altman in his best mode – overlapping dialogue, sharp cameos – at a smart society wedding. The setting is the posh Chicago suburb of **Lake Forest**, where the palatial residence used for the reception is the **Armour House, 1500 West Kennedy Road** (*© 847.615.3254, www.armourhouse.com*).

WEDDING SINGER, THE
(1998, dir: Frank Coraci)
Drew Barrymore, Adam Sandler, Steve Buscemi.
● **LOS ANGELES, CALIFORNIA**

Eighties-set feelgood comedy, filmed around Sierra Madre, the town east of Pasadena famous as Santa Mira, the setting for Don Siegel's original *Invasion of the Body Snatchers*. Drew Barrymore's home is the **Tucker House**, an old converted schoolhouse at **43 Sierra Place, Sierra Madre**, east of LA. The wedding receptions use the ballrooms of the **Ambassador Hotel, 3400 Wilshire Boulevard**, midtown LA (see the 1954 *A Star is Born* for details).

WEEKEND AT BERNIE'S
(1989, dir: Ted Kotcheff)
Andrew McCarthy, Jonathan Silverman, Catherine Mary Stewart.
● **NORTH CAROLINA; NEW YORK CITY**

Broad, one-note black farce, along the lines of *The Trouble With Harry*, with McCarthy and Silverman covering up the death of their boss while enjoying the highlife in his beach house. The insurance office in which the two boys work is the **Metropolitan Life Insurance Building, 1 Madison Avenue**, between 23rd and 25th Streets, New York. Hampton Island was actually filmed in North Carolina, not far from the East Coast filming centre of Wilm-

ington. Most of the movie was shot on **Bald Head Island**, about 30 miles south of Wilmington at the mouth of the Cape Fear River. The lighthouse, where Silverman gets temporarily blinded, is the **Old Baldy Light**. Bernie's ultramodern beach house was built specially for the movie (and dismantled after shooting) on the **Fort Fisher Recreation Area**, between Bald Head Island and **Carolina Beach State Park**, which is where the corpse of Bernie ends up 'waterskiing'.

WEIRD SCIENCE
(1985, dir: John Hughes)
Anthony Michael Hall, Ilan Mitchell-Smith, Kelly LeBrock.
● **ILLINOIS**

Horny teen computer nerds create femme-fantasy Kelly LeBrock, but the premise goes nowhere in another Hughes teen-farce, shot – where else? – around Chicago. The boys' neighbourhood (the standard fictitious Hughes setting of 'Shermer, Il') is **Highland Park**, north of the city. The mall, where the lads get the last laugh, riding off with LeBrock, is **Northbrook Court Mall, 2172 Northbrook Court, Northbrook** in the city's North Shore district. The car chase is downtown Highland Park.

WENT THE DAY WELL? (aka *Forty-eight Hours*)
(1942, dir: Alberto Cavalcanti)
Leslie Banks, Elizabeth Allan, Frank Lawton.
● **BUCKINGHAMSHIRE**

During WWII, a small English village is taken over by German fifth columnists in this excellent, low key propaganda piece, from a Graham Greene story, which still packs a punch. The fictitious village of Bramley End (though not the manor house, which filmed elsewhere) is **Turville**, off the B482 about five miles west of High Wycombe, Buckinghamshire. Pretty much unchanged to this day, the village is overlooked by the windmill from *Chitty Chitty Bang Bang*, and was

The policeman's cottage, Bramley End: Turville

The village of Bramley End: Turville

Leslie Banks' cottage in Bramley End: Turville

also the scene of the haunted wedding in the classic British chiller *Dead of Night*.

WEREWOLF OF LONDON
(1935, dir: Stuart Walker)
Henry Hull, Warner Oland, Valerie Hobson.
● CALIFORNIA

There's no London in this chiller from the era of Universal classics, which were made on the Universal back-lot in LA. Botanist Dr Glendon (Hull) gets the fateful lycanthrope bite while searching for a mysterious plant in Tibet. The opening Tibetan scenes are **Vasquez Rocks County Park, Escondido Road**, near Newhall, north of LA (see *Blazing Saddles* for details).

WEST SIDE STORY
(1961, dir: Robert Wise; Jerome Robbins)
Natalie Wood, Rita Moreno, Richard Beymer.
● NEW YORK CITY

Robert Wise's filming of the greatest Broadway musical of all time fizzes with the energy of Jerome Robbins' choreography, but suffers from some dreadful miscasting and a clumping staginess in the studio scenes. The opening 20 minutes, filmed by (the subsequently replaced) Robbins, show what might have been. They used the real about-to-be demolished slum tenements on the West Side, the area now occupied by the Lincoln Center for the Performing Arts. But after the exhilarating introduction it's off to the studio, with great music, cramped sets and naff filters.

WESTERNER, THE
(1940, dir: William Wyler)
Gary Cooper, Walter Brennan, Fred Stone.
● ARIZONA

Walter Brennan won an Oscar as Judge Roy Bean, and stole the show from a less-than-happy Cooper. The movie was shot in the town of **Goldwyn** (guess who it was named after) near Tucson, Arizona. Built as a replica of an early Texan town, movie mogul Sam Goldwyn promised to use it as a permanent set for all his Westerns.

WESTWORLD
(1973, dir: Michael Crichton)
Yul Brynner, Richard Benjamin, James Brolin.
● LOS ANGELES, CALIFORNIA

Long before *Jurassic Park*, writer Crichton tackled the theme of technology running amok, and this time as director too. The Roman World of the technically advanced theme park is **Greenacres**, the lavish Beverly Hills spread of ledge-dangling comic Harold Lloyd. The estate, which in 1928 covered twenty acres and included 12 themed gardens, had by the seventies been reduced to five acres. The 44-room house has 26 bathrooms and, for a while after the actor's death in 1971, was open to the public as a museum. No longer. Seen also in *The Godfather*, it's at **1740 Greenacres Place, Beverly Hills**. The Western landscapes are **Red Rock Canyon**, near Ridgecrest in central California (see *Jurassic Park* for details).

WHALES OF AUGUST, THE
(1987, dir: Lindsay Anderson)
Lillian Gish, Bette Davis, Vincent Price.
● MAINE

The incredible Lillian Gish, who first came to prominence in DW Griffith's *Birth of a Nation*, is paired with Bette Davis – who proved just too much for her – in Lindsay Anderson's gentle drama set on **Cliff Island**, off the coast of Portland, Maine. The house is the **Pitkin House**, a private home on **The Bluffs**, on the south coast of the island. Cliff Island is small. It has no guesthouse or hotel – or bank. The Casco Bay Line ferry takes around an hour and a half to make the crossing from Portland (*www.cascobaylines.com*).

WHAT EVER HAPPENED TO BABY JANE?
(1962, dir: Robert Aldrich)
Bette Davis, Joan Crawford, Victor Buono.
● LOS ANGELES, CALIFORNIA

The Hudson sisters' mansion: South McCadden Place, Hancock Park

Sold at the time as a psycho-horror, the movie has since turned out to be an all-time camp classic, as the two great screen queens of the thirties and forties were teamed for the first time in a low-budget schlocker. It was made by Warner Bros, but by the early sixties the two stars were seen as has-beens and the production was shunted off the lot to the ramshackle Producers Studio (now the independent Raleigh Studios), 650 North Bronson at Melrose Avenue, while the entire WB lot was given over to the big prestige production, *Gypsy*. Momma's boy pianist Edwin Flagg was to have been played by Peter Lawford, but President Kennedy's bro-in-law got cold feet and was thankfully replaced by the wonderfully fey Victor Buono.

Set in a fast-decaying Hollywood, where Bette drives her battered old Merc along **Wilcox Avenue**, and at **Sunset** and **La Brea**. She calls in at the, now gone, Western Costume Co, which stood at 5339 Melrose Avenue. The beach, where Crawford finally croaks, is **Paradise Cove** on Zuma Beach, Malibu, north of LA. The old mansion, where the Hudson sisters live in a mutually-dependent hate-hate relationship, is **172 South McCadden Place** between West First and West Second Streets, **Hancock Park**, south of Hollywood.

The TV remake, *Whatever Happened to...*, with real-life sisters Lynn and Vanessa Redgrave, used a house a couple of blocks east at – coincidentally – 501 South Hudson Avenue.

WHAT PRICE HOLLYWOOD?
(1932, dir: George Cukor)
Constance Bennett, Lowell Sherman, Neil Hamilton.
● **LOS ANGELES, CALIFORNIA**

The old Brown Derby: Café Mecca, Brown Derby Plaza, Wilshire Boulevard

Constance Bennett gets married: First United Methodist Church

In Cukor's early version of *A Star Is Born*, Constance Bennett works in the original hat-shaped Brown Derby restaurant. Long closed, you can see the dome of the Derby, now painted silver, on **Brown Derby Plaza, 3377 Wilshire Boulevard** at Alexandria, where it's now called **Café Mecca**. The original restaurant (there were other, more conventional, Derbys later) was built in 1926 as a coffeeshop by Gloria Swanson's hubby, Herbert Somborn. Bennett marries at **First United Methodist Church**, Highland Avenue at the northwest corner of Franklin Avenue, Hollywood. Still towering over Hollywood, you can see the church in *The Godfather*, behind Grauman's Chinese when Tom Hagen arrives in Hollywood. And it's to **Grauman's Chinese Theatre, 6925 Hollywood Boulevard**, that the director takes Bennett to a première.

WHAT'S EATING GILBERT GRAPE?
(1993, dir: Lasse Hallström)
Johnny Depp, Leonardo DiCaprio, Juliette Lewis.
● **TEXAS**

Domestic drama has Depp dealing with disturbed younger brother DiCaprio and his grossly obese mother. Set in the fictitious Endora, Iowa, it was actually made in Texas, in the town of **Manor**, just east of state capital Austin. The town square is nearby **Lockhart**, seen also in *Waiting For Guffman*. The Grape house was on **Hodde Lane**, outside Pflugerville, but nothing remains after the conflagration at the climax of the movie.

WHAT'S NEW, PUSSYCAT?
(1965, dir: Clive Donner)
Peter O'Toole, Peter Sellers, Woody Allen.
● **FRANCE**

The title was allegedly Warren Beatty's chat-up line (that *worked*?) in what started out as a quasi-biographical movie about Beatty's prodigious womanising, scripted by stand-up comic Woody Allen. But Beatty bailed out, O'Toole stepped in as the sex-addicted magazine editor, and Allen's script gets buried under Sellers' wildly out-of-control hamming and Donner's 'zany' direction. Nevertheless, it's an opportunity to marvel at the indulgence of the sixties, and the Burt Bacharach-Hal David score is a classic.

Filmed mainly around the city of lurve, Paris, where O'Toole bumps into Allen playing chess at **La Closerie des Lilas, 171 boulevard du Montparnasse** at boulevard St Michel (*℃ 01.40.51.34.50; metro: Port Royal or Vavin*), and promptly takes his queen. The Lilas is one of the city's legendary artsy Left Bank hangouts, slightly separate from other famed literary bars – the Dôme, Rotonde and Select, seen in *A Bout de Souffle* – possibly why it was a favourite of Ernest Hemingway. Helpfully, the favourite seats of the famous (or once-famous) are picked out with brass plaques.

If you fancy a weekend in the country, confident you won't bump into rampant ex-partners, sex-starved love goddesses or crazed shrinks, you can stay at Chateau Chantel, the retreat at which everyone is destined to collide in a farcical frenzy. It's the **Chateau de Chaumontel, 21 rue André Vassord, Chaumontel** (*℃ 01.34.71.0030, www.chateau-chaumontel.fr*), about 20 miles north of Paris.

WHAT'S UP DOC?
(1972, dir: Peter Bogdanovich)
Barbra Streisand, Ryan O'Neal, Kenneth Mars.
● **SAN FRANCISCO, CALIFORNIA**

The Hotel Bristol: Hilton Hotel, O'Farrell Street

The car chase: Alta Plaza Park

Bogdanovich's heavy-handed retread of thirties screwball comedies was shot around San Francisco. The Hotel Bristol, where wacky Barbra Streisand causes no end of trouble for meek geologist Ryan O'Neal, is the **Hilton San Francisco, 333 O'Farrell Street** at Mason Street (*℃ 415.771.1400*). The car chase is a joy but, much to the chagrin of the city, has left permanent cracks in the steps on the south side of **Alta Plaza Park**, on **Steiner Street** at Clay Street.

WHEN HARRY MET SALLY...
(1989, dir: Rob Reiner)
Billy Crystal, Meg Ryan, Carrie Fisher.
● **NEW YORK CITY; CHICAGO, ILLINOIS; LOS ANGELES, CALIFORNIA**

It's oh-so-predictable that Crystal and Ryan are finally going to get it together, but the journey's plenty of fun. They actually meet up in the Main Quad of the **University of Chicago, University Avenue** at 58th Avenue. After driving from the university, Ryan drops Crystal off at **Washington Arch, Washington Square Park** in Greenwich Village, New York. Years later, the two meet up at **Shakespeare & Co Booksellers, 2259 Broadway** at

"I'll have what she's having...": Katz's Delicatessen, East Houston Street, East Village

Harry finally declares his love at the New Year party: Puck Building, Lafayette Street

81st Street on the West Side, and they visit the **Metropolitan Museum of Art, Fifth Avenue** at 82nd Street. The café, where Ryan demonstrates how to fake it in the movie's most famous scene, is **Katz's Delicatessen, 205 East Houston Street** at Ludlow Street in the East Village. The restaurant, which has a sign: 'You are sitting at the table where Harry met Sally', also features in the excellent *Donnie Brasco*.

Harry and Sally help make up a foursome at **Cafe Luxembourg, 200 West 70th Street** near Amsterdam Avenue, and singalong to the karaoke machine at the home of the executive toy, **The Sharper Image, 4 West 57th Street**. Filming also took place at **West 96th Street Station** on the Upper West Side. The New Year party, where Crystal finally declares his love, is in the **Puck Building, 295 Lafayette Street**, though the entrance into which Crystal runs is the **Park Plaza Hotel, 607 South Park View Street** overlooking Macarthur Park in Los Angeles (see *New York New York* for details).

WHERE EAGLES DARE
(1969, dir: Brian G Hutton)
Richard Burton, Clint Eastwood, Mary Ure.
● AUSTRIA

Bluff, double bluff and multiple bluff in this clever Alistair MacLean adventure, which has Burton and Eastwood

The fake Nazis arrive in Austria: Werfen

Schloss Adler: Schloss Hohenwerfen, Werfen

posing as Nazis to rescue top military brass from the impregnable Schloss Adler in southern Germany. The village they arrive in is **Werfen**, about 20 miles south of Salzburg in the Salzach Valley, Austria (*rail: Werfen*). The mountaintop fortress looming over the village is the 11th century **Schloss Hohenwerfen**. But don't worry, you won't have to take a scary cable-car ride. In fact, there is no cable car. The castle, now a falconry centre and museum, is accessible by a short, if steep, road from the village.

WHISKY GALORE! (aka *Tight Little Island*)
(1948, dir: Alexander Mackendrick)
Basil Radford, Joan Greenwood, Gordon Jackson.
● SCOTLAND

Based on real events, when the SS *Politician*, carrying 50,000 cases of Scotch, was wrecked in 1941 on the Isle of Eriskay in the Outer Hebrides. In the movie, the island becomes Todday, and was filmed on the island of **Barra** in the Hebrides.

WHISTLE DOWN THE WIND
(1961, dir: Bryan Forbes)
Alan Bates, Hayley Mills, Bernard Lee.
● LANCASHIRE

Before the Lloyd-Webber musical transposed the story to the southern States, screenwriters Keith Waterhouse and Willis Hall already shifted the location for this story of a holed-up escapee being mistaken for Christ, from the pony-and-jodhpurs Home Counties to the gritty north of England. The film was shot on location in the village of **Downham**, off the A59, about ten miles northwest of Burnley, Lancashire. It's pretty much unchanged. You can still find the carpark, where the Salvation Army band played ("Do

"We three kings...": Pendle Hill

The village: Downham

you want a kitten? It's not dead."). Bostock's farm itself is nearby on **Pendle Hill**. In reality **Worsaw End Farm**, it's still instantly recognisable, both the farmhouse (the kitchen interiors were the only studio shots in the film) and the barn – though a shelter has since been added to the door. The original tractor, driven by Bernard Lee, is still here, rusting away.

The farm's current owner, a

The farmhouse: Worsaw End Farm

The barn: Worsaw End Farm

The ending: Worsaw End Farm

child at the time of filming, was denied the opportunity of appearing as one of the 'disciples' by a sudden bout of appendicitis. Even the trees silhouetted on Pendle Hill (as the children sing "We three kings…") can still be seen.

WHITE HEAT
(1949, dir: Raoul Walsh)
James Cagney, Edmond O'Brien, Virginia Mayo.
● LOS ANGELES, CALIFORNIA

Classic hardboiled gangster pic. The final chase leads through downtown LA, past City Hall. The climactic finale at the oil refinery ("Made it Ma, top of the world!") is the old Torrance Refinery, almost completely rebuilt in 1965, now the **Exxon Mobil Refinery, 3700 West 190th Street** at Figueroa, **Torrance**, southern LA.

WHITE HUNTER, BLACK HEART
(1990, dir: Clint Eastwood)
Clint Eastwood, Jeff Fahey, Charlotte Cornwell.
● AFRICA; BUCKINGHAMSHIRE

Eastwood's Irish estate: West Wycombe House

Eastwood as a thinly-disguised John Huston, on location in Africa to shoot both a film and an elephant, shot in Zimbabwe and Zambesi. Eastwood's Irish estate is **West Wycombe House**, two-and-a-half miles west of High Wycombe, south of the A40, Buckinghamshire (*www.west-wycombe-estate.co.uk*). The house can also be seen in *House of Mirth* and *Les Visiteurs*. See *The Music Lovers* for details.

WHITE MEN CAN'T JUMP
(1992, dir: Ron Shelton)
Wesley Snipes, Woody Harrelson, Rosie Perez.
● LOS ANGELES, CALIFORNIA

Too much basketball and trash talk getting in the way of the plot? Or too much plot getting in the way of the basketball and trash talk? Sports-movie specialist Shelton (*Bull Durham*) was never going to please everyone with his bickering buddy movie, as swaggering Sidney (Snipes) and nerdy Billy (Harrelson) hustle their way across the courts of LA. Billy rolls up, naturally enough, at the sporty beachfront of **Venice Beach**, where he first wrongfoots Sidney with his goofball persona on the ball courts.

Billy himself gets scammed down in Watts, near the famous Watts Towers, arriving at the old **Watts Train Station, 103rd Street**. The bad-tempered Brotherhood Tournament and the climactic game (yes, of course Billy can

jump) are the courts of **Lafayette Park, Wilshire Boulevard** between Hoover Street and Lafayette Park Place, where the swishy thoroughfare curves right

The basketball courts: Lafayette Park, Wilshire Boulevard

into the scuzzy downtown district near MacArthur Park.

After Billy's long-suffering girlfriend Gloria (Perez) wins big-time on *Jeopardy*, the couple move into the gorgeously 1930s streamline-deco **Hotel Shangri-La, 1301 Ocean Avenue** at Arizona Avenue (© *310.394.2791, www.shangrila-hotel.com*), overlooking Palisades Park, **Santa Monica**.

WHITE PALACE
(1990, dir: Luis Mandoki)
James Spader, Susan Sarandon, Eileen Brennan.
● MISSOURI

Spader is a young yuppie falling for older waitress Sarandon in this low-key, well-acted class- and age-gap drama, filmed in St Louis, Missouri. The White Palace burger house was the White Knight Diner, now the **Super Sandwich Shop, 1801 Olive Street** (© *314.621.5949*). The ad agency, where Spader works, is on **Laclede's Landing** on the St Louis Riverfront. The bachelor party was filmed in the **Lemp Mansion, 3322 DeMenil Place** (© *314.664.8024, www.lempmansion.com*). The New York restaurant, where the couple are finally reunited, is also St Louis. It's **Duff's Restaurant, 392 North Euclid Avenue** (© *314.361.0522*).

WHO FRAMED ROGER RABBIT
(1988, dir: Robert Zemeckis)
Bob Hoskins, Christopher Lloyd, Joanna Cassidy.
● LONDON; CALIFORNIA; ESSEX

No, there is no question mark, as it's considered bad luck in a film title. No need to have worried here, though, with Zemeckis' irresistable blend of animation and live action. Set in 1947 LA, but – since the production was based at Elstree Studios in Hertfordshire (where the Ink and Paint Club, the

Eddie Valiant's office: South Hope Street

LA in the 30s: Hope Street

interior of Eddie's office and the Terminal Bar sets were built) – locations are divided between California and the UK.

The Acme Factory: Dimco Building, Wood Lane, Shepherds Bush

The movie house: Gray's State Theatre

Maroon Cartoons, home of Roger Rabbit (voiced by Charles Fleischer), is the **Ren-Mar Studios, 846 North Cahuenga Boulevard**, north of Melrose Avenue, **Hollywood** (previously the Desilu Studios of Lucille Ball and Desi Arnaz, where *I Love Lucy* was taped). Eddie Valiant (Hoskins) takes the old Pacific Electric Red Car to his office on **Hope Street**, between 11th and 12th Streets, downtown LA, heavily disguised behind scads of period dressing. Much of the street has since been demolished but (in mid-2004) Eddie's office still stands, at **1130 South Hope Street**.

The Acme Factory on the border of Toontown, where Marvin Acme is killed by the falling safe and Judge Doom (Lloyd) finally gets his just desserts, can be seen in west London. It's the **Dimco Building, Wood Lane**, opposite Macfarlane Road, between **Shepherds Bush** and White City, W12.

Eddie and Roger escape from Judge Doom at the Terminal Bar and scoot off down Hope Street in the animated Yellow Cab Benny (Fleischer again), finally shaking off the pursuing weasels by leaping onto the **Glendale-Hyperion Viaduct**, on **Hyperion Avenue-Glendale Boulevard**, over I-5 and the Los Angeles River, in **Los Feliz**, way northeast of downtown.

The cinema, in which they hide out, is back in the UK. It's the, now closed, 2,000 seat **Gray's State Theatre, George Street, Grays** in Essex. The wonderful thirties movie palace was the largest single-screen auditorium still operating in Europe at the time, and has since been a nightclub but is currently closed.

The entrance to Toontown, where Eddie finally overcomes his hatred of Toons and pours away the Wild Turkey, is the **Griffith Park Tunnel**, between Western Canyon Road and Vermont Canyon Road, north of the Observatory. The tunnel was also featured in *War Games* and Zemeckis' first two *Back to the Future* movies.

WHO'S AFRAID OF VIRGINIA WOOLF?
(1966, dir: Mike Nichols)
Elizabeth Taylor, Richard Burton, George Segal.
● **MASSACHUSETTS**

Burton and Taylor are, for once, perfect together in Mike Nichols' rivetting movie of Edward Albee's play. Interiors were shot on a closed set at Warner's Burbank Studio. The campus setting is **Smith College, Northampton**, on I-91, north of Springfield, Massachusetts, where Burton-Taylor's home is the **Tyler Annex**.

WICKED LADY, THE
(1945, dir: Leslie Arliss)
Margaret Lockwood, James Mason, Griffith Jones.
● **NORFOLK**

Lady Skelton's stately pile: Blickling Hall

Margaret Lockwood is the wicked Lady Skelton, stealing husbands, poisoning aged retainers and moonlighting as a highway robber in this Restoration romp. Scandalous in its time for the plunging necklines, scenes had to be reshot for the trembling innocents of the USA. Lady Skelton's stately pile, Maryiot Cells, supposedly at Maiden Worthy in Buckinghamshire, is **Blickling Hall**, northwest of Aylsham in Norfolk. The redbrick Jacobean mansion is open to the public on various days of the week between March and October (✆ *01263.738030, www.nationaltrust.org.uk/places/blickling; admission charge*).

WICKER MAN, THE
(1973, dir: Robin Hardy)
Edward Woodward, Christopher Lee, Britt Ekland.
● **SCOTLAND**

Savagely cut down before release, and with some shaky performances, *The Wicker Man* has nevertheless achieved cult status since its initial release as a B-feature with *Don't Look Now*. Its success lies in the gameplaying of the clever plot and wicked script of Anthony Shaffer (*Sleuth*). Woodward is the puritanically Christian cop sent to investigate pagan rites on a remote Scottish isle. There is a real Summerisle, but it's way to the north of where this movie filmed. The near-tropical (warmed by the gulf stream) island estate of Lord Summerisle (so kindly thanked in the movie's credits – and as bogus as Eve Channing in *Sleuth*'s) is an amalgam of around 25 separate locations, all of them on the Scottish mainland.

The opening aerial shots were filmed en route to the Isle of Skye, though the harbour, where Woodward's seaplane touches down, is **Plockton**, a small town off the A890, at the mouth of Loch Carron, about 55 miles west of Inverness, on the west coast of Ross and Cromarty. The production was based at **Newton Stewart**, on the River Cree, north of Wigtown Bay in Galloway. Much of the filming was done here, including the schoolhouse and the inn. 20 miles southeast, at **Kirkcudbright** on the A711, you'll find the ruined church and the sweetshop. The Green Man Inn is a conflation of two locations: inside it's the **Ellan Gowan Hotel, Creetown**; the exterior is **Cally Estate office, Gatehouse of Fleet**. The schoolhouse and the old kirk are at **Anwoth**.

The exterior of Lord Summerisle's castle is **Culzean Castle**, a fine Adam house, just off the A719, 12 miles southwest of Ayr. It's open to the public from the end of March to the end of October (✆ *01655.760274; admission charge*). The interior, though, is **Lord Stair's Castle**, near **Wigtown** a few miles south of Newton Stewart. This was a tad too grand for the film – Lord Summerisle's palatial drawing room is Lord Stair's foyer. The tour of Summerisle's garden is in **Logan Botanic Garden, Port Logan**, 10 miles south of Stranraer.

The wicker man itself was built on the **Machars Peninsula**, the area of land between Luce and Wigtown Bays, south of Newton Stewart, around **St Ninian's Cave**, near the southern tip, off the A747.

WILD ANGELS, THE
(1966, dir: Roger Corman)
Peter Fonda, Nancy Sinatra, Bruce Dern.
● **CALIFORNIA**

The interior of the church: Little Country Church, North Argyle Avenue, Hollywood

Corman's biker movie, with real Hell's Angels in the cast, earned an inevitable cult reputation as a result of being banned in the UK for several years. It's set around LA, at **Venice Beach**; around the oil rigs of **San Pedro**; along the bike trails of **Palm Canyon** at Palm Springs; and at **Mecca**, in the desert south of I-10, near the Salton Sea.

The interior of the church, where the sacrilegious wake is held (the scene that was probably responsible for the ban), is the **Little Country Church, North Argyle Avenue**, Hollywood. The cemetery is the park at **Idyllwild**, off Route 74 in the San Bernardino National Forest, southwest of Palm Springs.

WILD AT HEART
(1990, dir: David Lynch)
Nicolas Cage, Laura Dern, Willem Dafoe.
● **TEXAS; CALIFORNIA**

The bloody murder: Park Plaza Hotel

Wilfully bizarre fantasy, a sick, violent road movie patterned on *The Wizard of Oz*, set around **El Paso** and **New Orleans** and, while there is some filming in Texas and Louisiana, much of the film was shot in California: **Palmdale**, north of LA, is where Bobby Peru (Dafoe) sells Sailor (Cage) a booby-trapped holdup job. The vast, vaulted lobby of the opening scenes, where Sailor bloodily brains a guy on the staircase, is the lobby of the **Park Plaza Hotel, 607 South Park View Street**, downtown LA (see *New York New York* for details). The mansion of Mr Reindeer is the **Castle Green Apartments, 99 South Raymond Avenue, Pasadena** (see *The Sting* for details), while the bar where Sailor does his Elvis number was a C&W bar in north Hollywood.

WILD BUNCH, THE
(1969, dir: Sam Peckinpah)
William Holden, Robert Ryan, Ernest Borgnine.

● **MEXICO**

Peckinpah's masterpiece, conjuring poetry from dust and blood, was filmed in Mexico. The town of Starbuck is **Parras**, one of the oldest towns in north Mexico, some 600 miles north of Mexico City, midway between Saltillo and Torreon on Route 40. The ever-present dust of the Mexican desert required a camera mechanic to be permanently on duty dismantling and cleaning the cameras.

Pike puts the wounded Buck out of his misery at the **Duranzo Arroyo, Torreon**. And it's here, too, behind the Perote Winery, that the bounty hunters bed down for the night. Angel's village is **El Rincon del Motero**. Old man Sykes waits at **El Romeral** with horses for the bunch to return from Starbuck. The robbery of the munitions train involved the use of a period locomotive on a rail spur south of **La Goma**.

The blowing up of the bridge, and the river crossing, take place on the **Rio Nazas** just south of Torreon. The climactic massacre, supposedly in the town of Agua Verde, took eleven days to film, at the **Hacienda Cienga del Carmen**.

WILD STRAWBERRIES
(1957, dir: Ingmar Bergman)
Victor Sjostrom, Ingrid Thulin, Gunnar Bjornstrand.
● **SWEDEN**

Archetypal fifties Bergman, with veteran movie director Sjostrom as an elderly professor travelling a physical and mental journey through a series of nightmares. Mostly studio-bound, but part of the 'phantom carriage' ride, when the carriage careers round a corner, was shot in a deserted Old Town. The professor recites a poem at a lunch overlooking **Lake Vattern**, and eventually arrives at the university in **Lund**, just north of Malmo at the southern tip of Sweden.

WILD WOMEN OF WONGO
(1958, dir: James L Wolcott)
Jean Hawkshaw, Johnny Walsh, Adrienne Bourbeau.
● **FLORIDA**

Just to prove that you don't always need the perverse genius of Ed Wood to produce one of the Worst Movies of All Time. The beautifully manicured island of Wongo is **Silver Springs** at Ocala, Florida.

WILDE
(1998, dir: Brian Gilbert)
Stephen Fry, Jude Law, Jennifer Ehle.
● **LONDON; DORSET; OXFORDSHIRE; HAMPSHIRE; HERTFORDSHIRE; SPAIN**

Stephen Fry in the role he was born to play, an explicitness missing from earlier versions and the use of striking period locations compensate for the familiarity of the flamboyant writer's fall from grace.

The Cadogan Hotel: South Audley Street

Ross consoles Wilde's ex-lover: Jamaica Wine Lodge, Cornhill

The startling Western opening, at Leadville, Colorado, is the desert at **Alicante** on the southeast coast of Spain, though the interior of the tin mine, where Wilde charms the miners, was constructed at Grip House Studios near London.

The exterior of Wilde's West End apartment is the central courtyard of the recently renovated **Somerset House** in the **Strand**, a familiar location seen as New York in Tim Burton's *Sleepy Hollow* and as St Petersburg in *GoldenEye* among many other appearances. The imposing frontage of the St James Theatre, where *Lady Windermere's Fan* opens, is the **Palace Theatre, Cambridge Circus**, but the interior and the bar are **Richmond Theatre, The Green**, Richmond (see *Evita* for full details).

Addle Hill, off Carter Lane, to the south of St Paul's Cathedral, is the street where Wilde gets the first intimations of his true sexuality as he watches a bunch of working class youths (well, the group does include Orlando Bloom). The elaborate Victorian shopfront was added to the undistinguished modern southwest corner, and the highly decorated Venetian-style building on **Carter Lane** is real enough. Originally the St Paul's Choir School, it's now a **YMCA**.

Spoiled and petulant opportunist Bosie (Law) confides his fear of blackmail to Wilde alongside the River Cherwell in the grounds of **Magdalen College**, Oxford, which actually was Wilde's alma mater (see that other period gay romance, *Maurice*, for details of this location). Meanwhile, Wilde's wife, Constance (Ehle), hints at marital problems to Lady Mount-Temple on the beach overlooked by the spectacular natural arch of **Durdle Door**, west of West Lulworth between Weymouth and Swanage on the B3070 in Dorset (*rail: Wool*), a location also seen in John Schlesinger's *Far From the Madding Crowd*. And at **Swanage** is the pier where Wilde takes his kids fishing while suffering from a cold.

The Queensberry country home, where Bosie gets a dire warning from his mother, is **Knebworth House** near Stevenage in Hertfordshire (see Tim Burton's *Batman* for details). Oscar relates the story of *The Selfish Giant* to his children at the country retreat where he can write in peace. The charming estate is **Houghton Lodge Gardens**, a cottage ornée just south of **Stockbridge**, about 12 miles east of Salisbury in Hampshire. The garden is open to the public from March to September (© *01264.810177*; *admission charge*).

The hotel where Wilde and Bosie make up

The prison: Oxford Gaol, New Road, Oxford

after their blazing row is another familiar location, **Luton Hoo**, near Luton, Hertfordshire (see *Four Weddings and a Funeral* for details). The law court exteriors are **Middle Temple, Lincoln's Inn**, London. Reading Gaol, where Wilde is incarcerated, is **HM Prison Oxford, New Road**, alongside Castle Mound. Period interiors were filmed at London's **Athenaeum Club**; the **National Liberal Club** in Whitehall (seen also in *The Elephant Man*); and **25-26 Tredegar Square** in Bow, E3.

Period interiors: Tredegar Square, Bow

The drinking den in which Robbie Ross (Michael Sheen) consoles Wilde's discarded love John Gray (Ioan Gruffudd), is the **Jamaica Wine Lodge, St Michael's Alley, Cornhill**, E3, an odd-looking terracotta pub tucked away in the heart of the City, built in 1652 as England's first coffee house. The ornate red-brick hotel where Wilde is arrested in the film is **2 South Audley Street** (see the interior in *Howards End*), behind the Hilton Hotel in Mayfair. The Cadogan Hotel, 75 Sloane Street at Pont Street in Chelsea (© *020.7235.7141, www.cadogan.com*), where Wilde was actually arrested, is still thriving, but it stands on a busy and modernised street.

It's back to Spain again for the Italian cemetery where Wilde visits his wife's grave, and the French sidewalk café, where he decides to meet Bosie again, which can both be found in **Granada**.

WILLIAM SHAKESPEARE'S ROMEO & JULIET

(1996, dir: Baz Luhrmann)
Leonardo DiCaprio, Claire Danes, Pete Postlethwaite.
● **MEXICO**

Baz Luhrmann's brashly imaginative reinvention of the Shakespeare play sets the action in Verona Beach, using settings in Mexico. Sycamore Grove, the beachfront where the Montagues hang out and where Mercutio is killed, is the coastal village of **Veracruz**, on the Gulf of Mexico, about 200 miles east of Mexico City. Romeo's banishment sees him holed up in a trailer in the barren badlands of **Texcoco**.

The Capulet mansion is **Castillo de Chapultepec** in Chapultepec Park, Mexico City. Built from 1780 to 1840, this palace was the summer house of Mexican presidents until 1940, when it became a national museum of history. St Peter's, the modern gothic concrete church where Romeo and Juliet wed in secret, and where they die together at the movie's end, is the **Immaculate Heart of Mary Church, Colonia Guerrero** in Mexico City.

WILLY WONKA AND THE CHOCOLATE FACTORY

(1971, dir: Mel Stuart)
Gene Wilder, Jack Albertson, Peter Ostrum.
● **GERMANY**

Musical version of Roald Dahl's kiddie fantasy, shot in **Munich**. The ending (with the flying glass elevator) was filmed at **Nördlingen, Bavaria**.

WINCHESTER '73
(1950, dir: Anthony Mann)
James Stewart, Shelley Winters, Dan Duryea.
● **ARIZONA**

The classic Western filmed in **Tucson, Old Tucson** and **Nogales**, Arizona.

WIND, THE
(1928, dir: Victor Seastrom)
Lillian Gish, Lars Hanson, Montagu Love.
● **CALIFORNIA**

City girl Gish goes to live out on the prairie, and murders a potential rapist in this overwhelming (and recently-restored) silent classic, using the desert around the town of **Mojave**, Route 14 north of LA.

WIND AND THE LION, THE
(1975, dir: John Milius)
Sean Connery, Candice Bergen, Brian Keith.
● **SPAIN**

Roosevelt reads the letter from the Raisuli: La Rotonda, Westin Palace Hotel, Madrid

In turn-of-the-century Tangier, widowed Eden Pedecaris (Bergen, a last-minute replacement for Faye Dunaway) and her two children are kidnapped by the Raisuli, an unlikely Scottish Berber (Connery). The old-fashioned boy's own epic-culture-clash adventure owes more to David Lean's *Lawrence of Arabia* (even sharing some of the same locations) than to historical accuracy – the real Pedecaris was a man, there were no kids and no gun battle.

Set in Morocco, the film was shot entirely in Spain. The Moroccan rif is the desert at **Bahia de los Genoveses, San Jose** on **Cabo del Gato** (Cape of the Cat) near to Almeria, southern Spain, which previously provided desert backgrounds for *Lawrence* as well as many Sergio Leone Westerns. **Almeria** itself is the town invaded by US Marines.

The Moorish palaces can be seen in **Seville**. Fez, the seat of the Sultan of Morocco, is Seville's **Alcázar, Plaza del Triunfo, Santa Cruz** (© *95.450.2323*). Despite appearances, the Alcázar is not technically a Moorish palace at all. The work of Moorish craftsmen, it was built in the 1360s for Spanish monarch Pedro the Cruel, and is the home of Spanish royalty. The US Vice Consul, delivering a gift of lions, is escorted through the sumptuously decorated **Salón de Embajadores** (Hall of the Ambassadors), where Carlos V married Isabel of Portugal in 1526. The Tangier palace of the Bashaw (Vladek Sheybal), ultimately captured by US marines, is the **Mudejar Pavilion**, the **Museo de Artes y Costumbres Populares**

(Museum of Art and Popular Traditions), **Plaza of the Americas** (south of the Plaza de Espana, seen in both *Lawrence* and *Star Wars Episode II*), in the **Parque de Maria Luisa, Avenida de Isabel la Catolica**. The Pavilion became Jerusalem for *Lawrence of Arabia*.

The US scenes were filmed in **Madrid**. The railway station, where 'Teddy' Roosevelt (Keith) goes on the stump, is in Madrid; the hunting camp in Yellowstone, where the Pres shoots a grizzly, is the countryside north of the city, where Milius would later film *Conan the Barbarian*. The movie ends with Roosevelt in DC at the foot of his stuffed and mounted bear, reading the letter from the Raisuli which explains the film's title. The pillared rotunda is **La Rotonda**, the glass-domed restaurant of Madrid's **Westin Palace Hotel, Plaza de las Cortes 7** (© *91.360.8000, www.westinpalacemadrid.com*).

WINGS
(1927, dir: William A Wellman)
Charles 'Buddy' Rogers, Richard Arlen, Clara Bow.
● **TEXAS**

The first ever Academy Award for Best Picture went to this WWI aerial melodrama. The flying sequences, filmed at **Carey Air Field** in **San Antonio**, Texas, are still breathtaking. A 100-foot tower was built to house the camera for some of the shots. There was help from the Air Service Ground School at Brooks Field and the Advanced Flying School at Kelly Field.

WINGS OF THE DOVE, THE
(1997, dir: Iain Softley)
Helena Bonham Carter, Linus Roache, Alison Elliott.
● **LONDON; HERTFORDSHIRE; SURREY; VENICE, ITALY**

Love takes second place to financial expediency in a beautifully photographed version of the Henry James tragedy. Helena Bonham Carter's London home is **10 Carlton House Terrace**, above the Mall in Westminster. The

Alison Elliott visits the Basilica San Marco

opening party, where she meets cynical aristo Alex Jennings, is the Great Hall of **Syon House, Brentford** (see *Accident* for details). Jennings' country castle, where he takes pot-shots at bunnies from the roof, is **Knebworth House**, Knebworth (see Tim Burton's *Batman* for details). Bonham Carter meets her lover Linus Roache and duped American heiress Alison Elliott at the **Serpentine Gallery** in Hyde Park, but the park which stands in for central London for most of the time is **Painshill**

Elliott and Roache in the little piazza: Campo Dei SS Apostoli

Elliott's palazzo: Palazzo Barbaro, Canal Grande

Picnic on the church steps: Santa Maria della Salute

Park, Portsmouth Road, Cobham (*admission charge*), about 20 miles southwest of the capital in Surrey. The newspaper office, where Roache inveighs against social injustice, is the Library of the **Freemason's Hall, Great Queen Street**, WC2 (*open daily, except Sunday, for guided tours*). Bonham Carter tends her mother's grave at **Brompton Cemetery, Old Brompton Road, Earls Court**, SW5, the last resting place of singer Richard Tauber and of suffragette Emmeline Pankhurst, which was also seen in *GoldenEye*, the bizarre 1992 thriller *Afraid of the Dark* and in spy spoof *Johnny English*.

On a trip to Venice, Bonham Carter, Roache and Elliot picnic on the steps of **Santa Maria della Salute** at the mouth of Canal Grande, and sightsee in **Piazza San Marco** and the **Basilica San Marco**. Elliott's Venetian palazzo is **Palazzo Barbaro** (also known as Palazzo Leporelli), on the Canal Grande at Ponte dell'Accademia, where Henry James actually wrote *The Wings of the Dove*. Elliott and Roach walk in the tiny piazza, **Campo Dei SS Apostoli**. The luxurious coffee house, where Roache spies Jennings and realises there's trouble afoot, is **Caffe Florian**, Piazza San Marco, where Gwyneth Paltrow also experiences dark forebodings in *The Talented Mr Ripley*.

WISE BLOOD

(1979, dir: John Huston)
Brad Dourif, Harry Dean Stanton, Ned Beatty.
● **GEORGIA**

Just when he was about to be dismissed as a has-been, Huston always seemed to storm back with a beaut. This story of religious heresy was shot around the town of **Macon**, Georgia.

WISH YOU WERE HERE

(1987, dir: David Leland)
Emily Lloyd, Tom Bell, Clare Clifford.
● **SUSSEX**

Loosely based on the early life of Cynthia Payne, this story of a feisty young girl growing up in the prudish fifties was made in **Worthing** and **Bognor** on the south coast of Sussex.

WITCHES OF EASTWICK, THE

(1987, dir: George Miller)
Susan Sarandon, Cher, Michelle Pfeiffer.
● **MASSACHUSETTS; CALIFORNIA**

Little Compton, Rhode Island, was the chosen location

Jack Nicholson's mansion: Castle Hill, Ipswich

for George Miller's film of the John Updike novel, until the locals found out about the sacrilegious nature of the script. The town council eventually voted in favour of the film, but by then Warner Bros had upped and found **Cohasset**, Massachusetts. The church is the **First Parish Unitarian Church, 23 North Main Street**. Jack Nicholson's mansion is **Castle Hill, 290 Argilla Road, Ipswich** (*© 978.356.4351*), about 30 miles north of Boston, though the interior is the familiar **Greystone Mansion, 905 Loma Vista Drive, Beverly Hills** (see *The Loved One* for full details).

WITCHFINDER GENERAL (aka *The Conqueror Worm*)

(1968, dir: Michael Reeves)
Vincent Price, Rupert Davies, Ian Ogilvy.
● **SUFFOLK; BUCKINGHAMSHIRE**

Director Reeves wanted Donald Pleasence for the role of Matthew Hopkins, who made a lucrative career in the 17th century searching out witches. The studio insisted on the more bankable Price, and after a running battle with the veteran star the 24-year-old director extracted a performance for once more sinister than camp, and produced a genuine English classic, violent, bleak and beautiful. This was the last of Reeves' three movies (the others are *The Sorcerers*, with Boris Karloff, and *Revenge of the Blood Beast*). The talented director died of a drug overdose in 1969.

Based on a true story, the film uses some of the real locations, including the church at **Brandeston**, ten miles northeast of Ipswich in Suffolk, where the priest John Lowes really was tried by water and executed for witchcraft.

The witch burning was filmed on the site of real witch burnings in the town square of **Lavenham**, on the A1141, 15 miles west of Ipswich. The coastal scene, where Ian Ogilvy questions the fishermen, is **Dunwich**, on the coast north of Orford. The magistrate's house, site of Lowes' trial by water, is the moat of **Kentwell, Long Melford**, on the A134, three miles north of Sudbury, Suffolk – also seen as Toad Hall in the 1996 *Wind in the Willows* (*© 01787.310207, www.kentwell.co.uk*).

The escape of the Witchfinder's henchmen is **Langley Park**, on the A412, north of Slough in Buckinghamshire; while the ambush of the soldiers is the oft-used **Black Park**, alongside Pinewood Studios, familiar from many Bond and Hammer movies.

The fortified tower, where vengeful Richard Marshall bloodily dispatches Hopkins, is **Orford Castle, Orford**, 13 miles southeast on the B1084 on the River Alde. Built by Henry II around 1173, it was a pretty advanced design for its time, and was an important royal residence until being handed over to the Earl of Norfolk in 1280. It's open to the public (*© 03944.50472*).

WITHNAIL & I
(1987, dir: Bruce Robinson)
Richard E Grant, Paul McGann, Richard Griffiths.
● **LONDON; CUMBRIA; BUCKINGHAMSHIRE**

Withnail orders drinks: The Mother Black Cap, Tavistock Crescent

Crow Cragg: Sleddale Hall

Bruce Robinson's sixties-set comedy has acquired a vast cult following over the years. Set in Camden Town, most of the London scenes were actually filmed in Notting Hill, including the squalid flat, which has since been demolished. The film's Mother Black Cap pub (presumably a conflation of Camden's Black Cap and Mother Red Cap – now the World's End), where Withnail (Grant) orders "Two large gins, two pints of cider, ice in the cider," was until recently one of the Babushka chain. It has now been relaunched as – **The Mother Black Cap, 41 Tavistock Crescent** at St Luke's Grove, W11 (*© 020.7727.9250*). Facing the end of St Luke's Road, it's had a radical makeover since finding fame as Camden's woozy old Irish boozer. The wolf enclosure is in Camden, though the wolves have now gone. It's **Regents Park Zoo**, by the **Gloucester Gate** entrance from the Outer Circle.

The grand London home of Uncle Monty (Griffiths) is **West House, 35 Glebe Place**, tucked away in a crook of the street off Bramerton Street, SW3, in Chelsea.

Crow Cragg, where the pair end up "on holiday by mistake", is **Sleddale Hall**, a derelict cottage alongside Wet Sleddale Reservoir just west from the A6, near Shap, about 12 miles south of Penrith, Cumbria (*rail: Penrith*).

Crow Cragg: Sleddale hall

The Penrith Tea Rooms: Cox and Robinson, Market Place, Stony Stratford

There's a limited bus service from Penrith to Shap. About a mile south of Shap, a narrow road runs west to Wet Sleddale, and from that, about two miles of footpath lead to Sleddale Hall. Although the cottage overlooks Wet Sleddale Reservoir, that's not the spectacular body of water seen in the movie.

There seem to be plenty of *Withnail* fans who head to Penrith to find the King Henry pub and the Penrith Tea Rooms without realising that these scenes were filmed in Buckinghamshire.

The King Henry in Penrith: The Crown, Market Place, Stony Stratford

The town square is **Market Square, Stony Stratford**, not far from Milton Keynes (*rail: Wolverton*). The King Henry is **The Crown, 9 Market Place**, but the really sad news is that there is no tea room and you'll not be able to order the finest wines known to humanity. The premises is now a chemist shop, **Cox and Robinson, 1 Market Place**, on the opposite corner to the Crown.

The grand London home of Uncle Monty: West House, Glebe Place

WITNESS
(1985, dir: Peter Weir)
Harrison Ford, Kelly McGillis, Lukas Haas.
● **PENNSYLVANIA**

When a small Amish boy witnesses a murder, a whole mess of police corruption is uncovered, and good cop Ford has to go into hiding with the austere religious commu-

Lukas Haas is fascinated by the angelic statue: 30th Street Station

nity. In the original script, the opening murder took place at Philadelphia bus station, but the state film commission suggested the more photogenic **30th Street Railway Station**, where young Lukas Haas is entranced by the concourse's vast angel statue. The café where Harrison Ford neglects to say grace and where Haas enjoys a hot dog, is now **Xando Coffee Bar, 235 South 15th Street** at Locust Street, a designer-heavy orange, purple and lime coffee shop. The rest of the

Haas enjoys a hot dog: Xando Coffee Bar, 15th Street

Kelly McGillis waits as Lukas Haas witnesses murder: 30th Street Station

movie was actually shot in Amish country: in Lancaster County, Eastern Pennsylvania, with the cooperation of more liberal members of the community. The farm, where Ford hides out, is **Paul Krantz Farm**, near **Strasburg**, a few miles south of Lancaster, about 50 miles west of Philadelphia. The tourist-riddled town that Ford visits is the racily-named **Intercourse**, ten miles east of Lancaster, where he makes a phonecall outside **WL Zimmerman & Sons** general store.

WITNESS FOR THE PROSECUTION

(1957, dir: Billy Wilder)
Charles Laughton, Tyrone Power, Marlene Dietrich.
● LOS ANGELES, CALIFORNIA; LONDON

Robarts and Miss Plimsoll are driven through the gates of New Square, Lincoln's Inn Fields, Holborn

Laughton steals the show as defence barrister Sir Wilfrid Robarts in Wilder's irresistible film of the tricksy Agatha Christie courtroom drama. Although made in Hollywood, second unit shots establish the London setting. The murder trial of Leonard Vole (Power) is held at **The Old Bailey**, more properly known as the **Central Criminal Court**, EC4, in the City of London. One of those iconic landmarks seen in stock shots to indicate a major legal case, it is similarly featured in Hitchcock's 1947 *The Paradine Case*. Robarts and his fussing nurse Miss Plimsoll (Laughton's real-life wife, Elsa Lanchester) are driven through the imposing gates of **New Square, Lincoln's Inn Fields, Holborn**, a quietly civilised square of gentlemanly solicitors' chambers, seemingly from another age. The square itself, seen in *A Fish Called Wanda* and *Tom Jones*, was recreated in the studio.

WO HU CANG LONG (aka *Crouching Tiger, Hidden Dragon/Ngo Foo Chang Lung*)

(2000, dir: Ang Lee)
Yun Fat Chow, Michelle Yeoh, Zhang Ziyi.
● CHINA

The desert scenes are the Gobi Desert in China's **Xinjiang Province**. The **Summer Palace** is four hours from Beijing. The bamboo forest is in **Zhejiang Province**, southern China. The stately home and courtyard, where Li Mu Bai (Chow) and Yu Shu Lien (Yeoh) meet, was constructed in the Beijing Film Studios. There was also filming at the **Forbidden City**, Beijing.

WOLF

(1994, dir: Mike Nichols)
Jack Nicholson, Michelle Pfeiffer, James Spader.
● NEW YORK CITY; NEW YORK; LOS ANGELES, CALIFORNIA

Considering the talent involved, this is a disappointing attempt to rework the werewolf myth in contemporary Manhattan. There are a couple of familiar locations:

Christopher Plummer's estate is **Old Westbury Gardens, 71 Old Westbury Road, Old Westbury**, Long Island, which is probably more familiar as the Townsend house in Hitchcock's *North by Northwest*. And Nicholson's publishing company isn't in New York at all, but over on the West Coast in LA. It's the **Bradbury Building, 304 South Broadway** at Third Street, downtown LA, seen in plenty of movies, most

Nicholson's hotel: Mayflower Hotel, Central Park West

famously *Blade Runner*. The upscale hotel Nicholson moves into can be found on New York's West Side. It's the **Mayflower Hotel, 15 Central Park West** at 61st Street.

WOLFEN

(1981, dir: Michael Wadleigh)
Albert Finney, Diane Venora, Edward James Olmos.
● NEW YORK CITY

Stylish and bloody eco-horror, from the director of *Woodstock*, has strangely-accented cop Finney investigating a race of superwolves, descended from native American hunters, who live by scavenging on the Big Apple's down-and-outs. The Van de Veers and their chauffeur get chomped at **Battery Park**. Finney lives in a surprisingly elegant mansion block on **Staten Island**, from where he flies in by helicopter to investigate the deaths. The wolfen inhabit the blighted urban wastes of the **South Bronx**.

The Van de Veers' glitzy apartment is in the **Chase Manhattan Bank Building, 1 Chase Manhattan Plaza**, in Lower Manhattan. The strange black and white sculpture outside is Jean Dubuffet's A Group of Four Trees. After a scare in the south Bronx, Finney and Venora head for **Chumley's**, a former speakeasy (you need to look for it – there's still no sign), **86 Bedford Street**, between Grove and Barrow Streets in Greenwich Village (seen also in Woody Allen's *Sweet and Lowdown*). Wolf-loving Dr Ferguson works out of **Central Park Zoo**, Fifth Avenue at East 64th Street. Finney questions Olmos in a dizzying scene atop the arch of the **Manhattan Bridge** high above the East River, after a queasy climb up the huge suspension wires. The climactic bloody wolf attack, with the Police Chief's head gaily bouncing off the car, is staged in front of the grandiose Parthenon-style **Federal Hall, 26 Wall Street** at Nassau Street.

WOMAN IN RED, THE

(1984, dir: Gene Wilder)
Gene Wilder, Charles Grodin, Kelly LeBrock.
● SAN FRANCISCO, CALIFORNIA

The Seven Year Itch revisited, as middle-aged married man Wilder gets smitten by impossible sex object LeBrock. Set in San Francisco, where Wilder's house is one of the group of 'Painted Ladies', the Gingerbread houses on **Steiner Street** between Hayes Street and Fulton Street. The apartment block, where Wilder teeters on the ledge, is the **Brocklebank Apartments, 1000 Mason Street** (see *Vertigo*, where the Brocklebank features as Kim Novak's apartment, for details).

WOMEN IN LOVE

(1969, dir: Ken Russell)
Glenda Jackson, Alan Bates, Oliver Reed.
● DERBYSHIRE; YORKSHIRE; SWITZERLAND

The grand house of Alan Bates and Eleanor Bron: Kedleston Hall, Derby

The best filming of a Lawrence novel, with Glenda Jackson getting her first Oscar. The grand house of Alan Bates and Eleanor Bron is **Kedleston Hall**, four miles northwest of Derby on the Derby-Hulland Road, Derbyshire. This neo-classical masterpiece was built in 1759 for Sir Nathaniel Curzon by Robert Adam, who also designed the superb interior. The circular saloon, where Eleanor Bron's cultural performance gets sabotaged, is based on the design of a Roman temple (© *01332.842191; open April to November, admission charge*). Shortlands, the Crich house of Oliver Reed, where Christopher Gable drowns during the party, is **Elvaston Castle, Borrowash Road, Elvaston**, Derby. The park is currently open (© *01332.571342, www.elvastoncastle.org.uk*), but there are plans to turn the house into a hotel. Other locations were found around Derbyshire and Sheffield. The snowy climax is **Zermatt**, at the foot of the Matterhorn, Switzerland.

WONDER BOYS

(2000, dir: Curtis Hanson)
Michael Douglas, Tobey Maguire, Frances McDormand.
● PITTSBURGH, PENNSYLVANIA

One-time wonderboy writer Douglas can't bring himself to complete his novel. Douglas' home is in Pittsburgh's Friendship district. His college is the **Carnegie-Mellon University**, with filming in **Baker Hall** and the **Fine Arts Building**. The Hi-Hat Club exterior is in Pittsburgh's historic African-American Hill District, but the interior is the **Modern Restaurant Cafe and Bar, 862 Western Avenue**, in the North Side neighbourhood. Filming also took place in **Pittsburgh International Airport** and in the **Beaver** district.

WONDERFUL LIFE

(1964, dir: Sidney J Furie)
Cliff Richard, The Shadows, Melvyn Hayes.
● CANARY ISLANDS; LONDON

Cliff and his backing group the Shads are sacked cruise line entertainers, who manage to get employed in the movies. Hey, just like real life! Made in the Canary Islands and at Elstree Studios, with the bonus of a musical number on a boat in the Thames.

WOODSTOCK

(1970, dir: Michael Wadleigh)

Jimi Hendrix, The Who, Richie Havens.
● NEW YORK

The giant split-screen documentary record of the legendary four-day rock concert (edited by the young Martin Scorsese) wasn't filmed at Woodstock at all. The concert had grown too large for its original location, which is upstate New York on Route 212 near the Catskills. The final venue, Max Yasgur's 38-acre farm, was in **Bethel**, some 50 miles southwest on Route 17B.

WORKING GIRL

(1988, dir: Mike Nichols)
Melanie Griffith, Sigourney Weaver, Harrison Ford.
● NEW YORK CITY

Office worker Griffith finally betters bitch-boss Weaver to make it in the Big Apple in this Oscar-nominated comedy. The opening shot of Griffith and Joan Cusack (both Oscar nominees) was stolen during the morning rush hour as the **Staten Island Ferry** arrives at New York's **Battery Park**. A 20-minute ride with fabulous views of the Lower Manhattan skyline, the ferry is now free.

Petty-Marsh, the broker house where they work, is a composite of four different locations: the huge secretarial pool is a set constructed on the 21st floor of **1 State Street Plaza** on Manhattan's southern tip overlooking Battery Park; the club room was filmed at the **Midday Club**; the company's lobby was that of 7 World Trade Center; while the reading floor is that of **LF Rothschild Company**.

The offices of the Trask Company are the 1907 Beaux Arts-style United States Custom House, now the **Museum of the Native American, Broadway** at Bowling Green, Lower Manhattan, seen also in *Batman Forever* and *Ghostbusters II*. Weaver's Manhattan town house is an early 19th century private home on **Irving Place**, south from Gramercy Park between Third and Park Avenues.

The fictitious Union Club, site of the Trask wedding reception, is also a composite. The exterior is the familiar **Carnegie Mansion**, home of the Cooper-Hewitt Museum, **2 East 91st Street** at Fifth Avenue on the East Side, while the interior was shot just across the street in the 1904 Burden Mansion, now the **Convent of the Sacred Heart, 1 East 91st Street** (see *The Anderson Tapes* for details).

WORLD ACCORDING TO GARP, THE

(1982, dir: George Roy Hill)
Robin Williams, Mary Beth Hurt, Glenn Close.
● NEW YORK; NEW JERSEY; CONNECTICUT

Confused and tiresome film of John Irving's complex novel, with Robin Williams' Garp struggling to become a writer, Glenn Close as Jenny Fields, his bizarre proto-feminist mother, and John Lithgow as a sex-changed ex-footballer.

The beachfront home of Close's parents is a private estate on **Fishers Island**, New York State. Long fought over by New York and Connecticut, Fishers Island was eventually awarded to New York in 1879, despite being much closer to the New England state – the locals prefer to identify with Connecticut. The island is a remote summer getaway for the very, very rich. The Everett Steering School, where Garp grows up, is the expansive green 600-acre campus of **Millbrook School, School Road, Millbrook**, about 12 miles northeast of Poughkeepsie, Route 44, in the Hudson Valley, upstate New York (seen also in *Regarding Henry*).

The home Jenny Fields buys for Garp and his wife is **2 Brassie Road, Eastchester** on Route 22, north of New York City on the road to White Plains. A façade was constructed at the end of the runway of **Lincoln Park Airport**, off I-80, in northern New Jersey, for the scene where a plane crashes into the front of the house.

Also in Lincoln Park is the college where Garp's wife teaches, **Rutgers University Campus**. Fields is assassinated in front of the town hall of **Madison**, New Jersey, the **Hartley Dodge Memorial Building, King's Road** at Green Avenue. Filming also took place at **Norwich**, Connecticut; and in New York State at **Roslyn**, **Long Island** and **Tuckahoe**.

WORLD IS NOT ENOUGH, THE

(1999, dir: Michael Apted)
Pierce Brosnan, Robert Carlyle, Sophie Marceau.
● LONDON; SURREY; BUCKINGHAMSHIRE; HERTFORDSHIRE; WILTSHIRE; AZERBAIJAN; FRANCE; SPAIN; TURKEY; SCOTLAND; WALES

Third in the increasingly confident Brosnan Bonds, given a little more weight than usual by a top-drawer cast and the director of *Gorillas in the Mist*. The opening teaser is set against the backdrop of Frank O Gehry's stunning, titanium-plated **Guggenheim Museum**, on the Nerrión River in the centre of **Bilbao** (*www.guggenheim-bilbao.es*). But when test audiences felt a bit short-changed with a single stunt, the titles were shunted back to include the Thames boat chase as part of the pre-credits sequence. In a move which garnered plenty of publicity, the movie opens at the real MI6 headquarters on the Thames at **Vauxhall Bridge**. The subsequent boat chase (much cut down) was shot, not so much on the Thames, as on nearby waterways and docks. The rollover is the **Royal Victoria Dock** at Canning Town – actually over the Thames from the chase's climax. West of the Dockland Light Railway's Crossharbour Station, in the shadow of the London Arena, is **Glengall Bridge** across **Millwall Inner Dock**, the bridge which Bond dives under as it closes, on the Isle of Dogs – the great loop in the Thames, which Bond appears to use as a shortcut. Then it's back west, toward Wapping, to **Tobacco Dock** on the tiny **Ornamental Canal** at **Wapping Lane**. The commercial redevelopment of the dock seems to have failed, with the shopping complex currently deserted and dusty. It's on the right-angle bend of the

The boat chase from the real MI6 HQ, Vauxhall

Ornamental Canal that the traffic wardens (a dated cameo by long-forgotten, minor celebs from reality-TV) get drenched as Bond's Q boat

Bond dives under the bridge: Glengall Bridge across Millwall Inner Dock, Isle of Dogs

leaps up the canal's steps and tears through the London Canoe Club clubhouse (specially built for the movie) alongside the pirate ships of Tobacco Dock. A crafty cut has Bond's boat tearing ashore at **Chatham High Street**, in Kent, before emerging opposite the then uncompleted **Millennium Dome, Greenwich**.

The temporary MI6 HQ in Scotland is made up of two separate locations. The funeral scene uses the chapel at **Stowe School** in Buckinghamshire (see *Indiana Jones and the Last Crusade* for details), though Castle Thane itself really is north of the border. It's **Eilean Donan Castle**, at **Dornie** near the Kyle of Lochalsh, probably most familiar from *Highlander* (℡ *01599.555202, www.eileandonancastle.com*).

The vast, sprawling oilfields of Azerbaijan are the real thing, at **Baku** on the Caspian Sea, though closer shots are of the familiar old standby **Black Park**, near to the Pinewood Studios, and **Hankley Common, Tilford Road** south of Tilford in Surrey. The oil pipeline site itself is at **Cuenca**, central Spain (but don't go looking for the beautiful little chapel, which was only a set).

The skiing sequence, supposedly in the Caucasus Mountains, where the paragliders attack, is high on the slopes of Mont Blanc near **Chamonix** on the Italian-French border.

From here on Azerbaijan is largely fake. The exterior of Electra's Baku palace is a mansion on the Bosphorus in Istanbul, while its interior is **Luton Hoo**, Luton (see *Four Weddings and a Funeral* for details), a veteran location seen in *Eyes Wide Shut*, Pink Panther sequel *A Shot in the Dark* and *Wilde*, among many other films. And it provides more backdrops here too, as the casino bar. The casino itself is the RAF officers' mess at **Horton**, Buckinghamshire. The airport from which Bond makes his nighttime escape is **Northolt Airport**.

The Kazakhstan site, where Bond meets Christmas, is **Bardenas Reales** near Tudela in Spain, while the gleaming pipeline terminal is the **Motorola Building** at **Swindon** in Wiltshire. The pipeline itself is in the mountains of **Snowdonia** in Wales, but the explosion from which Bond and Christmas escape was faked in Black Park.

M is imprisoned in **Kiz Kulesi – Maiden's Tower** – an 11th century lighthouse at the mouth of the Bosphorus at Istanbul, Turkey.

WRONG MAN, THE

(1957, dir: Alfred Hitchcock)
Henry Fonda, Vera Miles, Anthony Quayle.
● NEW YORK CITY; NEW YORK

Few bravura flourishes (even the famous cameo is reduced to a serious prologue) as Hitchcock explores his favourite theme of guilt in untypically sombre docu-style. Based on a true story – jazz muso Christopher 'Manny' Balestrero (Fonda) is wrongly arrested for armed robbery – the film was shot, wherever possible, on the real locations.

The Stork Club, where Manny plays bass, was a hangout for the stars (Sinatra, Monroe – and J Edgar Hoover – were regulars from 1934 to 1965). It stood at 3 East 53rd Street, but was demolished in the mid-sixties to make way for Samuel Paley Plaza.

Balestrero's neighbourhood is **Jackson Heights**, northern Queens, where the home of the real Christopher Balestrero was on **74th Street** (in the film the address is given as 4024 78th Street). It's at the Prudential Insurance Office – above the bus station in the Victor Moore Arcade, 74th Street at Broadway – that a counter clerk mistakenly identifies Manny. It was demolished in 2001. As more witnesses testify to his guilt, Manny is hauled off to the **110th Precinct, 94-41 43rd Avenue, Elmhurst**, and held at **City Prison, 1 Court Square, Long Island City**.

Manny tries vainly to establish an alibi at his holiday retreat, **Edelweiss Farm**, Cornwall, Route 9W by the Hudson just north of West Point Military Academy. As circumstantial evidence mounts Mrs Balestrero (Miles) is driven to the verge of a breakdown and treated at **Greenmont Sanatorium, North Highland Avenue, Ossining**, Route 9, east of the Hudson River north of New York.

Look out during the movie for the 'real' culprit: outside the Stork Club, in the Victor Moore Arcade, and in one of the liquor stores where the cops take Manny.

WUTHERING HEIGHTS
(1939, dir: William Wyler)
Laurence Olivier, Merle Oberon, David Niven.
● **LOS ANGELES, CALIFORNIA; YORKSHIRE**

The first major screen adaptation of Emily Brontë's novel, with location shooting near **Chatsworth**, California. Kilos of heather were imported from northern England and replanted in California to match up with location shots of the Yorkshire moors. The ducks and geese look cute, and are remarkably quiet. That's because they had their vocal chords snipped to prevent extraneous noise on the soundtrack.

X

X-FILES, THE
(1998, dir: Rob Bowman)
David Duchovny, Gillian Anderson, Martin Landau.
● CALIFORNIA; LONDON; WASHINGTON DC;
BRITISH COLUMBIA, CANADA

Mulder meets Kurtzweil: Casey's Bar,
South Grand Avenue

The stamping ground of the original TV series was Vancouver, where the first six series were shot (and you can find plenty of *X-Files* tours of the city), but the big screen version moved south to California. The Dallas Federal Building, blown up at the beginning of the movie, was the old Unocal Building, now the **LA Center Studios, 1202 West Fifth Street** at Beaudry Street, downtown LA (which houses film location offices). The FBI lab was on the 26th floor. The 'bee domes' in the cornfield are at **Bakersfield**, in the desert north of LA, as is the desert epilogue – supposedly in Tunisia at Foum Tatouine – a jokey reference to the *Star Wars* desert location.

Mulder (Duchovny) meets Kurtzweil (Landau) in **Casey's Bar, 613 South Grand Avenue**, downtown Los Angeles (seen also in Michelle Pfeiffer weepie *The Deep End of the Ocean*). Kurtzweil's apartment, where Mulder discovers the cops already searching, is the **Mira Monte Apartments** in LA.

The Somerset home of the Well-Manicured Man (John Neville) is in California, at **380 South San Rafael Avenue, Pasadena**, the Tudor-style mansion seen in *Topper*, *Dead Again* and *Rush Hour*. But when he's summoned to attend the meeting of elders, that really is London. The entrance is **Queen Alexandra's House, Kensington Gore**, SW7, alongside the **Albert Hall** in Kensington. The interior, however, is once more back in Pasadena. It's the **Athenaeum**, the dining club of the California Institute of Technology, at **551 South Hill Avenue** in Pasadena (a frequently used location, seen in *Beverly Hills Cop* and *True Romance* among others). The railway crossing scene is at

The meeting of elders, exterior: Queen
Alexandra's House, Kensington Gore...

...though the interior is the Athenaeum,
South Hill Avenue

Soledad Canyon at Saugus, just north of LA, also the location for Steven Spielberg's classic road movie *Duel*. Mulder and the Well-Manicured Man drive by the **Department of Agriculture Building** in DC. While the Cigarette-Smoking Man (William B Davis) watches, the unconscious Scully (Anderson) is loaded onto the plane at **LAX (Los Angeles International Airport)**. The hospital is the **St Mary Medical Center, 1050 Linden Avenue** in Long Beach, California.

The Antarctic location is a glacier above the ski resort of **Whistler**, British Columbia.

X-MEN
(2000, dir: Bryan Singer)
Patrick Stewart, Ian McKellen, Hugh Jackman.
● ONTARIO, CANADA

Set mainly around New York, Singer's dark, intelligent comic-strip adaptation was made almost entirely in Ontario. The opening concentration camp scene, 'Poland, 1944', used the old **Gooderham & Worts distillery, Mill Street** toward the Toronto waterfront, an abandoned complex whose empty

The concentration camp: Gooderham &
Worts distillery, Toronto

The interior of Dr Xavier's academy:
Casa Loma, Toronto

warehouses are frequently used as makeshift studios (*Blues Brothers 2000*, *Chicago*, *The Long Kiss Goodnight*, *Mimic*, *The Recruit* and *Three Men and a Baby* are among many movies shot here). The lowlife bar in northern Alberta where Wolverine (Jackman) is first discovered is also the old distillery.

Also in central Toronto is the dazzling metal and glass centre of the senate hearings, the **Metro Hall Council Chamber, St John Street**, and the Ellis Island meeting

Dr Xavier's, exterior: Parkwood Estate, Oshawa, Toronto

Cyclops' motorbike: The Stables, Casa Loma, Toronto

The interior of Dr Xavier's academy, schoolroom: Casa Loma, Toronto

The senate hearing: Metro Hall, St John Street, Toronto

place for the Conference of World Leaders, which is **Central Commerce Collegiate, 570 Shaw Street**, west of the city.

The stretch of road where Wolverine's truck is attacked is east of Toronto in the nature conservation area, the **Rouge River Valley Park**. Further east still, in the city of **Oshawa**, you'll find 'Mutant High', Dr Xavier's School for Gifted Youngsters, supposedly in Westchester, in reality the **Parkwood Estate, 270 Simcoe Street North** (© 905.433.4311; admission charge), which you might recognise from the Adam Sandler comedy *Billy Madison* or Shirley MacLaine's *Mrs Winterbourne*. The interior of the school, though, is **Casa Loma, 1 Austin Terrace** at Spadina Road (© 416.923.1171; admission charge), a turn-of-the-century mock-Medieval folly overlooking northern Toronto. The building is a frequent film location (see it in David Cronenberg's *Dead Ringers* and in Jean-Claude Van Damme actioner *Maximum Risk*), and here you'll find the study of Dr Xavier (Stewart), the conservatory where mutant children learn to channel their skills, and the old stables, where Cyclops' bike is stashed.

The lair of militant leader Magneto (McKellen) was constructed in a forest clearing at the **Greenwood Conservation Area** in **Hamilton**, about 40 miles southwest of Toronto. Westchester Railway Station, where Cerebro traces Rogue, and Magneto uses his electromagnetic powers to levitate the police cars, is also Hamilton, the **CNR (Canadian National Railway) Station, James Street North, Hamilton**, which was also the location of the spectacular shoot-out in *The Long Kiss Goodnight*. Liberty Island is actually **Spencer Smith Park** in **Burlington**, east of Hamilton, while some of the interior shots of the statue are the **Bridgeman Transformer Station**.

X2 (aka *X-Men 2*)
(2003, dir: Bryan Singer)
Patrick Stewart, Hugh Jackman, Ian McKellen.
● **ONTARIO, BRITISH COLUMBIA, CANADA; ALBERTA, CANADA; CALIFORNIA; LONDON**

The superior sequel moves from East Coast to West Coast, forsaking Toronto for Vancouver, where the underground

lair of Stryker was built in the Mammoth Studios, a former Sears department store and warehouse, boasting the largest soundstage in North America.

Xavier's school itself seems to have undergone a little mutation. It's now **Hatley Castle, Royal Roads University, Colwood** (which is also featured in TV's *Poltergeist: The Legacy* and *Smallville*). And late reshoots meant that the school mutates once again, for the final scene. The exterior is an outtake (of Toronto's Parkwood Estate) from the first movie, and the interior, with Xavier reading *The Once and Future King* to the kids, is the British Cinematographers' office at Shepperton Studios near London.

Pyro flips out after being provoked by local lads – foreshadowing his defection to the mutants' militant wing – on a trip to the science museum. You won't be able to visit the musem, however, as it was created in Vancouver's public convention centre, the **Plaza of Nations, 750 Pacific Boulevard**, on the False Creek waterfront at Concord Pacific Place. Jean Grey and Storm head up to Boston. The church in which they discover Nightcrawler is **St Andrew's-Wesley Church, 1012 Nelson Street** at Burrard Street, downtown Vancouver.

The snowbound Alkali Lake dam is between Upper and Lower Kananaskis Lakes in the **Peter Lougheed Provincial Park** near **Kananaskis**, Alberta, although for the dambursting, a 60-foot model was built in Van Nuys, north of LA. Another additional scene, after the Vancouver shoot had wrapped, is the transformation of Senator Kelly into Yuriko. The DC capital building is the pillared court at the west entrance to **Los Angeles City Hall, 200 North Spring Street**, downtown LA.

X – THE MAN WITH X-RAY EYES (aka *The Man With X-Ray Eyes*)
(1963, dir: Roger Corman)
Ray Milland, John Hoyt, Diana Van Der Vlis.
● **LOS ANGELES, CALIFORNIA**

Corman naturally makes the most of a microbudget in this story of another Dr Xavier (Milland), a scientist who develops x-ray vision, only to be driven bonkers by what he sees. The Las Vegas scenes were shot on soundstages and around LA. The x-ray visions of transparent buildings were achieved by photographing construction sites from the same angle over a period of time, then reversing the shots so the buildings appear to dissolve.

The fairground, where Xavier earns a living as 'Mentalo' after being chucked out of the hospital research department, was on **Long Beach Pier**, though naturally the interiors were recreated in the studio.

XXX
(2002, dir: Rob Cohen)
Vin Diesel, Samuel L Jackson, Asia Argento.
● **CALIFORNIA; TAHITI; AUSTRIA; CZECH REPUBLIC; WEST VIRGINIA**

Director Cohen signals his intentions early on, offing a smoothly tuxedoed secret agent at a Rammstein gig. Time for a new breed of hero, as extreme sportster Xander Cage (Diesel) is unwillingly recruited as a superagent for the

Xander Cage faces a test from Augustus Gibbons: Pann's Cafe, La Tijera Boulevard, Baldwin Hills

21st century. I can't help feeling, though, that Bond has a bit more life left in him.

Cage demonstrates attitude with a live webcast as he steals the Corvette of tightass "Senator Dick" from the country club at **Westlake Village**, north of Malibu. No crime of profit, of course; Cage is teaching the no-fun politician a lesson, and catapults the motor off a bridge. It was a long drive. You'll find **Foresthill Bridge** spanning the North Fork of the American River in **Auburn**, northeast of Sacramento, northern California. A breathtaking 728 feet above the river – plans to flood the valley were never brought to completion – allows Cage's spectacular base jump.

Unwittingly sussed out as a potential recruit, Cage faces a test from Augustus Gibbons (Jackson) in **Pann's Cafe, 6710 La Tijera Boulevard** at La Cienega Boulevards and Centinella Avenue, Baldwin Hills (© *310.337.2860, www.panns.com*), a classic fifties coffee shop built in 1958, restored in 1991 and now recognised as an LA landmark. (By the way, it's not, as some have claimed, the café seen in *Pulp Fiction*.) The next test finds Cage facing that old favourite, a vicious central American drug lord. The Colombian drug plantation was built at **Lake Piru**, north of LA.

The real mission takes Cage to **Prague** in the Czech Republic, where he stays on **Liliova Street** in **Stare Mesto** (the Old Town). No martinis or roulette wheels here. The front for Anarchy 99, bent on the destruction of life as we know it, is a string of rave clubs, but you needn't go looking for them. The nightclub of the opening scene was a de-sanctified, 150-year-old church in **Celna**, in the eastern Czech Republic; while the Orbital techno rave was staged in an electronic testing station to the north of Prague.

Anarchy 99's fortified HQ is real enough. It's the **State Castle of Vranov nad Dyji, 671 03 Vranov nad Dyji** (© *515.296.215*), in the Znojmo district (though the magic of FX moves it into the mountains north of Prague). Back in Prague itself, the vaulted basement of the abandoned **Patanka Brewery** became the Czech police HQ.

One place you will want to visit is the magnificent art nouveau restaurant, in which Cage reveals to Yelena (Argento) he's a secret agent. It's the **Francouzska Restaurace** (French Restaurant) of the recently restored art nouveau **Obecni Dum** (Municipal House), **Mamesti Republiky 5** (© *222.002.770*). Escaping an assassination attempt, Cage is bundled off to meet up with Gibbons in the **Tyl Theatre, Zelezna ulice 11** (Zelezna Street) at Havirska Street (see *Amadeus* for details), though the exterior seen is the **Rudolfinium, Palachovo namesti 1** (1 Palach Square), the London club in *The League of Extraordinary Gentlemen*.

The climax is staged on the **Vltava River**, where stunt-man Harry O'Connor was killed flying into the **Palacky Bridge** during a retake of the parascending stunt. Gibbons watches from **Karluv Most** (the Charles Bridge, seen in *Mission: Impossible* and *Van Helsing*) as Cage disarms Anarchy's dastardly device.

Some of the stunt work was filmed elsewhere: sky surfing above **Lake Tahoe**, northern California; and the snowmobiles and snowboarding at **Kaunertal** in the Austrian Tyrol. The tropical island on which Xander Cage and Yelena finally get to rest up is the tropical paradise of **Bora Bora**, French Polynesia (*www.borabora-island.com*).

Y

Y TU MAMÁ TAMBIÉN (aka *And Your Mother Too*)
(2001, dir: Alfonso Cuarón)
Gael García Bernal, Diego Luna, Maribel Verdú.
● MEXICO

The unlikely premise – older married woman ups sticks and takes to the road with a couple of hormonally-driven teens to find a mythically perfect beach – only makes sense at the downbeat conclusion. Director Cuarón went on to bring depth and darkness to the *Harry Potter* franchise.

The setting is **Mexico City**, where Julio (Bernal) has to collect car keys from his sister at the **National University**, in the 1950s University City campus, south of the city. Finding the campus was taken over by political unrest, Cuarón weaves the demo into the film.

The privileged kids leave the city behind and travel southeast through **Oaxaca**, Mexico's poorest state. The legendary (and fictitious) beach, Boca del Cielo, is at **Bahias de Huatulco**, about 70 miles east of Puerto Escondido on Mexico's southern coast. The resort is an attempt to mix tourist infrastructure with an ecological conservation area (*baysofhuatulco.com.mx*). The first beach at which they arrive is **Cacaluta**, one of the nine secluded bays at the resort, and fairly inaccessible. The beach with the bar where the three end up dancing together is **San Agustin**, the westernmost bay, reached by a dirt road from highway 200, Carretera Costera, near Huatulco International Airport.

YANKS
(1979, dir: John Schlesinger)
Richard Gere, Lisa Eichhorn, William Devane.
● LANCASHIRE; YORKSHIRE; CHESHIRE; WALES

GIs bringing a glimpse of romance, and not a little resentment, to a Lancashire town during WWII in Schlesinger's disappointingly clichéd tearjerker. The opening scene is actually Yorkshire. The GI convoy is seen on **Southowram Bank, Halifax**, leading up to Bank Top. The army camp is also east of the Pennines – **Steeton Ordinance Camp, Steeton**, an abandoned army facility a couple of miles northwest of Keighley. And a packed **Keighley Railway Station** is the site of the final goodbyes as the GIs leave for active service.

The picturesque village itself is **Dobcross**, near Saddleworth, east of Oldham, Lancashire. To the south, upper-crust Helen (Vanessa Redgrave) gets advice from her friends at **Stamford Golf Club, Huddersfield Road, Carrbrook**, near Stalybridge, Cheshire, alongside – oops! – some very 60s cooling towers. **Market Street**, in **Stalybridge** itself, was decked out with sandbags and an ARP (Air Raid Precautions) centre. Further south still, the New Year dance, which degenerates into a brawl, is in **Hyde Town Hall, Corporation Street, Hyde**, and the marvellous deco cinema, where Matt (Gere) enjoys his first date with Jean (Eichhorn) was in **Stockport**. It was the Davenport Theatre, Burton Road between Hazel Grove and Stockport town centre, built in 1937.It was demolished in 1999.

Helen guiltily chickens out of a weekend with Captain John (Devane) at the **Grand Hotel, Happy Valley Road**, overlooking the Victorian pier at **Llandudno** on the North Wales coast. Maybe she thinks John is a Nazi spy – her grasp of geography as she points directions to England and Ireland is decidedly dodgy. 'Denry' Machin holidayed at the same resort in Ronald Neame's 1952 adaptation of Arnold Bennett's *The Card*.

YEAR OF LIVING DANGEROUSLY, THE
(1982, dir: Peter Weir)
Mel Gibson, Sigourney Weaver, Linda Hunt.
● PHILIPPINES; NEW SOUTH WALES, AUSTRALIA

The film's actual setting of Indonesia was obviously out from the start, and production began in the Philippines, but threats from Islamic fundamentalists soon closed the production down. The production relocated to the comparative safety of Australia, largely around Sydney. The café and wharf are **Metro Manila**, with more filming at **Chatswood**, a northern suburb of Sydney.

YING XIONG (aka *Hero*)
(2002, dir: Yimou Zhang)
Jet Li, Tony Leung Chiu-wai, Maggie Cheung.
● CHINA

Yimou Zhang, who made *Raise the Red Lantern*, ventures for the first time into epic martial arts territory, and the results are never less than ravishing. The huge Qin palace, where Nameless (Li) spins his dubious tale for the suspicious King of Qin (Daoming Chen), is a set – the largest in China – built for Chen Kaige's *The Emperor and the Assassin*, at Hengdian TV & Movie City (Orient Hollywood), 1 Wansheng South Street, Hangzhou (*© 86.579.6555668*), a nine-square-mile complex. The rain-soaked chess house, where Nameless fights Sky (Donnie Yen) was also built at Hengdian. The complex is a major tourist attraction and you can book a tour from Shanghai.

The attack on the school, where Nameless is trying to learn the secret of Broken Sword's calligraphy, was filmed at **Dangjin Mountain** in **Akesai**, near old **Dunhuang City** (about six miles from the current Dunhuang), in northwest China, toward Mongolia. This is also where you'll find the amazing wind-blasted desert rock formations, or 'yadan,' (evocatively dubbed 'Devil City' by the local inhabitants), which are also featured in Peter Pau's 2002 *The Touch*, with Michelle Yeoh and Ben Chaplin. Virtually inaccessible until roads were built for the making of the films, the area is now promoted as a tourist destination. Since the location is over 2000 metres above sea-level,be aware of potential problems with thin oxygen and powerful UV radiation.

The dazzling fight between Nameless and Broken Sword (Chiu-wai) above the lake is at **Jiu Zhai Gou** (Nine Villages Valley), a popular tourist destination in the Min

Shan mountain range, about 200 miles north of Cheng-du (12 hours by bus), in the southwest province of Sichuan. There are certain restrictions when visiting, as the area is a nature reserve, but the breathtaking array of lakes and waterfalls are worth the journey. The lake – where the pavilion for Flying Snow's body was built for the film – is **Jian Zhu Hai** (Cold Bamboo Sea), surrounded by cold arrow bamboo (the foodstuff of giant pandas) and China fir trees. Filming the complex fight was limited to two hours a day, between ten and noon, the only time the lake's surface is perfectly still.

Just to the south, where two valleys merge into Shuzheng Gully, you can see the waterfall, at which Broken Sword and Flying Snow (Cheung) meet in the 'green' sequence. It's the 98-feet-high **Nuorilang Falls** ('nuorilang' is "magnificent and splendid" in the Tibetan language). More scenes filmed at the yellow grassy marshland near another lake, **Chang Hai** (Long Sea).

The elegiac fight between Flying Snow and Moon (Zhang Ziyi) among fluttering autumnal leaves, is an ancient oak grove in **Inner Mongolia**. Timing was everything: an employee, stationed out in Mongolia, called the director the moment the leaves turned a perfect shade of gold.

YOU ONLY LIVE TWICE
(1967, dir: Lewis Gilbert)
Sean Connery, Tetsuro Tamba, Akiko Wakabayashi.
● **JAPAN; GIBRALTAR; BAHAMAS; SCOTLAND; SPAIN**

Bond gets killed off before the opening credits, but – surprise! – it's only a ruse. He's buried at sea in Hong Kong Harbour, but what happens to the buildings and the hills and the teeming boats after the initial establishing shot? The burial was actually shot aboard HMS *Tenby*, safely anchored in **Gibraltar Harbour**, while the undersea rescue was across the Atlantic in the Bahamas.

Bond's mission takes him to Japan, dispatched to Tokyo to see Mr Henderson – played by Blofeld-in-waiting Charles Gray. The headquarters of Osato Chemicals is Tokyo's **Hotel New Otani, 4-1 Kioi-cho, Chiyoda-ku** (*© 3.3265.1111, www1.newotani.co.jp/en/tokyo*), a vast luxury block built in 1964 in time for the Olympic Games.

Bond dodges SPECTRE agents at the docks of **Kobe**, an industrial port near to Osaka (and, more recently, badly damaged in a disastrous earthquake). His crashlanding of Helga Brandt's plane, somewhere in Japan, is actually at **Finmere** in Scotland. Back in Japan, the helicopter flight was filmed above the village of **Ebino**, where aerial photographer Johnny Jordon lost a leg when the blades of another helicopter came too close. The sequence was later completed in the skies above **Torremolinos**, Spain.

The Ninja training school, where Bond limbers up and turns Japanese, is **Himeji Castle**, the White Heron Castle on a bluff overlooking the town of **Himeji**, 33 miles west of Kobe (take a virtual tour of the castle at *www.himeji-castle.gr.jp/index/english*). It's about ten minutes from Himeji Station, from where you can see it clearly. There were a few problems with the press when it was claimed

one of the steel darts became embedded in the venerable landmark's wooden wall. You can also see Himeji Castle in Kurosawa's epics *Kagemusha* and *Ran*. The extinct volcano, beneath which Blofeld establishes his hideout, can be found in **Kirishima National Park** near to Kagoshima (from where there's a frequent train service, though there's a deal of walking and climbing if you want to explore the fantastic volcanic landscape), at the southern tip of Kyushu, the southern island of Japan. The interior is a vast $1 million set constructed under canvas on an outdoor site at Pinewood.

YOUNG FRANKENSTEIN
(1974, dir: Mel Brooks)
Gene Wilder, Peter Boyle, Marty Feldman.
● **LOS ANGELES**

Frankenstein and his creation perform 'Puttin' on the Ritz': Mayfair Theatre, Santa Monica Boulevard

Loving pastiche of the Universal horror movies of the thirties, which even utilises props and lab equipment from the 1931 *Frankenstein*. The lecture theatre, where Frankenstein teaches, is **Hoffman Hall, University of Southern California** in the Exposition Park area, south of downtown LA. The theatre, where Frankenstein and his creation perform 'Puttin' on the Ritz', is the **Mayfair Theatre, 212-216 Santa Monica Boulevard** at Third Street, Santa Monica. The theatre has remained closed since being damaged in the Northridge earthquake. It seems to be undergoing renovation at present.

YOUNG GUNS
(1988, dir: Christopher Cain)
Emilio Estevez, Kiefer Sutherland, Lou Diamond Phillips.
● **NEW MEXICO**

Brat pack Western, filmed in New Mexico, at the **Bonanza Creek Movie Ranch, 15 Bonanza Creek Lane, Santa Fe** (*www.bonanzacreekranch.com*), seen also in *All the Pretty Horses, Butch Cassidy and The Sundance Kid, Easy Rider, The Man From Laramie* and *Silverado*. Also at **Galisteo, Ojo Caliente, Rancho de las Golondrinas, 334 Los Pinos Road** (*© 505.471.2261, www.golondrinas.org*), a living museum 15 miles south of Santa Fe; and at **Tesuque Pueblo**, ten miles north of Santa Fe in the foothills of the Sangre de Cristo Mountains, generally open to the public (*© 505.983.2667, www.indianpueblo.org/ipcc/tesuquepage.htm*). The wedding scene was filmed in the orchard of **Hacienda Galisteo**, a restored adobe home, which you can rent (© 505.466.2111). The circular building is the recently renovated **Round Barn, Ojo Caliente Mineral Springs**, built as a dairy in 1924. There was also filming at **Cerrillos Village**, a small town on I-14 between Santa Fe and Albuquerque. Look out for a tiny uncredited cameo by Tom Cruise as a bewhiskered bad guy.

The sequel was shot around **White Sands National Monument** and **Santa Fe**, New Mexico; **Tumacacori National Monument**; **Willcox Playa** and **Old Tucson**, Arizona.

YOUNG SHERLOCK HOLMES (aka *Young Sherlock Holmes and the Pyramid of Fear*)
(1985, dir: Barry Levinson)
Nicholas Rowe, Alan Cox, Sophie Ward.
● BERKSHIRE; OXFORDSHIRE; KENT; LEICESTERSHIRE; LONDON

Brompton School, gates: Brasenose College, Oxford

Disappointingly witless and FX-heavy story of Holmes and Watson's schooldays from producer Spielberg, director Barry Levinson – responsible for *Diner* and *Rain Man* – and writer Chris Columbus (director of *Home Alone*). The fictional Brompton School is an elaborate composite. The exterior is **Brasenose College, Radcliffe Square** opposite the Radcliffe Camera in Oxford, with the tower of St Mary the Virgin in the background. Once through the gates, the school quad is the quad of **Eton College, Eton**, Berkshire (for details of Eton see *Chariots of Fire*). But when Holmes and Watson look up to see Waxflatter demonstrating his flying machine, the crenellated towers are those of **Belvoir Castle** near Grantham in Leicestershire. Belvoir, the seat of the Dukes of Rutland, was built 1816 on the site of a Norman castle. It's seven miles west of Grantham between the A52 and the A607 and open to the public from the beginning of April to the end of September, except Mondays and Fridays (© 01476.871000; www.belvoircastle.com; admission charge).

Brompton School, quad: Eton College, Eton

The school gym, where Holmes fences with schoolmaster Rathe, is the **Barons Hall** of **Penshurst Place** – "Are you alright, Penshurst?" asks Rathe of one of the schoolboys. Penshurst Place is one of the finest 14th century

Brompton School, towers: Belvoir Castle

manor houses in England, with a rare, authentic Tudor garden, in Penshurst village a couple of miles east of Hever Castle (*rail: Penshurst*). Currently the home of the

Brompton School, gym: Barons Hall, Penshurst Place

Viscount de l'Isle, former Governor General of Australia, the house is open from the beginning of April to the beginning of October (© 01892.870307, www.penshurstplace.com). The castellated home of Cragwitch is Belvoir Castle once again. And once again **Shad Thames**, on the South Bank of the Thames, London SE1, and now redeveloped as shops and restaurants, stands in for Victorian London.

Z

Z
(1969, dir: Costa-Gavras)
Yves Montand, Irene Papas, Jean-Louis Trintignant.
● ALGERIA

Costa-Gavras' political thriller, though set in an unnamed country, was based on events in Greece under the rule of the Colonels, but was made in Algeria.

ZABRISKIE POINT
(1970, dir: Michelangelo Antonioni)
Rod Taylor, Mark Frechette, Daria Halprin.
● CALIFORNIA; ARIZONA; NEVADA

Antonioni's sixties Italian movies remain as cool as a sharp black suit. The Swinging London-set *Blowup*, saw the director slipping into a pair of white jeans and just about getting away with it, but with *Zabriskie Point* he donned kaftan and beads. Big mistake. The resulting film tells us that there are a lot of billboards in California, the scenery is very nice, businessmen are not, and revolutionary students talk endless drivel. Harrison Ford was in the movie, but his part was cut. Glimpse him in the background of the jail scene.

The film ran wildly over budget, proved incomprehensible to MGM bosses, and the director's working methods flummoxed the Hollywood crew. Antonioni brought in an Italian crew, but US union rules meant that for every Italian, there had to be an American equivalent on the payroll, standing around doing nothing.

Much of the movie was shot around LA. The office of heartless capitalist Lee Allen (Taylor) was the old Mobil Oil Building, 612 Flower Street at Wilshire Boulevard, downtown LA, where, at a cost of thousands of dollars, an extra storey was added to the roof. It has since been redeveloped into the luxury Pegasus Apartments. The fabulous black and gold deco tower seen through Allen's window is the **Eastern Columbia Building, 849 South Broadway** (see *Predator 2* for details). Allen's business meeting is in Phoenix, Arizona, and the famous slo-mo exploding house – covered by seventeen cameras – is also near Phoenix. The city's air traffic was held up during the filming of this profound scene, which reminds us that rich Americans have homes full of consumer goods.

Atmosphere is everything, though, and the film does look wonderful, particularly once it gets out into the desert, around **Blythe**, California, and **Overton**, Nevada. Greatest of all, of course, is the wondrous **Death Valley** and **Zabriskie Point** itself. The dizzying overlook, named for a Dutch businessman who mined borax in the area, is on the eastern fringe of Death Valley near the Nevada border, on Route 190 between the tiny town of Death Valley Junction (a location for David Lynch's *Lost Highway* and *The Hitcher*) and the Death Valley Visitor Center. The breathtaking sea of yellow and grey canyons is used for the movie's surreal orgy.

ZAZIE DANS LE MÉTRO
(1960, dir: Louis Malle)
Catherine Demongeot, Philippe Noiret, Vittorio Caprioli.
● PARIS, FRANCE

When precocious, and somewhat foulmouthed, Zazie (Demongeot) arrives in Paris only to find the Metro closed by a strike, she embarks on a series of increasingly bizarre adventures. At the time, Louis Malle's zany slapstick was undeniably innovative (predating Richard Lester's freeform anarchy), but whether you find it hilariously charming or gruesomely winsome is a matter of taste. Zazie is met from the train by her eccentric Uncle Gabriel (Noiret) at **Gare de l'Est**. The vertiginous clowning on the stairs and superstructure of the **Eiffel Tower** is impressive, but eventually tiresome. Zazie leads the lecherous Trouscaillon (Caprioli) on a goose-chase through Paris to the double-decker **Pont Bir Hakeim** (seen in *Last Tango in Paris* and Malle's earlier *L'Ascenseur Pour l'Echafaud*), where there's a surreal cameo from Sacha Distel.

ZELIG
(1983, dir: Woody Allen)
Woody Allen, Mia Farrow, Garrett Brown.
● NEW JERSEY; NEW YORK

Fake documentary about Leonard Zelig (Allen), a fictitious media celeb with a chameleon-like ability to adapt his personality to his surroundings. Filmed around New Jersey, in **Englewood**, **Alpine**, **Paramus**, **Weehawken**, **Saddle River**, **Jersey City** and **Union City**. Filming also took place at the **Old Promenade, Long Beach**, Nassau County, Long Island.

ZORBA THE GREEK
(1964, dir: Michael Cacoyannis)
Anthony Quinn, Alan Bates, Lila Kedrova.
● CRETE

Anthony Quinn teaches Alan Bates all about life, in this filming of Nikos Kazantzakis' novel, shot around **Chania**, on the northern coast of Crete. The beach is **Stavros Beach**, on the Akrotiri Peninsula, east of the town.

ZULU
(1964, dir: Cy Endfield)
Stanley Baker, Michael Caine, James Booth.

The desert orgy: Zabriskie Point, Death Valley

● SOUTH AFRICA

Star Stanley Baker himself produced this account of the last stand of the British garrison against 4,000 warriors of the Zulu nation at Rorke's Drift in 1879. The movie was shot in South Africa, with the cooperation of Chief Buthelezi, who actually appears in the movie playing his ancestor Cetewayo. The actual location of Rorke's Drift, alongside the Buffalo River, had changed beyond recognition so the movie was shot 10,000 feet above Durban against the backdrop of the country's longest mountain range, the Drakensburg Mountains, in the **Royal Natal National Park**, southeast South Africa.

GAZETTEER

* **ALGERIA:** BATTAGLIA DI ALGERI, LA; SHELTERING SKY, THE; Z

* **ANTARCTICA:** SCOTT OF THE ANTARCTIC

* **ARGENTINA:** DIARIOS DE MOTOCICLETA; EVITA; MISSION, THE

* **AUSTRALIA:** "CROCODILE" DUNDEE; MURIEL'S WEDDING; ON THE BEACH

NEW SOUTH WALES: ADVENTURES OF PRISCILLA, QUEEN OF THE DESERT, THE; BABE; CARS THAT ATE PARIS, THE; CHANT OF JIMMIE BLACKSMITH, THE; MAD MAX 2; MAD MAX BEYOND THUNDERDOME; MATRIX, THE; MATRIX RELOADED, THE; MATRIX REVOLUTIONS, THE; MISSION: IMPOSSIBLE 2; MY BRILLIANT CAREER; STAR WARS EPISODE II: ATTACK OF THE CLONES; STAR WARS EPISODE III: REVENGE OF THE SITH; STRICTLY BALLROOM; YEAR OF LIVING DANGEROUSLY, THE

NORTHERN TERRITORY: ADVENTURES OF PRISCILLA, QUEEN OF THE DESERT, THE

QUEENSLAND: DEAD CALM; THIN RED LINE, THE

SOUTH AUSTRALIA: ADVENTURES OF PRISCILLA, QUEEN OF THE DESERT, THE; GALLIPOLI; MAD MAX BEYOND THUNDERDOME; PICNIC AT HANGING ROCK; SHINE

VICTORIA: MAD MAX; PICNIC AT HANGING ROCK; ROMPER STOMPER; STRICTLY BALLROOM

* **AUSTRIA:** BAD TIMING; CHITTY CHITTY BANG BANG; DAY OF THE JACKAL, THE; GÖTTERDAMMERUNG; GREAT RACE, THE; HELP!; LIVING DAYLIGHTS, THE; NIGHT PORTER, THE; SOUND OF MUSIC, THE; THIRD MAN, THE; THREE MUSKETEERS, THE; WHERE EAGLES DARE; XXX

* **AZERBAIJAN:** WORLD IS NOT ENOUGH, THE

* **BAHAMAS:** COCOON; FOR YOUR EYES ONLY; HELP!; NEVER SAY NEVER AGAIN; SILENCE OF THE LAMBS, THE; SPY WHO LOVED ME, THE; THUNDERBALL; YOU ONLY LIVE TWICE

* **BELGIAN CONGO:** KING SOLOMON'S MINES

* **BELGIUM:** C'EST ARRIVÉ PRES DE CHEZ VOUS; LUST FOR LIFE; TOTO LE HEROS

* **BORA BORA:** MUTINY ON THE BOUNTY (1962)

* **BRAZIL:** EMERALD FOREST, THE; FITZCARRALDO; MOONRAKER

* **CAMBODIA:** LARA CROFT TOMB RAIDER

* **CAMEROONS:** GREYSTOKE: THE LEGEND OF TARZAN, LORD OF THE APES

* **CANADA:** ATLANTIC CITY; DOCTOR ZHIVAGO; ONCE UPON A TIME IN AMERICA; SPY WHO LOVED ME, THE

ALBERTA: DAYS OF HEAVEN; LEGENDS OF THE FALL; LITTLE BIG MAN; RIVER OF NO RETURN; SUPERMAN; SUPERMAN III; UNFORGIVEN; X2

BRITISH COLUMBIA: BLADE; FINAL DESTINATION; INSOMNIA (2002); LEGENDS OF THE FALL; LITTLE WOMEN (1994); LOOK WHO'S TALKING; MCCABE AND MRS MILLER; NEVERENDING STORY, THE; ROCKY IV; ROXANNE; SCARY MOVIE; THING, THE (1982); X-FILES, THE; X2

MONTRÉAL, QUÉBEC: JÉSUS DE MONTRÉAL

NOVA SCOTIA: MY LITTLE EYE

ONTARIO: AMERICAN PSYCHO; BRIDE OF CHUCKY; BRUCE ALMIGHTY; COCKTAIL; CRASH; DEAD RINGERS; FLY, THE (1986); FRESHMAN, THE; IN THE MOUTH OF MADNESS; LONG KISS GOODNIGHT, THE; NAKED LUNCH, THE; NETWORK; NIAGARA; RECRUIT, THE; SEA OF LOVE; SUPERMAN II; SWEET HEREAFTER, THE; 3 MEN AND A BABY; TO DIE FOR; URBAN LEGEND; VIDEODROME; X-MEN; X2

QUÉBEC: AVIATOR, THE; CATCH ME IF YOU CAN; HOTEL NEW HAMPSHIRE, THE; I CONFESS; RABID; SCANNERS; SHIVERS; TERMINAL, THE

TORONTO, ONTARIO: CHICAGO; GOOD WILL HUNTING;

HURRICANE, THE; MOONSTRUCK; MY BIG FAT GREEK WEDDING; SCANNERS

VANCOUVER, BRITISH COLUMBIA: CARNAL KNOWLEDGE; I, ROBOT

* **CANARY ISLANDS:** LAND THAT TIME FORGOT, THE; MOBY DICK; WONDERFUL LIFE

* **CAYMAN ISLANDS:** FIRM, THE

* **CHILE:** DIARIOS DE MOTOCICLETA; SPY KIDS

* **CHINA:** ARMAGEDDON; DAHONG DENGLONG GAOGAO GUA; EMPIRE OF THE SUN; KILL BILL: VOLUME 1; KILL BILL: VOLUME 2; LAST EMPEROR, THE; SHI MIAN MAI FU; WO HU CANG LONG; YING XIONG

HONG KONG: AROUND THE WORLD IN EIGHTY DAYS (1956); CHUNGKING EXPRESS; ENTER THE DRAGON; LARA CROFT TOMB RAIDER: THE CRADLE OF LIFE; MAN WITH THE GOLDEN GUN, THE; RUSH HOUR; SAND PEBBLES, THE; SPY GAME

* **COLOMBIA:** MISSION, THE

* **COSTA RICA:** 1492: CONQUEST OF PARADISE; SPY KIDS 2: ISLAND OF LOST DREAMS

* **CUBA:** DIARIOS DE MOTOCICLETA

* **CZECH REPUBLIC (see also CZECHOSLOVAKIA):** KNIGHT'S TALE, A; LEAGUE OF EXTRAORDINARY GENTLEMEN, THE; MISSION: IMPOSSIBLE; VAN HELSING; XXX

PRAGUE: BOURNE IDENTITY, THE

* **CZECHOSLOVAKIA (see also CZECH REPUBLIC and SLOVAKIA):** AMADEUS; CLOSELY OBSERVED TRAINS; NOSFERATU, PHANTOM DER NACHT

* **DENMARK:** ANASTASIA (1956); BABETTE'S FEAST; BREAKING THE WAVES; TOPAZ

* **DOMINICAN REPUBLIC:** GODFATHER PART II, THE

* **EGYPT:** DEATH ON THE NILE; GALLIPOLI; KABHI KHUSHI KABHIE GHAM...; MALCOLM X; SPY WHO LOVED ME, THE; TEN COMMANDMENTS, THE (1956)

* **ENGLAND:**

AVON: CANTERBURY TALES, THE; MUSIC LOVERS, THE; REMAINS OF THE DAY, THE; TITFIELD THUNDERBOLT, THE

BEDFORDSHIRE: BATMAN; EYES WIDE SHUT; FOUR WEDDINGS AND A FUNERAL; MUMMY RETURNS, THE; NEVER SAY NEVER AGAIN

BERKSHIRE: ALIEN; ARABESQUE; CARRY ON AGAIN DOCTOR; CARRY ON DICK; CARRY ON LOVING; CARRY ON REGARDLESS; CHARIOTS OF FIRE; DRACULA (1958); ELIZABETH; EMPIRE OF THE SUN; FRENCH LIEUTENANT'S WOMAN, THE; GENEVIEVE; HARRY POTTER AND THE PHILOSHER'S STONE; LAND THAT TIME FORGOT, THE; LARA CROFT TOMB RAIDER; LOCK, STOCK AND TWO SMOKING BARRELLS; MADNESS OF KING GEORGE, THE; MURDER BY DEATH; MUSIC LOVERS, THE; QUATERMASS XPERIMENT, THE; ROCKY HORROR PICTURE SHOW, THE; SHAKESPEARE IN LOVE; THEATRE OF BLOOD; VIEW TO A KILL, A; YOUNG SHERLOCK HOLMES

BUCKINGHAMSHIRE: BATMAN BEGINS; BLITHE SPIRIT; BRAZIL; BRIDGET JONES'S DIARY; BRIEF ENCOUNTER; CARRY ON AT YOUR CONVENIENCE; CARRY ON CAMPING; CARRY ON DICK; CARRY ON – DON'T LOSE YOUR HEAD; CARRY ON GIRLS; CARRY ON UP THE KHYBER; CHARIOTS OF FIRE; CHITTY CHITTY BANG BANG; CLOCKWORK ORANGE, A; CURSE OF FRANKENSTEIN, THE; DARLING; DEAD OF NIGHT; DEVIL RIDES OUT, THE; DRACULA (1958); EMMA; FOUR WEDDINGS AND A FUNERAL; GENEVIEVE; GOLDFINGER; HELP!; ISADORA; KABHI KHUSHI KABHIE GHAM...; LAYER CAKE; LOLITA (1962); MONTY PYTHON'S THE MEANING OF LIFE; MUMMY; MUMMY RETURNS, THE; MURDER, SHE SAID; MUSIC LOVERS, THE; NEVER SAY NEVER AGAIN; NIGHT TO REMEMBER, A; ON HER MAJESTY'S SECRET SERVICE; 101 DALMATIANS; PLAGUE OF THE ZOMBIES, THE; ROBIN HOOD: PRINCE OF

THIEVES; RULING CLASS, THE; SLEEPY HOLLOW; SUPERMAN II; THUNDERBALL; TO THE DEVIL A DAUGHTER; TIME BANDITS; TOMORROW NEVER DIES; WENT THE DAY WELL?; WHITE HUNTER, BLACK HEART; WITCHFINDER GENERAL; WORLD IS NOT ENOUGH, THE

CAMBRIDGESHIRE: FULL METAL JACKET; MAURICE; NIGHTCOMERS, THE; REVOLUTION

CHESHIRE: PATTON; ROBIN HOOD; YANKS

CORNWALL: DIE ANOTHER DAY; DRACULA (1979); KNIGHTS OF THE ROUND TABLE; SCOTT OF THE ANTARCTIC; STRAW DOGS; THIEF OF BAGDAD, THE; THREE MUSKETEERS, THE; TREASURE ISLAND (1950); TWELFTH NIGHT

COUNTY DURHAM: BILLY ELLIOT; HARRY POTTER AND THE CHAMBER OF SECRETS

CUMBRIA: BRAZIL; JULIA; MAHLER; 28 DAYS LATER; WITHNAIL & I

DERBYSHIRE: ELIZABETH; GOODBYE MR CHIPS (1939); JANE EYRE (1996); WOMEN IN LOVE

DEVON: FRENCH LIEUTENANT'S WOMAN, THE; HARRY POTTER AND THE GOBLET OF FIRE; HOWARDS END; ISADORA; KNIGHTS OF THE ROUND TABLE; MATTER OF LIFE AND DEATH, A (1946); REMAINS OF THE DAY, THE; REVOLUTION; SENSE AND SENSIBILITY

DORSET: BROWNING VERSION, THE; DAMNED, THE; EMMA; FAR FROM THE MADDING CROWD; FRENCH LIEUTENANT'S WOMAN, THE; SLEUTH; TOM JONES; WILDE

DURHAM: HARRY POTTER AND THE PHILOSOPHER'S STONE

ESSEX: CANTERBURY TALES, THE; FOUR WEDDINGS AND A FUNERAL; HIGH HOPES; KABHI KHUSHI KABHIE GHAM...; QUATERMASS II; WHO FRAMED ROGER RABBIT

GLOUCESTERSHIRE: BARRY LYNDON; BRIDGET JONES'S DIARY; CANTERBURY TALES, THE; HARRY POTTER AND THE CHAMBER OF SECRETS; HARRY POTTER AND THE PHILOSOPHER'S STONE; IF....; MAURICE

HAMPSHIRE: DIE ANOTHER DAY; EMMA; FOUR WEDDINGS AND A FUNERAL; INN OF THE SIXTH HAPPINESS, THE; MAN FOR ALL SEASONS, A; MISSION: IMPOSSIBLE; MODESTY BLAISE; MUSIC LOVERS, THE; OH MR PORTER; RULING CLASS, THE; THAT'LL BE THE DAY; TOMMY; 28 DAYS LATER; WILDE

HERTFORDSHIRE: ABOMINABLE DR PHIBES, THE; ANASTASIA (1956); BATMAN; CLOCKWORK ORANGE, A; CURSE OF THE CRIMSON ALTAR; DEVIL RIDES OUT, THE; DIRTY DOZEN, THE; DRACULA AD 1972; FOUR WEDDINGS AND A FUNERAL; GOLDENEYE; GREYSTOKE: THE LEGEND OF TARZAN, LORD OF THE APES; HARRY POTTER AND THE GOBLET OF FIRE; HARRY POTTER AND THE PRISONER OF AZKABAN; HOURS, THE; IF....; IN WHICH WE SERVE; JASSY; LOLITA (1962); MAHLER; MURDER ON THE ORIENT EXPRESS; NIGHT OF THE DEMON; QUATERMASS II; SATANIC RITES OF DRACULA, THE; SAVING PRIVATE RYAN; SCHOOL FOR SCOUNDRELS; SHADOWLANDS; SHAKESPEARE IN LOVE; SHOT IN THE DARK, A; SLEEPY HOLLOW; SPY GAME; TASTE THE BLOOD OF DRACULA; TOMMY; TOMORROW NEVER DIES; TOPSY-TURVY; 2001: A SPACE ODYSSEY; VAMPIRE LOVERS, THE; VILLAGE OF THE DAMNED (1960); WILDE; WINGS OF THE DOVE, THE; WORLD IS NOT ENOUGH, THE

ISLE OF MAN: WAKING NED

ISLE OF WIGHT: MRS BROWN

KENT: BRAZIL; CANTERBURY TALE, A; COLLECTOR, THE; DRAUGHTSMAN'S CONTRACT, THE; FOLLOW THAT CAMEL; GREAT EXPECTATIONS (1946); HAMLET (1990); KABHI KHUSHI KABHIE GHAM...; KIND HEARTS AND CORONETS; LAST ORDERS; MUMMY, THE; ROOM WITH A VIEW, A; YOUNG SHERLOCK HOLMES

LAKE DISTRICT, CUMBRIA: DAM BUSTERS, THE; PARADINE CASE, THE; TOMMY

LANCASHIRE: BRIEF ENCOUNTER; ENTERTAINER, THE; KIND OF LOVING, A; MONTY PYTHON'S THE MEANING OF LIFE; RICHARD III; TASTE OF HONEY, A; WHISTLE DOWN THE WIND; YANKS

LEICESTERSHIRE: HOURS, THE; SHADOWLANDS; YOUNG SHERLOCK HOLMES

LINCOLNSHIRE: DAM BUSTERS, THE; EMERALD FOREST, THE; RULING CLASS, THE

LIVERPOOL, MERSEYSIDE: BACKBEAT; HUNT FOR RED OCTOBER, THE; IN THE NAME OF THE FATHER

LONDON: ABOMINABLE DR PHIBES, THE; ABOUT A BOY; ACCIDENT; AFRICAN QUEEN, THE; ALFIE (1966); ALIENS; ALL OR NOTHING; AMERICAN WEREWOLF IN LONDON, AN; ANNE OF THE THOUSAND DAYS; ARABESQUE; AROUND THE WORLD IN EIGHTY DAYS (1956); BACKBEAT; BAD TIMING; BATMAN; BATMAN BEGINS; BEDAZZLED (1967); BEDAZZLED (2000); BEND IT LIKE BECKHAM; BILLION DOLLAR BRAIN; BILLY ELLIOT; BILLY LIAR; BLACKMAIL; BLOWUP; BLUE LAMP, THE; BOUNTY, THE; BRAZIL; BRIDGET JONES'S DIARY; BRIEF ENCOUNTER; BRITANNIA HOSPITAL; BUNNY LAKE IS MISSING; CARRY ON REGARDLESS; CHAPLIN; CHARGE OF THE LIGHT BRIGADE, THE (1968); CLOCKWORK ORANGE, A; COLLECTOR, THE; CRYING GAME, THE; DANCE WITH A STRANGER; DARLING; DAY OF THE JACKAL, THE; DAY OF THE TRIFFIDS, THE; DAY THE EARTH CAUGHT FIRE, THE; DIE ANOTHER DAY; DIRTY PRETTY THINGS; DOCTOR IN THE HOUSE; DR NO; DRACULA AD 1972; 84 CHARING CROSS ROAD; ELEPHANT MAN, THE; EMPIRE OF THE SUN; END OF THE AFFAIR, THE; ENTERTAINING MR SLOANE; EVITA; EYES WIDE SHUT; FAHRENHEIT 451; FALLEN IDOL, THE; FIFTH ELEMENT, THE; FISH CALLED WANDA, A; FOR YOUR EYES ONLY; FOUR WEDDINGS AND A FUNERAL; FRENCH LIEUTENANT'S WOMAN, THE; FRENZY; FULL METAL JACKET; GANDHI; GENEVIEVE; GEORGY GIRL; GOLDENEYE; GREAT EXPECTATIONS (1946); GREYSTOKE: THE LEGEND OF TARZAN, LORD OF THE APES; HARD DAY'S NIGHT, A; HARRY POTTER AND THE CHAMBER OF SECRETS; HARRY POTTER AND THE PHILOSOPHER'S STONE; HARRY POTTER AND THE PRISONER OF AZKABAN; HEAT AND DUST; HELLRAISER; HELP!; HIGH HOPES; HOURS, THE; HOWARDS END; HUDSON HAWK; HUNGER, THE; IPCRESS FILE, THE; ISADORA; IT ALWAYS RAINS ON SUNDAY; ITALIAN JOB, THE (1969); JUBILEE; KABHI KHUSHI KABHIE GHAM...; KID FOR TWO FARTHINGS, A; KILLING OF SISTER GEORGE, THE; KNACK... AND HOW TO GET IT, THE; KRAYS, THE; LADYKILLERS, THE; LARA CROFT TOMB RAIDER; LARA CROFT TOMB RAIDER: THE CRADLE OF LIFE; LAST ORDERS; LAWRENCE OF ARABIA; LAYER CAKE; LEATHER BOYS, THE; LEGALLY BLONDE; LIFE AND DEATH OF COLONEL BLIMP, THE; LIVING DAYLIGHTS, THE; LOCH NESS; LOCK, STOCK AND TWO SMOKING BARRELS; LONG GOOD FRIDAY, THE; LOOK BACK IN ANGER; LOVE ACTUALLY; MADNESS OF KING GEORGE, THE; MAN WHO KNEW TOO MUCH, THE (1934); MAN WHO KNEW TOO MUCH, THE (1956); MAURICE; MISSION: IMPOSSIBLE; MODESTY BLAISE; MONA LISA; MONTY PYTHON'S THE MEANING OF LIFE; MORGAN – A SUITABLE CASE FOR TREATMENT; MUMMY RETURNS, THE; MURDER ON THE ORIENT EXPRESS; MURDER, SHE SAID; MUSIC LOVERS, THE; MY BEAUTIFUL LAUNDRETTE; NAKED; NIGHT OF THE DEMON; NINETEEN EIGHTY-FOUR; NOTTING HILL; OCTOPUSSY; OMEN, THE; 101 DALMATIANS; PARADINE CASE, THE; PASSENGER, THE; PASSPORT TO PIMLICO; PATRIOT GAMES; PEEPING TOM; PERFORMANCE; PINK FLOYD — THE WALL; PRICK UP YOUR EARS; PRIVATE LIFE OF SHERLOCK HOLMES, THE; QUADROPHENIA; QUATERMASS XPERIMENT, THE; RED SHOES, THE; REPULSION; RICHARD III; ROBIN HOOD: PRINCE OF THIEVES; ROOM WITH A VIEW, A; RULING CLASS, THE; SABOTAGE; SATANIC RITES OF DRACULA, THE; SATURDAY NIGHT AND SUNDAY MORNING; SCANDAL; SEANCE ON A WET AFTERNOON; SECRETS & LIES; SENSE AND SENSIBILITY; SERVANT, THE; SHADOWLANDS; SHAKESPEARE IN LOVE; SHAUN OF THE DEAD; SHINE; SHIRLEY VALENTINE; SID AND NANCY; SLEEPY HOLLOW; SLIDING DOORS; SMALLEST SHOW ON EARTH, THE; SNATCH; SORCERERS, THE; SPY GAME; STAGE FRIGHT; SUNDAY, BLOODY SUNDAY; 10 RILLINGTON PLACE; TASTE OF HONEY, A; THEATRE OF BLOOD; THIRD MAN, THE; TITFIELD THUNDER-BOLT, THE; TOM JONES; TOMMY; TOMORROW NEVER DIES; TRAINSPOTTING; TROY; 28 DAYS LATER; VELVET GOLDMINE; VERA DRAKE; VICTIM; VIEW TO A KILL, A; WATERLOO ROAD; WHO FRAMED ROGER RABBIT; WILDE; WINGS OF THE DOVE, THE; WITHNAIL & I; WITNESS FOR THE PROSECUTION; WONDERFUL LIFE; WORLD IS NOT ENOUGH, THE; X-FILES, THE; X2; YOUNG SHERLOCK HOLMES

MANCHESTER: HOBSON'S CHOICE; IN THE NAME OF THE FATHER; RAINING STONES; TASTE OF HONEY, A

MERSEYSIDE: CHARIOTS OF FIRE; SCANDAL; SHIRLEY VALENTINE

MIDDLESEX: BOUNTY, THE; CLOCKWORK ORANGE, A; CURSE OF THE CRIMSON ALTAR; ELIZABETH; EMMA; FRANKENSTEIN MUST BE DESTROYED; HARRY POTTER AND THE PHILOSOPHER'S STONE; LAVENDER HILL MOB, THE; MADNESS OF KING GEORGE, THE; NIGHT TO REMEMBER, A; OCTOPUSSY; PRIME OF MISS JEAN BRODIE, THE; RICHARD III; SHIRLEY VALENTINE; THIRTY-NINE STEPS, THE; TOMORROW NEVER DIES

NORFOLK: FULL METAL JACKET; GO-BETWEEN, THE; JULIA; REVOLUTION; SHAKESPEARE IN LOVE; TOMB OF LIGEIA, THE; WICKED LADY, THE (1945)

NORTHAMPTONSHIRE: THUNDERBALL

NORTHUMBERLAND: ALIEN ³; CUL-DE-SAC; DEVILS, THE; ELIZABETH; HARRY POTTER AND THE PHILOSOPHER'S STONE; IVANHOE; MACBETH (1971); ROBIN HOOD: PRINCE OF THIEVES

NOTTINGHAMSHIRE: SATURDAY NIGHT AND SUNDAY MORNING; SCANDAL; SONS AND LOVERS

OXFORD, OXFORDSHIRE: FISH CALLED WANDA, A

OXFORDSHIRE: ACCIDENT; ARABESQUE; BLOOD ON SATAN'S CLAW; GREYSTOKE: THE LEGEND OF TARZAN, LORD OF THE APES; HAMLET (1996); HARRY POTTER AND THE CHAMBER OF SECRETS; HARRY POTTER AND THE PHILOSOPHER'S STONE; HEAVEN'S GATE; HOWARDS END; JULIA; KABHI KHUSHI KABHIE GHAM...; MADNESS OF KING GEORGE, THE; MAN FOR ALL SEASONS, A; SAVING PRIVATE RYAN; SHADOWLANDS; SHAKESPEARE IN LOVE; SPY GAME; TITFIELD THUNDERBOLT, THE; TOMORROW NEVER DIES; WILDE; YOUNG SHERLOCK HOLMES

SHROPSHIRE: GONE TO EARTH; HOWARDS END

SOMERSET: REMAINS OF THE DAY, THE; SENSE AND SENSIBILITY; TOM JONES

SUFFOLK: CANTERBURY TALES, THE; LARA CROFT TOMB RAIDER; TOMORROW NEVER DIES; WITCHFINDER GENERAL

SURREY: ACCIDENT; AMERICAN WEREWOLF IN LONDON, AN; CARRY ON – DON'T LOSE YOUR HEAD; CARRY ON SERGEANT; DARLING; DR STRANGELOVE OR: HOW I LEARNED TO STOP WORRYING AND LOVE THE BOMB; FISH CALLED WANDA, A; FOUR WEDDINGS AND A FUNERAL; GLADIATOR; GOLDENEYE; HARRY POTTER AND THE PRISONER OF AZKABAN; HOWARDS END; LAWRENCE OF ARABIA; LAYER CAKE; LONELINESS OF THE LONG DISTANCE RUNNER, THE; MUMMY, THE; NIGHT TO REMEMBER, A; OMEN, THE; PINK FLOYD — THE WALL; RULING CLASS, THE; TOPSY-TURVY; VERA DRAKE; WINGS OF THE DOVE, THE; WORLD IS NOT ENOUGH, THE

SUSSEX: BARRY LYNDON; BLACK NARCISSUS; BRIGHTON ROCK; CANTERBURY TALES, THE; CARRY ON AT YOUR CONVENIENCE; CARRY ON GIRLS; CHAPLIN; END OF THE AFFAIR, THE; INNOCENTS, THE; LEATHER BOYS, THE; LOOT; MADNESS OF KING GEORGE, THE; MONA LISA; MOULIN ROUGE (1952); OH! WHAT A LOVELY WAR; QUADROPHENIA; RICHARD III; ROBIN HOOD: PRINCE OF THIEVES; VIEW TO A KILL, A; WISH YOU WERE HERE

TYNESIDE, NORTHUMBERLAND: GET CARTER (1971)

WARWICKSHIRE: DEATH ON THE NILE; HAUNTING, THE (1963)

WEST COUNTRY (see also AVON, CORNWALL, DEVON, DORSET, SOMERSET): HARD DAY'S NIGHT, A

WILTSHIRE: BARRY LYNDON; BOUNTY, THE; DOCTOR DOLITTLE (1967); FAR FROM THE MADDING CROWD; HARRY POTTER AND THE PHILOSOPHER'S STONE; HELP!; MADNESS OF KING GEORGE, THE; MAURICE; MRS BROWN; MUSIC LOVERS, THE; NIGHT OF THE DEMON; NINETEEN EIGHTY-FOUR; REMAINS OF THE DAY, THE; ROBIN HOOD: PRINCE OF THIEVES; SAVING PRIVATE RYAN; SCANDAL; SENSE AND SENSIBILITY; 28 DAYS LATER; WORLD IS NOT ENOUGH, THE

WORCESTER, WORCESTERSHIRE: HOWARDS END

WORCESTERSHIRE: THIRTY-NINE STEPS, THE

YORKSHIRE: BARRY LYNDON; BILLY LIAR; CHARIOTS OF FIRE; ELIZABETH; ENTERTAINER, THE; FULL MONTY, THE; HARRY POTTER AND THE CHAMBER OF SECRETS; HARRY POTTER AND THE PHILOSOPHER'S STONE; JANE EYRE (1996); KES; LITTLE VOICE; PINK FLOYD — THE WALL; PRIVATE FUNCTION, A; PRIVATE LIFE OF SHERLOCK HOLMES, THE; RAILWAY CHILDREN, THE; ROBIN HOOD: PRINCE OF THIEVES; ROOM AT THE TOP; THIS SPORTING LIFE; WOMEN IN LOVE; WUTHERING HEIGHTS (1939); YANKS

☆ **FIJI:** BLUE LAGOON, THE; CAST AWAY

☆ **FINLAND:** BILLION DOLLAR BRAIN; DOCTOR ZHIVAGO

☆ **FRANCE:** AMANTS, LES; AMANTS DU PONT NEUF, LES; AMERIKANISCHE FREUND, DER; ARMAGEDDON; L'ATALANTE; BELLE ET LA BÊTE, LA; BOOT, DAS; BOUCHER, LE; C'EST ARRIVÉ PRES DE CHEZ VOUS; CET OBSCUR OBJET DU DÉSIR; CHITTY CHITTY BANG BANG; CYRANO DE BERGERAC; DANGEROUS LIAISONS; DANTON; DAY OF THE JACKAL, THE; DEJEUNER SUR L'HERBE; DIRTY ROTTEN SCOUNDRELS; DOUBLE VIE DE VÉRONIQUE, LA; DUELLISTS, THE; ENFANTS DU PARADIS, LES; ET DIEU... CREA LA FEMME; FAHRENHEIT 451; FRENCH CONNECTION, THE; GERMINAL; GOLDENEYE; GRAND BLEU, LE; GRANDE ILLUSION, LA; ISADORA; JEWEL OF THE NILE, THE; JOUR DE FÊTE; JOURNAL D'UNE FEMME DE CHAMBRE, LE; JULES ET JIM; JULIA; LACOMBE, LUCIEN; LE MANS; LION IN WINTER, THE; LONGEST DAY, THE; LUST FOR LIFE; MA NUIT CHEZ MAUD; MISSION: IMPOSSIBLE; MON ONCLE; MOONRAKER; NEVER SAY NEVER AGAIN; ONCE UPON A TIME IN AMERICA; ORPHÉE; RAIDERS OF THE LOST ARK; RED SHOES, THE; RÈGLE DU JEU, LA; ROBIN HOOD: PRINCE OF THIEVES; RONIN; TESS; TESTAMENT D'ORPHÉE, LE; 37°2 LE MATIN; THUNDERBALL; TIREZ SUR LE PIANISTE; TO CATCH A THIEF; TOMORROW NEVER DIES; TOPAZ; TROIS COULEURS: BLEU; TRZY KOLORY: BIALY; VACANCES DE MONSIEUR HULOT, LES; VIEW TO A KILL, A; VIKINGS, THE; WHAT'S NEW, PUSSY-CAT?; WORLD IS NOT ENOUGH, THE

HAUTE-SAVOIE: GENOU DE CLAIRE, LE

LOIRE: AU REVOIR LES ENFANTS

MARSEILLES: A BOUT DE SOUFFLE

NICE: Á PROPOS DE NICE; NUIT AMERICAINE, LA

PARIS: A BOUT DE SOUFFLE; L'AGE D'OR; AGE OF INNOCENCE, THE; ALPHAVILLE; ANASTASIA (1956); AROUND THE WORLD IN EIGHTY DAYS (1956); ASCENSEUR POUR L'ECHAFAUD; BELLE DE JOUR; BÊTE HUMAINE, LA; BIG FISH; BOUDU SAUVÉ DES EAUX; BOURNE IDENTITY, THE; BRAZIL; CHARADE; CHARME DISCRET DE LA BOURGEOISIE, LE; CHIEN ANDALOU, UN; CONFORMISTA, IL; DERNIER METRO, LE; DIVA; DOORS, THE; FABULEUX DESTIN D'AMÉLIE POULAIN, LE; FEMME EST UNE FEMME, UNE; FRANTIC; GIGI; HAINE, LA; HOTEL DU NORD; INTERVIEW WITH THE VAMPIRE: THE VAMPIRE CHRONICLES; KILLING ZOE; LAST TANGO IN PARIS; LAVENDER HILL MOB, THE; LÉON; LOVE AND DEATH; MARATHON MAN; MOULIN ROUGE (1952); MURDER ON THE ORIENT EXPRESS; QUATRE CENTS COUPS, LES; SAMOURAÏ, LE; SUBWAY; TRAPEZE; TRIAL, THE; ZAZIE DANS LE MÉTRO

PROVENCE: JEAN DE FLORETTE

ST TROPEZ: CAGE AUX FOLLES, LA

☆ **GALAPAGOS ISLANDS:** MASTER AND COMMANDER: THE FAR SIDE OF THE WORLD

☆ **GERMANY:** AMERIKANISCHE FREUND, DER; BARRY LYNDON; BOOT, DAS; BOURNE SUPREMACY, THE; CABARET; CHITTY CHITTY BANG BANG; DIAMONDS ARE FOREVER; FABULEUX DESTIN D'AMÉLIE POULAIN, LE; GÖTTERDAMMERUNG; GREAT ESCAPE, THE; IM LAUF DER ZEIT; NAME OF THE ROSE, THE; NOSFERATU; NOSFERATU, PHANTOM DER NACHT; PASSENGER, THE; ROLLERBALL; TOMORROW NEVER DIES; TORN CURTAIN; 28 DAYS LATER; VIKINGS, THE; WILLY WONKA AND THE CHOCOLATE FACTORY

BERLIN: HIMMEL ÜBER BERLIN, DER; LOLA RENNT; METROPOLIS; OCTOPUSSY; PIANIST, THE

HAMBURG: BACKBEAT; BEND IT LIKE BECKHAM

MUNICH: ANGST ESSEN SEELE AUF; ANNÉE DERNIÈRE À MARIENBAD, L'; PATHS OF GLORY

WUPPERTAL: ALICE IN DEN STADTEN

✴ **GIBRALTAR:** LIVING DAYLIGHTS, THE; YOU ONLY LIVE TWICE

✴ **GREECE:** BOURNE IDENTITY, THE; CAPTAIN CORELLI'S MANDOLIN; FOR YOUR EYES ONLY; GRAND BLEU, LE; GUNS OF NAVARONE, THE; LARA CROFT TOMB RAIDER: THE CRADLE OF LIFE; MEDITERRANEO; NEVER ON SUNDAY; OTELLO; PATTON; SHIRLEY VALENTINE; ZORBA THE GREEK

✴ **GRENADINES, THE:** PIRATES OF THE CARIBBEAN: THE CURSE OF THE BLACK PEARL

✴ **GUATEMALA:** MOONRAKER; STAR WARS EPISODE IV: A NEW HOPE

✴ **HOLLAND see NETHERLANDS**

✴ **HUNGARY:** CYRANO DE BERGERAC; EVITA; HUDSON HAWK; LOVE AND DEATH; SPY GAME

✴ **ICELAND:** BATMAN BEGINS; DIE ANOTHER DAY; LARA CROFT TOMB RAIDER; VIEW TO A KILL, A

✴ **INDIA:** APARAJITO; ARABIAN NIGHTS; ARMAGEDDON; AROUND THE WORLD IN EIGHTY DAYS (1956); BOURNE SUPREMACY, THE; CLOSE ENCOUNTERS OF THE THIRD KIND; GANDHI; HEAT AND DUST; KIM; MONSOON WEDDING; OCTOPUSSY; PASSAGE TO INDIA, A; PATHER PANCHALI; SALAAM BOMBAY!; SHAKESPEARE WALLAH

✴ **IRAN:** ARABIAN NIGHTS

✴ **IRAQ:** EXORCIST, THE

✴ **IRELAND:** ANGEL; ANGELA'S ASHES; BARRY LYNDON; BRAVEHEART; BUTCHER BOY, THE; COMMITMENTS, THE; CRYING GAME, THE; EXCALIBUR; ITALIAN JOB, THE (1969); HENRY V (1944); LION IN WINTER, THE; MICHAEL COLLINS; MOBY DICK; MY LEFT FOOT; QUIET MAN, THE; RYAN'S DAUGHTER; SAVING PRIVATE RYAN

DUBLIN: DEAD, THE; EDUCATING RITA; IN THE NAME OF THE FATHER

✴ **ISRAEL:** JESUS CHRIST SUPERSTAR; OMEN, THE; SCHINDLER'S LIST

✴ **ITALY:** AGONY AND THE ECSTASY, THE; AMADEUS; AMARCORD; AVANTI!; BEAT THE DEVIL; BEN HUR (1926); BEN HUR (1959); BOURNE IDENTITY, THE; BOURNE SUPREMACY, THE; DAY OF THE JACKAL, THE; DEATH IN VENICE; DESERTO ROSSO, IL; ENGLISH PATIENT, THE; FELLINI SATYRICON; FOR YOUR EYES ONLY; GIARDINO DEI FINZI-CONTINI, IL; GODFATHER PART II, THE; GÖTTERDAMMERUNG; HANNAH AND HER SISTERS; HUDSON HAWK; ISADORA; JASON AND THE ARGONAUTS; LAST EMPEROR, THE; MIDSUMMER NIGHT'S DREAM, A (1999); MIGHTY APHRODITE; MODESTY BLAISE; MUCH ADO ABOUT NOTHING; MY OWN PRIVATE IDAHO; NOVECENTO; ONCE UPON A TIME IN AMERICA; OTHELLO (1951); OTHELLO (1995); OTTO E MEZZO; PASSION OF THE CHRIST, THE; PINK PANTHER, THE; PLEIN SOLEIL; ROMEO AND JULIET; SALÒ; STAR WARS EPISODE I: THE PHANTOM MENACE; STAR WARS EPISODE II: ATTACK OF THE CLONES; STRADA, LA; STRATEGIA DEL RAGNO; STROMBOLI; TALENTED MR RIPLEY, THE; VANGELO SECONDO MATTEO, IL; VITA E BELLA, LA; VITELLONI, I; WATERLOO

CAPRI: MEPRIS, LE

FLORENCE: DARLING; HANNIBAL; ROOM WITH A VIEW, A

MILAN: TEOREMA; TRIAL, THE

PARMA: PRIMA DELLA RIVOLUZIONE

ROME: ACCATTONE; L'AVVENTURA; CONFORMISTA, IL; DOLCE VITA, LA; L'ECLISSE; FELLINI'S ROMA; FISTFUL OF DOLLARS, A; GANGS OF NEW YORK; GODFATHER PART III, THE; LADRI DI BICICLETTE; MEPRIS, LE; NIGHT PORTER, THE; OMEN, THE; ROMAN HOLIDAY; SOTTO GLI OCCHI DELL'ASSASSINO; STAZIONE TERMINI; TRIAL, THE

SICILY: L'AVVENTURA; CANTERBURY TALES, THE; CINEMA PARADISO; GATTOPARDO, IL; GODFATHER, THE; GODFATHER PART II, THE; GODFATHER PART III, THE; GRAND BLEU, LE; MAURICE; PATTON; STAR WARS EPISODE III: REVENGE OF THE SITH

TURIN: ITALIAN JOB, THE (1969)

✴ **VENICE:** DON'T LOOK NOW; FROM RUSSIA WITH LOVE; INDIANA JONES AND THE LAST CRUSADE; ITALIAN JOB, THE (2003); LARA CROFT TOMB RAIDER; MOONRAKER; SENSO; SUMMER MADNESS; WINGS OF THE DOVE, THE

✴ **JAMAICA:** LEGENDS OF THE FALL; LIVE AND LET DIE; PAPILLON; 20,000 LEAGUES UNDER THE SEA

✴ **JAPAN:** AROUND THE WORLD IN EIGHTY DAYS (1956); BLACK RAIN; GODZILLA, KING OF THE MONSTERS (1955); KAGEMUSHA; KAKUSHI TORIDE NO SAN-AKUNIN; KILL BILL: VOLUME 1; KUMONOSU-JO; LAST SAMURAI, THE; LOST IN TRANSLATION; RAN; SPY WHO LOVED ME, THE; YOU ONLY LIVE TWICE

✴ **JORDAN:** INDIANA JONES AND THE LAST CRUSADE; LAWRENCE OF ARABIA; MUMMY RETURNS, THE

✴ **KENYA:** BORN FREE; KING SOLOMON'S MINES; LARA CROFT TOMB RAIDER: THE CRADLE OF LIFE; OUT OF AFRICA

✴ **LIBYA:** ICE COLD IN ALEX

✴ **MACAU:** INDIANA JONES AND THE TEMPLE OF DOOM; MAN WITH THE GOLDEN GUN, THE

✴ **MALAYSIA:** ANNA AND THE KING

✴ **MALTA:** ALEXANDER; GLADIATOR; LEAGUE OF EXTRAORDINARY GENTLEMEN, THE; MIDNIGHT EXPRESS; SPY WHO LOVED ME, THE; TROY

✴ **MARTINIQUE:** THOMAS CROWN AFFAIR, THE (1999)

✴ **MAURITANIA:** FIFTH ELEMENT, THE

✴ **MEXICO:** ALTERED STATES; BORN ON THE FOURTH OF JULY; BRING ME THE HEAD OF ALFREDO GARCIA; BUTCH CASSIDY AND THE SUNDANCE KID; CATCH 22; CLOSE ENCOUNTERS OF THE THIRD KIND; DESPERADO; EL; HONDO; IN COLD BLOOD; KILL BILL: VOLUME 2; LADY FROM SHANGHAI, THE; LICENCE TO KILL; LONG GOODBYE, THE; MAGNIFICENT SEVEN, THE; MAJOR DUNDEE; MAN CALLED HORSE, A; MARIACHI, EL; MASTER AND COMMANDER: THE FAR SIDE OF THE WORLD; NIGHT OF THE IGUANA, THE; ONCE UPON A TIME IN MEXICO; PAT GARRETT AND BILLY THE KID (1941); PREDATOR; RAMBO: FIRST BLOOD PART II; ROMANCING THE STONE; 10; THREE KINGS; TITANIC; TOMORROW NEVER DIES; TRAFFIC; TREASURE OF THE SIERRA MADRE, THE; TROY; TWO MULES FOR SISTER SARA; UNIVERSAL SOLDIER; WILD BUNCH, THE; WILLIAM SHAKESPEARE'S ROMEO & JULIET; Y TU MAMÁ TAMBIÉN

✴ **MONACO:** GOLDENEYE; RED SHOES, THE; TO CATCH A THIEF

✴ **MOROCCO:** ALEXANDER; BAD TIMING; BLACK HAWK DOWN; GLADIATOR; JEWEL OF THE NILE, THE; KUNDUN; LAST TEMPTATION OF CHRIST, THE; LAWRENCE OF ARABIA; LIVING DAYLIGHTS, THE; MAN WHO KNEW TOO MUCH, THE (1956); MAN WHO WOULD BE KING, THE; MUMMY, THE; MUMMY RETURNS, THE; OTHELLO (1951); PATTON; PRICK UP YOUR EARS; SPY GAME; TIME BANDITS

✴ **NEPAL:** ARABIAN NIGHTS

✴ **NETHERLANDS:** ALICE IN DEN STADTEN; BRIDGE TOO FAR, A; DIAMONDS ARE FOREVER; LUST FOR LIFE; MODESTY BLAISE; NOSFERATU, PHANTOM DER NACHT

AMSTERDAM: LAYER CAKE

✴ **NEW ZEALAND:** BAD TASTE; BOUNTY, THE; BRAINDEAD; LAST SAMURAI, THE; LORD OF THE RINGS: THE FELLOWSHIP OF THE RING, THE; LORD OF THE RINGS: THE RETURN OF THE KING, THE; LORD OF THE RINGS: THE TWO TOWERS, THE; MIDNIGHT RUN; PIANO, THE; KING KONG (2005)

✴ **NIGER:** SHELTERING SKY, THE

✴ **NORTH AFRICA:** ARABIAN NIGHTS; PASSENGER, THE

✴ **NORTH ATLANTIC:** TITANIC

✴ **NORWAY:** INSOMNIA (1997); REVOLUTION; SCOTT OF THE ANTARCTIC; STAR WARS EPISODE V: THE EMPIRE STRIKES BACK; VIKINGS, THE

✴ **PERU:** AGUIRRE, WRATH OF GOD; DIARIOS DE

MOTOCICLETA; FITZCARRALDO; GRAND BLEU, LE

✳ **PHILIPPINES:** APOCALYPSE NOW; BORN ON THE FOURTH OF JULY; PLATOON; YEAR OF LIVING DANGEROUSLY, THE

✳ **POLAND:** DOUBLE VIE DE VÉRONIQUE, LA; KANAL; PIANIST, THE; POPIOL Y DIAMENT; SCHINDLER'S LIST; TROIS COULEURS: BLEU; TRZY KOLORY: BIALY

✳ **PORTUGAL:** ON HER MAJESTY'S SECRET SERVICE

✳ **PUERTO RICO:** GOLDENEYE; LORD OF THE FLIES; SPECIES

✳ **ROMANIA:** COLD MOUNTAIN

✳ **RUSSIA:** ALEXANDER NEVSKY; ANDREI ROUBLEV; BATTLESHIP POTEMKIN; BOURNE SUPREMACY, THE; CAST AWAY; GOLDENEYE

✳ **RWANDA:** GORILLAS IN THE MIST

✳ **ST LUCIA:** SUPERMAN

✳ **SARDINIA:** SPY WHO LOVED ME, THE

✳ **SAUDI ARABIA:** MALCOLM X

✳ **SCOTLAND:** BATTLE OF THE SEXES, THE; BRAVEHEART; BREAKING THE WAVES; CARRY ON REGARDLESS; CARRY ON UP THE KHYBER; CHARIOTS OF FIRE; DUELLISTS; FROM RUSSIA WITH LOVE; GREGORY'S GIRL; GREYSTOKE: THE LEGEND OF TARZAN, LORD OF THE APES; HAMLET (1990); HARRY POTTER AND THE CHAMBER OF SECRETS; HARRY POTTER AND THE GOBLET OF FIRE; HARRY POTTER AND THE PHILOSOPHER'S STONE; HARRY POTTER AND THE PRISONER OF AZKABAN; HIGHLANDER; I KNOW WHERE I'M GOING!; JOURNEY TO THE CENTER OF THE EARTH (1959); KIDNAPPED; LOCAL HERO; LOCH NESS; LONG GOOD FRIDAY, THE; MISSION: IMPOSSIBLE; MRS BROWN; MONTY PYTHON AND THE HOLY GRAIL; PRIME OF MISS JEAN BRODIE, THE; PRIVATE LIFE OF SHERLOCK HOLMES, THE; ROB ROY; SHALLOW GRAVE; SPY WHO LOVED ME, THE; 39 STEPS, THE; TRAINSPOTTING; 2001: A SPACE ODYSSEY; WHISKY GALORE!; WICKER MAN, THE; WORLD IS NOT ENOUGH, THE; YOU ONLY LIVE TWICE

✳ **SEYCHELLES:** EMMANUELLE

✳ **SLOVAKIA (see also CZECHOSLOVAKIA):** DRAGONHEART

✳ **SOLOMON ISLANDS:** THIN RED LINE, THE

✳ **SOUTH AFRICA:** MALCOLM X; RYAN'S DAUGHTER; ZULU

✳ **SOUTH PACIFIC:** HELL IN THE PACIFIC

✳ **SPAIN:** ABRE LOS OJOS; L'AGE D'OR; AROUND THE WORLD IN EIGHTY DAYS (1956); CET OBSCUR OBJET DU DÉSIR; CHIMES AT MIDNIGHT; CONAN THE BARBARIAN; DAY OF THE TRIFFIDS, THE; DIE ANOTHER DAY; DJANGO; DOCTOR ZHIVAGO; EL CID; EMPIRE OF THE SUN; FALL OF THE ROMAN EMPIRE, THE; FISTFUL OF DOLLARS, A; FOR YOUR EYES ONLY; 1492: CONQUEST OF PARADISE; INDIANA JONES AND THE LAST CRUSADE; LAWRENCE OF ARABIA; NEVER SAY NEVER AGAIN; PANDORA AND THE FLYING DUTCHMAN; PASSENGER, THE; PATTON; SPARTACUS; STAR WARS EPISODE II: ATTACK OF THE CLONES; THREE MUSKETEERS: THE QUEEN'S DIAMONDS, THE; TIME BANDITS; TRISTANA; WILDE; WIND AND THE LION, THE; WORLD IS NOT ENOUGH, THE; YOU ONLY LIVE TWICE

✳ **SRI LANKA:** BRIDGE ON THE RIVER KWAI, THE; INDIANA JONES AND THE TEMPLE OF DOOM

✳ **SUDAN:** FOUR FEATHERS, THE (1939)

✳ **SWEDEN:** ELVIRA MADIGAN; FACE, THE; FANNY AND ALEXANDER; PERSONA; SCOTT OF THE ANTARCTIC; SJUNDE INSEGLET, DET; SMILES OF A SUMMER NIGHT; SOMMAREN MED MONIKA; THROUGH A GLASS, DARKLY; TROLLFLÖJTEN; VARGTIMMEN; VIRGIN SPRING, THE; VISKNINGAR OCH ROP; WILD STRAWBERRIES

✳ **SWITZERLAND:** CHAPLIN; GOLDENEYE; GOLDFINGER; ON HER MAJESTY'S SECRET SERVICE; ROLLERBALL; SPY WHO LOVED ME, THE; STAR WARS EPISODE III: REVENGE OF THE SITH; TROIS COULEURS: ROUGE; VIEW TO A KILL, A; WOMEN IN LOVE

✳ **TAHITI:** BOUNTY, THE; MUTINY ON THE BOUNTY (1935); MUTINY ON THE BOUNTY (1962); XXX

✳ **TAIWAN:** SAND PEBBLES, THE

✳ **TANGANYIKA:** KING SOLOMON'S MINES; MOGAMBO

✳ **TANZANIA:** HATARI!; OUT OF AFRICA

✳ **THAILAND:** ALEXANDER; BEACH, THE; DEER HUNTER, THE; GOOD MORNING, VIETNAM; KILLING FIELDS, THE; MAN WITH THE GOLDEN GUN, THE; STAR WARS EPISODE III: REVENGE OF THE SITH; TOMORROW NEVER DIES

✳ **TUNISIA:** ENGLISH PATIENT, THE; MONTY PYTHON'S LIFE OF BRIAN; RAIDERS OF THE LOST ARK; STAR WARS EPISODE I: THE PHANTOM MENACE; STAR WARS EPISODE II: ATTACK OF THE CLONES; STAR WARS EPISODE III: REVENGE OF THE SITH; STAR WARS EPISODE IV: A NEW HOPE

✳ **TURKEY:** ARMAGEDDON; CHARGE OF THE LIGHT BRIGADE, THE (1968); FROM RUSSIA WITH LOVE; MIDNIGHT EXPRESS; MURDER ON THE ORIENT EXPRESS; TOPKAPI; WORLD IS NOT ENOUGH, THE

✳ **UGANDA:** AFRICAN QUEEN, THE; KING SOLOMON'S MINES; MOGAMBO

✳ **UKRAINE:** SHI MIAN MAI FU; WATERLOO

✳ **UNITED STATES OF AMERICA:**

ALABAMA: BIG FISH; CLOSE ENCOUNTERS OF THE THIRD KIND; MISSISSIPPI BURNING; UNDER SIEGE

ALASKA: INSOMNIA (2002); STAR TREK VI: THE UNDISCOVERED COUNTRY; THING, THE (1982)

ARIZONA: ALICE DOESN'T LIVE HERE ANY MORE; BACK TO THE FUTURE, PART III; BALLAD OF CABLE HOGUE, THE; BILL & TED'S EXCELLENT ADVENTURE; BUS STOP; DEAD MAN; DEATH WISH; DUEL IN THE SUN; EASY RIDER; EL DORADO; ELECTRA GLIDE IN BLUE; EXORCIST II: THE HERETIC; GUNFIGHT AT THE O.K. CORRAL; JERRY MAGUIRE; JOHNNY GUITAR; JUNIOR BONNER; KARATE KID, THE; MARS ATTACKS!; MIDNIGHT RUN; NATURAL BORN KILLERS; NUTTY PROFESSOR, THE (1963); OKLAHOMA!; OUTLAW — JOSEY WALES, THE; PLANET OF THE APES (1968); RAISING ARIZONA; RED RIVER; STAR WARS EPISODE VI: RETURN OF THE JEDI; RIO BRAVO; SEARCHERS, THE; STAR IS BORN, A (1976); STAR TREK: FIRST CONTACT; STARGATE; STARMAN; STIR CRAZY; SUPERMAN III; SUPERVIXENS; THIEF OF BAGDAD, THE; THREE KINGS; TOMBSTONE; 2001: A SPACE ODYSSEY; U TURN; UNFORGIVEN; WESTERNER, THE; WINCHESTER '73; ZABRISKIE POINT

ARKANSAS: CLIENT, THE; FIRM, THE

ATLANTIC CITY, NEW JERSEY: ATLANTIC CITY

BALTIMORE, MARYLAND: CRY-BABY; DINER; FEMALE TROUBLE; HAIRSPRAY

BOSTON, MASSACHUSETTS: GOOD WILL HUNTING

CALIFORNIA: A.I. ARTIFICIAL INTELLIGENCE; ADVENTURES OF ROBIN HOOD, THE; AIRPORT; ALL QUIET ON THE WESTERN FRONT; ALL THE KING'S MEN; AMERICAN BEAUTY; AMERICAN GIGOLO; AMERICAN GRAFFITI; AMERICAN PIE 2; AMERICAN SPLENDOR; ANNA KARENINA; ARACHNOPHOBIA; ARMY OF DARKNESS; AROUND THE WORLD IN EIGHTY DAYS (1956); AUSTIN POWERS: THE SPY WHO SHAGGED ME; AVIATOR, THE; BACK TO THE FUTURE PART II; BACK TO THE FUTURE PART III; BAD DAY AT BLACK ROCK; BAGDAD CAFE; BEDAZZLED (2000); BIRDMAN OF ALCATRAZ, THE; BIRDS, THE; BIRDY; BLACK RAIN; CASINO; CHAPLIN; CHARGE OF THE LIGHT BRIGADE, THE (1936); CHARLIE'S ANGELS; CHARLIE'S ANGELS: FULL THROTTLE; CHINA SYNDROME, THE; CLASH BY NIGHT; CLOSE ENCOUNTERS OF THE THIRD KIND; COCOON; COLOR PURPLE, THE; CON AIR; COOGAN'S BLUFF; COOL HAND LUKE; DAYS OF WINE AND ROSES; DEAD, THE; DEFIANT ONES, THE; DEVIL IN A BLUE DRESS; DIAMONDS ARE FOREVER; DIE HARD II: DIE HARDER; DOCTOR DOLITTLE (1967); DOCTOR DOLITTLE (1998); DOORS, THE; DUEL; DUEL IN THE SUN; EAST OF EDEN; EMPIRE OF THE SUN; ERIN BROCKOVICH; EVERY WHICH WAY BUT LOOSE; EXPLORERS; FAMILY PLOT; FAST AND THE FURIOUS, THE; FEW GOOD MEN, A; FIVE EASY PIECES; FOG, THE (1979); FOR WHOM THE BELL TOLLS; 48 HOURS; FOUL PLAY; FRIENDLY PERSUASION; FROM DUSK TILL DAWN; FROM HERE TO ETERNITY; GLENN MILLER STORY, THE; GO WEST; GODFATHER PART II, THE; GOLD RUSH,

THE; GONE WITH THE WIND; GRADUATE, THE; GRAPES OF WRATH, THE; GREAT DICTATOR, THE; GREAT RACE, THE; GREATEST STORY EVER TOLD, THE; GREED; GRIFTERS, THE; GROSSE POINTE BLANK; GUNGA DIN; HIGH NOON; HIGH PLAINS DRIFTER; HIGH SIERRA; HILLS HAVE EYES, THE; HITCHER, THE; HOUSE; HOWLING, THE; HULK; HUNT FOR RED OCTOBER, THE; I KNOW WHAT YOU DID LAST SUMMER; IN THE HEAT OF THE NIGHT; INDECENT PROPOSAL; INDEPENDENCE DAY; INDIANA JONES AND THE TEMPLE OF DOOM; INNERSPACE; ISLAND OF LOST SOULS; IT'S A MAD MAD MAD MAD WORLD; JAY AND SILENT BOB STRIKE BACK; JOHNNY BELINDA; JOY RIDE; JURASSIC PARK; JURASSIC PARK III; KILL BILL: VOLUME 1; KILL BILL: VOLUME 2; KILLING FIELDS, THE; KIM; KING SOLOMON'S MINES; KISS ME DEADLY; KISS ME, STUPID; LADY FROM SHANGHAI, THE; LASSIE COME HOME; LAWRENCE OF ARABIA; LEAVING LAS VEGAS; LITTLE BIG MAN; LIVES OF A BENGAL LANCER, THE; LONG RIDERS, THE; LOST BOYS, THE; LOST HIGHWAY; LOST HORIZON; LOST WORLD: JURASSIC PARK, THE; LOVE BUG, THE; MAGNIFICENT OBSESSION; MAGNOLIA; MALTESE FALCON, THE (1941); MAN ON THE MOON; MATRIX RELOADED, THE; MATRIX REVOLUTIONS, THE; MRS DOUBTFIRE; MOONRAKER; MOST DANGEROUS GAME, THE; MUTINY ON THE BOUNTY (1935); NATIONAL VELVET; NIXON; NORTH BY NORTHWEST; NOTHING SACRED; O BROTHER, WHERE ART THOU?; OCEAN'S ELEVEN (2001); OF MICE AND MEN; OLD SCHOOL; ON THE BEACH; ONE-EYED JACKS; OPPOSITE OF SEX, THE; OUT OF SIGHT; OUTLAW – JOSEY WALES, THE; OX-BOW INCIDENT, THE; PARENT TRAP, THE (1961); PATRIOT GAMES; PEGGY SUE GOT MARRIED; PERFECT STORM, THE; PHANTASM; PIRATES OF THE CARIBBEAN: THE CURSE OF THE BLACK PEARL; PLACE IN THE SUN, A; PLAN 9 FROM OUTER SPACE; PLANES, TRAINS & AUTOMOBILES; PLANET OF THE APES (1968); PLANET OF THE APES (2001); PLAY MISTY FOR ME; PLAYER, THE; POINT BLANK; POLLYANNA; POSEIDON ADVENTURE, THE; PREDATOR 2; RAIDERS OF THE LOST ARK; RAIN MAN; RAINMAKER, THE; REBECCA; RED DRAGON; REPLACEMENT KILLERS, THE; RIDE THE HIGH COUNTRY; RIVER'S EDGE; ROAD TO MOROCCO; ROAD TO PERDITION; ROAD TRIP; ROCK, THE; RULES OF ATTRACTION, THE; SABOTEUR; SCARFACE; SCREAM; SCREAM 2; SCREAM 3; SEARCHERS, THE; SECONDS; SHADOW OF A DOUBT; SHELTERING SKY, THE; SHORT CUTS; SIDEWAYS; SISTER ACT; SLEEPER; SPARTACUS; SPECIES; SPEED; SPIDER-MAN; SPIDER-MAN 2; STAGECOACH; STAND BY ME; STAR IS BORN, A (1954); STAR TREK: NEMESIS; STAR TREK: THE MOTION PICTURE; STAR TREK IV: THE VOYAGE HOME; STAR TREK V: THE FINAL FRONTIER; STAR TREK VI: THE UNDISCOVERED COUNTRY; STAR TREK: GENERATIONS; STAR TREK: FIRST CONTACT; STAR TREK: INSURRECTION; STAR WARS EPISODE IV: A NEW HOPE; STAR WARS EPISODE VI: RETURN OF THE JEDI; STARGATE; SUDDEN IMPACT; SUMMER OF '42; SUPERMAN; SUSPICION; SWEET DREAMS; TARGETS; TARZAN AND HIS MATE; TEEN WOLF; TEN COMMANDMENTS, THE (1923); TERMINAL; THE TERMINATOR 2: JUDGEMENT DAY; TERROR, THE; THELMA & LOUISE; THEM!; THEY DRIVE BY NIGHT; THX 1138; TOP GUN; TOPAZ; TORN CURTAIN; TOWERING INFERNO, THE; TRAFFIC; TRAMP, THE; TREASURE ISLAND (1934); TREMORS; TRIP, THE; TRUE GRIT; TRUE LIES; UNDER CAPRICORN; VANISHING, THE; VERTIGO; VIEW TO A KILL, A; WAR GAMES; WAR OF THE WORLDS, THE (2005); WE WERE SOLDIERS; WEREWOLF OF LONDON; WHO FRAMED ROGER RABBIT; WILD ANGELS, THE; WILD AT HEART; WIND, THE; WITCHES OF EASTWICK, THE; X-FILES, THE; X2; XXX; ZABRISKIE POINT

CHICAGO, ILLINOIS: BATMAN BEGINS; BREAKFAST CLUB, THE; CANDYMAN; CHICAGO; CHILD'S PLAY; FERRIS BUELLER'S DAY OFF; HENRY: PORTRAIT OF A SERIAL KILLER; HIGH FIDELITY; HOME ALONE; HOME ALONE 2: LOST IN NEW YORK; HUDSUCKER PROXY, THE; MIDNIGHT RUN; MIRACLE ON 34TH STREET (1994); MY BEST FRIEND'S WEDDING; MY BIG FAT GREEK WEDDING; SLEEPLESS IN SEATTLE; SPIDER-MAN 2; STING, THE; UNION STATION; UNTOUCHABLES, THE; WAYNE'S WORLD; WEDDING, A; WHEN HARRY MET SALLY…

COLORADO: AROUND THE WORLD IN EIGHTY DAYS (1956); BADLANDS; BUTCH CASSIDY AND THE SUNDANCE KID; CAT BALLOU; CHEYENNE AUTUMN; CITY SLICKERS; DIE HARD II: DIE HARDER; DUMB AND DUMBER; EVERY WHICH WAY BUT LOOSE; HOW THE WEST WAS WON; IN COLD BLOOD;

INDIANA JONES AND THE LAST CRUSADE; SEARCHERS, THE; SLEEPER; STARMAN; THELMA & LOUISE; TRUE GRIT; VANISHING POINT

CONNECTICUT: BOOMERANG; ICE STORM, THE; LAST HOUSE ON THE LEFT, THE; SECONDS; SLEEPERS; STEPFORD WIVES, THE (1975); STRANGERS ON A TRAIN (1951); VALLEY OF THE DOLLS; WAR OF THE WORLDS, THE (2005); WORLD ACCORDING TO GARP, THE

DALLAS, TEXAS: JFK; ROBOCOP

DELAWARE: DEAD POETS SOCIETY

DETROIT, MICHIGAN: BEVERLY HILLS COP; TRUE ROMANCE

FLORIDA: ANALYZE THIS; ANY GIVEN SUNDAY; APOLLO 13; ARMAGEDDON; BAD BOYS; BODY HEAT; BODYGUARD, THE; CADDYSHACK; CAPE FEAR (1991); COCOON; CREATURE FROM THE BLACK LAGOON; DAY OF THE DEAD; EDWARD SCISSORHANDS; GODFATHER PART II, THE; GREATEST SHOW ON EARTH, THE; HOURS, THE; JAWS 2; JEEPERS CREEPERS; KEY LARGO; LICENCE TO KILL; MATINEE; MIDNIGHT COWBOY; MOONRAKER; OCEAN'S ELEVEN (2001); ONCE UPON A TIME IN AMERICA; OUT OF SIGHT; RED DRAGON; SCARFACE; THUNDERBALL; TIGERLAND; TO DIE FOR; TRUE LIES; TRUMAN SHOW, THE; WILD WOMEN OF WONGO

GEORGIA: BIG FISH; CAPE FEAR (1962); DELIVERANCE; DRIVING MISS DAISY; FORREST GUMP; FRIED GREEN TOMATOES AT THE WHISTLE STOP CAFÉ; GLORY; LONG RIDERS, THE; MANHUNTER; ROAD TRIP; SCREAM 2; SMOKEY AND THE BANDIT; WE WERE SOLDIERS; WISE BLOOD

HAWAII: BLUE HAWAII; BODY HEAT; DONOVAN'S REEF; FEET FIRST; FROM HERE TO ETERNITY; GODZILLA (1998); JURASSIC PARK; JURASSIC PARK III; KING KONG (1976); LOST WORLD: JURASSIC PARK, THE; MISTER ROBERTS; MUTINY ON THE BOUNTY (1962); PEARL HARBOR; POINT BREAK; PUNCH-DRUNK LOVE; RAIDERS OF THE LOST ARK; SOUTH PACIFIC; THROW MOMMA FROM THE TRAIN

IDAHO: BUS STOP; HEAVEN'S GATE; NAPOLEON DYNAMITE; PALE RIDER

ILLINOIS: BLUES BROTHERS, THE; COLOR OF MONEY, THE; FIVE EASY PIECES; FUGITIVE, THE; GROUNDHOG DAY; IN THE HEAT OF THE NIGHT; LEAGUE OF THEIR OWN, A; MEET THE PARENTS; MISSION: IMPOSSIBLE; NATURAL BORN KILLERS; NORTH BY NORTHWEST; ORDINARY PEOPLE; PLANES, TRAINS & AUTOMOBILES; RISKY BUSINESS; ROAD TO PERDITION; WEIRD SCIENCE

INDIANA: BREAKING AWAY; LEAGUE OF THEIR OWN, A; NATURAL BORN KILLERS; RAIN MAN; ROAD TO PERDITION; SOME CAME RUNNING

IOWA: FIELD OF DREAMS; STARMAN; STRAIGHT STORY, THE; TWISTER

KANSAS: CARNIVAL OF SOULS; DANCES WITH WOLVES; IN COLD BLOOD; PAPER MOON; PICNIC

KENTUCKY: ASPHALT JUNGLE, THE; COAL MINER'S DAUGHTER; GOLDFINGER; HOW THE WEST WAS WON; LAWN DOGS; LEAGUE OF THEIR OWN, A; RAIN MAN; RAINTREE COUNTY

LAS VEGAS, NEVADA: AUSTIN POWERS: INTERNATIONAL MAN OF MYSTERY; CASINO; CON AIR; DIAMONDS ARE FOREVER; GODFATHER, THE; INDECENT PROPOSAL; MARS ATTACKS!; OCEAN'S ELEVEN (1960); OCEAN'S ELEVEN (2001); PRIZZI'S HONOR

LONG ISLAND, NEW YORK: BODYGUARD, THE; GODFATHER, THE; GOODFELLAS; MEET THE PARENTS

LOS ANGELES, CALIFORNIA: ACE IN THE HOLE; ADAM'S RIB; ADDAMS FAMILY, THE; ADVISE AND CONSENT; AFRICAN QUEEN, THE; AIRPLANE!; ALICE DOESN'T LIVE HERE ANY MORE; ALL THE PRESIDENT'S MEN; ALMOST FAMOUS; ALTERED STATES; AMERICAN HISTORY X; AMERICAN PIE; AMERICAN WEDDING; ANNIE HALL; APOLLO 13; ARMAGEDDON; AS GOOD AS IT GETS; ASPHALT JUNGLE, THE; ASSAULT ON PRECINCT 13 (1976); AUSTIN POWERS IN GOLDMEMBER; AUSTIN POWERS: INTERNATIONAL MAN OF MYSTERY; BACK TO THE FUTURE; BARTON FINK; BATMAN FOREVER; BEACH BLANKET BINGO; BEAST FROM TWENTY

THOUSAND FATHOMS, THE; BEING JOHN MALKOVICH; BEING THERE; BEVERLY HILLS COP; BIG LEBOWSKI, THE; BIG SLEEP, THE (1946); BIRTH OF A NATION, THE; BLADE; BLADE RUNNER; BLAZING SADDLES; BLOCKHEADS; BLUES BROTHERS, THE; BODYGUARD, THE; BOMBSHELL; BONFIRE OF THE VANITIES, THE; BOOGIE NIGHTS; BOUND; BOYZ N THE HOOD; BREATHLESS; BRIDE OF THE MONSTER; BRUCE ALMIGHTY; BUCKET OF BLOOD, A; BUFFY THE VAMPIRE SLAYER; BUSY BODIES; CAR WASH; CARRIE; CASABLANCA; CATCH ME IF YOU CAN; CHINATOWN; CITIZEN KANE; CLUELESS; COLLATERAL; COLLECTOR, THE; COUNTY HOSPITAL; CREATURE FROM THE BLACK LAGOON; CRUEL INTENTIONS; DAREDEVIL; DARKMAN; DAY AT THE RACES, A; DAY OF THE LOCUST, THE; DEAD MEN DON'T WEAR PLAID; DIE HARD; D.O.A. (1950); DONNIE DARKO; DOUBLE INDEMNITY; DRACULA (1931); DRIVER, THE; DUCK SOUP; E.T. THE EXTRA-TERRESTRIAL; EARTHQUAKE; EASY RIDER; ED WOOD; ERASER-HEAD; EXORCIST II: THE HERETIC; FABULOUS BAKER BOYS, THE; FACE/OFF; FAREWELL MY LOVELY (1944); FAREWELL MY LOVELY (1975); FAST TIMES AT RIDGEMONT HIGH; FEET FIRST; FERRIS BUELLER'S DAY OFF; FIGHT CLUB; FISHER KING, THE; FOREIGN CORRESPONDENT; FORREST GUMP; FRANKENSTEIN (1931); GALAXY QUEST; GARDEN STATE; GET SHORTY; GHOST; GHOSTBUSTERS; GIGI; GO; GODFATHER, THE; GODS AND MONSTERS; GOING MY WAY; GONE IN 60 SECONDS (1974); GONE IN 60 SECONDS (2000); GREASE; GREEN MILE, THE; HALLOWEEN; HALLOWEEN H20: 20 YEARS LATER; HEAT; HEATHERS; HORSE FEATHERS; HOUSE OF USHER; THE; HOUSE ON HAUNTED HILL, THE; HOW GREEN WAS MY VALLEY; HUNCHBACK OF NOTRE DAME, THE (1939); HUSTLER, THE; IMITATION OF LIFE; IN A LONELY PLACE; IN THE LINE OF FIRE; INTERNAL AFFAIRS; INVASION OF THE BODY SNATCHERS (1956); ITALIAN JOB, THE (2003); IT'S A WONDERFUL LIFE; JACKIE BROWN; JAZZ SINGER, THE; JERK, THE; JERRY MAGUIRE; KARATE KID, THE; KEY LARGO; KILLERS, THE; KILLING ZOE; KING KONG (1933); KING OF KINGS (1927); L.A. CONFIDENTIAL; L.A. STORY; LAST ACTION HERO; LAST SAMURAI, THE; LAVENDER HILL MOB, THE; LEGALLY BLONDE; LETHAL WEAPON; LETHAL WEAPON 2; LETHAL WEAPON 4; LITTLE SHOP OF HORRORS, THE; LONG GOODBYE, THE; LOVED ONE, THE; MADIGAN; MANCHURIAN CANDIDATE, THE (1962); MAN IN THE IRON MASK, THE (1939); MAN WITH TWO BRAINS, THE; MARATHON MAN; MASK, THE; MEAN STREETS; MEMENTO; MEN IN BLACK; MILDRED PIERCE; MILLION DOLLAR BABY; MILLION DOLLAR HOTEL; MINORITY REPORT; MR BLANDINGS BUILDS HIS DREAM HOUSE; MR SMITH GOES TO WASHINGTON; MOMMIE DEAREST; MOVE OVER, DARLING; MULHOLLAND DR; MUSIC BOX; MY LITTLE EYE; MYRA BRECKINRIDGE; NAKED GUN: FROM THE FILES OF POLICE SQUAD!, THE; NAKED GUN 33 1/3: THE FINAL INSULT, THE; NEW YORK NEW YORK; NIGHTMARE ON ELM STREET, A; NOT ANOTHER TEEN MOVIE; NOW, VOYAGER; OCEAN'S ELEVEN (1960); OCEAN'S ELEVEN (2001); ON THE TOWN; ONE FROM THE HEART; PANIC ROOM; PAPER MOON; PARALLAX VIEW, THE; PEARL HARBOR; PEE-WEE'S BIG ADVENTURE; PEOPLE VS LARRY FLYNT, THE; PHANTOM OF THE PARADISE; PHONE BOOTH; PIT AND THE PENDULUM, THE; PLANES, TRAINS & AUTOMOBILES; POLTERGEIST; PRETTY IN PINK; PRETTY WOMAN; PRINCE OF DARKNESS; PRIZZI'S HONOR; PSYCHO (1960); PULP FICTION; PUNCH-DRUNK LOVE; RAGING BULL; RAY; REALITY BITES; REBEL WITHOUT A CAUSE; REPO MAN; RESERVOIR DOGS; RING, THE; ROBOT MONSTER; ROCKY; ROCKY II; ROCKY III; RUSH HOUR; S.W.A.T.; SAFETY LAST; SAND PEBBLES, THE; SAYONARA; SE7EN; SEVEN BRIDES FOR SEVEN BROTHERS; SEVEN YEAR ITCH, THE; SHAMPOO; SHE'S ALL THAT; SID AND NANCY; SOCIETY; SOPHIE'S CHOICE; SOUND OF MUSIC, THE; SPLASH; STAR IS BORN, A (1937); STAR IS BORN, A (1976); STARSHIP TROOPERS; STING, THE; STRANGERS ON A TRAIN (1951); STREETCAR NAMED DESIRE, A; SUNSET BLVD.; SWINGERS; 10; TEN COMMANDMENTS, THE (1956); TERMINATOR, THE; TERMINATOR 3: RISE OF THE MACHINES; THEY LIVE BY NIGHT; THEY SHOOT HORSES, DON'T THEY?; THING, THE (1951); THIS IS SPINAL TAP; THROW MOMMA FROM THE TRAIN; TO KILL A MOCKINGBIRD; TOPPER; TOUCH OF EVIL; TRAINING DAY; TREASURE OF THE SIERRA MADRE, THE; TRUE ROMANCE; UNION STATION; USUAL SUSPECTS, THE; VALLEY OF THE DOLLS; VAN HELSING; VANILLA SKY; VIVA LAS VEGAS; WAR OF THE ROSES, THE; WAR OF THE WORLDS,

THE (1953); WAY WE WERE, THE; WAYNE'S WORLD; WE FAW DOWN; WEDDING SINGER, THE; WESTWORLD; WHAT EVER HAPPENED TO BABY JANE? (1962); WHAT PRICE HOLLYWOOD?; WHEN HARRY MET SALLY...; WHITE HEAT; WHITE MEN CAN'T JUMP; WITNESS FOR THE PROSECUTION; WOLF; WUTHERING HEIGHTS (1939); X – THE MAN WITH X-RAY EYES; YOUNG FRANKENSTEIN

LOUISIANA: BEGUILED, THE; CLIENT, THE; HUSH... HUSH, SWEET CHARLOTTE; INTERVIEW WITH THE VAMPIRE: THE VAMPIRE CHRONICLES; JFK; LIVE AND LET DIE; LONG, HOT SUMMER, THE; MILLER'S CROSSING; MONSTER'S BALL; OUT OF SIGHT; PELICAN BRIEF, THE; RAY; SEX, LIES, & VIDEOTAPE; SOUTHERN COMFORT; STEEL MAGNOLIAS

MAINE: CAROUSEL; FORREST GUMP; PEYTON PLACE; WHALES OF AUGUST, THE

MARYLAND: BLAIR WITCH PROJECT, THE; CRY-BABY; DIE HARD WITH A VENGEANCE; PATRIOT GAMES; PINK FLAMINGOS; RED DRAGON; SERIAL MOM; SLEEPLESS IN SEATTLE; TIN MEN; TWELVE MONKEYS

MASSACHUSETTS: ALTERED STATES; CARNAL KNOWLEDGE; FIELD OF DREAMS; FIRM, THE; GLORY; JAWS; JAWS 2; LAST DETAIL, THE; LEGALLY BLONDE; LITTLE WOMEN (1994); LOVE STORY; MYSTIC RIVER; OLD SCHOOL; PERFECT STORM, THE; PORTRAIT OF JENNIE; ROAD TRIP; THOMAS CROWN AFFAIR, THE (1968); WHO'S AFRAID OF VIRGINIA WOOLF?; WITCHES OF EASTWICK, THE

MEMPHIS, TENNESSEE: FIRM, THE; MYSTERY TRAIN; PEOPLE VS LARRY FLYNT, THE

MIAMI, FLORIDA: ACE VENTURA, PET DETECTIVE; BELLBOY, THE; GOLDFINGER; THERE'S SOMETHING ABOUT MARY

MICHIGAN: AMERICAN PIE 2; ANATOMY OF A MURDER; DIE HARD II: DIE HARDER; 8 MILE; EVIL DEAD, THE; EVIL DEAD II; GROSSE POINTE BLANK; MIDNIGHT RUN; OUT OF SIGHT; ROAD TO PERDITION

MIDWAY ISLAND: MISTER ROBERTS

MINNEAPOLIS, MINNESOTA: MALLRATS

MINNESOTA: AIRPORT; FARGO; SIMPLE PLAN, A

MISSISSIPPI: BABY DOLL; O BROTHER, WHERE ART THOU?; MISSISSIPPI BURNING; RAINTREE COUNTY

MISSOURI: IN COLD BLOOD; INTRUDER, THE; MANHUNTER; PAPER MOON; PLANES, TRAINS & AUTOMOBILES; WHITE PALACE

MONTANA: HEAVEN'S GATE; LITTLE BIG MAN; THING, THE (1951); UNTOUCHABLES, THE

NEBRASKA: BOYS' TOWN; ELECTION; TERMS OF ENDEARMENT

NEVADA: AMAZING COLOSSAL MAN, THE; BALLAD OF CABLE HOGUE, THE; CHARLEY VARRICK; GO; GODFATHER, THE; GODFATHER PART II, THE; GREATEST STORY EVER TOLD, THE; HIGH PLAINS DRIFTER; IN COLD BLOOD; INDEPENDENCE DAY; IRON HORSE, THE; JOY RIDE; KISS ME, STUPID; LEAVING LAS VEGAS; LETHAL WEAPON 4; MAGNOLIA; MIDNIGHT RUN; MISERY; MISFITS, THE; MOONRAKER; PLACE IN THE SUN, A; RAIN MAN; ROMANCING THE STONE; SABOTEUR; SHOOTIST, THE; SHOWGIRLS; SISTER ACT; STAR TREK: GENERATIONS; STARMAN; STIR CRAZY; SWINGERS; TOP GUN; VANISHING POINT; VIVA LAS VEGAS; ZABRISKIE POINT

NEW HAMPSHIRE: LAST DETAIL, THE; LITTLE WOMEN (1933); ON GOLDEN POND

NEW HAVEN, CONNECTICUT: ALL ABOUT EVE

NEW JERSEY: AMITYVILLE HORROR, THE (1979) ANALYZE THIS; BEAUTIFUL MIND, A; BIG; BIRDY; BROADWAY DANNY ROSE; CATCH ME IF YOU CAN; CHASING AMY; CLERKS; COLOR OF MONEY, THE; CREEPSHOW; DESPERATELY SEEKING SUSAN; DOGMA; FRIDAY THE 13TH; GARDEN STATE; GODFATHER PART III, THE; GOODFELLAS; HURRICANE, THE; JAY AND SILENT BOB STRIKE BACK; KING OF MARVIN GARDENS, THE; LÉON; LONG KISS GOODNIGHT, THE; MALLRATS; MANHATTAN; MARNIE; MEN IN BLACK; OCEAN'S ELEVEN (2001); ON THE WATER-FRONT; ONCE UPON A TIME IN AMERICA; PURPLE ROSE OF CAIRO, THE; RADIO DAYS; REVERSAL OF FORTUNE; ROUNDERS; ROYAL TENENBAUMS, THE; SCHOOL OF ROCK;

SHAFT (2000); STARDUST MEMORIES; SWEET AND LOW-DOWN; VILLAGE, THE; WAR OF THE WORLDS, THE (2005); WORLD ACCORDING TO GARP, THE; ZELIG

NEW MEXICO: ACE IN THE HOLE; ARMAGEDDON; CITY SLICKERS; EASY RIDER; EVERY WHICH WAY BUT LOOSE; GRAPES OF WRATH, THE; JOURNEY TO THE CENTER OF THE EARTH (1959); KING SOLOMON'S MINES; LONELY ARE THE BRAVE; MAN FROM LARAMIE, THE; MAN WHO FELL TO EARTH, THE; NATURAL BORN KILLERS; SPIDER, THE; SUPERMAN; TRAFFIC; 21 GRAMS; VAMPIRES; YOUNG GUNS

NEW ORLEANS, LOUISIANA: ANGEL HEART; BIG EASY, THE; CAT PEOPLE; CINCINNATI KID, THE; EASY RIDER; JFK; PRETTY BABY; STREETCAR NAMED DESIRE, A

NEW YORK CITY: ACROSS 110TH STREET; ADAM'S RIB; AFTER HOURS; ALICE IN DEN STADTEN; ALL ABOUT EVE; ALMOST FAMOUS; ALTERED STATES; AMATEUR; AMERICAN PSYCHO; AMERICAN SPLENDOR; AMERIKANISCHE FREUND, DER; ANDERSON TAPES, THE; ANGEL HEART; ANNIE HALL; APARTMENT, THE; ARMAGEDDON; ARTHUR; AS GOOD AS IT GETS; BAD LIEUTENANT; BAD TIMING; BEAST FROM TWENTY THOUSAND FATHOMS, A; BEING JOHN MALKOVICH; BELL, BOOK AND CANDLE; BIG; BLACK RAIN; BOILER ROOM; BONFIRE OF THE VANITIES, THE; BOURNE SUPREMACY, THE; BREAKFAST AT TIFFANY'S; BROADWAY DANNY ROSE; BULLETS OVER BROADWAY; CARLITO'S WAY; CARNAL KNOWLEDGE; CATCH ME IF YOU CAN; CHASING AMY; CITY SLICKERS; CLOCKERS; COOGAN'S BLUFF; COTTON CLUB, THE; CRIMES AND MISDEMEANORS; "CROCODILE" DUNDEE; CRUISING; DAREDEVIL; DEATH WISH; DESPERATELY SEEKING SUSAN; DIE HARD WITH A VENGEANCE; DO THE RIGHT THING; DOG DAY AFTERNOON; DONNIE BRASCO; DOORS, THE; DRESSED TO KILL; DRILLER KILLER; 8 MILE; 84 CHARING CROSS ROAD; ELECTION; ESCAPE FROM NEW YORK; EXORCIST, THE; FAME; FATAL ATTRACTION; FISHER KING, THE; FRENCH CONNECTION, THE; FRESHMAN, THE; GHOST; GHOSTBUSTERS; GODFATHER, THE; GODFATHER PART II, THE; GODFATHER PART III, THE; GOODFELLAS; GREAT GATSBY, THE; HESTER STREET; HIGHLANDER; HOME ALONE 2: LOST IN NEW YORK; HOURS, THE; HOUSE ON 92ND ST., THE; HOW TO MARRY A MILLIONAIRE; HUDSON HAWK; HUNGER, THE; HUSBANDS AND WIVES; HUSTLER, THE; ICE STORM, THE; INDEPENDENCE DAY; JERRY MAGUIRE; JOHNNY SUEDE; KING KONG (1933); KING KONG (1976); KING OF NEW YORK; KRAMER VS KRAMER; LAST ACTION HERO; LAST DETAIL, THE; LAST HOUSE ON THE LEFT, THE; LÉON; LIGHT SLEEPER; LIVE AND LET DIE; LOST WEEKEND, THE; LOVE AFFAIR (1939); LOVE STORY; MADIGAN; MALCOLM X; MAN WHO FELL TO EARTH, THE; MANCHURIAN CANDIDATE, THE (1962); MANHATTAN; MANHATTAN MURDER MYSTERY; MARATHON MAN; MEAN STREETS; MEN IN BLACK; MIDNIGHT COWBOY; MIDNIGHT RUN; MIRACLE ON 34TH STREET (1947); MIRACLE ON 34TH STREET (1994); MO' BETTER BLUES; MOONSTRUCK; NAKED CITY, THE; NETWORK; NEW JACK CITY; NEW YORK STORIES; NINE 1/2 WEEKS; NORTH BY NORTHWEST; NOTHING SACRED; ODD COUPLE, THE; ON THE TOWN; ONCE UPON A TIME IN AMERICA; PANIC ROOM; PELICAN BRIEF, THE; PHANTOM OF THE PARADISE; PHONE BOOTH; PORTRAIT OF JENNIE; PRIZZI'S HONOR; PRODUCERS, THE (1967); Q – THE WINGED SERPENT; QUIZ SHOW; RADIO DAYS; RAGING BULL; REQUIEM FOR A DREAM; REVERSAL OF FORTUNE; ROMANCING THE STONE; ROSEMARY'S BABY; ROUNDERS; ROYAL TENENBAUMS, THE; SABOTEUR; SATURDAY NIGHT FEVER; SCARFACE; SCENT OF A WOMAN; SCHOOL OF ROCK; SEA OF LOVE; SECONDS; SERPICO; SEVEN YEAR ITCH, THE; SHAFT (1971); SHAFT (2000); SHE'S GOTTA HAVE IT; SID AND NANCY; SINGLE WHITE FEMALE; SIX DEGREES OF SEPARATION; SLEEPERS; SLEEPLESS IN SEATTLE; SOTTO GLI OCCHI DELL'ASSASSINO; SPIDER-MAN; SPIDER-MAN 2; SPLASH; STIR CRAZY; STRANGERS ON A TRAIN (1951); SUMMER OF SAM; SUNSHINE BOYS, THE; SUPERMAN; SWEET SMELL OF SUCCESS; TAKING OF PELHAM ONE TWO THREE, THE; TALENTED MR RIPLEY, THE; TAXI DRIVER; THOMAS CROWN AFFAIR, THE; THREE DAYS OF THE CONDOR; 3 MEN AND A BABY; TOOTSIE; TOPAZ; TRADING PLACES; 12 ANGRY MEN; UNDER THE CLOCK; USUAL SUSPECTS, THE; VALLEY OF THE DOLLS; VANILLA SKY; WAIT UNTIL DARK; WALL STREET; WARRIORS, THE; WAY WE WERE, THE; WEEKEND AT BERNIE'S;

WEST SIDE STORY; WHEN HARRY MET SALLY...; WOLF; WOLFEN; WORKING GIRL; WRONG MAN, THE

NEW YORK: AGE OF INNOCENCE, THE; ANALYZE THIS; ARTHUR; BASKET CASE; BATMAN FOREVER; BEAUTIFUL MIND, A; BIG; BOOMERANG; BRUCE ALMIGHTY; CAT ON A HOT TIN ROOF; CITIZEN KANE; CRUEL INTENTIONS; FATAL ATTRACTION; FLESH EATERS, THE; FUGITIVE KIND, THE; HANNAH AND HER SISTERS; KING OF COMEDY, THE; LEAGUE OF THEIR OWN, A; MALCOLM X; MAN ON THE MOON; MEET THE PARENTS; MIGHTY APHRODITE; NATURAL, THE; NEW JACK CITY; NORTH BY NORTHWEST; PLANES, TRAINS & AUTOMOBILES; PURPLE ROSE OF CAIRO, THE; QUIZ SHOW; RAGING BULL; REVERSAL OF FORTUNE; ROBOCOP; SABRINA (1954); SCENT OF A WOMAN; SCHOOL OF ROCK; SLEEPERS; SPANKING THE MONKEY; SPLENDOR IN THE GRASS; STRANGERS ON A TRAIN (1951); SUPERMAN II; SWEET AND LOWDOWN; THEY DIED WITH THEIR BOOTS ON; THOMAS CROWN AFFAIR, THE (1999); TOOTSIE; TRADING PLACES; 20,000 YEARS IN SING SING; USUAL SUSPECTS, THE; WAR OF THE WORLDS, THE (2005); WAY DOWN EAST; WAY WE WERE, THE; WOLF; WOODSTOCK; WORLD ACCORDING TO GARP, THE; WRONG MAN, THE; ZELIG

NORTH CAROLINA: BEING THERE; BLUE VELVET; BULL DURHAM; COLOR PURPLE, THE; CROW, THE; DIRTY DANCING; EVIL DEAD II; FUGITIVE, THE; HANNIBAL; HUNT FOR RED OCTOBER, THE; I KNOW WHAT YOU DID LAST SUMMER; LAST OF THE MOHICANS, THE; MANHUNTER; STARMAN; WEEKEND AT BERNIE'S

NORTH DAKOTA: FARGO

OHIO: AMERICAN SPLENDOR; DEER HUNTER, THE; RAIN MAN; SHAWSHANK REDEMPTION, THE; TRAFFIC

OKLAHOMA: AROUND THE WORLD IN EIGHTY DAYS (1956); GRAPES OF WRATH, THE; OUTSIDERS, THE; RAIN MAN; RUMBLE FISH; TWISTER

OREGON: A.I. ARTIFICIAL INTELLIGENCE; DEAD MAN; DRUGSTORE COWBOY; FIVE EASY PIECES; GENERAL, THE; GREAT RACE, THE; MY OWN PRIVATE IDAHO; NATIONAL LAMPOON'S ANIMAL HOUSE; NORTHWEST PASSAGE; ONE FLEW OVER THE CUCKOO'S NEST; POINT BREAK; RING, THE; SHINING, THE; SHORT CIRCUIT; STAND BY ME; STAR WARS EPISODE V: THE EMPIRE STRIKES BACK

PENNSYLVANIA: AGE OF INNOCENCE, THE; BLOB, THE (1958); CREEPSHOW; DAWN OF THE DEAD (1978); DAY OF THE DEAD; DEER HUNTER, THE; DOGMA; FLASHDANCE; GREATEST SHOW ON EARTH, THE; HAIRSPRAY; KING OF MARVIN GARDENS, THE; MARNIE; ROBOCOP; SIGNS; TRADING PLACES; TWELVE MONKEYS; UNBREAKABLE; VILLAGE, THE; WITNESS

PHILADELPHIA, PENNSYLVANIA: BIRDY; ERASERHEAD; PHILADELPHIA; ROCKY; ROCKY II; ROCKY III; SIXTH SENSE, THE

PHOENIX, ARIZONA: GRIFTERS, THE; PSYCHO (1960)

PITTSBURGH, PENNSYLVANIA: NIGHT OF THE LIVING DEAD; SILENCE OF THE LAMBS, THE; WONDER BOYS

RHODE ISLAND: DUMB AND DUMBER; GREAT GATSBY, THE; HIGH SOCIETY; LOLITA (1962); THERE'S SOMETHING ABOUT MARY; TRUE LIES

ST LOUIS, MISSOURI: ESCAPE FROM NEW YORK

SAN DIEGO, CALIFORNIA: ALMOST FAMOUS; ATTACK OF THE KILLER TOMATOES!; SOME LIKE IT HOT

SAN FRANCISCO, CALIFORNIA: ALL ABOUT EVE; BASIC INSTINCT; BULLITT; CHAN IS MISSING; CONVERSATION, THE; DARK PASSAGE; DIRTY HARRY; D.O.A. (1950); ESCAPE FROM ALCATRAZ; INTERVIEW WITH THE VAMPIRE: THE VAMPIRE CHRONICLES; INVASION OF THE BODY SNATCHERS (1978); KILLER ELITE, THE; PAL JOEY; SUDDEN FEAR; TITANIC; WHAT'S UP DOC?; WOMAN IN RED, THE

SEATTLE, WASHINGTON: FABULOUS BAKER BOYS, THE; IT HAPPENED AT THE WORLD'S FAIR; SINGLES; SLEEPLESS IN SEATTLE

SOUTH CAROLINA: ABYSS, THE; BIG CHILL, THE; COLD MOUNTAIN; DIE HARD WITH A VENGEANCE; FORREST GUMP; PATRIOT, THE; SWAMP THING

SOUTH DAKOTA: ARMAGEDDON; DANCES WITH WOLVES; HOW THE WEST WAS WON; NORTH BY NORTHWEST; STARSHIP TROOPERS

TENNESSEE: CAST AWAY; CLIENT, THE; COAL MINER'S DAUGHTER; EVIL DEAD, THE; GREEN MILE, THE; IN THE HEAT OF THE NIGHT; NASHVILLE; RAINMAKER, THE; RAINTREE COUNTY; ROAD TRIP; STARMAN; SWEET DREAMS; THIS IS SPINAL TAP; 21 GRAMS; U.S. MARSHALS

TEXAS: ALAMO, THE; ANY GIVEN SUNDAY; APOLLO 13; ARMAGEDDON; BLOOD SIMPLE; BONNIE AND CLYDE; BORN ON THE FOURTH OF JULY; BOYS DON'T CRY; CAST AWAY; CROW, THE; DAZED AND CONFUSED; GETAWAY, THE; GIANT; HUD; IN COLD BLOOD; LAST PICTURE SHOW, THE; LOCAL HERO; LONG RIDERS, THE; MIDNIGHT COWBOY; PARIS, TEXAS; PEE-WEE'S BIG ADVENTURE; PERFECT WORLD, A; PHANTOM OF THE PARADISE; PROBLEM CHILD; REALITY BITES; ROBOCOP 2; RUSHMORE; SLACKER; SOUTHERN COMFORT; SPY KIDS; SPY KIDS 3-D: GAME OVER; SPY KIDS 2: ISLAND OF LOST DREAMS; SUGARLAND EXPRESS, THE; TERMS OF ENDEARMENT; TEXAS CHAIN SAW MASSACRE, THE; TRAFFIC; TRIP TO BOUNTIFUL, THE; TWISTER; WHAT'S EATING GILBERT GRAPE?; WILD AT HEART; WINGS

UTAH: AUSTIN POWERS IN GOLDMEMBER; BUTCH CASSIDY AND THE SUNDANCE KID; CARNIVAL OF SOULS; CHEYENNE AUTUMN; CON AIR; DUMB AND DUMBER; ELECTRA GLIDE IN BLUE; FOOTLOOSE; FORREST GUMP; FORT APACHE; GALAXY QUEST; GREATEST STORY EVER TOLD, THE; HOW THE WEST WAS WON; HULK; INDIANA JONES AND THE LAST CRUSADE; JEREMIAH JOHNSON; JEWEL OF THE NILE, THE; JOY RIDE; MISSION: IMPOSSIBLE 2; NAPOLEON DYNAMITE; OCTOPUSSY; OUTLAW – JOSEY WALES, THE; PLANET OF THE APES (2001); RIO GRANDE; ROMANCING THE STONE; SEARCHERS, THE; SEVEN BRIDES FOR SEVEN BROTHERS; SPECIES; STAGECOACH; THELMA & LOUISE; THIS BOY'S LIFE; VANISHING POINT

VERMONT: BEETLEJUICE; TROUBLE WITH HARRY, THE; WAY DOWN EAST

VIRGINIA: COAL MINER'S DAUGHTER; DIRTY DANCING; HANNIBAL; LAST DETAIL, THE; MINORITY REPORT; MISSION: IMPOSSIBLE; PATRIOT GAMES; SILENCE OF THE LAMBS, THE; SOMMERSBY; SPY GAME; WAR OF THE WORLDS, THE (2005)

WASHINGTON DC: ADVISE AND CONSENT; ALL THE PRESIDENT'S MEN; ARMAGEDDON; BEING THERE; CLOSE ENCOUNTERS OF THE THIRD KIND; DAY THE EARTH STOOD STILL, THE; DIE HARD II: DIE HARDER; EXORCIST, THE; FEW GOOD MEN, A; FIRM, THE; FORREST GUMP; FRENCH CONNECTION, THE; GREATEST SHOW ON EARTH, THE; HANNIBAL; IN THE LINE OF FIRE; INDEPENDENCE DAY; JFK; LAST DETAIL, THE; MANHUNTER; MARS ATTACKS!; MINORITY REPORT; MR SMITH GOES TO WASHINGTON; NIGHT OF THE LIVING DEAD; NIXON; PELICAN BRIEF, THE; PEOPLE VS LARRY FLYNT, THE; RECRUIT, THE; RED DRAGON; SPY GAME; STRANGERS ON A TRAIN (1951); TOPAZ; TRAFFIC; TRUE LIES; X-FILES, THE

WASHINGTON: DEAD MAN; DEER HUNTER, THE; HUNT FOR RED OCTOBER, THE; LASSIE COME HOME; LONG KISS GOODNIGHT, THE; MY OWN PRIVATE IDAHO; OFFICER AND A GENTLEMAN, AN; PARALLAX VIEW, THE; RING, THE; 10 THINGS I HATE ABOUT YOU; TWIN PEAKS: FIRE WALK WITH ME; VANISHING, THE; WAR GAMES; WAR OF THE ROSES, THE

WEST VIRGINIA: DEER HUNTER, THE; SWEET DREAMS; XXX

WISCONSIN: BLUES BROTHERS, THE; SIMPLE PLAN, A; STRAIGHT STORY, THE

WYOMING: CHEYENNE AUTUMN; CLOSE ENCOUNTERS OF THE THIRD KIND; DANCES WITH WOLVES; ROCKY IV; SHANE; STAR TREK: THE MOTION PICTURE; STAR TREK V: THE FINAL FRONTIER; STARSHIP TROOPERS; VANISHING, THE

✳ **VENEZUELA:** ARACHNOPHOBIA

✳ **VIRGIN ISLANDS:** DINOSAURUS; TRADING PLACES

✳ **WALES:** AMERICAN WEREWOLF IN LONDON, AN; ARABESQUE; BACKBEAT; CARRY ON UP THE KHYBER; CITADEL, THE; DAM BUSTERS, THE; DIE ANOTHER DAY; INN OF THE SIXTH HAPPINESS, THE; JABBERWOCKY; LARA CROFT TOMB RAIDER: THE CRADLE OF LIFE; LION IN WINTER, THE;

MACBETH (1971); MOBY DICK; ROBIN HOOD; TIGER BAY; TIME BANDITS; WORLD IS NOT ENOUGH, THE; YANKS

✳ **WEST INDIES:** DOCTOR DOLITTLE (1967); DR NO

✳ **YUGOSLAVIA (now SERBIA and MONTENEGRO):** CROSS OF IRON; FIDDLER ON THE ROOF; ISADORA; MURDER ON THE ORIENT EXPRESS; SOPHIE'S CHOICE; TRIAL, THE

✳ **ZAIRE:** AFRICAN QUEEN, THE

✳ **ZAMBESE:** WHITE HUNTER, BLACK HEART

✳ **ZIMBABWE:** CRY FREEDOM; WHITE HUNTER, BLACK HEART

ALTERNATIVE TITLES INDEX

A

AMERICAN FRIEND, THE see **AMERIKANISCHE FREUND, DER**

ALICE IN THE CITIES see **ALICE IN DEN STADTEN**

AMÉLIE see **FABULEUX DESTIN D'AMÉLIE POULAIN, LE**

AND GOD... CREATED WOMAN see **ET DIEU... CREA LA FEMME**

AND YOUR MOTHER TOO see **Y TU MAMÁ TAMBIÉN**

ASHES AND DIAMONDS see **POPIOL Y DIAMENT**

B

BATTLE OF ALGIERS see **BATTAGLIA DI ALGERI, LA**

BEAUTY AND THE BEAST see **BELLE ET LA BÊTE, LA**

BEFORE THE REVOLUTION see **PRIMA DELLA RIVOLUZIONE**

BETTY BLUE see **37°2 LE MATIN**

BICYCLE THIEVES, THE see **LADRI DI BICICLETTE**

BIG BLUE, THE see **GRAND BLEU, LE**

BIG CARNIVAL, THE see **ACE IN THE HOLE**

BIG HEART, THE see **MIRACLE ON 34TH STREET (1947)**

BIG TIME OPERATORS see **SMALLEST SHOW ON EARTH, THE**

BIRDS OF A FEATHER see **CAGE AUX FOLLES, LA**

BLAZING SUN see **PLEIN SOLEIL**

BLONDE BOMBSHELL see **BOMBSHELL**

BOAT, THE see **BOOT, DAS**

BOUDU SAVED FROM DROWNING see **BOUDU SAUVÉ DES EAUX**

BREATHLESS see **A BOUT DE SOUFFLE**

BUTCHER, THE see **BOUCHER, LE**

C

CARRY ON – FOLLOW THAT CAMEL see **FOLLOW THAT CAMEL**

CHARLIE THE TRAMP see **TRAMP, THE**

CHILDREN OF PARADISE see **ENFANTS DU PARADIS, LES**

CLAIRE'S KNEE see **GENOU DE CLAIRE, LE**

CLOCK, THE see **UNDER THE CLOCK**

CLOSELY WATCHED TRAINS see **CLOSELY OBSERVED TRAINS**

COBWEB CASTLE see **KUMONOSU-JO**

CONFORMIST, THE see **CONFORMISTA, IL**

CONQUEROR WORM, THE see **WITCHFINDER GENERAL**

CONTEMPT see **MEPRIS, LE**

COUNT DRACULA AND HIS VAMPIRE BRIDE see **SATANIC RITES OF DRACULA, THE**

CREEPING UNKNOWN, THE see **QUATERMASS XPERIMENT, THE**

CRIES AND WHISPERS see **VISKNINGAR OCH ROP**

CROUCHING TIGER, HIDDEN DRAGON see **WO HU CANG LONG**

CURSE OF THE DEMON see **NIGHT OF THE DEMON**

D

DAMNED, THE see **GÖTTERDAMMERUNG**

DANNY BOY see **ANGEL**

DAY FOR NIGHT see **NUIT AMERICAINE, LA**

DEAD ALIVE see **BRAINDEAD**

DESERT ATTACK see **ICE COLD IN ALEX**

DIARY OF A CHAMBERMAID, THE see **JOURNAL D'UNE FEMME DE CHAMBRE**

D (continued)

DISCREET CHARM OF THE BOURGEOISIE, THE see **CHARME DISCRET DE LA BOURGEOISIE, LE**

DOUBLE LIFE OF VÉRONIQUE, THE see **DOUBLE VIE DE VÉRONIQUE, LA**

E

EARTH VERSUS THE SPIDER see **SPIDER, THE**

ECLIPSE, THE see **ECLISSE, L'**

EIGHT AND A HALF see **OTTO E MEZZO**

8 1/2 see **OTTO E MEZZO**

EMPIRE STRIKES BACK, THE see **STAR WARS EPISODE V: THE EMPIRE STRIKES BACK**

ENEMY FROM SPACE see **QUATERMASS II**

F

FALL OF THE HOUSE OF USHER, THE see **HOUSE OF USHER, THE**

FEAR EATS THE SOUL see **ANGST ESSEN SEELE AUF**

FEDERICO FELLINI'S 8 1/2 see **OTTO E MEZZO**

FORTY-EIGHT HOURS see **WENT THE DAY WELL?**

FOUR HUNDRED BLOWS, THE see **QUATRE CENTS COUPS, LES**

FRANTIC see **ASCENSEUR POUR L'ECHAFAUD**

G

GARDEN OF THE FINZI-CONTINIS, THE see **GIARDINO DEI FINZI-CONTINI, IL**

GODSON, THE see **SAMOURAÏ, LE**

GONE IN SIXTY SECONDS see **GONE IN 60 SECONDS (1974)**

GONE IN SIXTY SECONDS see **GONE IN 60 SECONDS (2000)**

GOSPEL ACCORDING TO ST. MATTHEW, THE see **VANGELO SECONDO MATTEO, IL**

GRAND ILLUSION see **GRANDE ILLUSION, LA**

GUNS IN THE AFTERNOON see **RIDE THE HIGH COUNTRY**

H

HARRY POTTER AND THE SORCERER'S STONE see **HARRY POTTER AND THE PHILOSOPHER'S STONE**

HATE see **HAINE, LA**

HER MAJESTY, MRS BROWN see **MRS BROWN**

HERO see **YING XIONG**

HIDDEN FORTRESS, THE see **KAKUSHI TORIDE NO SAN-AKUNIN**

HORROR OF DRACULA see **DRACULA (1958)**

HOUNDS OF ZAROFF, THE see **MOST DANGEROUS GAME, THE**

HOUR OF THE WOLF see **VARGTIMMEN**

HOUSE OF FLYING DAGGERS see **SHI MIAN MAI FU**

HUIT ET DEMI see **OTTO E MEZZO**

HUMAN BEAST, THE see **BÊTE HUMAINE, LA**

I

INDISCRETION OF AN AMERICAN WIFE see **STAZIONE TERMINI**

J

JESUS OF MONTRÉAL see **JÉSUS DE MONTRÉAL**

JOHN CARPENTER'S VAMPIRES see **VAMPIRES**

JUDAS WAS A WOMAN see **BÊTE HUMAINE, LA**

K

KINGS OF THE ROAD see **IM LAUF DER ZEIT**